THIRD EDITION

EMPLOYMENT LAW FOR BUSINESS

Dawn D. Bennett-Alexander
University of Georgia

Laura Pincus Hartman
DePaul University

Irwin
McGraw-Hill

Boston, Massachusetts   Burr Ridge, Illinois   Dubuque, Iowa   Madison, Wisconsin
New York, New York   San Francisco, California   St. Louis, Missouri

Irwin/McGraw-Hill

A Division of The McGraw·Hill Companies

EMPLOYMENT LAW FOR BUSINESS

Published by Irwin/McGraw-Hill, an imprint of The McGraw-Hill Companies, Inc. 1221 Avenue of the Americas, New York, NY, 10020. Copyright © 2001, 1998, 1995, by The McGraw-Hill Companies, Inc. All rights reserved. No part of this publication may be reproduced or distributed in any form or by any means, or stored in a data base or retrieval system, without the prior written consent of The McGraw-Hill Companies, Inc., including, but not limited to, in any network or other electronic storage or transmission, or broadcast for distance learning. Some ancillaries, including electronic and print components, may not be available to customers outside the United States.

This book is printed on acid-free paper.

2 3 4 5 6 7 8 9 0 FGR/FGR 0 9 8 7 6 5 4 3 2 1 0

ISBN 0-07-231403-6

Vice president/Editor-in-chief: *Michael W. Junior*
Sponsoring editor: *Andy Winston*
Editorial assistant: *Sara Strand*
Marketing manager: *Brad Schultz*
Project manager: *Paula Krauza*
Production supervisor: *Gina Hangos*
Coordinator freelance design: *Laurie Entringer*
Supplement coordinator: *Susan Lombardi*
New media: *Barb Block*
Designer: *Michael Warrell*
Compositor: *ElectraGraphics, Inc.*
Typeface: *10/12 Times Roman*
Printer: *Quebecor Printing/Fairfield*

Library of Congress Cataloging-in-Publication Data

Bennett-Alexander, Dawn.
     Employment law for business / Dawn D. Bennett-Alexander, Laura Pincus Hartman.—
3rd ed.
        p.   cm.
     Includes index.
     ISBN 0-07-231403-6
     1. Labor laws and legislation—United States.   2. Discrimination in employment—Law and legislation--United States.   I. Hartman, Laura Pincus.   II. Title.
KF3455 .B46   2001
344.7301—dc21   00–027780

http://www.mhcollege.com

To:

Dawn D. Bennett-Alexander, Esq., is an award-winning tenured associate professor of Employment Law and Legal Studies at the University of Georgia's Terry College of Business and an attorney admitted to practice in the District of Columbia and six federal jurisdictions. She is a *cum laude* graduate of the Howard University School of Law and a *magna cum laude* graduate of the Federal City College, now the University of the District of Columbia. She was cofounder and cochair, with her coauthor, of the Employment and Labor Law Section of the Academy of Legal Studies in Business; present coeditor of the section's Employment and Labor Law Quarterly; past coeditor of the section's newsletter; and past president of the Southeastern Academy of Legal Studies in Business. Bennett-Alexander taught employment law in the University of North Florida's MBA program from 1982–87 and has been conducting employment law seminars for managers and supervisors since 1985. Prior to teaching, Bennett-Alexander worked at the Federal Labor Relations Authority, the White House Domestic Council, the US Federal Trade Commission, Antioch School of Law, and as law clerk to the Honorable Julia Cooper Mack (retired) at the highest court in the District of Columbia, the D.C. Court of Appeals. Bennett-Alexander publishes widely in the employment law area, is a noted ex-

pert on employment law issues, was asked to write the first ever sexual harassment entry for *Grolier Encyclopedia,* edited the National Employee Rights Institute's definitive book on federal employment, has been widely quoted on TV, radio, and in the print press, including *USA Today,* the *Wall Street Journal, Fortune* magazine, and is a founder of Practical Diversity, consultants on diversity and employment law issues. Bennett-Alexander is a 2000–2001 recipient of the Fulbright Scholar Fellowship through which she will teach law in Ghana and conduct research on race and gender in employment in a homogeneous society.

Laura Pincus Hartman, J.D., is an associate professor of legal studies and ethics at DePaul University and is DePaul's Assistant Vice-President for Academic Program Development. She recently held the Grainger Chair of Business Ethics at the University of Wisconsin–Madison and was the director of Executive Education for its Human Resource Management and Development programs. Hartman is also past director of DePaul University's Institute for Business and Professional Ethics and held the Wicklander Chair in Professional Ethics at DePaul's Kellstadt Graduate School of Business, where she won the University's Excellence in Teaching award and was chair of the university's Public Service Council. Hartman has also served as an adjunct professor of business law and ethics at Northwestern's Kellogg Graduate School of Management.

Hartman's teaching responsibilities have included Business Ethics, Employment Law, Human Resource Management, Business Law, Antitrust Law, and Corporate Communication and Crisis Management, among other courses. Hartman graduated *magna cum laude* from Tufts University and the University of Chicago Law School and is a member of the Illinois bar. She is cofounder and past cochair (with Dawn) of the Employment and Labor Law Section of the Academy of Legal Studies in Business, was coeditor of the section's *Employment and Labor Law Newsletter,* and served as president of the Midwest Academy of Legal Studies in Business for the 1994–1995 term.

Hartman has done extensive research on the ethics of the employment relationship, employee rights, and employer responsibilities and has published the first business school textbook in the field, *Employment Law for Business,* as well as *Perspectives in Business Ethics* and other textbooks. She has also published articles in, among other journals, the *Academy of Management Executive, Hofstra Law Review,* the *Columbia Business Law Journal,* the *Journal of Business Ethics, Business Ethics Quarterly,* the *Harvard Journal of Law & Technology,* the *American Business Law Journal,* the *Labor Law Journal,* the *Journal of Individual Employment Rights,* and the *Journal of Legal Studies Education.*

Preface to the First Edition

If a disabled employee could perform the job requirements when hired, but the job has progressed and the employee is no longer able to perform, must the employer keep her on?

- Is an employer liable when a supervisor sexually harasses an employee, but the employer knew nothing of it?
- Is an employer liable for racial discrimination because she terminates a black male who refuses to abide by the "no-beard" rule?
- Can an employer be successfully sued for "reverse discrimination" by an employee who feels harmed by the employer's affirmative action plan?
- How far can an employer go in instituting a dress code?
- If an employer has two equally qualified applicants from which to choose and prefers the white one to the black one, is it illegal discrimination for the employer to hire the white applicant, or must the employer hire the black one?
- Must an employer send to training the employee who is in line to attend, if that employee will retire shortly?
- Must an employer keep an employee

known to be HIV positive when other employees fear for their own health because of their exposure to the HIV-positive employee?

- Is it a violation of wage and hour laws for an employer to hire his 13-year-old daughter to pick strawberries during the summer?
- Is an ex-employer liable for defamation if he gives a negative recommendation about an ex-employee to a potential employer who inquires?
- Must an employer disclose to employees that chemicals with which they work are potentially harmful?
- Can an employer stop employees from forming a union?

These types of questions, which are routinely decided in workplaces everyday, can have devastating financial and productivity consequences if mishandled by the employer. Yet few employers or their managers and supervisors are equipped to handle them well. That is why this textbook was created.

Between fiscal years 1970 when newly enacted job discrimination legislation cases started to rise and 1983, the number of federal discrimination suits grew from fewer than 350 per year to around

9,000 per year. This is an astonishing 2,166 percent growth in the volume of discrimination suits, compared with only 125 percent growth in general federal civil cases for the same period. A major factor in this statistic is that the groups protected by Title VII of the Civil Rights Act of 1964 and similar legislation, including minorities, women, and white males over 40, now constitute over 70 percent of the total workforce. Add to that number those protected by laws addressing disability, wages and hours, unions, workplace environmental right-to-know laws, tort laws, occupational safety and health and tort laws, and the percentage increases even more. There was a 95.7 percent increase from 1969's 45.84 million such employees to 1989's 89.70 million employees.

It is good that employers and employees alike are now getting the benefits derived from having a safer, fairer workplace and one more reflective of the population's diversity. However, this is not without its attendant challenges. One of those challenges is reflected in the statistics given above. With the advent of workplace regulation by the government, particularly the Civil Rights Act of 1964, there is more of an expectation by employees of certain basic rights in the workplace. When these expectations are not met, and the affected population comprises more than 70 percent of the workforce, problems and their attendant litigation will be high.

Plaintiffs won 57% of lawsuits brought for wrongful termination based on race, gender, and disability discrimination in the seven-year period between 1988 and 1995. The median compensatory damage award was more than $100,000. Much of the litigation and liability arising in the area covered by these statistics is avoidable. Many times the only difference between an employer being sued or not is a manager or supervisor who recognizes that the decision being made may lead to unnecessary litigation and thus avoids it.

We have seen what types of employment law problems are most prevalent in the workplace from our extensive experience in the classroom, in our research and writing, as well as in conducting over the years many employment seminars for managers, supervisors, business owners, equal employment opportunity officers, human resources personnel, general counsels, and others. We have seen how management most often strays from appropriate considerations and treads on thin legal ice, exposing them to potential increased liability. We came to realize that many of the mistakes were based on ignorance rather than malice. Often it was simply not knowing that a decision was being handled incorrectly.

Becoming more aware of potential liability does not mean the employer is not free to make legitimate workplace decisions. It simply means that those decisions are handled appropriately in ways that lessen or avoid liability. The problem does not lie in not being able to terminate the female who is chronically late for work, because the employer thinks she will sue for gender discrimination. Rather, the challenge lies in doing it in a way that precludes her from being able to file a successful claim. It does not mean the employer must retain her, despite her failure to adequately meet workplace expectations and requirements. It means simply that the employer must make certain the termination is beyond reproach. If the employee has performed in a way that results in termination, this should be documentable and, therefore, defensible.

Termination of the employee under such circumstances should present no problem, assuming similarly situated employees have been treated consistently in the same manner. The employer is free to make the management decisions necessary to run the business, but she or he simply does so correctly.

Knowing how to do so correctly doesn't just happen. It must be learned. We set out to create a textbook aimed at anyone who would, or presently does, manage people. Knowing what is in this book is a necessity. For those already in the workplace, your day is filled with one awkward situation after another—for which you wish you had the answers. For those in school, you will soon be in the workplace, and in the not-too-distant future you will likely be in a position managing others. We cannot promise answers to every one of your questions, but we can promise that we will provide the information and basic considerations in most areas that will help you arrive at an informed, reasonable, and defensible answer about which you can feel more comfortable. You will not walk away feeling as if you rolled the dice when you made a workplace decision, then wait with anxiety to see if the decision will backfire in some way.

In an effort to best inform employers of the reasoning behind legal requirements and to provide a basis for making decisions in "gray areas," we often provide background in relevant social or political movements, or both, as well as in legislative history and other relevant considerations. Law is not created in a vacuum, and this information gives the law context so the purpose is more easily understood. Often understanding why a law exists can help an employer make the correct choices in interpreting the law when making workplace decisions with no clear-cut answers.

Legal cases are used to illustrate important concepts; however, we realize that it is the managerial aspects of the concepts with which you must deal. Therefore, we took great pains to try to rid the cases of unnecessary "legalese" and procedural matters that would be more relevant to a lawyer or law student. We also follow each case with questions designed to aid in thinking critically about the issues involved from an employer's standpoint, rather than from a purely legal standpoint. We understand that *how* employers make their decisions has a great impact on the decisions made. Therefore, our case-end questions are designed as critical-thinking questions to get the student to go beyond the legal concepts and think critically about management issues. This process of learning to analyze and think critically about issues from different points of view will greatly enhance student decision-making abilities as future managers or business owners. Addressing the issues in the way they are likely to arise in life greatly enhances that ability.

It is one thing to know that the law prohibits gender discrimination in employment. It is quite another to recognize such discrimination when it occurs and govern oneself accordingly. For instance, a female employee says she cannot use a "filthy" toilet, which is the only one at the work site. The employer can dismiss the complaint and tell the employee she must use the toilet, and perhaps later be held liable for gender discrimination. Or the employer can think of what implications this may have, given that this is a female employee essentially being denied a right that male employees have in access to a usable toilet. The employer then realizes there may be a problem and is more likely to make the better decision.

This seemingly unlikely scenario is based on an actual case, which you will later read. It is a great example of how simple but unexpected decisions can create liability in surprising ways. Knowing the background and intent of a law often can help in situations where the answer to the problem may not be readily apparent. Including the law in your thinking can help the thought process for making well-founded decisions.

We also have included boxed items from easily accessible media sources that you come across every day, such as *People* magazine and the *USA Today* newspaper. The intent is to demonstrate how the matters discussed are interesting and integrated into everyday life, yet they can have serious repercussions for employers.

Much of today's litigation results from workplace decisions arising from unfortunate ideas about various groups, and from lack of awareness about what may result in litigation. We do not want to take away anyone's right to think whatever they wish about whomever they wish, but we do want to teach that those thoughts may result in legal trouble when they are acted on.

Something new and innovative must be done if we are to break the cycle of insensitivity, and myopia that results in spiraling numbers of unnecessary lawsuits. Part of breaking this cycle is language and using terminology that more accurately reflects those considerations. We have, therefore, in a rather unorthodox move, taken the offensive and created a path, rather than followed one.

For instance, the term *sex* is used in this text to mean sex only in a purely sexual sense. The term *gender* is used to distinguish males from females. With the increasing use of sexual harassment as a cause of action, it became confusing to continue to speak of "sex" as meaning gender, particularly when it adds to the confusion to understand that sex need *not* be present in a sexual harassment claim, but gender differences *are* required. For instance, to say that a claim must be based on "a difference in treatment based on sex" leaves it unclear as to whether it means gender or sexual activity. Since it actually means gender, we have made such clarifications. Also, use of the term *sex* in connection with gender discrimination cases, the majority of which are brought by women, continues to inject sexuality into the equation of women and work. This, in turn, contributes to keeping women and sexuality connected in an inappropriate setting (employment). Further, it does so at a time when there is an attempt to decrease such connections and, instead, concentrate on the applicant's qualifications for the job.

So, too, with the term *homosexuality.* In this text, the term *affinity orientation* is used, instead. The traditional term emphasizes, for one group and not others, the highly personal yet generally irrelevant issue of the employee's sexuality. The use of the term sets up those within that group for consideration as different (usually interpreted to be "less than"), when they may well be qualified for the job and otherwise acceptable. With sexuality being highlighted in referring to them, it becomes difficult to think of them in any other light. The term also continues to pander to the historically more sensational or titillating aspects of the applicant's personal life choices and uses it to color their entire life when all that should be of interest is ability to do the job. Using more appropriate terminology will hopefully keep the focus on that ability.

The term *"disabled"* is used, rather than *"handicapped,"* to conform to the more enlightened view taken by the Americans with Disabilities Act of 1990. It gets away from the old notion that those who were differently abled went "cap in hand" looking for handouts. Rather, it recognizes the importance of including in employment these 43 million Americans who can contribute to the workplace.

There is also a diligent effort to use gender-inclusive or neutral terminology—for example, police officers, rather than policemen; firefighters, rather than firemen; servers, rather than waiters or waitresses; flight attendants, rather than stewards or stewardesses. We urge you to add to the list and use such language in your conversations. To use different terminology for males and females performing the same job reflects a gender difference when there is no need to do so. If, as the law requires, it is irrelevant because it is the job itself on which we wish to focus, then our language should reflect this.

It is not simply a matter of terminology. Terminology is powerful. It conveys ideas to us about the matter spoken of. To the extent we change our language to be more neutral when referring to employees, it will be easier to change our ingrained notions of the "appropriateness" of traditional employment roles based on gender, sexuality, or other largely irrelevant criteria and make employment discrimination laws more effective.

This conscious choice of language also is not a reflection of temporal "political correctness" considerations. It goes far beyond what terming something "politically correct" tends to do. These changes in terminology are substantive and nontrivial changes that attempt to have language reflect reality, rather than have our reality shaped and limited by the language we use. Being sensitive to the matter of language can help make us more sensitive to what stands behind the words. That is an important aid in avoiding liability and obeying the law.

The best way to determine what an employer must do to avoid liability for employment decisions is to look at cases to see what courts have used to determine previous liability. This is why we have provided many and varied cases for you to consider. Much care has been taken to make the cases not only relevant, informative, and illustrative but also interesting, up-to-date, and easy to read. There is a good mix of new cases, along with the old "standards" that still define an area. We have assiduously tried to avoid legalese and intricate legal consideration. Instead, we emphasize the legal managerial aspects of cases—that is, what does the case mean that management should or should not do to be best protected from violating the law?

We wanted the textbook to be informative, readable, and a resource, to encourage critical and creative thinking about workplace problems, and to sensitize you to the need for effective workplace management. We think we have accomplished our goal. We hope the text is as interesting and informative for you to read and use as it was exciting and challenging for us to write.

We *sincerely* would like to know what you think. We urge you to write and let us know—good or bad—your thoughts.

Dawn D. Bennett-Alexander
Terry College of Business
University of Georgia
202 Brooks Hall
Athens, GA 30602-6255
(706) 542-4290
E-mail: dawndba@terry.uga.edu
Laura P. Hartman
Executive Offices
DePaul University
55 E. Jackson Blvd.
Chicago, IL 60604-2787
(312) 362-6569
E-mail: lhartman@wppost.depaul.edu

Preface to the Third Edition

My, how time flies and things just keep getting better! When we first published this book in 1995, there were virtually no courses in employment law in the country. Our publisher believed so much in our mantra, "If we write it, they will come," that they promised to allow the book to go into second edition even if the first edition did not meet their modest projections. They took the long view and agreed to try to hang in there with us until the market caught on. Well, the first edition outstripped all projections, and the second edition did even better. It caught on. Then it zoomed. Once there was a text to use, the classes came and people understood how incredibly important this subject matter is to anyone managing people today. As we enter the new millennium, our population becoming ever more diverse, we must do more than pay lip service to the issue of diversity. Rather, we must understand that it will be increasingly vital to the very continued existence of business as we know it. We are pleased to be able to aid students, managers, and others in their quest for understanding these issues and avoiding unnecessary liability.

Thank you for helping to make our dream—a textbook that would give students, managers, human resources professionals and others the answers they needed in language they could understand and relate to—a successful reality. We feel like many of you were there with us from the first edition and have made this incredible journey into a new discipline with us. We very much appreciate your support in every way.

With this third edition, we have listened to your suggestions, which we encourage, and have incorporated a great many of them. In addition to updating the material, in this edition we have added pedagogical tools that we think will be even more helpful in using the textbook:

- There are many new cases.
- We have added case cites to many chapter-end questions.
- We have added more website notations.
- We have added nonlegal writings in selected areas to help you focus on some of the less obvious issues which greatly underscore the subject matter.
- We have put our website notations on a webpage dedicated to the text which can be easily updated.
- Look for this icon near topics that have additional Internet resources on the book's website (www.mhhe.com/emplaw).

We hope you have as much enjoyment reading the text as we had writing it. Either way, let us know.

Dawn D. Bennett-Alexander, Esq.
Athens, GA
April 20, 2000

The authors would like to honor and thank the following individuals, without whose assistance and support this text would never have been written: McGraw-Hill Higher Education editorial support, including Craig Beytien, executive editor, for having the insight and courage to sign the first employment law text of its kind before many others were able to see the vast but undeniable merit of doing so; and Sara Strand, editorial assistant. For their contributions to making the third edition better than ever, special thanks to Mark O. Flaherty, Old Dominion University; Denise Leigh, Phoenix Community College (Gainesville, FL); Lewis Tanner, University of Georgia; Anne Levy, Michigan State University; and a *very* special thank you to Diane Bradley, trial attorney extraordinaire for the District of Columbia office of the U.S. Equal Employment Opportunity Commission and adjunct professor of Employment Law at the University of Maryland. Diane's contributions to this edition, particularly chapter 3, were insightful, cogent, timely and selfless. Thank you *very much* Diane. Finally, we would like to thank the scholars who have class tested and reviewed this manuscript, including the following:

Curt Behrens	*Northern Illinois University*
George Biles	*American University*
Michael Garrison	*North Dakota State University*
Andrea Giampetro-Meyer	*Loyola College of Maryland*
John Gray	*Loyola College of Maryland*
Marsha Hass	*College of Charleston*
Roger Johns	*Eastern New Mexico State University*
Eileen Kelly	*Louisiana State University*
Nancy Kubasek	*Bowling Green State University*
Tony McAdams	*University of Northern Iowa*
James Morgan	*California State University–Chico*
Gregory Mosier	*Oklahoma State University*
Patricia Pattison	*University of Wyoming*
Kenneth Schneyer	*Johnson & Wales University*
Benjamin Weeks	*St. Xavier College*

Bennett-Alexander: I would like to thank (1) my co-author, Laura Pincus Hartman, one of my very favorite people in the whole world, for her wonderful enthusiasm, intellect, energy, support, and hard work; (2) my daughters Jenniffer Dawn Bennett Alexander, Anne Alexis Bennett Alexander and Tess Alexandra Bennett Harrison for being my special gifts from above and for knowing that my favorite thing in the whole world is being their Mama—even though they drive me crazy; (3) Linda F. Harrison, without whose laughter the world would be a much different, less fun, place and for whom I have only five words: "Oh! What *kind* of eggs?"; (4) my siblings, Brenda Bennett Watkins, Gale C. Bennett Harris, Barbara Jean Bennett Bethea and Rev. Dr. William H. Bennett II, for their unwavering confidence, love, support and laughs; (5) my department chair, Dr. Sandra G. Gustavson, who continues to be so supportive in so many ways; (6) the thousands of managers, supervisors, employers and employees who have shared their experiences and insights over the years; (7) my colleagues from across the country who have been so supportive of this text; and last but not least, (8) my students, who are a never-ending source of utter wonder, insight, and fun for me. Do we have a good time, or what?

This text is immeasurably richer for having the contributions of each of you.

DDB-A

I, Laura, am grateful for the assistance of a multitude of individuals who have helped to bring the third edition of this text to fruition. First, I would like to commend the efforts of my assistant Kimberly Tenerelli who methodically, precisely, and never begrudgingly cite-checked and helped to update this new edition. Without her attention to detail, her careful consideration of the context, and her patience with my requests, this book would be significantly different and inferior. I am also beholden to Robyn Berkley for her input and materials in connection with the segment on probationary employees and to Richard Henquinet for his assistance with the ADA accommodations material. On a more personal note, I couldn't imagine going through this life without the nurturing friendship, support, and coaxing of my co-author, Dawn. I am also continually astonished at the graces that have allowed me to share my life with my husband, David, and my daughters, Rachel and Emma. Everyone should be so blessed.

LPH

CONTENTS

I THE REGULATION OF THE EMPLOYMENT RELATIONSHIP

1 THE REGULATION OF EMPLOYMENT

Chapter Outline

S C E N A R I O S

S C E N A R I O   1

Emma Bina is working as a research scientist at a laboratory when she is approached with an employment offer from a competing laboratory. The competing lab director offers Emma nearly double her present salary and superior research equipment and opportunities. The lab director tells Emma that she can remain employed with the new company as long as she does satisfactory work. Emma accepts the offer, sells her house, takes her dog and cats and moves to the new state, buys a new house, and settles in. Emma's first two evaluations are superior. Then, six months after arriving, Emma is terminated and the employer offers no explanation. Emma sues for unlawful termination. Does she win? Why or why not?

S C E N A R I O   2

Mark Richter is about to retire as a candy salesperson when he closes on a deal the candy company has been trying to land for a long time. Just before Mark is to collect his substantial commission, he is terminated. Does Mark have a basis on which to sue for unlawful termination?

S C E N A R I O   3

Jenna Zitron informs her employer that she has been summoned to serve jury duty for a week. Though rescheduling her duties is not a problem, Jenna is told by her employer that, if she serves jury duty rather than trying to be relieved of it, she will be terminated. Jenna refuses to lie to be relieved of jury duty. Does Jenna have a basis on which to sue for unlawful termination?

Introduction to the Regulatory Environment

How is the employer regulated? How much can Congress or the courts tell an employer how to run its business, whom it should hire or fire, or how it should treat its employees?

If an employer wants to hire someone to work every other hour every other week, it should be free to do so as long as it can locate an employee who is willing to enter into such an agreement. Or, if an employer requires that all employees wear a purple chicken costume throughout the workday, there is no reason why that requirement could not be enforced if the employer can find employees to accept the agreement.

The freedom to contract is crucial to freedom of the market; an employee may choose to work or not to work for a given employer, and an employer may choose to hire or not to hire a given applicant.

As a result, though the employment relationship is regulated to some extent, Congress tries to avoid telling employers how to deal with their employees or dictating whom the employer should or should not hire. It is unlikely that Congress would enact legislation that would require employers to hire certain individuals or groups of individuals (like a pure quota system) or that would prevent employers and employees from freely negotiating the responsibilities of a given job. For example, employers have historically had the right to discharge an employee whenever they wished to do so.

However, Congress has passed employment-related laws where it believes that the employee is not on equal footing with the employer. For example, Congress has passed laws that require minimum wages as well as statutes that direct employers not to use certain criteria, such as race or gender, in arriving at specific employment decisions. On the other hand, Congress has also allowed municipalities to favor certain contractors over others as a result of their minority status, in an effort to correct past discrimination.

EXHIBIT 1–1   Myths about the Regulation of Employment

1. You have a right to your job.
2. Once you're hired, your employer may not fire you except if there's a good reason.
3. As an employer, you may not terminate someone unless that worker does something bad.
4. You have someone working for you whom you really do not get along with; you may not fire that person for that reason alone.
5. As an employer, you may have a rule that, if any employee reports the wrongdoings of the firm to the government, she or he will be terminated.

Is Regulation Necessary?

There are those scholars, however, who do not believe that regulation of discrimination and other areas of the employment relationship is necessary. President Ronald Reagan acknowledged this general philosophy when he enacted Executive Order 12291 in 1981. That order provided that no regulatory action be undertaken *unless the potential benefits to society outweigh the potential costs.* Proponents of this view believe that the market will work to encourage rational, nonbiased behavior.

For example, Title VII of the Civil Rights Act of 1964 prohibits discrimination based on race and gender among other characteristics. Some economists have argued that rational individuals interested in profit maximization will never hesitate to hire the most qualified applicants, regardless of their race. Status-dependent decisions are inefficient, since they are generally based on the incorrect and naive belief that members of one class are less meritorious than others. If these employers, instead, were to allow prejudices to govern or influence their employment decisions, they may overlook the most qualified applicant because that applicant was black or a woman. In that way, they would hire less-qualified individuals and employ a less-efficient workforce.

In an unregulated and competitive market, economic forces are working to minimize discrimination. In a market of many sellers, one can expect the intensity of the prejudice against blacks to vary considerably. Some sellers will have only a mild prejudice against blacks. These sellers will not forgo as many advantageous transactions with blacks as their more prejudiced competitors (unless the law interferes). Their costs, therefore, will be lower and this will enable them to increase their share of the market. The lease-prejudiced sellers will come to dominate the market in much the same way as people who are least afraid of heights come to dominate occupations that require working at heights; they demand a smaller premium for working at such a job.

However, opponents of this position contend that discrimination continues because often employers are faced with the choice of two *equally* qualified applicants for a position. In that case, the prejudiced employer suffers no decrease in efficiency of her or his firm as a result of choosing the white or male applicant over the minority or female applicant.

The second argument against the need for regulation in the area of discrimination is that if all or most employers preferred hiring employees from majority classes, such as white males, the cost of white male employment would rise. Consequently, it would become more profitable to hire qualified minority employees at a lower cost. The demand for these low-cost minority employees would also rise, and minority employees would be able to command a higher wage. Soon, the wage for minority employees and white employees would be close to equal.

The problem with this analysis is that, as the cost of hiring minority workers increases, prejudiced employers are less likely to hire the minority applicants in favor of the slightly more expensive white applicants. The price of minority work will then decrease, and minority employees will suffer an endless roller coaster of low wages, heightened demand, slightly increased wages, lower demand, low wages. This is where regulation offers a solution. Prejudice in the regulated workplace is restricted. Therefore, distinctions in treatment, pay, and other benefits between employees are based only on merit and not on personal biases. According to Title VII and other acts, employers are *not* restricted from maintaining the most qualified workforce possible, which is the specific aim of the statutes. Consequently, employment regulation may, in fact, promote efficiency in the workplace.

It is critical that employers understand the regulatory environment in which employment decisions are made or questioned. Increasingly, managers and corporate officers have been named as defendants in actions by employees and have been held personally liable for violations of various statutes including Title VII. The following is an explanation of the regulatory structure of the law relating to employment, including the balance between state and federal law. However, it must be noted that, in addition to the legal restrictions on employment decisions, strong nonregulatory factors also exert influence on management determinations and business judgment. These factors include public interest groups as well as societal pressure, pressure exerted by consumers or clients, media pressure, and ethical responsibilities.

VAN STEENBURGH V. RIVAL COMPANY
171 F.3d 1155 (8th Cir. 1999)

An employee sued under Title VII alleging constructive discharge because of sexual harassment. The court agreed.

Wollman, J.

In 1988, Van Steenburgh began working at Rival's manufacturing plant. She had a good working relationship with her supervisor, Larry Esser. However, after Esser told the married Van Steenburgh that he was interested in seeing her socially, their professional relationship deteriorated. Esser's conduct included repeatedly confronting Van Steenburgh in private and proposing that she engage in a romantic relationship with him; touching Van Steenburgh on numerous occasions; asking her to go somewhere to "be alone" with him; putting his arms around her and telling her he wished he could "take her away from her husband"; and staring at Van Steenburgh, entering her office uninvited, and repeatedly asking her to have an affair with him. In addition, while the two were playing cards with their spouses, Esser grabbed Van Steenburgh's leg under the table. During one incident, Esser grabbed her and put his arms around her but she pushed him away. He became angry with her. In another incident in March 1995, Esser put one arm around her, and put one hand on her breast. He said he would stop harassing her if he could "just touch [her] down there."

Van Steenburgh formally complained about Esser's conduct to Carol Bottcher, the plant manager, in May 1992 and in early 1994. Bottcher verbally warned Esser once but failed to make any written record of the complaints. When the harassment continued after Bottcher's warning, Van Steenburgh complained repeatedly about Esser and Bottcher to another supervisor, Tommy Toliver. Toliver insisted there was nothing he could do about Esser's conduct or Bottcher's failure to act, and he indicated that Bottcher would not take more severe action against Esser.

In June 1995, in front of others, Esser informed Van Steenburgh that another co-worker would be placed above her on the production line. Immediately after the incident, Van Steenburgh informed Toliver that she believed Esser had spoken to her in a hostile manner to humiliate her and to retaliate against her in front of her supervisors and co-workers. Toliver said that he believed her but that nothing could be done because Bottcher would not believe the story. Later that day, Van Steenburgh quit her employment at Rival. Van Steenburgh filed a complaint against Rival with the Equal Employment Opportunity Commission.

* * * *

To demonstrate constructive discharge, a plaintiff must show that the harassment was severe enough that a reasonable person in the same position would have found the working conditions intolerable. We conclude that Van Steenburgh made such a showing. She presented evidence of a pattern of harassment that continued for more than five years. Esser repeatedly propositioned Van Steenburgh, physically accosted her on numerous occasions, and made increasingly serious threats of retaliation. A reasonable person in Van Steenburgh's position would have found the conditions at Rival intolerable.

. . . This was adequate to demonstrate that Van Steenburgh had a lack of recourse against the harassment within Rival's organization. Therefore, there was sufficient evidence to support the jury's finding of constructive discharge.

* * * *

We REVERSE the district court's grant of judgment as a matter of law. We REMAND for an articulation of the reasons for granting a new trial that will enable us to conduct the meaningful review of that ruling. . . .

Case Questions

1. How would you respond to the argument, "If the conduct was so severe, why did she wait two years to complain again about the conduct?"

2. As an employer, how could you protect yourself against constructive discharge of this nature?

3. The court said that it was constructive discharge if the harassment was "severe enough that a reasonable person in the same position would have found the working conditions intolerable." As you'll see in a later chapter on sexual harassment, that is similar to the definition of hostile environment sexual harassment. Accordingly, should it be true that every time someone quits on the basis of sexual harassment, it should be constructive discharge?

YOHO V. TECUMSEH PRODUCTS CO.
—F.Supp.2d—, 1999 WL 203514 (E.D.Wisc. 1999)

An employee filed a complaint for discrimination and constructive discharge when she was constantly harassed after her husband was arrested for molesting their daughter. Even though the teasing and harassment took place over an extremely long period of time, the court did not find sufficient basis for constructive discharge.

Ms. Yoho and her husband, Gerald, were employed with Tecumseh. In June 1995 the husband was arrested and charged with sexually molesting his and Yoho's daughter. He pled guilty and was sentenced in April 1996. The incident was reported in a newspaper article, and the article appeared at the plant on two occasions within a few days of the date it was published in at least three places: a clipboard by her assembly line, on a metal cabinet on another assembly line, and in her mailbox. A second article was printed when he was sentenced and was posted in the workplace on two occasions: on a box of castings and the entire newspaper containing the article in a blueprint drawer where Yoho did not work. Yoho was told by another employee that the newspaper was being passed throughout the workplace and she complained to her supervisor. On 10 occasions during June 1995 to April 1996, Yoho learned of graffiti written inside the stalls of the men's restrooms that made vulgar references to Yoho or her daughter. Yoho reported the graffiti to her supervisor.

When she threatened to quit, the plant manager asked her to reconsider. The plant manager decided to transfer her from her position on second shift to the same position on first shift "to try to get her away from the graffiti." Yoho agreed. The next week following the transfer, she learned that more graffiti about her daughter had appeared in all the stalls of the men's restroom. She immediately quit.

Yoho also claims that employees made sexual comments in the workplace. She could not remember specific dates or specific language other than something to the effect of, "What was it? You didn't give it to him enough?" Yoho filed a discrimination complaint and a constructive discharge complaint.

Reynolds, J.

* * * *

Hostile Work Environment Claim

Title VII creates liability only for discrimination because of sex; it does not cover all workplace harassment. We have never held that workplace harassment . . . is automatically discrimination because of sex merely because the words used have sexual content or connotations. The critical issue . . . is whether members of one sex are exposed to disadvantageous terms or conditions of employment to which members of the other sex are not exposed. In addition, the alleged conduct must be severe or pervasive.

* * * *

The alleged sexual comments by co-workers are insignificant to this decision. With one exception, Yoho can give absolutely no specifics about the comments and therefore may not rely on them to support her hostile work environment claim.

The newspaper articles, which are typical reports, are not sexually offensive on their face, and Yoho gives no persuasive argument to support her position that such articles consitute "sexual harassment." One article was placed in her mailbox, while others were found at various locations around the plant, some in areas where Yoho did not work. Yoho claims that the articles were "used for an evil purpose," but there is no indication that they were posted because of Yoho's sex.

The sexual writings occurred over a period of fourteen to fifteen months. All but one were written in the men's restrooms (which is not Yoho's work environment). Yoho knew about this graffiti, and went to look at it on five occasions only because other employees told her about it (in a nonhostile manner). Yoho asserts that the graffiti was directed at her in her capacity as the only female line supervisor, with no male supervisors subjected to similar acts. However, there was sexual graffiti regarding Yoho's male supervisor, as well as graffiti about other male employees, in the men's restrooms; Yoho's allegation that she was treated differently than her male counterparts is therefore weakened. Yoho's primary argument in support of her claim that she was harassed because she is a woman is that her predecessor (to the supervisor position on the cam shaft line), a female, was sexually harassed. However, that employee resigned as a supervisor in 1989 (six years before Yoho became a supervisor), and attests that she never experienced any conduct she considered to be discrimination or harassment. Yoho also takes the position that plant management, who were all male, found the graffiti vulgar, extremely offensive, which to some extent works against her claim that she was harassed because of her gender. Finally, Yoho testified in her deposition that the graffiti concerning her daughter, as well as the articles about her husband, were "personal" harassment, not harassment "directed at [her] sexually."

* * * *

Given the nature and frequency of the incidents, Yoho cannot show that the harassment was sufficiently offensive or pervasive; nor has she presented adequate evidence to create an inference that the majority of the incidents were discrimination because of her sex. While the actions Yoho complains of may be considered in poor taste and extremely insensitive, the court concludes that they do not constitute harassment actionable under Title VII.

Constructive Discharge Claim

To prevail on her constructive discharge claim, Yoho must establish that (1) the conditions at Tecumseh were so intolerable that a reasonable person would have been compelled to resign; and (2) the working conditions were intolerable in a discriminatory way.

For the same reasons discussed with respect to Yoho's hostile work environment claim, her constructive discharge claim will be dismissed.

* * * *

Conclusion

Defendant Tecumseh Products Company's motion for summary judgment is GRANTED and this action is DISMISSED.

Case Questions

1. Do you agree with the court's decision? Why or why not?

2. What else do you think could have happened that would encourage the court to have found constructive discharge? How would you change the facts to create a situation of constructive discharge?

3. Compare and contrast this case with the previous case of constructive discharge, *Van Steenburgh* v. *Rival Company*.

Background—The Employment-at-Will Doctrine

Initially, the theoretical underpinnings of the American employer–employee relationship was one based on a patriarchal system played in the English feudal system. When employers were the wealthy landowners who owned the land and had people work the land for them, employers supplied virtually all the employees' needs, took care of disputes that arose, and allowed the employees to live out their lives on the land after they could no longer be the productive employees they once were. The employer took care of the employees as parents would offspring.

When we moved from an agrarian society toward a more industrialized one, the employee–employer relationship was now farther removed than before, but the underlying theory was still maintained. The employee could work for the employer as long as the employee wished, and leave when the employee no longer wished to work for the employer (therefore, the employees worked at their own will). The reverse was also true. The employer employed the employee for as long as the employer wished, and, when the employer no longer wished to have the employee in his or her employ, the employee had to leave.

Both parties were free to leave at virtually any time for any reason. Of course, if there was a contract between the parties, either as a collective bargaining agreement or an individual contract, the relationship was not governed by the will of the parties, but rather by the contract. Government employees generally were not at-will employees, either, since there were limitations imposed on the government–

employer through rules governing the federal employment relationship and how it could be terminated.

When protective employment legislation began to come into the equation, the employer's rights to hire and fire were circumscribed to a great extent. While an employer was free to terminate an employee for no particular reason, it could not terminate a worker based on race, gender, religion, national origin, age, or disability. Providing protection for historically discriminated-against groups by way of such laws as Title VII, the Age Discrimination in Employment Act, the Americans with Disabilities Act, and other such protective legislation also had the predictable effect of making all employees feel more like their position as employees embraced certain "rights" to which they were entitled as employees. Where virtually no employees sued employers before protective legislation, subsequent to legislation, employees afforded such protection were suing employers under the law. It gave employees the perception that the employment relationship had certain rights attached to it, for which they were willing to fight.

With women, minorities, older employees, disabled employees, and veterans given protected status under the laws, it was not long before those who were not afforded specific protection began to sue employers, based on their perception that it "just wasn't right" for an employer to be able to terminate them for any reason the employer wanted to, outside the protected categories. To them it was beside the point that they did not fit neatly into a protected category. They had been "wronged" and they wanted their just due. An employee could be fired if the employer didn't like the employee's green socks, or the way the employee wore his hair, or because the employee "blew it" on attempting to get his first account after being hired. There was no recourse because, since the relationship was at will, the employer could fire the employee for whatever reason the employer wished, as long as it was not a violation of the law.

Visualize a whole luscious, delectable pie of your favorite type. That pie represents the employer's rights in the workplace. At first, virtually the whole pie belonged to the employer. The employer could do practically anything the employer wished to do regarding the right to hire, fire, pay, or legislate employee activities in the workplace. Then Congress began passing laws that limited in some way the employer's prerogatives. The pie gets smaller and smaller as more and more of the pie is "eaten away" by laws. There are both state and federal laws governing wages and hours, child labor laws, equal employment laws, equal pay laws—all of which govern such areas as wages the employer will pay, time limits on how long employees can work, limits on the age employees must be, and prohibitions on reasons the employer can refuse to hire or terminate or discipline employees. If an employer was unionized, there was even less pie left. Employers who had their mouths set on having the whole pie ended up with much less than they envisioned. Then along comes the weakening of the employment-at-will concept, and much of the pie the employer thought was left is taken away. The amount of pie left to the employer is enough to be a filling portion, but much less than the employer initially thought he or she would have for disposal.

With employment at will, a legal issue will arise generally where the employee is more than likely not someone who fits within one of the other categories covered by protective legislation. They certainly can be, but most of the time they are not. As a practical matter, when an employee is not covered by any of the equal employment opportunity legislation and still wishes to sue the employer, the employee brings suit on the basis of unjust dismissal or wrongful termination. The employee feels that there is an unjust reason for his or her dismissal and brings suit against the employer, to be reinstated or for compensatory and punitive damages for the losses suffered in being unjustly dismissed. Unjust dismissal cases have been brought for such reasons as being terminated for signing a union card, filing workers' compensation claims, refusing to assist the employer in committing a crime, refusing to commit a crime on the employer's behalf, refusing to forgo suit against the employer for a valid legal claim against the employer, refusal to avoid jury duty, refusal to falsify records, refusal to lie in testifying in a case involving the employer, reporting wrongdoing or illegal activity by the employer, and termination at a time when the employee was about to receive a substantial bonus from the employer. For a long time, where the facts could be litigated under both theories, the critical difference between bringing suit under Title VII and bringing suit for unlawful discharge was that the employee in the unlawful discharge suit had the possibility of jury trial, and damages were unlimited, rather than being limited by the statutes under which the suits were brought. Since the passage of the Civil Rights Act of 1991, this is no longer an important distinction. Under the Civil Rights Act of 1991, claimants are permitted to have jury trials under most circumstances, and, while certain damages are limited, damages are no longer limited to make-whole relief under Title VII.

Probably because the law also began to include certain basic rights in its concept of the employment relationship, and because of the basic unfairness involved in some of the situations that the court was asked to decide, courts all over the country began making exceptions to the at-will doctrine. The at-will doctrine is dealt with on a state-by-state basis, because each state is free to deal with this area as it sees fit. Therefore, the changes in the at-will doctrine vary from state to state. Congress has entertained proposals to deal with the at-will doctrine on the federal level, but, as of yet, none has been successful. The Commission on Uniform State Laws, in August of 1991, issued a model termination act that states may use. The intent is to make terminations so uniform across the country that there will be some predictability and consistency where now there is only a patchwork of laws and case law. The model act will be discussed later in the chapter.

The state-by-state approach to addressing the exceptions to the at-will doctrine has created a crazy quilt of laws across the country. In some states the at-will doctrine has virtually no exceptions and, therefore, remains virtually intact as it always was. In other states the courts have created judicial exceptions to the at-will doctrine that apply in certain limited circumstances. In still other states, the state legislatures have passed laws providing legislative exceptions to the at-will doctrine.

Exceptions to the At-Will Doctrine

Employment at will is still the basic law in many states; however, after seeing case after case with results such as those above, the employment-at-will doctrine several years ago began to erode. There have been several judicial exceptions to the rule created by courts. The rule has become that, even though an employer can terminate an employee for any legal reason, if the reason is one that is determined to be an exception to the at-will doctrine, the employee cannot be terminated for that reason or it constitutes unjust dismissal for which the employee can receive damages or reinstatement.

Courts and state legislation have been fairly consistent in holding that exceptions will be permitted where the employer breaches an implied covenant of good faith and fair dealing, where an implied promise to the employee was breached, or where breach of an implied contract with the employee or the discharge is in violation of some recognized public policy. Keep in mind that if the employee and employer have an individual contract or a collective bargaining agreement, then the employment relationship is governed by the agreement. If the employer is the government, then the employment relationship regarding dismissals is governed by appropriate government regulations. It is the other 65 percent of the workforce that is covered by the employment-at-will doctrine.

The Worker Adjustment and Retraining Notification Act

The Worker Adjustment and Retraining Notification (WARN) Act generally requires that 60 days' advance notice of a "plant closing" or "mass layoff" be given to affected employees. If an employer does not comply with the requirements of the WARN Act notices, employees can recover pay and benefits for the period for which notice was not given, up to a maximum of 60 days. All but small employers and public employers are required to provide written notice of a "plant closing" or "mass layoff" no less than 60 days in advance.

The number of employees is a key factor in determining whether the WARN Act is applicable. Only an employer who has 100 or more full-time employees or has 100 or more employees who, in the aggregate, work at least 4,000 hours per week are covered by the WARN Act. In counting the number of employees, US workers at foreign sites, temporary employees, and employees working for a subsidiary as part of the parent company must be considered in the calculation.

There are three exceptions to the 60-day notice requirements. The first, referred to as the "faltering company" exception, involves an employer who is actively seeking capital and who in good faith believed that giving notice to the employees would have precluded the employer from obtaining the need capital. The second exception occurs when the required notice is not given due to a "sudden, dramatic, and unexpected" business circumstance not reasonably foreseen and outside the employers' control. The last exception is for actions arising out of a "natural disaster" such as a flood, earthquake, or drought.

Violation of Public Policy

One of the most popular exceptions that states have been fairly consistent in recognizing either through legislation or court cases has been the exception to the at-will doctrine based on the employer's dismissal of the employee constituting a violation of public policy (as determined by the legislature or courts). For a terminated employee to sustain a cause of action against her or his employer on this basis, the ex-employee must show that the employer's actions were motivated by bad faith, malice, or retaliation. Forty-four states allow this exception. The violations of public policy usually arise from the employee being terminated for acts such as refusing to violate a criminal statute on behalf of the employer or at the employer's request, exercising a statutory right, fulfilling a statutory duty, or disclosing violations of statutes by an employer.

For instance, a state may have a law that says that qualified citizens must serve jury duty unless they come within one of the statutory exceptions. The employer does not want the employee to miss work by serving jury duty. The employee serves jury duty and is terminated by the employer. The employee sues the employer for unjust dismissal. The employer counters with the at-will doctrine, which states that the employer can terminate the employee for any reason the employer wishes to use. Many courts have then held that the employer's termination of the employee under these circumstances constitutes a violation of public policy. That is, by the legislature passing such a law requiring jury duty service, it thus has been legislatively determined that serving jury duty is a public policy that should be upheld. Thus, terminating the employee for fulfilling that statutory duty is a violation of public policy by the employer. For the court to allow an employer to terminate an employee who upholds this public policy would be inconsistent with the public policy exhibited by the statute; therefore, the employer's termination of the employee will not be upheld.

Scenario

In one Washington State Supreme Court case, the court ruled that an employer violated public policy when it fired an armored-truck driver after the driver left the vehicle in order to rescue a robbery hostage. In that case, the driver was making a routine stop at a bank. When he saw the bank's manager running from the bank followed by a man wielding a knife, he locked the truck's door and ran to her rescue. While the woman was saved, the driver was fired for violating his employer's policy prohibiting him from leaving his vehicle. The court held that his termination violated the public policy encouraging such "heroic conduct." Understanding the confusion sometimes left in the wake of decisions surrounding public policy, the court noted that "this holding does not create an affirmative legal duty requiring citizens to intervene in dangerous life threatening situations. We simply observe that society values and encourages voluntary rescuers when a life is in danger. Additionally, our adherence to this public policy does nothing to invalidate [the firm's] work rule regarding drivers' leaving the trucks. The rule's importance cannot be understated, and drivers do subject themselves to a great risk of harm by leaving the driver's compartment. Our holding merely forbids [the firm] from firing [the driver] when he broke the rule because he saw a woman who faced imminent life-threatening harm, and he reasonably believed his intervention was necessary to save her life. Finally, by focusing on the narrow public policy encouraging citizens to save human lives from life threatening situations, we continue to protect employers from frivolous lawsuits."[1]

While the courts that have adopted the exception agree that the competing interests of employers and society require that the exception be recognized, as evidenced by the Gardner case, above, there is considerable disagreement in connection with what *is* the public policy and what constitutes a violation of the policy. In one of the leading cases in this area, the Illinois court stated that "the Achilles heel of the principle lies in the definition of public policy."

Some states have included "whistle-blowing" under the public policy theory. In whistle-blowing, the employee is terminated after blowing the whistle on the employer for some wrongdoing the employer is allegedly engaged in and may even want to involve the employee in. The employee is fired for reporting the employer's wrongdoings. As a matter of fact, in 1982 Congress enacted the Federal Whistleblower Statute, which prohibits retaliatory action against defense contractor employees who disclose information pertaining to a violation of the law governing defense contracts. The statute is administered by the Department of Defense and is enforced solely by that department; that is, an individual who suffers retaliatory action under this statute may not bring a private suit (common law recovery in certain states continues to exist and is the subject of this section). The statute states specifically that:

> An employee of a defense contractor may not be discharged, demoted, or otherwise discriminated against as a reprisal for disclosing to a Member of Congress or an authorized official of the Department of Defense or of Justice information relating to a substantial violation of law related to a defense contract (including the competition for or negotiation of a defense contract).

In addition, in 1989 Congress amended the Civil Service Reform Act of 1978 to include the Whistleblowers Protection Act, which expands the protection afforded to federal employees who report government fraud, waste, and abuse. The act applies to all employees appointed in the civil service who are engaged in the performance of a federal function and are supervised by a federal official. Employees of federal contractors, therefore, are not covered by the Act since they are hired by the contractor and not the government itself.

A number of states also have enacted whistle-blowing statutes, including California, Connecticut, Iowa, Maine, Michigan, Minnesota, New York, Rhode Island, South Dakota, and Utah. State whistle-blowing statutes are generally more broad in their terms than the antiretaliation provisions contained in civil rights laws and other statutes and that protect workers who report a variety of forms of violations. On the other hand, the majority of state statutes protect only those employees who work in the public sector, so private sector employees are left with little recourse after a re-

---

[1]*Gardner v. Loomis Armored, Inc.,* 128 Wash. 2d 931, 913 P.2d 377 (1996).

taliatory discharge unless the statute forming the basis of their complaint contains a specific antiretaliation provision (see Exhibit 1–2).

If there is a statute permitting an employee to do a certain thing or to pursue certain rights, the employer must be careful not to terminate employees for engaging in such activity. Examples of this type of legislation include state statutes permitting the employee to file a workers' compensation claim for on-the-job injuries sustained by the employee. The employee files the claim and is terminated by the employer for doing so. If the employee sues for unjust dismissal or retaliatory discharge, and the state is one that recognizes the public policy exception to the at-will doctrine, the employee will win.

PALMATEER V. INTERNATIONAL HARVESTER COMPANY
85 Ill.2d 124, 421 N.E.2d 876 (1981)

Ray Palmateer had worked for International Harvester (IH) for 16 years at the time of his discharge. Palmateer sued IH for retaliatory discharge, claiming that he was terminated because he supplied information to local law enforcement authorities regarding a co-worker's criminal activities and for offering to assist in the investigation and trial of the co-worker if necessary.

Simon, J.

[The court discusses the history of the tort of retaliatory discharge in Illinois and explains that the law will not support the termination of an at-will employment relationship where the termination would contravene public policy.] But the Achilles heel of the principle lies in the definition of public policy. When a discharge contravenes public policy in any way, the employer has committed a legal wrong. However, the employer retains the right to fire workers at will in cases "where no clear mandate of public policy is involved."

There is no precise definition of the term. In general, it can be said that public policy concerns what is right and just and what affects the citizens of the State collectively. It is to be found in the State's constitution and statutes and, when they are silent, in its judicial decisions. Although there is no precise line of demarcation dividing matters that are the subject of public policies from matters purely personal, a survey of cases in other States

involving retaliatory discharge shows that a matter must strike at the heart of a citizen's social rights, duties, and responsibilities before the tort will be allowed.

It is clear that Palmateer has here alleged that he was fired in violation of an established public policy. There is no public policy more basic, nothing more implicit in the concept of ordered liberty than the enforcement of a State's criminal code. There is no public policy more important or more fundamental than the one favoring the effective protection of the lives and property of citizens.

No specific constitutional or statutory provision requires a citizen to take an active part in the ferreting out and the prosecution of crime, but public policy nevertheless favors citizen crime-fighters. Public policy favors Palmateer's conduct in volunteering information to the law enforcement agency. Palmateer was under a statutory

---

EXHIBIT 1–2   States with Only Public Sector Whistle-blower Protection Statutes

States with Only Public Sector Whistle-blower Protection Statutes

Alaska, Arizona, Colorado, Delaware, Georgia,[2] Indiana, Kansas, Kentucky, Maryland,[1] Missouri, Oklahoma, Oregon, Pennsylvania,[3] South Carolina, South Dakota, Texas, Utah, Washington,[4] West Virginia, Wisconsin[2]

[1] Maryland restricts coverage to employees and classified-service applicants within the executive branch of state government.

[2] Georgia and Wisconsin exclude employees of the office of the governor, the legislature, and the courts.

[3] Pennsylvania's law excludes teachers, although school administrators are covered. Pennsylvania also has a separate law governing public-utility employees.

[4] Washington has separate laws covering state employees and local government employees.

States with Both Private and Public Sector Whistle-blower Protection

California, Connecticut,[2] Florida, Hawaii, Illinois, Iowa, Louisiana, Maine, Michigan, Minnesota,[1] New Hampshire,[1] New Jersey, New York, North Carolina, North Dakota, Ohio, Rhode Island, Tennessee[3]

[1] The laws in Minnesota and New Hampshire specifically exclude independent contractors.

[2] Connecticut has separate laws extending whistleblower protection to public service, nuclear-power, and state and local employees who report hazardous conditions.

[3] Tennessee has two whistleblower laws, one that covers only local school-system employees, and the other covering any employee who reports, or refuses to participate in, illegal activities.

—Separate laws in Nevada cover state employees and peace officers.

—Montana also protects public and private-sector whistleblowers through its Wrongful Discharge from Employment Act.

Source: The Bureau of National Affairs, Inc., Individual Employment Rights Manual, No. 133, 505:28–29 (Jan. 1995).

---

duty to further assist officials when requested to do so.

The foundation of the tort of retaliatory discharge lies in the protection of public policy, and there is a clear public policy favoring investigation and prosecution of criminal offenses. Palmateer has stated a cause of action for retaliatory discharge.

Case Questions

1. Is there a difference between the court's protection of an employee who reports a rape by a co-worker, or the theft of a car, and an employee who is constantly reporting the theft of the company's paper clips and pens?

2. Should the latter employee in the above question be protected? Consider that the court in *Palmateer* remarked that "the magnitude of the crime is not the issue here. It was the General Assembly who decided that the theft of a $2 screwdriver was a problem that should be resolved by resort to the criminal justice system."

3. What are other areas of public policy that might offer protection to terminated workers?

GREEN V. RALEE ENGINEERING COMPANY
78 Cal.Rptr.2d 16 (Cal. 1998)

An employee was terminated after calling attention to the fact that parts that had failed inspection were still being shipped to purchasers. He sued for wrongful discharge, asserting a public policy exception to the at-will employment rule. The court agreed that the termination violated public policy.

Chin, J.

Richard Green was a quality control inspector for Ralee Engineering Company, a fuselage and wing component manufacturer who supplied parts to airplane assembly companies. One of Green's responsibilities included inspecting parts before they were shipped to the assembly companies. Green noticed that Ralee Engineering was shipping parts to assembly companies even when those parts failed the inspections his team had performed. During a two-year period, Green called this practice to the attention of his immediate superiors and various management personnel, including the company president. Citing a lack of business, Green was dismissed from Ralee in 1991 after serving the company for 23 years. Green admitted he was an at-will employee but filed a wrongful discharge suit for alleging that a number of less-experienced inspectors than Green were retained and that the real reason for his dismissal was retaliation for his objections to the defective parts. Green argued that the discharge fell within the nationally well-recognized exception to the at-will employment providing tort damages where an employee was discharged for a reason that violated an important public policy.

May administrative regulations be a source of fundamental public policy that limits an employer's right to discharge an otherwise at-will employee? Although our legislature has determined that an employment contract is generally terminable at either party's will, we have created a narrow exception to this rule by recognizing that an employer's right to discharge an at-will employee is subject to limits that fundamental public policy imposes. At-will employees may recover tort damages from their employers if they can show they were discharged in contravention of fundamental public policy.

Employees who assert wrongful discharge claims must show that the important public interests they seek to protect are "tethered to fundamental policies that are delineated in constitutional or statutory provisions." Here, we address a related, albeit narrow issue. We must decide whether particular administrative regulations implementing the Federal Aviation Act of 1958, a public safety statute that created the Federal Aviation Administration (FAA), should be included as a source of fundamental public policy that limits an employer's right to discharge an at-will employee. Like the Court of Appeal, we conclude they should.

We continue to believe that, aside from constitutional policy, the legislature, and not the courts, is vested with the responsibility to declare the public policy of the state. Recognizing this important distinction, however, does not allow us to ignore the fact that statutorily authorized regulations that effectuate the legislature's purpose to ensure commercial airline safety are "tethered to" statutory provisions. . .

* * * *

Defendant argues principally that, even if we assume it did everything plaintiff claimed, its conduct violated no public policy embodied in a constitutional or statutory provision. Consequently, defendant argues, plaintiff's discharge fails to qualify as a wrongful discharge.

As we explain, we agree with the Court of Appeal in concluding that the federal safety regulations promulgated to address important public safety concerns may serve as a source of fundamental public policy. The regulations satisfy our requirement that the action be tethered to fundamental policies delineated in a statutory or constitutional provision. . .

* * * *

Public policy cases fall into one of four categories: the employee (1) refused to violate a statute; (2) performed a statutory obligation; (3) exercised a constitutional or statutory right or privilege; or (4) reported a statutory violation for the public's benefit. . . . In order to provide an exception to the at-will mandate, the policy must be "public" in that it "affects society at large" rather than the individual, must have been articulated at the time of discharge, and must be "fundamental" and "substantial."

The limitation on public policy sources (that they must be supported by either constitutional or statutory provisions) grew from our belief that "public policy as a concept is notoriously resistant to precise definition, and that courts should venture into this area, if at all, with great care and due deference to the judgment of the legislative branch" in order to avoid judicial policy-making. . . .

* * * *

. . . The question we now address is whether important public safety regulations governing commercial airline safety may provide a basis for declaring a public policy in the context of a retaliatory discharge action.

Federal regulations promoting the proper manufacture and inspection of component airline parts advance the important public policy objectives. In the Federal Aviation Act of 1958 Congress declared the public interest in commercial air safety. . . .

* * * *

Plaintiff performed the FAA-required inspections on the parts intended for use in Boeing aircraft to further a fundamental policy: "to ensure that each article produced conforms to the type design and is in a condition for safe operation." Therefore, this regulation-based fundamental public policy may serve as the foundation for plaintiff's claim. It furthers important safety policies affecting the public at large and does not merely serve either the employee's or employer's personal or proprietary interest. As we noted, "[t]here is no public policy more important or more fundamental than the one favoring the effective protection of the lives and property of citizens."

* * * *

We emphasize that not all administrative regulations can support such claims, but only those that implicate substantial public policies. It is insufficient for employees to allege that they were discharged for refusing to violate a statute or follow a statutory duty; they must also allege that the statute in question was designed to protect the public or advance some substantial public policy goal. Employees must do the same when alleging a discharge for refusing to follow administrative regulations that implement an important statutory objective. In the case of both statutes and regulations based on statutes, courts must distinguish between those that promote a "clearly mandated public policy" and those that do not. . . .

We conclude that the public policy behind federal regulations concerning airline safety has a basis in statutory provisions, consistent with our rule that the public policy giving rise to a wrongful termination action have a basis in a constitutional or statutory provision. Congress has specifically directed the FAA to assign, maintain, and enhance safety and security as the highest priorities in air commerce and to regulate air commerce "in a way that best promotes its safety." Our judicial decisions favor protecting employees who vindicate important public policy interests. Allowing defendant to discharge plaintiff with impunity after he sought to halt or eliminate its alleged inspection practices would only undermine the important and fundamental public policy favoring safe air travel. By including significant administrative safety regulations promulgated to serve important FAA mandates as a source of fundamental public policy limiting an employer's right to discharge an otherwise at-will employee, we effectively guarantee that employers do not exercise their right to terminate their employees at will in a way that undermines more important public safety objectives. AFFIRMED and REMANDED.

Case Questions

1. Not all of the justices agreed with this opinion. Do you agree with the majority's opinion? Why or why not?

2. Do you think an important factor in this case was the airline industry and the fact that safety of air travel was an issue?

3. The court notes that it should determine what policy should be considered "public policies" in relation to these types of causes of action. Do you agree? Who do you think should determine such public policies—the courts, the legislature (state or federal), employers, or employees?

In determining what exactly constitutes public policy, one should look to two factors: clarity and impact. In evaluating the clarity, or substantiality, of the policy, the employer should look to both the definiteness and weight of the policy. For instance, a statute that specifically protects individuals from discharge if they leave work to tend to a family emergency clearly articulates a public policy in that regard. On the other hand, if the basis for the employee's claim of public policy is one line in the legislative history of the statute, which was not later incorporated into the statute, such a policy may not have the same clarity of mandate as would the former.

Generally, courts require that the statement of public policy be rooted in a statutory or constitutional provision. In that way, courts are able to maintain some type of consistency among cases. This allows managers some degree of predictability in terms of the consequences of their employment decisions.

In evaluating the impact of the policy, the employer should look to the impact of the discharge on the policy. For instance, will this discharge discourage others from exercising their rights, or discourage compliance with that policy, and, therefore, frustrate the policy itself? Further, is the satisfaction of that policy dependent on the cooperation of the employees, and such cooperation would also be impacted? Accordingly, the focus in the latter inquiry is not on the effect of the discharge on this individual employee, but on society as a whole and the future impact of the policy. As noted by one scholar in this area, the burden on the individual discharged employee is insufficient to support a cause of action, because it is offset by the employer's legitimate interests in maximizing employee control, efficiency, and productivity.

Other reasons for termination that, at first blush, appear to be solid bases for claims of wrongful termination are not so protected. For example, where an

Public Policy determined by:
1. Statutes or constitutional provisions.
2. Impact of the discharge on the policy.

employee was discharged for seeking the assistance of an attorney after receiving a poor evaluation, the Seventh Circuit court held that the termination was proper. Or where an employee is discharged for performing acts that one would like to believe society should encourage, such acts are not necessarily protected. The determination will depend on the precedent of the jurisdiction in which the termination occurs.

While some states allow these exceptions articulated above, but do not allow for an extension of the doctrine beyond that, other states remain reticent in their denial of the public policy exception to at-will employment. For instance, the appellate court in New York held that an employee who was terminated for refusing to participate in illegal schemes designed to defraud the IRS, and for reporting these activities to a supervisor, could not maintain an action for wrongful discharge.

Supporting this line of court decisions is the principle that any modification to at-will employment should come from the legislature, either state or federal. Where there is a clear statement of public policy from the legislature, these courts are more likely to allow the public policy exception; however, where no clear mandate exists, the courts posit that any declaration of public policy would entail stepping over the line that divides the formation of law and the application of law.

Breach of Implied Covenant of Good Faith and Fair Dealing

Implied in every contract is a duty of good faith and fair dealing in its performance and its enforcement. This requirement should not be confused with a contractual requirement of "good cause" prior to termination. A New York court defined the duty as follows:

> In every contract there is an implied covenant that neither party shall do anything which will have the effect of destroying or injuring the right of the other party to receive the fruits of the contract, which means that in every contract there exists an implied covenant of good faith and fair dealing. While the public policy exception to the at-will doctrine looks to the law to judge the employer's actions and deems them violations of public policy or not, the breach of implied covenant of good faith looks instead to the actions between the parties to do so.

Covenant of good faith and fair dealing
Implied contractual obligation to act in good faith in the fulfillment of each party's contractual duties.

Where the implied **covenant of good faith and fair dealing** is recognized as an exception to the at-will doctrine, courts have implied that any agreement between the employer has inherent in it, unless specifically contracted out, a promise that the parties will deal with each other fairly and in good faith. Thus, with an implied covenant of good faith and fair dealing, the employer and employee may have entered into a contract of employment, but the particulars of why and when an employee could be terminated were not specifically included by the parties. The employee is then terminated for what the employee feels is an unwarranted reason. The court looks to the contract and the matter is not covered by the contract. The court then looks to the facts to see if, in interpreting what the contract does in fact cover, it is likely that the situation presented is in keeping with that.

Only 13 states consistently recognize this covenant as an exception to at-will employment. Some states allow the cause of action but limit the damages awarded to those that would be awarded under a breach of contract claim, while other states allow the terminated employee to recover higher tort damages.

In connection with scenario 2, discussed at the beginning of the chapter, Mark Richter may have a claim against his employer for breach of the covenant of good faith and fair dealing. Mark's employer is, in effect, denying Mark the fruits of his labor.

Scenario

Critics of this implied agreement argue that, where an agreement is specifically nondurational, there should be no expectation of guaranteed employment of any length. As long as both parties are aware that the relationship may be terminated at any time, it would be extremely difficult to prove that either party acted in bad faith in terminating the relationship. Courts have supported this contention in holding that the implied covenant does not recognize the balance between the employee's interest in maintaining her or his employment and the employer's interest in running its business as it sees fit. "The absence of good cause to discharge an employee does not alone give rise to an enforceable claim for breach of a condition of good faith and fair dealing." To the contrary, employers may terminate an individual for any reason, as long as the true reason is not contradictory to public policy.

COOMBS V. GAMER SHOE CO.
778 P.2d 885 (Mont. 1989)

David Coombs began working for Gamer Shoe Company in 1977 and was promoted to store manager soon thereafter, then later to buyer of children's and men's shoes. In August 1986, because of poor economic conditions, Gamer decided to close the store at which Coombs worked at the end of the lease and to reduce wages until that time. After the store was closed, no one was hired to replace Coombs as a buyer. Coombs felt that Gamer should have found a place for him within some other part of the company, since he was a loyal and satisfactory employee, and that the implied covenant of good faith and fair dealing required this result. The court disagreed and found that Gamer acted appropriately.

Harrison, J.

Even if the implied covenant of good faith and fair dealing governs the employment relationship, an employer may still terminate an employee as long as the employer gives a fair and honest reason.

In the instant case, it is undisputed that

Gamer had for some period of time experienced financial difficulties that necessitated closing several stores including [Coombs's] store. Although appellant argues that respondent should have made a more particularized proof regarding economic necessity, facts and figures certainly are not required when all parties admit that the business was in trouble and the business actually closed. Coombs knew of the economic difficulties of Gamer in general and of [Coombs's] store in particular. For some time prior to his termination, he knew that [his] store might close and that his job was in jeopardy.

Although Gamer did tell Coombs that it would try to find a place for him, Coombs testified that these assurances were not promises and did not guarantee him continuing employment with Gamer. Coombs also concedes that he had no right to continued employment based on seniority. As well, Coombs testified that Gamer did not terminate him for cause. In short, the record establishes that Gamer discharged Coombs for legitimate economic reasons. Therefore, Gamer did not violate the covenant of good faith and fair dealing implied in its employment relationship with Coombs.

Case Questions

1. What elements would have been necessary for Coombs to prove in order to uphold a breach of the implied covenant of good faith and fair dealing? Are there any other possible bases for his claim of wrongful discharge?

2. Can you think of circumstances where a company *would* have an obligation to relocate someone after having terminated her or his position?

3. Under what circumstances would Gamer's promise to Coombs that it would "try to find a place for him" be an enforceable agreement?

Breach of Implied Contract

Implied contract
A contract that is not expressed, but, instead, is created by other words or conduct of the parties involved.

In some cases, the court may take a written employment contract and impose on that existing contract an implied covenant of good faith and fair dealing. But what happens when the parties are not acting pursuant to a specific contractual agreement, yet there seems to be an injustice done? That is where **implied contracts** come in. The court finds such contracts from several different sources. Primarily, it creates them from the acts of the parties. What acts will lead the court to find an implied contract vary from situation to situation.

It behooves employers to beware of this area. In recent years, courts have been willing to find contracts implied from statements made during preemployment interviews about the candidate becoming a "permanent" employee or from conversations quoting yearly or other periodic salaries. In such cases, when the employee has been terminated in less than the time quoted in the salary (e.g., telling the employee the job pays $50,000 per year), then the employee has been able to maintain an action for the remainder of the salary, on the theory that there was an implied contract created of a year's duration. The employee being released before the year is up, for other than good cause, results in liability for the salary remaining on the year's contract.

Torosyan v. Boehringer Ingelheim Pharmaceuticals, Inc.
662 A.2d 89 (Conn. 1995)

After being given assurances of job security, an applicant was hired, then later terminated. The employee sued for a breach of an implied contract, using statements made by the employer as the basis of his claim. The court permitted the cause of action to survive a motion to dismiss.

Peters, C.J.

* * * *

At the outset, we note that all employer–employee relationships not governed by express contracts involve some type of implied "contract" of employment. "There cannot be any serious dispute that there is a bargain of some kind; otherwise, the employee would not be working." To determine the contents of any particular implied contract of employment, the factual circumstances of the parties' relationship must be examined in light of legal rules governing unilateral contracts.

Pursuant to the legal principles governing such contracts, in order to find that an implied contract of employment incorporates specific representations orally made by the employer or contained in provisions in an employee manual, the trier of fact is required to find the following subordinate facts. Initially, the trier of fact is required to find that the employer's oral representations or issuance of a handbook to the employee was an "offer"—i.e., that it was a promise to the employee that, if the employee worked for the company, his or her employment would thereafter be governed by those oral or written statements, or both. If the oral representations and/or the handbook constitute an "offer," the trier of fact then is required to find that the employee accepted that offer. Subsequent oral representations or the issuance of subsequent handbooks must be evaluated by the same criteria. To be incorporated into the implied contract of employment, any such representation or handbook must constitute an offer to modify the preexisting terms of employment by substituting a new implied contract for the old. Furthermore, the proposed modifications, like the original offers, must be accepted.

Typically, an implied contract of employment does not limit the terminability of an employee's employment but merely includes terms specifying wages, working hours, job responsibilities and the like. Thus "[a]s a general rule, contracts of permanent employment, or for an indefinite term, are terminable at will."

* * * *

. . . The plaintiff testified that certain statements were made to him in the context of an employment interview in direct response to his inquiries about job security. One of those statements was that if the plaintiff did a good job, the defendant would take care of him. Another statement was that the plaintiff's employment would be governed by an employment manual. The offer letter sent to the plaintiff neither stated that it contained the entire terms of the employment offer nor disclaimed any guarantees of job security. The defendant's oral representations were material to the plaintiff's decision to move from California and accept employment with the defendant. The employee manual was provided to the plaintiff on the first day of work, and he immediately proceeded to read it to ensure that it was consistent with the defendant's representations. The manual explicitly qualified the defendant's right to discharge with the words "for cause." The manual also stated that every employee could speak to an executive officer about "job-related problems which [he or she] may feel cannot be worked out successfully with [his or her] immediate supervisor or manager." Finally, after reading the manual, the plaintiff continued to work for the defendant for several years.

* * * *

Because the defendant does not allege that there was "just cause" for the discharge in the absence of actual falsification of documents by the plaintiff, we AFFIRM the trial court's determination in this case that there was no cause for the plaintiff's discharge.

Case Questions

1. Do you agree with the court's decision? Why or why not?

2. If the employer had later distributed a new manual that specifically stated that all workers were subject to "at will" employment, would this case have been decided differently?

3. What can companies do to avoid liability like that found in the above case?

Notwithstanding some of the court's comments in the above case, the Superior Court in North Carolina held to the contrary:

> This court has repeatedly held that in the absence of a contractual agreement between an employer and an employee establishing a definite term of employment, the relationship is presumed to be terminable at the will of either party, without regard to the quality of performance of either party . . . 'If you do your job, you'll have a job,' is not sufficient to make this indefinite hiring terminable only for cause. *Kurtzman v. Applied Analytical Inds., Inc.* 1997 WL 699199 (Sup. Ct. N.C. 1997).

In addition, the court noted that there should be no exception based on an employee's decision to move her or his residence or other burdens that the new position might have placed on the employee.

Scenario

Regarding scenario 1, Emma Bina may have a claim against her new employer based on a breach of an implied employment contract. Emma accepted her position with the understanding that, in exchange for sacrificing her previous position and the sale of her house, and so on, she would be employed as long as she performed satisfactory work. Her work was more than satisfactory, yet she still lost her job. If this could have been avoided (i.e., the company did not go bankrupt or something similar), she might have a claim. (The majority of courts would agree with the Torosyan case above.)

Employment Policy Manuals. Employment policy manuals may, in fact, be a form of implied contract. Employers use policy manuals as a means of organizing workplace policies and communicating them to employees. Employment policy manuals are the most logical way to handle the matter of workplace policies, because they present the employee, manager, and supervisor with one central place to search for policies when issues arise. However, aside from the convenience, they may present problems when it comes to unwittingly creating contracts of employment that take the employer out of the employment-at-will situation in which the employer maintains such a modicum of control over terminating the employee and, instead, places the employee in the implied contract situation, which may not be to the employer's advantage. Nobody wants to become bound to a contract when they are not even aware that they are doing so.

Court cases in 34 states have held that the rules and regulations set forth in the employee handbook or personnel manual may form a contract between the employer and employee, and the employee, by accepting the employment, becomes bound by the policies, as does the employer. The employer's failure to then abide by the policies may be cause of subsequent litigation and liability toward an employee harmed by the employee's failure to do so. Employers should be careful when making policy statements in the manual, such as that employees will only be terminated for good cause, or that, once the employees successfully complete their probationary period, they then become "permanent" employees. These have been held to be statements that created binding agreements between the employer and employee, and the employer's later termination of the employee, being inconsistent with those statements, has resulted in liability.

STEVE HICKS V. METHODIST MEDICAL CENTER
593 N.E.2d 119 (Ill. App. 3d Dist. 1992)

Plaintiff Steven Hicks was terminated in violation of his employee handbook. Defendant Methodist Medical Center claimed that it was allowed to modify the handbook at any time pursuant to a disclaimer found in the book. The District Court entered judgment for the employer and Hicks appealed.

Gorman, J.

Defendant's handbook contained a disclaimer. In order to negate any promises made in contract provisions, a disclaimer must be conspicuous. The disclaimer itself was located at page 38 of the handbook. It was not highlighted, printed in capital letters, or in any way prominently displayed. Furthermore, the disclaimer was not entitled "Disclaimer," but was located under a section headed "Revisions." This disclaimer was not conspicuous and so did not negate the promises made in the handbook's provisions. We hold that a contract existed. [The court affirmed the lower court's opinion on other grounds.]

JONES V. LAKE PARK CARE CENTER, INC.
569 N.W.2d 369 (Iowa 1997)

An employee who was not terminated in conformity with the procedures specified in the employee manual sued her employer for breach of an implied contract created by the manual. The court agreed with the employee.

Becky Jones started working as an administrator in the care center at Lake Park, Iowa, a 51-bed nursing home with approximately 40 employees. The nursing home was sold to Pamela and James Rogers in July of that year. Pamela Rogers was the licensee and the Care Center operated the facility.

Shortly after the Rogerses purchased the Lake Park facility, they created a handbook. The handbooks were distributed to all staff members including Becky. Each employee was asked to sign and return a receipt to the administrator to acknowledge receiving a handbook. The 24-page handbook contained a welcome, general policies on hiring, schedules, time cards, paydays, resignation, benefits, disciplinary action, additional miscellaneous policies, and an organizational chart. All the employees received the handbook and returned a signed receipt. Becky signed a receipt. The receipts were placed in each employee's personnel file at the Care Center.

The employee manual provided for progressive discipline if an employee violated workplace rules. However, when Becky was terminated, she was given only a termination notice. Becky brought an action against her employer, claiming that the Care Center breached its employment contract with her and the Rogerses intentionally interfered with the employment contract.

Andreasen, J.

* * * *

In Iowa, employment relations are presumed to be at-will. As a general rule, if no employment contract exists, either party may terminate the relationship for any lawful reason at any time. Two exceptions to the general rule are: (1) when a discharge violates a well-established and defined public policy, and (2) when an implied contract of employment is created by a handbook or employee policy manual guaranteeing that discharge will occur only under certain circumstances.

An implied contract of employment can arise from an employee handbook if: (1) the handbook is sufficiently definite in its terms to create an offer, (2) it is communicated to and accepted by the employee so as to create an acceptance, and (3) the employee provides consideration. The Rogers do not contend the handbook was not communicated to Becky or that she did not provide consideration. They do, however, deny that the terms of the handbook were sufficiently definite so as to create a contract. . . .

* * * *

Becky argued, and the trial court agreed, the language of the handbook was sufficiently definite to create an employment contract. As a result, Becky insists the progressive discipline policy gave her contractual rights that the Rogers violated by summarily terminating her. To determine whether the language of an employee handbook creates a contract we look at the following factors:

(1) Is the handbook in general and the progressive disciplinary procedures in particular mere guidelines or a statement of policy, or are they directives?

(2) Is the language of the disciplinary procedures detailed and definite or general and vague?

(3) Does the employer have the power to alter the procedures at will or are they invariable?

The key to determining whether a contract has been created is whether a reasonable employee upon reading the handbook would believe they had been guaranteed certain protections by their employer. Here, the handbook stated it was "to be regarded as binding on both the employee and management." The "disciplinary actions" section of the handbook began with the statement:

> The purpose of these rules is to define the employee's rights, not to restrict them. They exist to protect the best interest of all employees. The rules are itemized, along with the corrective action for each group of rules, to assure the employees are treated fairly and with consistency.

The progressive discipline policy divides offenses into four groups. Three of the four groups contain a statement to the effect that the list of offenses was not intended to be all inclusive. Specific disciplinary actions were prescribed for each group. The disciplinary steps to be taken for each infraction and any subsequent violations were summarized in a table. The language used in the policy constitutes more than mere guidelines. It requires specific action to be taken for different levels of violations and, thus, meets the first and second factors of definiteness.

The Care Center reserved the right to change or revoke the employee handbook. The reservation of that right might indicate an employee should not rely on the procedures outlined in the handbook. However, until management exercised its authority to change the terms of the handbook,

the employee's reliance on its provisions was reasonable because the handbook was "binding" on both the employee and management. Merely reserving the right to change the provisions is not sufficient to defeat the creation of an implied contract. To ensure no implied contract is created by a handbook, the employer would be wise to include an appropriately drafted disclaimer. Here, no disclaimer was included in the handbook. We find there was sufficient evidence to support the court's finding that an implied contract of employment was created by the handbook.

Next, we must consider whether there is evidence that this employment agreement was breached. The handbook listed various infractions and to which group they belonged. The gravity of the violations is the distinguishing feature separating one group of violations from another. For example, failing to maintain acceptable standards of personal hygiene is a group one violation while theft of company property is a group four violation.

The stated reason for Becky's termination was "inability to provide continuity in the facility by failure to provide effective leadership." Under the terms of the progressive disciplinary policy, the first three groups required a written warning. Becky did not receive such a warning. Instead, she was summarily discharged. There is substantial evidence in the record that the Care Center breached its employment contract with Becky.

Case Questions:

1. Shouldn't an employee be bound by anything written in an employee handbook when the employee signs an acknowledgment that she or he has read the book completely, no matter what page a disclaimer is on?

2. As an employer, how would you draft and print a disclaimer so that you would be certain it was enforceable?

3. Do you believe it is fair for an employer to insert a clear disclaimer allowing it to modify the employee handbook at a moment's notice?

Introduction to Wrongful Discharge

Compensatory damages
Money damages given to a party to compensate for direct losses due to an injury suffered.

Punitive damages
Money damages designed to punish flagrant wrongdoers and to deter them and others from engaging in similar conduct in the future.

At-will employment
An employment relationship where there is no contractual obligation to remain in the relationship; either party may terminate the relationship at any time, for any reason, as long as the reason is not prohibited by law, such as for discriminatory purposes.

Constructive discharge
Occurs when the employee is given no reasonable alternative but to terminate the employment relationship; considered an involuntary act on the part of the employee.

In May 1992, 124 million dollars was awarded in a wrongful discharge case. Five million dollars was awarded to an employee in California in 1991. Do these sound like judgments you want to have to pay to employees or ex-employees out of the coffers of your business? Probably not. You can think of far better ways to spend your money. After all, you're in business to *make* money, not to hand it away. But these judgments, rather than becoming less frequent, are becoming more so. They will be joined by the new **compensatory** and **punitive damages** that can now be awarded under Title VII. Employers that wish to give the "old heave ho" to their employees had better make sure the employee doesn't land in a pile of cash. The reason for much of this has been erosion of the at-will doctrine.

If there is no agreement or contract to the contrary, employment is considered to be **at will;** that is, either the employer or the employee may terminate the relationship at their will, as long as the reason for the termination was not prohibited by statute, such as a discharge on the basis of the employee's gender or race. Nevertheless, even where a discharge involves no discrimination nor a breach of contract, the termination may still be considered wrongful and the employer may be liable (called "wrongful discharge" or "unjust dismissal"). Therefore, in addition to ensuring that workplace policies do not wrongfully discriminate against employees on the basis of gender, race, religion, national origin, age, or disability, the employer must also beware of situations in which the employer's policy or action in a particular case can form the basis for unjust dismissal. Since such bases can be so diverse, the employer must be vigilant in watching this area, and employees must be fully aware of their rights, even though the relationship is considered at will.

Constructive Discharge

The "discharge" addressed in this chapter may be the usual firing case or may be based on constructive discharge. **Constructive discharge** exists where the employee is given no alternative but to quit her or his position; that is, the act of leaving was not truly voluntary. Therefore, while the employer did not, in fact, fire the worker, it was the actions of the employer that *caused* the worker to leave. Constructive discharge usually evolves from circumstances where an employer knows that it cannot really terminate an employee for one reason or another. So, to avoid being taken to court for wrongful termination, it creates an environment where the employee has no choice but to leave. If courts were to allow this type of treatment, those laws that restrict employers from wrongful termination, such as Title VII, would have no effect.

The test for constructive discharge is whether the employer made the working conditions *so intolerable that no reasonable employee should be expected to endure.* A minority of courts hold that the former employee must also show that the employer created the intolerable working conditions *with the specific intent of forcing the employee to quit.* To find constructive discharge, the circumstances complained of must be aggravated; aggravation may occur where there is one horrible event or a number of minor instances of hostile behavior.

Wrongful Discharge Based on Other Tort Liability

A tort is a violation of a duty, other than one owed when the parties have a contract. Where a termination happens because of intentional and outrageous conduct on the part of the employer and causes emotional distress to the employee, the employee may have a tort claim for a wrongful discharge in approximately half of the United States. For example, in one case, an employee was terminated because she was having a relationship with a competitor's employee. The court determined that forcing the employee to choose between her position at the company and her relationship with a male companion constituted outrageous conduct.

One problem exists in connection with a claim for physical or emotional damages under tort theories. In many states, an employee's damages are limited by workers' compensation laws. Where an injury is work-related, such as emotional distress as a result of discharge, these statutes provide that the workers' compensation process is a worker's exclusive remedy. An exception exists where a claim of injury is based solely on emotional distress; in that situation, many times workers' compensation will be denied. Therefore, in those cases, the employee may proceed against the employer under a tort claim. To avoid liability for this tort, the employer should ensure that the process by which an employee is terminated is respectful of the employee as well as mindful of the interests of the employer.

Where a discharge acts to defame the employee, there may be sufficient basis for a tort action for defamation. To sustain a claim for defamation, the employee must be able to show that (1) the employer made a false and defamatory statement about the employee, (2) the statement was communicated to a third party without the employee's consent, and (3) the communication caused harm to the employee. Claims of defamation usually arise where an employer makes statements about the employee to other employees or her or his prospective employers. This issue is covered in Chapter 16 relating to the employee's privacy rights and employer references.

Finally, where the termination results from a wrongful invasion of privacy, an employee may collect damages. For instance, where the employer wrongfully invades the employee's privacy, searches her purse, and consequently terminates her, the termination may be wrongful.

The Model Uniform Employment Termination Act

In August of 1991, the National Conference of Commissioners of Uniform State Laws issued the Model Uniform Employment Termination Act (UETA). The purpose was to attempt to bring some degree of uniformity to the patchwork of state laws addressing this area. While "uniform" acts are not required to be adopted by states, the purpose of drafting these types of laws is to offer suggestions for compromises of the various interests involved. Once a uniform act is proposed, states may either adopt the uniform act, adopt a similar version of the act, draft their own dissimilar statute, or adopt no statute at all.

For example, there is Uniform Commercial Code that regulates the sale of goods. Many states have adopted the Code in its entirety, while other states have adopted the majority of the Code and have included amendments of their own. The UETA, if adopted by a state, would supplant the case law for unlawful terminations with a uniform approach.

Because each state is free to develop employment-at-will on its own, the concept varies from state to state. A uniform act would promote predictability and uniformity of decisions. If it was adopted by the states there would not, for instance, be an employee permitted to recover for unjust dismissal because of whistle-blowing in one state, and, with the same facts, not be able to do so in another.

The most radical provision of the UETA states that an employer may not discharge an employee without good cause. In return, the employee would no longer have the right to bring a claim against the employer in court on the basis of wrongful discharge, but, instead, would be required by the UETA to pursue arbitration or some other form of state administrative procedure. "Good cause" in this context has been interpreted by the drafters of the UETA to mean a reasonable basis for discharge, including fighting, theft, intoxication or drug use, insubordination, incompetence, and excessive absenteeism or tardiness.

The act provides that the good cause requirement may also be satisfied if the employer can demonstrate its legitimate economic need for the discharge. Specifically, the act does not allow a termination in violation of a public policy derived from constitutional or statutory law, or a retaliatory termination of an employee who has blown the whistle on the employer. The employer and employee may, by express oral or written agreement, agree that the employee's failure to meet specified business-related standards of performance or the employee's commission or omission of specified business-related acts will constitute good cause for termination under the act. These standards would be effective only if they were consistently enforced and were not applied to a particular employee in a disparate manner without justification.

To qualify for UETA protection, the employee must have been working for the employer for no less than one year prior to the termination and for an average of 20 hours per week during the six-month period prior to the termination. Employers are to post a copy of the act or an approved summary in a prominent place in the work area. Violations of this provision may result in a civil fine. Employers may not retaliate against employees for, in any way, pursuing their rights under this act, including testifying, filing a claim, or otherwise.

While many scholars argue that the impact of the UETA would be greatly beneficial to employees and employers alike, no state has yet adopted the act. In fact, some legal pundits have been known to call it the "Menace to Employment Tranquility Act." The primary complaint about the act is that it is arbitrary—instead of providing for stability and predictability, the act requires interpretation and does *not* provide for simple resolution. One scholar notes, "Instead of providing a responsive and integrative solution to perceived defects in the at-will doctrine as applied, META proposes a regime that would compromise substantive claims, emasculate managerial discretion and beneficently bestow a cause of action to every employee subject to the Act." [Note: Mary Jean Navaretta, "The Model Employment Termination Act—More Aptly the Menace to Employment Tranquility Act: A Critique," 25 *Stetson Law Review* 1027 (1996).]

Management Considerations

Given the possibility of punitive damage awards in wrongful discharge actions, employers are cautioned regarding their interpretation and implementation of the at-will employment arrangement. Not only may a different arrangement exist—given implied contracts as well as contracts that arise from express statements within employment policy manuals and other literature produced by the employer—but the public policy exception may further modify the nature of the employer's rights to terminate at will. An employer is prohibited from acting in a manner that undermines public policy, however defined. Where the employer discharges an at-will employee, either for just cause or for no reason at all, the employer's actions are protected.

However, when the employee is terminated for exercising a protected right, for performing a public duty, for refusing to commit a crime or an immoral or unethical act, or for exposing the employer's or a co-worker's wrongdoings, the termination may be wrongful, and the employer may be liable for the payment of economic damages, as well as compensation for emotional distress and suffering.

To prevent temporary workers and independent contractors from being legally treated as employees, a firm must carefully structure the working relationship in a contract so as to limit the firm's control over the worker. The more control that the firm has over the worker and the more aspects of the employment relationship for which the firm has responsibility, the more likely the firm will be considered the employer of a temporary employee or independent contractor.

Employment at will is an area that is fraught with the potential of liability for employers. Not only can employees suing in this area often sue for compensatory and punitive damages, but the employees who can do so are not limited to an identifiable group such as women, or Asians, or the disabled—it can be any employee. It makes the employer's actions toward every employee take on even more added significance. The employer should *always* deal with employees honestly to limit this liability as much as possible. States are not uniform in their acceptance of the at-will erosions making headway into the at-will doctrine in recent years. Liability can change, literally from day to day. Not only may a case decided today change the existing law in the employer's state, this increasing erosion makes the idea of uniform laws all the more appealing to states.

Be careful of statements made to interviewees regarding promises of why an employee will be dismissed, or regarding salary or permanent status. Ensure that contracts for dismissed employees cannot be implied from acts the employer has done, like setting up the expectation of permanent employment by longevity, consistently great evaluation, and the like. It may mean, for the employer, that the employer has even less flexibility than desirable in this area. However, the employer's ability to control is most conclusive in determining liability.

Management Tips

- No matter the size of your firm, as long as you have hired one individual to work for you, you are considered an employer and potentially subject to numerous federal and other regulations.

- You are always allowed to hire the best person for a job; the law merely states that you may not make this decision based on prejudice or stereotypes. In order to avoid a wrongful discharge suit and, more importantly, to ensure the ethical quality of your decisions, don't fire someone for some reason that violates basic principles of dignity, respect, or social justice.

- You have the right to fire an employee for *any* reason as long as it is not for one of the specific reasons prohibited by law. On the other hand, if you don't have sufficient documentation or other evidence of the appropriate reason for your decision, a court might infer that your basis is discriminatory.

- While it is inconvenient, to say the least, when an employee reports wrongdoing occurring at your firm, under most circumstances, you may not retaliate against that person. Be sure to avoid even the *appearance* of retaliation, as the actual motivation for employment decisions is often difficult to prove.

- Since statements in an employee manual may be construed in some circumstances as contractual promises, review all documentation *as if* you will be bound to it as a contract.

- Have sufficient training for all employees who will conduct interviews, since the firm may be bound by promises made to applicants during interviews if the applicant relies on the promise in accepting a position.

Summary

- When an employer decides to terminate an employee, there is always a reason for the termination. That reason need not be fair, or even justified; the only restriction is that it should not be made on *improper* bases.

- To ensure that the discharge decision is not wrongful and to protect against a claim of wrongful discharge, employers should establish a discharge procedure to be followed in the course of every termination.

  1. The supervisor with the authority to make the termination decision should draft written responses to the following questions:

—What is the nature of the action to be taken?

—What is the factual basis for this action?

—Is there any evidence of this factual basis, oral or written?

—If this action is based on the employee's behavior, did the employee obtain permission or give notice of her or his intent to engage in this behavior prior to doing so? (For instance, if the employee needed to take time off for a stated purpose, did she or he first receive permission to do so?) [If permission has been granted, termination based on this behavior may constitute outrageous conduct.]

—If this action is based on the employee's behavior, is this behavior of the type in which she or he has a right or obligation to engage by law (such as jury duty, testifying pursuant to a subpoena, etc.)?

—If this action is based on the employee's behavior, is this a type of behavior that an employer ought to encourage (such as assisting in the investigation of a crime)?

—If this action is based on the employee's behavior, did this behavior harm us, as a firm? [Termination would be subject to greater scrutiny.]

—Is this action based on an omission or refusal to act on the part of the employee? If so, did the employee refuse to act in such a manner that could be construed as unethical, immoral, illegal, or humiliating?

2. Once the supervisor has responded to the above questions, the supervisor and an individual specifically chosen to review discharge decisions should review the responses to address whether they may give rise to liability. Where the potential exists, the employer is now better equipped to determine the costs and benefits of the anticipated action.

3. After a review of the facts and the supervisor's responses, it is in the employer's best interests to investigate the events leading to the discharge and to solicit a response from the employee relating to the possibility of termination. It allows the employee to feel as if she or he has had the opportunity to be heard. It also ensures that all of the relevant facts have been brought to the surface.

4. After the hearing, the supervisor and the termination "specialist" should review the information in light of earlier decisions and appropriate business judgment; consistency is crucial and the best defense.

Chapter-End Questions

1. Employer fired employee because employer did not like employee's husband, who was a rather loud and obnoxious type. When he came to office parties, he routinely wore everyone's nerves to a frazzle. Employee has no contract with employer and is not in a union. Does she have a cause of action for unjust dismissal?

2. For the following questions, think about them from the point of view of violation of public policy or breach of a covenant of good faith and fair dealing, and see what the outcome would be.

   a. Employee is discharged after advising the employer that he intended to file a medical claim under the company's group health insurance plan. (*Price v. Carmack Datsun, Inc.,* 485 N.E.2d 359 (Ill. 1985).)

   b. Employee reports patient abuse situations to the news media and is subsequently terminated. (*Rozier v. St. Mary's Hospital,* 411 N.E.2d 50 (Ill. App. Ct. 1980).)

   c. Employee starts a fight at work. The other employee, in self-defense, protects herself by fighting back. Both are terminated. Does the employee who was defending herself have a cause of action for unjust dismissal? (*McLaughlin v.*

Barclays American Corp., 385 S.E.2d 498 (N.C. 1989).)

d. A company's lawyer is terminated when he refuses to remove, from the company's files, documents that would be harmful to the company if they were given to opposing counsel under a discovery order in litigation the company is involved in. (*Herbster v. Northern American Co. for Life and Health Ins.,* 501 N.E.2d 343 (Ill. App. Ct. 1986), cert. denied, 484 U.S. 850 (1987).)

e. Employee is terminated because she married a coworker. (*McCluskey v. Clark Oil & Refining Corp.,* 498 N.E.2d 559 (Ill. App. Ct. 1986).)

f. Employee discovers that his supervisor is involved in a wrongdoing. The supervisor terminates the employee to prevent the employee from disclosing her wrongdoing to higher-level management. (*Adler v. American Standard Corp.,* 830 F.2d 1303 (4th Cir. 1987).)

g. Employee, a bartender, refuses to serve alcohol to intoxicated patron, though it is not a violation of state law to serve intoxicated patrons. Employee is terminated. (*Woodson v. AMF Leisureland,* 842 F.2d 699 (3d Cir. 1988).)

h. Employee is licensed to perform certain medical procedures, but he is terminated for refusing to perform a procedure he is not licensed to perform. (*O'Sullivan v. Mallon,* 390 A.2d 149 (N.J. Super. Ct. Law Div. 1978).)

i. Three woman were employed by a hotel chain, which required that its employees submit to polygraph examinations on demand. The three women signed an acknowledgment of that policy prior to taking their positions. However, when requested to do so, the three women refused to submit to the polygraph test and were discharged. The hotel is located in West Virginia, which, though it has no statute relating to the use or prohibition of polygraph tests, recognized one's protectable interest in privacy. The women sue the hotel for discharge in violation of public policy. (*Cordle v. General Hugh Mercer Corp.,* 325 S.E.2d 111 (W.Va. 1984).)

3. Dr. Pierce was hired by Ortho Pharmaceutical as an at-will employee to research drugs. After she was hired, she was assigned to perform research related to a drug called "loperamide," a foul-tasting medicine designed to assist in the treatment of diarrhea. Dr. Pierce voiced objections to the design of the drug, because saccharin was added to disguise its flavor; Dr. Pierce believed that saccharin should not be used, due to concerns relating to its safety. Believing that her assistance with this project would violate her Hippocratic oath as a doctor, she refused to participate in the testing of loperamide on humans. Eventually, Dr. Pierce resigned from the company, claiming constructive discharge for her failure to continue working on loperamide, which she believed was not only against public policy but also against her own personal code of ethics. Ortho Pharmaceuticals, however, claimed that there was no violation of public policy, especially given the fact that the Food and Drug Administration would have had to test and approve the drug prior to its dissemination to the public. What result? (*Pierce v. Ortho Pharmaceutical Corp.,* 417 A.2d 505 (N.J. 1980).)

4. Benecke and Schielke are former auditors for Lockheed. While working for Lockheed, they raised some concerns that their employer's CB5 mainframes were subjected to improper heating, resulting in cracks and warped areas. They were subsequently told by their supervisor not to investigate their

concerns. In violation of that direction, the two employees hired a metallurgist at their own expense to test the material in the mainframes. The tests reported defects in the material.

After a later meeting with the chairman of Lockheed and again voicing their concerns, they were discharged on the grounds that they had failed to conduct a formal audit of their allegations and had taken company property for testing without authorization. The former employees sued Lockheed for discharge in violation of public policy. (*Benecke, et al. v. Lockheed Corp.*, L.A. Superior Ct., C621967.)

5. Geary, a salesperson, complained of possible safety issues in connection with certain steel products produced by his employer, United States Steel Corporation. Geary voiced his concerns not only to his supervisors but all the way to the vice president of sales. The product was subsequently investigated and removed from the market. Thereafter, Geary was terminated. U.S. Steel's stated reason for the termination was that Geary ignored his employer's reporting structure and made a nuisance of himself in doing so; in addition, the employer noted that Geary was not responsible for or an expert in product safety. Geary, however, claims that he acted only in the best interests of his employer and the public. Who will prevail in a suit alleging wrongful discharge? (*Geary v. U.S. Steel Corp.*, 319 A.2d 174 (Penn. 1974).)

6. Grange was hired as a licensed practical nurse by Mount Desert Island Hospital. About seven months after he began working at the hospital, Grange began voicing complaints about his working conditions, as well as what he considered to be inept managerial policies. He also drafted written complaints, placed them in the hospital's suggestion box, and approached his supervisor. When he received little response, he sent a letter to the editor of the area newspaper detailing his complaints. The letter stated, "There is a high degree of frustration and resentment amongst the workers . . . Indeed, when only one nurse is out of work sick, the situation can become intolerable. Only very minimal patient care is given and safety standards are stretched to the limit and beyond . . . Please print this letter for the sake of public interest and free speech." Grange also circulated a petition among hospital employees, requesting an investigation of working conditions at the hospital. Over 100 employees signed the petition. The board of trustees thereafter and as a result decided to cancel its capital fund drive.

Grange left the hospital of his own accord but later attempted to obtain summer employment there and was refused. Grange claims that he was not hired in violation of public policy and in retaliation for his earlier activities. Are his activities protected? (*NLRB v. Mount Desert Island Hospital*, 695 F.2d 634 (1st Cir. 1982).)

7. The Duprees, Terry and Jerry, are former employees of UPS. They both started working for UPS as hourly union employees and were protected by union laws against being fired except "for cause." They were both promoted to managerial positions, which they accepted on the representation that they would retain job security since managerial positions were not provided with union protection. Soon after her promotion, Terry Dupree alleged that a senior manager, Pepper Simmons, was sexually harassing her. A few months after Terry Dupree's allegation, Simmons allegedly discovered that Terry was dating Jerry, who was in the same managerial level as Terry. Simmons, according to the Duprees, vowed to "get his job," and Jerry Dupree was soon fired for violating the UPS fraternization policy. The

Duprees say that it was their understanding that this policy only governed relations between supervisors and hourly employees, not relations between two supervisors. Terry Dupree filed a sexual harassment against Simmons, on which UPS took no disciplinary action. After Terry filed this complaint, her supervisors began "writing her up" for infractions of company policy. After several infractions, the UPS management offered her $12,000 to resign. She refused and was fired. Oklahoma recognizes a cause of action arising from the termination of an at-will employee against an employer in "cases in which the discharge is contrary to a clear mandate of public policy as articulated by constitutional, statutory or decisional law." What result? (*Dupree v. United Parcel Service, Inc.,* 956 F.2d 219 (10th Cir. 1992).)

8. Michael Corrigan received a written offer of employment on September 7, 1990, from Cactus International Trading Company outlining a compensation plan, commissions, profit sharing, insurance, benefits, leave time, and vacations. Corrigan accepted the job offer and, on September 14, 1990, he resigned from his previous employment. Cactus trained Corrigan and promised to provide him tile samples and other materials necessary to carry out his responsibilities as regional manager. However, once Corrigan started his job, Cactus failed to supply him with the necessary materials. On October 9, 1990, Corrigan was terminated. Corrigan filed a breach of contract and failure to deal fairly and in good faith actions against Cactus, and Cactus is urging the court to dismiss Corrigan's complaint with sanctions on the grounds that Corrigan was an at-will employee and that Cactus did not have an employment contract with him. What result?

(*Corrigan v. Cactus International Trading Co.,* 771 F.Supp 262 (N.D.Ill 1991).)

9. Patricia Meleen, a chemical dependency counselor, brought charges alleging wrongful discharge, defamation, and emotional distress against the Hazelden Foundation, a chemical dependency clinic, in regard to her discharge due to her alleged sexual relations with a former patient. Hazelden's written employment policies prohibited unprofessional and unethical conduct, including sexual contact between patients and counselors. A former patient alleged that Meleen had initiated a social and sexual relationship with him within one year of his discharge. A committee appointed by Hazelden told Meleen of the allegation against her and suspended her with pay in spite of Meleen's denial that she was involved in any improper relations or sexual contact with the former patient. Hazelden offered Meleen a nonclinical position, and, when she refused, she was dismissed. Is the dismissal wrongful? (*Meleen v. Hazelden Foundation,* 928 F.2d 795 (8th Cir. 1991).)

10. Judy Boyle was a lab helper for Vista Eyewear Company. As a lab assistant, she was responsible for hand-edging, hardening, and testing the eyeglasses manufactured and sold by the company. One of the eyeglass tests required by the FDA was a chem/drop-ball test that tested the glasses for resistance to breaking or shattering, or both. Mrs. Boyle claims that this test was not conducted by Vista, even though she and her coworkers were required to fill out a form for each pair of glasses confirming that the test had been conducted. Mrs. Boyle talked to David Baker, the president and co-owner of Vista, and he reassured her that he had ample insurance to cover any potential liabilities. Boyle reported the lack of testing

to the FDA, but Baker had another employee, Bob Bond, testify to the FDA that this charge was not true. Boyle was discharged a few weeks later for an unrelated reason. Does she have a claim for unjust dismissal? (*Boyle v. Vista Eyewear, Inc.,* 700 S.W.2d 859 (W.D.Mo. 1985).)

11. Max Huber was the agency manager at Standard Insurance's Los Angeles office. He was employed as an at-will employee, and his contract did not specify any fixed duration of guaranteed employment. Huber was discharged by the company after eight years, because of his alleged negative attitude, the company's increasing expense ratio, and the agency's decreasing recruiting. Huber provided evidence that he had never received negative criticism in any of his evaluations, and that his recruiting had been successful. Huber demonstrated that, even though the company had a decrease in recruitment during his employment, he himself had a net increase of contracted agents of 1,100 percent. Huber claims that he was discharged because he was asked to write a letter of recommendation about his supervisor, Canfield, whose termination was being considered. Johnson, Canfield's supervisor, was disappointed with the positive recommendation that Huber wrote, because it made Canfield's termination difficult to execute. Johnson is alleged to have transferred Huber to expedite Canfield's termination, and he eventually discharged Huber in retaliation for the positive letter of recommendation. If Huber files suit, what result? (*Huber v. Standard Insurance Co.,* 841 F.2d 980 (9th Cir. 1988).)

12. Wallis, a 55-year-old, was laid off from his job; but his employer agreed to pay him a specific sum of money for 10 years following his layoff if Wallis promised not to compete against him. Wallis and his employer did not have a written contract, but Wallis agreed to this deal on good faith. After a few payments, Wallis's employer stopped sending him the payments, and Wallis filed suit claiming that his employer breached its implied covenant of good faith and fair dealing. What result? (*Wallis v. Superior Court,* 160 Cal. App. 3d 1109 (4th Dist.Ca., 1984).)

2 THE EMPLOYER– EMPLOYEE RELATIONSHIP: DEFINITIONS AND DISTINCTIONS

Chapter Outline

S C E N A R I O S

S C E N A R I O   1

An employer intends to fill two positions. The first requires someone with computer programming experience to program all new company computers and serve as a technical assistant. What are the benefits of hiring someone "in-house," rather than from outside, and what obligations will the employer take on by doing so? Or, instead, what duties or obligations can the employer avoid by hiring outside assistance?

The second position available is temporary; the employer is looking for someone to take over a specific project, which has an expected completion date of six months. The employer does not want to hire a full-time employee and pay benefits, and so on, merely to obtain assistance with this project. In addition, the employer wants to give this person full responsibility for the project; the employer is not concerned with the process taken to complete the job, merely that it is done correctly and on time. Will this person be considered an employee or an independent contractor?

S C E N A R I O   2

A company employs a worker who is not as productive as expected. The payroll taxes as well as the benefits, which the company is required by law to provide, cost the company more than the employee's work produces in profits. The 61-year-old worker is given notice of termination, based on inadequate performance. He suggests that he, instead, be allowed to retire, and then be hired as an independent contractor on a project-by-project basis, so he retains a source of income and the company is not obligated to him except for his salary. Is this an acceptable solution?

S C E N A R I O   3

A consulting firm employs four people as consultants and two as secretaries, all on a part-time basis. Which of the many federal and state employment regulations apply to the employer? What are the employer's responsibilities to the employees?

Introduction to the Issue

The issue of whether an individual or business is an employer, a principal, or some other legal entity when contracting with another individual who is to perform work is extremely important. So, too, is the issue of whether the person hired is considered to be an employee, an independent contractor, or some other legal entity. Unfortunately, there is not complete uniformity surrounding the issue. Whether someone is an employer depends on the context, the statute being used, if any, the purpose of the relationship, and so on.

In this chapter, we will examine who is an employer and an employee and how it is decided. We will also learn what difference it makes to be considered either of the various legal entities that one becomes when performing work for another.

EXHIBIT 2–1   Myths about Who Is an Employee and Who Is Not

1. An employee is anyone who is paid to work.
2. As long as a person chooses how she will perform her job, she is an independent contractor and not an employee.
3. The one who hires the worker is liable for anything that the employee does in the course of his or her employment.
4. If someone is an employee under one statute, that person is considered an employee under all employment-related statutes.
5. If someone is considered an employer for purposes of one statute, he or she is considered an employer for all statutes.
6. It is always better to hire someone as an independent contractor, rather than as an employee.
7. If a mistake is made in categorizing one's workers, it's no big deal.

Origins in Agency Law

The law relating to the employment relationship is based on the traditional law of master and servant, which evolved into the law of agency. It may be helpful to briefly review the fundamentals of the law of agency in order to gain a better perspective on the legal regulation of the employment relationship that follows.

In an agency relationship, the party for whom another acts and from whom she or he derives authority to act is known and referred to as a "principal," while the one who represents the principal is known as an "agent." The agent is like a substitute appointed by the principal with power to do certain things. The agent is considered as the representative of the principal and acts for, in the place of, the principal. Similarly, an employee is the agent of the employer, the principal. The employee is the representative of the employer and acts in its place.

In an employment–agency relationship, the employee–agent is under a specific duty to the principal to act only as *authorized*. As a rule, if an agent exceeds her authority or places the property of the principal at risk without authority, the principal is now responsible for all loss or damage naturally resulting from the agent's unauthorized acts. An agent is subject to a duty to properly conduct himself in the discharge of the agency transaction and he is liable for injuries resulting to the principal from his unwarranted misconduct.

Accordingly, if an employee acts in a way that exceeds her authority, the employer may still be liable to a third party (though the employee would then be liable back to the employer because she exceeded her authority). For instance, assume an employee of a construction company has the authority to charge building supplies at the local hardware store for use in the firm's projects. If that employee went into the hardware store and charged supplies to the firm but then later used those supplies to build her daughter's clubhouse, the construction company (the principal) would still owe the hardware store (the third party) for the supplies since the employee (the agent) represented the company in the purchase, though the employee (the agent) would be liable to the company for the price of the inappropriately purchased supplies.

Throughout the entire relationship, the principal has the obligation toward the agent to exercise good faith in their relationship, and the principal has to use care to prevent the agent from coming to any harm during the agency relationship. This requirement translates into the employer's responsibility to provide a safe and healthy working environment for the workers.

In addition to creating these implied duties for the employment relationship, the principal–agent characterization is important to the working relationship for other reasons, explained in the next section.

Why Is It Important to Determine Whether a Worker Is an Employee?

You are hired by a company to do a job. Are you its employee or an **independent contractor?** While most workers may have no doubt about which they are, the actual answer may vary, depending on the statute, case law, or other analysis to be applied. The courts, employers, and the government are unable to agree on one definition of "employee" and "employer," so it varies, depending on the situation and the law being used. The distinction between the two is significant for tax law compliance and categorization, for benefit plans, for cost reduction plans, and for discrimination claims. For instance, Title VII applies to employers and prohibits them from discriminating against employees. It does not, however, cover discrimination against independent contractors. In addition, employers will not be liable for most torts committed by an independent contractor within the scope of the working relationship.

In addition, the definition of employee is all the more important as companies hire supplemental or contingent workers on an independent-contractor basis to cut costs. An employer's responsibilities generally increase when someone is an employee. This section of the chapter will discuss the implications of this characterization and why it is important to determine whether a worker is an employee. The next section will present the different ways to determine employment status.

Employer Payroll Deductions

Recall that an independent contractor is someone who performs work for the principal in a relationship where the principal does not control how the job is done. The principal does not oversee the independent contractor or give orders, other than what the final product is to be and what the principal wants. The independent contractor is then free to perform the requested service or act as he or she sees fit. This is in

Independent contractor
Generally, a person who contracts with a principal to perform a task according to her or his own methods, and who is not under the principal's control regarding the physical details of the work.

Scenario

Scenario

contrast to an employee over whom the employer has much more control about how the job is executed.

Also, an employer paying an employee is subject to different requirements than when paying an independent contractor. In general, for employees it is the employer's duty to pay Social Security (FICA), the FICA excise tax, Railroad Retirement Tax Act (RRTA) withholding amounts, federal unemployment compensation (FUTA), IRS federal income tax withholdings, Medicare, and state taxes. In addition, it is the employer's responsibility to withhold a certain percentage of the employee's wages for federal income tax purposes.

On the other hand, an independent contractor must be responsible for the payment of such taxes on his or her own. The principal merely pays the fee to the contractor, and the contractor then pays the taxes at a later date, usually through four estimated payments per year. Thus, the principal is able to avoid the tax expenses and bookkeeping costs associated with such withholdings.

Benefits

When you have taken jobs in the past, were you offered a certain number of paid vacation or sick days, a retirement plan, a parking spot, a medical or dental plan? These are known as benefits, and they cost the employer money outside of the wages the employer must pay the employee. In an effort to attract and retain superior personnel, employers offer employees a range of benefits that generally are not required to be offered, such as dental, medical, pension, and profit-sharing plans. Independent contractors have no access to these benefits.

The Employee Retirement Income Security Act of 1974 (ERISA) was enacted to protect employee benefit plan participants from retirement plan abuses by administrators; and the Fair Labor Standards Act of 1938 (FLSA) was enacted to establish standards for minimum wages, overtime pay, employer recordkeeping, and child labor. Where a worker is considered an employee, ERISA protects the employee's benefits, while the FLSA regulates the amount of money an employee must be paid per hour, and overtime compensation. A willful misclassification under FLSA may result in imprisonment and up to a $10,000 fine, imposed by the Department of Labor.

Discrimination and Affirmative Action

Can an independent contractor sue the employer for gender discrimination? No, Title VII and other related antidiscrimination statutes only protect *employees* from discrimination by employers. Employers are able to avoid discrimination and wrongful discharge claims where the worker is an independent contractor. (See below for discussion on coverage by various statutes of employers.)

However, this safe harbor for employers may be getting a bit more dangerous, if Texas courts have anything to say about it. In a 1999 decision, the Texas Supreme Court held that a firm may be sued by an individual who is *not* an employee of the firm when the company is in a position where it can exert control over a worker's "employment opportunities." While this is not the law in most states, it may indicate a trend.

Additionally, the National Labor Relations Act protects only employees and not independent contractors from unfair labor practices. Note, however, that independent contractors may be considered to be *employers,* so they may be subject to these regulations from the other side of the fence.

Cost Reductions

It would seem to be a safe statement that an objective of most employers is to reduce cost and to increase profit. Employees are more expensive to employ, due to the above regulations that require greater expenditures on behalf of employees, as well as the fact that others must be hired to maintain records of the employees. In addition, by hiring independent contractors, the cost of overtime is eliminated (the federal wage and hour laws do not apply to independent contractors) and the employer is able to avoid any work-related expenses, such as tools, training, or traveling. The employer is also guaranteed satisfactory performance of the job for which the contractor was hired, because it is the contractor's contractual obligation to adequately perform the contract with the employer, while the employee is generally able to quit without incurring liability (the at-will doctrine). If there is a breach of the agreement between the employer and the independent contractor, the independent contractor stands to lose not only the job but may also be liable for resulting damages. An employee is usually compensated for work completed with less liability for failure to perfectly perform.

In addition, the employee may actually cause the employer to have greater liability exposure. An employer is **vicariously liable** if the employee causes harm to a third party while the employee is in the course of employment. For instance, if an employee is driving a company car from one company plant to another, and, in the course of that trip sideswipes another vehicle, the employer may be liable to the owner of the other vehicle. While the employee may be required to indemnify or reimburse the employer for any liability incurred as a result of the negligence, generally the third party goes after the employer, because the employee does not have the funds to pay the liability. The employer could sue the employee for this reimbursement but, more likely, will write it off as an expense of doing business.

Finally, some managers contend that independent contractors are more motivated and, as a result, have a higher level of performance as a consequence of their freedom to control their own work and futures.

On the other hand, there may be situations where, notwithstanding the decrease in the amount of benefits that the employer must provide, independent contractors may still be more expensive to employ. This situation may exist where the employer finds that it is cheaper to have its employees perform certain types of work that are characteristically expensive to contract. Often a large firm will find it more profitable to employ a legal staff, and pay their benefits and salaries, than to employ a law firm every time a legal question arises. Or a school may find it less expensive to

Vicarious liability
The imposition of liability on one party for the wrongs of another. Liability may extend from an employee to its employer on this basis if the employee is acting within the scope of her or his employment at the time the liability arose.

maintain a full janitorial staff than to employ a professional cleaning crew whenever something needs to be taken care of at the school.

Failure to Appropriately Categorize Worker

Workers and employers alike make mistakes about whether a worker is an independent contractor or an employee. If a worker is found to be classified as an independent contractor, but later found to constitute an employee, the punishment by the IRS is harsh. The employer is not only liable for its share of FICA and FUTA but is also subject to an additional penalty equal to 20 percent of the FICA that should have been withheld. In addition, the employer is liable for 1.5 percent of the wages received by the employee. These penalty charges apply if there have been 1099 forms (records of payments to independent contractors) compiled for the worker. If, on the other hand, the forms have not been completed, the penalties increase to 40 percent of FICA and 3 percent of wages. Where the IRS determines that the worker was *deliberately* classified as an independent contractor to avoid paying taxes, the fines and penalties can easily run into six figures for even the smallest business.

In addition to potential IRS violations, the employer may be liable for violations of the National Labor Relations Act of 1935 (NLRA). Liability may include reinstatement and back pay to employees fired in violation of the NLRA under the mistaken belief that they were independent contractors. The employer may also be liable under the Fair Labor Standards Act of 1938 (FLSA) for amounts of unpaid wages or overtime compensation and for attorneys' fees and costs. Under the Employee Retirement Income Security Act of 1974 (ERISA) an employer may be liable for accrued but unpaid benefits. In addition, there is possible liability under the Social Security Act of 1935 and under state workers' compensation and unemployment compensation laws.

The fines for each violation are substantial. For example, any person who willfully violates the FLSA is subject to a fine of $10,000 and six months' imprisonment. Additionally, the tax advantages of a qualified retirement or fringe benefit plan to employers or employees may be lost as a result of misclassification.

Why is the IRS so intent on ensuring that improper classification does not occur? The IRS estimates that it loses over $2 billion a year in uncollected taxes that should have been paid by employers or the independent contractors whom they have hired. In 1989 alone, 76,000 workers were reclassified from independent contractors to employees; in some fields, misclassification rates run as high as 92 percent. As one scholar has written, IRS agents are told, "Go forth and find employees!" The IRS will generally attempt to "match" workers who claim to be independent contractors with their companies. If an independent contractor earned more than $10,000 from one source during a one-year period, the independent status of that individual is suspect.

The IRS is particularly interested in situations where a company is forced by rising costs to downsize. In doing so, many of its older workers choose to accept early retirement. Older workers, however, are often those more experienced and who have developed expertise in various areas of the company. Companies search for ways to use these "experts" without violating pension plan restrictions regarding recalling employees. Hiring them as independent contractors appears to be an efficient, cost-saving mechanism. Nevertheless, the IRS has successfully challenged the employment of these workers as independent contractors where they are hired to perform services *substantially similar* to those they rendered as employees of the firm. In an analogous situation, any individual who is hired as an independent contractor to perform in a capacity substantially similar to that performed by a company's own employees will be subject to IRS challenge.

But there is hope for correct classification: the 1978 Revenue Act forms a safe harbor for employers who have consistently classified a class of workers as independent contractors. Section 530 cites four criteria required to claim a worker as an independent contractor.

First, the business must have never treated the worker as an employee for the purposes of employment taxes for any period (i.e., the company has never withheld income or FICA tax from its payments, and so on). Second, all federal tax returns with respect to this worker were filed consistent with the worker being an independent contractor. Third, the company has treated all those in positions substantially similar to that of this worker as independent contractors. And fourth, the company has a reasonable basis for treating the worker as an independent contractor. Such a reasonable basis may include a judicial precedent or published IRS ruling, a past IRS audit of the company, or long-standing industry practices. Where these conditions have been satisfied, the employer is not liable for misclassification.

How Do You Determine Whether a Worker Is an Employee?

Courts have offered varied interpretations of whether someone is an employee. Generally, which interpretation is used depends on the factual circumstances presented by each case, as well as which law is at issue.

Scenario

A consistently cited case that illustrates the effect of the difference between classification as an independent contractor and as an employee is *Lemmerman v. A.T. Williams Oil Co.,* in which an eight-year-old boy frequently performed odd jobs for the Wilco Service Station at which his mother was employed. He was paid $1 a day to perform such services as stocking shelves and sweeping up. One day the boy fell and cut his hand. The boy sought damages in the form of lost wages, pain, and suffering. The main issue in this case was whether he was an employee. If he was an employee, then his sole remedy was in the form of workers' compensation; however, if he was, instead, an independent contractor, Wilco would lose the protection of the workers' compensation limits and would be liable in tort for additional amounts. Over a strong dissenting opinion, the court in *Lemmerman* determined that the boy was actually an employee of the defendant and, therefore, could not recover beyond a standard workers' compensation claim.

While many laws refer to similar definitions of "employee" or "independent contractor," other laws or regulations may rely on an entirely different test to answer the issue. Congress has responded by stating that employees are those not classified as independent contractors. The House has further explained that an employee is "one who works for another." The National Labor Relations Act states that "the term 'employee' shall not include . . . any individual having the status of an independent contractor" but does not define independent contractor.

Several tests have been developed and are commonly used by courts to classify employees and independent contractors. These tests include the common-law test of agency, which focuses on the right of control, the Internal Revenue Service (IRS) 20-factor analysis, and the economic reality analysis. Several courts also use a hybrid approach, using one test that combines factors from other tests. Following the definition and explanation of each test will be a case utilizing that specific approach. When reading the cases, think of the differences and similarities of each test and its strength and weaknesses.

Under the common-law agency test, a persuasive indicator of independent contractor status is the ability to control the manner in which the work is performed. This test was derived from the law involving domestic relations of the "master and servant." Where the master had control over the servant, the worker was considered the master's servant, employed by and connected to that master, more similar to common-law property rights than contract rights. Today, the contract or agency principles apply rather than property principles. The element of control has persisted in today's interpretation of who constitutes an employee and who is an independent contractor. The right to control remains the predominant factor.

Under the common-law agency approach, the employer need not actually control the work, but must merely *have the right or ability* to control the work for a worker to be classified an employee. Although this is a strong indication that the worker is an employee, other factors usually are considered. For example, it has been held that an employee is one who works for wages or salary and is under direct supervision. An independent contractor has benefited as one who does a "job for a price, decides how the work will be done, usually hires others to do the work, and depends for their income not upon wages, but upon the difference between what they pay for goods, materials and labor and what they receive for the end result, that is upon profits."

The common-law test is specifically and consistently used to determine employee status in connection with FUTA and FICA taxes, in determining whether an employee is a statutory employee (discussed later in this chapter), as well as in federal income tax withholding.

NATIONWIDE INSURANCE CO. V. DARDEN
112 S.Ct. 1344 (1992)

Darden worked as an agent for Nationwide Insurance Company pursuant to a contract which stated, among other terms, that Darden would sell only Nationwide policies and that he would forfeit his entitlement to retirement plan benefits if he sold insurance for Nationwide's competitors within one year of his termination and 25 miles of his previous business location. After his termination, he began working for one of those competitors, and Nationwide determined that he was therefore disqualified from receiving his retirement benefits. Darden sued under the Employee Retirement Income Security Act (ERISA). The district court granted summary judgment to Nationwide as Darden was not an employee and therefore not a proper ERISA plaintiff. The court of appeals reversed the lower court's ruling, and the Supreme Court evaluated which definition of employee was most appropriate for an ERISA claim.

Souter, J.

We have often been asked to construe the meaning of "employee" where the statute containing the term does not helpfully define it. Most recently we confronted this problem in *Community for Creative Non Violence v. Reid,* a case in which a sculptor and a nonprofit group each claimed copyright ownership in a statue the group had commissioned from the artist. The dispute ultimately turned on whether, by the terms of the Copyright Act, the statue had been "prepared by an employee within the scope of his or her employment." Because the Copyright Act nowhere defined the term "employee," we unanimously applied the "well established" principle that, "where Congress uses terms that have accumulated settled meaning under the common law, a court must infer, unless the statute otherwise dictates, that Congress means to incorporate the established meaning of those terms. In the past, when Congress has used the term 'employee' without defining it, we have concluded that Congress intended to describe the conventional master-servant relationship as understood by the common law agency doctrine."

So, too, it should stand here. ERISA's nominal definition of "employee" as "any individual employed by an employer" is completely circular and explains nothing . . . Thus, we adopt a common law test for determining who qualifies as an "employee" under ERISA. Since the common law test contains no shorthand formula or magic phrase that can be applied to find the answer, all of the incidents of the relationship must be assessed and weighed with no one factor being decisive.

To be sure, the traditional agency law criteria offer no paradigm for determinacy. But their application generally turns on factual variables within an employer's knowledge, thus permitting categorical judgments about the "employee" status of claimants with similar job descriptions. REVERSED AND REMANDED.

Case Questions

1. If someone were to ask you to define "employee," according to the "established definition" as described by the Court, how would you respond?

2. Do you agree that the definition offered by ERISA, "any individual employed by an employer," is circular if "employer" is clearly defined?

3. Do you think that the average employer will be clear regarding which workers are employees and which are not, using the criteria for the common law test described in this chapter?

IRS Test
List of 20 factors to which the IRS looks to determine whether someone is an employee or an independent contractor. The IRS compiled this list from the results of judgments of the courts relating to this issue.

Under the IRS 20-factor analysis, the IRS, in training material issued in July 1996, explained that "this Twenty Factor Test is an analytical tool and **not** the legal test used for determining worker status. The legal test is whether there is a right to direct and control the means and details of the work" (emphasis in original). [Dept. of Treasury, Internal Revenue Service, "Employee or Independent Contract?" Training 3320-102 (July 96)]. However, the following 20 factors have been consistently and continually articulated by courts, regulatory agencies, commentators, and scholars as critical to the determination of the status of an individual worker. When these factors are satisfied, courts are more likely to find "employee" status. In addition, the IRS stated that these 20 factors are not inclusive but that "every piece of information that helps determine the extent to which the business retains the right to control the worker is important."

1. *Instructions.*   A worker who is required to comply with other persons' instructions about when, where, and how to perform the work is ordinarily considered to be an employee.

2. *Training.*   Training a worker indicates that the employer exercises control over the means by which the result is accomplished.

3. *Integration.*   When the success or continuation of a business depends on the performance of certain services, the worker performing those services is subject to a certain amount of control by the owner of the business.

4. *Services rendered personally.*   If the services must be rendered personally, the employer controls both the means and the results of the work.

5. *Hiring, supervising, and paying assistants.*   Control is exercised if the employer hires, supervises, and pays assistants.

6. *Continuing relationships.*   The existence of a continuing relationship between the worker and the employer indicates an employer–employee relationship.

7. *Set hours of work.*   The establishment of hours of work by the employer indicates control.

8. *Full time required.*   If the worker must devote full time to the employer's business, the employer has control over the worker's time. An independent contractor is free to work when and for whom he chooses.

9. *Doing work on the employer's premises.*   Control is indicated if the work is performed on the employer's premises.

10. *Order or sequenced set.*   Control is indicated if a worker is not free to choose his own pattern of work but must perform services in the sequence set by the employer.

11. *Oral or written reports.*   Control is indicated if the worker must submit regular oral or written reports to the employer.

12. *Furnishing tools and materials.*   If the employer furnishes significant tools, materials, and other equipment, an employer–employee relationship usually exists.

13. *Payment by hour, week, or month.*   Payment by the hour, week, or month points to an employer–employee relationship, provided that this method of payment is just not a convenient way of paying a lump sum agreed on as a cost of a job. However, hourly pay may not be evidence that a worker is an employee if it is customary to pay an independent contractor by the hour (an attorney, for example). An independent contractor usually is paid by the job or on a straight commission.

14. *Payment of business or traveling expenses.*   Payment of the worker's business or traveling expenses, or both, is indicative of an employer–employee relationship. However, this factor is less important because companies do reimburse independent contractors.

15. *Significant investment.*   A worker is an independent contractor if she or he invests in facilities that are not typically maintained by employees, such as the maintenance of an office rented at fair value from an unrelated party. An employee depends on the employer for such facilities.

16. *Realization of profit or loss.*   A worker who can realize a profit or loss (in addition to the profit or loss ordinarily realized by employees) through management of resources is an independent contractor. The worker who cannot is generally an employee.

17. *Working for more than one firm at a time.*   If a worker performs more than *de minimis* services for a number of unrelated persons at the same time, she or he is usually considered an independent contractor.

18. *Making service available to the general public.*   A worker is usually an independent contractor if the services are made available to the general public on a regular or consistent basis.

19. *Right to discharge.*   The right of the employer to discharge a worker indicates that he or she is an employee.

20. *Right to terminate.*   A worker is an employee if the right to end the relationship with the principal is available at any time he wishes without incurring liability.

In the following case, the court considered the 20 factors established by the IRS in determining whether Hospital Resource Personnel (HRP) correctly classified their works as independent contractors. The court, in considering the 20 factors, decided that HRP correctly classified its workers as independent contractors.

HOSPITAL RESOURCE PERSONNEL, INC., v. UNITED STATES
68 F.3d 421 (11th Cir. 1995)

The court analyzes whether temporary nurses provided to hospitals are employees or independent contractors.

Barkett, J.

HRP is a business which provides specialized nurses to hospitals in need of temporary additional staffing. HRP contracts with approximately fifteen hospitals and does not prescribe the work that the nurses are to perform at the hospitals, nor does it furnish the nurses with uniforms, transportation, journals, sick pay, vacation pay, pensions, bonuses, medical insurance, or licenses. In addition, HRP permits the nurses to be employed directly by the hospitals or to register with other similar nursing agencies or registries. The nurses may choose when, where, and how often they work. HRP pays the nurses according to the number of hours worked at the client hospitals, making the payments on a regular basis, daily or weekly, as the nurses complete a particular job or project.

HRP has never withheld federal income or social security taxes from the compensation it pays to the nurses on its registry. Instead, it has always treated the nurses as independent contractors who are not subject to withholding, and at the end of each year has furnished them with information returns on Form 1099, listing all payments made during the year.

Following an audit, the IRS assessed employment taxes, plus penalties and interest, in excess of $1,144,000, against HRP for all quarters of the years 1988, 1989, and 1990. The IRS disagreed with HRP's characterization of the nurses as independent contractors, declaring instead that they were employees subject to withholding. . . .

* * * *

The IRS has compiled a non-exclusive list of twenty factors to aid in analyzing the status of workers. Those indicative of employee status include: (1) instructions from the employer; (2) training; (3) integration of worker's services into employer's business; (4) worker's services rendered personally; (5) a continuing relationship between worker and employer; (6) set hours of work; (7) mandatory full-time employment; (8) work on employer's premises; (9) set order of tasks; (10) oral or written reports; (11) payment by the hour, week, or month; and (12) right to discharge for reasons other than nonperformance. Those indicative of independent contractor status include: (13) worker's right to hire, supervise, and pay assistants; (14) payment of own business and/or travel expenses; (15) furnishing own tools and materials; (16) significant investment; (17) realization of profit or loss; (18) right to work for more than one firm at a time; (19) right to make service available to the general public; and (20) right to terminate without incurring liability. Although no one factor is definitive on its own, collectively the factors define the extent of an employer's control over the time and manner in which a worker performs. This control test is fundamental in establishing a worker's status.

HRP presented undisputed evidence that it does not control the manner and means of the nurses' work: HRP does not instruct or train the nurses; it does not mandate full-time employment; it neither schedules the tasks nor sets the number of hours the nurses must work; and it is the nurses themselves who provide transportation, incidental expenses, uniforms, tools, and materials. In addition, while HRP does require the nurses to provide their services personally and pays them on set time intervals (hourly), the nurses do not work on HRP's premises, and they are free to provide their services directly to hospitals and to register with other similar nursing agencies. . . .

⁕ ⁕ ⁕ ⁕

We agree with the district court's conclusion that the undisputed facts satisfy many of the twenty factors set forth by the IRS, and therefore that HRP, as a matter of law, did not control the manner in which the nurses performed their work.

Accordingly, we hold that HRP was exempt from employment taxes under §§ 530(a)(2)(A) and (1)(B) because of its reasonable reliance on Revenue Ruling 61-196, judicial precedent, and common law in treating the nurses as independent contractors.

AFFIRMED in part; VACATED in part (regarding a jurisdictional issue); and REMANDED.

Case Questions

1. What factor did the court consider the most important when determining the classification?

2. What was at stake for HRP in classifying its workers as employees or independent contractors?

3. On what did HRP originally rely in classifying its workers as independent contractors? Why must a court use a test, such as the IRS 20 factors when determining whether an employer classified its workers correctly?

Finally, under the economic realities test, courts consider whether the worker is economically dependent on the business or, as a matter of economic fact, is in business for himself or herself. In applying the economic realities test, courts look to the degree of control exerted by the alleged employer over the worker, the worker's opportunity for profit or loss, the worker's investment in the business, the permanence of the working relationship, the degree of skill required by the worker, and the extent the work is an integral part of the alleged employer's business. Typically, all of these factors are considered as a whole with none of the factors being determinative.

In the following case, rig welders filed an action against Flint Engineering and Construction Company for overtime compensation under the Fair Labor Standards Act (FLSA). The workers believed they were employees rather than independent contractors and thus entitled to overtime compensation. The court used the economic realities test in determining the classification of the workers.

BAKER, ET. AL. V. FLINT ENGINEERING & CONSTRUCTION COMPANY
137 F.3d 1436 (10th Cir. 1998)

Workers who provide their own equipment, supplies, and repairs but who are directed by a foreman are analyzed to determine whether they are employees or independent contractors.

Briscoe, J.

Flint is routinely hired as a general contractor by oil and gas companies to build natural gas pipelines and compressor stations which transport natural gas from the wellheads to the owner's main processing plants. When Flint is hired, Flint subcontracts with a variety of workers, including rig welders, to assist in completion of the project.

Rig welders provide their own welding equipment, which is typically mounted on flat-bed pickup trucks. Rig welders are also responsible for costs of stocking their welding rigs with supplies, as well as for necessary repairs to the rigs. Rig welders do not bid on jobs and do not have contractor's licenses that would enable them to do so. Flint simply hires rig welders at a set hourly rate to work on particular projects. Flint does not negotiate the hourly rate, and sometimes pays on a "straight contract" basis at approximately $27 to $30 per hour, and sometimes on a "split check" basis at a rate of $10 per hour for labor and $17 per hour for rig rental.

Rig welders are supervised by Flint foremen and are required to arrive, take breaks, and leave at times specified by the foremen. They are not allowed to complete their work when they want and, in most cases, it would be impossible for them to do so because they must coordinate their work with the other crafts and because other equipment and workers are necessary to move pipe for welding. Rig welders are not provided project blueprints. Instead, the foremen map out what pipes they want built and in what order. The foremen do not establish the welding specifications and standards, nor do they tell rig welders

how to weld or how long a particular weld should take. Rig welders would be unemployed after completion of a project if they did not seek work on new projects.

Prior to July 1, 1991, Flint considered rig welders as independent contractors and asked each rig welder to sign a document entitled "Agreement with Independent Contractor," which basically stated the intent of the relationship was that of independent contractor rather than employer–employee and as such, the workers were responsible for any employment taxes and insurance. Flint treats the majority of other workers on each project as employees.

The workers filed an action claiming violations of the FLSA. The district court concluded that the workers were employees and entered a final judgment in favor of the workers. . . .

* * * *

In determining whether an individual is covered by the FLSA, "our inquiry is not limited by any contractual terminology or by traditional common law concepts of 'employee' or 'independent contractor.'" Instead, the economic realities of the relationship govern, and "the focal point is 'whether the individual is economically dependent on the business to which he renders service . . . or is, as a matter of economic fact, in business for himself.'" The economic reality test includes inquiries into whether the alleged employer has the power to hire and fire employees, supervises and controls employee work schedules or conditions of employment, determines the rate and method of payment, and maintains employment records.

In applying the economic reality test, courts generally look at (1) the degree of control exerted by the alleged employer over the worker; (2) the worker's opportunity for profit or loss; (3) the worker's investment in the business; (4) the permanence of the working relationship; (5) the degree of skill required to perform the work; and (6) the extent to which the work is an integral part of the alleged employer's business. . . . None of the factors alone is dispositive; instead, the court must employ a totality-of-the-circumstances approach. . . .

* * * *

The district court found Flint's "degree of control over the rig welders, and the Plaintiffs' lack of independence over setting their work hours, work crews and other details of their welding work, is more consistent with employee rather than independent contractor status." R.I. 272. After carefully reviewing the record on appeal, we conclude this finding is not clearly erroneous.

. . . Flint's foremen tell the rig welders when to report to work, when to take breaks, on what portion of the project they will be working, and when their workday ends. The record indicates rig welders cannot perform their work on their own schedule; rather, pipeline work has assembly-line qualities in that it requires orderly and sequential coordination of various crafts and workers to construct a pipeline. The record further indicates plaintiffs work on only one project at a time and do not offer services to third parties while a project is ongoing. Indeed, the hours plaintiffs are required to work on a project (10 to 14 hours a day, six days a week), coupled with driving time between home and often remote work sites each day, make it practically impossible for them to offer services to other employers. In short, very little about plaintiffs' work situation makes it possible to view plaintiffs as persons conducting their own businesses.

In analyzing the second factor, . . . if plaintiffs could bid on jobs at a set amount and correspondingly set their own hours or schedule, they would have the opportunity for profit or loss.

However, plaintiffs are hired on a per-hour basis rather than on a flat-rate-per-job basis. There is no incentive for plaintiffs to work faster or more efficiently in order to increase their opportunity for profit. Moreover, there is absolutely no risk of loss on plaintiffs' part. "In short, the [rig welders] ha[ve] no control over the essential determinants of profits in a business, and no direct share in the success of the business."

* * * *

. . . The investment, "which must be considered as a factor is the amount of large capital expenditures, such as risk capital and capital investments, not negligible items, or labor itself." Courts have generally held that the fact that a worker supplies his or her own tools or equipment does not preclude a finding of employee status. In making a finding on this factor, it is appropriate to compare the worker's individual investment to the employer's investment in the overall operation.

. . . Plaintiffs' investments are disproportionately small when compared to Flint's investment in the overall business. Several witnesses testified that Flint routinely had hundreds of thousands of dollars of equipment at each work site. Compared to Flint's investment in the overall business, plaintiff's investments are not so significant as to indicate they are independent contractors.

* * * *

. . . Although plaintiffs exhibit characteristics generally typical of independent contractors as regards the short duration of their employment relationships and their frequent relocation to find employment, these characteristics of plaintiffs' employment are clearly due to the intrinsic nature of oil and gas pipeline construction work rather than any choice or decision on the part of plaintiffs. We conclude it is appropriate to characterize plaintiffs' relationship with Flint as "permanent and exclusive for the duration of" the particular job for which they are hired.

. . . In light of the fact that the plaintiffs do not exercise any initiative or make any judgment decisions on the job site, the court finds that plaintiffs' skills are not indicative of independent contractor status.

. . . As noted by the district court, plaintiffs are highly skilled but they did not exercise those skills in any independent fashion in their employment with Flint. Although plaintiffs are not told by Flint how to complete a particular weld, they are told by Flint foremen when and where to weld. Accordingly, the fact that plaintiffs use special skills does not necessarily indicate they are independent contractors.

. . . The evidence in the record on appeal clearly indicates rig welders' work is an important, and indeed integral, component of oil and gas pipeline construction work.

Our final step is to review the findings on each of the above factors and determine whether plaintiffs, as a matter of economic fact, depend upon Flint's business for the opportunity to render service, or are in business for themselves. The question is whether plaintiffs are economically dependent upon Flint during the time period they work for Flint, however long or short that period may be. . . .

* * * *

We agree with the district court that this is not the type of "profit" typically associated with an independent contractor. [A]n independent contractor has the ability to make a profit or sustain a loss due to the ability to bid on projects at a flat rate and to complete projects as it sees fit. Here, plaintiffs have neither the ability to bid on projects nor to complete their work in an independent fashion.

Ultimately, we conclude that plaintiffs are employees of Flint, rather than independent contractors, for purposes of the FLSA. . . . The only substantial difference between plaintiffs and the other workers on the job site is that plaintiffs are required to supply equipment to perform their jobs. AFFIRMED.

Case Questions

1. Do you think the outcome of the case would have been different if the court utilized one of the other tests in determining the classification of the worker as an employee or independent contractor?

2. When the court is considering the factors in the economic reality test, must all factors be consistent with a classification or are the factors weighed?

3. The court found dispositive the fact that the rig welders could not work for anyone other than Flint while performing their job; contrast this with the tax code which states physicians are independent contractors. Couldn't it be argued that a doctor can only work for one hospital at a time and cannot work at another simultaneously?

EXHIBIT 2–2

The IRS, in its training materials, offers this case study on the question of whether someone is an employee or an independent contractor (*modified slightly by the author*):

A computer programmer is laid off when company X downsizes. Company X agrees to pay the programmer $10,000 to complete a one-time project to create a certain product. It is not clear how long it will take to complete the project, and the programmer is not guaranteed any minimum payment for the hours spent on the project. The programmer does the work on a new high-end computer, which was purchased by the company. The programmer works at home, but may attend meetings of the software development group at the firm. Company X provides the programmer with no instructions beyond the specifications for the product itself. The programmer and Company X have a written contract, which provides that the programmer is considered to be an independent contractor, is required to pay her own taxes, and receives no benefits from Company X.

Is she an employee?

ZINN V. MCKUNE
143 F.3d 1353 (10th Cir. 1988)

In this case, the plaintiff was hired by a state contractor to work as a nurse in a prison clinic. The worker contends that she is an employee while the employer contends that she was an independent contractor. The court agrees with the employer.

Kelly, J.

Jerilyn Zinn was hired by Prison Health Services (PHS) as a correctional nurse assigned to the prison clinic at the Osawatomie Correctional Facility. From 1992 to 1995, Zinn was responsible for the day-to-day operation of the clinic. The contract between PHS and the Department of Corrections expressly provided that both PHS and its employees were independent contractors, and explicitly negated the existence of any agency, employment or servant relationship between PHS and the Department of Corrections. Accordingly, PHS exercised control over the hiring, firing, wages and benefits of PHS personnel like Ms. Zinn. The contract granted the Department discretion to request removal of PHS personnel assigned to work in a Department prison facility under the contract. If the Department's concerns

about a PHS employee were not resolved, PHS agreed to remove the employee from the facility.

In 1995, Deputy Warden Rudy Stupar requested that Mark Boyd, Health Services Administrator of PHS, reassign Zinn, citing four specific examples of "inappropriate behavior." PHS subsequently offered Zinn reassignment to other prison clinics in Wyandotte or Lansing, but Ms. Zinn accepted neither offer because she claimed she was physically unable to perform the duties of either position. PHS placed Zinn on disability leave without pay in March 1995.

Ms. Zinn filed a charge of discrimination with the Kansas Human Rights Commission against the Department as well as PHS alleging violations of the Americans with Disabilities Act (ADA), the Age Discrimination in Employment

Act (ADEA), and sex discrimination and retaliation in violation of Title VII of the Civil Rights Act of 1964. The defendants sought summary judgment against Ms. Zinn, arguing, among other things, that the Department was not Ms. Zinn's employer. The district court granted defendants' motion, holding that Ms. Zinn presented "no evidence from which a trier of fact could conclude that she was an employee of the [Department] for Title VII purposes." She appeals from the district court's grant of summary judgment in favor of the employer.

* * * *

We agree with the parties that *Lambertsen v. Utah Dept. of Corrections* provides the analysis for determining whether Ms. Zinn is an employee of the Department for purposes of Title VII. In *Lambertsen,* we held that the skeletal definitions of "employer" and "employee" provided in 42 U.S.C. § 2000e(b) and (f) should be fleshed out by applying common-law agency principles to the facts and circumstances surrounding the working relationship of the parties. Though the main focus of *Lambertsen's* hybrid inquiry is whether and to what extent a putative employer has the "right to control the 'means and manner' of the worker's performance," other factors inform the analysis, including

(1) the kind of occupation at issue, with reference to whether the work usually is done under the direction of a supervisor or is done by a specialist without supervision; (2) the skill required in the particular occupation; (3) whether the employer or the employee furnishes the equipment used and the place of work; (4) the length of time the individual has worked; (5) the method of payment, whether by time or by job; (6) the manner in which the work relationship is terminated; (7) whether annual leave is afforded; (8) whether the work is an integral part of the business of the employer; (9) whether the worker accumulates retirement benefits; (10) whether the employer pays Social Security taxes; and (11) the intention of the parties.

The *Lambertsen* calculus requires us to look to the totality of circumstances surrounding the working relationship between the parties; no single factor is determinative.

Apart from the issue of supervision and evaluation, it is uncontroverted that Ms. Zinn was an employee of PHS and received compensation and benefits from PHS, not the Department. PHS provided services to the Department as an independent contractor, and PHS employees, merely by fulfilling terms of the Department–PHS service contract, did not thereby become Department employees. Ms. Zinn suggests otherwise. We believe it is apparent that is not the case. No evidence establishes the requisite degree of control over Ms. Zinn's professional nursing services necessary to support a finding that Ms. Zinn was an employee of the Department. Though some elements, in isolation and not in accordance with *Lambertsen,* might appear consistent with an employment relationship, no reasonable jury could find an employment relationship existed based on the totality of the circumstances, and summary judgment is thus proper.

Though valid penological measures imposed to ensure safety and security within a facility may require a worker to fulfill certain conditions, those conditions do not rise to the level of "control" for purposes of determining a worker's employment status with the correctional facility itself. Much of the evidence Ms. Zinn cites in an attempt to establish the Department's control over the means and manner of her work performance reflects the Department's penological interest in ensuring security and safety within the facility. For example, the memoranda upon which Ms. Zinn relies to establish her manager's supervisory control over her relate to inmate access to the clinic, restocking of the first aid kits, maintaining a "sharps" inventory, and beginning sick call at a time when the facility is adequately staffed. The Department's interest in controlling who and what goes into and out of the clinic and at what time clearly relates to the safety and security of the prison, as does its interest in maintaining an accurate "sharps" inventory and adequate medical supplies throughout the prison. Similarly, Ms. Zinn's performance of on-site nursing duties using Department facilities and equipment serves the Department's interest in operating the correctional facility in a manner which ensures the safety and security of employees and inmates alike. Finally, the Department's interests in controlling Ms. Zinn's working hours and access to the facility serve these same purposes. Ms. Zinn's reliance on these factors is thus misplaced.

Moreover, many of the terms and conditions that Ms. Zinn relies upon were part and parcel of the agreement governing the relationship between the Department and PHS. The contract provides that PHS and its employees will be considered independent contractors by the Department and expressly denies the creation of an agency, employee or servant relationship with PHS or its employees, but requires all PHS personnel to abide by the Department's Employee Rules of Conduct. The contract also grants the Department the ability to control the format of documentation in medical records prepared by PHS personnel. The Department's imposition of these requirements on PHS, its independent contractor, in order to facilitate the clinic's operation does not make Ms. Zinn, admittedly an employee of PHS, also an employee of the Department. The contract language simply indicates the parties intended the Department to retain control over its facility and, to that end, to a limited extent over PHS personnel. Thus, Ms. Zinn's reliance on the contract's provisions and the Department's compliance with them proves nothing . . .

* * * *

Finally, Ms. Zinn argues that the services she provided to the Department were integral to the Department's business because the Department must provide adequate medical care to prisoners. While Ms. Zinn's performance of a traditional government function as an employee of a private contractor is pertinent to other inquiries, we do not believe, considering the totality of the circumstances, that Ms. Zinn has proffered sufficient evidence to support a finding that she was an employee of the Department. The evidence presented by Ms. Zinn indicates that her relationship with the Department was defined by the terms of the PHS–Department contract and by the Department's valid interests in security and safety. In all other respects, PHS controlled the manner and means of her work performance. This is not a case where an individual independent contractor claims to be an employee of an entity. Rather, it is a case where an employee of one entity necessarily contends, despite her admission to the contrary, that she is also the employee of another. The summary judgment evidence simply does not support this difficult position. Because Ms. Zinn has not presented evidence which would allow a reasonable jury to find for her on this issue, the district court properly granted summary judgment on Ms. Zinn's Title VII claims.

Case Questions

1. Do you agree that Zinn was not an employee of the department? What is the strongest argument for your side?

2. If you disagree with the court and believe that Zinn was an employee of the department, how would you suggest the defendant could have protected itself?

3. Do you think this was a fair decision? Why or why not?

The question of employment status would be made easier if the statutes that regulate employment and employment-related issues actually defined "employee." In fact, some do; however, many of the definitions are vague in some respects. Title VII, for instance, protects employees and applicants for employment from certain prohibited, discriminatory actions of employers. However, Title VII defines employee as one employed by an employer, with some exclusions related to public office. Volunteer workers are generally not protected by Title VII, but it does apply to volunteer workers where the employer is otherwise subject to the statute and where the volunteer's position generally leads to paid work with the same employer (i.e., where the work is viewed as a training or apprenticeship program). Title VII applies here because the volunteer program is viewed as an employment opportunity, and discrimination, therefore, would constitute denial of an employment opportunity. In addition, the Court of Appeals for the Second Circuit recently held in *Pietras v. Board of Fire Commissioners* that a volunteer firefighter constituted an employee for purposes of Title VII since she received a number of job-related benefits, including a retirement pension.

The mere fact that a worker does not receive cash in payment for work does not mean that he or she is not an employee. A worker may be paid in other compensation, such as clothing, food, or shelter. For instance, a hotel may hire someone as a gardener and, in lieu of paying her standard wages, allow her to live at the hotel as long as she continues working there. This payment is sufficient to constitute compensation, and the worker may be considered to be an employee, depending on other factors.

Statutory employees
Individuals who are deemed to be employees by statutes, no matter what the circumstances of their employment.

Additionally, there are some who are considered **statutory employees** by Congress. This means that, whether they would otherwise be considered employees, they have been deemed to be employees by statute. For instance, officers of corporations are automatically defined as employees for FUTA, FICA, and income tax withholding purposes. Notwithstanding this specific distinction, problems arise where the classification as "officer" is not so clear cut. A life insurance salesperson, on the other hand, is considered a statutory employee for FICA purposes, but not in connection with FUTA. This distinction is critical in that profession as the insurance salesperson is, therefore, not considered an employee for purposes of imposing the 2 percent floor on employee business expenses.

Another example of statutory treatment is a real estate agent, who is statutorily treated as an independent contractor only where she or he satisfies two conditions: first, he or she must receive all or substantially all of the real estate–related remuneration as a result of real estate *sales,* rather than on the basis of hours worked; second, the agent and his or her contractor must have a written agreement that provides that the agent is not an employee for federal tax purposes. Further, in the Tax Reform Act of 1978, Congress classified engineers, designers, drafters, computer programmers, and systems analysts who work for technical services firms as employees. Similarly, the tax code states that physicians, lawyers, veterinarians, public stenographers, auctioneers, and others who follow an independent trade, business, or profession in which they offer their services to the public are not employees. (26 CFR. §31.3401(c)-1(e).)

Contingent or Temporary Workers

When utilizing contingent and temporary workers, an employer must be cognizant of the advantages and disadvantages. (See Exhibit 2–3.) Although contingent or temporary workers provide a cost savings as a short-term benefit, depending on their classification they could be entitled to protection under the employment laws. Also, the IRS is looking seriously at the way employers classify their employees. It is important to be sure the classification given is the true classification.

EXHIBIT 2–3   Contingent Workers

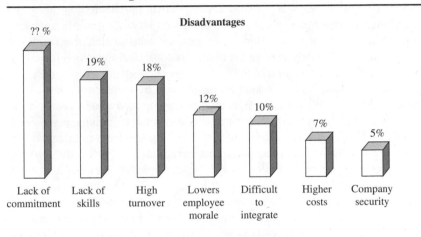

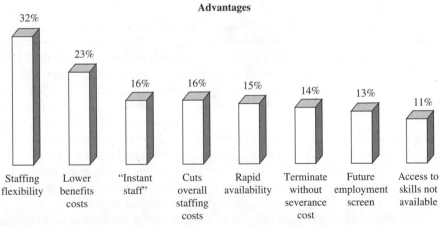

Reprinted with the permission of *HR Magazine*, published by the Society for Human Resource Management, Alexandria, Va.

Employment Probation

Probationary employee
Individual who is considered an employee under the Common Law Test but still may not be granted the full rights and benefits of an employee.

There are certain circumstances where an individual is considered an employee under the Common Law Test, but still may not be granted the full rights and benefits of an employee. These individuals are called **probationary employees.** There are three situations where probation may occur: initial employment of rehire probation, promotion or transfer probation, and disciplinary probation. In these situations, the probationary employee, though called an employee, is not treated the same as a "regular" employee.

The most common form of probation is initial employment or rehire probation. Sometimes, a firm's policies, employment contract, or established workplace practice limit the benefits to which a probationary hire has access, including the denial of medical benefits, lower pay, or the inability to use a grievance procedure in challenging a management decision. During the probationary period, the employee might also be required to demonstrate the ability to do the job for which they were hired. Upon successful completion of the probationary period, the probationary employee is entitled to have all rights and benefits allowed by company policy.

Promotion or transfer probation is similar to initial employment probation in that the promoted employee must demonstrate the ability to perform the new job adequately during the probationary period before they are considered to be in that position on a regular basis. However, promotion or transfer probation differs from initial probation because these employees are already considered regular nonprobationary employees, may not be denied certain benefits such as health care, and may not be immediately dismissed for the inability to perform the new job. In fact, some companies' employees who are promoted but do not pass probation may be able to return to their previous position without any negative ramifications for their status in the company.

Disciplinary probation is a period of conditional employment during which a regular employee has restricted rights due to a disciplinary problem such as insubordination, harassment, and chronic lateness and absenteeism, for example. Typically, disciplinary probation is one of the stages in a progressive discipline policy. Under disciplinary probation, the employee is informed of specific terms and conditions for continued employment; if she or he fails to satisfy those terms, they are terminated.

Probationary periods can vary in duration for 30 days to the discretion of the employer, although typically periods last from 60–90 days. Probationary periods can also be extended at the discretion of the employer; however, reasons for the extension and the terms and conditions of the extension period should be clearly stated.

Unionized and government employers, who are not covered under the employment-at-will doctrine due to their employment contract with their workers, may use probation as a means to screen employees and reserve the right to fire them if they cannot do the job for which they were hired. Piggybacking off of unionized and government employers, private employers are using probationary employment to maintain some degree of management prerogative in an at-will relationship. The courts have granted employers broad authority to administer probation programs; however, courts do curtail probation programs where an employer is shown to have behaved in a capricious, arbitrary, or discriminatory manner. An example of the broad discretion courts give employers is that employers have been allowed to hold probationary employees to a more rigorous performance standard than nonprobationary employees, assuming those standards are applied in a fair and consistent manner to all employees under probationary status.

Even though employers do not need just cause for terminating a probationary employee, it does not mean these employees have no rights whatsoever. Probationary employees are still protected by Title VII and are also covered under the Age Discrimination in Employment Act and the Americans with Disabilities Act. The Equal Employment Opportunity Commission considers probation simply another form of a selection test; consequently, organizations are held accountable by the EEOC for protecting probationary employees under any legislation affecting the employee selection process.

In order to ensure that a probation system is not considered to be discriminatory or unfairly applied, employers should

- ensure that the terms and conditions differentiating probationary from regular employees are clear and communicated to the employees,
- have an accurate and legal performance evaluation system for all employees and document all evaluations, and
- apply all rules, policies, and procedures in a fair and consistent manner and in compliance with current employment law.

These rules of thumb will help minimize an organization's legal exposure as well as protect the rights of both probationary and non-probationary workers.

Who Constitutes an Employer?

Courts and regulatory agencies have not experienced great difficulty in defining the term *employer.* Depending on the applicable statute or provision, an employer is one who employs or uses others to do her work, or to work on her behalf. Most statutes specifically include in this definition employment agencies, labor organizations, and joint labor–management committees. Issues may arise where an entity claims to be a private membership club (exempt from Title VII prohibitions) or a multinational company that may or may not be subject to application of various US laws. Or, a determination must be made whether the employer receives federal funds or maintains federal contracts for coverage under the Rehabilitation Act of 1973, among others. The most exacting issue is usually how many employees an employer must have in order to be subject to a given statute. However, it is crucial for employers to be familiar with those statutes to which it is subject and those from which it is immune.

The Civil Rights Act of 1866

The Civil Rights Act (CRA) of 1866 regulates the actions of all individuals or entities who enter into a contract to employ another. An employer under the CRA of 1866 is one with 15 or more employees.

Title VII of the Civil Rights Act of 1964

Scenario

Title VII applies to all firms or their agents engaged in an industry affecting commerce that employ 15 or more employees for each working day in each of 20 or more weeks in the current or preceding calendar year. Title VII exempts from its regulation government-owned corporations, Indian tribes, and bona fide private membership clubs. "Commerce," in this context, is defined as trade, traffic, transportation, transmission, or communication among the states, between a state and any other place, within the District of Columbia, or within a possession of the United States. "Industry affecting commerce" means any activity, business, or industry in commerce or in which a labor dispute would hinder or obstruct commerce or the free flow of commerce. Lack of *intent* to affect commerce is no defense to coverage.

"Working day" is generally computed by counting the number of employees maintained on the payroll in a given week, as opposed to the number of employees who work on any one day.

Note, however, this form of calculation is merely the majority approach; other courts have found that part-time employees who work for any part of each day of the work week should be counted, while part-time employees who work full days for only a portion of the work week should not be counted.

Title VI of the Civil Rights Act of 1964

Title VI applies the race, color, and national origin proscriptions of Title VII to any program or activity that receives federal financial assistance. States and state agencies are also covered under the Civil Rights Restoration Act of 1987. Title VI applies where the financial assistance to the program or activity has as its primary objective the provision of employment.

The Department of Education, one of the larger federal funding agencies, cites four categories of programs that will be covered by Title VI: projects under the Public Works Acceleration Act; work-study programs under the Vocational Education Act of 1963; programs under other funding statutes that are limited to, or in which a preference is given to, students or others training for employment; and assistance to rehabilitation facilities under the Vocational Rehabilitation Act.

Unless it falls within one of the five exemptions, a government contractor is also prohibited from discriminating on the bases of race, color, religion, gender, or national origin by Executive Order 11246. The order exempts (1) employers with contracts of less than $10,000 from the requirement to include an equal employment opportunity clause in each of their contracts; (2) contracts for work performed outside the United States by employees not recruited within the United States; (3) contracts with state and local governments by providing that the EEO requirements do not apply to any agency of that government that is not participating in the work of the contract; (4) religious educational institutions that hire only people of that religion; and (5) preferences offered to Native Americans living on or near a reservation in connection with employment on or near the reservation; (6) certain contracts on the basis of national interest or security reasons.

Age Discrimination in Employment Act of 1967

The Age Discrimination in Employment Act (ADEA) applies to all entities or their agents that employ 20 or more employees on each working day for 20 or more weeks during the current or preceding calendar year. In addition to an exemption similar to that of Title VII for government-owned corporations, the ADEA also exempts American employers who control foreign firms where compliance with the ADEA in connection with an American employee would cause the foreign firm to violate the laws of the country in which it is located. The ADEA does *not* exempt Indian tribes or private membership clubs, like Title VII.

Rehabilitation Act of 1973

The Rehabilitation Act provides that covered agencies may not discriminate against otherwise qualified disabled individuals, and it applies not only to all entities, programs, and activities that receive federal funds, and government contractors, but also to all programs and activities of any Executive agency as well as the US Postal Service. Federal funding may include grants, loans, contracts, provision of personnel, or real or personal property. A covered federal contractor is one who maintains a contract with the federal government in excess of $2,500 for the provision of personal property or nonpersonal services. A contract may include any agreement between any department, agency, establishment, or instrumentality of the federal government and any person. It does not include employment contracts where the parties to the agreement are employer and employee. There is no requirement similar to that of Title VI that the assistance must be for the provision of employment.

Management Considerations

For reasons cited earlier in this chapter, an employer may hire someone with the intent of establishing an employment relationship or an independent contractor relationship. A variety of protections available to the employer allow the employer some measure of control over this seemingly arbitrary categorization process. However, none will guarantee a court determination of employee or independent contractor status.

First, as in most relationships, a written document will help to identify the nature of the association between the parties and their rights and obligations, provided that the role of the worker is consistent with the duties of an employee or independent contractor. While the classification made in this document is not binding in any way on the courts or the IRS, it may serve as persuasive evidence about the parties' intentions.

If the person is hired as an employee, and it is so stipulated in the document, the written agreement may be considered an employment agreement. The employer should be careful to discuss whether the employment duration will remain at will or for a specified time period.

If the employer intends to hire the worker as an independent contractor, the agreement should articulate the extent of the worker's control over her or his performance and the outcome to be produced pursuant to the contract. Further, where the agreement recites particular hours to be worked, rather than a deadline for completion, it is more likely that the worker will be considered an employee.

Included in the written agreement should be a discussion of who is responsible for the payment of income taxes and benefits and for the division of responsibility for office expenses and overhead, such as tools, supplies, and office rent.

Second, the independent contractor should be paid on the basis of the nature of the job completed, rather than the hours worked to complete it.

Third, no training should be offered to an independent contractor; courts hypothesize that the reason an employer would hire outside help is to reduce these costs. On the other hand, where an employer provides extensive training and support, it is likely that the employer seeks to reap a benefit from this investment in the long run through continued service of its employee.

Fourth, where additional assistance is required, an independent contractor will be made to supply that extra assistance, while an employer would be the party to provide the aid if the worker is an employee. The employer may offer to guarantee a loan to the contractor to allow her or him to obtain the assistance, or new tools, or other equipment if necessary without threatening the independent contractor status.

Finally, where the risk of misclassification is great—for instance, where the failure to correctly categorize the worker may result in large financial penalties—the

Management Tips

- Always evaluate the status of your workers; don't assume employee or independent contractor status for any worker.
- Employment status is relevant to employer payroll and other financial issues; therefore, misclassification may be costly to the employer.
- While an employer is not liable to independent contractors for discrimination based on Title VII, the independent contractor may have other causes of action. Therefore, hiring an independent contractor is not a safe harbor from liability.
- If your intent is to hire an individual as an independent contractor, ensure that, among other factors, the worker has complete control over the manner in which the work will be done, uses her or his own supplies, is paid by the project rather than by the hour, and sets her or his own hours to complete the project.

EXHIBIT 2–4

Form **SS-8** (Rev. July 1993) Department of the Treasury Internal Revenue Service	**Determination of Employee Work Status for Purposes of Federal Employment Taxes and Income Tax Withholding** OMB No. 1545-0004 Expires 7-31-96

Paperwork Reduction Act Notice

We ask for the information on this form to carry out the Internal Revenue laws of the United States. You are required to give us this information. We need it to ensure that you are complying with these laws and to allow us to figure and collect the right amount of tax.

The time needed to complete and file this form will vary depending on individual circumstances. The estimated average time is: **recordkeeping**, 34 hr., 55 min., **learning about the law or the form,** 6 min. and **preparing and sending the form to IRS,** 40 min. If you have comments concerning the accuracy of these time estimates or suggestions for making this form more simple, we would be happy to hear from you. You can write to both the **Internal Revenue Service,** Attention: Reports Clearance Officer, T:FP, Washington, DC 20224; and the **Office of Management and Budget,** Paperwork Reduction Project (1545-0004), Washington, DC 20503. **DO NOT** send the tax form to either of these offices. Instead, see **General Information** for where to file.

Purpose

Employers and workers file Form SS-8 to get a determination as to whether a worker is an employee for purposes of Federal employment taxes and income tax withholding.

General Information

This form should be completed carefully. If the firm is completing the form, it should be completed for **ONE** individual who is representative of the class of workers whose status is in question. If a written determination is desired for more than one class of workers, a separate Form SS-8 should be completed for one worker from **each** class whose status is typical of that class. A written determination for any worker will apply to other workers of the same class if the facts are not materially different from those of the worker whose status was ruled upon.

Please return Form SS-8 to the Internal Revenue Service office that provided the form. If the Internal Revenue Service did not ask you to complete this form but you wish a determination on whether a worker is an employee, file Form SS-8 with your District Director.

Caution: Form SS-8 is **not** a claim for refund of social security and Medicare taxes or Federal income tax withholding. Also, a determination that an individual is an employee does not necessarily reduce any current or prior tax liability. A worker must file his or her income tax return even if a determination has not been made by the due date of the return.

Name of firm (or person) for whom the worker performed services	Name of worker
Address of firm (include street address, apt. or suite no., city, state, and ZIP code)	Address of worker (include street address, apt. or suite no., city, state, and ZIP code)
Trade name	Telephone number (include area code) Worker's social security number ( ) – –
Telephone number (include area code) Firm's taxpayer identification number ( ) –	

Check type of firm for which the work relationship is in question:
☐ **Individual**   ☐ **Partnership**   ☐ **Corporation**   ☐ **Other** (specify) ▶

Important Information Needed to Process Your Request

This form is being completed by: ☐ **Firm**   ☐ **Worker**

If this form is being completed by the worker, the IRS **must** have your permission to disclose your name to the firm.

Do you object to disclosing your name and the information on this form to the firm? . . . .   ☐ **Yes**   ☐ **No**
If you answer "Yes," the IRS cannot act on your request. **DO NOT complete the rest of this form unless the IRS asks for it.**

Under section 6110 of the Internal Revenue Code, the information on this form and related file documents will be open to the public if any ruling or determination is made. However, names, addresses, and taxpayer identification numbers must be removed before the information can be made public.

Is there any other information you want removed? . . . .   ☐ **Yes**   ☐ **No**
If you check "Yes," we cannot process your request unless you submit a copy of this form and copies of all supporting documents showing, in brackets, the information you want removed. Attach a separate statement telling which specific exemption of section 6110(c) applies to each bracketed part.

This form is designed to cover many work activities, so some of the questions may not apply to you. You must answer ALL items or mark them "Unknown" or "Does not apply." If you need more space, attach another sheet.

Total number of workers in this class. (Attach names and addresses. If more than 10 workers, attach only 10.) ▶ _____

This information is about services performed by the worker from _____ to _____
                                            (month, day, year)   (month, day, year)

Is the worker still performing services for the firm? . . . .   ☐ **Yes**   ☐ **No**

If "No," what was the date of termination? ▶ _____
                                        (month, day, year)

Cat. No. 16106T   Form **SS-8** (Rev. 7-93)

EXHIBIT 2–4 (continued)

Form SS-8 (Rev. 7–93)   Page **2**

1a Describe the firm's business ....

2a If the work is done under a written agreement between the firm and the worker, attach a copy. ....

3a Is the worker given training by the firm? . . . . ☐ Yes   ☐ No
   If "Yes": What kind? ....
   How often? ....

4a The firm engages the worker:
   ☐ To perform and complete a particular job only
   ☐ To work at a job for an indefinite period of time
   ☐ Other (explain) ....

5a State the kind and value of tools, equipment, supplies, and materials furnished by:
   The firm ....
   ....
   The worker ....
   ....

6a Will the worker perform the services personally? . . . . ☐ Yes   ☐ No

7 At what location are the services performed? ☐ Firm's ☐ Worker's ☐ Other (specify) ....

8a Type of pay worker receives:
   ☐ Salary   ☐ Commission ☐ Hourly wage   ☐ Piecework ☐ Lump sum   ☐ Other (specify) ....

9a Is the worker eligible for a pension, bonus, paid vacations, sick pay, etc.? . . . . ☐ Yes   ☐ No
   If "Yes," specify ....

10a Approximately how many hours a day does the worker perform services for the firm? ....
   Does the firm set hours of work for the worker? . . . . ☐ Yes   ☐ No
   If "Yes," what are the worker's set hours? _____ am/pm to _____ am/pm (Circle whether am or pm)

11a Can the firm discharge the worker at any time without incurring a liability? . . . . ☐ Yes   ☐ No
   If "No," explain ....

12a Does the worker perform services for the firm under:
   ☐ The firm's business name   ☐ The worker's own business name ☐   Other (specify) ....

13 Is a license necessary for the work? . . . . ☐ Yes   ☐ No ☐ Unknown
   If "Yes," what kind of license is required? ....
   By whom is it issued? ....
   By whom is the license fee paid? ....

14 Does the worker have a financial investment in a business related to the services performed? ☐ Yes   ☐ No ☐ Unknown
   If "Yes," specify and give amounts of the investment ....

15 Can the worker incur a loss in the performance of the service for the firm? . . . . ☐ Yes   ☐ No
   If "Yes," how? ....

16a Has any other government agency ruled on the status of the firm's workers? . . . . ☐ Yes   ☐ No
   If "Yes," attach a copy of the ruling.

17 Does the worker assemble or process a product at home or away from the firm's place of business? . ☐ Yes   ☐ No
   If "Yes":
      Who furnishes materials or goods used by the worker? ☐ Firm   ☐ Worker
      Is the worker furnished a pattern or given instructions to follow in making the product? . . . . . ☐ Yes   ☐ No
      Is the worker required to return the finished product to the firm or to someone designated by the firm? . ☐ Yes   ☐ No

Answer items 18a through n only if the worker is a salesperson or provides a service directly to customers.

18a Are leads to prospective customers furnished by the firm? . . . . ☐ Yes   ☐ No ☐ Does not apply

19 Attach a detailed explanation of any other reason why you believe the worker is an independent contractor or is an employee of the firm.

Under penalties of perjury, I declare that I have examined this request, including accompanying documents, and to the best of my knowledge and belief, the facts presented are true, correct, and complete.

Signature ▶   Title ▶   Date ▶

If this form is used by the firm in requesting a written determination, the form must be signed by an officer or member of the firm.
If this form is used by the worker in requesting a written determination, the form must be signed by the worker. If the worker wants a written determination about services performed for two or more firms, a separate form must be completed and signed for each firm.
Additional copies of this form may be obtained from any Internal Revenue Service office or by calling 1-800-TAX-FORM (1-800-829-3676).

*U.S. Government Printing Office: 1993 — 343-034/80171

This form was edited for emphasis.

employer may choose to obtain an advance ruling from the IRS regarding the nature of the relationship. This is accomplished through the filing of IRS Form SS-8 (see Exhibit 2–4).

Summary

• Why is the definition of "employee" important? The distinction between employees and independent contractors is crucial from a financial perspective. Because many regulations require different responsibilities from employers of employees and independent contractors, it is imperative that an employer be confident of the classification of its employees.

• How does an employer make the distinction between employees and independent contractors? The classification of employees may vary depending on the statute that is to be applied or on the court in which a given case is scheduled to be heard. However, the common thread is generally the right of the employer to control the actions of the worker. Where this is present, the worker is likely to be considered an employee. Other factors to be considered include those that are part of the "economic realities" test, which evaluates the economics of the employment situation. Finally, some workers may be classified statutorily as employees, making the distinction all the easier.

• Who is an "employer"? The definition of employer is generally agreed on. An employer is usually thought to be one who employs or uses others (either employees or independent contractors, or both) to do its work, or to work on its behalf.

Chapter-End Questions

1. Rogers is a firefighter who serves on a volunteer basis for a municipal fire department. The department is a Title VII employer. While Rogers claims that she is entitled to relief because she was discriminated against on the basis of her gender, the department contends that it is not liable because she is not an employee of the department. On investigation, the EEOC learns that many of the department's regular firefighters initially performed work as volunteers with the department prior to hiring, though such volunteer work is not a prerequisite to regular work, and there are firefighters who do not share that experience. However, the EEOC also finds that volunteers are given preferential treatment when competing for vacancies over applicants with no volunteer experience. If the discrimination charge has foundation, is the department subject to liability?

2. Roy and Robert Harvey were in business with a logging company, Careful Cutters, that was a partnership between Roy Harvey's daughter and son-in-law. Careful Cutters did almost all of its work for Roy Harvey; they did have to petition for each job, but they were always awarded the bid. Careful Cutters kept a different set of books than Roy Harvey's business, and they employed their own employees as needed. Roy and Robert Harvey also did not have any control over the operation of Careful Cutters. The Employment Division of Oregon filed an action that Roy and Robert Harvey did not pay unemployment taxes for the employees of Careful Cutters. Can

Careful Cutters be considered an employee of Roy and Robert Harvey or is it an independent contractor? (*Harvey v. Employment Division,* 674 P.2d 1204 (Ore. App. 1984).)

3. Calvin Ehehalt is a firefighter for the New Jersey Fire Department, but he has also been a licensed basketball official for New Jersey for about 20 years. On the average, he officiates about 25–30 basketball games a year for various schools. On one occasion, he was hired by a school to officiate two specific games at $15 a game. During one of these games, Ehehalt suffered an injury to his teeth, and he filed suit against the school for his dental injury. Is Ehehalt considered an employee of the school, which would make the school responsible for his injury on the job, or is Ehehalt an independent contractor? (*Ehehalt v. Livingston Board of Education,* 371 A.2d 752 (N.J. 1977).)

4. James Morris owned and operated Dillon Flying Service, a charter air service in Dillon, Montana. On April 8, 1988, he was flying gubernatorial candidate Jim Waltermire on a campaign trip on a plane donated by Montana Forward, a company unrelated to Dillon Flying Service, when the plane crashed and Morris was killed. Morris had flown for Waltermire on two previous occasions for the rate of $25 per hour or $100 per day plus expenses; however, his acceptance of the jobs was based on his availability. Morris's widow claimed a suit for workers' compensation death benefits against State Compensation Mutual Fund (State Fund), but her claim was denied on the grounds that Morris was an independent contractor and not an employee of Montana Forward at the time of his death. Do you agree? (*Morris v. Montana Forward,* 799 P.2d 1063 (Mont. 1990).)

5. Ramona and Robert Graham were asked by Fuller White Chevrolet to deliver two trucks to a company 388 miles away from the dealer's place of business. The directions given to the Grahams were to take the shortest routes, not use any gravel roads, not to drive any new truck over 50 mph for the first 100 miles, and to check oil and add necessary oil before delivering the trucks. They were to receive 10 cents a mile. Although the Grahams weren't payroll employees of Fuller White Chevrolet, they had delivered trucks for the dealer several times for about two years. On this specific trip, Robert Graham was involved in an automobile accident in which he was injured. Is he eligible for workers' compensation? (*Fuller White Chevrolet Company v. Graham,* 355 P.2d 557 (Okla. 1960).)

6. John Jones is a 63-year-old carpenter who had worked mostly on his own for the past 12 years. Jones was asked by Dwight Holland, manager of the T.M. Deal Lumber Company of Dodge City, to do some repairs for Mike Gebhart, manager of the Dodge City Airport. Gebhart lived in a house that was owned and furnished to him by the city. Gebhart met Jones, told him about the ceiling repairs that needed to be done, and asked him to order any needed materials from T. M. Deal Lumber Company and to charge these materials to the city. Jones hired another man to help him with the repairs, and he used his own tools and equipment in doing the work. While Jones was fixing the ceiling, he fell and suffered a broken pelvis and a dislocated kidney. Is Dodge City responsible for providing Jones with workers' compensation or is Jones considered an independent contractor, which would make him ineligible for the compensation? (*Jones v. Dodge City,* 402 P.2d 108 (Kan., 1965).)

7. Price, a homebuilder, agreed to install siding on the Otts's residence. Though Yvonne

Otts, Price's sister, knew nothing about painting houses, she chose the color of the paint and purchased some of the materials while Otts purchased others. The parties agreed that Price would do the job without any charge for labor, but that the Otts would reimburse him for the cost of the materials he purchased. Wimpey, Price's brother-in-law, was employed by Price and volunteered to help Price with this job, even though he would not be paid for his labor. Price and Wimpey constructed a scaffold using some leftover boards in the Otts's garage; but after several days of work, the scaffold gave way due to rotten boards and Wimpey fell to the ground, suffering disabling injuries to his legs. Wimpey argues that the Otts are liable to compensate him for his injuries as he was an employee of the Otts. What result? (*Wimpey v. Otts,* 427 S.E.2d 34 (Ga. 1993).)

8. Spivey was a retired carpenter who occasionally drove automobiles from one location to another for automobile dealers. Generally, the dealership would contact Spivey to drive various automobiles to locations designated by the dealerships. Spivey was hired by an Acura dealer to drive a car from Raleigh to Fayetteville. Because several cars needed to get to Fayetteville at the same time, several of Spivey's friends were also hired. Spivey was unaware of the route to Fayetteville and planned to follow one of the dealer's employees, who was driving a van at the head of the motorcade. The van was intended to bring the drivers home from Fayetteville. As Spivey was driving the car out of the lot, he ran into Brewer, a pedestrian. Brewer filed suit against Acura, which defended itself claiming that Spivey was not its employee. Are they correct? (*Brewer v. Spivey,* 423 S.E.2d 95 (N.C. 1992).)

9. Lutz was injured as a result of an accident between himself and Cybularz, a newspaper deliverer for *The Inquirer,* as well as several other journals. *The Inquirer* made up approximately one-half of Cybularz's daily deliveries. Cybularz would purchase newspapers wholesale from the publishers, then deliver them to his customers, who would pay Cybularz directly. In connection with *The Inquirer,* the publisher would drop off the newspapers at Cybularz's garage, where Cybularz would pick them up and deliver them. *The Inquirer* considered that Cybularz "worked under them" and he was not permitted to deliver *The Inquirer* at the same time as delivery of other newspapers. Cybularz would be terminated if he did not deliver the papers in the manner specified by *The Inquirer.* Lutz subsequently filed an action against Cybularz and *The Inquirer* to compensate him for his injuries. Is *The Inquirer* liable to Lutz? (*Lutz v. Cybularz,* 607 A.2d 1089 (Penn. 1992).)

10. Between 1980 and 1988, Torres was a self-employed gardener doing business under the name of Jose Torres Gardening Service. From 1984 to 1988, as part of his gardening business, Torres performed weekly gardening services at several homes in Torrence, California, including the Reardons' home. In early 1988, the Reardons discussed with Torres the possibility of employing him to trim a 70-foot tree in their front yard. The Reardons dictated precisely where the tree was to be cut, how much should be left, where the trimmings should be placed, how to finish the cut ends, and when the cutting should take place. The Reardons were not at home when Torres arrived to perform the trim. At one point, a next door neighbor asked Torres why he did not use safety lines, and Torres responded that he did not need them. When Torres began to cut a large branch that

overhung the neighbor's garage, the neighbor came out to help hold a line that would keep the branch from falling on the garage. The neighbor pulled the line too early and Torres fell from the tree, suffering injuries. Torres filed suit against the Reardons. What result? (*Torres v. Reardon,* 5 Cal.Rptr.2d 52 (2d Dist. 1992).)

II REGULATION OF DISCRIMINATION IN EMPLOYMENT

Cages. Consider a birdcage. If you look very closely at just one wire in the cage, you cannot see the other wires. If your conception of what is before you is determined by this myopic focus, you could look at that one wire, up and down the length of it, and be unable to see why a bird would not just fly around the wire any time it wanted to go somewhere. Furthermore, even if, one day at a time, you myopically inspected each wire, you still could not see why a bird would have trouble going past the wires to get anywhere. There is no physical property of any one wire, nothing that the closest scrutiny could discover, that will reveal how a bird could be inhibited or harmed by it except in the most accidental way. It is only when you step back, stop looking at the wires one by one, microscopically, and take a macroscopic view of the whole cage, that you can see why the bird does not go anywhere; and then you will see it in a moment. It will require no great subtlety of mental powers. It is perfectly obvious that the bird is surrounded by a network of systematically related barriers, no one of which would be the least hindrance to its flight, but which, by their relations to each other, are as confining as the solid walls of a dungeon.

From "Oppression," by Marilyn Frye, *The Politics of Reality,* reprinted in *Race, Class and Gender: An Anthology,* Margaret L. Anderson and Patricia Hill Collins, 1992, Wadsworth Press. Used by permission.

3 TITLE VII OF THE CIVIL RIGHTS ACT OF 1964

Chapter Outline

S C E N A R I O S

S C E N A R I O   1

Jack feels he has been discriminated against by his employer, based on national origin. After a particularly tense incident one day, Jack leaves work and goes to his attorney and asks the attorney to file suit against the employer for violation of Title VII of the Civil Rights Act of 1964. Will the attorney do so?

S C E N A R I O   2

Jill, an interviewer for a large business firm, receives a letter from a consulting firm inviting her to attend a seminar on Title VII issues. Jill feels she doesn't need to go since all she does is interview applicants, who are then hired by someone else in the firm. Is Jill correct?

S C E N A R I O   3

The same letter Jill received from the consulting firm is received by Gerald, one of the officers of the local labor organization. Gerald, like Jill, does not see the need to attend, since he is not an employer but, rather, works for a labor organization. Is Gerald's thinking correct?

Statutory Basis

Title VII of the Civil Rights Act of 1964
(a) It shall be an unlawful employment practice for an employer—

(1) to fail or refuse to hire or to discharge any individual, or otherwise to discriminate against any individual with respect to his compensation, terms, conditions, or privileges of employment, because of such individual's race, color, religion, sex, or national origin; or

(2) to limit, segregate, or classify his employees or applicants for employment in any way which would deprive or tend to deprive any individual of employment opportunities or otherwise adversely affect his status as an employee, because of such individual's race, color, religion, sex, or national origin. Title VII of the Civil Rights Act of 1964, as amended, 42 U.S.C.A. sec. 2000e et seq., sec. 703 (a)

A Historic Rights Act

Title VII of the Civil Rights Act of 1964 is the single most important piece of legislation that has helped to shape and define employment law rights in this country. It was an ambitious piece of social legislation, the likes of which had never been attempted here, so passage of the law was not an easy task.

EXHIBIT 3–1   June 1961 (pre–Title VII) Newspaper Want Ad

The exhibit below is typical of the index to want ads from the classified section found in newspapers in the United States before Title VII was passed in 1964.

Index to Want Ads

Announcements
1—Funeral Notices
2—Funeral Notices, Colored
3—Cemetery Lots, Crypts
4—Cards of Thanks
5—In Memoriam
6—Florists
7—Lodge Notices
8—Local Notices
10—Nursery and Baby Sitters
11—Personals
12—Personal Interests
13—Lost and Found

Business Services
A—Air Conditioning, Heating
C—Building, Contracting
E—Cement, Brick, Stone Work
F—Septic Tanks
G—Appliance Repair
J—Electrical Work
L—Exterminating
N—Furniture Repairs, Refinishing
O—Grading, Excavating
R—Landscaping, Tree Service
S—Moving, Trucking, Storage
U—Painting, Decorating, Plastering
V—Roofing, Sheet Metal
W—Plumbing
X—Slip Covers, Draperies
Y—Dressmaking, Tailoring
Z—Miscellaneous Services

Male Employment
14—Male Help Wanted
15—Male Employment Agencies
16—Situations Wanted, Male
17—Male, Female Help Wanted

Instructions
18—Business Schools
19—Trade or Home Study Schools
20—Private Institutions

Female Employment
22—Female Help Wanted
23—Female Employment Agencies
24—Situations Wanted, Female

Colored Employment
26—Help Wanted Male, Colored
27—Employment Agency Male, Colored
28—Situations Wanted Male, Colored
29—Help Wanted Female, Colored
30—Employment Agency Female, Colored
31—Situations Wanted Female, Colored

Financial
40—Business Opportunities
41—Money to Loan
42—Investments
43—Wanted to Borrow

Livestock
44—Farm Livestock
45—Riding Horses and Equipment
46—Dogs and Puppies
47—Miscellaneous Pets
48—Pet Supplies, Services

Merchandise
50—Miscellaneous for Sale
51—Articles for Rent
52—Household Goods
53—Antiques
54—Musical Merchandise
55—Radio, TV, Recording
56—Auctions
58—Machinery, Tools
59—Building Materials
60—Farm Equipment, Supplies
61—Seeds, Plants, Nurseries
65—Office Equipment, Supplies
66—Business Equipment
67—Swaps
72—Wanted to Buy

Rentals
74—Hotels, Motels
75—Rooms
76—Room and Board
77—Housekeeping Rooms
78—Furn. Apts.: Duplexes
79—Unfur. Apts.: Duplexes
80—Furnished Houses
81—Unfurnished Houses
84—Suburban

85—Resorts
86—Office, Desk Space
87—Stores, Building, Land
88—Wanted to Rent
89—For Rent, Colored
91—Resorts, Colored

Real Estate
93—Realty Loans, Insurance
94—Homes, Area 1
96—Homes, Area 2
98—Homes, Area 3
100—Homes, Area 4
102—Homes, Area 5
104—Homes, Area 6
105—Suburban
106—Realty Exchange
107—Home Sites
108—Income Property
109—Commercial Property
110—Other Cities Realty
111—Farms and Lands
112—Resorts
113—Realty, Colored
114—Miscellaneous Realty
115—Wanted Realty
116—Realty Auctions

Transportation
118—Boats, Motors, Needs
120—Aviation and Services
121—Mobile Homes
122—Trucks, Trailers, Buses
123—Motorcycles, Motor Scooters
124—Auto Parts, Services
125—Car, Truck Rentals
126—Antique Classic Autos
127—Wanted, Automotive
128—Auto Loans, Insurance
129—Imported or Sports Cars
130—Auto for Sale

While the law prohibits discrimination on the basis of race, color, gender, national origin, or religion, it was racial discrimination that was the moving force for the law. Blacks had been brought to America from Africa to be slaves. After slavery ended 300+ years later, the country struggled to forge a new relationship with blacks with whom they had no relationship other than ownership or blacks serving their needs. When the civil rights legislation was debated in Congress and eventually passed in 1964, the country was deeply divided in trying to move away from its 99-year post–Civil War history of its treatment of blacks—a history that included everything from benign neglect to legally sanctioned discrimination, called "Jim Crow" laws. There were laws regulating the separation of blacks and whites in every facet of life from birth to death. Laws prohibited blacks and whites from marrying, going to school together, and working together. Every facility imaginable was segregated, including movies, restaurants, hospitals, cemeteries, libraries, funeral homes, swimming pools, housing developments, parks, colleges, public transportation, recreational facilities, social organizations, and stores.

The doctrine of separate but equal educational facilities had fallen 10 years before in 1954, with the US Supreme Court's decision in *Brown v. Topeka Board of Education.*[1] Citizens were challenging infringements upon the right of blacks to vote. There were boycotts, "freedom rides," and sit-in demonstrations for the right to nonsegregated public accommodations, transportation, municipal parks, swimming pools, libraries, and lunch counters. There was racial unrest, strife, marches, and civil disobedience on as close to a mass scale as this country has ever experienced. Something had to give.

In an impressive show of how important societal considerations can be in shaping law, the 1964 Civil Rights Act was passed soon after the historic March on Washington in August of 1963. It was at this march that the late Rev. Dr. Martin Luther King, Jr., gave his famous "I Have a Dream" speech on the steps of the Lincoln Memorial. In the largest march of its kind ever held in this country, hundreds of thousands of people of all races, creeds, colors, and walks of life traveled from around the world to show legislators that legalized racism was no longer tolerable in a society that considered itself to be civilized.

Title VII, the employment section of the act, is only one title of a much larger piece of legislation. The Civil Rights Act of 1964 created the legal basis for nondiscrimination in housing, education, public accommodations, federally assisted programs, and employment. Since employment in large measure defines the availability of the other matters, the case law in Title VII of the Civil Rights Act quickly became the most important arbiter of rights under the new law. In President John F. Kennedy's original message to Congress on introducing the act in 1963, he stated: "There is little value in a Negro's obtaining the right to be admitted to hotels and restaurants if he has no cash in his pocket and no job."

The face of the workplace has changed dramatically since the passage of the

---

[1] 347 U.S. 483 (1954).

act (see Exhibit 3–1). More women and minorities than ever before are engaged in meaningful employment. While Title VII applies equally to everyone, because of the particular history behind the law it gave new rights to women and minorities, who had only limited legal recourse available for job discrimination before the act. With the passage of Title VII, the door was opened to prohibiting job discrimination and creating expectations of fairness in employment. It was not long before legislation followed providing similar protection from discrimination based on age, Vietnam veteran status, and disability.

State and local governments passed laws paralleling Title VII and the other protective legislation. Sometimes the laws added categories, such as marital status, affinity orientation, receipt of public benefits, or others as prohibited categories of discrimination. The new expectations did not stop there. As we saw in the chapter on employment at will, others not included in the coverage of the statutes came to have heightened expectations about the workplace and their role within it and were willing to pressure legislators and sue employers in pursuit of these perceived rights.

For employers, Title VII meant that the workplace was no longer a place in which decisions regarding hiring, promotion, and the like could go unchallenged. Now there were prohibitions on some of the factors that had previously been a part of many employers' hiring considerations. Employers had been feeling the effects of federal regulation in the workplace for some time. Among others, there were wage and hour and child labor laws regulating minimum ages, wages, and permissible work hours that employers could impose, and there were labor laws protecting collective bargaining. Now came Title VII, regulating to some extent the bases an employer could use to hire or promote employees.

After enactment, Title VII was amended several times to further strengthen it. There were amendments in 1972 and 1978, with the passage of the Equal Employment Opportunity Act of 1972 and the Pregnancy Discrimination Act of 1978. The 1972 amendment expanded Title VII's coverage to include government employees and to strengthen the enforcement powers of the enforcing agency created by the law, the Equal Employment Opportunity Commission (EEOC). The 1978 amendment added discrimination on the basis of pregnancy as a type of gender discrimination.

In its most far-reaching overhaul since its passage, the act was also amended by the Civil Rights Act of 1991. This amendment added jury trials, compensatory and punitive damages (where appropriate), and several other provisions, further strengthening the law.

The EEOC is now the lead agency for job discrimination and handles most matters of employment discrimination arising under federal laws, including age and disability. The EEOC has implemented regulations that govern agency procedures and requirements under the law, and it provides guidelines to employers for dealing with employment discrimination laws. The EEOC's regulations can be found in the Code of Federal Regulations. E.g., 29 CFR Part 1604.1–9, Guidelines on Discrimination Because of Sex; 29 CFR Part 1604.10, Guideline on Discrimination

---

EXHIBIT 3–2   Civil Rights Act of 1991

When the Civil Rights Act of 1991 was signed into law by President George Bush on November 21, 1991, it was the end of a fierce battle that had raged for several years over the increasingly conservative decisions of the US Supreme Court in civil rights cases. The new law was a major overhaul for Title VII. The law's nearly 30-year history was scrutinized. It is significant for employers that, when presented the opportunity, Congress chose to strengthen the law in many ways, rather than lessen its effectiveness. Among other things, the new law for the first time in Title VII cases:

- Permitted:
  —Jury trials where compensatory or punitive damages are sought.
  —Compensatory damages in religious, gender, and disability cases (such damages were already allowed for race and national origin under related legislation).
  —Punitive damages for the same.
  —Unlimited medical expenses.
- Limited the extent to which "reverse discrimination" suits could be brought.
- Authorized expert witness fees to successful plaintiffs.
- Codified the disparate impact theory.
- Broadened protections against private race discrimination in 42 USC section 1981 cases.
- Expanded the right to bring actions challenging discriminatory seniority systems.
- Extended extraterritorial coverage of Title VII to US citizens working for US companies outside the United States, except where it would violate the laws of the country.
- Extended coverage and established procedures for Senate employees.
- Established the Glass Ceiling Commission.
- Established the National Award for Diversity and Excellence in American Executive Management (known as the Frances Perkins–Elizabeth Hanford Dole National Award for Diversity and Excellence in American Executive Management) for businesses who "have made substantial efforts to promote the opportunities and development experiences of women and minorities and foster advancement to management and decision-making positions within the business."

---

because of sex, pregnancy and childbirth; 29 CFR Part 1606, Guidelines on Discrimination Because of National Origin; 29 CFR Part 1607, Employee Selection Procedures; 29 CFR Part 1613.701–707, Guidelines on Discrimination Because of Disability; 45 CFR Part 90, Guidelines on Discrimination Because of Age.

Most employers have come to accept the reality of Title VII. Some have gone beyond acceptance and grown to appreciate the diversity and breadth of the workplace that the law engenders. The best way to avoid violations of employment discrimination laws is to know and understand its requirements. That is what the following sections and chapters will help you do.

Keep the opening selection, "Cages," in mind as you go through this section of the text. Most of us look at things microscopically. That is, we tend to see only the situation in front of us, and don't give much thought to the larger picture it fits into. But it is this larger picture in which we operate. It is the one the law considers when enacting legislation, the courts consider in deciding cases, and the one an employer should be considering when developing workplace policies or responding to workplace situations. Often, a situation, in and of itself, may seem to us to have little or no significance. "Why are they whining about this?" we say; "Why can't they just go along?" But we are often missing the larger picture and how this situation may fit into it. Like the birdcage in the opening selection, each thing, in and of itself, may not be a big deal, but put each of these things together, and a picture is revealed of a very different reality for those who must deal with the "wires."

Many of the situations you see in the following chapters are "wires" which Title VII tries to eradicate in an effort to break down the seemingly impenetrable invisible barriers we have erected around issues of race, gender, disabilities, ethnicity, religion, and affinity orientation. As you go through the cases and information, think not only about the micro picture of what is going on in front of you, but also the larger macro picture that it fits into. Sometimes what makes little sense in one setting, makes all the sense in the world in the other.

What does this all mean? Let's look at an example. A female who works in a garage comes in one day and there are nude photos of females all around the shop. She complains to the supervisor and he tells her that the men like the photos and if she doesn't like it, just don't look at them. The guys she works with begin to really rib her about complaining. They tell her she's a "weenie" and "can't cut the mustard" and "can't hang with the big boys." "What's the big deal?" you say. "Why didn't she just shut up and ignore the photos?"

Well, in and of itself the photos may not seem like much. But when you look at the issue in context, it looks quite different. Research shows that in workplaces in which nude photos, adult language, sexual jokes, and so on, are present, women tend to be paid less and receive fewer and less significant raises, promotions, and training. It is not unlikely that the environment that supports such photos doesn't clearly draw lines between the people in the photos and females at work. Case after case bears it out. So the photos themselves aren't really the whole issue. It's the micro picture. But the macro picture is the objectification of women and what contributes to women being viewed as less than and not as capable in a workplace in which they may well be just as capable as anyone else. What might have seemed like harmless joking or photos in the micro view, takes on much more significance in the macro view and has much more of a potential negative impact on the work experience of the female employee.

Again, as you go through the following chapters, try to look at the micro as well as the macro picture. You will get help from the case-end questions, which get you to try to view what you have read in a larger context. Again, it is this context which will be under scrutiny when the policies of a workplace form the basis of a lawsuit. Thinking about that context beforehand and making policies consistent with it give the employer a much greater chance of avoiding embarrassing and costly litigation.

The Structure of Title VII

What Is Prohibited under Title VII

Title VII prohibits discrimination in hiring, firing, training, promotion, discipline, or other workplace decisions on the basis of an employee or applicant's race, color, gender, national origin, or religion. Included in the prohibitions are discrimination in pay, terms and conditions of employment, training, layoffs, and benefits. Virtually any workplace decision can be challenged by an applicant or employee who falls within the Title VII categories.

EXHIBIT 3–3   Title VII Provisions

An employer cannot discriminate on the basis of:
- Race
- Color
- Gender
- Religion
- National origin

In making decisions regarding:
- Hiring
- Firing
- Training
- Discipline
- Compensation
- Benefits
- Classification
- Or other terms or conditions of employment

Who Must Comply

Title VII applies to employers, unions, and joint labor and management committees making admission, referral, training, and other decisions, and to employment agencies and other similar hiring entities making referrals for employment. It applies to all private employers employing 15 or more employees, and to federal, state, and local governments. In opening scenario 3, Gerald has reason to attend the training because Title VII applies to labor unions as well as employers.

Who Is Covered

Title VII applies to public (governmental) and private employees alike. Unlike labor laws that do not apply to managerial employees or wage and hour laws that exempt

EXHIBIT 3–4   Who Must Comply

- Employers engaged in interstate commerce if they have:
  —Fifteen or more employees for each working day in each of 20 or more calendar weeks in the current or preceding calendar year.
- Labor organizations of any kind that exist to deal with employers concerning labor issues, engaged in an industry affecting commerce.
- Employment agencies that, with or without compensation, procure employees for employers or opportunities to work for employees.

certain types of employees, Title VII covers all levels and types of employees. The Civil Rights Act of 1991 further extended Title VII's coverage to US citizens employed outside the United States for American employers. Non-US citizens are protected in the United States but not outside the United States.

Who Is Not Covered

Exemptions under Title VII are limited. Title VII permits businesses operated on or around Native American Indian reservations to give preferential treatment to Native Americans. The act specifically states that it does not apply to actions taken with respect to someone who is a member of the Communist party or other organization required to register as a Communist-action or Communist-front organization. The law permits religious institutions and associations to discriminate when performing their activities. For instance, a Catholic priest could not successfully sue under Title VII alleging religious discrimination for not being hired to lead a Jewish synagogue.

EXHIBIT 3–5   Employees Who Are Not Covered by Title VII

- Employees of employers having less than 15 employees.
- Employees whose employers are not engaged in interstate commerce.
- Non-US citizens employed outside the United States.
- Employees of religious institutions, associations, or corporations hired to perform work connected with carrying on religious activities.
- Members of Communist organizations.

DAWAVENDEWA V. SALT RIVER PROJECT AGRICULTURAL IMPROVEMENT AND POWER DISTRICT
154 F3d 1117 (9th Cir. 1998)

A Native American sued under Title VII after he was not hired because he was not of the preferred Native American tribal affiliation. The court had to determine if the Title VII Native American preference provision permitted discrimination on the basis of tribal affiliation among Native Americans. The court determined that Title VII's Native American preference provision only permitted distinctions between Native Americans and non-Native Americans, not between one tribe of Native American and another.

Reinhardt, J.

The private employer operates a power plant in northeast Arizona under a lease agreement with the Navajo Nation. Under the agreement, there is a preference for "local Navajos," defined as members of the tribe living on land within tribal jurisdiction. If local Navajo labor was not available or if the quality of work was not acceptable to the employer, they could hire "in order of preference, first qualified non-local Navajos, and second, non-Navajos."

Applicant, a member of the Hopi tribe, lives within three miles of the Navajo reservation. He applied for an operator trainee position and alleged that his test scores ranked ninth out of the top 20 applicants. According to the applicant, he would have been hired if he were a member of the Navajo Nation or married to a Navajo. The employer refused to consider the applicant for the job, and the applicant sued under Title VII for national origin discrimination.

The purpose of the Indian Preferences exemption is to authorize an employer to grant preference to all Indians (who live on or near a reservation) to permit the favoring of Indians over non-Indians. The exemption is not designed to permit employers to favor members of one Indian tribe over another, let alone to favor them over all other Indians.

REVERSED.

Filing Claims under Title VII

Claimant or charging party
The person who brings an action alleging violation of Title VII.

Employees who feel they have been the victim of employment discrimination may file a charge or claim with the EEOC. An employee filing such a claim is called a **"claimant"** or a **"charging party."** Employers should be aware that it costs an employee nothing but time and energy to go to the nearest EEOC office and file a claim. By law, the EEOC must handle every claim it receives. To discourage claims, employers should ensure that their policies and procedures are legal, fair, and consistently applied.

For employers, the good news is that the vast majority of charges are quickly sifted out of the system for one reason or another. For instance, in fiscal year 1998, of the 58,124 charges filed with EEOC, 4.4 percent were settled, 26.5 percent had administrative closures (failure of the claimant to pursue the claim, loss of contact with the claimant, etc.), 62.1 percent resulted in findings of no reasonable cause, and reasonable cause was found in only 4.2 percent of the charges. However, the monetary value of the recovery by EEOC was $257.3 million.

Nonfederal government employee claims must be filed within 180 days of the discriminatory event. For federal employees, claims must be filed with their employing agency within 30 days of the event.

The reason for the fairly short statute of limitations is an attempt to ensure that the necessary parties and witnesses are still available and that events are not too remote to recollect accurately. Violations of Title VII may also be brought to the EEOC's attention because of its own investigation or by information provided by employers meeting their **recordkeeping and reporting requirements** under the law.

State Law Interface in the Filing Process.   Since most states have their own fair employment practice laws, they also have their own state and local enforcement agencies for employment discrimination claims. These agencies may contract with the EEOC to be what is called a **"706" agency** (named for section 706 of the act). These agencies receive and process claims of discrimination for the EEOC in addition to carrying on their own state business.

Title VII's intent is that claims be **conciliated** if possible. Local agencies serve as a type of screening process for the more serious cases. If the complaint is not satisfactorily disposed at this level, it may eventually be taken by the EEOC and, if necessary, litigated. State and local agencies have their own procedures, which are similar to those of the EEOC.

If an employee files his or her claim with the EEOC when there is a 706 agency in the jurisdiction, the EEOC must defer the complaint to the 706 agency for 60 days before investigating. The employee can file the complaint with the EEOC, but the EEOC sends it to the 706 agency, and EEOC will not move on the claim for 60 days.

If the employee files with the 706 agency, then the complaint is filed by the 706 agency with the EEOC up to 300 days after the alleged discrimination or 30 days after notice of termination of local proceedings by the 706 agency, whichever comes first. In further explaining the process, reference will only be made to the EEOC as the enforcing agency involved.

Proceeding through the EEOC.   After the complaint is filed with the EEOC, within 10 days the EEOC serves notice of the charge with the employer (called **"respondent"** or **"responding party"**). Title VII also includes **antiretaliation provisions.** It is a separate offense for an employer to retaliate against an employee for pursuing rights under Title VII. Noting that retaliation claims had doubled since

Recordkeeping and reporting requirements
Title VII requires that certain documents must be maintained and periodically reported to EEOC.

706 agency
State agency that handles EEOC claims.

Conciliation
Attempting to reach agreement on a claim through discussion, without resort to litigation.

Respondent/ responding party
Person to whom an EEOC claim is directed, usually the employer.

Antiretaliation provisions
Provisions making it illegal to treat an employee adversely because the employee pursued his or her rights under Title VII.

Reasonable cause
Basis for finding illegal discrimination existed.

1991, in late 1998 the EEOC issued retaliation guidelines to provide its view on what constitutes retaliation for pursuing Title VII rights and how it will view such claims by employees.

After the filing of a complaint and notice to the respondent, until recently the EEOC would then investigate the complaint by talking with the parties and any other necessary witnesses in an attempt to find out if there was **reasonable cause** for the discrimination alleged. However, on February 11, 1999, the EEOC launched its expanded mediation program, adopted after extensive investigation determined that it would be helpful in streamlining agency procedures and making them less expensive, thus preserving EEOC's resources to address major issues.

Under the new mediation procedures, which EEOC says will significantly change the way it does business, the EEOC will screen all new charges for mediation referral. Complex and weak cases will not be referred for mediation. The agency estimates that it will refer to mediation 70 to 80 percent of the charges filed. Both parties will be sent letters offering mediation, and the decision to do so is voluntary for both parties. Each side has 10 days to respond to the offer. If both parties elect mediation, the charge must be mediated within 60 days for in-house mediation or 45 days for external mediation.

If the parties choose to mediate, then during mediation, they will have the opportunity to present their positions, express their opinions, provide information, and express their request for relief. Any information disclosed during this process is not to be revealed to anyone, including EEOC employees. If the parties reach agreement, that agreement is as binding as any other settlement agreement.

EEOC specialist
Employee of EEOC agency who reviews complaints for merit.

No cause
Finding that no basis for illegal discrimination existed.

Right-to-sue letter
Letter given by EEOC to claimants, permitting them to pursue their claim in court.

Exhaustion of administrative remedies
Going through the established administrative procedure before being permitted to seek judicial review of an agency decision.

Conciliation.   If the parties choose not to mediate the charge or the mediation is not successful, the charge is referred back to EEOC for the usual handling. That is, after filing the complaint, the EEOC will then investigate the complaint by talking with the employer and employee and any other necessary witnesses. If the EEOC finds there is reasonable cause for the employee to charge the employer with discrimination, it will attempt to have the parties conciliate the matter. That is, the EEOC will bring the parties together in a fairly informal setting, usually with an EEOC employee called an **"EEOC specialist."**

The EEOC specialist will set forth what has been found during the investigation and discuss with the parties the ways the matter can be resolved. Often the employee is satisfied if the employer simply agrees to provide a favorable letter of recommendation. The majority of claims filed with the EEOC are adequately disposed of at this stage of the proceedings.

No Cause Finding.   After investigation, if the EEOC finds there is **no cause** for the employee's discrimination complaint, the employee is notified by an EEOC **right-to-sue letter.** If the employee wants to pursue the matter further, the employee is now free to do so, having **exhausted the administrative remedies.** The employee can then bring suit against the employer in federal court within 90 days of receiving the right-to-sue letter.

Judicial Review

If no conciliation is reached, the EEOC may eventually file a civil action in federal district court. As we have seen, if the EEOC originally found no cause and issued the complaining party a right-to-sue letter, the employee can take the case to court, seeking **judicial review.** Title VII requires that courts give EEOC decisions *de novo* **review.** A court can only take a Title VII discrimination case for judicial review after the EEOC has first disposed of the claim. Thus, in opening scenario one, Jack cannot immediately file a discrimination lawsuit against his employer because Jack has not yet gone through the EEOC process.

The case is handled entirely new, as if there had not already been an investigation and a finding by the EEOC. Employees proceeding with a no cause letter are also free to develop the case however they wish without being bound by EEOC's determination. If a party is not satisfied with the court's decision and has a basis upon which to appeal, the case can be appealed up to, and including, the US Supreme Court, if it agrees to hear the case.

Remedies

If the employee wins the case, the employer may be liable for **back pay** of up to two years before filing the charge with the EEOC, for **front pay** for future earnings that the employee would have received absent discrimination, for reinstatement to his or her position, for **retroactive seniority,** for injunctive relief, if applicable, and for attorney fees. Until passage of the Civil Rights Act of 1991, remedies for discrimination under Title VII were limited to **make-whole relief** and injunctive relief.

The Civil Rights Act of 1991 added **compensatory damages** and **punitive damages** as available remedies. Punitive damages are permitted when it is shown that the employer's action was malicious or was done with reckless indifference to federally protected rights of the employee. They are not allowed under the **disparate/adverse impact** or unintentional theory of discrimination (to be discussed shortly) and may not be recovered from governmental employers. Compensatory damages may include future pecuniary loss, emotional pain, suffering, inconvenience, mental anguish, loss of enjoyment of life, and other nonpecuniary losses.

There are certain limitations on the damages under the law. Gender discrimination (including sexual harassment) and religious discrimination have a $300,000 cap total on compensatory and punitive damages. The cap depends on the number of employees the employer has (see Exhibit 3–8). Juries may not be told of the caps on liability. Since race and national origin discrimination cases can also be brought under 42 USC section 1981, which permits unlimited compensatory damages, the limitations do not apply to these categories.

With the addition of compensatory and punitive damages possible in Title VII cases, litigation is likely to increase. It is now more worthwhile for employees to sue. The possibility of money damages also makes it more likely that employers will settle more suits rather than risk large damage awards. The best defense to costly litigation and liability is solid workplace policies.

Scenario

Judicial review
Court review of an agency's decision.

De novo **review**
Complete new look at administrative case by the reviewing court.

Back pay
Money awarded for time employee was not working (usually due to termination) because of illegal discrimination.

Front pay
Money awarded for time a claimant would have been in a job had illegal discrimination not occurred.

Retroactive seniority
Seniority that dates back to the time the claimant was treated illegally.

Make-whole relief
Attempts to put claimant in position he or she would have been in had there been no discrimination.

Compensatory damages
Money awarded to compensate the injured party for direct losses.

Punitive damages
Money over and above compensatory damages, imposed by court to punish defendant and to act as a deterrent.

Disparate/adverse impact
Effect of facially neutral policy is deleterious for Title VII group.

EXHIBIT 3–6   **The Procedure for Bringing a Claim within the EEOC**

- Employee goes to 706 agency office and files EEOC complaint.
- Agency sends notice to employer responding party accused of discrimination.
- Parties receive referral to mediation (if appropriate).
- If both elect mediation, charge is mediated.
- If parties agree in mediation, agreement is binding.
- If mediation is not successful or parties choose not to mediate, EEOC schedules a meeting with the parties.
- Parties meet and try to conciliate.
- If agreement is reached, claim ends.
- If no agreement is reached, claim is investigated by 706 agency.
- 706 agency makes determination of cause or no cause.
- If no cause, employee is notified and given right-to-sue letter.
- If cause, 706 agency notifies employer of proposed remedy.
- If employer disagrees, he or she appeals decision to next agency level.

EXHIBIT 3–7   **Remedies under Title VII**

- Back pay
- Front pay
- Reinstatement
- Seniority
- Retroactive seniority
- Injunctive relief
- Compensatory damages
- Punitive damages
- Attorney fees

EXHIBIT 3–8   **Compensatory and Punitive Damages Caps**

For employers with:
- 15 to 100 employees, there is a cap of $50,000.
- 101 to 200 employees, there is a cap of $100,000.
- 201 to 500 employees, there is a cap of $200,000.
- More than 500 employees, there is a cap of $300,000.

Jury Trials

The Civil Rights Act of 1991 also added jury trials to Title VII. From the creation of Title VII in 1964 until passage of the 1991 Civil Rights Act 27 years later, jury trials were not permitted under Title VII. Jury trials are now permitted under Title VII at the request of either party when compensatory and punitive damages are sought.

There is always less predictability about case outcomes when juries are involved. Arguing one's cause to a judge who is a trained member of the legal profession is quite different from arguing to a jury of 6 to 12 jurors, all of whom come with their own backgrounds, prejudices, and predilections. Employers now have even more incentive to ensure that their policies and actions are well-reasoned, business-related, and justifiable—especially since employees have even more incentive to sue.

Theoretical Bases for Title VII Lawsuits

In alleging discrimination, an employee **plaintiff** may use either of two theories to bring suit under Title VII: disparate treatment or disparate impact. The suit must fit into one theory or the other to be recognized under Title VII. A thorough understanding of each will help employers to make sounder policies that avoid litigation and enhance the workplace. Since cases will be our vehicle for viewing Title VII, we will speak of the parties as plaintiff and **defendant.** In virtually all situations, the employee has first filed a claim with the EEOC, and the case has eventually been taken to court by the employee plaintiff.

Plaintiff
One who brings a civil action.

Defendant
One against whom a case is brought.

Disparate Treatment

Disparate treatment is the Title VII theory used in cases of individual discrimination. The plaintiff employee (or applicant) bringing suit alleges that the defendant employer treats the employee differently than other similarly situated employees. Further, the employee alleges that the reason for the difference is the employees' race, religion, gender, color, or national origin. Disparate treatment is considered intentional discrimination, but the plaintiff need not actually know that unlawful discrimination is the reason for the difference. That is, the employee need not prove that the employer actually said that race, gender, and so on was the reason for the decision. As you will see in the following case, the US Supreme Court has come up with a set of indicators that leave intentional discrimination as the only plausible explanation when all other possibilities are eliminated.

Disparate treatment
Treating similarly situated employee differently because of prohibited Title VII factor.

McDonnell Douglas Corp. v. Green
411 U.S. 792 (1973)

Green, an employee of McDonnell Douglas and a black civil rights activist, engaged with others in "disruptive and illegal activity" against his employer in the form of a traffic stall-in. The activity was done as part of Green's protest that his discharge from McDonnell Douglas was racially motivated, as were the firm's general hiring practices. McDonnell Douglas later rejected Green's reemployment application on the ground of the illegal conduct. Green sued, alleging race discrimination. The case is important because it is the first time the US Supreme Court set forth how to prove a disparate treatment case under Title VII. In such cases the employee can use an inference of discrimination drawn from a set of inquiries the Court set forth.

Powell, J.

The critical issue before us concerns the order and allocation of proof in a private, nonclass action challenging employment discrimination. The language of Title VII makes plain the purpose of Congress to assure equality of employment opportunities and to eliminate those discriminatory practices and devices which have fostered racially stratified job environments to the disadvantage of minority citizens.

The complainant in a Title VII trial must carry the initial burden under the statute of establishing a **prima facie case** of racial discrimination. This may be done by showing (i) that he belongs to a racial minority; (ii) that he applied and was qualified for a job for which the employer was seeking applicants; (iii) that, despite his qualifications, he was rejected; and (iv) that, after his rejection, the position remained open and the employer continued to seek applicants from persons of complainant's qualifications. The facts necessarily will vary in Title VII cases, and the specification of the prima facie proof required from Green is not necessarily applicable in every respect to differing factual situations.

In the instant case, Green proved a prima facie case. McDonnell Douglas sought mechanics, Green's trade, and continued to do so after Green's rejection. McDonnell Douglas, moreover,

does not dispute Green's qualifications and acknowledges that his past work performance in McDonnell Douglas's employ was "satisfactory."

The burden then must shift to the employer to articulate some legitimate, nondiscriminatory reason for the employee's rejection. We need not attempt to detail every matter which fairly could be recognized as a reasonable basis for a refusal to hire. Here McDonnell Douglas has assigned Green's participation in unlawful conduct against it as the cause for his rejection. We think that this suffices to discharge McDonnell Douglas's burden of proof at this stage and to meet Green's prima facie case of discrimination.

But the inquiry must not end here. While Title VII does not, without more, compel the rehiring of Green, neither does it permit McDonnell Douglas to use Green's conduct as a pretext for the sort of discrimination prohibited by Title VII. On remand, Green must be afforded a fair opportunity to show that McDonnell Douglas's stated reason for Green's rejection was in fact pretext. Especially relevant to such a showing would be evidence that white employees involved in acts against McDonnell Douglas of comparable seriousness to the "stall-in" were nevertheless retained or rehired.

McDonnell Douglas may justifiably refuse to

rehire one who was engaged in unlawful, disruptive acts against it, but only if this criterion is applied alike to members of all races. Other evidence that may be relevant to any showing of pretext includes facts as to the McDonnell Douglas's treatment of Green during his prior term of employment; McDonnell Douglas's reaction, if any, to Green's legitimate civil rights activities; and McDonnell Douglas's general policy and practice with respect to minority employment.

On the latter point, statistics as to McDonnell Douglas's employment policy and practice may be helpful to a determination of whether McDonnell Douglas's refusal to rehire Green in this case conformed to a general pattern of discrimination against blacks. The District Court may, for example, determine, after reasonable discovery that "the [racial] composition of defendant's labor force is itself reflective of restrictive or exclusionary practices." We caution that such general determinations, while helpful, may not be in and of themselves controlling as to an individualized hiring decision, particularly in the presence of an otherwise justifiable

reason for refusing to rehire. In short, on the retrial Green must be given a full and fair opportunity to demonstrate by competent evidence that the presumptively valid reasons for his rejection were in fact a cover up for a racially discriminatory decision. VACATED and REMANDED.

Case Questions

1. Do you think the Court should require actual evidence of discrimination in disparate treatment cases rather than permitting an inference? What are the advantages? Disadvantages?
2. Practically speaking, is an employer's burden really met after the employer "articulates" a legitimate nondiscriminatory reason for rejecting the employee?
3. Does the Court say that Green must be kept on in spite of his illegal activities? Discuss.

The effect of the *McDonnell Douglas* inquiries is to set up a legal test of all relevant factors that are generally taken into consideration in making employment determinations. Once those considerations have been ruled out as the reason for failure to hire the applicant, the only factor left to consider is the applicant's membership in one of Title VII's prohibited categories (i.e., race, color, gender, religion, or national origin).

The *McDonnell Douglas* Court recognized that there would be scenarios under Title VII other than failure to rehire (i.e., failure to promote or train, discriminatory discipline, and so on) and its test would not be directly transferrable to them, but it could be modified accordingly. For instance, the issue may not be a refusal to rehire; it may, instead, be a dismissal. In such a case, the employee would show the factors as they relate to dismissal.

If an employer makes decisions in accordance with these requirements, it is less likely that the decisions will later be successfully challenged by the employee. Disparate treatment cases involve an employer's variance from the normal scheme of things, to which the employee can point to show he or she was treated differently. Employers should therefore consistently treat similarly situated employees similarly. If there are differences, ensure that they are justifiable.

Think carefully before deciding to single out an employee for a workplace

Prima facie case
Alleging facts that fit each requirement of a cause of action.

action. Is the reason for the action clear? Can it be articulated? Based on the information the employer used to make the decision, is it reasonable? Rational? Is the justification job related? If the employer is satisfied with the answers to these questions, the decision is probably defensible. If not, the employer should reexamine the considerations for the decision, find its weakness, and determine what can be done to address the weakness. The employer will then be in a much better position to defend the decision and show it is supported by legitimate, nondiscriminatory reasons.

Disparate Impact

Facially neutral policy
Workplace policy applies equally to all appropriate employees.

While disparate treatment is based on an employee's allegations that she or he is treated differently as an individual, disparate impact cases are generally statistically based group cases. An employee alleges that the employer's policy, while neutral on its face **(facially neutral),** has a disparate or adverse impact on a protected Title VII group. If such a policy impacts protected groups more harshly than majority groups, illegal discrimination may be found.

The disparate impact theory was established by the Supreme Court in 1971 in the *Griggs* case, below. *Griggs* is generally recognized as the first important case under Title VII, setting forth how Title VII was to be interpreted by courts. Even though the law became effective in 1965, it was not until *Griggs* that it was taken seriously by most employers. *Griggs* has since been codified into law by the Civil Rights Act of 1991. Notice the difference between the theories in the decision of the case below involving disparate impact and the previous case involving disparate treatment.

GRIGGS V. DUKE POWER CO.
401 U.S. 424 (1971)

Until the day Title VII became effective, it was the policy of Duke Power Co. that blacks be employed in only one of its five departments: the Labor Department. The highest paid black employee in the Labor Department made less than the lowest paid white employee in any other department. Blacks could not transfer out of the Labor Department into any other department. The day Title VII became effective, Duke instituted a policy requiring new hires to have a high school diploma and passing scores on two general intelligence tests in order to be placed in any department other than Labor and a high school diploma to transfer to other departments from Labor. Two months later, Duke required that transferees from the Labor or Coal Handling Departments who had no high school diploma pass two general intelligence tests. White employees already in other departments were grandfathered in under the new policy and the high school diploma and intelligence test requirements did not apply to them. Black employees brought this action under Title VII of the Civil Rights Act of 1964, challenging the employer's requirement of a high school diploma and the passing of intelligence tests as a condition of employment in or transfer to jobs at the power plant. They alleged the requirements are not job related and have the effect of disqualifying blacks from employment or transfer at a higher rate than whites. The US Supreme Court held that the act dictated that job requirements which have a disproportionate impact on groups protected by Title VII be shown to be job related.

Burger, J.

We granted the writ in this case to resolve the question of whether an employer is prohibited by Title VII of the Civil Rights Act of 1964, from requiring a high school education or passing of a standardized general intelligence test as a condition of employment in or transfer to jobs when (*a*) neither standard is shown to be significantly related to successful job performance, (*b*) both requirements operate to disqualify Negroes at a substantially higher rate than white applicants, and (*c*) the jobs in question formerly had been filled only by white employees as part of a longstanding practice of giving preference to whites.

What is required by Congress [under Title VII] is the removal of artificial, arbitrary, and unnecessary barriers to employment when the barriers operate invidiously to discriminate on the basis of racial or other impermissible classifications.

The act proscribes not only overt discrimination but also practices that are fair in form, but discriminatory in operation. The touchstone is business necessity. If an employment practice which operates to exclude Negroes cannot be shown to be related to job performance, the practice is prohibited.

On the record before us, neither the high school completion requirement nor the general intelligence test is shown to bear a demonstrable relationship to successful performance of the jobs for which it was used. Both were adopted without meaningful study of their relationship to job performance ability.

The evidence shows that employees who have not completed high school or taken the tests have continued to perform satisfactorily and make progress in departments for which the high school and test criteria are now used.

Good intent or absence of discriminatory intent does not redeem employment procedures or testing mechanisms that operate as "built-in head winds" for minority groups and are unrelated to measuring job capability.

The facts of this case demonstrate the inadequacy of broad and general testing devices as well as the infirmity of using diplomas or degrees as general measures of capability. History is filled with examples of men and women who rendered highly effective performance without the conventional badges of accomplishment in terms of certificates, diplomas, or degrees. Diplomas and tests are useful servants, but Congress has mandated the commonsense proposition that they are not to become masters of reality.

Nothing in the act precludes the use of testing or measuring procedures; obviously they are useful. What Congress has forbidden is giving these devices and mechanisms controlling force unless they are demonstrably a reasonable measure of job performance. Congress has not commanded that the less qualified be measured or preferred over the better qualified simply because of minority origins. Far from disparaging job qualifications as such, Congress has made such qualifications the controlling factor, so that race, religion, nationality, and sex become irrelevant. What Congress has commanded is that any tests used must measure the person for the job and not the person in the abstract. REVERSED.

Case Questions

1. Does this case make sense to you? Why? Why not?

2. The Court said the employer's intent does not matter here. Should it? Explain.

3. What would be your biggest concern as an employer who read this decision?

Griggs stood as good law until 1989 when the US Supreme Court decided *Wards Cove Packing Co. v. Atonio.*[2] In that case the Court held that the burden was on the employee to show that the employer's policy was *not* job related. In *Griggs* the burden was on the *employer* to show that the policy *was* job related. This increase in the employee's burden was taken as a setback in what was considered to be settled civil rights law. It moved Congress to immediately call for *Griggs* and its 18-year progeny to be enacted into law so it would no longer be subject to the vagaries of whoever was sitting on the US Supreme Court. The Civil Rights Act of 1991 did this.

Screening device
Factor used to weed out applicants from the pool of candidates.

Disparate impact cases can be an employer's nightmare. No matter how careful an employer tries to be, a policy, procedure, or **screening device** may serve as the basis of a disparate impact claim if the employer is not vigilant in watching for its indefensible disparate impact. Even the most seemingly innocuous policies can turn up unexpected cases of disparate impact. Employers must guard against analyzing policies or actions for signs of intentional discrimination, yet missing those with a disparate impact. Ensure that any screening device is explainable and justifiable as job related and does not have a disparate impact on Title VII groups.

Four-fifths rule
Minority must do at least 80 percent or four-fifths as well as majority on screening device or presumption of disparate impact arises, and device must then be shown to be job related.

What Constitutes a Disparate Impact?   While we have talked about disparate impact in general, we have not yet discussed what actually constitutes a disparate impact. Any time an employer uses a factor as a screening device to decide who receives the benefit of any type of employment decision—from hiring to termination, from promotion to training, from raises to employee benefit packages—it can be the basis for disparate impact analysis.

Recall that Title VII does not mention disparate impact. On August 25, 1978, several federal agencies, including the EEOC and the Departments of Justice and Labor, adopted a set of uniform guidelines to provide standards for ruling on the legality of employee selection procedures. The Uniform Guidelines on Employee Selection Procedures takes the position that there is a 20 percent margin permissible between the outcome of the majority and the minority under a given screening device. This is known as the **four-fifths rule.** Disparate impact is statistically demonstrated when the selection rate for groups protected by Title VII is less than 80 percent or four-fifths that of the higher scoring majority group.

For example, 100 women and 100 men take a promotion examination. One hundred percent of the women and 50 percent of the men pass the exam. The men have

---

[2] 490 U.S. 642 (1989).

only performed 50 percent as well as the women. Since the men did not pass at a rate of at least 80 percent of the women's passage rate, the exam has a disparate impact on the men. The employer would now be required to show that the exam is job related. If this can be shown to the satisfaction of the court, then the job requirement will be permitted even though it has a disparate impact. Even then the policy may still be struck down if the men can show there is a way to accomplish the employer's goal in using the exam, without it having a disparate impact on them.

The guideline is only a rule of thumb. The US Supreme Court stated in *Watson v. Ft. Worth Bank and Trust*[3] that it has never used mathematical precision to determine disparate impact. What is clear is that the employee is required to show that the statistical evidence is significant and has the effect of selecting applicants for hiring and promotion in ways adversely affecting groups protected by Title VII.

The terminology regarding scoring is intentionally imprecise, because the "outcome" depends on the nature of the screening device. The screening device can be anything that distinguishes one employee from another for workplace decision purposes. It may be a policy of hiring only ex-football players as barroom bouncers (most females would be precluded from consideration since most of them have not played football); requiring a minimum passing score on a written or other examination; physical attributes such as height and weight requirements; or of another type of differentiating factor. Disparate impact's coverage is very broad and virtually any policy may be challenged.

If the device is a written examination, then the outcomes compared will be test scores of one group (usually whites) versus another (usually blacks). If the screening device is a no-beard policy, then the outcome will be the percentage of black males affected by the medical condition, which is exacerbated if they shave, versus the percentage of white males so affected. If it is a height and weight requirement, it will be the percentage of females or members of traditionally shorter ethnic groups who can meet that requirement versus the percentage of males or majority members who can do so. The hallmark of these devices is that they appear neutral on their face. That is, they apply equally to everyone. Yet on closer examination, there is a harsher impact on a group with Title VII protection.

Disparate Impact and Subjective Criteria.   When addressing the issue of the disparate impact of screening devices, subjective and objective criteria are a concern. Objective criteria are factors that are able to be quantified by anyone, such as whether the employee made a certain score on a written exam. Subjective criteria are, instead, factors based on someone's personal thoughts or ideas (i.e., a supervisor's opinion as to whether the employee being considered for promotion is "compatible" with the workplace).

Initially it was suspected that subjective criteria could not be the basis for disparate impact claims, since the Supreme Court cases only involved objective factors, such as height and weight, educational requirements, test scores, and the like. In *Watson v. Fort Worth Bank,* the Supreme Court, for the first time, determined that subjective criteria could also be the basis for a disparate impact claim.

---

[3] 487 U.S. 977 (1988).

In *Watson,* a black employee had worked for the bank for years and was constantly passed over for promotion in favor of white employees. She eventually brought suit, alleging racial discrimination in that the bank's subjective promotion policy had a disparate impact upon black employees. The bank's policy was to promote employees based on the recommendation of the supervisor (all of whom were white). The Supreme Court held that the disparate impact analysis could indeed be used in determining illegal discrimination in subjective criteria cases.

Preemployment Interviews and Employment Applications.   Quite often questions asked during idle conversational chat during preemployment interviews or included on job applications may unwittingly be the basis for Title VII claims. Such questions or discussions should therefore be scrutinized for their potential impact, and interviewers should be trained in potential trouble areas to be avoided. If the premise is that the purpose of questions is to elicit information to be used in the evaluation process, then it makes sense to the applicant that if the question is asked, the employer must want to use the information. It may seem like innocent conversation to the interviewer, but if the applicant is rejected, then whether or not the information was gathered for discriminatory purposes, the applicant has the foundation for alleging that it illegally impacted the decision-making process. See Exhibit 3–9, only questions relevant to legal considerations for evaluating the applicant should be asked. There is virtually always a way to solicit legal, necessary information without violating the law or exposing the employer to potential liability.

For example, applications often ask the marital status of the applicant. Since there is often discrimination against married women holding certain jobs, this question has a potential disparate impact on married female applicants. If the married female applicant is not hired, she can allege that the reason was because she was a married female. This may have nothing whatsoever to do with the reason for her rejection, but since the employer asked the question, the argument can be made that it did. In truth, employers often ask this question because they want to know whom to contact in case of an emergency should the applicant be hired and suffer an on-the-job emergency. Simply asking who should be contacted in case of emergency, or not soliciting such information until after the applicant is hired, gives the employer exactly what the employer needs without risking potential liability by asking questions about gender or marital status that pose a risk. That is why in opening scenario 2, Jill, as one who interviews applicants, is in need of training, just as those who actually hire applicants.

Scenario 2

Defenses for Title VII Claims.   Once an employee provides prima facie evidence that the employer has discriminated, the employer has the opportunity to present evidence of several things for his or her defense:

• That employee's evidence is not true—that is, this is not the employer's policy as alleged, or that it was not applied as the employee alleges, that employee's statistics regarding the policy's disparate impact are incorrect and there is no disparate impact, or that the treatment employee says she or he received did not occur.

EXHIBIT 3–9   Disparate Impact Screening Devices

Court cases have determined the following screening devices have a disparate impact:

- Credit status—gender, race.
- Arrest record—race.
- Unwed pregnancy—gender, race.
- Height and weight requirements—gender, national origin.
- Educational requirements—race.
- Marital status—gender.
- Conviction of crime unrelated to job performance—race.

- In a disparate impact claim, that the practice is job related and consistent with **business necessity.** For instance, an employee challenges the employer's policy of requesting credit information and demonstrates that, because of shorter credit histories, fewer women are hired than men. The employer can show that it needs the policy because it is in the business of handling large sums of money and hiring only those people with good and stable credit histories is thus a business necessity. Business necessity may not be used as a defense to a disparate treatment claim.

- That the basis for employer's intentional discrimination is a **bona fide occupational qualification (BFOQ)** reasonably necessary to the employer's particular business. This is available only for disparate treatment cases involving gender, religion, and national origin, and is not available for race or color or for disparate impact cases. BFOQ is legalized discrimination and, therefore, very narrowly construed by the courts.

To have a successful BFOQ defense, the employer must be able to show that the basis for preferring one group over another goes to the essence of what the employer is in business to do, and that predominant attributes of the group discriminated against are at odds with that business. For instance, it has been held that, because bus companies and airlines are in the business of safely transporting passengers from one place to another, and driving and piloting skills begin to deteriorate at a certain age, a maximum age requirement for hiring is an appropriate BFOQ for bus drivers and pilots. The evidence supporting the qualification must be credible, and not just the employer's opinion. The employer must also be able to show it would be impractical to determine if each member of the group who is discriminated against could qualify for the position.

As you can see from the following case, not every attempt to show a BFOQ is successful. Weigh the business considerations in the following case against the dictates of Title VII, and think about how you would decide the issue.

Business necessity
Defense to a disparate impact case based on the employer's need for the policy as a legitimate requirement for the job.

Bona fide occupational qualification (BFOQ)
Permissible discrimination if legally necessary for employer's particular business.

WILSON V. SOUTHWEST AIRLINES COMPANY
517 F. Supp. 292 (N.D. Tex. Dallas Div. 1981)

A male sued Southwest Airlines after he was not hired as a flight attendant because he was male. The airline argued that being female was a BFOQ for being a flight attendant. The court disagreed.

Memorandum Opinion

Southwest conceded that its refusal to hire males was intentional. The airline also conceded that its height–weight restrictions would have an adverse impact on male applicants, if actually applied. Southwest contends, however, that the BFOQ exception to Title VII's ban on gender discrimination justifies its hiring only females for the public contact positions of flight attendant and ticket agent. The BFOQ window through which Southwest attempts to fly permits gender discrimination in situations where the employer can prove that gender is a "bona fide occupational qualification reasonably necessary to the normal operation of that particular business or enterprise." Southwest reasons it may discriminate against males because its attractive female flight attendants and ticket agents personify the airline's sexy image and fulfill its public promise to take passengers skyward with "love." The airline claims maintenance of its females-only hiring policy is crucial to its continued financial success.

Since it has been admitted that Southwest discriminates on the basis of gender, the only issue to decide is whether Southwest has proved that being female is a BFOQ reasonably necessary to the normal operation of its particular business.

As an integral part of its youthful, feminine image, Southwest has employed only females in the high customer contact positions of ticket agent and flight attendant. From the start, Southwest's attractive personnel, dressed in high boots and hot-pants, generated public interest and "free ink." Their sex appeal has been used to attract male customers to the airline. Southwest's flight attendants, and to a lesser degree its ticket agents, have been featured in newspaper, magazine, billboard, and television advertisements during the past 10 years. According to Southwest, its female flight attendants have come to "personify" Southwest's public image.

Southwest has enjoyed enormous success in recent years. From 1979 to 1980, the company's earnings rose from $17 million to $28 million when most other airlines suffered heavy losses.

The broad scope of Title VII's coverage is qualified by Section 703(e), the BFOQ exception Section 703(e) states:

(e) Notwithstanding any other provision of this subchapter,

(1) It shall not be an unlawful employment practice for an employer to hire . . . on the basis of his religion, gender, or national origin in those certain instances where religion, gender, or national origin is a bona fide occupational qualification reasonably necessary to the normal operation of that particular business or enterprise.

The BFOQ defense is not to be confused with the doctrine of "business necessity" which operates only in cases involving unintentional discrimination, when job criteria which are "fair in form, but discriminatory in operation" are shown to be "related to" job performance.

This Circuit's decisions have given rise to a two step BFOQ test: (1) does the particular job under consideration require that the worker be of one gender only; and if so, (2) is that requirement reasonably necessary to the "essence" of the employer's business. The first level of inquiry is designed to test whether gender is so essential to job performance that a member of the opposite gender simply could not do the same job.

To rely on the bona fide occupational qualification exception, an employer has the burden of proving that he had reasonable cause to believe, that is a factual basis for believing, that all or substantially all women would be unable to perform safely and efficiently the duties of the job involved. The second level is designed to assure that the qualification being scrutinized is one so important to the operation of the business that the business would be undermined if employees of the "wrong" gender were hired. . . . The use of the word "necessary" in section 703(e) requires that we apply a business necessity test, not a business convenience test. That is to say, discrimination based on gender is valid only when the essence of the business operation would be undermined by not hiring members of one gender exclusively.

Applying the first level test for a BFOQ to Southwest's particular operations results in the conclusion that being female is not a qualification required to perform successfully the jobs of flight attendant and ticket agent with Southwest. Like any other airline, Southwest's primary function is to transport passengers safely and quickly from one point to another. To do this, Southwest employs ticket agents whose primary job duties are to ticket passengers and check baggage, and flight attendants, whose primary duties are to assist passengers during boarding and deboarding, to instruct passengers in the location and use of aircraft safety equipment, and to serve passengers cocktails and snacks during the airline's short commuter flights. Mechanical, nongender-linked duties dominate both these occupations. Indeed, on Southwest's short-haul commuter flights there is time for little else. That Southwest's female personnel may perform their mechanical duties "with love" does not change the result. "Love" is the manner of job performance, not the job performed.

Southwest's argument that its primary function is "to make a profit," not to transport passengers, must be rejected. Without doubt the goal of every business is to make a profit. For purposes of BFOQ analysis, however, the business "essence" inquiry focuses on the particular service provided and the job tasks and functions involved, not the business goal. If an employer could justify employment discrimination merely on the grounds that it is necessary to make a profit, Title VII would be nullified in short order.

In order not to undermine Congress' purpose to prevent employers from "refusing to hire an individual based on stereotyped characterizations of the genders," a BFOQ for gender must be denied where gender is merely useful for attracting customers of the opposite gender, but where hiring both genders will not alter or undermine the essential function of the employer's business. Rejecting a wider BFOQ for gender does not eliminate the commercial exploitation of sex appeal. It only requires, consistent with the purposes of Title VII, that employers exploit the attractiveness and allure of a gender-integrated workforce. Neither Southwest, nor the traveling public, will suffer from such a rule. More to the point, it is my judgment that this is what Congress intended.

Case Questions

1. What should be done if, as here, the public likes the employer's scheme?

2. Do you think the standards for BFOQs are too strict? Explain.

3. Should a commercial success argument be given more weight by the courts? How should that be balanced with concern for Congress's position on discrimination?

Make sure that you understand the distinction the court made in *Southwest Airlines* between the essence of *what* an employer is in business to do, and *how* the employer does it. People often neglect this distinction and cannot understand why business owners cannot simply hire whoever they want (or not, as the case may be) if it has a marketing scheme it wants to pursue. Perhaps the Playboy Club bunnies will make it clearer.

After the success of *Playboy* magazine, Playboy opened several Playboy clubs in which the servers were dressed as Playboy bunnies. The purpose of the clubs was not to serve drinks as much as it was to extend *Playboy* magazine and its theme of beautiful women dressed in bunny costumes into another form for public consumption. *Playboy* magazine and its concept was purely for the purpose of adult male entertainment. The bunnies serving drinks were not so much drink servers as they were Playboy bunnies in the flesh rather than on a magazine page. That is what the business of the clubs was all about. Though it later chose to open up its policies to include male bunnies, being female was a BFOQ for being a bunny server in a Playboy club.

Contrast this with Hooters restaurants, where Hooters asserted that its business is serving spicy chicken wings. Since males can serve chicken wings just as well as females, being female is not a BFOQ for being a Hooters server. However, if Hooters had said the purpose of its business is to provide males with scantily clad female servers for entertainment purposes, as it was with the Playboy clubs, then being female would be a BFOQ.

In a disparate impact case, once the employer provides evidence rebutting the employee's prima facie case by showing business necessity or other means of rebuttal, the employee can show that there is a means of addressing the issue that has less of an adverse impact than the challenged policy. If this is shown to the court's satisfaction, then the employee will prevail and the policy will be struck down.

Knowing these requirements provides the employer with valuable insight into what is necessary to protect himself or herself from liability. Even though disparate impact claims can be difficult to detect beforehand, once they are brought to the employer's attention by the employee, they can be used as an opportunity to revisit the policy. With flexible, creative, and innovative approaches, the employer is able to avoid many problems in this area.

The Bottom-Line Defense.   We initially said that disparate impact is a statistical theory. Employers have often tried to avoid litigation under this theory by taking measures to ensure that the relevant statistics will not exhibit a disparate impact. In an area in which they feel they may be vulnerable, such as in minorities' passing scores on a written examination, they may make decisions to use criteria that make it appear as if minorities do at least 80 percent as well as the majority so the prima facie elements for a disparate impact case are not met. This attempt at an end run around Title VII was soundly rejected by the US Supreme Court in *Connecticut v. Teal* (see page 99). Note that this is also very often the reason you hear someone say there are "quotas" in a workplace. They are there *not* because the law requires them—it doesn't—but rather because the employer has self-imposed them to try to avoid liability. *Not* a good idea. The best policy is to have an open, fair employment process.

CONNECTICUT V. TEAL
457 U.S. 440 (1982)

Unsuccessful black promotion candidates sued the employer for race discrimination. Employees alleged that even though the employer's final promotion figures showed no disparate impact, the employer's process of arriving at the bottom line figures should be subject to scrutiny for disparate impact. The Supreme Court agreed.

Brennan, J.

Black employees of a Connecticut state agency were promoted provisionally to supervisors. To attain permanent status as supervisors, they were first required to receive a passing score on a written examination. There was a disparate impact, in that blacks passed at a rate of approximately 68 percent of the passing rate for whites. The black employees who failed the examination were thus excluded from further consideration for permanent supervisory positions. They then brought an action against the state of Connecticut and certain state agencies and officials, alleging violation of Title VII of the Civil Rights Act of 1964 by requiring, as an absolute condition for consideration for promotion, that applicants pass a written test that disproportionately excluded blacks and was not job related. Before trial, Connecticut made promotions from the eligibility list, with an overall result that 22.9 percent of the black candidates were promoted but only 13.5 percent of the white candidates—thus no disparate impact resulted from the final promotions.

We consider here whether an employer sued for violation of Title VII of the Civil Rights Act of 1964 may assert a "bottom-line" theory of defense. Under that theory, as asserted in this case, an em-

ployer's acts of racial discrimination in promotions effected by an examination having disparate impact would not render the employer liable for the racial discrimination suffered by employees barred from promotion if the "bottom-line" result of the promotional process was an appropriate racial balance. We hold that the "bottom-line" does not preclude employees from establishing a prima facie case, nor does it provide the employer with a defense to such a case.

A nonjob-related test that has a disparate racial impact, and is used to "limit" or "classify" employees, is "used to discriminate" within the meaning of Title VII, whether or not it was "designed or intended" to have this effect and despite an employer's efforts to compensate for its discriminatory effect.

Employer's claim of disparate impact from the examination, a pass-fail barrier to employment opportunity, states a prima facie case of employment discrimination under Title VII despite their employer's nondiscriminatory "bottom line," and that "bottom line" is no defense to this prima facie case.

Having determined that employees' claim comes within the terms of Title VII, we must address the suggestion of the employer and some *amici curiae* ["friends of the court"—nonparties who wish to have their positions considered by the Supreme Court in its deliberation of an issue] that we recognize an exception, either in the nature of an additional burden on employees seeking to establish a prima facie case or in the nature of an affirmative defense, for cases in which an employer has compensated for a discriminatory pass-fail barrier by hiring or promoting a sufficient number of black employees to reach a nondiscriminatory "bottom line." We reject this suggestion, which is in essence nothing more than a request that we redefine the protections guaranteed by Title VII.

Section 703(a)(2) prohibits practices that would deprive or tend to deprive "any individual of employment opportunities." The principal focus of the statute is the protection of the individual employee, rather than the protection of the minority group as a whole.

The Court has stated that a nondiscriminatory "bottom line" and an employer's good-faith efforts to achieve a nondiscriminatory workforce, might in some cases assist an employer in rebutting the inference that particular action had been intentionally discriminatory: Proof that a workforce was racially balanced or that it contained a disproportionately high percentage of minority employees is not wholly irrelevant on the issue of intent when that issue is yet to be decided. But resolution of the factual question of intent is not what is at issue in this case. Rather, employer

seeks simply to justify discrimination against the employees on the basis of their favorable treatment of other members of the employees' racial group. Under Title VII, a racially balanced work force cannot immunize an employer from liability for specific acts of discrimination.

It is clear beyond cavil that the obligation imposed by Title VII is to provide an equal opportunity for each applicant regardless of race, without regard to whether members of the applicant's race are already proportionately represented in the workforce.

Congress never intended to give an employer license to discriminate against some employees on the basis of race or gender merely because he favorably treats other members of the employees' group. In sum, the employer's nondiscriminatory "bottom line" is no answer, under the terms of Title VII, to the employees' prima facie claim of employment discrimination. AFFIRMED and REMANDED.

Case Questions

1. After being sued but before trial, why do you think that the agency promoted a larger percentage of blacks than whites when a larger percentage of whites actually passed the exam?

2. Should the employees have been allowed to sue if the bottom line showed no discrimination?

3. How could the employer here have avoided liability?

Teal demonstrates that Title VII requires equal employment *opportunity,* not simply equal *employment.* This is *extremely* important to keep in mind. It is *not* purely a "numbers game" as many employers, including Connecticut, have interpreted the law. Under the Civil Rights Act of 1991, it is an unfair employment practice for an employer to adjust the scores of, or to use different cutoff scores for, or otherwise alter the results of, an employment-related test on the basis of a prohibited category as was done in *Teal.*

Employers' policies should ensure that everyone has an equal chance at the job, based on qualifications. The *Teal* employees had been in their positions on a provisional basis for nearly two years before taking the examination. Thus, the employer had nearly two years of actual job performance that it could consider to determine the applicant's promotability. Instead, an exam was administered, requiring a certain score, which exam the employer could not show to be related to the job. Of course, the logical question is "then why give it?" Make sure you ask yourself that question before using screening devices that may operate to exclude certain groups on a disproportional basis. If you cannot justify the device, you take an unnecessary risk by using it.

An Important Note

One of the prevalent misconceptions about Title VII is that all an employee must do is file a claim, and the employer is "automatically" deemed to be liable for discrimination. This is not true. Discrimination claims under Title VII and other employment discrimination legislation must be proved just as any other lawsuits. It is not enough for an employee to think he or she is being discriminated against. The employee must offer evidence to support the claim. As shown in *Ali,* below, not doing so has predictable results. As you read *Ali,* however, keep in mind the inadvisability of the questionable parts of the encounter between the employer and the employee.

ALI V. MOUNT SINAI HOSPITAL
68 Empl. Prac. Dec. (CCH) P44,188 (6-12-96)

Employee sued the employer for racial discrimination in violation of Title VII, for discriminatory enforcement of the employer's dress code. She alleged she was disciplined for violating the code, but whites were not. The court found that the employee had offered no evidence of discriminatory enforcement, so the court had no choice but to find in favor of the employer.

Gershon, J.

It is undisputed that, at all relevant times, the Hospital had a detailed three-page dress code for all of its nursing department staff, including unit clerks. It expressly provided that "the style chosen be conservative and in keeping with the professional image in nursing" and that the "Unit clerks wear the blue smock provided by the Hospital with conservative street clothes." The wearing of boots, among other items of dress, was expressly prohibited. With regard to hair, the dress code provided that "it should be clean and neatly groomed to prevent interference with patient care" and only "plain" hair barrettes and hairpins should be worn. As plaintiff acknowledges, "The hallmark of said code was that the staff had to dress and groom themselves in a conservative manner."

It is also undisputed that Ms. Ali violated the dress code. Ms. Ali reported to work at the CSICU wearing a red, three-quarter length, cowl-necked dress and red boots made of lycra fabric which went over her knees. Over her dress, Ms. Ali wore the regulation smock provided by the Hospital. She wore her hair in what she says she then called a "punk" style. She now calls it a "fade" style, which she describes as an "Afro hairstyle." It was shorter on the sides than on the top and was in its natural color, black. According to Dr. Shields, Ms. Ali's hair was not conservative because it "was so high" and "you noticed it right away because it was high and back behind the ears and down. It certainly caused you to look at her. It caused attention." Deposition of Dr. Elizabeth Shields: Her hair "had to be at least three to five inches high down behind her ears." This description by Dr. Shields has not been disputed.

According to the employee, Dr. Shields approached her and asked her to look in the mirror and see what looks back at her. Ali responded that she looked beautiful. Ms. Ali testified that Dr. Shields told her that "I belong in a zoo, and then the last thing she said was I look like I [am] . . . going to a disco or belong in a disco or something to that effect." Dr. Shields testified: "I told her about the whole outfit. She had red boots, red dress, in the unit. This is the post open heart unit. People come out of here after just having cracked their chest. We were expected to be conservative."

Title VII makes it an unlawful employment practice for an employer "to fail or refuse to hire or to discharge any individual, or otherwise to discriminate against any individual with respect to his compensation, terms, conditions, or privileges of employment, because of such individual's race, color, religion, sex, or national origin . . . ." Defendants seek summary judgment dismissing the complaint on the ground that plaintiff cannot make a prima facie showing that they engaged in discriminatory conduct.

To establish a prima facie case of individualized disparate treatment from an alleged discriminatory enforcement of the dress code, plaintiff must show that she is a member of a protected class and that, at the time of the alleged discriminatory treatment, she was satisfactorily performing the duties of her position. This she has done. However, her prima facie showing must also include a showing that Mount Sinai Hospital had a dress code and that it was applied to her under circumstances giving rise to an inference of discrimination.

Reviewing all of the evidence submitted on the motion, employee does not raise an issue of fact as to whether the enforcement of the code against her was discriminatory. There is no dispute that employee was in violation of the dress code. Her claim is that the dress code was enforced against her but not against others, who also violated its requirements, but were not black. The problem is the utter lack of evidence supporting this position.

Employee offers no evidence that the dress code was not enforced against other Hospital employees as it was against her. Dr. Shields' testimony that the dress code had been enforced against other nurses was not disputed. Although Ms. Ali identified certain caucasian women whom she believed were in violation of the code, she failed to set forth any evidence to show a lack of enforcement.

All that employee's testimony establishes is that she was unaware of the enforcement of the dress code against others. Following a full opportunity for discovery, employee has not proffered any additional evidence to support her claim of disparate treatment. On this record, there is no reason to believe that she will be able to offer at trial evidence from which a jury could reasonably conclude that there was racially discriminatory enforcement of the dress code.

It is not enough that Ms. Ali sincerely believes that she was the subject of discrimination; "[a] plaintiff is not entitled to a trial based on pure speculation, no matter how earnestly held." Summary judgment is appropriate here because employee has failed to raise an issue of fact as to whether the dress code was enforced against her under circumstances giving rise to an inference of discrimination. Motion to dismiss GRANTED.

Case Questions

1. What do you think of the way in which Ali was approached by Dr. Shields about her

violation of the dress code? Does this seem advisable to you?

2. How much of a role do you think different cultural values played in this situation? Explain.

3. What can the employer do to avoid even the appearance of unfair enforcement of its dress policy in the future?

Management Tips

Since potentially all employees can bind the employer by their discriminatory actions, it is important for all employees to understand the law. This will not only greatly aid them in avoiding acts which may cause the employer liability, but it will also go far in creating a work environment in which discrimination is less likely to occur. Through training, make sure that all employees understand:

- What Title VII is.
- What Title VII requires.
- Who Title VII applies to.
- How the employees' actions can bring about liability for the employer.
- What kinds of actions will be looked at in a Title VII proceeding.
- That the employer will not allow Title VII to be violated.
- That all employees have a right to a workplace free of illegal discrimination.

Summary

- Title VII prohibits employers, unions, joint labor–management committees, and employment agencies from discriminating in any aspect of employment on the basis of race, color, religion, gender, or national origin.

- Title VII addresses subtle as well as overt discrimination; disparate treatment as well as disparate impact; and discrimination that is intentional as well as unintentional.

- The law allows for compensatory and punitive damages, where appropriate, as well as jury trials.

- The employer's best defense is an offense. A strong, top-down policy of nondiscrimination can be effective in setting the right tone and getting the message to managers and employees alike that discrimination in employment will not be tolerated.

- Strong policies, consistently and appropriately enforced, as well as periodic training and updating as issues emerge, and even as a means of review, are most helpful.

- To the extent that an employer complies with Title VII, it can safely be said that workplace productivity will benefit, as will the employer's coffers, because unlawful employment discrimination can be costly to the employer in more ways than one.

Chapter-End Questions

1. What is the name of the party who files a complaint with the EEOC? The name of the party accused of discrimination?

2. How long does a private employee have to file a claim with the EEOC or be barred from doing so?

3. Lin Teung files a complaint with the EEOC for national origin discrimination. His jurisdiction has a 706 agency. When Teung calls up the EEOC after 45 days to see how his case is progressing, he learns that the EEOC has not yet moved on it. Teung feels the EEOC is violating its own rules. Is it?

4. Althea, black, has been a deejay for a local Christian music station for several years. The station gets a new general manager and within a month he terminates Althea. The reason he gave was that it was inappropriate for a black deejay to play music on a white Christian music station. Althea sues the station. What is her best theory for proceeding?

5. Melinda wants to file a sexual harassment claim against her employer but feels she cannot do so because he would retaliate against her by firing her. She also has no money to sue him. Any advice for Melinda?

6. Jenniffer, Anne, and Tess, all members of the US arm of the Communist party, work for Hard and Tough Steel Company. They wish to file a gender discrimination action against Steel Company because their supervisor, Willie, is giving them a "hard time" and is treating them differently because they are women. The one male in the shop, Jamal, is treated more favorably. Will the women likely be successful if they file claims?

7. Sharon works for Valentine Investigative Services (VIS), a private detective firm. VIS's staff also includes three investigators and a computer expert. Sharon is being sexually harassed by Art, the firm's owner. What are Sharon's rights under Title VII?

8. An employer, the owner of a chain of day care centers, has a policy of hiring only females as teachers in his centers, because he feels they are better nurturers. If Tony, a male, sued the employer for refusal to hire, under what theory would Tony proceed?

9. Day Care Center has a policy stating that no employee can be over 5 foot 4, because the employer thinks children feel more comfortable with people who are closer to them in size. Does Tiffany, who is 5 foot 7, have a claim? If so, under what theory could she proceed?

10. During the interview Gale had with Leslie Accounting Firm, Gale was asked whether she had any children, whether she planned to have any more children, to what church she belonged, and what her husband did for a living. Are these questions illegal?

4 TITLE VII: THE BEGINNING OF THE EMPLOYMENT RELATIONSHIP

Chapter Outline

SCENARIOS

SCENARIO 1

Carmine Escobida is asked to fill two new positions at his company. The first requires complicated engineering knowledge; the second has no prerequisites, and no opportunity for advancement without a college degree. Carmine wants to hire younger workers so they will be more likely to have a long tenure at the firm. The advertisement for the positions placed in a newspaper of general circulation requests résumés from "recent college graduates," engineering degrees preferred. Is Carmine's firm subject to any liability based on this advertisement?

SCENARIO 2

Tammy Hartman, personnel manager at a large service firm, has not been allocated much money for recruitment. Because of the reputation of her company, it constantly receives unsolicited résumés from qualified applicants without the use of advertising. After reviewing the numbers, Tammy discovers her firm is 87 percent white and 95 percent male. Should Tammy suggest a change in the firm's recruitment practices?

SCENARIO 3

Sarah Stollman hires someone for the position of messenger/clerk at her company. Prior to being hired, the applicant completed a basic application form. The form asked whether the applicant had ever been convicted of a felony, and he had responded that he had not. After working at the company for two months, the employee admitted stealing $500 from the wallet of another employee. Thereafter, Sarah finds out that he was convicted of grand theft of an automobile four years earlier. The employee whose money was stolen sues the company for negligent hiring. Does Sarah suggest a change in the firm's hiring procedures?

Management Concerns in Recruitment

The human resources of a firm are among its most valuable assets; consequently, the utmost discretion must be used in their selection process. The law recognizes this and permits employers much leeway in choosing employees. Virtually the only restrictions on an employer's right to hire are the laws that protect certain groups from employment discrimination (as will be discussed). History has demonstrated a need for such protection. As we will see, discrimination in employment, whether intentional or unintentional, is allowed unless it is based on an impermissible category, such as gender, race, and the like. Employers looking for a salesperson may discriminate against applicants who cannot get along well with others; employers hiring computer technicians may discriminate on the basis of computer training; and other individuals may be discriminated against for permissible reasons.

While laws that protect employees from discrimination are not actually the subject of this chapter, because there has been so much regulation under those laws, it is difficult to speak any longer of establishing the employment relationship without heavily drawing on those laws. We will briefly mention some of these laws where appropriate to establish the employment relationship, but fuller coverage will be given in the chapters devoted to such coverage.

Establishing the employment relationship begins with recruitment. Employers use a variety of techniques to locate suitable applicants. Once the employer has a group from which to choose, information gathering begins. This stage consists of soliciting information from the applicant through forms, interviews, references, and testing. Targeting recruitment and selection has been found to be the most effective way to reduce employment discrimination charges. While testing will be addressed in the following chapter, this chapter will discuss regulation of the means by which employers establish the employment relationship.

Exhibit 4–1   Myths about Hiring Your Employee or Getting Your Job

1. The best way to promote workplace unity is to get hiring suggestions only from those who already work there.
2. As long as an advertisement is placed somewhere in the city where hiring is to be done, an employer cannot be accused of selective recruiting.
3. The purpose of this interview is for the employer to find out information about the employee. The employer can hide information about itself.
4. There's nothing wrong with promoting only from within; after all, it raises employee morale and encourages devotion.
5. The only problem with nepotism (favoring family members in hiring decisions) is that present employees may resent the hired family member, and believe he or she got the job because of the familial connection.

Recruitment

Recruitment practices are particularly susceptible to claims of discrimination as barriers to equal opportunity. If applicants are denied access to employment opportunities on the basis of membership in a protected class, they may have a claim against the potential employer for discriminatory practice. Recruitment, as with every other phase of the employment process, is subject to government regulation, including Title VII of the Civil Rights Act of 1964, the Rehabilitation Act of 1973 (if a federal agency, employer, or contractor), the Americans with Disabilities Act of 1990 (if a private sector employer), the Age Discrimination in Employment Act of 1967, the Immigration Reform and Control Act of 1986, and various state laws relating to fair employment practices.

In part, these statutes require that an employer not only recruit from a diverse audience but also design employment announcements that will encourage a diverse group of applicants. How does the employer obtain its applicant pool? Does it place an advertisement in a local newspaper, advertise on the radio in a given neighborhood, ask certain people to submit résumés, ask current employees for suggestions? Does the advertisement contain gender-specific language that would discourage certain groups from applying for the position? Each of these possibilities has potential hazards. When the employer utilizes recruitment practices that result in an adverse impact on a group protected by antidiscrimination statutes, that practice may be wrongful even if the employer had no intent to discriminate.

Federal Statutory Regulation of Recruitment

As mentioned, to prevent liability, there are several laws employers must be aware of when recruiting employees (see Exhibit 4–2).

State Employment Law Regulation

Many states have enacted legislation specifically aimed at expansion of the federal statutes above. For instance, many states have human rights acts that include in their protections the prohibitions against discrimination based on marital status or affinity orientation. The statutes generally establish a state human rights commission, which hears claims brought under the state act. Several other states have enacted legislation that closely mirrors Title VII but covers a larger number of employers. In the case below, the court addresses the marital status provision of the Minnesota statute.

PULLAR V. INDEPENDENT SCHOOL DISTRICT NO. 701, HIBBING
582 N.W.2d 273 (Minn. App. Ct. 1998)

Pullar, a female, applied for a teaching position that involved coaching after school hours. The school district refused to hire her because she had young children whose needs, the principal claimed, were incompatible with the coaching responsibilities. Instead, it hired another woman with less teaching and coaching experience and no young children. Puller brought an action against the school district, alleging sex discrimination in violation of the Minnesota Human Rights Act (MHRA). The complaint also alleged that the school district "ha[d] frequently hired males for teaching positions that involved coaching responsibilities."

The lower court dismissed the complaint for failure to state a discrimination claim under the Minnesota act, finding it did not sufficiently allege that the school district had a hiring policy that treated women and men with young children differently.

Holtan, J.

The district court dismissed Pullar's complaint for failure to state an employment discrimination claim under the MHRA upon a finding that it did not sufficiently allege that the district had an employment policy that treated similarly situated men and women differently. We disagree.

The complaint alleges that the school district denied Pullar employment in favor of another female because she had young children whose needs were incompatible with a teaching position that involved coaching after school hours. The complaint also alleges that the school district had hired men for those positions in the past. Those allegations permit an inference that the school district, relying on stereotypical characterizations of the proper domestic role of women, took adverse employment action against Pullar that it would not have taken had Pullar been a man. That inference is sufficient to establish a prima facie case of discrimination under the MHRA.

The school district claims that Pullar's complaint should be dismissed because it alleges a claim of discrimination based on familial status and the MHRA does not prohibit familial status discrimination in the employment context. Although it is true that in the employment context the MHRA does not prohibit discrimination based on the status of having children alone, the MHRA does prohibit an employment practice that treats men and women with children differently. Cases interpreting Title VII have referred to that type of discrimination as "sex-plus" discrimination.

* * *

Like Title VII, the MHRA must be construed to prohibit employment practices that discriminate against women on the basis of familial status when the discrimination results in unequal treatment of the sexes, even though the MHRA does not enumerate familial status as a protected class in the employment context. Contrary to the school district's claim, therefore, Pullar's complaint states a claim under the MHRA.

The school district also claims that, to establish a prima facie case of sex discrimination, the complaint must allege that it hired a man instead of hiring Pullar. We disagree. To establish a prima facie case of discrimination in hiring under Minnesota law, Pullar need not allege that she was denied employment in favor of a man. She need only allege that the employment opportunities she sought "remained available or were given to other persons with her qualifications." . . . The fact that the school district denied Pullar employment in favor of another female, therefore, has no bearing on whether or not the complaint states a prima facie case of discrimination based on sex. The complaint need only establish that a prohibited factor, in this case, stereotypical characterizations of the proper role of women with children, played a determinative role in the employer's decision. Pullar's complaint establishes that.

Because the complaint alleges that the school district had one hiring policy for women with young children and a different hiring policy for men, it alleges a claim under the MHRA even though the MHRA does not prohibit familial status discrimination in employment and the school district denied an applicant employment in favor of a member of the same gender. We therefore REVERSE the district court's judgment dismissing the complaint.

Case Questions

1. If an employer knows that an applicant will have problems meeting the responsibilities, why can't they be proactive and decide not to hire the applicant due to the problems the applicant will encounter meeting her responsibilities?

2. Why do you think some applicants bring claims under the state human rights act rather than Title VII?

3. In this case, what must an applicant show in the complaint in order to avoid being dismissed for lack of stating a claim under the Minnesota Human Rights Act?

EXHIBIT 4–2

Title VII of the Civil Rights Act of 1964

Section 703(a)(1)   It shall be an unlawful employment practice for an employer to fail or refuse to hire . . . any individual or otherwise to discriminate against any individual with respect to his [sic] compensation, terms, conditions, or privileges of employment, because of such individual's race, color, religion, sex, or national origin.

Section 704(b)   It shall be an unlawful employment practice for an employer, . . . to print or cause to be printed or published any notice or advertisement relating to employment by such an employer indicating any preference, limitation, specification, or discrimination based on race, color, religion, sex, or national origin, except that such a notice or advertisement may indicate a preference, limitation, specification, or discrimination based on religion, sex, or national origin when religion, sex, or national origin is a bona fide occupational qualification for employment.

Vocational Rehabilitation Act of 1973 and the Americans with Disabilities Act of 1990

While covered in depth in Chapter 14, the Rehabilitation Act and the Americans with Disabilities Act protect otherwise qualified individuals with disabilities. The former regulates the employment practices of federal contractors, agencies, and employers, while the latter act applies similar standards to private sector employers of 25 (15, effective July 1993) employees or more.

The Rehabilitation Act specifically provides that, in connection with recruitment, contractors and their subcontractors who have contracts with the government in excess of $2,500 must design and commit to an affirmative action program with the purpose of providing employment opportunities to disabled applicants. Affirmative action recruitment programs may include specific recruitment plans for universities for the disabled, designing positions that will easily accommodate a disabled employee, and adjusting work schedules to conform to the needs of certain applicants.

Age Discrimination in Employment Act of 1967

All employers of 20 or more employees are subject to the act, which prohibits discrimination against an individual 40 years of age or older, unless age is a bona fide occupational qualification. In addition, the act states that:

> *"Section 4(e)*   It shall be unlawful for an employer . . . to print or publish, or cause to be printed or published, any notice or advertisement relating to employment . . . indicating any preference, limitation, specification or discrimination based on age."

Immigration Reform and Control Act of 1986

IRCA is slightly different in its regulation of recruitment. IRCA applies to all employers. IRCA's purpose is to eliminate work opportunities that attract illegal aliens to the United States. With regard to discrimination based on national origin, the act provides that employers of four or more employees determine the eligibility of each individual they intend to hire, prior to the commencement of employment. In this way, IRCA condones discrimination against illegal aliens in recruitment. Note that while IRCA applies to all employers, its discrimination provisions apply only to those with four employees or more.

Common Law

Employers should be careful of statements and promises made during the recruitment process. A company representative who makes an intentional or negligent misrepresentation, which encourages an applicant to take a job, may be liable to that applicant for harm that results. Misrepresentations may include claims regarding the terms of the job offer, including the type of position available, the salary to be paid, the job requirements, and other matters directly relating to the representation of the offer.

To be successful in a misrepresentation action, the applicant must show that the employer misrepresented a material fact, either intentionally or with recklessness about its truth or falsity, that the applicant reasonably relied on this representation in arriving at the decision to accept the offer, and that she or he was damaged by this reliance.

For example, assume an applicant is told by her employer at the time when she is hired that she will automatically receive a raise at her six month review. Based on this representation, the applicant accepts an offer. Six months pass and she does not receive the promised raise. She would be able to sue her employer for the misrepresentation that induced her to take the job.

Additionally, the misrepresentation need not actually be a false statement: where a statement creates a false impression, the employer may also be liable for fraud. Or, where the employer is aware that the applicant is under a mistaken belief about the position or the company, the employer's silence may constitute misrepresentation.

Where the employer hides certain bits of information, the employer's silence may again be considered misrepresentation. For instance, an employer needs someone to serve as an assistant to the president of the company. The president has a reputation for being unpleasant to his assistants and for constantly firing them. Employer, therefore, solicits applications for a general administrative position, "with specific duties to be assigned later," knowing the hiree will spend the majority of time working for the president.

Someone applies for the job and states during his interview that he would like the position, and he is glad that it is not the assistant to the president position for which they were interviewing last month. He is hired, and, even though he has an excellent offer from another company for more money, decides to take the job because he likes the work environment. Later he is told that he will be spending a large part of his workday with the president. The employee could sue employer for misrepresentation, even though the employer did not respond to his statement about the president during the interview.

In a strange turn of events, one employer in California may end up being liable to a number of employees' *spouses* for misrepresentations made during recruitment regarding the firm's expectations for growth. In *Meade v. Cedarapids, Inc.,* (9th Cir. 1999), the Ninth Circuit Court of Appeals reversed a lower court's granting of a summary judgment in the employer's favor. The court of appeals held instead that a genuine issue of material fact existed as to whether the company made false

EXHIBIT 4–3

Fraud
1. Misrepresentation.
2. Of a material fact.
3. With the intent to deceive or recklessness about truth or falsity.
4. On which the applicant reasonably relies.
5. To her or his detriment.

Misrepresentation
1. False statement.
2. True statement creating a false impression.
3. Silence where:
   - It is necessary to correct applicant's mistaken belief about material facts.
   - There is active concealment of material facts.
   - It is necessary to correct an employer's statement that was true at the time made but subsequently became false.

Material Facts
1. Statement of fact.
2. Which will influence.
3. A reasonable person.
4. Regarding whether to enter into a contract.

Note that opinions are not material facts, because it would be generally unreasonable to rely fully on the opinion of another in arriving at a decision.

misrepresentations and whether the employees justifiably relied upon them. In connection with the spouses' arguments, the court held that the spouses will have to prove that the company made representations to their husbands under the circumstances that entitled the spouses to believe that the company had authorized the husbands to communicate the representations to them.

The court noted that couples usually make decisions as a family unit, and "it is likely that the process of deciding whether to relocate for a new job involves convincing the spouse that the positive qualities of the new job outweigh the difficulties caused to the family." The concurrence remarked that "a marriage is a partnership, and major decisions such as whether the family will pull up roots and move to a different city are normally made by the partners jointly. Only a very foolish employer will try to persuade a prospective employee to relocate without addressing the concerns of the spouse." Given this holding, employers should be all the more cautious about representations—there may be more possible plaintiffs than they think.

Employers may also be liable for fraud in recruitment when misstatements are used to discourage potential applicants from pursuing positions. For instance, an employer who wishes to maintain a male-dominated workforce may intentionally present an excessively negative image of the position or the company in an effort to persuade females not to apply. If all candidates are offered the same information, there may be no basis for a discrimination claim. However, if only the female applicants receive this discouraging outlook, the practice presents to the female applicants a "chilling" effect and the employer may be subject to claims of gender discrimination.

Application of Regulation to Recruitment Practices

Advertisements.   Statutes and the common law claim of fraud protect applicants from discriminatory recruitment practices, ranging from a refusal to interview Hispanics to a job notice that is only posted in the executive suite where it will be seen primarily by white males. Assume, for instance, that an employer advertises in a newspaper, which is circulated in a neighborhood that has an extremely high Asian population with very few other minorities represented; also, that the employer can expect to see almost all of its applications from Asians and few, if any, applications from other groups. While there may be no intent to discriminate, the effect of the practice is an unbalanced workforce with a disparate impact on non-Asians.

Scenario

In connection with scenario 1, recall that Carmine is concerned about placing an advertisement requesting résumés from "recent college grads." Older workers may claim that they are discouraged from applying due to the language—they are less likely to be "recent" college grads. On the other hand, language such as this does not constitute a *per se* violation. Instead, the applicant would have to establish a prime facie case of age discrimination. Though terminology such as this seems to be a minor concern to some, courts have found that it may lead to a belief that stereotyping or pigeonholing of one gender or a certain age group in certain positions is condoned by the law. Consider Dominick's supermarket's experience when it named the second-in-command of its deli section the "Second Deli Man," notwithstanding whether the person was male or female. Maybe someone at Dominick's noticed the inconsistency this might create but probably no one expected a class-action suit by 1,500 women alleging gender discrimination! While this was only one of numerous pieces of evidence, it may have made a difference in encouraging a settlement.

Word-of-Mouth Recruiting.   The same discriminatory effect may occur where an employer obtains its new employees from referrals from within its own workforce, or "word-of-mouth" recruiting. Generally most people know and recommend others similar to themselves. Word-of-mouth recruiting generally results in a homogeneous workplace.

This type of recruiting is not necessarily harmful where precautions are taken to ensure a balanced applicant pool or where it is necessary for ensuring hire of the safest and most competent workers. Benefits to this type of recruitment include the preliminary screening accomplished by the current employees before they even recommend the applicant for the position, and the propensity for long-term service and loyalty among the new hires. Since they already have bonds to the company, a family attitude toward the firm resulting in increased productivity is more easily developed. The practice is only subject to suspicion if it results in adverse impact against members of protected classes.

The following two cases present the court's analysis of word-of-mouth recruiting efforts.

EQUAL EMPLOYMENT OPPORTUNITY COMMISSION V. CHICAGO MINIATURE LAMP WORKS

947 F.2d 292 (7th Cir. 1991)

The employer hired employees for entry-level positions through word of mouth. Since there were only one or two black employees in entry-level positions, there were very few black applicants.

The EEOC claimed that Chicago Miniature Lamp Works (Miniature) discriminated against blacks in its recruitment and hiring of its entry-level workers. Miniature's principal method of obtaining new entry-level workers was almost exclusively on word of mouth in order to fill its entry-level job openings. Employees would simply tell their relatives and friends about the nature of the job—if interested, these persons then would come to Miniature's office and complete an application form. Miniature did not tell or encourage its employees to recruit in this manner. The evidence indicates that the only time Miniature initiated this word of mouth process was when it adopted an affirmative action plan. At that time, Miniature asked one or two black employees to recruit black applicants from among their relatives and friends. Evidence indicated that 1 person was hired for every 15 who applied. Because of the success of this process, Miniature never advertised for these jobs, and only rarely used the State of Illinois unemployment referral service.

Between 1978 and 1981, Miniature hired 146 entry-level workers. Nine of these workers (6 percent) were black. The trial court concluded that "the statistical probability of Chicago Miniature's hiring so few blacks in the 1978–81 period, in the absence of racial bias against blacks in recruitment and hiring, is virtually zero." The trial court also concluded that racial bias was the reason for the disparities between the percentage of blacks in Miniature's entry-level workforce for the years 1970–1981 and the percentage of black entry-level workers in Chicago. However, the court of appeals reversed.

Cummings, J.

* * *

. . . Congress intended a delicate balance, strongly condemning discrimination on account of a protected characteristic, yet recognizing that racial imbalances in the workforce may result from legitimate, nondiscriminatory factors. A recognition of this tension informs our analysis in this case.

The district court found Miniature liable based on both a disparate treatment and a disparate impact model. Although it is clear that the same set of facts can support both theories of liability, it is important to treat each model separately because each has its own theoretical underpinnings. The disparate treatment model is based most directly on Title VII's statutory language and requires an inquiry into the defendant's state of mind. The defendant is liable under this model when the plaintiff can prove that the defendant subjectively intended to discriminate against the plaintiff on account of a protected trait.

In a disparate impact case, however, motive is irrelevant. "Under the Act, practices . . . neutral on their face, and even neutral in terms of intent, cannot be maintained if they operate to 'freeze' the status quo of prior discriminatory employment practices." The line between disparate impact and disparate treatment cases is most blurred in "pattern and practice" cases such as this one, because statistics can be used to prove both disparate treatment and disparate impact.

A. Disparate Treatment

A prima facie case for a pattern or practice of disparate treatment can be established by "statistical evidence demonstrating substantial disparities in the application of employment actions as to minorities . . . buttressed by evidence of general policies or specific instances of discrimination." The plaintiff must prove "more than the mere occurrence of isolated or 'accidental' or sporadic discriminatory acts." Instead, the plaintiff must show that racial discrimination was the "standard operating procedure—the regular rather than the unusual practice."

As part of its attempt to separate its recruiting and hiring practices, Miniature argues that it did not recruit and therefore, as a matter of logic, it could not have recruited discriminatorily. We reject this simplistic syllogism. . . .

* * *

. . . Miniature has recruited; it made an intentional decision to rely on word of mouth to attract applicants for its entry-level openings. Miniature knew how workers were learning of its employment opportunities. When it adopted an affirmative action plan in 1977, it made an effort to tell its black employees to contact their friends and relatives in order to increase the effectiveness of its word-of-mouth network in the black community. Miniature also used other recruiting procedures at times. It used newspaper advertisements to attract clerical and secretarial applicants. On occasion it used a job referral service. But Miniature obviously intentionally chose not to use these two forms of recruiting for its entry-level workers.

* * *

We reject defendant's claim that "Miniature cannot be held liable because it did not commit any act." It was the trial court's finding that Miniature's overall entry-level hiring decisions were made with racial animus. It is true that the trial court focused on Miniature's reliance on word of mouth as evidence of its discriminatory intent. . . . Miniature's passive reliance on word of mouth to generate applicants must be given minimal weight because it involved no affirmative act by Miniature. Drawing the inference of intent from "non-action" is necessarily more difficult than drawing the inference of intent from particular actions. This is especially true since intent means more than knowledge that a certain action (or non-action) will cause certain discriminatory results. Intent means a subjective desire or wish for these discriminatory results to occur.

A pattern or practice of disparate treatment is shown through a combination of "statistical evidence demonstrating substantial disparities . . . buttressed by evidence of general policies or specific instances of discrimination." . . .

Miniature argues that the EEOC's statistics are clearly erroneous because they do not include the following considerations: relative commuting distance, shift preference, and lack of an English fluency requirement. The EEOC responds that any attack on its statistical evidence should be precluded, since Miniature did not include these variables in its own statistical analysis.

* * * *

It is clear that Miniature was held liable because there were relatively few blacks in its applicant pool as compared to the number of entry-level black workers in Chicago. The EEOC's statistical expert used a very simple demographic model. The applicant's race was the only variable considered in the model, and Miniature's racial composition was compared with the racial composition of Chicago as a whole.

* * * *

The trial court erred in concluding that Miniature was liable under Title VII for disparate treatment of blacks. This is one of those rare cases where the statistical evidence credited by the lower court does not support liability. Anecdotal evidence of intentional discrimination, only tangentially relied upon by the lower court, also fails to carry the day for the EEOC.

B. Disparate Impact

When conducting its disparate impact analysis, the trial court again focused on the statistics put forward by the EEOC's expert and on Miniature's reliance on word-of-mouth recruiting. Underscoring the basic similarity in the two approaches, the court began by stating that the "EEOC's statistics are not open to rebuttal under the disparate-impact model any more than under the disparate-treatment model." The district court recognized that under a disparate-impact approach a plaintiff must identify a particular practice that caused the disparate impact. In this case, the district court considered the "particular practice" to be reliance on word-of-mouth recruiting. Since "Chicago Miniature has not even sought to offer any evidence tending to show its reliance on word-of-mouth recruiting is business-related," the court concluded that the EEOC's disparate impact case was established and unrebutted.

We concluded above that it was clearly erroneous for the trial court to rely on the statistical evidence put forward by the EEOC. Since the EEOC relied on the same evidence to uphold liability under its disparate impact claim that it relied upon for its disparate treatment claim, it was also clearly erroneous for the trial court to support its findings of disparate impact with this statistical evidence.

There is another reason that the holding of disparate impact liability against Miniature can-

not stand. In a disparate impact case, "plaintiff is . . . responsible for isolating and identifying the specific employment practices that are allegedly responsible for any observed statistical disparities." The EEOC does not allege that Miniature affirmatively engaged in word-of-mouth recruitment of the kind where it told or encouraged its employees to refer applicants for entry-level jobs. Instead, it is uncontested that Miniature passively waited for applicants who typically learned of opportunities from current Miniature employees. The court erred in considering passive reliance on employee word-of-mouth recruiting as a particular employment practice for the purposes of disparate impact. The practices here are undertaken solely by employees. Therefore, disparate impact liability against Miniature must be reversed.

As stated above, the reliance on word of mouth to obtain applicants for jobs does not insulate an employer from a finding of disparate treatment of minorities. However, for the purposes of disparate impact, a more affirmative act by the employer must be shown in order to establish causation. "[A] Title VII plaintiff does not make out a case of disparate impact simply by showing that, 'at the bottom line,' there is a racial imbalance in the work force." The EEOC here, in essence, is attacking Miniature's overall hiring procedure by pointing to the "bottom line" results; it has not made the more focused allegation required by *Wards Cove* that a specific, affirmative employment practice caused the disparity between entry-level workers at Miniature and entry-level workers throughout Chicago.

There is no doubt that racial discrimination in employment remains widespread in Chicago. Without probative evidence of discriminatory intent, however, Miniature is not liable when it passively relies on the natural flow of applicants for its entry-level positions. Miniature's entry-level hiring practices were straightforward, simple, and effective. The EEOC's misspecified statistical model that ignored commuting distance and language fluency requirements, when unaccompanied by more probative anecdotal testimony, cannot support a ruling that Miniature violated Title VII by discriminating against blacks. Therefore, the trial court erred in finding Miniature liable under Title VII. Its disparate treatment and disparate impact findings were clearly erroneous because they credited statistics that did not take into account applicant preference and because the anecdotal evidence presented at trial was not sufficiently probative. In addition, the EEOC's disparate impact theory fails because the EEOC did not specifically identify a particular practice by the employer that caused any disparity. REVERSED.

Case Questions

1. Would an unbalanced workforce due to word-of-mouth recruiting alone ever constitute disparate treatment?

2. Consider your and the court's response to the above question. Would your decision be different if it could be shown that, in a certain small, all-white firm, recruiting was done only using word of mouth and this effort resulted in only white applicants?

3. How would you balance the advantages of word-of-mouth recruiting against the possibility of discriminatory impact?

EEOC v. Consolidated Service System
989 F.2d 233 (7th Cir. 1993)

Defendant is a small janitorial firm in Chicago owned by Mr. Hwang, a Korean immigrant, and staffed mostly by Koreans. The firm relied mainly on word-of-mouth recruiting. Between 1983 and 1987, 73 percent of the applicants for jobs and 81 percent of the hires were Korean, while less than 1 percent of the workforce in the Chicago area is Korean. The district court found that these discrepancies were not due to discrimination.

Posner, J.

We said that Consolidated is a small company. The EEOC's lawyer told us at argument that the company's annual sales are only $400,000. We mention this fact not to remind the reader of David and Goliath, or to suggest that Consolidated is exempt from Title VII (it is not), or to express wonderment that a firm of this size could litigate in federal court for seven years (and counting) with a federal agency, but to explain why Mr. Hwang relies on word of mouth to obtain employees rather than reaching out to a broader community less heavily Korean. It is the cheapest method of recruitment. Indeed, it is practically costless. Persons approach Hwang or his employees—most of whom are Korean too—at work or at social events, and once or twice Hwang has asked employees whether they know anyone who wants a job. At argument the EEOC's lawyer conceded, perhaps improvidently but if so only slightly so, the Hwang's recruitment posture could be described as totally passive. Hwang did buy newspaper advertisements on three occasions—once in a Korean-language newspaper and twice in the *Chicago Tribune*—but as these ads resulted in zero hires, the experience doubtless only confirmed him in the passive posture. The

EEOC argues that the single Korean newspaper ad, which ran for only three days and yielded not a single hire, is evidence of discrimination. If so, it is very weak evidence. The Commission points to the fact that Hwang could have obtained job applicants at no expense from the Illinois Job Service as further evidence of discrimination. But he testified that he had never heard of the Illinois Job Service and the district judge believed him.

If an employer can obtain all the competent workers he wants, at wages no higher than the minimum that he expects to have to pay, without beating the bushes for workers—without in fact spending a cent on recruitment—he can reduce his costs of doing business by adopting just the stance of Mr. Hwang. And this is no mean consideration to a firm whose annual revenues in a highly competitive business are those of a mom and pop grocery store. Of course if the employer is a member of an ethnic community, especially an immigrant one, this stance is likely to result in the perpetuation of an ethnically imbalanced workforce. Members of these communities tend to work and to socialize with each other rather than with people in the larger community. The social and business network of an immigrant community racially and culturally distinct from the majority of Americans is bound to be largely confined to that community, making it inevitable that when the network is used for job recruitment the recruits will be drawn disproportionately from the community.

No inference of *intentional* discrimination can be drawn from the pattern we have described, even if the employer would prefer to employ people drawn predominantly or even entirely from his own ethnic or, here, national-origin community. Discrimination is not preference or aversion; it is acting on the preference or aversion. If the most efficient method of hiring adopted *because* it is the most efficient (not defended because it is efficient—the statute does not allow an employer to justify intentional discrimination by reference to efficiency), just happens to produce a workforce whose racial or religious or ethnic or national-origin or gender composition pleases the em-

ployer, this is not intentional discrimination. The motive is not a discriminatory one. "Knowledge of a disparity is not the same thing as an intent to cause or maintain it." Or if, though the motives behind adoption of the method were a mixture of discrimination and efficiency, Mr. Hwang would have adopted the identical method of recruitment even if he had no interest in the national origin of his employees, the fact that he had such an interest would not be a "but for" cause of the discriminatory outcome and again there would be no liability. There is no evidence that Hwang is biased in favor of Koreans or prejudiced against any group underrepresented in his work force, except what the Commission asks us to infer from the imbalance in that force and Hwang's passive stance.

If this were a disparate-impact case (as it was once, but the Commission has abandoned its claim of disparate impact), and, if, contrary to *EEOC v. Chicago Miniature Lamp Works,* word of mouth recruitment were deemed an employment practice and hence was subject to review for disparate impact, as assumed in *Clark v. Chrysler Corp.,* then the advantages of word of mouth recruitment would have to be balanced against its possibly discriminatory effect when the employer's current work force is already skewed along racial or other disfavored lines. But in a case of disparate treatment, the question is different. It is whether word of mouth recruitment gives rise to an inference of intentional discrimination. Unlike an explicit racial or ethnic criterion or, what we may assume without deciding amounts to the same thing, a rule confining hiring to relatives of existing employees in a racially or ethnically skewed work force, as in *Thomas v. Washington County School Board,* word of mouth recruiting does not compel an inference of intentional discrimination. At least it does not do so where, as in the case of Consolidated Services Systems, it is clearly, as we have been at pains to emphasize, the cheapest and most efficient method of recruitment, notwithstanding its discriminatory impact. Of course, Consolidated had some non-Korean applicants for employment, and if it had never hired any this would support, perhaps decisively, as inference of discrimination. Although the respective percentages of Korean and of non-Korean applicants hired were clearly favorable to Koreans (33 percent to 20 percent), the EEOC was unable to find a single person out of the 99 rejected non-Koreans who could show that he or she was interested in a job that Mr. Hwang ever hired for. Many, perhaps most, of these were persons who responded to the ad he placed in the *Chicago Tribune* for a contract that he never got, hence never hired for.

The Commission cites the statement of Consolidated's lawyer that his client took advantage of the fact that the Korean immigrant community offered a ready market of cheap labor as an admission of "active" discrimination on the basis of national origin. It is not discrimination, and it is certainly not active discrimination, for an employer to sit back and wait for people willing to work for low wages to apply to him. The fact that they are ethnically or racially uniform does not impose upon him a duty to spend money advertising in the help-wanted columns of the *Chicago Tribune*. The Commission deemed Consolidated's "admission" corroborated by the testimony of the sociologist William Liu, Consolidated's own expert witness, who explained that it was natural for a recent Korean immigrant such as Hwang to hire other recent Korean immigrants, with whom he shared a common culture, and that the consequence would be a workforce disproportionately Korean. Well, of course. People who share a common culture tend to work together as well as marry together and socialize together. That is not evidence of illegal discrimination.

In a nation of immigrants, this must be reckoned an ominous case despite its outcome. The United States has many recent immigrants, and today as historically they tend to cluster in their own communities, united by ties of language, culture, and background. Often they form small businesses composed largely of relatives, friends, and other members of their community, and they ob-

tain new employees by word of mouth. These small businesses—grocery stores, furniture stores, clothing stores, cleaning services, restaurants, gas stations—have been for many immigrant groups, and continue to be, the first rung on the ladder of American success. Derided as clannish, resented for their ambition and hard work, hated or despised for their otherness, recent immigrants are frequent targets of discrimination, some of it violent. It would be a bitter irony if the federal agency dedicated to enforcing the antidiscrimination laws succeeded in using those laws to kick these people off the ladder by compelling them to institute costly systems of hiring. There is equal danger to small black-run businesses in our central cities. Must such businesses undertake in the name of nondiscrimination costly measures to recruit nonblack employees?

Although Consolidated has been dragged through seven years of federal litigation at outrageous expense for a firm of its size, we agree with the Commission that this suit was not frivolous. The statistical disparity gave the Commission a leg up, and it might conceivably have succeeded in its disparate-impact claim but for our intervening decision in *EEOC v. Chicago Miniature Lamp Works,* supra. Had the judge believed the Commission's witnesses, the outcome even of the disparate-treatment claim might have been different. The Equal Access to Justice Act was intended, one might have thought, for just such a case as this, where a groundless but not frivolous suit is brought by the mighty federal government against a tiny firm; but Consolidated concedes its inapplicability. We do not know on what the concession is based—possibly on cases like *Escobar Ruiz v. INS,* on rehearing, holding the Act inapplicable to statutes that have their own fee-shifting statutes—but other cases, such as *Gavette v. Office of Personnel Management,* are contra. It may not be too late for Consolidated to reconsider its concession in light of our holding in *McDonald v. Schweiker,* supra, regarding the deadline for seeking fees under the Act.

AFFIRMED.

Case Questions

1. If the court in *Consolidated* ruled that, even though the statistics told another story, there was no evidence of "intentional" discrimination, would an unbalanced workforce due to word-of-mouth recruiting alone ever constitute disparate treatment?

2. Consider your and the court's response to the above question. Would your decision be different if it could be shown that, in a certain small, all-white firm, recruiting was done only using word of mouth and this effort resulted in only white applicants. Would your decision remain the same?

3. If this case were tried as a disparate impact case, as discussed by the court, how would you balance the advantages of word-of-mouth recruiting against the possibility of a discriminatory impact?

Nepotism.   Nepotism is the practice of hiring members of the same family, and some employers rely on this to locate the most appropriate candidates. Such employers theorize that, if the mother and the firm are a "good fit," then the daughter may also work out well. Therefore, the least costly method of locating additional employees may be to ask current employees whether their family members may be interested in a position. This practice also results in homogeneity, as the company becomes a conglomerate of a number of homogeneous families, with greatest likelihood of discrimination resulting from a disparate impact.

Nepotism policies are not, *per se,* illegal. When an employee or applicant challenges the policy, the court will determine whether it has an adverse impact on a protected class. If so, it will be found illegal unless the employer has a strong justification in favor of its business necessity.

An antinepotism policy (one stating that the company will *not* hire family members) may also be discriminatory where it is not applied across the board. For example, if the antinepotism policy provides that a wife may be hired if her husband is a current employee, but does not provide the parallel provision for the hiring of husbands of current employees, the policy may be discriminatory. Similar problems exist where the policy is only enforced at one level of the company. Where the line workers in a firm are primarily Hispanic and management is primarily white, an antinepotism policy for line workers that does not apply to management would result in disparate impact.

Courts have consistently upheld general antinepotism policies that provide that the company will not hire the *spouse* of a current employee, as long as there is no evidence of disparate impact, or that the policy applies to employees at all levels of employment.

Promoting from Within.   While promoting from within the company is not in and of itself illegal, it also has the potential for discriminatory results, depending on the process used and the makeup of the workforce. Some employers use a secretive process, quietly soliciting interest in a position from a few upper-level employees selected on recommendations from their supervisors. The employer then conducts interviews with the candidates and extends an offer. After the employee accepts the offer, a notice is posted announcing the promotion. If women and minorities are not well represented in a firm, such a process may result in a disparate impact against them, even where the purpose of the employer is merely to locate and promote the most qualified candidate.

Employers are more likely to post a notice of position availability in which all employees are offered the opportunity to compete for open positions. The employer is less vulnerable to attack for discriminatory policies as long as the workforce is relatively balanced so there is equal employment opportunity.

Venue Recruiting.   Employers may decide to conduct recruiting at a university or high school. Similar precautions must be taken to attract diverse applicants in a locale that may be either purposefully or unintentionally uniform. The same effect may result when an employer recruits with a preference for experienced applicants for entry-level jobs—for instance, recruiting firefighters and specifying a preference for applicants with experience in volunteer fire departments. The court held that this recruitment practice was wrongful, because volunteer fire departments tended to be hostile to minorities and to women as firefighters. Preference for firefighters with this experience, therefore, would lead to few, if any, women and minorities being hired. Employers should be aware of the composition of their workforce on women and minorities, but also the composition of the sources of their recruitment.

Walk-in Applicants.   Recruiting may not be necessary where the company is constantly receiving unsolicited applications. Depending on the professional, potential employees may send their résumés to prospective employers in hopes of locating an open position, or of persuading them to create one. While this strategy may be effective in locating employees and reducing costs of actual formal recruiting, the company may find that its reputation attracts only one type of employee, while others are intimidated by, are unaware of, or are uninterested in the firm. Equal employment opportunity is again lost.

Neutral Solicitation.   While selecting an appropriate source from which to choose applicants is crucial, it is also important to fashion the process to encourage diverse applicants. For instance, an advertisement that requests "recent college grads" may discourage older workers from applying and result in an adverse impact on them. Or a job announcement that states the employer is looking for "busboys" or "servicemen" may deter females from applying. Other terms that at first appear innocuous are discouraging to one group or another as well, including *draftsman, saleswoman, repairman, waiter, host,* and *maid.* The announcement or solicitation should invite applications from all groups and should not suggest a preference for any one class of individual.

Consider Tammy Hartman's concern about her uneven workforce as a result of her firm's hiring practices. Her firm hires based on walk-in applications. Since her firm is evidently attracting more of one type of applicant than others, she may want to consider using additional types of application solicitations.

Scenario

Résumé Collection Concerns.   Since applicants acquire certain rights simply by virtue of being applicants (such as the right under Title VII to sue for discrimination if rejected for inappropriate reasons), it is critical to control the processing of applications. If, for instance, you receive an inquiry by e-mail from the daughter of one of your friends, does this constitute an application? Is this woman an applicant? If you are not involved in this hiring process, the best response may be simply to leave the e-mail or attached résumé unopened (if possible!) and to forward it to the appropriate human resources individual.

Once an application is received, federal employers or contractors have a duty to keep records and collect information regarding compliance with selection or affirmative action requirements and other obligations. Other employers should retain this information, as well, since (1) some statutes have record-keeping requirements, such as the Age Discrimination in Employment Act, and (2) one of the ways to refute an applicant's claim of discrimination is through statistical analysis of the applicant pool.

Since "applicant" is not defined by any of the enforcement bodies such as the EEOC or Department of Justice, it is a good idea for employers to do so for themselves. This definition could be useful in later litigation, if the situation arises. One example of a definition of an applicant is anyone who fills out one of the company's application forms. Those who do not fill out the prescribed form are *not* considered applicants. In this way, the firm has greater control over this pool and, therefore, over its obligations.

Preferential Treatment

Preferential treatment, or, more generally, affirmative action, may be required by federal law, depending on the employer, on the number of employees, and on the type of position available. This chapter will introduce the regulation of preferential treatment under various statutes while the chapter on affirmative action will address the substantive questions surrounding the extent to which employers have satisfied the requirements discussed here.

The difference between preferential treatment and affirmative action, as those terms are used in this section, is that *preferential treatment* means simply a preference offered to members of a certain class that is not offered to members of other classes; *affirmative action* provides for the most equal opportunity possible to members of various groups historically not having been provided equal opportunity, and may include preferential treatment, education programs, referral services, or preemployment preparation or training for certain groups.

Title VII does not require that preferential treatment is given to any specific protected class. In fact, the statute states that preferential treatment cannot be used to remedy the existing number or percentage imbalance of a protected group. However, if a protected group has been discriminated against by the employer, the employer can consider this as a *factor* in its hiring decision. Title VII states:

Nothing in this title shall be interpreted to require any employer . . . to grant preferential treatment to any individual or to any group because of the race, color, religion, sex, or national origin of such individual or group on account of an imbalance which may exist with respect to the total number or percentage of persons of any race, color, religion, sex or national origin employed . . . in comparison with the total number or percentage of any persons of such race, color, religion, sex or national origin in any community. *(Section 703(j).)*

The Rehabilitation Act requires affirmative action programs for the employment of disabled employees, though not specifically preferential treatment. The act distinguishes between small contractors, those with contracts between $2,500 and $50,000, and large contractors, those with contracts of $50,000 or more. The action required of the smaller employer is limited to posting notices of the obligation to be nondiscriminatory in its hiring practices. The larger employer must maintain a more specific written action plan, including a review of job requirements to confirm that those requirements acting as barriers to disabled applications are actually job related; a commitment to making reasonable accommodations for those employees who require them; recruitment at institutions that train disabled individuals; and other activities that, collectively, demonstrate the employer's commitment to hiring disabled employees.

The Vietnam Era Veterans' Readjustment Assistance Act of 1974 provides that government contractors with contracts of $10,000 or more must undertake affirmative action programs for the purpose of employing and advancing disabled and qualified veterans who were on active duty between August 5, 1964, and May 7, 1975. Similar to the Rehabilitation Act, those contractors who have contracts of $50,000 or more must design and maintain a written affirmative action program.

Executive Order 11246, as amended, regulates the activities of those who have contracts of $10,000 or more with the federal government. The order was signed before Title VII was enacted and requires similar employment actions (i.e., the order prohibits a covered employer from basing any employment decision on race, color, religion, sex, or national origin). Contractors with contracts of over $50,000 must design and implement affirmative action programs whenever women or minorities are "underutilized," or underrepresented, in the workforce. *Underutilization* is defined by Revised Order No. 4 as "having fewer minorities or women in a particular job group than would reasonably be expected by their availability." The plan must also establish timetables for elimination of the disparity and address the satisfaction of these goals in the program.

Finally, the Civil Service Reform Act of 1978 provides that all federal government agencies implement programs designed to create "a federal workforce reflective of the Nation's diversity." This general statement of intent provides the basis for involuntary affirmative action programs discussed in the affirmative action chapter.

The Office of Federal Contract Compliance Programs (OFCCP), which administers the Executive Order, offers several recruitment suggestions to ensure that an affirmative action program does not unduly discriminate in reverse (i.e., discriminate against white males in favor of minorities and women). For instance, the

OFCCP recommends that the employer obtain applicant referrals from a medley of organizations that would likely be able to refer minorities or women such as the Job Corps, the Urban League, the National Organization for Women, and the Professional Women's Caucus. It is further recommended that the organization invite a representative of these groups to the place of employment and instruct the representatives regarding the necessary requirements for each available position, as well as the formal recruiting and referral procedures. Women and minorities within the company may also be a valuable source of applicant referrals, and such referrals should be encouraged. Finally, inclusion of current female and minority employees in the recruitment process is essential.

Information Gathering and Selection

Once the employer has recruited a group of applicants, on what basis does the employer reach a final conclusion regarding the employment of any given applicant? The employer weighs the appropriateness of the applicant—given her or his experience, education, fit with the company, and other information gained through interviews, reference checks, and application forms—with the needs of the company and any negative information on the candidate discovered in the course of the information gathering. The gathering of this information is a timely, yet important, process that is subject to suspicion by applicants as a result of its potential for the invasion of privacy and discriminatory treatment. While the extent to which an employer is prohibited from delving into private information about an employee on the basis of invasion of privacy is discussed in the chapter on privacy, this section will examine that information that the employer may or may not obtain based on a potential for discrimination.

The Application Process

The hiring process usually begins with an application for employment. Most of us at some point have filled out an employment application. Did you ever stop to think about whether the employer actually had a right to ask these questions? Under most circumstances, the application requests information that will serve as the basis for later screening out applicants, because of education or experience requirements. Questions that are business related and used for a nondiscriminatory purpose are appropriate. The form will generally ask for name, address, educational background, work experience, and other qualifications for the position; but it may additionally request your date of birth, nationality, religion, marital status, children, or ethnicity.

There are only a few questions that are strictly prohibited by federal law from being asked on an application and during the interview process. Any questions concerning disability, specific health inquiries, and workers' compensation history are prohibited by the Americans with Disabilities Act of 1990. Other questions regarding age, sex, religion, marital status, nationality, and ethnicity are not prohibited by federal law but they are dangerous. Questions relating to these areas must be related to the position for which the applicant applies in order for an employer to be able to ask such questions. If they are not related and it can be shown these inquiries are being made to discriminate against applicants, the employers could be facing liability. Furthermore, even if the employer does not base its employment decision on the responses of these inquiries, where the selection process results in a disparate impact against a protected group, the employer could also be liable.

Nevertheless, research has shown that companies frequently violate guidelines promulgated by the EEOC regarding appropriate application and interview questions. You may even be thinking right now that you have answered these questions on some form in the past. The areas of inquiry that are most often violated include education (where not business-justified and where questions relate to religious affiliation of the school, and so on), arrest records, physical disabilities, and age. Even the most innocuous remark may be inappropriate. For instance, an employer is advised not to ask questions regarding the name of the applicant, other than what it is (it may be perceived as national origin discrimination). Questions relating to other names by which the applicant may be known are proper, while questions regarding the origins of an interesting surname or whether it is a maiden name are improper (it may be perceived as marital status discrimination).

Moreover, while most applicants are used to filling in the response to a question regarding gender on an application, an employer actually has no right to that knowledge unless gender is a bona fide occupational qualification. As hair and eye color may lead to an inference regarding the applicant's race or color, these questions, too, may be inappropriate, but not *per se* illegal if it is a bona fide qualification.

While the previous discussion has focused on potential for employer wrongdoing, what happens when an applicant includes misstatements on her or his application? According to a recent Supreme Court decision, *McKennon v. Nashville Banner Publ. Co.,* 115 S.Ct. 879 (1995), an employer need not hire someone once the misstatement or misconduct has been discovered, or may fire someone for that reason. Often, this situation will come up after someone has been fired for another, allegedly wrongful reason. The "after-acquired evidence" of the misstatements is admissible to show the court that, whether or not the employer had unlawful reasons for the action, it also had this legal justification for the action. In *McKennon,* the court held that a discharge in violation of the ADEA was acceptable where the employer would have terminated the employment anyway because of a breach of confidentiality.

The Interview

The second step in the process is usually an interview with a representative of the employer. Discrimination may occur during the interview in the same manner in which it is present on application forms. If it would be improper to ask a question on the application, it is just as improper to ask for the same information in an interview.

Questions are not the only source of discrimination during an interview. In a recent study conducted by the Urban Institute, researchers found that black applicants were treated more harshly during interviews than white applicants with identical qualifications. Researchers submitted pairs of applications of black and white applicants for available positions. The researchers found that blacks were treated more favorably than whites in 27 percent of the interview situations, while they were treated less favorably than whites in half of the interviews. Black applicants suffered greater abuses, including longer waiting times, shorter interviews, and being interviewed by a greater number of individuals. White applicants were found to be more likely to receive a job offer. All of this occurred under controlled circumstances where the applications of the pairs were kept equal in terms of qualifications and experience. An interview must, therefore, not only be nondiscriminatory in terms of the information solicited but also in terms of the process in which it is conducted.

There are four areas of potential problems in connection with the interview. First, the employer must ensure that the interview procedures do not discourage women, minorities, or other protected groups from continuing the process. Second, employers should be aware that all-white or all-male interviewers, or interviewers who are not well trained, may subject the employer to liability. Third, the training of the interviewers is crucial to avoid biased questions, gender-based remarks, and unbalanced interviews. Fourth, the evaluation of the applicant subsequent to the interview should follow a consistent and evaluative process rather than reflect arbitrary and subjective opinions.

Background or Reference Check, Negligent Hiring

Negligence
The failure to do something in such a way or manner as a reasonable person would have done the same thing; or doing something that a reasonable person would not do. Failing to raise one's standard of care to the level of care that a reasonable person would use in a given situation.

Once the applicant has successfully completed the interview process, the next step for the employer is to check the applicant's background and references. This is how the employer discovers whether what is contained in the application and is said during the interview are true. The *Small Business Report* found that 80 percent of job applications contain false information regarding prior work history, while 30 percent of the information related to educational background is false. On the other hand, as job responsibilities decrease, the employer is less likely to verify all of the information provided by the applicant. A check, therefore, is crucial to verify the information given on the application and in the interview.

It is important, as well, to ensure that no undiscovered information would disqualify the applicant from employment or may subject other employees, clients, or customers to a dangerous situation and the employer to a claim of negligent hiring. An employer is liable for negligent hiring where an employee causes damage that could have been prevented if the employer had conducted a reasonable and responsible background check on the employee. The person injured may claim that the negligence of the employer placed the employee in a position where harm could result, and, therefore, the employer contributed to that harm. Since 30 percent of workplace attacks are committed by co-workers or ex–co-workers, this is a critical area of caution.[1]

---

[1]Dawn Anfuso, "Deflecting Workplace Violence," *Personnel Journal* 73, no. 10 (October 1994), pp. 66–77.

Exhibit 4–4

Tips for Tracing Lies: 20 Tips for Catching Résumé Fraud, by Christopher J. Bachler

1. Carefully note the order of the material given on the résumé. What's given up front is generally what the applicant wishes to emphasize. But what's hidden below may well be more revealing.

2. Concentrate on the most important points in the applicant's résumé. Diverting attention to too many insignificant details draws focus away from key areas.

3. Does the applicant's history follow a logical sequence? For example, has there been a consistent upward progression during the career? Or has there been a downward trend? People don't tend to leave better jobs for poorer ones.

4. Look for conflicting details or overlapping dates.

5. Look for gaps in dates. It's common for applicants who wish to cover something up to try to omit it.

6. Look for omissions of any kind.

7. Pay attention to what the applicant doesn't say as much as to what he or she does say. You'll probably find the most valuable information in those areas your applicant doesn't want to discuss.

8. Get particulars about various subjects. For example, if the applicant says he or she studied business at Harvard, find out what courses he or she took. Casually ask some questions about the campus or physical environment—just to determine if he or she really was there. People who are dishonest will probably stumble on questions like those.

9. Be sure to discuss all key points.

10. Question the applicant about details as you review the résumé. It will be much harder for him or her to remember false information.

11. Probe the applicant's reasons for leaving past jobs, or for jumping from school to school.

12. How quick and sharp are the applicant's answers? Do they sound rehearsed? An honest person has no need to hesitate or rehearse.

13. Does the applicant look you in the eye? Notice body language.

14. Ask the applicant if he or she minds if you verify information. Then assure him or her that you will need to verify every detail. Imposters likely will drop out at that point.

15. Ask colleagues to sit in on your interview. Your associates may catch vital signs or details that you might miss. They might also think of revealing questions to ask.

16. When confirming information by phone, begin by asking for the company operator. That will help you be sure that the place you're calling is a genuine company. Then move on to the personnel department, and then to the particular manager indicated.

17. Send something in the mail. That will enable you to determine if the address given is genuine.

18. Ask references you're given for other references. The applicant is bound to provide only favorable references. But those sources may be aware of others.

19. If the applicant sought the help of a résumé service or other career placement service, ask him or her why. The reasons may be legitimate. But they may also be revealing.

20. If the résumé isn't very clear, or if it has been produced by a professional service, consider asking the applicant to redo it in his or her own way.

Workforce online, reprinted from *Personnel Journal,* June 1995, Vol. 74, No. 6, p. 55.

For instance, in one case an applicant for an over-the-road truck driving position had a criminal record for rape and sexual misconduct, but no driving violations. However, the applicant stated on his application that he had no prior criminal convictions or traffic offenses. The employer verified the statement regarding traffic offenses and found it to be true, but did not investigate the statement regarding criminal convictions. The applicant was hired by the employer. While on a scheduled work route for the employer, he picked up a hitchhiker and raped her. The victim sued the employer for negligent hiring, since the employer was shown to be aware that truck drivers pick up hitchhikers but neglected to ensure that its truck drivers were harmless.

To carefully and adequately check on an applicant's references, the employer has several options. First, the employer may contact the reference in person, by telephone, or by letter and request a general statement about whether the information stated in the application and interview is correct. For example, the employer may contact a prior employer of the applicant to confirm that the applicant actually worked there during the time period stated on the application, in the position identified, and at the salary named. Second, the contact might be much more specific, posing questions about the applicant's abilities and qualifications for the available position. Third, the employer may undertake an independent check of credit standing through a credit reporting agency, military service and discharge status, driving record, criminal record, or other public information to obtain the most complete information on the applicant.

There are problems inherent in each form of query.

• Most employers are willing to verify the employment of past employees, but obtaining this limited information may not necessarily satisfy the standard of care required to avoid a claim of negligent hiring.

• Certain information is not available to employers and is protected by state law. For instance, if an employer asks about the applicant's prior criminal arrest record, or even certain convictions, in one of several states that statutorily protect disclosure of this type of information, the employer may be subject to a claim of invasion of privacy or other statutory violations.

• There may also be the basis for a claim of disparate impact where it can be shown that those of one protected class are arrested more often than others. In that

---

Exhibit 4–5

To state a claim for negligent hiring, the plaintiff must show:
1. The existence of an employer–employee relationship.
2. The employee's incompetence or inappropriateness for the position assumed.
3. The employer's actual or constructive knowledge of such incompetence or inappropriateness, or the employer's ability.
4. That the employee's act or omission caused the plaintiff's injuries.
5. That the employer's negligence in hiring or retaining the employee was the proximate cause of the plaintiff's injuries (i.e., on investigation, the employer could have discovered the relevant information and prevented the incident from occurring).

EXHIBIT 4–6

Where an employer is having a difficult time obtaining information from a prior employer of an applicant for a position, author Edward Andler offers the following advice:

Introduce yourself:

If reference answers:

- Mr/Ms/ _____, my name is _____ with the XYZ Company.
- We are in the process of hiring _____. Before we will extend an offer, we need to verify her/his background. She/he has asked that we contact you as her/his personal/employment reference.
- I would like to spend a few minutes with you. Is this a convenient time to talk? When would be the best time/day? At work/home?
- Everything we talk about is confidential and will be treated that way.

If reference will not cooperate:

- Ask if she/he would like a personal call from the candidate authorizing her/him to speak with you.

Fallback (comment):

- I cannot understand why we're having a problem getting you to talk with us, because we're just trying to help _____ get a new job. Who can I talk with to clear this matter up?

From E. C. Andler, *Winning the Hiring Game* (Traverse City, MI: Smith Collins, 1992).

case, asking about an arrest record where the offense is not necessarily related to job performance may result in adverse impact. Note that arrests and convictions are not the same. Employers are more limited in inquiring about arrest records than about convictions relevant to the job.

- The Fair Credit Reporting Act requires that an employer notify the applicant in writing of its intention to conduct an investigative consumer report, and to inform the applicant of the information it seeks. It further requires the employee to obtain written authorization to obtain the report.

- The reference and background information gathering process is a lengthy one and may be unmanageable, given the employer's position requirements.

- Employers may not be willing to offer any further information than that the applicant worked at that company for a time. Employers have cause for concern, given the large number of defamation actions filed against employers based on references (see Chapter 17; Exhibit 4–6).

The most effective means by which to avoid this potential stumbling block is to request that the applicant sign a statement on the application form, which states that former employers are released from liability for offering references on her or his behalf. In the course of making a request for a reference from those former employers, the release should be sent to the former employer along with a copy of the applicant's entire application.

POE V. DOMINO'S PIZZA, INC.
139 F.3d 617 (8th Cir. 1998)

When a woman was abducted and raped by a Domino's employee, she investigated and found that this employee had a criminal record for a previous sexual assault and abuse which Domino's failed to discover. On this basis, she sued Domino's alleging that it was negligent in hiring the employee and in not checking his background thoroughly. The court held that, since the woman was not a Domino's customer, there was no special relationship creating a duty of Domino's to protect her.

Gina Poe brought this lawsuit against Domino's Pizza after she was abducted and raped by James Sturtz, a Domino's employee. Sturtz was hired by Domino's in early 1994. He was distributing pizza coupons door-to-door near the college Poe attended. She was waiting at her bus stop when Sturtz approached her and asked if he could give her a ride. Poe declined. When Sturtz explained he worked for Domino's and that it would be okay for her to ride with him, showing her the coupons he was passing out, Poe got into the car. Sturtz drove to a remote area and at knifepoint raped Poe. Sturtz had a previous conviction for sexual assault and abuse and lied on his application form stating he had never been convicted of a felony. Poe alleged negligent hiring for failing to check Sturtz's criminal background thoroughly. She also accused Domino's of negligent supervision for violating its own policy by not supervising Sturtz while he was distributing coupons. The District Court granted Domino's motion for summary judgment. Poe appealed.

Arnold, Richard S.

* * * *

The plaintiff concedes that Mr. Sturtz was not acting within the scope of his employment when he committed the acts complained of. The theory of respondeat superior is therefore not available as a basis of liability in this case. Plaintiff proceeds on a theory of negligent hiring. The Iowa courts hold that a special relationship must exist in order for the plaintiff to prevail in a negligent-hiring case. Whether a duty exists is a matter for the court to determine.

The District Court reviewed three factors to determine whether a special relationship existed: whether the plaintiff and the employee were in places where each had a right to be when the wrongful act occurred; whether the plaintiff met the employee as a direct consequence of the employment; and whether the employer would re-

ceive some benefit, even if only a potential or indirect benefit, from the meeting of the employee and the plaintiff had the wrongful act not occurred. The Court held that Domino's did not cause the meeting between Ms. Poe and Mr. Sturtz, that the meeting did not arise out of Mr. Sturtz's employment, and that Domino's received no benefit from the meeting. Ms. Poe was not a customer of Domino's, nor was she an owner or resident of a house where Mr. Sturtz was going to leave an advertisement for Domino's.

Ms. Poe claims there was a special relationship because Domino's considers all members of the public to be potential customers and encourages its drivers to have frequent contact with targeted customers such as college students. She also argues that Mr. Sturtz lured her into his car by telling her he worked for Domino's and by showing her the coupons he was distributing. The District Court found this unpersuasive, and, under Iowa law, so do we. Ms. Poe was not a customer, and she was not one to whom Domino's owed a duty because of its coupon distribution. She got into Mr. Sturtz's car for the purpose of getting a ride to her destination. We believe the District Court correctly held there was no special relationship. Ms. Poe had no more connection with Domino's than any other member of the general public that Mr. Sturtz might have victimized. **Held for Domino's.**

Case Questions

1. Would you analyze the three factors of a special relationship the same way in which the court did? Why or why not?

2. How do you respond to the argument that Domino's did not check Sturtz's references? Shouldn't they be held responsible for their negligence in not taking responsible care to ensure the accuracy of the application?

3. What can employers do to prevent suits like this?

The amount of background and reference checking necessary to be shielded from a claim of negligent hiring varies from situation to situation. A position that provides for absolutely no contact with clients, customers, or other employees may necessitate a quick check of the information contained on the application, while a position that requires a great deal of personal contact would require an investigation into the applicant's prior experiences, and so on. An employer must exercise reasonable care in hiring applicants who may pose a risk to others as a result of their employment and the employer's negligent failure to obtain more complete

EXHIBIT 4–7

So how does the employer protect itself? Precaution.

During the interview process:

- Obtain releases from all applicants allowing the employer to check on previous employment.
- Request that all applicants obtain copies of their personnel files from previous employers.

Before a position is offered to the candidate:

- Investigate the employment record, including all gaps, missing data, and positions held.
- Review educational records carefully. Contact the institutions listed to verify their existence, the years attended, the course of study, and, most importantly, actual graduation with degree.
- Check references, especially when several are reluctant to speak. This may be viewed as a warning beacon that they do not have much good to say or have no desire to support the candidate. (On the other hand, ensure that this unwillingness is not the result of a bad relationship with the person. Allow the candidate the opportunity to explain.)

After the candidate is hired:

- Maintain clear, consistent policies relating to employment decisions.
- Follow up on the implementation and enforcement of these policies.

information. The standard of care to be met is what would be exercised by a reasonable employer in similar circumstances. If an employer had no means by which to learn a dangerous propensity, or if discovery of this information would place a great burden on the employer, a court is more likely to deny a claim for negligent hiring.

In connection with scenario 3, Sarah may be well advised to modify her hiring practices in order to ensure that they would uncover facts such as an applicant's prior felony convictions. Failure to do so might result in liability on the basis of negligent hiring, as discussed above.

Certain states have recently enacted Employment Record Disclosure Acts which insulate an employer from liability as a result of offering a reference for a previous employee. In other words, an employer who provides information to a new employer about a previous employee may not be sued for defamation as long as there is a good-faith belief in the truth of the statement made. While the restrictions on what information may be lawfully transmitted vary from state to state, this new legislation will allow previous employers to be more free about their concerns regarding past employees.

Reference Checks: Potential for Defamation?

Various states have passed some form of law relating to reference checks or created a general statutory privilege making employers immune from liability when giving information regarding a former employer unless (1) the claims made were false or (2) the employer did not act in good faith. Some of the states that have such laws include California, Georgia, Illinois, Oklahoma, and West Virginia.

However, this protection does not go so far as to protect an employer who issues a negative reference in retaliation for a title VII claim by a former employee. For example, in *Robinson v. Shell Oil Company,* a former employee claimed that his employer had given a negative reference to a prospective employer *because* he had filed a charge of race discrimination with the EEOC after he was terminated. The court ruled that former employees have the same right as current employees to sue on grounds that they were retaliated against for exercising their Title VII rights.

Due to an increasing risk of lawsuits as a result of reference checks, many employers have adopted an official policy of providing only name, position held, and salary. However, employers should be aware that, should an employer choose not to provide reference information on prior employees, it could be facing lawsuits and liability from the new or prospective employer who sought the reference. In one case, a former employer settled for an undisclosed amount after allegedly sending an incomplete referral letter that neglected to mention that the former employee had been fired for bringing a gun to work. The employee was subsequently hired by an insurance company and went on a rampage, killing three and wounding two of his co-workers, before killing himself.[2]

---

[2]17 Daily Lab. Rep. No. 193 (Oct. 5, 1995).

One possible safeguard an employer can utilize is requiring written release from former employees before any information is released. However, the written release should be voluntary, should allow the former employee to discuss the waiver with an attorney, and should include the employee's agreement not to contest his or her termination or the contents of the personnel file.

Uniform Guidelines on Employee Selection Procedures

The Uniform Guidelines on Employee Selection Procedures were enacted in 1978 in an attempt to assist employers to comply with Title VII. The guidelines provide a framework for determining the proper use of tests and other selection procedures. The guidelines have several significant provisions that affect employer practices.

The guidelines are based on the concept that any selection procedure resulting in a disparate impact (discussed in detail in the chapter on Title VII) will be considered discriminatory. The guidelines, therefore, attempt to offer a benchmark for whether adverse impact exists. Disparate impact is said to exist where a selection rate for any protected class is less than 80 percent of the rate for the group with the highest rate of selection (the four-fifths rule).

While test validation is discussed in the preceding chapter, the most significant aspect of the guidelines relating to testing is that there is no requirement to validate the tests where no adverse impact results or has been shown. A considerable portion of the guidelines relates to the validation of selection instruments.

In addition, where two or more selection procedures are available, which serve the employer's legitimate interest in an efficient and trustworthy manner, and which are substantially equal for their stated purpose, the employer is directed to use the procedure that has been shown to have a lesser adverse impact.

Documentation of Failure to Hire?

No federal statute or guideline requires that employers document the reasons for failing to hire any specific applicant. However, it may be in the best interests of the employer to articulate the reasons in order to avoid the presumption of inappropriate reasons. In addition, since a claim under Title VII or other statutes may come long after the decision was made, documentation will help an employer recall the particular reasons why a certain applicant was rejected so that she or he is not left, perhaps on the witness stand, to say "I don't remember!" Moreover, the individuals who originally made the decision about this candidate may no longer be with the firm. Finally, a firm may choose to document in order to supplement statistical data proving a lack of discrimination. This paper trail may serve to prove that others who were similarly situated were treated the same way, not differently. For instance, in a gender discrimination action, the documentation may demonstrate that no one with a certain low level of experience was hired, male or female.

On the other hand, documentation may also serve to demonstrate facts to which the employer does not want to be bound. Once the reason for failing to hire is on

EXHIBIT 4–8

Possible lawful reasons for choosing to reject a candidate:

1. No positions available.
2. Not interested in positions available.
3. Not qualified for positions available.
4. Not qualified for position being sought.
5. Better qualified persons were hired instead.
6. Cannot work hours offered.
7. Rejected our job offer.
8. Unable to communicate effectively in the English language (if required for position).
9. Obviously under the influence of drugs or alcohol during the employment interview.
10. Did not return for follow-up interview or otherwise failed to complete the preemployment process.
11. Employment interview revealed no interest in type of work.

paper, the employer is now bound to use that, alone, as the reason for the decision. Further, while any one decision may seem appropriate, systematic documentation of these decisions may demonstrate a pattern of adverse impact that one might not notice if nothing is ever recorded.

The decision about whether to put on paper reasons for failing to hire is best left to individual employers who may choose to record this information, while instituting a monitoring system that will catch any areas of potential vulnerability. This is not to say that employers should use paper or choose not to use it as a form of "cover-up;" instead, employers may discover problem areas and respond appropriately and lawfully to them once observed. As long as an employer's policies about hiring are consistently applied and are reasonable, there should be no problems—whether recorded in writing or not.

Administration

To ensure compliance with the prohibitions in federal regulation, Title VII established the Equal Employment Opportunity Commission (EEOC) and charged it with the administration of the Act, as well as the ADEA, the Equal Pay Act, and the ADA. The EEOC requires that employers who employ 100 or more workers must annually file Form EEO-1, which reports the number of women, African-Americans, Asian-Americans, Native Americans, and Hispanic-Americans in comparison to the nonminority males in various positions. The information contained in these reports forms the basis for later statistical analyses relating to workforce composition and adverse impact suits.

Management Tips

- If you are looking for the most qualified candidate, make sure that you are advertising in *all* of the places where that candidate might look for employment—not just the obvious places where you are sure to find the same type of workers as those that already work for you.

- Be wary of representations about the firm that are made during recruitment interviews. While, of course, you want to encourage the best candidates to work for your firm, sometimes glowing accounts of life at the firm might cross the line to misrepresentations. Also, be cautious about promises made to prospective employees as these might be construed as part of the individual's contract with the firm.

- While word of mouth recruiting, nepotism, and promoting from within may seem to be the easiest methods for locating a new employee, these methods are also likely to produce new employees quite similar to your present employees. Make sure that you employ additional methods to ensure diversity in the applicant pool.

- Take a look at your written applicant form. Does it ask for any information that is not relevant to the candidate's potential ability to do the job? Is there any information upon which you are prohibited from basing an employment decision, such as age?

- Background checks are relevant to most positions. If you fail to conduct a check, you might be liable for any actions that you would have learned about in the check, such as previous workplace violence. From a cost-benefit perspective, conducting the check usually wins.

Summary

- Employers believe that freedom of contract should permit them to hire whom they please. However, such statutes as Title VII and IRCA require the employer to ensure that all qualified employees are provided with equal employment opportunity and that decisions to hire are based solely on appropriate concerns and not on prejudice or bias that is neither supported nor relevant to business necessities.

- An ethic of nondiscrimination must permeate the hiring process from advertising the position to drafting the application form to making the decision to hire.

- One of the most effective means by which an employer can protect itself from claims of discrimination in the recruitment/application process is to have a clear view of the job to be filled and who is the best person to fill that job (i.e., an ade-

quate, specific job description for each position within the company).

- After the employer has conducted the analysis, she should implement those results by reviewing the written job descriptions to ensure that they are clear and specific in line with the analysis; all nonessential job requirements should be deleted or defined as nonessential, and minimum requirements should be listed.

- Employers are cautioned, however, that the court or enforcement agency will look first to the actual job performance, then only to the description to the extent that it accurately reflects what the employee really does in that position. If the employer fails to include a function in the description, that may be used as an admission that the function is nonessential. If the function is nonessential, it is likely that an employment decision made on that basis will be suspect.

• Employers should ensure that recruitment procedures seek not only to obtain the most diversified applicant pool by reaching diverse communities but also encourage diverse applicants through the language used and the presentation of the firm.

• Finally, employers should establish efficient, effective procedures to guarantee that they know *who* they are hiring. If an employer wants a certain type of person to fill a position, ensure that the one hired is such a person. Failure to do so may result in liability under a theory of negligent hiring.

Chapter-End Questions

1. In the process of its recruitment of Peters, Security Pacific informed Peters that the company was doing "just fine" and Peters would have "a long tenure" at Security Pacific, should he accept the position offered. In doing so, Security Pacific concealed its financial losses and the substantial, known risk that the project on which Peters was hired to work might soon be abandoned and Peters laid off. Peters accepts the position and moves from New Orleans to Denver to begin his new job. Two months later, Peters is laid off as a result of Security Pacific's poor financial condition. Does Peters have a cause of action?

2. Oakland Scavenger Company instituted a policy pursuant to which ownership of company stock was restricted to family members, all of whom were of Italian ancestry. Prior to the institution of this new rule, the company had a policy that only stockholders were eligible for the upper-level, and more lucrative, jobs in the company. While the company did not dispute the disparate impact that this policy had on Hispanic and black employees, it attempted to justify its position by claiming that the purpose of the new rule was to protect its family members. Several black and Hispanic employees file suit. Who wins and why? (*Bonilla v. Oakland Scavenger Co.,* 697 F.2d 1297 (9th Cir. 1982).)

3. The manager of an apartment complex owned by KMS Investments used a key during his off-duty hours to enter a tenant's apartment and to forcibly rape the tenant at knife point. In the investigation that followed the event, it was discovered that KMS had not checked the manager's references and had not inquired about a lengthy gap in employment. The tenant sued KMS Investments for compensatory damages. Is the employer liable? (*Ponticas v. K.M.S. Investments,* 331 N.W.2d 907 (Minn. 1983).)

4. Clara Watson, a black woman, worked for Fort Worth Bank & Trust as a teller. Four years after working as a teller, she applied for the position of supervisor of the main lobby tellers, but her application was rejected, and a white male was selected for the job. Watson then applied for the position of supervisor of the drive-in section of the bank, and her application was rejected again, in favor of a white woman. Watson filed a discrimination suit based on disparate treatment, but the bank presented legitimate and nondiscriminatory reasons for each of her rejections. However, the bank did not have any objective formal criteria for evaluating any of the positions for which Watson applied; the bank relied mostly on the subjective judgments of the supervisors and on short interviews with these

supervisors. All four of the supervisors involved in Watson's promotion decisions were white. Is the bank's selection process adequate? (*Watson v. Ft. Worth Bank & Trust,* 487 U.S. 977 (1988).)

5. Cone Mills Corporation had several recruiting procedures that gave preferential treatment to applicants who had either family members or friends working for the company. One of these procedures was to give priority to applicants who had family employed by the company; the other procedure was to have an unwritten policy that walk-in applications had to be renewed every two weeks. This created a situation where only those walk-in applicants who had friends or family in the company would renew their applications, because they would be the only ones informed of this unwritten informal rule, which was not present in any manual or policy. These recruiting procedures were charged to be discriminatory toward blacks in general, especially black women, because the informal network responsible for recruiting new employees was unavailable to them. The company claims that its procedures were not designed to be discriminatory; they were merely a method of creating a loyal family atmosphere within the plants. Is the company's argument effective? (*Lea v. Cone Mills Corp.,* 301 F.Supp. 97 (D.N.C. 1969).)

6. The WT Grant Company recruited new "over-the-road" (OTR) drivers predominantly by word-of-mouth solicitation and recommendations by current employees. Barnett, a black man who was rejected for the OTR position, filed suit against the company on the basis that the company's word-of-mouth recruitment was excluding employment opportunities for blacks as evidenced by the all-white OTR

driver workforce. The company claimed that the lack of blacks on the OTR driver workforce was due to the lack of interest on the part of blacks in these positions, not the recruitment methods. There were other divisions in the company that utilized advertising and other recruitment alternatives, and the workforces in these divisions were much more racially mixed. The company claims that each division needs to be treated differently and denies any intention of discrimination. Is the recruitment technique allowed? (*Barnett v. W. T. Grant Co.,* 518 F.2d 543 (4th Cir. 1975).)

7. United Air Lines placed an ad for flight attendants in a New Orleans newspaper. This ad was placed under the heading "Help Wanted—Females Only." There was no additional ad placed under the "Help Wanted—Males Only" column. In the ad, United did verify its status as an equal opportunity employer. After reading this ad, Clarence Hailes, a white male, filed charges against United on the basis that the ad was sexually discriminatory toward the male gender. He claimed that the ad's location, the use of the term *stewardesses,* and the lack of attention paid to the male gender made this ad a discriminatory ad. Hailes had never applied for the steward position at United, and he had never contacted United for any form of employment in the past. United claimed that Hailes cannot be considered an aggrieved party in this case, because he had not been discriminated against in any way. Hailes claimed that he had applied for this position before with another airline and had been rejected because of his sex, and he did not apply to United because he predicted the same outcome. How does the court decide? (*Hailes v. United Air Lines,* 464 F.2d 1006 (5th Cir. 1972).)

8. Brown was interviewed by the personnel department of the North Houston Pole Line Company but, during the interview, the interviewer failed to obtain information about Brown's driving record. Nevertheless, after a 20-minute interview, Brown was hired. One week later, he caused a several-car pileup. One of the victims sued both the pole company for negligent hiring and Brown, who had received five traffic tickets for moving violations in the previous year. Is the employer liable? (*McAllister v. North Houston Pole Line Co.,* 667 S.W.2d 829 (Tex. Ct. App. 1983).)

9. Phillips, an African-American woman, applied for a position as secretary at the Mississippi legislature as a "walk-in" applicant. Phillips worked in the same building, which was made up of approximately 80 percent African-American employees. She stopped by the office one day to ask if the office was hiring clerical help. She was told that the office was and she was given an application to fill out. After not hearing a response from the office regarding the position, she called and learned that a white woman with similar qualifications had filled the position, even though Phillips applied before this woman. The office defended itself, claiming only that it has a practice of not contacting walk-in applicants for positions. Phillips claims that this policy disfavors African-American applicants who work in the building and is, therefore, illegal based on disparate impact. What result?

10. O & G is a wire company that offers line positions in its factory at extremely low pay and in what would be considered by most to be poor working conditions. To obtain new workers, O & G relies exclusively on word of mouth from its predominantly Polish workforce. Parents tell their children, and friends tell friends. Given that the majority of the Polish-born workforce has received technical training in school in Poland, O & G is continually provided with a supply of workers who can graduate to more skilled positions without the need of a formal training program. Keller, an Asian man, files an action against O & G, claiming that its practice of not advertising its open positions and merely relying on word of mouth discriminates against non-Polish workers. Is he correct?

5   AFFIRMATIVE ACTION

Chapter Outline

S C E N A R I O S

S C E N A R I O   1

Employer is concerned that her workplace has only a few blacks, Hispanics, and women in upper-level management and skilled labor jobs. Most unskilled labor and clerical positions are held by women and minorities. Employer decides to institute a program that will increase the numbers of minorities and women in management and skilled labor positions. Is this permissible? Do you have all relevant facts needed to decide?

S C E N A R I O   2

Union has not permitted blacks to become a part of its ranks because of opposition from union members. Black employees sue to join. The court orders appropriate remedies. The union still resists blacks as members. Eventually the court orders that the union admit a certain number of blacks by a certain time or be held in contempt of court. Is this an appropriate or permissible remedy?

S C E N A R I O   3

An employer is found by a court to have discriminated. As part of an appropriate remedy, employer is ordered to promote one female for every male that is promoted, until the desired goal is met. Male employees who were next in line for promotions sue the employer, alleging reverse discrimination in that the new promotees are being hired on the basis of gender, and the suing employees are being harmed because of their gender. Who wins and why?

Statutory Basis

Except in the contracts exempted in accordance with Section 204 of this Order, all Government contracting agencies shall include in every Government contract hereafter entered into the following provisions:

During the performance of this contract, the contractor agrees as follows:

(1) The Contractor will not discriminate against any employee or applicant for employment because of race, color, religion, sex, or national origin. The contractor will take affirmative action to ensure that applicants are employed, and that employees are treated during employment, without regard to their race, color, religion, sex, or national origin. Such action shall include, but not be limited to, the following: employment, upgrading, demotion, or transfer; recruitment or recruitment advertising; layoff or termination; rates of pay or other forms of compensation; and selection for training, including apprenticeship. [202, Executive Order 11246.]

If the court finds that respondent has intentionally engaged in or is intentionally engaging in an unlawful employment practice charged in the complaint, the court may enjoin the respondent from engaging in such unlawful employment practice, and order such affirmative action as may be appropriate, which may include, but is not limited to, reinstatement or hiring of employees . . . or any other equitable relief as the court deems appropriate. [Section 706(g) of Title VII of the Civil Rights Act of 1964, 42 USC 2000e, sec. 706(g).]

Several other pieces of more limited protective employment legislation, such as the Rehabilitation Act and the Vietnam Era Veterans Readjustment Act, also contain affirmative action provisions.

The Design and Unstable History

Important Note.   *Due to the nature of this chapter's topic, we feel compelled to give a cautionary note to readers before they get into the substance of the chapter. After discussing the issue with thousands of students, employers, and employees all over the country over the years, we have learned that affirmative action can be a difficult subject for people to deal with. Parties tend to come to the table with very strong views and misconceptions which can easily manifest themselves in closing our minds to information, being defensive, or perceiving an agenda whether or not one is present. As such, and based on the kind of feedback we have received over the years, we feel it necessary to say from the outset that* **nothing** *in the chapter should be taken as a disparagement of white males or anyone else. Right up front we'll say that our experience is that quite often white males in particular feel that a discussion of affirmative action automatically means painting them as "the bad guy." That is not our intent nor our action.*

In this chapter, while engaging in the necessary look at the history of affirmative action and race in this country in order to put the issue in its proper perspective, it can be easy to become defensive and protective of our positions. That gets us nowhere. In order to accomplish our goal of learning what affirmative action is, how it applies to the workplace, and how to avoid liability on the issue, we must keep in mind that history is a **fact.** *Describing how things were before Title VII, or even how they may still be today in some sectors, is fact,* **not** *a qualitative judgment about those facts.*

As you read the information in this chapter, remember that this dance (of race and its effects) was going on long before most of you got here and you had nothing to do with starting it. The purpose of the chapter is to provide accurate information about affirmative action and what the law requires, not to urge you to have a particular personal opinion about it. After reading the information you can determine for yourself how you feel about the issue. However, your determination will now be based on fact rather than misconceptions. That can only happen if you take the chapter in the spirit in which it is written; to provide information, not to disparage any group whatsoever. Again, we feel compelled to say this up front because our experience tells us that it is a big part of what is there for readers when they begin the chapter. Fortunately, it is rarely there afterwards.

Introduction

Pretend that you are a judge in a gender discrimination case. Evidence is presented by both sides, and the jury determines that the employer has been excluding women from the workplace for years. Those who were hired were not promoted even though they were qualified. As the judge, you must now come up with a remedy for the situation. What would you design to remedy the illegal discrimination? Would you require the employer to give jobs to the excluded women? To promote those who weren't promoted? Give the employer a deadline so that he doesn't drag his feet for the next 20 years? Maybe money damages for the harm they suffered? Make the employer apologize? Those might be helpful. But the main thing that you want to do, and by law are required to do, is to find an appropriate remedy for the situation. Ordering the employer to include those who have been shown to have been excluded is the most logical.

That is what affirmative action is.

Surprised? Bet you are. Affirmative action is probably the single most misunderstood concept in employment law. Most people think it is a law that requires employers to take jobs from qualified white males and give them to minorities and females regardless of their qualifications. Not so. But you wouldn't necessarily know that by listening to legislators or reading the papers—and certainly not from listening to your friends' and families' stories. With all you hear about race-based scholarships, would it surprise you to know that each year twice as many scholarships are given out on the basis of religion as race? That's not nearly as appealing an issue for politicians and media as race, so it is race you hear the most about.

In this chapter we'll clear up the misconceptions. We'll learn what affirmative action is, what it is not, who it affects, and what the law requires. From the outset you should realize that affirmative action does not apply to all employers. For the most part it applies to those with 50 or more employees who have contracts with the federal government to provide the government with goods or services worth $50,000 or more. As a part of that contract the government requires the employer to agree not to discriminate in the workplace and further, to engage in affirmative action if it is found to be needed (discussed later in the chapter). Keep in mind that affirmative action regulations do not apply to everyone, but only to just over 20 percent of the workforce. Despite what you think or may have heard, it is not a law that affects everyone, and it certainly does not require anyone to give up his or her job to someone who is not even qualified to hold it.

Affirmative action
Intentional inclusion of women and minorities in the workplace based on a finding of their previous exclusion.

Noise. There is a lot of it around the concept of **affirmative action.** It can be difficult to turn off the noise and determine what is real and what is not. Did you ever hear someone say, "We *have* to hire a black" or "We *have* to hire a woman"? Such a statement is likely rooted somewhere in the concept of affirmative action. While there may be truth somewhere in the statement, it is probably far from what it appears to be. Many, mistakenly, think affirmative action is a law that takes qualified whites or men out of their jobs and gives the jobs to unqualified minorities or women, or that affirmative action is an entitlement program that provides unqualified women

---

EXHIBIT 5–1   Affirmative Action Myths

Here are some common misconceptions about affirmative action gathered from students, employees, managers, supervisors, and business owners over the years. See if you recognize any of them.

- Affirmative action requires employers to remove qualified whites and males from their jobs and give these jobs to minorities and women whether they are qualified or not.
- Affirmative action prevents employers from hiring white males who are more qualified for the job.
- Under affirmative action, all an employee must be is a female or a minority to be placed in a job.
- Most employees who obtain jobs under affirmative action plans are unqualified for the job.
- Workplace productivity and efficiency always suffer under affirmative action plans.
- There should be no affirmative action because the best person is always the one who gets the job.

or minorities with jobs while qualified whites or males, or both, are shut out of the workplace.

This is not so. It is one thing to say an employer "had to hire a woman." It is quite another to say, "Because the court found that the employer has discriminated against women in its hiring and promotion policies, it is required to remedy the situation by hiring and promoting qualified female applicants." The latter is what affirmative action is designed to do; the former is how many employers interpret it. This is not surprising given the unstable history of the concept.

The misunderstanding, as well as the impact of affirmative action requirements, has been the basis for increasing concern and consternation by employers and employees alike. At its simplest, affirmative action involves the employer bringing qualified women and minorities (or others statutorily mandated) into a workplace from which it has been determined that they are excluded, in order to make the workplace more reflective of the population from which the employees are drawn. This would ordinarily happen on its own in the absence of discrimination or its vestiges. This intentional inclusion must be premised on one of several bases we will discuss—usually as a result of a court finding of discrimination, underrepresentation, or a manifest racial or gender imbalance in the workplace which cannot be accounted for in any other way. Initiating an effort to intentionally include employees previously excluded is quite different from saying that workplace discrimination is prohibited. The former is the active approach required by Executive Order 11246, the latter, Title VII's passive approach.

So-called **reverse discrimination** has often been considered the flip side of affirmative action. When an employer is taking race or gender into account to achieve an affirmative action **goal,** others not in that group allege they are harmed by the employer's consideration of race or gender, or both, in hiring or in promotion decisions. Thus the employer is alleged to have discriminated in the reverse, against the suing employees.

Reverse discrimination
Majority group member alleges adverse affect of affirmative action.

Goal
Appropriate representation of women and minorities in the workplace, based on their availability in the workforce from which they are drawn.

As the years passed after protective employment legislation was enacted—and after employees entering the workplace grew farther and farther away from understanding the circumstances that created the need for the legislation and its remedies (as referenced in the chapters on race discrimination and Title VII)—employees, and many times the employers, understood less and less about the underlying reasons for the need for the remedial action provided by affirmative action. There are several reasons for this.

- The first significant employment affirmative action case was not decided by the US Supreme Court until *Weber* in 1979, 15 years after the Civil Rights Act of 1964 was enacted.
- During the 1980s when many of the initial affirmative action cases were decided by the Supreme Court and much of the public opinion was formed, there was vast difference of opinion in national leadership over the issue of affirmative action. The presidential administrations of the 1980s, which were an important part of setting a tone for national policy and legislation, were hostile to the concept and often blasted Supreme Court decisions and enforcement officials. Even within the administrations there were frequent public disagreements by officials of relevant agencies, such as the Department of Labor, Department of Justice's Civil Rights Division, the EEOC, and the US Office of Civil Rights. (See Exhibit 5–2.) Employers, observing this interaction and being aware of the hostility, indecisiveness, infighting, and ambiguity, were understandably confused. With resistance to the idea from top government officials, business often felt no particular need to embrace the concept.
- In the view of many, the economy worsened and massive layoffs, removal of jobs to non-US markets, the fight for remaining jobs, shrinking union rolls, and resulting workplace uncertainty made employees even more hostile to anything they thought smacked of unfairness, threatened job security, or both.
- The media, in its quest for the convenient "soundbite," rarely took the time to explain to the public significant Supreme Court decisions in ways that helped them understand their reasoning or impact. "The US Supreme Court today determined that employers were required to hire qualified, available blacks after it was found that they were severely underrepresented in the workplace because of years of proven discrimination by the employer," became "Employers are required to hire blacks." Predictably, people were upset.
- Vote-sensitive politicians, in response to their constituents' understandable displeasure (given the above portrayal of the concept) at having affirmative action "invade their workplace and threaten their jobs," denounced Supreme Court decisions that rarely reflected the criticism leveled at them. This further reinforced the negative view of the concept.
- Employers, watching this, and receiving one message from national leadership, another from enforcing agencies and courts, and not sure of what they should do, but wanting to avoid lawsuits, took the "safe" way out and interpreted the message as "we have to hire certain groups." Frequently, without regard to qualifications, but to avoid perceived trouble, they did so. Female and minority employees, many times improperly used by their employers to fill a "minority position" or a "fe-

EXHIBIT 5–2   1980s Media Statements Regarding Affirmative Action

After the seminal US Supreme Court cases on affirmative action in 1978 and 1979, it was in the 1980s that the concept was really shaped and molded by fallout from the Court's decisions. You can see from the statements below how incredibly divisive the issue was, even for the federal administrators and others with responsibility in the area.

3/4/85. "Department of Justice is asking public sector employers to change their negotiated consent decrees [which DOJ had previously pressed for] to eliminate preferential treatment to nonvictims of discrimination." (BNA Daily Labor Report No. 42.)

4/4/85. "[Dept. of] Justice moves to eliminate quotas called 'betrayal' by Birmingham mayor, in testimony before the Subcommittee on Civil and Constitutional Rights of the House Judiciary Committee. Cites 'remarkable progress' made in bringing blacks into the city's fire and police departments." (BNA Daily Labor Report No. 74.)

5/6/85. "Challenges Mount to Department of Justice's Anti-Quota Moves." (BNA Daily Labor Report No. 87.)

9/16/85. "Congress recently ordered an audit of the U.S. Civil Rights Commission and the EEOC, headed by Clarence Pendleton, Jr., and Clarence Thomas, respectively, to find out if financial and personnel troubles are hurting the way both federal panels are enforcing civil rights laws." (*Jet* magazine, p. 16.)

10/17/85. "Attorney General Meese acknowledges that review of Executive Order 11246 is proceeding at Cabinet level, but dismisses charges that Administration officials are at odds over question of affirmative action." (BNA Daily Labor Report No. 201.)

11/29/85. "Majority of Senate is on record as opposing efforts by Attorney General Meese and others in Administration to alter Executive Order 11246 to prohibit goals and timetables for minority hiring." (BNA Daily Labor Report No. 230.)

5/12/86. "Business Applauded for Opposing Changes in Affirmative Action Order." (BNA Daily Labor Report No. 91.)

7/7/86. "Civil Rights Groups Applaud Supreme Court [for *Cleveland Firefighters* and *Sheet Metal Workers* decisions upholding affirmative action]; Department of Justice Vows to Continue Bid to Revise Executive Order 11246." (BNA Daily Labor Report No. 129.)

7/7/86. "Labor Department says 'we don't see anything in these cases to suggest a legal necessity to change either the executive order or the OFCCP program.'" (BNA Daily Labor Report No. 129.)

6/4/87. "OFCCP Enforcement Activity Scored by House Labor Staff: Alleged Lack of OFCCP Enforcement Activity Criticized by House Labor Staff." (BNA Daily Labor Report No. 106.)

6/5/87. "DOL Official Defends OFCCP's Performance Against Charges of Declining Enforcement." (BNA Daily Labor Report No. 107.)

7/2/89. "Civil Rights: Is Era Coming to an End? Decades of Change Called into Question by [Supreme Court] Rulings." (*Atlanta Journal and Constitution,* A–1.)

male position," were the object of resentment aimed at them, rather than at the employer who made the employment decision.

These factors accounted for much of the historical consternation and ill will surrounding affirmative action. For the past few years, affirmative action has been in the forefront of national debate again. This is due in large part to what culminated in the November 1996 passage of California's Proposition 209, the California Civil Rights Initiative. The statewide referendum now bans affirmative action in public hiring, contracting, and education. Other states followed, with Florida being the latest to challenge affirmative action. Presently, the mere mention of the term in many settings is enough to cause heated discussion and debate about its merit, or lack thereof.

Efforts to eliminate affirmative action in employment, government contracts, university admissions, and other areas come primarily from those who feel it has outlived its usefulness and causes only ill will among majority employees. Many think of it as "punishment" to redress slavery and feel they should not have to bear the burden of something for which they had no responsibility. (See Exhibit 5–6.)

As you will see, however, affirmative action is only used when there is a demonstrated underrepresentation or finding of discrimination. It is designed to remedy *present-day* employment inequities based on race or gender. A new seven-volume study released on October 1, 1999, by Harvard University and the Russell Sage Foundation found that racial stereotypes and attitudes "heavily influence the labor market, with blacks landing at the very bottom." The researchers found that "race is deeply entrenched in the country's cultural landscape—perhaps even more than many Americans realize or are willing to admit." The week after Proposition 209 was passed in California, based largely on the idea that affirmative action was no longer necessary to remedy discrimination, news stories broke in the national media alleging that Texaco Oil Company executives disparaged minority workers by using derogatory names for them and joking about their progress in the workplace, at a meeting in which they discussed destroying evidence, purging their files, shredding documents, and concealing evidence in a pending racial discrimination lawsuit by 1,500 black employees. A meeting of the most senior finance department officers was allegedly to discuss "the development of women and minorities within the department" and to "hide" documents from the plaintiffs. Tapes of the meeting, made to help the notetaker keep accurate minutes, were turned over to the plaintiffs in the discrimination suit.

Lawyers for the Texaco employees asked the court to order sanctions against Texaco for the alleged destruction and withholding of documents in the lawsuit, and a grand jury convened to look into the allegations. Less than two weeks after disclosure of the tapes, Texaco agreed to pay $176.1 million to settle the race discrimination lawsuit—the largest ever racial discrimination suit settlement. Attitudes such as those allegedly manifested on the tapes or found by the Harvard study find their way into the workplace and affect minority and female employees working there. That, in turn, leads to the need for assistance such as an affirmative action plan to remedy the situation.

If we could think of one thing that bothers us the most about affirmative action, it is that we view our country as based on fairness and achievement being based on the effort we put forth. Affirmative action seems to fly in the face of this because it appears that women and blacks or other minorities get something without any effort. All they have to do is be born female or black and show up and they get the job. Based on this premise, it makes absolutely perfect sense to greatly resent affirmative action.

However, when we view the premise, as well as the intent of the affirmative ac-

EXHIBIT 5–3   **Affirmative Action Tidbits**

Research has discovered some interesting information about affirmative action. Take a look
and think about whether research indicates that affirmative action has outlived its
usefulness.

- According to the US Census, 23 percent of the workforce is minority, up from 10.7% in
  1964.
- The National Committee for Pay Equity calculates that in 1975 the average black man's
  paycheck was about 74.3 percent of his white counterpart's. By 1997 that ratio was 75.1
  percent. In 1975, the median salary for a Latino man was 72.1 percent of a white man's. By
  1997, it was 61.4 percent. In 1975 the average white woman's salary was 57.5 percent of a
  white man's. By 1997 it was 71.9 percent. Black and Hispanic women's wages improved
  also, but not nearly as much.
- Black men with professional degrees receive 79 percent of the salary paid to white men
  with the same degrees and comparable jobs. Black women earn 60 percent.
- A study conducted by the US Department of Labor found that women and minorities have
  made more progress breaking through the glass ceiling at smaller companies. Women
  comprise 25 percent of the managers and corporate officers in smaller establishments,
  while minorities represent 10 percent. But among *Fortune* 500 companies, women held 18
  percent of the managerial jobs, with minorities holding 7 percent.
- The federal Glass Ceiling Commission found that white women made up close to half
  the workforce, but hold only 5 percent of the senior level jobs in corporations. Blacks
  and other minorities account for less than 3 percent of top jobs (vice president and
  above).
- The Glass Ceiling Commission found that a majority of chief executives acknowledge that
  the federal guidelines have been crucial in maintaining their commitment to a diverse
  workforce. It is estimated that only 30–40 percent of American companies are committed
  to affirmative action programs purely for business reasons, without any federal pressure.
  Most medium-sized and small companies, where job growth is greatest and affirmative
  action gains biggest, have adopted affirmative action only grudgingly, and without
  guidelines, they are most likely to toss it overboard.
- Studies show that there is little correlation between what black and white workers score on
  employment tests and how they perform in the workplace.
- A February 1995 Census Bureau survey of 3,000 businesses asked them to list the things
  they consider most important when hiring workers. The employers ranked test scores as
  eighth on a list of eleven factors. Job testing did not come into wide usage in the United
  States until after the civil rights movement.
- The Glass Ceiling Commission research reported in March 1995 that stereotyping and
  prejudice still rule many executives suites. Women and minorities are frequently routed into
  career paths like customer relations and human resources, which usually do not lead to the
  top jobs.
- Cecelia Conrad, associate professor of economics at Barnard College in New York,
  examined whether affirmative action plans had hurt worker productivity. She found "no
  evidence that there has been any decline in productivity due to affirmative action." She also
  found no evidence of improved productivity due to affirmative action.
- A 1993 study of Standard and Poor's 500 companies found firms that broke barriers for
  women and minorities reported stock market records nearly 2.5 times better than
  comparable companies that took no action.

tion law more closely, we find that we are missing some crucial pieces. First of all, we assume that because we may not see discrimination in our own lives, it does not exist. We assume that everyone is at the same place and will have the same general experience when it comes to applying for a job, being promoted, and so on. However, as much as we might like for them to, statistics don't bear this out. Discrimination still exists. (See Exhibit 5–3.) Affirmative action is meant to address the present-day vestiges of discrimination.

In all of the years we have taught Title VII in predominantly white universities, without a doubt the biggest surprise that white students experience in the class is the shock of discovering that there really is discrimination and that it is as pervasive as it is. One of the things we have found to be most helpful in this area in our own classes is to have students bring in news articles each day on any area of discrimination they wish. Before taking the class they have never given much thought to the idea of discrimination. Many students think that when they hear people complain of discrimination, the complainants are whining and being overly sensitive. After all, the students believe, they live in the same world and never see such things, so they must not exist. But, sharing these articles each day, they come to realize that discrimination does, in fact, exist, and on a much greater scale than they have ever imagined. Learning about the history of discrimination in this country, and seeing the present-day impact, makes students realize that there really is a need for legislation after all. Things which they were not aware of were going on long before today and they greatly impact the world in which the students live. This gives them a very different view of the situation. In fact, most students come into class thinking affirmative action is awful and should be done away with, but after learning the reality, they leave angry that it doesn't do more to address the problem!

Research indicates that while the main target of affirmative action foes is race, white females have been the largest group benefitted, making gender rather than race the basis for most gains. Actually, when the anti–affirmative action arguments are analyzed, it is apparent that the real problem lies not in the concept itself, but its misuse.

Throughout the chapter, keep this thought in mind: If Alaska is 99 percent Inuit (Eskimo), then, all things being equal, that will be reflected at all or most levels of their employment spectrum. All things being equal, it would look odd if Alaska is 99 percent Inuit and there are only 5 percent Inuits holding managerial level jobs but 100 percent of the unskilled labor jobs. Of course, the reality is that it is rare to have a workforce that has so little diversity. Among other things, there will also be differing skill levels and interests within the workforce from which the employees are drawn. However, the example is instructive for purposes of illustrating how a workplace should reflect the available workforce from which its employees are drawn. If there is a significant difference, which cannot be accounted for otherwise, the difference between availability and representation in the workplace should be addressed. In essence, this is affirmative action.

Affirmative action also arises in other contexts such as college admissions, the granting of government contracts, and set-asides. However, these are beyond the scope of this text, which only addresses the employment setting.

Executive Order 11246

Though Title VII has an affirmative action component as part of its statutory remedies, affirmative action actually stems from a requirement imposed by Executive Order 11246 and its amendments. Under the executive order, those employers who contract to furnish the federal government with goods and services (called federal contractors) must agree not to discriminate in the hiring, termination, promotion, pay, and so on of employees on the basis of race, color, religion, gender, or national origin.

The first forerunner to E.O. 11246 was Executive Order 8802, signed by President Franklin D. Roosevelt on June 25, 1941. It applied only to defense contracts and was issued to combat discrimination during World War II "as a prerequisite to the successful conduct of our national defense production effort." This executive order underwent several changes before the present version was signed into law by President Lyndon B. Johnson on September 24, 1965.

In addition to prohibiting discrimination in employment, the executive order requires that employers agree to take steps to ensure adequate representation of women and minorities in their workplace. In cases where the employer refuses to remedy disparities found, he or she is **debarred** from further participation in government contracts. This is a rare occurrence, since most employers eventually comply with OFCCP's suggestions for remedying disparities.

Debar
Prohibit a federal contractor from further participation in government contracts.

The executive order is enforced by the Office of Federal Contract Compliance Programs (OFCCP) in the US Department of Labor, which issues extensive regulations implementing the executive order (41 CFR Chapter 60). OFCCP's enforcement addresses only the employer's participation in federal government contracts and contains no provisions for private lawsuits by employees. Employees seeking redress must do so through their state's fair employment practice laws, Title VII, or similar legislation discussed in Chapter 3. However, employees may file complaints with OFCCP, which the secretary is authorized to receive and investigate, and may sue the Secretary of Labor to compel performance of executive order requirements.

Title VII prohibits discrimination in employment, but it does not impose affirmative duties on the employer. However, as a part of the remedies provided under Title VII, courts may order affirmative action.

Employers who contract with the federal government to provide goods and services of $10,000 or more must agree to comply with the executive order. In addition, contractors and subcontractors agree to:

• Post in conspicuous places, available to employees and applicants, notices provided by the contracting officer setting forth the provisions of the nondiscrimination clause.

• Include in all the contractor's solicitations or advertisements for employees a statement that all qualified applicants will receive consideration for employment without regard to race, color, religion, gender, or national origin.

• Include a statement of these obligations in all subcontracts or purchase orders, unless exempted, which will be binding on each subcontractor or vendor.

• Furnish all information and reports required by the executive order and the implementing regulations, and permit access to the contractor's or subcontractor's books, records, and accounts by the contracting agency and the Secretary of Labor for purposes of investigation to ascertain compliance with the executive order and its regulations.

Affirmative action plan
A contractor's plan containing goals for inclusion of women and minorities in the workplace and timetables for accomplishing the goals.

Workforce analysis
Appraisal of the workplace for representation of women and minorities in all types and levels of employment.

Under-representation or **underutilization**
Significantly fewer minorities or women in the workplace than relevant statistics indicate are available.

Timetables
Time limit attached to affirmative action goals.

Under the implementing regulations, Executive Order 11246 increases compliance requirements based on the amount of the contract. For the smallest contracts the employer agrees that, in addition to not discriminating in employment, it will post notices that it is an equal opportunity employer. If a contractor or subcontractor has 50 or more employees and a nonconstruction contract of $50,000 or more, the contractor must develop a written **affirmative action plan** for each of his or her establishments within 120 days of the beginning of the contract.

Large contractors must also perform a **workforce analysis.** In this analysis the employer–contractor must indicate how many women and minorities are in each of several employment categories, ranging from unskilled workers to managerial employees. The employer must also compare the percentage of women and minority employees in these positions with the percentage of such employees available in the workforce from which the employer's workforce is drawn.

Underrepresentation or **underutilization** is defined in the OFCCP regulations as "having fewer minorities or women in a particular job group than would reasonably be expected by their availability." (See Exhibit 5–4.) If the assessment indicates that the employer has an underrepresentation in a given category—for instance, too few women in upper-level management—then the employer must set forth a plan of corrective action, which includes goals as to how many employees are needed to correct the underrepresentation, and **timetables** for accomplishing the goals. This plan of corrective action is called an "affirmative action plan" because it represents a plan of action the employer will affirmatively pursue to address deficiencies found to exist in the workplace. Employers submit annual reports to the OFCCP giving the results of their affirmative action programs.

The concept of "availability" is not based on the mere presence of women and minorities in a given geographic area. Rather, it is based on the availability of women and minorities qualified for the particular job. Simply because women are 35 percent of the general population does not mean that they are all qualified to be doctors, professors, skilled craft workers, or managers. Availability for jobs as managers would only consider those qualified to fill the positions.

EXHIBIT 5–4   Determining Underutilization for Affirmative Action Purposes

Under federal regulations, in making the utilization analysis of jobs at the employer's facility and determining whether minorities and females are being underutilized in any job group, the contractor will consider at least all of the following factors (separately for minorities and women):

Minorities:

  (i) The minority population of the labor area surrounding the facility;
  (ii) The size of the minority unemployment force in the labor area surrounding the facility;
  (iii) The percentage of the minority workforce as compared with the total workforce in the immediate labor area;
  (iv) The general availability of minorities having requisite skills in the immediate labor area;
  (v) The availability of minorities having requisite skills in an area in which the contractor can reasonably recruit;
  (vi) The availability of promotable and transferable minorities within the contractor's organization;
  (vii) The existence of training institutions capable of training persons in the requisite skills; and
  (viii) The degree of training which the contractor is reasonably able to undertake as a means of making all job classes available to minorities.

In determining whether women are being underutilized in any job group, the contractor will consider at least all of the following factors:

  (i) The size of the female unemployment force in the labor area surrounding the facility;
  (ii) The percentage of the female workforce as compared with the total workforce in the immediate labor area;
  (iii) The general availability of women having requisite skills in the immediate labor area;
  (iv) The availability of women having requisite skills in an area in which the contractor can reasonably recruit;
  (v) The availability of women seeking employment in the labor or recruitment area of the contractor;
  (vi) The existence of training institutions capable of training persons in the requisite skills; and
  (vii) The degree of training which the contractor is reasonably able to undertake as a means of making all job classes available to women.

CFR 60-2.11 Required utilization analysis; 43 FR 49249, Oct. 20, 1978; 43 FR 51400, Nov. 3, 1978.

Penalties for Noncompliance

The Secretary of Labor or the appropriate contracting agency can impose on the employer a number of penalties for noncompliance, including:

• Publishing the names of nonconforming contractors or labor unions.

• Recommending to the EEOC or the Department of Justice that proceedings be instituted under Title VII.

• Requesting that the Attorney General bring suit to enforce the executive order in cases of actual or threatened substantial violations of the contractual EEO clause.

• Recommending to the Department of Justice that criminal proceedings be initiated for furnishing false information to a contracting agency or the Secretary of Labor.

• Canceling, terminating, or suspending the contract, or any portion thereof, for failure of the contractor or subcontractor to comply with the nondiscrimination provisions of the contract (this may be done absolutely, or continuance may be conditioned on a program for future compliance approved by the contracting agency).

• Debarring the noncomplying contractor from entering into further government contracts until the contractor has satisfied the secretary that it will abide by the provisions of the order.

The Secretary of Labor must make reasonable efforts to secure compliance by conference, conciliation, mediation, and persuasion before requesting the US Attorney General to act or before canceling or surrendering a contract. While a hearing is required before the secretary can debar a contractor, it may be granted before any other sanction is imposed, if appropriate. As a practical matter, the more severe penalties are rarely used, because contractors are generally not so recalcitrant toward OFCCP orders. An employer would do well to conduct a voluntary **equal employment opportunity (EEO) audit** from time to time, to monitor the workplace and discover potential problems before they worsen. The longer the problem exists, the more likely it is to be viewed as intentional illegal action by the employer.

Equal employment opportunity (EEO) audit
Periodic check for inclusion of women and minorities in the workplace.

Judicial Affirmative Action Plan Requirements

Courts have played an important role in shaping the concept of affirmative action. The initial cases, *Bakke* and *Weber,* provided important information on how the courts view affirmative action plans when they come into question because someone who feels harmed by them sues alleging "reverse discrimination." While there are no specific requirements as to what form an affirmative action plan must take (see Exhibit 5–5), if the plan is in keeping with the requirements set forth below, the employer has little to fear from such suits—although the monetary and energy costs in dealing with them are great.

The first affirmative action case to reach the court, *Bakke,* involved affirmative action in medical school admissions, rather than employment; however, the case is viewed as the one that opened the affirmative action debate, and much of its reasoning was used in subsequent cases. In reading the cases, pay particular attention to the underlying bases the Court uses to find affirmative action acceptable or unacceptable, recognizing that, in effect, it is permitting judicially endorsed discrimination.

REGENTS OF THE UNIVERSITY OF CALIFORNIA V. BAKKE
438 U.S. 265 (1978)

A white male applying to medical school was rejected for admission and sued after discovering other, less-qualified students were admitted under a special admissions program. The Supreme Court struck down the program but did not outlaw such plans in general and said that race is a factor that can be considered in such programs.

Powell, J.

After having no blacks, Mexican-Americans, Native Americans, only three Asians, and no disadvantaged students in its first class when it opened in 1968, the faculty of the medical school of the University of California at Davis (Davis) devised a special admissions program to increase the representation of "disadvantaged students." Davis then had two admissions programs for the entering class of 100 students at the times relevant here—the regular admissions program and the special admissions program.

Bakke applied to Davis in 1973 and 1974 and was considered under the general admissions program. He was rejected both times. In both years, special admit applicants were admitted with lower scores than those of Bakke. After his second rejection, Bakke filed this action, alleging, among other things, a violation of Title VI of the Civil Rights Act of 1964 [among other things, prohibiting discrimination on the basis of race or color in programs receiving federal assistance], and the Equal Protection Clause of the Fourteenth Amendment to the US Constitution.

Davis views its program as establishing a "goal" of minority representation in the medical school. Bakke, echoing the courts below, labels it a racial quota. This semantic distinction is beside the point: The special admissions program is undeniably a classification based on race and ethnic background. To the extent that there existed a pool of at least minimally qualified minority applicants to fill the 16 special admissions seats, white applicants could compete only for 84 seats in the entering class, rather than the 100 open to minority applicants. Whether this limitation is described as a quota or a goal, it is a line drawn on the basis of race and ethnic status.

The guarantees of the Fourteenth Amendment extend to all persons. Its language is explicit: "No State shall . . . deny to any person within its jurisdiction the equal protection of the laws." The guarantee of equal protection cannot mean one thing when applied to one individual and something else when applied to a person of another color. If both are not accorded the same protection, then it is not equal.

Davis urges us to adopt for the first time a more restrictive view of the Equal Protection Clause and hold that discrimination against members of the white "majority" cannot be suspect if its purpose can be characterized as "benign." If Davis's purpose is to assure within its student body some specified percentage of a particular group merely because of its race or ethnic origin, such a preferential purpose must be rejected—not as insubstantial, but as facially invalid. Preferring members of any one group for no reason other than race or ethnic origin is discrimination for its own sake. This the Constitution forbids. The State certainly has a legitimate and substantial interest in ameliorating, or eliminating where feasible, the disabling effects of identified discrimination.

We have never approved a classification that aids persons perceived as members of relatively victimized groups at the expense of other innocent individuals in the absence of judicial, legislative, or administrative findings of constitutional or statutory violations. After such findings have been made, the governmental interest in preferring members of the injured groups at the expense of others is substantial, since the legal rights of the victims must be vindicated. In such a case, the extent of the injury and the consequent remedy will have been judicially, legislatively, or administratively defined. Also, the remedial action usually remains subject to continuing oversight to assure that it will work the least harm possible to other innocent persons competing for the benefit. Without such findings of constitutional or statutory violations, the government has no compelling justification for inflicting such harm.

Davis Medical School does not purport to have made, and is in no position to make, such findings. Its broad mission is education, not the formulation of any legislative policy or the adjudication of particular claims of illegality. Hence, the purpose of helping certain groups whom the faculty of the Davis Medical School perceived as victims of "societal discrimination" does not justify a classification that imposes disadvantages upon persons like Bakke, who bear no responsibility for whatever harm the beneficiaries of the special admissions program are thought to have suffered.

Davis also has as a goal of its special admissions program the attainment of a diverse student body. This clearly is a constitutionally permissible goal for an institution of higher education. The atmosphere of "speculation, experiment, and creation"—so essential to the quality of higher education—is widely believed to be promoted by a diverse student body. It is not too much to say that the "nation's future depends upon leaders trained through wide exposure" to the ideas and mores of students as diverse as this Nation of many peoples. The contribution of diversity is substantial.

Physicians serve a heterogeneous population. An otherwise qualified medical student with a particular background—whether it be ethnic, geographic, culturally advantaged or disadvantaged—may bring to a professional school of medicine, experiences, outlooks, and ideas that enrich the training of its student body and better equip its graduates to render with understanding their vital service to humanity.

Ethnic diversity, however, is only one element in a range of factors a university properly may consider in attaining the goal of a heterogeneous student body. Although a university must have wide discretion in making the sensitive judgments as to who should be admitted, constitutional limitations protecting individual rights may not be disregarded.

Davis's argument that reserving a specified number of seats in each class for minorities is the only effective means of attaining diversity in the student body is seriously flawed. The diversity that furthers a compelling state interest encompasses a far broader array of qualifications and characteristics of which racial or ethnic origin is but a single though important element. Davis's special admissions program, focused *solely* on ethnic diversity, would hinder rather than further attainment of genuine diversity.

The experience of other university admissions programs, which take race into account in achieving the educational diversity valued by the First Amendment, demonstrates that the assignment of a fixed number of places to a minority group is not a necessary means toward that end. An illuminating example is found in the Harvard College program which uses race as only one factor among others such as economics, ethnicity, and geography, used to diversify its student body. Ethnicity or race may tip the scales for a student deemed capable of performing the work, just as race or life spent on a farm may, and there is no specified number Harvard shoots for in any given year.

In such an admission program, race or ethnic background may be deemed a "plus" in a particular applicant's file, yet it does not insulate the individual from comparison with all other candidates for the available seats. An admissions program operated in this way is flexible enough to consider all pertinent elements of diversity in light of the particular qualifications of each applicant and to place them on the same footing for consideration, although not necessarily according them the same weight.

This kind of program treats each applicant as an individual in the admissions process. His qualifications would have been weighed fairly and competitively, and he would have no basis to complain of unequal treatment under the Fourteenth Amendment.

In summary, it is evident that the Davis special admissions program involves the use of an explicit racial classification never before countenanced by this Court. It tells applicants who are not Negro, Asian or Chicano that they are totally excluded from a specific percentage of the seats in an entering class. No matter how strong their qualifications, qualitative and extracurricular, including their own potential for contribution to educational diversity, they are never afforded the chance to compete with applicants from the preferred groups for the special admissions seats. At the same time, the preferred applicants have the opportunity to compete for every seat in the class.

The fatal flaw in Davis' preferential program is its disregard of individual rights as guaranteed by the Fourteenth Amendment. Such rights are not absolute. But when a State's distribution of benefits or imposition of burdens hinges on an-

cestry or the color of a person's skin, that individual is entitled to a demonstration that the challenged classification is necessary to promote a substantial state interest. Davis has failed to carry this burden. For this reason that portion of the lower court's judgment holding Davis' special admission program invalid under the Fourteenth Amendment is AFFIRMED.

Case Questions

1. The court said that a classification that imposes disadvantages on people like Bakke who bear no responsibility for whatever harm beneficiaries of special admit programs suffered is not justifiable. If people like Bakke benefit from the harm done, but had no role in doing the harm, what can be done to either keep him from benefitting or keep those harmed from not being further harmed by the benefit?

2. Do you agree with the Court that it is an important factor for a school to have diversity among its student body to enhance the educational experience of all? Why or why not?

3. If you were an employer and felt, as the university here did, that diversity was important, what would you do to increase it in your workplace?

When dealing with the issue of affirmative action and job requirements, keep in mind that there was little use of testing and scores before Title VII came along. Why do you think they became so widely used after Title VII?

Even though *Bakke* involved a medical school's admission policy, the analysis is similar for affirmative action plans in employment. The *Bakke* case is a seminal case in affirmative action because the court did not dismiss the concept of voluntary affirmative active plans, but instead held that race or ethnicity could be used by the state as a basis for different treatment where there was a compelling state interest furthered by doing so, such as remedying past discrimination. It also indicated the requirements that such public sector plans must meet to be acceptable.

The next big questions after *Bakke* were whether a similar analysis applied (1) if the affirmative action plan involved private, rather than state, action and (2) if the plan involved a workplace, rather than an admissions, program. The opportunity to have those questions answered came the next year in *Weber.*

United Steelworkers of America, AFL-CIO v. Weber
443 U.S. 193 (1979)

A white employee sued under Title VII alleging race discrimination, in that the union and employer adopted a voluntary affirmative action plan reserving for black employees 50 percent of the openings in a training program until the percentage of black craft workers in the plant approximated the percentage of blacks in the local labor force. The Supreme Court held that the program was permissible, in that Title VII did not prohibit voluntary race-conscious affirmative action plans undertaken to eliminate a manifest racial imbalance, the measure is only temporary, and it did not unnecessarily trample the rights of white employees.

Brennan, J.

In 1974, the union and Kaiser entered into a master collective bargaining agreement covering terms and conditions of employment at 15 Kaiser plants. The agreement included an affirmative action plan designed to eliminate conspicuous racial imbalances in Kaiser's craftwork force, which was almost exclusively white. The plan was to eliminate this racial imbalance by reserving for black employees 50% of the openings in in-plant craft-training programs until the percentage of black craftworkers in a plant is commensurate with the percentage of blacks in the local labor force.

This litigation arose from the operation of the affirmative action plan at Kaiser's Gramercy plant where, prior to 1974, only 1.83% of the skilled craftworkers were black, even though the local workforce was approximately 39% black. Pursuant to the national agreement, rather than continue its practice of hiring trained outsiders, Kaiser established a training program to train its production workers to fill craft openings. Pursuant to the master collective bargaining agreement, trainees were selected on the basis of seniority,

with the proviso that at least 50% of the trainees were to be black until the percentage of black skilled craftworkers in the Gramercy plant approximated the percentage of blacks in the local labor force. During the first year of the plan, 7 black and 6 white craft trainees were selected, with the most senior black trainee having less seniority than several white production workers whose bids for admission to the program were rejected. Weber was one of those workers.

After being turned down for the training program when blacks with less seniority were admitted, Weber sued, alleging that, because the affirmative action program had resulted in junior black employees receiving training in preference to more senior white employees, Weber, and others similarly situated, had been discriminated against in violation of sections 703(a) and (d) of Title VII of the Civil Rights Act of 1964 which made it unlawful to discriminate on the basis of race in the hiring and selection of apprentices for training programs.

The question is whether Congress, in Title VII, left employers and unions in the private sector free to take such race-conscious steps to eliminate manifest racial imbalances in traditionally segregated job categories. We hold that Title VII does not prohibit such race-conscious affirmative action plans.

Weber argues that since *McDonald* [see Chapter 6] settled that Title VII forbids discrimination against whites as well as blacks, and since the affirmative action plan here discriminates against whites solely because they are white, the plan therefore violates Title VII.

Weber's argument is not without force. But it overlooks the significance of the fact that the plan is an affirmative action plan voluntarily adopted by private parties to eliminate traditional patterns of racial segregation. In this context, Weber's reliance upon a literal construction of sections 703(a) and (d) and *McDonald* is misplaced. It is a familiar rule that a thing may be within the letter of the statute and yet not within the statute, because not within its spirit nor within the intention of its makers. The prohibition against racial discrimination in sections 703(a) and (d) of Title VII must therefore be read against the background of the legislative history of Title VII and the historical context from which the Act arose. Examination of those sources makes clear that an interpretation of the sections that forbade all race-conscious affirmative action would "bring about an end completely at variance with the purpose of the statute" and must be rejected.

Congress's primary concern in enacting the prohibition against racial discrimination in Title VII of the Civil Rights Act of 1964 was with "the plight of the Negro in our economy." Before 1964 blacks were largely relegated to "unskilled and semi-skilled jobs." Because of automation the number of such jobs was rapidly decreasing. As a consequence, "the relative position of the Negro worker [was] steadily worsening. In 1947 the non-white employment rate was only 64% higher than the white race; in 1962 it was 124%." Congress considered this a serious social problem and feared that the goal of the Civil Rights Act—the integration of blacks into the mainstream of society—could not be achieved unless the trend were

reversed. It further recognized that this would not be possible unless blacks were able to secure jobs "which have a future."

Accordingly, it was clear to Congress that "[t]he crux of the problem [was] to open employment opportunities for Negroes in occupations which have been traditionally closed to them", and it was to this problem that Title VII's prohibition against racial discrimination in employment was primarily addressed.

It plainly appears from the House Report accompanying the Civil Rights Act that Congress did not intend wholly to prohibit private and voluntary affirmative action efforts as one method of solving this problem. The Report provides: "No bill can or should lay claim to eliminating all of the causes and consequences of racial and other types of discrimination against minorities. There is reason to believe, however, that national leadership provided by the enactment of Federal legislation dealing with the most troublesome problems *will create an atmosphere conducive to voluntary or local resolution of other forms of discrimination.*" H.R. Rep. No. 914, 88th Cong., 1st Sess., pt. 1, p. 18 (1963); U.S. Code Cong. & Admin. News 1964, pp. 2355, 2393. (Emphasis supplied.)

Given this legislative history, we cannot agree with Weber that Congress intended to prohibit the private sector from taking effective steps to accomplish the goal that Congress designed Title VII to achieve. The very statutory words intended as a spur or catalyst to cause "employers and unions to self-examine and to self-evaluate their employment practices and to endeavor to eliminate, so far as possible, the last vestiges of an unfortunate and ignominious page in this country's history," cannot be interpreted as an absolute prohibition against all private, voluntary, race conscious affirmative action efforts to hasten the elimination of such vestiges. It would be ironic if a law triggered by a Nation's concern over centuries of racial injustice and intended to improve the lot of those who had "been excluded from the American dream for so long," constituted the first legislative prohibition of all voluntary, private, race-conscious efforts to abolish traditional patterns of racial segregation and hierarchy.

The purposes of the plan mirror those of the statute. Both were designed to break down old patterns of racial segregation and hierarchy. Both were structured to "open employment opportunities for Negroes in occupations which have been traditionally closed to them."

At the same time, the plan does not unnecessarily trammel the interests of the white employees. The plan does not require the discharge of white workers and their replacement with new black hirees. Nor does the plan create an absolute bar to the advancement of white employees; half of those trained in the program will be white. Moreover, the plan is a temporary measure; it is not intended to maintain racial balance, but simply to eliminate a manifest racial imbalance. Preferential selection of craft trainees at the Gramercy plant will end as soon as the percentage of black skilled craftworkers in the Gramercy plant approximates the percentage of blacks in the local labor force.

We conclude, therefore, that the adoption of the Kaiser–USWA plan for the Gramercy plant falls within the area of discretion left by Title VII to the private sector voluntarily to adopt affirmative action plans designed to eliminate conspicuous racial imbalance in traditionally segregated job categories. Accordingly, the judgment of the Fifth Circuit is REVERSED.

Case Questions

1. Does this decision make sense to you? Why? Why not?

2. If, because of discrimination, blacks were not in a workplace for as long as whites and, therefore, did not have as much seniority as whites, does it seem reasonable to allow blacks with less seniority than whites to join the training program? If not, can you think of an alternative?

3. As a manager in a firm that is thinking of instituting a voluntary affirmative action plan, what factors would you consider?

Many employers were surprised by *Weber,* since the year before the Court struck down a voluntary affirmative action plan in *Bakke.* In viewing the language for yourselves, you should be able to see the differences in the cases. While both concerned affirmative action plans, there were considerable differences, beyond even public versus private employers. Some of these differences and the Court's reasoning got lost in news coverage. The reason the Court's language is included here is for you to analyze for yourself the considerations the Court used in reaching its decisions. Both decisions endorsed the concept of affirmative action, but the requirements were not met in *Bakke* and were in *Weber,* thus giving different, though not inconsistent, outcomes. *Weber* is the basis for opening scenarios one and three.

After reading *Weber,* you now realize that in opening scenario one, it is permissible for an employer to have a voluntary affirmative action plan, but certain factors must be present in order to justify the plan to a court. In opening scenario one, we do not have all the relevant facts to determine if the employer can take the affirmative action measures the employer wishes. For instance, we do not know why there are such small numbers of minorities and women in upper-level management and skilled labor jobs. We do not know if it is because there is a history of discrimination and exclusion, or that there simply are not sufficient numbers of women and minorities available in the workforce.

1
Scenario

In opening scenario three, we know from *Weber* that an employer can have a one-for-one affirmative action promotion plan as part of a judicial remedy for past discrimination, and if the *Weber* requirements are met, the employer is protected from liability for discrimination against employees alleging they are adversely impacted by implementation of the plan.

Seven years later, in the case of *Wygant v. Jackson Board of Education,*[1] and consistent with language in *Bakke* and *Weber,* the Supreme Court upheld the concept of affirmative action (in *Wygant,* preferential protection against layoffs) for public employees, though it held that the requirements of demonstrating a compelling state interest and narrowly tailoring the plan to meet the objective had not been met in this particular case. This answered the question of whether the Court's analysis in *Bakke,* involving a preferential admissions policy for a public university, also applied to an affirmative action plan in a public workplace. It did. It also answered the question left after *Weber* as to whether the acceptance of voluntary affirmative action in private employment also applied to public employment. It did.

Johnson v. Transportation Agency, Santa Clara County, California,[2] a 1987 Supreme Court decision which relied heavily on *Weber,* determined that, under circumstances similar to those in *Weber,* but involving a public employer, rather than private, and gender, rather than race, the employer could appropriately take gender into account under its voluntary affirmative action plan as one factor of a promotion decision. The Court said the plan, voluntarily adopted to redress a "conspicuous imbalance in traditionally segregated job categories" represented a "moderate, flexible, case-by-case approach to effecting a gradual improvement in the representation of minorities and women." The plan was acceptable, because:

1. It did not unnecessarily trammel male employees' rights or create an absolute bar to their advancement.
2. It set aside no positions for women (as did *Bakke*) and expressly stated that its goals should not be construed as quotas to be met.
3. It unsettled no legitimate, firmly rooted expectation of employees.
4. It was only temporary in that it was for purposes of attaining, not maintaining a balanced workforce.
5. There was minimal intrusion into the legitimate, settled expectations of other employees.

Who Can Receive Benefits under Affirmative Action Plans?

The question often arises as to who can receive the benefit of affirmative action plans. Can the plan benefit individuals who were not the actual victims of the employer's discriminatory practices? In the following *Sheet Metal Workers* case, the

[1]476 U.S. 267 (1986).
[2]480 U.S. 616.

EXHIBIT 5–5   Affirmative Actions

While there are guidelines as to what may or may not be legally acceptable as affirmative action designed to intentionally include women and minorities in the workplace, there are no specific requirements about what affirmative action must be taken. As a result, employers' means of addressing affirmative action have varied greatly. Keep in mind the Supreme Court's characterization of plans that are acceptable when viewing the following ideas employers have used. Just because employers have used these methods does not mean they are always legal. Sometimes they may simply be convenient.

- *Advertising for applicants in nontraditional sources.*   Employers solicit minority and female applicants through resources such as historically black colleges and universities, women's colleges, minority and female civic, educational, religious, and social organizations, including the NAACP, National Urban League, La Raza, American Indian Movement, National Organization for Women, and other such groups.

- *One-for-one hiring, training, or promotion programs.*   One minority or female is hired, trained, or promoted for every white or male until a certain desired goal is reached. This is usually only used in long-standing, resistant cases of underrepresentation.

- *Preferential layoff provisions.*   As in *Wygant,* in recognition of the reality that many female and minority employees would be lost if layoffs are conducted based on seniority and, thereby, affirmative action gains lost, employers institute plans that are designed to prevent the percentage of minorities and women from falling below a certain point. Some minorities and women with less seniority may be retained, while those with more are laid off.

- *Extra consideration.*   Women and minorities are considered along with all other candidates, but extra consideration is paid to their status as women and minorities, and, all other factors being equal, they may be chosen for the job.

- *Lower standards.*   Women and minorities may be taken out of the regular pool of candidates and given different, usually less stringent, standards for qualifying for the position. Natural questions are why the higher standards are imposed if the job can be performed with lesser qualifications and why should someone who is not qualified under the higher, "normal" standards be given the job? This is *not* a good approach.

- *Added points.*   Much like with a veteran's preference, the employer has a rating system giving points for various criteria, and women and minorities receive extra points because they are women or minorities.

- *Minority or female "positions."*   In an effort to meet affirmative action goals, employers create and fund positions that are designed to be filled only by women or minorities. These positions may or may not be needed by the employer.

Some of the approaches are more desirable than others, because they are less likely to result in "reverse discrimination" suits or more likely to result in qualified minority or female employees. Affirmative action plans walk a fine line between not holding women and minorities to lower standards than other employees, while, at the same time, not permitting the standards to be arbitrary and likely to unnecessarily or unwittingly screen out female or minority candidates. The 1991 Civil Rights Act made it unlawful to "adjust the scores of, use different cutoff scores for, or otherwise alter the results of, employment related tests" on the basis of race, color, religion, gender, or national origin. Since there are few rules, employers can be creative, within the guidelines provided by law. Now that you have seen some of the affirmative action schemes employers have used, which seem most suited to accomplish the goals of affirmative action, while having the least adverse impact on other employees?

Supreme Court held that there need not be a showing of discrimination against the particular individual (employee, applicant, promotion candidate, and the like) as long as the affirmative action plan meets appropriate requirements set forth in Exhibit 5–5, and the individual fits into the category of employees the plan was designed to benefit. This approach recognizes that the employer's policy may result in discouraging certain people from ever even applying for a job because they know it would be futile.

While the notion of providing relief for nonspecific victims of discrimination may appear somewhat questionable, the case below is the type of situation that justifies such action. As you read the case, think of how you would have handled the situation if you were the employer. Also think of whether you would have allowed the situation to go on for so long if you were the court. This case is the basis for opening scenario two.

2
Scenario

LOCAL 28, SHEET METAL WORKERS V. E.E.O.C.
478 U.S. 421 (1986)

The union and its apprenticeship committee were found guilty of discrimination against Hispanics and blacks and were ordered to remedy the violations. They were found numerous times to be in contempt of the court's order and after 18 years the court eventually imposed fines and an affirmative action plan as a remedy. The plan included benefits to persons not members of the union. The Supreme Court held the remedies to be appropriate under the circumstances.

Brennan, J.

Local 28 represents sheet metal workers employed by contractors in the New York City metropolitan area. The Local 28 Joint Apprenticeship Committee (JAC) is a labor–management committee which operates a 4-year apprenticeship training program designed to teach sheet metal skills. Apprentices enrolled in the program receive training both from classes and from on the job work experience. Upon completing the program, apprentices become journeyman members of Local 28. Successful completion of the program is the principal means of attaining union membership.

In 1964, the New York State Commission for Human Rights determined that the union and JAC had excluded blacks from the union and apprenticeship program in violation of state law. The

Commission, among other things, found that the union had never had any black members or apprentices, and that "admission to apprenticeship is conducted largely on a nepot[is]tic basis involving sponsorship by incumbent union members," creating an impenetrable barrier for nonwhite applicants. The union and JAC were ordered to "cease and desist" their racially discriminatory practices. Over the next 18 years and innumerable trips to court, the union did not remedy the discrimination.

To remedy the contempt and the union's refusal to comply with court orders, the court imposed a 29% nonwhite membership goal to be met by a certain date, and a $150,000 fine to be placed in a fund designed to increase non-white membership in the apprenticeship program and the union. The fund was used for a variety of purposes, including:

- Providing counseling and tutorial services to non-white apprentices, giving them benefits that had traditionally been available to white apprentices from family and friends.
- Providing financial support to employers otherwise unable to hire a sufficient number of apprentices.
- Providing matching funds to attract additional funding for job-training programs.
- Creating part-time and summer sheet metal jobs for qualified non-white youths.
- Extending financial assistance to needy apprentices.
- Paying for non-white union members to serve as liaisons to vocational and technical schools with sheet metal programs in order to increase the pool of qualified non-white applicants for the apprenticeship program.

The union appealed the remedy. Principally, the parties maintain that the Fund and goal exceeds the scope of remedies available under Title VII because it extends race-conscious preferences to individuals who are not the identified victims of their unlawful discrimination. They argue that section 706(g) authorizes a district court to award preferential relief only to actual victims of unlawful discrimination. They maintain that the goal and Fund violates this provision since it requires them to extend benefits to black and Hispanic individuals who are not the identified victims of unlawful discrimination. We reject this argument and hold that section 706(g) does not prohibit a court from ordering, in appropriate circumstances, affirmative race-conscious relief as a remedy for past discrimination. Specifically, we hold that such relief may be appropriate where an employer or a labor union has engaged in persistent or egregious discrimination, or where necessary to dissipate the lingering effects of pervasive discrimination.

The availability of race-conscious affirmative relief under section 706(g) as a remedy for a violation of Title VII furthers the broad purposes underlying the statute. Congress enacted Title VII based on its determination that racial minorities were subject to pervasive and systematic discrimination in employment. It was clear to Congress that the crux of the problem was "to open employment opportunities for Negroes in occupations which have been traditionally closed to them and it was to this problem that Title VII's prohibition against racial discrimination was primarily addressed." Title VII was designed to achieve equality of employment opportunities and remove barriers that have operated in the past to favor an identifiable group of white employees over other employees. In order to foster equal employment opportunities, Congress gave the lower courts broad power under section 706(g) to fashion the most complete relief possible to remedy past discrimination.

In most cases, the court need only order the employer or union to cease engaging in discriminatory practices, and award make-whole relief to the individuals victimized by those practices. In some instances, however, it may be necessary to require the employer or union to take affirmative steps to end discrimination effectively to enforce Title VII. Where an employer or union has engaged in particularly longstanding or egregious discrimination, an injunction simply reiterating Title VII's prohibition against discrimination will often prove useless and will only result in endless enforcement litigation. In such cases, requiring a recalcitrant employer or unions to hire and to admit qualified minorities roughly in proportion to the number of qualified minorities in the workforce may be the only effective way to ensure the full enjoyment of the rights protected by Title VII.

Further, even where the employer or union formally ceases to engage in discrimination, informal mechanisms may obstruct equal employment opportunities. An employer's reputation for discrimination may discourage minorities from seeking available employment. In these circumstances, affirmative race-conscious relief may be the only means available to assure equality of employment opportunities and to eliminate those discriminatory practices and devices which have fostered racially stratified job environments to the disadvantage of minority citizens. Affirmative action promptly operates to change the outward and visible signs of yesterday's racial distinctions and thus, to provide an impetus to the process of dismantling the barriers, psychological or otherwise, erected by past practices.

Finally, a district court may find it necessary to order interim hiring or promotional goals pending the development of nondiscriminatory hiring or promotion procedures. In these cases, the use of numerical goals provides a compromise between two unacceptable alternatives: an outright ban on hiring or promotions, or continued use of a discriminatory selection procedure.

We have previously suggested that courts may utilize certain kinds of racial preferences to remedy past discrimination under Title VII. The Courts of Appeals have unanimously agreed that racial preferences may be used, in appropriate cases, to remedy past discrimination under Title VII. The extensive legislative history of the Act supports this view. Many opponents of Title VII argued that an employer could be found guilty of discrimination under the statute simply because of a racial imbalance in his workforce, and would be compelled to implement racial "quotas" to avoid being charged with liability. At the same time, supporters of the bill insisted that employers would not violate Title VII simply because of racial imbalance, and emphasized that neither the EEOC nor the courts could compel employers to adopt quotas solely to facilitate racial balancing. The debate concerning what Title VII did and did not require culminated in the adoption of section 703(j), which stated expressly that the statute did not require an employer or labor union to adopt quotas or preferences simply because of a racial imbalance.

Although we conclude that section 706(g) does not foreclose a court from instituting some sort of racial preferences where necessary to remedy past discrimination, we do not mean to suggest such relief is always proper. The court should exercise its discretion with an eye towards Congress' concern that the measures not be invoked simply to create a racially balanced work force. In the majority of cases the court will not have to impose affirmative action as a remedy for past discrimination, but need only order the employer or union to cease engaging in discriminatory practices. However, in some cases, affirmative action may be necessary in order effectively to enforce Title VII, such as with persistent or egregious discrimination or to dissipate the effects of pervasive discrimination. The court should also take care to tailor its orders to fit the nature of the violation it seeks to correct.

Here, the membership goal and Fund were necessary to remedy the union and JAC's pervasive and egregious discrimination and its lingering effects. The goal was flexible and thus gives a strong indication that it was not being used simply to achieve and maintain racial balance, but rather as a benchmark against which the court could gauge the union's efforts. Twice the court adjusted the deadline for the goal and has continually approved changes in the size of apprenticeship classes to account for economic conditions preventing the union from meeting its targets. And it is temporary in that it will end as soon as the percentage of minority union members approximates the percentage of minorities in the local labor force. Similarly the fund is scheduled to terminate when the union achieves its membership goal and the court determines it is no longer needed to remedy past discrimination. Also, neither the goal or the fund unnecessarily trammels the interests of white employees. They do not require any union members to be laid off, and does not discriminate against existing union members. While whites seeking admission into the union may be denied benefits extended to non-white counterparts, the court's orders do not stand as an absolute bar to such individuals; indeed a majority of new union members have been white. Many of the provisions of the orders are race-neutral (such as the requirement that the JAC assign one apprenticeship for every four journeymen workers) and the union and JAC remain free to adopt the provisions of the order for the benefit of white members and applicants. Accordingly, we AFFIRM.

Case Questions

1. Is it clear to you why a court would be able to include in its remedies those who are not directly discriminated against by an employer? Explain.

2. If you were the court and were still trying to get the union to comply with your order 18 years after the fact, what would you have done?

3. As an employer, how could you avoid such a result?

Reverse Discrimination

Reverse Discrimination Lawsuit or claim brought by majority member who feels adversely affected by the use of an affirmative action plan.

So-called **reverse discrimination** has often been considered the flip side of affirmative action. When an employer is taking race or gender into account under an affirmative action plan in order to achieve an affirmative action **goal,** someone not in the excluded group alleges she is harmed by the employer's consideration of race or gender, or both, in hiring or promotion decisions.

For example, an employer finds an underrepresentation of women in managerial positions in the workplace and develops an affirmative action plan for their inclusion. As part of that plan, one qualified female employee is to be chosen for a managerial training program for each male chosen. The employer chooses one male, then one female. The male employee who feels he would have been chosen next if there were no affirmative action plan requiring a woman to be chosen sues the employer, alleging reverse discrimination. That is, that but for his gender, he would have been chosen for the position the female received.

Despite what you may have heard, reverse discrimination accounts for only about 3 percent of the charges filed with EEOC, and most of those claims result in no-cause findings.

As you learned in our discussion of the requirements for an employer to have an affirmative action plan, once the plan is deemed necessary because there is an underrepresentation that cannot be accounted for in virtually any way other than exclusion of certain groups, even unwittingly, then consideration of race or gender becomes a necessary part of the remedy. The law builds in protections for employees who feel they may be adversely affected by ensuring that the plan is only given protection if it complies with the legal requirements.

One of the arguments frequently made in reverse discrimination cases is that affirmative action requires the "sons to pay for the sins of the fathers" and that "Slavery is over. Why can't we just forget it and move on?" Keep in mind that affirmative action is not about something that happened nearly 150 years ago. It is about underrepresentation in the workplace *today.* Also keep in mind that it is not punishment in any way, but rather a remedy for discrimination or its vestiges, *which has already been found to exist.* As for the "sins of the fathers," keep in mind that to the extent that blacks and women were, for the most part, *legally* excluded from the workplace from the beginning of this country's existence until 1964, and their intentional inclusion only began to become a significant issue in the late 1970s to early 1980s, this gave those who were in the workplace for all those years before a huge head start on experience, training, presence, trustworthiness, perception of fitness for the position, seniority, perception of appropriateness for the job, and so on.

These factors come into play each time an applicant or employee applies for a job, promotion, training, or other benefit. Without the applicant intentionally doing anything that may ask for more favorable or less favorable consideration (depending on the group to which the applicant belongs), because of years of ingrained history, it happens. While it may not be intentional, or even conscious, it has a definite harmful impact on groups traditionally excluded from the workplace—an impact that research has proved to be present time and again. For instance, despite the anecdotal evidence of reverse discrimination situations we may hear about from our friends or colleagues, the US Department of Labor's 1995 Glass Ceiling Report found that though antidiscrimination laws have made a significant impact in bringing women and minorities into the workplace in entry-level positions, there are still significant workplace disparities. Given that, it should come as no surprise that, according to the Glass Ceiling Commission Report, while white men are only 43 percent of the *Fortune* 2000 workforce, they hold 95 percent of the senior management jobs. In addition, women are only 8.6 percent of all engineers, less than one percent of carpenters, 23 percent of lawyers, 16 percent of police, and 3.7 percent of firefighters. White men are 33 percent of the US population, but 65 percent of physicians, 71 percent of lawyers, 80 percent of tenured professors, and 94 percent of school superintendents.

As you learned in the preceding section, affirmative action must be viewed as a remedy aimed at an excluded *group,* not just an individual. It must also be viewed macroscopically rather than microscopically. That is, it must be viewed in the larger context of what has taken and is taking place in our country regarding race and gender issues, not just what happens in one particular instance. Looking at the issue macroscopically gives quite a different picture than looking at the issue microscopically. While you may not have created the problems of discrimination, or even feel that you contribute to them, discrimination has been the history of our country, and statistics bear out that its repercussions are still with us. While we would all love to live in a color-blind society where merit is the only factor considered in the workplace, the truth is, research shows that we aren't there yet. Affirmative action steps in as a measure to help remedy this situation. Nevertheless, as you can see from the *Johnson* case below, reverse discrimination remains an important tool in effectuating rights under Title VII, as well as further defining its parameters.

Johnson v. Transportation Agency, Santa Clara County, California

480 U.S. 616 (1987)

A female was promoted over a male pursuant to an affirmative action plan voluntarily adopted by the employer to address a traditionally segregated job classification in which women had been significantly underrepresented. A male employee who also applied for the job sued, alleging it was illegal discrimination under Title VII for the employer to consider gender in the promotion process. The US Supreme Court upheld the promotion under the voluntary affirmative action plan. It held that since it was permissible for a public employer to adopt such a voluntary plan, the plan was reasonable, and the criteria for the plan had been met, gender could be considered as one factor in the promotion.

Brennan, J.

In December 1978, the Santa Clara County Transit District Board of Supervisors adopted an Affirmative Action Plan (Plan) for the County Transportation Agency. The Plan implemented a County Affirmative Action Plan, which had been adopted because "mere prohibition of discriminatory practices is not enough to remedy the effects of past practices and to permit attainment of an equitable representation of minorities, women and handicapped persons." Relevant to this case, the Agency Plan provides that, in making promotions to positions within a traditionally segregated job classification in which women have been significantly underrepresented, the Agency is authorized to consider as one factor the sex of a qualified applicant.

In reviewing the composition of its work force, the Agency noted in its Plan that women were represented in numbers far less than their proportion of the County labor force in both the Agency as a whole and in five of seven job categories. Specifically, while women constituted 36.4% of the area labor market, they composed only 22.4% of Agency employees. Furthermore, women working at the Agency were concentrated largely in EEOC job categories traditionally held by women: women made up 76% of Office and Clerical Workers, but only 7.1% of Agency Officials and Administrators, 8.6% of Professionals, 9.7% of Technicians, and 22% of Service and Maintenance Workers. As for the job classification relevant to this case, none of the 238 Skilled Craft Worker positions was held by a woman. The Plan noted that this underrepresentation of women in part reflected the fact that women had not traditionally been employed in these positions, and that they had not been strongly motivated to seek training or employment in them "because of the limited opportunities that have existed in the past for them to work in such classifications." The Plan also observed that, while the proportion of ethnic minorities in the Agency as a whole exceeded the proportion of such minorities in the County work force, a smaller percentage of minority employees held management, professional, and technical positions.

The Agency stated that its Plan was intended to achieve "a statistically measurable yearly improvement in hiring, training and promotion of minorities and women throughout the Agency in all major job classifications where they are underrepresented." As a benchmark by which to evaluate progress, the Agency stated that its long-term goal was to attain a work force whose composition reflected the proportion of minorities and women in the area labor force. Thus, for the Skilled Craft category in which the road dispatcher position at issue here was classified, the Agency's aspiration was that eventually about 36% of the jobs would be occupied by women.

The Agency's Plan thus set aside no specific number of positions for minorities or women, but authorized the consideration of ethnicity or sex as a factor when evaluating qualified candidates for jobs in which members of such groups were poorly represented. One such job was the road dispatcher position that is the subject of the dispute in this case.

The Agency announced a vacancy for the promotional position of road dispatcher in the Agency's Roads Division. Twelve County employees applied for the promotion, including Joyce and Johnson. Nine of the applicants, including Joyce and Johnson, were deemed qualified for the job, and were interviewed by a two-person board. Seven of the applicants scored above 70 on this interview, which meant that they were certified as eligible for selection by the appointing authority. The scores awarded ranged from 70 to 80. Johnson was tied for second with a score of 75, while Joyce ranked next with a score of 73. A second interview was conducted by three Agency supervisors, who ultimately recommended that Johnson be promoted.

James Graebner, Director of the Agency, concluded that the promotion should be given to Joyce. As he testified: "I tried to look at the whole picture, the combination of her qualifications and Mr. Johnson's qualifications, their test scores, their expertise, their background, affirmative action matters, things like that . . . I believe it was a combination of all those."

The certification form naming Joyce as the person promoted to the dispatcher position stated that both she and Johnson were rated as well qualified for the job. The evaluation of Joyce read: "Well qualified by virtue of 18 years of past clerical experience including 3½ years at West Yard plus almost 5 years as a [road maintenance worker]." The evaluation of Johnson was as follows: "Well qualified applicant; two years of [road maintenance worker] experience plus 11 years of Road Yard Clerk. Has had previous outside Dispatch experience but was 13 years ago." Graebner testified that he did not regard as significant the fact that Johnson scored 75 and Joyce 73 when interviewed by the two-person board.

Johnson filed a complaint with the EEOC alleging that he had been denied promotion on the basis of sex in violation of Title VII.

In reviewing the employment decision at issue in this case, we must first examine whether consideration of the sex of applicants for Skilled Craft jobs was justified by the existence of a "manifest imbalance" that reflected underrepresentation of women in "traditionally segregated job categories." In determining whether an imbalance exists that would justify taking sex or race into account, a comparison of the percentage of minorities or women in the employer's work force with the percentage in the area labor market or general population is appropriate in analyzing jobs that require no special expertise or training programs designed to provide expertise. Where a job requires special training, however, the comparison should be with those in the labor force who possess the relevant qualifications. The requirement that the "manifest imbalance" relate to a "traditionally segregated job category" provides assurance both that sex or race will be taken into account in a manner consistent with Title VII's purpose of eliminating the effects of employment discrimination, and that the interests of those employees not benefitting from the plan will not be unduly infringed.

It is clear that the decision to hire Joyce was made pursuant to an Agency plan that directed that sex or race be taken into account for the purpose of remedying underrepresentation. The Agency Plan acknowledged the "limited opportunities that have existed in the past," for women to find employment in certain job classifications "where women have not been traditionally employed in significant numbers." As a result, observed the Plan, women were concentrated in traditionally female jobs in the Agency, and represented a lower percentage in other job classifications than would be expected if such traditional segregation had not occurred. Specifically, 9 of the 10 Para-Professionals and 110 of the 145 Office and Clerical Workers were women. By contrast, women were only 2 of the 28 Officials and Administrators, 5 of the 58 Professionals, 12 of the 124 Technicians, none of the Skilled Craft Workers, and 1—who was Joyce—of the 110 Road Maintenance Workers. The Plan sought to remedy these imbalances through "hiring, training and promotion of . . . women throughout the Agency in all major job classifications where they are underrepresented."

The Agency adopted as a benchmark for measuring progress in eliminating underrepresentation the long-term goal of a work force that mirrored in its major job classifications the percentage of women in the area labor market. Even as it did so, however, the Agency acknowledged that such a figure could not by itself necessarily justify taking into account the sex of applicants for positions in all job categories. For positions requiring specialized training and experience, the Plan observed that the number of minorities and women "who possess the qualifications required for entry into such job classifications is limited." The Plan therefore directed that annual short-term goals be formulated that would provide a more realistic indication of the degree to which sex should be taken into account in filling particular positions. The Plan stressed that such goals "should not be construed as 'quotas' that must be met," but as reasonable aspirations in correcting the imbalance in the Agency's work force. These goals were to take into account factors such as "turnover, layoffs, lateral transfers, new job openings, retirements and availability of minorities, women and handicapped persons in the area work force who possess the desired qualifications or potential for placement." The Plan specifically directed that, in establishing such goals, the Agency work with the County Planning Department and other sources in attempting to compile data on the percentage of minorities and women in the local labor force that were actually working in the job classifications constituting the Agency work force. From the outset, therefore, the Plan sought annually to develop even more refined measures of the underrepresentation in each job category that required attention.

As the Agency Plan recognized, women were most egregiously underrepresented in the Skilled Craft job category, since none of the 238 positions was occupied by a woman. In mid-1980, when Joyce was selected for the road dispatcher position, the Agency was still in the process of refining its short-term goals for Skilled Craft Workers in accordance with the directive of the Plan. This process did not reach fruition until 1982, when the Agency established a short-term goal for that year of 3 women for the 55 expected openings in that job category—a modest goal of about 6% for that category.

The Agency's Plan emphasized that the long-term goals were not to be taken as guides for actual hiring decisions, but that supervisors were to consider a host of practical factors in seeking to meet affirmative action objectives, including the fact that in some job categories women were not qualified in numbers comparable to their representation in the labor force.

By contrast, had the Plan simply calculated imbalances in all categories according to the proportion of women in the area labor pool, and then directed that hiring be governed solely by those figures, its validity fairly could be called into question. This is because analysis of a more specialized labor pool normally is necessary in determining underrepresentation in some positions. If a plan failed to take distinctions in qualifications into account in providing guidance for actual employment decisions, it would dictate mere blind hiring by the numbers, for it would hold supervisors to "achievement of a particular percentage of minority employment or membership . . . regardless of circumstances such as economic conditions or the number of available qualified minority applicants. . . ."

The Agency's Plan emphatically did not authorize such blind hiring. It expressly directed that numerous factors be taken into account in making hiring decisions, including specifically the qualifications of female applicants for particular jobs. The Agency's management had been clearly instructed that they were not to hire solely by reference to statistics. The fact that only the long-term goal had been established for this category posed no danger that personnel decisions would be made by reflexive adherence to a numerical standard.

Furthermore, in considering the candidates for the road dispatcher position in 1980, the Agency hardly needed to rely on a refined short-term goal to realize that it had a significant problem of underrepresentation that required attention. Given the obvious imbalance in the Skilled Craft category, and given the Agency's commitment to eliminating such imbalances, it was plainly not unreasonable for the Agency to determine that it was appropriate to consider as one factor the sex of Ms. Joyce in making its decision. The promotion of Joyce thus satisfies the first requirement since it was undertaken to further an affirmative action plan designed to eliminate Agency work force imbalances in traditionally segregated job categories.

We next consider whether the Agency Plan unnecessarily trammeled the rights of male employees or created an absolute bar to their advancement. The Plan sets aside no positions for women. The Plan expressly states that "[t]he 'goals' established for each Division should not be construed as 'quotas' that must be met." Rather, the Plan merely authorizes that consideration be given to affirmative action concerns when evaluating qualified applicants. As the Agency Director testified, the sex of Joyce was but one of numerous factors he took into account in arriving at his decision. The Plan thus resembles the "Harvard Plan" approvingly noted in *Regents of University of California v. Bakke,* which considers race along with other criteria in determining admission to the college. As the Court observed: "In

such an admissions program, race or ethnic background may be deemed a 'plus' in a particular applicant's file, yet it does not insulate the individual from comparison with all other candidates for the available seats." Similarly, the Agency Plan requires women to compete with all other qualified applicants. No persons are automatically excluded from consideration; all are able to have their qualifications weighed against those of other applicants.

In addition, Johnson had no absolute entitlement to the road dispatcher position. Seven of the applicants were classified as qualified and eligible, and the Agency Director was authorized to promote any of the seven. Thus, denial of the promotion unsettled no legitimate, firmly rooted expectation on the part of Johnson. Furthermore, while Johnson was denied a promotion, he retained his employment with the Agency, at the same salary and with the same seniority, and remained eligible for other promotions.

Finally, the Agency's Plan was intended to attain a balanced work force, not to maintain one. The Plan contains 10 references to the Agency's desire to "attain" such a balance, but no reference whatsoever to a goal of maintaining it. The Director testified that, while the "broader goal" of affirmative action, defined as "the desire to hire, to promote, to give opportunity and training on an equitable, non-discriminatory basis," is something that is "a permanent part" of "the Agency's operating philosophy," that broader goal "is divorced, if you will, from specific numbers or percentages." The Agency acknowledged the difficulties that it would confront in remedying the imbalance in its work force, and it anticipated only gradual increases in the representation of minorities and women. It is thus unsurprising that the Plan contains no explicit end date, for the Agency's flexible, case-by-case approach was not expected to yield success in a brief period of time.

Express assurance that a program is only temporary may be necessary if the program actually sets aside positions according to specific numbers. This is necessary both to minimize the effect of the program on other employees, and to ensure that the plan's goals "[are] not being used simply to achieve and maintain . . . balance, but rather as a benchmark against which" the employer may measure its progress in eliminating the underrepresentation of minorities and women. In this case, however, substantial evidence shows that the Agency has sought to take a moderate, gradual approach to eliminating the imbalance in its work force, one which establishes realistic guidance for employment decisions, and which visits minimal intrusion on the legitimate expectations of other employees. Given this fact, as well as the Agency's express commitment to "attain" a balanced work force, there is ample assurance that the Agency does not seek to use its Plan to maintain a permanent racial and sexual balance.

In evaluating the compliance of an affirmative action plan with Title VII's prohibition on discrimination, we must be mindful of "this Court's and Congress's consistent emphasis on 'the value of voluntary efforts to further the objectives of the law.'" The Agency in the case before us has undertaken such a voluntary effort, and has done so in full recognition of both the difficulties and the potential for intrusion on males and nonminorities. The Agency has identified a conspicuous imbalance in job categories traditionally segregated by race and sex. It has made clear from the outset, however, that employment decisions may not be justified solely by reference to this imbalance, but must rest on a multitude of practical, realistic factors. It has therefore committed itself to annual adjustment of goals so as to provide a reasonable guide for actual hiring and promotion decisions.

The Agency earmarks no positions for anyone; sex is but one of several factors that may be taken into account in evaluating qualified applicants for a position. As both the Plan's language and its manner of operation attest, the Agency has no intention of establishing a work force whose permanent composition is dictated by rigid numerical standards.

We therefore hold that the Agency appropriately took into account as one factor the sex of Diane Joyce in determining that she should be promoted to the road dispatcher position. The decision to do so was made pursuant to an affirmative action plan that represents a moderate, flexible, case-by-case approach to effecting a gradual improvement in the representation of minorities and women in the Agency's work force. Such a plan is fully consistent with Title VII, for it embodies the contribution that voluntary employer action can make in eliminating the vestiges of discrimination in the workplace. Accordingly, the judgment of the Court of Appeals is AFFIRMED.

Case Questions

1. What do you think of the court's decision in this case? Does it make sense to you? Why/why not?

2. If you disagree with the court's decision, what would you have done, as the employer, instead?

3. Are the court's considerations for how to institute an acceptable affirmative action program consistent with how you thought affirmative action worked? Explain.

There is no requirement of quotas under Executive Order 11246 or under Title VII. In fact, the law specifically says it is not to be interpreted as such. Virtually the only time quotas are permitted is when there has been a longstanding violation of the law and there is little other recourse. The *Sheet Metal Workers* case demonstrated this with the union's resistance over an 18-year period, resulting in the imposition of quotas.

Goals to remedy underrepresentation should not be confused with quotas. As long as an employer can show legitimate, good faith effort to reach affirmative action goals, quotas will not be imposed as a remedy for underrepresentation.

EXHIBIT 5–6   Opposing Views of Affirmative Action
Which side makes most sense to you?

Con—Clarence Pendleton, chair of the US Commission on Civil Rights.

Human resource management departments are "the major force companies have for getting rid of preference (hiring) plans and for not letting the 'new racism' take hold," Clarence Pendleton told his packed luncheon-time audience at a recent monthly meeting of the Metropolitan New York City American Society of Personnel Administrators.

"New racism," Pendleton explained, is a lot like old racism. New racists typically are vociferous supporters of civil rights, but want different treatment for minorities, such as goals, timetables and quotas. "New racists think of blacks as a commodity," he commented, "and, therefore, they set numbers as goals."

Preferential treatment, which Pendleton characterized as "neo-slavery," leads automatically to different results for classes of people. With no equality of results, he said.

Pendleton, who is often and loudly criticized for his conservative Republican beliefs, made no apologies for his work with the Reagan Administration. He defended the civil rights record of the Administration, claiming that "we are not turning our backs on civil rights. Discriminatory affirmative action programs are dead, but those who have been discriminated against should be made whole."

He suggested that a best-selling book could be a compendium of the Civil Rights Act of 1964. "Read it," he challenged his audience, "and you will find that nowhere does the Act call for preferential treatment. The faster we get preferential treatment out of politics, the faster we are going to get to a color-blind society."

Too many black leaders "are peddling pain with federal preference programs, but they don't demand education," Pendleton charged.

And that's where HR professionals come into Pendleton's plan. He challenged the audience to "develop a profile on what it takes to move into corporate America without preferences. Let us know what training and support is necessary to get minorities into the economic system. Tell us—'Here's what it takes to get prepared.' Pass that information on to educators."

He asked that professionals support schools and to fight for a reduced minimum wage for teens. "Affirmative action without jobs isn't doing a thing for the 59 percent of black youth who are unemployed and are not qualified for jobs which exist."

"It's time to remove all the chains," he said. "And you in human resources play a major role in the development of public policy. We need a majestic national river of employees, and not these ethnic creeks."

Reprinted with the permission of *HR Magazine,* published by the Society for Human Resource Management, Alexandria, VA.

Valuing Diversity/Multiculturalism

Once affirmative action plans accomplished (at least to a limited degree) their purpose of bringing nontraditional employees into the workplace, employers discovered that this, in and of itself, was not enough. Employees coming into workplaces

EXHIBIT 5–6 (concluded)

Pro—Richard Womack, director, Office of Civil Rights for the AFL-CIO.

It is all well and good to promote the concept of equality in hiring and promotion, but centuries of discrimination against minorities and women have put them at a disadvantage in the workplace that must first be corrected through aggressive action.

Addressing a June 5 plenary session of the 15th annual American Association of Affirmative Action conference, Womack told several hundred conferees that the challenge facing equal employment and affirmative action officers today is to decide how to proceed "until we reach the day when we can say we have a color-blind society."

Womack likened the state of today's workforce to a football game where the dominant team, which has mounted a huge lead by cheating and putting 15 players on the field, decides to stop cheating and pare its team down to eleven players with just three minutes left to play. "For those three minutes the two teams may be equal, but the cheating that preceded the equality will doom the other team to certain failure," Womack said.

White males have had the advantage of preference in the workplace for years. "Now it's time to do the same thing for women and minorities." Noting that his remarks may be viewed by some as "harsh," Womack said that protected groups must be given preference in order to put all workers on the same level playing field. "After whites used race as a basis for slavery and a standard for the exclusion to education and advancement, why now should we be colorblind? There is too much damage to undo."

Womack urged the EEO officers to provide opportunity to minorities and women in the same manner that white males have in the past. "White males have historically taken care of other whites," Womack said.

Affirmative action is an "imperfect tool" to be used to correct past discrimination and suffers from a perception problem, Womack said. "You mention affirmative action to whites and they conjure up images of incompetent blacks who have been given jobs that should have gone to qualified whites," Womack told the conference. Blacks, on the other hand, view affirmative action as "a paltry effort of reduced bias—a dent in whites favoring whites," he said.

The concept and use of goals and timetables also face perception problems, Womack said. The federal government and corporations alike set goals and timetables for everything from collection of taxes to the implementation of new products or procedures, he noted. "So why are goals and timetables so horrible in the employment context?" Womack asked.

Reprinted with permission from *Daily Labor Report,* No. 107, pp. A-10–A-11 (June 6, 1989). Copyright 1989 by the Bureau of National Affairs, Inc. (800/372-1033) http://www.bna.com

that were not used to their presence found the workplace often hostile in subtle, but very real ways.

While the hostilities may have been subtle, the impact on their work lives was not. Employees found they did not move up as quickly as other, more traditional, employees. They may also not be included in workplace activities, may be reprimanded more often, not receive the same opportunities, and thus have higher turnover rates. Even subtle differences in their treatment meant the difference between progressing in the workplace and remaining stagnant.

Faced with workplaces filled with new kinds of people, employers sought answers. The search became even more immediate after the release of the Hudson Institute's "Workforce 2000" study for the US Department of Labor in 1987.

EXHIBIT 5–7

> Did you ever think about how much culture affects us, and how we differ culturally? Not only
> does it impact big things like our holidays, clothing, and so on, but it shapes much smaller
> things.
> A recent list of tips to travelers abroad issued by the Chinese government warned: "Don't squat
> when waiting for a bus or a person. Don't spit in public. Don't point at people with your
> fingers. Don't make noise. Don't laugh loudly. Don't yell or call to people from a distance.
> Don't pick your teeth, pick your nose, blow your nose, pick at your ears, rub your eyes, or
> rub dirt off your skin. Don't scratch, take off your shoes, burp, stretch or hum."

According to the study, the United States was about to face its largest wave of immigration since World War II, and, unlike the last big wave that was 90 percent European, this one would be about 90 percent Asian and Latin American.

The idea of **valuing diversity** began to take root. Valuing diversity is being sensitive to and appreciative of differences among groups that may be different from the "mainstream" and using those differences, yet basic human similarities, as a positive force to increase productivity and efficiency. For the past few years, employers all over the country have sponsored workplace programs to sensitize employees to differences among people in the workplace. Being made aware of these differences in various racial, ethnic, religious, and other groups has helped employees learn to better deal with them. Chances are, at some point in your career, you will be exposed to the concept of valuing diversity. It will greatly increase your value to the employer to do so. See Exhibits 5–7, 5–8.

Valuing diversity
Learning to accept and appreciate those who are different from the majority and value their contributions to the workplace.

EXHIBIT 5–8   Valuing Diversity

> Make a circle with your thumb and forefinger. What does it mean? In America we know it
> primarily as meaning "okay." But how many of us know that it may also mean the equivalent
> of "flipping someone the bird," "give me coin change," "I wish to make love with you," or "I
> wish you dead, as my mortal enemy?" The objective act has not changed, yet the meaning
> has. The interpretation the act is given depends on the cultural conditioning of the receiver.
> Welcome to multiculturalism. Knowing what is meant becomes a necessity in processing the
> act, otherwise the act has little meaning. Culture is what provides that information and, thus,
> meaning for virtually everything we do, say, wear, eat, value, and where and in what we live,
> sit, and sleep. Imagine how many other acts we engage in every day which can be
> misinterpreted based upon differences in cultural conditioning. Yet our cultural conditioning is
> rarely given much thought. Even less is given to the culture of others. That will not be true
> much longer.

EXHIBIT 5–8   (continued)

In the Fall 1992 issue of the magazine of the American Assembly of Collegiate Schools of Business, the accrediting body of schools of business, the cover story and lead article was "Teaching Diversity: Business Schools Search for Model Approaches." In the article, it stated that "without integrating a comprehensive diversity message into the entire curriculum, the most relevant management education cannot occur." Multiculturalism is learning to understand, appreciate, and value (*not* just "tolerate") the unique aspects of cultures different from one's own. The end product is learning to value others who may be different, for what they contribute, rather than rejecting them simply because they are different.

The concept of "culture" encompasses not only ethnicity, but also gender, age, disability, affinity orientation and other factors which may significantly affect and in many ways, define, one's life. Multiculturalism is learning that "different from" does not mean "less than." It is getting in touch with one's cultural conditioning and working toward inclusion, rather than conformity.

Learning to value diversity opens people up to more. A major workplace concern is maximizing production and minimizing liability. Multiculturalism and valuing diversity contribute to this. To the extent that each person, regardless of cultural differences, is valued as a contributor in the workplace, he or she is less likely to sue the employer for transgressions (or perceived transgressions) stemming from not being valued. To the extent they are valued for who they are and what they can contribute in society, they are much less likely to end up engaging in acts such as the Los Angeles riots causing death and destruction in the spring of 1992 after the Rodney King verdict.

The U.S. Department of Labor's Workforce 2000 study conducted by the Hudson Institute and released in 1987 held a few surprises that galvanized America into addressing the issue of multiculturalism. According to the widely cited study, by the year 2000 we will experience the greatest influx of immigrants since World War II. At the same time, the percentage of women entering the workforce is increasing. The net result, according to the study, is that 85% of the net growth in the workforce will be comprised of women and non-Europeans. For the first time, white males will be a minority in the workforce. This need not be viewed as a threatening circumstance, but rather an opportunity for innovation and progress.

These factors, alone, reveal that the workplace (and by implication, schools, universities, recreational facilities and everything else) will be very different from before. It will no longer do to have a white, European, male, standard of operation. Others will be pouring into the workplace and will come with talent, energy, ideas, tenacity, imagination and other contributions the U.S. has always held dear as the basis for the "American Dream." They will come expecting to be able to use those qualities to pursue that dream. They will come feeling that they have much to offer and are valuable for all their uniqueness and the differences they may have from "the norm." And what will happen? There is no choice but to be prepared. It is a simple fact that the workplace cannot continue to operate in the same way and remain productive.

Studies have shown that when the same problem is given to homogeneous groups and heterogeneous groups to solve, the heterogeneous groups come up with more effective solutions. When people feel valued for who they are and what they can contribute, rather than feeling pressed into conformity as if who they are is not good enough, they are more productive. Energy, and creativity can be spent on the task at hand, rather than on worrying about how well they fit into someone's idea of who they should be. A significant number of the problems we face as a society and on which is spent millions in precious tax dollars, comes from rejecting multiculturalism and not valuing diversity. If people were judged for who they are and what they contribute, there would not be a need for a civil rights act, affirmative action plans, riot gear, human rights commissions, etc.

EXHIBIT 5–8   (concluded)

There are, or course, naysayers on the topic of multiculturalism such as those who think it is just an attempt at being "politically correct." It has been said that the term "politically correct" is an attempt to devalue, trivialize, demean and diffuse the substantive value of the issues spoken of; that once something is deemed to be an issue of "political correctness," then there is no need to worry about the real import or impact of it, because it is only a passing fad which need not be taken seriously, as it will die its own natural death soon enough.

Multiculturalism is here to stay. People have evolved to the point where it will not go away. Self-worth and valuing oneself is a lesson that it takes many a long time to learn. Once learned, it is hard to give up. And, of course, why should it be given up? Again, "different from" does not mean "less than." Learning to value others as unique human beings whose cultures is an integral part of who they are, rather than something to be shed at the work or school door, and learning to value the differences rather than to try to assimilate them, will benefit everyone.

Reprinted with permission from April 1994 *Wisconsin Lawyer,* the official publication of the State Bar of Wisconsin.

EXHIBIT 5–9

As managers, part of your duties will be to try to limit the legal liability of your employer. There will be many reasons for this, and one of them will be avoiding discrimination claims. Below are some tips for helping to do so.

A Checklist for Eliminating Barriers to Diversity

✓ Think about and recognize your own cultural biases. Are you making assumptions about people who are different from you? Are you denying or ignoring differences that exist?

✓ Learn more about different cultures within your own organization—make friends with someone from a different cultural background. Recognize that we tend to promote and surround ourselves with people who are like us.

✓ Enhance communication by focusing on the whole person and the content of the message. Some people become distracted or biased by others' gestures, appearance, accent and so on.

✓ Understand that diversity is a bottom-line business issue. To stay competitive, companies need to be reflective of the changing demographics and cultures of the marketplace.

Nine Steps to Fostering Diversity

1) Aggressively recruit qualified, diverse candidates.
2) Speak out about inappropriate behavior.
3) Include employees and volunteers in decision making.
4) Introduce diversity education within the workplace.
5) Mentor a diverse student or colleague.
6) Share diversity development strategies with colleagues.
7) Incorporate diversity into all aspects of the workplace.
8) Review policies and practices for hindrance of diversity.
9) Broaden your definition of diversity to be inclusive of white males.

By Rachel Patrick, American Bar Association. Reprinted with permission from the *Wisconsin Bar Journal,* April 1994, page 11.

Management Tips

Affirmative action can be a bit tricky. Keeping in mind these tips can help avoid liability for instituting and implementing a plan.

- Ensure that the hiring, promotion, training, and other such processes are open, fair, and available to all employees on an equal basis.
- If an affirmative action plan is to be adopted voluntarily, work with the union (if there is one) and other employee groups to try to ensure fairness and get early approval from the constituencies affected to ward off potential litigation.
- Make sure voluntary affirmative action plans meet the judicial requirements of
  - being used to redress a conspicuous imbalance in traditionally segregated job categories
  - being moderate, flexible, and gradual in its approach
  - being temporary in order to attain, not maintain a balanced workforce
  - not unnecessarily trammeling employees' rights or creating an absolute bar to their advancement
  - unsettling no legitimate, firmly rooted expectations of employees
  - presenting only a minimal intrusion into the legitimate, settled expectations of other employees.
- Provide training about the plan so that all employees understand its purpose and intent. Try to allay fears from the outset to ward off potential litigation. The more employees know and understand what is being done, the less likely they are to misunderstand and react adversely. Even so, keep in mind that some employees will still dislike the plan. Reiterating top-level management's commitment to equal employment opportunity will stress the seriousness of management's commitment.
- Implement periodic diversity and related training. This not only provides a forum for employees to express their views about diversity issues, but it also provides information on learning how to deal with their co-workers as diversity issues arise.

Summary

- Affirmative action is intentional inclusion of women, minorities, and others traditionally excluded in the workplace after demonstrated underrepresentation of these historically disadvantaged groups.
- Affirmative action plans may arise voluntarily, as a remedy in a discrimination lawsuit, or as part of an employer's responsibilities as a contractor or subcontractor with the government.
- Employers should conduct voluntary periodic equal employment opportunity audits to monitor their workforce for gender, minority, and other inclusion. If there is underrepresentation, the employer should develop a reasonable, nonintrusive, flexible plan within appropriate guidelines.
- Such plans should not displace nonminority employees or permit people to hold positions for which they are not qualified, simply to meet affirmative action goals. This view should not be encouraged or tolerated.
- A well-reasoned, flexible plan with endorsement at the highest levels of the workplace,

applied consistently and diligently, will greatly aid in diminishing negativity surrounding affirmative action and in protecting the employer from adverse legal action.

Chapter-End Questions

1. What is the monetary floor an employer/federal government contractor must meet to have Executive Order 11246 imposed?

2. Anne is employed by Bradley Contracting Company. Bradley has a $1.3 million contract to build a small group of outbuildings in a national park. Anne alleges that Bradley Contracting has discriminated against her, in that she has not been promoted to skilled craft positions with Bradley because it thinks that it is inappropriate for women to be in skilled craft positions and that most of the male skilled craftworkers are very much against having women in such positions. Knowing that Bradley Contracting has a contract with the federal government, Anne brings suit against Bradley under Executive Order 11246 for gender discrimination. Will she be successful? Why or why not?

3. Can employers lawfully consider race or gender when making hiring or promotion decisions? Explain.

4. If so, may it only be used to remedy identified past discrimination? Discuss.

5. Must such discrimination have been committed by the employer or can the discrimination have been committed by society in general? Explain.

6. May preferential treatment be used to benefit those who did not actually experience discrimination? Discuss.

7. Can race or gender be the only factor in an employment decision?

8. If race or gender can be the only factor in an employment decision, how long can it be a factor?

9. What is the difference between an affirmative action goal and a quota? Is there a difference?

10. What is the proper comparison to determine if there is an underrepresentation of women or minorities in the workplace?

6   RACE DISCRIMINATION

Chapter Outline

S C E N A R I O S

S C E N A R I O   1

An employer has a "no beard" policy, which applies across the board to all employees. A black employee tells the employer he cannot shave without getting severe facial bumps from ingrown hairs. The employer replies that the policy is without exception and the employee must comply. The employee refuses and is later terminated. The employee brings suit under Title VII on the basis of race discrimination. Does he win? Why? Why not?

S C E N A R I O   2

Two truck driver employees are found to have stolen goods from the cargo they were carrying. The black employee is retained and reprimanded. The white employee is terminated. The white employee sues the employer for race discrimination under Title VII. Who wins and why?

S C E N A R I O   3

A black female employee is terminated during a downsizing at her place of employment. The decision was made to terminate the two worst employees, and she was one of them. The employer had not told the employee of her poor performance nor given her any negative feedback during evaluations to enable her to assess her performance and govern herself accordingly. In fact, there were specific orders not to give her any negative feedback. The employee sues for racial discrimination, alleging it was a violation of Title VII for the employer not to give her appropriate negative feedback during evaluations to prevent her from being put in the position of being terminated. Does the employee win? Why? Why not?

Statutory Basis

It shall be an unlawful employment practice for an employer—

(1) to fail or refuse to hire or to discharge any individual, or otherwise to discriminate against any individual with respect to his compensation, terms, conditions, or privileges of employment, because of such individual's race, color . . . or

(2) to limit, segregate, or classify his employees or applicants for employment in any way which would deprive or tend to deprive any individual of employment opportunities or otherwise adversely affect his status as an employee, because of such individual's race, color . . . 42 U.S.C. 2000e-2(a).

Below the "Glass Ceiling"

"It ain't paranoia if it's real." The single most common reason that discrimination continues unabated in so many quarters today is that those in the majority often simply refuse to believe that it exists. Used to thinking of discrimination in terms of rude, overt acts, employers often miss the more subtle manifestations, which are nonetheless devastating. We have only to look at much of the research to see that it still exists. The statistics in Exhibits 6–1 and 6–4 regarding racial disparities in employment, wages, education, and other areas cannot all be attributed to mere happenstance.

Employees who report race discrimination are frequently faced with employers who simply cannot believe that it happened. They think the employee is being "overly sensitive" or is simply mistaken. The manager therefore frequently does nothing. This only compounds the problem.

While most of the country expressed shock when the *New York Times* reported in November of 1996 the disparaging racial remarks and comments taken from tapes of Texaco Oil Company executives who met and openly discussed disposing of documents requested in a federal discrimination lawsuit brought by 1,400 black Texaco employees, few blacks were surprised. Earlier in the year the EEOC had determined that Texaco had failed to promote black employees based on race. The revelations about Texaco only confirmed what many minorities suspected based on their own experiences in the workplace.

So, too, did allegations the next week by a former Avis car rental manager that franchise owner John Dalton gave his employees detailed instruction on ways to deny car rentals to black customers. The seven-year Avis manager alleged that Dalton docked the pay of employees who refused to comply and denied bonuses if employees rented cars to blacks. Dalton was alleged to have a strict policy against hiring blacks and instructed employees to mark blacks' applications with yellow Post-it notes indicating race, age, and gender. Once again, many nonminorities were shocked by these nationally reported allegations, but few minorities were. It was simply life as they live it.

Unless we admit that race discrimination still exists, we will not be able to work on abating it. There is no indication from the race discrimination lawsuits still being filed and won under Title VII that race discrimination no longer exists in the workplace.

On the other hand, there are companies that do believe and understand the impact of race in the workplace and they govern themselves accordingly. In May of 1999, the *Wall Street Journal* reported that after a study of 31,000 of their jobs in the United States showed discrepancies, Eastman Kodak Co. agreed to pay about $13 million in retroactive and current pay raises to 2,000 female and minority employees in New York and Colorado. The pay raise allocation was not in response to a threatened lawsuit or a settlement to a prior action. Employees had raised the issue when they complained to supervisors the year before, so Kodak conducted the study and determined it would make the raises, which did not even prevent them from receiving their routine performance-based raises.

As we saw in the previous chapters, the driving force for the Civil Rights Act of 1964 was addressing discrimination because of race. While much of the discrimination now occurring in the workplace is not as overt as it was before Title VII (see Exhibit 6–2), research indicates that race is still very much a factor in employment. See Exhibits 6–1, 6–4.

EXHIBIT 6–1   Equal?

According to US Census data, and updates:

- more blacks attend college and work than ever before
- of those, black men earn nearly one-third less than whites in professional, specialty, and sales jobs
- average black college graduates earn roughly $5,000 less than white college graduates
- those blacks with master's degrees have a higher unemployment rate than whites with only bachelor's degrees
- the median income of black men is about 75 percent of white men
- black unemployment was twice that of whites in the days when Bull Conner loosed vicious dogs on peaceful civil rights demonstrators in the South in the early 1960s. It was still that in 1995. *USA Today,* June 19, 1995, p. 11A
- according to a US Census Bureau report issued on September 30, 1999, the median income for white households was $42,439; Hispanics, $28,330; blacks, $25,351
- as of September 30, 1999, per capita (individual) income for whites was $22,952; blacks, $12,957; Hispanics, $11,434
- nearly half of white Bostonians surveyed in a recent study said blacks and Hispanics are less intelligent than whites, and blacks are harder to get along with than other ethnic groups
- a 5-year, 7-volume study by the Russell Sage Foundation, released on October 1, 1999, found that "racial stereotypes and attitudes heavily influenced the labor market, with blacks landing at the very bottom"

Department of Labor Glass Ceiling Studies in 1991 and 1995 of barriers to full management participation in the workplace by women and minorities found that minorities had made strides in entering the workplace, but a "glass ceiling" exists, beyond which minorities rarely progress. The study found that minorities plateau at a lower corporate level than women, who plateau at a lower level than white males.

Monitoring for equal access and opportunity was almost never considered a corporate responsibility or a part of the planning and developmental programs and policies of the employer, nor as part of participation with regard to senior management levels. Neither employee appraisals nor total compensation systems were usually monitored. Most companies had inadequate records regarding equal employment opportunity and affirmative action responsibilities in recruitment, employment, and developmental activities for management-level positions.

Such factors militate against serious consideration of full participation by all sectors of the work population and prevent the employer from being presented in the best light should lawsuits arise. If an employer analyzed and monitored workplace information based on the Glass Ceiling considerations, much race discrimination could be discovered and addressed before it progressed to the litigation stage.

History and its present-day effects account for much of the discrimination. Africans arrived in this country in 1619, before the Mayflower. Their initial experience was as free people who were contracted as indentured servants. After the first

EXHIBIT 6–2

The exhibit below, adapted from an actual newspaper classified ad section from 1961, is typical of want ads found in newspapers before Title VII was passed in 1964. For publication purposes names and phone numbers have been omitted. It is now illegal to advertise for males, females, or racial groups.

Male Help Wanted

SOUTH ATLANTA

PERMANENT position for 2 young men 18-35, must be ambitious, high school graduate, and neat appearing. $85 week guaranteed, plus bonus. Opportunity to earn in excess of $100 per week. Must have desire to advance with company. For interview call...

ATTN YOUNG MEN

18-25, SINGLE, free to travel, New York and Florida, returns for clearing house for publishers. New car, transportation furnished. Expense account to start. Salary plus commission. We train you. Apply...

10 BOYS

14 OR OVER. Must be neat in appearance to work this summer. Salary 75 cent per hour. Will be supervised by trained student counselor. Apply...

MAN experienced in selling and familiar with the laundry and dry cleaning business needed to sell top brands of supplies to laundries and dry cleaning plants. This is an excellent opportunity for a man who is willing to work for proper rewards. Salary and comm. Reply to...

EXPERIENCED dairy man to work in modern dairy in Florida. Must be married, sober, and reliable. Salary $60 per week for 6 days with uniform, lights and water—furnished. Excellent house. Write...

SALESMEN

THIS corporation provides its salesmen with a substantial weekly drawing account. New men are thoroughly trained in the field with emphasis directed toward high-executive income bracket. Men experienced in securities, encyclopedias, and other intangibles who can stand rigid investigation, are dependable, and own late-model car. Reply to...

Situations Wanted, Female   24

SECRETARY—RECEPTIONIST (experienced). Ex-Spanish teacher desires diversified permanent position. Responsible, personable, like people, unencumbered. Can travel.

EXPERIENCED executive secretary with college degree, top skills, currently employed—seeks better position with opportunity for advancement and good salary.

SECRETARY desires typing at home, evenings, and weekends.

COLORED EMPLOYMENT

Help Wanted Male, Colored   26

CURB BOYS

DAY or night shift. No experience necessary. Good tips. Apply in person only.

HOUSEMAN, chauffeur. Must be experienced. Recent references, driver's license, health card required. Must be sober, reliable. Write...

RESTAURANT COOK

FOR frying and dinner cooking. Age 22-35. Must be sober, dependable and well-experienced. Salary $250-$275 for good man. Apply...

SOBER, experienced service station porter. No Sundays. Top pay.

PART-TIME lawn and yard maintenance man.

EXP service station porter, 6-day wk. Good sal.

KITCHEN porters, also ware washers. Apply...

Situations Wanted, Male, Col.   28

YOUNG man wants job. Short order and plain cooking, experienced.

Help Wanted, Female, Col.   29

MAID, free to travel with family, $35 to $50 week. Free room and board.

LAUNDRY MARKER—Experienced. 40 hours—pay hourly basis.

SHIRT girl. Experienced.

SHIRT girl, Experienced. Good pay. Good hours. Apply in person.

WAITRESS, experienced, for lunch counter. Over 40. Call...

Situation Wanted, Female, Col.   31

COOK-MAID (experienced)—desires Monday, Wednesday, Friday. References and health card.

MAID wants 5 days week. References.

GIRL WANTS 5 DAYS

MAID wants 5 days work. Will live-in.

MID-TEEN girl desires maid or office work.

EXHIBIT 6–3   Profile: Thurgood Marshall (1908–1993) Associate Justice of the US Supreme Court 1967–1992

Thurgood Marshall was born in Baltimore, Maryland, the son of a steward and a school teacher. He graduated from Lincoln University and from Howard University Law School in 1933. While at Howard, Marshall attracted the attention of Dean Charles Houston, a noted black lawyer and chief legal planner for the NAACP. When he met Marshall, Houston was about to begin a campaign challenging the constitutionality of racial segregation laws in the United States. After law school Marshall practiced law for a brief period, joined the NAACP as a staff attorney, then took over as chief counsel after Houston in 1938.

When Marshall assumed leadership of the NAACP legal program, racial segregation pervaded every aspect of life in the United States—its legality was hardly questioned, and blacks were not considered full partners in the American republic. The 13th, 14th, and 15th Amendments and the laws enacted to give meaning to their promise of black equality had been emptied of content by decisions of the US Supreme Court. The most influential decision, *Plessy v. Ferguson,* 1896, was understood to give broad approval to providing separate public facilities and services for blacks. The political power of the Southern states was such that neither congress nor the president would support legislation to outlaw lynching, much less to end racial segregation. Marshall and his colleagues determined, therefore, to concentrate their efforts on the courts. Their early cases aimed at documenting the inequalities—for example, in per pupil spending and teacher pay—that made the segregated public facilities and education offered to blacks by the Southern and border states not equivalent to those provided to whites. It was thought that such litigation might lead to significant short-term improvement in the facilities with which blacks were provided. However, the NAACP's ultimate goal and grand design was to persuade the Supreme Court that racial segregation as such was unconstitutional, that regardless of the facilities offered to blacks it inevitably relegated them to a position of inferiority and second-class citizenship.

After World War II the pace of litigation quickened, and the Supreme Court struck down particular instances of racial discrimination in interstate travel, primary elections, housing, and criminal justice. Eventually litigation efforts were concentrated on education. By 1954 when Marshall argued *Brown v. Board of Education,* dealing with public school segregation, extensive documentation had been accumulated demonstrating that, as the Court ultimately found, "separate educational facilities are inherently unequal." Soon after, civil rights lawyers won a series of cases that made clear that *Brown* had undermined any constitutional basis for the government to make invidious distinctions in the allocation of goods, services, or benefits on the basis of race.

During his years with the NAACP, Marshall earned a reputation as a tough, shrewd legal tactician with a deceptively easygoing personal style. Southern senators attempted to block his appointment to the US court of appeals in 1961, but the nomination was confirmed in 1962. In 1965, President Lyndon B. Johnson named Marshall solicitor-general, and in 1967 Johnson appointed him an associate justice of the Supreme Court.

On the Supreme Court, Marshall usually supported positions taken by civil libertarians, equal rights advocates, and those who construe the procedural guarantees of the Bill of Rights to protect criminal defendants. In the 1970s when many ground-breaking liberal decisions of the later 1950s and the 1960s were restricted by a new conservative majority of justices appointed by President Richard M. Nixon, Marshall became one of the Court's more vocal dissenters, especially in cases such as the *Bakke* decision outlawing reverse racial quotas, where he believed the Court had retreated from a commitment to eliminate racism in public life.

Adapted from "Thurgood Marshall" by Michael Meltsner, *Collier's Encyclopedia,* vol. 15.

Copyright © 1983 by Macmillan Educational Company. Reprinted by permission of the publisher.

40 years or so, this changed, and slavery came into existence. While some blacks were free, slavery as an integral part of American life lasted for over 200 years until the Emancipation Proclamation in September of 1862. With a slight pause (11 years) for Reconstruction after the Civil War, the next 99 years saw Black Codes and Jim Crow laws legalize and codify racial discrimination. It was not until the passage

of the Civil Rights Act of 1964, that this country was first forced to deal with blacks as equals.

Thus, for virtually their entire history in this country, blacks were dealt with in one way, with societal laws and mores totally built around this approach. Then came the Civil Rights Act of 1964, attempting to change this 200+ year history in one fell swoop.

When race has been as ingrained in a culture as it has been in the United States, it is predictable that it is taking a rather long while to rid the workplace of the vestiges of race discrimination. The effects of racially based considerations and decisions linger long after the actual intent to discriminate may have dissipated.

This is even truer when, as is the case for millions of white Americans, they can go for virtually their whole lives living where they wish, having friends of their choosing, and never having to seriously consider the issue of race. Suddenly it must be confronted in the workplace, to which they have come with all of their life experiences and media-influenced stereotypes of which they may not even be aware. This is, in part, why intent is not required to show some types of discrimination (i.e., disparate impact). Exposure to how race discrimination can unwittingly arise should prepare the employer for recognizing and combatting it effectively in the workplace. The more you know, the better.

General Considerations

Title VII was enacted primarily in response to discrimination against blacks in this country, but the act applies equally to all. Though, as we saw in Chapter 5 on affirmative action, there are times when it appears the law does not equally protect rights of nonminorities, this is done only in a remedial context with strict safeguards in place. The case below demonstrates that racial discrimination may occur against any group and is equally prohibited under Title VII. Note that the decision is written by Justice Thurgood Marshall, who strenuously fought on the US Supreme Court, and even before, to end racial discrimination (See Exhibit 6–3). The *McDonald* case, below, is the basis for opening scenario two.

Scenario

McDONALD V. SANTA FE TRAIL TRANSPORTATION
427 U.S. 273 (1976)

Two white employees and one black employee misappropriated cargo from one of the employer's shipments. The two white employees were discharged and the black employee was not. The white employees sued the employer for race discrimination. The Court held that Title VII is not limited to discrimination against members of any particular race and applies equally to whites and blacks.

Marshall, J.

Santa Fe Transportation employees, McDonald, Laird and Jackson were separately and together accused by their employer of misappropriation of 60-gallon cans of antifreeze which were part of a shipment they were carrying for one of Santa Fe's customers. Six days later, McDonald and Laird, white, were fired by the employer. Jackson, black, was not. We hold that this unequal discipline based on race violates Title VII even though the employees bringing suit are white.

Title VII of the Civil Rights Act of 1964 prohibits the discharge of "any individual" because of "such individual's race." Its terms are not limited to discrimination against any particular race. Thus, although we were not there confronted with racial discrimination against whites, we described the Act in *Griggs v. Duke Power Co.* as prohibiting "[d]iscriminatory preference for any [racial] group, minority or majority."

This conclusion is in accord with uncontradicted legislative history to the effect that Title VII was intended to "cover white men and white women and all Americans," 110 Cong. Rec. 2578 (1964), and create an "obligation not to discriminate against whites," *id.,* at 7218.

Santa Fe, while conceding that "across-theboard discrimination in favor of minorities could never be condoned consistent with Title VII," contends nevertheless that "such discrimination in isolated cases which cannot reasonably be said to burden whites as a class unduly," such as is alleged here, "may be acceptable." We cannot agree. There is no exception in the terms of the Act for isolated cases; on the contrary, "Title VII tolerates no racial discrimination, subtle or otherwise." Santa Fe disclaims that the actions challenged here were any part of an affirmative action program, and we emphasize that we do not consider here the permissibility of such a program, whether judicially required or otherwise prompted.

While Santa Fe may decide that participation in a theft of cargo may render an employee unqualified for employment, this criterion must be applied alike to members of all races, and Title VII is violated if, as employees allege, it is not. Thus, we conclude that the district court erred in dismissing the employees' Title VII claims and we REVERSE and REMAND.

Case Questions

1. Does it seem consistent with Title VII for the Court to hold as it did? Why or why not?

2. Do you agree with the employer's "isolated case" argument? Explain.

3. How does this holding square with what you know of affirmative action?

Recognizing Race Discrimination

Often employers are held liable for race discrimination because they treated employees of a particular race differently without even realizing they were building a case of race discrimination for which they could ultimately be liable. As the case below demonstrates, intent may be established by direct evidence of discrimination by the employer even when an employer may discriminate for what it considers to be justifiable reasons.

As you read the case below, think about whether you would have handled things differently to avoid the result the court reached here. *Vaughn* is the basis for opening scenario three.

Scenario

EXHIBIT 6–4

Below is an excerpt from a report issued in February 1999 by the esteemed Professor Alfred W. Blumrosen of Rutgers Law School about the state of discrimination in Georgia as gathered by an analysis of EEO-1 Reports. These reports are required to be submitted to the EEOC each year by employers with 100 or more employees, federal contractors with 50 or more employees and smaller establishments in special cases. The reports show the composition of the employer's workforce as to gender, race, national origin and occupational group and cover about half of all employees in the private sector (about 47 million). The purpose of the study was "to measure the *current* extent of discrimination against women and minorities, to describe the employers engaged in such practices, and to count the number of women and minority workers who are harmed. Analyzing the 1997 reports for Georgia offers a "detailed, objective means of detecting serious and sustained employment discrimination and monitoring the nation's progress in overcoming it." The Georgia report covers about 3.1 million workers, 47 percent of whom are women and 36 percent of whom are members of racial and ethnic minority groups. Professor Blumrosen's final report will cover the entire nation. Reading the excerpt of his report is instructive in answering whether present-day discrimination exists.

Our analysis further reveals that substantial employment discrimination *against women* continues to operate in Georgia, with the state ranking in the lowest quarter of states in a 50-state comparison. In 1997, such discrimination was directly observed in 960 private-sector business establishments in the state. *These employers represent 28.4 percent—more than one in four—among the establishments examined.* These establishments appear to discriminate against women in 20.5 percent of the employment situations we had data to analyze.

Our analysis further reveals that substantial employment discrimination *against racial and ethnic minorities* also continues to operate in Georgia, with the state ranking in the lowest quarter of states in a 50-state comparison. In 1997, such discrimination was directly observed in 1,345 private sector business establishments in the state. *These employers represent 38.4 percent—more than one in three—among the establishments examined.* These establishments appear to discriminate against minorities in 28.2 percent of the employment situations we had data to analyze.

The discrimination directly harmed 19,819 women and 31,973 minorities who, in the absence of such discrimination, would have been employed by these establishments or would have been employed by them in higher-level, better paid positions. When this rate is applied to all business establishments in the state, we estimate that *more than 103,000 women and more than 160,000 minorities statewide are currently experiencing workplace discrimination.* These victims of discrimination come from all walks of life, from factory workers and secretaries to professionals and managers. They reside in both urban and rural areas and work in many different industries. The discrimination affects not only the workers involved but also their families and their children.

These findings make clear that the "playing field" is *not* level for women and minorities in the workplace today. The employers identified by our statistical analysis operate in ways that are different from other employers in the same industry and location. They provide significantly less opportunity to women and minorities than other, comparable firms. The United States Supreme Court ruled 20 years ago that, when an employer's employment patterns "stick out like a sore thumb" compared to similar employers, then that employer is presumed to be engaged in *intentional discrimination*—that is, discrimination that is embedded in its regular course of business. Our analysis of the information in these employer's own reports reveals more than one Georgia private employer in four apparently discriminating against women, and one in three apparently discriminating against minorities.

EXHIBIT 6–4   Concluded

This finding, in turn, carries implications for public and private activities undertaken to improve the situation. These actions include efforts to eliminate discrimination through *enforcement of civil rights laws,* by litigation and by the complaint processes of the EEOC, Georgia Commission on Equal Opportunity, and similar agencies. *The findings are consistent with the need for continuing, expanding, and strengthening of such enforcement activities.*

Public and private activities to address discrimination also *include "affirmative action,"* by which we mean any approaches, other than simple determination of a discriminatory practice, adopted to correct for past discrimination or prevent discrimination from recurring in the future. Our findings suggest that *this approach continues to be relevant in Georgia,* not merely to address the effects of past discrimination but to address discrimination that operates currently. Such actions are particularly necessary when, as our findings suggest, such discrimination continues to be "the regular operating practice" of a significant number of employers, rather than merely the hostile acts of a few individuals. (Emphasis in original)

Employment Discrimination Against Women and Minorities in Georgia, Employment Discrimination Report Number 4, by Alfred W. Blumrosen, Marc Benedick, Jr., John J. Miller, Ruth Blumrosen, February 1999. Used by permission

---

VAUGHN V. EDEL
918 F.2d 517 (5th Cir. 1990)

During a retrenchment, a black female was terminated for poor performance. She alleged race discrimination in that her employer intentionally determined not to give her necessary feedback about her performance which would have helped her perform better and perhaps avoid dismissal. The court upheld the employee's claim.

Wiener, J.

Emma Vaughn, a black female attorney, became an associate contract analyst in Texaco's Land Department in August of 1979. Her supervisors were Robert Edel and Alvin Earl Hatton, assistant chief contract analyst. In Vaughn's early years with Texaco, she received promotions and was the highest ranked contract analyst in the department.

The events leading to this dispute began on April 16, 1985, the day after Vaughn returned from a second maternity leave. On that day, Edel complained to Vaughn about the low volume of her prior work and the excessive number of people who visited her office. Vaughn later spoke with Roger Keller, the head of the Land Department, about Edel's criticism of her.

In a memorandum concerning this discussion, Keller wrote that he had told Vaughn that he had been told that Vaughn's productivity "was very low"; that he "had become aware for some time of the excessive visiting by predominantly blacks in her office behind closed doors"; and that "the visiting had a direct bearing on her productivity." Keller then told Vaughn, as he noted in his memo, that "she was allowing herself to become a black matriarch within Texaco" and "that this role was preventing her from doing her primary work for the company and that it must stop."

Keller's remarks offended Vaughn, so she sought the advice of a friend who was an attorney in Texaco's Legal Department. Keller learned of this meeting and of Vaughn's belief that he was prejudiced. To avoid charges of race discrimination, Keller told Vaughn's supervisor, Edel, "not [to] have any confrontations with Ms. Vaughn about her work." Keller later added that "if he [Edel] was dissatisfied, let it ride. If it got serious, then see [Keller]."

Between April 1985 and April 1987 when Vaughn was fired, neither Edel nor Hatton (one of two supervisors) expressed criticism of Vaughn's work to her. During this period all annual written evaluations of Vaughn's work performance (which, incidentally, Vaughn never saw) were "satisfactory." Vaughn also received a merit salary increase, though it was the minimum, for 1986. Keller testified that for several years he had intentionally overstated on Vaughn's annual evaluations his satisfaction with her performance because he did not have the time to spend going through procedures which would result from a lower rating and which could lead to termination.

In 1985–86 Texaco undertook a study to identify activities it could eliminate to save costs. To meet the cost-reduction goal set by the study, the Land Department fired its two "poorest performers," one of whom was Vaughn, as the "lowest ranked" contract analyst. The other employee fired was a white male.

In passing Title VII, Congress announced that "sex, race, religion, and national origin are not relevant to the selection, evaluation, or compensation of employees."

When direct credible evidence of employer discrimination exists, employer can counter direct evidence, such as a statement or written document showing discriminatory motive on its face, "only by showing by a preponderance of the evidence that they would have acted as they did without regard to the [employee's] race."

Vaughn presented direct evidence of discrim-

ination. Keller testified that to avoid provoking a discrimination suit he had told Vaughn's supervisor not to confront her about her work. His "black matriarch" memorandum details the events that led Keller to initiate this policy. Keller also testified to deliberately overstating Vaughn's evaluations in order not to start the process that might eventually lead to her termination. This direct evidence clearly shows that Keller acted as he did solely because Vaughn is black.

Although Vaughn's race may not have directly motivated the 1987 decision to fire her, race did play a part in Vaughn's employment relationship with Texaco from 1985–1987. Texaco's treatment of Vaughn was not color-blind during that period. In neither criticizing Vaughn when her work was unsatisfactory nor counselling her how to improve, Texaco treated Vaughn differently than it did its other contract analysts because she was black. As a result, Texaco did not afford Vaughn the same opportunity to improve her performance and perhaps her relative ranking, as it did its white employees. One of those employees was placed on an improvement program. Others received informal counselling. The evidence indicates that Vaughn had the ability to improve. As Texaco acknowledges, she was once its highest ranked contract analyst.

Had her dissatisfied supervisors simply counselled Vaughn informally, such counselling would inevitably have indicated to Vaughn that her work was deficient. Had Keller given Vaughn the evaluation that he believed she deserved, Texaco's regulations would have required his placing her on a ninety-day work improvement program, just as at least one other employee—a white male—had been placed. A Texaco employee who has not improved by the end of that period is fired.

When an employer excludes black employees from its efforts to improve efficiency, it subverts the "broad overriding interest" of Title VII—"efficient and trusty workmanship assured through fair and racially neutral employment and personnel decisions." Texaco has never stated any reason, other than that Vaughn was black, for treating her as it did. Had Texaco treated Vaughn in a color-blind manner from 1985–1987, Vaughn may have been fired by April 1987 for unsatisfactory work; on the other hand, she might have sufficiently improved her performance so as not to be one of the two lowest ranked employees, thereby avoiding termination in April 1987.

Because Texaco's behavior was race-motivated, Texaco has violated Title VII. Texaco limited or classified Vaughn in a way which would either "tend to deprive [her] of employment opportunities or otherwise adversely affect [her] status as an employee" in violation of the law.

Case Questions

1. Do you agree with the court's decision? Why or why not?

2. How would you have handled this matter if you were the manager?

3. What do you think of Edel's remark about Vaughn becoming the "black matriarch" of Texaco? What does it signify to you? What attitudes might it reflect that may be inappropriate in the workplace? What concern, if any, might be appropriate?

An employer who has not considered the issue of race may well develop and implement policies that have a racially discriminatory impact, without ever intending to do so. The "no-beard" case below is a good example of this. It is also a good example of why disparate impact cases must be recognized, if Congress's legislative intent of ridding the workplace of employment discrimination is to be at all successful. *Bradley* is the basis for opening scenario one. *Bradley* also clearly demonstrates why the more an employer knows about diverse groups, the better. Here, it could have saved the employer.

Scenario

BRADLEY V. PIZZACO OF NEBRASKA, INC., D/B/A DOMINO'S
939 F.2d 610 (8th Cir. 1991)

Employee brought a race discrimination case against his employer after being discharged for failure to comply with the employer's policy requiring employees to be clean-shaven. The court held that the policy had a disparate impact on blacks and violated Title VII.

Fagg, J.

Domino's grooming policy prohibits employees from wearing beards. Pizzaco, a Domino's franchisee, hired Bradley to deliver pizzas, but fired him within two weeks because he would not remove his beard. Bradley is a black man who suffers from pseudofolliculitis barbae (PFB), a skin disorder affecting almost half of all black males. The symptoms of PFB—skin irritation and scarring—are brought on by shaving, and in severe cases PFB sufferers must abstain from shaving altogether. Domino's policy, however, provides for no exceptions. As Pizzaco's owner explained, "You must be clean-shaven to work for Domino's."

This case then, is about a facially neutral employment policy that discriminates against black males when applied. Title VII forbids employment policies with a disparate impact unless the policy is justified by legitimate employment goals. Through expert medical testimony and studies, the EEOC demonstrated Domino's policy necessarily excludes black males from the company's workforce at a substantially higher rate than white males. In so doing, the EEOC has shown Domino's facially neutral grooming requirement operates as a "built-in headwind" for black males. *Griggs,* 401 U.S. at 432.

The record shows PFB almost exclusively affects black males and white males rarely suffer from PFB or comparable skin disorders that may prevent a man from appearing clean-shaven. Dermatologists for both sides testified that as many as forty-five percent of black males have PFB. The EEOC's dermatologist offered his opinion that approximately twenty-five percent of all black males cannot shave because of PFB.

Domino's also contends that EEOC failed to show black males with PFB who could not shave were turned away or were fired for failing to comply with Domino's no-beard policy. We disagree.

There is no requirement that disparate impact claims must always include evidence that actual job applicants were turned down for employment because of the challenged discriminatory policy. The reason is self-evident: a discriminatory work policy might distort the job applicant pool by discouraging otherwise qualified workers from applying. PFB prevents a sizable segment of the black male population from appearing clean-shaven, but does not similarly affect white males. Domino's policy—which makes no exceptions for black males who medically are unable to shave because of a skin disorder peculiar to their face—effectively operates to exclude these black males from employment with Domino's. REVERSE in part, AFFIRM in part, and REMAND.

Case Questions

1. If you had been the manager would you have been surprised at this case outcome? Explain.

2. Why do you think Pizzaco had a no-beard policy? What purpose did it serve? Was there another way to get what Pizzaco may have wanted by instituting the policy?

3. Did stereotypes play a role in this policy? What role should stereotypes play in developing workplace policies?

If the employer in *Bradley* had simply asked the employee to provide documentation for his condition from a reputable and reliable source, such as a dermatologist or barber, the outcome may have been different. The employer would have had a basis for providing an exception to the rule in these particular circumstances, while still maintaining the general rule for other employees. While not satisfied that everyone does not have to obey the policy, the employer at least feels satisfied that sufficient justification was provided to excuse this employee. Other employees seeing the employee treated differently would feel reasonably comfortable knowing that the difference in treatment is based on justifiable medical reasons. If the employer had been flexible, rather than dismissing the employee's assertions out of hand, he undoubtedly could have avoided the result in this case. As a manager, make sure you try to consider all angles before making a decision. It is especially important to consider the realities of those who belong to groups with whom you may not be familiar.

Below is another unusual manifestation of racial discrimination that might well slip by a manager, just as it did in this case. In the case below, the action was not brought by the blacks discriminated against by the employer, but rather, the white manager who was trying *not* to discriminate, when her company wanted her to do so.

CHANDLER V. FAST LANE, INC.
868 Fed. Supp. 1138 (E.D. Ark, W. Div. 1994)

A white employee brought suit against her employer for constructive dismissal under Title VII and other statutes, alleging that she was forced to leave her job when the employer would not allow her to hire and promote blacks. The employer argued that since its policies discriminated only against blacks, the white employee had no right to sue under Title VII. The court disagreed and permitted the case to be brought.

Eisele, J.

In the complaint filed with the Court, Chandler (who is white) alleges that she was the victim of a discriminatory employment practice at the hands of her employers. Chandler, a former manager of employers' restaurant, claims that her employer thwarted her efforts to employ and promote African-American employees, and that as a result the conditions of her employment became so intolerable that she was forced to resign. The employer argues that because they are alleged to have adopted discriminatory hiring and promotional practices targeted only at African-Americans, a white person has no standing to assert a Title VII claim premised upon these policies.

It is true that only individuals whom employers are claimed to have failed or refused to hire or promote were African-Americans. However, by focusing on the "fail or refuse to hire" provision of 2000e-2(a)(1), employers' argument misperceives the unlawful employment practice alleged by Chandler. Chandler does not claim that she

was a target of employers' allegedly anti–African-American employment practices. Rather, Chandler argues that employers' insistence that she enforce these practices violated her fundamental right to associate with African-Americans, and as a consequence employer committed a separate violation by engaging in an unlawful employment practice that "otherwise discriminate[d] against an[ ] individual," namely Chandler.

Although the Court recognizes that Chandler's Title VII claim is somewhat novel, it is of the opinion that such a claim, if proven, would state a cause of action under Title VII. A white person's right to associate with African-Americans is protected by Sec. 1981. Therefore, the Court concludes that an employer's implementation of an employment practice that impinges upon this right is actionable under Title VII.

Additionally, Chandler's allegations are sufficient to establish a Title VII claim under a separate provision of the statute. The relevant provision of Title VII is found in §42 U.S.C.A. §2000e- 3(a), which provides in pertinent part:

> It shall be an unlawful employment practice for an employer to discriminate against any of his employees . . . because [s]he has opposed any practice made an unlawful employment practice by [Title VII].

In order to establish a prima facie case under the "opposition" clause of §2000e-3(a), an employee must show: (1) that she was engaged in an opposition activity protected under Title VII; (2) that she was a victim of adverse employment action; and (3) that a causal nexus exists between these two events. The Court has no doubt that an employee who exercises her authority to promote and employ African-Americans engages in protected "opposition" to her employer's unlawful employment practice which seeks to deprive African-Americans of such benefits. Thus, Chandler's allegations are clearly sufficient to meet the first requirement of a §2000e-3(a) claim. The Court further concludes that employers' insistence that Chandler enforce such an employment practice, if proven, would certainly cause an "adverse employment action" to be visited upon her. Title VII forbids an employer from requiring its employees "to work in a discriminatorily hostile or abusive environment," and included within this prohibition is the right of white employees to a work environment free from discrimination against African-Americans, or any other class of persons. Indeed, subjecting an employee to such a hostile working environment may result in an actionable constructive discharge, a result that is especially likely under facts similar to those presently alleged. Under Title VII, a constructive discharge occurs whenever it is reasonably foreseeable that an employee will resign as a result of her employer's unlawful employment practice, and it is plainly foreseeable that an employee might choose to resign rather than to acquiesce in or enforce her employer's discriminatory and illegal employment practice.

The Court is therefore satisfied that employers' efforts to hinder Chandler from hiring and promoting African-Americans, and their insistence that she discriminate against such persons, if proven, would result in an actionable Title VII claim. Indeed, "[u]nder the terms of §2000e-3(a), requiring an employee to discriminate is itself an unlawful employment practice." Accordingly, it is therefore ordered that employers' motion to dismiss is DENIED.

Case Questions

1. What do you think of the employer's argument that since its policies discriminated against blacks, the white employee should not be able to bring a suit for discrimination? Explain.

2. Do you understand the court's reasoning that the white employee was being discriminated against by not being able to hire and promote black employees? Explain.

3. What reason can you think of as to why the employer had the policy of not hiring or promoting blacks? Do you think it makes good economic sense? (Consider all facets of economics, including the possibility of litigation over the policies.)

Racial Harassment

In addition to an employer being liable for race discrimination under Title VII, the employer may also be liable for racial harassment in the workplace. The employer is responsible for such activity if the employer himself or herself is the one who perpetrates the harassment, or if it is permitted in the workplace by the employer or supervisory employees. Actions for racial harassment, like those of race discrimination under Title VII, may be brought under the same alternative statutes as race discrimination, as appropriate—that is, the post–Civil War statutes, state human rights or fair employment practice laws, or constitutional provisions.

As shown by the case below, racial harassment has as its basis the employer imposing on the harassed employee different terms or conditions of employment based on race. The employee is required to work in an atmosphere in which severe and pervasive harassing activity is directed at the employee because of the employee's race or color. As we shall see later with sexual harassment, the employer's best approach to racial harassment is to maintain a workplace in which such activity is not permitted or condoned in any way, to take all racial harassment complaints seriously, and to take immediate corrective action, if necessary, after investigation. As the case below demonstrates, an employer must do this to avoid liability.

DANIELS V. WORLDCOM CORP.
1998 U.S. Dist. LEXIS 2335 (N. D. Tex. 1998)

Employees sued the employer under Title VII and state civil causes of action when jokes with racial undertones were sent to them and other employees on their workplace computers. While the court dismissed the actions based on legal problems with the case, the case is instructive for demonstrating how racial harassment can arise in the workplace, and even changes with technology.

Solis, J.

Angela Daniels and Dimple Ballou allege that they were racially discriminated against while working at WorldCom, Inc. Specifically, they assert that four electronic mail [e-mail] jokes sent by a non-managerial employee of WorldCom were racially harassing. Further, the employees assert that WorldCom was negligent for allowing the e-mail system to be used to send the jokes and that WorldCom retaliated against them for reporting the jokes.

On January 21, 1997, Cathy Madzik, a non-managerial employee at WorldCom, sent a joke to Daniels and two other co-workers across the company's e-mail system. After receiving this and construing the joke as having racial undertones, Daniels sent a message to Madzik objecting to the joke's contents. Three days later, Madzik sent

three more jokes to Daniels and others. Daniels was offended by what she perceived as racial undertones in one of the jokes.

At some point shortly after receiving these jokes, Daniels complained to the manager of the Information Systems Department, Dianne Summers. Daniels also took her concerns to Tom Adams, the Human Resources Manager at WorldCom's Dallas facility. After learning of Daniels' concerns and discussing the situation with the Human Resources Department, Summers issued a "strong verbal warning" to Madzik and placed a written reprimand in her personnel file. On or about January 27, 1997, Summers held a staff meeting which Daniels and Ballou attended. At the close of this meeting, Summers dismissed Madzik and warned the remaining individuals not to use the e-mail system for non-business purposes. On January 29, 1997, Adams held a meeting during which Daniels and Ballou were also allowed to voice their displeasure about the jokes. Adams also addressed the appropriate use of the company e-mail system. In addition to the two meetings discussed above, Summers requested several workers at WorldCom, including Daniels and Ballou, to review the company's Electronic Mail Policy. Daniels and Ballou filed suit on February 27, 1997.

Daniels and Ballou assert that WorldCom was negligent in allowing employees to use the e-mail system to send racially discriminatory jokes. To the extent that they claim an allegation of common-law negligence, this claim fails as a matter of law because WorldCom acted reasonably. Within ten days of the employees' complaints regarding the e-mail jokes, supervisors at WorldCom organized two meetings to discuss the proper use of the company's e-mail system. Further, Summers verbally reprimanded Madzik and issued a written warning regarding improper use of e-mail. Finally, WorldCom had an established policy regarding the use of e-mail and Summers attached a copy of this policy on February 4, 1997, for the employees in her department to review. Based on all of this evidence, WorldCom acted reasonably and employees' common-law claim of negligence fails as a matter of law. Employer's motion to dismiss is GRANTED.

Case Questions

1. Does it surprise you that there would be liability on the part of the employer for harassing e-mails sent from a workplace computer? Explain.

2. Do you agree with the court that the employer quickly and appropriately addressed the problem here so that liability should not attach?

3. If you were the manager to whom the employees came reporting the e-mail jokes, what would you have done?

A Word about Color

EXHIBIT 6–5

> The National Survey of Black Americans across the country published in a recent issue of the *American Journal of Sociology* found that "the fairer one's pigmentation (skin color), the higher his or her occupational standing." Researchers found that a light complexion Black, on average, had a 50 percent higher income than darker Blacks, regardless of educational, occupational or family background.

Jet, January 20, 1992, p. 28.

Color is one of the five categories included in Title VII as a prohibited basis for discrimination. Despite the findings reflected in Exhibit 6–5, however, few cases have been brought using color as a basis for discrimination, and those only in the late 1980s. However, it should be noted that color may be a basis for discrimination in employment.

Employers should be aware of this and guard against it, as with the other categories. In both cases, it was a black supervisor who was alleged to have discriminated against a black employee. Employers should not miss the possibility of this problem by thinking there can be no discrimination since two people of the same race are involved.

If you think color doesn't matter, think about whether it was a mere coincidence that the first-ever black Miss America, Vanessa Williams, was light skinned with green eyes and long hair. Was America ready for Miss America to be dark brown with short, kinky natural hair? No. It didn't appeal to their cultural sensibilities of what beauty is. That is why blacks and other ethnic groups still hold their own beauty pageants. It is not for purposes of segregation. Rather, it is to have a pageant that uses the standards of beauty that arise from, and are appreciated by the group itself, rather than the one generally imposed by the larger society.

The recent flap over the third US president, Thomas Jefferson's alleged 38-year-long relationship with his slave Sally Hemmings also reflected this color issue. When several of the Hemmings descendants who claimed to be the descendants of the relationship between Jefferson and Hemmings appeared in public and looked "whiter" than many whites, there was initially widespread public disbelief. If color did not matter, this simply would not have occurred.

Whether or not you agree with the idea of beauty pageants or separate ones, or even that color matters, the point is that skin color exists and has value (negative or positive) in our society that may be reflected in the workplace. Make sure you are aware that Title VII covers color and be mindful of the subtle, though not necessarily conscious role it may play in how we deal with others.

As the case below demonstrates, liability is still possible, though for other reasons it was not imposed here.

WALKER V. SECRETARY OF THE TREASURY, INTERNAL REVENUE SERVICE
742 F. Supp. 670 (N.D. Ga., Atlanta Div. 1990).

A light-skinned black employee sued her employer alleging discrimination by her supervisor based on color. The employee alleged that the supervisor, a brown-skinned black, said and did derogatory things to her because the supervisor resented the employee's lighter skin color. The court recognized that color could be a basis for discrimination under Title VII, but held that the employee failed to demonstrate that the employer had discriminated since there were legitimate nondiscriminatory reasons for the dismissal.

May, J.

Employee, a lighter-skinned black female, filed a complaint alleging, among other things, that she had been terminated by her darker-skinned black female supervisor because of employee's lighter colored skin, in violation of Title VII of the Civil Rights Act of 1964.

The employer maintains that employee's termination was based upon her poor performance, poor attitude and misconduct. Employee argues that these reasons were a mere pretext and that she was actually terminated because of her supervisor's color-based prejudice. We hold that employee failed to meet her burden by proving by a preponderance of the evidence that her termination was the result of a violation of Title VII rather than the stated reasons of poor performance and attitude.

The only significant evidence that employee offered that, if true, would tend to prove that her supervisor did indeed have feelings of prejudice toward her are some derogatory personal comments that her supervisor allegedly made to her, such as: "you need some sun"; "you think you're bad, you ain't about nothing, you think you're somebody, I can do what I want to do to you"; "why don't you go back to where you belong?"; and "why did you come down here?" However, this court holds that employee has failed to prove by a preponderance of the evidence that the comments were in fact made.

But even if the comments were made, employee failed to prove that they were uttered for any reason other than the personal animosity that the two individuals might have had for each other. It appears undisputed that there was a personality conflict between the employee and her supervisor, and that her supervisor was not wholly innocent in the propagation of the conflict. However, a personality conflict alone does not establish invidious discrimination. There is ample evidence in the record to support the supervisor's contention that the reason for the personality conflict, and likewise the subsequent termination of employment, was employee's performance on the job.

Employee has failed to prove by a preponderance of the evidence that she was terminated because of invidious discrimination on the basis of color on the part of her supervisor. Conversely, the employer has offered legitimate reasons for employee's termination which the court finds nonpretextual. JUDGMENT for DEFENDANT.

Case Questions

1. Do you think the court was correct in interpreting Title VII to permit a color discrimination case to be brought by a black employee against a black supervisor? Why or why not?

2. If you were the manager here, what would you have done to deal with employee and her supervisor?

3. Since the statements were insufficient to show discrimination, what else do you think employee could have used to satisfy the court? Do you think the case would have been decided differently if the supervisor was a different race than the employee? Explain.

The Reconstruction Civil Rights Acts

Title VII was not the first piece of legislation aimed at prohibiting racial discrimination. The previous laws did not apply to as broad a range of employers as Title VII and did not provide a full and comprehensive statutory scheme for addressing the problems they were directed to. As a result, litigation was not as active or effective as it is under Title VII. Keep in mind that the time limit on bringing lawsuits under Title VII is rather short, so a claimant who misses the Title VII filing deadline can still use other laws, including this one which does not have such limitations.

42 U.S.C. Section 1981

Section 1981. Equal Rights under the Law

All persons within the jurisdiction of the United States shall have the same right in every State and Territory to make and enforce contracts . . . as is enjoyed by white citizens.

This provision of the post–Civil War statutes has been used to a limited extent in the past as a basis for employees suing employers for racial discrimination in employment. In 1975, the Court held that section 1981 prohibits purely private discrimination in contracts, including employment contracts. In *Patterson,* below, the limitations of section 1981 become evident. *Patterson* was nullified by the Civil Rights Act of 1991. As you read the case for historical and analytical purposes, see if you can determine why Congress would want to overrule the Supreme Court's decision by the 1991 legislation. *Patterson* was specifically chosen for inclusion here to demonstrate how seemingly small, insignificant matters can accumulate and provide a solid picture of discriminatory treatment leading to liability.

PATTERSON V. MCLEAN CREDIT UNION
491 U.S. 164 (1989)

A black female alleged racial discrimination in violation of section 1981 in that she was treated differently from white employees and not promoted, on the basis of race. The Court held that section 1981 was not available to address this problem since the case did not involve the making of a contract, but rather, its performance.

Kennedy, J.

Patterson, a black female, worked for the McLean Credit Union (MCU) as a teller and file coordinator for ten years. She alleges that when she first interviewed for her job, the supervisor, who later became the president of MCU, told her that she would be working with all white women and that they probably would not like working with her because she was black. According to Patterson, in the subsequent years, it was her supervisor who proved to have the problem with her working at the credit union.

Patterson alleges that she was subjected to a pattern of discrimination at MCU which included her supervisor repeatedly staring at her for minutes at a time while she performed her work and not doing so to white employees; not promoting her or giving her the usually perfunctory raises which other employees routinely received; not arranging to have her work reassigned to others when she went on vacation, as was routinely done with other employees, but rather, allowing Patterson's work to accumulate during her absence; assigning her menial, non-clerical tasks such as sweeping and dusting, while such tasks were not assigned to other similarly situated employees; being openly critical of Patterson's work in staff meetings, and that of one other black employee, while white employees were told of their shortcomings privately; telling Patterson that it was known that "blacks are known to work slower than whites, by nature" or, saying in one instance, "some animals [are] faster than other animals"; repeatedly suggesting that a white would be able to perform Patterson's job better than she could; unequal work assignments between Patterson and other similarly situated white employees, with Patterson receiving more work than others; having her work scrutinized more closely and criticized more severely than white employees; despite her desire to "move up and advance," being offered no training for higher jobs during her ten years at the credit union, while white employees were offered training, including those at the same level, but with less seniority (such employees were later promoted); not being informed of job openings, nor interviewed for them, while less senior whites were informed of the positions and hired; and when another manager recommended to Patterson's supervisor a different black to fill a position as a data processor, the supervisor said that he did not "need any more problems around here," and would "search for additional people who are not black."

When Patterson complained about her workload, she was given no help, and in fact was given more work and told she always had the option of quitting. Patterson was laid off after ten years with MCU. She brought suit under 42 U.S.C. section 1981, alleging harassment, failure to promote and discharge because of her race.

None of the racially harassing conduct which McLean engaged in involved the section 1981 prohibition against refusing to make a contract with Patterson or impairing Patterson's ability to enforce her existing contract rights with McLean. It is clear that Patterson is attacking conditions of employment which came into existence after she formed the contract to work for McLean. Since section 1981 only prohibits the interference with the making or enforcement of contracts because of race, performance of the contract is not actionable under section 1981.

Section 1981's language is specifically limited to making and enforcing contracts. To permit race discrimination cases involving post-formation actions would also undermine the de-

tailed and well-crafted procedures for conciliation and resolution of Title VII claims. While section 1981 has no administrative procedure for review or conciliation of claims, Title VII has an elaborate system which is designed to investigate claims and work toward resolution of them by conciliation rather than litigation. This includes Title VII's limiting recovery to backpay, while section 1981 permits plenary compensatory and punitive damages in appropriate cases. Neither party would be likely to conciliate if there is the possibility of the employee recovering the greater damages permitted by section 1981. There is some overlap between Title VII and section 1981, and when conduct is covered by both, the detailed procedures of Title VII are rendered a dead letter, as the plaintiff is free to pursue a claim by bringing suit under section 1981 without resort to those statutory prerequisites.

Regarding Patterson's failure to promote claim, this is somewhat different. Whether a racially discriminatory failure to promote claim is cognizable under section 1981 depends upon whether the nature of the change in positions is such that it involved the opportunity to enter into a new contract with the employer. If so, then the employer's refusal to enter the new contract is actionable under section 1981. AFFIRMED in part, VACATED in part, and REMANDED.

Case Questions

1. Do you think justice was served in this case? Explain. Why do you think Patterson waited so long to sue?

2. If you had been the manager when Patterson was initially interviewed, would you have made the statement about whites not accepting her? Why or why not?

3. When looking at the list of items Patterson alleged McLean engaged in, do any seem appropriate? Why do you think it was done or permitted?

The Civil Rights Act of 1991 contained provisions specifically addressed to *McLean.* The act overturned *McLean*'s holding that section 1981 does not permit actions for racial discrimination during the performance of the contract, but only in making or enforcing the contract. Note that the limitation on damages the Court spoke of as part of Title VII's administrative scheme no longer applies. The Civil Rights Act of 1991 now permits recovery of compensatory and punitive damages. How do you think this squares with the Court's statement that "Neither party would be likely to conciliate if there is the possibility of the employee recovering the greater damages permitted by section 1981"?

Other Reconstruction Civil Rights Acts

Section 1983. Civil Action for Deprivation of Rights

Every person who, under color of any statute, ordinance, regulation, custom, or usage, of any State or Territory, subjects, or causes to be subjected, any citizen of the United States or other person within the jurisdiction thereof to the deprivation of any rights, privileges, or immunities secured by the Constitution and laws, shall be liable to the party injured in an action at law, suit in equity, or other proper proceeding for redress.

The Civil Rights Act of 1871, codified as 42 U.S.C. section 1983, protects citizens from deprivation of their legal and constitutional rights, privileges, and immunities, **under color of state law.** That is, someone acting on behalf of the state cannot deprive people of their rights. An example would be the police officers who were videotaped beating Rodney King during his arrest in Los Angeles in 1991. While performing their duties as government employees, they were alleged to have deprived King of his rights by using excessive force and thus depriving him of his rights as if it were a legitimate part of their duties.

Under color of state law Government employee is illegally discriminating against another as if it is a legitimate part of his or her duties.

In the employment area, section 1983 cases arise when, for instance, a city fire department or municipal police department discriminates against an employee on the basis of race, gender, or one of the other bases protected under federal or state law.

Neither the 14th Amendment nor section 1983 may be used for discrimination by private employers. They both redress actions by government personnel. The government may not be sued without its permission because of the 11th Amendment to the Constitution, so, the action is brought against the government official in his or her individual and official capacity.

Section 1985. Conspiracy to Interfere with Civil Rights—Preventing Officer from Performing Duties

Depriving persons of rights or privileges

(3) If two or more persons in any State or Territory conspire or go in disguise on the highway or on the premises of another, for the purpose of depriving, either directly or indirectly, any person or class of persons of the equal protection of the laws, or of equal privileges and immunities under the laws; in any case of conspiracy set forth in this section, if one or more persons engaged therein do, or cause to be done, any act in furtherance of the object of such conspiracy, whereby another is injured in his person or property, or deprived of having and exercising any rights or privileges of a citizen of the

Management Tips

Race discrimination can seem elusive. Many of us tend to think it no longer exists, or that others feel as neutral as we do about race. That is not necessarily so. Because a manager can be unaware of the presence of race discrimination, he or she can miss it until litigation arises. Think back to the *Patterson* case. Remember that many of the things Patterson alleged as part of a discriminatory pattern of treatment toward her would have been insignificant in and of themselves. However, taken together, the list becomes quite significant. Be aware of what goes on in the workplace and "don't miss the forest for the trees." The following tips may prove useful.

- Believe that race discrimination occurs and be willing to acknowledge it when it is alleged.
- Make sure that there is a top-down message that the workplace will not tolerate race discrimination in any form.
- Don't shy away from discussing race when the issue arises.
- Provide a positive, nonthreatening, constructive forum for the discussion of racial issues. Don't let the only time a discussion of race arises be in the midst of an allegation of racial discrimination.
- Be aware of cultural differences which may be based, at least in part, on race, when doing things as simple as deciding how to celebrate special events in the workplace. Be inclusive regarding what music will be played, what food will be served, what recreation will be offered, what clothes will be worn, and other factors. These all form a part of the atmosphere in which an employee must work and experience workplace leisure. If people do not see themselves reflected in the workplace culture, they will not feel a part of it. If they feel isolated, they are more likely to experience other factors leading to discrimination and ultimately to litigation. If this seems like a small matter to you, imagine yourself showing up at a gathering at work, and the music, decorations, food, and clothing were all Japanese. There's sushi to eat, saki to drink, and everyone is speaking Japanese. You'd probably feel a bit out of your element and would quickly realize how those seemingly simple things make a big impact.
- When an employee reports discrimination based on race, don't let the first move be to tell the employee he or she must be mistaken. Investigate it as any other matter would be investigated.
- Be willing to treat the matter as a misunderstanding if it is clear that is what has taken place. There is no use in making a federal case (literally) out of a matter that could be handled much more simply. Do not, however, underplay the significance of what occurred.
- Offer support groups if there is an expressed need.
- Offer training in racial awareness and sensitivity.
- Constantly monitor workplace hiring, termination, training, promotion, raises, and discipline to ensure that they are fair and even-handed. If there are differences in treatment among races, be sure they are legally justifiable and explainable.

United States, the party so injured or deprived may have an action for the recovery of damages, occasioned by such injury or deprivation, against any one or more of the conspirators.

Section 42 U.S.C., section 1985, known as the Ku Klux Klan Act, addresses conspiracies to interfere with or deprive the civil rights of others. For instance, it was used to convict the murderers of three student civil rights activists in Mississippi in 1964 who were killed for trying to help blacks register to vote. It is not used as much as the other post–Civil War statutes for employment because of the types of facts needed are so specific and, for the most part, we've moved away from such acts. Title VII is used more than all of them. It is only under Title VII that an employee can file a charge with the EEOC, its enforcing agency, and have the case handled free of charge. The other cases must be brought by the employee suing the employer in court—many times a formidable task when the employee has often been discharged from employment and may have no funds to pursue litigation.

Unlike actions under Title VII, cases brought under the Reconstruction era statutes have no administrative structure to file complaints and have them addressed in an agency proceeding. These cases must be brought by the employees on their own. They are not used as much as Title VII, but they are viable options where appropriate.

Employees can also sue under the state or federal constitution for a denial of equal protection or under state tort laws for defamation, intentional infliction of emotional distress, assault, or any other tort the facts support.

An employer who must remedy racial discrimination may not avoid doing so because of the possibility of a "reverse discrimination" suit by employees alleging they were adversely affected. If an employer institutes a judicially imposed or voluntary affirmative action plan, which can withstand judicial scrutiny for the reasons set forth in the affirmative action chapter, the employer will not be liable to employees for "reverse discrimination."

Summary

- Title VII prohibits discrimination on the basis of race.
- The employer must ensure that every employee has an equal opportunity for employment and advancement in the workplace, regardless of race.
- Employers must be vigilant to guard against the more stubborn, subtle manifestations of race discrimination.
- Racial discrimination may be by way of disparate treatment or disparate impact.
- Disparate treatment may be shown by direct or indirect evidence of discrimination.
- Disparate impact may be more difficult to discern, so employers need to closely scrutinize workplace policies and procedures to prevent unintended disparate impact leading to liability.
- Race can never be a bona fide occupational qualification.

Chapter-End Questions

1. Plaintiff, a black firefighter, brings an action against the fire department for racial discrimination. The employee alleges that each time he is transferred from one fire station to another, he must take his bed with him, on orders of the fire chief. The chief defends on the basis that it is a legitimate decision, because white firefighters would not want to sleep in the same bed in which a black firefighter slept. Who wins and why?

2. A white college receptionist is fired when it is found that she told a black college applicant that the applications for admissions are distinguished by race by the notation of a small *RH* in the corner of black applicants' applications. "RH," she says, is her supervisor's term for "raisin heads," which he calls blacks. Is the employee entitled to reinstatement?

3. It is discovered that, at a health club, the owner has been putting a notation on the application of black membership applicants that reads "DNWAM," which means "do not want as member." In addition, the black membership applicants are charged higher rates for the club fee and are much less likely to be financed as other nonblack applicants. Can the black applicants bring a successful action under Title VII?

4. A black female employee is told that she cannot come to work with her hair in decorative braids traditionally worn in Africa, and if she continues to do so, she will be terminated. Does the employee have a claim under Title VII?

5. Bennie's Restaurant chain routinely hires blacks, but it only assigns them to the lower-paying jobs as kitchen help, rather than as higher-paid servers, salad bar helpers, or managers. Bennie's says it does not discriminate because it has many black employees. If suit is brought by the black employees, who will likely win?

6. A prominent black professor takes an unpaid leave of absence to protest the fact that his extremely prominent university has failed to ever hire any black females in tenure-track (regular, permanent) positions on the faculty. When he does not return after two years, he is terminated. He sues the university, alleging constructive discharge, in that the situation created by the school's policies made it an unlivable situation for him. Is this an effective argument? Explain.

7. Ken recruits applicants for several prominent companies. Often when the companies call for Ken's services, they strongly hint that they do not wish to hire blacks, so Ken never places blacks with those companies. Is Ken liable for illegal discrimination?

8. Brie owns a six-person beauty salon. One day a black customer comes in and wants a wash and set. Brie has a cold and does not wish to give it to the customer, so she tells her that Jerre will take care of her. Jerre starts protesting, in front of the other customers, that she is not going to do the customer's hair, because "she doesn't do black hair" and "she [Jerre] is from New Hampshire." The customer, totally humiliated and crying, leaves the premises. Is Brie liable under Title VII?

9. Jill, the owner of a construction business, says her construction crew will not work if she hires black crew members, so Jill does not do so. Is this a defense to a Title VII action?

10. When Cynthia tries out for a job as a cheerleader for a large southern school, she is not chosen. Cynthia thinks it is because she is an Asian-American, even though she was born in Pittsburgh of third-generation Asian-Americans. If Cynthia proves this is true, does she have a cause of action under Title VII?

7 GENDER DISCRIMINATION

Chapter Outline

S C E N A R I O S

S C E N A R I O   1

A discount department store has a policy requiring that all male clerks be attired in coats and ties and all female clerks wear over their clothing a smock provided by the store, with the store's logo on the front. A female clerk complains to her supervisor that making her wear a smock is illegal gender discrimination. Is it? Why or why not?

S C E N A R I O   2

A male applies for a position as a server for a restaurant in his hometown. The restaurant is part of a well-known regional chain named for an animal whose name is a colloquial term for a part of the female anatomy. Despite several years of experience as a server for comparable establishments the male is turned down for the position, which remains vacant. The applicant is instead offered a position as a kitchen helper. The applicant notices that all servers are female and most are blonde. All servers are required to wear very tight and very short shorts, with T-shirts with the restaurant logo on the front, tied in a knot below their, usually ample, breasts. All kitchen help and cooks are male. The applicant feels he has been unlawfully discriminated against because he is a male. Do you agree? Why or why not?

S C E N A R I O   3

An applicant for a position of secretary informs the employer that she is pregnant. The employer accepts her application but never seriously considers her for the position because she is pregnant. Is this employment discrimination?

Statutory Basis

It shall be an unlawful employment practice for an employer—

(1) to fail or refuse to hire or to discharge any individual, or otherwise to discriminate against any individual with respect to his compensation, terms, conditions, or privileges of employment, because of such individual's . . . sex [gender] . . . 42 U.S.C. 2000e-2 (a).

(1) No employer . . . shall discriminate between employees on the basis of sex by paying wages to employees . . . at a rate less than the rate at which he pays wages to employees of the opposite sex . . . for equal work on jobs the performance of which requires equal skill, effort, and responsibility, and which are performed under similar working conditions, except where such payment is made pursuant to (i) a seniority system; (ii) a merit system; (iii) a system which measures earnings by quantity or quality of production; or (iv) a differential based on any other factor other than sex . . . Equal Pay Act, 29 U.S.C.A. §206(d).

(k) The term "because of sex" or "on the basis of sex" includes, but is not limited to, because of or on the basis of pregnancy, childbirth, or related medical conditions; and women affected by pregnancy, childbirth, or related medical conditions shall be treated the same for all employment-related purposes, including receipt of benefits under fringe benefit programs, as other persons not so affected but similar in their ability or inability to work . . . Pregnancy Discrimination Act, 42 U.S.C. §2000e.

Note: Reread the Preface regarding the use of gender terminology before reading this chapter.

Does It Really Exist?

It can be hard to recognize gender discrimination when it plays itself out in the workplace. A woman is required by her employer to wear two-inch heels to work. Doing so causes her to develop bunions on her feet, which can only be removed by surgery. After surgery she is ordered by her doctor to wear flat shoes for two months. Her employer refuses to permit her to do so. Left with no alternative, she quits. The employer imposes no such requirement or its attendant problems on male employees. When you realize that the employer's two-inch heels policy cost the woman her job and had she been male, this would not have happened, it becomes more obvious that the policy is discriminatory. Remember the wires of the bird cage.

It is not difficult to discriminate on the basis of gender if one is not sensitive to the issues involved. (See Exhibit 7–9.) Once again, as with race discrimination, vigilance pays off. This chapter will address gender discrimination in general, including pregnancy discrimination, fetal protection policies, and the Family and Medical Leave Act. Sexual harassment, another type of gender discrimination, will be considered in the next chapter. Gender discrimination covers both males and females, but because of the unique nature of the history of gender in this country, it is females who feel the effects of gender discrimination in the workplace more so than men, and most EEOC gender claims are filed by women.

Women are the single largest group of beneficiaries under affirmative action. They seem to be gaining in all facets of life. Who, you think to yourself, would be dumb enough to discriminate against women these days? It can be hard to believe that gender discrimination still exists when you go to school and work with so many people of both genders; you don't feel like *you* view gender as an issue, and it just seems like everything is okay. But even the professionals can be caught off guard. In February 1999, the media reported that a gender discrimination charge that started with eight female stockbrokers at Merrill Lynch alleging various forms of gender inequality, particularly economic discrimination, had ballooned to 900 women and was still growing. "It's been a flood. I've been stunned. We were expecting 200–300 claims, but the calls are still coming in," said one of the lawyers representing the women.

What makes us think gender discrimination is still alive and well? Let's take a look. Nearly half the workforce is female. At the same time women are nearing the halfway mark in the workforce; they represent two-thirds of all poor adults. Nearly 80 percent of female employees work in traditional "female" jobs—as secretaries, administrative support workers, and salesclerks. Statistics show that 16 percent of the female workforce is employed as professionals, but 10 percent of them are actually nurses or K-12 teachers—traditionally "pink collar" female strongholds. Women in such jobs earn about $3,446 less a year than women who work in male-dominated fields. Even the men who work in these female-dominated jobs make less. They earn about $6,259 less per year than their male counterparts in male-dominated occupations. On average, women working full time earn 74 cents for every dollar men earn, $148 less each week. For black females the gap is even wider: they earn only 64 cents for each dollar men earn, or $210 less each week. If the gender wage gap closed today, the average woman would earn $4,229 more each year, according to a recent study by the AFL–CIO and the Institute for Women's Policy Research.

The 1991 Civil Rights Act called for the establishment of a Glass Ceiling Commission to investigate the barriers to female and minority advancement in the workplace and suggest ways to combat the situation. In March 1995, the US Department of Labor released a study by the bipartisan commission. Findings were based on information obtained from independent studies, existing research, public hearings, and focus groups. The commission reported that while women have gained entry into the workforce in substantial numbers, once there they face all but invisible barriers to promotion into top ranks. "Glass ceilings" prevent them from moving up higher in the workplace. "Glass walls" prevent them from moving laterally into areas that lead to higher advancement. Research indicates that many professional women hold jobs in such areas as public relations, human resources management, and law—areas that are not prone to provide the experience management seeks when it determines promotions to higher level positions.

Segregation by both race and gender among executives and management ranks is widespread. A survey of top managers in *Fortune* 1000 industrial and *Fortune* 500 service firms found that 97 percent are white males. As part of their findings, a survey by Korn/Ferry International found 3 to 5 percent of top managers are women. Of those, 95 percent are white, non-Hispanic. Further, women and minorities are trapped in low-wage, low-prestige and dead-end jobs, the commission said.

It is therefore not difficult to see why, in a *New York Times* poll of women about "the most important problem facing women today," job discrimination won overwhelmingly. Despite the gains made in the workplace, "the proportion of women complaining of unequal employment opportunities jumped more than 10 points from the 1970s, and the number of women complaining of unequal barriers to job advancement climbed even higher." Eighty to 95 percent of women said they suffered from job discrimination and unequal pay.

Our country, like many others, has a history in which women's contributions to the workplace have historically been precluded, denied, or undervalued. Prior to the 1964 Civil Rights Act, it was common for states to have laws that limited or prohibited women from working at certain jobs under the theory that such laws were for the protection of women. Unfortunately, those jobs also tended to have higher wages. The effect was to prevent women from entering into, progressing within, or receiving higher wages in the workplace. In *Muller v. Oregon,*[1] which upheld protective

---

[1] 208 US 412 (1908).

EXHIBIT 7–1

Dear Abby: As I begin my second year of medical school, I need some advice on how to respond to those ignorant people who assume that, since I am female, I am studying to be a nurse. Men and women alike are guilty of this.

Please don't get me wrong, I have just as much respect for nurses—they work as hard as some physicians, but women are seldom given the credit they deserve. I once heard this statement: "Oh, so you're in medical school? My sister is a nurse, too!"

I cannot tell you how angry this makes me. Many of my female classmates also feel this way. Do you have a response that expresses our feelings without offending the speaker?—Ms. Future Doctor in L.A.

Dear Future Doctor: Anyone who is confused about the role of a student in medical school should be told that future physicians are trained in medical schools, and future nurses are trained in nursing schools.

Dear Abby: After reading the letter from "Ms. Future Doctor," I felt the need to write and give another view on career sexual stereotypes.

I am 27, a registered nurse for four years, and I am a MALE. I am frequently asked, "When will you become a doctor?" Or, "You're doing this just to put yourself through medical school, right?" Also, "What's the matter, couldn't you get into medical school?"

When I first started my schooling to become a nurse, I considered medical school, but the further I got into nursing, the more I enjoyed being a nurse. I enjoy comforting a patient in pain, teaching my patients about their diseases, and holding the hand of someone who is frightened and hurting. These feelings are experienced by every nurse, and being male did not exclude me from doing them. (Most doctors are too busy.) I still work hard being a competent and compassionate nurse.

More males are choosing nursing as a career, and we need to shed our preconceived notions about who nurses are and what they look like.—Mr. Nurse in Tampa

legislation for women and justified them being in a class of their own for employment purposes, the US Supreme Court stated that a woman must "rest upon and look to her brother for protection . . . to protect her from the greed as well as the passions of man." This is precisely the view our laws took until the Civil Rights Act of 1964.

After women came into the workplace in unprecedented numbers out of necessity during World War II and performed traditional male jobs admirably, it became more difficult to maintain the validity of such arguments. This type of protective legislation was specifically outlawed by Title VII, and the glass ceiling and walls notwithstanding, women have made tremendous strides in the workplace over the past 30-odd years. In evaluating those strides, keep in mind that women were starting from scratch since there was little or nothing to prevent workplace discrimination, so gaining entry into the workplace and the statistics reflected by that should, of course, be high.

Despite the fact that many of the strides made by women were made with the help of male judges, employers, legislators, and others, much of the cause of the figures is attitudinal. Workplace policies generally reflect attitudes of management. A 1990 national poll of chief executives at *Fortune* 1000 companies, showed more than 80 percent acknowledged that discrimination impedes female employees' progress, yet less than 1 percent regarded *remedying* gender discrimination as a goal that their personnel departments should pursue. In fact, when the companies' human resources officers were asked to rate their departments' priorities, women's advancement ranked last.

Gender was inserted into the civil rights bill at the last moment by Judge Howard Smith, a southern legislator and civil rights foe who was confident that, if gender discrimination was included in the bill, then the bill legislating racial equality would surely be defeated. He was wrong. However, because of the ploy, there was little legislative debate on the gender category, so there is little to guide the courts in interpreting what Congress intended by prohibiting gender discrimination. To date, it has been determined that gender discrimination also includes discrimination due to pregnancy and sexual harassment, but not because of affinity orientation or being transsexual.

The goal of a manager, supervisor, human resources employee, or business owner is to have workplace policies that maximize the potential for every employee to contribute to the productivity and growth of the workplace, while minimizing or eliminating irrelevant, inefficient, and nonproductive policies that prevent them from doing so. The underlying consideration to keep in mind when developing, enforcing, or analyzing policies is that, no matter what we may have been taught about gender by cultural or societal mores, gender alone is considered by the law as irrelevant to one's ability to perform a job. By law, it is the person's ability to perform, not his or her gender, that must be the basis of workplace decisions. (See Exhibits 7–1, 7–3.) As we shall see, there may be very limited exceptions to this rule if a BFOQ exists. It is not only the law, but it is in the best interest of any employer who is serious about maximizing production, efficiency, and profits to recognize that gender discrimination, whether subtle or overt, is just plain bad business. After all, workplace turnover, morale and defending against lawsuits cost the employer money, time, and energy better spent elsewhere. (See Exhibit 7–6.)

The aim of this chapter is to provide information about obvious gender discrimination and what factors must be considered in making determinations about the policies in "gray areas." This chapter provides the tools to use when developing, applying, or analyzing policies that may result in gender discrimination claims.

Gender Discrimination in General

Title VII and state fair-employment practice laws regarding gender cover the full scope of the employment relationship. Unless it is a BFOQ, gender may not be the basis of any decision related to employment. This includes:

• *Advertising* for available positions and specifying a particular gender as being preferred (see Exhibit 7–2).

EXHIBIT 7–2   Pre-Title VII Newspaper Want Ads for Females

The classified ad below is typical of those found in newspapers in the United States before Title VII was passed in 1964. For publication purposes, all names and phone numbers have been omitted. Title VII made it illegal to advertise for jobs based on gender this way.

FEMALE EMPLOYMENT	**A REFRESHING CHANGE**
Female Help Wanted 23	FROM your household chores! Use those old talents of yours and become a part-time secretary. You can earn that extra money you have been needing by working when you want. XXX has temporary positions open in all locations in town and you can choose what and where you want. TOP HOURLY RATES…NO FEE
ATTRACTIVE, NEAT APPEARING, RELIABLE YOUNG LADIES FOR permanent employment as food waitresses. Interesting work in beautiful surroundings. Good salary plus tips. UNIFORMS FURNISHED. Vacation with pay. Age 21-35 years. For interview appointment phone…	**Opening Soon…WAITRESSES…NO EXPERIENCE NECESSARY** Will train neat, trim, and alert applicants to be coffee house and cocktail waitresses. Apply at once.
SETTLED white woman who needs home to live in.	**CLERK FOR HOTEL** CLERK for medium-size, unusually nice motor hotel. 6-day wk. Hours 3-11. Experience not necessary. Must be mature, neat, and refined. Call…
LADY to run used furniture store on…	
GIRL FRIDAY If you are a qualified executive secretary, dependable, and would like a solid connection with a growing corporation, write me your qualifications in confidence…	

EXHIBIT 7–3   Gender Myths

Due to the particular historical development of gender in our country, there are many myths about gender that affect how those of a given gender are perceived. These myths impact how we view employees of a given gender in the workplace. See if any are familiar.

- Women are better suited to repetitive, fine motor skill tasks.
- Women are too unstable to handle jobs with a great deal of responsibility or high pressure.
- Men are better in the workplace because they are more aggressive.
- Men do not do well at jobs requiring nurturing skills, such as day care, nursing, elder care, and the like.
- When women marry they will get pregnant and leave their jobs.
- When women are criticized at work, they will become angry or cry.
- A married woman's income is only extra family income.

EXHIBIT 7–4

An *Esquire* magazine poll asked men: "If you received $1.00 for every sexist thought you had in the past year, how much richer would you be today? The median answer was $139.50.

Parade Magazine, December 1991, p. 5.

• Asking questions on an *application* that are only asked of one gender. For example, for background-check purposes asking the applicant's maiden name, rather than simply asking all applicants if there is another name they may have used.

• Asking questions in an *interview* that are only asked of one gender. For example, asking female interviewees if they have proper day care arrangements for their children and not asking male interviewees who also have children. Or asking

EXHIBIT 7–5   On the Lighter Side

Women are often accused of being humorless when it comes to gender issues. While the issue of gender discrimination is far from funny, it doesn't mean we can't laugh at ourselves. To wit, the following e-mail:

Is your computer a he or a she?

A college professor who was previously a sailor, was very aware that ships are addressed as "she" and "her." He often wondered [by] what gender computers should be addressed.

To answer that question, he set up two groups of computer experts. The first was composed of women, and the second of men. Each group was asked to recommend whether computers should be referred to in the feminine gender, or the masculine gender. They were asked to give four reasons for their recommendations.

The group of women reported that the computers should be referred to in the masculine gender because:

1. In order to get their attention, you have to turn them on.
2. They have a lot of data, but they are still clueless.
3. They are supposed to help you solve problems, but half the time they are the problem.
4. As soon as you commit to one, you realize that if you had waited a little longer, you could have had a better model.

The men, on the other hand, concluded that computers should be referred to in the feminine gender because:

1. No one but the Creator understands their internal logic.
2. The native language they use to communicate with other computers is incomprehensible to everyone else.
3. Even your smallest mistakes are stored in long-term memory for later retrieval.
4. As soon as you make a commitment to one, you find yourself spending half your paycheck on accessories for it.

Thanks to Dr. Andy Walters, Hobart and William Smith Colleges. Used with permission.

female applicants about reproductive plans and not asking males. (Yes, people actually do such things.)

• *Requiring one gender to work different hours or job positions* for reasons not related to their ability or availability for the job. For example, not permitting women to work at night.

• *Disciplining* one gender for an act for which the other gender is not disciplined. For example, chastising a female employee who is late for work because of reasons related to her children, while not similarly chastising a male employee who is late because of a sick dog.

• Providing or not providing *training* for one gender, while doing so for another. For example, requiring all female employees to be trained on word processing equipment, no matter what position they hold in the company, while not requiring that males undergo the same training. Or, alternatively, providing training opportunities for career advancement to male employees and not to female employees who equally qualify for the training.

• Establishing *seniority systems* specifically designed to give greater seniority to one gender over another. For example, instituting a new seniority system that bases seniority on how long an employee has been working for the employer, rather than how long the employee has been working in a particular department with the intent that, if the employer ever needs to lay off employees for economic reasons, more males will be able to retain their positions because females have been in the workplace a shorter time and thus have less seniority.

• *Paying* employees different wages based on gender, though the job one employee performs is the same or substantially the same as another. This may also violate the Equal Pay Act, which prohibits discrimination in compensation on the basis of gender.

• Providing different *benefits* for one gender than for another. For example, providing spouses of male employees with coverage for short-term disabilities including pregnancy, while not providing female employees with similar coverage for short-term disabilities for their spouses.

• Subjecting one gender to different *terms or conditions of employment.* For example, requiring female associates in an accounting firm to dress, talk, or act "feminine," when no comparable requirement is imposed on males aspiring to partnership.

• *Terminating* the employment of an employee of one gender for reasons that would not serve as the basis for termination for an employee of the other gender. For example, terminating a female employee for fighting on the job, when males engaged in similar activity are retained.

Clearly the antidiscrimination provisions are comprehensive. The law is broad enough to cover virtually every decision or policy that could possibly be made in the workplace. The scope of antidiscrimination laws is intentionally undefined, so that decisions can be made on a case-by-case basis. Some of the examples above are not illegal *per se.* Rather, they elicit gender or gender-related information that can form

EXHIBIT 7–6

Jury Tells NBA to Pay Female Referee $7.85 Million

Read what happened when a female rose to number two on the list of those in line to officiate
in the NBA, only to be repeatedly passed over.

For years, Sandra Ortiz-Del Valle had dreamed of becoming a referee in the National Basketball
Association, but she never got any closer than officiating a few preseason games for the New
Jersey Nets. Convinced that she was a victim of sex discrimination, she sued the league.

Thursday, a federal jury in Manhattan agreed, finding that the league had denied her a job
because she was a woman and awarding her $7.85 million in damages.

The verdict, which includes an award of $7 million in punitive damages, marks the first time
the league has lost a discrimination case in court, said one of its lawyers.

Ortiz-Del Valle, 46, who teaches physical education and coaches basketball at Humanities High
School in New York City, sobbed as the verdict was announced. "The best ref is what I
wanted to be," she said afterward. "I didn't go into it just because I wanted to break the doors
down."

During the six-day trial, the league's lawyers strongly disputed the discrimination allegations,
and called as witnesses Violet Palmer and Dee Kanter, who made history this season when
they became the first women to officiate regular-season games in the NBA or any other major
professional team sport.

Palmer and Kanter both testified that they had been hired on merit and that they did not believe
the league discriminated in hiring.

NBA attorney Mishkin called the verdict "a bizarre sort of result."

"Here is a finding that the NBA discriminates against women in the hiring of officials, and we
are the only league that has them," he said. But Ortiz-Del Valle's lawyers introduced
documents that showed that the NBA had given her high marks as a referee.

One such document, a scouting report to Darell Garretson, the chief of the league's officiating
staff, from Aaron C. Wade, another league official, described Ortiz-Del Valle as being in good
physical condition, having "excellent basketball officiating skills" and being "very
knowledgeable about the rules."

"I would not hesitate to recommend that at sometime in the near future she be considered to
enter our training program," Wade wrote.

Ortiz-Del Valle's lawyers asserted that the league gave her varying reasons for denying her a
job, which they called a pretext for discrimination. "The NBA has no formal admission
process for potential referees," said one of her lawyers, "which means, if the man at the top
wants to discriminate against women, it's very easy."

The league maintained that Ortiz-Del Valle was treated no differently than male candidates and
that she was not hired because she failed to upgrade the level of competition in her officiating
schedule despite being asked to and she was out of shape after 1993.

Ortiz Del-Valle was born in Harlem, graduated from Bronx High School of Science and City
College of New York, where she played forward and center on the women's basketball team.

She said that she had all the qualifications to be an NBA referee, including officiating in top
men's amateur and professional basketball leagues for 17 years. In fact, in 1991, she worked a
U.S. Basketball League game and became the first woman in history to officiate a men's
professional basketball game. The uniform and whistle she used in the game are on exhibit at
the Naismith Memorial Basketball Hall of Fame in Springfield, Mass.

She said she also officiated in men's leagues on the Jersey Shore, in Westchester County and in
the New York Pro-Am league.

But NBA officials kept setting up new obstacles to hiring her, she said, questioning her

EXHIBIT 7–6　Concluded

qualifications and the level of competition in the games she refereed. She filed a complaint in 1995 and sued the league the next year.

"I got tired of doing everything they asked, and realized that other people I had trained were getting a start," she said, referring to men who had officiated with her and were hired by the league. "It was like they kept moving the basket," she said.

Note: A judge later reduced the jury award to $350,000: $250,000 in punitive damages, $79,926 in lost wages, and $20,000 for emotional distress.

the basis of illegal gender-based employment decisions—or at least make it appear as if that is the case.

The law takes a case-by-case approach to gender discrimination, so it is imperative to know what factors will be considered in analyzing whether gender discrimination has occurred. To the extent that these factors are considered when developing or implementing policies, it is less likely that illegal considerations or criteria will be used in making workplace decisions and policies. (See Exhibit 7–7.)

Recognizing Gender Discrimination

When analyzing employment policies or practices for gender discrimination, first check to see if it is obviously so. See if the policy excludes members of a particular gender from the workplace or some workplace benefit. An example is a policy that recently appeared in a newspaper story on local restaurants. One owner said that he did not hire males as servers because he thought females were more pleasant and

EXHIBIT 7–7

We often discriminate against others without even realizing it. Since only those things prohibited by law are considered illegal, not all discrimination is actionable. Look at the items below.

- Very attractive men and women earn at least 5% more per hour than people with average looks.
- Plain women earn an average of 5% less than women with average looks.
- Plain men earn 10% less than average men.
- Most employers pay overweight women 20% less per hour than women of average weight.
- Overweight males earn 26% more than underweight co-workers.
- Of men with virtually identical résumés, the taller man will be hired 72% of the time.
- Men who are 6'2" or taller receive starting salaries 12% greater than men under 6 feet.

better at serving customers. As the following case demonstrates, employers such as the restaurant owner, unaware of how their policies may have negative legal repercussions, may engage in obvious gender discrimination.

MILLIGAN-JENSEN V. MICHIGAN TECHNOLOGICAL UNIV.
767 F. Supp. 1403 (WD Mich., N. Div. 1991)

A female public safety officer (PSO) at Michigan Technological University brings suit for gender discrimination after being treated differently because of her gender. The court found the employer liable.

Hillman, J.

In this case there was a substantial amount of direct evidence that defendant took plaintiff employee's gender into account in her employment and termination. Employer initially welcomed Milligan-Jensen's application, telling her that the department would be receptive to her application because "their woman" had just quit and "they had to hire a female." Two months later, after Milligan-Jensen updated her application, the employer wrote, "We are interested in interviewing female applicants for the position of PSO."

Milligan-Jensen came to work as a PSO. The employer assigned her a badge number that every female before her had previously had. Initially she was assigned another badge number, but her supervisor, Louis Fredianelli, changed it to the "female" number because he said, whenever he called for her, he got the other person assigned that number because he was used to using the number for the female officer. Fredianelli, who made the decision to terminate the employee, criticized her uniform and dress even though he admitted that she was helpless to change the mandatory clothes, which are designed for men to wear. Further, Fredianelli treated the employee differently from a male co-worker when each of them committed the same infraction of the rules of not wearing a hat.

Milligan-Jensen's evaluations were mostly marginal, even though a comparable employee received better ratings. When another officer announced his retirement and Milligan-Jensen asked Fredianelli for his shift, she was asked by Fredianelli, who became angry, what was wrong with the job that she had. He declared, "You've got the lady's job. Don't you like it?" On the same day Fredianelli wrote two notes which he placed in employee's file. One said that she asked why she has the dayshift job and he told her it was the "female's job." Two weeks after Fredianelli's "lady's job" remark, employee was terminated. When she asked why, she was told it was because she did not complete her progress reports to satisfaction and spent too much time in the office.

Direct evidence of discrimination usually entails a general comment about a minority group in society. The courts infer from such a remark that the defendant had discriminatory animus toward the particular plaintiff in the particular job. Here, no inference is necessary: Fredianelli's "lady's job" remark was directed specifically at plaintiff and directly related to her job. The court can only surmise that someone infected by discriminatory animus would be "mad and upset" by such a question. After making the discriminatory remark, Fredianelli documented it. The remark is direct evidence of Fredianelli's discriminatory state of mind toward plaintiff. The uniform criticism, disparate treatment, and badge episode are also direct evidence that Fredianelli's state of mind was affected by employee's gender.

Because Milligan-Jensen made a showing of intentional discrimination, the burden shifts to the employer to convince the court by a preponderance of the evidence that the decision would have been the same absent consideration of the unlawful factor. This is difficult because more than one motive nearly always occupies a decisionmaker's mind. As a result, when the court finds that a substantial motivating factor of a decision was unlawful, the burden is then placed squarely on the decisionmaker's shoulders to prove that the identical decision would have been made absent the unlawful motive.

Here, a number of factors suggest that Fredianelli's discrimination terminally infected employee's employment as a PSO. From the testimony, it appears that Fredianelli decided that plaintiff was going to be terminated as early as a month before it occurred. At that time, there were already indications of Fredianelli's discriminatory state of mind toward employee. Thus, the increase in critical notes to her file and heightened watch over her job performance indicate that Fredianelli was simply building a file so that he would have justification to terminate her. Further, on the day he made the "lady's job" comment, he put in employee's file a note about her spending too much time in the office. Two weeks later in her termination meeting, he told her she was being fired for this reason.

Thus, Fredianelli's decision to dismiss employee was infected by his desire to retaliate for her complaint about his acts of discrimination. It is clear that Fredianelli was motivated by discriminatory animus and in the end, by a desire to retaliate against employee.

The next question is whether the employer proved by a preponderance of the evidence that the employment decisions concerning employee would have been identical absent the unlawful motivation. This court cannot separate the good from the bad, the times when Fredianelli's mind was infected by discrimination and the times when he treated employee as he would have treated any other employee. Employer bore the burden of persuading the court that gender discrimination did not infect the decision to dismiss employee. Employer failed to carry its burden. Therefore, based on all of the above, the court concludes that employer did in fact discriminate against employee on the basis of gender in violation of Title VII. JUDGMENT for PLAINTIFF.

Case Questions

1. Would you have said some of the things that Fredianelli said to Milligan-Jensen? Which things and why or why not?

2. Do you think the police department intended to discriminate? Explain.

3. How would you have avoided this situation?

Not all cases may be as easy to recognize as gender discrimination when making workplace decisions or policies. (See Exhibit 7–8.) It is easier to realize there is gender discrimination when the policy says "no women hired as guards" than when, as with the case on page 217, there is a policy, neutral on its face, saying all applicants must meet a certain height and weight requirement to be guards, yet most women do not generally meet the requirement.

EXHIBIT 7–8   Illegal or Unfair?

Several courts have wrestled with the issue of what constitutes gender discrimination under Title VII. One issue that has arisen several times is whether it is illegal gender discrimination under Title VII if a female who is having a relationship with a supervisor receives a job or promotion over a qualified male who applies for the position. In *Womack v. Runyon,* 77 FEP Cases 769 (11th Cir. 1998), Paul Womack, having excellent credentials, experience, and training, applied for a carrier supervisor position in Waycross, Georgia. He was unanimously selected as the best qualified candidate by a review board, but O. M. Lee, the newly appointed postmaster of Waycross, instead appointed his (Lee's) paramour, Jeanine Bennett. In rejecting Womack's Title VII claim of gender discrimination, the court held that Title VII did not cover claims of favoritism, saying that such decisions may not be fair, but they are not illegal under Title VII. According to a 1990 EEOC policy guidance, "Title VII does not prohibit . . . preferential treatment based upon consensual romantic relationships. An isolated instance of favoritism toward a paramour . . . may be unfair, but it does not [amount to] discrimination against women or men in violation of Title VII, since both [genders] are disadvantaged for reasons other than their genders."

DOTHARD V. RAWLINSON
433 U.S. 321 (1977)

After her application for employment as an Alabama prison guard was rejected because the applicant, Rawlinson, failed to meet the minimum 120-pound weight, 5'2" height requirement of an Alabama statute, Rawlinson sued. She challenged the statutory height and weight requirements and a regulation establishing gender criteria for assigning prison guards to "contact" positions (those requiring close physical proximity to inmates) as violative of Title VII of the Civil Rights Act of 1964. The Supreme Court found gender discrimination.

Stewart, J.

At the time she applied for a position as a correctional counselor trainee, Rawlinson was a 22-year-old college graduate whose major course of study had been correctional psychology. She was refused employment because she failed to meet the minimum 120-pound weight requirement established by an Alabama statute. The statute stated that the applicant shall not be less than five feet two inches nor more than six feet ten inches in height, shall weigh not less than 120 pounds nor more than 300 pounds. Variances could be granted upon a showing of good cause, but none had ever been applied for by the Board and the Board did not apprise applicants of the waiver possibility. While this suit was pending the Board adopted Administrative Regulation 204 establishing gender criteria for assigning correctional counselors to maximum-security institutions for "contact positions." Rawlinson amended her complaint by adding a challenge to Regulation 204 as violative of Title VII of the Civil Rights Act of 1964 and the Fourteenth Amendment.

Like most correctional facilities in the U.S., Alabama's prisons are segregated on the basis of gender. Inmate living quarters are for the most part large dormitories, with communal showers and toilets that are open to the dorms and hallways. Two of the facilities carry on extensive farming operations, making necessary a large number of strip searches for contraband when prisoners re-enter the prison buildings. A prison guard's primary duty within these institutions is to maintain security and control the inmates by continually supervising and observing their activities.

At the time this litigation was in the district court, women applicants could under Regulation 204 compete equally with men for only about 25% of the correctional counselor jobs available in the Alabama prison system because of the gender and "contact" restrictions. In considering the effect of the minimum height and weight standards on this disparity in rate of hiring between genders, the district court found that when the height and weight restrictions are combined, Alabama's statutory standards would exclude 41.13% of the female population while excluding less than 1% of the male population.

In enacting Title VII, Congress required "the removal of artificial, arbitrary, and unnecessary barriers to employment when the barriers operate invidiously to discriminate on the basis of racial or other impermissible classification." *Griggs v. Duke Power Co.* The District Court found the minimum height and weight requirements constitute the sort of arbitrary barrier to equal employment opportunity that Title VII forbids. Alabama asserts that the district court erred both in finding the standards discriminate against women, and in its refusal to find that, even if they do, these standards are justified as "job related."

This claim does not involve an assertion of purposeful discriminatory motive. It is asserted, rather, that these facially neutral qualification standards work in fact disproportionately to exclude women from eligibility for employment by the Alabama Board of Corrections.

We turn to Alabama's argument that they have rebutted the prima facie case of discrimination by showing that the height and weight requirements are job related. These requirements, they say, have a relationship to strength, a sufficient but unspecified amount of which is essential to effective job performance as a correctional counselor. In the district court, however, they failed to offer evidence of any kind in specific justification of the statutory standards.

If the job-related quality that the Board identifies is bona fide, their purpose could be achieved by adopting and validating a test for applicants that measures strength directly. But nothing in the present record even approaches such a measurement.

The district court was not in error in holding that Title VII of the Civil Rights Act of 1964 prohibits application of the statutory height and weight requirements to Rawlinson and the class she represents. AFFIRMED in part, REVERSED in part, and REMANDED.

Case Questions

1. What purpose did the height and weight requirement serve? Do you think it was made to intentionally discriminate against women?

2. How could management have avoided this outcome?

3. In your view, should women's access to male prisoners be limited as described here? Why or why not?

EXHIBIT 7–9   **Gender-Neutral Language?**

> In November of 1991, attorney Harry McCall, arguing before the US Supreme Court, stated: "I
> would like to remind you gentlemen" of a legal point. Associate Supreme Court Justice
> Sandra Day O'Connor asked, "Would you like to remind me, too?" McCall later referred to
> the Court as "Justice O'Connor and gentlemen." Associate Justice Byron White told McCall,
> "Just 'Justices' would be fine."

Newsweek, November 25, 1991, p. 17.

"Gender-Plus" Discrimination

There are some situations in which the employer's policy may permit the hiring of
women, but not if there are other factors present. For example, no hiring of women
who are pregnant, married, over a certain age, have children under a certain age, or
are unmarried with children. This is **"gender-plus" discrimination.** Of course, the
problem is that such policies are not neutral at all, because males are not subject to
the same limitations. (See Exhibit 7–10.)

"Gender-plus"
discrimination
Employment
discrimination
based on gender
and some other
factor such as
marital status or
children.

    The *Phillips* case below was the first Title VII case to reach the US Supreme
Court and is still widely cited. It is a *per curiam* or summary decision, rather than a
full court opinion, such as the one rendered a short while later in *Griggs v. Duke
Power Co.,* but it provides insight into the considerations the Court will use in deciding gender-plus discrimination cases.

PHILLIPS V. MARTIN MARIETTA CORP.
400 U.S. 542 (1971)

A female applicant was denied employment because of the employer's policy
against hiring women with preschool-aged children. There was no policy against
hiring men with such children. The Supreme Court held the employer's policy violated Title VII.

Per Curiam

Martin Marietta informed Ida Phillips that it was
not accepting job applications from women with
pre-school-age children. As of the time of this action, Martin Marietta employed men with pre-
school-age children. At the time Phillips applied,
70–75% of the applicants for the position she
sought were women; 75–80% of those hired for
the position, assembly trainee, were women,
hence no question of bias against women as such
was presented.

    Section 703(a) of the Civil Rights Act of
1964 requires that persons of like qualifications

be given employment opportunities irrespective of their gender. The Court of Appeals therefore erred in reading this section as permitting one hiring policy for women and another for men—each having pre-school-age children. The existence of such conflicting family obligations, if demonstrably more relevant to job performance for a woman than a man, could arguably be a basis for distinction under 703(3) [BFOQ] of the Act. But that is a matter of evidence tending to show that the condition in question is a BFOQ reasonably necessary to the normal operation of that particular business or enterprise. The record before us, however, is not adequate for resolution of these important issues. VACATED and REMANDED.

Mr. Justice Marshall, concurring.

While I agree that this case must be remanded for a full development of the facts, I cannot agree with the Court's indication that a BFOQ reasonably necessary to the normal operation of Martin Marietta's business could be established by a showing that some women, even the vast majority, with pre-school-age children have family responsibilities that interfere with job performance and that men do not usually have such responsibilities. Certainly, an employer can require that all of his employees, both men and women, meet minimum performance standards, and he can try to insure compliance by requiring parents, both mothers and fathers, to provide for the care of their children so that job performance is not interfered with.

The Court has fallen into the trap of assuming that the Act permits ancient canards about the proper role of women to be the basis for discrimination. Congress, however sought just the opposite result.

Even characterizations of the proper domestic roles of the genders was not to serve as predicates for restricting employment opportunity. The exception for a BFOQ was not intended to swallow that rule.

Case Questions

1. Why do you think the employer instituted the rule discussed here? Does it actually address the employer's concern?

2. Can you think of a better way for management to handle its concerns about preschool parents?

3. Does Justice Marshall's position make sense to you? Why or why not?

The Court evidently took Justice Marshall's concerns seriously, because in the years after *Martin Marietta* it has not permitted BFOQs to be used in the way he warned against. Keep in mind that, while BFOQs are permitted as a lawful means of discriminating based on gender, they are very narrowly construed. The employer is under a heavy duty to show that the gender requirement is reasonably necessary for the employer's business.

Gender Issues

As we have seen, there are many issues included under the umbrella of illegal gender discrimination. Following are some that are more prevalent. Keep in mind that many things we take for granted and dismiss as "that's just the way things are" may be illegal in the workplace.

Exhibit 7–10

Breast-Feeding: A Gender-Plus Issue?

In May of 1999, a federal judge in the southern district of New York (Manhattan) dismissed a gender discrimination and disability suit brought by Alicia Martinez, a cable television producer, alleging that after returning from maternity leave, her employer, MSNBC cable, failed to provide her with a "safe, secure, sanitary and private" spot to pump breast milk during work breaks and harassed her for complaining. *Martinez v. NBC, Inc. and MSNBC,* 98 Civ. 4842 (S.D. N.Y. 1999).

Regarding the ADA claim, Judge Kaplan said it was "preposterous to contend a woman's body is functioning abnormally because she is lactating." As to the Title VII claim, the court said this was not "sex plus" discrimination because "to allow a claim based on sex-plus discrimination here would elevate breast milk pumping—alone—to a protected status," and that could only be done by Congress. It was not plain gender discrimination under Title VII because "The drawing of distinctions among persons of one gender on the basis of criteria that are immaterial to the other, while in given cases perhaps deplorable, is not the sort of behavior covered by Title VII."

Note that an argument similar to the latter was struck down by Congress in enacting the Pregnancy Discrimination Act, where the court determined it was not illegal gender discrimination to treat pregnant employees differently, since only females could become pregnant. Keep an eye on what happens with breast-feeding in the workplace. Some states have already enacted laws providing protection for nursing mothers and many others are considering legislation.

Gender Stereotyping

Much discrimination on the basis of gender is in some way based on **gender stereotypes.** That is, workplace decisions are based on ideas of how a particular gender should act, dress, or what roles they should perform. An employer may terminate a female employee who is too "abrasive," or not hire a female for a job as a welder because it is "men's work." Stereotypes generally have little or nothing to do with an individual employee's qualifications or ability to perform, thus decisions based on stereotypes are prohibited by Title VII. (See Exhibits 7–8 and 7–11.)

As we will see in *Hopkins,* stereotyping frequently leads to actions that form

Gender stereotypes
The assumption that most or all members of a particular gender must act a certain way based on preconceived notions of a few people.

Exhibit 7–11

"Hey, didja hear the one about the blond bimbo?" Well, you won't hear it here. Whether or not jokes playing on stereotypes of women make you laugh, they might affect your judgments of women. About 100 male and female college students who heard sex-stereotyped jokes before watching female lecturers later rated the women in a more stereotyped fashion than did students who heard non-sexist jokes. "This study suggests we should be on guard about (stereotyped humor)," says co-author Christine Weston, Boston University.

USA Today, August 24, 1993, p. D-1.

the basis of unnecessary liability for the employer. It is senseless for employers to allow managers and supervisors who hold such views to cause liability that unnecessarily costs the whole company money.

PRICE WATERHOUSE V. HOPKINS
490 U.S. 228 (1989)

Ann Hopkins, a female associate who was refused admission as a partner in an accounting firm, brought a gender discrimination action against the firm. The US Supreme Court held that the evidence was sufficient to show that illegal gender stereotyping played a part in evaluating Hopkins' candidacy.

Brennan, J.

In a jointly prepared statement supporting her candidacy, the partners in Hopkins' office showcased her successful 2-year effort to secure a $25 million contract with the Department of State, labeling it "an outstanding performance" and one that Hopkins carried out "virtually at the partner level." None of the other partnership candidates had a comparable record in terms of successfully securing major contracts for the partnership.

The partners in Hopkins' office praised her character and her accomplishments, describing her as "an outstanding professional" who had a "deft touch," a "strong character, independence, and integrity." Clients appeared to have agreed with these assessments. Hopkins "had no difficulty dealing with clients and her clients appeared to be very pleased with her work" and she "was generally viewed as a highly competent project leader who worked long hours, pushed vigorously to meet deadlines, and demanded much from the multidisciplinary staffs with which she worked."

Virtually all of the partners' negative comments about Hopkins—even those of partners supporting her—had to do with her "interpersonal skills." Both supporters and opponents of her candidacy indicate she was sometimes "overly aggressive, unduly harsh, difficult to work with, and impatient with staff."

There were clear signs, though, that some of the partners reacted negatively to Hopkins' personality because she was a woman. One partner described her as "macho"; another suggested that she "overcompensated for being a woman"; a third advised her to take "a course at charm school." Several partners criticized her use of profanity; in response, one partner suggested that those partners objected to her swearing only "because it['s] a lady using foul language." Another supporter explained that Hopkins "ha[d] matured from a tough-talking somewhat masculine hard-nosed manager to an authoritative, formidable, but much more appealing lady partner candidate." But it was the man who bore responsibility for explaining to Hopkins the reasons for the Policy Board's decision to place her candidacy on hold who delivered the coup de grace; in order to improve her chances for partnership, Thomas Beyer advised, Hopkins should "walk more femininely, talk more femininely, dress more femininely, wear make-up, have her hair styled, and wear jewelry."

Dr. Susan Fiske, a social psychologist and Associate Professor of Psychology at Carnegie-Mellon University, testified at trial that the partnership selection process at Price Waterhouse was likely influenced by gender stereotyping. Her testimony focused not only on the overtly gender-based comments of partners but also on gender-neutral remarks, made by partners who knew Hopkins only slightly, that were intensely critical of her. One partner, for example, baldly stated that Hopkins was "universally disliked" by staff and another described her as "consistently annoying and irritating"; yet these were people who had had very little contact with Hopkins. According to Fiske, Hopkins's uniqueness (as the only woman in the pool of candidates) and the subjectivity of the evaluations made it likely that sharply critical remarks such as these were the product of gender stereotyping.

An employer who acts on the basis of a belief that a woman cannot be aggressive or that she must not be, has acted on the basis of gender. Although the parties do not overtly dispute this last proposition, the placement by Price Waterhouse of "sex stereotyping" in quotation marks throughout its brief seems to us an insinuation either that such stereotyping was not present in this case or that it lacks legal relevance. We reject both possibilities. A number of the partners' comments showed gender stereotyping at work. As for the legal relevance of gender stereotyping, we are beyond the day when an employer could evaluate employees by assuming or insisting that they matched the stereotype associated with their group, for "[i]n forbidding employers to discriminate against individuals because of their gender, Congress intended to strike at the entire spectrum of disparate treatment of men and women resulting from sex stereotypes." An employer who objects to aggressiveness in women but whose positions require this trait places women in the intolerable and impermissible Catch-22: out of a job if they behave aggressively and out of a job if they don't. Title VII lifts women out of this bind.

Remarks at work that are based on gender stereotypes do not inevitably prove that gender played a part in a particular employment decision. The plaintiff must show that the employer actually relied on her gender in making its decision. In making this showing, stereotyped remarks can certainly be evidence that gender played a part. REVERSED and REMANDED.

Case Questions

1. What were Price Waterhouse's fatal flaws?
2. Does Hopkins' treatment here make good business sense? Explain.
3. How would you avoid the problems in this case?

Do any of the stereotypes below, taken from actual cases, sound familiar? Note that they do not only address gender.

- "Older employees have problems adapting to changes and to new policies."
- One had to be wary around "articulate black men."
- Would not consider "some woman" for the position, questioned plaintiff about future pregnancy plans, and asked whether her husband would object to her "running around the country with men."
- Female employee who spent time talking to other black employees was becoming "the black matriarch" within the company.
- A lesser job position was sufficient for women and that no woman would be named to the higher position.
- If it were his company, he would not hire any black people.
- He was "not going to hire a black leasing agent."

Grooming Codes

The issue of gender stereotypes may be closely linked to that of grooming codes. Courts recognize that employers need to be able to control this aspect of the workplace, and some flexibility is permitted. As *Willingham* demonstrates, Title VII does not prohibit an employer from using gender as a basis for reasonable grooming codes.

HARPER V. BLOCKBUSTER ENTERTAINMENT CORPORATION
139 F. 3d 1385 (11th Cir. 1998)

Male employees sued employer under Title VII and Florida Civil Rights Act, alleging that employer's grooming policy which prohibited men, but not women, from wearing long hair, discriminated against them on the basis of gender. The court held that the grooming policy did not violate Title VII or Florida law.

Carnes, J.

The plaintiffs in this case are four males formerly employed by Blockbuster Entertainment Corp. ("Blockbuster"). They brought this suit against Blockbuster under Title VII and the Florida Civil Rights Act alleging that Blockbuster's grooming policy discriminated against them on the basis of their gender and that they were wrongfully terminated in retaliation for protesting that policy. After the district court granted Blockbuster's motion to dismiss the employees' complaint, the employees appealed. For the reasons discussed below, we affirm the district court's order dismissing employees' complaint.

In May of 1994, Blockbuster implemented a new grooming policy that prohibited men, but not women, from wearing long hair. The employees, all men with long hair, refused to comply with the policy. They protested the policy as discriminatory and communicated their protest to supervisory officials of Blockbuster. Two of the employees were the subject of media stories concerning their protest of the policy. All of the employees were subsequently terminated by Blockbuster because they had refused to cut their

hair and because they had protested the grooming policy.

The employees timely filed a charge with the EEOC. After the EEOC issued right to sue letters, the employees filed a complaint alleging gender discrimination under Title VII. Blockbuster moved to dismiss the complaint. The district court granted the motion, and this appeal followed. We affirm the dismissal.

The employees allege that Blockbuster's grooming policy discriminates on the basis of gender in violation of Title VII. In *Willingham v. Macon Telegraph Pub. Co.,* our predecessor court held that differing hair length standards for men and women do not violate Title VII, a holding which squarely forecloses the employees' discrimination claim. [In *Willingham,* the court stated:

> Willingham argues that the Telegraph discriminates among employees based upon their gender in that female employees may wear their hair any length they choose, while males must limit theirs to a length deemed acceptable by the Telegraph. He therefore asserts that he was denied employ-

ment because of his gender because were he a girl with identical length hair and comparable job qualifications, he (she) would have been employed.

We conclude that the undisputed discrimination practiced by the Macon Telegraph is not based upon gender, but rather upon grooming standards, and thus not a violation of Title VII. We perceive the intent of Congress to have been the guarantee of equal job opportunity for males and females. Providing such opportunity is where the emphasis rightly lies. This is to say that Title VII should lie to reach any device or policy of any employer which serves to deny acquisition and retention of a job or promotion in a job to an individual *because* the individual is either male or female. Equal employment *opportunity* may be secured only when employers are barred from discriminating against employees on the basis of immutable characteristics, such as race and national origin. Similarly, an employer cannot have one hiring policy for men and another for women if the distinction is based on some fundamental right. But a hiring policy that distinguishes on some other ground, such as grooming codes or length of hair, is related more closely to the employer's choice of how to run his business than to equality of employment opportunity. We perceive that a line of distinction must be drawn between distinctions grounded on such fundamental rights as the right to have children as in *Phillips v. Martin Marietta* and those interfering with the manner

in which an employer exercises his judgment as to the way to operate a business. Hair length is not immutable and in the situation of an employer vis-à-vis employee, enjoys no constitutional protection. If the employee objects to the grooming code he has the right to reject it by looking elsewhere for employment or alternatively he may choose to subordinate his preference by accepting the code along with the job.

We adopt the view, therefore, that distinctions in employment practices between men and women on the basis of something other than immutable or protected characteristics do not inhibit employment *opportunity* in violation of 703(a) of Title VII. Congress sought only to give all persons equal access to the job market, not to limit an employer's right to exercise his informed judgment as to how best to run his shop.] AFFIRMED.

Case Questions

1. Do you agree with the court? Why or why not?

2. In your view, how can the court reach its decision simply by saying Title VII only deals with immutable characteristics? Were the discriminatory factors in *Hopkins* immutable (i.e., wear more jewelry, have hair styled, dress more femininely, etc.)? What is the distinction?

3. If you were an employer, what policy would you adopt? Why?

Courts have also upheld grooming codes that required, among other things, male supermarket clerks to wear ties, female employees not to wear pants, a female attorney to "tone down" her "flashy" attire, and male and female flight attendants to keep their weight down. Not permitted were a weight restriction policy applied only to the exclusively female category of flight attendants, but not the category of male directors of passenger service, when both were in-flight employees. Or requiring male employees to wear "normal business attire" and women to wear uniforms, though both performed the same duties. The court found "there is a natural tendency to assume that the uniformed women have a lesser professional status than their male colleagues attired in normal business clothes." This is the basis for opening scenario one, and the reason the female clerk made to wear the smock would have a viable claim for gender discrimination.

A gender-based grooming policy, which subjects one gender to different conditions of employment, would also not be allowed—for instance, where the scant uniform the female lobby attendant was required to wear made her the object of lewd comments and sexual propositions from male entrants. Or where a manager required female employees to wear skirts when the "head honcho" visited, because he "liked to look at legs." It is not a defense for an employer to argue that the employee knew about the grooming code when he or she came into the workplace. If the code is illegal, it is illegal, period. Agreeing to it makes it no less so.

Customer or Employee Preferences

Often an employer differentiates in a work assignment between male and female employees because of the preference of customers, clients, or other employees. Many times the work to which one gender is not privy presents a loss of valuable revenue or a professionally beneficial opportunity for that employee. Such considerations may be formidable in client-driven businesses, such as law, brokerages, accounting, sales, and other professions. If a customer does not wish to have a female audit his or her books, can her accounting firm legally refuse to let her service the client? Is an employer in violation of Title VII if the employer does not permit an employee of a given gender to deal with a customer because the customer does not wish to have a person of that gender do so and the employee is thereby denied valuable work experience or earning potential? What if the male employees don't want a female to work with them?

The answer is yes, the employer is in violation of Title VII and can be held liable to the employee for gender discrimination. Gender-based customer preference is not a legitimate and protected reason to treat otherwise qualified employees differently.

Hooters is an Atlanta-based restaurant chain known for its buffalo wings and scantily clad (very short shorts and T-shirts tied around the middle, revealing a bare midriff), generally well-endowed, female servers. Recently it came to light that Hooters refuses to hire males as servers. The conventional wisdom is that despite Hooters' claims that it is a family restaurant and "Hooters" refers to its owl logo, "Hooters" is a not-so-subtle reference to female breasts, and the servers are as or more important than the food it serves. This is further supported by the servers' outfits, the fact that Hooters is known for its "Hooters' Girls," complete with pin-up calendars and a 10-page Playboy magazine spread in April 1994, and its "more than a mouthful" logo which few believe refers to chicken wings or owls.

Hooters alleges that customers want only female servers. In 1996, Hooters launched a "no to male servers" billboard campaign featuring husky male servers clad in the Hooters' attire. So far, Hooters' serving staff is still female, but litigation is pending.

The Hooters situation is the basis for opening scenario two. If Hooters can show that the gender of the servers is an integral part of its product or service, refusing to hire males is not illegal gender discrimination. Since they had claimed to be a family restaurant, it was difficult to argue also that their marketing ploy is one of delivering sexy, female servers along with its food menu. If they are a family restaurant interested primarily in serving buffalo wings to the public, gender is not a BFOQ and it would be gender discrimination not to hire male servers. They later said they were just a "neighborhood" restaurant, but this would not change this analysis.

This issue of customer preference may cause special problems now that the Civil Rights Act of 1991 applies Title VII to US citizens employed by American-owned or controlled companies doing business outside the United States. An employer in a country whose mores may not permit women to deal professionally with men must still comply with Title VII unless doing so would cause the company to violate the law of the country in which the business is located.

Logistical Considerations

In some workplaces, males and females working together can present logistical challenges. For instance, what is done about female sports reporters going into male sports players' locker rooms or a female firefighter sleeping at a fire station, or when there are no bathrooms at a construction site? It arose in the context of construction workers in the case below. Note how the employer can take little for granted in making workplace decisions, as even the seemingly smallest decisions can be the basis of a time-consuming and expensive lawsuit.

LYNCH V. FREEMAN
817 F.2d 380 (6th Cir. 1987)

A female carpenter's apprentice sued her employer for gender discrimination, alleging the failure to furnish adequate sanitary toilet facilities at her worksite. The court found the unsanitary facilities violated Title VII.

Lively, J.

The portable toilets were dirty, often had no toilet paper or paper that was soiled, and were not equipped with running water or sanitary napkins. In addition, those designated for women had no locks or bolts on the doors and one of them had a hole punched in the side.

To avoid using the toilets, Lynch began holding her urine until she left work. Within three days after starting work she experienced pain and was advised that the practice she had adopted, as well as using contaminated toilet paper, frequently caused bladder infections.

The powerhouse, which had large, clean, fully equipped restrooms, was off limits to construction workers. Lynch testified that some of the men she worked with used them regularly and were not disciplined. In late December 1979 or early January 1980, knowing the restrooms were off limits, Lynch began using the powerhouse restrooms occasionally, after her doctor diagnosed her condition as cystitis, a type of urinary infection. When the infection returned in February, Lynch began using a restroom in the powerhouse regularly and she had no further urinary tract infections. Lynch was eventually fired for insubordination in using the powerhouse toilet.

The lower court found that the toilets were poorly maintained. The cleaning was accomplished by pumping out the sewage. This process often left the toilets messy, with human feces on the floors, walls, and seats. The contractors were to scrub down the toilets afterwards, but it appears they often failed to do so. Paper covers were not provided, and the toilet paper, if any, was sometimes wet and/or soiled with urine. No running water for washing one's hands was available near the toilets, although a chemical hand cleaner could be checked out from the "gang-boxes."

The lower court found it credible that most women were inhibited from using the toilets. Further, the inhibitions described were not personal peculiarities, but that Lynch and others reasonably believed that the toilets could endanger their health. Lynch introduced credible medical expert testimony to demonstrate that women are more vulnerable to urinary tract infections than are men.

On the basis of that evidence, the court concluded that all increased danger of urinary tract infections may be linked to the practice of females holding their urine and to the use of toilets under the circumstances where the female's bacteria-contaminated hands came into contact with her external genitalia or where a female's perineal area comes into direct contact with bacteria-contaminated surfaces.

Few concerns are more pressing to anyone than those related to personal health. A prima facie case of disparate impact is established when a plaintiff shows that the facially neutral practice has a significantly discriminatory impact. Any employment practice that adversely affects the health of female employees while leaving male employees unaffected has a significantly discriminatory impact. The burden then shifts to the employer to justify the practice which resulted in this discriminatory impact by showing business necessity; that is, that the practice of furnishing unsanitary toilet facilities at the work site substantially promotes the proficient operation of business.

Title VII is remedial legislation, which must be construed liberally to achieve its purpose of eliminating discrimination from the workplace. Although Lynch was discharged for violating a rule, she did so in order to avoid the continued risk to her health which would have resulted from obeying the rule. The employer created an unacceptable situation in which Lynch and other female construction workers were required to choose between submitting to a discriminatory health hazard or risking termination for disobeying a company rule. Anatomical differences between men and women are "immutable characteristics," just as race, color, and national origin are immutable characteristics. When it is shown that employment practices place a heavier burden on minority employees than on members of the majority, and this burden relates to characteristics which identify them as members of the protected group, the requirements of a Title VII disparate impact case are satisfied. REVERSED and REMANDED.

Case Questions

1. Are you surprised by this outcome? Why or why not?
2. Does the outcome make sense to you? Explain.
3. What would you have done if you were the employer in this situation?

An employer may not forgo hiring those of a certain gender because of the logistical problems it may cause unless it involves an unreasonable financial burden—usually a matter difficult for an employer to show. These challenges must be resolved in a way that does not discriminate against the employee based on gender. Generally it is not exceedingly difficult, although it may take thinking about the workplace in a different way. In one situation the employer said he could not hire females because there was only one restroom on the premises. However, if there is no state sanitation or building code prohibiting it, there is no requirement that males and females use separate restrooms as long as privacy is maintained.

Equal Pay and Comparable Worth

> (1) No employer . . . shall discriminate between employees on the basis of sex by paying wages to employees . . . at a rate less than the rate at which he pays wages to employees of the opposite sex . . . for equal work on jobs the performance of which requires equal skill, effort, and responsibility, and which are performed under similar working conditions, except where such payment is made pursuant to (i) a seniority system; (ii) a merit system; (iii) a system which measures earnings by quantity or quality of production; or (iv) a differential based on any other factor other than sex . . . **Equal Pay Act,** 29 U.S.C.A §206(d).

Despite the statute quoted above, according to wage data, on average, women earn 74 cents for every dollar earned by men. This is up from 60 cents in 1979. Younger women make 80 cents for every dollar a man makes in the same age group. While Title VII prohibits discrimination in employment including in the area of compensation, even before Title VII there was legislation protecting employees against discrimination in compensation solely on the basis of gender. The year before Title VII was passed, the Equal Pay Act (EPA), actually part of the Fair Labor Standards Act (FLSA) governing wages and hours in the workplace, became law. In 1998, wage discrimination claims accounted for 8 percent of all charges filed with the EEOC.

Under the act, employers subject to the minimum wage provisions of the FLSA may not use gender as a basis for paying lower wages to an employee for equal work "on jobs the performance of which requires equal skill, effort, and responsibility, and which are performed under similar working conditions." There are exceptions. Differences in wages are permitted if based on seniority or merit systems, on systems that measure earnings by quantity or quality of production, or on a differential based on "any other factor other than [gender]."

To comply with the Equal Pay Act, the employer may not reduce the wage rate of the higher-paid employees. According to Bureau of Labor Statistics figures, the pay gap that was supposed to be closed by the legislation actually widened nine times from one year to the next since passage of the EPA.

The EPA overlaps with Title VII's general prohibition against discrimination in employment on the basis of gender. Title VII's Bennett Amendment was passed so that the exceptions permitted by the EPA would also be recognized by Title VII. The EPA also has a longer statute of limitations (two years from the time of the alleged violation, which may be raised to three years for willful violations, rather than 180 days under Title VII). Perhaps due to the fact that Title VII was passed very soon after the EPA, and more generally proscribed discrimination in employment, there has been less activity under the EPA than under Title VII. However, the prohibitions on pay discrimination should be considered no less important. (See Exhibit 7–12.)

POLLIS V. THE NEW SCHOOL FOR SOCIAL RESEARCH
132 F.3d 115 (2nd Cir. 1997)

A professor sued her college for, among other things, willful violation of the Equal Pay Act. The jury held in her favor and the college appealed. The court of appeals held that evidence that the professor complained about discrepancies between her salary and salaries of male professors on many occasions, but that the college did not rectify the situation was sufficient to show reckless or willful violation of the Equal Pay Act by the college.

Leval, J.

The New School for Social Research ("New School") appeals the judgment of the District Court entered pursuant to jury verdict, awarding damages to Dr. Adamantia Pollis, a retired professor of political science. Among other things, the New School contests the sufficiency of evidence in support of the jury's finding of willfulness, with respect to its violation of the Equal Pay Act, in paying Pollis less than comparable male faculty members. We affirm the jury's finding that the New School's violation of the Equal Pay Act was willful or reckless.

Pollis was hired as a professor of political science at the Graduate Faculty of the New School in 1964. She was granted tenure in 1966, and promoted to full professor in 1976. During her employment at the New School, she twice served as chair of the political science department. Her primary areas of specialty were human rights and Greek politics. According to evidence Pollis submitted at trial, during a 19-year period, her salary was lower than the salaries of five male teachers who were comparable to her.

The Equal Pay Act is violated if an employer

whose employees are subject to the Fair Labor Standards Act pays wages to an employee "at a rate less than the rate at which he pays wages to employees of the opposite sex . . . for equal work on jobs the performance of which requires equal skill, effort, and responsibility, and which are performed under similar working conditions. . . ." 29 U.S.C. § 206(d). A violation occurs when an employer pays lower wages to an employee of one gender than to substantially equivalent employees of the opposite gender in similar circumstances. A plaintiff need not prove that the pay disparity was motivated by an intention to discriminate on the basis of gender. The New School contends that there is insufficient evidence to support the jury's finding that the New School willfully violated the Equal Pay Act.

A defendant's violation of the Equal Pay Act is willful or reckless if "the employer either knew or showed reckless disregard for the matter of whether its conduct was prohibited by the statute." A plaintiff need not show that an employer acted with intent to discriminate or in bad faith. Pollis testified that on multiple occasions over several years, she complained to New School decisionmakers about discrepancies between her salary and the salaries of male professors. Responses she received indicated an awareness on the part of the administration that her salary level was below that of comparable male teachers. Nonetheless, the school continued to pay Pollis less than comparable male teachers.

This evidence—that the New School knew that Pollis was paid less than comparable males, but did not rectify the situation—is sufficient to support the jury's finding of reckless or willful violation of the Equal Pay Act. Therefore, compensatory damages for the Equal Pay Act violation should have been calculated by reference to the three-year limitations period for willful viola-

tions, and the resulting compensatory award should be doubled pursuant to the Fair Labor Standards Act's liquidated damages provision. AFFIRMED IN PART, VACATED IN PART, and REMANDED.

Case Questions

1. What do you think accounted for the difference in Pollis's salary?

2. If you were the department chair responsible for such things, how would you have avoided this situation?

3. Why do you think the school did not rectify the situation even after the salary differences became clear?

Though there has traditionally been less activity under the Equal Pay Act than under Title VII, this is in the process of changing. In April of 1999, the EEOC and the Department of Labor approved two memoranda of understanding to enable them to better enforce the laws prohibiting discrimination in compensation. In a rare move, a week later on April 13, the EEOC held its monthly meeting in Philadelphia rather than Washington, DC, to hear testimony from individuals representing a broad range of interests on the issue of discrimination in the payment of wages. Ida L. Castro, EEOC Chair, said . . . Women and minorities deserve equal pay for equal work. We plan to step up our efforts in this area through stronger enforcement of the laws covering wage discrimination, coupled with increased education, enhanced outreach, and better customer service. The EEOC is committed to educating employers, employees, and the public about their rights and responsibilities in order to promote voluntary compliance and create workplaces which are free of discrimination. The Clinton administration has proposed giving the EEOC an extra $14 million to hire investigators to handle EPA violations.

Under the EPA it is the content of the job, not the job title or description, that controls the comparison of whether the jobs are substantially the same. For instance, if a hospital's male "orderlies" and female "aides" perform substantially the same job, they should receive the same pay, despite the difference in job title.

In *County of Washington v. Gunther,*[1] the Court held that Title VII's Bennett Amendment only incorporated the four EPA exceptions into Title VII, not the "substantially equal" requirement; therefore, the jobs compared in a Title VII unequal pay action need not be substantially equal. Thus, under Title VII, employees have attempted to bring **comparable worth** cases in which higher-paid predominantly male jobs with similar value to the employer are compared in order to challenge lower wage rates for jobs held mostly by women. Federal courts have, however,

Comparable worth
A Title VII action for pay discrimination based on gender, in which jobs held mostly by women are compared with comparable jobs held mostly by men who are paid more than the women, to determine if there is gender discrimination.

---

[1]452 U.S. 161 (1981).

Exhibit 7–12

Hardly a Dead Issue

A national study undertaken by the AFL–CIO and the Institute for Women's Policy Research reveals very interesting insights into the issue of pay equality among American workers. Almost two-thirds of *all* working women responded to the 1997 survey. When looking at the findings and thinking about the issue of wage equality, keep in mind that the women responding provided half or more of their families' incomes.

- Ninety-four percent of working women described equal pay as "very important"; two of every five cited pay as the biggest problem women face at work.

- Women who work full-time are paid only 74 cents for every dollar men earn—$148 less each week. A Census Bureau study issued October 1, 1999, found the amount had decreased to 73 cents.

- Women of color who work full-time are paid only 64 cents for every dollar men earn— $210 less each week.

- Working families lose $200 billion of income annually to the wage gap—an average yearly loss of more than $4,000 for each working woman's family because of unequal pay, even after accounting for differences in education, age, location and the number of hours worked.

- If married women were paid the same as comparable men, their family income would rise by nearly 6 percent, and their families' poverty rates would fall from 2.1 percent to 0.8 percent.

- If single working mothers earned as much as comparable men, their family incomes would increase by nearly 17 percent, and their poverty rates would be cut in half, from 25.3 percent to 12.6 percent.

- If single women earned as much as comparable men, their incomes would rise by 13.4 percent and their poverty rates would be reduced from 6.3 percent to 1 percent.

- Working families in Ohio, Michigan, Vermont, Indiana, Illinois, Montana, Wisconsin, and Alabama pay the heaviest price for unequal pay to working women, losing an average of roughly $5,000 in family income each year.

- Family income losses due to unequal pay for women range from $326 million in Alaska to $21.8 billion in California.

- Women who work full-time are paid the least, compared with men, in Indiana, Louisiana, Michigan, Montana, North Dakota, Wisconsin, and Wyoming, where women earn less than 70 percent of men's weekly earnings.

- Women of color fare especially poorly in Louisiana, Montana, Nebraska, Oregon, Rhode Island, Utah, Wisconsin, and Wyoming, earning less than 60 percent of what men earn.

- Even where women fare best compared with men—in Arizona, California, Florida, Hawaii, Massachusetts, New York, and Rhode Island—women earn little more than 80 percent as much as men.

- Women earn the most in comparison to men—97 percent—in Washington, DC, but the primary reason women appear to fare so well is the very low wages of minority men.

- For women of color, the gender pay gap is smallest in Washington, DC; Hawaii; Florida; New York; and Tennessee, where they earn more than 70 percent of what men overall in those states earn.

- The 25.6 million women who work in predominantly female jobs lose an average of $3,446 each per year; the 4 million men who work in predominantly female occupations lose an average of $6,259 each per year.

1999 AFL-CIO and The Institute for Women's Policy Research (IWPR).

generally rejected Title VII claims based on comparable worth. Take a look at the *AFSCME* case, below, to see some of the considerations involved.

AMERICAN FEDERATION OF STATE, COUNTY, AND MUNICIPAL EMPLOYEES, AFL–CIO (AFSCME) v. STATE OF WASHINGTON
770 F.2d 1401 (9th Cir. 1985)

The state of Washington conducted studies of prevailing market rates for jobs and wages in order to determine the wages for various state jobs. Under market rates, female-dominated jobs were paid lower wages than male-dominated jobs. The state then compared jobs for comparable worth and after finding that female-dominated job salaries were generally about 20 percent less than wages in male-dominated jobs, legislated that it would begin basing its wages on comparable worth rather than the market rate, over a 10-year period. State employees wanted the scheme to go into effect immediately, and a class of state employees in job categories at least 70 percent female brought a Title VII suit against the state alleging it was a violation of Title VII for the state to know of the wage differences and not remedy the situation immediately. The lower court held for the employees and the state appealed. The court of appeals held that the state's decision to base compensation on the competitive market rather than on a theory of comparable worth did not establish its liability under the disparate impact analysis of Title VII, and the state's participation in a market system did not allow an inference of discriminatory motive in order to establish its liability under a disparate-treatment theory, since the state did not create the market disparity and was not shown to have been motivated by illegal gender-based considerations in setting its salaries. Therefore, the employees did not prove liability under Title VII, and the lower court decision was reversed. Note that since the jobs being compared were not the "same or substantially the same," as required by the Equal Pay Act, the employees were constrained to bring suit under Title VII.

Kennedy, J.

It is evident from the legislative history of the Equal Pay Act that Congress, after explicit consideration, rejected proposals that would have prohibited lower wages for comparable work, as contrasted with equal work. In the instant case, the district court found a violation of Title VII, premised upon both the disparate impact and the disparate treatment theories of discrimination.

AFSCME's disparate impact argument is based on the contention that the State of Washington's practice of taking prevailing market rates into account in setting wages has an adverse impact on women, who, historically, have received lower wages than men in the labor market. Disparate impact analysis is confined to cases that challenge a specific, clearly delineated employment practice applied at a single point in the job selection process.

The instant case does not involve an employment practice that yields to disparate impact analysis. The decision to base compensation on the competitive market, rather than on a theory of comparable worth, involves the assessment of a number of complex factors not easily ascertainable, an assessment too multifaceted to be appropriate for disparate impact analysis. Unlike a specific, clearly delineated employment policy contemplated by precedent such as those requiring a height and weight requirement or a certain score on an exam, the compensation system in question resulted from surveys, agency hearings, administrative recommendations, budget proposals, executive actions, and legislative enactments. A compensation system that is responsive to supply and demand and other market forces is not the type of single practice that suffices to support a claim under disparate impact theory. Such cases are controlled by disparate treatment analysis. Under these principles and precedents, we must reverse the district court's determination of liability under the disparate impact theory of discrimination.

Under the disparate treatment theory, our review of the record indicates failure by AFSCME to establish the requisite element of intent by either circumstantial or direct evidence.

AFSCME contends discriminatory motive may be inferred from the Willis study, which finds the State's practice of setting salaries in reliance on market rates creates a sex-based wage disparity for jobs deemed of comparable worth. AFSCME argues from the study that the market reflects a historical pattern of lower wages to employees in positions staffed predominantly by women, and it contends the State of Washington perpetuates that disparity, in violation of Title VII, by using market rates in the compensation system. The inference of discriminatory motive which AFSCME seeks to draw from the State's participation in the market system fails, as the State did not create the market disparity and has not been shown to have been motivated by impermissible sex-based considerations in setting salaries.

The requirement of intent is linked at least in part to culpability. That concept would be undermined if we were to hold that payment of wages according to prevailing rates in the public and private sectors is an act that, in itself, supports the inference of a purpose to discriminate. Neither law nor logic deems the free market system a suspect enterprise. Economic reality is that the value of a particular job to an employer is but one factor influencing the rate of compensation for that job. Other considerations may include the availability of workers willing to do the job and the effectiveness of collective bargaining in a particular industry. Employers may be constrained by market forces to set salaries under prevailing wage rates for different job classifications. We find nothing in the language of Title VII or its legislative history to indicate Congress intended to abrogate fundamental economic principles such as the laws of supply and demand or to prevent employers from competing in the labor market. While the Washington legislature may have the discretion to enact a comparable worth plan if it chooses to do so, Title VII does not obligate it to eliminate an economic inequality that it did not create. Title VII was enacted to ensure equal opportunity in employment to covered individuals, and the State of Washington is not charged here with barring access to particular job classifications on the basis of sex.

We have recognized that in certain cases an inference of intent may be drawn from statistical evidence. We have admonished, however, that statistics must be relied on with caution. Though the comparability of wage rates in dissimilar jobs may be relevant to a determination of discriminatory animus, job evaluation studies and comparable worth statistics alone are insufficient to establish the requisite inference of discriminatory motive critical to the disparate treatment theory. The weight to be accorded such statistics is determined by the existence of independent corroborative evidence of discrimination. We conclude the independent evidence of discrimination presented by AFSCME is insufficient to support an inference of the requisite discriminatory motive under the disparate treatment theory.

AFSCME offered proof of isolated incidents of sex segregation as evidence of a history of sex-based wage discrimination. The evidence consists of "help wanted" advertisements restricting various jobs to members of a particular sex. These advertisements were often placed in separate "help wanted—male" and "help wanted—female" columns in state newspapers between 1960 and 1973, though most were discontinued when Title VII became applicable to the states in 1972. At trial, AFSCME called expert witnesses to testify that a causal relationship exists between sex segregation practices and sex-based wage discrimination, and that the effects of sex segregation practices may persist even after the practices are discontinued. However, none of the individually named plaintiffs in the action ever testified regarding specific incidents of discrimination. The isolated incidents alleged by AFSCME are insufficient to corroborate the results of the Willis study and do not justify an inference of discriminatory motive by the State in the setting of salaries for its system as a whole. Given the scope of the alleged intentional act, and given the attempt to show the core principle of the State's market-based compensation system was adopted or maintained with a discriminatory purpose, more is required to support the finding of liability than these isolated acts, which had only an indirect relation to the compensation principle itself.

We also reject AFSCME's contention that, having commissioned the Willis study, the State of Washington was committed to implement a new system of compensation based on comparable worth as defined by the study. Whether comparable worth is a feasible approach to employee compensation is a matter of debate. Assuming,

however, that like other job evaluation studies it may be useful as a diagnostic tool, we reject a rule that would penalize rather than commend employers for their effort and innovation in undertaking such a study. The results of comparable worth studies will vary depending on the number and types of factors measured and the maximum number of points allotted to each factor. A study that indicates a particular wage structure might be more equitable should not categorically bind the employer who commissioned it. The employer should also be able to take into account market conditions, bargaining demands, and the possibility that another study will yield different results.

We hold there was a failure to establish a violation of Title VII under the disparate treatment theory of discrimination, and reverse the district court on this aspect of the case as well. The State of Washington's initial reliance on a free market system in which employees in male-dominated jobs are compensated at a higher rate than employees in dissimilar female-dominated jobs is not in and of itself a violation of Title VII, notwithstanding that the Willis study deemed the positions of comparable worth. Absent a showing of discriminatory motive, which has not been made here, the law does not permit the federal courts to interfere in the market-based system for the compensation of Washington's employees. REVERSED.

Case Questions

1. Do you think that using comparable worth is an effective way to determine salaries?
2. Why do you think male-dominated jobs tend to pay less than female-dominated jobs, if both have virtually the same value to the employer?
3. What would you do to avoid this situation?

Employers should be aware of any pay differentials between specific males and females, as well as between jobs that are held primarily by males and those held primarily by females. Employers should perform periodic audits to ensure that they are not operating under gender-based pay differentials, which may prompt employees to sue for wage discrimination.

Gender as a BFOQ

Title VII permits gender to be used as a bona fide occupational qualification (BFOQ) under certain limited circumstances. Under the EEOC guidelines, a BFOQ may be used when there is a legitimate need for authenticity such as for the part of a female in a theater or film production. More often than not, when employers have attempted to use BFOQ as a defense to gender discrimination, courts have found the defense inapplicable. As the case below demonstrates, it is not always females who are kept out of the workplace because of gender.

E.E.O.C. v. Audrey Sedita, d/b/a Women's Workout World
755 F. Supp. 808 (N. Dist. Ill. E.D. 1991)

The employer, Women's Workout World (WWW), refused to hire males as managers, assistant managers, or instructors in employer's exercise studio. Employer argued that being a female was reasonably necessary for the particular business. The court did not agree.

Williams, J.

The employer asserts that the jobs at issue require a substantial amount of physical contact with members' bodies and that they are exposed to nudity in the club locker room, shower, and bathroom, during orientation sessions when they show club facilities to new members. They argue that it would be impossible for WWW to reassign job duties in order to avoid intruding on members' privacy interests, since the conduct which infringes on privacy interests amounts to the essence of the jobs in question.

EEOC argues that the essence of the jobs in question does not require employees to intimately touch health club members, or force employees to be exposed to nudity of members. They suggested

WWW could hire male employees by changing the duties of the jobs in question, such as hiring females to assist clients who objected to being touched by males, posting a schedule to inform clients of when male employees would be on duty, or letting clients take themselves through the locker rooms.

The BFOQ exception is meant to be an extremely narrow exception to the general prohibition of discrimination on the basis of gender. Hence, a defendant asserting a BFOQ defense has a heavy burden in terms of justifying his employment practice. An employer asserting a privacy-based BFOQ defense must satisfy a three-part test. First, the employer must assert a factual basis for believing that hiring any members of one gender would undermine the business operation. Second, the employer must prove that the customer's privacy interest is entitled to protection under the law, and third, that no reasonable alternatives exist to protect those interests other than the gender-based hiring policy.

WWW contends a factual basis for their hiring policy exists because their clients have consciously chosen to join an all-female health club. They present the owner's testimony that members have, in the past, been disturbed by the presence of males in the club.

We find that WWW failed to prove either that a factual basis exists for their discriminatory hiring policies, or that no reasonable alternatives exist to protect their customers' privacy interests other than sex-based hiring.

A defendant in a privacy rights case may satisfy its burden of proving a factual basis for sex-based hiring policies by showing that the clients or guests of a business would not consent to service of the opposite gender and would stop patronizing the business if members of the opposite gender were allowed to perform the service. This, WWW has failed to do. Also, WWW has previously hired males as "class givers," suggesting that there is no basis in the law for their present refusal to hire men. The EEOC's evidence of feasibility exists in the nation's other health clubs, which hire both genders, and allow members to be served both by assistants of their own gender and by members of the opposite gender.

The purpose of WWW's business operation is to provide individualized fitness and exercise instruction to the club's women members. Hence, WWW must prove that they cannot achieve their business purpose without engaging in single-gender hiring. In response to EEOC's alternatives, WWW produced nothing more than the owner's assertions that the alternatives were not feasible because of the views of her clientele, and the difficulties of accommodating men in the health club. This is not strong enough to prove that no alternatives were feasible. WWW needed to provide evidence to prove their argument such as data on costs, studies on the feasibility of changing their present operation, or projections on the impact of such changes in terms of lost profits.

The motion for PARTIAL SUMMARY JUDGMENT for EEOC is GRANTED.

Case Questions

1. Do you agree with the court's decision? Why or why not? Do you think the outcome would have been the same if the genders were reversed and females were prevented from working at the club?

2. If you were the employer in this case, what would you do?

3. Do you think Title VII was made to address these types of situations; that is, where a private commercial enterprise wishes to have a particular clientele served a particular way? Explain.

Pregnancy Discrimination

The Supreme Court determined in *General Electric Co. v. Gilbert,*[1] that discrimination on the basis of pregnancy was not gender discrimination under Title VII. Two years later Congress passed the Pregnancy Discrimination Act (PDA) amending Title VII's definitions to include discrimination on the basis of pregnancy. Despite the fact that women comprise nearly 50 percent of the workforce, and statistics show

---

[1]429 U.S. 125 (1976).

Exhibit 7–13

The news article below shows what can happen when employees are not included in protective legislation. The employer here did not have at least 15 employees, so Title VII did not apply. Under the state's fair employment practice law, pregnancy was not a protected category. When the employee brought her case alleging that her termination as an at-will employee violated the state's public policy against discrimination, the court did not agree. Read on . . .

Having a Child? You're Fired, Some Employers Insist

When Lisa Bailey was pregnant with her baby daughter, Ashley, her boss at Scott-Gallaher Inc. in Coverdale, Va., had something other than congratulations in mind, according to a lawsuit she filed.

While she was home during a doctor-ordered leave because of complications related to the pregnancy, she was fired. And six weeks after Ashley was born, her boss, Ron Scott, told her, according to documents in the court case, that she lost her job "because she was no longer dependable since she had delivered a child; that Bailey's place was at home with her child; that babies get sick sometimes and Bailey would have to miss work to care for her child, and that he needed someone more dependable."

The description of what happened went unchallenged—and unproven, according to an attorney for the company—in the eventual decision on Bailey's case.

A state court judge in Roanoke ruled Bailey hadn't been wrongfully fired. The dismissal was acceptable under Virginia laws covering "employment at will"—jobs that aren't protected by a union contract, according to Circuit Court Judge Clifford R. Weckstein.

Although Virginia law says "at will" workers cannot be fired based on their sex, the judge ruled Virginia's legislature has not spelled out specifically that firing a woman because she is pregnant or has given birth constitutes sex discrimination.

"Enlightened public policy might very well prohibit the sort of actions about which Bailey complains in this case," the judge wrote. "It is not the place of the judiciary, however, to adopt and articulate public policy of this sort," he said, but rather is up to the General Assembly.

The ruling means that "becoming pregnant or giving birth is grounds for termination of employment in Virginia," said Bailey's attorney, Terry N. Grimes. Grimes said he expects Bailey will appeal.

To some attorneys familiar with the origins of the Pregnancy Discrimination Act, adopted by Congress in 1978, it sounds like a blast from the past.

"This decision is, unfortunately, 20 years behind the times and will have a hard time being upheld upon appeal," said Helen Norton, director of equal-opportunity programs for the Women's Legal Defense Fund.

The Pregnancy Discrimination Act, which Congress adopted to clarify that pregnancy should be included in the definition of illegal discrimination, excluded small employers such as the Roanoke-area heavy-equipment leasing company for which Bailey worked. Some states have amended their fair-employment laws specifically to make pregnancy discrimination illegal— but not Virginia.

"Is it fair to small employers, where federal statutes expressly excluded them from coverage because they are so small, then to turn around and—on the basis of something so nebulous as public policy—potentially saddle them with a liability that could wipe out their business?" said Clinton S. Morse, who represented Scott-Gallaher.

"Do I think that small employers ought to be allowed to discriminate on the basis of pregnancy?"s He asked rhetorically. "My only rejoinder there is that I certainly would understand if the legislature wanted to pass a specific statute that prohibited that. That would at least make clear to small employers what the rules of the game are," he said.

EXHIBIT 7–13   Concluded

Ron Scott, president of Scott-Gallaher, said it wasn't sex discrimination, but declined to discuss the case further, "I'm just taking a lot of licks, but I can't comment on it," he said.

As Bailey's case demonstrates, claims of pregnancy discrimination haven't disappeared as a result of laws intended to prohibit it. Complaints of pregnancy discrimination filed with the Equal Employment Opportunity Commission have been creeping up—from 3,000 in fiscal 1991 to 3,191 in fiscal 1995.

Most of the complaints involve a firing, according to Elaine Herskowitz, senior attorney adviser with the EEOC's office of legal counsel. She said 66 percent of all pregnancy discrimination complaints involve claims that women were dismissed illegally, compared with 47 percent of all discrimination charges.

Even so, pregnancy discrimination nowadays often takes more subtle forms, said Donna R. Lenhoff, general counsel of the Women's Legal Defense Fund. For instance, a male manager may assume a pregnant worker will want to return to work part time, without consulting the worker.

"I think it often takes the form of a more subtle 'mommy track,'" she said. "I think in general those prejudices have not been eradicated but have gone underground somewhat. People alter their expectations of new mothers as opposed to new fathers."

Bailey did, in fact, appeal the decision. The Virginia Supreme Court (*Bailey v. Scott-Gallaher, Inc.,* 253 Va. 121 (1997)) disagreed with the lower court and permitted Bailey to sue her employer based on gender discrimination being a violation of Virginia public policy, even though she was an at-will employee.

©1996, *The Washington Post.* Reprinted by permission.

that about 75 percent of those of childbearing age will have children sometime during their work life, pregnancy discrimination is still a serious workplace concern.

Many employers have maternity leave policies to address this more-than-likely event, but others, particularly smaller employers, do not. Based on traditional notions about the inappropriateness of women in the workplace in general, or pregnant women in particular, some employers are actually hostile to pregnant employees and run the very real risk of being sued for pregnancy discrimination. (See Exhibit 7–13.)

The PDA prohibits an employer from using pregnancy, childbirth, or related medical conditions as the basis for treating an employee differently if that employee can perform the job. This is why in opening scenario 3, it is illegal for the employer to evaluate the pregnant employee differently than it would any other. Employers illegally treat employees differently in many ways. For instance, the employer:

Scenario

- Refuses to hire pregnant applicants.
- Terminates an employee on discovering the employee's pregnancy.
- Does not provide benefits to pregnant employees on an equal basis with short-term disabilities of other employees.
- Refuses to allow a pregnant employee to continue to work even though the employee wishes to do so and is physically able to do so.
- Does not provide the employee with lighter duty if needed, when such accommodations are made for employees with other short-term disabilities.

• Eliminates the pregnant employee by moving her to a new job title with the same pay, then eliminates the position in a job restructuring or a reduction in force.

• Evaluates the employee as not having performed as well or as much as other employees when the basis for the evaluation is the employer's own refusal or hesitation to assign equal work to the employee, because the employee is pregnant and the employer feels the need to "lighten" the employee's load, though the employee has not requested such.

• Does not permit the pregnant employee to be a part of the normal circle of office culture so she becomes less aware of matters of importance to the office or current projects, resulting in more likelihood that the employee will not be able effectively to compete with those still within the circle.

ZAKEN V. BOERER
964 F.2d 1319 (2nd Cir. 1992)

Employee's performance was above average until employer found out employee was pregnant, at which time she was terminated. Court held for employee.

Cardamone, J.

Defendant, Bonnie Boerer, was the chief executive officer of Bonnie Boerer & Company and the owner of 98% of its stock. Boerer had owned the now-defunct company since 1983. Boerer designed clothing which was then manufactured by her Hong Kong corporation and sold through her New York City showroom where plaintiff, Zaken was employed. Boerer controlled almost every aspect of her business and had ultimate decision-making power with respect to all corporate activities including personnel decisions. Boerer made the final decision to terminate Zaken.

Zaken was hired in September 1988 as a sales manager of the company's large size clothing division in their New York office. When Zaken was hired, she was brought on at a salary of $46,000 per year and promised a bonus at the end of the year (1988). At the time she was hired, Zaken did not realize that she was replacing Robin Weinberg, who had been discharged during her fifth month of pregnancy.

Shortly after beginning employment in Sep-

tember, Zaken learned that she was pregnant and told this to her supervisor in October. Zaken planned to work as long as possible before the baby was born, then return as soon as possible after delivery. When Zaken told her supervisor she was pregnant, he told her that she should not tell Boerer or anyone else at the company she was pregnant, and suggested it would be best if he broke the news to Boerer at a later time.

At the end of December 1988, Boerer returned to her New York office from the Orient where she had been overseeing her product line since Zaken was hired in September. It was then that Boerer learned of Zaken's pregnancy.

Zaken was not given her bonus at the end of 1988. When Zaken asked why, she was told by her supervisor that Boerer had decided Zaken was "not qualified" for her sales position. Zaken testified that she told her supervisor then that she believed Boerer was discriminating against her because of her pregnancy.

A month later, on January 23, 1989, Zaken's

supervisor told Zaken that Boerer had decided to terminate Zaken, who was now five months pregnant. When Zaken asked why she was being fired, her supervisor told her that Boerer had decided Zaken was "not qualified" as a sales manager. The supervisor testified that he also told Zaken that he had fought to convince Boerer not to fire Zaken. In Zaken's subsequent recommendation letter, the supervisor stated that Zaken's "administrative skills, attention to detail, work ethics and ability to communicate were outstanding."

Zaken brought suit alleging that she was denied a bonus and her employment was terminated because she was pregnant, in violation of Title VII of the Civil Rights Act of 1964, as amended, and New York's Human Rights Law. At the trial, Zaken's predecessor, Weinberg, testified that she had also been discharged by Boerer when she was five months pregnant after working for Boerer for a little over a year.

She testified that at the time she was terminated, she had a very good sales record and before becoming pregnant, had received very positive comments from Boerer. Weinberg had received a bonus after working for Boerer for only five months, and a raise after eight months. After Boerer discovered she was pregnant, Weinberg testified, Boerer became cold and hostile and terminated Weinberg a few months later. Weinberg also testified that, at the time of her hiring interview, Boerer asked whether Weinberg planned to have children and told Weinberg she hoped Weinberg would not become pregnant while Weinberg was employed by Boerer's company.

Boerer insisted in her testimony that she fired Zaken because Zaken was not qualified to fill the sales manager position and Weinberg because of excessive absenteeism, low productivity and dishonesty. Boerer also testified that she employed about 30 people in her New York showroom, of whom 24 were women and 5 had become pregnant during their employment without losing their jobs.

Plaintiff need not show pregnancy was the primary reason for defendant's decision to discharge plaintiff and deny her a bonus, but only that it was a factor relied upon by defendant. Moreover, the trial court's statement could have been interpreted to require that pregnancy had to be the factor that "prompted" the defendant to deny plaintiff a bonus and terminate her employment, rather than simply a factor that made a difference in these decisions.

The jury should have been instructed that if it found Zaken had demonstrated by a preponderance of the evidence that her pregnancy played a part in Boerer's decision, then it should find for Zaken unless Boerer demonstrated by a preponderance of the evidence that the same decision would have been made even if pregnancy would not have been one of the factors contributing to it. REVERSED and REMANDED.

Case Questions

1. Point out some of the things that you think Boerer and the supervisor should not have done in this case. How would you have handled it differently?

2. Can you think of reasons why Boerer may have terminated pregnant employees, if she did as Zaken alleged?

3. Do you think that the type of business had an impact here? That is, the fashion industry, rather than some other workplace? Should it?

If the employee is temporarily unable to perform the duties of the job because of pregnancy, then the inability to perform should be the issue, not the fact that the employee is pregnant. The employee should therefore be treated just as any other employee who was temporarily unable to perform job requirements. Whatever arrangements the employer generally makes in such circumstances must be extended to the pregnant employee. Note, however, that the EEOC has ruled that an employer's adherence to a facially neutral sick leave policy and its consequent refusal to provide pregnant employees with a reasonable leave of absence, in the absence of a showing of business necessity, discriminates on the basis of gender because of its disproportionate impact on women. EEOC Dec. No. 74-112, 19 FEP Cases 1817 (4/15/74); EEOC Guidelines, 29 CFR section 1604.10(c). Pregnancy can, of course, be used as a BFOQ.

Parental Leave Policies

Leave Requirement

(a)(1) Entitlement to leave.—an eligible employee shall be entitled to a total of 12 workweeks of leave during any 12-month period for one or more of the following:

(A) Because of the birth of a son or daughter of the employee and in order to care for such son or daughter.

(B) Because of the placement of a son or daughter with the employee for adoption or foster care.

(C) In order to care for the spouse, or a son, daughter, or parent, of the employee, if such spouse, son, daughter, or parent has a serious health condition.

(D) Because of a serious health condition that makes the employee unable to perform the functions of the position of such employee. The Family and Medical Leave act of 1993, 29 U.S.C. §2601 et seq.

Closely related to the issue of pregnancy discrimination is protection of employees who take time off work to have a baby or to adopt.

On February 5, 1993, President Clinton signed into law the first piece of legislation of his administration: The Family and Medical Leave Act (FMLA). The act guarantees employees who have been on the job at least a year up to 12 weeks of unpaid leave per year for a birth, adoption, or care of sick children, spouses, or parents, and the same or an equivalent job upon their return. The act applies to employers with 50 or more employees within a 75-mile radius. Employees must have worked for their employer for at least one year and for at least 1,250 hours during the 12 months preceding the time off. They must give the employer at least 30 days' notice when practical (such as for a birth).

Employers may require employees to first use vacation or other leave before applying for the unpaid leave, but employees must be compensated for the vacation days as they normally would. Where both members of the couple work for the same employer, the employer can restrict the couple to a total of 12 weeks leave per year. Employers must continue to provide employees with health insurance during their leave and may exclude the highest-paid 10 percent of their employees.

Employers can also require medical confirmation of an illness, which the US Department of Labor, which has issued regulations on the act, defines as requiring at least one night in the hospital. Complaints may be filed with the Wage and Hour

Division of the Labor Department, or the employee can file a lawsuit if he or she feels the employer violated the act. (See Exhibit 7–14.)

In 1997, Congress declined to grant President Clinton's request to extend the FMLA to permit employees to take up to 24 hours of unpaid leave each year to fulfill certain family obligations such as attending parent–teacher conferences, taking a child to the doctor, finding child care, or to care for elderly relatives.

The FMLA affects about 5 percent of US employers and about 40 percent of US employees. The number of employees who will be able to take 12 weeks without pay is significantly fewer than those who are covered by the law. However, since its passage, over 20 million employees have used the FMLA. On February 12, 2000, President Clinton proposed a $20 million plan to help parents with the economic incentive to use the FMLA. A 1996 study showed that the most significant reason employees did not exercise their rights under the law was because of the expected loss of income. His plan, if implemented by Congress, would help this. In March 1999, the US Department of Labor reported that after adding 200 new FMLA inspectors, it had resolved 3,795 complaints in 1998, a 42 percent increase over 1997. Employees not being reinstated to their jobs after taking leave was the main reason for FMLA complaints, followed by denial of leave and the employer's interference with the employee's right to leave under the law.

As the case below reveals, it is important that an employer's FMLA policies not only comply with the law but also be clearly communicated to the employee, or the employer may lose FMLA protections.

FRY V. FIRST FIDELITY BANCORPORATION
67 Empl. Prac. Dec. (CCH) ¶43,943 (E.D. Penn. 1996)

Employer had a policy of allowing employees to take an additional 4 weeks of unpaid leave after taking 12 weeks of FMLA leave. The employer did not, however, notify the employee that doing so would mean that she would no longer maintain her FMLA right to reinstatement after the first 12 weeks. The court held that this lack of notification of rights under the law violated the FMLA.

Troutman, J.

In this claim for interference with FMLA rights, Fry alleges that the employer violated the FMLA by failing to return her to her previous position or to train her for a comparable position after she returned to work from a leave occasioned by the birth of her child. The dispute arises entirely from the employer's policy of permitting an eligible employee to take an additional 4 weeks of family leave, but counting the first 12 weeks thereof as the amount of leave required under the FMLA. As a result, the employer contends that the employee, who elected to take consecutively the full 16 weeks offered by the employer, forfeited the FMLA entitlement to reinstatement to her former, or a comparable position.

The employee argues that she was unaware of her employer's method of calculating the family leave period required by the FMLA in that the employer failed to provide adequate notice thereof as required by DOL's FMLA regulations. We conclude that adequate notice to employees concerning their FMLA right to reinstatement in light of any additional leave permitted by the employer is necessary to enable them to exercise their statutory right to reinstatement by electing to request only 12 weeks of family leave, if the employer's policy so provides. Conversely, if an employer fails to provide its employees with the required notice of its FMLA policies and procedures, it can interfere with the employees' exercise of their FMLA right to reinstatement by depriving them of the opportunity to choose to remain within the protection of the FMLA.

The FMLA regulation provides, in pertinent part, as follows:

> a) If an employer has any written guidance to employees concerning employee benefits or leave rights, such as in an employee handbook, information concerning FMLA entitlements and employee obligations under the FMLA must be included in the handbook or other documents.
>
> c) In addition, when an employee provides notice of the need for FMLA leave, the employer shall provide the employee with notice detailing the specific expectations and obligations of the employee and explaining any consequences of a failure to meet these obligations. Such specific notice should include, as appropriate:
>
> 1) That the leave shall be counted against their annual FMLA leave entitlement.

It appears to the Court that the obligation under subsection (a) to provide notice concerning FMLA rights in an employee handbook encompasses an obligation to provide such essential information as a forfeit of FMLA reinstatement rights if an employee's leave exceeds the statutory minimum of 12 weeks, notwithstanding the employer's offer of an additional 4 weeks of family leave.

The section of defendant's employee handbook which purports to set forth its FMLA family leave policy states that an employee may be eligible for 16 weeks of family leave. In explaining defendant's reinstatement provisions, however, the handbook makes no mention, either explicitly or implicitly, of defendant's policy of limiting reinstatement to the same or a comparable position to those who elect to take no more than the 12 weeks provided by the FMLA, which has the substantive effect of designating as FMLA leave the first 12 weeks of leave. Moreover, said handbook section also specifically states that its policy is designed to provide an employee with rights equal to or greater than those mandated by the FMLA. Thus, as a result of the employer's omission from the handbook of its policy concerning the designation of FMLA leave and the explicit statement therein that it intends to confer rights equal to or greater than FMLA rights, an employee could be misled into believing that he or she retains full FMLA rights even if he or she takes the full 16 weeks of leave offered by the employer. It is clear, therefore, that the handbook omits essential information concerning an employee's FMLA rights and the employer's FMLA policies. Hence, the employer's handbook does not comport with the notice provisions of the regulations.

A lapse in compliance with the regulations does not automatically amount to a statutory violation. Rather, a violation of the handbook notice provision is actionable only if the inadequate notice effectively interfered with the employee's statutory rights. Since an employer is obligated to provide specific notice of FMLA rights at the time an employee requests leave, and the leave will be counted against an employee's FMLA leave entitlement, any inadequacy in an employee handbook FMLA notice can be cured by providing complete and adequate notice of FMLA rights at the time the leave is requested. The motion to dismiss is DENIED.

Case Questions

1. As a manager, can you understand why the employee was not notified about the policy?

2. Since the employer's policy was contained in an employee handbook, does it seem that there should be a heavier burden on the employer to make sure the policy is correctly reflected in the written material?

3. If the employer need not have provided the extra four weeks of leave, but did so anyway, does it seem self-defeating for the employer not to have notified employees of it and thereby incur liability?

EXHIBIT 7–14

Unfortunately, while the FMLA applies to both mothers and fathers, there are still societal impediments to fathers taking advantage of their rights under the law. Many don't do so because they feel they will be perceived as not being committed to their jobs if they take off for the birth or adoption of a child. If you think the teasing and jokes don't matter, read on.

Working Dads Fear 'Slacker' Label

There were snide comments and many, many jokes. And when Maryland state trooper Kevin Knussman won his four-year legal fight this week against the bosses who denied him parental leave, only a couple of colleagues called to congratulate him.

Knussman's victory highlights the rights of working fathers to take time off with their babies. But his isolation shows how balancing a job and family remains a silent struggle for many men.

"Much of the progress (for working fathers) is still going on underground," says James Levine, a leading researcher on fatherhood and co-author of the book "Working Fathers."

Fearing—often with reason—that they'll be labeled slackers, fathers cobble together sick days and vacation time to create leave time after a baby is born. When they want to go to a school play, they dash for the door, under cover of attending a "late meeting." Progress has been made, albeit slowly, in accepting men's growing desire to be involved parents.

Asked 15 years ago how much unpaid parental leave time was reasonable for men to take, 63 percent of business leaders at large companies said "none." Even 40 percent of executives at companies with a parental leave policy at the time nixed the idea of actually using it, according to Catalyst, a non-profit group that studies women in business.

Today, half a million men take some sort of parental leave each year to care for a new child, under the auspices of the 1993 federal Family and Medical Leave Act. That compares with 1.4 million women. A total of 20 million people have taken leave under the federal law.

Knussman, a helicopter paramedic, sued the state police after he was denied 12 weeks leave following the birth of his daughter in 1994. He was given 10 days off, but sought more time because his wife experienced childbirth complications.

A jury awarded him $375,000 in damages for mental anguish, in the first sex discrimination case under the Family Leave Act. Attorneys for the state police said they may appeal.

"There's still a presumption that women are going to be the primary caretaker," said Sara Mandelbaum, an ACLU lawyer who represented Knussman. "Those studies are hard to change, especially a male-dominated organization like the state police."

Money also plays a role. A few companies, including Merrill Lynch and the software maker Lotus Development Corp., offer paid leaves for men. But most don't, and since men are major breadwinners, it's hard for them to take unpaid time off.

EXHIBIT 7–14 Concluded

For now, many men choose to do what they can, when they can. Still, Knussman is glad he took
a stand. After he filed his suit, the state police gave him a full 12 weeks off following the
birth of his second child.

"Biting the hand that feeds you is never easy," he said by telephone as his daughters giggled in
the background. But taking three months off was "just a great, great time. I will never, ever
regret that."

Courtesy of the Associated Press.

Fetal Protection Policies

**Fetal-protection
policies**
Policies an
employer institutes
to protect the fetus
or reproductive
capacity of
employees.

The issue of **fetal protection policies** will be given attention here because of the
unique gender employment problems involved. Fetal protection policies are policies
adopted by an employer that limit or prohibit employees from performing certain jobs
or working in certain areas of the workplace because of the potential harm presented to
pregnant employees, their fetuses, or the reproductive system or capacity of employees.

The problem with these policies is that, as in *Johnson,* below, many times, even
though there is a danger presented to male employees, the policies only exclude females (and do so very broadly), and the jobs from which the females are excluded
pay more or have more promotion potential.

UAW v. JOHNSON CONTROLS, INC.
499 U.S. 187 (1991)

A group of employees challenged the employer's policy barring all women except
those whose infertility was medically documented from jobs involving actual or potential lead exposure exceeding Occupational Safety and Health Administration
(OSHA) standards. The Court found the policy to be gender discrimination.

Blackmun, J.

In this case we are concerned with an employer's
gender-based fetal-protection policy. May an employer exclude a fertile female employee from
certain jobs because of its concern for the health
of the fetus the woman might conceive? Our answer is no.

Employees involved in the suit include Elsie
Nelson, a 50-year-old divorcee, who suffered a

loss in compensation when she was transferred
out of a job where she was exposed to lead, Mary
Craig who chose to be sterilized in order to avoid
losing her job, and Donald Penny, who was denied a request for leave of absence for the purpose
of lowering his lead level because he intended to
become a father.

The bias in Johnson Control's policy is obvious. Fertile men, but not fertile women, are given the choice as to whether they wish to risk their reproductive health for a particular job. Johnson Control's fetal-protection policy explicitly discriminates against women on the basis of their gender. The policy excludes women with childbearing capacity from lead-exposed jobs and so creates a facial classification based on gender.

The policy classifies on the basis of gender and childbearing capacity, rather than fertility alone. The employer does not seek to protect the unconceived children of all its employees. Despite evidence in the record about the debilitating effect of lead exposure on the male reproductive system, Johnson Controls is concerned only with the harms that may befall the unborn offspring of its female employees. Johnson Control's policy is facially discriminatory because it requires only a female employee to produce proof that she is not capable of reproducing.

Our conclusion is bolstered by the Pregnancy Discrimination Act of 1978 in which Congress explicitly provided that, for purposes of Title VII, discrimination "on the basis of sex" included discrimination "because of or on the basis of pregnancy, childbirth, or related medical conditions." The PDA has now made clear that, for all Title VII purposes, discrimination based on a woman's pregnancy is, on its face, discrimination because of her gender. Johnson Controls has chosen to treat all its female employees as potentially pregnant; that choice evinces discrimination on the basis of gender.

An employer may discriminate on the basis of gender in those certain instances where religion, gender or national origin is a BFOQ reasonably necessary to the normal operation of that particular business or enterprise. We conclude that the language of both the BFOQ provision and the PDA, which amended it, as well as the legislative history and case law, prohibit employers from discriminating against a woman because of her capacity to become pregnant unless her reproductive potential prevents her from performing the duties of her job. We have said before, an employer must

direct its concerns about a woman's ability to perform her job safely and efficiently to those aspects of the woman's job-related activities that fall within the "essence" of the particular business.

Johnson Controls cannot establish a BFOQ. Fertile women, as far as appears on the record, participate in the manufacture of batteries as efficiently as anyone else. Johnson Controls' professed moral and ethical concerns about the welfare of the next generation do not suffice to establish a BFOQ of female sterility. Nor can concerns about the welfare of the next generation be considered a part of the "essence" of Johnson Controls' business. It is word play to say that the job at Johnson Controls is to make batteries without risk to fetuses in the same way the job at an airline is to fly planes without crashing. Decisions about the welfare of future children must be left to the parents who conceive, bear, support and raise them rather than to the employers who hire those parents.

A word about tort liability and the increased cost of fertile women in the workplace is perhaps necessary. It is correct to say that Title VII does not prevent an employer from having a conscience. The statute, however, does prevent genderspecific fetal-protection policies. These two aspects of Title VII do not conflict. More than 40 states currently recognize a right to recover for a prenatal injury based either on negligence or on wrongful death. According to Johnson Controls, however, the company complies with the lead standard developed by OSHA and warns its female employees about the damaging effects of lead. It is worth noting that OSHA gave the problem of lead lengthy consideration and concluded that "there is no basis whatsoever for the claim that women of childbearing age should be excluded from the workplace in order to protect the fetus or the course of the pregnancy." 43 Fed. Reg. 52952, 22996 (1978). Instead, OSHA established a series of mandatory protections, which, taken together, "should effectively minimize any risk to the fetus and newborn child." Without negligence, it would be difficult for a court to find liability on the part of the employer. If, under general tort principles, Title VII bans gender-specific fetal-protection policies, the employer fully informs the woman of the risk, and the employer has not acted negligently, the basis for holding an employer liable seems remote at best.

Our holding today that Title VII, as so amended, forbids gender-specific fetal-protection policies is neither remarkable nor unprecedented. Concern for a woman's existing or potential offspring historically has been the excuse for denying women equal employment opportunities. Congress and the PDA prohibited discrimination on the basis of a woman's ability to become pregnant. We do no more than hold that the PDA means what it says.

It is no more appropriate for the courts than it is for individual employers to decide whether a woman's reproductive role is more important to herself and her family than her economic role. Congress has left this choice to the woman as hers to make. REVERSED and REMANDED.

Case Questions

1. Do you agree with the Court that the welfare of the child should be left to the parents, not the employer?

2. What do you find most troublesome about the decision, if anything? Explain.

3. As an employer, what would you do in this situation?

Management Tips

As you have seen from the chapter, gender discrimination can manifest itself in many forms, some of which may take the employer by surprise. Following these tips can help keep the surprises to a minimum.

- Let employees know from the minute they come to work for the employer that gender bias will not be tolerated in any way. Give them examples of unwanted behavior.
- Back up the strong gender message with appropriate enforcement.
- Take employee claims of gender discrimination or bias seriously.
- Promptly and thoroughly investigate all complaints, keeping privacy issues in mind.
- Don't go overboard in responding to offenses found to be substantiated by investigation. Make sure the "punishment fits the crime."
- Conduct periodic training to keep communication lines open and to act as an ongoing reminder of the employer's antibias policy.
- Conduct periodic audits to make sure gender is not adversely affecting hiring, promotion, and raises in the workplace.
- Review workplace policies to make sure there are no hidden policies or practices that could more adversely impact one gender than another.
- In dealing with gender issues, keep in mind that none of the actions need make the workplace stilted and formal. Employees can respect each other without discriminating against each other.

Summary

• Discrimination on the basis of gender is illegal and not in keeping with good business practices of efficiency and maximizing resources.

• Gender discrimination has many manifestations, including discrimination in hiring, firing, compensation, training, fetal-protection policies, and client preferences.

• In determining whether employment policies are gender biased, look at the obvious, but also look at the subtle bias that may arise from seemingly neutral policies adversely impacting a given gender, such as height and weight requirements. Both are illegal.

• Where employees must be treated differently, ensure that the basis for differentiation is grounded in factors not gender-based but, instead, address the actual limitation of the employee or applicant's qualifications.

• Under the PDA, employers must treat a pregnant employee who is able to perform the job just as they treat any other employee with a short-term disability.

• Because of health and other considerations, an employer may use pregnancy as a BFOQ and may have policies excluding or limiting pregnant employees if there is a reasonable business justification for such policies.

• If there are legitimate bases for treating pregnant employees differently, an employer has ample flexibility to make necessary decisions.

• Outmoded ideas regarding pregnant employees may not be the basis of denying them equal employment opportunities.

• Covered employers must provide covered employees with leave under the FMLA.

• Fetal-protection policies may not operate to discriminate against employees and fail to extend to them equal employment opportunities.

Chapter-End Questions

1. A food-service manager of a facility in serious disrepair was consistently rated as a favorable employee and received salary increases. However, when the company lost the facility account, she lost her job, even though male employees in equivalent positions with lower performance ratings received new assignments. The former employee filed suit against the company for gender discrimination. Will she win? (*Suggs v. ServiceMaster Educ. Food Management,* 72 F.3d 1228 (6th Cir. 1996).)

2. Employee says she was forced to quit her job because of her status as a mother of young children. She claimed that her female supervisor created a hostile work environment that violated Title VII. She was replaced by another mother. Does she win?

(*Fuller v. GTE Corp./Contel Cellular, Inc.,* 926 F. Supp. 653 (M.D. Tenn 1996).)

3. Employer faced a terrible dilemma. He had only one promotion to give, but he was torn between giving it to the single female and the male who had a family and, the employer thought, most needed and could best use the money. He finally decided to give the promotion to the male and told the female he gave it to the male because the male was a family man and needed the money. If the female employee sues, will she win? (*Taylor v. Runyon,* 175 F.3d 861 (11th Cir. 1999).)

4. An accounts receivable supervisor was laid off by her employer after taking an extended disability leave for pregnancy. She claimed that the employer discriminated against her

on the basis of sex and ability to bear children, stating that two male employees were retained and her replacement was a childless, 40-year-old unmarried female. She files suit, alleging gender discrimination. The employer said it was a legitimate layoff. What should the court consider in determining whether the employer's argument is true? (*Leahey v. Singer Sewing Co.*, 694 A.2d 609 (N.J. Super. 1996).)

5. Employee is dismissed when she becomes pregnant while she is having an affair with a married co-worker. The employer said that employee violated its norms of conduct by committing the crime of adultery. The father of the child is dismissed also. Is employee's dismissal a violation of the PDA? (*Cumpiano v. Banco Santander Puerto Rico*, 902 F.2d 148 (1st Cir. 1990).)

6. A cable company closed its door-to-door sales department and released all employees of that department after settling a discrimination complaint by one of the department's employees. The employee's mother, sister, and two close friends had also been employed in the department. Eighteen months later, the company resumed its door-to-door sales, but refused to rehire three of the former employees connected with the employee who had previously sued. The former employees sue, alleging gender discrimination. Will they be successful in their suit? Explain. (*Craig v. Suburban Cablevision, Inc.*, 660 A.2d 505 (N.J. 1995).)

7. A power company began employing women as meter readers, and the job classification went from all-male to all-female within a few years. The labor union which represented bargaining unit employees negotiated a new collective bargaining agreement that froze wages in the meter reader classification and lowered the wage for new hires. There was evidence that the company president made comments concerning the desirability of housewives to read meters and that he admitted that the contract was unfavorable to women. A number of women in the meter reader category filed a state court lawsuit against the employer and union for gender discrimination on the basis of state law and wage discrimination under federal law. The employer argued that the federal labor law preempted the state law gender discrimination complaint, therefore the gender complaint should be dismissed. Is the state law preempted? (*Donajkowski v. Alpena Power Co.*, 556 N.W.2d 876 (Mich. App. 1996).)

8. On employee's first day on the job, employer withdraws an offer of employment as a medical claims examiner after learning that employee is four months pregnant. Is this a violation of the PDA? Does it matter if the point at which employee would be taking leave would likely have been the beginning of her paying small claims without close supervision? (*Ahmad v. Loyal American Life Ins. Co.*, 767 F. Supp. 1114 (S.D. Ala. S. Div. 1991).)

9. Employer decides to shut down one of its three plants because the employees at that plant are almost exclusively women. The males who worked at the plant and lost their jobs as a result of the closing wish to sue for gender discrimination under Title VII. If they do, will they be successful? (*Allen v. American Home Foods, Inc.*, 644 F. Supp. 1553 (N.D. Ind. 1986).)

10. Employer terminates female employee because employer's daughter-in-law feels the female employee is having an affair with her husband, the employer's son, who is also employed by employer. Female employee sues for gender discrimination. Does she win?

8 SEXUAL HARASSMENT

Chapter Outline

S C E N A R I O S

S C E N A R I O   1

A female employee tells her supervisor that she is disturbed by the workplace display of nude pictures, calendars, and cartoons. He replies that, if she is bothered, she should not look. The employee suspects this is a form of sexual harassment. Do you agree? Why or why not?

S C E N A R I O   2

A male and female employee have engaged in a two-year consensual personal relationship, which ends. The male continues to attempt to get the female to go out with him on dates. When she does not, she is eventually fired by the male, who is her supervisor. She sues, alleging sexual harassment. Who wins and why?

S C E N A R I O   3

An employee routinely compliments employees about their appearance, hair, and body. Is this sexual harassment? Why or why not?

Statutory Basis

It shall be unlawful employment practice for an employer—

(1) to fail or refuse to hire or to discharge any individual, or otherwise to discriminate against any individual with respect to his compensation, terms, conditions, or privileges of employment, because of such individual's . . . sex [gender]. . . . 42 U.S.C. 2000e2(a)

Unwelcome sexual advances, requests for sexual favors, and other verbal or physical conduct of a sexual nature constitute sexual harassment when (1) submission to such conduct is made either explicitly or implicitly a term or condition of an individual's employment, (2) submission to or rejection of such conduct by an individual is used as the basis for employment decisions affecting such individual, or (3) such conduct has the purpose or effect of unreasonably interfering with an individual's work performance or creating an intimidating, hostile, or offensive working environment. 29 C.F.R. Section 1604.11 (a)

Since Eden . . . and Counting

"Navy blue dress, white spot. Cigars. Altoid breath mints. Black beret." You could probably say that from one end of the globe to the other, and before you got to the third item you would hear "Monica Lewinsky." Oklahoma isn't any longer just the lead song in a musical of the same name. It's also the place where Anita Hill, who took on the US Senate, resided and taught law school. Mitsubishi doesn't just bring to mind cars anymore. It also conjures up visions of masses of employees (given the day off with pay and transported to the site by company-arranged buses) demonstrating outside of the Chicago office of the EEOC, protesting the charges of several women who claimed Mitsubishi's rampant atmosphere of sexual harassment violated Title VII.

Impeachment of a president, resignation of starred generals and other high-level military personnel, resignation of company presidents and long-term legislators, televised hearings of US Supreme Court justices, have all been part of our national consciousness and abrupt introduction to, and education in, the area of sexual harassment.

It seems like such a short time ago that most of us were blissfully unaware that the legal cause of action of sexual harassment even existed. Though it had been around for more than 10 years, most people knew very little about it. Until, that is, it was thrust into the limelight when then-University of Oklahoma law professor Anita Hill took her seat at the table before the Senate Judiciary Committee in the confirmation hearings for associate justice of the US Supreme Court, Clarence Thomas. Hill had worked for Thomas when he was head of the EEOC about 10 years before.

When Thomas came up for confirmation, friends of Hill reported to the committee that she had at one time revealed to them details of unprofessional exchanges with Thomas that could have amounted to sexual harassment. The committee contacted Hill and made clear that she would either testify about the matter and set the record straight herself or leave them to their own devices of discovery. Hill chose to testify, and the country hasn't been the same since.

Hill's testimony over the next several days, and Thomas's barely concealed anger about it, were painful for the millions of Americans who sat glued to their television sets during those unbelievable autumn days in 1991. People who had never even heard the term *sexual harassment* now had implacable opinions about it. From barber shops to executive suites, and everywhere in between, *everyone* discussed the pros and cons of not only Hill's and Thomas's veracity, but also the concept of sexual harassment itself. Men who had thought nothing of what they considered harmless sexually suggestive jokes, comments, and gestures suddenly felt themselves looked upon as virtual lechers. Women who had found themselves on the receiving end of such attentions now discovered that those attentions might actually be illegal. Eight months after the Hill–Thomas hearings, sexual harassment complaints filed with the EEOC increased by more than 50 percent. Ninety percent of the charges were from women. In the elections of 1992, called the "Year of the Woman," unprecedented numbers of female politicians rode the backlash wave of women who wanted to change "politics as usual" after witnessing the Senate's poor treatment of Hill during the hearings.

Almost overnight, the country's offices and workplaces went from friendly to foul. It had to be seen to be believed. It was a matter that captivated the national consciousness much the way the Lewinsky affair did in 1998, only there was an immediate, acerbic, often acrimonious air to it. Lines were drawn in offices, bars, universities, churches, and homes all across the country, and people took their places on one side or the other and held their ground.

Whew! Scary, huh? Why do we bother to tell you all this instead of launching right into a narrative on sexual harassment? Because it is important for you to understand the context of this issue. Sexual harassment law is not something that has been around forever that we've grown accustomed to and learned to live with over hundreds of years or even in the 30+ years since Title VII was born. Even though it may seem like old hat today, it's still pretty new in the legal sense. It is still evolving. The US Supreme Court didn't hear its first sexual harassment case until 1986, and the next one didn't come until seven years later. All of a sudden there were four decisions in the Court's 1997–98 term. An unprecedented bonanza!

We also told you the background of sexual harassment because there's a lot of baggage that comes with the issue. Often, managers, supervisors, and employees don't recognize sexual harassment when it occurs because they still don't "get it." Our society preaches sexual permissiveness on the one hand, through music, movies, television, advertising, and so forth, but when it comes to the workplace, the rules are different (See Exhibit 8–1), and some people don't make the transition very well. Sexual harassment isn't confined only to one segment of society. Some of the largest judgments or most embarrassing cases have been against such august bastions as Wall Street brokerage firms, otherwise upstanding law firms, finance houses, prestigious universities, Hollywood shows, large nonprofits and, of course, the presidency of the United States. No one is exempt.

But does it really exist? Is it really widespread? Should we really be concerned? Is it that big a deal? Well, let's see.

In one of the first, and still one of the most comprehensive studies ever conducted on the issue, the US Merit Systems Protection Board in 1980 conducted a study of sexual harassment among federal employees. It was found that over 40 percent of them had reported incidents of sexual harassment. The study was repeated seven years later and the results were nearly the same (42 percent). A survey by *Working Woman* magazine of 160 of the *Fortune* 500 companies, showed that nearly 40 percent of the companies surveyed had received at least one sexual harassment complaint in the past 12 months. A *New York Times* poll found that 4 of every 10 women reported having experienced sexual harassment. The *National Law Journal* reported that 60 percent of female attorneys nationally said they had experienced some form of sexual harassment. A *Parade Magazine* poll discovered that 70 percent of the women polled who served in the military said they had been sexually harassed, as had 50 percent of the women who worked in congressional offices on Capitol Hill. Despite the numbers, only about 5 percent of the incidents of sexual harassment are reported.

Those who experience sexual harassment "pay all the intangible emotional costs inflicted by anger, humiliation, frustration, withdrawal, [and] dysfunction in family life."[1] In *Robinson v. Jacksonville Shipyards, Inc.,*[2] the court found, based on expert testimony, that:

---

[1] *Ellison v. Brady,* 924 F.2d 872, 881, n. 15 (9th Cir. 1991), quoting from the MSPB update study, "United States Merit Systems Protection Board, Sexual Harassment in the Federal Government: An Update" at 42 (1988).

[2] 760 F. Supp. 1486, 1506–07 (M.D. Fla., 1991).

EXHIBIT 8–1   Mixed Messages . . . and Not Everyone Agrees with Title VII

Sometimes, trying to stamp out sexual harassment in the workplace can seem like an unwinnable battle, given the greater context in which we live. The excerpt below gives a compelling view of that context. But, as we discussed in the introduction to sexual harassment, the concept of sexual harassment does carry baggage, and not everyone agrees that something should be done about stamping it out.

Sex is everywhere you look in America. No escaping it. Newsstands spill over with glossy photos of bikini-popping babes. Radio jocks like Don Imus and Howard Stern dole out sexually tinged humor to go with your morning coffee. There are sexual fantasy telephone lines advertised on matchbook covers. Pay TV channels show male and female stripteasers and porn films day and night. Condoms are handed out like bubble gum, even to kids, sometimes courtesy of the Board of Education. Porn CD-ROMs like *Virtual Valerie* are big sellers.

Sex screams at us from the sides of buses with their underwear ads, and from TV sets carrying afternoon soap operas. But let anyone complain, and the affected interests, backed by the civil libertarians, scream censorship.

Except. Except in the workplace. Don't pin a *Penthouse* centerfold onto your office wall. Don't repeat to a co-worker an off-color joke about the guy in the White House. And for heaven's sake, don't leave *Virtual Valerie* on your office desk.

Do any of these things and the federal government suddenly forgets about the First Amendment. It could easily slap your employer with a six-figure lawsuit because you've created a "hostile environment" in the workplace.

"Outside of work, we face an incredibly permissive society," notes Louis DiLorenzo, a senior partner at Bond, Schoeneck & King, in Syracuse, NY, which represents companies in sexual harassment cases. "Yet we're told, at work, make sure no one talks about race or sex."

Of all the crusades Washington has ever embarked upon, the current commitment to stamp out sex in the workplace surely ranks among the daffiest.

Reprinted by permission of *Forbes* Magazine © 2000, *Forbes* 1996.

[v]ictims of sexual harassment suffer stress effects from the harassment. Stress as a result of sexual harassment is recognized as a specific, diagnosable problem by the American Psychiatric Association. Among the stress effects suffered is "work performance stress," which includes distraction from tasks, dread of work, and an inability to work. Another form is "emotional stress," which covers a range of responses, including anger, fear of physical safety, anxiety, depression, guilt, humiliation, and embarrassment. Physical stress also results from sexual harassment; it may manifest itself by sleeping problems, headaches, weight changes, and other physical ailments. A study by the Working Women's Institute found that 96 percent of sexual harassment victims experienced emotional stress, 45 percent suffered work performance stress, and 35 percent were inflicted with physical stress problems.

Sexual harassment has a cumulative, eroding effect on the victim's well-being. When women feel a need to maintain vigilance against the next incidence of harassment, the stress is increased tremendously. When women feel that their individual complaints will not change the work environment materially, the ensuing sense of despair further compounds the stress.

Regarding tangible costs, according to the classic 1987 MSPB update study, sexual harassment cost the federal government $267 million from May 1985 to May

1987 for losses in productivity, sick leave costs, and employee replacement costs. The *Working Woman* magazine survey found the actual cost of sexual harassment in the responding companies to be $6.7 million in low productivity, absenteeism, and employee turnover. In addition, along with the nontangible price they pay, MSPB found that employees who are sexually harassed pay medical expenses, litigation expenses, job search expenses, and the loss of valuable sick leave and annual leave.

Whether it occurs through joking, e-mails, touching, unwanted requests for dates, denials of job opportunities, or some other means, sexual harassment is not just kidding or a joke or workplace fraternization. It is illegal as a form of gender discrimination that violates Title VII of the 1964 Civil Rights Act. But it is not only illegal: given the toll it takes on the workplace, it is simply not good business. Since it is purely personal on the part of the harasser, it makes little sense for an employer not to take simple steps to prevent this totally unnecessary liability. It has become even less justifiable in the face of the 1991 Civil Rights Act permitting jury trials and compensatory and punitive damages. The spectre of class action suits also looms since *Jensen v. Eveleth Taconite Co.*[3] certified a class of female miners in a sexual harassment suit for the first time and others have followed suit, including the Mitsubishi Corporation.

The Civil Rights Act was passed in 1964, but it was the mid to late 1970s before courts began to seriously recognize sexual harassment as a form of gender discrimination under Title VII. In 1980, soon after the first few significant sexual harassment cases were decided, the EEOC issued guidelines on sexual harassment.

Exhibit 8–2

Dear Ann Landers: I am married. I am also the boss. I have several competent women employees who come on to me in subtle ways. They wear see-through blouses in the office, which I consider in poor taste. I do not wear see-through pants to work. Their thigh-high short skirts may be fashionable but when they sit down I am afraid to look for fear of what might be showing.

If I were to bring up this subject, they might charge me with "sexual harassment," so once they are hired and their work skills are up to par, there is very little I can do. The law is now on their side.

I often wonder if these women are trying to trap me into making passes at them. When I once mentioned "appropriate clothing" in the office, they pointed out that they dress like everyone else in the building—which is true.

I am proud to say that in the 28 years I've been married, cheating never once crossed my mind. Why, then, do these women come on to me? I don't flirt and am very businesslike. Of course, I could not ask my secretary to type this letter, so please excuse the mistakes.—Business Man, USA.

Permission to reprint granted by Ann Landers/Creators Syndicate.

---

[3] 139 F.R.D. 657 (D. Minn. 1991).

The guidelines, quoted at the beginning of this chapter, are not law in the sense of Title VII but carry a great deal of weight when it comes to how courts will view and analyze the issue.

Where Do Sexual Harassment Considerations Leave the Employer?

The letter to Ann Landers in Exhibit 8–2 evidences a common frustration with and ignorance of sexual harassment issues. The intent of the law is *not* that the workplace either become totally devoid of sexuality, or be given completely over to employees who would misuse the law. Consensual relationships are *not* forbidden, and employees may date consistent with appropriate company policy. It is only when the activity directed toward an employee is *unwelcome* and imposes terms or conditions different for one gender than another that it becomes a problem. For instance, a female employee might be required as a condition of employment to date her supervisor, while the male employees have no such condition imposed.

Sexual Harassment in General

There are two theories on which an action for sexual harassment may be brought: **quid pro quo** and **hostile environment sexual harassment.** The first generally requires the employer to require something of the harassee as a condition of employment. The second addresses an offensive work environment to which one gender is subjected, but not the other. While there are two different types of sexual harassment and each has its own requirements, the US Supreme Court recently said that the distinction need not be rigid. In *Burlington Industries, Inc. v. Ellerth,*[4] the supervisor made threats to the harassee, but did not carry them out. The harassee brought suit on the theory of quid pro quo sexual harassment, but rather than deny relief because there had been no loss of a tangible job benefit which would impose liability on the employer, the Court said that the terms *quid pro quo* and *hostile environment* are not controlling for purposes of determining employer liability for harassment by a supervisor. Rather, they are helpful in making rough demarcations between Title VII cases in which sexual harassment threats are carried out and where they are not or are absent altogether.

In order to see the context within which sexual harassment operates, and many of the ideas that underlie courts' consideration of the issue, take a look at both the majority decision in the following case as well as the dissent. Read the case with the idea in mind that you are looking at the competing interests at issue as society continues to struggle with this sometimes difficult issue. Note that the dissent in *Rabidue* has pretty much become the majority view in the way courts now approach the issue of sexual harassment, but the case is instructive in forcing you to think about the "subtext" of sexual harassment claims and why there is often so much acrimony around the issue.

Quid pro quo sexual harassment Sexual harassment in which the harasser requests sexual activity from the harassee in exchange for workplace benefits.

Hostile environment sexual harassment Sexual harassment in which the harasser creates an offensive or intimidating environment for the harassee.

---

[4] 524 U.S. 742 (1998).

RABIDUE V. OSCEOLA REFINING CO.
805 F.2d 611 (6th Cir. 1986)

An employee asserted gender discrimination and sexual harassment in violation of Title VII due to "vulgarity" and nude posters in the workplace. The court rejected her claim. However, the case is probably cited more for the dissent than the majority opinion. The dissenting view is now the one that generally prevails in sexual harassment cases. The majority opinion helps you see the evolution of sexual harassment claims from the more provincial view, to the more enlightened position now taken by the courts.

Krupansky, J.

Rabidue was a credit manager and office manager. Her charge of sexual harassment arose primarily as a result of her unfortunate acrimonious working relationship with Douglas Henry, a supervisor of the company's key punch and computer sections. Henry exercised no supervisory authority over Rabidue nor Rabidue over him. Henry was an extremely vulgar and crude individual who customarily made obscene comments about women generally, and, on occasion, directed such obscenities, to Rabidue. Management was aware of Henry's vulgarity, but it had been unsuccessful in curbing his offensive personality traits. Rabidue, and other female employees, were annoyed by Henry's vulgarity. In addition to Henry's obscenities, other male employees from time to time displayed pictures of nude or scantily clad women in their offices and/or work areas, to which Rabidue and other women employees were exposed. Rabidue was discharged from her employment at the company as a result of her many job-related problems, including her irascible and opinionated personality and her inability to work harmoniously with co-workers and customers.

Rabidue to have prevailed in her cause of action against Osceola on this record must have proved that she had been subjected to unwelcome verbal conduct and poster displays of a sexual nature which had unreasonably interfered with her work performance and created an intimidating, hostile, or offensive working environment that affected seriously her psychological well-being.

The record disclosed that Henry's obscenities, although annoying, were not so startling as to have affected seriously the psyches of the plaintiff or other female employees. The evidence did not demonstrate that Henry's vulgarity substantially affected the totality of the workplace. The sexually oriented poster displays had a negligible effect on Rabidue's work environment when considered in the context of a society that condones and publicly features and commercially exploits open displays of written and pictorial erotica at the newsstands, on prime-time television, at the cinema, and in other public places. In sum, Henry's vulgar language and the sexually oriented posters did not result in a working environment that could be considered intimidating, hostile, or offensive under the guidelines. AFFIRMED.

Keith, Circuit Judge, concurring in part, dissenting in part.

I dissent, for several reasons, as I believe the majority erroneously resolves Rabidue's substantive claims.

First, after review of the entire record I am firmly convinced, that although supporting evidence exists, the court is mistaken in affirming the findings that Osceola's treatment of Rabidue evinced no anti-female animus and that gender-based discrimination played no role in her discharge. The overall circumstances of Rabidue's workplace evince an anti-female environment. For seven years plaintiff worked at Osceola as the sole woman in a salaried management position. In common work areas Rabidue and other female employees were exposed daily to displays of nude or partially clad women belonging to a number of male employees at Osceola. One poster, which remained on the wall for eight years, showed a prone woman who had a golf ball on her breasts with a man standing over her, golf club in hand, yelling "Fore." And one desk plaque declared "Even male chauvinist pigs need love." Plaintiff testified the posters offended her and her female co-workers.

In addition, Henry regularly spewed anti-female obscenity. He routinely referred to women as "whore," "cunt," "pussy," and "tits." Of plaintiff, Henry specifically remarked "All that bitch needs is a good lay" and called her "fat ass." Plaintiff arranged at least one meeting of female employees to discuss Henry and repeatedly filed written complaints on behalf of herself and other female employees who feared losing their jobs if they complained directly. Osceola Vice President Charles Meutzel stated he knew that employees were "greatly disturbed" by Henry's language. However, because Osceola needed Henry's computer expertise, Meutzel did not reprimand or fire Henry. In response to subsequent complaints about Henry, a later supervisor testified that he gave Henry "a little fatherly advice" about Henry's prospects if he learned to become "an executive type person."

In addition to tolerating this anti-female behavior, Osceola excluded Rabidue, the sole female in management, from activities she needed to perform her duties and progress in her career. Unlike male salaried employees, she did not receive free lunches, free gasoline, a telephone credit card or entertainment privileges. Nor was she invited to the weekly golf matches. Without addressing Osceola's disparate treatment of Rabidue, the district court dismissed these perks and business activities as fringe benefits. After Rabidue became credit manager, Osceola prevented her from visiting or taking customers to lunch as all previous male credit managers had done. Upon requesting such privileges, Rabidue's supervisor replied that it would be improper for a woman to take a male customer to lunch and that she might have car trouble on the road. On another occasion, he asked her "how would it look for me, a married man, to take you, a divorced woman, to the West Branch Country Club in such a small town?" Osceola saw no problem in male managers entertaining female clients regardless of marital status. Rabidue's later supervisor stated to another female worker, "[Rabidue] is doing a good job as credit manager, but we really need a man on that job," adding "She can't take customers out to lunch."

Rabidue was consistently accorded secondary status. At a meeting to instruct clerical employees of their duties after a corporate takeover, Rabidue was seated with female hourly employees. The male salaried employees, apparently pre-informed of the post-takeover procedures, stood at the front of the room. There are many other instances in the record of how Rabidue was treated differently in negative ways because of her gender. I conclude that the misogynous language and decorative displays tolerated at the workplace, the primitive views of working women expressed by Osceola supervisors and Osceola's treatment for their only female salaried employee clearly evinces anti-female animus.

Nor do I agree with the majority's holding that a court considering hostile environment claims should adopt the perspective of the reasonable person's reaction to a similar environment. In my view, the reasonable person perspective fails to account for the wide divergence between most women's views of appropriate sexual conduct and those of men. I would have courts adopt the perspective of the reasonable victim which simultaneously allows courts to consider salient sociological differences as well as shield employers from the neurotic complaint.

The majority also mandates that we consider

the "prevailing work environment," the obscenity that pervaded the environment before and after Rabidue came there and her reasonable expectations upon "voluntarily" entering the environment. The majority suggests through these factors that a woman assumes the risk of working in an abusive anti-female environment. Moreover, the majority contends that such work environments somehow have an innate right to perpetuation and are not to be addressed under Title VII. In my view, Title VII's precise purpose is to prevent such behavior and attitudes from poisoning the work environment of classes protected under the Act. As I believe no woman should be subjected to an environment where her sexual dignity and reasonable sensibilities are visually, verbally, or physically assailed as a matter of prevailing male prerogative, I dissent.

Nor can I agree with the majority's notion that the effect of pin-up posters and misogynous language in the workplace can have only a minimal effect on female employees and should not be deemed hostile or offensive "when considered in the context of a society that condones and publicly features and commercially exploits open displays of erotica." "Society" in this scenario must primarily refer to the unenlightened; I hardly believe reasonable women condone the pervasive degradation and exploitation of female sexuality perpetuated in American culture. In fact, pervasive societal approval thereof and of other stereotypes stifles female potential and instills the debased sense of self worth which accompanies stigmatiza-

tion. The presence of pin-ups and misogynous language in the workplace can only evoke and confirm the debilitating norms by which women are primarily and contemptuously valued as objects of male sexual fantasy. That some men would condone and wish to perpetuate such behavior is not surprising. However, the relevant inquiry at hand is what the reasonable woman would find offensive, not society, which at one point also condoned slavery. I conclude that sexual posters and anti-female language can seriously affect the psychological well-being of the reasonable woman and interfere with her ability to perform her job.

In conclusion, I dissent because the record shows that Osceola's treatment of Rabidue evinces anti-female animus and that Rabidue's gender played a role in her dismissal. I also believe the hostile environment standard set forth in the majority opinion shields and condones behavior Title VII would have the courts redress.

Case Questions

1. Do you think the majority decision or the dissent is closer to your view of sexual harassment? Why?

2. Do you agree that the dissent's factors about how Rabidue had been treated by management is a basis for hostile environment?

3. If you were management and needed Henry's expertise, what would you have done about his actions?

Scenario

There were courts that followed the majority in *Rabidue,* and those that preferred the dissent. Those preferring the dissent were more prevalent, and ultimately prevailed when the US Supreme Court decided *Harris v. Forklift Systems, Inc.*[5] *Harris* was also a Sixth Circuit decision with facts similar to *Rabidue's.* That is why the employee would be correct in opening scenario one.

---

[5] 510 U.S. 17 (1993).

EXHIBIT 8–3   Trading Places

Sexually harassed at work, a California man is awarded $1 million

When Sabino Gutierrez asked his boss, Maria Martinez for a few days off back in 1986 to visit his native Mexico, she promptly approved the vacation. As a token of his appreciation, he brought her back a gift of two embroidered pillowcases. When Martinez, who was personnel manager at Cal-Spas, a hot-tub manufacturing company in Pomona, Calif., dropped by Gutierrez's office to thank him personally for the gift, she closed the door and embraced him. He thought she was going to give him a peck on the cheek. "But the kiss," says Gutierrez, "was coming straight to the mouth." He says his supervisor told him, "I want to give you my thanks this way."

That, according to Gutierrez, 33, was the beginning of a six-year campaign of sexual harassment during which he was subjected to the advances of Martinez, 39, almost daily. He says the torment included unwanted caresses, kissing, fondling of genitals and demands for sex. In her defense, Martinez, who is married and the mother of two children, contends that it was Gutierrez who was coming on to her, as well as to other women at the company. "He walked around here like a peacock," she says. "Nobody stood in this man's way." Last week, though, a Los Angeles jury found that Martinez had indeed sexually harassed Gutierrez and awarded him more than $1 million in damages. The decision is the largest award ever handed down in the United States for a male victim of sexual harassment.

Nonetheless, the facts of the case are far from cut-and-dried. Gutierrez, then a division manager at Cal-Spas, admits that after Martinez's initial advances, he had sex with her—once—in the summer of 1988. "It got to the point where I had to do it to keep her happy," he says. After that, he says, he managed to fend her off despite her continuing overtures. Still, says Gutierrez, he was afraid to reject Martinez outright for fear of losing his job.

The real crisis came in May 1990, Gutierrez says, when he fell in love and became engaged in the span of a few weeks. When Martinez heard, says Gutierrez, she offered her congratulations—then stormed out of his office and slammed the door. The next day, he testified, she vowed to get revenge. During the next several months, she humiliated him by tearing down his office and paring away his duties.

The low point came when she stripped him of all his managerial responsibilities. "She was treating me like a sweeper," he says. "It's terrible even to remember this." According to Martinez, though, the only source of stress for Gutierrez was his own incompetence on the job, which she attributed to his being promoted beyond his capabilities. As for the allegations of harassment, Martinez, who like Gutierrez emigrated from Mexico, scoffs at the notion. "Look at me," she says, incredulous, "I'm a well-educated woman. I've been married for 15 years. I have two children. I grew up with *very* high morals in my family."

At the trial, Gutierrez's lawyer produced a few witnesses who could corroborate his accounts of harassment. But in the end, a key factor for the 10-woman, two-man jury was the demeanor of the accused and her accuser. While Gutierrez, who has a 22-month-old son, Geovanni, with wife Angelica and now works at another spa company in Ontario, Calif., came across as genuine and sympathetic, Martinez appeared calculating and defensive. "I found him to be very credible right from the beginning," says jury forewoman Clara Riles. By contrast, "it was like [Martinez] had an agenda and she was following that agenda."

The long-term implications of the decision are hard to gauge. If nothing else, the case put some women's rights advocates in the unusual position of arguing against a woman. Yet, in their eyes, the verdict was a solid victory for their cause, since they believe it will strengthen harassment protection for everyone. "The message is that this country is not about justice for some, but about justice for all," says noted feminist lawyer Gloria Allred, whose firm represented Gutierrez. "And that includes men."

In *Harris,* a female managerial employee was subject to several embarrassing and demeaning actions by Charles Hardy, president of Forklift, who admitted to the acts but considered it "joking." Women were requested to retrieve coins from his front pants pockets; he threw objects on the ground in front of Harris and other females and asked them to pick them up; he made sexual innuendoes about Harris and other women's clothing; in front of others, he suggested that he and Harris negotiate her raise at the Holiday Inn; he told her on several occasions "you're a woman, what do you know?" "we need a man as the rental manager," and that she was a "dumb ass woman." After Harris requested that Hardy curtail his activities because she was offended, he promised to stop, but then he resumed. Harris quit after Hardy asked her again, in front of others while she was arranging a deal with a customer, "what did you do, promise the guy . . . some [sex] Saturday night?" The US Supreme Court rejected the notion that such activity in the workplace does not violate Title VII. The Court did not determine the issue of a "reasonable victim" versus "reasonable person" test, but made clear that such activity was totally inappropriate and created a hostile environment.

Most sexual harassment takes place between males and females, with the male as the harasser and the female as the harassee. But the gender of the harasser need not be male. Males can be sexually harassed, just as females can be sexually harassed. Unfortunately, because society views males and sex so differently from females and sex, many males do not bring cases for fear of ridicule (See Exhibit 8–3). Males who are being sexually harassed and wish to put a stop to it often find themselves the object of workplace jokes, teasing, and questioned sexuality, so they forgo filing claims. In *Showalter,* below, males alleged sexual harassment when they were forced to have sex with their supervisor's secretary in order to keep their jobs.

SHOWALTER V. ALLISON REED GROUP, INC.
767 F. Supp. 1205 (DC RI 1991)

Two male employees allege sexual harassment in violation of Title VII of the Civil Rights Act of 1964, because their manager forced them to engage in sexual activities with his secretary by threatening them with the loss of their jobs if they did not comply. The court found sexual harassment even though the harassees were male.

Lagueux, J.

Employees allege that a series of several sexual incidents occurred on the Techni-Craft premises beginning the summer of 1988 and lasting until June or July of 1989. Defendants Smith and Marsella deny that most of it ever occurred, as does the Allison Reed Group.

Smith, the general manager, was having a sexual liaison with his secretary, Marsella. Employee Showalter alleges that in the Spring of 1988, Smith began talking incessantly and obsessively about Marsella to Showalter. The talks were of a sexual nature and usually described to

Showalter Smith's sexual relationship with Marsella, including showing Showalter nude photos, pornographic drawings, and X-rated letters, all involving Marsella. By the end of the summer, Smith began telling Showalter that Marsella was interested in Showalter and prodding Showalter to join his sexual liaison with Marsella. Showalter declined on the ground that he was married, but Smith immediately told Showalter that he and Marsella were also married, but what their spouses didn't know wouldn't hurt them. Angrily, Smith told Showalter that Marsella controlled the hiring and firing decisions at Techni-Craft, and that if he valued his job he would follow Smith's demands. Smith continued to press Showalter to engage in a ménage-à-trois, and reminded Showalter of Smith's extensive connections in the jewelry business in Rhode Island, implying that Showalter would be shut out of the jewelry business if he did not comply with Smith's request. Smith also told Showalter that he had to please Marsella in order for everything between Smith and Marsella "to be okay." At one point, Smith also threatened Showalter with the loss of his medical benefits if he failed to participate in the sexual activity. Smith knew that this was especially important to Showalter because Showalter's son had a heart defect and had undergone three open heart surgeries.

Showalter first acceded to Smith's demands in September 1988 when Smith orchestrated an after hours strip-tease performance by Marsella on company premises. Before the actual event Smith gave Showalter explicit instructions outlining the various sexual activity Smith expected Showalter to engage in with Marsella and him. This occurred at least twice and each time Showalter was unable to maintain an erection to do what was demanded of him, and was berated by Smith and Marsella. Showalter was also forced to observe and engage in other sexual activity at

Techni-Craft from September 1988 to June 1989, including during work hours and after work hours. Smith tried to get Showalter to bring his wife into the activity in the Spring of 1989, but Showalter resisted. [Employee] Phetosomphone [Fet´-ō-som´-fō-nee] was also forced by Smith to engage in sexual activity at Techni-Craft and observe it between Smith and Marsella. He feared he would lose his job if he did not accede.

Here, Showalter and Phetosomphone were clearly the victims of both hostile environment sexual harassment and quid pro quo sexual harassment. For the quid pro quo sexual harassment, the employees were clearly required to trade the requested sexual activity for the privilege of keeping their jobs. The hostile environment sexual harassment occurred and drastically altered the conditions of plaintiffs' employment and created a hostile and abusive work environment. The frequency and nature of the unwelcome sexual activity certainly was severe and pervasive. Sexual advances were made to plaintiffs for months and the harassment completely infected the work environment. JUDGMENT for PLAINTIFFS on this issue.

Case Questions

1. What can an employer do to protect against liability for sexual harassment in situations such as this, where the person responsible for the workplace is the perpetrator?

2. Do you think males who complain of sexual harassment are less likely to be believed? Why or why not? Do you think they are less likely to sue? Explain.

3. Should it make any difference that the request for sex with Showalter did not come directly from Marsella, the person who wanted to engage in the activity with him, but rather came from Smith? Explain.

As a final preliminary matter, Title VII does not protect employees from discrimination on the basis of affinity orientation, but the US Supreme Court recently held, after many, many lower court cases to the contrary, that even though both the harasser and the harassee are the same gender, a harassee can bring a sexual harassment claim and be protected by Title VII. Of course, the reason for the harassment cannot be because the harassee is gay or lesbian, since that is not covered by Title VII, but there will not be a presumption that if both parties are the same gender the claim is not covered by Title VII.

ONCALE V. SUNDOWNER OFFSHORE SERVICES, INC.
523 US 75 (1998)

Employee sued for sexual harassment under Title VII after being harassed by his co-workers. For the first time, the US Supreme Court dealt with the question of whether there can be a sexual harassment claim under Title VII if the harassers and the harassee are the same gender. The Court determined that Title VII's exclusion of discrimination on the basis of affinity orientation did not prevent a cause of action for sexual harassment under Title VII even when the harasser and harassee are both the same gender.

Scalia, J.

This case presents the question whether workplace harassment can violate Title VII's prohibition against "discriminat[ion] . . . because of . . . sex," when the harasser and the harassed employee are of the same sex.

Oncale was working for Sundowner Offshore Services on a Chevron U.S.A., Inc., oil platform in the Gulf of Mexico. He was employed as a roustabout on an eight-man crew which included John Lyons, Danny Pippen, and Brandon Johnson. Lyons, the crane operator, and Pippen, the driller, had supervisory authority. On several occasions, Oncale was forcibly subjected to sex-related, humiliating actions against him by Lyons, Pippen and Johnson in the presence of the rest of the crew. Pippen and Lyons also physically assaulted Oncale in a sexual manner, and Lyons threatened him with rape. Oncale's complaints to supervisory personnel produced no remedial action; in fact, the company's Safety Compliance

Clerk, Valent Hohen, told Oncale that Lyons and Pippin "picked [on] him all the time too," and called him a name suggesting homosexuality. Oncale eventually quit—asking that his pink slip reflect that he "voluntarily left due to sexual harassment and verbal abuse." When asked at his deposition why he left Sundowner, Oncale stated "I felt that if I didn't leave my job, that I would be raped or forced to have sex." The district court held that "Mr. Oncale, a male, has no cause of action under Title VII for harassment by male co-workers." The Fifth Circuit affirmed.

Title VII of the Civil Rights Act of 1964 not only covers "terms" and "conditions" in the narrow contractual sense, but "evinces a congressional intent to strike at the entire spectrum of disparate treatment of men and women in employment." "When the workplace is permeated with discriminatory intimidation, ridicule, and insult that is sufficiently severe or pervasive to alter the conditions of the victim's employment and create an abusive working environment, Title VII is violated."

Title VII's prohibition of discrimination "because of . . . sex" protects men as well as women, and in the related context of racial discrimination in the workplace we have rejected any conclusive presumption that an employer will not discriminate against members of his own race. "Because of the many facets of human motivation, it would be unwise to presume as a matter of law that human beings of one definable group will not discriminate against other members of that group." We hold today that nothing in Title VII necessarily bars a claim of discrimination "because of . . . sex" merely because the plaintiff and the defendant are of the same sex.

Courts have had little trouble with that principle in cases where an employee claims to have been passed over for a job or promotion. But when the issue arises in the context of a "hostile environment" sexual harassment claim, the state and federal courts have taken a bewildering variety of stances. Some, like the Fifth Circuit in this case, have held that same-sex sexual harassment claims are never cognizable under Title VII. Other decisions say that such claims are actionable only if the plaintiff can prove that the harasser is homosexual (and thus presumably motivated by sexual desire). Still others suggest that workplace harassment that is sexual in content is always actionable, regardless of the harasser's sex, sexual orientation, or motivations.

We see no justification in the statutory language or our precedents for a categorical rule excluding same-sex harassment claims from the coverage of Title VII. As some courts have observed, male-on-male sexual harassment in the workplace was assuredly not the principal evil Congress was concerned with when it enacted Title VII. But statutory prohibitions often go beyond the principal evil to cover reasonably comparable evils, and it is ultimately the provisions of our laws rather than the principal concerns of our legislators by which we are governed. Title VII

prohibits "discriminat[ion] . . . because of . . . sex" in the "terms" or "conditions" of employment. Our holding that this includes sexual harassment must extend to sexual harassment of any kind that meets the statutory requirements.

Respondents contend that recognizing liability for same-sex harassment will transform Title VII into a general civility code for the American workplace. But that risk is no greater for same-sex than for opposite-sex harassment, and is adequately met by careful attention to the requirements of the statute. Title VII does not prohibit all verbal or physical harassment in the workplace; it is directed only at "discriminat[ion] . . . because of . . . sex." We have never held that workplace harassment, even harassment between men and women, is automatically discrimination because of sex merely because the words used have sexual content or connotations. "The critical issue, Title VII's text indicates, is whether members of one sex are exposed to disadvantageous terms or conditions of employment to which members of the other sex are not exposed."

Courts and juries have found the inference of discrimination easy to draw in most male–female sexual harassment situations, because the challenged conduct typically involves explicit or implicit proposals of sexual activity; it is reasonable to assume those proposals would not have been made to someone of the same sex. The same chain of inference would be available to a plaintiff alleging same-sex harassment, if there were credible evidence that the harasser was homosexual. But harassing conduct need not be motivated by sexual desire to support an inference of discrimination on the basis of sex. A trier of fact might reasonably find such discrimination, for example, if a female victim is harassed in such sex-specific and derogatory terms by another woman as to make it clear that the harasser is motivated by general hostility to the presence of women in the workplace.

A same-sex harassment plaintiff may also, of course, offer direct comparative evidence about how the alleged harasser treated members of both sexes in a mixed-sex workplace. Whatever evidentiary route the plaintiff chooses to follow, he or she must always prove that the conduct at issue was not merely tinged with offensive sexual connotations, but actually constituted "discrimination[ion] . . . because of . . . sex."

And there is another requirement that prevents Title VII from expanding into a general civility code: The statute does not reach genuine but innocuous differences in the ways men and women routinely interact with members of the same sex and of the opposite sex. The prohibition of harassment on the basis of sex requires neither asexuality nor androgyny in the workplace; it forbids only behavior so objectively offensive as to alter the "conditions" of the victim's employment. "Conduct that is not severe or pervasive enough to create an objectively hostile or abusive work environment—an environment that a reasonable person would find hostile or abusive—is beyond Title VII's purview." We have always regarded that requirement as crucial, and as sufficient to ensure that courts and juries do not mistake ordinary socializing in the workplace—such as male-on-male horseplay or intersexual flirtation—for discriminatory "conditions of employment."

We have emphasized, moreover, that the objective severity of harassment should be judged from the perspective of a reasonable person in the plaintiff's position, considering "all the circumstances." In same-sex (as in all) harassment cases, that inquiry requires careful consideration of the social context in which particular behavior occurs and is experienced by its target. A professional football player's working environment is not severely or pervasively abusive, for example, if the coach smacks him on the buttocks as he heads onto the field—even if the same behavior would reasonably be experienced as abusive by the coach's secretary (male or female) back at the office. The real social impact of workplace behavior often depends on a constellation of surrounding circumstances, expectations, and relationships which are not fully captured by a simple recitation of the words used or the physical acts performed. Common sense, and an appropriate sensitivity to social context, will enable courts and juries to distinguish between simple teasing or roughhousing among members of the same sex, and conduct which a reasonable person in the plaintiff's position would find severely hostile or abusive. In light of our holding, the case is REVERSED and REMANDED.

Case Questions

1. Do you understand why the Court allowed Oncale to prevail here, despite the fact that the sexual harassment was between males? Explain.

2. What about the idea of men "roughhousing" and otherwise interacting with each other in ways that may cause claims to arise: as the employer, what would you do to lessen liability exposure?

3. As an employer, how would you be able to distinguish between activity directed at an employee because he or she was gay or lesbian, which is not protected by Title VII, and activity which is not, which is protected by Title VII?

Quid Pro Quo Sexual Harassment

In quid pro quo sexual harassment, the employee is required to engage in sexual activity in exchange for workplace entitlements or benefits such as promotions, raises, or continued employment. This is the more obvious type of sexual harassment and is not generally difficult to recognize. In the *Jones* case on page 267, you get to see for yourself whether you think President Clinton's actions toward Paula Jones met the legal requirements for quid pro quo sexual harassment. You undoubtedly saw much in the press about it, but now you get to analyze the case for yourself using the facts as alleged, and the law as it stands. See what you think.

JONES V. CLINTON
990 F. Supp. 657 (E.D. Ark. W. Div. 1998)

In what is probably the most famous sexual harassment case in history, Paula Jones, a former Arkansas state employee, filed suit against a state trooper and a sitting president of the United States, claiming that a sexual advance the president made while serving as governor of Arkansas amounted to sexual harassment. The decision of whether the case could be brought against a sitting president went all the way to the US Supreme Court, and the Court saw no impediment to such a suit.[1] When the case proceeded in the district court, it was dismissed, with the court holding that Jones failed to establish a basis for quid pro quo or hostile work environment sexual harassment because the actions of the president, even if taken to be true, did not meet the requirements of Title VII. In December of 1998, the Eighth Circuit Court of Appeals dismissed Jones's appeal of this case,[2] leaving this decision intact.

Of course, you heard of the case, and you probably had thoughts of your own about the court's decision. In fact, I'd be willing to bet you thought the court was wrong in dismissing the case. Most people did. But now you get to read and analyze the facts for yourself, rather than through a media account. See if you still feel the same way after reading Judge Susan Webber Wright's decision. The quotation marks in the parts of the opinion in which the court sets forth what the parties allege indicate that the information was taken from documents submitted to the court by the parties.

Wright, J.

Jones seeks civil damages from William Jefferson Clinton, President of the United States, and Danny Ferguson, a former Arkansas State Police osfficer, for alleged actions beginning with an incident in a hotel suite in Little Rock, Arkansas. In addressing the issues in this case, the Court has viewed the record in the light most favorable to plaintiff Jones and has given her the benefit of all reasonable factual inferences, which is required at this stage of the proceedings.

This lawsuit is based on an incident that is said to have taken place on the afternoon of May 8, 1991, in a suite at the Excelsior Hotel in Little Rock, Arkansas. President Clinton was Governor of the State of Arkansas at the time, and Jones was a State employee with the Arkansas Industrial Development Commission ("AIDC"), having begun her State employment on March 11, 1991. Ferguson was an Arkansas State Police officer assigned to the Governor's security detail.

According to the record, then-Governor Clinton was at the Excelsior Hotel on the day in

---

[1]520 U.S. 681 (1997).

[2]James V. Clinton, 138 F. 3d 758 (8th Cir. 1998).

question delivering a speech at an official conference being sponsored by the AIDC. Jones states that she and another AIDC employee, Pamela Blackard, were working at a registration desk for the AIDC when a man approached the desk and informed her and Blackard that he was Trooper Danny Ferguson, the Governor's bodyguard. She states that Ferguson made small talk with her and Blackard and that they asked him if he had a gun as he was in street clothes and they "wanted to know." Ferguson acknowledged that he did and, after being asked to show the gun to them, left the registration desk to return to the Governor. The conversation between Jones, Blackard, and Ferguson lasted approximately five minutes and consisted of light, friendly banter; there was nothing intimidating, threatening, or coercive about it.

Upon leaving the registration desk, Ferguson apparently had a conversation with the Governor about the possibility of meeting with Jones, during which Ferguson states the Governor remarked that Jones had "that come-hither look," i.e. "a sort of [sexually] suggestive appearance from the look or dress." He states that "some time later" the Governor asked him to "get him a room, that he was expecting a call from the White House and . . . had several phone calls that he needed to make," and asked him to go to the car and get his briefcase containing the phone messages. Ferguson states that upon obtaining the room, the Governor told him that if Jones wanted to meet him, she could "come up."

Ferguson states that Jones informed him that she would like to meet the Governor, remarking that she thought the Governor "was good-looking [and] had sexy hair," while Jones states that Ferguson asked her if she would like to meet the Governor and that she was "excited" about the possibility.

Jones states that Ferguson later reappeared at the registration desk, delivered a piece of paper to her with a four-digit number written on it, and said that the Governor would like to meet with her in this suite number. She states that she, Blackard, and Ferguson talked about what the Governor

could want and that Ferguson stated, among other things, "We do this all the time." Thinking that it was an honor to be asked to meet the Governor and that it might lead to an enhanced employment opportunity, Jones states that she agreed to the meeting and that Ferguson escorted her to the floor of the hotel upon which the Governor's suite was located.

Jones states that upon arriving at the suite and announcing herself, the Governor shook her hand, invited her in, and closed the door. She states that a few minutes of small talk ensued, which included the Governor asking her about her job and him mentioning that Dave Harrington, Jones' ultimate superior within the AIDC and a Clinton appointee, was his "good friend."

Jones states that the Governor then "unexpectedly reached over to [her], took her hand, and pulled her toward him, so that their bodies were close to each other." She states she removed her hand from his and retreated several feet, but that the Governor approached her again and, while saying, "I love the way your hair flows down your back" and "I love your curves," put his hand on her leg, started sliding it toward her pelvic area, and bent down to attempt to kiss her on the neck, all without her consent. Jones states that she exclaimed, "What are you doing?," told the Governor that she was "not that kind of girl," and "escaped" from the Governor's reach "by walking away from him." She states she was extremely upset and confused and, not knowing what to do, attempted to distract the Governor by chatting about his wife. Jones states that she sat down at the end of the sofa nearest the door, but that the Governor approached the sofa where she had taken a seat and, as he sat down, "lowered his trousers and underwear, exposed his penis (which was erect) and told [her] to 'kiss it.'" She states that she was "horrified" by this and that she "jumped up from the couch" and told the Governor that she had to go, saying something to the effect that she had to get back to the registration desk. Jones states that the Governor, "while fondling his penis," said, "Well, I don't want to make you do anything you don't want to do," and then pulled up his pants and said, "If you get in trouble for leaving work, have Dave call me immediately and I'll take care of it." She states that as she left the room (the door of which was not locked), the Governor "detained" her momentarily, "looked sternly" at her, and said, "You are smart. Let's keep this between ourselves." (Jones did not mention this in earlier court documents.)

Jones states that the Governor's advances to her were unwelcome, that she never said or did anything to suggest to the Governor that she was willing to have sex with him, and that during the time they were together in the hotel suite, she resisted his advances although she was "stunned by them and intimidated by who he was." She states that when the Governor referred to Dave Harrington, she "understood that he was telling her that he had control over Mr. Harrington and over her job, and that he was willing to use that power." She states that from that point on, she was "very fearful" that her refusal to submit to the Governor's advances could damage her career and even jeopardize her employment.

Jones states that when she left the hotel suite, she was in shock and upset but tried to maintain her composure. She states she saw Ferguson waiting outside the suite but that he did not escort her back to the registration desk and nothing was said between them. Ferguson states that five or ten minutes after Jones exited the suite he joined the Governor for their return to the Governor's Mansion and that the Governor, who was working on some papers that he had spread out on the desk, said, "She came up here, and nothing happened."

Jones states she returned to the registration desk and told Blackard some of what had happened. Blackard states that Jones was shaking and embarrassed. Following the conference, Jones states she went to the workplace of a friend, Debra Ballentine, and told her of the incident as well. Ballentine states that Jones was upset and crying. Later that same day, Jones states she told her sister, Charlotte Corbin Brown, what had happened and, within the next two days, also told her

other sister, Lydia Corbin Cathey, of the incident. Brown's observations of Jones' demeanor apparently are not included in the record. Cathey, however, states that Jones was "bawling" and "squalling," and that she appeared scared, embarrassed, and ashamed.

Ballentine states that she encouraged Jones to report the incident to her boss or to the police, but that Jones declined, pointing out that her boss was friends with the Governor and that the police were the ones who took her to the hotel suite. Ballentine further states that Jones stated she did not want her fiance to know of the incident and that she "just want[ed] this thing to go away." Jones states that what the Governor and Ferguson had said and done made her "afraid" to file charges.

Jones continued to work at AIDC following the alleged incident in the hotel suite. One of her duties was to deliver documents to and from the Office of the Governor, as well as other offices around the Arkansas State Capitol. She states that in June 1991, while performing these duties for the AIDC, she encountered Ferguson who told her that Mrs. Clinton was out of town often and that the Governor wanted her phone number and wanted to see her. Jones states she refused to provide her phone number to Ferguson. She states that Ferguson also asked her how her fiance, Steve, was doing, even though she had never told Ferguson or the Governor his name, and that this "frightened" her. Jones states that she again encountered Ferguson following her return to work from maternity leave and that he said he had "told Bill how good looking you are since you've had the baby." She also states that she was "accosted" by the Governor in the Rotunda of the Arkansas State Capitol when he "draped his arm over her, pulled her close to him and held her tightly to his body," and said to his bodyguard, "Don't we make a beautiful couple: Beauty and the Beast?" Jones additionally states that on an unspecified date, she was waiting in the Governor's outer office on a delivery run when the Governor entered the office, patted her on the shoulder, and in a "friendly fashion" said, "How are you doing, Paula?"

Jones states that she continued to work at AIDC "even though she was in constant fear that [the Governor] would retaliate against her because she had refused to have sex with him." She states this fear prevented her from enjoying her job. Jones states that she was treated "very rudely" by certain superiors in AIDC, including her direct supervisor, Clydine Pennington, and that this "rude treatment" had not happened prior to her encounter with the Governor. She states that after her maternity leave, she was transferred to a position which had much less responsibility and that much of the time she had nothing to do. Jones states that she was not learning anything, that her work could not be fairly evaluated, and that as a result, she could not be fairly considered for advancement and other opportunities. She states that Pennington told her the reason for the transfer was that her prior position had been eliminated, but that she later learned this was untrue, as her former position was being occupied by another employee. Jones states that she repeatedly expressed to Pennington an interest in transferring to particular positions at a higher "grade" which involved more challenging duties, more potential for advancement, and more compensation, but that Pennington always discouraged her from doing so and told her she should not bother to apply for those positions. She goes on to state that her superiors exhibited hostility toward her by moving her work location, refusing to give her meaningful work, watching her constantly, and failing to give her flowers on Secretary's Day in 1992, even though all the other women in the office received flowers.

Jones voluntarily terminated her employment with AIDC on February 20, 1993, in order to move to California with her husband, who had been transferred. She states that in January 1994, while visiting family and friends in Arkansas, she was informed of an article in *The American Spectator* magazine that she claims referred to her alleged encounter with the Governor at the Excelsior Hotel and incorrectly suggested that she had engaged in sexual relations with the Governor. Jones states that she also encountered Ferguson in a restaurant during this same time and that he indicated he was the source for the article and that he knew she had refused the Governor's alleged advances because, he said, "Clinton told me you wouldn't do anything anyway, Paula."

On February 11, 1994, at an event attended by the media, Jones states that she publicly asked President Clinton to acknowledge the incident mentioned in the article in *The American Spectator,* to state that she had rejected his advances, and to apologize to her, but that the President responded to her request for an apology by having his press spokespersons deliver a statement on his behalf that the incident never happened and that he never met Jones. Thereafter, on May 6, 1994, Jones filed this lawsuit.

To make a prima facie case of quid pro quo sexual harassment, Jones must show, among other things, that her refusal to submit to unwelcome sexual advances or requests for sexual favors resulted in a tangible job detriment.

Apparently recognizing the infirm ground upon which her assertions of tangible job detriments rest (which will be discussed later), Jones first argues that a showing of a tangible job detriment is not an essential element of an action for quid pro quo sexual harassment under Title VII. The Court rejects this argument as it conflicts with the Eighth Circuit's requirement that a refusal to submit to unwelcome sexual advances or requests for sexual favors resulted in a tangible job detriment, and conflicts with the majority of the other circuits on this point as well.

While it is true that the Seventh Circuit concluded that a "clear and unambiguous" quid pro quo threat that "clearly conditions concrete job benefits or detriments on compliance with sexual demands" can constitute an actionable claim "even if the threat remains unfulfilled," Jones acknowledges that no one, including Governor Clinton, ever told her that if she refused to submit to his alleged advances it would have a negative effect on her job, that she had to submit to his alleged advances in order to receive job benefits, or that the Governor would use his relationship with

AIDC Director Dave Harrington to penalize her in her job. She merely states that "read[ing] between the lines," she "knew what [the Governor] meant" when he allegedly indicated in the hotel suite that Harrington was his good friend. Be that as it may, the Governor's alleged statements do not in any way constitute a clear threat that clearly conditions concrete job benefits or detriments on compliance with sexual demands.

Based on the foregoing, the Court finds that a showing of a tangible job detriment is an essential element of plaintiff's quid pro quo sexual harassment claim. It is that issue to which the Court now turns.

As evidence of tangible job detriments (or adverse employment action), Jones claims the following occurred after she resisted Governor Clinton's alleged advances on May 8, 1991: (1) she was discouraged from applying for more attractive jobs and seeking reclassification at a higher pay grade within the AIDC; (2) her job was changed to one with fewer responsibilities, less attractive duties and less potential for advancement—and the reason given for the change proved to be untrue; (3) she was effectively denied access to grievance procedures that would otherwise have been available to victims of sexual harassment; and (4) she was mistreated in ways having tangible manifestations, such as isolating her physically, making her sit in a location from which she was constantly watched, making her sit at her workstation with no work to do, and singling her out as the only female employee not to be given flowers on Secretary's Day. The Court has carefully reviewed the record in this case and finds nothing in Jones' employment records, her own testimony, or the testimony of her supervisors showing that Jones' reaction to Governor Clinton's alleged advances affected tangible aspects of her compensation, terms, conditions, or privileges of employment.

Jones' claim that she was discouraged from applying for more attractive jobs and seeking reclassification at a higher pay grade within the AIDC does not demonstrate any "tangible" job detriment as she has not identified a single specific job which she desired or applied for at AIDC but which she had been discouraged from seeking. When asked for such specific information, Jones merely testified that the unidentified jobs she sought were "a grade higher" but that her supervisor "would always discourage me and make me believe that I could grow within the administrative services, which in fact I didn't. I got degrade—downgraded." She further states that those "few" times that she would talk to her supervisor and receive discouragement, she "would go ahead and fill out an application maybe or something." There is no record of Jones ever applying for another job within AIDC, however, and the record shows that not only was Jones' position never downgraded, her position was reclassified upward from a Grade 9 classification to a Grade 11 classification, thereby increasing her annual salary.

Indeed, it is undisputed that Jones received every merit increase and cost-of-living allowance for which she was eligible during her nearly two-year tenure with the AIDC and consistently received satisfactory job evaluations. Specifically, on July 1, 1991, less than two months after the alleged incident that is the subject of this lawsuit, Jones received a cost-of-living increase and her position was reclassified from Grade 9 to Grade 11; on August 28, 1991, she received a satisfactory job evaluation from her supervisor, Clydine Pennington; and on March 11, 1992, the one-year anniversary of her hire date with AIDC, Jones received another satisfactory evaluation from Pennington and Cherry Duckett, Deputy Director of AIDC, which entitled her to a merit raise. In addition, Jones was given a satisfactory job review in an evaluation covering the period of March 1992 until her voluntary departure from the AIDC in February 1993. Jones signed this review on February 16, 1993, and would have received another merit increase one month later in accordance with this review had she elected to continue her employment at AIDC.

It is Jones' burden to come forward with "specific facts" showing that there is a genuine issue for trial, and the Court finds that her testimony on this point, being of a most general and nonspecific nature (and in some cases contradictory to the record), simply does not suffice to create a genuine issue of fact regarding any tangible job detriment as a result of her having allegedly been discouraged from seeking more attractive jobs and reclassification.

Equally without merit is Jones' assertion that following her return from maternity leave in September 1992, she suffered a tangible job detriment when her job was changed to one with fewer responsibilities, less attractive duties and less potential for advancement. These matters do not constitute a tangible job detriment as it is undisputed that there was no diminution in Jones' salary or change in her job classification following her return from maternity leave and, further, that her last review at AIDC following her return was positive and would have entitled her to another merit increase had she not resigned her position in order to move to California with her husband. Changes in duties or working conditions that cause no materially significant disadvantage, such as diminution in title, salary, or benefits, are insufficient to establish the adverse conduct required to make a prima facie case.

Although Jones states that her job title upon returning from maternity leave was no longer that of purchasing assistant and that this change in title impaired her potential for promotion, her job duties prior to taking maternity leave and her job duties upon returning to work both involved data input; the difference being that instead of responsibility for data entry of AIDC purchase orders and driving records, she was assigned data entry responsibilities for employment applications. That being so, Jones cannot establish a tangible job detriment. A transfer that does not involve a demotion in form or substance and involves only minor changes in working conditions, with no reduction in pay or benefits, will not constitute an adverse employment action, "[o]therwise every trivial personnel action that an irritable . . . employee did not like would form the basis of a discrimination suit." Whether or not the reasons given for the change were untrue, Jones' allegations describe nothing "more disruptive than a mere inconvenience or an alteration of job responsibilities." Jones offers no evidence that her previous position conferred some type of status or prestige not conferred in her subsequent position, and she offers no evidence that the change in her duties impaired her ability to advance in her career.

Finally, the Court rejects Jones' claim that she was subjected to hostile treatment having tangible effects when she was isolated physically, made to sit in a location from which she was constantly watched, made to sit at her workstation with no work to do, and singled out as the only female employee not to be given flowers on Secretary's Day. Jones may well have perceived hostility and animus on the part of her supervisors, but these perceptions are merely conclusory in nature and do not, without more, constitute a tangible job detriment. Absent evidence of some more tangible changes in duties or working conditions that constitute a material employment disadvantage, of which the Court has already determined does not exist, general allegations of hostility and personal animus are not sufficient to demonstrate any adverse employment action that constitutes the sort of ultimate decision intended to be actionable under Title VII.

Similarly, Jones' allegations regarding her work station being moved so that she had to sit directly outside Pennington's office and, at times, not having work to do (Jones makes this allegation even though she testified that following her return from maternity leave, she input data pursuant to her new responsibilities "all day long") describe nothing more than minor or de minimis personnel matters which, again without more, are insufficient to constitute a tangible job detriment or adverse employment action.

Although it is not clear why Jones failed to receive flowers on Secretary's Day in 1992, such an omission does not give rise to a federal cause of action in the absence of evidence of some more tangible change in duties or working conditions that constitute a material employment disadvantage.

In sum, the Court finds that a showing of a tangible job detriment or adverse employment action is an essential element of quid pro quo sexual harassment claim and that Jones has not demonstrated any tangible job detriment or adverse employment action for her refusal to submit to the Governor's alleged advances. The President is therefore entitled to summary judgment on Jones' claim of quid pro quo sexual harassment.

The Court now turns to Jones' hostile work environment claim. Unlike quid pro quo sexual harassment, hostile work environment harassment arises when "sexual conduct has the purpose or effect of unreasonably interfering with an individual's work performance or creating an intimidating, hostile, or offensive working environment." To prevail on a hostile work environment cause of action, a plaintiff must establish, among other things, that she was subjected to unwelcome sexual harassment based upon her sex that affected a term, condition, or privilege of employment. The behavior creating the hostile working environment need not be overtly sexual in nature, but it must be " 'unwelcome' in the sense that the employee did not solicit or invite it, and the employee regarded the conduct as undesirable or offensive." The harassment must also be sufficiently severe or pervasive "to alter the conditions of employment and create an abusive working environment."

In assessing the hostility of an environment, a court must look to the totality of the circumstances. Circumstances to be considered include "the frequency of the discriminatory conduct; its severity; whether it is physically threatening or humiliating, or a mere offensive utterance; and whether it unreasonably interferes with an employee's work performance." No single factor is determinative, and the court "should not carve the work environment into a series of discrete incidents and then measure the harm occurring in each episode." Jones' allegations of adverse employment action are without merit.

Jones received every merit increase and cost-of-living allowance for which she was eligible during her nearly two-year tenure with the AIDC, her job was upgraded from Grade 9 to Grade 11 (thereby increasing her salary), she consistently received satisfactory job evaluations, and her job responsibilities upon her return from maternity leave were not significantly different from prior to her taking leave and did not cause her any materially significant disadvantage. These facts are clearly established by the record and dispel the notion that she was subjected to a hostile work environment.

Jones certainly has not shown under the totality of the circumstances that the alleged incident in the hotel and her additional encounters with Ferguson and the Governor were so severe or pervasive that it created an abusive working environment. She admits that she never missed a day of work following the alleged incident in the hotel, she continued to work at AIDC another nineteen months (leaving only because of her husband's job transfer), she continued to go on a daily basis to the Governor's Office to deliver items and never asked to be relieved of that duty, she never filed a formal complaint or told her supervisors of the incident while at AIDC, and she never consulted a psychiatrist, psychologist, or incurred medical bills as a result of the alleged incident. In addition, Jones has not shown how Ferguson's alleged comments, whether considered alone or in conjunction with the other alleged conduct in this case, interfered with her work, and she acknowledges that the Governor's statement about him and her looking like "beauty and the beast" was made "in a light vein" and that his patting her on the shoulder and asking her how she was doing was done in a "friendly fashion."

While the alleged incident in the hotel, if true, was certainly boorish and offensive, the Governor's alleged conduct does not constitute sexual assault. This is thus not one of those exceptional cases in which a single incident of sexual harassment, such as an assault, was deemed sufficient to state a claim of hostile work environment sexual harassment. See to the contrary, *Crisonino v. New York City Housing Auth.,* 985 F.Supp. 385 (S.D.N.Y.1997) (supervisor called plaintiff a "dumb bitch" and "shoved her so hard that she fell backward and hit the floor, sustaining injuries from which she has yet to fully recover").

Considering the totality of the circumstances, it simply cannot be said that the conduct to which Jones was allegedly subjected was frequent, severe, or physically threatening, and the Court finds that defendants' actions as shown by the record do not constitute the kind of sustained and nontrivial conduct necessary for a claim of hostile work environment.

In sum, the Court finds that the record does not demonstrate conduct that was so severe or pervasive that it can be said to have altered the conditions of Jones' employment and created an abusive working environment. Accordingly, the President is entitled to summary judgment on Jones' claim of hostile work environment sexual harassment.

For the foregoing reasons, the Court finds that the President's and Ferguson's MOTIONS FOR SUMMARY JUDGMENT should both be and hereby are GRANTED. There being no remaining issues, the court will enter JUDGMENT DISMISSING THIS CASE.

Case Questions

1. Do you agree with Judge Wright that Jones did not present sufficient evidence to support a claim for quid pro quo sexual harassment by Clinton? Explain.

2. Does this single incident seem severe enough to you to constitute sexual harassment under the law? Explain. What role does the fact that it was the governor who is now the president, play in your decision, if any?

3. Did your opinion of the case change after reading the case for yourself? Why/why not? In explaining your answer, be sure to use logic and analysis of the facts as presented, rather than your "gut reaction" and emotion.

An employer can limit a supervisor's ability to abuse power by choosing supervisory employees carefully and having in place a system with adequate monitors and checks. It greatly decreases morale for employees to witness quid pro quo harassment by the supervisor, thus lowering workplace productivity. In fact, a recent court even held that the other employees witnessing such activity may bring a cause of action of their own.

Hostile Environment Sexual Harassment

The more difficult sexual harassment issues have been in the area of hostile environment because employers are confused about what activity constitutes the offense. Part of the difficulty lies in the fact that many of the causes that may serve as a basis for liability have until now gone unchallenged. However, a closer look at what courts have held to constitute a hostile environment lends more predictability.

To sustain a finding of hostile environment sexual harassment, it is generally required that:

- The harassment be unwelcome by the harassee.
- The harassment be based on gender.
- The harassment be sufficiently severe or pervasive to create an abusive working environment.
- The harassment affect a term, condition, or privilege of employment.
- The employer had actual or constructive knowledge of the sexually hostile working environment and took no prompt or adequate remedial action.

In light of these requirements, it becomes clear why simply giving polite compliments or calling a female "dear" as in opening scenario 3 is not sexual harassment as many fear. It involves much more.

Scenario

Now knowing what you do about the requirements of the law, it should also be clear why Jones' claim was dismissed. It simply did not meet the legal requirements of a cause of action for sexual harassment. You may consider the president's actions inappropriate, disappointing, boorish, not in keeping with the conduct you expect from someone holding the office of president of the United States (then governor), and you may even consider his actions immoral. However, none of these is the same as his actions being legally sufficient to meet the requirements set forth by law for the cause of action of sexual harassment. It is important to be able to see the difference.

The case below was the first case to reach the US Supreme Court. See if you can now distinguish between quid pro quo and hostile environment sexual harassment.

MERITOR SAVINGS BANK, FSB v. VINSON
477 U.S. 57 (1986)

An employee alleged sexual harassment even though she lost no tangible job benefits. The Court determined that quid pro quo was not the only type of sexual harassment. For the first time, the US Supreme Court determined that this kind of situation constituted hostile environment sexual harassment.

Rehnquist, J.

Mechelle Vinson worked at Meritor Savings Bank, initially as a teller-trainee, but was later promoted to teller, head teller and assistant branch manager, admittedly based upon merit. Sidney Taylor was the bank branch manager and the person who hired Vinson. Vinson alleged that in the beginning Taylor was "fatherly" toward her and made no sexual advances, but eventually he asked her to go out to dinner. During the course of the meal Taylor suggested that he and Vinson go to a motel to have sexual relations. At first she refused, but out of what she described as fear of losing her job, she eventually agreed. Taylor thereafter made repeated demands upon Vinson for sexual activity, usually at the branch, both during and after business hours. She estimated that over the next several years she had intercourse with him some 40 or 50 times. In addition, she testified that Taylor fondled her in front of other employees, followed her into the women's restroom when she went there alone, exposed himself to her, and even forcibly raped her on several occasions. These activities ceased in 1977 when Vinson started going with a steady boyfriend.

Courts have applied Title VII protection to racial harassment and nothing in Title VII suggests that a hostile environment based on discriminatory *sexual* harassment should not be likewise prohibited. The Guidelines thus appropriately drew from, and were fully consistent with, the existing case law.

Of course, not all workplace conduct that may be described as "harassment" affects a "term, condition, or privilege" of employment within the meaning of Title VII. For instance, mere utterance of an ethnic or racial epithet which engenders offensive feelings in an employee would not affect the condition of employment to a sufficiently significant degree to create an abusive working environment. For sexual harassment to be actionable, it must be sufficiently severe or pervasive to alter the conditions of the victim's employment and create an abusive working environment. Vinson's allegations in this case—which include not only pervasive harassment, but also criminal conduct of the most serious nature—are plainly sufficient to state a claim for hostile environment sexual harassment.

The District Court's conclusion that no actionable harassment occurred might have rested on its earlier finding that if Vinson and Taylor had engaged in intimate or sexual relations, that relationship was a voluntary one. But the fact that sex-related conduct was "voluntary" in the sense that the complainant was not forced to participate against her will, is not a defense to a sexual harassment suit brought under Title VII. The gravamen of any sexual harassment claim is the alleged sexual advances were "unwelcome." While the question

whether particular conduct was indeed unwelcome presents difficult problems of proof and turns largely on credibility determinations committed to the trier of fact, the District Court in this case erroneously focused on the "voluntariness" of Vinson's participation in the claimed sexual episodes. The correct inquiry is whether Vinson, by her conduct, indicated that the alleged sexual advances were unwelcome, not whether her participation in sexual intercourse was voluntary.

The district court admitted into evidence testimony about Vinson's "dress and personal fantasies." The court of appeals stated that testimony had no place in the litigation, on the basis that Vinson's voluntariness in submitting to Taylor's advances was immaterial to her sexual harassment claim. While "voluntariness" in the sense of consent is not a defense to such a claim, it does not follow that a complainant's sexually provocative speech or dress is irrelevant as a matter of law in determining whether she found particular sexual advances welcome. To the contrary, such evidence is obviously relevant. The EEOC Guidelines emphasize that the trier of fact must determine the existence of sexual harassment in light of "the record as a whole" and the "totality of circumstances," such as the nature of the sexual advances and the context in which the alleged incidents occurred.

In sum we hold that a claim of "hostile environment" sexual harassment gender discrimination is actionable under Title VII. AFFIRMED.

Case Questions

1. As a manager, what would you have done if Vinson had come to you with her story?
2. Under the circumstances, should it matter that Vinson "voluntarily" had sex with Taylor? That she received her regular promotions?
3. How would you determine whom to believe?

In *Meritor* it is clear that the supervisor's actions changed the terms and conditions of Vinson's employment. There is a big difference between the ongoing, pervasive actions of Vinson's supervisor and what happened to Paula Jones in the previous case. Be sure that you understand that in a hostile environment action, the action must be more than someone committing a boorish, stupid, inappropriate act. The act must come up to the standards the courts and the EEOC have set forth for the cause of action. Contrary to what you may have been led to believe by the press or other information you've received, not every act, though reprehensible, will do so; thus, not every act, though committed against the employee's wishes, constitutes sexual harassment as set forth by law.

Unwelcome Activity

The basis of hostile environment sexual harassment actions is unwanted activity by the harasser. If the activity is wanted or welcome by the harassee, there is no sexual harassment. Even if the activity started off being consensual, if one employee calls a halt to it and the other continues, it can become sexual harassment, as in opening scenario 2. In making the determination of whether the harasser's activity was welcome, the actions used as a basis for the determination can be direct or indirect. In the case below the court had no trouble in determining that harassee welcomed the activity of harasser, if, in fact, it took place at all. It also demonstrates that there is more to winning a sexual harassment case than alleging simply that sexual harassment occurred.

Scenario

McLean v. Satellite Technology Services, Inc.
673 F. Supp. 1458 (E.D. Mo. 1987)

An assistant salesperson contends she was wrongfully terminated after she spurned romantic advances by her supervisor. The court found no sexual harassment because it held that the supervisor's actions, if they occurred, were not unwelcome.

Gunn, J.

McLean alleges she was at a business seminar meeting in Florida with Manning, who was making a presentation. McLean was to observe so she would ultimately be able to conduct a seminar. After one day's work, McLean, Manning, and another Satellite employee had dinner and went to the hotel's hot tub. Manning suggested to McLean that she should review his presentation, so he went to her hotel room. McLean claims that while they were in the room, with her dressed in a swimsuit and towel, and Manning in shorts and a shirt, they sat on the couch together and while Manning talked about his presentation, he put his arm around her back, touched her leg, and made an effort to kiss her once. McLean testified the effort was easily rebuffed and Manning then left the room. Manning denies making any advances to McLean. Following the trip McLean alleges

Manning was cool to her. She attributes this and her subsequent dismissal to her rebuff of his advances.

The court finds that there was a multitude of legitimate business reasons for terminating McLean and that her discharge was not based upon sexual harassment. It is undisputed that McLean was anything but demure, that she possessed a lusty libido and was no paragon of virtue. From the beginning of her short term of employment with Satellite in November of 1985, to its end in February 1986, she displayed a remarkable lust for those of the opposite sex. She displayed her body through semi-nude photos or by lifting her skirt to show her supervisor an absence of undergarments. Also, during work hours, she made offers of sexual gratification or highly salacious comments to employees, customers and competitors alike, though warned by Manning not to do so. There was uncontroverted evidence of acceptance of her offers.

Though specifically ordered by her supervisor, Manning, to refrain from an obviously flirtatious telephone relationship with an employee of a customer, McLean flouted the order and carried on the dalliance. It was McLean's activities at a trade show in Las Vegas, Nevada, on February 22–23, 1986 that finally led to McLean's discharge. At the trade show, McLean missed meetings she was expected to attend, was not at her job station a large percentage of the time and continued her libidinous behavior, acknowledging she was "intimate" with an employee of a customer at least two or three times, entertaining him in her hotel room during the period of the trade show. This was despite orders from her supervisor to abstain from promiscuity with customers or dealers.

On her return from Las Vegas, McLean was summarily discharged from her employment by the president of Satellite. His basis was McLean's performance at the Last Vegas trade show as related by Satellite's chief operating officer who was there and observed McLean's actions. Specifically, she was dismissed for missing work and meetings in Las Vegas.

The court specifically finds that there was no sexual harassment of McLean by her supervisor. From McLean's character, it is apparent that she would have welcomed rather than rejected Manning's advance, if he did indeed do so. But the court finds that Manning made no sexual advance. McLean was not subjected to any unwelcome sexual harassment. Indeed, it is McLean who bears the responsibility for whatever sexually suggestive conduct is involved in this case. Satellite has stated nonpretextual, legitimate and absolutely nondiscriminatory reasons for its discharge of McLean. She was insubordinate, and displayed total disrespect for her supervisor, which would serve as a legitimate basis for termination. It is also abundantly clear that McLean was terminated because of her poor work performance, attitudes, and habits, e.g., excessively long lunch hours, personal phone calls, entertaining nonbusiness visitors during working hours, and being inattentive to her work, particularly at the Las Vegas trade show. As such, her termination was proper. JUDGMENT FOR DEFENDANT, COSTS TO BE PAID BY PLAINTIFF.

Case Questions

1. Do you agree with the court's assessment of the evidence? Why or why not?

2. If you were McLean's supervisor and she exhibited the behavior alleged, what could you have done?

3. Do you think the court would have held the same way if McLean had been a male? Explain. Do you think a male employee would have been ordered by his supervisor to "abstain from promiscuity with customers"? Would it be gender discrimination to give such orders to employees of one gender and not the other? Explain.

There may also be a finding that the harassee did not welcome the activity by the harasser. Evidence can be direct, such as the harassee telling the harasser to discontinue the offending activity, or indirect, such as the harassee using body language, eye signals, and the like to show disapproval of the harasser's actions. Employees should be told to make it clear to a harasser that the activity is unwelcome, otherwise the signals may become confused and the harasser thinks his actions are wanted by the harassee. In Exhibit 8–4 you can see how some employers are trying to address the issue in novel ways.

In another type of welcomeness issue, the Hooters restaurant chain was involved in several cases which, among other things, brought up the question of unwelcomeness parameters. Hooters is an Atlanta-based chain of 230 restaurants in 41 states and 9 countries. It is noted for its buffalo chicken wings and scantily clad female servers. At least seven lawsuits have been filed by female servers who were allegedly illegally fired or forced to quit because of sexual harassment.

The suits allege that the environment created by management for female servers was hostile, starting with the name Hooters, which is a slang term for women's breasts. Servers, who are required to wear uniforms of revealing shorts and T-shirts, alleged that they were required to endure an atmosphere of sexually offensive remarks, touching, and other conduct by both management and customers. For example, the sign on entering Hooters reads "Men: no shirt, no shoes: no service. Women: no shirt: free food."

An important issue in the lawsuits has been whether, as the company argued, the women assumed the risk of the activities directed at them by agreeing to work for the company. That is, whether the conduct was welcomed by the fact that the servers worked for a company whose concept encouraged such behavior. What do you think? Should it matter, if as it turns out, the requirement is illegal under Title VII? Check out the Hooters website and see if you agree, as Hooters argued, that it is merely a neighborhood restaurant (previously they had argued they were a family restaurant), complete with a children's menu. There is at least some truth to this. One of our students said his Little League baseball coach took the all male team to Hooters to celebrate the student's 12th birthday and they *loved* it. The coach was his dad!

Severe and Pervasive Requirement

One of the most troublesome problems with hostile environment is determining whether the harassing activity is **severe and pervasive** enough to amount to an unreasonable interference with an employee's ability to perform. Built into the elements of hostile environment sexual harassment is a requirement that the offending activity be sufficiently severe and pervasive. That is, the activity is not an isolated occurrence that is not serious enough to warrant undue concern. The more frequent or serious the occurrences, the more likely it is that the severe and pervasive requirement will be met. As we saw earlier in the *Jones* case the isolated incident was not sufficiently severe to meet this requirement.

Compare the following case, where events over a two-day period met the requirement for one employee but not her sister, to the *Jones* case, and see if you can

Severe and pervasive activity Harassing activity based on gender, which is more than an occasional act or so serious that it is the basis for liability.

EXHIBIT 8–4

Wanna fool around? Sign on the dotted line, please . . .
"Love Contracts": The newest way to try to avoid employer liability for sexual harassment

---

In the face of increasingly expensive and embarrassing sexual harassment litigation, there have been all sorts of attempts to lessen employer liability. See how you like the newest workplace idea. You may recall hearing about a similar plan imposed upon the students by the administration at a large midwestern university a few years ago.

"Love Contract" Help Fend Off Harassment Suits

No matter how many training sessions or awareness workshops they conduct, companies still find themselves facing sexual harassment claims. Alarmingly, claims keep going higher up the chain of command, increasingly hitting CEOs. And when such a suit reaches a top executive, it's not just a department in trouble, but the entire company itself.

The latest trend in fending off sexual harassment suits is a "love contract." Teresa Butler, managing partner in the Atlanta office of employment law firm Littler Mendelson, explains.

Can you talk about the "love contract" and how it works?

It's really only intended for higher-level executives. This isn't something we advise employers to put in their handbooks, and we don't recommend that all supervisors issue them to subordinates. We talk about this for CEOs and officers, top-level executives, and maybe directors; that's a judgment call for the company. It's basically for people who have broad power in the workplace—not the average first-level supervisor.

What's included in the contract?

The love contract does three things. First it restates the voluntary nature of the relationship. The CEO, or whoever is in this situation, issues the agreement to a subordinate employee, basically explaining to the individual, "I want to have this relationship with you. My understanding is you want to have this relationship with me. But I'm concerned that over time you might believe that the continuation of this relationship—even though you don't want it anymore—might be necessary for you to be successful here. As you know, we have a harassment policy, and I want you to understand that I'm aware of that policy and would never allow [the end of the relationship] to influence my decision making with regard to your employment." So the agreement is actually a formal contract. It restates the voluntary nature of the relationship.

What else should a love contract do?

Secondly, it affirms that the parties will use the company's sexual harassment policies if a problem arises, and it confirms the existence of those policies and [procedures]. It also states that if the policies aren't used, it's fair to assume there isn't a problem. And thirdly, the parties agree if work-related disputes arise, they'll resolve their differences using alternative dispute resolution (ADR) rather than resorting to the courts. Some might want to use that third piece and some might not, but we recommend ADR from a legal standpoint.

How are these contracts useful?

Often these relationships go bad at some point; one party wants to end it and the other doesn't. And then there's retaliatory conduct by the other, sometimes by the subordinate in the form of a sexual harassment complaint. So this contract is a method for the top-level executives to just say out loud what is actually the case. It's assurance for the company and the individuals that everybody understands what the rules are.

Exhibit 8–4   Concluded

How legally defensible is a love contract?

The first response we typically hear, especially from lawyers, is: How could this possibly be enforceable? The idea is this person can always come back and say this was coerced, that he or she was forced to sign this agreement. That's a risk you take with any contractual relationship because an employee is always in a subordinate role to the employer. If you take that to its logical end, you might as well say you could never have an enforceable contract with an employee.

So can they raise that issue?

Of course they can. But are you better off with the contract than without it? Yes. I think it's a pretty tough argument for an individual who signs this agreement to say that he or she was coerced into having this consensual relationship that you'll be able to [prove] the person had. There's usually evidence in these cases of a consensual relationship: You've got birthday cards, receipts for dinner, letters and other types of communications that the subordinate employee has clearly engaged in on a voluntary basis.

"Love Contract" Sample Letter

Dear [Name of Object of Affection]:

As we discussed, I know that this may seem silly or unnecessary to you, but I really want you to give serious consideration to the matter as it is very important to me. [Add other materials as appropriate]

I very much value our relationship and I certainly view it as voluntary, consensual and welcome, and I have always felt that you feel the same. However, I know that sometimes an individual may feel compelled to engage in or continue in a relationship against their will out of concern that it may affect the job or working relationships.

It is very important to me that our relationship be on an equal footing and that you be fully comfortable that our relationship is at all times fully voluntary and welcome. I want to assure you that under no circumstances will I allow our relationship or, should it happen, the end of our relationship, to impact on your job or our working relationship. Though I know you have received a copy of [our company's name] sexual harassment policy, I am enclosing a copy [Add specific reference to policy as appropriate] so that you can read and review it again. Once you have done so, I would greatly appreciate your signing this letter below, if you are in agreement with me.
[Add personal closing]
Very truly yours,
[Name]

I have read this letter and the accompanying sexual harassment policy, and I understand and agree with what is stated in both this letter and the sexual harassment policy. My relationship with [name] has been (and is) voluntary, consensual and welcome. I also understand that I am free to end this relationship any time, and in doing so, it will not adversely impact on my job.
[Signature of Object of Affection]

Source: Teresa Butler, Littler Mendelson, Atlanta, 888-LITTLER; Gillian Flynn, *Workforce magazine* March, 1999, pp. 106–108. Used with permission.

understand the difference. Also, look at the sister's situation here and see if you understand why, like *Jones,* the facts were insufficient to meet the severe and pervasive requirement of sexual harassment claims.

Regarding the "unreasonable interference" requirement, in *Harris v. Forklift Sys.,* the Supreme Court decided that sexual harassment claims do not require findings of severe psychological harm to be actionable. The Court said that "so long as the environment would reasonably be perceived, and is perceived, as hostile or abusive, there is no need for it also to be psychologically injurious."

In the case below, events over a two-day period were determined to meet the requirement for one employee, but not for her sister. See if you agree with the different conclusions or can understand the difference in the court's decision about one sister versus the other.

Ross v. Double Diamond, Inc.

672 F. Supp. 261 (N.D. Tex. 1987)

Two discharged employees, sisters, brought this action against their former employer, alleging that he violated Title VII by creating a sexually harassing work environment, then constructively discharging them because they reported it and also because of their gender. The court found a hostile environment for acts occurring during a two-day period for one sister, Beverly Ross, but not the other, Sheila Stroudenmire.

Mahon, J.

Within the first hour that twenty-year old Ross was on her new job at Double Diamond, her supervisor, Larry Womack, asked her if she "fooled around," to which she answered no. A short time later, Womack asked Ross to bring him a cup of coffee. When she entered his office with the coffee, he told her he wanted to take her picture. She protested, he insisted, and Ross agreed for fear of Womack's reaction if she continued to refuse. Womack then told Ross to pull up her dress for the picture. Still afraid of his reaction to her refusal, she pulled her dress up two inches above her knee and Womack took the picture. A short time later Ross asked for the picture and Womack refused to give it to her.

Later that day Womack called Ross on the phone and asked her to pant heavily for him. Ross immediately hung up. Still later the same day, Ross entered Womack's office during a meeting to give a message to one of the attendees. A salesman, Larry West, placed a Polaroid camera on the floor directly under Ross and took a picture up Ross's dress. The salesmen at the meeting laughed. Ross attempted to take the camera, but Womack prevented it. Ross asked for the picture and Womack refused, told her the picture did not develop and that she could not look for it in the trash can. Womack later called Ross on the phone and again asked her to pant heavily into the phone. Ross immediately hung up.

The next day, when Ross came into Womack's office to bring him coffee, he told her to come over to him by the desk. She did so and Womack pulled her onto his lap. A salesman came into the office. The salesman testified that Ross was on Womack's lap and Womack had his arms around Ross's waist and Ross was feverishly trying to pull away. After the salesman came in, Womack, who the salesman said looked "perverted," released his hold on Ross.

During this same day, Ross's sister, Stroudenmire, came to work for her first day of work as a sales trainee. She heard some employees laughing while looking at a picture in Womack's office. She told Ross and they went into the office to obtain the picture. Two salesmen were laughing at a picture, but slipped it into Womack's desk drawer when the two came in. Stroudenmire removed the picture from the drawer. It was the one taken up Ross's dress. Ross left the office in tears and went to the ladies' room. Later that day Womack called Ross into his office and told her to "bend over" and clean something off the wall. She refused to do so and started to leave. Womack proceeded to close the door to prevent her from leaving and trapped Ross against the door. Ross escaped by crawling out from under Womack's arm. Womack later entered a room in which Stroudenmire was studying and told her that he bet she liked to wear black boots and carry a whip in the bedroom. Womack also segregated Stroudenmire from the other sales trainees who were studying together, refused to allow her to take materials home to study with, and threatened in a loud voice to have Stroudenmire's husband fired and to make Stroudenmire and her husband lose their home because Stroudenmire reported Womack's activities to his supervisor. Stroudenmire and Ross called the sheriff and told him of the threats and asked him to come to Double Diamond. When he came and inquired as to what was going on, Womack said they were just having fun. Ross and Stroudenmire soon after left their jobs after being told they could not take the rest of the afternoon off or if they did so, they could not return.

To determine severity or pervasiveness the court should consider several things. First, the nature of the unwelcome sexual acts or words. Generally unwelcome physical touching is more offensive than unwelcome verbal abuse. However, this is only a generalization and in specific situations, the type of language used may be more offensive than the type of physical touching. Second, a court should consider the frequency of the offensive encounters. It is less likely that a hostile work environment exists when, for instance, the offensive encounters occur once every year than if the encounters occur once every week. Third, the court would consider the total number of days over which all the offensive meetings occur. Lastly, the court should consider the context in which the sexually harassing conduct occurred. The court emphasizes that none of these factors should be given more weight than others. In addition, the nonexistence of one of these factors does not, in and of itself, prevent a Title VII claim. The trier of fact must consider the totality of the circumstances.

Because of its importance in this case, the court chooses to elaborate on the reasons why a short duration of sexual harassment does not prohibit a Title VII claim. The courts are looking for a pattern of sexual harassment inflicted upon an employee because of her gender because this type of activity is a pattern of behavior that inflicts disparate treatment upon a member of one gender with respect to terms, conditions, or privileges of employment. Sexual harassment need not exist over a long period for it to be considered a pattern. If the sexual harassment is frequent and/or intensely offensive, a pattern can be established over a short period of time.

The court finds that the acts and communications perpetrated against Ross at Double Diamond are sufficiently severe or pervasive to alter the conditions of Ross's employment and create an abusive work environment.

This is not so with Stroudenmire. Title VII is not a shield which protects people from all sexual discrimination. The type of conduct listed above does not rise to the level of harassment which is actionable. It is not sufficiently severe and pervasive to alter the conditions of employment or create an abusive work environment. JUDGMENT for ROSS.

Case Questions

1. Do you agree with the court's decision about Stroudenmire? Ross? Explain.

2. As the manager, what would you have done about Womack?

3. Do you agree that there was sufficient severity and pervasiveness in the two-day period here? Specifically, what makes you reach your conclusion?

Whether an environment is hostile or abusive can be determined only by looking at all the circumstances. These may include the frequency of the discriminatory conduct, its severity, whether it is physically threatening or humiliating or a mere offensive utterance, and whether it unreasonably interferes with an employee's work performance. According to the Court, no single factor is determinative.

Perspective Used to Determine Severity

Reasonable person standard
Viewing the harassing activity from the perspective of a reasonable person in society at large.

Reasonable victim standard
Viewing the harassing activity from the perspective of a reasonable person experiencing the harassing activity.

Until recently the determination of whether the harasser's activity was sufficiently severe and pervasive was generally based on a **reasonable person standard,** which is supposed to be a gender-neutral determination. That is, the activity would be judged as offensive (or not) based on whether the activity would offend a reasonable person under the circumstances. Since this "neutral" standard generally turned out to be instead a male standard, the EEOC issued a policy statement in which it required that the victim's perspective must also be considered, so as not to perpetuate stereotypical notions of what behavior is acceptable to those of a given gender. Sound familiar? It is the concept argued by Judge Keith in the *Rabidue* dissent. This notion, labeled the "reasonable woman" or **"reasonable victim" standard,** has been used increasingly by courts and should be given serious consideration when evaluating harassing activity. If the victim is a male, it would, of course, be a "reasonable man" standard. In *Ellison v. Brady,* the court adopted a "reasonable woman" standard for analyzing whether the harasser's behavior was severe and pervasive enough to create a hostile work environment, and it explains why viewing severity and pervasiveness from this perspective may render different results. The US Supreme Court has not addressed the "reasonable victim" versus "reasonable person" dichotomy as a direct issue, but in *Oncale* it said "the objective severity of harassment should be judged from the perspective of a reasonable person *in the plaintiff's position;"* which sounds like the reasonable victim standard.

ELLISON V. BRADY
924 F.2d 872 (9th Cir. 1991)

An employee brought a sexual harassment suit because, among other things, her co-worker kept sending her personal letters. The court found that while some may think it only a small matter, viewed from the employee's perspective as a female in a society in which females are often the victims of violence, the action was offensive and a violation of Title VII.

Beezer, J.

The case presents the important issue of what test should be applied to determine whether conduct is sufficiently severe or pervasive to alter the conditions of employment and create a hostile working environment.

Ellison worked as a revenue agent for the IRS in San Mateo, California. During her initial training in 1984 she met Sterling Gray, another trainee also assigned to that office. The two never became friends and did not work closely together. Gray's desk was twenty feet from Ellison's, two rows behind and one row over.

In June of 1986 when no one else was in the office, Gray asked Ellison to go to lunch. She accepted. They went past Gray's house to pick up his son's forgotten lunch and Gray gave Ellison a tour of his house. Ellison alleges that after that June lunch, Gray began to pester her with unnecessary questions and hang around her desk.

On October 9, when Gray asked Ellison out for a drink after work, she declined, but suggested lunch the following week. Ellison did not want to have lunch alone with him and she tried to stay away from the office during lunch time. The next week Gray asked her out to lunch and she did not go.

On October 22, 1986 Gray handed Ellison a note written on a telephone message slip which read: "I cried over you last night and I'm totally drained today. I have never been in such constant termoil (sic). Thank you for talking with me. I could not stand to feel your hatred for another day." Ellison was shocked at the note, became frightened and left the room. Gray followed Ellison into the hallway and demanded that she talk to him. Ellison left the building. While Gray reported this to her supervisor and asked to try to handle it herself, she asked a male co-worker to talk to Gray and tell him she was not interested in him and to leave her alone. The next day, Gray called in sick. Ellison did not work the following day, Friday, and on Monday started a four week training session in Missouri.

While Ellison was at the training session, Gray mailed her a card and a three page, typed, single spaced letter. Ellison described the letter as "twenty times, a hundred times weirder" than the prior note. In part, Gray wrote:

> I know that you are worth knowing with or without sex. . . . Leaving aside the hassles and disasters of recent weeks. I have enjoyed you so much over these past few months. Watching you. Experiencing you from O so far away. Admiring your style and elan. . . . Don't you think it odd that two people who have never even talked together, alone, are striking off such intense sparks . . . I will [write] another letter in the near future.

Ellison stated that she thought Gray was "crazy. I thought he was nuts. I didn't know what he would do next. I was frightened." Ellison immediately called her supervisor and reported this and told her she was frightened and wanted one of them transferred. Gray was told many times over the next few weeks not to contact Ellison in any way. On November 24 Gray transferred to the San Francisco office. Ellison returned from Missouri in late November. After three weeks in San Francisco, Gray filed a grievance to return to San Mateo and as part of the settlement in Gray's favor, he agreed to be transferred back provided he spend four more months (a total of six months) in San Francisco and promise not to bother Ellison. When Ellison learned of Gray's request to return in a letter from her supervisor indicating Gray would return after a six month separation, she said she was "frantic" and filed a formal sexual harassment complaint with IRS. The letter to Ellison also said that they could revisit the issue if there was further need.

Gray sought joint counseling. He wrote another letter to Ellison seeking to maintain the idea that he and Ellison had a relationship.

We do not agree with the standard set forth in *Rabidue.* We believe that Gray's conduct was sufficiently severe and pervasive to alter the conditions of Ellison's employment and create an abusive working environment. We believe that, in evaluating the severity and pervasiveness of sexual harassment, we should focus on the perspective of the victim. If we examined whether a reasonable person would engage in allegedly harassing conduct, we would run the risk of reinforcing the prevailing level of discrimination. Harassers could continue to harass merely because a particular discriminatory practice was common, and victims of harassment would have no remedy.

We therefore prefer to analyze harassment from the victim's perspective. A complete understanding of the victim's view requires, among other things, an analysis of the different perspectives of men and women. Conduct that many men consider unobjectionable may offend many women. See, e.g., *Lipsett v. University of Puerto Rico,* 864 F.2d 881, 898 (1st Cir. 1988) ("A male supervisor might believe, for example, that it is legitimate for him to tell a female subordinate that she has a 'great figure' or 'nice legs.' The female subordinate, however, may find such comments

offensive"); Yates, 819 F.2d at 637, n.2 ("men and women are vulnerable in different ways and offended by different behavior"). See also, Ehrenreich, Pluralist Myths and Powerless Men: The Ideology of Reasonableness in Sexual Harassment Law, 99 Yale L. J. 1177, 1207–1208 (1990) (men tend to view some forms of sexual harassment as "harmless social interactions to which only overly-sensitive women would object"); Abrams, Gender Discrimination and the Transformation of Workplace Norms, 42 Vand. L. Rev. 1183, 1203 (1989) (the characteristically male view depicts sexual harassment as comparatively harmless amusement).

We realize that there is a broad range of viewpoints among women as a group, but we realize that many women share common concerns which men do not necessarily share. For example, because women are disproportionately victims of rape and sexual assault, women have stronger incentives to be concerned with sexual behavior. Women who are victims of mild forms of sexual harassment may understandably worry whether a harasser's conduct is merely a prelude to violent sexual assault. Men, who are rarely victims of sexual assault, may view sexual conduct in a vacuum without a full appreciation of the social setting or the underlying threat of violence that a woman may perceive.

In order to shield employers from having to accommodate the idiosyncratic concerns of the rare hyper-sensitive employee, we hold that a female plaintiff states a prima facie case of hostile environment sexual harassment when she alleges conduct that a reasonable woman would consider sufficiently severe or pervasive to alter the conditions of employment and create an abusive working environment. Of course, where male employees allege that co-workers engage in conduct which creates a hostile environment, the appropriate victim's perspective would be that of a reasonable man.

We adopt the perspective of a reasonable woman primarily because we believe that a gender-blind reasonable person standard tends to be male-biased and tends to systematically ignore the experiences of women. The reasonable woman standard does not establish a higher level of protection for women than men. Instead, a gender-conscious examination of sexual harassment enables women to participate in the workplace on an equal footing with men. By acknowledging and not trivializing the effects of sexual harassment on reasonable women, courts can work towards ensuring that neither men nor women will have to "run a gauntlet of sexual abuse in return for the privilege of being allowed to work and make a living."

We note that the reasonable woman victim standard we adopt today classifies conduct as unlawful sexual harassment even when harassers do not realize that their conduct creates a hostile working environment. Well-intentioned compliments by co-workers or supervisors can form the basis of a sexual harassment cause of action if a reasonable victim of the same gender as plaintiff would consider the comments sufficiently severe or pervasive to alter a condition of employment and create an abusive working environment. That is because Title VII is not a fault-based tort scheme. Title VII is aimed at the consequences or effects of an employment practice and not the motivation of co-workers or employers.

The facts of this case illustrate the importance of considering the victim's perspective. Analyzing the facts from the alleged harasser's viewpoint, Gray could be portrayed as a modern-day Cyrano de Bergerac wishing no more than to woo Ellison with his words. There is no evidence that Gray harbored ill-will toward Ellison. He even offered in his "love letter" to leave her alone if she wished [though he said he would not be able to forget her]. Examined in this light, it is not difficult to see why the district court characterized Gray's conduct as isolated and trivial.

Ellison, however, did not consider the acts to be trivial. Gray's first note shocked and frightened her. After receiving the three-page letter, she became really upset and frightened again. She immediately requested that she or Gray be transferred. Her supervisor's prompt response suggests that she too did not consider the conduct trivial. When Ellison learned that Gray arranged to return to San Mateo, she immediately asked to transfer and she immediately filed an official complaint.

We cannot say as a matter of law that Ellison's reaction was idiosyncratic or hypersensitive. We believe that a reasonable woman could have had a similar reaction. After receiving the first bizarre note from Gray, a person she barely knew, Ellison asked a co-worker to tell Gray to leave her alone. Despite her request, Gray sent her a long, passionate, disturbing letter. He told her he had been "watching" and "experiencing" her, he made repeated references to sex; and he said he would write again. Ellison had no way of knowing what Gray would do next. A reasonable woman could consider Gray's conduct, as alleged by Ellison, sufficiently severe and pervasive to alter a condition of employment and create an abusive working environment.

Sexual harassment is a major problem in the workplace. Adopting the victim's perspective ensures that courts will not "sustain ingrained notions of reasonable behavior fashioned by the offenders." Congress did not enact Title VII to codify prevailing sexist prejudices. To the contrary, "Congress designed Title VII to prevent the perpetuation of stereotypes and a sense of degradation which serve to close or discourage employment opportunities for women." We hope that over time both men and women will learn what conduct offends reasonable members of the other gender. When employers and employees internalize the standard of workplace conduct we establish today, the current gap in perception between the genders will be bridged. REVERSED and REMANDED.

Case Questions

1. Do you agree with the court's use of the "reasonable victim" standard? Explain.

2. Do you think the standard creates problems for management? If so, what are they? If not, why not?

3. Do you think Ellison was being "overly sensitive?" What would you have done if you had been the supervisor to whom she reported the incidents?

"Sexual" Requirement Explained

While the harassment of the employee must be based on gender, oddly enough it need not involve sex, requests for sexual activity, sexual comments, or other such activity. Often a female entering a workplace with few or no other females is verbally harassed about "doing men's work," "taking away the job a man should have," or simply working at a traditionally male job. This, despite the lack of sexual overtones, could well constitute sexual harassment. In the case below, the sexual activity was only a small part of what the females who came into the traditionally male job were subjected to in being harassed. Notice how little of what they went through conforms to what we usually think of as sexually based hostile environment. This "non-sex" requirement is also one of the reasons it is better to use the term *gender* in sexual harassment discussions so that sex in the traditional sense, and gender, meaning whether one is male or female, are clearly differentiated and the discussion is less confusing.

ANDREWS V. CITY OF PHILADELPHIA
895 F.2d 1469 (3d Cir. 1990)

Two female police officers, Andrews and Conn, filed a Title VII action against their employer and supervisors for sexual harassment. The court found sufficient basis for hostile environment sexual harassment even though sex, per se, was not the basis of the activity directed toward them.

Rosenn, J.

While employees were assigned to the Auto Investigation Division (AID) of the Philadelphia police department, males dominated the division and according to Andrews, the AID squadroom was charged with sexism. Women were regularly referred to in an offensive and obscene manner and they personally were addressed by obscenities.

There was evidence that the language was commonplace in police headquarters, but also testimony that one of the plaintiffs, a twelve-year police veteran, "had never been called some of the names that [she] was called in AID." There was also evidence of pornographic pictures of women displayed in the locker room on the inside of a locker which most often was kept open. Plaintiffs contend that the language and pictures embarrassed, humiliated, and harassed them.

Both employees further claimed that their files often disappeared from their desks, or were ripped or sabotaged. When Conn reported the sabotage, she was told by her supervisor, "You know, you're no spring chicken. You have to expect this working with the guys." Male officers who were to assist them in their work often hindered them or refused to help, although the men would help each other. The women experienced vandalism of their personal property, with Andrews having her car thrice vandalized while parked on the AID lot, with tires slashed, car scratched and windshield wipers removed; soda was poured into her typewriter; someone tore the cover off Andrews' book needed to keep track of investigations. Someone spit on Conn's coat, cut the band off her hat, and scratched her car. A roll of film Conn was using in an investigation disappeared before it was dispatched for developing.

Both employees also received obscene phone calls at their unlisted home phone numbers which AID had access to. One of the time periods for the calls was after the lawsuit was filed. One caller told the daughter of Andrews that her mother was sleeping with Conn, and that "those bitches ain't getting no money because they think they trying to get money but they not going to get none." During one of the conversations Andrews heard someone say "Yoh, sarge" in the background. Conn testified that the calls made her very scared and nervous and unable to function emotionally. She was also harassed by co-workers placing sexual devices and pornographic magazines in her desk drawer and gathering around and laughing at her reaction. When she reported this to her superior, he remained unresponsive. Another time a caustic substance was placed inside Andrews' shirt in her locker in the women's locker room. Andrews' back was severely burned by what was later determined to be a lime substance. Lime was found in other clothing in the locker and on the handle. Andrews also says that lewd pictures were posted on the walls and that she was embarrassed by pornographic pictures placed in her personal desk drawer.

Some of Conn and Andrews' complaints were investigated, others were not, but nothing significant came of any investigations. In both cases there was some sexually-based activity directed toward the women, such as suggestive remarks or tones used in connection with them.

We believe that the trial court too narrowly construed what type of conduct can constitute sexual harassment. Great emphasis was put on the lack of sexual advances, innuendo, or contact. In the lower court's opinion, evidence was extremely minimal and would not, standing alone, support a finding of a sexually hostile work environment, noting the lack of evidence of direct sexual harassment. To the extent that the court ruled that overt sexual harassment is necessary to establish a sexually hostile environment, we are constrained to disagree.

To make out a case under Title VII it is only necessary to show that gender is a substantial factor in the discrimination, and that if the plaintiff had been a man she would not have been treated in the same manner. To constitute impermissible discrimination, the offensive conduct is not necessarily required to include sexual overtones in every instance or that each incident be sufficiently severe to detrimentally affect a female employee. Intimidation and hostility toward women because they are women can obviously result from conduct other than explicitly sexual advances. *Meritor* appears to support this proposition as well, "Title VII affords employees the right to work in an environment free from discriminatory intimidation, ridicule and insult." The Supreme Court in no way limited this concept to intimidation or ridicule of an explicitly sexual nature.

More specifically, we hold that the pervasive use of derogatory and insulting terms relating to women generally and addressed to female employees personally may serve as evidence of a hostile environment. Similarly, so may the posting of pornographic pictures in common areas and in the plaintiff's personal work spaces.

Although the employer's attorney argues

vigorously that a police station need not be run like a day care center, it should not, however, have the ambience of a nineteenth century military barracks. We realize that it is unrealistic to hold an employer accountable for every isolated incident of sexism; however, we do not consider it an unfair burden of an employer of both genders to take measures to prevent an atmosphere of sexism to pervade the workplace.

On remand, the trial judge should look at all incidents to see if they produce a work environment hostile and offensive to women of reasonable sensibilities. The evidence in this case includes not only name calling, pornography, displaying sexual objects in desks, but also the re-current disappearance of plaintiffs' case files and work products, anonymous phone calls, and destruction of other property. The court should view this evidence in its totality, as described above, and then reach a determination. VACATED and REMANDED.

Case Questions

1. Why do you think the employer did nothing much to remedy this situation?

2. Do you think sexual overtones should have been required here?

3. What would you have done if you were the manager?

A common element of hostile environment sexual harassment cases that may lack an actual sexuality factor is "anti-female animus" exhibited by the harasser toward those of harassee's gender. This is manifested through, for instance, the use of derogatory terms when referring to women. Recall that the *Rabidue* dissent said it was exhibited, among other things, by workplace references to women or female employees as "bitches," "cunts," "pussy," or "whores." Courts have also found it in derogatory statements to or about women in the context of their jobs, such as "women have shit for brains," "should be barefoot and pregnant," "should not be surgeons because it takes them too long to bathe and put on makeup," "could never stand up to union representatives," "are unstable when they are 'in heat' [having their menstrual cycle, said to a female doctor]," or "all she needs is a good lay." Often anti-female animus is accompanied by sexually based activity, but need not be to be considered hostile environment sexual harassment. Harassee's complaint should not be dismissed simply because it does not involve sexually-related activity.

Employer Liability for Sexual Harassment

In this important recent US Supreme Court case, the Court discussed employer liability for sexual harassment. The Court not only provided employers with a defense they could use when sued by an employee who had not acted reasonably in seeking to avoid harm, but also ammunition for an employee who could allege that the employer did not use reasonable measures to prevent sexual harassment.

FARAGHER V. CITY OF BOCA RATON
524 US 775 (1998)

Former city lifeguard sued the city under Title VII for sexual harassment based on the conduct of her supervisors. The Supreme Court held that an employer is subject to vicarious liability under Title VII for actionable discrimination caused by a supervisor, but the employer may raise an affirmative defense that looks to the reasonableness of the employer's conduct in seeking to prevent and correct harassing conduct and to the reasonableness of employee's conduct in seeking to avoid harm. The Court held that the employer was vicariously liable here because it failed to exercise reasonable care to prevent harassing behavior.

Souter, J.

This case calls for identification of the circumstances under which an employer may be held liable under Title VII of the Civil Rights Act for the acts of a supervisory employee whose sexual harassment of subordinates has created a hostile work environment amounting to employment discrimination. We hold that an employer is vicariously liable for actionable discrimination caused by a supervisor, but subject to an affirmative defense looking to the reasonableness of the employer's conduct as well as that of a plaintiff victim.

Between 1985 and 1990, while attending college, petitioner Beth Ann Faragher worked part time and during the summers as an ocean lifeguard for the Marine Safety Section of the Parks and Recreation Department of respondent, the City of Boca Raton, Florida (City). During this period, Faragher's immediate supervisors were Bill Terry, David Silverman, and Robert Gordon. In June 1990, Faragher resigned. In 1992, Faragher brought an action against Terry, Silverman, and the City, asserting claims under Title VII, and Florida law. The complaint alleged that Terry and Silverman were agents of the City, and that their conduct created a "sexually hostile atmosphere" that amounted to discrimination in the "terms, conditions, and privileges" of her employment at the beach by repeatedly subjecting

Faragher and other female lifeguards to "uninvited and offensive touching," by making lewd remarks, and by speaking of women in offensive terms.

Throughout Faragher's employment with the City, Terry served as Chief of the Marine Safety Division, with authority to hire new lifeguards (subject to the approval of higher management), to supervise all aspects of the lifeguards' work assignments, to engage in counseling, to deliver oral reprimands, and to make a record of any such discipline. Silverman and Gordon were captains and responsible for making the lifeguards' daily assignments, and for supervising their work and fitness training. The lifeguards and supervisors were stationed at the city beach. The lifeguards had no significant contact with higher city officials like the Recreation Superintendent.

In February 1986, the City adopted a sexual harassment policy, which it stated in a memorandum from the City Manager addressed to all employees. In May 1990, the City revised the policy and reissued a statement of it. Although the City may actually have circulated the memos and statements to some employees, it completely failed to disseminate its policy among employees of the Marine Safety Section, with the result that Terry, Silverman, Gordon, and many lifeguards were unaware of it.

Faragher did not complain to higher management about Terry or Silverman. In April 1990, however, two months before Faragher's resignation, Nancy Ewanchew, a former lifeguard, wrote to Richard Bender, the City's Personnel Director, complaining that Terry and Silverman had harassed her and other female lifeguards. Following investigation of this complaint, the City found that Terry and Silverman had behaved improperly, reprimanded them, and required them to choose between a suspension without pay or the forfeiture of annual leave.

Since our decision in *Meritor,* Courts of Appeals have struggled to derive manageable standards to govern employer liability for hostile environment harassment perpetrated by supervisory employees. While indicating the substantive contours of the hostile environments forbidden by Title VII, our cases have established few definite rules for determining when an employer will be liable for a discriminatory environment that is otherwise actionably abusive.

A "master is subject to liability for the torts of his servants committed while acting in the scope of their employment." Restatement §219(1). This doctrine has traditionally defined the "scope of employment" as including conduct "of the kind [a servant] is employed to perform," occurring "substantially within the authorized time and space limits," and "actuated, at least in part, by a purpose to serve the master," but as excluding an intentional use of force "unexpectable by the master."

A justification for holding the offensive behavior within the scope of Terry's and Silverman's employment was well put in Judge Barkett's dissent: "[A] pervasively hostile work environment of sexual harassment is never (one would hope) authorized, but the supervisor is clearly charged with maintaining a productive, safe work environment. The supervisor directs and controls the conduct of the employees, and the manner of doing so may inure to the employer's benefit or detriment, including subjecting the employer to Title VII liability."

It is by now well recognized that hostile environment sexual harassment by supervisors (and, for that matter, co-employees) is a persistent problem in the workplace. An employer can, in a general sense, reasonably anticipate the possibility of such conduct occurring in its workplace, and one might justify the assignment of the burden of the untoward behavior to the employer as one of the costs of doing business, to be charged to the enterprise rather than the victim. As noted, developments like this occur from time to time in the law of agency.

We agree with Faragher that in implementing Title VII it makes sense to hold an employer vicariously liable for some tortious conduct of a supervisor made possible by abuse of his supervisory authority. The agency relationship affords contact with an employee subjected to a supervisor's sexual harassment, and the victim may well be reluctant to accept the risks of blowing the whistle on a superior. When a person with supervisory authority discriminates in the terms and conditions of subordinates' employment, his actions necessarily draw upon his superior position over the people who report to him, or those under them, whereas an employee generally cannot check a supervisor's abusive conduct the same way that she might deal with abuse from a co-worker. When a fellow employee harasses, the victim can walk away or tell the offender where to go, but it may be difficult to offer such responses to a supervisor, whose "power to supervise—[which may be] to hire and fire, and to set work schedules and pay rates—does not disappear . . . when he chooses to harass through insults and offensive gestures rather than directly with threats of firing or promises of promotion." Recognition of employer liability when discriminatory misuse of supervisory authority alters the terms and conditions of a victim's employment is underscored by the fact that the employer has a greater opportunity to guard against misconduct by supervisors than by common workers; employers have greater opportunity and incentive to screen them, train them, and monitor their performance.

In order to accommodate the principle of vicarious liability for harm caused by misuse of supervisory authority, as well as Title VII's equally basic policies of encouraging forethought by employers and saving action by objecting employees, we adopt the following holding in this case and in *Burlington Industries, Inc. v. Ellerth,* also decided today. An employer is subject to vicarious liability to a victimized employee for an actionable hostile environment created by a supervisor with immediate (or successively higher) authority over the employee.

When no tangible employment action is taken, a defending employer may raise an affirmative defense to liability or damages, subject to proof by a preponderance of the evidence. The defense comprises two necessary elements: (a) that the employer exercised reasonable care to prevent and correct promptly any sexually harassing behavior, and (b) that the plaintiff employee unreasonably failed to take advantage of any preventive or corrective opportunities provided by the employer or to avoid harm otherwise.

While proof that an employer had promulgated an antiharassment policy with complaint procedure is not necessary in every instance as a matter of law, the need for a stated policy suitable to the employment circumstances may appropriately be addressed in any case when litigating the first element of the defense. And while proof that an employee failed to fulfill the corresponding obligation of reasonable care to avoid harm is not limited to showing an unreasonable failure to use any complaint procedure provided by the employer, a demonstration of such failure will normally suffice to satisfy the employer's burden under the second element of the defense. No affirmative defense is available, however, when the supervisor's harassment culminates in a tangible employment action, such as discharge, demotion, or undesirable reassignment.

Applying these rules here, it is undisputed that these supervisors "were granted virtually unchecked authority" over their subordinates, "directly controll[ing] and supervis[ing] all aspects of [Faragher's] day-to-day activities." It is also clear that Faragher and her colleagues were "completely isolated from the City's higher management."

While the City would have an opportunity to raise an affirmative defense if there were any serious prospect of its presenting one, it appears from the record that any such avenue is closed. The City entirely failed to disseminate its policy against sexual harassment among the beach employees and its officials made no attempt to keep track of the conduct of supervisors like Terry and Silverman. The City's policy did not include any assurance that the harassing supervisors could be bypassed in registering complaints. Under such circumstances, we hold as a matter of law that the City could not be found to have exercised reasonable care to prevent the supervisors' harassing conduct. Unlike the employer of a small workforce, who might expect that sufficient care to prevent tortious behavior could be exercised informally, those responsible for city operations could not reasonably have thought that precautions against hostile environments in any one of many departments in far-flung locations could be effective without communicating some formal policy against harassment, with a sensible complaint procedure. REVERSED and REMANDED.

Case Questions

1. How could the city have avoided this outcome? Explain.

2. Do you think that it would have made sense for the city to consider the particulars of the circumstances here, such as that these were lifeguards, in a remote location, who by the nature of the job would be dressed in fairly little clothing, and who, because of the environment (the beach and recreational facilities) might need a different approach to sexual harassment than, say, office employees? Explain.

3. What do you think of the Court's affirmative defense given to employers and employees? What are the pros and cons?

EXHIBIT 8–5   Maine Has First Sexual Harassment Law

---

26 Maine Revised Statutes Sections 806, 807

In an effort to ensure a workplace free of sexual harassment, Maine was the first state to pass a sexual harassment law. Connecticut passed such a law in May 1992 and was followed by other states, including Rhode Island, Massachusetts, Vermont, and Connecticut. While the EEOC guidelines are voluntary on the part of employers, Maine's law, which took effect October 9, 1991, imposes affirmative duties on all employers, whether or not they have been found to have violated Maine's human rights law. The law, which in large part tracks the EEOC guidelines, requires employers to provide employees with information regarding sexual harassment, including:

- A statement that it is illegal.
- Defining sexual harassment under the state law.
- Descriptions of sexual harassment using examples.
- Descriptions of the internal complaint process available to employees.
- The availability of legal recourse and complaint process through the state's Human Rights Commission.
- Directions on how to contact the Commission.
- The availability of protection against retaliation for invoking rights under the discrimination law.

The employer must provide this information in three ways:

- Posting a poster (which cannot exceed a 6th grade literacy level and may be purchased from Maine's Human Rights Commission) in a prominent and accessible location in the workplace.
- Providing employees each year with an individual written notice about sexual harassment delivered in a manner to ensure its receipt, such as with employees' pay.
- If the employer has 15 or more employees, the employer must conduct an education and training program for all new employees within one year of the employee starting work. Additional training is required for supervisory and managerial employees within a year of commencing work to ensure that those employees take immediate and appropriate corrective action addressing sexual harassment complaints.

CBC Employment Alert, August 15, 1991, pp. 2–3, © 1994 by Clark Boardman Callahan, a division of Thomson Legal Publishing, Inc.

There is a difference in liability for harassment based on the position of the harasser and his or her relationship to the employer. If the sexual harassment is committed by a supervisory employee, the employer is liable for the supervisor's actions whether the employer knows or should have known or even warned the employee not to commit such acts (as with an anti–sexual harassment policy). The supervisor is the employer's agent and representative, and the acts of the supervisor are the acts of the employer. Considering the potential for holding the employer liable, employers should carefully choose supervisory employees.

If the harasser is a nonsupervisory co-worker, the employer is responsible if the employer knew or should have known of the harassment (through its agents—the supervisory employees) and took no steps to curtail or prevent it. This would include an employee reporting harassing activity to a supervisor and the supervisor failing to take appropriate steps to handle the matter. Often the supervisor will ignore the employee's complaint or will joke about it. This can be taken as notice that the employer knew of the activity and failed to take immediate appropriate corrective action. This should be avoided at all costs. In *Robinson* below, the court addresses this situation and gives excellent guidance to employers regarding how their actions will be perceived by a court. (Later, see Exhibit 8–5.)

On June 18, 1999, the EEOC issued a policy guidance based on the Supreme Court's decisions in *Faragher* and *Burlington Industries, Inc. v. Ellerth,*[6] a similar sexual harassment case which was decided the same day by the Court. The guideline is based on the EEOC's determination that the Supreme Court decisions are premised on two principles: an employer is responsible for the acts of its supervisors, and employers should be encouraged to prevent harassment, while employees should be encouraged to avoid or limit the harm from harassment. Under the guideline, employers are subject to liability if a supervisor's actions result in tangible job loss to the harassee. If they do not, the employer may be able to avoid liability for sexual harassment claims by establishing an affirmative defense that includes proving two necessary elements: (1) the employer exercised reasonable care to prevent and/or correct promptly any harassing behavior and (2) the employee unreasonably failed to take advantage of corrective opportunities provided by the employer or to avoid harm otherwise.

ROBINSON V. JACKSONVILLE SHIPYARDS, INC.
760 F. Supp. 1486 (M.D. Fla. Jacksonville Div. 1991)

An employee brought this action against her employer because of the prevalence of nude photos, posters, reading material, plaques and other nude representations in the workplace. She alleged that this, and the harassing activity toward her constituted hostile environment sexual harassment in violation of Title VII of the Civil Rights Act of 1964. After an exhaustive 59-page, extremely detailed opinion, the court held for the employee and discussed the employer's handling of its sexual harassment complaints.

Melton, J.

The shipyard had very few female skilled employees, so males greatly outnumbered females in the workplace. The employees bringing the complaint were skilled female craftworkers who had been subjected to a full range of harassing activity in the workplace including repeated requests for sexual activity, lewd comments, propositions, jokes, nude photos, posters, magazines

---

[6] 524 U.S. 742 (1998).

and sexual teasing, all of the most egregious kind.

In addressing the employer's response to the harassing activity in the workplace, the court finds that the policies and procedures at JSI for responding to complaints of harassment are inadequate. The company has done an inadequate job of communicating with employees and supervisors regarding the nature and scope of sexually harassing behavior. This failure is compounded by a pattern of unsympathetic response to complaints by employees who perceive that they are victims of harassment. This pattern includes an unwillingness to believe the accusations, an unwillingness to take prompt and stern remedial action against admitted harassers, and an express condonation of behavior that is and encourages sexually harassing conduct (such as the posting of nude and partially nude women). In some instances, the process of registering a complaint about sexual harassment became a second episode of sexual harassment.

JSI cannot stand on an "ostrich defense" that it lacked knowledge of many of the complaints, because its handling of sexual harassment complaints deterred reporting and it did not conduct adequate investigation of the complaints it did receive. JSI received reports at the supervisory level and at the line level concerning incidents of sexual harassment. Additionally, many supervisory personnel admitted that they knew of the sexually oriented pictures throughout the workplace. JSI concedes it had reports of this and those reports should have alerted them to the need to conduct a more thorough investigation of conditions in the shipyards. Such a duty arises when reports show that the workplace may be charged with a sexually hostile atmosphere.

JSI instead ignored the warning signs of a hostile environment. The evidence reveals a supervisory attitude that sexual harassment is an incident-by-incident matter; records were not maintained that would have permitted an analysis of sexual harassment complaints to determine the level of sexual hostility in the workplace. Under these circumstances, the court concludes that JSI received adequate actual knowledge of the state of the work environment, but, like an ostrich, the company elected to bury its head in the sand rather than learn more about the conditions to which female employees, Robinson in particular, were subjected.

The court additionally imposes constructive knowledge on JSI for the sexually hostile state of its work environment. Constructive knowledge is measured by a practical threshold. An employer escapes liability for isolated and infrequent slurs and misogynist behaviors because even a reasonably prudent employer cannot exercise sufficient control over the workplace to put an end to such conduct; conversely, an employer incurs liability when harassing behavior happens frequently enough that the employer can take steps to halt it. The sexually harassing behaviors described here are too pervasive to have escaped the notice of a reasonably alert management. Moreover, the extent to which co-workers and supervisory personnel actually knew of the existence of sexually harassing behaviors is a good barometer of the company's constructive knowledge. The testimony establishes that Robinson's plight was widely known. To the extent that JSI contends that the physical size of its work environment diminished its ability to monitor incidents of sexual harassment, the company must realize that its expansive size may increase its burden in providing a workplace free of discrimination, but that expanse does not decrease the responsibility in its task. JUDGMENT for PLAINTIFF on the Title VII issue.

Case Questions

1. How would you have handled this workplace if you had been manager?

2. Do you think the court imposed too heavy a burden on the employer for monitoring the workplace?

3. Should the "ostrich defense" be permitted?

Liability for hostile environment sexual harassment by nonemployees is judged by the same standard as for co-workers. That is, the employer will be liable when the employer knows or should have known of the harassment through its supervisors and failed to take appropriate corrective action. It may seem unfair to hold an employer responsible for the actions of someone like a computer repairer who routinely comes to service the company's machines. However, it makes sense on close inspection. Once made aware of the situation by the harassee, the employer can speak to the repairer and request that the offending behavior be curtailed, speak to the repairer's supervisor, request that a different repairer service the computers, or even cancel the contract altogether, as appropriate. The employer is also responsible for an outsiders' harassment if the employer set up a situation encouraging harassing activity, such as requiring employees to dress in skimpy uniforms.

Remember that it is a defense to liability if an employer can show that the harassee unreasonably failed to avail himself or herself of any mechanism the employer had in place for preventing or correcting sexual harassment. Likewise, it is helpful if a harassee can show that the employer had unreasonable means of preventing or correcting sexual harassment (for instance, the only one to whom claims are reported is the harasser). This makes it more important than ever for an employer to have an anti–sexual harassment policy as well as effective training, monitoring, and reporting of sexual harassment. The EEOC has determined that since harassment of any kind is the only type of discrimination carried out by a supervisor for which an employer can avoid liability, that limitation is to be narrowly construed.

Other Important Considerations

There are several other important miscellaneous matters you should be aware of that are often at issue in sexual harassment claims.

Determining the Truth of Allegations

The number one problem managers have with responding to sexual harassment complaints is determining the truth of sexual harassment allegations. Appropriate investigation should provide the employer a basis on which to decide and to appropriately respond. Both parties, as well as any witnesses, should be questioned. The investigator's objective is to find out the "who," "what," "when," "where," and "how" of the allegations as quickly and as discreetly as possible. Employees should be involved only on a "need to know" basis. When all appropriate evidence is gathered, like the members of a jury the employer must determine what took place. The employer bases the determination on who seems most credible, whose version of the alleged incidents is more likely to be closer to the truth, what interests the parties have in telling their version of the events, and any credible corroboration presented. The common problem of the employer's discomfort with making judgments should not prevent moving quickly and appropriately on complaints.

The EEOC's June 1999 Policy Guidance on Harassment provides insight into how credibility determinations are to be made. According to the EEOC, while none of the following is necessarily determinative, factors to consider in determining credibility include:

- **Inherent plausibility:** Is the testimony believable on its face? Does it make sense?
- **Demeanor:** Did the person seem to be telling the truth or lying?
- **Motive to falsify:** Did the person have a reason to lie?
- **Corroboration:** Is there **witness testimony** (such as testimony of eyewitnesses, people who saw the person soon after the alleged incidents, or people who discussed the incidents with him or her at or around the time that they occurred) or **physical evidence** (such as written documentation) that corroborates the party's testimony?
- **Past record:** Did the alleged harasser have a history of similar behavior in the past?

Retaliation and Employee Privacy

Often harassees report sexual harassment and, out of fear of retaliation, want the employer to provide relief without informing the alleged harasser of the complaint or of the complainant's identity. Harassees should be informed that the alleged harasser must be told of the complaint for the employer to effectively address it, but that retaliation will not be tolerated, as the law has separate retaliation provisions.

Corrective Action

The guidelines state that the employer must take "immediate and appropriate corrective action" to remedy sexual harassment. What is most appropriate depends on the facts. Consideration should be given to such factors as the employment position of the employees, the activity involved, the duration, the seriousness of the actions, the employer's anti–sexual harassment policy, the alleged harasser's prior experience with sexual harassment, and so on. While the remedy must be calculated to stop the harassment and must not have the effect of punishing the harassee neither should it be out of proportion to the act. Make sure "the punishment fits the crime."

Damages and Jury Trials

Under the Civil Rights Act of 1991, an employee suing for sexual harassment can now ask for up to $300,000 in compensatory and punitive damages (and unlimited medical damages) and request a jury trial. Both these factors greatly increase the employer's potential liability for sexual harassment and make avoiding liability for this unnecessary activity even more imperative.

EXHIBIT 8–6   Example of an Anti–Sexual Harassment Policy

In the *Jacksonville Shipyards* case, as part of the court's order, it required the employer to adopt an anti–sexual harassment policy, which it included in an appendix. It is reproduced below, with changes, as appropriate to generalize the policy, rather than have it be specific to JSI.

XYZ Company Anti–sexual Harassment Policy

Statement of Policy.   Title VII of the Civil Rights Act of 1964 prohibits employment discrimination on the basis of race, color, gender, religion, or national origin. *Sexual harassment is included among the prohibitions.*

Sexual harassment, according to the federal Equal Employment Opportunity Commission (EEOC), consists of unwelcome sexual advances, requests for sexual favors, or other verbal or physical acts of a sexual or sex-based nature where (1) submission to such conduct is made either explicitly or implicitly a term or condition of an individual's employment; (2) an employment decision is based on an individual's acceptance or rejection of such conduct; or (3) such conduct interferes with an individual's work performance or creates an intimidating, hostile, or offensive working environment.

It is also unlawful to retaliate or take reprisal in any way against anyone who has articulated any concern about sexual harassment or discrimination, whether that concern relates to harassment of or discrimination against the individual raising the concern or against another individual.

Examples of conduct that would be considered sexual harassment or related retaliation are set forth in the Statement of Prohibited Conduct, which follows. These examples are provided to illustrate the kind of conduct proscribed by this policy; the list is not exhaustive.

XYZ Company and its agents are under a duty to investigate and eradicate any form of sexual harassment, gender discrimination, or retaliation. To further that end, XYZ Company has issued a procedure for making complaints about conduct in violation of this policy and a schedule for violation of this policy.

Sexual harassment is unlawful, and such prohibited conduct exposes not only XYZ Company but individuals involved in such conduct to significant liability under the law. Employees at all times should treat other employees respectfully and with dignity in a manner so as not to offend the sensibilities of a coworker. Accordingly, XYZ's management is committed to vigorously enforcing its Anti–sexual Harassment Policy at all levels within the company.

Statement of Prohibited Conduct.   The management of XYZ Company considers the following conduct to represent some of the types of acts which violate XYZ's Anti–sexual Harassment Policy:

A. *Physical assaults of a sexual nature, such as:*

(1) rape, sexual battery, molestation, or attempts to commit these assaults; and

(2) intentional physical conduct, which is sexual in nature, such as touching, pinching, patting, grabbing, brushing against another employee's body, or poking another employee's body.

B. *Unwanted sexual advances, propositions, or other sexual comments, such as:*

(1) sexually oriented gestures, noises, remarks, jokes, or comments about a person's sexuality or sexual experience directed at or made in the presence of any employee who indicates or has indicated in any way that such conduct in his or her presence is unwelcome;

(2) preferential treatment or promise of preferential treatment to an employee for submitting to sexual conduct, including soliciting or attempting to solicit any employee to engage in sexual activity for compensation or reward; and

(3) subjecting, or threats of subjecting, an employee to unwelcome sexual attention or conduct or intentionally making performance of the employee's job more difficult because of that employee's gender.

EXHIBIT 8–6   Continued

C. *Sexual or discriminatory displays or publications anywhere in XYZ's workplace by XYZ's employees, such as:*

(1) displaying pictures, posters, calendars, graffiti, objects, promotional materials, reading materials, or other materials that are sexually suggestive, sexually demeaning, or pornographic, or bringing into the XYZ work environment or possessing any such material to read, display, or view at work.

A picture will be presumed to be sexually suggestive if it depicts a person of either gender who is not fully clothed or in clothes that are not suited to or ordinarily accepted for the accomplishment of routine work in and around the workplace and who is posed for the obvious purpose of displaying or drawing attention to private portions of his or her body;

(2) reading or otherwise publicizing in the work environment materials that are in any way sexually revealing, sexually suggestive, sexually demeaning, or pornographic; and

(3) displaying signs or other materials purporting to segregate an employee by gender in any area of the workplace (other than restrooms and similar semiprivate lockers/changing rooms).

D. *Retaliation for sexual harassment complaints, such as:*

(1) disciplining, changing work assignments of, providing inaccurate work information to, or refusing to cooperate or discuss work-related matters with any employee because that employee has complained about or resisted harassment, discrimination, or retaliation; and

(2) intentionally pressuring, falsely denying, lying about, or otherwise covering up or attempting to cover up conduct such as that described in any item above.

E. *Other acts:*

(1) The above is not to be construed as an all-inclusive list of prohibited acts under this policy.

(2) Sexual harassment is unlawful and hurts other employees. Any of the prohibited conduct described here is sexual harassment of anyone at whom it is directed or who is otherwise subjected to it. Each incident of harassment, moreover, contributes to a general atmosphere in which all persons who share the victim's gender suffer the consequences. Sexually oriented acts or gender-based conduct have no legitimate business purpose; accordingly, the employee who engages in such conduct should be and will be made to bear the full responsibility for such unlawful conduct.

Schedule of Penalties for Misconduct.   The following schedule of penalties applies to all violations of this policy, as explained in more detail in the Statement of Prohibited Conduct.

Where progressive discipline is provided for, each instance of conduct violating the policy moves the offending employee through the steps of disciplinary action. In other words, it is not necessary for an employee to repeat the same precise conduct in order to move up the scale of discipline.

A written record of each action taken pursuant to the policy will be placed in the offending employee's personnel file. The record will reflect the conduct, or alleged conduct, and the warning given, or other discipline imposed.

(A) *Assault:*

Any employee's first proven offense of assault or threat of assault, including assault of a sexual nature, will result in dismissal.

(B) *Other acts of harassment by coworkers:*

An employee's commission of acts of sexual harassment, other than assault, will result in nondisciplinary oral counseling upon alleged first offense; written warning, suspension, or discharge upon the first proven offense, depending upon the nature and severity of the misconduct; and suspension or discharge upon the second proven offense, depending upon the nature and severity of the misconduct.

(C) *Retaliation:*

Alleged retaliation against a sexual harassment complainant will result in nondisciplinary oral counseling. Any form of proven retaliation will result in suspension or discharge upon the

---

EXHIBIT 8–6   Continued

---

first proven offense, depending upon the nature and severity of the retaliatory acts, and
discharge upon the second proven offense.

(D) *Supervisors:*

A supervisor's commission of acts of sexual harassment (other than assault) with respect to any
employee under that person's supervision will result in nondisciplinary oral counseling upon
alleged first offense, final warning or dismissal for the first offense, depending upon the
nature and severity of the misconduct, and discharge for any subsequent offense.

Procedures for Making, Investigating, and Resolving Sexual Harassment and Retaliation Complaints

A. *Complaints:*

XYZ Company will provide its employees with convenient, confidential, and reliable
mechanisms for reporting incidents of sexual harassment and retaliation. Accordingly, XYZ
designates at least two employees in supervisory or managerial positions to serve as
investigative officers for sexual harassment issues. The names, responsibilities, work
locations, and phone numbers of each officer will be routinely and continuously posted so
that an employee seeking such name can enjoy anonymity and remain inconspicuous to all of
the employees in the office in which he or she works

The investigative officers may appoint "designees" to assist them in handling sexual harassment
complaints. Persons appointed as designees shall not conduct investigations until they have
received training equivalent to that received by the investigative officers. The purpose of
having several persons to whom complaints may be made is to avoid a situation where an
employee is faced with complaining to the person, or a close associate of the person, who
would be the subject of the complaint.

Complaints of acts of sexual harassment or retaliation that are in violation of the sexual
harassment policy will be accepted in writing or orally, and anonymous complaints will be
taken seriously and investigated. Anyone who has observed sexual harassment or retaliation
should report it to a designated investigative officer. A complaint need not be limited to
someone who was the target of harassment or retaliation. Only those who have an immediate
need to know, including the investigative officers and/or his/her designee, the alleged target of
harassment or retaliation, the alleged harasser(s) or retaliator(s), and any witnesses will or
may find out the identity of the complainant. All parties contacted in the course of an
investigation will be advised that all parties involved in a charge are entitled to respect and
that any retaliation or reprisal against an individual who is an alleged target of harassment or
retaliation, who has made a complaint, or who has provided evidence in connection with a
complaint is a separate actionable offense as provided in the schedule of penalties. This
complaint process will be administered consistent with federal labor law when bargaining unit
members are affected.

B. *Investigations:*

Each investigative officer will receive thorough training about sexual harassment and the
procedures herein and will have the responsibility for investigating complaints or having an
appropriately trained and designated XYZ investigator do so.

All complaints will be investigated expeditiously by a trained XYZ investigative officer or
his/her designee. The investigative officer will produce a written report, which, together with
the investigation file, will be shown to the complainant upon request within a reasonable time.
The investigative officer is empowered to recommend remedial measures based upon the
results of the investigation, and XYZ management will promptly consider and act upon such
recommendation. When a complaint is made, the investigative officer will have the duty of
immediately bringing all sexual harassment and retaliation complaints to the confidential
attention of the office of the president of XYZ, and XYZ's EEO officer. The investigative and

Exhibit 8–6   Continued

EEO officers will each maintain a file on the original charge and follow up investigation. Such files will be available to investigators, to federal, state, and local agencies charged with equal employment or affirmative action enforcement, to other complainants who have filed a formal charge of discrimination against XYZ, or any agent thereof, whether that formal charge is filed at a federal, state, or local law level. The names of complainants, however, will be kept under separate file.

C. *Cooperation:*

An effective sexual harassment policy requires the support and example of company personnel in positions of authority. XYZ agents or employees who engage in sexual harassment or retaliation or who fail to cooperate with company-sponsored investigations of sexual harassment or retaliation may be severely sanctioned by suspension or dismissal. By the same token, officials who refuse to implement remedial measures, obstruct the remedial efforts of other XYZ employees, and/or retaliate against sexual harassment complainants or witnesses may be immediately sanctioned by suspension or dismissal.

Procedures and Rules for Education and Training.   Education and training for employees at each level of the workforce are critical to the success of XYZ's policy against sexual harassment. The following documents address such issues: the letter to be sent to all employees from XYZ's chief executive officer/president; the Anti–sexual Harassment Policy; Statement of Prohibited Conduct; the Schedule of Penalties for Misconduct; and Procedures for Making, Investigating, and Resolving Sexual Harassment Complaints. These documents will be conspicuously posted throughout the workplace at each division of XYZ, on each company bulletin board, in all central gathering areas, and in every locker room. The statements must be clearly legible and displayed continuously. The anti–sexual harassment policy under a cover letter from XYZ's president will be sent to all employees. The letter will indicate that copies are available at no cost and how they can be obtained.

XYZ's anti–sexual harassment policy statement will also be included in the Safety Instructions and General Company Rules, which is issued in booklet form to each XYZ employee. Educational posters using concise messages conveying XYZ's opposition to workplace sexual harassment will reinforce the company's policy statement; these posters should be simple, eye-catching, and graffiti resistant.

Education and training include the following components:

1. *For all XYZ employees:* As part of the general orientation, each recently hired employee will be given a copy of the letter from XYZ's chief executive officer/president and requested to read and sign a receipt for the company's policy statement on sexual harassment so that they are on notice of the standards of behavior expected. In addition, supervisory employees who have attended a management training seminar on sexual harassment will explain orally at least once every six months at general meetings attended by all employees the kind of acts that constitute sexual harassment, the company's serious commitment to eliminating sexual harassment in the workplace, the penalties for engaging in harassment, and the procedures for reporting incidents of sexual harassment.

2. *For all female employees:* All women employed at XYZ will participate on company time in annual seminars that teach strategies for resisting and preventing sexual harassment. At least a half-day in length, these seminars will be conducted by one or more experienced sexual harassment educators, including one instructor with work experience in the trades for skilled employees in traditionally male-dominated jobs.

3. *For all employees with supervisory authority of any kind over other employees:* All supervisory personnel will participate in an annual, half-day-long training session on gender discrimination. At least one-third of each session (of no less than one and one-half hours) will be devoted to education about workplace sexual harassment, including training (with

EXHIBIT 8–6   Concluded

dcmonstrative evidence) as to exactly what types of remarks, behavior, and pictures will not be tolerated in the XYZ workplace. The president of XYZ will attend the training sessions in one central location with all company supervisory employees. The president will introduce the seminar with remarks stressing the potential liability of XYZ and individual supervisors for sexual harassment. Each participant will be informed that they are responsible for knowing the contents of XYZ's anti–sexual harassment policy and for giving similar presentations at meetings of employees.

4. *For all investigative officers:* The investigative officers and their designees, if any, will attend annual full-day training seminars conducted by experienced sexual harassment educators and/or investigators to educate them about the problems of sexual harassment in the workplace and the techniques for investigating and stopping it.

Tort and Criminal Liability

In addition to bringing an action under Title VII, harassees may also bring civil actions in state court—or if permitted, federal court—based on state laws that may also be violated by the actions of the alleged harasser recall that in *Meritor,* the first sexual harassment case to come before the U.S. Supreme Court, the bank manager was alleged to have fondled plaintiff in public, followed her to and entered the ladies' restroom with her, and engaged in unwelcome sexual intercourse, including while in the bank's vault. These acts, while constituting sexual harassment under Title VII, also could form the basis for the tort actions of:

Assault—intentionally putting the victim in fear or apprehension, or both, of immediate unpermitted bodily touching.

Battery—intentional unpermitted bodily touching.

Intentional infliction of emotional distress—an intentional outrageous act that goes outside the bounds of common decency, for which the law will provide a remedy.

False imprisonment—intentionally preventing the harassee's exit from a confined space.

Intentional interference with contractual relations—intentionally causing the harassee to be unable to perform her employment contract as agreed upon.

These cases are generally heard by juries, and there is the possibility of unlimited compensatory and punitive damages. In addition, the harasser's action could also form the basis of criminal prosecution for, at a minimum, criminal assault, battery, and rape. Of course, the criminal cases would be against the harasser, rather than the employer, and would result in punishment for the harasser, rather than money damages to the harassee.

Management Tips

Sexual harassment doesn't have to be the employer's worst nightmare. Don't ever expect to have absolute control over every employee in the workplace, but following the tips below can substantially decrease the chances of a recalcitrant employee causing liability.

Zero tolerance should be the rule for sexual harassment. The EEOC and courts take the position that the best thing an employer can do to effectively keep sexual harassment complaints to a minimum—and to minimize liability for sexual harassment complaints that do occur—is to take a preventive approach. This may include the employer:

- Making sure, from the top down, that all employees understand that sexual harassment in the workplace simply will not be tolerated. *Period.*
- Adopting an anti–sexual harassment policy discouraging such activity. This should be separate from the general antidiscrimination policy.
- Creating and disseminating information about an effective reporting mechanism for harassees.
- Providing employees with training or information apprising them of what sexual harassment is and of what specific activities are appropriate and inappropriate in the workplace.
- Ensuring that reported incidents of sexual harassment are taken seriously by supervisors and others involved in reporting.
- Ensuring that immediate appropriate corrective action is taken against harassers.
- Developing a strong anti–sexual harassment policy and make sure that each and every employee is aware of it.
- After developing the policy, don't let it sit in a drawer somewhere. Use it.
- Not leaving employees hanging as to what the policy means and not assuming that everyone understands sexual harassment. Effective training as to what constitutes sexual harassment, and what is and is not permissible in the workplace will go a very long way toward decreasing potential liability.
- Ensuring that the training employees receive is effective and answers their questions and concerns.
- Keeping in mind that creating an atmosphere in which sexual harassment is not tolerated is a big part of what the EEOC and courts want employers to do. Operationalize this on a real-life basis. That is, when employees engage in activity that helps to create an atmosphere that accepts harassing activity, challenge it. Don't tolerate the jokes, sneers, leers, gestures, and so forth.
- Taking all sexual harassment complaints seriously. Do not tell the employee to "get over it," or that it is to be expected.
- Promptly investigating all sexual harassment claims and only circulating information on a need-to-know basis.
- If investigation warrants discipline for the harasser, making sure it is commensurate with the policy violation. Termination is not the response to every sexual harassment claim.
- Working to keep the workplace friendly and open. Having a workplace free of sexual harassment does not mean employees can't still have a pleasant time at work.

Summary

- Consensual activity is not a violation of Title VII.

- Unwelcome sexual advances that cause one gender to work under conditions or terms of employment different from those of the other gender constitute sexual harassment for which the employer may be liable.

- Employers will be responsible only if the sexual harassment is severe and pervasive.

- Activity does not have to be sexual in nature to constitute sexual harassment.

- Employers should treat all sexual harassment complaints seriously and act on them quickly.

- Prevention is imperative to avoid sexual harassment claims and lessen liability. The employer must make it clear that sexual harassment will not be tolerated. This should be clearly stated and followed up and monitored by appropriate mechanisms.

- Employers need a strong anti–sexual harassment policy which is vigorously enforced.

Chapter-End Questions

1. Dave comes into the office and says to Sue, "Good morning! You look great today! Ooops, I'd better not say that. That's sexual harassment." Is Dave correct? Explain.

2. Employee, a 33-year-old unmarried male, is frequently teased by the other males in his plant about being unmarried and still living at home with his mother. Is this sexual harassment? (*Goluszek v. Smith,* 697 F. Supp. 1452 (N.D. Ill. 1988).

3. Employee sues employer for sexual harassment, because her supervisor once touched her on her back and made an "untoward" statement to her. Will she win? (*Strickland v. Sears Roebuck and Co.,* 693 F. Supp. 403 (E.D. Va. 1988)). Explain.

4. Two employees, Marge and Ben, are having a relationship that later turns sour. When Marge does not get the promotion she goes up for, she sues the employer for sexual harassment, alleging it was committed by her ex-boyfriend Ben, who has, since their breakup, left Marge alone. Will Marge win her suit? (*Koster v. Chase Manhattan Bank,* 687 F. Supp. 848 (S.D. N.Y. 1988)).

5. Dennis comes up to his supervisor, Mae, at a Christmas party and tells Mae he wants to sue for sexual harassment. Mae asks what happened. Dennis says that Linda came over to him and tweaked his cheek and called him sweetie. Dennis pursues the case. Does he win? Why or why not?

6. Is it possible for a subordinate to sexually harass a supervisor? Explain.

7. A female employee has an operation on her breast and, when she returns to work, a male employee "jokingly" asks to see the scar. Actionable sexual harassment? (*Keziah v. W. M. Brown Son, Inc.,* 683 F. Supp. 542 (W.D. N.C. 1988)).

8. Joan, a female manager, asks Margaret, one of her subordinates, out on a date. When Margaret refuses, Joan becomes mean to her at work and rates Margaret's work poorly on her next evaluation. Margaret wants to bring a sexual harassment claim, but feels she cannot do so since her boss is female. Is Margaret correct?

9. At the door of church each Sunday as his church members are leaving, Rev. Bill

kisses the females on the cheek and calls them names like "honey" and "sweetheart." Is this sexual harassment?

10. Trudy comes to Pat, her supervisor, and tells her that Jack has been sexually harassing her by making suggestive remarks, comments, and jokes, constantly asking her for dates, and by using every available opportunity to touch her. Pat has been friends with Jack for a long time and can't imagine Jack would do such a thing. Pat is hesitant to move on Trudy's complaint. What should Pat do?

9   Affinity Orientation Discrimination

Chapter Outline

SCENARIOS

SCENARIO 1

A third-year female law student is given an offer to come to work for a law firm after graduation. She accepts the offer. Later, the lawyers at the law firm find out that the law student is planning on engaging in a symbolic ceremony of commitment with another female. The ceremony is private and does not have the legal effect of marriage. The law firm takes back its "offer" (actually now a contract) after it discovers the law student is a lesbian. The law student sues for employment discrimination. Does she win? Why or why not?

SCENARIO 2

A male airline pilot is terminated after he puts in a request for medical leave, in accordance with company policy, to have sexual reassignment surgery to change him anatomically from male to female. Is this illegal discrimination? Why or why not?

SCENARIO 3

Sylvio's immediate supervisor, Leroy, has been giving Sylvio sexually suggestive looks and making sexually suggestive comments. Sylvio is feeling extremely uncomfortable about it and fears for his job. However, Sylvio thinks that because both he and Leroy are males, there can be no sexual harassment. Is Sylvio correct?

Statutory Basis

It shall be an unlawful employment practice for an employer—

(1) to fail or refuse to hire or to discharge any individual, or otherwise to discriminate against any individual with respect to his compensation, terms, conditions, or privileges of employment, because of such individual's . . . sex. 42 U.S.C. 2000e-2(a).

Affinity orientation
Whom one is attracted to for personal and intimate relationships.

The above does *NOT* prohibit discrimination on the basis of **affinity orientation.**

Nor shall any State deprive any person of life, liberty, or property, without due process of law; nor deny to any person within its jurisdiction the equal protection of the laws. Amendment XIV of the US Constitution.

Out of the Closet

"Look," the angry gentleman in the audience said gruffly as I walked into the room and up to the stage in preparation for conducting a training session. "Does this diversity training mean that I have to deal with homosexuals? Because if it does, I'm not doing it, because homosexuality is against my religion and I just don't think it's right."

Whew! All of this and I hadn't yet fortified myself with a morning cup of coffee. "Well, good morning to you too!" I said with a smile.

Same-gender affinity[1] orientation pushes a lot of buttons in society in general, and the workplace is just a microcosm of society. Though a bit gruff, this employee's greeting was a manifestation of that. I had seen this enough to know that this employee spoke for many others when he made his statement. The good thing is, he got it out onto the table where we could talk about it, put it into perspective, and fit it into what his employer wanted this program to accomplish: less exposure to liability for violations of the law on this and other bases of discrimination. Since we understand that this sentiment is a fairly common one, let's take a bit of time up front to discuss it and give you some things to keep in mind as you go through the chapter and think about the subject matter.

Discrimination on the basis of affinity orientation is not included in Title VII, but many local and state laws include it as part of prohibited bases for employment discrimination, so we include coverage here. It is also one of the types of discrimination that may call into question ideas we hold dear and wish to protect, so we may think of this type of discrimination differently—as more justifiable—than we do other types. In order to prevent those thoughts from turning into actions that lead to litigation and liability for the employer, we must learn to view the matter of employment discrimination on the basis of affinity orientation in its proper perspective.

As you read the chapter, keep this thought in the front of your mind: The intent of this chapter is not to get you to "accept" homosexuality. This chapter is not about going against your religious dictates, moral obligations, or conscience. You are free to believe whatever you want. Rather, this chapter is about what the law requires in this area and what will lessen or prevent costly liability from attaching for violations of the law.

Before choosing to engage in activity that may cause the employer liability for discrimination and get you fired, keep in mind that this is the *employer's* workplace, not yours. Employees don't have the right to engage in activities that will cause unnecessary liability for the employer. Since this is the employer's workplace, the employer gets to call the shots. If the employer has hired someone you don't like, for whatever reason, you have to decide what it's worth to you. Do you create trouble for the employer and run the risk of getting fired, or do you conduct yourself in a professional manner and keep your personal issues to yourself and collect a check? If you feel like you can't do the latter, then seek employment elsewhere. But if you choose to stay, you have no right to impose your personal beliefs on the workplace in a way that increases the employer's liability.

If you think your religious beliefs don't permit same-gender affinity orientation, then don't take your **gay** or **lesbian** co-worker to lunch. Don't take him or her home

Gay
A male attracted to other males; collective generic term for a mix of both gays and lesbians.

Lesbian
Female attracted to females.

---

[1] Also included in this general discussion are those of bi-gender affinity orientation. Since their workplace problems stem from exercise of their same gender component, they are not specifically delineated here separately.

for dinner. But refusing to work with him or her as required or otherwise treating the co-worker in ways that discriminate and expose the *employer* to liability is simply not an option. It might help to think about whether you discriminate against other employees who do things that are against your religion. If you also refuse to deal with co-workers who are alcoholics, fornicators, adulterers, or engage in other activity against your religious beliefs, the religious justification is consistent. For most, it rarely is. Working with someone who is gay or lesbian does not mean you "accept homosexuality" any more than working with adulterers means you "accept adultery." Many people put affinity orientation into another category that permits them to treat it differently. That may be fine for your personal life, but work is work, and your personal life is your personal life, and the considerations for one are not always the same as the considerations for the other. When it's a matter of business and someone else's pocket that will suffer, you have to rein in your personal feelings. Again, if all else fails, and you just can't bring yourself to think of this differently, you ought to find another job where you'd be more comfortable.

With that out of the way, let's explore this area and see what's here.

Despite the stereotypes of gay males as florists, designers, or interior decorators, a survey by the Chicago marketing research firm, Overlooked Opinions, found that more gay males work in science and engineering than in social services, 40 percent more are employed in finance and insurance than in entertainment and the arts, and 10 times as many work in computers as in fashion. (See Exhibit 9–1.) Once, gays and lesbians in the workplace were virtually invisible, but diverse circumstances have begun to change that in dramatic ways.

Recent issues such as the impact of AIDS in the workplace, the military's "don't ask, don't tell" policy, the 1992 presidential election in which President Bill Clinton voiced support for gays (he later appointed over 150 gays and lesbians in his administration, including an ambassador and cabinet-level positions (see Exhibit 9–4.)), and Colorado's attempted constitutional ban on protection for gays and lesbians put the issue of gays and lesbians on the national agenda for the first time. On April 25, 1993, the Cable News Network (CNN) broadcast day-long national television coverage of the convergence of nearly a million people, gay and straight, on Washington, DC, for the March on Washington for Lesbian, Gay, and Bi Equal Rights and Liberation. It was clear that it was one of the largest marches ever held, and that gays and lesbians could no longer be ignored. Since that time, states have seen a spate of legislation about gays and lesbians, and courts have seen cases on issues ranging from parental rights to military discharges, from domestic partner benefits to gay marriage, and from hate crimes to workplace discrimination.

Earning a living is a necessity for most people, so the issue of gays and lesbians is increasingly surfacing in the workplace and has become one an employer must deal with. There is an increasing realization that gays and lesbians are everywhere and should be judged for who they are as people, not for the singular measure of the private matter of sex. With the rules changing almost daily, and more state and local legislation both for and against civil rights for gays, it has become imperative for employers to know what their potential legal liability is in this area.

A fairly recent development has been the emergence of nondiscrimination poli-

EXHIBIT 9–1   Heterosexual Myths

Questionnaire

The questions below provide a somewhat humorous yet insightful look at some of the more frequent assumptions surrounding gays and lesbians, which affect how they may be perceived in the workplace and society at large. The approach of reversing the questions subtly challenges commonly held heterosexually based notions.

1. What do you think caused your heterosexuality?
2. When and how did you first decide you were heterosexual?
3. Is it possible your heterosexuality is just a phase you may grow out of?
4. Is it possible your heterosexuality stems from a neurotic fear of others of the same gender?
5. Heterosexuals have histories of failures in gay relationships. Do you think you may have turned to heterosexuality out of fear of rejection?
6. If you've never slept with a person of the same gender, how do you know you wouldn't prefer that?
7. To whom have you disclosed your heterosexual tendencies? How do they react?
8. Your heterosexuality doesn't offend me as long as you don't try to force it on me. Why do you people feel compelled to seduce others into your sexual orientation?
9. Why do you insist on being so obvious and making a public spectacle of your heterosexuality by holding hands or kissing in public? Can't you just be what you are and keep it quiet?
10. How would the human race survive if everyone were heterosexual like you, considering the menace of overpopulation?
11. Why do heterosexuals place so much emphasis on sex?
12. How can you be heterosexual if you've never had sex?

Adapted from Martin Rochlin, PhD, by Dr. Miranda Pollard, University of Georgia.

cies and gay and lesbian employee support groups within companies. Now listed among such companies are Apple, Digital Equipment, AT&T, Boeing, Coors, Du Pont, Hewlett-Packard, Lockheed, Sun Microsystems, Pacific Gas and Electric Company, Disney Co., J. P. Morgan, Goldman Sachs, Merrill Lynch, and USWest, to name a few. The groups tackle such issues as workplace hostility, extending employee benefits to domestic partners, making sure that partners are welcome at company social functions, and generally making the workplace more hospitable to gays and lesbians.

Some companies sponsor their gay and lesbian employees at events like Gay Pride, a nationwide celebration each June, culminating in a parade comprised of many types of contingents, including businesses. Companies provide employees with such things as novelty items to be passed out to attendees or T-shirts with slogans, such as "ABC Company Supports Its Gay and Lesbian Employees." (See Exhibit 9–2.)

Gay Pride Month is not just a fun time. It is the commemoration of the unfortunate events of June 1969. Being gay or lesbian is often a life-threatening proposition, but it was even more so then. As a result, most gays and lesbians led an extremely closeted existence and often congregated in gay bars in order to be sure of the safety of their surroundings. Since gays and lesbians were considered social outcasts of the highest order, they did not want to risk their own lives, or embarrass their families and friends by being honest about who they were. Fearing discovery made them a very vulnerable group who rarely fought against their circumstances. Gay bars were routinely raided by police officers and the patrons hauled off to jail for one minor infraction or another. Fearing publicity, most patrons went quietly.

In June 1969, this changed. When plainclothes police raided the Stonewall Inn in New York's Greenwich Village, there was uncharacteristic resistance by the bar patrons and people on the street that resulted in a weekend of riots. The next year in New York, the first legislative hearings on gay issues were held, as was the first parade to commemorate the events at Stonewall. The resistance at Stonewall in 1969 is considered the beginning of the modern gay rights movement. Over the years the commemoration has grown and spread as more people, gay and straight, determine that being gay should not equal being vulnerable to discrimination or death. Each June there are now Gay Pride Month celebrations across the country. On June 11, 1999, President Clinton issued a proclamation declaring June 1999 as Gay Pride Month.

The Clinton administration's first US Department of Transportation secretary, Federico Peña, held a lunch hour gay pride day ceremony for department employees, stating, "We need to draw on the talents of everyone. It's not about special privileges. It's about equal treatment." AT&T handed out slick, three-color brochures during the 1993 march on Washington. (See Exhibit 9–2) providing information for gay and lesbian AT&T employees about AT&T and its policies and attitudes regarding them. Each year there is a National Conference on Gay Issues in the Workplace held for human resources professionals needing guidance in this area.

The issue of gays in the workplace can surface in some surprising ways, making it all the more compelling for an employer to be aware of the possibilities of the issues arising and take them into consideration when making policy in this area. Apple computer company was thinking of moving its operations to Williamson County, Texas. The city council refused to vote Apple concessions as an incentive to move there after it discovered that Apple had domestic partnership benefits for its employees. Apple refused to take away these benefits, and the city council finally voted to give Apple the concessions. The Walt Disney Company took a real beating from conservatives when it extended benefits to domestic partners of its employees. The company chose to continue the benefits. Anheuser-Busch recently took flak for its ads featuring two men holding hands, but the ads continued.

Based on the potential for increased productivity and the possibility of litigation or other business problems, some employers conclude that the safer practice is to base workplace decisions solely on an employee's ability to effectively perform the job, rather than on his or her affinity orientation. If the employee's conduct interferes with the workplace, it may be the basis for a legitimate adverse employment decision, but this is not the same as the employee's affinity orientation. The focus should not be on the employee's *status* as gay or lesbian but, rather, on the employee's workplace *performance.*

The above notwithstanding, affinity orientation is *not* a protected category under Title VII of the Civil Rights Act. It has been judicially and administratively

EXHIBIT 9–2

IT'S

GREAT

TO BE GAY

AT

AT&T

PROVIDED

BY THE

LESBIAN,

BISEXUAL &

GAY UNITED

EMPLOYEES

AT AT&T

LEAGUE

HISTORY OF LEAGUE

In 1987 a handful of AT&T employees returned home from the March on Washington inspired, energized and convinced that they could change their part of the world . . . that they could make AT&T a place that welcomed ALL its employees!

Meeting in restaurants and private homes, they formed an informal support group called LEAGUE. In 1988, these brave people brought LEAGUE to the corporation where it was recognized as the two-way communication vehicle between the decision-makers and the AT&T gay community. Soon, word about LEAGUE came out on informal gay bulletin boards across the country . . . chapters sprang up in Denver, then New Jersey, then Ohio and Illinois! In 1992, LEAGUE National was created and bound the loosely associated chapters together to form a common voice, with a common vision: To share the AT&T values, we commit ourselves to advancing changes that will help people respect and value lesbian, bisexual and gay employees and further AT&T's quest for excellence and customer satisfaction. Today there are over 20 LEAGUE chapters across the country that provide its members:

- Advocacy and access to all levels of management
- Professional development courses and conferences
- Workplace community support via electronic mail and regular meetings
- The "Safe Place" ™ program
- Help with community service projects
- Social and networking opportunities
- Resources for solving workplace issues
- Opportunities to educate the AT&T community via homophobia workshops and speaking engagements.

LEAGUE has become a proud and visible leader in the global business community, offering an example for other gay employee resource groups to follow.

EXHIBIT 9–2   Concluded

I LOVE WORKING FOR AT&T BECAUSE...

...I have something special here: a non-discrimination policy, the respect of my management, the support of fellow lesbian, bisexual, gay and straight co-workers, the empowerment to help make AT&T a better place for everyone and the freedom to bring my partner to Family Day at my office.

Rich Mielke, Network Systems, LEAGUE, N. Illinois

...I can aspire toward my professional goals without compromising my personal values or pretending to be someone I'm not. It's inspiring to see gay role models and rewarding to be one in a corporation that takes valuing the diversity of its workforce as seriously as its other business imperatives.

Linda Escalante, Mgr.-Int'l Sales Support, LEAGUE, N. Jersey

...I can finally be open about who I am. I feel very supported by AT&T knowing that if anyone gives me a hard time because of my sexual orientation, more education will take place. I am a much more powerful manager now that I am open about who I am. My personal and professional relationships are moving to deeper levels as I share more of myself with others.

Don Shuart, Programmer/Analyst, LEAGUE, Atlanta

...I believe that our management is honestly committed to understanding our issues and to promoting a healthy, diverse work place and that this will give us a competitive advantage in the decades to come.

Bill Thacker, Quality Engineer, LEAGUE, Columbus

...while recognizing that this is not a perfect place to work, AT&T is committed to making it an attractive, supportive place for all employees. I feel safe being out at work because people around me make it a supportive, caring place.

Terry Teeter, QA Specialist, LEAGUE, Central Florida

...it has taught me the true value of a supportive community on the job. When my life partner became ill with AIDS seven years ago, I "came out" to my boss and my co-workers in order to help them understand why I might suddenly be absent to deal with a health crisis at home. My boss cried and offered me her complete support. When my partner died a year later, about half of the workers in our office—secretaries, paralegals and attorneys—came to his memorial service. I knew then that I was "at home" and "with family" here at AT&T and have felt even closer to my colleagues in the years since.

Glenn Stover, Senior Attorney, LEAGUE, At-Large

...since my involvement with LEAGUE-Atlanta, I've gained a deeper self-respect and found that the people I work with respect me more as a person. I used to live my life in fear of what a few people may have thought of me rather than accepting the positive support that I now know was out there all along. After 25 years with the company, I now know that AT&T really is its people.

Jane Darby, Quality Specialist, LEAGUE, Atlanta

Reprinted with permission of AT&T.

Gender/sexual reassignment surgery
The surgery required to change a person's gender.

Transsexual
Someone who undergoes a change from one gender to another.

Bi-gender affinity orientation
Someone attracted to both genders.

determined that gender discrimination under Title VII does not include discrimination on the basis of affinity orientation, **gender/sexual reassignment surgery (transsexuals), bi-gender affinity orientation** (bisexuality), or effeminacy in males. Those who are terminated or not hired solely on the basis of affinity orientation have no claim for relief under this law. This was reaffirmed once again when Congress failed to pass the Employment Nondiscrimination Act (ENDA) in 1997. ENDA would have basically extended Title VII's reach to include discrimination on the basis of affinity orientation, without, of course, the affirmative action aspect. Corporations endorsing ENDA include NYNEX Corp., Polaroid, Bethlehem Steel Corp., Harley-Davidson, Merrill Lynch, Quaker Oats, and Microsoft, to name a few. A 1997 US Government Accounting Office report on states with antidiscrimination laws protecting gays and lesbians found that the laws had not generated a significant amount of litigation.

This is not to say that employers are totally free to discriminate against gay, lesbian, or bisexual employees. To date, legislation has been passed protecting gays and lesbians from workplace discrimination in over 100 municipalities and eleven

EXHIBIT 9–3   Antidiscrimination Laws Banning Discrimination against Gays and Lesbians

- There are job protection statutes in Washington, DC, Massachusetts, Nevada, New Hampshire, Wisconsin, California, Connecticut, New Jersey, Minnesota, Vermont, Hawaii, and Rhode Island.
- There is an executive order prohibiting discrimination in the federal civilian workforce and mandating that security clearances no longer be denied based on affinity orientation.
- At least 14 states have executive orders.
- At least 71 cities and countries have civil rights ordinances.
- At least 41 cities or counties have council or mayoral proclamations banning discrimination in public employment.

Jurisdictions include:

Berkeley, CA	Toledo, OH
Davis, CA	Minneapolis, MN
Laguna Beach, CA	St. Louis, MO
Los Angeles, CA	Albany, NY
Oakland, CA	Alfred, NY
Sacramento, CA	Ithaca, NY
San Diego, CA	New York, NY
San Francisco, CA	Tompkins County, NY
West Hollywood, CA	Watertown, NY
Washington, DC	Columbus, OH
Key West, FL	Yellow Springs, OH
Miami Beach, FL	Portland, OR
Champaign, IL	Harrisburg, PA
Chicago, IL	Lancaster, PA
Ames, IA	Philadelphia, PA
Iowa City, IA	Pittsburgh, PA
New Orleans, LA	Austin, TX
Howard County, MD	Alexandria, VA
Rockville, MD	Seattle, WA
Detroit, MI	Madison, WI

Source: Human Rights Campaign.

states (Wisconsin, California, Nevada, Massachusetts, Hawaii, Connecticut, New Jersey, Minnesota, Vermont, Rhode Island, and New Hampshire). (See Exhibit 9–3.)

In addition to rights that may be provided by state and local legislation, gay and lesbian public employees adversely affected by an employment decision based on affinity orientation may, under appropriate circumstances, use state constitutions or the 1st, 5th, or 14th Amendments of the US Constitution as a basis for suit, as well as the constitutional right to privacy. This applies to federal, state, and local employees. These lawsuits have traditionally been decided in the employer's favor, but recent decisions have impacted this trend and increasingly recognize the rights of gays and lesbians.

Gay and lesbian employees may also bring tort actions, such as intentional

---

EXHIBIT 9–4   Lesbian Confirmed for No. 2 HUD Post

While Achtenberg is no longer with HUD, take a look at a news article from the time of her appointment to see the issues of concern.

President Clinton on Monday won Senate confirmation of a lesbian to be assistant secretary of Housing and Urban Development after a barbed, three-day debate.

By a vote of 58–31 Roberta Achtenberg, a member of the San Francisco Board of Supervisors, becomes the first open lesbian appointed to the upper echelons of government.

"She is the showpiece of the homosexual movement," said Sen. Jesse Helms, R–N.C., during the debate. "I wish every American could have seen (her) . . . with her partner kissing and hugging as they led that gay pride parade."

The Christian Action Network made sure senators who wanted to see could: It sent every member a videotape of Achtenberg and partner Mary Mogan, a municipal court judge, riding in a white convertible in San Francisco's 1992 Gay Pride Parade.

Senate offices reported receiving thousands of calls from opponents urged on by traditional value proponents like conservative minister Pat Robertson, who urged viewers of his *700 Club* TV show to call.

"I think clearly, some members of the Republican party have a vested interest in demonizing lesbian and gay people for fund-raising purposes," said Gregory King, who is a spokesman for the Human Rights Campaign Fund, a [gay and lesbian] lobby group . . .

Supporters noted that Achtenberg received numerous awards for her community service and as San Francisco city supervisor was a moderate office-holder who sought to help a diverse range of people.

Sen. Barbara Boxer, D–Calif., urged her colleagues not to "vote against a person's private life."

"Today, we have a chance to turn our back to prejudice," said Sen. Dianne Feinstein, D–Calif., and former mayor of San Francisco. "Today we can vote down the politics of hate and take a small step to make sure our government is representative of all the people it seeks to serve."

Copyright 1993, USA TODAY. Reprinted with permission.

Note: Achtenberg resigned in 1995 to run for elected office in San Francisco.

---

infliction of emotional distress, intentional interference with contractual relations, invasion of privacy, or defamation. The outcome depends on the particular circumstances, but employers should be mindful of the possibility of civil suits with unlimited damages.

Employers should also be aware of the possibility of several closely related matters that may arise in affinity orientation cases and cause liability based on the protected category of gender—for instance, stereotyping as discussed in Chapter 7. Judging employees based on an idea of how they measure up to qualities a given gender should or should not possess (i.e., females who are "too aggressive" or "too macho" or males who are "too effeminate"), rather than on legitimate job requirements, may result in liability for gender discrimination, rather than affinity orientation, and should be avoided where possible (see *Williamson,* later in this chapter). Similarly, if an employer knowingly hires lesbians but not gay men, this could be the basis for gender discrimination.

So, unlike the rest of the categories we have discussed, affinity orientation is not nearly as settled as other types of employment discrimination. The patchwork quilt of constitutional, state, and local laws and ordinances, as well as the public relations and political aspects of the issue, make it one in which careful thought to policy is critical. We are in the rare position of seeing an entirely new area of law unfold. As exciting as this is, it can have traps for the unwary employer. Sticking with only relevant qualifications and watching trends in case law and legislation at all levels will greatly aid in making policy decisions much less likely to result in liability.

Seeing how the Court handles this issue, as in *Romer* below, is instructive in trying to shape policies consistent with its pronouncements.

ROMER V. EVANS
517 U.S. 620 (1996)

The state of Colorado amended its constitution with a provision prohibiting all legislative, executive, or judicial action designed to provide any protection from discrimination against gays and lesbians. The US Supreme Court declared the amendment to be unconstitutional in that it violated the Equal Protection Clause.

Kennedy, J.

The enactment challenged in this case is an amendment to the Constitution of the State of Colorado, adopted in a 1992 state-wide referendum. The parties and the state courts refer to it as "Amendment 2." The impetus for the amendment and the contentious campaign that preceded its adoption came in large part from ordinances that had been passed in various Colorado municipalities. For example, the cities of Aspen and Boulder, and the City and County of Denver each had enacted ordinances which banned discrimination in many transactions and activities, including housing, employment, education, and public accommodations, and health and welfare services. What gave rise to the statewide controversy was the protection the ordinances afforded persons discriminated against by reason of their sexual orientation. Amendment 2 repeals these ordinances to the extent they prohibit discrimination on the basis of "homosexual, lesbian or bisexual orientation, conduct, practices or relationships."

Yet Amendment 2, in explicit terms, does more than repeal or rescind these provisions. It prohibits all legislative, executive or judicial action at any level of state or local government designed to protect the named class, a class we shall refer to as homosexual persons or gays and lesbians. The amendment reads:

> "No Protected Status Based on Homosexual, Lesbian, or Bisexual Orientation. Neither the State of Colorado, through any of its branches or departments, nor any of its agencies, political subdivisions, municipalities or school districts, shall enact, adopt or enforce any statute, regulation, ordinance or policy whereby homosexual, lesbian or bisexual orientation, conduct, practice or relationships shall constitute or otherwise be the basis of or entitle any person or class of persons to have or claim any minority status, quota preferences, protected status or claim of discrimination. This Section of the Constitution shall be in all respects self-executing." Colo. Const., Art. II, § 30b.

The State's principal argument in defense of Amendment 2 is that it puts gays and lesbians in the same position as all other persons. So, the

State says, the measure does no more than deny homosexuals special rights. This reading of the amendment's language is implausible.

Sweeping and comprehensive is the change in legal status effected by this law. So much is evident from the ordinances that the Colorado Supreme Court declared would be void by operation of Amendment 2. Homosexuals, by state decree, are put in a solitary class with respect to transactions and relations in both the private and governmental spheres. The amendment withdraws from homosexuals, but no others, specific legal protection from the injuries caused by discrimination, and it forbids reinstatement of these laws and policies.

In any event, even if, as we doubt, homosexuals could find some safe harbor in laws of general application, we cannot accept the view that Amendment 2's prohibition on specific legal protections does no more than deprive homosexuals of special rights. To the contrary, the amendment imposes a special disability upon those persons alone. Homosexuals are forbidden the safeguards that others enjoy or may seek without constraint. They can obtain specific protection against discrimination only by enlisting the citizenry of Colorado to amend the state constitution or perhaps, on the State's view, by trying to pass helpful laws of general applicability. This is so no matter how local or discrete the harm, no matter how public and widespread the injury. We find nothing special in the protections Amendment 2 withholds. These are protections taken for granted by most people either because they already have them or do not need them; these are protections against exclusion from an almost limitless number of transactions and endeavors that constitute ordinary civic life in a free society.

Amendment 2 confounds the normal process of judicial review. It is at once too narrow and too broad. It identifies persons by a single trait and then denies them protection across the board. The resulting disqualification of a class of persons from the right to seek specific protection from the law is unprecedented in our jurisprudence.

It is not within our constitutional tradition to enact laws of this sort. Central both to the idea of the rule of law and to our own Constitution's guarantee of equal protection is the principle that government and each of its parts remain open on impartial terms to all who seek its assistance.

A second and related point is that laws of the kind now before us raise the inevitable inference that the disadvantage imposed is born of animosity toward the class of persons affected. "[I]f the constitutional conception of 'equal protection of the laws' means anything, it must at the very least mean that a bare . . . desire to harm a politically unpopular group cannot constitute a *legitimate* governmental interest." Even laws enacted for broad and ambitious purposes often can be explained by reference to legitimate public policies which justify the incidental disadvantages they impose on certain persons. Amendment 2, however, in making a general announcement that gays and lesbians shall not have any particular protections from the law, inflicts on them immediate, continuing, and real injuries that outrun and belie any legitimate justifications that may be claimed for it. We conclude that, in addition to the farreaching deficiencies of Amendment 2 that we have noted, the principles it offends, in another sense, are conventional and venerable; a law must bear a rational relationship to a legitimate government purpose, and Amendment 2 does not.

The primary rationale the State offers for Amendment 2 is respect for other citizens' freedom of association, and in particular the liberties of landlords and employers who have personal or religious objections to homosexuality. Colorado also cites its interest in conserving resources to fight discrimination against other groups. The breadth of the Amendment is so far removed from these particular justifications that we find it impossible to credit them. We cannot say that Amendment 2 is directed to any identifiable legitimate purpose or discrete objective. It is a status-based enactment divorced from any factual context from which we could discern a relationship to legitimate state interests; it is a classification of persons undertaken for its own sake, something the Equal Protection Clause does not permit.

We must conclude that Amendment 2 classifies homosexuals not to further a proper legislative end but to make them unequal to everyone else. This Colorado cannot do. A State cannot so deem a class of persons a stranger to its laws. Amendment 2 violates the Equal Protection Clause, and the judgment of the Supreme Court of Colorado is AFFIRMED.

Case Questions

1. What do you think of the "special rights" argument? Does it make sense to you? Explain.

2. What would you do as an employer who didn't want to hire gays and lesbians in your workplace, given this case?

3. Now that you've seen how the US Supreme Court stands on the issues in *Romer,* what would you do when establishing policies on gays and lesbians in your workplace?

Affinity Orientation as a Basis for Adverse Employment Decisions

As you will see from the cases below, not all affinity orientation issues arise in the same contexts. The employee may be the basis of employer concern because the employee, among other things:

- Is gay or lesbian (i.e., status or orientation).
- Exhibits inappropriate workplace behavior, such as detailed discussions of intimate sexual behavior or improperly propositioning others in the workplace.
- Wears clothing, jewelry, or make-up in violation of workplace grooming codes.
- Undergoes gender reassignment surgery.
- Is in the presurgery adjustment stages of such gender reassignment surgery.
- Is living as a member of the opposite gender.
- Has primary relationships with those of the same gender.

Note that some of the activity presents a problem no matter who the employee is. An employer should not tolerate from any employee inappropriate workplace behavior, such as improperly propositioning other employees. A distinction should also be made between status or orientation as a gay or lesbian on the one hand, and, on the other, activity that may be inappropriate. Basing decisions and policies on actions is more defensible than basing them on status. Each of the above contexts of gay or lesbian issues presents its own unique issues.

In the following case, the courts set forth the reasoning for not extending Title VII protection to discrimination on the basis of affinity orientation. Notice that it is directed toward status, more so than any particular activity in which the employee may have engaged. It is this basic approach that underlies why the employee would not be protected in opening scenario one.

DeSantis v. Pacific Telephone & Telegraph Co., Inc.
Strailey v. Happy Times Nursery School, Inc.
Lundin and Buckley v. Pacific Tel. & Tel. Co., Inc.
608 F.2d 327 (9th Cir. 1979)

Gays and lesbians brought these actions claiming their employers and former employers discriminated against them in employment decisions because they were gay and lesbian. The cases were consolidated because of the similarity of issues involved. The court of appeals dismissed the cases.

Choy, J.

Employee Strailey, a male, was fired by the Happy Times Nursery School after two years as a teacher. He alleged he was fired because he wore a small gold ear-loop to school before the beginning of the school year.

DeSantis, Boyle and Simard, all males, claimed that Pacific Telephone & Telegraph (PT&T) impermissibly discriminated against them because they were gay. DeSantis alleged he was not hired when a PT&T supervisor concluded he was gay. Boyle was continually harassed by his coworkers and had to quit to preserve his health after only three months because his supervisor did nothing to alleviate this condition. Finally, Simard was forced to quit under similar conditions after almost four years of employment with PT&T, but he was harassed by his supervisors as well. In addition, his personnel file has been marked as not eligible for rehire, and his applications for employment were rejected by PT&T in 1974 and 1976. All three alleged that PT&T officials have publicly stated that they would not hire gays and lesbians. EEOC rejected all claims for lack of jurisdiction.

The employees then filed suit in court on behalf of themselves and others similarly situated seeking declaratory, injunctive and monetary relief under Title VII and 42 U.S.C. Section 1985. They also asked that the district court order EEOC to process charges based on affinity orientation. The district court dismissed their complaint and held that the court lacked jurisdiction to compel the EEOC to alter its interpretation of Title VII and that the claimants did not have viable claims under either Title VII or section 1985.

Lundin and Buckley, both females, were operators with PT&T. They filed suit in federal court alleging that PT&T discriminated against them because of their known lesbian relationship and eventually fired them. They also alleged they endured numerous insults by PT&T employees because of their relationship. The district court dismissed their suit as not stating a claim upon which relief could be granted.

Employees argue first that the district courts erred in holding that Title VII does not prohibit discrimination on the basis of affinity orientation. They claim that in prohibiting certain employment discrimination on the basis of "gender," Congress meant to include discrimination on the basis of affinity orientation. They add that in trial they could establish that discrimination against such employees disproportionately affects men and that this disproportionate impact and correlation between discrimination on the basis of affinity orientation and discrimination on the basis of gender requires that affinity orientation be considered a subcategory of the gender category of Title VII.

Congress has not shown any intent other than to restrict the term gender to its traditional meaning. Therefore, this court will not expand Title VII's application in the absence of Congressional mandate. The manifest purpose of Title VII's prohibition against gender discrimination in employment is to insure that men and women are treated equally, absent a bona fide relationship between the qualifications for the job and the person's gender. Based on similar readings of the legislative history and the principle that "words used in statutes are to be given their ordinary meaning," the EEOC has concluded "that when Congress used the word 'sex' in Title VII, it was referring to a person's 'gender' and not to 'sexual practices.'" EEOC Dec. No. 76-75 (1976) Employment Practice Guide (CCH) section 6495 at 4266. We conclude that the prohibition against gender discrimination does not include same gender affinity orientation.

Employees further argue that recent decisions dealing with disproportionate impact require that discrimination against gays and lesbians fall within the purview of Title VII. They contend that recent decisions like *Griggs v. Duke Power Co.,* establish that any employment criterion that affects one gender more than the other violates Title VII. They quote from *Griggs* at 431, that "what is required by Congress is the removal of artificial, arbitrary and unnecessary barriers to employment when the barriers operate invidiously to discriminate on the basis of racial or other impermissible classifications." They claim that they can prove that discrimination against gays and lesbians disproportionately affects males both because of the greater likelihood of an employer discovering males with such orientation compared to females similarly situated.

Assuming that the employees can otherwise satisfy the requirements of *Griggs,* we do not believe that *Griggs* can be applied to extend Title VII protection to those in employees' position. In finding that the disproportionate impact of educational tests on blacks violated Title VII when they were not job related, the Supreme Court in *Griggs* sought to effectuate a major congressional purpose in enacting Title VII: protection of blacks from employment discrimination. Our objective is to ascertain the congressional intent and give effect to the legislative will. Congress did not intend to protect affinity orientation and has repeatedly refused to extend such protection. Employees now ask us to employ the disproportionate impact decisions as an artifice to "bootstrap" Title VII protection for this group under the guise of protecting men generally.

This we are not free to do. Adoption of this bootstrap device would frustrate congressional objectives, not effectuate congressional goals as in *Griggs.* It would achieve by judicial "construction" what Congress did not do and has consistently refused to do on many occasions. We conclude that the *Griggs* disproportionate impact theory may not be applied to extend Title VII protection to affinity orientation.

Employees next contend that recent decisions have held that an employer generally may not use different employment criteria for men and women. They claim that if a male employee prefers males, he will be treated differently from a female who prefers males. They conclude that the employer thus uses different employment criteria for men and women and violates *Phillips v. Martin-Marietta Corp.,* 400 U.S. 542 (1971). We must again reject employees' efforts to "bootstrap" Title VII protection for their group. While we do not express approval of an employment policy that differentiates according to affinity orientation, we note that, whether dealing with men or women, the employer is using the same criterion: it will not hire or promote a person who prefers sexual partners of the same gender. Thus the policy does not involve different decisional criteria for the genders.

Employees argue that EEOC has held that discrimination against an employee because of the race of the employee's friends may constitute discrimination based on race in violation of Title VII. They contend that analogously discrimination because of gender of the employee's sexual partner should constitute discrimination based on gender. They have not, however, alleged that the employers have policies of discriminating against employees because of the gender of their friends. That is, they do not claim that the employers will terminate anyone with male (or female) friends. They claim instead that the employees discriminate against employees who have a certain type of relationship—i.e., a same-gender affinity orientation—with certain friends. As noted earlier, that relationship is not protected by Title VII. Thus, assuming it would violate Title VII for an employer to discriminate against employees be-cause of the gender of their friends, the employees' claims do not fall within the purported rule. AFFIRMED.

Case Questions

1. The court said that the employer was discriminating against the parties because of their choice of sexual partners. Notwithstanding the way the issue has historically been treated, does this seem to be a valid basis for judging an applicant for employment? Explain.

2. Do you agree with the parallels that the parties attempted to draw, between race discrimination and discrimination on the basis of affinity orientation? Discuss.

3. As a manager, what would you have done in these cases? Why?

Employees, realizing the effect of *DeSantis,* which has been widely used as precedent in other jurisdictions, have often tried to get around the Title VII limitation on affinity orientation by attempting to allege some other recognized basis for discrimination under Title VII. As you will see in the following case, it may not work. When the employer terminates the employee for a combination of reasons, some protected and some not, liability may ensue. For instance, if an employer terminates a black female after the employer finds that she is a lesbian, the employee cannot use her status as a lesbian as the basis for a claim under Title VII. However, the employee could allege discrimination based on her gender or race as a basis for suit, but would have to prove this was the basis for termination. On the other hand, look at Exhibit 9–5 to see how much the workplace is changing.

Allegations and actual proof to the satisfaction of EEOC or the court are two very different things. The employee may not be able to prove a case of race or gender discrimination because the evidence simply is not present. To be fully protected in the decision to terminate, an employer must be certain there are no facts that will support the other categories the employee may allege as a basis for suit. The following case illustrates the use of both protected and unprotected status as a basis for a discrimination suit and how the courts analyze such a case.

EXHIBIT 9–5   New Push to Recruit Gay Students

On Wall Street, a New Push to Recruit Gay Students

Facing a Tight Labor Market, Banks Adopt a New Tactic to Lure Top Prospects

By RACHEL EMMA SILVERMAN
Staff Reporter of THE WALL STREET JOURNAL

For the first time, major Wall Street financial firms are targeting recruiting efforts at gay and lesbian business students.

Goldman Sachs Group Inc. has wined and dined gay M.B.A. students at fine restaurants in New York's Chelsea and Boston's Back Bay neighborhoods. J.P. Morgan & Co. and American Express Co. co-hosted a dinner for gay students in the plush corporate dining room of J.P. Morgan's Wall Street headquarters.

In an unusually tight job market, employers everywhere are searching for new hiring tactics. "It makes good sense for us," says Michael Golden, a J.P. Morgan spokesman. "We're trying to get the talent wherever we can find it."

But there's more to the pursuit of gay students than a shrinking candidate pool. Increasingly vocal gay employees at some Wall Street firms have been pressing their employers to create workplaces more hospitable to gays. That includes stepped-up recruitment.

At J.P. Morgan, for example, gay employees formed Gleam, for Gay and Lesbian Employees at Morgan. One of the group's top goals was to make the hiring process more welcoming for gay recruits, says Tricia Vivado, a Gleam member who works as a vice president in fixed-income financing. Gay employees at Goldman Sachs and Merrill Lynch & Co. are also forming networks with the goal of mobilizing and attracting gay workers.

Another new force: openly gay business students who are prodding companies to pay more attention to gay issues in the workplace. Goldman Sachs organized its recruitment dinners after Harvard Business School's gay student group suggested the idea.

Reaching Out

Some financial companies that have non-discrimination policies on sexual orientation and offer benefits to domestic partners:

- **BankAmerica Corp.**
- **Bankers Trust Corp.**
- **Charles Schwab & Co.**
- **Chase Manhattan Bank Corp.**
- **Fannie Mae**
- **FleetBoston Financial**
- **J.P. Morgan & Co.**
- **Merrill Lynch**
- **Prudential**
- **Scudder Kemper Investments**
- **Wells Fargo & Co.**

Source: Human Rights Campaign

By actively courting gay students, Wall Street firms are doing what top management consulting firms have done for several years. McKinsey & Co.'s gay recruiting events, featuring renowned speakers, draw scores of students, including undergraduates. Their events are a "well-oiled machine," says Harvard business student Imtiyaz Hussein.

At the November dinner hosted by J.P. Morgan and American Express, employees spoke with almost 50 gay students from top Eastern business schools about what it's like being gay around clients and colleagues. Students wondered how open they should be on resumes and in interviews, said attendee Liz Zale, a Columbia M.B.A. student. "It was inspiring," she said.

"I had the impression that it was not impossible to be gay and work on Wall Street, but it was certainly a challenge," says Sean Hennessey, a Harvard Business School student who attended events hosted by Goldman

EXHIBIT 9–5   Concluded

A Push to Recruit Gay Students

Sachs and others. "The dinners went a long way to make me feel more comfortable." He is now considering working in investment banking this summer.

Some students say, however, that the dinners focus too much on gay issues, and not enough about the firm's other activities. "These dinners should provide an opportunity to learn about the firm in general, not just about gay and lesbian life," says Andrew Fiala, a Wharton M.B.A. student.

One downside to niche recruiting is the risk of tokenism. Students say they want to be hired for their skills—not because of their sexual orientation. "Most gay candidates want to be judged solely on abilities—don't choose me because I'm gay but because I'm good," says Walter Schubert, CEO of Gfn.com, a gay-oriented financial services company in New York.

For that reason, some firms say they won't specifically target gays for recruiting. "We don't break down our recruiting effort by sexual orientation. We have a very open, merit-based recruitment philosophy that has nothing to do with anything other than the merit of the candidate . . . and I don't anticipate that changing," says Jeanmarie McFadden, a spokeswoman for Morgan Stanley Dean Witter & Co.

Still, gay students will want the "environment they're working in to be embracing and welcoming," says Mr. Schubert. That means having gay-friendly policies in place, like domestic-partner benefits and corporate nondiscrimination policies. Goldman Sachs introduced global domestic-partner benefits on Jan. 1 and J.P. Morgan has had such benefits since December, 1997—the first major Wall Street firm to offer such a perk.

As more companies in consulting and investment banking are targeting gay students, the competition for candidates from this group is heating up. "The field is getting more crowded. Everyone's doing a targeted gay and lesbian dinner," says an overextended Mr. Hussein, the Harvard student.

To woo dinner-weary gay students, some companies are experimenting with other techniques. Monitor Co., a Cambridge, Ma., consulting firm, for example, flew about 20 gay M.B.A. candidates to Boston last winter to attend a special weekend workshop on "difficult conversations" that may occur when a participant reveals his or her sexual identity to a parent or employer. "We had to think about difficult conversations we've had in the past and be prepared to talk about them. A lot were gay and lesbian issues—but not all," says Wharton's Mr. Fiala.

Do these events translate into hires? Consulting firms with expanded efforts already see an increase in the numbers of gay recruits. About five of McKinsey's 32 1999 summer associates in the New York office were gay students who had attended its recruiting events, says Peter Allen, one of the summer associates. Several already have been offered permanent posts, including Mr. Allen. To further step up their recruiting efforts, a number of top consulting and investment firms will participate at "Working Out," a conference and career fair for gay M.B.A. students to be held in Philadelphia next month.

Recruiting events are just a beginning step for gay students looking for companies where they'll feel comfortable. One second-year Columbia M.B.A. student who will be working at Goldman Sachs after graduation says that the dinners tipped his decision to work at the firm. "If I can avoid it, I don't want to be in an environment where I have to hide who I am," he says.

Still, he asked not to be identified for this story, choosing to wait until he is "more aware of what the internal culture is like" at the firm.

Courtesy of The Wall Street Journal, February, 2000.

WILLIAMSON V. A. G. EDWARDS & SONS, INC.
876 F.2d 69 (8th Cir. 1989)

A gay black male who wore makeup to work brought suit alleging his dismissal was illegally based upon race in violation of Title VII of the Civil Rights Act of 1964. The court disagreed and held for the employer.

Per Curiam

Employee Williamson worked for the employer from November 1979 until May 1985 when he was discharged for his disruptive and inappropriate conduct at work. Williamson alleged that his supervisor, Bruce Morgan, falsely accused him of disrupting the workflow by continuing to discuss the details of his gay lifestyle in the workplace and harassing another employee, and that similarly situated white employees who behaved as he did were not disciplined. The lower court found that the employee's complaint and deposition clearly indicated that Williamson believed he had been treated differently because of his affinity orientation and not his race. On appeal Williamson argues that the lower court erred in failing to consider his allegations that similarly situated white employees working in the same department as Williamson, were not harassed or terminated as he had been.

Title VII does not prevent discrimination on the basis of affinity orientation. *DeSantis v. Pacific Tel. & Tel. Co.,* 608 F.2d 327 (9th Cir. 1979). Although employee stated that he believed he was treated differently because he was black, he failed to allege facts sufficient to establish that other similarly situated white employees were treated differently. He did not claim that the other white employees who also allegedly were gay behaved as he did in openly discussing their lives while at work, but only compared his behavior in that regard to the behavior of other heterosexuals. Although he alleged he was reprimanded for wearing makeup at work while two other white males, allegedly gay were only reprimanded for wearing jewelry, there is no indication in the record that the other two men wore any makeup. Accordingly, we AFFIRM.

Case Questions

1. How would you have handled this issue if you had been the manager?
2. Do you accept the argument that, if things were as the employee alleged, it was racial discrimination?
3. What do you think of the court saying that heterosexuals openly discussed their lives at work but it was not the same as the gay employee doing so? Should they be treated any differently? Why? Why not?

It was previously stated that employers should not base workplace decisions on stereotyped ideas of gender any more than necessary. *Williamson* indicates when it may be necessary (i.e., when a male is wearing makeup). As mentioned in the section on dress codes in Chapter 7 on gender, employers have the flexibility to impose reasonable rules about workplace appearance. The Washington Supreme Court ruled that Boeing Company had sufficient basis for terminating a male engineer who was undergoing gender reassignment surgery. Boeing attempted to accommodate the employee by permitting him to wear "unisex" clothing; but the employee was terminated when he added pink pearls to such an outfit and insisted on using the women's bathroom.

Male employees have also tried to argue that their effeminacy should not be a basis on which employers can refuse to hire them or to terminate them from their jobs. This argument rarely succeeds and courts routinely side with the employer. The court in *DeSantis* stated:

> Employee Strailey contends he was terminated by the Happy Times Nursery School because the school felt that it was inappropriate for a male teacher to wear an earring to school. He claims that the school's reliance on a stereotype—that a male should have a virile, rather than an effeminate, appearance—violates Title VII. This does not fall within Title VII. We hold that discrimination because of effeminacy, like discrimination because of [affinity orientation], does not fall within the purview of Title VII.

Same-Gender Sexual Harassment

Re-read the *Oncale* case in Chapter 8. Since Title VII does not include a prohibition against discrimination on the basis of affinity orientation, an important question in the past few years has been whether an employee sexually harassed by someone of the same gender could bring an action under Title VII. Some courts said no because they considered any sexual harassment between employees of the same gender to be homosexual in nature (regardless of the nature of the harassment) and since Title VII excluded affinity orientation coverage, a harassee had no cause of action.

Other courts looked at the nature of the harassment and allowed a cause of action if it was not based on affinity orientation (rather than presuming that because it was between employees of the same gender it *must* be). And there were many other variations on the theme. In the *Oncale* case in Chapter 8, the US Supreme Court finally made sense of it all.

Under the *Oncale* decision, the Court preserved Title VII's exclusion of discrimination on the basis of affinity orientation by holding that the sexual harassment of an employee by someone of the same gender is prohibited unless it can be shown that it was actually based on affinity orientation. That is, if a female employee can show that a female harassed her by calling her awful names, undermining her work productivity, spreading lies about her, and so on, then she can bring a claim under Title VII. If, however, the harassee is a lesbian and the harassment is in the form of doing something like constantly calling her a lesbian, directing teasing, joking, and comments on homosexuality toward her, or persistently asking for dates or making sexual comments, then the harassee would not have a cause of action under Title VII. The first situation is plain old sexual harassment even though the parties are both the same gender, and is covered by Title VII. The second is harassment based on affinity orientation and it is not covered. What the Supreme Court did is to not presume that every harassment between employees of the same gender is based on same-gender affinity orientation.

Transsexual Discrimination

Think the issue of transsexuals is far fetched? In one of the cases below, a company was faced with the requests so frequently (at least 9 times) that it developed a carefully crafted policy. As you can imagine, the issue presents rather interesting, confusing, and complicated workplace challenges.

Nonetheless, it is a workplace issue that must be addressed. The argument has been made by transsexuals who have had gender reassignment surgery that they should be afforded the protection of Title VII, because they have changed their gender status from male to female or vice versa and now are being discriminated against in employment because they are of a particular gender. Courts have not upheld this position. As stated in the case below, the basis for opening scenario 2, it is not the status of the employee as a member of the gender to which they have been reassigned that has created the problem. That is, a male who is terminated on becoming a female is not discriminated against because he is a female as contemplated by Title VII. Rather, he is discriminated against because he changed from male to female. These are considered two very different arguments, with the former being provided Title VII protection, but not the latter.

Scenario

ULANE V. EASTERN AIRLINES, INC.
742 F.2d 1081 (7th Cir. 1984)

Employee, a male airline pilot, underwent a gender change operation and became a female. After being terminated by the airline, he brought suit. The court upheld the termination, concluding that the matter was not protected by Title VII.

Wood, J.

Employee, Ulane, became a licensed pilot in 1964 serving in the US Army from that time until 1968 with a record of combat missions in Viet Nam for which he received the Air Medal with eight clusters. Upon discharge in 1968, Ulane began flying for Eastern. With Eastern he progressed from Second to First Officer, and also served as a flight instructor, logging over 8,000 flight hours.

Ulane was diagnosed a transsexual in 1979. Transsexualism is a condition that exists when a physiologically normal person experiences discomfort or discontent about nature's choice of his or her gender and prefers to be the other gender. This discomfort is generally accompanied by a desire to utilize hormonal, surgical, and civil procedures to allow the individual to live in his or her preferred gender role. The diagnosis is appropriate only if the discomfort has been continuous for at least two years, and is not due to a mental disorder such as schizophrenia. This is to be distinguished from homosexuals who are sexually attracted to persons of the same gender and transvestites, who are generally male heterosexuals who cross-dress, i.e., dress as females, for sexual arousal rather than social comfort. Both homosexuals and transvestites are content with the gender into which they were born.

Ulane explains that although embodied as a male, from early childhood she felt like a female. She first sought psychiatric and medical assistance in 1968 while in the military. Later she began taking female hormones as part of her treatment, and eventually developed breasts from the hormones. In 1980 she underwent "sex reassignment surgery" and afterwards was issued a revised birth certificate indicating she was female and the FAA certified her for flight status as a female. Eastern was not aware of Ulane's transsexuality, her hormone treatments, or her psychiatric counseling until she attempted to return to work after her reassignment surgery. Eastern knew Ulane only as one of its male pilots.

The district court found Eastern discharged Ulane because she was a transsexual, and that Title VII does not prohibit discrimination on this basis. While we do not condone discrimination in any form, we are constrained to hold that Title VII does not protect transsexuals. AFFIRMED.

Case Questions

1. As the manager to whom Ulane reported after surgery, how would you have handled this?

2. Why do you think Eastern terminated Ulane?

3. What should be the significance of Ulane's prior flight history and experience? In your view, how should it be analyzed with the other relevant factors here?

Employees have also argued that being a transsexual is a disability which must be accommodated. The "pink pearls" case below rejected that view in Washington state. It also provides great insight into how an employer can approach these issues to best provide protection against liability for discrimination.

JANE DOE V. THE BOEING COMPANY
121 Wash. 2d 8 (1993)

A biological male employee who was planning to have gender reassignment surgery sued his employer, Boeing, for employment discrimination, alleging an unaccommodated disability. She was discharged by Boeing for wearing "excessively" feminine attire (pink pearls) in violation of company directives. The Washington Supreme Court found that Boeing had done enough to reasonably accommodate the employee, even though it had no duty to do so under Washington's law against discrimination.

Guy, J.

Jane Doe was hired as a Boeing engineer in 1978. At the time of hire, Doe was a biological male and presented herself as such on her application for employment. In 1984, after years of struggling with her sexual identity, Doe concluded that she was a transsexual. Transsexualism is also known in the psychiatric and medical communities as gender dysphoria.

Doe's treating physician confirmed Doe's self-assessment and diagnosed Doe as gender dysphoric. In April 1984, Doe began hormone treatments, as prescribed by Dr. Smith, as well as electrolysis treatments. In December 1984, Doe legally changed her masculine name to a feminine name.

In March 1985, Doe informed her supervisors, management and co-workers at Boeing of her transsexualism and of her intent to have sex reassignment surgery. Doe informed Boeing of her belief that in order to qualify for sex reassignment surgery, she would have to live full time, for 1 year, in the social role of a female. Doe based her belief on discussions with her treating psychologist and her physician about a treatment protocol for transsexuals known as the Harry Benjamin International Gender Dysphoria Standards (Benjamin Standards). Benjamin Standard 9 states: "Genital sex reassignment shall be preceded by a period of at least 12 months during which time the patient lived full-time in the social role of the genetically other sex."

Upon being notified of Doe's intentions, Boeing informed Doe that while Doe was an anatomical male, she could not use the women's rest rooms or dress in "feminine" attire. Boeing informed Doe that she could dress as a woman at work and use the women's rest rooms upon completion of her sex reassignment surgery.

While Doe was an anatomical male, Boeing permitted Doe to wear either male clothing or unisex clothing. Unisex clothing included blouses, sweaters, slacks, flat shoes, nylon stockings, earrings, lipstick, foundation, and clear nail polish. Doe was instructed not to wear obviously feminine clothing such as dresses, skirts, or frilly blouses. Boeing applied its unwritten dress policy to all employees, which included eight other transsexuals who had expressed a desire to have sex reassignment surgery while working for Boeing. Both Doe's psychologist and treating physician testified that what Doe was allowed to wear at Boeing was sufficiently feminine for Doe to qualify for sex reassignment surgery.

Between June and late September 1985, Boeing management received approximately a dozen anonymous complaints regarding Doe's attire and use of the women's rest rooms. On October 25,

1985, following the receipt of a complaint about Doe using the women's rest room, Boeing issued Doe a written disciplinary warning. The warning reiterated Boeing's position on acceptable attire and rest room use and stated that Doe's failure to comply with Boeing's directives by November 1, 1985, would result in further corrective action, including termination. During this "grace" period, Doe's compliance with Boeing's "acceptable attire" directive was to be monitored each day by Doe's direct supervisor. Doe was told that her attire would be deemed unacceptable when, in the supervisor's opinion, her dress would be likely to cause a complaint were Doe to use a men's rest room at a Boeing facility. No single article of clothing would be dispositive. Doe's overall appearance was to be assessed.

Doe's transsexualism did not interfere with her ability to perform her job duties as a software engineer at Boeing. There was no measurable decline in either her work group's performance or in Doe's own job performance. There was no testimony to indicate that Boeing's dress restrictions hindered Doe's professional development.

On November 4, 1985, the first day Doe worked after the grace period, Doe wore attire that her supervisor considered acceptable. Doe responded that she was disappointed that her attire was acceptable, and that she would "push it" the next day. By "push it," Doe testified that she meant she would wear more extreme feminine attire. The next day, Doe came to work wearing similar attire, but she included as part of her outfit a strand of pink pearls which she refused to remove. This outfit was similar to one she had been told during the grace period was unacceptable in that the addition of the pink pearls changed Doe's look from unisex to "excessively" feminine. Doe was subsequently terminated from her position at Boeing as a result of her willful violation of Boeing's directives. Doe filed a handicap discrimination action against Boeing pursuant to Washington's Law Against Discrimination (hereafter Act) RCW49.60. The trial court held that Doe was "temporarily handicapped" under its construction of the law. The Court of Appeals reversed, finding Boeing failed to accommodate Doe. We reverse the Court of Appeals.

This case presents two issues for review. First, is Jane Doe's gender dysphoria a "handicap" under RCW 49.60.180? We hold that Doe's gender dysphoria is not a handicap under the Act. The definition of "handicap" for enforcement purposes in unfair practice cases under RCW 49.60.180, as defined in WAC 162-22-040, requires factual findings of both (1) the presence of an abnormal condition, and (2) employer discrimination against the plaintiff because of that condition. While gender dysphoria is an abnormal condition, we hold that Doe was not "handicapped" by her gender dysphoria because Boeing did not discharge her because of that condition.

Second, did Boeing have to provide Doe's preferred accommodation under RCW 49.60.180? We hold that the scope of an employer's duty to reasonably accommodate an employee's abnormal condition is limited to those steps necessary to enable the employee to perform his or her job. We hold that Boeing's actions met this standard and did not discriminate against Doe by reason of her abnormal condition.

It is uncontested that gender dysphoria is an abnormal, medically cognizable condition with a prescribed course of treatment. Assuming the presence of an abnormal condition, the next inquiry is whether the employer discriminated against the employee because of that condition. Boeing did not discriminate against Doe because of her condition. Boeing discharged Doe because she violated Boeing's directives on acceptable attire, not because she was gender dysphoric. Doe was treated in a respectful way by both her peers and supervisors at Boeing. Doe's supervisor consistently rated her work as satisfactory on her performance evaluations. While complaints were filed with Boeing management about Doe's use of the women's rest room, the record is void of any evidence that Doe suffered harassment because of her use of the rest room or because of her attire.

Inasmuch as Boeing did not discharge Doe based on her abnormal condition but on her refusal to conform with directives on acceptable attire, we must turn our attention to whether Boeing discriminated against Doe by failing to reasonably accommodate her condition of gender dysphoria.

We recognize that employers have an affirmative obligation to reasonably accommodate the sensory, mental, or physical limitations of such employees unless the employer can demonstrate that the accommodation would impose an undue hardship on the conduct of the employer's business. The issue before us is whether Boeing had a duty to accommodate Doe's preferred manner of dress prior to her sex reassignment surgery. We hold that the scope of an employer's duty to accommodate an employee's condition is limited to those steps reasonably necessary to enable the employee to perform his or her job.

Doe contends that Boeing's dress code failed to accommodate her condition and, thus was discriminatory. We disagree. The record substantially supports the trial court's findings that Boeing reasonably accommodated Doe in the matter of dress by allowing her to wear unisex clothing at work. Despite this accommodation, Doe determined unilaterally, and without medical confirmation, that she needed to dress as a woman at her place of employment in order to qualify for sex reassignment surgery. We find substantial support for the trial court's finding that Doe had no medical need to dress as a woman at work in order to qualify for her surgery.

[P]laintiff's experts declined to state that any particular degree of feminine dress was required in order for plaintiff to fulfill any presurgical requirements. In fact, the evidence was uncontradicted that the unisex dress permitted by Boeing . . . would not have precluded plaintiff from meeting the Benjamin Standards presurgical requirement of living in the social role of a woman. The trial court's findings are well supported by the testimony of Doe's own treating physician and psychologist, as well as other medical evidence.

Doe argues, however, that the trial court's

findings on this point are irrelevant since Boeing did not have the benefit of such medical testimony prior to enforcing its dress policy. We disagree. The trial court found that Boeing's policy on accommodation of transsexuals was developed with input from Boeing's legal, medical, personnel and labor relations departments. The Boeing medical department consulted with outside experts in the field and reviewed the literature on transsexualism. The trial court also held that Boeing has a legitimate business purpose in defining what is acceptable attire and in balancing the needs of its work force as a whole with those of Doe. The record supports the trial court's findings of fact and conclusions of law that Boeing developed and reasonably enforced a dress policy which balanced its legitimate business needs with those of its employees.

Doe further argues that, as a gender dysphoric, her perceived needs should have been accommodated. We disagree. The Act does not require an employer to offer the employee the precise accommodation he or she requests. Her perceived need to dress more completely as a woman did not impact her job performance. Doe's condition had no measurable effect on either Doe's job performance or her work group's performance. That is not to say that Doe did not have emotional turmoil over the changes that were taking place in her life, but that turmoil did not prevent her from performing her work satisfactorily. Based on the record, there was no need for any further action by Boeing to facilitate Doe in the performance of job-related tasks.

Doe also argues that Boeing failed to accommodate her unique condition because its dress policy was uniformly applied.

In determining what is a reasonable accommodation, the evaluation must begin with the job specifications and how those tasks are impacted by the abnormal condition. In the case of trauma or physical deterioration, the answers are generally apparent and the issue becomes one of whether the accommodation is reasonable, not what is the accommodation. In Doe's case, the analysis is not so simple. Doe's job performance was unchanged by reason of her condition. Based on the record, there was no accommodation that Boeing could have provided that would have aided Doe in the performance of her work. How she dressed or appeared had no impact on the physical or mental requirements of her employment responsibilities.

Doe's gender dysphoria did not impede her ability to perform her engineering duties. Therefore, Boeing had no duty to provide any further accommodation to Doe beyond what it provided for all employees. REVERSED.

Case Questions

1. What do you think the real problem was here? If you say that it was Jane trying to push too hard, explore what that really means. How responsible should the employer be for the discomfort of other employees? What about when the discomfort arises from long-held beliefs based on misinformation, which society may have taken for granted until now? Would it be different if the issue was race instead of affinity orientation (i.e., employees did not want to deal with employees of other races in the workplace and were uncomfortable doing so)? Explain.

2. Are you surprised that Boeing had eight other employees to deal with on this issue? Explain. Are you surprised that an employer dealt with this issue with the depth that Boeing did? Why do you think it did so?

3. Doe evidently kept going to the female toilet, but it was the pink pearls that got her fired. Any thoughts as to why? Explain.

Employment Benefits

In the past few years, one of the most active issues regarding affinity orientation and the workplace has been that of employment benefits. Many things that other employees take for granted are major hurdles for gays and lesbians. For instance, bereavement leave routinely granted for the death of a loved one is often not provided to gays and lesbians when their partners die. Sick leave routinely granted to take care of a family member is often not given when the family is the gay or lesbian employee's life partner. (See Exhibits 9–6, 9–7.)

    In recent years, cities like Atlanta, Georgia; Ithaca, New York; Madison, Wisconsin; and West Hollywood, California, provided for the registration of unmarried couples (gay or straight) as domestic partners. Partners generally must be able to prove that for a specified length of time they have lived together and given mutual aid and support. Upon proof of the jurisdiction's requirements, partners may qualify for certain benefits. For instance, Delta Airlines expanded its definition of "family" to whom frequent flyer miles can be transferred to include registered gay partners. In June 1994, Vermont became the first state to offer health benefits to domestic partners of state workers. Other jurisdictions followed. More than 2,800 private companies and city governments now permit their employees to include domestic partners in their health insurance coverage. Included among them are Goldman Sachs and J. P. Morgan, both major Wall Street investment firms. As the labor market continues to tighten, such benefits are used as a marketing tool to attract employees.

    While there are employers who treat gay and lesbian employees much like any

---

EXHIBIT 9–6   Workplace Issues for Gays and Lesbians

- *Nondiscrimination policies.*   Corporate antidiscrimination policies are a primary concern for lesbians and gays who don't have state or local civil rights ordinances protecting them. A basic statement that employees are given the same opportunity to enter, advance, and succeed in an organization sets the tone for how that organization relates to lesbians and gays.
- *Bereavement leave for domestic partners.*   Many corporations have policies granting employees paid leave to attend the funerals of spouses and immediate members of the family. These policies don't help unmarried domestic partners of gays or straights. This is a particularly important issue, given the devastating impact of the AIDS crisis.
- *Vacation leave transfer.*   Another issue is the enormous financial burden placed on employees with AIDS. Other employees often want to help these employees by donating their earned vacation time. Gay and lesbian groups are lobbying companies to consider allowing employees to offer support in this way.
- *Benefits for domestic partners.*   Earning health care benefits for their partners is an important goal for lesbian and gay employees. They're asking corporations to respect alternative families and recognize their benefit needs, and they argue that the family partner of an unmarried employee is just as likely to need health insurance as is the spouse of a married employee. Gays and lesbians also are asking for parental leave benefits when appropriate.

G K Kronenberger, "Out of the Closet," *Workforce Magazine,* June 1991, p. 40.

EXHIBIT 9–7   Domestic Partner Law Debate: Domestic Partner Law Protects Personal Wishes

USA Today **Editorial: Our View**

Shouldn't you be able to decide who should care for you in crisis or [should] benefit if you die?

Unmarried couples should keep an eye on California. A bill awaiting the governor's signature would bring some needed changes to Californians' lives. The concept could, and should, spread to other states.

There's nothing earthshaking about the bill. In fact, it's surprising no state yet offers three basic protections to unmarrieds:

- The right to have your partner visit if you're hospitalized
- The right to have your partner act as guardian if you're incapacitated
- And the right to leave your money and property to whom you wish in your will, avoiding nasty court battles with relatives

Spouses, of course, already have these rights. But there are plenty of couples—nearly half a million in California alone—who aren't married, 93% of them heterosexual. Many will marry later; some never will, for a variety of reasons. And for gay couples, marriage is out of the question.

Domestic partner programs have expanded rapidly in the past decade. Two states and several cities grant full health benefits to employees' partners.

Others offer domestic partner registration, which offers varying degrees of legal protection. Ordinances in Minneapolis, Minn., and West Hollywood, Calif., for example, allow hospital visitation. In other places, registration provides psychological benefits but not legal ones.

How important is legal recognition of a partnership? Anyone who pooh-poohs it could use a lesson from Karen Thompson and Sharon Kowalski. The two women, teachers in Minnesota, began living together in 1979. In 1983, Kowalski was injured in an accident caused by a drunken driver. She was brain damaged and comatose for five months.

Thompson battled Kowalski's parents over guardianship, and when the parents won in 1985, they banned Thompson from even visiting their daughter. The case went to the Minnesota Court of Appeals, and Thompson, who had built a wheelchair-accessible home for Kowalski, finally gained custody in 1991.

When it comes to the law, spouses and blood relatives come first regardless of the wishes of the victim. That's why legislation such as the one in California [is] so important.

[It allows] people to say, in effect, "Hey, world. This is my life partner. This is the person I want when I'm sick or need to be taken care of, and it's the person I want taken care of if I die first."

The California proposal is such a little step in the legal scheme of things, but it's an important one.

Growth of Benefits

More than 2800 firms and organizations offer some type of domestic partner benefits. Two states, Vermont and New York, have granted health and dental benefits to domestic partners of state employees. Some cities with similar provisions:

Health benefits: Ann Arbor and East Lansing, Mich.; Berkeley, Calif.; Cambridge, Mass.; Seattle, Wash.; New York, N.Y.

Registration and/or sick and bereavement leave: Atlanta, Ga.; Madison, Wis.; Takoma Park, Md.; Los Angeles, Calif.; West Palm Beach, Fla.

Source: Copyright 1994, USA Today. Reprinted with permission.

EXHIBIT 9–7   Concluded

Opposing View

This law isn't necessary. Stop this campaign to legitimize cohabitation.

Hold on to your checkbook, because the liberal/left is pushing another nearsighted social experiment called "domestic partners," which will cost taxpayers and redefine the institution of marriage.

The goal of the homosexual special interest lobby is to change the public policy of this nation by expanding the definition of marriage and family to include two homosexuals or heterosexuals living together. This new quasi-marital union impacts the way our judges make their rulings on issues that relate to marriage and family, and it devalues the concept of marriage.

So far, courts have denied marital status to cohabiting homosexuals. But this could change. If government expands the definition of marriage, the courts will then be compelled to force businesses to pay benefits for the domestic partners of employees just like benefits for employees' spouses. And governments could be forced to use scarce tax dollars for benefits for domestic partners of government employees. Most states allow consenting adults to live together, but that doesn't mean taxpayers should have to subsidize this arrangement.

Also, domestic partnerships weaken the institution of marriage and encourage relationships without the responsibility of marriage. Some may argue this new legislation promotes monogamous relationships, but these laws typically allow for a new "partner" every six months and erode the cultural support for the permanency of marriage.

Homosexual activists are good at marketing. They have tried to mainstream themselves by garnering some senior citizens' support. But domestic partners is an unnecessary shotgun approach to remedy some senior-citizen concerns.

Moreover, medical facilities already allow visitation in intensive care units and hospital rooms by friends or relatives. Existing law allows a testator to will property to anyone—friend or stranger. Existing law allows any "interested person" to file petitions or receive notice regarding conservatorship or guardianship.

The man/woman marriage relationship is best for society.

Rev. Louis P. Sheldon, chairman of Traditional Values Coalition, Anaheim, Calif.

Courtesy of the Rev. Louis P. Sheldon, chairman of Traditional Values Coalition, Anaheim, Ca.

other employees when it comes to these issues, others do not. Lately, gay and lesbian employees have been fighting back. In the case below, lesbians sued their employer to have the right to include their long-term life partners on their insurance policies. They won.

TANNER V. OREGON HEALTH SCIENCES UNIVERSITY
971 P.2d 435 (Ore. 1998)

Three lesbian university employees sued when the university denied insurance benefits to their domestic partners. The Oregon Court of Appeals held that the university's denial of insurance benefits to the employees' domestic partners violated the Oregon constitution's privileges and immunities clause.

Landau, J.

At issue in this case is the lawfulness of Oregon Health Science University's (OHSU) denial of health and life insurance benefits to the unmarried domestic partners of its homosexual employees. Plaintiffs, who are three lesbian employees of OHSU and their domestic partners, initiated this action for judicial review of State Employees' Benefits Board (SEBB) orders affirming the lawfulness of the denial and for declaratory and injunctive relief. Plaintiffs contend that OHSU's actions violate Article I, section 20, of the Oregon Constitution, which prohibits granting privileges or immunities not equally belonging to all citizens.

Article I, section 20, of the Oregon Constitution provides:

> "No law shall be passed granting to any citizen or class of citizens privileges or immunities, which, upon the same terms, shall not equally belong to all citizens."

Article I, section 20 generally is understood to express two separate prohibitions. The clause "forbids inequality of privileges or immunities not available upon the same terms, first, to any citizen, and second, to any class of citizens." In this case, employees contend that they are members of a class of citizens—homosexual couples—to whom certain privileges—insurance benefits—are not made available.

There is no question but that employees are members of a true class. That class—unmarried homosexual couples—is not defined by any statute nor by the practices that are the subject of employees' challenges. Moreover, the class clearly is defined in terms of ad hominem, personal, and social characteristics. The question then is whether employees are members of a suspect class. Here, too, we have no difficulty concluding that employees are members of a suspect class. Sexual orientation, like gender, race, alienage, and religious affiliation is widely regarded as defining a distinct, socially recognized group of citizens, and certainly it is beyond dispute that homosexuals in our society

have been and continue to be the subject of adverse social and political stereotyping and prejudice.

Because employees are members of a suspect class to which certain privileges and immunities are not made available, we must determine whether the fact that the privileges and immunities are not available to that class may be justified by genuine differences between the class and those to whom the privileges and immunities are made available. Stated perhaps more plainly, we must determine whether the fact that the domestic partners of homosexual OHSU employees cannot obtain insurance benefits can be justified by their homosexuality. The parties have suggested no such justification, and we can envision none.

OHSU's defense is that it determined eligibility for insurance benefits on the basis of marital status, not sexual orientation. According to OHSU, the fact that such a facially neutral classification has the unintended side effect of discriminating against homosexual couples who cannot marry is not actionable under Article I, section 20. We are not persuaded by the asserted defense. Article I, section 20, does not prohibit only intentional discrimination. OHSU has taken action with no apparent intention to treat disparately members of any true class of citizens. Nevertheless, its actions have the undeniable effect of doing just that. OHSU's intentions in this case are not relevant. What is relevant is the extent to which privileges or immunities are not made available to all citizens on equal terms.

OHSU insists that in this case privileges and immunities are available to all on equal terms: All married employees—heterosexuals and homosexuals alike—are permitted to acquire insurance benefits for their spouses. That reasoning misses the point, however. Homosexual couples may not marry. Accordingly, the benefits are not made available on equal terms. They are made available on terms that, for gay and lesbian couples, are a legal impossibility.

We conclude that OHSU's denial of insurance benefits to the unmarried domestic partners of its homosexual employees violated the Oregon Constitution and that the trial court correctly entered judgment in favor of plaintiffs on that ground. AFFIRMED.

Case Questions

1. While this case was pending, the employer decided to revise its policies to extend insurance coverage to gays and lesbians. Why do you think they did so?

2. List what you consider to be the five best reasons for not extending benefits to gay and lesbian employees. Explain. Now give the arguments for why these reasons may not be good ones. Which do you prefer? Why?

3. Do you understand why the court would hold that the Oregon constitution's privileges and immunities clause requires that the employer not extend benefits to one group that it will not extend to another unless it can show there is a valid reason for the differentiation? Can you think of a valid reason here?

Management Considerations

Since affinity orientation is not a protected category under Title VII, employers have more flexibility in making workplace policies and decisions on this issue. The approach the employer takes will depend in large part on the employer's own views and preferences. Those employers who prefer the benefits of a diverse workplace—and who wish to maximize the potential the employee has for growth and contribution within the workplace—will likely choose to deal with the affinity orientation issue in a less restrictive manner.

Such employers will likely not have policies that have a hard and fast rule of "no gays or lesbians allowed." Rather, they will judge all employees on the basis of work-related criteria.

If some action of the lesbian or gay employee presents an issue, it should be dealt with as a legitimate workplace issue, rather than one that arose solely because of the employee's affinity orientation. The fact that the employee happens to be gay or lesbian should not be treated as the "why," any more than it would be if the employee were not gay or lesbian. It is irrelevant to the activity. The focus is on the conduct itself, not on the affinity orientation of the actor. It greatly reduces the potential for liability to deal with all employees this way.

Employers who decide to have a policy that treats gays and lesbians as full contributors to the workplace should ensure that the message goes out to gay and lesbian employees from the very top. It is more likely to be accepted, appreciated, and understood and therefore will be more likely to accomplish its purpose. Other employees will be more likely to comport themselves consistently with the policy if it comes from the top of the hierarchy. It should be made clear that not only will the employer not discriminate on the basis of affinity orientation, but that it will not be tolerated from other employees, particularly in the form of harassment of gays and lesbians.

The employer who does not prefer this approach may have more latitude under the law (depending on the jurisdiction in which the employer is located) not to take this view, than they would, say, about having women in the workplace, or having Jews, or blacks, or Hispanics. Some employers may even wish to take an adverse workplace decision involving a gay or lesbian employee to court to maintain maximum control over areas not as heavily regulated as the other protected categories. That is the employer's personal choice, but at least the employer now knows both sides of the issue. (See Exhibit 9–7.)

Most employers take a middle-ground position. That is, they do not have a specific policy of either support or prohibition, but they deal with issues as they arise on a case-by-case basis. Again, because the law is not as restrictive for this category of employees as it is for others and does not extend the same Title VII protections, the employer potentially (again, depending on the state the employer is in) has more leeway to choose the management approach that best suits his or her needs or desires.

The caution to be heeded is that simply because Title VII or the majority of state fair-employment practice laws do not prohibit discrimination on the basis of affinity orientation does not mean that it is not prohibited by relevant state or local laws relating to closely connected issues, such as privacy, right to free speech, interference with contractual relations, and so on. And the laws are changing every day. Employers concerned about workplace decisions should, at the very least, check such laws or case law in their jurisdiction before making final decisions.

Even if the law is on the employer's side, the employer may wish to consider other possible repercussions of restrictive employment policies in this area. An example of this is the Cracker Barrel restaurant chain headquartered in Tennessee. Cracker Barrel operates a number of restaurants around the country. With no apparent motivating event, the company announced that it would no longer employ people "whose sexual preferences fail to demonstrate normal heterosexual values which have been the foundation of families in our society." Pursuant to this policy, Cracker Barrel dismissed its gay and lesbian employees.

After doing so, it was the subject of vigorous opposition, mainly by the gay and lesbian community. Many of Cracker Barrel's restaurants have been picketed and denounced by vocal protesters. Gays and lesbians have bought stock to be able to have a say in its policies. Even though the law may permit Cracker Barrel's actions, some employers may wish to avoid the controversy exhibited here, particularly if there is no pressing need to address the issue.

Management Tips

Policies and decisions in the affinity orientation area are rapidly evolving. The patchwork of state, federal, local, public, and private laws and policies we have discussed present the employer with the challenge of trying to do what is required for each jurisdiction, when, in fact, the requirements may be quite different. However, there are conclusions which can be drawn about creating policy in the midst of such seeming chaos. In order to provide the maximum protection from liability for affinity orientation–related issues, there are several things an employer can do:

- hire using only relevant, work-related criteria;
- keep inquiries about applicants' personal lives at a minimum, and make sure the information is relevant;
- have a policy ensuring all employees respect in the workplace and ensure that all employees are aware of the policy and what it it means;
- no matter what the employer's policy about gays in the workplace, the respect policy should protect everyone from things like unsolicited negative statements about immutable and other characteristics such as race, religion, gender, and affinity orientation;
- take prompt action whenever there are complaints of violations of the policy or it sends the message that the policy is meaningless;
- deciding what position to take on affinity orientation–related issues for policy purposes can be done proactively before the issue arises, or defensively to meet the issue when it comes about; the latter has the benefit of specificity, the former the advantage of deliberate, strategic thinking;
- be aware of the potential impact on gays and lesbians of workplace policies regarding issues like bereavement leave, benefits, bringing significant others to office functions, accepting personal calls during work hours, display of personal items at work (i.e., photos, cards, political buttons, and so forth);
- if the employer decides to institute policies inclusive of gays and lesbians, ensure that they are fair and evenly handled.

Summary

- Affinity orientation is not protected by Title VII.

- Several states and municipalities have passed protective legislation. Constitutional protection may also apply to public employees.

- Employers in most jurisdictions have more leeway in this area to make employment decisions without regard to the same legal strictures applicable to other categories of employees included within Title VII.

- The safer approach is to base employment decisions on the person's qualifications and fitness for the job, rather than on questionably relevant characteristics about their personal life.

Chapter-End Questions

1. Applicant applies for a position with Ace Corporation. During the interview, Ace suspects that applicant is gay. When asked why the suspicion, Ace says that the male applicant acted effeminately. Ace decides not to hire the applicant, who is otherwise qualified. Does the applicant have a cause of action against Ace?

2. When the FBI learns that Mary, its FBI agent, is a lesbian, Mary is fired. Mary goes to an attorney to find out about the possibility of suing to get her job back. What does the attorney likely tell her?

3. As a manager, an employee comes to you and tells you that he has a hunch that one of the other employees is probably gay. What do you do?

4. Charlie, the manager, does not like it that Chester wears an earring and orders Chester to get rid of it or run the risk of termination. Chester refuses. Can Charlie terminate Chester?

5. Bill has gender reassignment surgery and changes to a female and is now Billie. Upon her return to work, Billie is terminated. Can the employer legally terminate Billie for this?

6. Maureen brings her same gender partner of 14 years to a company picnic. One of the other employees treats Maureen poorly after realizing she is a lesbian. Does Maureen have any recourse?

7. In a state that has a human rights law, including affinity orientation, Sereta, a secretary in a law firm, comes to work in Doc Marten-type brogan boots, a flannel shirt, and a pair of jeans. The chief personnel officer terminates Sereta when she refuses to change clothes. Sereta brings an action for affinity orientation discrimination. Does she win?

8. Cy is terminated from his position as chief cartographer for the US Mapping Agency, a department of the federal government, when it is discovered that he is gay. Does Cy have any recourse?

9. Derry owns his own business and employs about 75 people. Derry is a very "macho" male and detests gay men. Derry has several lesbians working in his company and is not bothered by their presence. When a gay male who is not hired sues Derry for gender discrimination, what is the outcome?

10. In a state that prohibits discrimination on the basis of affinity orientation in its human rights provisions, Sheila is terminated when she is supposed to be at her desk but is found having sex with Donna in the broom closet of their workplace. Will Sheila's termination likely be upheld?

10 RELIGIOUS DISCRIMINATION

S C E N A R I O S

S C E N A R I O   1

In his preemployment interview, Mosley stated that he would not work on Saturdays because that is the day of his sabbath. As a result, he is not hired. Is this religious discrimination?

S C E N A R I O   2

Three months after coming to work for Steel Bank, Jon joins a religious group whose sabbath is on Tuesdays. Members of the religion are not to work on the sabbath. Jon refuses to work on Tuesdays. He is terminated. Jon sues the employer, alleging religious discrimination. The employer defends by saying that (1) Jon was not of this religion when he was hired, (2) Tuesday is not a valid sabbath day, and (3) any religious group that celebrates a sabbath on Tuesday is not a valid religion and the employer does not have to honor it. Are any of these valid defenses?

S C E N A R I O   3

While she was off on maternity leave, the church fires Rev. Pamela Combs on the basis of her gender and her pregnancy. She sues, will she win?

Statutory Basis

It shall be an unlawful employment practice for an employer—

(1) to fail or refuse to hire or to discharge any individual, or otherwise to discriminate against any individual with respect to his compensation, terms, conditions, or privileges of employment, because of such individual's . . . religion . . . or

(2) to limit, segregate, or classify his employees or applicants for employment in any way which would deprive or tend to deprive any individual of employment opportunities or otherwise adversely affect his status as an employee, because of such individual's religion . . . 42 U.S.C. 20002-2(a).

Congress shall make no law respecting an establishment of religion, or prohibiting the free exercise thereof . . . First Amendment to the U.S. Constitution.

Posings and Imposings

Religion has unique significance in our country's creation and development. In the 16th century, when the Catholic Church did not allow King Henry VIII to divorce his wife, Catherine of Aragon, and to marry Anne Boleyn, Henry broke with Rome. This led to the establishment of a separate national church in England under the

EXHIBIT 10–1   World Religions

Group	Adherents	Percent of World Pop.
Major world religions		
Christianity	1,548,500,000	32.4%
Islam	817,000,000	17.1
Hinduism	647,500,000	13.5
Buddhism	295,600,000	6.2
Judaism	17,800,000	0.4
Total	3,326,400,000	69.6%
Other broad religious groupings		
Chinese folk religions	188,000,000	3.9%
New Asian religions	106,400,000	2.2
Tribal religions	91,200,000	1.9
Total	385,600,000	8.0%
Regional and smaller religious groups		
Sikhism	16,100,000	0.34%
Shamanism	12,200,000	0.26
Spiritism	6,700,000	0.14
Confucianism	5,200,000	0.11
Bahaism	4,400,000	0.09
Jainism	3,300,000	0.07
Shintoism	3,200,000	0.07
Parsiism (Zoroastrianism)	500,000	0.01
Total	51,600,000	1.1%
Unaffiliated		
Nonreligious	805,900,000	16.9%
Atheist	210,500,000	4.4
Total	1,026,400,000	21.3%
Total	**4,781,200,000**	**100.0%**

THE UNIVERSAL ALMANAC © by John W. Wright. Reprinted with permission of
Andrews McMeel Publishing. All rights reserved.

supreme headship of the king. Henry VIII was allowed to divorce Catherine (he
eventually took six wives) and marry Anne, whom he ordered beheaded in 1536.

The aftermath of Henry's maneuvers was that the church became inextricably
woven with the government, and religious freedom was virtually nonexistent. The
right to practice religion freely and not be required to blindly accept the government's state-imposed religious beliefs was a large part of what made America break
away from Great Britain and its Church of England more than a century later.

Rejecting the tyranny of this state-imposed religion, religious freedom was
included in the US Constitution, and freedom of religion has always been highly
valued and closely held and has enjoyed a protected position in American law. Title
VII embodies this in the employment arena by prohibiting discrimination in (see

EXHIBIT 10–2 Religious Affiliations in the United States

FAMILY/Denomination	Local congregations	Total clergy	Total membership	% of total affiliated
ALL RELIGIOUSLY AFFILIATED	346,092	532,697	147,499,662	100.0%
CHRISTIAN CHURCHES	342,576	526,082	138,585,662	94.0%
ROMAN CATHOLIC CHURCH	23,561	53,382	52,893,217	35.9%
BAPTIST CHURCHES	97,004	146,818	28,224,395	19.1%
Southern Baptist Convention	37,072	63,200	14,613,618	
National Baptist Convention, USA, Inc.	26,000	27,500	5,500,000	
National Baptist Convention of America	11,398	28,574	2,668,799	
American Baptist Churches in the USA	5,864	7,678	1,576,483	
Baptist Bible Fellowship International	3,449	4,500	1,405,900	
Progressive Natl. Baptist Convention, Inc.	655	863	521,692	
General Assoc. of Regular Baptist Churches	1,571	2,045	300,839	
American Baptist Association	1,705	1,760	250,000	
National Primitive Baptist Convention, Inc.	606	636	250,000	
Baptist Missionary Association of America	1,359	2,450	228,125	
Conservative Baptist Assoc. of America	1,140	—	225,000	
Free Will Baptists, National Assoc. of	2,483	2,895	205,546	
Baptist General Conference	762	1,700	131,480	
Liberty Baptist Fellowship	267	374	130,000	
Others (10 denominations)	2,673	2,643	216,913	
METHODIST CHURCHES	52,704	53,554	13,343,996	9.0%
United Methodist Church	37,876	37,808	9,192,172	
African Methodist Episcopal Church	6,200	0,550	2,210,000	
African Methodist Episcopal Zion Church	6,057	6,396	1,195,173	
Christian Methodist Episcopal Church	2,340	2,650	718,922	
Others (4 denominations)	231	150	27,729	
LUTHERAN CHURCHES	18,739	27,153	8,455,747	5.7%
Evangelical Lutheran Church in America	11,041	16,929	5,318,844	
Lutheran Church—Missouri Synod	5,897	8,044	2,630,588	
Wisconsin Evangelical Lutheran Synod	1,180	1,497	416,493	
Others (9 denominations)	621	683	89,822	
PENTECOSTAL CHURCHES	41,501	80,431	7,901,625	5.4%
Church of God in Christ	9,982	10,425	3,709,661	
Assemblies of God	10,886	26,837	2,135,104	
Church of God (Cleveland, Tenn.)	5,346	9,638	505,775	
United Pentecostal Church International	3,410	6,984	500,000	
Church of God in Christ, International	300	1,600	200,000	
International Church of the Foursquare Gospel	1,250	3,482	186,213	
Pentecostal Holiness Church, International	1,461	3,422	113,000	
Others (24 denominations)	8,866	18,043	551,872	
REFORMED CHURCHES	22,513	36,527	5,733,828	3.9%
Presbyterian Church (USA)	11,531	19,514	3,007,322	
United Church of Christ	6,406	10,071	1,676,105	
Reformed Church in America	928	1,636	340,359	
Christian Reformed Church in North America	650	1,077	219,988	
Presbyterian Church in America	913	1,702	188,083	
Others (12 denominations)	2,085	2,527	301,971	
ORTHODOX CHURCHES	1,746	2,236	4,459,177	3.0%
Greek Orthodox Archdiocese of North and South America	535	655	1,950,000	
Orthodox Church in America	440	531	1,000,000	
Armenian Church of America, Diocese of the	66	61	450,000	
Antiochan Orthodox Christian Archdiocese of North America	120	180	280,000	
Coptic Orthodox Church	28	28	115,000	
American Carpatho-Russian Orthodox Greek Catholic Church	70	66	100,000	
Others (14 denominations)	487	715	564,177	
LATTER-DAY SAINTS CHURCHES	9,575	45,614	4,057,131	2.8%
Church of Jesus Christ of Latter-day Saints	8,396	28,598	3,860,000	
Reorganized Church of Jesus Christ of Latter-day Saints	1,094	16,585	192,077	
Others (2 denominations)	85	431	5,054	

FAMILY/Denomination	Local congregations	Total clergy	Total membership	% of total affiliated
CHRISTIAN CHURCHES AND CHURCHES OF CHRIST	23,151	12,282	3,793,915	2.6%
Churches of Christ	13,364	—	1,623,754	
Christian Church (Disciples of Christ)	4,221	6,806	1,106 692	
Christian Churches and Churches of Christ	5,566	5,476	1,063,469	
EPISCOPAL CHURCHES	7,175	14,235	2,516,240	1.7%
Episcopal Church	7,054	14,111	2,504,507	
Others (2 denominations)	121	124	11,733	
HOLINESS CHURCHES	14,843	22,395	1,398,557	0.9%
Church of the Nazarene	5,018	8,667	530,912	
Christian and Missionary Alliance	1,691	2,154	238,734	
Church of God (Anderson, Ind.)	2,296	3,313	188,662	
Wesleyan Church	1,704	2,596	109,196	
Christian Congregation, Inc.	1,450	1,455	105,478	
Others (13 denominations)	2,684	4,210	225,575	
JEHOVAH'S WITNESSES	8,336	—	752,404	0.5%
CHURCH OF CHRIST, SCIENTIST	—	—	700,000[1]	0.5%
ADVENTIST CHURCHES	4,641	6,236	698,521	0.5%
Seventh-Day Adventists	4,055	5,481	666,199	
Others (4 denominations)	586	755	32,322	
SALVATION ARMY	1,092	5,195	432,893	0.3%
ROMAN RITE CHURCHES	308	316	347,092	0.2%
Polish National Catholic Church of Amer.	162	141	282,411	
North American Old Roman Catholic Church	133	150	62,611	
Others (2 denominations)	13	25	2,070	
MENNONITE CHURCHES	2,365	3,168	239,681	0.2%
Mennonite Church	989	2,399	91,167	
Old Order Amish Church	696	—	62,640	
Others (9 denominations)	680	769	85,874	
BRETHREN CHURCHES	1,545	2,718	216,217	0.1%
Church of the Brethren	1,059	1,963	155,967	
Others (3 denominations)	486	755	60,250	
UNITARIAN UNIVERSALIST ASSOCIATION	956	1,069	173,167	0.1%
FRIENDS (QUAKER) CHURCHES (5 denominations)	1,395	1,095	120,320	0.1%
MISCELLANEOUS CHURCHES	9,426	11,658	1,127,539	0.8%
Community Churches, International Confederation of	350	350	200,000	
Independent Fundamental Churches of America	1,019	1,366	120,446	
Congregational Christian Churches, National Association of	464	826	108,115	
Christian Brethren (also known as The Plymouth Brethren)	1,150	500	98,000	
Evangelical Free Church of America	880	1,484	95,722	
Evangelical Covenant Church	570	930	86,079	
Others (37 denominations)	4,993	6,202	419,177	
OTHER CHRISTIANS (UNREPORTED)	—	—	1,000,000[1]	0.7%
OTHER RELIGIONS	3,516	6,615	8,914,000	6.0%
JEWS	3,416	6,500	5,814,000	3.9%
MUSLIMS	—	—	2,500,000[1]	1.7%
BUDDHIST CHURCHES OF AMERICA	100	115	100,000	0.1%
OTHER NON-CHRISTIANS (UNREPORTED)	—	—	500,000[1]	0.3%

1. Estimates–denominations/organizations do not report membership. Sources: Christianity–*Yearbook of American and Canadian Churches 1988.* An estimated 1 million people are members of very small denominations or independent congregations not accounted for in the *YACC.* Judaism–*Yearbook of American and Canadian Churches 1988.* Number represents the total of all who are considered members of the Jewish cultural community. Islam-based on *The World Christian Encyclopedia, 1985* estimated for North America. Number represents the total of all who are considered members of the Islamic cultural community. Other–*Universal Almanac* estimate. Number includes 100,000 Buddhists not affiliated with Buddhist Churches of America and members of other non-Christian religious organizations.

Exhibits 10–1 and 10–2) employment based on religion—either its practices or beliefs. While litigation on the basis of religious discrimination does not occur as frequently as some of the other categories (it accounted for 2.2 percent of EEOC claims filed in 1998), or may not have as high a profile, it is just as important a concern for employers. The percentage of claims may seem small, but the more important factor is that there has been a steady increase in claims since 1993.

Federal and state constitutional guarantees of due process, equal protection, and freedom of religion also provide protection for federal, state, and local government employees. If the employer is a governmental entity, the employer must avoid workplace policies that have the effect of tending to establish or to interfere with the practice of the employee's religion. In determining whether the employer has discriminated on the basis of religion, the court must sometimes first address whether even deciding the issue entangles the government excessively in the practice of religion. Title VII is the only legislation specifically prohibiting religious discrimination in employment, and consideration is given to constitutional issues where necessary.

Unlike the other categories included in Title VII, there is not an absolute prohibition against discrimination on the basis of religion. Rather, for the first time under Title VII, we see that a category has built into it a **duty to reasonably accommodate** the employee's religious conflict unless to do so would cause the employer **undue hardship.** There is no such reasonable accommodation requirement for race, gender, color, or national origin, but there is under the Americans with Disabilities Act (ADA) as we shall see in that chapter. However, the nature of the accommodation in the ADA is quite different.

To a great extent, religious organizations are exempt from the prohibitions in Title VII. As a general rule, they can discriminate so that, for instance, a Catholic church may legitimately refuse to hire a Baptist minister as its priest. That is, religion is recognized as a basis for a BFOQ reasonably necessary to the normal operation of that particular business or enterprise under section 703(e)(1) of Title VII. That is why, in scenario 3, the minister loses. Her firing is considered an exception to Title VII and the church can do as it wishes. If the church has nonsectarian activities, such as running a day care center, bookstore, or athletic club, it may enjoy the same broad type of freedom to discriminate, since these activities may have religion or propagation of the religion as an integral part of their activity. Employers should be cautioned that the specific facts play an important role in making this determination.

Duty to reasonably accommodate
The employer's duty to try to find a way to avoid conflict between workplace policies and an employee's religious practices or beliefs.

Undue hardship
A burden imposed on an employer, by accommodating an employee's religious conflict, that would be too onerous for the employer to bear.

3
Scenario

CORPORATION OF THE PRESIDING BISHOP OF THE CHURCH OF JESUS CHRIST OF LATTER-DAY SAINTS V. AMOS
483 U.S. 327 (1987)

Employees who were terminated from their jobs with church-owned corporations for failure to qualify as church members brought suit for religious discrimination. The US Supreme Court held that applying the religious exemption to Title VII's prohibition against religious discrimination in employment to secular nonprofit activities of religious organization did not violate the US Constitution's Establishment Clause.

White, J.

Section 702 of the Civil Rights Act of 1964 exempts religious organizations from Title VII's prohibition against discrimination in employment on the basis of religion. ["Title VII shall not apply . . . to a religious corporation, association, educational institution, or society with respect to the employment of individuals of a particular religion to perform work connected with the carrying on by such corporation, association, educational institution, or society of its activities."] The question presented is whether applying the exemption to the secular nonprofit activities of religious organizations violates the Establishment Clause of the First Amendment. The District Court held that it does. We reverse.

The Deseret Gymnasium (Gymnasium) in Salt Lake City, Utah, is a nonprofit facility, open to the public, run by religious entities associated with The Church of Jesus Christ of Latter-day Saints (Church), an unincorporated religious association sometimes called the Mormon or LDS Church.

Employee Mayson worked at the Gymnasium for some 16 years as an assistant building engineer and then as building engineer. He was discharged in 1981 because he failed to qualify for a temple recommend, that is, a certificate that he is a member of the Church and eligible to attend its temples. Temple recommends are issued only to individuals who observe the Church's standards in such matters as regular church attendance, tithing, and abstinence from coffee, tea, alcohol, and tobacco.

Mayson brought an action against the Church alleging, among other things, discrimination on the basis of religion in violation of §703 of the Civil Rights Act of 1964. The Church moved to dismiss this claim on the ground that §702 shields them from liability. The employees contended

that if construed to allow religious employers to discriminate on religious grounds in hiring for nonreligious jobs, the exemption of §702 violates the Establishment Clause.

"This Court has long recognized that the government may (and sometimes must) accommodate religious practices and that it may do so without violating the Establishment Clause." It is well established, too, that "[t]he limits of permissible state accommodation to religion are by no means co-extensive with the noninterference mandated by the Free Exercise Clause." There is ample room under the Establishment Clause for "benevolent neutrality which will permit religious exercise to exist without sponsorship and without interference." At some point, accommodation may devolve into "an unlawful fostering of religion," but these are not such cases, in our view.

Under the analysis in *Lemon v. Kurtzman,* 403 U.S. 602 (1971), the court first held that §702 has the permissible secular purpose of assuring it is a permissible legislative purpose to alleviate significant governmental interference with the ability of religious organizations to define and carry out their religious missions. Employees argue that there is no such purpose here because §702 provided adequate protection for religious employers prior to the 1972 amendment, when it exempted only the religious activities of such employees from the statutory ban on religious discrimination. We may assume for the sake of argument that the pre-1972 exemption was adequate in the sense that the Free Exercise Clause required no more. Nonetheless, it is a significant burden on a religious organization to require it, on pain of substantial liability, to predict which of its activities a secular court will consider religious. The line is hardly a bright one, and an organization might understandably be concerned that a judge would not understand its religious tenets and sense of mission. Fear of potential liability might affect the way an organization carried out what it understood to be its religious mission.

After a detailed examination of the legislative history of the 1972 amendment, the District Court concluded that Congress's purpose was to minimize governmental "interfer[ence] with the decision-making process in religions." We agree that this purpose does not violate the Establishment Clause.

The second requirement under *Lemon* is that the law in question have a "principal or primary effect . . . that neither advances nor inhibits religion." Undoubtedly, religious organizations are better able now to advance their purposes than they were prior to the 1972 amendment to §702. But religious groups have been better able to advance their purposes on account of many laws that have passed constitutional muster. A law is not unconstitutional simply because it allows churches to advance religion, which is their very purpose. For a law to have forbidden "effects" under *Lemon,* it must be fair to say that the government itself has advanced religion through its own activities and influence.

The District Court appeared to fear that sustaining the exemption would permit churches with financial resources impermissibly to extend their influence and propagate their faith by entering the commercial, profit-making world. The cases before us, however, involve a nonprofit activity instituted over 75 years ago in the hope that "all who assemble here, and who come for the benefit of their health, and for physical blessings, [may] feel that they are in a house dedicated to the Lord." Dedicatory Prayer for the Gymnasium. This case therefore does not implicate the apparent concerns of the District Court. Moreover, we find no persuasive evidence in the record before us that the Church's ability to propagate its religious doctrine through the Gymnasium is any greater now than it was prior to the passage of the Civil Rights Act in 1964. In such circumstances, we do not see how any advancement of religion

achieved by the Gymnasium can be fairly attributed to the government, as opposed to the Church. In the present cases, Mayson was not legally obligated to take the steps necessary to qualify for a temple recommend, and his discharge was not required by statute. We find no merit in his contention that §702 "impermissibly delegates governmental power to religious employees and conveys a message of governmental endorsement of religious discrimination."

We find unpersuasive the District Court's reliance on the fact that §702 singles out religious entities for a benefit. Although the Court has given weight to this consideration in its past decisions, it has never indicated that statutes that give special consideration to religious groups are per sé invalid. That would run contrary to the teaching of our cases that there is ample room for accommodation of religion under the Establishment Clause. Where, as here, government acts with the proper purpose of lifting a regulation that burdens the exercise of religion, we see no reason to require that the exemption comes packaged with benefits to secular entities.

We are also unpersuaded by the District Court's reliance on the argument that §702 is unsupported by long historical tradition. There was simply no need to consider the scope of the §702 exemption until the 1964 Civil Rights Act was passed, and the fact that Congress concluded after eight years that the original exemption was unnecessarily narrow is a decision entitled to deference, not suspicion.

Mayson argues that §702 offends equal protection principles by giving less protection to the employees of religious employers than to the employees of secular employers. In cases such as these, where a statute is neutral on its face and motivated by a permissible purpose of limiting governmental interference with the exercise of religion, we see no justification for applying strict scrutiny to a statute that passes the *Lemon* test. The proper inquiry is whether Congress has chosen a rational classification to further a legitimate end.

We have already indicated that Congress acted with a legitimate purpose in expanding the §702 exemption to cover all activities of religious employers. To dispose of employees' equal protection argument, it suffices to hold—as we now do—that as applied to the nonprofit activities of religious employers, §702 is rationally related to the legitimate purpose of alleviating significant governmental interference with the ability of religious organizations to define and carry out their religious missions.

It cannot be seriously contended that §702 impermissibly entangles church and state; the statute effectuates a more complete separation of the two and avoids intrusive inquiry into religious belief. The statute easily passes muster under the third part of the *Lemon* test. REVERSED and REMANDED.

Case Questions

1. Are you surprised at the outcome of this case? Why?
2. As a church employer in your religion, what reason would you give for requiring that the building engineer be of the same religion?
3. Are you able to draw a bright line between excessive interference with church business and the government wanting to ensure employment protection for all? Explain.

Section 703(e)(2) of Title VII states that it is not an unlawful employment practice for a school, college, university, or other educational institution to hire or employ employees of a particular religion if the institution is in whole or in substantial part owned, supported, controlled, or managed by a particular religion or by a religious corporation, association, or society or if its curriculum is directed toward the propagation of a particular religion.

Not very long ago it was fairly routine for employers to be nearly as adamant about not hiring those of certain religious faiths as it was about not hiring people of a certain race, ethnic background, or gender. The issue has usually been more covertly handled, but it existed extensively, nonetheless. Title VII was enacted to remedy such practices.

The more frequent basis for lawsuits today is that an employee is not hired or is terminated because of some religious practice that comes into conflict with the employer's workplace policies. The employee may wish not to work on a particular day because it is the employee's sabbath. Or the employee may wish to dress a certain way for religious reasons, or to take certain days off for religious holidays or observances. When it conflicts with the employer's policies and the employee refuses to accede, the employee is terminated and Title VII comes into play.

Frequently the employer discovers religious information through questions on an employment application or during a preemployment interview, either of which relates to notifying a religious figure or taking employee to a particular hospital in the event of on-the-job injury. To eliminate the appearance of illegal consideration of religion in hiring, employers should instead, ask such questions after hire.

In this chapter, we will learn what is meant by religious discrimination, what the duty to accommodate involves, and how far an employer can go in handling management considerations when religious conflict is at issue.

What Is Religion?

Title VII originally provided no guidance as to what it meant by the word *religion*. In the 1972 amendments to Title VII, Congress addressed the issue. In section 701 providing definitions for terms within Title VII, section (j) states that "The term 'religion' includes all aspects of religious observance and practice, as well as belief, unless an employer demonstrates that he is unable to reasonably accommodate an employee's or prospective employee's religious observance or practice without undue hardship on the conduct of the employer's business."

The question frequently arises: "What if I never heard of the employee's religion. Must I still accommodate it?" The answer is based on two considerations: Whether the belief is closely held and whether it takes the place of religion in the employee's life. The latter requirement means that even atheism has been considered a "religion" for Title VII purposes.

The religious belief need not be a belief in a religious deity as we generally know it. However, courts have determined that groups like the Ku Klux Klan are not religious organizations even though their members have closely held beliefs. The employer need not previously know of, or have heard of, or approve of the employee's religion in order to be required to accommodate it for Title VII purposes. Also, the employer cannot question the sincerity of the belief merely because it appears to the employer unorthodox.

In the case below, the Supreme Court held that the employee need not be a member of an organized religion at all. The case involves the Free Exercise Clause of the First Amendment to the US Constitution, made applicable to the states by the 14th Amendment, but the considerations are similar to those of Title VII.

FRAZEE V. ILLINOIS DEP'T. OF EMPLOYMENT SECURITY, ET AL.
489 U.S. 829 (1989)

Unemployment compensation was denied to an applicant who refused a temporary retail position because he would not work on Sundays for religious reasons. The Court held that the fact that the applicant did not belong to a particular religious organization did not mean he could not claim his religious freedom had been abridged.

White, J.

Frazee refused a temporary retail position offered him by Kelly Services because the job would have required him to work on Sunday. Frazee told Kelly that, as a Christian, he could not work on "the Lord's day." Frazee applied to the Illinois Department of Employment Security for unemployment benefits claiming there was good cause for his refusal to work on Sunday. His application was denied. Frazee appealed the denial of benefits to the Department's Board of Review, which also denied his claim. The Board of Review stated: "When a refusal of work is based on religious convictions, the refusal must be based upon some tenets or dogma accepted by the individual of some church, sect, or denomination, and such a refusal based solely on an individual's personal belief is personal and noncompelling and does not render the work unsuitable."

To the Illinois court, Frazee's position that he was "a Christian" and as such felt it wrong to work on Sunday was not enough. For a Free Exercise Clause claim to succeed, said the Illinois Appellate Court, "the injunction against Sunday labor must be found in a tenet or dogma of an established religious sect. Frazee does not profess to be a member of any such sect."

The courts below did not question his sincerity, and the State concedes it. Furthermore, the Board of Review characterized Frazee's views as "religious convictions," and the Illinois Appellate Court referred to his refusal to work on Sunday as based on a "personal professed religious belief."

Frazee asserted that he was a Christian, but did not claim to be a member of a particular Christian sect. It is also true that there are assorted Christian denominations that do not profess to be compelled by their religion to refuse Sunday work, but this does not diminish Frazee's protection flowing from the Free Exercise Clause. Undoubtedly, membership in an organized religious denomination, especially one with a specific tenet forbidding members to work on Sunday, would simplify the problem of identifying sincerely held religious beliefs, but we reject the notion that, to claim the protection of the Free Exercise Clause, one must be responding to the commands of a particular religious organization. Here, Frazee's refusal was based on a sincerely held religious belief. Under our cases, he was entitled to invoke First Amendment protection. REVERSED and REMANDED.

Case Questions

1. As the employer here, how could you stay within the law and still have a policy in the best interest of your company?

2. If you were Kelly Services, what would you have done to avoid a conflict with Frazee?

3. As an employer, would you be concerned about how you could tell when an employee had a right to be protected under the law and when an employee was simply trying to get out of work? What would you do about it?

Perhaps the single, most-asked question in this area is: "Must I accommodate the employee's religious conflict if it did not exist when the employee was hired?" The answer is yes. The duty attaches to the conflict itself, not to when the conflict arises.

Religious Conflicts

Workplace conflict between employee religious practices at odds with workplace policies is probably the most frequent type of religious discrimination case. That is, it is not so much that the employer dislikes a particular religion and refuses to hire members of that religion. Rather, it is that the employee may engage in some religious practice that is not compatible with the workplace. For instance, the employer may have a no-beard policy, but the employee's religion forbids shaving; the employer may have a policy forbidding the wearing of headgear, but the employee's

Exhibit 10–3   The Lord at Work

Mandatory prayer meetings pit Christian boss against atheist worker

Jake Townley can't understand it–why this atheist from Arizona complained about these weekly devotional meetings, why anyone would. It's *paid* work time. Nobody's asking him to do anything except show up, just like all Townley Manufacturing employees are required to do. The meetings only last half an hour. They're harmless. They've been a Townley tradition for 25 years.

Until this Louis Pelvas came along.

Pelvas, a machinist in the Townley plant in Arizona, objected to the prayer meetings. He filed a complaint of religious discrimination with the Equal Employment Opportunity Commission raising questions about religion in the workplace. Questions Jake Townley thinks the government has no right asking.

Townley is seated on one of about 50 metal folding chairs in the Townley Manufacturing Company workshop in Candler [Florida]. It is 7 A.M. Tuesday, time for the weekly devotional meeting held at this and five other Townley Manufacturing plants in the United States.

The working men file through the door slow and easy, the way people amble into church on Sundays. The preacher sits, Bible in hand, by the welding station. The meeting begins. A man strums a red electric guitar and sings: "I won't walk without Jesus and I won't talk without Jesus . . ."

After the song, one manager speaks briefly about production schedules. Another manager talks just as quickly about safety regulations. Then the preacher rests his large hands on the lectern.

"Good morning," he says. "Praise the Lord."

He points out "Brother and Sister Townley," the company owners, and speaks of their blessed mission of gospel-sharing and toolmaking. He begins conversationally, as if he were addressing the family at the dinner table, but then picks up steam. "God is the one what that breathes in us the breath of life, he made us, he created us, he loves us. . . ." The preacher's words rise from his belly, his voice swells. He cups his arms toward the ceiling. Tears moisten his cheeks.

The workers sit motionless, a sea of wooden faces. Twenty minutes pass. The preacher closes with a prayer. The men bow their heads.

Seconds later, the men are at their stations and Townley looks proud: That wasn't so bad, now was it?

The Townleys think they have a right to keep it that way.

But that may not be possible. The EEOC sued Townley Manufacturing, charging its policy of requiring attendance at devotional meetings violates Title VII of the Civil Rights Act of 1964.

Townley says the case will determine whether owners of private, for-profit companies can operate their businesses according to their religious beliefs.

The EEOC says Title VII requires employers to accommodate an employee's religious beliefs and practices unless it presents undue hardship.

All newly hired employees must read and sign an employee handbook, which states that all employees must attend weekly "non-denominational" services; missing them is grounds for termination. Profanity is also prohibited, and the handbook encourages employees to keep track of "how our politicians stand on various issues and to vote for those candidates who support a realistic and stable government policy toward business."

"We run the business according to Christian principles," Townley says. "Everyone may not agree with it, but we feel the Lord gave us the business and it's inseparable from what we do."

Pelvas says his family never went to church. "I was always brought up to the fact that religion and politics should never enter industry."

EXHIBIT 10–3   Concluded

If he had known the meetings would start in Eloy, [Arizona] he says, "I don't believe I would ever have taken the job."

Townley pressured the manager to comply with company policy, and pretty soon one atheist and a roomful of Hispanic Catholics got weekly doses of Bible readings. Pelvas asked to be allowed to work, instead, but was told to show up, even if he didn't pay attention.

Pelvas acquiesced. He listened to music from an ear plug attached to a radio. Sometimes he read. Company business was never discussed, he says. Nor were the services "non-denominational."

"It was strictly born-again services. There were three different preachers. All three of 'em would start off with what a bad person they was—alcohol, woman chaser—and they must have seen the light because they're all different now. I'm 60-some years old, and I haven't seen the light yet."

"I went along with 'em for quite a while until I got disgusted with the whole thing."

The other employees wouldn't object because they were afraid of being fired, Pelvas said. Besides, they didn't mind "listening to some yo-yo blabber away as long as they're gettin' paid for it—I can't blame 'em for that."

Two men, two views: America means freedom *of* religion; America means freedom *from* religion.

St. Petersburg Times, April 24, 1988, p. 1F.
Note: The EEOC decided in favor of Pelvas. 859 F.2d 610 (9th Cir. 1988).

religion requires the wearing of some sort of head cover; the employer may have a policy forbidding the wearing of long hair on males, but the employee's religion forbids the cutting of male hair except in certain limited circumstances; the employer may have a policy that all employees must work on Saturdays, but the employee's religious sabbath may be on Saturday and followers may be forbidden to work on the sabbath.

In fact, sometimes the conflict comes not with the employee's religion, but with that of the employer. In Exhibit 10–3 the atheist employee is upset at having to attend mandatory fundamentalist Christian workplace church services at the manufacturing plant in which he is employed.

As more and more employees come into the workplace who are not of the "traditional" religions with which an employer may be more familiar, employers will need to learn to effectively handle the religious differences which arise. The key is to make sure that the basis for the conflict is a religious one and then to try to work out an accommodation. Once the employer is aware of the conflict, the employer must attempt a good faith accommodation of the religious conflict and employee must assist in that attempted accommodation. If none can be worked out and the employer has tried everything available that does not present an undue hardship, then the employer has fulfilled his or her Title VII obligation and there is no liability, even if the employee's religious conflict cannot be accommodated. Of course, because of the diversity of religious conflicts that are possible, there is no single set of rules that can be given to handle all religious conflicts.

GOLDMAN V. WEINBERGER
475 U.S. 503 (1986)

A member of the military, an Orthodox Jew and ordained rabbi, brought suit against the Secretary of Defense claiming that application of Air Force regulation to prevent him from wearing his yarmulke infringed upon his First Amendment freedom to exercise his religious belief. The Supreme Court held that the First Amendment did not prohibit a regulation that prevented the wearing of a yarmulke by a member of the military while on duty and in uniform.

Rehnquist, J.

Petitioner S. Simcha Goldman contends that the Free Exercise Clause of the First Amendment to the United States Constitution permits him to wear a yarmulke while in uniform, notwithstanding an Air Force regulation mandating uniform dress for Air Force personnel. The District Court for the District of Columbia permanently enjoined the Air Force from enforcing its regulation against Goldman and from penalizing him for wearing his yarmulke. The Court of Appeals for the District of Columbia Circuit reversed on the ground that the Air Force's strong interest in discipline justified the strict enforcement of its uniform dress requirements. We granted certiorari because of the importance of the question and now affirm.

Goldman is an Orthodox Jew and ordained rabbi. In 1973, he was accepted into the Armed Forces Health Professions Scholarship Program and placed on inactive reserve status in the Air Force while he studied clinical psychology at Loyola University of Chicago. During his three years in the scholarship program, he received a monthly stipend and an allowance for tuition, books, and fees. After completing his Ph.D. in psychology, Goldman entered active service in the United States Air Force as a commissioned officer, in accordance with a requirement that participants in the scholarship program serve one year of active duty for each year of subsidized education. Goldman was stationed at March Air Force Base in Riverside, California, and served as a clinical psychologist at the mental health clinic on the base.

Until 1981, Goldman was not prevented from wearing his yarmulke on the base. He avoided controversy by remaining close to his duty station in the health clinic and by wearing his service cap over the yarmulke when out of doors. But in April 1981, after he testified as a defense witness at a court-martial wearing his yarmulke but not his service cap, opposing counsel lodged a complaint with Colonel Joseph Gregory, the Hospital Commander, arguing that Goldman's practice of wearing his yarmulke was a violation of Air Force Regulation (AFR) 35-10. This regulation states in pertinent part that "[h]eadgear will not be worn . . . [w]hile indoors except by armed security police in the performance of their duties."

Colonel Gregory informed Goldman that wearing a yarmulke while on duty does indeed violate AFR 35-10, and ordered him not to violate this regulation outside the hospital. Although virtually all of Goldman's time on the base was spent in the hospital, he refused. Later, after Goldman's attorney protested to the Air Force General Counsel, Colonel Gregory revised his order to prohibit Goldman from wearing the yarmulke even in the hospital. Goldman's request to report for duty in civilian clothing pending legal resolution of the issue was denied. The next day he received a formal letter of reprimand, and was warned that failure to obey AFR 35-10 could subject him to a court-martial. Colonel Gregory also withdrew a recommendation that Goldman's application to extend the term of his active service be approved, and substituted a negative recommendation. Goldman then sued the Secretary of Defense and others, claiming that the application of AFR 35-10 to prevent him from wearing his yarmulke infringed on his First Amendment freedom to exercise his religious beliefs.

Our review of military regulations challenged on First Amendment grounds is far more deferential than constitutional review of similar laws or regulations designed for civilian society. The military need not encourage debate or tolerate protest to the extent that such tolerance is required of the civilian state by the First Amendment; to accomplish its mission the military must foster instinctive obedience, unity, commitment, and esprit de corps. The essence of military service "is the subordination of the desires and interests of the individual to the needs of the service."

These aspects of military life do not, of course, render entirely nugatory in the military context the guarantees of the First Amendment. But "within the military community there is simply not the same [individual] autonomy as there is in the larger civilian community." In the context of the present case, when evaluating whether military needs justify a particular restriction on religiously motivated conduct, courts must give great deference to the professional judgment of military authorities concerning the relative importance of a particular military interest. Not only are courts "ill-equipped to determine the impact upon discipline that any particular intrusion upon military authority might have," but the military authorities have been charged by the Executive and Legislative Branches with carrying out our Nation's military policy. "[J]udicial deference . . . is at its apogee when legislative action under the congressional authority to raise and support armies and make rules and regulations for their governance is challenged."

The considered professional judgment of the Air Force is that the traditional outfitting of personnel in standardized uniforms encourages the subordination of personal preferences and identities in favor of the overall group mission. Uniforms encourage a sense of hierarchical unity by tending to eliminate outward individual distinctions except for those of rank. The Air Force considers them as vital during peacetime as during war because its personnel must be ready to provide an effective defense on a moment's notice; the necessary habits of discipline and unity must be developed in advance of trouble. We have acknowledged that "[t]he inescapable demands of military discipline and obedience to orders cannot be taught on battlefields; the habit of immediate compliance with military procedures and orders must be virtually reflex with no time for debate or reflection."

To this end, the Air Force promulgated AFR 35-10, a 190-page document, which states that "Air Force members will wear the Air Force uniform while performing their military duties, except when authorized to wear civilian clothes on duty." The rest of the document describes in minute detail all of the various items of apparel that must be worn as part of the Air Force uniform. It authorizes a few individualized options with respect to certain pieces of jewelry and hairstyle, but even these are subject to severe limitations. In general, authorized headgear may be worn only out of doors. Indoors, "[h]eadgear [may] not be worn . . . except by armed security police in the performance of their duties." A narrow exception to this rule exists for headgear worn during indoor religious ceremonies. In addition, military commanders may in their discretion permit visible religious headgear and other such apparel in designated living quarters and nonvisible items generally.

Goldman contends that the Free Exercise Clause of the First Amendment requires the Air Force to make an exception to its uniform dress requirements for religious apparel unless the accouterments create a "clear danger" of undermining discipline and esprit de corps. He asserts that in general, visible but "unobtrusive" apparel will not create such a danger and must therefore be accommodated. He argues that the Air Force failed to prove that a specific exception for his practice of wearing an unobtrusive yarmulke would threaten discipline. He contends that the Air Force's assertion to the contrary is mere ipse dixit [a bare assertion], with no support from actual experience or a scientific study in the record, and is contradicted by expert testimony that religious exceptions to the policy are in fact desirable and will increase morale by making the Air Force a more humane place.

But whether or not expert witnesses may feel that religious exceptions to AFR 35-10 are desirable is quite beside the point. The desirability of dress regulations in the military is decided by the appropriate military officials, and they are under no constitutional mandate to abandon their considered professional judgment. Quite obviously, to the extent the regulations do not permit the wearing of religious apparel such as a yarmulke, a practice described by Goldman as silent devotion akin to prayer, military life may be more objectionable for him and probably others. But the First Amendment does not require the military to accommodate such practices in the face of its view that they would detract from the uniformity sought by the dress regulations. The Air Force has drawn the line essentially between religious apparel that is visible and that which is not, and we hold that those portions of the regulations challenged here reasonably and evenhandedly regulate dress in the interest of the military's perceived need for uniformity. The First Amendment therefore does not prohibit them from being applied to Goldman even though their effect is to restrict the wearing of the headgear required by his religious beliefs. The judgment of the Court of Appeals is AFFIRMED.

Case Questions

1. Do you agree with the Court's decision? Explain.

2. What do you think of Goldman's argument that wearing the yarmulke will help morale? Does that seem a valid argument for permitting the apparel exception?

3. Can you think of other types of clothing that people may want to wear as part of their religious practice that may present the same situation as here? Do you understand why it should not be permitted? Explain.

We chose to include this case for several reasons. First, it presents a conflict between religious practice (wearing a yarmulke) and work (being a member of the military). It also allows you to see the US Supreme Court's position on matters military and how they interact with Title VII and other protective legislation. As we are discussing Title VII, students frequently ask us how the military can have the rules it has, which seem to be at odds with Title VII. Our answer is that the Court tends to view the military as being in a class all its own for most purposes. The need for cohesion, instant and unquestioning obedience, esprit de corps, morale, and other such interests as the Court discussed in the case, usually end up with the Court deferring to the military when there are conflicts, for the reasons set forth in the *Goldman* opinion.

We also wanted you to understand that the right to be free of religious discrimination is not absolute. There are limitations to the right where there may be overriding considerations such as the military cohesion in *Goldman* or the undue hardship in Title VII.

Not every conflict involving religion will necessarily be a religious conflict recognized by the law. In *Lumpkin* below, the legitimate nondiscriminatory basis for termination was not deemed a religious conflict at all, even though it involved religion to an extent.

LUMPKIN V. JORDAN
49 Cal. App. 4th 1223 (1996)

A minister who was a member of the San Francisco Human Rights Commission was terminated after making public statements to the press about homosexuality being an abomination, a position at odds with the work of the Commission. The minister sued the city for religious discrimination under California's civil rights laws (comparable to Title VII). The court held for the city, deciding that the termination was not based on religion, but rather on the minister's position being at odds with the position he held on the Commission.

Champlin, J.

This case concerns the alleged unlawful removal of Reverend Lumpkin from the City's Human Rights Commission (the Commission). Mayor Jordan, then Mayor of the City, appointed Reverend Lumpkin to serve as a member of the Commission. At the time of his appointment, Reverend Lumpkin was a Baptist minister who served as Pastor of the Ebenezer Baptist Church. Mayor Jordan and Reverend Lumpkin had known one another for over 15 years and, at the time of the appointment, Mayor Jordan was aware that Reverend Lumpkin was a Baptist minister.

Later the *San Francisco Chronicle* quoted Reverend Lumpkin as saying: "It's sad that people have AIDS and what have you, but it says right there in the scripture that the homosexual lifestyle is an abomination against God. So I have to preach that homosexuality is a sin." These remarks provoked a public controversy surrounding Reverend Lumpkin's membership on the Commission.

After meeting with Reverend Lumpkin, Mayor Jordan issued a press release announcing that he would not remove Reverend Lumpkin from the Commission. In this statement, Mayor Jordan stated that Reverend Lumpkin "has a solid and unambiguous record as a member of the Human Rights Commission. As a commissioner he has protected and advanced gay and lesbian civil rights."

In reaction to Mayor Jordan's announcement, the San Francisco Board of Supervisors adopted a resolution calling for Reverend Lumpkin's resignation or removal from the Commission. The resolution demanded that Mayor Jordan "restore public confidence in the role and mission of the Commission, especially with regards to the ability of the Commission to consider complaints and lead the community toward equality and respect for all lesbian and gay San Franciscans."

Reverend Lumpkin was interviewed during a live broadcast of a television news show, Mornings on 2. After the interviewer identified Reverend Lumpkin as a member of the Commission, he asked him if he believed homosexuality to be an "abomination." Reverend Lumpkin replied,

"Sure, I believe, I believe everything the Bible sayeth." The following exchange ensued:

"Interviewer: Leviticus also says that a man who sleeps with a man should be put to death. Do you believe that? Reverend Lumpkin: That's what it sayeth. Interviewer: Do you believe that? Reverend Lumpkin: That's—I said that's what the Book sayeth."

Later that day, after learning of the interview, Mayor Jordan asked Reverend Lumpkin to resign from the Commission. In a press release explaining his decision, Mayor Jordan stated: "While religious beliefs are constitutionally protected and cannot be the grounds to remove anyone from elected or appointed public office, the direct or indirect advocacy of violence is not, cannot and will not be condoned by this administration. . . . On the grounds of religious freedom and an unblemished record as a Human Rights Commissioner, I have supported Reverend Lumpkin for holding fundamentalist beliefs which are not my own. We part company when those beliefs imply that attacks against anyone can be justified by the scripture or on any other grounds."

Mayor Jordan met with Reverend Lumpkin, who refused to resign. After this meeting, Mayor Jordan announced his decision to remove Reverend Lumpkin from the Commission.

After his removal from the Commission, Reverend Lumpkin brought suit against Mayor Jordan, alleging that he had been terminated "solely because of his religious beliefs" in violation of the FEHA. The second cause of action alleged that defendants, acting under color of state law, deprived Reverend Lumpkin of the right to exercise his constitutionally protected religious beliefs as guaranteed by 42 United States Code section 1983.

Reverend Lumpkin's removal from the Commission did not violate his freedom of expression. The court reasoned that he was a policymaker with the Jordan administration and "Reverend Lumpkin's televised remarks regarding homosexuality could reasonably have been interpreted by the Mayor as undermining the very policies of the Commission to promote good will toward all people."

Reverend Lumpkin's removal did not violate his rights under the Free Exercise Clause. The court found that Mayor Jordan's interest in preventing disruption of the goals of his administration outweighed Reverend Lumpkin's right to religious expression. The court's opinion points out that "critical to this analysis is the fact that Reverend Lumpkin was not removed solely for exercising his constitutional rights. He is, and at all times was, free to hold and to profess his religious beliefs; however, when the expression of those beliefs clashed with the goals of the Jordan Administration and undermined the public confidence in the ability of the Commission to effect its goals, the Mayor was justified in removing him."

Finally, the court's order held that Reverend Lumpkin's removal did not violate the Establishment Clause. The court explained that Reverend Lumpkin's removal could not reasonably be construed as sending a message either endorsing or disapproving of religion and that "his removal was based on secular concerns." The court emphasized that Reverend Lumpkin "was not removed because he believed in the inerrancy of the Bible; rather, he was removed because his religious beliefs were at odds with the goals of the Commission and disrupted Mayor Jordan's administration." AFFIRMED.

Case Questions

1. Do you agree that this case was not about religious discrimination? Explain.

2. Can you think of some other way to have handled this matter? Explain.

3. Do you agree with the minister that he could continue to do his job with no problems, despite the feelings he expressed to the media? Explain.

Employer's Duty to Reasonably Accommodate

Unlike the other categories under Title VII, the prohibition against religious discrimination is not "absolute." An employer can discriminate against an employee for religious reasons if not doing so causes the employer undue hardship. When the employer discovers a religious conflict between the employer's policy and the employee's religion, the employer's first responsibility is to attempt accommodation. If this is not possible, the employer can implement the policy even though it has the effect of discriminating against the employee on the basis of religion.

The duty to reasonably accommodate is not a static concept. Due to the nature of religious conflicts and the fact that they can arise in all types of contexts and in many different ways, there is not one single action an employer must take to show that she or he has reasonably accommodated conflicting religious considerations. It depends on the circumstances and will vary from situation to situation. For example:

- The employer owns a sandwich shop. The employer's policy entitles employees to eat all the restaurant food they wish during their lunch break. Employee's religion does not allow eating meat. Aside from the meat used for sandwiches, the employer has little else, other than sandwich trimmings like lettuce and tomatoes. The employee alleges it is religious discrimination to provide the benefits of lunch that the employee cannot eat for religious reasons while other employees receive full free lunches. The duty to accommodate may be as simple as the employer arranging to have peanut butter and jelly, eggs, or a variety of vegetables or pasta available for the employee.

- The employer requires employees to work six days per week. An employee cannot work on Saturdays due to a religious conflict. The accommodation may be that the employee switches days with an employee who does not wish to work on Sundays—a day that the employee with the religious conflict is available to work.

- Employer grocery store has a policy requiring all counter clerks to be clean-shaven, to present the employer's view of a "clean-cut" image to the public. Employee cannot shave for religious reasons. The accommodation may be that the employer switches the employee to a job the employee can perform, which does not require public contact, such as stocking shelves or handling paperwork.

If it can be shown that the employer reasonably accommodated the employee, then the employer is relieved of liability under Title VII. In the *Wilson* case, the court found the accommodation to be reasonable, but also found that the employee's claim of the problematic activity was not based on religious requirements.

WILSON V. U.S. WEST COMMUNICATIONS
58 F.3d 1337 (8th Cir. 1995)

Employee was terminated when she refused to remove or cover a button she wore on her clothing depicting a graphic anti-abortion message which caused immediate and emotional reactions from coworkers. She brought suit against the employer claiming religious discrimination in violation of Title VII, claiming her religious "living witness" commitment required further accommodation. The court held that the employer reasonably accommodated the employee.

Gibson, J.

Wilson worked for U.S. West for nearly 20 years before U.S. West transferred her to another location as an information specialist, assisting U.S. West engineers in making and keeping records of the location of telephone cables. This facility had no dress code.

In late July 1990, Wilson, a Roman Catholic, made a religious vow that she would wear an anti-abortion button "until there was an end to abortion or until [she] could no longer fight the fight." The button was two inches in diameter and showed a color photograph of an eighteen to twenty-week old fetus. The button also contained the phrases "Stop Abortion," and "They're Forgetting Someone." Wilson chose this particular button because she wanted to be an instrument of God like the Virgin Mary. She believed that the Virgin Mary would have chosen this particular button. She wore the button at all times, unless she was sleeping or bathing. She believed that if she took off the button she would compromise her vow and lose her soul.

Wilson began wearing the button to work in August 1990. Another information specialist asked Wilson not to wear the button to a class she was teaching. Wilson explained her religious vow and refused to stop wearing the button. The button caused disruptions at work. Employees gathered to talk about the button. U.S. West identified Wilson's wearing of the button as a "time robbing" problem. Wilson acknowledged that the button

caused a great deal of disruption. A union representative told Wilson's supervisor, Mary Jo Jensen, that some employees threatened to walk off their jobs because of the button. Wilson's co-workers testified that they found the button offensive and disturbing for "very personal reasons," such as infertility problems, miscarriage, and death of a premature infant, unrelated to any stance on abortion or religion.

In early August 1990, Wilson met with her supervisors, Jensen and Gail Klein, five times. Jensen and Klein are also Roman Catholics against abortion. Jensen and Klein told Wilson of co-workers' complaints about the button and an anti-abortion T-shirt Wilson wore which also depicted a fetus. Jensen and Klein told Wilson that her co-workers were uncomfortable and upset and that some were refusing to do their work. Klein noted a 40 percent decline in the productivity of the information specialists since Wilson began wearing the button.

Wilson told her supervisors that she should not be singled out for wearing the button because the company had no dress code. She explained that she "just wanted to do [her] job," and suggested that co-workers offended by the button should be asked not to look at it. Klein and Jensen offered Wilson three options: (1) wear the button only in her work cubicle, leaving the button in the cubicle when she moved around the office; (2) cover the button while at work; or (3) wear a different button with the same message but without the photograph. Wilson responded that she could neither cover nor remove the button because it would break her promise to God to wear the button and be a "living witness." She suggested that management tell the other information specialists to "sit at their desks and do the job U.S. West was paying them to do."

On August 22, 1990, Wilson met with Klein, Jensen, and the union's chief steward. During the meeting, Klein again told Wilson that she could either wear the button only in her cubicle or cover the button. Klein explained that, if Wilson continued to wear the button to work, she would be sent home until she could come to work wearing proper attire.

In an August 27, 1990 letter, Klein reiterated Wilson's three options. He added that Wilson could use accrued personal and vacation time instead of reporting to work. Wilson filed suit but later dismissed the action when U.S. West agreed to allow her to return to work and wear the button pending an investigation by the Nebraska Equal Opportunity Commission.

Wilson returned to work on September 18, 1990, and disruptions resumed. Information specialists refused to go to group meetings with Wilson present. The employees complained that the button made them uneasy. Two employees filed grievances based on Wilson's button. Employees accused Jensen of harassment for not resolving the button issue to their satisfaction. Eventually, U.S. West told Wilson not to report to work wearing anything depicting a fetus, including the button or the T-shirt. U.S. West told Wilson again that she could cover or replace the button or wear it only in her cubicle. U.S. West sent Wilson home when she returned to work wearing the button and fired her for missing work unexcused for three consecutive days. Wilson sued U.S. West, claiming that her firing constituted religious discrimination.

The court considered the three offered accommodations and concluded that requiring Wilson to leave the button in her cubicle or to replace the button were not accommodations of Wilson's

sincerely held religious beliefs because: (1) removing the button at work violated Wilson's vow to wear the button at all times; and (2) replacing the button prohibited Wilson from wearing the particular button encompassed by her vow. However, the court concluded that requiring Wilson to cover the button while at work was a reasonable accommodation. The court based this determination on its factual finding that Wilson's vow did not require her to be a living witness. The court reasoned that covering the button while at work complied with Wilson's vow but also reduced office turmoil. The court also concluded that, even if Wilson's vow required Catholic Voice, she said nothing about being a living witness. Klein testified that he never heard Wilson use the word witness in explaining her vow, but rather, that he understood Wilson's vow was to "wear the button until abortions were ended." Accordingly, the district court's finding is supported by the evidence and is not clearly erroneous.

We next consider Wilson's argument that the district court erred as a matter of law in concluding that U.S. West offered to reasonably accommodate Wilson's religious views. Wilson argues that her religious beliefs did not require her or any other employee to miss or rearrange work schedules, as typically causes a reasonable accommodation dispute. She argues that it was her co-workers' response to her beliefs that caused the workplace disruption, not her wearing the button. Wilson contends that U.S. West should have focused its attention on her co-workers, not her. Wilson's brief states: "Quite frankly, . . . Klein and Jensen should have simply instructed the troublesome co-workers to ignore the button and get back to work."

The district court, however, succinctly answered Wilson's argument: Klein was unable to persuade the co-workers to ignore the button. Although Wilson's religious beliefs did not create scheduling conflicts or violate dress code or safety rules, Wilson's position would require U.S. West to allow Wilson to impose her beliefs as she chooses. Wilson concedes the button caused substantial disruption at work. To simply instruct Wilson's co-workers that they must accept Wilson's insistence on wearing a particular depiction of a fetus as part of her religious beliefs is antithetical to the concept of reasonable accommodation.

Moreover, U.S. West did not oppose Wilson's religious beliefs, but rather, was concerned with the photograph. The record demonstrates that U.S. West did not object to various other religious articles that Wilson had in her work cubicle or to another employee's anti-abortion button. It was the color photograph of the fetus that offended Wilson's co-workers, many of whom were reminded of circumstances unrelated to abortion. Indeed, many employees who opposed Wilson's button shared Wilson's religion and view on abortion.

Wilson also argues that requiring her to cover the button is not a reasonable accommodation. She argues that the accommodation offered required her to abandon her religious beliefs, and therefore, that the accommodation was no accommodation at all. Having affirmed the finding that Wilson's religious vow did not require her to be a living witness, we summarily reject this argument. U.S. West's proposal allowed Wilson to comply with her vow to wear the button and respected the desire of co-workers not to look at the button. Hence, the district court did not err in holding that U.S. West reasonably accommodated Wilson's religious beliefs.

Finally, Wilson argues that the district court erred in concluding that her suggested proposals would be an undue hardship for U.S. West.

The Supreme Court held that an employer is not required to select the employee's proposal of reasonable accommodation and that any reasonable accommodation by the employer is sufficient to comply with the statute. "The employer violates the statute unless it 'demonstrates that [it] is unable to reasonably accommodate . . . an employee's . . . religious observance or practice without undue hardship on the conduct of the employer's business.'" When the employer reasonably accommodates the employee's religious beliefs, the statutory inquiry ends. The employer need not show that the employee's proposed accommodations would cause an undue hardship. Undue hardship is at issue "only where the employer claims that it is unable to offer any reasonable accommodation without such hardship."

Because we hold that U.S. West offered Wilson a reasonable accommodation, our inquiry ends, and we need not consider Wilson's argument that her suggested accommodations would not cause undue hardship.

We recognize that this case typifies workplace conflicts which result when employees hold strong views about emotionally charged issues. We reiterate that Title VII does not require an employer to allow an employee to impose his religious views on others. The employer is only required to reasonably accommodate an employee's religious views. AFFIRMED.

Case Questions

1. What do you think of the co-worker reaction to Wilson's button? Does it seem reasonable? Explain.

2. What do you think of Wilson's response to her supervisors that those who did not like the button should simply be told not to look at it? Does this seem to be a reasonable response for the employer to make? Explain.

3. If you were the employer here, what would you have done about Wilson?

If an accommodation cannot be found, as *Williams,* below, demonstrates, the employer's duty is discharged. It is the basis for opening scenarios 1 and 2. The important factor is to attempt an accommodation rather than simply dismissing the conflict without trying.

① Scenario ② Scenario

WILLIAMS V. SOUTHERN UNION GAS COMPANY
529 F.2d 483 (10th Cir. 1976)

Employee was terminated for not working on Saturday. His reason for not doing so was that it was against his religion to work on his sabbath. The court found that accommodating this religious conflict would cause the employer an undue hardship; therefore the termination did not violate Title VII.

McWilliams, J.

When Williams went to work for Southern Union in 1962 he was informed that it was a company policy that all employees should be available for work seven days a week 24 hours per day inasmuch as it was a public utility and was obligated to provide continuous and uninterrupted natural gas service to the general public. It was also Southern Union's policy, however, to schedule its employees for only five days of work each week, eight hours per day. Williams in 1962 did not belong to any church and hence was under no prohibition, religious or otherwise, from working any day in the week.

During the fall of 1969 Williams became a member of the Worldwide Church of God. He informed his supervisor of his conversion and advised him that he would no longer be able to work between Friday at sundown and Saturday at sundown. The supervisor, Al Dean, explained that it would be difficult to promise that Williams would never be called on to work on a Saturday, but that he would do what he could. Coincidentally, or otherwise, at the time of his conversion Williams' regular work week was from Sunday through Thursday, with both Friday and Saturday off. It would appear that for obvious reasons most all employees desired to have Saturday off. At his supervisor's suggestion Williams checked back with his minister and was informed that he could work on Saturdays if there were an emergency, but that since this was a matter between Williams and his God, he (Williams), and not his employer, would have to make the decision as to whether a true emergency existed.

From the date of his conversion in the fall of 1969 until October 3, 1970, Williams was never asked to work on Saturday. During the fall of 1970 Williams was assigned to work on the Dogie Canyon project in northwest New Mexico, a rather isolated location. This was a new pipeline about 25 miles long that was to expand the capacity of the pipeline system which took natural gas from the production area of the San Juan Basin and supplied the Los Alamos–Santa Fe area with natural gas. This project was running somewhat behind schedule and Southern Union, at least, was of the view that the pipeline had to be completed, purged of air, and brought up to pressure by Saturday, October 3, 1970.

On Wednesday, September 30, 1970, Williams went to Dean and told him that the next day, Thursday, was a special religious holiday in his church and that he would have to have the day off. Dean agreed that Williams could take Thursday off, but explained that the pipeline would have to be pressured up by Saturday, and that if the work were not completed by Friday night Williams would have to work Saturday. Williams testified that he made no protest at this time about the possibility of Saturday work, as he thought the project might very possibly be completed by Friday, and any confrontation would thereby be avoided.

Williams took Thursday off. Unfortunately for Williams, the job was not completed on Friday, and Friday evening Williams called Dean at the latter's home and told Dean that he would not report for work on Saturday morning, as he had been directed. Dean's response was that if Williams didn't show up he would be fired. Dean himself was scheduled to go on vacation starting Saturday. When Williams didn't show up for work on Saturday, Dean delayed the start of his vacation and completed the work himself. There was no one else with the expertise who could be called. It was in this factual setting that Dean fired Williams.

42 U.S.C. 2000e-2(a) provides that it is an unlawful employment practice for an employer to discriminate against an employee because of his religion. Under a regulation promulgated in 1966 an employer was allowed to establish a "normal work week" which would be generally applicable to all employees even though such would not operate uniformly in its effect upon the religious observances of all employees. In 1967 the following regulation which now appears as 29 C.F.R. 1605.1 (1975) was promulgated:

> Observation of the Sabbath and other religious holidays.
>
> (a) Several complaints filed with the Commission have raised the question whether it is discrimination on account of religion to discharge or refuse to hire employees who regularly observe Friday evening and Saturday, or some other day of the week, as the Sabbath or who observe certain special religious holidays during the year and, as a consequence, do not work on such days.

> (b) The Commission believes that the duty not to discriminate on religious grounds, required by section 703(a)(1) of the Civil Rights Act of 1964, includes an obligation on the part of the employer to make reasonable accommodations to the religious needs of employees and prospective employees where such accommodations can be made without undue hardship on the conduct of the employer's business. Such undue hardship, for example, may exist where the employee's needed work cannot be performed by another employee of substantially similar qualifications during the period of absence of the Sabbath observer.

> (c) Because of the particularly sensitive nature of discharging or refusing to hire an employee or applicant on account of his religious beliefs, the employer has the burden of proving that an undue hardship renders the required accommodations to the religious needs of the employee unreasonable.

The foregoing regulation was given legislative approval when Congress amended the definition of religion, as that term is read in the Act, to read as follows:

> The term "religion" includes all aspects of religious observance and practice, as well as belief, unless an employer demonstrates that he is unable to reasonably accommodate to an employee's or prospective employee's religious observance or practice without undue hardship on the conduct of the employer's business. 42 U.S.C. 2000e(j).

Under the applicable statute and regulations the question before the trial court was whether Southern Union demonstrated that it was unable to reasonably accommodate to Williams' religious practice without undue hardship in the conduct of its business. The key phrases are "reasonably accommodate" and "undue hardship." The trial court's findings are not clearly erroneous and we affirm.

Most of the civil rights cases concerning those who celebrate the Sabbath on Saturday involve situations where the employer attempts to compel the employee to work on Saturdays as a part of his normal work week. Such is not true in the instant case. On the contrary Williams' normal work week was Sunday through Thursday. Furthermore, Southern Union did not ask Williams to perform work on a Saturday until approximately one year after his conversion. Williams' boss earlier explained that he could not promise Williams that he would never be asked to work on Saturday, and that he might well be asked to work in an emergency situation. The very nature of Southern Union's business required that service be available to the public 24 hours a day, 7 days per week. Someone was going to have to work on Saturdays, even though all employees understandably preferred Saturday off. Indeed, Williams himself recognized that his religion did not preclude him from working on Saturdays in the event of a special emergency. However, Williams insisted that he, rather than his employer, had the exclusive right to determine just what constituted an emergency.

Getting down to the events which immediately preceded Williams' discharge. Southern Union was engaged in certain pipeline construction which it felt had to be completed by Saturday, October 3, 1970. The record is such as to permit the inference that completion of the pipeline by that date was of critical importance. And such fact we deem to be of great significance and distinguishes the instant case from other cases cited to us by counsel, i.e., we are not concerned here with the employer's effort to compel Williams to work on a Saturday as a part of his normal work week; rather this is a situation where the employer was faced with an emergency situation in an isolated work area where there was no reserve of manpower who were qualified to complete the project and could be called in on a moment's notice. Williams, apparently without giving notice advised his boss on Wednesday that he was taking off Thursday, a regular work day, for a special religious holiday. Whether this absence in anywise contributed to the failure to complete the project by Friday, is not disclosed by the record. In any event, the project was not completed by Friday and it was only in this circumstance that Southern Union for the first time asked Williams to work on Saturday.

When Williams refused, his boss had to delay his long scheduled vacation in which he was to meet someone from out of town at a remote location for an elk hunt, and he completed the job himself.

The phrases "reasonably accommodate" and "undue hardship" are relative terms and cannot be given any hard and fast meaning. In a sense the case boils down to a determination as to whether Southern Union acted reasonably under all the circumstances. On the one hand it had a duty to at least try to accommodate Williams' religious practices. On the other hand it also had a duty not only to serve the consuming public on a continuous and uninterrupted basis but also to adhere to employment practices that were fair to its other employees. In our view whether Southern Union in the instant case acted in a reasonable manner is a matter upon which reasonable minds might conceivably differ. Such fact, however, does not permit us to substitute our judgment for that of the trial court. It was the trial judge who heard the testimony and saw the various witnesses. He is the one who draws the inferences and finds the facts. He found that to have accommodated William's refusal to work on Saturday, October 3, 1970, would have placed an undue hardship on the Southern Gas and the conduct of its business, and as a result, Southern was justified in discharging Williams because of his refusal to work. In such circumstances we should not disturb his determination of the matter. Judgment AFFIRMED.

Case Questions

1 Do you agree with the court that the employer's duty was discharged in this case?

2. If you had been the employer, what would you have done when Williams came to you after his conversion, and later (if you decided to keep him on) when he requested the Thursday off?

3. As an employer, what questions would you ask yourself before deciding on a policy to handle religious conflicts?

Even where an employee's activity is religiously based, it need not be accommodated if doing so presents real problems for the employer. In *Chalmers,* below, the court refused to find a basis for accommodation, even though the employee claimed she was doing what her religion dictated she do.

CHALMERS V. TULON COMPANY OF RICHMOND
101 F. 3d 1012 (4th Cir. 1996)

The supervisory employee sued for religious discrimination and a failure to accommodate after being terminated for sending employees letters at home about their personal and religious lives. One employee received the letter while ill at home on leave after delivering a baby out of wedlock, and the other employee's wife opened the letter and became distraught because she thought the references in the letter meant her husband was having an affair. The court held that there was no duty to accommodate the terminated employee's religious practice of sending such letters.

Motz, J.

Chalmers, a supervisor, has been a Baptist all of her life, and in June 1984 became an evangelical Christian. At that time, she accepted Christ as her personal savior and determined to go forth and do work for him. As an evangelical Christian, Chalmers believes she should share the gospel and looks for opportunities to do so.

Chalmers felt that her supervisor, LaMantia, respected her, generally refraining from using profanity around her, while around other employees who did not care, "he would say whatever he wanted to say." She felt that she and LaMantia had a "personal relationship" and that she could talk to him. Chalmers stated that "in the past we have talked about God." Chalmers further testified that "starting off" she and LaMantia had discussed religion about "everytime he came to the service center . . . maybe every three months" but "then, towards the end maybe not as frequently." LaMantia never discouraged these conversations, expressed discomfort with them, or indicated that they were improper. In one of these conversations,

LaMantia told Chalmers that three people had approached him about accepting Christ.

Two or three years after this conversation, Chalmers "knew it was time for [LaMantia] to accept God." She believed LaMantia had told customers information about the turnaround time for a job when he knew that information was not true. Chalmers testified that she was "led by the Lord" to write LaMantia and tell him "there were things he needed to get right with God, and that was one thing that . . . he needed to get right with him."

Accordingly, on Labor Day, September 6, 1993, Chalmers mailed the following letter to LaMantia at his home:

Dear Rich:

The reason I'm writing you is because the Lord wanted me to share somethings [sic] with you. After reading this letter you do not have to give me a call, but talk to God about everything.

One thing the Lord wants you to do is get your life right with him. The Bible says in Romans 10:9vs that if you confess with your mouth the Lord Jesus and believe in your heart that God hath raised him from the dead, thou shalt be saved. vs 10 - For with the heart man believeth unto righteousness, and with the mouth confession is made unto salvation. The two verse are [sic] saying for you to get right with God now.

The last thing is, you are doing somethings [sic] in your life that God is not please [sic] with and He wants you to stop. All you have to do is go to God and ask for forgiveness before it's too late.

I wrote this letter at home so if you have a problem with it you can't relate it to work.

I have to answer to God just like you do, so that's why I wrote you this letter. Please take heed before it's too late.

In his name,
Charita Chalmers

On September 10, 1993 when Chalmers' letter arrived at LaMantia's home, he was out of town on Tulon business and his wife opened and read the letter in his absence. Mrs. LaMantia became distraught, interpreting the references to her husband's improper conduct as indicating that he was committing adultery. In tears, she called Chalmers and asked her if LaMantia was having an affair with someone in the New Hampshire area where LaMantia supervised another Tulon facility. Mrs. LaMantia explained that three years before she and LaMantia had separated because of his infidelity. Chalmers told Mrs. LaMantia that she did not know about any affair because she was in the Richmond area. When Mrs. LaMantia asked her what she had meant by writing that there was something in LaMantia's life that "he needed to get right with God," Chalmers explained about the turnaround time problem. Mrs. LaMantia responded that she would take the letter and rip it up so LaMantia could not read it. Chalmers answered, "Please don't do that, the Lord led me to send this to Rich, so let him read it." The telephone conversation then ended.

Mrs. LaMantia promptly telephoned her husband, interrupting a Tulon business presentation, to accuse him of infidelity. LaMantia, in turn, called the Richmond office and asked to speak with Chalmers; she was in back and by the time she reached the telephone, LaMantia had hung up. Chalmers then telephoned the LaMantias' home and, when she failed to reach anyone, left a message on the answering machine that she was sorry "if the letter offended" LaMantia or his wife and that she "did not mean to offend him or make him upset about the letter."

LaMantia also telephoned Craig A. Faber, Vice President of Administration at Tulon. LaMantia told Faber that the letter had caused him personal anguish and placed a serious strain on his marriage. LaMantia informed Faber that he felt he could no longer work with Chalmers. LaMantia recommended that Tulon management terminate Chalmers' employment.

While investigating LaMantia's complaint, Faber discovered that Chalmers had sent a second letter, on the same day as she sent the letter to LaMantia, to another Tulon employee. That employee, Brenda Combs, worked as a repoint operator in the Richmond office and Chalmers was her direct supervisor. Chalmers knew that Combs was convalescing at her home, suffering from an undiagnosed illness after giving birth out of wedlock. Chalmers sent Combs the following letter:

Brenda,

You probably do not want to hear this at this time, but you need the Lord Jesus in your life right now.

One thing about God, He doesn't like when people commit adultery. You know what you did is wrong, so now you need to go to God and ask for forgiveness.

Let me explain something about God. He's a God of Love and a God of Wrath. When people sin against Him, He will allow things to happen to them or their family until they open their eyes and except [sic] Him. God can put a sickness on you that no doctor could ever find out what it is. I'm not saying this is what happened to you, all I'm saying is get right with God right now. Romans 10:9;10vs says that is [sic] you confess with your mouth the Lord Jesus and believe in your heart that God has raised him from the dead thou shalt be saved. For with the heart man believeth unto righteousness; and with the mouth confession is made unto salvation. All I'm saying is you need to invite God into your heart and live a life for Him and things in your life will get better.

That's not saying you are not going to have problems but it's saying you have someone to go to.

Please take this letter in love and be obedient to God.

In his name,

Charita Chalmers

Upon receiving the letter Combs wept. Faber discussed the letter with Combs who told him that she had been "crushed by the tone of the letter." Combs believed that Chalmers implied that "an immoral lifestyle" had caused her illness and found Chalmers' letter "cruel." Combs, in a later, unsworn statement, asserted that although the letter "upset her" it did not "offend" her or "damage her working relationship" with Chalmers.

Faber consulted with other members of upper management and concluded that the letters caused a negative impact on working relationships, disrupted the workplace, and inappropriately invaded employee privacy. On behalf of Tulon, Faber then sent Chalmers a memorandum, informing her that she was terminated from her position. The memorandum stated in relevant part:

> We have decided to terminate your employment with Tulon Co. effective today, September 21, 1993. Our decision is based on a serious error in judgment you made in sending letters to LaMantia and Combs, which criticized their personal lives and beliefs. The letters offended them, invaded their privacy, and damaged your work relationships, making it too difficult for you to continue to work here.
>
> We expect all of our employees to show good judgment, especially those in supervisory positions, such as yours. We would hope you can learn from this experience and avoid similar mistakes in the future.

As a result of the preceding events, Chalmers filed suit, alleging that Tulon discriminated against her based on her religion, in violation of Title VII. She contended that her letter writing constituted protected religious activity that Tulon, by law, should have accommodated with a lesser punishment than discharge.

In a religious accommodation case, an employee can establish a claim even though she cannot show that other (unprotected) employees were treated more favorably or cannot rebut an employer's legitimate, non-discriminatory reason for her discharge. This is because an employer must, to an extent, actively attempt to accommodate an employee's religious expression or conduct even if, absent the religious motivation, the employee's conduct would supply a legitimate ground for discharge.

Tulon's proffered reasons for discharging Chalmers—because her letters, which criticized her fellow employees' personal lives and beliefs, invaded the employees' privacy, offended them and damaged her working relationships—are legitimate and nondiscriminatory. Examination of the letters indicates that Chalmers knew that her conduct might distress her co-workers (e.g., her statement in the letter to Combs—"You probably do not want to hear this"). Additionally, the damage to her working relationship with LaMantia, arising from the marital discord her letter caused, is attributable to Chalmers whether or not it was intended or foreseeable (had she not invaded LaMantia's privacy by sending the letter to his home and included vague references to immoral conduct, Mrs. LaMantia would not have been upset).

To establish a prima facie religious accommodation claim, a plaintiff must establish that: "(1) he or she has a bona fide religious belief that conflicts with an employment requirement; (2) he or she informed the employer of this belief; (3) he or she was disciplined for failure to comply with the conflicting employment requirement."

Chalmers has alleged that she holds bona fide religious beliefs that caused her to write the letters. Tulon offers no evidence to the contrary. The parties agree that Tulon fired Chalmers because she wrote the letters. Accordingly, Chalmers has satisfied the first and third elements of the prima facie test. However, in other equally important respects, Chalmers' accommodation claim fails.

Chalmers cannot satisfy the second element of the prima facie test. She has forecast no evidence that she notified Tulon that her religious beliefs required her to send personal, disturbing letters to her co-workers. Therefore she did not allow the company any sort of opportunity to attempt reasonable accommodation of her beliefs.

Chalmers concedes that she did not expressly notify Tulon that her religion required her to write letters like those at issue here to her co-workers, or request that Tulon accommodate her conduct. Nonetheless, for several reasons, she contends that such notice was unnecessary in this case.

Initially, Chalmers asserts that Tulon never explicitly informed her of a company policy against writing religious letters to fellow employees at their homes and so she had "no reason to request an accommodation." However, companies cannot be expected to notify employees explicitly of all types of conduct that might annoy co-workers, damage working relationships, and thereby provide grounds for discharge. As noted previously, Chalmers implicitly acknowledged in the letters themselves that they might distress her co-workers. Moreover, she conceded that, as a supervisor, she had a responsibility to "promote harmony in the workplace."

Although a rule justifying discharge of an employee because she has disturbed co-workers requires careful application in the religious discrimination context (many religious practices might be perceived as "disturbing" to others), Chalmers, particularly as a supervisor, is expected to know that sending personal, distressing letters to co-workers' homes, criticizing them for assertedly ungodly, shameful conduct, would violate employment policy. Accordingly, the failure of the company to expressly forbid supervisors from disturbing other employees in this way, provides Chalmers with no basis for failing to notify Tulon that her religious beliefs require her to write such letters.

Alternatively, Chalmers contends that the notoriety of her religious beliefs within the company put it on notice of her need to send these letters. In her view, Chalmers satisfied the notice requirement because Tulon required "only enough information about an employee's religious needs to permit the employer to understand the existence of a conflict between the employee's religious practices and the employer's job requirements."

Knowledge that an employee has strong religious beliefs does not place an employer on notice that she might engage in any religious activity, no matter how unusual. Chalmers concedes that she did not know of any other employee who had ever written distressing or judgmental letters to co-workers before, and that nothing her co-workers had said or done indicated that such letters were acceptable. Accordingly, any knowledge Tulon may have possessed regarding Chalmers' beliefs could not reasonably have put it on notice that she would write and send accusatory letters to co-workers' homes.

Chalmers also contends that the letters themselves provided notice that her religious beliefs compelled her to write them. But giving notice to co-workers at the same time as an employee violates employment requirements is insufficient to provide adequate notice to the employer and to shield the employee's conduct.

In a similar vein, Chalmers appears to contend that because Tulon was necessarily aware of the religious nature of the letters after her co-workers received them and before her discharge, Tulon should have attempted to accommodate her by giving her a sanction less than a discharge, such as a warning. This raises a false issue. There is nothing in Title VII that requires employers to give lesser punishments to employees who claim, after they violate company rules (or at the same time), that their religion caused them to transgress the rules.

Part of the reason for the advance notice requirement is to allow the company to avoid or limit any "injury" an employee's religious conduct may cause. Additionally, the refusal even to attempt to accommodate an employee's religious requests, prior to the employee's violation of employment rules and sanction, provides some indication, however slight, of improper motive on the employer's part. The proper issue, therefore, is whether Chalmers made Tulon aware, prior to her letter writing, that her religious beliefs would cause her to send the letters. Since it is clear that she did not, her claims fail.

In sum, Chalmers has not pointed to any evidence that she gave Tulon—either directly or indirectly—advance notice of her need for accommodation. For this reason, Chalmers has failed to establish a prima facie case of discrimination under the religious accommodation theory.

If we had concluded that Chalmers had established a prima facie case, Chalmers' religious accommodation claim would nonetheless fail. This is so because Chalmers' conduct is not the type that an employer can possibly accommodate, even with notice.

Chalmers concedes in the letters themselves that she knew the letters to her co-workers, accusing them of immoral conduct (in the letter to Combs, suggesting that Combs' immoral conduct caused her illness), might cause them distress. Even if Chalmers had notified Tulon expressly that her religious beliefs required her to write such letters, i.e. that she was "led by the Lord" to write them, Tulon was without power under any circumstances to accommodate Chalmers' need.

Typically, religious accommodation suits involve religious conduct, such as observing the Sabbath, wearing religious garb, etc., that result in indirect and minimal burdens, if any, on other employees. An employer can often accommodate such needs without inconveniencing or unduly burdening other employees.

In a case like the one at hand, however, where an employee contends that she has a religious need to impose personally and directly on fellow employees, invading their privacy and criticizing their personal lives, the employer is placed between a rock and a hard place. If Tulon had the power to authorize Chalmers to write such letters, and if Tulon had granted Chalmers' request to

write the letters, the company would subject itself to possible suits from Combs and LaMantia claiming that Chalmers' conduct violated their religious freedoms or constituted religious harassment. Chalmers' supervisory position at the Richmond office heightens the possibility that Tulon (through Chalmers) would appear to be imposing religious beliefs on employees.

Thus, even if Chalmers had notified Tulon that her religion required her to send the letters at issue here to her co-workers, Tulon would have been unable to accommodate that conduct.

We do not in any way question the sincerity of Chalmers' religious beliefs or practices. However, it is undisputed that Chalmers failed to notify Tulon that her religious beliefs led her to send personal, disturbing letters to her fellow employees accusing them of immorality. It is also undisputed that the effect of a letter on one of the recipients, LaMantia's wife, whether intended or not, caused a co-worker, LaMantia, great stress and caused him to complain that he could no longer work with Chalmers. Finally, it is undisputed that another employee, Combs, told a company officer that Chalmers' letter upset her (although she later claimed that her working relationship with Chalmers was unaffected). Under these facts, Chalmers cannot establish a religious accommodation claim. Accordingly, the district court's order granting summary judgment to Tulon is AFFIRMED.

Case Questions

1. Is there any way the employer could have avoided this situation? Explain.

2. If the employee had initially told the employer of her plan to write the letters and the employer had told her not to send them, would the outcome be any different if she had done so anyway?

3. What would you have done if your employee's wife called as Ms. LaMantia did?

Employee's Duty to Cooperate in Accommodation

The US Supreme Court has held that, in attempting to accommodate the employee, all that is required is that the employer make any reasonable accommodation and this need not necessarily be the *most* reasonable accommodation. The employee must also be reasonable in considering accommodation alternatives. In *Vargas,* which follows, the employer attempted to accommodate the employee's conflict and the employee refused to compromise. The employer's only alternative may involve demoting the employee. This is not forbidden if all other alternatives present the employer with an undue hardship. EEOC and courts will look to the following factors in determining whether the employer has successfully borne the burden of reasonably accommodating the employee's religious conflict:

- Whether the employer made an attempt at accommodation.
- The size of the employer's workforce.
- The type of job in which the conflict is present.
- The employer's checking with other employees to see if anyone was willing to assist in the accommodation.
- The cost of accommodation.
- The administrative aspects of accommodation.

Each factor will be considered and weighed as appropriate for the circumstances. If on balance the employer has considered the factors appropriate for the employer's particular circumstances and accommodation was not possible, there is usually no liability for religious discrimination.

VARGAS V. SEARS, ROEBUCK & COMPANY
1998 U.S. Dist. LEXIS 21148 (E.D. Mich. 1998)

A Mexican-American who practiced traditional Native American religion, which considers the wearing of long hair on men to be sacred, sued his employer when he was terminated for refusing to cut his hair or to wear it tucked into his shirt as an accommodation. The court held that the employee was required to try to help in making the accommodation, and the employee had not done so. The court therefore granted the employer's motion to dismiss the employee's complaint.

Rosen, J.

Vargas was employed as a salesperson in Ann Arbor, Michigan's Briarwood Mall Sears store from October 1994 until February 1996. He worked on the selling floor in the Sears "Brand Central" home electronics department. When he was hired in the fall of 1994, Vargas was given a copy of the "Sears Associate Handbook," which provides, in pertinent part that all associates were to be neatly dressed in professional, businesslike clothing and for men, beards and contemporary hair styles are acceptable, but should be maintained in a neat, trimmed manner. When Vargas was hired by Sears in the fall of 1994, his hair was collar-length, and therefore, according to Sears, in compliance with store policy.

Vargas' supervisor Kevin Jones confronted Vargas about his hair in late summer 1995 when Vargas had his hair in a short pony tail. Jones did not discipline or direct Vargas to do anything about his hair, but rather, merely advised him that Walter Crockrel, the General Store Manager, did not approve of male salespersons wearing their hair in ponytails. Vargas did not tell Mr. Jones that wearing his hair long or in a ponytail was part of his Native American religion.

Vargas testified in his deposition that he adheres to the practices and customs of Native American religion, that he participates in Native American religious ceremonies, including conducting sweat lodge ceremonies. He further testified that in Native American religious practice, many of the beliefs and practices are "personal," and although long hair is not a requirement of his religion, he believes that the practice of Native American religion is dependent upon "your own spiritual development and the sacrifices you want to make for that." Shortly after Jones had this conversation with Vargas, Jones was replaced by Zerry Rue as Vargas' supervisor.

Zerry Rue addressed Vargas' hair with him in October 1995 upon the direction of Walter Crockrel. On October 25, 1995 Rue gave Vargas a memo stating that his ponytail and hair length were not in compliance with Sears personal appearance policies, and that he had until November 1st to bring himself within compliance with the policies. It was in connection with Rue's memo that Sears was informed that Vargas objected to Sears' hair length policy on religious grounds. On October 30, 1995, Vargas' attorney, Jane Bassett, wrote Crockrel that

> [Vargas] is of Mexican-American descent and he practices traditional Native American reli-

gion. Traditionally, growing the hair long has sacred significance in Native American religion. A policy which unequivocally prohibits male employees to have long hair discriminates against men who practice traditional Native American religion.

Upon becoming aware that Vargas' religious beliefs precluded him from cutting his hair, Mr. Crockrel, Mr. Rue and Susan Wisniewski, Sears' Human Resources Director, met with Vargas in the first week of November 1995 in an attempt to accommodate his religious beliefs, and asked him to tuck his hair into the collar of his shirt or jacket. Sears had used this accommodation with another Native American employee, Tony Goulet, who also worked at the Briarwood Mall store.

Vargas flatly refused to even attempt to tuck his hair in. He stated "I felt that it was an inhumane accommodation that was not reasonable . . . It . . . put me in a position of ridicule and . . . didn't allow a conducive position for my spirit to be, you know, free. I felt that I was being made to do something that I didn't feel comfortable doing. I felt that this was another form of religious oppression. . . ."

At his deposition, Vargas, whose hair is now nearly waist-length, took the position that tucking his hair into his collar, no less than cutting his hair, would violate his religious convictions. He actually testified that any demand made upon him would violate his religious beliefs. It is undisputed, however, that during the course of his employment Vargas never told his employer that tucking his hair into his collar would violate his religious beliefs.

Despite Vargas' refusal to attempt to comply with Sears' proposed accommodation, Sears did not immediately terminate his employment. Rather, he was urged by his supervisor to go home and reconsider his position. Vargas eventually chose not to comply with Sears' proposed accommodation and thereby terminated his employment. At no time did Vargas offer any alternatives, but instead demanded that he be allowed to work and wear his hair any way he wanted.

In order for an employee to proceed with a claim of religious discrimination, he must first establish a prima facie case by establishing that (1) he holds a sincere religious belief that conflicts with an employment requirement; (2) he has informed the employer about the conflict; and (3) he was discharged or disciplined for failing to comply with the conflicting employment requirement. If an employee establishes a prima facie case, the burden shifts to the employer to show that it offered a reasonable accommodation to the employee or that it could reasonably accommodate the employee without incurring undue hardship.

Although the burden is on the employer to accommodate the employee's religious needs, the employee must make some effort to cooperate with an employer's attempt at accommodation. Where an employee "will not attempt to . . . cooperate with his employer in its conciliatory efforts, he may forgo the right to have his beliefs accommodated by his employer." An employee cannot shirk his duties to try to accommodate himself or to cooperate with his employer in reaching an accommodation by a mere recalcitrant citation of religious precepts. Nor can he thereby shift all responsibility for accommodation to his employer. Where an employee refuses to attempt to accommodate his own beliefs or to cooperate with his employer's attempt to reach a reasonable accommodation, he may render accommodation impossible. Moreover, any reasonable accommodation fulfills the employer's duty. The employee cannot reject the accommodation simply because he desires an alternative accommodation.

In this case, Vargas has not established a prima facie case of failure to accommodate. While Sears does not dispute that Vargas has religious beliefs that prohibit him from cutting his hair, it is clear from the record that Vargas was not terminated for failing to cut his hair. Vargas admitted in his deposition that he was given the option to tuck his hair into his collar to avoid termination of his employment. He, therefore, has not shown that he was discharged for failing to comply with an employment requirement that conflicted with his religious beliefs.

Although Vargas now takes the position that tucking his hair into his collar would also violate his religious beliefs, one of the elements that Vargas must satisfy in order to establish a prima facie case of religious discrimination is to establish that "he informed his employer about his [religious] conflict." There is no evidence whatsoever to establish that Vargas ever told any of his supervisors that his religion precluded him from tucking his hair into his collar. For all of the foregoing reasons, the Court finds that Vargas has failed to make out a prima facie claim of religious discrimination.

Moreover, even if the Court were to find that Vargas had established a prima facie claim, the Court finds that Sears attempted in good faith to reasonably accommodate Vargas' religious beliefs. As set forth above, where an employee refuses to attempt to accommodate his own beliefs or to cooperate with his employer's attempt to reach a reasonable accommodation, accommodation is deemed to be impossible. Vargas does not have the right to insist on his preferred accommodation. Vargas flatly refused to even attempt to comply with the accommodation of tucking his hair into his collar. He did not propose any alternative accommodation to his employer. In fact, Vargas testified that it was not "his job" to offer alternatives or cooperate in any accommodation proposals that were "imposed" on him or caused him any discomfort. Vargas' refusal to cooperate with Sears with respect to attempts to accommodate his religious beliefs precludes Vargas from challenging the sufficiency or "reasonableness" of Sears' offered accommodation.

For all of the foregoing reasons, Sears' Motion for Summary Judgment on Vargas' Title VII religious discrimination claim will be GRANTED.

Case Questions

1. Do you think that Sears' accommodation was sufficient? Explain.

2. Do you think Sears' policies adequately reflected its workforce? Explain.

3. What approach would you take to developing policies such as these?

What Constitutes Undue Hardship?

Just as reasonable accommodation varies from situation to situation, so, too, does what constitutes undue hardship. There are no set rules about what constitutes undue hardship since each employer operates under different circumstances. What may be hardship for one employer may not be for another. What constitutes an undue hardship is addressed by the EEOC and courts on an individual basis.

It is clear, however, that the undue hardship may not be a mere inconvenience to the employer. The EEOC has provided guidelines as to what factors it will consider in deciding whether the employer's accommodation would cause undue hardship.[1] Such factors include:

- The nature of the employer's workplace.
- The type of job needing accommodation.
- The cost of the accommodation.
- The willingness of other employees to assist in the accommodation.
- The possibility of transfer of the employee and its effects.
- What is done by similarly situated employers.
- The number of employees available for accommodation.
- The burden of accommodation on the union (if any).

The factors are similar to those used to determine if the employer has reasonably accommodated. Generally speaking, EEOC's interpretation of what constitutes undue hardship and reasonable accommodation has been more stringent than the interpretation of undue hardship by the courts. However, since the EEOC's guidelines are not binding, and court decisions are, employers must look to the interpretation by courts in their own jurisdictions. Courts have found, among other things, that it would be an undue hardship if an employer had to violate the seniority provision of a valid collective bargaining agreement, to pay out more than a "de minimis" cost (in terms of money or efficiency) to replace a worker who has religious conflicts, or to force other employees who do not wish to do so to trade places with the employee who has a religious conflict. The US Supreme Court's determination of what constitutes undue hardship was established in the following case, which still stands today. As you can see, it did not offer a very heavy burden on the employer.

---

[1] 29 C.F.R. 1605.1.

TRANS WORLD AIRLINES, INC. V. HARDISON
432 U.S. 63 (1977)

Employer was unable to accommodate employee's religious conflict of working on the sabbath, without undue hardship. The Court set forth the guidelines for determining what constitutes undue hardship.

White, J.

The employee, Hardison, was employed by Trans World Airlines (TWA), in a department that operated 24 hours a day throughout the year in connection with an airplane maintenance and overhaul base. Hardison was subject to a seniority system in a collective bargaining agreement between TWA and the International Association of Machinists & Aerospace Workers (union), whereby the most senior employees have first choice for job and shift assignments as they become available, and the most junior employees are required to work when enough employees to work at a particular time or in a particular job to fill TWA's needs cannot be found.

Because Hardison's religious beliefs prohibit him from working on Saturdays, attempts were made to accommodate him, and these were temporarily successful mainly because on his job at the time he had sufficient seniority regularly to observe Saturday as his Sabbath. But when he sought, and was transferred to, another job where he was asked to work Saturdays and where he had low seniority, problems began to arise. TWA agreed to permit the union to seek a change of work assignments, but the union was not willing to violate the seniority system, and Hardison had insufficient seniority to bid for a shift having Saturdays off. After TWA rejected a proposal that Hardison work only four days a week on the ground that this would impair critical functions in the airline operations, no accommodation could be reached, and Hardison was discharged for refusing to work on Saturdays.

We hold that TWA, which made reasonable efforts to accommodate Hardison's religious needs, did not violate Title VII, and each of the Court of Appeals' suggested alternatives would have been an undue hardship within the meaning of the statute as construed by the EEOC guidelines. The employer's statutory obligation to make reasonable accommodation for the religious observances of its employees, short of incurring an undue hardship, is clear, but the reach of that obligation has never been spelled out by Congress or by EEOC guidelines. With this in mind, we turn to a consideration of whether TWA has met its obligation under Title VII to accommodate the religious observances of its employees.

The Court of Appeals held that TWA had not made reasonable efforts to accommodate Hardison's religious needs. In its view, TWA had rejected three reasonable alternatives, any one of which would have satisfied its obligation without undue hardship. First, within the framework of the seniority system, TWA could have permitted Hardison to work a four-day week, utilizing in his place a supervisor or another worker on duty elsewhere. That this would have caused other shop functions to suffer was insufficient to amount to undue hardship in the opinion of the Court of Appeals. Second, also within the bounds of the collective-bargaining contract the company could have filled Hardison's Saturday shift from other available personnel competent to do the job, of which the court said there were at least 200. That this would have involved premium overtime pay was not deemed an undue hardship. Third, TWA could have arranged a "swap between Hardison and another employee either for another shift or for the Sabbath days." In response to the assertion that this would have involved a breach of the seniority provisions of the contract, the court noted that it had not been settled in the courts whether the required statutory accommodation to religious needs stopped short of transgressing seniority rules, but found it unnecessary to decide the issue because, as the Court of Appeals saw the record, TWA had not sought, and the union had therefore not declined to entertain, a possible variance from the seniority provisions of the collective-bargaining agreement. The company had simply left the entire matter to the union steward who the Court of Appeals said "likewise did nothing."

We disagree with the Court of Appeals in all relevant respects. It is our view that TWA made reasonable efforts to accommodate and that each of the suggested alternatives would have been an undue hardship within the meaning of the statute as construed by the EEOC guidelines.

It might be inferred from the Court of Appeals' opinion and from the brief of the EEOC in this Court that TWA's efforts to accommodate were no more than negligible. The findings of the District Court, supported by the record, are to the contrary. In summarizing its more detailed findings, the District Court observed:

"TWA established as a matter of fact that it did take appropriate action to accommodate as required by Title VII. It held several meetings with plaintiff at which it attempted to find a solution to plaintiff's problems. It did accommodate plaintiff's observance of his special religious holidays. It authorized the union steward to search for someone who would swap shifts, which apparently was normal procedure." It is also true that TWA itself attempted without success to find Hardison another job. The District Court's view was that TWA had done all that could reasonably be expected within the bounds of the seniority system.

We are also convinced, contrary to the Court of Appeals, that TWA itself cannot be faulted for having failed to work out a shift or job swap for Hardison. Both the union and TWA had agreed to the seniority system; the union was unwilling to entertain a variance over the objections of men senior to Hardison; and for TWA to have arranged unilaterally for a swap would have amounted to a breach of the collective-bargaining agreement.

Hardison and the EEOC insist that the statutory obligation to accommodate religious needs takes precedence over both the collective-bargaining contract and the seniority rights of TWA's other employees. We agree that neither a collective-bargaining contract nor a seniority system may be employed to violate the statute, but we do not believe that the duty to accommodate requires TWA to take steps inconsistent with the otherwise valid agreement. Collective bargaining, aimed at effecting workable and enforceable agreements between management and labor, lies at the core of our national labor policy, and seniority provisions are universally included in these contracts. Without a clear and express indication from Congress, we cannot agree with Hardison and the EEOC that an agreed-upon seniority system must give way when necessary to accommodate religious observances.

The Court of Appeals also suggested that TWA could have permitted Hardison to work a four-day week if necessary in order to avoid working on his Sabbath. Recognizing that this might have left TWA short-handed on the one shift each week that Hardison did not work, the court still concluded that TWA would suffer no undue hardship if it were required to replace Hardison either with supervisory personnel or with qualified personnel from other departments. Alternatively, the Court of Appeals suggested that TWA could have replaced Hardison on his Saturday shift with other available employees through the payment of premium wages. Both of these alternatives would involve costs to TWA, either in the form of lost efficiency in other jobs or higher wages.

To require TWA to bear more than a de minimis cost in order to give Hardison Saturdays off is an undue hardship. Like abandonment of the seniority system, to require TWA to bear additional costs when no such costs are incurred to give other employees the days off that they want would involve unequal treatment of employees on the basis of their religion. By suggesting that TWA should incur certain costs in order to give Hardison Saturdays off the Court of Appeals would in effect require TWA to finance an additional Saturday off and then to choose the employee who will enjoy it on the basis of his religious beliefs. While incurring extra costs to secure a replacement for Hardison might remove the necessity of compelling another employee to work involuntarily in Hardison's place, it would not change the fact that the privilege of having Saturdays off would be allocated according to religious beliefs. While the cost may seem small for one employee compared to TWA's resources, TWA may have many employees who need such accommodation.

Case Questions

1. In your opinion, were the alternatives suggested by the court of appeals viable for TWA? Why or why not?

2. Does it seem inconsistent to prohibit religious discrimination, yet say that collective bargaining agreements cannot be violated to accommodate religious differences? Explain.

3. If you had been Hardison's manager and he came to you with this conflict, how would you have handled it? Does that change now that you have seen the Court's decision? If so, how?

Religion as a BFOQ

Title VII permits religion to be a bona fide occupational qualification if it is reasonably necessary to the employer's particular normal business operations. It also specifically permits educational institutions to employ those of a particular religion if they are owned in whole or in substantial part by a particular religion. In *Pime,* the court looked at whether a historically Jesuit university could have Jesuit membership as a BFOQ for philosophy professors. Exhibit 10–4 discusses the issue of being male as a BFOQ for being a Catholic priest.

EXHIBIT 10–4　Catholic Bishops Split on Women Priests

Document on Women's Role in Church, Society Rejected

WASHINGTON—Nine years of sharp debate and soul searching over the ordination of women priests ended Wednesday as the United States' Roman Catholic bishops rejected a controversial statement on the role of women in society and the church.

On a 137–110 vote, 53 short of the required two-thirds of eligible voters needed for passage, the prelate sealed a tumultuous chapter in the history of the American church over the ordination of women.

But it did not close the book on the debate over admitting women to the priesthood.

While the letter, which was repeatedly revised, strongly reaffirmed the church's ancient tradition of an all-male priesthood, many advocates of women's ordination said the mere fact that the bishops were debating the issue was a victory.

Some bishops stressed that the vote against the letter was not a vote against banning women priests.

Those bishops, including Cardinal Joseph Bernardin of Chicago, said the missive was rejected because it was either too insensitive in dealing with the subject of women's ordination, or too weak in advancing a rationale for upholding a male priesthood.

Others said the letter had strayed from the bishops' original intent to address pressing social concerns affecting women, such as sexism and domestic violence, and had become too political and divisive.

It marked the first time that a proposed pastoral letter, an authoritative teaching of bishops, had been defeated in the United States.

The letter's defeat came on the eve of the Episcopal Church's plans tonight to consecrate the Rev. Jane Holmes Dixon as the second woman bishop in its history and the third in the 70 million member worldwide Anglican Communion.

Last week, the Church of England—mother church of the Anglican Communion, which broke with Rome in the 16th century—voted to admit women to its priesthood.

L B Stammer, *Palm Beach Post,* November 19, 1992, p. 1A. Copyright, 1992, Los Angeles Times. Reprinted by permission.

PIME V. LOYOLA UNIVERSITY OF CHICAGO
803 F.2d 351 (7th Cir. 1986)

The employee, Pime, brought suit against the university under Title VII for religious discrimination in the hiring of tenure track professors in their College of Arts and Sciences, Department of Philosophy. The Department passed a resolution reserving its next three vacancies in tenure track teaching positions for Jesuits, members of the Society of Jesus. The court held the Jesuit requirement to be a BFOQ and not violative of Title VII.

Fairchild, J.

Loyola asserts two affirmative defenses. First, it claimed that it could require its employees to be Jesuits (and thus Catholics) under 42 U.S.C 2000e-2(e) permitting an educational institution to employ persons of a particular religion if the institution is "in whole or in substantial part, owned, supported, controlled, or managed by a particular religion or by a particular religious corporation, . . . association, or society." It also claimed it could require those employees to be Jesuits according to 42 U.S.C. 2000e-2(e)(1) permitting an employer to employ an individual "on the basis of his religion, gender or national origin in those certain situations where religion, gender or national origin is a bona fide occupational qualification reasonably necessary to the normal operation of that particular business or enterprise." (BFOQ)

After a bench trial, the district court granted judgment in favor of Loyola, finding that being a Jesuit is a BFOQ. Employee challenges the finding of BFOQ. Loyola challenges the trial court's finding that it could not rely on subsection (e)(2).

The Society of Jesus is a religious order of the Roman Catholic Church. Its members, who are, with few exceptions, priests, are called Jesuits. The order has been characterized by interests and particular energy in the promotion of education, and has established twenty-eight universities in the United States. Jesuits are required to complete a protracted course of training and to make perpetual vows. Once they accept positions as professors they continue to incorporate their religious mission into their professional work.

Loyola University of Chicago has a long Jesuit tradition. Since 1909 its legal entity has been an Illinois not-for-profit corporation. Until 1970, it was governed by a Board of Trustees, all members of which were Jesuits. It has become a large university, consisting of ten schools and colleges, a medical center and a hospital. Presently 93% of the academic administrators are non-Jesuits, as are 94% of the teaching staff.

Every undergraduate must take three Philosophy courses. About 75% of the students come from Catholic backgrounds. There was testimony by the President that, "I'm convinced that of all the things we say about Loyola, the most effective single adjective in attracting students and alumni support and benefactors is its Jesuitness."

In the fall of 1978, there were 31 tenure track positions in the Philosophy Department. Seven had been held by Jesuits, but one had resigned and two more retirements were imminent. On October 12, the department chair reported to a meeting of the department and faculty as follows:

> We anticipate 3 full-time faculty openings in the Philosophy Department beginning September 1979. They are the position of Fr. Dehler and those of Fr. Grant and Fr. Loftus after they retire at the end of the current academic year.
>
> There are two different kinds of departmental needs which seem to bear heavily on the decisions as to the kind of persons we should seek to hire for these openings.
>
> 1. The first is a need which the Chair voiced two years ago just after Fr. Dehler's resignation. That is, the need for an adequate Jesuit presence in the Department. We are a philosophy Department in a University with a Jesuit tradition. It is mainly by reason of this tradition that philosophy has the importance it does in the education of Loyola undergraduates. Therefore, it behooves us, however strong we may feel about "the autonomy of philosophy," to acknowledge our association with this tradition. One very basic and obvious way of making such acknowledgments is by insisting upon an adequate Jesuit presence in the faculty of the Department. With the retirement of Father Grant and Father Loftus, we shall be left with 4 out of 31 faculty positions occupied by Jesuits. Four out of 31 is not an adequate Jesuit presence in the Department. In the judgment of the Chair, it would be highly desirable to fill all three openings with professionally competent Jesuit philosophers. And it is his recommendation that we do so if we can.

The second kind of departmental need is for faculty, especially qualified to teach courses in the following areas: *a.* Applied ethics, especially medical ethics. There is an increasing student demand for such courses and for additional undergraduate course offerings at the Medical School. *b.* Philosophy of Law. This is one of the most popular of our 300-level course offerings. It needs to be offered annually both at Lake Shore Campus and Water Tower Campus. *c.* Logic. There is an exceedingly heavy student enrollment at both Lake Shore Campus and Water Tower Campus. Additional sections of courses in logic should be offered in each campus.

Consequently, we should seek persons who have special competence and interest in teaching courses in these areas. The Chair's recommendation is that we seek to hire persons who will help teach in these two areas.

These two kinds of needs are different, though not incompatible. The Chair's recommendation as to hiring is the following:

That for each of these 3 positions we seek to hire a professionally competent Jesuit philosopher—preferably a young Jesuit with competence to teach in one or several of the following areas: *a)* applied ethics, especially medical ethics; *b)* philosophy of law; and *c)* logic; and that if we should be unable to hire such, we hire temporary full-time person(s) with special competence to teach in one or several of these areas.

Pime, a Jew, had been employed in 1976 as a part-time lecturer in the department. He taught several courses. He expected to receive his doctorate in June, 1979 and had received indications of approval of his work. He knew of the resolution of November 30, and asked the department chair when there would be a full-time tenure track position for him. The chair said he saw nothing in the way of a position for Pime in the next three or four years. Disappointed, Pime left Loyola after the spring semester.

There is no hint of invidious action against Pime on account of his religion. The faculty resolution excluded every non-Jesuit from consid-

eration, whether of the Catholic faith or otherwise. We shall assume, however, that because Pime's faith would prevent his being a Jesuit, he has a claim on discrimination on account of religion.

The BFOQ involved in this case is membership in a religious order of a particular faith. There is evidence of the relationship of the order to Loyola and that Jesuit "presence" is important to the successful operation of the university. It appears to be significant to the educational tradition and character of the institution that students be assured a degree of contact with teachers who have received the training and accepted the obligation which are essential to membership in the Society of Jesus. It requires more to be a Jesuit than just adherence to the Catholic faith, and it seems wholly reasonable to believe that the educational experience at Loyola would be different if Jesuit presence were not maintained. As priests, Jesuits perform rites and sacraments, and counsel members of the university community, including students, faculty and staff. One witness expressed the objective as keeping a presence "so that students would occasionally encounter a Jesuit."

It is true that it has not been shown that Jesuit training is a superior academic qualification, applying objective criteria, to teach the particular courses. It is also true that in looking at claims of BFOQ, courts have considered only the content of the particular jobs at issue. Yet it seems to us here the evidence supports the more general proposition that having a Jesuit presence in the Philosophy faculty is "reasonably necessary to the normal operation" of the enterprise, and that fixing the number at 7 out of 31 is a reasonable determination.

Case Questions

1. Does the decision make sense to you? Explain.

2. Since such a high percentage of Loyola's faculty and administrators are non-Jesuits, does

it seem as if an argument could be made that the school has thereby given up its legitimate claim to have being Jesuit be a BFOQ?

3. As an employer, do you think you would have to face dealing with the policy adopted here making other employees or applicants feel unwelcome? If so, what would you do?

Religious Harassment

One of the most active areas under religious discrimination lately has been religious harassment. Several factors have come together and caused many employees to decide that expressing their religious views in some way in the workplace is something they are compelled to do, either by their religious dictates or their own interpretations of them.

For instance, employees may feel they must, or wish to, display crosses or other religious artifacts at work, display religious tracts on their desk or pass them out to co-workers, hold Bible or other religious study groups during the workday, preach, teach, testify, or witness to their co-workers in order to act out their religion, and other such activities.

This activity surrounding the issue of religious harassment is due, in part, to matters peripheral to workplace religious discrimination. In 1990, the US Supreme Court rejected Native Americans' argument that they should be permitted the ritual use of peyote [a hallucinogenic drug] in their tribal religious ceremonies as a part of their First Amendment right to freedom of religion. With tremendous support from many quarters, in 1993 Congress passed the Religious Freedom Restoration Act (RFRA) in order to ensure the free exercise of religious practices. The Act was an attempt to restore the previous status quo under which religious practices must be accommodated unless a compelling governmental interest can be demonstrated and advanced in the least restrictive manner. In 1997, the US Supreme Court overturned RFRA as giving a governmental preference for religion, in violation of the First Amendment to the Constitution.

While the matter of religious practices in the workplace was not at issue in these cases or this legislation, the national attention and debate about it, along with a growing religious presence in political issues extended the religious practices issue to the workplace by extrapolation. When the religious practices were challenged, religious harassment claims rose.

Of course, with all different types of religions in the workplace, (see Exhibit 10–2) it is inevitable that there would be religious conflicts and that those with religions considered out of the ordinary, or with religious practices that co-workers consider extreme would be the subject of religious harassment. In addition, it is often the nonreligious employees who allege they are being harassed by religious employees. (See Exhibit 10–3). For instance, in a case filed in 1998 by information systems manager Rosamaria Machado-Wilson of DeLand, Florida, the employee alleged that she was fired after less than six months on the job after reporting religious harassment to the human resources office of her employer, BSG Laboratories. According to Machado-Wilson, a simple walk to the coffeepot sometimes meant "weaving past prostrate, praying co-workers and stopping for impromptu ceremonies spoken in tongues." She says she was forced to attend company prayer meetings and be baptized, employees were subjected to inquiries into and comments about their religious beliefs, and those found to be nonbelievers were fired.

Of course, since Title VII prohibits religious discrimination, it also prohibits religious harassment. The EEOC's guidelines on liability for workplace harassment issued in June of 1999 explicitly cover religious harassment. On August 14, 1997, President Clinton issued guidelines for the religious freedom of federal employees. The purpose of the guidelines is to accommodate religious observance in the workplace as an important national priority by striking a balance between religious observance and the requirements of the workplace. Under the guidelines, employees:

- Should be permitted to engage in private religious expression in personal work areas not regularly open to the public to the same extent that they may engage in nonreligious private expression.
- Should be permitted to engage in religious expression with fellow employees, to the same extent they may engage in comparable nonreligious private expression, subject to reasonable restrictions.
- Are permitted to engage in religious expression directed at fellow employees, and may even attempt to persuade fellow employees of the correctness of their religious views. But employees must refrain from such expression when a fellow employee asks that it stop or otherwise demonstrates that it is unwelcome.

In order to best prevent liability for religious harassment, employers should be sure to protect employees from those religious employees who attempt to proselytize others who do not wish to be approached about religious matters, as well as to protect employees with permissible religious practices who are given a hard time by those who do not. Making sure that employees are given comparable opportunities to use workplace time and resources for religious practices if given for secular ones is also an important consideration.

Union Activity and Religious Discrimination

As *Hardison* discussed, at times the religious conflicts that arise between the employee and the employer are caused by collective-bargaining agreement provisions, rather than by policies unilaterally imposed by the employer. It has been determined that, even though Title VII defines the term "religion" with reference to an employer having a duty to reasonably accommodate, unions are also under a duty to reasonably accommodate religious conflicts.

The most frequent conflicts are requirements that employees be union members or pay union dues. Union membership, payment of union dues, or engaging in concerted activity, such as picketing and striking, conflicts with some religious beliefs. Employees have also objected to the payment of union dues as violating their First Amendment right to freedom of religion and Title VII's prohibition against religious discrimination. Unions have claimed that applying the religious proscription of Title VII violates the Establishment Clause of the First Amendment to the US Constitution, ensuring government neutrality in religious matters.

Courts have ruled that union security agreements requiring that employees pay union dues within a certain time after the effective date of their employment or be discharged does not violate an employee's First Amendment rights. However, it violates Title VII for an employer to discharge an employee for refusal to join the union because of his religious beliefs.

Employees with religious objections must be reasonably accommodated, including the possibility of the alternative of keeping their job without paying union dues. However, the union could prove undue hardship if many of the employees chose to have their dues instead paid to a nonunion, nonsectarian charitable organization chosen by the union and the employer, since the impact on the union would not be insubstantial.

In *Tooley v. Martin-Marietta Corp.*[2s] Seventh Day Adventists who were prohibited by their religion from becoming members in, or paying a service fee to, a union offered to pay an amount equal to union dues to a mutually acceptable charity. The union refused and argued that to accommodate the employees violated the Establishment Clause ensuring governmental neutrality in matters of religion. The court said that the government could legitimately enforce accommodation of religious beliefs when the accommodation reflects the obligation of neutrality in the face of religious differences and does not constitute sponsorship, financial support, or active involvement of the sovereign in religious activities with which the Establishment Clause is mainly concerned. The Establishment Clause, typically applied to state legislation, such as in *Frazee,* on page 348, requires that the accommodation reflect a clearly secular purpose, have a primary effect that neither inhibits nor advances religion, and avoids excessive government entanglement with religion.

Whether the objection under Title VII is directed toward the employer or the union, a government employer still has a duty to reasonably accommodate the employee's religious conflict unless to do so would cause undue hardship or excessive entanglement with religion, or violate the Establishment Clause.

---

[2]648 F.2d 1239 (9th Cir. 1981)

Management Tips

One of the primary reasons employers get into trouble in this area is because they simply miss realizing the religious conflict when an employee notifies them, or they refuse to adequately address it if they do. Many of the conflicts can be avoided by following a few basic rules:

- take all employee notices of religious conflicts seriously;
- once an employee puts the employer on notice of a religious conflict, the employer should immediately try to find ways to avoid the conflict;
- ask the employee with the conflict for suggestions on avoiding the conflict;
- ask other employees if they can be of assistance, but make it clear that they are not required to do so;
- keep workplace religious comments and criticisms to a minimum;
- make sure all employees understand that they are not to discriminate against employees on the basis of religion;
- once an employee expresses conflict based on religion, do not challenge the employee's religious beliefs, though it is permissible to make sure of the conflict;
- make sure undue hardship actually exists if it is claimed;
- revisit issues such as Christmas bonuses and Christmas parties to see if it is more appropriate to use more inclusive language such as "holiday" to cover employees who do not celebrate the Christian Christmas;
- revisit the issue of granting leave for religious events and make sure it does not favor one religion over another, such as giving employees paid leave for Christmas, but requiring them to take their own leave for other religious holidays such as Rosh Hashana or Yom Kippur; and
- make sure food at workplace events is inclusive of all employees, regardless of religion, such as having kosher (or at least nonpork or seafood) items for Jewish employees, having alternatives to alcoholic beverages for those who do not drink for religious reasons, or having nonpork items for Muslims, and so on. Asking employees what religious dietary limitations they have or having employees bring a dish to share is an easy way to handle this.

Summary

- Employees are protected in the workplace in their right to adhere to and practice their religious beliefs, and employer cannot discriminate against them on this basis unless to do so would be undue hardship on the employer.
- Employer cannot question the acceptability of employee's religion or when the employee came to believe.

- Employer should be conscious of potential religious conflicts in developing and implementing workplace policies.
- The prohibition on religious discrimination is not absolute, as employer has only the duty to reasonably accommodate the employee's religious conflict unless to do so would cause the employer undue hardship.

• While employer must make a good faith effort to reasonably accommodate religious conflicts, if such efforts fail, employer will have discharged his or her legal duties under Title VII.

Chapter-End Questions

1. The *Christian Science Monitor* refused to hire Feldstein because he was not a Christian Scientist. The newspaper said they only hired those who were of the Christian Science religion, unless there are none qualified for a position. Is the newspaper's policy legal? Explain. (*Feldstein v. EEOC,* 547 F.Supp. 97 (D.C. Mass. 1982).)

2. Cynthia requested a two-week leave from her employer to go on a religious pilgrimage. The pilgrimage was not a requirement of her religion, but Cynthia felt it was a "calling from God." Will it violate Title VII if Cynthia's employer does not grant her the leave? Explain. (*Tiano v. Dillard Department Stores, Inc.,* 1998 WL 117864 (9th Cir. 1998).)

3. A Catholic police officer is given the opportunity to transfer to another police district after he refuses duty at an abortion clinic, where antiabortion demonstrations are being held, because he does not believe in abortions. He does not think this is a reasonable accommodation and sues for religious discrimination. Will the employer's accommodation be upheld by the court as reasonable? Why or why not? (*Rodriguez v. Chicago,* No. 97-3339 (7th Cir. 1998).)

4. Jacinto, a supervisor, repeatedly told offensive religious jokes in the presence of Jarman, an employee, and unjustly criticized Jarman's work. Another manager saw Jarman reading a Bible during his lunch break and directed a lower-level supervisor to tell him to stop. Jarman also says there was an increase in his workload and he was told to have a project finished by the end of the day, "or else." During this time, Jarman received positive job evaluations and his requests for overtime were routinely granted. Jarman eventually quits his job and sues for religious harassment. Will he win? (*Hernandez-Torres v. Intercontinental Trading, Inc.,* 78 FEP Cas. 90 (1st Cir. 1998).)

5. A Michigan Holiday Inn fired a pregnant employee because the "very Christian" staff members were very upset by her talk of having an abortion. Has the employer violated Title VII? (*Turic v. Holland Hospitality, Inc.,* No. 1-93-CV-379 (W.D. Mich. 1994).)

6. A Seventh Day Adventist whose religious faith required him to refrain from work from sunset Friday to sunset Saturday was allowed to bid on several jobs that would not have required that he work on his sabbath. Employee says the proffered positions are jobs that most other people didn't want, so he refused to bid on them, even though he would have received at least two of the positions. Because he did not participate in the special bidding procedure, he could be assigned to any position. The position he was assigned to required him to work on Friday evenings, so he resigned. When he brings suit for religious discrimination, will he win? (*Wright v. USPS,* 2 F.3d 214 (7th Cir. 1993).)

7. Employer has a strict policy of not allowing employees with beards to work in public contact positions. All managerial positions are public contact positions. Employer does not make exceptions to its policies for those

with religious objections to shaving, but it reasonably accommodates them by offering them other positions within the company. When employee applies for a driver position and is turned down, he sues employer. Does he win? *EEOC v. UPS,* 94 F.3d 314 (7th Cir. 1996).)

8. Brenda has been working in the public school system for many years, first as a teacher, then as an administrator. She was well-known within the system for work as choir director for several churches. She also performed this function in an extracurricular capacity for many schools. The work often necessitates Brenda taking time off to deal with the school activities. The time was not taken from her existing leave. While her work for the school system did not suffer, the new school superintendent tells Brenda that she is now to be charged leave time

when she performs such functions. Is this religious discrimination? Why or why not?

9. Betty, a public school teacher and a Baptist minister's wife, gives her elementary school students Christian terms as spelling words, decorates the classroom with religious items on Christian holidays, and engages the students in religious lectures. Jewish parents complain, and Betty's principal tells her to end the religious activity. Betty objects to the warning, saying "witnessing" this way is a part of her religion. What should the principal do?

10. Muslim employees who do not celebrate Christmas resent the fact that they must take off on the Christmas holidays, which they do not celebrate, but use their annual leave when they are off for their own religious holidays. As the employer, what do you tell them?

11 NATIONAL ORIGIN DISCRIMINATION

Chapter Outline

S C E N A R I O S

S C E N A R I O   1

Marietta, the owner of a manufacturing plant, is having personnel problems because most of her line of American workers are of Irish descent, and she recently introduced to the workforce a number of Italian-American workers. The tension has interfered with the performance of all workers, and she believes that it will ease if she terminates the Italian-American workers. What are her options?

S C E N A R I O   2

Kayla, a supervisor, recently hired a new manager, Alex, but has received complaints from customers that they cannot understand him when they speak to him on the telephone. Alex is a Rumanian employee visiting from the company's Rumanian office and is scheduled to remain with the firm for two years. Kayla is concerned that if she allows Alex to perform duties similar to other managers the firm will lose customers; however, she is unsure about the firm's liability for decreasing Alex's responsibilities as a result of his foreign accent.

Statutory Basis

Exhibit 11–1

Title VII, Civil Rights Act of 1964
Sec. 703(a)
It shall be an unlawful employment practice for an employer—
(1) to fail or to refuse to hire or to discharge any individual, or otherwise to discriminate against any individual with respect to his compensation, terms, conditions, or privileges of employment, because of such individual's . . . national origin.

Immigration Reform and Control Act of 1986
Sec. 274A(a)
(1) It is unlawful for a person or other entity:
　　(A) to hire or to recruit or refer for a fee for employment in the United States an alien knowing the alien is an unauthorized alien with respect to such employment, or
　　(B) to hire for employment in the United States an individual without [verification of employment eligibility].
(2) It is unlawful for a person or other entity, after hiring an alien for employment in accordance with paragraph (1), to continue to employ the alien in the United States knowing the alien is (or had become) an unauthorized alien with respect to such employment.
(3) A person or entity that establishes that it has complied in good faith with the [verification of employment eligibility] with respect to hiring, recruiting or referral for employment of an alien in the United States has established an affirmative defense that the person or entity has not violated paragraph (1)(A).

Exhibit 11–1   Concluded

> Sec. 274(B)(a)
> (1) It is an unfair immigration-related practice for a person or other entity to discriminate against any individual (other than an unauthorized alien) with respect to the hiring, or recruitment or referral for a fee, or the individual for employment or the discharging or the individual from employment—
>   (A) because of such individual's national origin, or
>   (B) in the case of a protected individual [a citizen or authorized alien], because of such individual's citizenship status.

Chez/Casa/Fala/Wunderbar Uncle Sam

America has always considered itself to be a melting pot. Under this theory, different ethnic, cultural, and racial groups came together in America, but differences were melted into one homogeneous mass composed of all cultures. Recently, this characterization has been revisited and other, more accurate terms have been proposed. They include such terms as a *salad bowl,* in which all the ingredients come together to make an appetizing, nutritious whole, but each ingredient maintains its own identity; or a *stew,* in which the ingredients are blended together, but maintain their distinct identity, with the common thread of living in America acting as the stew base that binds the stew's ingredients together.

While the words on the Statue of Liberty—"Give me your tired, your poor, your huddled masses yearning to breathe free"—have always acted as a beacon to those of other countries to find solace on our shores, the reality once they get here, even sometimes after being here for generations, is that they are often discriminated against, rather than consoled. National origin was included in Title VII's list of protected classes to ensure that employers did not base employment decisions on preconceived notions about employees or applications based on their country of origin.

On its face, national origin discrimination appears to be relatively simple to determine; however, it has surprising complexities. Employers have always been uncertain of the scope of Title VII's coverage in this area and what could be used as a defense to decisions based on national origin.

Exhibit 11–2   Myths about National Origin Discrimination

> 1. Citizenship and national origin are synonymous.
> 2. A restaurant may hire whomever it wishes to represent the national origin of the restaurant.
> 3. It is not illegal discrimination for an employer to require that employees speak only English at work.

Background

National origin discrimination protection
It is unlawful for an employer to limit, segregate, or classify employees in any way on the basis of national origin which would deprive them of the privileges, benefits, or opportunities of employment.

The **protection** offered by Title VII in connection with national origin is similar to that of gender or race. That is, it is an unlawful employment practice for an employer to limit, segregate, or classify employees in any way that would deprive them of employment opportunities because of national origin. An employer may not group its employees on the basis of national origin, make employment decisions on that basis, or implement policies or programs which, though they appear not to be based on an employee or applicant's country of origin, actually affect those with one national origin differently than those of a different group.

An employee may successfully claim discrimination on the basis of national origin if it is shown that:

1. He or she is a member of a protected class (i.e., articulate the employee's national origin).
2. He or she was qualified for the position for which she applied or in which she was employed.
3. The employer made an employment decision against this employee or applicant.
4. The position was filled by someone who was not a member of the protected class.

Each of the above will be discussed in turn.

Member of the Protected Class

National Origin
Individual's or her or his ancestor's place of origin (as opposed to citizenship), or physical, cultural, or linguistic characteristics of an origin group.

In connection with the first requirement, what is meant by "national origin"? While the term is not defined in Title VII, the EEOC guidelines on discrimination define **national origin** discrimination as "including, but not limited to, the denial of equal employment opportunity because of [an applicant or employee's] or his or her ancestor's place of origin; or because an applicant has the physical, cultural, or linguistic characteristics of a national origin group."

Note that the term includes protection against discrimination based only on country of origin, not on country of *citizenship*. Title VII protects employees who are not US citizens from employment discrimination based on the categories of the act, but it does not protect them from discrimination based on their status as aliens, rather than as US citizens. That is, it protects a Somali woman from gender discrimination, but not from discrimination on the basis of the fact that she is a Somali citizen, rather than an American citizen. The issue of citizenship as it relates to national origin is discussed later in this chapter.

Many national origin cases under Title VII involve claims of discrimination by those who were not born in America; however, American-born employees are also protected against discrimination on the basis of their *American* origin. For example, the court has held that the employer's conscious decision to decide whom to dismiss on the basis of the national origin of its employees (in an effort towards "affirmative action") was not acceptable, because that method tended to disfavor Americans, in favor of other nationalities.

In addition to national origin encompassing the employee's place of birth, it also includes ethnic characteristics or origins. For instance, it has been held that Cajuns, Gypsies, and Ukrainians are protected under Title VII. It may also serve as the basis for a national origin discrimination claim if the employee:

- Is identified with or connected to a person of a specific national origin, such as where someone suffers discrimination because he or she is married to a person of a certain ethnic heritage.
- Is a member of an organization that is identified with a national group.
- Is a participant in a school or religious organization that is affiliated with a national origin group.
- Has a surname that is generally associated with a national origin group.

Recall scenario 1 where Marietta is considering terminating all workers of one national origin as a result of ethnic conflicts in her workplace. This act, of course, would constitute a prima facie case of disparate treatment discrimination of those fired individuals under the above description.

Scenario

Qualification/BFOQs

The second factor that must be shown for an employee to claim national origin discrimination is that the applicant or employee is *qualified* for the position. That is, the claimant must show that he or she meets the job's requirements. The employer may rebut this contention by showing that national origin is a **bona fide occupational qualification** (BFOQ) for the job. That is, the employer may set forth why an employee's being of a specific national origin is necessary for the position applied for, in that it is a legitimate job requirement reasonably necessary for the employer's particular business. For instance, the employer may assert that it is necessary to have a server be Italian or Chinese to preserve the authenticity or ambience of an Italian or Chinese restaurant.

BFOQ
Bona fide occupational qualification.

English Fluency and Speaking Native Languages in the Workplace.   Employers have also had to address the matter of either requiring employees to be fluent in English or requiring that only English be spoken in the workplace, even when employees are speaking only among themselves. Employers have argued that fluency in English is a BFOQ, and, therefore, they should not be required to hire someone who is not fluent in English because of their national origin.

To best be protected from possible Title VII liability, the employer must be able to show that English fluency is required for the job, and that the requirement is necessary to maintain supervisory control of the workplace. Perhaps it may be required of an employee who has much communication with clients, or it may be a BFOQ where the employee could not speak or understand English sufficiently to perform required duties.

Scenario

For example, where a teacher was fluent in English but spoke with such a thick accent that her students had a difficult time understanding her, her discharge was upheld. On the other hand, if the employee is in a job requiring little speaking and the employee can understand English, the requirement may be more difficult to defend—for instance, requiring English fluency for a janitor who talks little, has little reason to speak to carry out the duties of the job, and who understands what is said to him or her. Unlike the teacher above, in scenario 2 Kayla is considering *decreasing* Alex's responsibilities due to his foreign accent, not terminating him. However, like the teacher, it is quite possible in this scenario to show that speaking clear English is a BFOQ, especially if it can be shown that customers have been complaining that they cannot understand him.

Closely related is the employer's policy requiring employees capable of speaking English to speak only English in the workplace. Courts have gone both ways on this. Some have held the policy to be discriminatory, excessively prohibitive, and a violation of Title VII. Others have held it is not national origin discrimination, since all employees, regardless of ancestry, were prohibited from speaking all but English on the job and that there is no statutory right to speak English at work. It has been held that speaking one's native language when the employee is bilingual is not an immutable characteristic that Title VII prohibits.

In general, English-only rules have been upheld (see *Garcia,* below); however, challenges to the rules have increased dramatically in recent years. In 1996, the EEOC received 77 complaints regarding English-only rules, while in 1998 there were 146 complaints. The EEOC takes the position that English-only rules *applied at all times* are presumptively discriminatory, although the courts have not always agreed with that approach. When a rule is applied only at certain times, it must be justified by a business purpose in order to avoid discrimination claims. Rules applied during work time *only* are less likely to be considered harassment and more likely to show a business purpose. When an employer is considering an English-only rule, it should take into consideration the legal considerations as well as the fact that such a rule can create an atmosphere of inferiority, isolation, and intimidation that may result in a discriminatory work environment.

GARCIA V. SPUN STEAK CO.
998 F. 2d 1480 (9th Cir. 1993)

Defendant, Spun Steak Co., employs 33 workers, 24 of whom are Spanish-speaking. Two of the Spanish-speakers speak no English. Plaintiffs Garcia and Buitrago are production line workers for the defendant and both are bilingual. After receiving complaints that some workers were using their second language to harass and to insult other workers, defendant enacted an English-only policy in the workplace in order to (1) promote racial harmony; (2) enhance worker safety because some employees who did not understand Spanish claimed that they were distracted by its use; and (3) enhance product quality because the USDA inspector in the plant spoke only English. Plaintiffs received warning notices about speaking Spanish during working hours, and they were not permitted to work next to each other for two months. They filed charges with the EEOC which found reasonable cause to believe that the defendant had violated Title VII. The District Court awarded summary judgment to the plaintiffs and Spun Steak appealed.

O'Scannlain, J.

The Spanish-speaking employees do not contend that Spun Steak intentionally discriminated against them in enacting the English-only policy. Rather, they contend that the policy had a discriminatory impact on them because it imposes a burdensome term or condition of employment exclusively upon Hispanic workers and denies them a privilege of employment that non-Spanish-speaking workers enjoy.

The employees argue that denying them the ability to speak Spanish on the job denies them the right to cultural expression. It cannot be gainsaid that an individual's primary language can be an important link to his ethnic culture and identity. Title VII, however, does not protect the ability of workers to express their cultural heritage at the workplace. Title VII is concerned only with disparities in the treatment of workers; it does not confer substantive privileges. It is axiomatic that an employee must often sacrifice individual self-expression during working hours. Just as a private employer is not required to allow other types of self-expression, there is nothing in Title VII which requires an employer to allow employees to express their cultural identity.

Next, the Spanish-speaking employees argue that the English-only policy has a disparate impact on them because it deprives them of a privilege given by the employer to native-English speakers: the ability to converse on the job in the language with which they feel most comfortable. It is undisputed that Spun Steak allows its employees to converse on the job. The ability to converse—especially to make small talk—is a privilege of employment, and may in fact be a significant privilege of employment in an assembly-line job. It is inaccurate, however, to describe the privilege as broadly as the Spanish-speaking employees urge us to do.

The employees have attempted to define the privilege as the ability to speak in the language of their choice. A privilege, however, is by definition given at the employer's discretion; an employer has the right to define its contours. Thus, an employer may allow employees to converse on the job, but only during certain times of the day or during the performance of certain tasks. The employer may proscribe certain topics as inappropriate during working hours or may even forbid the use of certain words, such as profanity.

Here, as is its prerogative, the employer has defined the privilege narrowly. When the privilege is defined at its narrowest (as merely the ability to speak on the job), we cannot conclude that those employees fluent in both English and Spanish are adversely impacted by the policy. Because they are able to speak English, bilingual employees can engage in conversation on the job. It is axiomatic that "the language a person who is multilingual elects to speak at a particular time is . . . a matter of choice." The bilingual employee can readily comply with the English-only rule and still enjoy the privilege of speaking on the job. "There is no disparate impact" with respect to a privilege of employment "if the rule is one that the affected employee can readily observe and nonobservance is a matter of individual preference."

This analysis is consistent with our decision in *Jurado v. Eleven-Fifty Corporation*. In *Jurado*, a bilingual disc jockey was fired for disobeying a rule forbidding him from using an occasional Spanish word or phrase on the air. We concluded that Jurado's disparate impact claim failed "because Jurado was fluently bilingual and could easily comply with the order" and thus could not have been adversely affected.

The Spanish-speaking employees argue that fully bilingual employees are hampered in the enjoyment of the privilege because for them, switching from one language to another is not fully volitional. Whether a bilingual speaker can control which language is used in a given circumstance is a factual issue that cannot be resolved at the summary judgment stage. However, we fail to see the relevance of the assertion, even assuming that it can be proved. Title VII is not meant to protect against rules that merely inconvenience some employees, even if the inconvenience falls regularly on a protected class. Rather, Title VII protects against only those policies that have a *significant* impact. The fact that an employee may have to catch himself or herself from occasionally slipping into Spanish does not impose a burden significant enough to amount to the denial of equal opportunity. This is not a case in which the employees have alleged that the company is enforcing the policy in such a way as to impose penalties for minor slips of the tongue. The fact that a bilingual employee may, on occasion, unconsciously substitute a Spanish word in the place of an English one does not override our conclusion that the bilingual employee can easily comply with the rule. In short, we conclude that a bilingual employee is not denied a privilege of employment by the English-only policy.

By contract, non-English speakers cannot enjoy the privilege of conversing on the job if conversation is limited to a language they cannot speak. As applied "[t]o a person who speaks only one tongue or to a person who has difficulty using another language than the one spoken in his home," an English-only rule might well have an adverse impact. Indeed, counsel for Spun Steak conceded at oral argument that the policy would have an adverse impact on an employee unable to

speak English. There is only one employee at Spun Steak affected by the policy who is unable to speak any English. Even with regard to her, however, summary judgment was improper because a genuine issue of material fact exists as to whether she has been adversely affected by the policy. She stated in her deposition that she was not bothered by the rule because she preferred not to make small talk on the job, but rather preferred to work in peace. Furthermore, there is some evidence suggesting that she is not required to comply with the policy when she chooses to speak. For example, she is allowed to speak Spanish to her supervisor. Remand is necessary to determine whether she has suffered adverse effects from the policy. It is unclear from the record whether there are any other employees who have such limited proficiency in English that they are effectively denied the privilege of speaking on the job. Whether an employee speaks such little English as to be effectively denied the privilege is a question of fact for which summary judgment is improper.

We do not foreclose the prospect that in some circumstances English-only rules can exacerbate existing tensions, or, when combined with other discriminatory behavior, contribute to an overall environment of discrimination. Likewise, we can envision a case in which such rules are enforced in such a draconian manner that the enforcement itself amounts to harassment. In evaluating such a claim, however, a court must look to the totality of the circumstances in the particular factual context in which the claim arises.

In holding that the enactment of an English-only while working policy does not inexorably lead to an abusive environment for those whose primary language is not English, we reach a conclusion opposite to the EEOC's long standing position. The EEOC Guidelines provide that an employee meets the prima facie case in a disparate impact cause of action merely by proving the existence of the English-only policy. Under the EEOC's scheme, an employer must always provide a business justification for such a rule. The EEOC enacted this scheme in part because of its conclusion that English-only rules may "create an atmosphere of inferiority, isolation and intimidation based on national origin which could result in a discriminatory working environment."

We do not reject the English-only rule Guideline lightly. We recognize that "as an administrative interpretation of the Act by the enforcing agency, these Guidelines . . . constitute a body of experience and informed judgment to which courts and litigants may properly resort for guidance." But we are not bound by the Guidelines. We will not defer to "an administrative construction of a statute where there are 'compelling indications that it is wrong.'"

In sum, we conclude that the bilingual employees have not made out a prima facie case and that Spun Steak has not violated Title VII in adopting an English-only rule as to them. Thus, we reverse the grant of summary judgment in favor of Garcia, Buitrago, and Local 115 to the extent it represents the bilingual employees, and remand with instructions to grant summary judgment in favor of Spun Steak on their claims. A genuine issue of ma-

terial fact exists as to whether there are one or more employees represented by Local 115 with limited proficiency in English who were adversely impacted by the policy. As to such employee or employees, we reverse the grant of summary judgment in favor of Local 115, and remand for further proceedings. REVERSED and REMANDED.

Case Questions:

1. Do you agree with the contention that denying a group the right to speak their native tongue denies them the right to cultural expression?

2. Do employees have a "right" to cultural expression in the workplace?

3. Do you agree with the court that an English-only rule is not abusive per se to those whose primary language is not English? Do you believe that it creates a "class system" of languages in the workplace and therefore inherently places one group's language above another's?

An employer, therefore, may properly enforce a limited, reasonable, and business-related, English-only rule against an employee who can readily comply. However, if the practice of requiring only English on the job is mere pretext for discrimination on the basis of national origin (i.e., the employer imposes the rule *in order to* discriminate, or the rule produces an atmosphere of ethnic oppression), such a policy would be illegal. This might be the case where an employer requires English to be spoken in all areas of the workplace, even on breaks or in discussions between employees during free time.

Scenario

Ruiz, et al. v. Hull, Governor of Arizona
957 P.2d 984 (Ariz. 1998)

Elected officials, state employees, and public school teachers brought action to challenge the constitutionality of an Arizona Constitution amendment which provides that English is the official language of the State of Arizona and that the state and its political subdivisions must "act" only in English. The trial court upheld the amendment. The plaintiffs wanted the court to find that the amendment violates the First and Fourteenth Amendments of the United States Constitution. It did.

Moeller, J.

Plaintiffs contend that the Amendment is a blanket prohibition against all publicly elected officials and government employees using any language other than English in the performance of any government business. Therefore, they reason that the Amendment is a content-based regulation of speech contrary to the First Amendment. Plaintiffs also argue that the Amendment constitutes discrimination against non-English-speaking minorities, thereby violating the Equal Protection Clause of the Fourteenth Amendment. [The] . . . defendants respond that the Amendment should be narrowly read and should be construed as requiring the use of English only with regard to "official, binding government acts." They argue that this narrow construction renders the Amendment constitutional.

At the outset, we note that this case concerns the tension between the constitutional status of language rights and the state's power to restrict such rights. On the one hand, in our diverse society, the importance of establishing common bonds and a common language between citizens is clear. We recognize that the acquisition of English language skills is important in our society. For instance, as a condition to Arizona's admission to the Union, Congress required Arizona to create a public school system and provided that "said schools shall always be conducted in English." . . . Congress has recognized the importance of understanding English in such matters as naturalization legislation and the need for the education of non-English-speaking students. Indeed, Arizona law mandates that school districts in which there are pupils who have limited English proficiency shall provide programs of bilingual instruction or English as a second language with a primary goal of allowing the pupils to become proficient in English in order to succeed in classes taught in English.

However, the American tradition of tolerance "recognizes a critical difference between encouraging the use of English and repressing the use of other languages." We agree with the Ninth Circuit's statement that Arizona's rejection of that tradition by enacting the Amendment has severe consequences not only for Arizona's public officials and employees, but also for the many thousands of persons who would be precluded from receiving essential information from government employee and elected officials in Arizona's governments. If the wide-ranging language of the prohibitions contained in the Amendment were to be implemented as written, the First Amendment rights of all those persons would be violated, a fact now conceded by the proponents of the Amendment, who, instead, urge a restrictive interpretation in accordance with the Attorney General's narrow construction discussed below.

* * *

[W]e reject the Attorney General's construction of the Amendment for three substantive reasons. First, the proffered narrowing construction does not comport with the plain working of the Amendment, and hence, with the plain meaning rule guiding our construction of statutes and provisions in the Arizona Constitution. Second, it does not comport with the stated intent of the drafters of the Amendment. Third, it suffers from both ambiguity and implausability. Therefore, the narrowing construction is rejected because the Amendment's clear terms are not "readily susceptible" to the constraints that the Attorney General attempts to place on them.

* * *

The Attorney General's interpretation would unnecessarily inject elements of vagueness into the Amendment. We feel confident that an average reader of the Amendment would never divine that he or she was free to use a language other than English unless one was performing an official act defined as "a decision or determination of a sovereign, a legislative council, or a court of justice."

Because we conclude that the narrow construction advocated by the Attorney General is untenable, we analyze the constitutionality of the Amendment based on the language of the Amendment itself.

* * *

. . . Assuming arguendo that the government may, under certain circumstances and for appropriate reasons, restrict public employees from using non-English languages to communicate while performing their duties, the Amendment's reach is too broad.

The First Amendment to the United States Constitution provides:

> Congress shall make no law respecting an establishment of religion, or prohibiting the free exercise thereof; or abridging the freedom of speech, or of the press; or the right of the people peaceably to assemble, and to petition the government for a redress of grievances.

The First Amendment applies to the states as well as to the federal government. The trial court held that the Amendment is content-neutral, and, therefore, does not violate the First Amendment. That ruling is flawed.

* * *

The Amendment violates the First Amendment by depriving elected officials and public employees of the ability to communicate with their constituents and with the public. With only a few exceptions, the Amendment prohibits all public officials and employees in Arizona from acting in a language other than English while performing governmental functions and policies. We do not prohibit government offices from adopting language rules for appropriate reasons. We hold that the Amendment goes too far because it effectively cuts off governmental communication with thousands of limited-English-proficient and non-English-speaking persons in Arizona, even when the officials and employees have the ability and desire to communicate in a language understandable to them. Meaningful communication in those cases is barred. Under such circumstances, prohibiting an elected or appointed governmental official or an employee from communicating with the public violates the employee's and the official's rights.

. . . We conclude that the Amendment violates the First Amendment.

* * *

The Amendment adversely affects non-English-speaking persons and impinges on their ability to seek and obtain information and services from government. Because the Amendment chills First Amendment rights that government is not otherwise entitled to proscribe, it violates the Equal Protection Clause of the Fourteenth Amendment. REVERSED and REMANDED.

Case Questions

1. How would this case have been handled differently if it involved a private employer rather than a public entity?

2. The EEOC has stated that an English-only speaking rule at a place of employment is unduly burdensome and a presumptively unnecessary condition of employment. Pursuant to EEOC guidelines, an employer may only establish such a rule where it can show business necessity as well as full and fair notice given to its employees. What type of policy would satisfy this requirement? Be specific.

3. Why do you think the other states' amendments regarding English-only restrictions withstood constitutional scrutiny and the Arizona amendment did not?

Adverse Employment Action and Dissimilar Treatment

Adverse employment action
Any action or omission that takes away a benefit, opportunity, or privilege of employment from an employee.

The third and fourth requirements will be addressed together because they often arise together. The third element of the prima facie case for national origin discrimination is that the employee is **adversely affected** by the employer's employment decision. This may include a demotion, termination, or removal of privileges afforded to other employees. The adverse effect may arise either because employees of the same national origin are treated differently (disparate treatment) or because the policy, though neutral, adversely impacts those of a given national origin (disparate impact).

The fourth element requires that the employee show her position was filled by someone who is not a member of her protected class, or, under other circumstances, that those who are not members of her protected class are treated differently than she. For example, assume an Asian employee is terminated after the third time he is late for work. There is a rule that employees will be terminated if they are late for work more than twice. However, the employer does not enforce the rule against the other employees, only against Asian employees. This would be a case of disparate treatment, because the employee could show that he was treated differently from other employees who were similarly situated but not members of his protected class.

Alternatively, disparate impact has been found, for example, with physical requirements, such as minimum height and weight. Such requirements may have a disparate impact on certain national origin groups as a result of genetic differences among populations and these requirements disproportionately precluded the groups from qualifying for certain jobs. These requirements violate Title VII and must be justified by business necessity. For instance, a requirement that a firefighter be at least five feet, seven inches tall was found to be unlawful where the average height of an Anglo man in the United States is five feet, eight inches, where Spanish-surnamed American men average five feet, four-and-a-half inches, and females average five feet, three inches. On the other hand, if the rule can be shown to be a business necessity, it may be allowed.

Prudencio v. Runyon, Postmaster General, United States Postal Service
986 F.Supp. 343 (Dist. Ct. W.D. Virginia 1997)

A brother and sister of Philippine origin took the US Postal Service (USPS) test, scored high marks, and were never hired during a four-year period, while other non-Philippines with lower scores were hired. They sued for national origin discrimination.

Michael, J.

The plaintiffs, Maritess and Robin Prudencio ("Prudencio"), are brother and sister. Both are of Asian (specifically, Philippine) origin. In 1989, both took a United States Postal Service ("USPS"

or "Post Office") qualifying examination in an effort to secure employment with the Post Office. Both of the plaintiffs passed the test; Maritess Prudencio received a score of 98.80 out of a possible score of 100 and Robin Prudencio got a score of 94.00. Upon receipt of such passing scores, the plaintiff's were qualified in all respects to be considered for employment.

After the test, in May 1989, the Post Office apparently placed job applicants' names on an eligibility "register" in Richmond from which names are drawn as and when positions become available at designated branches. Names were to be placed on the register in numerical order by the score each applicant received on the qualifying test. When a position opened up, a computer-generated list of names was to be produced in the order of the scores received on the test.

Between 1989 and November 1993, the Post Office never contacted the plaintiffs concerning their status for potential employment. Although on three separate occasions names were drawn, in which Maritess ranked within the applicants on three occasions and Robin met the scoring on two occasions, the plaintiffs were never on the hiring list. Of the four persons hired from the worksheet's list of names all had lower test scores than the plaintiffs; three of the persons hired were white, one was black, and none was Asian.

* * *

The applicants have alleged sufficient facts in their complaint to state a claim for discriminatory failure to hire. The Prudencios are members of a protected class because of their national origin (Philippine); they were qualified, by virtue of their high scores on the Post Office tests, for the job in the Charlottesville branch for which the USPS was seeking applicants; they were not hired despite their qualifications; and the positions remained open and the USPS continued to seek or accept applications. The employer filled the positions in question with persons of the applicants' qualifications, but from outside the Title VII protected class (i.e., the white persons hired). Moreover, in the administrative proceedings below, the Post Office admitted that the plaintiffs met all elements of the prima facie test.

The USPS objects . . . that the plaintiffs established a prima facie case of national origin discrimination. The defendant argues . . . [that] the USPS did not know that the Prudencios are of Asian ancestry and, thus, within a Title VII protected class. Of course, while knowledge of a job applicant's race by an employer is a prerequisite for intentional discrimination, the necessary knowledge (or constructive knowledge) is present here. As an initial matter, the Prudencios' father, possessing the same surname, has been employed by the Post Office they applied to in Charlottesville for over fifteen years. Additionally, the USPS acquired actual notice of the Prudencios' national origin when the plaintiffs personally appeared before postal employees to take the employment test in 1989 and again in 1993 to request copies of the "Individual Applicant Ranking Report." Because the burden of establishing a prima facie case of discrimination is not an "onerous" one, and because the USPS had either actual or constructive notice of the plaintiffs' protected national origin status, defendant's motion to dismiss or for summary judgment shall be denied. The Prudencios make out a classic prima facie case of employment discrimination under the *McDonnell Douglas* paradigm.

The defendant-employer must "articulate some legitimate, nondiscriminatory reason for the employee's rejection." Once a plaintiff has established a prima facie case of discrimination, "the employer must respond or lose."

* * *

Here, the Post Office's attempts to proffer two "legitimate nondiscriminatory reasons" that accounted for the omission of the Prudencios' names from the worksheet issued for the Charlottesville branch's vacancies. One such reason is that an administrative or computer error of some type in the Richmond office removed the Prudencios' names from the active list of applicants when the registry was automated; the Post Office headquarters in Richmond failed to forward the full list of qualified applicants to the branch office in Charlottesville where the ultimate hiring decision was made. Thus, because the Richmond Post Office, for whatever reason, omitted the plaintiffs' names from the registry, the Charlottesville branch was operating on a legitimate, nondiscriminatory basis when it failed to hire the Prudencios.

The plaintiffs argue, and the court agrees, however, that in addition to the above reason's overly syllogistic logic, the USPS cannot and does not know that an innocent error (administrative, computer, or otherwise) accounted for the plaintiffs' exclusion from the Charlottesville job candidates' list. Indeed, as the Post Office itself stated

> The Postal Service merely speculate[s] that the omission of the Plaintiffs' names from the hiring work sheets resulted from administrative or computer error. What actually caused the apparent error is not known.

In this court's view, the USPS's concession that it does not know the reason for the exclusion of the plaintiffs from the employment candidates' list is the logical and legal equivalent of proffering no reason for the omission. Because, as a matter of law, "no reason" cannot serve as a "legitimate, nondiscriminatory reason," the plaintiffs' prima facie showing of national origin discrimination remains unrebutted. Under the *McDonnell Douglas* framework, then, the Prudencios are entitled to judgment as a matter of law. Judgment GRANTED for the Prudencios.

Case Questions

1. Who has to prove a company discriminated against an employee or applicant? Do you agree with this?

2. Do you think this was an "honest mistake" by the Post Office? If so, how can the Post Office prove that it had unintentionally removed the plaintiffs from the list?

3. As an employer, what is the best way for you to protect the company from charges accusing the employer of hiring discrimination?

Guidelines on Discrimination Because of Religion or National Origin

Guidelines on Discrimination Because of Religion or National Origin
Federal guidelines that apply only to federal contractors or agencies, which impose on these employers an affirmative duty to prevent discrimination.

Federal agencies or employers who enter into contracts with a government agency are required by the **Guidelines on Discrimination Because of Religion or National Origin** to ensure that individuals are hired and retained without regard to their religion or national origin. These guidelines impose on the federal contractor an affirmative obligation to prevent discrimination. The provisions include the following ethnic groups: Eastern, Middle, and Southern European ancestry, including Jews, Catholics, Italians, Greeks, and Slavs. Blacks, Spanish-surnamed Americans, Asians, and Native Americans are specifically excluded from the guidelines' coverage because of their protection elsewhere in Office of Federal Contract Compliance Rules.

The guidelines provide that, subsequent to a review of the employer's policies, the employer should engage in appropriate outreach and positive recruitment activities to remedy existing deficiencies (i.e., affirmative action). Various approaches to this outreach requirement include the following:

1. Internal communication of the obligation to provide equal employment opportunity without regard to religion or national origin.

2. Development of reasonable internal procedures to ensure that the equal employment policy is fully implemented.

3. Periodic informing of all employees of the employer's commitment to equal employment opportunity for all persons, without regard to religion or national origin.

4. Enlistment of the support and assistance of all recruitment sources.

5. Review of employment records to determine the availability of promotable and transferable members of various religious and ethnic groups.

6. Establishment of meaningful contacts with religious and ethnic organizations and leaders for such purposes as advice, education, technical assistance, and referral of potential employees (many organizations send job announcements to these community groups when recruiting for positions).

7. Significant recruitment activities at educational institutions with substantial enrollments of students from various religious and ethnic groups.

8. Use of the religious and ethnic media for institutional and employment advertising.

Citizenship and the Immigration Reform and Control Act

As mentioned above, Title VII's prohibition against discrimination on the basis of national origin does not prohibit discrimination on the basis of citizenship. In fact, legal aliens (noncitizens residing in the United States) are often restricted from access to certain government or other positions by statute. For instance, in *Foley v. Connelie,* 435 U.S. 291 (1978), the Supreme Court held that a rule requiring citizenship was valid in connection with certain nonelected positions held by officers who participate directly in the formulation, execution, or review of broad public policy. This is called the "political function" exception for positions that are intimately related to the process of self-government. In cases where the restricted position satisfies this exception, discrimination against legal aliens is permitted. *Espinoza* is the seminal case in the area of discrimination on the basis of citizenship and sets forth the important considerations.

ESPINOZA V. FARAH MANUFACTURING CO.
414 U.S. 86 (1973)

Cecilia Espinoza, a lawful Mexican alien, applied for a position at Farah Manufacturing's San Antonio Division. She was denied the position, however, as a result of Farah's policy to hire only US citizens. The issue to be decided by the court is whether Title VII's proscription against discrimination on the basis of national origin protects against discrimination on the basis of citizenship.

Marshall, J.

The term "national origin" on its face refers to the country where a person was born, or, more broadly, the country from which his or her ancestors came.

There are other compelling reasons to believe that Congress did not intend the term "national origin" to embrace citizenship requirements. Since 1914, the Federal Government itself, through Civil Service Commission regulations, has engaged in what amounts to discrimination against aliens by denying them the right to enter competitive examination for federal employment. But it has never been suggested that the citizenship requirement for federal employment constitutes discrimination because of national origin. To interpret the term "national origin" to embrace citizenship requirements would require us to conclude that Congress itself has repeatedly flouted its own declaration of policy. This Court cannot lightly find such a breach of faith. Certainly Title VII prohibits discrimination on the basis of citizenship whenever it has the purpose or effect of discriminating on the basis of national origin. However, there is no indication in the record that Farah's policy against employment of aliens had the purpose or effect of discriminating against persons of Mexican national origin.

Douglas, J., dissenting

It is odd that the Court which holds that a State may not bar an alien from the practice of law or deny employment to aliens can read a federal statute that prohibits discrimination in employment on account of "national origin" so as to permit discrimination against aliens.

Alienage results from one condition only: being born outside the United States. Those born within the country are citizens from birth. It could not be more clear that Farah's policy of excluding aliens is *de facto* a policy of preferring those who were born in this country.

Case Questions

1. Which argument, the majority's or the dissent, do you find more compelling?

2. What implications does this case have for hiring practices in parts of the United States where aliens are prevalent?

3. If Espinoza could show that this policy, while arguably "facially neutral," actually impacts people of Mexican origin differently than people of American origin, wouldn't Espinoza have a claim for disparate impact?

The Immigration Reform and Control Act (IRCA), enacted in 1986 and amended by the Immigration Act of 1990, in contrast to Title VII *does* prohibit employers in certain circumstances from discriminating against employees on the basis of their citizenship or intended citizenship, and from hiring those not legally authorized for employment in the United States. However, IRCA does allow discrimination in favor of United States citizens as against legal aliens. While aliens are guaranteed various rights pursuant to the Constitution, citizenship confers certain benefits only to those who are citizens and not to those who are legal aliens in the United States. For instance, while rights pursuant to the National Labor Relation Act and Fair Labor Standards Act are provided to citizens and aliens alike, government-provided benefits, such as Medicare and Medicaid, are limited to citizens.

Employers not subject to Title VII's prohibitions because of their small size may still be sufficiently large to be covered by IRCA's antidiscrimination provisions; those employers with 4 through 14 employees are prohibited from discriminating on the basis of national origin; and employers with 4 or more employees may not discriminate on the basis of citizenship.

Two acceptable BFOQs are statutorily allowed under IRCA:

1. English-language skill requirements that are reasonably necessary to the normal operation of the particular business or enterprise.
2. Citizenship requirements specified by law, regulation, executive order, or government contracts, along with citizenship requirements that the US attorney general determines to be essential for doing business with the government.

The main difference between a proof of discrimination under Title VII and IRCA is that, in proving a case of disparate impact, Title VII does not require proof of discriminatory intent, while IRCA requires that the adverse action be knowingly and intentionally discriminatory. Therefore, innocent or negligent discrimination is a complete defense to a claim of discrimination under IRCA.

For example, consider a hypothetical firm, Talbort Industries, which was interviewing for customer service representatives in their large order processing department. They required all applicants to speak fluent English. Ching Lee applied and was denied employment due to his accent, which some thought was heavy. It turns out that only 3 applicants out of 20 of Asian descent obtained jobs at Talbort. Talbort explained to Lee that not many Chinese applicants apply and those who do have had strong accents. They claim customers have complained of not understanding these individuals. Does Lee have a claim under Title VII? Under IRCA? Without the showing of knowing and intentional discrimination, Talbort Industries could survive the IRCA claim if Lee could not prove they discriminated against him intentionally; however such knowledge and intention is not required under Title VII and Lee might prevail.

Alternate Basis for National Origin or Citizenship Discrimination

While it is probably the most popular basis for the claim of discrimination based on national origin, Title VII is not the only basis for such a claim. In *St. Francis College v. Al-Khazraji,* 481 U.S. 604 (1987), the Supreme Court held that section 42 USC 1981 encompassed national origin also. In this case, a US citizen who was born in Iraq sued under section 1981, alleging discrimination when he was denied tenure. The Court held that the law applied to "identifiable classes of persons who are subjected to intentional discrimination solely because of their ancestry or ethnic characteristics." The requirement for section 1981 actions is that the employee show he or she was discriminated against because of what they are (here, Iraqi) and not just because of their place of origin or religion.

CHACKO v. TEXAS A & M UNIVERSITY
960 F.Supp. 1180 (Dist. Ct. Tex. 1997)

Applicant was terminated from her job with Texas A & M University (TAMU) because she was not a US citizen. She sued under Title VII and 42 U.S.C. secs. 1981 and 1983 for national origin discrimination.

Crone, J.

. . . It is apparent that Chacko's Title VII claim is based upon her citizenship and not her national origin. Consequently, Chacko is unable to satisfy the first element of a prima facie case—membership in a protected class. Because citizenship discrimination does not fall within the ambit of Title VII, TAMU is entitled to summary judgment.

Chacko's §1981 claim, like her Title VII claim, is entitled "national origin discrimination." Chacko again, however, neither identifies her national origin nor adduces facts suggesting that she was terminated or was not hired due to her national origin. Instead, as noted above, her complaint avers nothing more than a claim based on her status as a noncitizen. The defendants argue that because Chacko has failed to provide any information concerning her national origin or race, she cannot prove that their alleged discrimination against her was based on her membership in a group protected under §1981.

It is well settled that §1981 prohibits private, as well as official, discrimination on the basis of race or national origin. Supreme Court precedent also establishes that §1981 prohibits official discrimination against aliens. The Supreme Court, however, has not addressed whether §1981 prohibits private discrimination on the basis of citizenship.

. . . As the court reasoned in *Cheung:*

> [w]hen Congress enacted section 1981(c), it was well-established that section 1981 prohibited public discrimination on the basis of citizenship. Section 1981 does not exempt private citizenship from its coverage, nor is there evidence in the legislative history that Congress did not intend to prohibit private citizenship discrimination. Accordingly, section 1981 must be construed to prohibit private discrimination on the basis of citizenship.

* * *

"To establish a prima facie case under section 1981, a plaintiff must produce direct or circumstantial evidence of purposeful discrimination by the defendant." . . . The criteria set forth in McDonnell Douglas Corp. are sufficient to establish a prima facie case under §1981 based on circumstantial evidence.

In the case at bar, Chacko, as a noncitizen, is a member of a protected class under §1981. Chacko was unquestionably qualified for the position at issue. At her deposition, Cook testified that Chacko was the most qualified applicant and ranked number one. With respect to the third or fourth element, it is undisputed that Chacko was not hired by TAMU or was discharged from the position of Sponsored Student Specialist. Finally, Chacko has demonstrated that TAMU hired an individual outside the protected class, Yurgensen-Jacks, a United States citizen, to fill the position. Thus, Chacko has adduced sufficient evidence to establish a prima facie case of citizenship discrimination.

The employer has articulated a legitimate, nondiscriminatory reason for its actions—the hiring process for the Sponsored Student Specialist position was deferred in order to initiate an investigation into claims regarding irregularities in the application procedure with respect to Chacko.

The next inquiry, therefore, is whether the proffered reason is merely pretextual. A plaintiff may succeed in demonstrating pretext "either directly by persuading the court that a discriminatory reason more likely motivated the employer or indirectly by showing that the employer's proffered explanation is unworthy of credence." According to the deposition testimony of another worker, when [it was] announced in the morning meeting on November 10, 1993, that Chacko had been or was being hired, [one of the employees] "blew up." When the worker was questioned as to what [that person] said, she responded:

> I really tried to block this out of my mind. He was just very angry and felt that it was unfair and un-American to hire a foreigner and that other peo-

ple—Americans were more qualified or at least should have been given the position.

Moreover, Chacko stated in her deposition that she was told that "a formal complaint had been lodged and that there was a problem with my being a foreigner." From these comments, it could be inferred that TAMU's articulated reason for its actions toward Chacko was merely a pretext for alienage discrimination. Thus, fact issues remain with respect to why Chacko either was terminated or was not hired by TAMU. Accordingly, in the absence of an affirmative defense, summary judgment is not appropriate, and Chacko may proceed to trial on her §1981 claim of citizenship discrimination. Judgment for Chacko.

Case Questions

1. Why do you think Title VII does not protect an individual from discrimination based on citizenship?

2. Do you think discrimination based on citizenship should be condoned or prohibited? Why or why not?

3. The court did not decide the issue of whether Chacko was discriminated against due to her citizenship. Do you think she was or was not? Why or why not?

Workforce 2000

In 1998, African Americans made up 11.3% of the workforce, Hispanics made up 10.4%, and Asians, Pacific Islanders, American Indians, and Alaska Natives made up 4.2%. It is projected that in 2008, African Americans will make up 11.5% of the workforce, Hispanics will make up 12.7%, and Asians, Pacific Islanders, American Indians, and Alaska Natives will make up 5.2%. (cite to: Howard N. Fullerton, Jr., "Civilian labor force 16 years and older by 1988, 1998, and projected 2008." http://stats.bls.gov/emplt986.htm, November 30, 1999.)

The number of African Americans in the workforce by 2008 is expected to increase by 19.5%, Asians, Pacific Islanders, American Indians, and Alaska Natives by 40.3%, and Hispanics by 36.8%. (Bureau of Labor Statistics. "Civilian labor force 16 years and older by sex, age, race, and Hispanic origin, 1988, 1998, and projected 2008." http://stats.bls.gov/news.release/ecopro.t05.htm, February 9, 2000.)

If the increases are anywhere near the projections, then entry, development, or promotion barriers to full use of the total diversity of the workplace will likely result in loss in the business's effectiveness and productivity. For any business wishing to be on the cutting edge, or simply to effectively use its resources and encourage the best performance from employees, adherence to Title VII's requirements regarding race and national origin should be viewed as a business imperative and not merely as compliance with the law.

The significance to managers of this protection is there must be a complete review of all policies that may have an impact on employees or applicants of diverse national origin. As stated above, this impact may not be obvious.

Employers must be cognizant of the varying needs of employees from different backgrounds. For instance, employers may address the perceived problem of bilingual employees in a number of ways, such as offering English-as-a-second-language classes or tutors for semibilingual employees. Not only would this foster less isolation and exclusion of the employee, but it would also create greater confidence and less intimidation when the employees are speaking English. This type of proactive approach may prevent problems in this area before they emerge.

Management Tips

- While a specific national origin may be a BFOQ, make sure that only individuals of that origin can do the specific job since courts have a high standard for BFOQs in this area.
- While English fluency may be required, you are not allowed to discriminate because of an accent (unless the accent makes it impossible to understand the individual). However, be cautious to evaluate the requirement of the job since there may be positions that do not actually require English speaking.
- If you are a federal contractor, remember that you have additional responsibilities to engage in outreach and positive recruitment activities under the Guidelines on Discrimination Because of Religion or National Origin.
- While you are not prohibited from discriminating on the basis of citizenship under Title VII, you may be prohibited from discriminating on this basis under IRCA. Before instituting a policy, consider the implication of both statutes.

Summary

• Title VII, the Civil Rights Act of 1964, makes it an unlawful employment practice for employers to limit, segregate, or classify employees in any way that would deprive them of employment opportunities based on their national origin.

• An employee or applicant must show the following to be successful in a claim of discrimination based on national origin discrimination.

1. The individual is a member of a protected class.
2. The individual was qualified for the position at issue.
3. The employer made an employment decision against the individual.
4. The position was filled by someone not in a protected class.

• National origin refers to an individual's ancestor's place of origin or physical, cultural, or linguistic characteristics of an origin group.

• An employer has a defense against a national origin discrimination claim if it can show that the national origin is a bona fide occupational qualification. However, in general, this is very difficult to do. An exception to the difficulty is the requirement of English fluency, if speaking English is a substantial portion of the individual's job.

• English-only rules applied at all times are presumptively discriminatory, according to the EEOC. If the employer is considering an English-only rule, it is recommended that the employer should:

1. Consider whether the rule is necessary.
2. Determine if the rule is a business necessity.
3. Consider if everybody is fluent in English.
4. Communicate the rule to employees.
5. Enforce the rule fairly.

• An alternative basis for national origin or citizenship discrimination is section 42 USC 1981.

• Guidelines on Discrimination Because of Religion or National Origin are federal guidelines that apply to federal contractors or agencies and impose on those employers an affirmative duty to prevent discrimination.

• The Immigration Reform and Control Act, unlike Title VII, prohibits, in certain circumstances, discrimination on the basis of citizenship. The act does allow for discrimination in favor of US citizens.

• Two statutorily allowed BFOQs under IRCA include:

1. English-language skill requirements that are reasonably necessary.
2. Citizenship requirements specified by law, regulation, executive order, government contracts, or requirements established by the US attorney general.

Chapter-End Questions

1. Which, if any, of the following scenarios would support an employee's claim of discrimination on the basis of national origin?
   a. A Dominican chambermaid in a hotel is denied promotion to front-desk duties primarily because of her inability to clearly articulate and to make herself adequately understood in English. (*Majia v. New York Sheraton Hotel,* 459 F.Supp. 375 (S.D.N.Y. 1978).)
   b. Applicant with a speech impediment is unable to pronounce the letter "r." The applicant therefore often has difficulty

being understood when speaking and is denied a position.

c. The owner of a manufacturing facility staffed completely by Mexicans refuses employment to a white American manager because the owner is concerned that the Mexicans will only consent to supervision by and receive direction from another Mexican.

d. An Indian restaurant seeks to fill a server position. The advertisement requests applications from qualified individuals of Indian descent to add to the authenticity of the restaurant. In the past, the restaurant found that its business declined when it used Caucasian servers, because the atmosphere of the restaurant suffered. An Italian applies for the position and is denied employment.

e. A company advertises for Japanese-trained managers, because the employer has found that they are more likely to remain at the company for an extended time, to be loyal and devoted to the firm, and to react well to direction and criticism. An American applies for the position and is denied employment in favor of an equally qualified Japanese-trained applicant, who happens to also be Japanese.

2. Hector Garcia, a bilingual Mexican-American, is a salesperson for Gloor Lumber and Supply, Inc. Management complimented Hector's work on several occasions and gave him a $250 bonus at the end of his first year. The company had a rule that the employees could not speak Spanish on the job (except during breaks) unless they were dealing with customers who could not speak English. On one occasion, Garcia was asked a question on the job by another Mexican-American employee, and when he replied in Spanish he was discharged. The employer claims Garcia's infraction of the rule was only one of the reasons for his discharge. The employer offered evidence of Garcia's general failure to perform other aspects of his job and claims that the compliments and bonus Garcia received were motivational tools used by the company to encourage him to perform better, not evidence that he was doing a good job. Garcia claims that the English-only rule is discrimination based on national origin. What do you think? (*Garcia v. Gloor,* 618 F.2d 264 (5th Cir. 1980).)

3. Calvin Roach, a native-born American of Acadian descent, was fired by Dresser Industrial. Roach claimed that he was fired because of his "Acadian" national origin ("Cajun" descent) and his association with Dresser employees of the same origin. Employer claims that, since there is not and never was such a country as Acadia, employee's claim of national origin discrimination is not covered under Title VII. Do you agree? (*Roach v. Dresser Ind. Valve & Instrument Division,* 494 F.Supp. 215 (W.D.La. 1980).)

4. Valentine Jurado, of Mexican-American and Native American descent, was a disc jockey for KIIS radio station. After broadcasting in English for several years, Jurado was asked by the program director to incorporate some "street" Spanish words into the program to attract more Hispanic listeners. A consultant was hired by the radio station to analyze the effects of Jurado's bilingual broadcasting on the listening audience. The consultant concluded that the attempt to increase the Hispanic audience had actually resulted in hurting the overall ratings of the station because it confused many of the listeners, and there was no quantifiable rise in the station's Hispanic audience. Jurado was told to stop speaking Spanish on the air, and he was fired the next day for refusing to comply with this order. Jurado claims that the English-only order disproportionately disadvantaged Hispanics and that he was also fired before being given a chance to

attempt to comply. (*Jurado v. Eleven-Fifty Corp.*, 813 F.2d 1406 (9th Cir. 1987).)

5. Ray Wardle was police officer for the Ute Indian tribe in Utah for more than 17 years; he was not a member of this tribe. After 17 years of service, he was discharged because the tribe was hiring a tribal member to fill his position. Wardle filed an action against the tribe, claiming that he was fired based purely on the basis of his national origin. Who will win? (*Wardle v. Ute Indian Tribe*, 623 F.2d 670 (10th Cir. 1980).)

6. Frontera, a Spanish-speaking employee, applied for a full-time position as a carpenter at the Cleveland airport. He had been hired previously as a temporary carpenter for the airport and had demonstrated that he was capable of sufficiently performing his duties as a carpenter. He also had not had any trouble communicating on the job. When he applied for the full-time position, he was required to take a test that was advertised and administered in English. Frontera failed the test and filed suit against the employer on the basis that the test discriminated against Spanish-speaking individuals. The Civil Service Commission claims that, because of a lack of training programs for carpenters, it needs to ensure proficiency, and the test is only designed to test knowledge of words and terms that a carpenter should definitely know. How should the court decide? (*Frontera v. Sindell*, 522 F.2d 1215 (6th Cir. 1975).)

7. Carino, born in the Republic of the Philippines and naturalized as a US citizen, was hired by the University of Oklahoma College of Dentistry as the supervisor of the dental lab. Even though Carino was hired as a supervisor, his job consisted more of technical expertise than supervisory skills. About a year after his employment began, the university changed his title from supervisor to lab technician (there was no change in his salary or responsibilities), but Carino was not informed of this title change. After another year, the college of dentistry hired a new supervisor, Mr. Wimpy, and changed Carino's title to senior maxillofacial technician. This change was labeled a promotion, and Carino received a raise in pay, but he was not informed of his second title change, either. Soon after this change took place, the faculty member who required maxillofacial products left the school and Carino's position became obsolete. Carino finally consulted the dean of the college of dentistry and discovered that he had been demoted and replaced as supervisor. Carino filed suit, claiming national origin discrimination. The college claims that Carino was hired primarily for his technical skills and was awarded the supervisory position to start him off at a higher salary, and that he was not qualified to be a supervisor because of his inability to effectively communicate due to his native accent. Will this be a sufficient argument by the school to justify what it did? (*Carino v. University of Oklahoma Board of Regents*, 750 F.2d 815 (10th Cir. 1985).)

8. In 1979, Xieng, a Cambodian, began working at Peoples National Bank in its management training program for minorities. The program involved a great deal of customer contact. In 1981, Xieng was awarded a certificate of successful completion of the program and received consistently positive performance appraisals. At the bank's suggestion, Xieng received English-language training and his tutor viewed his ability to communicate in English as "dramatically improved." However, in each of his reviews, Xieng's supervisors noted that his communication skills needed future improvement. In 1986, Xieng was passed over for promotion in favor of a white woman with no previous

experience in that position. What does the bank need to show to establish that the promotion decision does not violate Title VII? (*Xieng v. Peoples National Bank,* 821 P.2d 520 (Wash. 1991).)

9. Rush Presbyterian requires that employees in all job classifications be able to speak and write English. Garcia, a Latino, contends that this rule discriminates against those for whom English is not a first language. The court held that, because there was no evidence that Latinos had been excluded from Rush's workforce in greater numbers than people of other origins, there was no adverse impact on Latinos. Is this true? Couldn't Latinos have been discouraged from even applying and, therefore, those nonapplicants do not appear in the numbers presented in the court? Can you imagine that a rule requiring proficiency in English does not have an adverse effect on minorities? (*Garcia v. Rush Presbyterian,* 660 F.2d 1217 (7th Cir. 1981).)

12   AGE DISCRIMINATION

Chapter Outline

S C E N A R I O S

S C E N A R I O   1

In an effort to reduce costs across the board, Pilchard wishes to hire recent graduates of MBA programs who have little experience. His firm would be paying them above competitive salaries even if it offered them one-half the salaries of its present staff members who are over age 40. Should Pilchard terminate the older employees in favor of the younger, less-expensive workers?

S C E N A R I O   2

Beth, an employer, wants to hire someone for a strenuous job that requires a great deal of training, which will take place over the course of several years. The applicant who appears most qualified is 58 years old; however, Beth is concerned that the applicant will not be able to handle the physical demands of the position in the long run. Further, she is concerned that the applicant will only continue working for several more years before she retires. Does Beth hire the applicant, anyway?

Statutory Basis

EXHIBIT 12–1   Age Discrimination in Employment Act

Sec. 4 (a) It shall be unlawful for an employer—
(1) to fail or refuse to hire or to discharge any individual or otherwise discriminate against any individual with respect to his compensation, terms, conditions, or privilege of employment, because of such individual's age;
(2) to limit, segregate, or classify his employees in any way which would deprive or tend to deprive any individual of employment opportunities or otherwise adversely affect his status as an employee, because of such individual's age; or
(3) to reduce the wage rate of any employee in order to comply with this chapter.

Source: 20 U.S.C. §§623.

Oldie . . . but Goldie?

America is a culture in which youth is valued. It must be very strange indeed to those of other cultures, like the Japanese, who revere age and believe that with it comes wisdom and insight unobtainable by the young. In our culture, the general perception is that with youth comes energy, imagination, and innovation. With age

EXHIBIT 12–2   Myths about Older Workers and Age Discrimination

1. Older workers are less able to perform in most positions than younger workers, even given their experience.
2. In a reduction in force caused by economic reasons, employers should always terminate the older workers, since they are usually the highest paid.
3. If most people in a certain age group have a common weakness, it can be generalized that all in that group have the weakness, and age can be used as a job qualification.
4. If an employee is discriminated against because of youth, the employee has a claim under the Age Discrimination in Employment Act.
5. Employees must retire at age 65 in the United States.

comes decreasing interest, lack of innovation and imagination, and a lessening of the quality of the person.

Older employees suffer from these misperceptions in the workplace, subtle and subconscious though they may be. While statistics show that older workers are more reliable, harder working, more committed, and have less absenteeism than younger workers—all characteristics that employers say they value—the general perception of them as employees is exactly the opposite. This adversely affects employees who may not be treated as well, because they are perceived as less-desirable employees. In addition, older workers are now more likely to remain on the job than their counterparts earlier in this century. Fifteen percent of Americans over 65 (about 4.7 million) are working full or part time. While 47 percent of those workers claim that they do so because they need the money, more than 80 percent say that they do it because they like being with other people and want to be productive.[1]

The scenarios above are merely generalizations, but they are omnipresent in the workplace. Many employers feel older employees may be more expensive to retain because they have greater experience and seniority. Each year they may receive a raise until their salary becomes a burden on the firm. Management realizes that it could reduce costs by terminating older employees, who have more experience than may be necessary to perform the requirements of the position, and by hiring younger, less experienced employees.

This may seem to be a realistic and legitimate business decision but, once terminated, older workers are disadvantaged in the search for new employment. They are either viewed as overqualified or employers express concern about their ability to adequately perform. The concerns are usually based on preconceived stereotypical notions about the deterioration of the older worker's senses, physical capabilities, response time, and competence.

---

[1]Arthur Shostak, "Futures Poll on Americans, Work and Education," Drexel University Center for Employment Futures.

In addition, younger workers, as a group, may be better educated and better qualified when entering the workforce. Instead of making a time-consuming individualized determination of the abilities of each applicant, employers generalize about classes of workers and only choose employees from those classes they perceive as more desirable. While some of these generalizations may be grounded in fact, it is the act of generalizing, rather than making individualized conclusions, that constitutes the wrongful discrimination.

In this chapter, we will discuss older employees and the legal rights that the law provides for them through the Age Discrimination in Employment Act.

Regulation

Age Discrimination in Employment Act

Age Discrimination in Employment Act Prohibits discrimination in employment on the basis of age; applies to individuals who are at least 40 years old. Individuals who are not yet 40 years old are not protected by the act and *may* be discriminated against on the basis of their age.

Baseless discrimination against older workers occurs with such consistency that Congress was compelled to enact legislation to protect older workers from discrimination to prevent increased unemployment for those over 40. In 1967, Congress enacted the **Age Discrimination in Employment Act** (ADEA) for the express purpose of "promot[ing the] employment of older people based on their ability rather than age [and prohibiting] arbitrary age discrimination in employment." The act applies to employment by public and private employers and by unions and employment agencies, as well as by foreign companies with more than 20 workers located in the United States.

On its effective date, the act covered employees between the ages of 40 and 65. The upper limit was extended to 70 in 1978 and later removed completely. There is no longer an upper age limit, in recognition that an 80-plus-year-old may be just as qualified for a position as a 30-year-old and should have the opportunity to prove her or his qualifications and to obtain or retain employment based on them. With few exceptions, mandatory retirement has now become a dinosaur. It is also important to recognize that the act will become all the more critical as health care advances allow people to live more vital lives to longer ages. Many people today feel healthy enough to work long beyond the age at which most people used to retire.

Courts and Congress have recognized there is a trade-off for the required employment of qualified older workers. In *Graefenhain v. Pabst Brewing Co.,* 827 F.2d 13, n.8 (7th Cir. 1987), overruled on other grounds, 860 F.2d 834 (7th Cir. 1988), the court said:

> Although the ADEA does not hand federal courts a roving commission to review business judgments, the ADEA *does* create a cause of action against business decisions that merge with age discrimination. Congress enacted the ADEA precisely because many employers or younger business executives act as if they believe that there are good business reasons for discriminating against older employees. Retention of senior employees who can be replaced by younger lower-paid people frequently competes with other values, such as profits or conceptions of economic efficiency. The ADEA represents a

choice among these values. It stands for the propositions that this is a better country for its willingness to pay the costs for treating older employees fairly.

You may wonder, why wasn't age merely included as an amendment to Title VII since the laws have several similarities? Both are enforced by the EEOC, as well as through private actions. However, discrimination based on age is substantively different from discrimination based on factors covered by Title VII in two important ways. The ADEA is more lenient than Title VII regarding the latitude afforded employers' reasons for adverse employment decisions. The ADEA allows an employer to rebut a prima facie case of age discrimination by identifying any "reasonable factor other than age" that motivated the decision.

Second, the act only protects employees over 40 from discrimination. Unlike Title VII, there is no protection from "reverse" discrimination. In other words, an individual under 40 cannot file a claim under the act based on the claim that she was discriminated against because of her youth—that it was because she was too young. Note, however, that certain state laws or precedents allow for what might be considered a youth's "reverse-discrimination" claim under state age discrimination statutes. One New Jersey man who claimed he was fired from a bank vice president position because of his young age (25) was allowed to proceed in court in that state.

In order to ensure that appropriate and adequate information exists as to hiring practices in connection with age, the act has specific record-keeping provisions for employers. Employers are required to maintain the following information for **three years** for each employee and applicant, where applicable:

- Name
- Address
- Date of birth
- Occupation
- Rate of pay
- Compensation earned each week

Employers are required to maintain the following information for **one year** for each employee, and for both regular and temporary workers:

- Job applications, résumés, or other employment inquiries in answer to ads or notices, plus records about failure or refusal to hire.
- Records on promotion, demotion, transfer, selection for training, layoff, recall, or discharge of any employee.
- Job orders given to agencies or unions for recruiting personnel for job openings.
- Test papers.
- Results of physical exams that are considered in connection with any personnel action.
- Ads or notices relating to job openings, promotions, training programs, or opportunities for overtime.

The Burdens of Proof

The Employee's Prima Facie Case: Disparate Treatment.   An employee believes that his employer has made a decision about him on the basis of age. What does he do now? The employee may file an action against the employer under the ADEA and prove age discrimination on the basis of disparate treatment by utilizing the method of proof for Title VII cases originally set forth in *McDonnell Douglas Corp. v. Green* and later adapted to age discrimination claims under the ADEA. Under this approach, the employee must establish the following four elements to persuade the court that she or he even has a claim for age discrimination:

1. She is in the protected class.
2. She was terminated or demoted.
3. She was doing her job well enough to meet her employer's legitimate expectations.
4. Others not in the protected class were treated more favorably.

Member of the Protected Class.   To satisfy the first requirement of the prima facie case, the employee must merely show that she or he is 40 years old or older.

Adverse Employment Action.   The second requirement is proof that the employer made an employment decision that adversely affected the employee. This may include a decision not to hire the applicant or to terminate the employee.

Qualified for the position
Able to meet the employer's legitimate job requirements.

Qualified for the Position.   With the third requirement, the applicant must prove that he or she was **qualified for the position.** If applicant is not qualified, then the employer's decision regarding the applicant would be justified and the applicant's claim fails. The position requirements, however, must be legitimate requirements, and not merely devised for the purpose of terminating or refusing to hire older workers. Courts have allowed this requirement to be met by the employee simply by showing that the employee was never told that performance was unacceptable. The qualifications requirement is not a difficult one. Courts have even held that the fact that the employee was hired initially indicates that he or she has the basic qualifications.

Dissimilar Treatment.   In connection with the fourth requirement for a prima facie case of age discrimination, the employee or applicant must show that he was treated differently than other employees who are not in the protected class. This requires an employer to explain its actions if it terminates (or refuses to hire) an older qualified employee, while simultaneously hiring younger employees. For instance, where an employer terminates a 57-year-old worker and hires, in her place, a 34-year-old employee, and the 57-year-old employee can show that she remains qualified for her position, the employer must defend its decision.

This requirement has presented the most difficulty for courts. What if an 80-year-old is fired and replaced by a 78-year-old? Is this discriminatory action? The

EXHIBIT 12–3

The EEOC Interpretive Rules offer the following guidance:

When help wanted notices or advertisements contain terms and phrases such as "age 25 to
35," "young," "boy," "girl," "college student," "recent college graduate," or others of a
similar nature, such a term or phrase discriminates against the employment of older people,
and will be considered in violation of the act. Such specifications as "age 40 to 50," "age
over 50," or "age over 65" are also considered to be prohibited. Where such specifications
as "retired person" or "supplement your pension" are intended and applied so as to
discriminate against others within the protected group, they, too, are regarded as prohibited
unless one of the exceptions applies.

basic ADEA case is filed where an employee is replaced by or not hired in favor of
an employee who is *not* a member of the protected class. However, the Supreme
Court has held, in *O'Connor v. Consolidated Coin Caterers,* 116 S.Ct. 1307 (1996),
that a plaintiff can state a claim as long as she or he is replaced by someone younger,
even if the replacement is 40 years old or older.

One other provision of the ADEA merits special attention; section 4(e) makes
it unlawful to "print or publish or cause to be printed or published, any notice or
advertisement . . . indicating any preference, limitation, specification, or discrimination, based on age."

The court in *Hodgson v. Approved Personnel Serv., Inc.,* 529 F.2d 760 (4th Cir.
1975), found that, in determining whether an advertisement had a discriminatory effect on older individuals, "the discriminatory effect of an advertisement is determined not by 'trigger words' but rather by its context." That is, the ad is not considered discriminatory because of a word or words but rather whether the intent of
the ad is to discriminate against older individuals.

While the use of certain trigger words like "girl" or "young" does not establish
a *per se* ADEA violation, the context of the statement is therefore important to determine its discriminatory effect. For instance, the use of "recent college graduate"
is not discriminatory if a personnel agency merely intended to identify those services that it offered to that specific class of individuals. See Exhibit 12–3.

Employer's Defenses.   Once the employee has presented evidence relating to the
employer's actions, the burden of proof shifts to the employer to present a legitimate
and nondiscriminatory reason for its actions.

What does "articulate" mean in the *McDonnell Douglas* requirement that
the employer "articulate" a legitimate, nondiscriminatory reason for the adverse
employment decision? Courts have differed, with some holding that the employer
must merely identify a reason why the individual was terminated or not hired and
others requiring that the employer present evidence of its nondiscriminatory reason
and also persuade the court that the reason actually constitutes the basis for its
decision.

EXHIBIT 12–4

The employer may present a legitimate and nondiscriminatory reason for its actions in one of
several ways. The act states that:

It shall not be unlawful for an employer

(1) to take any action otherwise prohibited where age is a bona fide occupational
qualification reasonably necessary to the normal operation of the particular business, or
where the differentiation is based on reasonable factors other than age.

(2) to observe the terms of a bona fide seniority system or any bona fide employee benefit
plan such as a retirement, pension, or insurance plan.

(3) to discharge or otherwise discipline an individual for good cause.

Bona Fide Occupational Qualification.   If an employer is sued for age discrimination, the defense of BFOQ is available. In fact, age is one of the most consistently
applied BFOQs. The employer's proof of a bona fide occupational qualification
under the ADEA is slightly different and less exacting than under Title VII. Title
VII requires that the employer demonstrate that the essence of the business requires
the exclusion of the members of a protected class and all or substantially all of
the members of that class are unable to perform adequately in the position in
question. The EEOC follows the requirements of Title VII in connection with the
ADEA but adds one further possibility for the employer's proof. The EEOC identifies what the employer must prove in an age discrimination case brought under the
ADEA as:

1. The age limit is reasonably necessary to the essence of the employer's
business; and either

2. All or substantially all of the individuals over that age are unable to
perform the job's requirements adequately; or

3. Some of the individuals over that age possess a disqualifying trait that
cannot be ascertained except by reference to age.

The third element of the proof allows an employer to exclude an older worker
from a position that may be unsafe to *some* older workers. This defense would only
be accepted by a court where there is no way to individually assess the safety potential of a given applicant or employee.

For example, assume there existed a medical disorder that was prevalent among
those over 80 and was not discoverable under standard medical investigation. Assume also that this medical condition caused its sufferers to lose consciousness
without warning. An employer who refused to place those over 80 in the position of
a school bus driver would satisfy the proof of a BFOQ. Note that it is not enough
for an employer to simply think there is a condition related to age that supports a
BFOQ. The decision must be based on competent expert evidence of a connection
between age and the component of the job affected.

2

Scenario

When Congress passed the 1986 amendments to the ADEA prohibiting **mandatory retirement** on the basis of age for most workers, it included several temporary exemptions, notably one for tenured faculty in higher education. That exemption expired December 31, 1993. Mandatory retirement has been limited to two circumstances. First, a small number of high-level employees with substantial executive authority can be subjected to compulsory retirement at age 70. This exception is a very narrow one and does not allow for compulsory retirement policies for mid-level managers. Second, persons in selected occupations, such as police and fire-fighters, in which age is a bona fide occupational qualification have been subject to mandatory retirement. Regarding tenured faculty members, until recently, the ADEA did not prohibit compulsory retirement at age 70 for tenured faculty members at institutions of higher learning. This exception expired on December 31, 1993, making compulsory retirement ages for tenured faculty no longer permissible. However, some educators are pushing for reinstatement of the ADEA exemptions.

Mandatory retirement
Deemed illegal by the 1986 amendments to the ADEA, with few exceptions.

Reasonable Factor Other Than Age.   Is there discrimination if an employer who owns a steel manufacturing plant wants all of its employees to be super strong, just in case their strength is needed during the business day, even if each particular job may not require that much strength, for instance, an office position? This requirement may seriously impair the ability of an older worker to be hired. The employer's defense that the adverse action was taken as a result of "reasonable factors other than age" appears to allow employers to discriminate against protected persons for reasons that may have an adverse *effect* on older workers, such as dexterity or strength.

In fact, the EEOC regulations require that the factor be *job-related* if the distinction has a disparate impact on employees over 40. Reasonable factors, therefore, may include any requirement that does not have an adverse impact on older workers, as well as those factors that do adversely affect this protected class but are shown to be job-related. For example, if an employee is not performing satisfactorily and is terminated, her failure to meet reasonable performance standards would constitute a reasonable factor other than age.

In addition, if an employee is terminated as a result of his failure to maintain a certain speed on an assembly line, he may claim that this speed requirement adversely affects older workers, because they are not able to maintain similar speeds as younger workers. However, if the employer can show that speed of performance in this position is job related and necessary to the operations of the business, then the termination does not constitute an ADEA violation.

In scenario 2, the applicant's age appears to be of some concern; however the real issue is whether the applicant can do the strenuous job. If it can be shown that the applicant can perform all the necessary job functions, he should be hired because he is the most qualified. In the future, if he becomes unable to meet the demands of the job, his termination would be a result of his lack of ability, not his age. Furthermore, regarding the concerns about the applicant leaving after a few years, *any* employee can leave an employer at any time unless there is a contract. This is not only a concern with older individuals.

Scenario

PARRISH V. IMMANUEL MEDICAL CENTER

92 F.3d 727 (8th Cir. 1996)

A 66-year-old employee resigned after being summarily transferred to a new position and after her supervisor made age-based remarks. She sued for age discrimination and the jury found for the employee. The employer appealed but the judgment is upheld.

Beam, J.

Mary Ruth Parrish was hired as a registrar at Immanuel Medical Center (Immanuel) in 1979 at the age of 57. Although her position became computerized after she was hired, she did not have a problem learning the new technology and received satisfactory evaluations from her superiors, received no negative evaluations, and largely positive comments from her supervisors, save for an admonishment to refrain from criticizing fellow employees in the department.

Although Parrish was slower in admitting patients than many of the other registrars, she was also one of the most accurate workers in the department. When the computer system was upgraded and additional training was required, Mary attended day one of the two-day sessions but missed the second session because she was admitted to the hospital due to depression and anxiety. On at least one occasion, Mary's supervisor was said to have commented that younger registrars were having problems with the new computers.

When she returned to work a month later, Mary was assigned to a new position with new hours. Mary was not given the option of returning to her position as a part-time registrar and was presented the offer to transfer as an all-or-nothing proposition. The following day Mary did not report to work but called her supervisor to ask her to reconsider the transfer. The supervisor refused so Mary, at the age of sixty-six, resigned. Mary sued Immanuel, alleging that she was constructively discharged because of her age and her disability.

Immanuel contended that it legitimately sought to transfer Mary because of her inefficiency and her difficulties with the new computer system. The jury rejected Immanuel's explanation and found that Immanuel had discriminated against Mary due to her age and disability. A jury awarded Mary $21,218.15 in compensatory damages. Based on the jury's finding that Immanuel willfully violated the ADEA, the district court determined that Parrish was entitled to liquidated damages and accordingly entered final judgment for Parrish in the amount of $42,436.30.

* * *

We are satisfied that there is sufficient evidence to support the jury's finding of age discrimination. First of all, Parrish produced ample evidence from which a reasonable jury could conclude that Immanuel's stated reasons for transferring Parrish were pretextual. Immanuel alleges that Parrish was inefficient, slow, and incapable of adjusting to the new computers. Parrish proved, however, that she was an accurate and reliable employee during her ten years at Immanuel. She consistently received above average ratings on her yearly evaluations. Although her rate of production was slower than the average registrar, [a supervisor] did not think the problem significant enough to warrant more than a single comment. Moreover, there was undisputed evidence that Parrish was given only one day of training on the new computer system, and that all of the trainees were helping each other learn the new software on the first day of training. Several witnesses testified that they did not recall Parrish having significant problems learning the new system.

Erickson's comment to Parrish that even "younger registrars" were having difficulty with the computers also supports the jury's verdict. As the Supreme Court has noted, "[i]t is the very essence of age discrimination for an older employee to be fired because the employer believes that productivity and competence decline with old age." The ADEA was enacted to combat stereotypes regarding the ability of older employees to keep pace with changes in the workplace. From comments comparing Parrish's ability to learn computers to the abilities of younger registrars, reasonable minds could infer that the decision to create the new position for Parrish was based on such stereotypes.

Parrish produced ample evidence from which a jury could conclude that Immanuel constructively discharged Parrish not for its proffered reasons but because of her age. Consequently, the district court properly denied Immanuel's motion for judgment as a matter of law with respect to Parrish's age claim. Affirmed.

Case Questions

1. Should employers be able to terminate or transfer older workers when they cannot grasp new technology? What can employers do to protect themselves?

2. What do you think is the purpose of the ADEA? What do you think should be its purpose?

3. Do you believe that there is an age after which most people should not be allowed in certain positions? What type of positions? What age would you decide is appropriate for removing these people from the position? How would you decide?

As the case below demonstrates, the employer cannot simply assume things about older people that keeps them from holding certain positions. The employer must base such decisions on credible evidence.

WESTERN AIR LINES, INC. v. CRISWELL
472 U.S. 400 (1985)

Western Air Lines requires that its flight engineers, who are members of the cockpit crew but do not operate flight controls unless both the pilot and copilot become incapacitated, retire at age 60. The Federal Aviation Administration prohibits anyone from acting as a pilot or copilot after they have reached the age of 60. The respondents in this case include both pilots who were denied reassignment to the position of flight engineers at age 60 and flight engineers who were forced to retire at that age. The airline argued that the age 60 retirement requirement is a BFOQ reasonably necessary to the safe operation of the business. The lower court instructed the jury as follows: the airline could only establish age as a BFOQ if "it was highly impractical for [petitioner] to deal with each [flight engineer] over age 60 on an individualized basis to determine his particular ability to perform his job safely" and that some flight engineers "over 60 possess traits of a physiological, psychological or other nature which preclude safe and efficient job performance that cannot be ascertained by means other than knowing their age." The Supreme Court evaluated whether this instruction was appropriate and determined that it correctly stated the law.

Stevens, J.

As the district court summarized, the evidence at trial established that the flight engineer's "normal duties are less critical to the safety of flight than those of a pilot." The flight engineer, however, does have critical functions in emergency situations and, of course, might cause considerable disruption in the event of his own medical emergency.

The actual capabilities of persons over age 60, and the ability to detect diseases or a precipitous decline in their faculties, were the subject of conflicting medical testimony. Western's expert witness, a former FAA [Federal Aviation Administration] deputy federal air surgeon, was especially concerned about the possibility of a "cardiovascular event," such as a heart attack. He testified that "with advancing age the likelihood of onset of disease increases and that in persons over age 60 it could not be predicted whether and when such diseases would occur."

The plaintiff's experts, on the other hand, testified that physiological deterioration is caused by disease, not aging, and that "it was feasible to determine on the basis of individual medical examinations whether flight deck crew members, including those over age 60, were physically qualified to continue to fly." Moreover, several large commercial airlines have flight engineers over age 60 "flying the line" without any reduction in their safety record.

Throughout the legislative history of the ADEA, one empirical fact is repeatedly emphasized: the process of psychological and physiological degeneration caused by aging varies with each individual. "The basic research in the field of

aging has established that there is a wide range of individual physical ability regardless of age." As a result, many older workers perform at levels equal or superior to their younger colleagues.

In 1965, the Secretary of Labor reported to Congress that despite these well-established medical facts, "there is persistent and widespread use of age limits in hiring that in a great many cases can be attributed only to arbitrary discrimination against older workers on the basis of age and regardless of ability." Two years later, the President recommended that Congress enact legislation to abolish arbitrary age limits on hiring. Such limits, the President declared, have a devastating effect on the dignity of the individual and result in a staggering loss of human resources vital to the national economy.

The legislative history of the 1978 amendments to the ADEA makes quite clear that the policies and substantive provisions of the Act apply with especial force in the case of mandatory retirement provisions. The House Committee on Education and Labor reported: "Increasingly, it is being recognized that mandatory retirement based solely upon age is arbitrary and that chronological age alone is a poor indicator of ability to perform a job."

In *Usery v. Tamiami Trail Tours, Inc.,* the court of appeals for the Fifth Circuit was called upon to evaluate the merits of a BFOQ defense to a claim of age discrimination. Tamiami Trail Tours had a policy of refusing to hire persons over age 40 as intercity bus drivers. At trial, the bus company introduced testimony supporting its theory that the hiring policy was a BFOQ based upon safety considerations—the need to employ persons who have a low risk of accidents. The court concluded that "the job qualifications which the employer invokes to justify his discrimination must be *reasonably necessary* to the essence of his business—here, the safe transportation of bus passengers from one point to another. The greater the safety factor, measured by the likelihood of harm and the probable severity of that harm in case of an accident, the more stringent may be the job qualifications designed to insure safe driving."

In the absence of persuasive evidence supporting its position, Western nevertheless argues that the jury should have been instructed to defer to "Western's selection of job qualifications for the position of flight engineer that are reasonable in light of safety risks." This proposal is plainly at odds with Congress' decision, in adopting the ADEA, to subject management decisions to a test of objective justification in a court of law. The BFOQ standard adopted in the statute is one of "reasonable necessity," not reasonableness.

In adopting that standard, Congress did not ignore the public interest in safety. That interest is adequately reflected in instructions that track the language of the statute. When an employer establishes that a job qualification has been carefully formulated to respond to documented concerns for public safety, it will not be overly burdensome to persuade a trier of fact that the qualification is "reasonably necessary" to safe operation of the business. The uncertainty implicit in the concept of managing safety risks always makes it "reasonably necessary" to err on the side of caution in a close case. . . . Since the instructions in this case would not have prevented the airline from raising this contention to the jury in closing argument, we are satisfied that the verdict is a consequence of a defect in Western's proof, rather than a defect in the trial court's instructions.

Case Questions

1. What is the difference between the two cases cited in full above? What is the basis for the determination that an employer should or should not be required to test applicants on an individual basis?

2. Should an employer have available as a defense that the cost of the tests would impose a great burden on the employer? Why or why not?

3. What is the distinction the *Criswell* opinion makes between "reasonable necessity" and "reasonableness?"

Economic Concerns.   Would a company's desire to cut payroll costs constitute a reasonable factor other than age? As stated in the beginning of this chapter, it is likely to be more expensive under certain circumstances to maintain older workers than younger; so cutting the numbers of older workers may reduce costs in some firms.

Scenario

This issue is unique to ADEA discrimination claims as it is not more costly, for instance, to hire an Asian employee than a Caucasian employee. However, in many cases, it is more expensive to hire or to retain older workers since, among other reasons, they have more experience and thereby command a higher wage. Courts disfavor this justification for the termination of older workers. As stated by the Illinois district court in *Vilcins v. City of Chicago,* 1991 WL 74610 (N.D. Il. 1991), "[n]othing in the ADEA prohibits elimination of a protected employee's position for budgetary reasons. In fact, the case law establishes that economic or budgetary factors may provide valid reasons for discharging a protected employee. A termination allegedly based on economic factors may constitute impermissible discrimination, however, *when the economic reasons proffered serve merely to obscure the fact that age was the true determinant."* (Emphasis added.)

This brings to mind one of the most interesting case opinions in this area: *Metz v. Transit Mix, Inc.,* 828 F.2d 1202 (7th Cir. 1987). In that case, the appellate court noted that salary is often a direct function of seniority. Individual salary increases may occur on a yearly basis with no regard to the financial condition of the employer; consequently, those who have been employed for the longest times, and have accrued the most seniority, are also the highest paid employees. In disallowing the termination of older workers for financial reasons, the court then cited Willie Loman, the salesman who was fired after working for his boss for 34 years (in Arthur Miller's *Death of a Salesman*): "You can't eat the orange and throw the peel away—a man is not a piece of fruit." Courts have emphatically rejected business practices in which the "plain intent and effect was to eliminate older workers who had built up, through years of satisfactory service, higher salaries than their younger counterparts."

The court stated that, where salary is tied directly to seniority (and therefore age), seniority then serves as a "proxy" for age, supporting a claim of age discrimination. The court of appeals noted that one possible solution to the high-pay quandary for the continued employment of older workers is to offer the older worker the option of accepting a pay cut in lieu of termination. The pay cut, of course, must be warranted by business necessity, such as economic difficulties; but at least the older worker would be retained and not replaced by a younger worker who would be willing to accept the lower salary offered. Such an offer to the older worker would be evidence of the intent to reduce costs, as opposed to the intent to relieve the firm of its older workforce.

In addition, terminations pursuant to bona fide reductions in force, bankruptcy, or other legitimate business reasons are generally legal, even if the economic considerations that have necessitated the reduction in force require the termination of more older workers than younger employees. (See "Unique Problems Associated with a Reduction in Force," later in this chapter.)

The Hazens hired Walter Biggins in 1977 and fired him in 1986 when he was 62 years old. Biggins sued, alleging a violation of the ADEA. The Hazens claimed instead that they terminated him because he did business with their competitors. A jury rendered a verdict for Biggins and the appellate court agreed, relying on evidence that the Hazens really fired him in order to prevent his pension benefits from vesting (which would have happened in the few weeks following his termination). In this case, the Supreme Court determines whether a firing decision based on number of years served is "age-based."

HAZEN PAPER CO. V. BIGGINS
507 U.S. 604(1993)

O'Connor, J.

The Courts of Appeals repeatedly have faced the question whether an employer violates the ADEA by acting on the basis of a factor, such as an employee's pension status or seniority, that is empirically correlated with age. . . . We now clarify that there is no disparate treatment under the ADEA when the factor motivating the employer is some feature other than the employee's age.

* * *

In a disparate treatment case, liability depends on whether the protected trait (under the ADEA, age) actually motivated the employer's decision. The employer may have relied upon a formal, facially discriminatory policy requiring adverse treatment of employees with that trait. Or the employer may have been motivated by the protected trait on an ad hoc, informal basis. Whatever the employer's decision-making process, a disparate treatment claim cannot succeed unless the employee's protected trait actually played a role in that process and had a determinative influence on the outcome.

Disparate treatment, thus defined, captures the essence of what Congress sought to prohibit in the ADEA. It is the very essence of age discrimination for an older employee to be fired because the employer believes that productivity and competence decline with old age.

"Although age discrimination rarely was based on the sort of animus motivating some other forms of discrimination, it was based in large part on stereotypes unsupported by objective fact. . . . Moreover, the available empirical evidence demonstrated that arbitrary age lines were in fact generally unfounded and that, as an overall matter, the performance of older workers was at least as good as that of younger workers."

Thus the ADEA commands that "employers are to evaluate [older] employees . . . on their merits and not their age." The employer cannot rely on age as a proxy for an employee's remaining characteristics, such as productivity, but must instead focus on those factors directly.

When the employer's decision is wholly motivated by factors other than age, the problem of inaccurate and stigmatizing stereotypes disappears. This is true even if the motivating factor is correlated with age, as pension status typically is. Pension plans typically provide that an employee's accrued benefits will become nonforfeitable, or "vested," once the employee completes a certain number of years of service with the employer. On average, an older employee has had more years in the work force than a younger employee, and thus may well have accumulated more years of service with a particular employer. Yet an employee's age is analytically distinct from his years of service. An employee who is younger than 40, and therefore outside the class of older workers as defined by the ADEA, may have worked for a particular employer his entire career, while an older worker may have been newly hired. Because age and years of service are analytically distinct, an employer can take account of one while ignoring the other, and thus it is incorrect to say that a decision based on years of service is necessarily "age based."

The instant case is illustrative. Under the Hazen Paper pension plan, as construed by the Court of Appeals, an employee's pension benefits vest after the employee completes 10 years of service with the company. Perhaps it is true that older employees of Hazen Paper are more likely to be "close to vesting" than younger employees. Yet a decision by the company to fire an older employee solely because he has nine-plus years of service and therefore is "close to vesting" would not constitute discriminatory treatment on the basis of age. The prohibited stereotype ("Older employees are likely to be—") would not have figured in this decision, and the attendant stigma would not ensue. The decision would not be the result of an inaccurate and denigrating generalization about age, but would rather represent an accurate judgment about the employee—that he indeed is "close to vesting."

We do not mean to suggest that an employer lawfully could fire an employee in order to prevent his pension benefits from vesting. Such conduct is actionable under §510 of ERISA. But it would not, without more, violate the ADEA. That law requires the employer to ignore an employee's age (absent a statutory exemption or defense); it does not specify further characteristics that an employer must also ignore. . . .

We do not preclude the possibility that an employer who targets employees with a particular pension status on the assumption that these employees are likely to be older thereby engages in age discrimination. . . . Finally, we do not consider the special case where an employee is about to vest in pension benefits as a result of his age, rather than years of service, and the employer

fires the employee in order to prevent vesting. That case is not presented here. Our holding is simply that an employer does not violate the ADEA just by interfering with an older employee's pension benefits that would have vested by virtue of the employee's years of service.

Case Questions

1. Do you agree with the court that age and years of service are sufficiently distinct to allow for terminations based on years of service and to find no violation of the ADEA where the terminations result in a greater proportion of older workers being fired?

2. Aren't workers close to vesting more likely to be older workers? And, if so, then do you believe that an employer can use the category "close to vesting" to avoid liability under the ADEA?

3. If an employer did terminate a group of individuals on the basis of their being "close to vesting" with the intention to get rid of older workers, what type of evidence would the employees/plaintiffs be able to use to prove the unlawful intent?

There is no consensus in the federal courts on the question of whether there is a "high correlation" between compensation and age in any generic manner that would imply that compensation-based decisions would have a disparate impact on older workers as a general rule. An employer's decision based on salary which disproportionately affected older workers because of the high correlation between age and salary would be actionable age discrimination under a number of federal circuit court decisions. (See *Caron v. Scott Paper Co.,* 834 F.Supp. 33 (D.Maine 1993); *Camacho v. Sears, Roebuck de Puerto Rico,* 939 F.Supp. 113 (D. P.R. 1996.) On the other hand, federal courts which have examined the issue more recently, particularly in the wake of *Hazen Paper Co. v. Biggins,* have tended to hold that economic decisions do not give rise to liability for age discrimination, despite the disparate impact of such decisions on older workers. (See *Ellis v. United Airlines, Inc.,* 73 F.3d 999, 1009 (10th Cir. 1996) ("Of those courts that have considered the issue since Hazen, there is a clear trend toward concluding that the ADEA does not support a disparate impact claim").)

The split among courts of whether economic factors can be considered when terminating older workers can be traced to two fundamentally differing views about the goal of the age discrimination statutes. If the goal of the age discrimination statutes is to preclude decisions based on generalities about older workers which may have no basis as to individuals, then they certainly do not extend to decisions based on relative compensation rates between individual workers. In this view, age discrimination statutes were enacted to prevent employers from assuming that just because an individual attained a certain age, he or she no longer could do the job, or do it as well. This view was best articulated by the dissent in *Metz v. Transit Mix, Inc.,* which stated, "The Act prohibits adverse personnel actions based on myths, stereotypes, and group averages, as well as lackadaisical decisions in which employers use age as a proxy for something that matters (such as gumption) without troubling to decide employee-by-employee who can still do the work and who can't."

The other view is that age-discrimination statutes were enacted to protect older workers because of their status as older workers, since older workers, generally speaking, face unique obstacles late in their careers. Age discrimination law is thus seen as a kind of protective legislation designed to improve the lot of a people who are vulnerable as a class. If this view is correct, then holding that decisions based solely on salary may contravene laws precluding discrimination based on age makes sense.

Benefit Plans and Seniority Systems.   The ADEA specifically excludes bona fide retirement plans that distinguish based on age but are "not a subterfuge to evade the purpose of [the] Act." "Subterfuge" in this definition denotes those plans that are mere schemes for the purpose of evading the ADEA or the Older Workers' Benefit Protection Act (discussed below). The effect of the 1978 and 1986 amendments to the ADEA was to completely prohibit involuntary retirement plans when they are imposed on the sole basis of an employee's age.

"Voluntariness" of Plan.   To qualify as a bona fide voluntary retirement plan allowed by the act, the plan must be truly voluntary. Some employees have contended that there is no voluntary decision when they are given only a short time in which to reach a decision about whether to accept the retirement option. But a short time period in which to reach a decision does not necessarily render the decision involuntary. The determination of what qualifies as a bona fide plan must be made on a case-by-case basis.

It has been held that early retirement plans offered by employers are not bona fide pursuant to the act if a reasonable person would have felt compelled to resign under similar circumstances. However, even after several court decisions relating to the issues of voluntariness, and whether a plan was a subterfuge, employers are left without much direction in terms of the formulation of early retirement programs and other means of providing benefits.

"Same Actor" Defense.   A number of appellate courts, including the First, Second, Fourth, Fifth, Sixth, Seventh, Eighth, Ninth and Eleventh Circuits, have adopted a defense called the "same actor" defense to age discrimination claims. The circuit courts have applied various weights of strength or value of the defense when the hirer and firer are the same actor. These courts have held that, when the same "actor" both hires and fires a worker protected by the ADEA, there is a permissible inference that the employee's age was not a motivating factor in the decision. After all, if someone held discriminatory beliefs about older workers, why would that person have hired the worker in the first place? A Fourth Circuit Court reasoned that "claims that the employer animus exists in termination but not in hiring seem irrational. From the standpoint for the putative discriminator, it hardly makes sense to hire workers from a group one dislikes (thereby incurring the psychological costs of associating with them), only to fire them once they are on the job." (*Proud v. Stone,* 945 F.2d 796 (4th Cir. 1991).)

The Older Workers' Benefit Protection Act of 1990.   In 1990, Congress enacted the Older Workers' Benefit Protection Act (OWBPA), amending section 4(f) of the ADEA. The OWBPA concerns the legality and enforceability of early retirement incentive programs (called "exit incentive programs" in the act) and of waivers of rights under the ADEA, and it prohibits age discrimination in the provision of employee benefits. What this act really deals with are those situations where employees are offered amounts of money through retirement plans as incentives for leaving a company. In that way, the company is not terminating an older worker and, thereby, cannot in theory be held liable under the ADEA.

Many companies also request that an older worker sign a waiver, relinquishing the right to later question the plan by filing an age discrimination action. Once the waiver is signed and the worker accepts the benefits under the plan, the company would like to believe it is safe from all possible claims of discrimination. But this is not the case, as will be discussed.

The OWBPA codifies the EEOC's "equal cost principal," requiring firms to provide benefits to older workers that are at least equal to those provided to younger workers, unless the cost of their provision to older workers *greatly* exceeds the cost of provision to younger workers. Therefore, a firm may only offer different benefits to older and younger workers if it costs a significant amount more to provide those benefits to older workers. This section amends section 4 of the ADEA, which provides that adverse employment actions taken in observance of the terms of a bona fide employee benefit plan are partially exempt from question.

Waiver
The intentional relinquishment of a known right.

In connection with employee waivers of their rights to file discrimination actions under the ADEA, the OWBPA requires that every **waiver** must be "knowing and voluntary" to be valid. In order to satisfy this requirement, the waiver must meet all of the requirements below:

1. The waiver must be written in a manner calculated to be understood by an average employee.
2. The waiver must specifically refer to ADEA rights or claims (but may refer to additional acts, such as Title VII or applicable state acts).

3. The waiver only affects those claims or rights that have arisen prior to the date of the waiver (i.e., the employee is not waiving any rights that will be acquired after signing the waiver).

4. The waiver of rights to claims may only be offered in exchange for some consideration in addition to anything to which the individual is already entitled (this usually involves inclusion in an early retirement program).

5. The employee must be advised in writing to consult with an attorney prior to execution of the waiver (this does not mean that the employee must consult with an attorney, but must merely be advised of the suggestion).

6. The employee must be given a period of 21 days in which to consider signing a waiver, and an additional 7 days in which to revoke the signature. Note that where a waiver is offered in exchange for an early retirement plan, as opposed to some other consideration, the individual must have 45 days in which to consider signing the agreement.

7. If the waiver is executed in connection with an exit incentive (early retirement) or other employment termination program, the employer must inform the employee in writing of the exact terms and inclusions of the program.

The waiver may not bar the employee from filing a claim with the EEOC or participating in investigations by the EEOC. Therefore, the employee may testify on another's behalf if requested. The purpose of these provisions is basically to ensure that the employee entered into the agreement that waived her or his rights knowingly and voluntarily based on the "totality of the circumstances."

Even if the employee could have disputed the employer's enforcement of the waiver because of this provision, the employee cannot do so if she retains the additional benefits she received when she agreed to sign the waiver. Note that if an employee signs a defective waiver, the employee is *NOT* required to return any benefits received under the defective waiver. In addition, if the employer offers to individually negotiate the waiver (as opposed to offering a standard form to the employee on a take-it-or-leave-it basis), this may be able to serve as proof to the court that the employee knew what he was doing when he signed the document.

OUBRE v. ENTERGY OPERATIONS, INC.
118 S.Ct. 838 (1998)

An employee who received a severance agreement and signed a waiver discharging the employer from all claims later sued the employer for age discrimination. The court had to determine whether the waiver was effective.

Kennedy, J.

Dolores Oubre worked as a scheduler at a power plant in Louisiana run by her employer, Entergy Operations, Inc. In 1994, she received a poor performance rating. Oubre's supervisor met with her on January 17, 1995, and gave her the option of either improving her performance during the coming year or accepting a voluntary arrangement for her severance. She received a packet of information about the severance agreement and had 14 days to consider her options, during which she consulted with attorneys. On January 31, Oubre decided to accept. She signed a release, in which she "agree[d] to waive, settle, release, and discharge any and all claims, demands, damages, actions, or causes of action . . . that I may have against Entergy . . ." In exchange, she received six installment payments over the next four months, totaling $6,258.

Oubre filed this suit against Entergy alleging constructive discharge on the basis of her age in violation of the ADEA and state law. She has not offered or tried to return the $6,258 to the employer, nor is it clear she has the means to do so. The lower court agreed with the employer that Oubre had ratified the defective release by failing to return or offer to return the monies she had received. The Court of Appeals affirmed judgment for the employer and we reverse.

* * * *

In 1990, Congress amended the ADEA by passing the OWBPA. The OWBPA provides: "An individual may not waive any right or claim under [the ADEA] unless the waiver is knowing and voluntary. . . . [A] waiver may not be considered knowing and voluntary unless at a minimum" it satisfies certain enumerated requirements.

The statutory command is clear: An employee "may not waive" an ADEA claim unless the waiver or release satisfies the OWBPA's requirements. The policy of the Older Workers' Benefit Protection Act is likewise clear from its title: It is designed to protect the rights and benefits of older workers. The OWBPA implements Congress' policy via a strict, unqualified statutory stricture on waivers, and we are bound to take Congress at its word. Congress imposed specific duties on employers who seek releases of certain claims created by statute. Congress delineated these duties with precision and without qualification: An employee "may not waive" an ADEA claim unless the employer complies with the statute. Courts cannot with ease presume ratification of that which Congress forbids.

. . . The statute creates a series of prerequisites for knowing and voluntary waivers and imposes affirmative duties of disclosure and waiting periods. The OWBPA governs the effect under federal law of waivers or releases on ADEA claims and incorporates no exceptions or qualifications. The text of the OWBPA forecloses the employer's defense, notwithstanding how general contract principles would apply to non-ADEA claims.

The rule proposed by the employer (that the employee must first give back monies received before avoiding the release) would frustrate the statute's practical operation as well as its formal command. In many instances a discharged employee likely will have spent the monies received and will lack the means to tender their return. These realities might tempt employers to risk noncompliance with the OWBPA's waiver provisions, knowing it will be difficult to repay the monies and relying on ratification. We ought not to open the door to an evasion of the statute by this device.

Oubre's cause of action arises under the ADEA, and the release can have no effect on her ADEA claim unless it complies with the OWBPA. In this case, both sides concede the release the employee signed did not comply with the requirements of the OWBPA. Since Oubre's release did not comply with the OWBPA's stringent safeguards, it is unenforceable against her insofar as it purports to waive or release her ADEA claim. As a statutory matter, the release cannot bar her ADEA suit, irrespective of the validity of the contract as to other claims.

In further proceedings in this or other cases, courts may need to inquire whether the employer has claims for restitution, recoupment, or setoff against the employee, and these questions may be complex where a release is effective as to some claims but not as to ADEA claims. We need not decide those issues here, however. It suffices to hold that the release cannot bar the ADEA claim because it does not conform to the statute. Nor did the employee's mere retention of monies amount to a ratification equivalent to a valid release of her ADEA claims, since the retention did not comply with the OWBPA any more than the original release did. The statute governs the effect of the release on ADEA claims, and the employer cannot invoke the employee's failure to tender back as a way of excusing its own failure to comply. RE-VERSED and REMANDED.

Case Questions

1. Do you think the fact that an attorney was consulted before the acceptance of the offer is relevant in this case to determine whether the waiver was knowing and voluntary?

2. As an employer, what should you do to ensure the waiver an individual will be signing is valid?

3. Why do you think an employer must follow such strict guidelines when creating a waiver? Do you think the guidelines are correct? How would you change them?

After the Supreme Court decision in *Oubre,* above, the EEOC issued a notice of proposed rulemaking to address the issues raised in that case. The proposed regulations reflect the EEOC's position that:

1. An individual alleging that a waiver agreement was not knowing and voluntary under the ADEA is not required to tender back the consideration as a precondition for challenging that waiver agreement;

2. a covenant not to sue or any other condition precedent, penalty, or other limitation adversely affecting any individual's right to challenge a waiver agreement is invalid under the ADEA;

3. although in some cases an employer may be entitled to setoff, recoupment, or restitution against an individual who has successfully challenged the validity of a waiver agreement, such setoff, recoupment, or restitution cannot be greater than the consideration paid to the individual or the damages awarded to the individual, whichever is less; and

4. no employer may unilaterally abrogate its duties under a waiver agreement, even if one or more of the signatories to the agreement successfully challenges the validity of that agreement under the ADEA.

A firm must be cautious because individual negotiations may lead to slightly different agreements with various employees; and varying benefits among similar employees may constitute a violation of the Employee Retirement Income Security Act (ERISA).

The OWBPA also contains the following provisions in connection with early retirement plans, 29 U.S.C. §623:

1. Employers may set a minimum age as a condition of eligibility for normal or early retirement benefits.
2. A benefit plan may provide a subsidized benefit for early retirement.
3. A benefit plan may provide for Social Security supplements in order to cover the time period between the time when the employee leaves the firm and the time when the employee is eligible for Social Security benefits.
4. While severance pay cannot vary based on the employee's age, the employer may offset the payments made by the value of any retiree health benefits received by an individual eligible for immediate pension.

Thus, while an employer may not actually discriminate in the amount of the payments offered by the retirement plan on the basis of age, these provisions actually seem to allow for inconsistent payments to older and younger workers, under certain circumstances.

Note that no provision of the OWBPA prohibits an employer from revoking a retirement offer *while* the employee is considering it. So, for example, a firm could offer an employee a retirement package in a separation agreement; then, while the employee considers it, the firm could revoke it and offer a less attractive package. This could be abused, of course, if it is interpreted as a threat to encourage the worker to decide earlier than the 21-day limit.

Employee Retirement Income Security Act.   In 1974, Congress passed the Employee Retirement Income Security Act, which regulates private employee benefit plans. While ERISA specifically governs the operation of retirement plan provisions, among other benefits, and is therefore relevant to the issue of age discrimination, a complete discussion of its implications is found later in Chapter 19, devoted entirely to ERISA.

In short, however, ERISA's purpose is to protect employees from wrongful denial of all types of benefits, including retirement or pension benefits. Prior to ERISA's enactment, employers were able to discriminate against certain employees in their determination of eligibility for pension benefits and the amount of time one must work for the employer to be eligible for benefits. In addition, many employees suffered from the loss of their benefits when companies underwent management reorganizations, or when the company decided to terminate the plan only a short time before the employees' benefits were to vest. Other employees lost their benefits when they became sick and were forced to quit their job prior to the time at which their pension rights vested.

ERISA prevents such problems as these through its regulation of the determination of who must be covered by pension plans, vesting requirements, and the amount that the employer must invest for the benefit of its employees. In an effort to encourage compliance with this provision, ERISA also requires complete disclosure of the administration of the plan. Further, ERISA stipulates that an employee may not be excluded from a plan on account of age, as long as she or he is at least 21 years of age and is a full-time employee with at least one year of service.

ERISA does have some negative side effects. It has made the provision of benefit plans more costly for employers. In addition, no federal law requires employers to offer retirement plans.

Distinctions among Benefit Plans.   Can an employer simply decide to lower the amounts of benefits it offers its employees? Yes, as long as it is in line with requirements of ERISA. However, those reductions must be made across the board; the OWBPA limits the distinctions that an employer may make on the basis of age to only those that are justified by "age-based cost differences."

Many firms also have seniority systems that award benefits on the basis of seniority. Because experience seniority is often balanced in favor of older workers, not as many problems arise as a result of these systems. Those not themselves based in age discrimination are valid. In other words, those systems that disadvantage employees as they age are not protected by the ADEA.

Employee's Response: Proof of Pretext.   An ADEA case begins as employee proves the elements of the prima facie claim; then the employer has the chance to justify its decision using any of the above defenses. Now it is again the employee's turn; the employee must show that those reasons or that defense is pretextual. When a claim is pretextual, it means that it is not the true reason for the action, that there is some underlying motivation to which the employer has not admitted. To prove that the offered reason is pretext for an actual case of age discrimination, the employee need not show that age was the *only* factor motivating the employment decision, but only that age was a determining factor.

Where there is direct evidence of discrimination, proof of pretext is not required. This may occur where the employer admits to having based the employment decision on employee's age, or when a representative of the employer states that the employee is "too old," or that it would be cheaper to hire younger applicants.

The question of what constitutes direct evidence is not always clear. Despite the similarity between statements made by employers, however, statements regarding an applicant's or employee's race are taken more seriously than those about age. For instance, most courts would rule in employee's favor if it were determined that she was not hired pursuant to the manager's statement, "I don't want any more blacks in my unit." But it is questionable whether this same employer would be held guilty if the manager states, "We need some new ideas in this unit. Let's hire younger analysts." The statement may be viewed as merely descriptive.

An employee can also show pretext by proving that the offered reasons for the adverse employment action have no basis in fact, the offered reasons did not actually motivate the adverse employment action, or the offered reasons are insufficient to motivate the adverse action taken. The following case highlights those circumstances where a court may consider an employer's reasons to be pretextual.

Wilson v. AM General Corporation
1999 WL 50271 (7th Cir. 1999)

Sixty-year-old William Wilson was employed for thirteen years at AM General (AM). AM began a company-wide reduction in force (RIF), at which time Wilson was terminated. When he asked whether it was due to poor performance, his supervisor responded, "absolutely not." Wilson brought suit against AM under the ADEA alleging he was discharged because of his age. In depositions taken before trial, the same supervisor indicated the discharge was due to poor working relations with former supervisors and customers of AM. AM argued that Wilson lost his job because of the RIF *and* because of his poor relationships with fellow employees and customers. At trial, testimony was given regarding the supervisors with whom Wilson had poor working relations. Evidence demonstrated that these supervisors gave him excellent and outstanding performance ratings. With regard to the poor relationship with customers, contradictory testimony was given by both sides. A jury returned a verdict in favor of Wilson. AM appealed.

Coffey, J.

* * *

The employer seemingly admits that the employee established a prima facie case of age discrimination. The company next argues that AM General provided evidence of legitimate, nondiscriminatory reasons for the discharge—namely, the allegedly poor working relationships that Wilson had with co-workers . . . and customers. . . . Finally, and more importantly, AM General alleges that Wilson failed, as a matter of law, to demonstrate that AM General's proffered reasons for termination were mere pretexts for age discrimination. Thus, the sole issue before this Court is whether Wilson provided a sufficient evidentiary basis for a reasonable jury to find that AM General's "poor working relationships" justification was a pretext for discrimination. If so, we must affirm the trial judge's decision to send the case to the jury, and the jury's verdict.

An employee demonstrates pretext by offering evidence that the employer's "ostensible justification is 'unworthy of credence.'" The employee must offer evidence "tending to prove that the employer's proffered reasons are factually baseless, were not the actual motivation for the discharge in question, or were insufficient to motivate the discharge." An employee discharged in a RIF is not required to produce evidence tending to prove that the employer's explanation was a "lie" in the sense of its being a complete fabrication; instead, he must "establish that age 'tripped the balance' in favor of discharge." The ultimate question is "whether the same events would have transpired if the employee had been younger than 40 and everything else had been the same."

Generally, the employee has the burden of demonstrating that each proffered nondiscriminatory reason is pretextual. However, "[t]here may be cases in which the multiple grounds offered by the defendant . . . are so intertwined, or the pretextual character of one of them so fishy and suspicious, that the plaintiff may [prevail.]" If the employee produces evidence from which a reasonable jury could conclude that each reason is pretextual, the employee is entitled to a jury determination on that issue.

* * *

. . . The employee argues that he provided sufficient evidence at trial to rebut each proffered reason. Moreover, he argues that even if he did fail to rebut any one of the employer's alleged reasons for his discharge, he nevertheless presented evidence that the reasons given by AM General are collectively "fishy and suspicious" for they lack even a "smidgen" of documentary proof. Wilson further asserts that during the course of the trial, Wilson and AM General's representatives engaged in a battle of credibility on equal terms, and that the jury simply sided with Wilson on the question of AM General's motivations for terminating him.

AM General argues that Wilson's testimony rebutting AM General's nondiscriminatory reasons is insufficient to meet his burden. The company . . . argues that when an employer's nondiscriminatory reasons for terminating an employee as part of a RIF include the decision-maker's perception that the plaintiff had performance related problems, the issue is not the adequacy in fact of plaintiff's performance; rather, it is the honesty of the company's belief that plaintiff's performance was inadequate that controls. Moreover, AM General argues that Wilson's testimony alone, offered on his own behalf and without other evidence, is insufficient as a matter of law to sustain a jury verdict.

* * *

A reasonable jury might very well have believed (and, it turns out, did believe) Wilson was more credible than [his former supervisor].

Moreover, even if Wilson's testimony alone was insufficient as a matter of law, the jury could have found a combination of factors sufficiently "fishy and suspicious" to warrant a verdict for Wilson. A number of factors were relevant: the virtual nonexistence of AM General files regarding Wilson's employment record, including the reasons for his termination; the firm's failure to disclose the reasons for discharge at the exit interview, in spite of Wilson's direct query; Wilson's past exemplary performance ratings; and Wilson's testimony. When taken in combination, these factors were sufficient to allow a reasonable jury to question AM General's alleged nondiscriminatory reasons.

* * *

In sum, we are convinced that Wilson presented sufficient testimony and other evidence that a reasonable jury could have found that AM General's proffered reasons were pretextual. The judgment of the district court is AFFIRMED.

Case Questions

1. Do you think the reasons offered by the employer were pretextual? Why or why not?

2. Do you think that the burden shifting from employee to employer than back again to the employee is a good system? Why or why not?

3. What can an employer do to insulate itself from terminating individuals for reasons that can be perceived to be pretextual?

Employee's Prima Facie Case: Disparate Impact.   As explained in connection with other forms of discrimination, there are two claims an employee may make against the employer: disparate treatment and disparate impact. The former occurs where an employee is treated differently than other employees because she or he is a member of a protected class. For example, disparate treatment exists where an applicant is not hired because of her age. Disparate impact, on the other hand, exists where a policy or rule of an employer, though not discriminatory on its face, has a different effect on one group than on another. For example, a rule that required all bus drivers to have 20/20 vision may have the effect of limiting the number of older workers who can be bus drivers. Now, this rule is indeed discriminatory, in that it distinguishes between those who have good vision and those who do not. The question is whether the rule is wrongful. In the example, perhaps it is justified by business reasons, and perfectly acceptable.

Disparate impact was the basis for Ms. Geller's claim in *Geller v. Markham.* In that case, the Second Circuit court held that a policy that expressly prohibited the hiring of teachers at or above the "sixth step" of the salary schedule was wrongful. The employee presented evidence that 92.6 percent of all teachers over 40 years of age are at or above the sixth step, which the court held to be adequate proof of the disparate impact of the policy.

However, the Tenth Circuit Court, in *Ellis v. United Airlines,* 73 F.3d 999, (10th Cir. 1996), recently found that disparate impact claims are *not* actionable under the ADEA. In this case, applicants for the position of flight attendants were rejected because of their weight. They contended that weight standards adversely affected older women. The court held, basically, that it was too far a stretch to read the ADEA as covering "incidental and unintentional discrimination that results from employment decisions made for reasons other than age." At the time of publication, the DC and First Circuit have faced this issue but left it unresolved; the Second and Eighth Circuits allow ADEA claims for disparate impact, and the Seventh Circuit does not allow them.

The Use of Statistical Evidence

Courts allow the use of statistical evidence to prove discrimination on the basis of age, though it is generally more useful in disparate impact cases than it is in disparate treatment cases. However, the court in *Heward v. Western Electric Co.* explained the similarities in the application of statistics in disparate impact cases as compared to disparate treatment cases:

> The significance of companywide statistics is heightened in disparate *impact* cases because plaintiffs need only demonstrate statistically that particular companywide practices in actuality operate or have the effect of excluding members of the protected class. However, even in a disparate *treatment* class action or "pattern and practice" suit, only gross statistical disparities make out a prima facie case of discrimination.

In either case, statistical evidence is meticulously examined to ensure that the statistics shed some light on the case. There is a great deal of skepticism relating to statistical evidence in age discrimination cases precisely because of the fact that older workers are likely to be replaced by younger workers, merely as a result of attrition of the workforce. This is not true in cases brought under Title VII based on race or gender discrimination; therefore, statistics may be slightly more relevant to a determination under Title VII, because they may represent pure discrimination.

Where statistics are used to prove discriminatory effect, the Supreme Court has offered some guidance about their use. The Supreme Court has considered percentage comparisons and standard deviation analyses of those comparisons. "As a general rule,

. . . if the difference between the expected value and the observed number is greater than two or three standard deviations, then the hypothesis that the [selection process] was random would be suspect." In addition, the Court cautioned that the usefulness or weight of statistical evidence depends on all of the surrounding facts and circumstances, and, specifically, "when special qualifications are required to fill particular jobs, comparisons to the general population (rather than to the smaller group of individuals who possess the necessary qualifications) may have little probative value."

Remedies

The court may award a variety of remedies to a successful employee/plaintiff in an age discrimination action. However, where money damages such as back pay (what the employee would have received but for the violation) or front pay (which includes a reasonable and expected amount of compensation for work that the employee would have performed until the time of her expected retirement) are ascertainable and adequately compensate the employee for damages incurred, the court may *not* grant other **equitable relief.** Five circuits have ruled that compensation for pain and suffering is not available under the ADEA. Forms of equitable relief include reinstatement, promotions, or injunctions.

Where it has been proven the employer has acted with knowledge that its actions violate the ADEA, or in conscious disregard for compliance or consequences, the act allows the court the discretion to award **liquidated damages** equal to double the amount owed. Some courts, however, require that the violation be intentional as well as knowing to award increased damages. Moreover, a successful employee may recover reasonable attorneys' fees and costs.

Equitable relief
Relief that is not in the form of money damages, such as injunctions, reinstatement, promotion, and so on. Equitable relief is generally based on concepts of justice and fairness.

Liquidated damages
Increased damage award where party in error has acted with knowledge (and sometimes intent) that actions are in violation of the act or in willful disregard for the propriety of their actions under the act.

Unique Problems Associated with a Reduction in Force

A reduction in force (RIF) may occur when a company is forced to downscale its operations to address rising costs or the effects of a recession. A RIF is an intentional premeditated termination of one or more positions within a company caused by economic considerations. When management reaches the determination to conduct a RIF, discrimination issues arise if the terminations appear to be arbitrary. It is crucial that the discharges be made on the basis of an objective standard, both in purpose and effect.

Where an individual is terminated pursuant to a bona fide RIF, the employer's actions are protected. Courts generally absolve the employer from responsibility where the employer follows a specified procedure for the terminations, where objective criteria are used to determine which individuals shall be discharged, and where the entire position is eliminated or the work of the discharged older employee is not given to a retained younger employee, or both.

However, in stating a case of age discrimination where a RIF has occurred, the fourth prong of the traditional prima facie case no longer appropriately fits the factual situation: where a RIF has occurred, no one replaces the discharged employee. Therefore, in the event of a RIF, age discrimination may be proven where: (1) the employer refuses to allow a discharged (or demoted) employee to bump others with less seniority and (2) the employer hires younger workers when jobs become available after the employee was discharged (or demoted).

For example, in *White v. Westinghouse Electric Co.,* the court held that the plaintiff had articulated a prima facie case of age discrimination based on the fact that the employer retained three younger and equally qualified employees in the employee's department after the reduction in force. As long as the plaintiff is able to produce circumstantial or direct evidence of the employer's intention to discriminate in connection with the adverse action, the fourth prong has been satisfied. However, in *Leichihman v. Pickwick International,* the court said that:

> in a reduction in force case, there is no adverse inference to be drawn from an employee's discharge if his position and duties are completely eliminated. . . . If [the discharged employee] cannot show that [his employer] had some continuing need for his skills and services in that his various duties were still being performed, then the basis of his claim collapses.

In an effort not to terminate an employee but to continue to cut costs, can an employer unilaterally reduce the salary of a protected employee to more accurately reflect market wages? Section 4(a)(3) of the ADEA states that it is "unlawful for any employer . . . to reduce the wage rate of any employee in order to comply with this Act." The employer would be reducing the wage rate of the older worker to avoid terminating that employee. It is unclear whether the employer defenses cited under other provisions of the act apply to this section. If not, is the employer liable for a violation when cutting the salary? If the employer defenses are available, the issue remains whether the salary was cut "in order to comply with [the] Act." Courts have not yet reached a conclusion in connection with this issue.

Several courts, including the First, Fourth, Sixth, and Seventh circuits, have stated that age discrimination may be avoided by offering older workers the opportunity to work at the same job for reduced pay.

The court in *Marks v. Loral Corp,* on the facing page, referring to the ADEA statement that "[i]t shall be unlawful for an employer—(3) to reduce the wage rate of any employee to comply with this chapter," explained that, if an employer cannot cut costs by reducing the wages of older workers, it might be reasoned, then an employer cannot prefer lower paid workers when making layoff decisions. But, the court argued, the statute does not say that an employer cannot reduce wage rates to reduce costs. The court claimed it merely forbids reducing wage rates to comply with the age discrimination laws. The court found that an employer may not reduce an older worker's wage rate on the ground that it is required by age discrimination laws. The court stated, "the anti-wage reduction provision was clearly enacted simply to prevent the passage of the age discrimination laws themselves from precipitating wage reductions based on the idea that pay differentials between younger and older workers had to be equalized. In that sense the provision buttresses the general theme in the text of the federal statute that workers should be considered on their individual merits, and not as members of some age cohort."

MARKS V. LORAL CORPORATION ET AL.
57 Cal.App.4th 30 (1997)

In this case, the court considers whether age discrimination claims are subject to the disparate impact theory.

Sills, J.

Marks was originally employed by Ford Aerospace's (AFC) corporate finance department in Michigan. In 1990, Loral Corporation bought Ford Aerospace and Marks' employment transferred to Loral. Marks (then aged 48) filed an age discrimination complaint with the EEOC against AFC, charging that when AFC was sold to Loral, several of his younger peers had been offered jobs in Michigan, but he had not, though he preferred to work there.

While Loral Aerospace had no authority to direct any other division to employ any particular individual, the company's Newport Beach human resources officer tried to help Marks find a position at one of the other locations by revising his resume, informing other divisions that Loral would pay his relocation costs, sending his resume to other divisions, and allowing him to use company computers, resume services, fax machines and telephones after his termination. Ultimately, all members of the corporate finance staff willing to relocate found new positions, except for Marks and one other, who was also over 40 years old.

Marks was laid off in August 1992. He brought this suit claiming a violation of state and federal age discrimination laws, contending that his age was a factor in his not being able to secure another position with the company, particularly a position in Colorado Springs where several accounting positions were open. The case went to trial on claims of age discrimination and retaliation and the jury found in favor Loral. Marks appealed.

* * * *

For years now, the federal courts have struggled, in applying federal age discrimination law, with the problem of whether an employer's policy or practice which has a "disparate impact" on older workers generally constitutes illegal age discrimination. . . . In the present case, Marks argues that a particular jury instruction was improper because it told the jury that an employer was entitled to prefer lower paid workers to higher paid workers, even if that preference results in choosing younger workers. Marks contends that the instruction was not proper. If it were, he says, it would eliminate the "vast majority" of age discrimination cases because of the "high correlation" between age and salary level.

In this case we need not decide the broad question of whether "disparate impact analysis," as labor law mavens style it, can ever apply to age discrimination claims, under either federal or California law. We do, however, determine that the particular jury instruction here—which deals with the impact of compensation differentials in employer decision-making—was correct under both federal and state law: Employers may indeed prefer workers with lower salaries to workers with higher ones, even if the preference falls disproportionately on older, generally higher paid workers. Both the text and intent of the federal and state age discrimination statutes compel such a result. Moreover, when we look at the origins of the disparate impact doctrine, we find that, by its very nature, it was never intended to apply to something so basic to the running of any enterprise as its costs of doing business. There was thus no error in giving the instruction and the judgment must be affirmed.

The court instructed the jury that: "An employer is entitled to choose employees with lower salaries, even though this may result in choosing younger employees. If the choice is based on salary, there is no age discrimination." Marks now argues that the salary instruction was error because of the "high correlation" between age and salary. He raises the specter that, if the law allows employers to make decisions on the basis of salary, many age discrimination claims are simply going to disappear.

We will begin our analysis by granting, for the sake of argument, Marks' premise that there is a "high correlation" between compensation and age generally, so that compensation based decisions would have a disparate impact on older workers generally. . . .

Three reasons demonstrate that the view that the ADEA precludes decisions based on generalities about older workers which may have no relationship to individuals and does not extend to decisions based on relative compensation rates between individual workers should prevail: (1) The text of both the federal and state statutes indicates that price-based decisions are not within their ambit; (2) the legislative history is devoid of any intent to impose disparate impact analysis on age discrimination claims rooted in compensation differentials in either set of statutes, and, in fact, indicates an opposite intention; and (3) disparate impact analysis, properly understood, is fundamentally inapplicable to age discrimination claims based on compensation differentials.

* * *

. . . A differentiation based on salary is as "reasonable" a factor as is imaginable in a market economy.

* * * *

Unlike other facially neutral factors which might fall disproportionately on older workers, decision-making by cost—reliance on relative prices if you will—goes to the very core of the operation of a market economy.

* * * *

An objection to the use of price as a "reasonable factor" is that profitability has not been al-lowed to justify discrimination in other civil rights contexts. . . .

Salary differentials, however, present a matter qualitatively different from the usual disparate impact situation in a Title VII context. An action based on price differentials represents the very quintessence of a legitimate business decision. "In a for-profit enterprise, wrote Judge Gary Taylor in a recent federal decision, "the essence of employment decisions is whether an employee's salary is justified by that employee's productivity." As the dissent pointed out in the Metz case, "wages correspond precisely to the costs of doing business, and hence to profitability." . . .

Decisions based on salary therefore must, as Justice Rehnquist said in his dissent from the denial of a hearing of an early Second Circuit decision, come within the "reasonable factors other than age" language of the federal age discrimination statute.

The main "textual" argument which is advanced against the use of salary in the context of age discrimination claims is the phrase "otherwise adversely affect" as it appears in the federal age discrimination statute. Some courts have concluded that the phrase means "any policy having a more harmful effect on older people than on their co-workers."

There are two flaws in the "adversely affect" argument. The first is that it is based on a grammatically nonsensical reading of the federal text. Admittedly, the statute was not written by Hemingway. Nevertheless, it is not so convoluted that it cannot be understood. The text does not say, "It shall be unlawful for an employer—. . . to otherwise adversely affect an employee because of such individual's age." It says, "It shall be unlawful for an employer to limit, segregate or classify his employees in any way which would deprive or tend to deprive any individual of employment opportunities or otherwise adversely affect his status as an employee, because of such individual's age." We emphasize the words "his status as an employee" because those words show that the words "adversely affect" pertain to the verbs "limit, segregate or classify," and do not stand on their own. To read the phrase the way the *Camacho* and *Caron* courts did would mean that the "his" in the phrase, "his status as an employee," would refer to the employer, which makes no sense at all. The words "adversely affect" refer to actions which "affect" an employee's "status as an employee" because of "such individual's age."

The second flaw in the adverse affect argument is that it ignores the balance of the language from the federal age discrimination statute, all of which contradicts the idea that the statute was enacted to provide special protection for older workers as a group. In fact, the balance of the language favors the idea that the statute was enacted to protect individuals from being discriminated against because of their age, not because they share a characteristic with a protected class. The word "individual" appears no less than five times in the course of one sentence, delineating the nature of age discrimination.

The theme of this language is the protection of individuals from discrimination because of their age, not the protection of "older workers" by virtue of their status as older workers. The surrounding context of the phrase "adversely affect" deals with the impact of the "adverse" decision on "any individual."

* * *

. . . Age discrimination is something which protects individuals, not protected groups qua groups . . .

* * *

. . . The intent of the federal and state age discrimination statutes was to prevent employers from basing decisions on generalities, not to prevent employers from making perfectly sound economic decisions which have a disproportionate effect on older workers as a group.

* * *

The first principles of "disparate impact analysis," as articulated by the United States Supreme Court, do not apply to differentiations based on salary.

Because legal ideas are necessarily expressed in words, they sometimes take on a life of their own independent of their origins or intentions. Marks' argument suggests that such a process has taken place over the years with regard to the idea of "disparate impact" discrimination. Taking the phrase in the abstract, it is easy to see why Marks has challenged the salary instruction given here: Given that older workers are generally higher paid than younger workers, preferring lower paid to higher paid workers can show age discrimination because the preference has a "disparate impact" on older workers generally.

The error in the logic is reliance on an incomplete understanding of the legal idea of discrimination when discrimination is based on "disparate impact analysis." Disparate impact discrimination by definition involves a requirement or criterion which does not have a business justification. . . .

* * *

Given the emphasis on job relatedness, job performance, individualized assessment of ability to do a job, and business necessity, it is unfathomable that disparate impact analysis should apply to differentiation on the basis of salary. Such differentiation goes to the very essence of any enterprise.

* * *

We perceive no intent on the part of the Legislature to distinguish between companies that are failing, companies which are just keeping their heads above water, and companies which are rolling in money in this regard. There is not one age discrimination law for the marginally profitable, and another for the highly profitable. Parsing "business necessity" from the normal conduct of any business is unpersuasive in the extreme. Most fundamentally, all businesses, indeed all enterprises including government and nonprofit entities, have a legitimate interest in saving money—from the bankrupt to the most profitable. Companies once thought, like the

Titanic, to be unsinkable have come close, and even sunk into bankruptcy because they did not control costs. It may be easy for judges, looking at one year's income statement, to assert that a salary restructuring violates age discrimination laws because the company was making too much money at the time, but that is an extremely short-sighted and unrealistic view of "business necessity." Similarly, the question of how much profitability is "too much" and therefore takes a company out of some strict necessity rule involves courts in determinations for which they are manifestly ill-equipped. Business people, rather than judges, are presumed to know what is best for their own businesses. . . .

Case Questions

1. It can be stated that employees who grow with a company increase their earnings throughout the years. In addition, while their earnings grow, so does their age. Do you think it is fair for an employer to use salary as a basis for layoffs, knowing that there is a connection between age and earnings? Why or why not?

2. What are the arguments for and against the court's decision?

3. At this point, do older employees have a claim when arguing their layoffs were indirectly based on their age due to their salary?

The Supreme Court decision in *O'Connor v. Consolidated Coin Caterers,* cited in the previous case, is also noteworthy. The case concerned a situation where a protected individual was replaced by another protected individual. Although the ADEA limits its protection to those who are 40 or older, it prohibits discrimination against those protected employees on the basis of age, not class membership. It is irrelevant that one member of the protected class lost out to another member, so long as that person lost out because of her or his age. The latter is more reliably indicated by the fact that his replacement was substantially younger than by the fact that his replacement was not a member of the protected class. Regardless, upon remand to the Court of Appeals the court held that the employee failed to perform his job at a level that met employer's legitimate expectations, and the employer's nondiscriminatory reason for terminating employee was not pretextual.

Management Considerations

Generalizations, such as "older people have poorer vision" or "workers over 50 are less motivated than younger workers," may appear to be grounded in fact, based on the experiences of many firms. But adherence to these prejudiced principals during recruitment or retention of employees may cause more problems for the company than it prevents. As with other areas of protection against wrongful discrimination, managers are not precluded by the ADEA from hiring or retaining the most qualified individual; the act specifically requires that the employer do just that.

The employer may be losing a valuable and completely qualified employee simply because it incorrectly believes that all individuals over a certain age are not qualified for the available position. Instead of relying on vague generalizations concerning all individuals of advanced years, employers would do better to reevaluate the true requirements of the position, then test for those characteristics.

For instance, if an employee must have 20/20 vision to safely drive a taxicab, the taxi company will hire the most qualified individuals if it chooses the most competent and experienced from the pool of applicants and subjects these individuals to a vision test. In that way, the employer is sure to locate those workers who are, actually, the most *qualified* for the position, while not excluding an older worker based on a preconceived idea about failing vision. Or, if a position on an assembly line requires great dexterity and speed of movement, the employer should choose the most qualified applicants and allow them to perform the functions required of the position. If the older worker performs adequately, that applicant should be evaluated with no regard to her age.

In addition, several problems are unique to the employer's defense of a claim of discrimination as a result of a RIF. These problems arise as a result of the difficulty of complete documentation of employee performance.

First, employers generally do not retain intricate written analyses of performance. Consequently, when asked what are the particular problems associated with the employment of this individual, the employer must rely on the subjective oral reports of its supervisors or managers. The jury is then not only faced with the question of whether the adverse action was justified but also with whether the recollection of the managers is correct or merely fabricated for purposes of the litigation. In addition, the employer should ensure that the performance appraisals that *are* recorded reflect an objective evaluation of the employee's performance at that time. The evaluator must exercise caution in the area of the employee's future potential, because this is an area that may be related to age and comments may be suspect.

Second, managers and supervisors will likely evaluate an employee as compared to other employees. Therefore, a rating of "good" may be the worst rating given in a department. When the RIF later requires that certain employees be discharged, the employer is left with the obligation to justify the termination of an individual who, in fact, never received a poor evaluation. This is not a sympathetic position.

Finally, the employer may make a decision based on some factor other than performance, such as the fact that a retained employee's wife is in the hospital, or that the discharged worker had the opportunity to participate in an early retirement program, while the retained worker could not. Superior care should be exercised in reaching a conclusion regarding terminations where these issues serve as the bases for retention and discharge, because many determining factors could be viewed as age-based.

It is in both the employer's and the employee's interest to ensure that the employee periodically receives an objective, detailed performance appraisal. In this way, the employer protects against later claims that the employee was not informed of the employer's dissatisfaction with her or his work, and the employee can guarantee that the employer may only use valid justifications for its discharge decisions.

EXHIBIT 12–5

In settling a case based on age discrimination allegations brought by the Massachusetts Commission Against Discrimination on behalf of 2,000 workers, Bull NH Information Systems Inc. ("Bull Systems") agreed to implement six procedures. They seem to be appropriate considerations for any firm going through a period of downsizing:

1. Give notice to former employees of future job vacancies and the right to file a discrimination complaint if not rehired.
2. Treat seniority as a tie-breaker when making rehiring or termination decisions among equally qualified individuals.
3. Train supervisors on age discrimination law and require them to report suspected violations to the company's EEO officer.
4. Require senior management to review any decisions to lay off workers older than age 40 to ensure that age is not a factor in the decisions.
5. Review voluntary layoffs of workers age 40 or older to ensure that coercion or duress is not involved.
6. Change the internal complaint procedure to require prompt and thorough investigations of complaints.

Source: "More Ideas to Prevent Age Discrimination," http://www.workforceonline.com/digest/legal/CVS/19990305.html, citing AlignMark, January 1999, 258 Southhall Lane, Suite 400, Maitland, FL, 32751. 800/652-4587, as its source.

Management Tips

• Any job requirement on the basis of age must be subject to your highest scrutiny. There are extremely few BFOQs allowed on the basis of age alone. Instead, consider what you are actually concerned about and test for that characteristic. For instance, if you are concerned about the eyesight of your applicants or workers, conduct vision tests rather than follow a presumption that older workers will always be disqualified because of their eyesight.

• Reductions in force are prone to problems in connection with age discrimination as a result of higher salaries paid to older and more experienced workers. Review all termination decisions carefully in order to ensure fair and balanced procedures.

• Terminating an older worker and replacing her or him with another worker who is over 40 does *not* protect you from a charge of age discrimination.

• Review all recruiting literature to remove all age-based classifications like "looking for young upstarts to help build growing business."

• You may not terminate an older worker on the basis of age; if you must terminate a worker who is 40 or over, ensuring that you have appropriate documentation to justify dismissal creates a safe harbor.

• In drafting a waiver of discrimination claims for older workers to sign upon termination, review the form to ensure compliance with the OWBPA.

Summary

- Employees are protected against discrimination on the basis of their age under the ADEA, unless age is a bona fide occupational qualification.
- To prove a case of age discrimination, the employees must show that:

    1. They are 40 years of age or older.
    2. They suffered an adverse employment decision.
    3. They are qualified for the position (either that they meet the employer's requirements or that the requirements are not legitimate).
    4. They were replaced by someone younger.

- Once the employee has presented this information, the employer may defend its decision by showing that:

    1. Age requirement of a job is a bona fide occupational qualification. This can be done by showing
        a) the age limit is reasonably necessary to the employer's business and
        b) all or a substantial number of people over that age are unable to perform the requirements of the job adequately; or
        c) some of the people over that age possess a trait which disqualifies them for the position and it cannot be ascertained except by reference to age.
    2. The decision was made based on some other reasonable factor than age.
    3. The employee was not qualified for the position.
    4. The decision to leave was because of a voluntary retirement plan.
    5. The "same actor" defense may be used in some courts. The presumption is that when the same person hires and fires a worker protected by ADEA, there is a permissible inference that the employee's age was not a motivating factor in the decision to terminate.

- Once the employer presents its defense, the employee will have the opportunity to prove that this defense is mere pretext for the actual discrimination that exists.
- Federal courts are split as to whether an employer can terminate an older employee due to economic considerations.
- Benefit plans and seniority systems cannot be created for the purpose of evading the ADEA or the OWBPA.
- The OWBPA amended section 4(f) of the ADEA and places restrictions where employers offer employees amounts of money through retirement plans as incentives for leaving the company.
- The Employee Retirement Income Security Act (ERISA) regulates private employee benefit plans. It governs the operation of welfare and retirement plan provisions. (See Chapter 19 for a further discussion of ERISA.)
- There is a difference in the circuits whether disparate impact claims are actionable under the ADEA.
- There are a variety of remedies available to those discriminated against due to their age.
- A reduction in force (RIF) occurs when a company is forced to downscale its operations to address rising costs or the effects of a recession. When an individual is terminated pursuant to a bona fide RIF, the employer's actions are protected. In the event of a RIF, age discrimination may be proven when:

    1. The employer refuses to allow a discharged or demoted employee to bump others with less seniority.
    2. The employer hires younger workers when jobs become available.

Chapter-End Questions

1. Paul Schwager was discharged by Sun Oil Company of Pennsylvania after having worked for it for 19.5 years. Schwager claims that he was fired because of his age, but Sun Oil rebuts by stating that Schwager's discharge was a necessary action in the company's overall reorganizing process. Schwager introduced statistics showing that the average age of the employees retained was 35.0 and the average age of employees discharged was 45.7, to demonstrate that the reorganization was aimed at firing the older workers. Schwager also admitted as evidence a letter from Sun Oil's chairman of the board in which the chairman stated that the reorganization plan would provide "a better age distribution of executive personnel." After the reorganization scheme, the company's pension retirement fund liabilities decreased significantly because of the reduction of older workers. Sun Oil maintains that Schwager's age had nothing to do with his discharge, because he was the poorest performer of the district's sales personnel and his position was eliminated as part of the reorganization structure. (*Schwager v. Sun Oil Company of Pennsylvania,* 591 F.2d 58 (10th Cir. 1979).)

2. Byrl Prichard and James Johnson were two men over 50 who applied for positions as truck drivers with Ace Hardware Corporation. Neither of these men was selected for the available positions. They claim they were not hired due to their age, and the company claims that age was not a factor in its decisions. During the application evaluating process, Dallas Howell, the traffic manager, made a notation of "Age?" on both applications. A "No" was written next to this notation on each application after the interview. The company claims that "age"

did not mean the employee's age but the qualification level of the applicant. Howell claimed that Prichard was not qualified for the job, in addition to having a "bad attitude," and Johnson had failed the department of transportation tests. During this hiring period, every applicant over 50 had the same notation of "Age?" with a "No" next to it. (*Brennan v. Ace Hardware Corporation,* 495 F.2d 368 (8th Cir. 1974).)

3. Charles Grubb, 64 years old, was terminated from his laundry manager position at Foote Memorial Hospital. Foote Memorial Hospital had recently purchased the Sisters of Mercy Hospital and was in the process of reorganization when Grubb received his notice. When the hospital decided to eliminate Grubb's position, it made no attempt to determine whether Grubb possessed the skills necessary for other in-house positions and, instead, offered him the position of a truck driver. In addition, when Grubb was informed that his position was eliminated, he was told by his supervisor, "You can call this fired, kicked out, or whatever you want, but old man you're through." In addition, Grubb's supervisor had told him earlier that he was "too old and set in his ways" and that he ought to retire. Grubb's responsibilities were given to a woman who was 63 years old. Grubb claims that he was terminated as a result of age discrimination. (*Grubb v. Foote Memorial Hospital,* 533 F.Supp. 671 (E.D. Mich. 1981) mod. 741 F.2d 1486.).)

4. Howard Berkowitz, 57 years old, worked for Pomeroy's, a retail outlet in Pennsylvania. He was a hardworking, competent employee who was qualified for his position as a merchandising manager. When he was fired, his responsibilities were divided among the other three merchandising managers. All

three of these managers were younger than Berkowitz (34, 44, and 36). In addition, at the time the company was considering the termination decision, Berkowitz's supervisor said to him, "Howard Berkowitz, you've been around since the dinosaurs roamed the earth." Pomeroy's claims that Berkowitz was replaced because of the lackluster performance of the departments under his supervision. Berkowitz's departments, however, were those that were most likely to suffer during difficult times, and Pomeroy's had just been through one of its worst seasons ever. (*Berkowitz v. Allied Stores of Penn-Ohio, Inc.,* 541 F.Supp. 1209 (E.D. Pa. 1982).)

5. Stanford Downey was demoted from a position as director of safety and counseling for Southern Natural Gas Company to security manager in 1974 at the age of 58. He had been working at the company in the safety area since 1949. In addition to his demotion, he also suffered an effective freeze on his salary, which allowed him only one pay raise from 1974 to his retirement in 1978 in the amount of $85. In 1977, he requested a transfer to the position of director of safety and training at another facility, and he was recommended for the position by the personnel director. However, this request was denied and the position was given to a 33-year-old employee with three years' experience. The personnel director told him that he was not selected because he would only be there a couple of years before the replacement would have to undergo costly training due to Downey's advanced age. Downey files an age discrimination charge; what result? (*Downey v. Southern Natural Gas Company,* 649 F.2d 302 (5th Cir. 1981).)

6. Lyle Ver Planck was the postmaster in Costa Mesa. In 1976, while he was temporarily assigned out of the area, a supervisor position became available. Vincent Limongelli, age 49 and a postal employee since 1944, and five others applied for the position. A three-member advisory panel briefly interviewed each of the applicants. Limongelli was asked about his age and the number of years before he planned to retire. While the panel claims that age and retirement plans had no bearing on its decision, the members unanimously voted to appoint Nathan Ver Planck, Lyle's 39-year-old nephew, as supervisor. Does Limongelli have a basis for a claim? (*Limongelli v. Postmaster General of the United States,* 707 F.2d 368 (9th Cir. 1983).)

7. Forty-three-year-old Lawrence Jackson lost his job as a sales representative in Shell Oil's animal health business when Shell sold the business to Diamond Shamrock. The animal health employees were told, "The reason we cannot transfer you into other departments in Shell is because we can go out and hire younger people, better qualified, from college, and pay them $16,000 rather than $30,000." Shell claims that its legitimate nondiscriminatory reason for Jackson's termination was Diamond's desire to purchase the entity as a going concern, with all of the personnel force intact. To transfer a salesperson on request would encourage others to do so, which may have precluded the sale. However, one employee, less qualified but younger than Jackson, was allowed to transfer. Does Jackson have a claim for age discrimination? (*Jackson v. Shell Oil Co.,* 702 F.2d 197 (9th Cir. 1983).)

8. Can an employer be liable under any antidiscrimination statute for refusing to hire someone whom the employer thinks is overqualified? (*Taggart v. Time, Inc.,* 924 F.2d 43 (2d Cir. 1991).)

9. The oldest or nearly oldest in each department happened to be the employee

chosen by each unit supervisor to be laid off in a cutback. An employee filed suit and the employer claimed that (1) it had the right to terminate the oldest employees because they cost the most to the company and (2) there was no discrimination or intent to do so because each unit supervisor made her or his own decisions, so there was no concerted effort or decision to get rid of older employees. Are you persuaded by this defense?

10. Since 1975, Featherly had been the production supervisor of the crankshaft department at Teledyne. As a result of a reduction in force in 1987, the crankshaft and the gears departments were combined and Featherly's supervisors determined that he should be laid off because he did not have the versatility to supervise both departments. Consequently, Featherly's duties were given to Gilbert, production manager of the gears department. At the time of his termination, Featherly was 58 years old, with 25 years' seniority; Gilbert was 41 years old, with 12 years of supervisory experience. What does Featherly need to show to be successful on a claim of age discrimination against Teledyne? (*Featherly v. Teledyne Industries,* 486 N.W.2d 361 (Mich. 1992).)

13 DISABILITY DISCRIMINATION

Chapter Outline

S C E N A R I O S

S C E N A R I O   1

Thekla Tsonis is responsible for filling a vacant position at her firm. The position requires good interpersonal and communication skills and the ability to type, file, and travel on an as-needed basis. An applicant sits before her during an interview for the vacant position. Tsonis is relatively confident that the applicant satisfies the first three criteria. However, Tsonis is concerned about the fourth requirement, traveling on an as-needed basis, because the applicant is bound to a wheelchair due to a muscular disorder which does not affect her cognitive skills or her use of her arms and hands. A second applicant's performance evaluations come from her previous employer and are slightly lower than those received by the first applicant, and the applicant informed Tsonis that she is not fond of traveling. Does Tsonis hire the first applicant, even though she believes that the wheelchair will pose a problem with travel and other areas, or does she hire the second, fearing that the second may complain if the travel requirements become excessive?

S C E N A R I O   2

An employee discovers she tested HIV-positive for AIDS. The rest of the employees in her workplace refuse to work if the employee is retained. Can the employer dismiss the HIV-positive employee?

S C E N A R I O   3

Marquita applies for a position as a typist, but she has no arms past the elbow. Marquita types 80 words per minute with her toes. How should the employer handle this? Does Marquita have to be hired? If so, how can she be accommodated?

Statutory Basis

Americans with Disabilities Act of 1990, ¶602, §102

No covered entity shall discriminate against a qualified individual with a disability because of the disability of such individual in regard to job application procedures, the hiring, advancement, or discharge of employees, employee compensation, job training, and other terms, conditions, and privileges of employment.

Vocational Rehabilitation Act of 1973, ¶504 §794

No otherwise qualified individual with a disability in the United States . . . shall, solely by reason of her or his disability, be excluded from the participation in, be denied the benefits of, or be subjected to discrimination under any program or activity receiving Federal financial assistance or under any program or activity conducted by any Executive agency.

EXHIBIT 13–1   Myths about Disability Discrimination

1. A question on an application form about specific disabilities of an applicant is not improper.
2. If you would have to alter the working environment to accommodate a disabled applicant or employee, that person is not qualified for the position.
3. Disabled employees have many more rights to their jobs than do disabled applicants.
4. Disabled people generally are incapable of performing the jobs for which they apply.
5. If someone is not disabled, but others believe she or he is, that person is not protected against discrimination.
6. Disabled employees make poor workers.
7. If a disabled applicant applies for a job, the employer must hire that applicant.
8. HIV status is not a disability under the ADA.
9. Only physical disabilities are protected under the ADA.

Disproving Old Barriers

While Title VII assured certain groups of protection from discrimination in employment decisions, those groups with disabilities continued to face the frustration of physical and attitudinal employment barriers long after the passage of Title VII—employers refused to hire the disabled for fear that they would not be able to perform at the same level as other employees, or had fears based on the attitudes of co-workers. Disabled applicants found that they were required to prove themselves and their abilities to a much greater extent than did able-bodied applicants.

Approximately 43 million Americans have one or more physical or mental disabilities. Approximately 13.4% of the potential workforce in the United States is disabled; however, the unemployment rate for disabled Americans is estimated at 10.5%, compared to 4.3% for the general workforce. On the other hand, research has shown that, when properly placed, the performance of a disabled worker equals that of an able-bodied worker. It has also been shown that a disabled employee may in fact surpass co-workers as he or she overcomes the effects of his or her disability.

Employers have yet to recognize the potential lost by their underutilization of this valuable resource. Instead, many employment decisions regarding disabled applicants are grounded in naive prejudice. Often, managers reach inaccurate conclusions related to the scope of the disabled applicant's abilities and are apprehensive regarding the perceived costs of employing a disabled person. For instance, an employer who invites an applicant to her office for an interview based on a stellar résumé may be surprised to discover that the applicant is blind.

The employer may immediately jump to the conclusion that this blind applicant is not qualified for the position, which requires a great deal of reading. The employer, however, may be losing an excellent candidate merely because she failed to recognize possible accommodations of this disability, which may allow the applicant to make a meaningful addition to her staff. In fact, many disabled workers are

Exhibit 13–2

The following was written prior to the passage of the ADA.

The employment difficulties of Americans with disabilities deepened during the 1980s, according to new figures from the Census Bureau (www.census.org). This occurred despite the increased efforts and partial successes of Americans with disabilities to assert their rights to equal treatment in transportation, employment, voting, and within society in general. According to the new Census Bureau statistics, workers with disabilities saw their earnings fall further below the income of able-bodied workers as the decade progressed. In 1980, workers with disabilities earned 77% as much as the able-bodied; but, by 1987, they earned only 64%. And a smaller percentage of men with disabilities were working as the decade neared an end than in 1981: 30% in 1981, but only 23% [in 1989]. . . .

Specialists in disability issues are surprised by the negative implications of the new Census Bureau statistics. And they are not certain how to explain the figures, although they offer theories. . . . Philip Calkins, of the President's Committee on Employment of People with Disabilities . . . offers several:

- Health-care costs have really skyrocketed in the 1980s. The costs of health-care, and of health-care insurance, are a major reason why people with disabilities face discrimination in the work force.

- "The number of employees in government at all levels has declined" relative to the U.S. population. "Therefore, the number of places available in those protected areas has declined." With the decline in government jobs, which offer legal protection against discrimination, workers with disabilities increasingly may have been kept in lower paying jobs, experts theorize. This may be a reason for the growing income gap between American workers in general and those with disabilities.

- As America's budget squeeze has tightened during the decade of the 1980s, some of the trims in spending for social programs have cut back on programs that aid people with disabilities, and that help prepare them for employment.

R. Hey, *Christian Science Monitor,* July 16, 1990, p. 8, col. 1.

capable of performing the essential requirements of their position with little or no accommodation on the part of their employer.

To ensure that an employer is reaping the greatest benefit from its applicant pool, the employer should be "disability-blind" and evaluate each applicant on the basis of her or his competence. This is true during all stages of employment, including the interview, hiring, employee relations, transfer requests, performance reviews, disciplinary decisions, and termination decisions.

Regulation

In an effort to stem the discrimination against disabled employees and applicants, Congress enacted the Vocational Rehabilitation Act of 1973, which applies to the government and any firm that does business with the government. Section 504 of the act prohibits discrimination against otherwise qualified individuals with disabilities by any program or activity receiving federal assistance. The Rehabilitation Act seeks to alleviate the burdens that are specifically confronted by those with disabilities and to ensure that disabled employees or applicants encounter only the burdens that are encountered by those who are not disabled. Section 503 of the act further requires that, where a federal department or agency enters into a contract that exceeds $2,500 annually, the contractor is required to take affirmative action to employ and promote qualified disabled individuals. Federal contractors, therefore, must take proactive steps to change their hiring policies, recruit disabled employees, train disabled employees so they are likely to advance, and assist in their accommodation should they experience surmountable difficulties in their position.

Federal employers and contractors have the additional obligation to take steps to employ and to advance disabled workers, pursuant to the Rehabilitation Act's requirement of affirmative action. This may include positive steps to recruit disabled employees; modification of personnel practices to meet the needs of the disabled workforce, such as special training for individuals who will be interviewing disabled applicants; and the training of supervisors and managers to provide the strong internal support and an environment in which a disabled employee would feel welcome.

Section 503 of the Rehabilitation Act
Requires affirmative action on the part of federal contractors and agencies to recruit, hire, and train disabled workers.

Unfortunately, since it only applies to the government and federal contractors, the Vocational Rehabilitation Act was insufficient to prevent discrimination against private-sector employees and was inconsistently enforced against federal employers. While Congress passed other statutes relating to discrimination against the disabled since the Rehabilitation Act, this was done on a segmented basis. Disabled veterans were protected by one statute, and mine workers who had contracted black lung disease were protected by another; private sector employers remained immune from prosecution in this regard.

Seventeen years after Congress passed the Rehabilitation Act, President George Bush signed into law the **Americans with Disabilities Act** (ADA), which became effective in July 1992. The ADA applied Rehabilitation Act standards to private employers of 25 employees or more until 1994; now the act is enforceable against employers of 15 employees or more. While many employers have complained about the act based on its vague definitions and unclear requirements, the ADA was seen as the "Declaration of Independence" or "Emancipation Proclamation" for the disabled, and the most far-reaching civil rights law to have been passed since the Civil Rights Act of 1964. Even today, however, a majority of employers are unsure about many applications of the act.

Americans with Disabilities Act
Extends Rehabilitation Act protection to employees in the private sector, with few modifications.

In addition, the impact of the ADA has been less than its advocates had hoped. In 1998, the American Bar Association's Commission on Mental and Physical Disability Law reported that the employer-defendant was the successful party in 92% of cases brought by allegedly disabled employee-plaintiffs. (However, the study also noted that it excluded the results of settlements since they were so difficult to track.) Also in 1998, the first report of the Presidential Task Force on the Employment of Adults with Disabilities reported on some of the effects of the ADA. Specific to employment, the Task Force concluded that

. . . enforcement mechanisms of the ADA have not proven sufficient to begin narrowing the gap in employment rates between people with and without disabilities. Enforcement of existing legislation designed to eliminate disability-based discrimination in all aspects of life, including employment, is clearly inadequate. Enactment of potentially powerful legislative remedies, like the ADA, without commitment of resources to enforcement will not produce desired results. Both public and private assessments of the ADA suggest that the lack of enforcement, particularly with regard to employment, has diminished the impact that this landmark legislation might otherwise have had.

Although the results seem disappointing, the task force did ask the president to take action on several issues, including

- Increasing the number of adults with disabilities working for the federal government.
- Increasing employment options for persons with psychiatric disabilities.
- Supporting legislation which allows adults with disabilities to retain Medicare coverage when they return to work.

In an executive order of December 1998, President Clinton supported all of these measures and allocated funding for their implementation.

To understand the coverage of the act, it is important to understand its scope of protection. The ADA protects the disabled from three types of barriers: intentional discrimination for reasons of social bias against them, neutral standards with disparate impact on the disabled, and discrimination as a result of barriers to job performance that can be fully overcome by accommodation.

Generally, an employer may not reach any employment decision on the basis of the individual's disability; an employer may not classify an applicant or employee

Courtesy of the U.S. Department of Labor.

because of a disability in a way that adversely affects her or his opportunities or status. Employers may not make presumptions about what a class of disabled individuals may or may not be able to do. Employers may not impose standards or criteria that discriminate against or screen out employees or applicants on the basis of their disability, unless that criteria can be shown to be job-related and consistent with business necessity. Employers may not discriminate against qualified disabled applicants or employees in recruitment, hiring, promotion, training, layoffs, pay, terminations, position assignments, leave policies, or benefits.

How is the protection given to disabled individuals different from that afforded other minorities under Title VII and similar statutes? Under the ADA and the Rehabilitation Acts, employers must take *proactive steps* to make their workplaces amenable to the impaired worker, and they may not wait until a problem presents itself. For example, an employer is not merely required to restructure its workplace and job descriptions to allow disabled individuals access as applicants but also to implement mechanisms to retain those disabled workers once hired. This is because Congress has determined that the value of the resources to be provided by the disabled workforce greatly outweighs the costs of their employment.

How do these laws protect the disabled individual, and what must an employer do to ensure that she or he is in compliance? First, it is important to understand that the law merely protects the individual from discrimination based solely on her or his disability. The laws do not require an employer to hire a disabled person who is unable to perform the work required by the position. The operative word, however, is "required." Under the acts, the employer must ascertain the actual components of the position, the elements essential to the employee's performance, and which components are convenient but not essential to be performed by this individual. The employer should ensure that its position descriptions are up to date and job-specific, and that each description specifically outlines every responsibility of the job and discusses the qualifications that may be necessary to satisfy those responsibilities.

The general policy implemented by **the ADA and the Rehabilitation Act** is that, as long as the applicant or employee is otherwise qualified for the position, with or without reasonable accommodation, the acts prohibit any adverse employment decision that is made solely on the basis of the disability. An employer may not terminate an employee, for example, who is able to adequately perform merely because he uses a walker to assist in his mobility. An employee may be able to claim discrimination on the basis of her disability if she can prove:

1. That she is disabled.
2. That she is otherwise qualified for the position.
3. If an accommodation is required, that the accommodation is reasonable.
4. That she suffered an adverse employment decision, such as a termination or demotion.

Employers should keep in mind that there are state laws as well as the federal laws that protect employees from discrimination. Employees filing claims based on

ADA and Rehabilitation Acts protection
As long as an individual with a disability is otherwise qualified for a position, with or without reasonable accommodation, the employer may not make an adverse employment decision solely on the basis of the disability.

a disability may find greater relief in state courts, applying state laws. In some states, damages are higher for disability discrimination under state laws, and claims are easier to prove than in federal courts applying the federal laws.[1]

"Disability"

Disability
A physical or mental impairment that substantially limits one or more of the major life activities of an individual; a record of such impairment; or being regarded as having such an impairment.

A variety of terms are used in the disability discrimination area. What constitutes a disability? The ADA defines **disability** as "(a) a physical or mental impairment that substantially limits one or more of the major life activities of an individual; (b) a record of having such impairment; (c) or being regarded as having such an impairment." A "record" of impairment is discussed in the *Arline* case on page 458. In the third provision, the law protects those persons who are not actually disabled but who are instead *regarded* as having a disability. There is no definitive list of impairments that are considered to be disabilities. Courts are directed to reach determinations based on a case-by-case analysis. This determination is not made on the basis of the name or diagnosis of the employee's impairment but, instead, on the basis of the effect of the impairment on her or his life. Note also that some states even have laws that mandate that certain conditions be considered disabilities, thus eliminating this requirement of the plaintiff's proof.

Is an employee's claim that she or he is disabled or has a disabling disease sufficient to prove that the employee should be protected by the ADA or the Rehabilitation Acts? No. For instance, in one case, the employee sought to be covered by the Rehabilitation Act based on her obesity. Though courts have been split in connection with obesity, in this case the court said that, while obesity may lead to a condition resulting in a disability or physical impairment, the *mere* assertion, without more, is not enough to make someone a member of the protected class.

If an employee can take a medication to rid herself or himself of the disability, is this individual disabled? The Third Circuit was recently faced with this issue in *Taylor v. Phoenixville School District,*[2] where an individual who suffered from a bipolar disorder (manic depression) appeared completely recovered when taking medication. The court specifically held that "disabilities should be evaluated based on the plaintiff's unmedicated state . . . Whether an impairment 'substantially limits' a major life activity should be evaluated 'without regard to mitigating measures such as medicines, or assistive or prosthetic devices.'" In justifying its decision, the Third Circuit noted that "it makes little sense to insist that serious, chronic conditions like diabetes, epilepsy, or bipolar disorder cannot be disabilities unless they are so poorly controlled that it becomes all but inevitable that no reasonable accommodation is possible." Anticipating employers' fears of a deluge of claims based on this case, the court reassured in a footnote:

> Employers need not fear that discounting mitigating factors will establish a flood of new-found disabilities and demands for accommodations. First, many widely-treated

---

[1]See *City of Moorpark v. Ventura County Superior Court,* 959 P.2d 752 (ca. 1998) and *Dillard's v. Beckwith,* 989 P.2d 882 (Nev. 1999).

[2]1999 U.S. App. LEXIS 6067(3rd Cir. 1999).

conditions simply do not significantly restrict a person's functioning as compared to the average person's—even when those conditions are left untreated. If, on the other hand, a condition is disabling when untreated, but really is fully corrected by mitigating measures, then it is very unlikely that employers will need to make much in the way of accommodations, for by hypothesis, the condition imposes no restrictions on the employee.

The value of looking to the unmitigated condition is that it allows the ADA to encompass serious, chronic conditions like diabetes or bipolar disorder that, while capable of being controlled by medication, are not always perfectly controlled. Medical treatments for many chronic conditions can in some instances themselves create limitations. The problem with insisting that these uncontrolled symptoms must themselves be substantially limiting before accommodations are required is that once the symptoms of a serious, chronic condition are no longer kept in check, they can rapidly become totally disabling. As a result, employees with these disabilities would be denied the right to accommodations when modest accommodations could help them surmount significant although not substantially limiting symptoms. And "disability" status would only be achieved when their health had deteriorated so precipitously that no reasonable accommodation was possible. To take Taylor's case, she would not be legally entitled under the ADA to even the most simple accommodations for blood tests until she experienced the onset of another manic episode which could easily result in her becoming psychotic, requiring another commitment to an institution.

It might be thought that those who have serious, chronic conditions can turn to the "regarded as disabled" prong to establish a disability and obtain accommodations when symptoms or the side effects of treatments flare. However, aside from the fact that an employer may not regard the employee as disabled, it remains an open question in this circuit whether employees are entitled to accommodations if they can only satisfy the "regarded as" prong for demonstrating a disability.

However, in June 1999, the Supreme Court released three opinions that further articulate and delineate the law in this area, *Sutton v. United Air Lines, Murphy v. United Parcel Service, Inc.,* and *Albertsons, Inc. v. Kirkingburg.* These cases reach conclusions contrary to those reached by the Third Circuit. In *Sutton,* where the plaintiff's uncorrected vision was 20/200 or worse but could be corrected by eyeglasses to 20/20, the court specifically stated,

> Three separate ADA provisions, read in concert, lead to the conclusion that the determination whether an individual is disabled should be made with reference to measures, such as eyeglasses and contact lenses, that mitigate the individual's impairment . . . A "disability" exists only where an impairment "substantially limits" a major life activity, not where it "might," "could," or "would" be substantially limiting if corrective measures were not taken . . . It could also lead to the anomalous result that courts and employers could not consider any negative side effects suffered by the individual resulting from the use of mitigating measures, even when those side effects are very severe.[3]

Mental Impairments.   The issue of how to handle mental impairments has been a concern for employers and employees alike because of the increased possibility for fraudulent claims (due to the challenge of verification). To address concerns and to offer guidance on the issue, the EEOC issued its Enforcement Guidance on the

---

[3]*Sutton v. United Air Lines,* 1999 U.S. LEXIS 4371 (1999).

Americans with Disabilities Act and Psychiatric Disabilities in April 1997. Three key concepts are addressed in the guidelines. First, the guidelines include "interacting with others" as an example of a major life activity that, if substantially limited by mental impairment, would support a determination of an ADA disability, Second, among the methods for reasonable accommodation of psychiatric disabilities, the guidelines state that employers must consider requests for modified work schedules, individual office space, or changes in supervisory style. The third area on which the guidelines expand relates to an employer's uniformly applied workplace standards for dress, grooming, personal appearance, and behavior. An employee may claim that, due to a mental impairment, he or she cannot conform to certain standards. In this circumstance, the guidelines provide that, in order to avoid fraud, an employer is entitled to document the conduct, verify the disorder, and work toward a reasonable accommodation that will enable the employee to perform the essential functions of the job.

Accordingly, employers should have a process in place to obtain and to evaluate appropriate medical information. The employer can request further information, beyond a doctor's note, from an employee claiming a psychiatric disability by requesting permission from the employee to have the company doctor review his or her medical records. The company can then verify that the accommodation is medically necessary to enable the employee to do the job.

"Physical or Mental Impairment"; "Major Life Activity."   Generally, a person who suffers from a serious medical condition is limited in her or his major life activities. Breathing is impaired when one has emphysema; learning is impaired when one suffers from dyslexia. Functioning and procreation are impaired when one is HIV-positive. Employers, however, are offered little guidance by the acts; neither the ADA nor the Rehabilitation Act defines "physical or mental impairment" or "major life activities."

An employer must exercise caution in any determination of disability, because even working has been held to constitute a major life activity. While some employees have argued a "bootstrap" theory of coverage—that if an employer denies a position to an applicant on the basis of his impairment, such denial may be just the act necessary for the employee to prove that the impairment constitutes a disability—this is not generally accepted. The counterargument is that if working is considered a major life activity, the employer is not limiting the applicant from working *per se,* merely working in that position.

In fact, employers should determine whether the impairment the employee claims is one generally regarded as having a disabling effect. The determination of whether an applicant's employment is a major life activity would depend on the degree to which his employment options were limited. The factors most important to this analysis include:

The number and type of jobs from which the impaired applicant is
    disqualified.

The geographical area to which the applicant has reasonable access.

The applicant's job expectations and training.

The language of one court offers further guidance; a Hawaiian district court concluded that "an impairment that interfered with an individual's ability to do a

---

Impairment
[a]ny physiological disorder or condition . . . affecting one or more of the following body systems: neurological; musculoskeletal; special sense organs; respiratory, including speech organs; cardiovascular; reproductive; digestive; genito-urinary; hemic and lymphatic; skin; and endocrine; or any mental or psychological disorder" which substantially limits one of life's major activities. (From the Equal Employment Opportunity Commission regulations.)

Major life activities
"functions such as caring for one's self, performing manual tasks, walking, seeing, hearing, speaking, breathing, learning and working." (From the EEOC regulations.)

particular job, but did not significantly decrease that individual's ability to obtain satisfactory employment otherwise, was not *substantially* limiting within the meaning of the statute." Accordingly, a particular job for a particular employer cannot be a major life activity. If, on the other hand, the impairment completely prevents performing the type of work for which the applicant is trained, for any employer, such an impairment may constitute a disability. In the following case, the employer claimed that the employee was not disabled, as his medical restrictions only prohibited him from performing this job, not all jobs.

Otis v. Canadian Valley-Reeves Meat Co.
52 F.3d 338 (10th Cir. 1995)

Plaintiff was employed by defendant when he injured his back. When he returned to work, he was restricted in terms of how much he could lift. He requested a transfer but it was denied. Defendant claims that plaintiff is not substantially limited in a major life activity and therefore not covered by the ADA.

Kelly, J.

Plaintiff asserts he is disabled under the ADA because his back injury "Substantially limits one or more of [his] major life activities," including working. He claims he is disabled because he is unable to perform his previous job or the job he was assigned following his injury.

"To demonstrate that an impairment 'substantially limits' the major life activity of working, an individual must show 'significant . . . restrict[ion] in the ability to perform either a class of jobs or a broad range of jobs in various classes as compared to the average person having comparable training, skills and abilities.'" The inability to perform the duties of any one particular job does not qualify as a restriction on the major life activity of working.

Here, plaintiff has shown only that he cannot perform his previous job of meat loader due to the seventy-pound lifting restriction imposed by his physician. The evidence presented to the district court does not establish that plaintiff is restricted in any major life activity, including working.

Therefore, we affirm the district court's conclusion that plaintiff is not disabled within the meaning of the ADA.

Case Questions

1. Do you agree with the court's conclusion that the plaintiff must be restricted from performing an entire class of jobs or broad range of jobs in various classes in order to prevail?

2. If an individual is precluded from even one position that an able-bodied person could obtain, doesn't that seem to be a substantial impairment? If not, how would you define "class of jobs?"

3. Couldn't any one employer use this defense; in other words, couldn't each employer to whom this person applied for a position claim that the individual is simply unable to perform that *one* position for which he applied, thereby disallowing the claim?

"Substantially Limits."   The following case involves an employee who has a contagious disease. The court was required to determine whether this disease "substantially limited" the employee's major life activities.

SCHOOL BD. OF NASSAU COUNTY V. ARLINE
107 S.Ct. 1123 (1987)

Plaintiff, employee Arline, is a teacher who has tuberculosis. In this case, the Supreme Court determined that Arline was disabled pursuant to the definition of the Rehabilitation Act because her disability required hospitalization. The defendant employer argued that Arline was not terminated due to her disease but instead due to the threat that her relapses posed to the health of others. The court stated that the threat posed to others by one's disability is not distinct from the disability itself; therefore, the employee was considered to be disabled and the employer's actions were subject to scrutiny under the Rehabilitation Act.

Brennan, J.

In determining whether a particular individual is handicapped as defined by the [Rehabilitation] Act, the regulations promulgated by the Department of Health and Human Services are of significant assistance. As we have previously recognized, these regulations were drafted with the oversight and approval of Congress; they provide an important source of guidance on the meaning of section 504.

Within this statutory and regulatory framework, then, we must consider whether Arline can be considered a handicapped individual. According to the testimony of Dr. McEuen, Arline suffered tuberculosis "in an acute form in such a degree that it affected her respiratory system," and was hospitalized for this condition. Arline thus has a physical impairment as that term is defined by the regulations, since she had a "physiological disorder or condition affecting her respiratory system." This impairment was serious enough to require hospitalization, a fact more than sufficient to establish that one or more of her major life activities were substantially limited by her impairment. Thus, Arline's hospitalization for tuberculosis in 1957 suffices to establish that she has a "record of . . . impairment" within the meaning of [the regulations] and is therefore a handicapped individual.

Petitioners concede that a contagious disease may constitute a handicapping condition to the extent that it leaves a person with "diminished physical or mental capabilities," and concede that Arline's hospitalization for tuberculosis in 1957 demonstrates that she has a record of a physical impairment. Petitioners maintain, however, that Arline's record of impairment is irrelevant in this case, since the School Board dismissed Arline not because of her diminished capabilities, but because of the threat that her relapses of tuberculosis posed to the health of others.

We do not agree with petitioners that, in defining a handicapped individual under §504, the contagious effects of a disease can be meaningfully distinguished from the disease's physical effects on a claimant in a case such as this. Arline's contagiousness and her physical impairment each resulted from the same underlying condition, tuberculosis. It would be unfair to allow an employer to seize upon the distinction between the effects of a disease on others and the effects of a disease on a patient and use that distinction to justify discriminatory treatment.

Few aspects of a handicap give rise to the same level of public fear and misapprehension as contagiousness. Even those who suffer or have recovered from such noninfectious diseases as epilepsy or cancer have faced discrimination based on the irrational fear that they might be contagious. The Act is carefully structured to replace such reflexive reactions to actual or perceived handicaps with actions based on reasoned and medically sound judgments: the definition of "handicapped individual" is broad, but only those individuals who are both handicapped *and* otherwise qualified are eligible for relief. The fact that *some* persons who have contagious diseases may pose a serious health threat to others under certain circumstances does not justify excluding from the coverage of the Act all persons with actual or perceived contagious diseases. Such exclusion would mean those accused of being contagious would never have the opportunity to have their condition evaluated in light of medical evidence and a determination made as to whether they were "otherwise qualified." Rather, they would be vulnerable to discrimination on the basis of mythology—precisely the type of injury Congress sought to prevent. We conclude that the fact a person with a record of a physical impairment is also contagious does not suffice to remove that person from coverage under §504.

The remaining question is whether Arline is otherwise qualified for the job of elementary schoolteacher. The basic factors to be considered in conducting such an inquiry are well established. In the context of employment of a person handicapped with a contagious disease, we agree with *amicus* American Medical Association that this inquiry should include: "findings of facts,

based on reasonable medical judgment given the state of medical knowledge, about (a) the nature of the risk (how the disease is transmitted), (b) the duration of the risk (how long is the carrier infectious), (c) the severity of the risk (what is the potential to harm third parties), and (d) the probabilities the disease will be transmitted and will cause varying degrees of harm." The next step in the "otherwise qualified" inquiry is for the court to evaluate whether the employer could reasonably accommodate the employee under the established standards for that inquiry.

Because of the paucity of factual findings by the district court, we, like the court of appeals, are unable at this stage to resolve whether Arline is otherwise qualified for her job. We remand the case to the district court to determine whether Arline is otherwise qualified for her position.

Case Questions

1. Consider the similarities between the Court's analysis of the public reaction to contagiousness in Arline ("Few aspects of a handicap give rise to the same level of public fear and misapprehension as contagiousness") and the analysis it would have to undergo if Arline had AIDS as opposed to tuberculosis. Any differences? Where do you think any differences might be found in a court's analysis of an employee with HIV? (See *Doe v. Kohn Nast & Graf,* in this chapter.)

2. Is it realistic to think that, as the employer here argued, the contagious aspect of a disease can be divorced from the consideration of the public of having the disease itself? Will an employer always run the risk of being sued in such a situation?

3. What type of policy could you develop that would instruct your managers about how to handle an employee with a contagious disease?

Substantially limits
"unable to perform a major life activity that the average person in the general population can perform; or significantly restricted as to the condition, manner, or duration under which an individual can perform a major life activity."
(From the EEOC regulations.)

In 1986, the Department of Justice issued an opinion, which stated that, if fear of contagion is the basis for the termination, the employee is not considered disabled and is not protected under the Rehabilitation Act because the ability to communicate the disease to another is not a disability. The opinion made no distinction based on whether the fear of contagion is reasonable or unreasonable on the part of the employer. However, the Department of Justice opinion was in direct contravention of the Supreme Court's later determination in *Arline,* which specifically stated that chronic contagious diseases are considered to be protected disabilities. The Department of Justice thereafter issued a second memorandum, which reversed its earlier analysis in connection with HIV after Surgeon General Koop informed the Justice Department that physical impairment is almost always present. Do you believe that someone who is contagious due to a congenital disease, but who exhibits no physical impairment, is considered disabled under the act?

Many courts have been faced with the issue of HIV in the workplace and in academic institutions. For instance, in one case, the court held that the lower court's finding that there was a remote possibility of transmission of HIV from tears, saliva, and urine of an HIV-infected child did not support the segregation of this child from students in a classroom for regularly trainable mentally handicapped children.

Perception of Impairment.   The ADA definition of "disability" includes not only an actual impairment but also being *perceived* as having an impairment. Congress included an employee who is perceived as being disabled in the definition of disability because it was concerned with discrimination stemming from simple prejudice, and also from "archaic attitudes and laws" and from "the fact that the American people are simply unfamiliar and insensitive to the difficulties confront[ing] individuals with disabilities."

An employee or applicant is regarded as having an impairment if he or she has a physical or mental impairment that does not substantially limit major life activities, but which is treated as constituting a limit, as well as an impairment that substantially limits major life activities only as a result of the attitudes of others toward such impairment. An example of this type of perceived limitation would involve someone with a disfiguring facial scar that does not limit employment capabilities. If the employer discriminates against this person because of the negative reaction of its customers or clients, "the employer would be regarding the individual as disabled and acting on the basis of that perceived disability." Similarly, HIV-positive employees might be perceived as incapable of functioning while, in fact, no symptoms of the disease are yet manifested or inhibiting.

On the other hand, if an employer refuses to hire an applicant merely because the employer believes that person to be ugly, the applicant would probably not be considered disabled and would therefore not be covered by the ADA.

In one particularly interesting case, a telemarketer who was missing 18 teeth was fired from his position after only three days of training. Even though he had generally positive evaluations in the training program, the trainers reported that the gentleman mumbled on the phone. The worker claimed that he did not have a disability and that his missing teeth did not cause him to mumble; he filed an ADA claim based on his employer's *perception* that he was disabled. The district court held that, since the worker did not actually have a disability, he could not sustain a claim that his employer perceived him as disabled. Without finding whether mumbling would be considered a disability, the Seventh Circuit reversed, holding that, "If for no reason whatsoever an employer regards a person as disabled—for example, because of a blunder in reading medical records it imputes to him a heart condition he has never had—and takes an adverse action, it has violated the [ADA]." (Note that, on remand, the district court found that mumbling would not substantially limit a major life activity. Therefore, a decision based on a *perception* of mumbling could not be considered a violation of the ADA.)

NIELSEN V. MORONI FEED COMPANY, ET. AL.
162 F.3d 604 (10th Cir. 1998)

> When a company president went into some people's homes without permission, he was terminated. He sued under the ADA and the court had to determine if he had a qualified disability.

Ebel, J.

Nielsen worked for ten years as the President of Moroni Feed, a farming cooperative. In 1994, Moroni Feed received a report that Nielsen entered a board member's home without permission when no one was present. This was the second time that Nielsen had entered this home without permission. The Chairman of the Board discussed these incidents with Nielsen and Nielsen promised it would not occur again. At the time of termination, Moroni Feed had received a total of eight reports of Nielsen's unauthorized entry into private homes in the area.

Following one of the home-entering incidents, the Moroni Feed Board of Directors met to discuss the situation. Olson told the Board that Nielsen had confided in him that Nielsen had a "drug problem." Nielsen denied this. Some members of the Board subsequently met with a psychologist to discuss Nielsen's behavior; at this meeting members of the Board indicated that they perceived Nielsen to be suffering from a drug problem that was interfering with Nielsen's performance of his duties as President of the company. Some board members began to discuss the possibility of terminating Nielsen due to his deficient performances as President.

Nielsen said that members of the Board told him that they believed that he had a drug problem, that he was going into homes to steal drugs, and that the problem was set to be discussed at an upcoming Board meeting. Nielsen met with the Board at which time they indicated they were considering replacing him based on the unauthorized entries into private homes. The Board neither confirmed nor denied that its decision was based upon a perceived drug problem, but it requested that Nielsen be admitted to Dayspring, a drug treatment center, for evaluation. Nielsen agreed. After three days of evaluation, the Dayspring staff determined that Nielsen was not chemically dependent, and Nielsen was discharged.

Nielsen returned to Moroni Feed, reported his experiences at Dayspring to the Board, and was instructed to "get back to work." However, the next day he was terminated by a board member because Nielsen had lost the trust of the Board, the managers, and the membership of the co-op by the unauthorized access into others' homes. The Board ratified the decision.

Nielsen filed suit in federal district court, claiming discrimination in employment on the basis of a perceived disability, in violation of the Americans with Disabilities Act ("ADA"). The district court granted summary judgment and Nielsen appealed.

* * *

One area where the ADA and the Rehabilitation Act recognize a dichotomy between a disability and disability-caused misconduct is where the disability is related to alcoholism or illegal drug use. . . . Although . . . [some] cases [have] state[d] in general terms that a disability is protected while disability-caused misconduct is not, they all make this distinction in the context of alcoholism or illegal drug use. We too have noted such a distinction when alcoholism or illegal drug use is involved.

The reason this dichotomy exists in the context of alcoholism and illegal drug use is simple: both the ADA and the Rehabilitation Act clearly contemplate removing from statutory protection unsatisfactory conduct caused by alcoholism and illegal drug use. Specifically, the ADA states that a covered entity "may hold an employee who engages in the illegal use of drugs or who is an alcoholic to the same qualification standards for employment or job performance and behavior that such entity holds other employees, even if any unsatisfactory performance or behavior is related to the drug use or alcoholism of such employee. . . ." The Rehabilitation Act similarly removes unsatisfactory conduct caused by alcoholism from its purview, stating that the term "'individual with a disability' . . . does not include any individual who is an alcoholic whose current use of alcohol prevents such individual from performing the duties of the job in question or whose employment, by

reason of such current alcohol abuse, would constitute a direct threat to property or the safety of others."

* * *

Significantly, while the mere status of being an illegal drug user may invoke protection under the ADA, that protection does not extend to those "currently engaging in the illegal use of drugs." On the other hand, the ADA specifically exempts from [this] exclusion, and hence protects, an individual who

(1) has successfully completed a supervised drug rehabilitation program and is no longer engaging in the illegal use of drugs, or has otherwise been rehabilitated successfully and is no longer engaging in such use;

(2) is participating in a supervised rehabilitation program and is no longer engaging in such use; or

(3) is erroneously regarded as engaging in such use, but is not engaged in such use.

Because [this section] excludes erroneous perception of illegal drug use from being disallowed as a disability under [the exclusion], the ADA protects employees who are erroneously regarded as being current illegal drug users. However, the erroneous perception of being an illegal drug user is to be treated like any other perception of a disability, and is only to be considered a qualifying disability if the employer perceives the disability to substantially limit a major life activity.

Therefore, Nielsen could avoid summary judgment only by presenting evidence to the district court that, when taken in the light most favorable to Nielsen, would have allowed a reasonable jury to conclude (1) that Nielsen had a perceived disability protected under the ADA because Moroni Feed erroneously believed he was illegally using drugs and that the perceived use was severe enough to substantially limit one or more of his major life activities, and (2) that Moroni Feed terminated Nielsen on the basis of this perceived disability or conduct erroneously attributed to it.

. . . Nielsen has failed to produce any evidence that Moroni Feed erroneously believed he was illegally using drugs which use was severe enough to substantially limit one or more of his major life activities. While Nielsen did present evidence that at least some decision-makers at Moroni Feed at some point were concerned about his behavior and about his perceived addiction to prescription painkillers, Nielsen proffered no evidence that anyone at Moroni Feed believed this perceived drug addiction was severe enough to substantially limit one or more of his major life activities. Indeed, Nielsen failed to state explicitly what major life activities, if any, Moroni Feed regarded as substantially limited by the perceived drug addiction. Nielsen simply argued that Moroni Feed "fired him due to his perceived disability in violation of the ADA." Hence, in terms of substantial limitation of a major life activity, the most we can infer from Nielsen's argument is a contention that Moroni Feed fired him because it believed he suffered from a drug addiction severe enough to prevent him from performing his duties as President of the co-op. However, such a contention, even if true, falls well short of establishing that Moroni Feed regarded Nielsen as having a disability substantially limiting the only major life activity implicated by Nielsen's argument—namely, working.

. . . In order to demonstrate that an impairment "substantially limits" the major life activity of working, an individual must show "signifi-cant[] restrict[ion] in the ability to perform either a class of jobs or a broad range of jobs in various classes as compared to the average person having comparable training, skills and abilities." In other words, "[a]n impairment must substantially limit employment in general, not merely the particular job that the plaintiff may wish to hold.'" Therefore, in order to establish a disability under the 'regarded as' prong of the ADA with respect to the major life activity of working, an individual must show that the employer regarded him or her as being substantially limited in performing either a class of jobs or a broad range of jobs in various classes. Because Nielsen merely presented evidence suggesting that Moroni Feed no longer believed him capable of performing his duties as President of the co-op, but presented no evidence whatsoever that Moroni Feed believed any perceived illegal drug addiction on his part significantly restricted his "ability to perform either a class of jobs or a broad range of jobs in various classes," we must affirm the district court's entry of summary judgment.

In addition to Nielsen's failure to advance evidence that he had a qualified perceived disability because Moroni Feed believed he had an illegal drug addiction severe enough to substantially limit the major life activity of working, Nielsen also failed to advance evidence that Moroni Feed fired him on the basis of any perceived disability or conduct attributed to it. . . . While, as noted, Nielsen did present evidence that some at Moroni Feed at some point believed he was addicted to prescription painkillers, the record is clear that Nielsen was ultimately discharged, not because of an erroneous perception that he was addicted to prescription painkillers, but because of his unexplained conduct in entering uninvited into the homes of co-workers and co-op participants in the small community where Moroni Feed was located.

It is undisputed that for a considerable time Moroni Feed tried to work with Nielsen after receiving information that caused some of Moroni Feed's directors to believe he was addicted to painkillers. The co-op also directed him to a drug treatment center for evaluation. During none of this time was he discharged. It was only after the evaluation came back from Dayspring that he was not addicted to drugs and thus that his bizarre conduct of going into homes throughout the community uninvited could not be explained by drug addiction that Nielsen was terminated. The timing of Nielsen's discharge, and the references in the record about the deliberation of the Board, as well as the reasons articulated to Nielsen himself for the discharge, all make it clear beyond peradventure that Nielsen was discharged for his conduct, and that this conduct, at the time of his discharge, was not erroneously attributed to illegal drug use. Simply put, Nielsen's conduct was potentially quite disruptive to Moroni Feed, and when it was neither stopped nor explained, Moroni Feed determined it could no longer trust or tolerate a president who engaged in such conduct. Therefore, because Nielsen has failed to produce any evidence that Moroni Feed fired him on the basis of an erroneously perceived disability based on illegal drug use or conduct believed to be so caused, the district court properly granted Moroni Feed's

summary judgment motion. The judgment of the district court is AFFIRMED.

Case Questions

1. Do you think that Nielsen was fired based on a perceived disability? If so, how could Nielsen have presented his case to be more effective, eluding summary judgment?

2. Assuming the Board did fire Nielsen based on his perceived drug addiction, do you think the Board has a right to protect its interests and eliminate workers with drug or alcohol problems?

3. Why do you think the Board required Nielsen to undergo a drug evaluation?

"Otherwise Qualified"

The acts state that an employer may not terminate or refuse to hire an employee with a disability who is "otherwise qualified" to perform the essential requirements of his or her position. The determination of a position's essential functions ensures that disabled persons are not disqualified simply because they may have difficulty in performing tasks that bear only a marginal relationship to a particular job. In that way, employers protect themselves from liability and are able to most effectively utilize their human resources.

In one case, the court held that a civilian employee of the Navy failed to establish that she was qualified for her position due to her chronic fatigue syndrome. The court noted that "the accommodation plaintiff seeks is simply to be allowed to work only when her illness permits." The court held that the employee was not otherwise qualified, because she was not prepared to pull her full weight. In addition, an employer may not consider the possibility that an employee or applicant will become disabled or unqualified for the position in the future. If the applicant or employee is qualified *at the time the adverse employment action is taken,* the employer has violated the acts.[4]

Where the claim of disability is based on a disease, the court in the *Arline* case (excerpted in this chapter) held that the determination of whether an individual is "otherwise qualified" should be based on the following factors:

- The nature of the risk (how the disease is transmitted).
- The duration of the risk (how long the carrier is infectious).

---

[4]*Walders v. Garrett,* 765 F.Supp. 303 (D.C. Va. 1991).

- The severity of the risk (potential harm to third parties).
- The probability that the disease will be transmitted and will cause varying degrees of harm.

The Supreme Court's decision in the *Arline* case is important because it serves, by implication, as a proclamation that the acts safeguard the rights of employees with HIV or AIDS. Other decisions have echoed or forecasted the determination of the Supreme Court in connection with this definition. This is especially significant, given the high number of HIV-positive employees in the workforce today.

Scenario

The issue of the level of risk the disabled employee poses to herself or to others is crucial to the determination of whether the applicant is otherwise qualified for the position. The standard for balancing the risk of harm to others against the employer's duties under the acts is whether the employer can show there is a *direct threat* to the health and safety of the potential employee or others. For example, as it has been shown that HIV is not transmitted through casual but only through intimate contact, it is extremely unlikely that a showing of reasonable probability of infection can be made. Therefore, employers who take adverse employment actions based on the unreasonable complaints or fears of coemployees or customers relating to HIV would violate either the Rehabilitation Act or the ADA.

In March 1993, the northern district court of Illinois issued the first opinion in connection with a case brought under the ADA, *EEOC v. AIC Security Investigations Ltd.* In that case, Charles Wessel, the executive director of AIC, had been diagnosed with an inoperable malignant brain tumor. The evidence in the case suggested that he was still completely able and willing to perform the essential functions of his position. Nevertheless, the employer terminated him because it was concerned that, as his health declined, he would no longer be able to perform. The jury concluded that since he was otherwise qualified to perform his job, AIC's termination was in violation of the ADA and awarded Wessel $572,000.

The following two cases highlight the factors involved in a court's determination of whether an employee suffers from a disability covered by the ADA and whether the individual remains otherwise qualified for his position.

DOE V. KOHN NAST & GRAF
862 F.Supp. 1310 (E.D. Penn. 1994)

Defendant law firm terminated a plaintiff attorney because he had AIDS. Defendant claimed that plaintiff was not covered under the ADA because he was fully capable of performing as an attorney.

Gawthrop, J.

Defendants contend that the plaintiff cannot make out his prima facie case because he is not within the protected class. The thrust of the defense argument is that even though HIV-positive status, most assuredly, is not a happy medical condition with which to be diagnosed, it is not, in fact, disabling. Thus, they say, he is not protected by the statute. The defense argues that plaintiff is able to do just about anything that needs to be done; certainly he is capable of doing that in the context of a law office and courtroom, his chosen line of work, and that here at issue. Occupationally, rather than being disabled, he is perfectly able. To this, the plaintiff responds that his ability to procreate, at least successfully—that is, with uninfected progeny—is impaired irreparably by his malady, and that inability, disability, being a major life activity, brings him within the purview of the statute.

The defense argues that this really is not a relevant concern. Not in any way to be facetious, but plaintiff is not being hired to practice procreation, or to be a professional blood donor, for example. He is being hired to practice law. The defense argues that although he may have some dysfunction in an utterly unrelated area—a dysfunction familiar to millions of Americans, who happen to be sterile, but who nevertheless go about ably living their lives—to hold that that medical problem makes the act applicable to him would be to stretch the language and the purpose of the statute beyond the breaking point.

To analyze this, I must turn first to that language. The statute reads:

The term "disability" means, with respect to an individual—(A) a physical or mental impairment that substantially limits one or more of the major life activities of such individual; (B) a record of such impairment; or (C) being regarded as having such an impairment.

This plain language, although setting forth several specific criteria, provides no express guidance as to whether an HIV-infected person comes within the ambit of the act. In interpreting the meaning of a statute, substantial deference is due the interpretation given its provisions by the agency charged with administering that statute. The agency's interpretation must be given "controlling weight unless it is plainly erroneous or inconsistent with the regulation." Hence, for further guidance, I turn to the regulations defining the components of this statutory provision—(1) physical impairment and (2) substantially limits a major life activity.

Physical Impairment: The Equal Employment Opportunity Commission is the agency charged with administering Title I of the Americans with Disabilities Act, the subchapter proscribing employment discrimination. Its regulations define "physical impairment" as:

Any physiological disorder, or condition, cosmetic disfigurement, or anatomical loss affecting one or more of the following body systems: neurological, musculoskeletal, special sense organs, respiratory (including speech organs), cardiovascular, reproductive, digestive, genito-urinary, hemic and lymphatic, skin, and endocrine.

"Physiologic" is defined by Dorland's Medical Dictionary (27th ed. 1988) as "characteristic of or conforming to the normal functioning or state of the body or a tissue or organ." A physiological disorder is thus an abnormal functioning of the body or a tissue or organ. One can have one of the statutorily enumerated disabilities without being "disabled" in the usual, common, lay sense of the word. For example, the statute would apply to people who have high blood pressure, that being a hemic disorder, a proclaimed disability. Tens of millions of Americans walk around and live full and active lives, hypertense though they may be. To the lay eye, they hardly seem disabled, yet they have a "disability" within the statutory definition. That lay observation may have a certain common sense ring to it, but my role is not to construe the statute so that it might conform with a lay perception. Rather, I must read with care the definitions of disability that Congress and the EEOC, gave us, and decide whether this plaintiff's disease and its symptoms fall within one or more of those express statutory and regulatory definitions, as anomalous as the statutory result might seem to some.

Around the third week of September, 1992, plaintiff developed a fever and a rash. During September through December, 1992, plaintiff's doctor noticed that his patient lost a lot of weight. Towards the end of October and into November, plaintiff's skin became so dry and scaly that at least three people in the firm took note of it.

A skin disorder which is sufficiently noticeable to be remarked upon by several people is classifiable as a cosmetic disfigurement. Further, HIV itself "creates a physiological disorder of the hemic (blood) and lymphatic systems." Dr. Braffman, plaintiff's physician, testified that in late September, 1992, "a few lymph nodes in the neck" were swollen, although not visible to the naked eye. Each of these symptoms fall within the regulatory definition of "physical impairment."

Substantial limits on major life activities: The regulations spell out "major life activities" as:

Functions such as caring for oneself, performing manual tasks, walking, seeing, hearing, speaking, breathing, learning, and working.

The use of the words "such as" indicates that this list is illustrative and is not intended to be exclusive. In construing the statute, trying to figure out just what it means, I deem it significant that the Congress chose to use the broad term "life"— "major life activities." That encompasses a lot. Had the term "work-life," or "work" been used— "major work activities," for example—it would, of course, suggest that the disability would only be deemed relevant in the on-the-job context. Instead, the term "working" appears as just one example of the various major activities embraced within the full scope of one's life. It is clear, therefore, that the language of the statute does not preclude procreating as a major life activity, but may well include it.

A major life activity is substantially limited when an impaired person is:

(i) Unable to perform a major life activity that the average person in the general population can perform; or (ii) Significantly restricted as to the condition, manner or duration under which an individual can perform a particular major life activity as compared to the condition, manner or duration under which the average person in the general population can perform that same major life activity.

Plaintiff argues that because the regulations define a "physical impairment" to include a disorder or condition that affects the "reproductive" system, the ability to procreate is a "major life activity" within the plain meaning of the ADA. The factual record in this case is thin, indeed, as to whether HIV status is a disorder or condition that affects the "reproductive" system. No physicians testified as to that, and the parties seemed content to rely on administrative findings and the rulings of other judges such as that given in *Cain v. Hyatt.* That was a case involving a plaintiff with full-blown AIDS, in which Judge Broderick found in dictum that a person who is HIV-infected is substantially limited in a major life activity because of the significant risk of transmitting the HIV infection to a partner or a child, thereby endangering their lives.

The defendants' motion for summary judgment is bottomed largely upon the thesis that plaintiff's illness falls without the types of disability defined, described, and illustrated in the statute and the regulations. Nothing in the record—no evidence, medical or otherwise—counters the above statutory construction, reinforced by administrative and judicial findings, that being HIV-positive places one within the protection of the act. Upon a careful reading of the Act and its interpretive regulations, measured up against the record in this case, I conclude the plaintiff has a physical or mental impairment that substantially limits one or more of his major life activities, and thus has a disability within the meaning of the ADA. Accordingly, plaintiff has met his threshold burden of establishing his prima facie case of disability discrimination.

Case Questions

1. Do you agree with the judge's decision? Is there any problem with the defendant's analysis that, if someone is perfectly able to perform her or his job, then there is no disability?

2. The third prong of the definition of disability under the acts includes all of those perceived to be disabled. Should this include all stereotypes, or only those that seem reasonable? For instance, should left-handedness be a protected disability? Height? While an employer's bias against an employee or applicant, which is based on a certain physical or mental trait, may result in an adverse employment action against her, the trait does not necessarily constitute a disability. For example, an employer may have a prejudice against all persons with red hair and may refuse to hire anyone with such hair. This does not mean that a red-haired applicant who is denied a position is disabled; red hair is a characteristic, not a disorder. Can you think of others?

3. How should the courts determine the effect of a societal bias? For instance, if employers generally believe that persons with feet larger than a man's size 10 are clumsy, would a graceful man with size 12 feet be considered disabled? Consider *Blackwell v. US Dept. of the Treasury,* in which the district court held that transvestites are disabled under the Rehabilitation Act because many experience strong social rejection in the workplace. Note, however, that the ADA specifically excludes as disabilities transvestism, transsexualism, voyeurism, and gender identity disorders not resulting from physical impairments, or other sexual behavior disorders.

Note, however, the Fourth Circuit decided in *Doe v. Univ. of Maryland Medical System Corporation,* 50 F.3d 1261 (4th Cir. 1995), that HIV status is relevant to an employee's qualifications in a hospital setting. "The types of procedures in which Dr. Doe is engaged as a neurosurgical resident are not so clearly outside the characteristics of exposure-prone procedures identified by the CDC that we can conclude that deference to public health officials requires us to decide that Dr. Doe does not pose a significant risk." The court in this case decided that, even though the risk of contagion was minimal given Dr. Doe's responsibilities, it could not be eliminated by reasonable accommodation.

However, in the Supreme Court case *Bragdon v. Abbott,* which is not an employment case, the Court established guidance for determining when a person has a disability under the ADA and can therefore be applied in employment cases. Sidney Abbott, who was HIV positive, went to her dentist, Bragdon. He refused to treat her unless it was in the hospital due to his fear of her HIV status. Abbott sued claiming Bragdon discriminated against her based on her disability, HIV. The court considered whether Abbott met the definition of having an "impairment that substantially limits one or more life activities." The Court, relying heavily on medical information, stated she did because an HIV infection is a condition that is inherently disabling. The Court stated, "HIV infection must be regarded as a physiological disorder with a constant and detrimental effect on the infected person's hemic and lymphatic systems from the moment of infection." The Court also noted that HIV substantially limited reproduction, a major life activity. This case challenges many lower court decisions that have held a condition must more or less visibly interfere with the person's public life or economic life on a fairly consistent basis to be a disability under the ADA. However, the Court in *Bragdon* states, in effect, that there are some conditions that are inherent disabilities if they so greatly affect the human biological system, in this case the HIV virus.

COLLINS V. BLUE CROSS BLUE SHIELD OF MICHIGAN
579 N.W.2d 435 (Mich. Ct. App. 1998)

An employee was terminated for expressing homicidal ideas about her supervisor to a psychiatrist while on psychiatric disability leave. The court had to determine if the termination was a violation of the ADA. It determined that it was not.

Holbrook, J.

While employee Collins was on psychiatric disability leave from her employment with Blue Cross Blue Shield, she expressed homicidal ideas regarding her immediate supervisor to a psychiatrist assigned to evaluate her disability claim. Specifically, Collins stated that her supervisor, Jacobson, was "living on borrowed time," that Collins "had killed her a thousand times in her mind," and talked about "taking a .38 and blowing [Jacobson] away." She further indicated that "she had thought of killing her supervisor prior to the company strike and had decided not to when the department was dispersed to other areas." After she returned to work, Collins was terminated as a result of those statements. Collins claimed discrimination under the Americans with Disabilities Act (ADA) and the Michigan Handicappers' Civil Rights Act (HCRA). The matter was submitted to binding arbitration and . . . hearings were held before an arbitrator.

During the hearing, defendant acknowledged that plaintiff's statements to Dr. Wagner were the sole reason for plaintiff's termination. At the hearing, plaintiff testified that she did not recall making most of the statements attributed to her in Dr. Wagner's report, although she did acknowledge calling Jacobson a liar and a bitch. Dr. Wagner testified in a deposition that she would not characterize plaintiff's statements as "threats," but rather as expressions of plaintiff's thoughts. Dr. Wagner also stated that she would defer to the opinion of the treating physician, Dr. Griffin, with respect to whether plaintiff had recovered from her disability or whether she posed any actual threat to Jacobson. Dr. Griffin testified in her deposition that she never reported plaintiff's homicidal ideation because she did not believe that plaintiff would act on it or that she otherwise posed any threat to Jacobson.

The arbitrator ruled in plaintiff's favor with regard to both claims and ordered that plaintiff be reinstated with back pay to a "comparable, but not identical, position" under a different supervisor and at a different work site if possible. The award added that defendant had the right to satisfy itself that plaintiff did not present a threat to other employees by requiring plaintiff to be examined by another psychiatrist and to continue treatment if necessary.

* * * *

The gravamen of this appeal requires us to determine whether the arbitrator committed an error of law in ruling that plaintiff was discharged because of her disability, rather than for her homicidal ideation toward her supervisor. Although we do not dispute the arbitrator's finding of fact that plaintiff's homicidal ideation was a product of her psychiatric condition, we conclude that the arbitrator committed an error of law in ruling that defendant's discharge of plaintiff constituted discrimination under the ADA and the HCRA. We hold that plaintiff failed to establish a prima facie case of discrimination under the ADA or the HCRA because her homicidal ideation left her unqualified for employment with defendant and because defendant did not discharge her because of her disability.

* * * *

Defendant argues on appeal that, because plaintiff was discharged for her expressed homicidal ideation regarding her supervisor, not because of her disability, it did not act with discriminatory intent. Our review of the current state of the law regarding this issue supports defendant's argument that a disabled employee may be discharged for misconduct, even where the misconduct is a manifestation of the employee's disability. Recently, in *Palmer v. Cook Co. Circuit Court,* the Seventh Circuit Court of Appeals held that an ADA claim failed where the plaintiff had been discharged because of threats she made to her supervisor, not because of her diagnosed major depression/delusional disorder. Chief Judge Posner explained:

> There is no evidence that Palmer was fired because of her mental illness. She was fired because she threatened to kill another employee. The cause of the threat was, we may assume, her mental illness. . . . But if an employer fires an employee because of the employee's unacceptable behavior, the fact that [the] behavior was precipitated by a mental illness does not present an issue under the Americans with Disabilities Act. The Act does not require an employer to retain a potentially violent employee. Such a requirement would place the

employer on a razor's edge—in jeopardy of violating the Act if it fired such an employee, yet in jeopardy of being deemed negligent if it retained him and he hurt someone. The Act protects only "qualified" employees, that is, employees qualified to do the job for which they were hired; and threatening other employees disqualifies one.

A qualified individual with a disability is one who satisfies the requisite skill, experience, education, or other work-related requirements of the job and who can perform its essential functions with or without reasonable accommodation. Simply put, the ADA does not cover all disabled persons, but only those who can perform their jobs' essential functions with the aid of reasonable accommodation. Indeed, an express provision of the ADA allows employers to defend against a charge of discrimination by establishing certain employee "qualification standards" that are job-related, consistent with business necessity, and accomplished by reasonable accommodation. "Qualification standards" include "a requirement that an individual shall not pose a direct threat to the health and safety of other individuals in the workplace." "Direct threat" means "a significant risk to the health and safety of others that cannot be eliminated by reasonable accommodation."

Plaintiff argues that defendant impermissibly perceived her as a direct threat to workplace safety, despite the fact that she had never directly threatened her supervisor and despite the opinion of plaintiff's treating psychiatrist that plaintiff would not act on her homicidal ideation. While we acknowledge the distinction between expressing homicidal thoughts to a psychiatrist in the context of a disability benefit determination and directly threatening a co-worker—given that employees are not generally subject to discharge or discipline for mere thoughts or ideas—we are not persuaded that the distinction is controlling on these facts.

* * * *

Here, the facts are considerably more compelling. . . . Plaintiff's homicidal thoughts regarding

Ms. Jacobson were frighteningly specific and detailed, not vague or isolated. Indeed, plaintiff indicated to Dr. Wagner that her vehement bitterness toward Ms. Jacobson had culminated in a specific plan to kill her, but that plaintiff had decided not to when a strike intervened. We believe it is clear that employers must be afforded wide latitude to ensure a safe workplace for their employees. Where an employee's homicidal thoughts about a co-worker are either expressed in the workplace, or otherwise made known to others in the workplace, the law does not require the employer to establish that the employee would affirmatively act on her homicidal thoughts before discharging her. Thus, we conclude that defendant did not violate the ADA in discharging plaintiff, whom it considered a direct threat to workplace safety.

Finally, we acknowledge that an employer generally has a duty to make "reasonable accommodations" to enable a disabled employee to perform the essential functions of the job, if the employer can do this without "undue hardship." However, the duty of reasonable accommodation applies only where the disabled employee is otherwise qualified for the position. Here, because

plaintiff's homicidal thoughts left her unqualified for continued employment with defendant, we need not further address the issue of reasonable accommodation.

Accordingly, because plaintiff has failed to establish a prima facie case under either the ADA or the HCRA, her claims fail. The arbitrator committed substantial legal error in ruling otherwise; therefore, we vacate the circuit court order confirming the arbitrator's award.

The circuit court order confirming the arbitrator's award is VACATED.

Case Questions

1. If you were the employer in this situation, would you have handled this problem the same or differently?

2. Could you think of a situation where a threat would be protected by the ADA when spoken by a person with a disability?

3. Do you think a person with a disability should be held as accountable for their actions as a non-disabled person in the workforce?

"Essential Functions."   For an employer to determine whether one is otherwise qualified for his or her position, the employer must first ascertain what are the essential functions of that position. For example, some companies require that all employees have driver's licenses, "in case of emergencies." While this is a meritorious request, the ability to drive is not always a basic requirement of the positions themselves but, instead, is marginal to the objectives of each position. An applicant who cannot drive because of a disability is otherwise qualified for the position, unless the position specifically has driving as its integral purpose, such as a taxi driver or delivery person.

The term *essential* refers to those tasks that are fundamental, and not marginal or unnecessary, to fulfillment of the position objectives. Disabled persons may not be disqualified simply because they may have difficulty in performing tasks that bear only a marginal relationship to a particular job. How does an employer determine what job tasks are considered essential? Employers may not include in their job descriptions responsibilities that are incidental to the actual job, or duties that are not generally performed by someone in this position. The employer must look,

Essential functions of a position
The employer may not take an adverse employment action against a disabled employee based on the disability where the individual can perform the essential functions of the position: those tasks that are fundamental, not marginal or unnecessary, to the fulfillment of the position's objectives.

not to the means of performing a function but, instead, to the function desired to be accomplished. Some employers are shocked to find that an individual with disabilities may discover innovative and novel means to accomplish the same task. On the other hand, some individuals cannot perform the essential functions of their jobs no matter what accommodation they might request. For instance, in one case, as a result of his disability, a corrections officer did not have the physical ability to restrain inmates during an emergency. The court held that this ability was an essential function of his position and therefore he was not qualified under the ADA.[5]

Can a job function be *essential* where someone was in the position for 16 years and never performed this task? Is the frequency the function must be performed relevant to determining whether it is essential? In a recent Fourth Circuit case, the court determined that frequency is just one factor that a manager should look to in determining the essential functions of the position. *Champ v. Baltimore County, MD*[6] involved a police officer who sustained an arm injury and was put on light duty. Whole officers were not supposed to remain on light duty for more than 251 days; this officer continued to work in this capacity for 16 years. The Chief of Police then determined that all officers must be able to perform the full duties of a police officer. The court held that this officer could not perform the job's essential functions with or without reasonable accommodation and upheld the officer's termination.

One of the more perplexing issues to have developed since the ADA's inception is attendance. Some courts have characterized attendance as an "essential function."[7] Attendance, however, is not an essential function as defined by the ADA because it is not one of the "fundamental job duties of the employment position."[8] As the regulations make clear, essential functions are the duties to be performed.[9]

The concept of essential functions under the ADA and the Rehabilitation Acts differs slightly from the job-relatedness requirement for selection criteria under Title VII. Under Title VII, an employer has a defense to a claim of discrimination if it can show that the basis for the discrimination was the employee's failure to satisfy job-related requirements.

Under the ADA and the Rehabilitation Acts, however, the court will look one step further. The requirement may be job-related, but the court will look to whether that requirement is also consistent with business necessity. In addition, courts disfavor employers who make general exclusions on the basis of business necessity, unless it can be shown that all or substantially all of the individuals who satisfy that category of disability could not do the job, or the exclusion is justified by the high personal or financial risk involved, which cannot be protected against. For example,

---

[5]*Kees v. Wallenstein,* 1998 WL 813374, (9th Cir.).

[6]91 F.3d 129 (4th Cir. 1996).

[7]*Carr v. Reno,* 23 F.3d 525, 530; 3 AD Cas.(BNA) 434, 438 (D.C. Cir. 1994).

[8]29 C.F.R. 1630.2(n)(1) (1997).

[9]29 C.F.R. 1630.2(n)(2) (1997).

in *Davis v. Bucher,*[10] a categorical exclusion of methadone program participants and those with a history of drug addiction was ruled unlawful, as well as a general prohibition against epileptics in the workforce, in *Duran v. City of Tampa.*[11]

The ADA does not require employers to lower standards or to exclude from their position descriptions functions which are actually required of an employee in that position. It merely dictates that requirements be objectively determined, and not articulated for the purpose of excluding a disabled employee.

"Reasonable Accommodation"   "On occasion, the elimination of discrimination might involve some costs," states the Supreme Court in its decision in *Southeastern Community College v. Davis.*[12] An applicant or employee is otherwise qualified for the position if, with or without *reasonable accommodation,* the worker can perform the essential functions of the position. Reasonable accommodation in this context generally means the removal of unnecessary restrictions or barriers. **Reasonable accommodation** is further defined as what does not place an *undue burden* on the employer. Therefore, as one commentator wrote, "reasonable accommodation is but one side of the coin; undue hardship . . . is the other side." It is generally believed that these types of accommodation expenses are normally quite low, averaging approximately $261 per disabled employee.

An example of a reasonable accommodation is adapting a work space to the use of a wheelchair. If an employer has two applicants for an open position, one who requires the use of a wheelchair and another who has no disability, the employer may choose the applicant without a disability solely because of the need to modify the work space for the other applicant (i.e., to provide a reasonable accommodation). But, referring to the hypothetical situation at the introduction of this chapter, what if the wheelchair poses a greater burden than merely adapting a work space?

In that situation, the position for which the disabled applicant applied required a great deal of traveling. Unless there is some reason to believe that the disabled applicant would not be able to travel, the employer must afford her the opportunity. While accommodation may be necessary to allow her to travel, such as a modified schedule to allow her more time to get from one place to another, such accommodation would generally be considered reasonable and required.

Similarly, as in scenario 3, Marquita may need an accommodation to be able to type with her feet. For instance, moving the keyboard to the floor may enable her to perform her job. This may involve little or no expense and would most likely be considered a reasonable accommodation. As for whether the employer must hire Marquita, the employer is not required to hire her if she is not the most qualified individual for the job. However, if she is the best qualified and the accommodation is reasonable, which it appears to be, Marquita may have a claim for disability discrimination.

Reasonable accommodation An accommodation to the individual's disability that does not place an undue burden on the employer, which may be determined by looking to the size of the employer, the cost to the employer, the type of employer, and the impact of the accommodation on the employer's operations.

Scenario

---

[10]451 F.Supp. 791 (E.D. Pa. 1978).
[11]430 F.Supp. 75 (M.D. Fl. 1977).
[12]442 U.S. 397, n. 10 (1979).

EXHIBIT 13–3

How far does the employer have to go for the disabled employee or applicant? The EEOC has defined "reasonable accommodation" in its regulations as follows:

(1) The term "reasonable accommodation" means:

    (i) Any modification or adjustment to a job application process that enables a qualified individual with a disability to be considered for the position such qualified individual desires, and which will not impose an undue hardship on the covered entities business; or

    (ii) Any modification or adjustment to the work environment, or to the manner or circumstances under which the position held or desired is customarily performed, that enables a qualified individual with a disability to perform the essential functions of that position, and which will not impose an undue hardship on the operation of the covered entities business; or

    (iii) Any modification or adjustment that enables a covered entity's employee with a disability to enjoy the same benefits and privileges of employment as are enjoyed by its other similarly situated employees without disabilities, and which will not impose an undue hardship on the operation of the covered entities business.

(2) Reasonable accommodation may include but is not limited to:

    (i) making facilities used by employees readily accessible to and usable by individuals with disabilities, and

    (ii) Job restructuring; part-time or modified work schedules; reassignment to a vacant position; acquisition or modification of equipment or devices; appropriate adjustment or modification of examinations, training materials or policies; the provision of readers or interpreters; and other similar accommodations for individuals with disabilities.

An accommodation need not be the best possible solution, but it must be sufficient to meet the needs of the individual with the disability. An employee who suffers from a congenital upper respiratory disease may be unable to maintain consistent stamina or a high degree of effort throughout an entire workday. The requirement of reasonable accommodation does not mean that the employer must create a new job, modify a full-time position to create a part-time position, or modify the essential functions of the job. The EEOC's enforcement guidance stipulates, however, that a disabled employee is entitled to reassignment if he or she is qualified to fill a vacant position, *even if he or she can no longer perform the essential functions of her or his own position.* Moreover, the employee does not have to be the *most* qualified person entitled to fill the vacant position—the worker must only be *qualified* in order to be entitled to the position; and the burden is on the employer to notify the worker of open positions for which she or he is qualified. However, the employer does not have to give this employee preference in a reassignment that would be considered a promotion. (See also *Cassidy v. Detroit Edison Company,* on page 479.)

To accommodate an employee, the employer may have to redesign a job and eliminate those tasks not required by the purpose of the position. For instance, an employee who is unable to stand may not be able to reach certain supplies but can

EXHIBIT 13–4

The state of Oregon has offered the following guidelines to its employers in connection with the cost of "reasonable" accommodations. These guidelines highlight several possible accommodations and their costs, including the following:

(1) Maintenance Mechanic, Back Injury
   Obstacle: Cannot push or pull more than 100 lbs.
   Modification: Purchase of a torque multiplier wrench, which has a geared head and allows 400 or 500 pounds of torque within 100 pound effort. Cost: $1,130.

(2) Cemetery Grave Digger, Back Injury
   Obstacle: Cannot lift more than 50 lbs., and therefore cannot operate 90 lb. jackhammer.
   Modification: Purchase of pneumatic jackhammer attachment. Cost: $2,200.

(3) Logger, Hip Injury
   Obstacle: Cannot return to logging at all; could work in office setting, but cannot sit more than 1.5 hours per day.
   Modification: Hired as insurance adjuster by employer who purchased a "versatility" table (used as a desk), which can be easily lowered for sitting, raised for standing. Cost: $750.

(4) Operator of Packaging Machine, Repetitive Strain Injury, Carpal Tunnel Surgery on Wrists
   Obstacle: Limited use of right wrist; cannot return to factory position.
   Modification: Hired as receptionist/lab assistant by employer who would have had employee use syringe in lab work, but purchased pipetting machine to automatically pump solution into vials. Cost: $1,320.

(5) Clerical Specialist, Neck and Back Injury
   Obstacle: Cannot clutch telephone receiver between shoulder and head while searching computer for answers to callers' questions.
   Modification: Purchase of a headset that plugs into the phone. Cost: $50–100.

(6) Nurses' Aide, Neck Injury
   Obstacle: Cannot do tasks requiring flexion of the neck; cannot return to health care position.
   Modification: Hired to do general office clerical work; purchase of a portable ergonomic desk with a slanted work surface and a moveable holder for books or papers which allows writing without moving head. Cost: $75.

(7) Nurse-in-Charge, Back Injury
   Obstacle: Cannot lift or pull, and therefore could not move a patient into or out of bed, or onto a gurney.
   Modification: Purchase of a mobilizer patient transfer system, with a conveyor that "unwinds" or retracts from under the patient. Cost: $15,000.

Portions excerpted from the "Worksite Modification Digest," on the cost of "reasonable" accommodations. Oregon Dept. of Insurance and Finance, Workers' Compensation Division, Rehabilitation Review Section, 21 Labor and Industries Bldg., Salem, Oregon, 97310 (503/373-7939).

otherwise perform the necessary components of her position. The employer may be required to accommodate the employee by relocating the supplies to a lower level that is accessible to the employee. Other examples of accommodation may include switching a worker's shift time, testing air quality (where a worker has an allergy) or permitting the allergic worker to wear a mask. A blind receptionist might use a light probe to detect which telephone line to answer; deaf employees at a workplace

Exhibit 13–5

"New Tools Help Minneapolis Employers Accommodate Workers with Disabilities"

A central database of accommodations is one tool being used by ADA specialists to bring efficiency to the process of accommodating workers with disabilities. At American Express Financial Advisors in Minneapolis, ADA specialist Michelle Jourdan created a computer database that includes information on any item the company purchased to accommodate somebody with a disability, the item's cost, and how the accommodation is working.

To keep track of legal developments and other resources, Jordan worked with Karen Moore, an accommodation project leader for Northwest Airlines, which is also headquartered in the Minneapolis area, to set up a local business network. The two met at a conference on disability accommodation. They invited other disability compliance specialists to join, and new the group meets once a month for two hours to exchange ideas. All participants have some responsibility for ADA accommodations for their employers.

One effort the network is pursuing is developing a purchasing cooperation with vendors that could provide network members with better deals on devices, such as voice-activated software.

Excerpted from *The EEO Review Newsletter,* Issue 381, October 1998.

that uses buzzers on equipment would benefit from the use of indicator lights instead. On the other hand, an employer is not required to reassign or reallocate *essential* job functions. An accommodation is also unreasonable if it requires a "fundamental alteration" in the nature of the program or imposes financial or administrative costs on the employer.

One example of a job redesign request that was found to be an undue burden on the employer is found in *Guice-Mills v. Derwinski*.[13] In that case, the plaintiff, a head nurse at a hospital, suffered from severe depression, which subjected her to feelings of hopelessness, malaise, insomnia, inability to get up in the morning, extreme fatigue, and irritability. As a result of her syndrome, she was unable to arrive at the hospital prior to 10 AM, while her position required that she arrive at 8 AM. The employee requested that her position as head nurse be officially changed to allow her to begin work at 10 AM. The court held that the hospital was not required to accommodate the request because all head nurses were required to begin work at 8 AM as a matter of administrative necessity. The court instead found that the hospital's offer to reassign her to a position as a staff nurse so she could work a different shift was a reasonable accommodation.

Scenario 1 presents an issue of reasonable accommodation and concerns the definition of essential functions of a position. If Thekla Tsonis determines that travel is an *essential function* of the position, she may be able to justify "ability to travel" as a qualification for employment. Even if it is a real requirement, the wheelchair-bound applicant may be perfectly willing to travel. Tsonis should simply lay out the requirements of the position, then ask both applicants if there is any reason why they

1
Scenario

---

[13]967 F.2d. 794 (2nd Cir. 1992).

EXHIBIT 13–6 Examples of Accommodations

> Low technology possibilities:
>   Lap boards, delivered lunches, telephone amplifiers, computer screen magnifiers, door levers (instead of knobs), walking canes, automatic page turners.
> High technology possibilities:
>   Robotic devices, screen reading mechanisms, speech synthesizers, telecommunication devices for the deaf, remote control devices, voice-responsive computers.

would not be able to perform these functions, with or without reasonable accommodation. The wheelchair-bound applicant may need some accommodation, such as assistance getting to and from the airport or travel times that allow her or him to have extra time to arrive at the airport. These would probably be viewed as reasonable accommodations.

The Appendix to the EEOC's ADA regulations suggests the following hypothetical situations as examples of the weight to be given to each of the factors in an "undue hardship" determination.

> [A] small day care center might not be required to expend more than a nominal sum, such as that necessary to equip a telephone for use by a secretary with impaired hearing, but a large school district might be required to make available a teacher's aide to a blind applicant for a teaching job. Further, it might be considered reasonable to require a state welfare agency to accommodate a deaf employee by providing an interpreter while it would constitute an undue hardship to impose that requirement on a provider of foster care services.

Where the cost of the accommodation would result in an undue hardship and outside funding is not available, the disabled employee or applicant should be given the option of paying the portion of the cost that constitutes an undue hardship.

Update: Requests for Accommodation and Employer Responses.   The EEOC recently released a lengthy "Enforcement Guidance" to provide assistance to employers to help them better navigate and understand the EEOC's and the courts' perceptions and expectations concerning the employment of disabled individuals. The guidance clarifies how a disabled individual can request reasonable accommodations and how employers can reasonably accommodate such requests.

According to the enforcement guidance, when an ADA situation first arises, the disabled employee must provide notice to the employer of her disability and any resulting limitations. Courts have recognized that an employee has the initial duty to inform his employer of a disability before ADA liability is triggered for failing to provide an accommodation. An employee cannot keep secret his disability and then later sue for failure to accommodate. Nor are employers expected to be clairvoyant. As a general matter, the individual with a disability has the responsibility to inform her employer that an accommodation is needed.

EXHIBIT 13–7

In connection with the definition of "undue hardship," the EEOC regulations direct the following:

In determining whether an accommodation would impose an undue hardship on a covered entity, factors to be considered include:

  (i)   The nature and cost of the accommodation needed under this part;

  (ii) The overall financial resources of the facility or facilities involved in the provision of the reasonable accommodation, the number of people employed at such site, and the effect on expenses and resources;

  (iii) The overall financial resources of the covered entity, the overall size of the business of the covered entity with respect to the number of its employees, and the number, type, and location of its facilities;

  (iv) The type of operation or operations of the covered entity, including the composition, structure, and functions of the workforce of such entity, and the geographic separateness and administrative or fiscal relationship of the site or sites in question to the covered entity; and

  (v)   The impact of the accommodation upon the operation of the site, including the impact on the ability of other employees to perform their duties, and the impact on the site's ability to conduct business.

What suffices as a request for an accommodation? A key reasonable accommodation request, according to this guidance, "does not require the employee to speak any magic words . . . the employee need not mention the ADA or even the term accommodation."[14] The courts have also concluded that an employee who merely tells his supervisor that "his pain prevented him from working and that he requested leave under the Family and Medical Leave Act (FMLA)" is protected by the ADA.[15] A request simply asking for continued employment can be a sufficient request for accommodation. Nothing in the ADA requires an individual to use legal terms or to anticipate all of the possible information an employer may need in order to provide a reasonable accommodation. The ADA avoids a formulaic approach in favor of an interactive discussion between the employer and the individual with a disability, after the individual has requested a change due to a medical condition. However, some courts have required that individuals initially provide detailed information in order to trigger protection under the act.

In addition, the EEOC encourages employers to be receptive to any relevant information or requests they receive from a third party acting on the disabled individual's behalf because the reasonable accommodation process presumes open communication (in order to help the employer make an informed decision). The essence of the reasonable accommodation concept requires an employer to go out of its way,

---

[14]*Schmidt v. Safeway Inc.*, 864 F. Supp. 991, 997; 3 AD Cas. (BNA) 1141, 1146–47 (D. Or. 1994).

[15]*McGinnis v. Wonder Chemical Co.*, 5AD Cas. (BNA) 219 (E.D. Penn. 1995).

to maintain a disabled employee's employment. It is an interactive process. It requires participation by both the employee and the employer. As part of that interactive process, once the employer's responsibilities are triggered by appropriate notice from the employee, the employer may want to take the lead. The employer may want to initiate informal discussions about the need for and the scope of any possible accommodation. Communication is essential. The object is to identify the precise limitations resulting from the disability and potential reasonable accommodations that could overcome those limitations.

The EEOC and the courts have been tough on employers who have not been promptly receptive and responsive to disability situations. When determining whether or not there has been an unnecessary delay in responding to ADA situations, the courts consider these relevant factors: (1) the reason(s) for the delay, (2) the length of the delay, (3) how much the individual with a disability and the employer each contributed to the delay, (4) what the employer was doing during the delay, and (5) whether the required accommodation was simple or complex to provide. Employers who do not respond expeditiously to employee's requests tend to suffer greater legal consequences.

Undue Hardship.   Undue hardship is not limited to financial difficulty but may also include any accommodation that would be unduly costly, extensive, substantial, or disruptive, or that would fundamentally alter the nature or operation of the business. While employers may also attempt to show that they took an adverse employment action based on their fears relating to future absences or higher insurance costs, an undue hardship, or more than a *de minimis* cost that the employer should not have to bear, these are not acceptable defenses to a claim of discrimination. In a case dealing with an employer's concern that an obese employee would cost the employer higher health care amounts in the future, the New York high court held that this was not a valid defense even though obese people, as a class, *are* at a greater risk for certain health problems than others. See an additional case on a similar topic below.

CASSIDY V. DETROIT EDISON COMPANY
138 F.3d 629 (6th Cir. 1997)

The employee, Cassidy, began suffering allergic reactions to workplace substances after exposure to "stack gas." Over a period of time, the employer attempted accommodations that proved ineffective. The employee was eventually terminated, and she sued under the ADA. The court had to determine whether the employer had reasonably accommodated the employee and found that the employer had done so.

Suhrheinrich, J.

Cassidy worked as an assistant power plant operator at Detroit Edison Company (DEC) until she was exposed to "stack gas" on the job. As a result, she suffered numerous allergic reactions to a multitude of substances. To accommodate her breathing and allergy conditions, the company found an assignment for her in the area with the most filtered and clean air, the computer center. After time, Cassidy experienced more breathing difficulties from exposure in her work environment to cleaning chemicals, diesel fumes, food odors, paint fumes, and smoke. DEC accommodated her by scheduling her for straight day shifts, allowing her to leave when a known allergen would be present, testing the area to comply with environmental air standards, permitting her to wear a mask and use a breathing machine, and scheduling maintenance when she was not present. DEC also tested its facilities for fungus, bacteria, and mists to find an adequate work environment for her.

Still having breathing problems, Cassidy met with several of her doctors. DEC approved a three-month medical leave on the advice of her doctors. Prior to her return, DEC's chief medical officer requested Cassidy's physicians to specify appropriate restrictions. She submitted a return-to-work statement from one of her physicians stating she could return to a "workstation free of exposure to any agent that may trigger asthma or cause a drop in peak flow and that is well ventilated." An independent medical examiner examined Cassidy and recommended "a location that is reasonably free of irritants and also an area where she may have some control over the environment through use of desktop air purifiers."

During this time, Defendant's staff continued to assess available positions within the company to accommodate Plaintiff. After the chief medical officer reviewed the restrictions recommended by Cassidy's personal physician he concluded "[u]nder these restrictions there is no position available at Detroit Edison. However, if her physician would possibly modify these restrictions, we

might be able to make a position available for her." Upon finding no position available at the company with these restrictions, the company terminated her. Cassidy filed suit, alleging that her termination violated the ADA because the employer had failed to reasonably accommodate her disability. The district court found no genuine issue of material fact, that "[DEC] did all that it possibly could to accommodate [Cassidy] in light of her disability," and granted DEC's motion for summary judgment. Cassidy appealed.

* * * *

The employee contends that genuine issues of material fact exist as to whether the employer reasonably accommodated him because the employer did not consider reassignment to a vacant position. The employer responds that it attempted to reasonably accommodate the employee, but that Cassidy proposed only general and vague accommodations, such as a transfer to a position in an allergen-free environment, which did not exist within the company.

* * * *

An employee demonstrates disability for purposes of the ADA by showing a substantial limitation on a major life activity, not necessarily the major life activity of working. . . . In the present case, the district court found that Plaintiff was disabled because of her substantial limitation on her major life activity of breathing, not of working.

. . . A disabled employee who claims that he or she is otherwise qualified with a reasonable accommodation "bears the initial burden of proposing an accommodation and showing that [the] accommodation is objectively reasonable." An employer then has the burden of persuasion to show that an accommodation would impose undue hardship. The reasonableness of an accommodation is a fact issue.

* * * *

Under the ADA, an employer need only reassign the employee to a vacant position. Generally, transfer or reassignment of an employee is only considered when accommodation within the individual's current position would pose an undue hardship. An employer may reassign an employee to a lower grade and paid position if the employee cannot be accommodated in the current position and a comparable position is not available. However, a reassignment will not require creating a new job, moving another employee, promoting the disabled employee, or violating another employee's rights under a collective bargaining agreement.

The employer provided several reasonable accommodations, including: initially transferring Plaintiff to the computer department after her first asthmatic attack; allowing Plaintiff to work straight days; scheduling cleaning and maintenance to occur when Plaintiff was gone; allowing Plaintiff to leave when she may be exposed to allergens; allowing Plaintiff to use her prescribed breathing apparatus at work allowing Plaintiff to use paid and unpaid leave, and testing Plaintiff's work area. The district court noted that based on her physicians' vague recommendations, Plaintiff requested transfers to a vacant position in a well-ventilated and allergen-free workstation that would not "trigger asthma or cause a drop in peak flow." But because Plaintiff did not "identify the precise limitations resulting from the disability and potential reasonable accommodations that could overcome those limitations," the district court concluded that "Defendant did all that it possibly could to accommodate Plaintiff in light of her disability."

We agree with the district court. Plaintiff's proposed accommodation for essentially an allergen-free workplace, which Defendant attempted to locate within the company, was simply too vague to reasonably inform Defendant of a reasonable accommodation, or was otherwise simply unavailable. Defendant attempted numerous accommodations but finally concluded that there was no sufficiently allergen-free work environment within the company in which Plaintiff could perform her job. Plaintiff had the duty to propose an objectively reasonable accommodation. However, Plaintiff simply failed to create a genuine issue of material fact as to Defendant's assertions that no such allergen-free work environment existed within the company for Plaintiff. Further, Plaintiff also did not demonstrate that there were any vacant positions in such areas.

* * * *

Thus, based on Plaintiff's lack of specific proposed accommodation, Defendant's previous attempts to accommodate Plaintiff, and Defendant's conclusion that it did not have a position in the company that satisfied Plaintiff's vague restrictions, there is no genuine issue of material fact that Plaintiff failed to propose or identify an objectively reasonable accommodation. Therefore, Defendant is entitled to judgment as a matter of law. Accordingly, we AFFIRM.

Case Questions

1. Do you believe the employer made a good faith effort to reasonably accommodate the employee?

2. What do you think about the possibility of the employee working at home, since it did not appear she had breathing problems there? What if this caused animosity among co-workers that wanted to work at home for convenience but could not due to company policy?

3. Cost was not discussed in this opinion, but do you think there should be a dollar limit on the price of a reasonable accommodation?

In order to ease the financial burden of providing accommodation, the Internal Revenue Service offers several federal tax incentives to eligible small businesses (those with either 30 or fewer full-time employees or $1 million or less in gross receipts in the preceding tax year) that make these accommodations. First, they can take advantage of the Disabled Access Tax Credit—50 percent of eligible expenditures over $250 (but not over $10,250) made to provide access to the workplace for disabled workers. Second, any business may be eligible for a deduction for removing architectural or transportation barriers to disabled workers in the firm, up to $15,000 per year. (Eligible small businesses can take *both* of these deductions.) Finally, firms that hire workers who are "vocational rehabilitation referrals" certified by local employment agencies will be allowed a tax credit under the Work Opportunity Tax Credit (Internal Revenue Code, sec. 51).

Employee's Responsibility for "Interactive Process": Identification and Request for Reasonable Accommodation. Once an employee learns that she or he will need some form of accommodation in order to perform the essential functions of her or his position, the burden is on the employee to make a request for the accommodation. An employer is not charged with the responsibility to know each and every need of its workforce. Besides, the person who would know best how to meet the worker's needs *is the worker.* Except in unusual circumstances, an employee does not have a claim under the ADA for an employer's failure to accommodate unless that employee has made a request for reasonable accommodation that has been denied. Once the employee has made the request for accommodation, she or he has the responsibility to work with the employer to determine the most effective and efficient means by which to meet these needs. "The federal regulations implementing the ADA envision an interactive process that requires participation by both parties."[16]

In one case where an employer requested a medical form from a worker's doctor, the worker refused to provide the form. The worker claimed that she was concerned that the company would misuse the information provided in the form, while the employer asserted that it needed the requested information in order to determine her accommodation needs and to comply with insurance requirements. The Tenth Circuit Court held that the worker's ADA claim was barred because she failed to engage in the interactive process with her employer to determine a reasonable accommodation for her disability. "Even assuming such conduct by Neodata could support a claim under the ADA for failure to provide reasonable accommodation, that claim would only arise after Mrs. Templeton satisfied her duty "to notify the employer of the nature of her disability."

In fact, the EEOC's recent enforcement guidance on reasonable accommodations specifically states that employers have a right to request medical documentation of disabilities in order to best satisfy their duty to reasonably accommodate. The enforcement guidance, however, does not place *too* large a burden on workers

---

[16]*Templeton v. Neodata Services, Inc.,* 162 F.3d 617 (10th Cir. 1998).

for such "interaction." The request [for accommodation] may be in "plain English," and need not explicitly mention the ADA or the term "reasonable accommodation."

Disability Harassment

The ADA prohibits workplace harassment when it creates a hostile environment against disabled workers. While there have not been a great number of cases brought on this basis, there is evidence of a trend toward greater reporting and enforcement of the prohibition. In a federal case in the New Jersey court system, *Lanni v. State of New Jersey Dept. of Environmental Protection,* the plaintiff–employee claimed that he was subject to harassment and teasing as a result of his dyslexic learning disability. Co-workers reportedly made faces at Lanni and derogatory sounds when speaking to him, as well as committing some physical abuse. The jury awarded Lanni $277,000, finding an ADA violation.

In another case in Oregon, a worker who suffered from depression requested that he be separated from the individual who was the source of the harassment. The supervisor refused to separate the two workers, even after the alleged abuser called the plaintiff "mental," "delusional," and "out of his mind," when interviewed by the supervisor. Again, the plaintiff prevailed.

Effect on the Actions of Employers

Potential Liability of Employer

Protection.   The employer of an employee with a contagious disability may be liable to co-workers of the employee based on a variety of common law **tort** theories. While the only remedy available to the employee for common workplace injury is workers' compensation, the employer may be additionally liable to its employee for any intentional torts. The employer has both a statutory duty to provide a safe work environment according to federal regulations, as well as a similar common-law duty to refrain from an intentional wrong against the employee. This type of tort liability may arise based on the response of the employer to the news that an employee has a contagious disease. If the employer reacts in a manner that causes the employee severe emotional distress by its outrageous conduct, the employer would be liable in tort. In addition, unwarranted invasions of privacy, breaches of confidentiality, and defamation have been held to be bases for actions against employers. A tortious invasion of privacy occurs where the employer intentionally intrudes into an employee's private affairs, and the court finds that the intrusion would be highly offensive to a reasonable person.

How does this issue arise? Predictably, there have been several cases filed by employees who work with HIV-positive employees. Usually, the case will surface after the employee has made requests for additional protections. Pursuant to the Occupational Safety and Health Act, an employer must provide a safe workplace for its employees, free from conditions reasonably believed in good faith to be

Tort
A private (civil) wrong against a person or her or his property.

hazardous. Where an employer knowingly and willfully disregards the safety of its employees, the employer will be liable.

In California, for instance, a group of nurses requested gloves and masks when treating AIDS patients. The nurses were denied protection based on the California Labor Commission's finding that there was no health danger from working in an AIDS ward without protective clothing. The employees' fears must be based on an honest, good faith, and reasonable belief that their safety is threatened. Since the employer is therefore required to protect both the employee, by virtue of the ADA, and the complaining employees, by virtue of the National Labor Relations Act and the Occupational Safety and Health Act, the only answer must be complete education of the workforce to preclude any "good faith" belief that the employee with AIDS presents a health danger.

Disclosure.   The issue of whether the employee's co-workers have a right to information related to the employee's condition is an area of hot dispute. You may recall the newspaper stories that explained the American Medical Association was faced with complaints from patients regarding the doctors' responsibility to inform their patients if they have AIDS. The employer may only release information if she or he reasonably believes such disclosure to be necessary.

The EEOC stated in its 1997 guidelines that if employees ask questions about a worker with a disability, the employer must not disclose any medical information in response.

Management Considerations

The employer is restricted in its preemployment inquiries related to disabilities. Medical examinations may only be required after the employment offer has been extended, and only where all employees in that position category are subject to similar examinations. Employment may then be conditioned on passing the test. However, as previously stated, where the withdrawal of the offer is based on the discovery of a disability, that disability must be related to adequate performance of the job or business necessity, and there must exist no reasonable accommodation. All information obtained through medical examinations must be kept confidential by the employer. The employer should therefore establish separate files for this information and restrict their access.

The ADA apparently treats testing differently based on when the test is given. As mentioned above, no testing is allowed pre-offer. Once the offer has been made, but prior to employment, some testing might be acceptable. Once hired and employed, employers are far more restricted in terms of testing and the decisions that may be based on the results of testing. (See Chapter 15, Testing.) In one case that found its plaintiff in the middle category where employers have the greatest latitude in testing, the plaintiff alleged that the test violated the ADA. In *Rowles v. Automated Production System, Inc.,* the plaintiff was a worker who had been given an offer conditioned on a drug test. The worker, an epileptic, took medication to prevent seizures. Upon learning that this particular medication was on the list of prohibited drugs for which he would be tested, he refused to take the drug test and was fired. Rowles filed a claim under the ADA asserting a violation since the firm prohibited the use of legally prescribed drugs without any showing that testing for these drugs was job related or a business necessity.

The district court judge in *Rowles* held that since the policy prohibited the use of physician-prescribed medication, the policy was in direct violation of the ADA. In so holding, the judge granted partial summary judgment but still required the employee to show that the termination resulted from the illegal policy.

Not all preemployment inquiry issues are so clear. Imagine a situation where the interviewer notices an apparent disability that might interfere with the applicant's job performance. However, when asked if he can perform the essential functions of the position, the applicant replies that he can. The ADA is unclear as to whether the interviewer can inquire further about the applicant's disability given this response.

Many firms are now adopting educational programs so their managers become more aware of the needs of the disabled. In this way, firms can better prevent problems from arising once the disabled employee joins the workforce. This is of even greater necessity given the ADA's prohibition on preoffer medical examinations. A company may not require a medical examination before an offer has been extended, though it may make a verbal inquiry about whether the applicant is capable of performing the essential functions of the position in question. Only after that time may a company require an examination. Because of this prohibition, many firms employ disabled employees who did not appear to be disabled at the time the offer was extended.

Firms are also developing policies of direct referral of disabled employees to specially designated personnel directors. This director or counselor is aware of job possibilities and would be in the best position to suggest job content modifications and redesign potential. After assignment or reassignment, the counselor usually checks on the employee to ensure that the requirements of the position are appropriate to the needs of the employee, and that the employee is satisfying the needs of the firm. In addition, many firms conduct periodic reviews of their position descriptions to ensure that they encompass the essential functions of the position, as well as a review of their job application forms and procedures, facilities, personnel programs, and policies.

Finally, employers should be aware that the Internal Revenue Service offers a Targeted Jobs Tax Credit to employers against five-year wages paid to newly hired workers with disabilities, among others who have difficulty obtaining employment. The program is administered by the US Department of Labor.

It is evident that employers must establish cohesive guidelines to ensure their compliance in the area of disability discrimination. Guidelines have already been established by the courts in connection with claims by alcoholic employees, alleging a disability due to their alcoholism. These guidelines are very tough on employers.

In *Rodgers v. Lehman*[17], the court established a five-step directive for the benefit of employers dealing with alcoholic employees:

1. If the employer suspects alcoholism, she must inform the employee of counseling services.
2. If the alcoholism continues, the employer must give the employee a "firm choice" between treatment and discipline.
3. The employer must then provide outpatient treatment.
4. If this is unsuccessful, the employer must provide inpatient treatment.
5. Only if the first four steps fail can the employer legally discharge the employee.

Employers thus have the benefit of a statement by the courts about the proper means of handling such a case under the Rehabilitation Act (and, by inference, the ADA). Employers must follow similar directives in connection with the hiring and retention of employees with other disabilities.

The issue of smoking in the workplace has also become an issue. Many, if not all states have enacted legislation banning smoking in the workplace environment. An employer is forced to balance the rights of smokers without violating the laws intended to protect nonsmokers. But, is nicotine dependence or withdrawal a disability? Does smoking create a physiological or a psychological dependency requiring it to provide a reasonable accommodation for smokers? The answer has not been decided. Congress was silent on this issue and the Supreme Court has not had a case on point.

Nicotine dependence has been analogized to alcoholism, which has long been recognized as creating a dependency. With the large-scale tobacco litigation, more evidence is coming forward about the dependent nature of nicotine. Further, the American Psychiatric Association's Diagnostic and Statistical Manual of Mental Disorders, Fourth Edition, *DSM-IV,* lists nicotine dependence and withdrawal under the heading of nicotine use disorders. In addition, the EEOC's *Enforcement Guidance on the ADA* identifies the *DSM-IV* as a relevant reference for classifying mental disorders. (Note, however, that not all disorders listed in the manual rise to the level of disabilities protected by the ADA.) The EEOC Enforcement Guidance, issued in March 1997, provides more solid support for the position that nicotine withdrawal presents a substantially limiting mental impairment.

Not every smoker would have a claim, however; a claim would only be upheld if the nicotine dependence or withdrawal disabled the claimant in the performance of a major life activity. It has been noted that, in order to make a viable claim under the ADA, the disability must create a "substantial limitation"; that is, it must typically restrict the performance for at least several months. The rights of either recovering or current smokers have not been tested under the ADA.

Drug addiction is also an issue that employers are now facing with regard to

---

[17]869 F.2d 253 (4th Cir. 1989).

disabilities. While current drug use is not protected by the ADA, former illegal drug users, including individuals who either are participating in or have completed a drug rehabilitation program, are not excluded from protection under the ADA. Courts have recognized that, under certain circumstances, drug addiction *may* constitute a disability under the ADA and the Federal Rehabilitation Act. As with all disabilities, the former drug users must demonstrate they have a "disability"; that is, they must show that the past drug use limits a "major life activity" and it must have been sufficiently severe to be considered a drug addiction. An employee who is a recovering addict no longer using drugs may use the past drug addiction to argue that he or she has a disability based on a "record of such an impairment."

An increasing number of claims for discrimination that are rejected by a judge or jury have nonetheless cost the employer money in damages. Why? It seems that employers tend to retaliate against those employees who file discrimination claims. To avoid liability, managers should clearly understand that if they act on emotions created by the filing of a discrimination claim, those actions are likely to constitute unlawful retaliation. Even if the underlying charge of discrimination is unfounded, the person who brings the charge is protected from retaliation, whether or not the claim is found to be valid. A study released in June 1998 by the American Bar Association's Commission on Mental and Physical Disability Law found that people with a mental or physical disability who claim discrimination under the ADA usually lose. In more than 1,200 ADA cases filed since 1992, employers won 92 percent of the cases decided by a judge and 86 percent of cases resolved by the EEOC. However, the Supreme Court decision in *Bragdon v. Abbott,* noted on page 468, may have an impact on new cases filed under the ADA.

The hiring or retention determination in connection with a disabled employee comprises a three-step analysis. First, the employer must determine whether the

---

EXHIBIT 13–8

Examples of questions that *may not* be asked of an applicant for a position:

1. Please list any disabilities.
2. Have you ever filed a workers' compensation claim, and on what basis?
3. Do you have any disability(ies) that may prevent you from performing the requirements of this position?
4. How did you become disabled?
5. How often do you expect to miss work as a result of this disability?

Examples of questions that *may* be asked:

1. This job requires that you [be present for eight hours a day, five days a week], [lift 150 lb. bags], [stand for long periods of time], can you meet this requirement?
2. If the employer is aware of the disability, the employer may ask how the applicant intends to perform the essential functions of the position with or without accommodation.
3. The employer may request documentation of the need for a requested accommodation.

Exhibit 13–9

James Frierson, a professor in the College of Business at East Tennessee State University, suggests that companies conduct a 50-question self-audit in order to identify ADA compliance problem areas, and to preclude any potential hazards. Here are some of the questions that Frierson suggests a manager or owner should ask of their own business:

1. Does the company have a written policy concerning disabled job applicants and employees?

2. Does the company have a system to encourage employees to report their disabilities in order that accommodations can be provided?

3. Has the company notified unions and professional organizations with whom they have a contract of the company's disability policies?

4. Are procedures in place to ensure that all contractors who come into contact with company employees are complying with the ADA?

5. Have all written job descriptions been reviewed and revised to omit outdated or nonessential tasks and, where possible, to describe required job results, rather than methods?

6. Has the company designated individuals to be responsible for making reasonable accommodations? Does the designated individual understand the legal definition of a disabled person? Does the designated individual understand the legal duty of accommodation?

7. How are decisions documented when disabled individuals are not hired, retained, or promoted because the needed accommodation creates an undue hardship?

8. Do all managers who make employment decisions understand the A-B-C-D-E rule? (Frierson contends that disability lawsuits that are settled unfavorably for employers are most likely to occur when people with **A**IDS, **B**ad backs, **C**ancer, **D**iabetes, and **E**pilepsy are denied jobs because of a risk of future injury.)

9. Is the company's HR department or any other location where job applicants must go fully accessible to disabled people, including those who use wheelchairs?

10. Have all employment tests and procedures for taking the tests been reviewed to ensure that they accurately measure necessary skills and aptitudes?

11. Has the company created a separate, confidential file for employee health and medical information?

12. Are disabled and nondisabled employees who are in the same job classifications provided with the same fringe-benefit coverage?

James Frierson, "A Fifty-Question Self-Audit on ADA Compliance," *Employment Relations Today,* v19 N2. Reprinted by permission of John Wiley & Sons, Inc.

employee is "disabled." Second, the employer must determine whether the applicant is otherwise qualified for the position. Can the employee perform the essential requirements of his or her position with or without accommodation? Third, the employer must determine whether the accommodation that is necessary to allow the employee to perform his or her job effectively is "reasonable."

Would the accommodation impose an undue hardship on the employer in terms of cost or the compromise of the business environment? If the employer ascertains that the employee is disabled; that, with or without reasonable accommodation, the employee is qualified (for more information on drafting appropriate job descriptions, see Chapter 4); and that the accommodation does not impose an undue hardship, the accommodation must be given, and the employer may not take adverse action against the applicant based on that disability.

Management Tips

- Never assume the physical or intellectual limitations of a disabled worker or applicant. If you assume that someone can't perform certain functions, you may be creating limitations where none exist.

- Be sure to explore all possible reasonable accommodations for otherwise qualified applicants or employees. Failure to do so might result not only in legal liability but also costs connected with identifying and training alternative candidates. Often, a small accommodation will allow you to retain qualified and experienced disabled individuals.

- Engage in frank and open discussions. Determining the appropriate reasonable accommodation is a collaborative process. Candid communication is the key ingredient leading to successfully handling ADA matters.

- Consult with the employee. Ask questions. Ask the employee to offer suggestions. Asking the employee to provide additional information will lead you to more opportunities for best identifying and handling the accommodation.

- Document that dialogue. These are negotiations. They may or may not lead to litigation. Don't let the employee say that you remained silent once the employee asked for an accommodation. Confirm your efforts to accommodate in writing. This documentation is one of the best defenses against an employee's memory.

- Be proactive. Reasonable accommodation obligations require action and effort on the employer's part. Flexibility is critical to management's efforts.

- Negotiate. Make counterproposals. Be sure they are fair and reasonable. Remember, an employer is not required to provide the best accommodation, only a reasonable accommodation.

- Review all application materials to ensure that there are no inappropriate questions concerning irrelevant abilities.

- Review all job descriptions to make sure that the job requirements are actually required to complete the job; get rid of extraneous requirements that are not really essential to job performance.

- Since "disability" under the statutes includes someone who is perceived as being disabled, conduct training sessions with all management to educate them regarding what is actually a disability and what is not.

- You are not required to accommodate all disabilities. Consider all costs involved with providing accommodation and consider whether it would be an undue burden under the courts' precedents.

Summary

- As a manager, when faced with scenarios similar to those presented at the beginning of this chapter:

    —Determine whether the applicant is disabled. Does she or he fit into one of the three categories of disability:

    Disabled?
    Perceived Impairment?
    Record of Impairment?

    —Is the applicant otherwise qualified? What are the essential requirements of the position for which she or he applied? Can the applicant perform these functions with or without reasonable accommodation?

    —If the applicant needs accommodation in order to perform the essential functions, is the accommodation reasonable? Does it impose an undue burden upon the employer?

- If the employee can perform the essential requirements of the position without accommodation or with accommodation that is considered reasonable under the circumstances, then the employer is prohibited from discriminating against that employee on the basis of the disability.

Chapter-End Questions

1. Fields applies for a position as a labor relations specialist at the Department of Labor. Fields's medical examination, however, reveals that he suffers from "Borderline Personality Organization" with side effects of kleptomania and travel anxiety. The position for which Fields applied requires extensive travel for labor negotiations and representations before various committees. Additionally, Fields's kleptomania would weaken his reputation for integrity. Should the Department of Labor be required to accommodate Fields's disabilities? (*Fields v. Lynn,* 705 F.Supp. 1134 (D. Md. 1988), aff'd, 888 F.2d 1385 (4th Cir. 1989).)

2. Black is employed as a letter sorter by the Postal Service. After several years with the service, he develops carpel tunnel syndrome, a disease that paralyzes his wrists after several hours of sorting. Thereafter, Black is only able to sort letters for four hours a day, instead of the usual seven. The Postal Service claims that he cannot perform the essential functions of his position, while Black claims that he can perform these functions, just not for the entire day. What result? (*Black v. Frank,* 730 F.Supp. 1087 (S.D. Ala. 1990).)

3. Davis had been deaf since birth. She applied for a clerk position at the Postal Service. The Postal Service denied her application because she would not be able to answer the telephones, one of the duties of the position. It contended that asking other hearing clerks to take on Davis's telephone duties would lower employee morale and cause bitterness and dissent. In addition, it claimed that it would be inconvenient to other employees who would need to communicate with someone in the desired position. Is the Postal Service's claim sufficient to satisfy the undue hardship defense? (*Davis v. Frank,* 711 F.Supp. 447 (N.D. Ill. 1989).)

4. Halsey was hired as a vending machine serviceperson by Coca-Cola Bottling

Company. His duties included driving to various sites in his territory to service, replace, or retrieve vending machines. Due to a permanent degenerative condition of his retina, Halsey failed the vision test required to obtain a driver's license and was terminated by the company for failing to have a valid license. Halsey contends that he should be able to arrange for his own transportation and to retain his position. The company argues that it should be able to select who transports its equipment. Is a reasonable accommodation possible? (*Halsey v. Coca-Cola Bottling Co. of Mid-America, Inc.,* 410 N.W.2d 250 (Iowa 1987).)

5. Arneson was a claims representative employed by the Social Security Administration. He was diagnosed with apraxia, a neurological disorder that allows the sufferer to be easily distracted by activity around him, and an impaired ability to concentrate in general. The SSA relocated Arneson to the back of a room used by other workers and provided him with a special telephone headset and assistance in organizing his work. He was later terminated for unsatisfactory performance. Arneson claims that he was otherwise qualified for his position as long as he had the use of the headset, a quiet workplace, and clerical assistance to review all of his work. SSA contends that this would require hiring a second employee and that this would amount to an undue hardship. Is this true? (*Arneson v. Heckler,* 879 F.2d 393 (8th Cir. 1989).)

6. After violently assaulting his supervisor, Adams is diagnosed as suffering from a "maladaptive reaction to a psychosocial stressor," his argumentative supervisor. His employer terminates Adams for misconduct. Adams claims that all that was needed was "reasonable" accommodation: the transfer of either or both him and his supervisor elsewhere within the firm. Does Adams's problem constitute a disability? Does it limit a major life activity? If so, is this a reasonable request, assuming that such a move would prevent future misconduct by Adams? (*Adams v. Alderson,* 723 F.Supp. 1531 (D. D.C. 1989).)

7. Which of the following should be considered disabilities under the Rehabilitation or Americans with Disabilities Acts?
   a. Poor judgment, irresponsible behavior, or poor impulse control. (*Daley v. Koch,* 892 F.2d 212 (2d Cir. 1989).)
   b. Excessive weight, which exceeds position limits for position of flight attendant. (*Tudyman v. United Airlines,* 608 F.Supp. 739 (C.D. Ca. 1984).)
   c. Epilepsy, where the refusal to hire is based on the possibility of future injury. (*Mantolete v. Bolger,* 767 F.2d 1416 (9th Cir. 1985); *Reynolds v. Brock,* 815 F.2d 571 (9th Cir. 1987).)
   d. Cross-eyes, for the position of a postal worker who operates a sorting machine requiring detailed visual work. (*Jasany v. United States Postal Service,* 755 F.2d 1244 (6th Cir. 1985).)

8. Louise is employed at a department store and, due to her disability, requires a warm environment in which to work. This heat is uncomfortable to other employees and customers. Need the employer accommodate this request? What may be considered to be reasonable accommodation?

9. Leckelt was a licensed nurse hired by the Terrebone General Medical Center in Louisiana. In his capacity at the hospital, he routinely administered medication, orally and by injection, changed dressings, performed catheterizations, administered enemas, and started intravenous tubes. After

the board of the hospital was informed that Leckelt was the roommate of a hospital patient who was believed to have AIDS, the board requested that Leckelt submit to HIV antibody testing. Leckelt informed the hospital that, indeed, he had been tested but that he was not interested in sharing the results with the hospital, contrary to the policy of the hospital in connection with infectious disease reporting. Leckelt was informed that he was not to return to work until such time as he divulged the results of his exam, and he was likely to be discharged for insubordination. Leckelt refuses to inform the hospital of the results, is terminated, and files an action. What result? (*Leckelt v. Board of Commissioners of Hosp. Dist. No. 1,* 909 F.2d 820 (5th Cir. 1990).)

10. Agency Rent-A-Car hired Gimello as a management trainee in 1978, and he was promoted to office manager one month later. As a manager, Gimello received several bonuses for maintaining high sales levels and received consistently positive evaluations, except for two points. In 1981, he was described as needing a course in employee–public relations and six months later was told that he should soften his telephone skills and should manage dispatching more efficiently. Gimello was 5'8" and weighed 325 pounds (doctors would testify that the average weight for a man of his height is about 180 pounds). When Gimello was up for a new promotion, he was told that, because of his weight, he would not be able to travel from office to office, as the job required. Gimello files suit on the basis of disability discrimination and presents evidence from a doctor who defines obesity as a compilation of fat in body tissue caused by overeating, heredity, and metabolism but explains that distinguishing the cause in any given case is next to impossible. Does this failure to promote Gimello constitute disability discrimination? (*Gimello v. Agency Rent-A-Car,* 594 A.2d 264 (N.J. 1991).)

III REGULATION OF THE EMPLOYMENT ENVIRONMENT

14 TESTING

S C E N A R I O S

S C E N A R I O   1

Shefali Trivedi is the manager at a large food store and has hired many young employees to work for her on a part-time basis. During the past few weeks, she has noticed that she is missing a sizeable amount of her stock in many different areas. She has no idea where to begin a search for suspects but is convinced that it is an "inside" job, because her security during nonworking hours is excellent. Can she simply notify each of her employees that they will all be required to submit to a polygraph test to determine who is involved, or should she perform additional investigation and use the polygraph test only as a means of confirmation of suspicion?

S C E N A R I O   2

In addition, Shefali has not yet purchased computerized checkout scanners, and therefore all of the product prices must be input by hand to the store registers. Shefali has found in the past that certain employees are able to perform this task at a much more rapid pace than others. To maintain store efficiency, she decides to test all applicants relating to their ability to input prices into the register. After administering an on-site timed test, she finds that 12 white applicants, 2 black applicants, and 1 Hispanic applicant are represented among the top 15 performers. Shefali has five positions available. Will she be subject to liability for disparate impact discrimination if she proceeds to hire the five top performers, all of whom are white?

S C E N A R I O   3

As a store manager, Victoria Geguzys has been experiencing a problem with employees who consistently appear for work under the influence of either drugs or alcohol. Victoria does not remember if there is a strict store policy on the matter, but she does not want this type of behavior to continue. Does she inform her employees that there will now be random drug and alcohol testing and, if the results return positive, adverse action will be taken against them? She would also like to see a more teetotaling group of people hired when positions become available. Does she implement a policy that requires a drug or alcohol test and a physical as a prerequisite for hiring?

EXHIBIT 14–1   Myths about Testing in Employment

1. The Constitution will always protect an employee against unreasonable searches.
2. In the private employment sector, employers can pretty much do what they want in terms of testing.
3. Polygraphs are reliable.
4. If you test positive for drug or alcohol on an employment test, you will be terminated.
5. HIV testing is relevant to job performance.

Background

Preemployment testing
Testing that takes place before hiring, or sometimes after hiring but before employment, in connection with such qualities as integrity, honesty, drug and alcohol use, HIV, or other characteristics.

Preemployment testing began in the 1950s as a response to the inefficiencies that were purportedly present in American business. Since that time, preemployment testing has been considered a necessity to the selection process. The majority of selection tests originally given were conducted as a means of bettering the company's position in a competitive market. Testing was seen as the answer to workplace personnel problems, ineffective hiring programs, and the inappropriate job placement of hirees. Employers believed they would be more competitive if they could test applicants to "weed out" those who failed the tests. These tests became the wave of the future. However, many managers administered tests that had never been validated as indicators of performance, or were not specifically job related in any way. In 1990, former US Surgeon General C. Everett Koop estimated that between 14 and 25 percent of employees between the ages of 18 and 40 would test positive for illegal substances on any given day. Today, the estimated cost of substance abuse in the workplace in the form of lost productivity, medical claims, and accidents amounts to $142 billion per year. The enormity of this figure is one of the reasons why approximately 22 million employees were tested in 1992 alone.

Testing in the workplace has taken two forms: tests for the purpose of finding the best individual for a position and tests to ensure that the individual is free of difficulties. Examples of the former include achievement tests and personality indicators. The problem with this type of eligibility test is that, while it may appear facially neutral, it may have a disparate impact on a protected class. Pursuant to the Civil Rights Act of 1964, where adverse impact has been shown, the test may still be used if it has been professionally developed and validated (discussed later). If used properly, however, a validated test will not only determine for the employer the most appropriate applicant for the position but may also reduce the chance for discriminatory choices based on conscious or subconscious employer bias.

The latter form of examination refers to tests for ineligibility, such as for drug and alcohol abuse, and other impairments that may limit an applicant's ability to perform. Drug and alcohol addictions have become pervasive issues in our society. Highly publicized mishaps, such as the alcohol-related Exxon *Valdez* disaster and drug-related railway incidents, have added to our consternation. The problem of addiction has permeated almost every facet of our lives, including the workplace. Employers have institutionalized prevention programs, not only for the safety of their workers but also in an effort to ensure high productivity and quality output. As tech-

EXHIBIT 14–2   Balancing the Interests in the Testing Debate

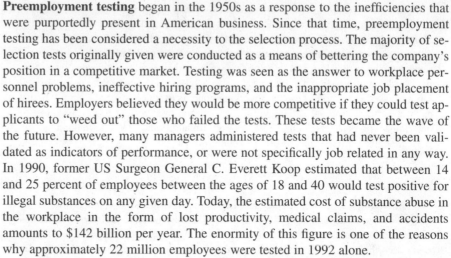

Employer's interest in securing a problem-free or substance-free workplace
versus
Employee's privacy rights and protections against self-incrimination

nology has improved, impairment tests have become more efficient, less expensive, and therefore more prevalent.

In an effort to protect individual employee rights, courts do a balancing test to determine the legality of ineligibility testing. "At some point, an individual's privacy interests trump an employer's efficiency concerns. That point is when the invasion of privacy is 'substantially and highly offensive to the reasonable person,'" one judge stated. The courts accordingly weigh the conflicting interest of the employer in securing a problem-free or substance-free workplace against the privacy rights of the employee and protections against self-incrimination.

As many of the protections afforded to the employee derive from the Constitution (4th Amendment protection against unreasonable searches and seizures, 5th Amendment right against self-incrimination, and 5th and 14th Amendments' protections of due process), government employees and contractors generally receive greater protection in these areas than do employees in the private sector. However, state constitutions can be a source of protection as well. While discussed to some extent in the following case, the issue of privacy rights is more completely discussed in Chapter 16. This chapter, instead, will be concerned with the potential for discrimination in the course of testing procedures and requirements, and the various statutes that protect against related discrimination.

NORMAN-BLOODSAW V. LAWRENCE BERKELEY LABORATORY
135 F.3d 1260 (9th Cir. 1998)

Employees of a research facility operated by Lawrence Berkeley Laboratory (LBL) brought an action against the employer, alleging nonconsensual testing for sensitive, personal medical information pursuant to general employee health examinations in violation of Title VII, the ADA, and the right to privacy guaranteed by the U.S. Constitution.

The employees claim that, without their knowledge, the employer tested blood and urine for intimate medical conditions, such as syphilis, sickle cell trait, and pregnancy, during the course of their mandatory employment entrance exam. They also claim that only black employees were tested for sickle cell trait and assert the obvious fact that only female employees were tested for pregnancy. They contend that they did not discover that the disputed tests had been conducted until approximately January 1995 and deny that they observed any signs indicating that such tests would be performed. LBL is a research facility jointly operated by state and federal agencies. LBL claims that the plaintiffs were informed of the tests conducted and moved for a motion to dismiss and summary judgment. The district court granted these motions and the plaintiffs appealed. The Circuit Court affirmed as to the ADA claims, but reversed as to the Title VII and state and federal privacy claims.

Reinhardt, J.

* * *

The constitutionally protected privacy interest in avoiding disclosure of personal matters clearly encompasses medical information and its confidentiality. Although cases defining the privacy interest in medical information have typically involved its disclosure to "third" parties, rather than the collection of information by illicit means, it goes without saying that the most basic violation possible involves the performance of unauthorized tests—that is, the non-consensual retrieval of previously unrevealed medical information that may be unknown even to plaintiffs. These tests may also be viewed as searches in violation of Fourth Amendment rights that require Fourth Amendment scrutiny. The tests at issue in this case thus implicate rights protected under both the Fourth Amendment and the Due Process Clause of the Fifth or Fourteenth Amendments.

* * *

The district court erred in dismissing the claims on the ground that any violation was de minimis, incremental, or overlapping.

* * *

One can think of few subject areas more personal and more likely to implicate privacy interests than that of one's health or genetic make-up. Furthermore, the facts revealed by the tests are highly sensitive, even relative to other medical information. . . . [T]he conditions tested for were aspects of one's health in which one enjoys the highest expectation of privacy.

. . . [T]here was little, if any, "overlap" between what plaintiffs consented to and the testing at issue here. Nor was the additional invasion only incremental. In some instances, the tests related to entirely different conditions. In all, the information obtained as the result of the testing was qualitatively different from the information that plaintiffs provided in their answers to the questions, and was highly invasive. That one has consented to a general medical examination does not abolish one's privacy right not to be tested for intimate, personal matters involving one's health—nor does consenting to giving blood or urine samples, or filling out a questionnaire. . . . Thus, the intrusion was by no means de minimis. Rather, if unauthorized, the testing constituted a significant invasion of a right that is of great importance, and labeling it minimal cannot and does not make it so.

LBL further contends that the tests in question, even if their intrusiveness is not de minimis, would be justified by an employer's interest in performing a general physical examination. This argument fails because issues of fact exist with respect to whether the testing at issue is normally part of a general physical examination. There would of course be no violation if the testing were authorized, or if the plaintiffs reasonably should have known that the blood and urine samples they provided would be used for the disputed testing and failed to object. However, as we concluded . . . material issues of fact exist as to those questions. Summary judgment in the alternative on the merits of the federal constitutional privacy claim was therefore incorrect.

* * *

The district court also dismissed the Title VII counts on the merits on the ground that plaintiffs had failed to state a claim because the "alleged classifications, standing alone, do not suffice to provide a cognizable basis for relief under Title VII" and because plaintiffs had neither alleged nor demonstrated how these classifications had adversely affected them.

* * * *

Despite defendants' assertions to the contrary, plaintiffs' Title VII claims fall neatly into a Title VII framework. . . .

. . . It is well established that Title VII bars discrimination not only in the "terms" and "conditions" of ongoing employment, but also in the "terms" and "conditions" under which individuals may obtain employment. Thus, for example, a requirement of preemployment health examinations imposed only on female employees, or a require-ment of preemployment background security checks imposed only on black employees, would surely violate Title VII.

In this case, the term or condition for black employees was undergoing a test for sickle cell trait; for women it was undergoing a test for preg-nancy. It is not disputed that the preplacement exams were, literally, a condition of employment: the offers of employment stated this explicitly. Thus, the employment of women and blacks at LBL was conditioned in part on allegedly uncon-stitutional invasions of privacy to which white and/or male employees were not subjected. An ad-ditional "term or condition" requiring an unconsti-tutional invasion of privacy is, without doubt, ac-tionable under Title VII. Furthermore, even if the intrusions did not rise to the level of unconstitu-tionality, they would still be a "term" or "condi-tion" based on an illicit category as described by the statute and thus a proper basis for a Title VII action. Thus, the district court erred in ruling on the pleadings that the plaintiffs had failed to assert a proper Title VII claim under §2000e-2(a)(1).

The district court also erred in finding as a matter of law that there was no "adverse effect" with respect to the tests as required under §2000e-2(a)(2). The unauthorized obtaining of sensitive medical information on the basis of race or sex would in itself constitute an "adverse ef-fect," or injury, under Title VII. Thus, it was error to rule that as a matter of law no "adverse effect" could arise from a classification that singled out particular groups for unconstitutionally invasive, non-consensual medical testing, and the district court erred in dismissing the Title VII claims on this ground as well. AFFIRMED IN PART, RE-VERSED IN PART, and REMANDED.

Case Questions

1. The court did not decide the final issues but only remanded it back to the trial court. If you were the judge, based on the facts presented, how would you decide the case?

2. Would it make a difference if the plaintiff consented to the testing?

3. Do you think the fact that these tests were not being conducted after 1995 had any affect on the court's decision? Why or why not? Should it?

Legality of Eligibility Testing

What do we mean by "eligibility testing"? **Eligibility testing** comprises those tests an employer administers to ensure that the potential employee is capable and qualified to perform the requirements of the position. Some tests are also used to determine who is most capable among applicants. These tests may include intelligence tests, tests of physical stamina, eye exams, tests for levels of achievement or aptitude, or tests for the presence of certain personality traits. Tests for ineligibility, on the other hand, test for disqualifying factors, such as drug and alcohol tests, polygraphs, and HIV testing.

Of course, a test may cross the line between the two. For instance, an employer may administer a preemployment, postoffer medical exam to determine whether the applicant is sufficiently healthy to perform the job requirements. If the individual fails the medical examination, the test has determined that she or he is not qualified for the position and, therefore, is ineligible.

Eligibility Testing
Tests an employer administers to ensure that the potential employee is capable and qualified to perform the requirements of the position.

Employers may conduct eligibility tests for a variety of reasons. For example, the position may require a unique skill for which the employer wishes to test the applicants. Those applicants who possess that skill will continue in the application process. Or perhaps the employer may need to ensure that the applicants meet minimum standards to satisfy requirements of the position. For instance, an eye exam may be required for all potential bus drivers, or an English language competency examination for all applicants for customer relations positions. These tests, however, may in their implementation have a disparate impact on members of a protected class. To illustrate, the employer's test for English language competency would have an adverse impact on individuals of non-English-speaking origin. Where discrimination on the basis of national origin has been shown, the employer may continue to use the test only where it can establish that the requirement is a bona fide occupational qualification.

Title VII specifically exempts professionally developed employment tests of eligibility from disparate impact claims of discrimination, as long as the test is not designed, intended, or used to discriminate on the basis of membership in a protected class. Therefore, if a test has been validated according to strict validation standards, Title VII does not prohibit its use, even where a disparate impact is present. For an eligibility test to be legally validated as an effective gauge of performance, an employer must show that the test is job-related and consistent with **business necessity**. In other words, providing evidence of validity involves showing that test scores can be used to determine appropriate and meaningful inferences about probable job-related behavior.

Business necessity
A character trait that is necessary for the essence of the business.

Scenario

Job analysis
information regarding the nature of the work associated with a job and the knowledge, skills and abilities required to perform that work.

For example, most people would agree a test of general math is probably related to successful performance as a cashier. Thus, even if this type of test had disparate impact against a particular group, it would be allowable if the employer provided **job analysis** data supporting its claim that math skills were required to perform the job. Suppose that a greeting card company found through various job analytic techniques that creativity is necessary for someone who designs greeting cards. Based on the job analysis data, this company most likely would be permitted to use an instrument which tests for creativity, even if it has adverse impact against a certain group. An employer should, however, be prepared to offer evidence the test instrument really does measure creativity. In general, the more abstract the trait the instrument purports to test, the more difficult it becomes to establish evidence of validity. Different approaches for establishing the validity of a test instrument are available and are discussed later. Note that a test still may be challenged if there exists a less discriminatory alternative.

The Seventh Circuit held in *Melendez v. Illinois Bell Telephone Co.*[1] that the employer's aptitude test had a disparate impact on Hispanic job applicants because there was no significant correlation between an applicant's test score and his or her ability to perform the duties of an entry-level manager. The plaintiff's expert testi-

---

[1]79 F.3d 661, 665–669 (7th Cir. 1996).

fied that the aptitude tests could "predict a person's job performance only 3 percent better than chance alone."

A job applicant or employees can show adverse affects by different methods but the most common approach is the "applicants–statistics" approach. The approach compares the percentage of minority applicants successfully passing a personality or aptitude test to the percentage of majority applicants.

Test Validity

In 1978, the EEOC, with the assistance of several other government agencies, developed the Uniform Guidelines on Employee Selection Procedures as a framework for employers in connection with the determination of the proper use of tests and other selection procedures. Where a selection test has been shown to have an adverse impact on a protected class, the guidelines identify three approaches to gathering evidence of validity; the choice of **validation** strategy depends on the type of inference the user wishes to draw from the test scores. The guidelines define an adverse impact on a protected class as any procedure that has a selection rate for any group of less than 80 percent of the selection rate of the group with the highest rate.

Validation
Evidence that shows a test evaluates what it says it evaluates.

Criterion-Related Validation

The most traditional type of validating a test is criterion-related/empirical statistical validity. The test must be shown to accurately predict job performance as evidenced by the ability to do the job. This form of validation collects data relating to job performance from a simulated exercise, or other on-the-job measures of performance. This data is known as the criterion, or criteria if more than one measure of job performance is used. Once the test in question has been administered, and criterion measures have been taken, statistical relationships between the criteria and test scores are examined. Evidence of validity is obtained if there exists a systematic relationship between the criteria and the test scores. The strength of the relationship helps to determine how accurately performance can be predicted from test scores. The guidelines explain that the criterion on which the test is based may include other measures than work proficiency, such as training time, supervisory ratings, regularity of attendance, and tenure. Whatever criteria are used, they must represent major or critical work behaviors as revealed by careful job analyses. In connection with criterion-based validation, it is important that the employer identify the proper criteria to be measured, identify the proper measurement, and establish a significant level of correlation between criterion measurement and job performance. Evidence for criterion-related validity can be obtained by one of two methods: predictive or concurrent. Predictive validity studies administer the test first and later collect criterion data. Concurrent studies collect both test and criterion data at the same time. Both types of studies then examine the statistical relationships between the two data sets. Concurrent studies are often used because predictive studies frequently prove to be less feasible.

Content Validation

A test that demonstrates content validity is one that has sufficiently sampled the knowledge and/or skills required by the specific position for job performance. To ensure content validity, the job domain must first be defined based on careful job analysis. This definition should identify important tasks, behaviors, and the knowledge the job requires. The test must then be judged against a representative sample of these tasks, behaviors, and knowledge. Employers should be particularly concerned with this type of validity during test construction, as it is easiest to ensure representativeness at this stage. In determining representativeness, it is also important to consider the format and response properties of test items: a test measuring a skill or ability should either closely approximate an observable work behavior or its product should closely approximate an observable work product. The closer the content and context of the test are to work samples or behaviors, the stronger the basis for content validity. Contrary to criterion validity, which attempts to predict performance, a test that demonstrates content validity specifically measures performance of certain position requirements.

Construct Validation

Evidence of construct validity is generally most useful when test scores are considered measures of a psychological characteristic such as reasoning ability, introversion (a personality characteristic), leadership behaviors, and others. These characteristics are theoretical constructions about behavior, and in an employment setting are about job-related behavior. Several issues must be considered when gathering evidence for construct validity. First, the construct must be shown to be important for job performance. As with content validity, this is done through the use of careful job analysis. In addition, the construct should be well defined, distinguished from other constructs, and should specify how the construct relates to other variables. Construct validity is determined by examining the intercorrelation of test items (i.e., ensuring the internal consistency of the test) and examining relationships with other measures of the same construct and with measures of different constructs. These relationships should be strong for measures of the same construct and weak for measures of distinct constructs.

Subgroup Norming

Traditionally, the EEOC has considered evidence of differential validation. In other words, a test must not only be valid for the overall population to be tested (i.e., be differentially valid), but also must be valid for each separate minority subgroup. In the past, this goal was achieved by making adjustments within a particular subgroup population to make scores equivalent across subgroup populations. However, this practice of subgroup norming, or "race norming" as it is sometimes called, was

Exhibit 14–3   Information Required to Be Maintained

Criterion Validation
User, location, and date(s) of studies.
Problem and setting.
Job analysis or review of job information.
Job titles and codes.
Criterion measures.
Sample description.
Description of selection procedure.
Techniques and results.
Alternative procedures investigated.
Uses and applications.
Source data.
Contact person.
Steps taken to assure accuracy and completeness.

Content Validation
User, location, and date(s) of studies.
Problem and setting.
Job analysis, content of the job.
Selection procedure and its content.
Relationship between the selection procedure and the job.
Alternative procedures investigated.
Uses and applications.
Contact person.
Steps taken to assure accuracy and completeness.

Construct Validation
User, location, and date(s) of studies.
Problem and setting.
Construct definition.
Job analysis.
Job titles and codes.
Description of selection procedure.
Relationship between the selection procedure and job performance.
Alternative procedures investigated.
Uses and applications.
Steps taken to assure accuracy and completeness.
Source data.
Contact person.

made illegal by the Civil Rights Act of 1991. The ban on subgroup norming is not limited to race as the means of defining subgroups; subgroups may also no longer be defined in terms of gender, religion, or national origin. Critics of subgroup norming say the practice is unfair because it essentially amounts to using different standards or cutoff scores for different groups. Advocates claimed the practice "leveled the playing field" and increased the employment opportunities of minorities and females.

The Uniform Guidelines on Employee Selection Procedures also require that, where there is evidence of an adverse impact, employers of 100 or more employees must maintain specific records in order to ascertain the validity of tests and their impact on various populations. The type of documentation required varies depending on the type of validity test required.

Job-Related Requirement

In addition to test validation, an employer must show that the specific trait for which the applicant is being tested is job related. For instance, in *Evans v. City of Evanston,* female applicants for firefighter positions claimed that the physical agility tests for the positions had a disparate impact on women. The defendant, however, presented evidence that the examination was rationally related to a legitimate purpose of the city. The court stated that, as long as the scoring system was fair, the test was acceptable, even if it did in fact impact women differently than men.

GRIGGS V. DUKE POWER CO.
401 U.S. 424 (1971)

Duke Power Company required that its employees either have a high school diploma or pass an intelligence test in order to continue employment or to transfer positions at the company. Section 703(h) of Title VII allows the use of a professionally developed ability test, as long as the test is not designed, intended or used to discriminate. This requirement, however, operated to exclude African-American workers from positions at Duke Power. The court found that if an employment practice that has a disparate impact on a protected class cannot be shown to be related to job performance, that practice is prohibited, notwithstanding the employer's lack of discriminatory intent.

Burger, C. J.

The court of appeals was confronted with a question of first impression, as are we, concerning the meaning of Title VII. After careful analysis, a majority of that court concluded that a subjective test of the employer's intent should govern, particularly in a close case, and that in this case there was no showing of discriminatory purpose in the adoption of the diploma and test requirements. On this basis, the Court of Appeals concluded there was no violation of the Act.

The objective of Congress in the enactment of Title VII is plain from the language of the statute. It was to achieve equality of employment opportunities and remove barriers that have operated in the past to favor an identifiable group of white employees over other employees. Under the Act, practices, procedures or tests neutral on their face, and even neutral in terms of intent, cannot be maintained if they operate to "freeze" the status quo of prior discriminatory employment practices.

What is required by Congress is the removal of artificial, arbitrary and unnecessary barriers to employment when the barriers operate invidiously to discriminate on the basis of racial or other impermissible classification.

The Act proscribes not only overt discrimination but also practices that are fair in form, but discriminatory in operation. The touchstone is business necessity. If an employment practice which operates to exclude Negroes cannot be shown to be related to job performance, the practice is prohibited.

On the record before us, neither the high school completion requirement nor the general intelligence test is shown to bear a demonstrable relationship to successful performance of the jobs for which it was used. Both were adopted, as the Court of Appeals noted, without meaningful study of their relationship to job performance ability. Rather, a vice-president of the company testified, the requirements were instituted on the company's judgment that they generally would improve the overall quality of the work force.

The evidence, however, shows that employees who have not completed high school or taken the tests have continued to perform satisfactorily and make progress in departments for which the high school and test criteria are now used.

The facts of this case demonstrate the inadequacy of broad and general testing devices as well as the infirmity of using diplomas or degrees as fixed measures of capability. History is filled with examples of men and women who rendered highly effective performance without the conventional badges of accomplishment in terms of certificates, diplomas or degrees. Diplomas and tests are useful servants, but Congress has mandated the commonsense proposition that they are not to become masters of reality.

Nothing in the Act precludes the use of testing or measuring procedures; obviously they are useful. What Congress has forbidden is giving these devices and mechanisms controlling force unless they are demonstrably a reasonable measure of job performance. Congress has not commanded that

the less qualified be preferred over the better qualified simply because of minority origins. Far from disparaging job qualifications as such, Congress has made such qualifications the controlling factor, so that race, religion, nationality and sex become irrelevant. What Congress has commanded is that any tests used must measure the person for the job and not the person in the abstract.

Case Questions

1. What did the Court mean by "a subjective test of the employer's intent"? How would this be different from an objective test?

2. If Duke Power argued that the diploma requirement or intelligence test was a business necessity, how do you think it could have shown this?

3. Would Duke Power have been successful in this showing?

ALBEMARLE PAPER CO. V. MOODY
422 U.S. 405 (1975)

Respondents in this case were a number of African-American employees of Albemarle Paper Company. They complained that the plant's employment testing program had a disparate impact on African-Americans and served to lock African-American employees in the lower paying job classifications. The testing program required applicants for employment in skilled labor positions to have a high school diploma and to pass two tests, the Revised Beta Examination (allegedly a measure of nonverbal intelligence) and the Wonderlic Personnel Test (allegedly a measure of verbal facility). The Supreme Court found that there was inadequate validation of the tests and that they may not be shown to be job related.

Stewart, J.

In *Griggs v. Duke Power,* this Court unanimously held that Title VII forbids the use of employment tests that are discriminatory in effect unless the employer meets "the burden of showing that any given requirement has a manifest relationship to the employment in question." This burden arises, of course, only after the complaining party or class has made out a prima facie case of discrimination—that is, has shown that the tests in question select applicants for hire or promotion in a racial pattern significantly different from that of the pool of applicants. If an employer does then meet the burden of proving that its tests are "job related," it remains open to the complaining party to show that other tests or selection devices, without a similarly undesirable racial effect, would also serve the employer's legitimate interest in "efficient and trustworthy workmanship." Such a showing would be evidence that the employer was using its tests merely as a "pretext" for discrimination. In the present case, however, we are concerned only with the question whether Albemarle has shown its tests to be job related.

The question of job relatedness must be viewed in the context of the plant's operation and history of the testing program. The plant, which now employs about 650 persons, converts raw wood into paper products. It is organized into a number of functional departments, each with one or more distinct lines of progression, the theory being that workers can move up the line as they acquire the necessary skills. The number and structure of the lines have varied greatly over time.

[The court explains the history of the use of the Beta Examination and the Wonderlic tests by Albemarle.] The Company made no attempt to validate the [Wonderlic] test for job relatedness, and simply adopted the national "norm" score of 18 as a cut-off point for new job applicants. After 1964, when it discontinued overt segregation in the lines of progression, the Company allowed Negro workers to transfer to the skilled lines if

they could pass the Beta and Wonderlic tests, but few succeeded in doing so. Incumbents in the skilled lines, some of whom had been hired before adoption of the tests, were not required to pass them to retain their jobs or their promotion rights. The record shows that a number of incumbents in high ranking job groups could not pass the tests.

Four months before this case went to trial, Albemarle engaged an expert in industrial psychology to "validate" the job relatedness of its testing program. He spent a half day at the plant and devised a "concurrent validation" study, which was conducted by plant officials, without his supervision. The expert then subjected the results to statistical analysis. The study dealt with 10 job groupings, selected from near the top of nine of the lines of progression. Jobs were grouped together solely by their proximity in the line of progression; no attempt was made to analyze jobs in terms of the particular skills they might require. All, or nearly all, employees in the selected groups participated in the study—105 employees in all, but only four Negroes.

On the basis of these results, the District Court found that "[t]he personnel tests administered at the plant have undergone validation studies and have been proven to be job related." Like the Court of Appeals, we are constrained to disagree.

The EEOC has issued Guidelines for employers seeking to determine, through professional validation studies, whether their employment tests are job related. The EEOC Guidelines are not administrative "regulations" promulgated pursuant to formal procedures established by the Congress. But, as this Court has heretofore noted, they do constitute "the administrative interpretation of the Act by the enforcing agency" and consequently are "entitled to great deference."

The message of these Guidelines is the same as that of the *Griggs* case—that discriminatory tests are impermissible unless shown, by professionally acceptable methods, to be "predictive of or significantly correlated with important elements of work behavior which comprise or are relevant to the job or jobs for which candidates are being evaluated."

Measured against the Guidelines, Albemarle's validation study is materially defective in several respects:

(1) Even if it had been otherwise adequate, the study would not have validated the Beta and Wonderlic test battery for all of the skilled lines of progression for which the two tests are, apparently, now required. The study showed significant correlations for the Beta Exam in only three of the eight lines.

(2) The study compared test scores with subjective supervisorial rankings. While they allow the use of supervisorial rankings in test validation, the Guidelines quite plainly contemplate that the rankings will be elicited with far more care than demonstrated here. Albemarle's supervisors were asked to rank employees by a "standard" that was extremely vague and fatally open to divergent interpretations.

(3) The Company's study focused, in most cases, on job groups near the top of the various lines of progression. In *Griggs,* the Court left open "the question whether testing requirements that take into account capability for the next succeeding position or related future promotion might be utilized upon a showing that such long-range requirements fulfill a genuine business need." The fact that the best of those employees working near the top of a line of progression score well on a test does not necessarily mean that test, or some particular cutoff score on that test, is a permissible measure of the minimal qualifications of new workers entering lower level jobs. In drawing any such conclusion, detailed consideration must be given to the normal speed of progression, to the efficacy of on-the-job training in the scheme of promotion, and to the possible use of testing as a promotion device, rather than as a screen for entry into low-level jobs. The District Court made no finding on these issues. The issues take on special importance in a case, such as this one, where incumbent employees are permitted to work at even high-level jobs without passing the Company's job battery.

(4) Albemarle's validation study dealt only with job-experienced, white workers; but the tests themselves are given to new job applicants, who are younger, largely inexperienced, and in many instances nonwhite.

For all these reasons, we agree with the Court of Appeals that the District Court erred in concluding that Albemarle had proven the job relatedness of its testing program and that the respondents were consequently not entitled to equitable relief. . . . Accordingly, the judgment [of the District Court] is vacated, and these cases are remanded to the District Court for proceedings consistent with this opinion.

Case Questions

1. What could or should Albemarle have done to ensure that the test validation would hold up in court?

2. Can you think of other situations or requirements that may serve to lock out one sector of the workforce?

3. What are some examples of employment tests, such as that used in this case, that may hold up in court?

Preparing selection testing programs which will be acceptable to the courts can become a complex and labor-intensive process. In *Rudder v. District of Columbia,*[2] African-American firefighters brought suit against the District of Columbia alleging that promotional examinations violated Title VII. After the firefighters established a prima facie case of discrimination for the sergeants' examination, the court found the examination to be valid and job related. However, this finding involved scrutiny of several issues with regard to the test, including the job analysis on which the test was based, the test itself, weighting of scores, methods and type of validation, test administration, and test reliability.

The comprehensive inquiry into the District of Columbia's test and its development suggest several issues that employers should be aware of in developing or using an employment-related testing program. First, employers must carefully conduct job analyses, ensuring adequate representation of minority groups when collecting data concerning jobs. Second, a specific strategy for validation is necessary, and adequate support must be obtained in order to be acceptable to the courts. Clear links between the information necessary to answer test questions and work performance should be shown. Third, attention to test administration and security can also be relevant, particularly if there is any chance that someone may cheat. Fourth, if there is more than one section or part to a test (i.e., using a test battery), the weighting of those parts in making the employment decision will also be taken into account by the courts. A specific rationale for the weights applied should be logical and based on job analysis data rather than an arbitrary assignment of weights. Finally, the test itself should be systematically developed using job analysis data and representative groups of job incumbents.

In *Rudder,* the District of Columbia developed its job knowledge test for sergeants in six phases. Three separate biracial groups of incumbents and officers were used to review material and determine criticality and importance of knowledge areas for firefighter officers. Officers also helped in writing the test items. Items were then analyzed and revised, and taken again to incumbents for review and assessment of content validity. This extensive process helped ensure content validity and job-relatedness for the test that was ultimately used for promotions.

Legality of Testing for Ineligibility

A variety of reasons encourages workplace testing for ineligibility. The employer may wish to reduce workplace injury or to provide a safer working environment. Drug testing has been shown to drastically reduce the number of workplace injuries and personal injury claims. Second, an employer may use tests to predict employee performance. Personnel costs related to drug use, workplace crimes, and personality conflicts lead to great increases in costs to the employer. Third, testing can reduce the employer's financial responsibility to the state workers' compensation sys-

---

[2]890 F.Supp. 23 (D. D.C. 1996).

tem. The use of an illegal substance, which contributes to the claimant's injury, may serve as a defense to the employer's liability.

Despite the fact that the Constitution only protects employees from invasive or wrongful state action, an employee may make a number of possible claims against testing. Portions of the constitutions or state statutes of certain states establish private sector requirements for workplace testing. For example, San Francisco has enacted an ordinance that requires reasonable suspicion based on evidence of job impairment or danger to others before testing is deemed appropriate. Mandatory or random testing would not be allowed in this jurisdiction.

There is also some support for a claim of common-law invasion of privacy in connection to private sector testing. In order to support a claim of invasion of privacy, the individual must show that her or his privacy was invaded by . . . (1) unreasonable intrusion upon her or his seclusion; (2) appropriation of her or his name or likeness; (3) unreasonable publicity of her or his private facts; and (4) publicity that unreasonably places the individual in a false light before the public. Of these causes of action, the ones most likely to arise in the employment context are intrusion and public disclosure of private facts. Some courts have adopted some or all of these causes of action while others have not.

Workers have also found support for claims based on reckless or negligent infliction of emotional distress. This would occur where the employee can show that the employer's intrusion into the employee's private affairs constitutes intentional (and in some states, even reckless or negligent) extreme and outrageous conduct, and would cause mental suffering, shame, or humiliation (be highly offensive) to a reasonable individual under similar circumstances. In determining the offensiveness or reasonableness of the invasion, courts will balance the employer's reason for the test with the extent or intrusiveness of the invasion of privacy.

In addition to a common law invasion of privacy argument, an employee may be able to state a claim for **defamation.** The employee must be able to show that the employer disseminated his or her intimate information to the public and that disclosure was not reasonably necessary to serve the employer's legitimate business interest in the fitness of the employee to perform her or his job. This latter requirement would allow dissemination of the information to those people who have a "need to know" the information to adequately perform their jobs. The exception is lost where the employer disclosed the information on the basis of its malice against the employee. Once the test has been administered, whether it is a physical, drug test, or polygraph, it is advisable for the employer to secure the chain of custody of any data, samples, or both and to confirm the results with other examinations.

Defamation
An intentional tort involving the publication of false statements about another.

Finally, the employee may have a common law cause of action for wrongful discharge in violation of public policy. An employee may base her claim on the argument that the court should not condone certain employer activities because those activities would directly contravene some clear public policy. In *Twigg v. Hercules Corporation,* the West Virginia Supreme Court held that, even though there was no state statute against drug testing, a strong public policy exists against testing. Therefore, since it was unclear whether the employee's job actually brought him into close physical contact with the explosive fuels produced by the employer, there was insufficient support for the testing. The court instead held there were only two exceptions to the policy against testing: (1) where conducted by an employer based on a reasonable good faith suspicion of an employee's drug usage and (2) where an employee's job responsibility involves public safety or the safety of others.

Generally, congruent with fundamental theories of employment law, a discharge resulting from an employee's failure to take a test for ineligibility is protected under the employment-at-will doctrine. The employment relationship is based on consent of both parties; if the employee does not wish to be subject to various requirements or conditions of employment, the employee may refuse and leave. If the employee, for instance, is uncomfortable with the idea of random drug testing, that employee may quit and work in an environment in which she or he is more comfortable.

Forms of Testing

Polygraphs

Polygraph
A lie detecting device that measures biological reactions to individuals when questioned.

One of the most newsworthy areas of testing is the **polygraph** or lie detector. In each year during the past decade, more than two million private sector employees were asked to take a lie detector test. While the actual number of polygraph tests administered is unknown, it is probative to learn that there are between 2,000–3,500 polygraphers practicing in the United States. There are at least nine schools of polygraph analysis that graduate hundreds more each year.

A polygraph test measures three physiological indicators of arousal: rate and depth of respiration, cardiovascular activity, and perspiration. The examiner asks a structured set of questions, and the subject is evaluated as honest or deceitful based on the pattern of arousal responses. The test has been criticized, however, because other catalysts than dishonesty may produce similar effects in an individual subject. For instance, if an individual is aware that the basis for the test is a concern regarding theft, she or he may become innocently aroused when asked questions relating to the theft. On the other hand, the individual who has actually committed the theft may not be concerned at all; if the person was capable of theft, she or he may be just as comfortable with deceit.

The desire of employers to use polygraphs is perplexing when one considers the reliability of these tests (or lack thereof). In 1983, the Congressional Office of Technology Assessment conducted a study of polygraph reliability. The office found there is a dearth of research or scientific evidence to prove the polygraph is valid for screening purposes. In fact, it has been found that accuracy rates range from 90 percent to 50 percent.

Because of the large number of false positives and inaccuracies of the polygraph test, a loud outcry from those wrongly accused of improper behavior has resulted in the enactment of the Federal Employee Polygraph Protection Act of 1988. This act, to a great extent, puts an end to polygraph use in selection and greatly restricts its use in many other employment situations. The act provides that an employer may not:

1. Directly or indirectly require, request, suggest, or cause any employee to take or submit to any lie detector test (e.g., a polygraph, deceptograph, voice-stress analyzer, psychological-stress evaluator, and any similar mechanical or electrical device used to render a diagnostic opinion about the honesty of an individual).

2. Use, accept, refer to, or inquire about the results of any lie detector test of any job applicant or current employee.

3. Discharge, discipline, discriminate against, or deny employment or promotion to (or threaten to take such adverse action against) any prospective or current employee who refuses, declines, or fails to take or submit to a lie detector test, or who fails such a test

However, certain employers are exempt from these regulations. These employers include:

1. Private employers whose primary business purpose is to provide security services. Prospective employees may be tested if the positions to which they are applying involve the protection of nuclear power facilities; shipments or storage of radioactive or other toxic waste materials; public transportation of currency, negotiable securities, precious commodities, or proprietary information.

2. Employers involved in the manufacture, distribution, or dispensing of controlled substances. Employers may administer polygraph tests to applicants for positions that would provide direct access to the manufacture, storage, distribution, or sale of a controlled substance.

3. Federal, state, and local government employers. The federal government may also test private consultants or experts under contract to the Defense Department, the National Security Agency, the Defense Intelligence Agency, the Central Intelligence Agency, and the Federal Bureau of Investigation.

According to the act, a private employer may also test current employees if the following four conditions exist. First, the test must be administered in connection with a workplace theft or incident investigation. Second, the employee must have had reasonable access to the missing property or loss incurred. Third, the employer must have reasonable suspicion that this particular employee was involved. Fourth, the employee must have been given written information regarding the basis for the investigation and for the suspicion that she or he is involved. Furthermore, an employer cannot discharge, discipline, or otherwise discriminate against the test taker in any manner on the basis of the polygraph test results or refusal to take a polygraph test, without additional supporting evidence. This is called the "investigation exemption." See Exhibit 14–5.

The act also provides that, except in limited settlement-related circumstances, employees may not waive their rights under the act, nor is an employer allowed to offer financial incentives to employees to take the test or to waive their rights.

Scenario

EXHIBIT 14–4

NOTICE

EMPLOYEE POLYGRAPH PROTECTION ACT

The Employee Polygraph Protection Act prohibits most private employers from using lie detector tests either for pre-employment screening or during the course of employment.

PROHIBITIONS

Employers are generally prohibited from requiring or requesting any employee or job applicant to take a lie detector test, and from discharging, disciplining, or discriminating against an employee or prospective employee for refusing to take a test or for exercising other rights under the Act.

EXEMPTIONS*

Federal, State and local governments are not affected by the law. Also, the law does not apply to tests given by the Federal Government to certain private individuals engaged in national security-related activities.

The Act permits *polygraph* (a kind of lie detector) tests to be administered in the private sector, subject to restrictions, to certain prospective employees of security service firms (armored car, alarm, and guard), and of pharmaceutical manufacturers, distributors and dispensers.

The Act also permits polygraph testing, subject to restrictions, of certain employees of private firms who are reasonably suspected of involvement in a workplace incident (theft, embezzlement, etc.) that resulted in economic loss to the employer.

EXAMINEE RIGHTS

Where polygraph tests are permitted, they are subject to numerous strict standards concerning the conduct and length of the test. Examinees have a number of specific rights, including the right to a written notice before testing, the right to refuse or discontinue a test, and the right not to have test results disclosed to unauthorized persons.

ENFORCEMENT

The Secretary of Labor may bring court actions to restrain violations and assess civil penalties up to $10,000 against violators. Employees or job applicants may also bring their own court actions.

ADDITIONAL INFORMATION

Additional information may be obtained, and complaints of violations may be filed, at local offices of the Wage and Hour Division, which are listed in the telephone directory under U.S. Government, Department of Labor, Employment Standards Administration.

THE LAW REQUIRES EMPLOYERS TO DISPLAY THIS POSTER WHERE EMPLOYEES AND JOB APPLICANTS CAN READILY SEE IT.

The law does not preempt any provision of any State or local law or any collective bargaining agreement which is more restrictive with respect to lie detector tests.

U.S. DEPARTMENT OF LABOR

EMPLOYMENT STANDARDS ADMINISTRATION
Wage and Hour Division
Washington, D.C. 20210

★U.S.GPO:1991-0-522-762

WH Publication 1462
September 1988

EXHIBIT 14–5

Employers are required by the Act to offer certain information to all individuals who may be subject to a polygraph. The information required is as follows:

SAMPLE NOTICE TO EXAMINEE

Section 8(b) of the Employee Polygraph Protection Act, and Department of Labor regulations (29 CFR 801.22) require that you be given the following information before taking a polygraph examination:

1.(a) The polygraph examination area [does] [does not] contain a two-way mirror, a camera, or other device through which you may be observed.

(b) Another device, such as those used in conversation or recording, [will] [will not] by used during the examination.

(c) Both you and the employer have the right, with the other's knowledge, to record electronically the entire examination.

2.(a) You have the right to terminate the test at any time.

(b) You have the right, and will be given the opportunity, to review all questions to be asked during the test.

(c) You may not be asked questions in a manner which degrades, or needlessly intrudes.

(d) You may not be asked any questions concerning: Religious beliefs or opinions; beliefs regarding racial matters; political beliefs or affiliations; matters relating to sexual behavior; beliefs, affiliations, opinions, or lawful activities regarding unions or labor organizations.

(e) The test may not be conducted if there is sufficient written evidence by a physician that you are suffering from a medical or psychological condition or undergoing treatment that might cause abnormal responses during the examination.

3.(a) The test is not and cannot be required as a condition of employment.

(b) The employer may not discharge, dismiss, discipline, deny employment or promotion, or otherwise discriminate against you based on the analysis of a polygraph test, or based on your refusal to take such a test without additional evidence which would support such action.

(c)(1) In connection with an ongoing investigation, the additional evidence required for an employer to take adverse action against you, including termination, may be (A) evidence that you had access to the property that is the subject of investigation, together with (B) the evidence supporting the employer's reasonable suspicion that you were involved in the incident or activity under investigation.

(2) Any statement made by you before or during the test may serve as additional supporting evidence for an adverse employment action, as described in 3(b) above, and any admission of criminal conduct by you may be transmitted to an appropriate government law enforcement agency.

4.(a) Information acquired from a polygraph test may be disclosed by the examiner or by the employer only:

(1) To you or any other person specifically designated in writing by you to receive such information:

(2) To the employer that requested the test:

(3) To a court, governmental agency, arbitrator, or mediator that obtains a court order:

(4) To a U.S. Department of Labor official when specifically designated in writing by you to receive such information.

(b) Information acquired from a polygraph test may be disclosed by the employer to an appropriate governmental agency without a court order where, and only insofar as, the information disclosed is an admission of criminal conduct.

5. If any of your rights or protections under the law are violated, you have the right to file a complaint with the Wage and Hour Division of the U.S. Department of Labor, or to take action in court against the employer. Employers who violate this law are liable to the affected examinee, who may recover such legal or equitable relief as may be appropriate, including employment, reinstatement, and promotion, payment of lost wages and benefits, and reasonable costs, including attorney's fees. The Secretary of Labor may also bring action to restrain violations of the Act, or may assess civil money penalties against the employer.

6. Your rights under the Act may not be waived, either voluntarily or involuntarily, by contract or otherwise, except as part of a written settlement to a pending action or complaint under the Act and agreed to and signed by the parties.

I acknowledge that I have received a copy of the above notice and that it has been read to me.

_____
(Date)

_____
(Signature)

Reprinted from 53 Fed. Reg. 204 (October 21, 1988)

EXHIBIT 14–6

The following is from the instruction booklet for the Institute for a Drug Free America's Drug Screening Kit, which is designed for parents who want to determine if their children are using illegal drugs. Parents tape-record the session then forward it to the institute for analysis. The instructions say:

Select the room in your home that has the fewest distractions. Have the subject sit across the table facing the examiner. The dominant family member must do the screening. Do not have any other family members in the room while giving the test—one examiner and one subject only.

Ask the subject to take a seat and adjust the microphone. Explain to the subject that he or she is to wait until you have completed each question and then answer with a simple "yes" or "no." Do not let the subject try and explain the answers. Turn the tape recorder on, press "record," and ask the subject to state his or her name. Be friendly. Look at the subject and say, "I want you to tell me the truth."

After the subject responds, say, "THE TEST . . . IS ABOUT . . . TO BEGIN!"

1. Is your name _____? (Subject's name)
2. Do you live in _____? (Your state)
3. Are you 100 years old?
4. Have you taken any illegal drugs in the past 30 days?
5. Do you like the color blue?
6. Have you consumed any alcoholic beverage in the last 30 days?
7. Do you like the color green?
8. Do you have any friends taking illegal drugs?
9. Have you answered these questions truthfully?

Violations of the act are subject to fines as high as $10,000 per violation, as well as reinstatement, employment, or promotion, and the payment of back wages and benefits to the adversely affected individual. The Wage and Hour Division of the Employment Standards Administration of the Department of Labor has the authority to administer the Employee Polygraph Protection Act. Pursuant to the act, the Department of Labor has issued the poster in Exhibit 14–4 for workplace distribution.

In addition to the regulations promulgated by Congress, 33 states have statutes that either prohibit or restrict the use of polygraph examinations for use in employment decisions. Where a state law is more restrictive than the federal act, the act does not preempt the statute.

BLACKWELL V. 53RD-ELLIS CURRENCY EXCHANGE
852 F.Supp. 646 (N.D. Ill. 1994)

Yvonne Blackwell worked for the 53rd-Ellis Currency Exchange, Inc., as a cashier. At the time Yvonne was working for the exchange, a notary seal was discovered missing from the office. The owner of the exchange (Mr. Miller) announced that every employee would be required to take a polygraph test to see who had taken the seal, as well as to investigate various cash shortages. Yvonne took the test, and she was informed that she had passed immediately afterward. Two weeks later, Yvonne was fired. According to Miller, Yvonne was fired for cashing several forged checks, misrepresenting the verification of a cashier's check and "acting uncivilly" toward Miller. Yvonne filed suit, claiming violations of the Employee Polygraph Protection Act based, in part, on Miller's failure to meet the requirements for the ongoing investigation exemption in that Miller did not have a reasonable suspicion of her involvement in the alleged activity.

Plunkett, J.

The Employee Polygraph Protection Act of 1988

The EPPA generally prohibits most private employers' use of polygraph tests either for pre-employment screening or for random testing during the course of employment. Section 2006 spells out six exemptions from the general prohibition on administering polygraph tests. The exemption at issue here is the fourth one, namely, the "Limited exemption for ongoing investigations."

* * *

Subsection 2007(b) sets out an examinee's rights both pre-test and during all phases of the process.

. . . An employer is liable under the EPPA if the employer administers a polygraph test without meeting each one of the requirements set out in the statute. Because Plaintiff admits that the first two requirements are met, Plaintiff is entitled to summary judgment only if there is no genuine issue of fact with regard to Defendant's failure to meet at least one of the latter three requirements.

Plaintiff first argues that the dictates of section 2006(3) have not been met because Defen-

dants did not have a "reasonable suspicion" that Plaintiff was involved in the incident or activity under investigation. Plaintiff asserts that Defendants lacked the requisite reasonable suspicion about her involvement in the incidents because all employees were asked to submit to the test, other employees had access to the missing items, and no specific allegations have been made that Plaintiff more than any other employee was involved in the disappearance of the missing items. Defendant's response seems to be that all employees were requested to take the test because all employees had access to the missing items. Whether Plaintiff can prevail on this issue turns on the interpretation of "reasonable suspicion."

The EPPA does not define the term "reasonable suspicion." The statute merely states that an employer may request an employee to submit to a polygraph test if *inter alia,* "the employer has a reasonable suspicion that the employee was involved in the incident or activity under investigation." Thus, we look to the legislative history of the Act and the interpretive regulations promulgated by the Department of Labor for guidance on the term's intended meaning.

According to the legislative history, Congress intended "reasonable suspicion" to refer to

> some observable articulable basis in fact *beyond the predicate loss and access required for testing.* This could include such factors as the demeanor of the employee or discrepancies which arise during the course of an investigation. And while access alone does not constitute a basis for reasonable suspicion, the totality of the circumstances surrounding such access, such as its unauthorized or unusual nature, may constitute an additional factor.

The regulations promulgated by the Department of Labor provide further insight into the term's meaning. Regulation 801.12(f) (1) mirrors the language found in the legislative history that reasonable suspicion refers to an "observable, articulable basis in fact which indicates that a particular employee was involved in, or responsible for, an economic loss." The regulation further emphasizes that "[a]ccess in the sense of possible or potential opportunity, standing alone, does not constitute a basis for 'reasonable suspicion.'"

The regulations illustrate the limited circumstances in which reasonable suspicion may be predicated on access alone.

> [I]n an investigation of a theft of an expensive piece of jewelry, an employee authorized to open the establishment's safe no earlier than 9 A.M. in order to place the jewelry in a window display case, is observed opening the safe at 7:30 A.M. In such a situation, the opening of the safe by the employee one and one-half hours prior to the specified time may serve as the basis for reasonable suspicion. On the other hand, in the example given, if the employer asked the employee to bring the piece of jewelry to his or her office at 7:30 A.M., and the employee then opened the safe and reported the jewelry missing, *such access, standing alone, would not constitute a basis for reasonable suspicion that the employee was involved in the incident unless access to the safe was limited solely to the employee. If no one other than the employee possessed the combination to the safe, and all other possible explanations for the loss are ruled out, such as a break-in, the employer may formulate a basis for reasonable suspicion based on sole access by one employee.*

The employer has the burden of establishing that the specific individual to be tested is "reasonably suspected" of involvement in the specific economic loss or injury for the requirement in section [200]7(d) (3) to be met."

Defendants have failed to establish that there is a genuine issue regarding the requisite "reasonable suspicion" that Plaintiff was involved in the missing notary seals and/or the cash shortages at 53rd-Ellis. Miller's deposition testimony and Defendant's entire argument indicate that reasonable suspicion was premised solely upon the fact that Plaintiff had access to the missing notary seals and to the cash. Defendants do not—and could not consistent with the uncontested facts—argue that Plaintiff had sole access.

The fact that Plaintiff had access to the missing items is not enough. The legislative history of the EPPA and the Department of Labor's regulations state in no uncertain terms that mere access is not enough to establish the reasonable suspicion required under 29 U.S.C. section 2006(d) (3). Because all Defendants offer is Plaintiff's access, and because mere access to stolen items is as a matter of law an insufficient foundation for reasonable suspicion under the EPPA, Defendants have not met their burden under Rule 56 to "designate specific facts" that show that there is a genuine issue of fact. We "need not scour the record" to find such an issue if Defendants fail to do so.

Plaintiff is entitled to summary judgment on the issue of liability. The EPPA exemption for ongoing investigations into economic loss or injury to business is only available if the employer fulfills every one of the requirements set forth in section 2006. Defendants have not shown that there is a genuine issue for trial on the issue of reasonable suspicion. Hence, Defendants cannot, as a matter of law, prevail on the liability issue.

Case Questions

1. What additional facts would you look for to support reasonable suspicion in a case such

as this (beyond merely having access to the stolen items)?

2. Do you believe that the burden on employers under the EPPA is too great?

3. Do you believe that the EPPA adequately protects employees from unfair tests?

Integrity and Personality Tests

Because employers have been restricted in their use of polygraph tests, many have resorted to subjective tests that purport to measure honesty or integrity through analysis of written or oral answers to numerous questions.

Integrity tests are believed to measure a wide variety of constructs, such as honesty, integrity, propensity to steal, attitudes, and counterproductivity. There is general agreement among experts that integrity tests can predict a number of outcomes of interest to employers, and that they have validity levels comparable to many other kinds of tests used in employment settings. In addition, the tests have not been shown to have a consistently adverse impact on any one protected group. However, like the polygraph, integrity tests are likely to have many false positives, and are difficult to validate (e.g., some have used polygraph tests or past criminal behavior).

While the validity of such tests in discovering useful employment-related information remains at issue, the tests have not been shown to have a consistently adverse impact on any one protected group.

Personality tests have also become a viable option in preemployment selection screening. As with other nontraditional selection strategies, these tests have proven to be free from discriminatory selection results. Personality tests should not be confused with intelligence tests, which have suffered a great deal of criticism in connection with their potential for disparate impact discrimination against various minority groups. It is generally agreed that a basic intelligence test is too blunt an instrument with which to determine any specific employment-related results.

Personality tests have recently been shown to reasonably predict job performance behaviors across a variety of jobs (for example, service job and military personnel) using various criteria of performance (e.g., tenure and supervisory performance ratings). However, employers must be sure their tests cover relevant dimensions of personality using a reliable and valid instrument. Some employers have resorted to dubious measures, such as handwriting analysis and other nontraditional forms of employee selection. Because of the use of these methods, several states severely restrict or prohibit various personality tests.

Soroka v. Dayton Hudson Corp.
235 Cal.App.3d 654 (1991)

Appellants Sibi Soroka, Sue Urry, and William D'Arcangelo sued Dayton Hudson claiming that its practice of requiring Target Store security officer applicants to pass a psychological screening (called the "Psychoscreen") discriminated on the basis of race, gender, religion, and physical handicap. The appellants took the test. Soroka was hired; Urry, a Mormon, and D'Arcangelo were not hired. The main functions of the store security officers (SSO) are to observe, apprehend, and arrest shoplifters. The SSOs carry handcuffs and are allowed to use force against a suspect in self-defense. Target contends that good judgment and emotional stability are important skills for the SSOs. The purpose of the Psychoscreen, Target argues, is to screen out applicants who are emotionally unstable, who may put customers or employees in jeopardy, or who will not take direction or follow store procedures.

The test used is a combination of two different accepted psychological tests. The resulting test includes questions about the applicant's religious attitudes, such as "my soul sometimes leaves my body. . . . I have no patience with people who believe there is only one true religion. . . . Everything is turning out just like the prophets of the Bible said it would." The test also includes questions regarding the applicant's sexual preference, such as "I have been in trouble one or more times because of my sex behavior. . . . I am very attracted to members of my own sex. . . . I like to talk about sex . . . Many of my dreams are about sex matters." Although the tests are scored by outside consultants and applicants are rated as to emotional stability, interpersonal style, addiction potential, dependability and reliability, and socialization, Target does not receive individual responses to the questions. Hiring decisions may be made on the basis of these recommendations, although the recommendations may be overridden.

Reardon, J.

Soroka . . . argues that Target has not demonstrated that its Psychoscreen questions are job-related, that is, that they provide information relevant to the emotional stability of its SSO applicants. Having considered the religious belief and sexual orientation questions carefully, we find this contention . . . persuasive.

Although the state right of privacy is broader than the federal right, California courts construing article I, section I of the California constitution have looked to federal precedents for guidance. Under the lower federal standard, employees may not be compelled to submit to a violation of their right to privacy unless a clear, direct nexus exists between the nature of the employee's duty and the nature of the violation. We are satisfied that this nexus requirement applies with even greater force under article I, section I.

. . . we turn to the voter's interpretation of article I, section I. The ballot argument, the only legislative history for the privacy amendment, specifically states that one purpose of the constitutional right of privacy is to prevent businesses from "collecting unnecessary information about us." It also asserts that the right to privacy would "preclude the collection of *extraneous or frivo-*

lous information." Thus, the ballot language requires that the information collected be necessary to achieve the purpose for which the information has been gathered.

The California Supreme Court has also recognized this nexus requirement. When it found that public employees could not be compelled to take a polygraph test, it criticized the questions asked as both highly personal and unrelated to any employment duties. It found that a public employer may require its workers to answer some questions but only those that specifically, directly, and narrowly relate to the performance of the employee's official duties.

While Target unquestionably has an interest in employing emotionally stable persons to be SSOs, testing applicants about their religious beliefs and sexual orientation does not further this interest. To justify the invasion of privacy resulting from the use of the Psychoscreen, Target must

demonstrate a compelling interest and must establish that the test serves a job-related interest. [The court found that Target did not do so.]

Case Questions

1. Why do you think Target administered this test? What did it learn about each applicant as a result of the test?

2. Is there any relevance between the responses to the questions asked and the individual's ability to perform the job?

3. If Target's main purpose was to determine emotional stability, what other method could it have used to obtain this information about its applicants?

One of the difficulties in using personality or other less objective testing techniques for employment purposes is the concept of **face validity.** Face validity is concerned with whether a test appears to measure what it is supposed to measure. No statistical properties are involved. While not a technical or legally recognized form of validity, face validity can often be important in avoiding legal action based solely on the test taker's perception of what the test assesses. As in *Soroka* above, even if the questions in the Psychoscreen had not invaded the privacy of the test takers, the appellants might still have brought legal action based on the apparent lack of relationship to the job. Simply because a test is an accepted psychological measure does not make that test relevant to a particular job, nor does it validate its use in any situation.

Face validity
A test which looks well suited to its purpose.

Currently there are reliable personality measures available which avoid using the type of items used in the Psychoscreen that seem a particular invasion of privacy. Employers must be aware of the types of items used on any tests and their relationship to the job in order to shield themselves from legal liability.

Physical Ability Testing

Whereas tests of general skills are often used to find out whether job applicants have the mental ability to perform a certain job, and integrity tests are used as an indicator of whether an applicant will engage in counterproductive behaviors such as theft, physical ability tests are administered to applicants seeking particularly physically demanding jobs. This type of test is used to increase the likelihood candidates will be able to perform the essential physical functions of the job in question. Because the ADA calls for the testing of essential functions, general tests of fitness may no longer be an appropriate means of testing for physical fitness. For instance, physical ability tests in the past might have required applicants to perform sit-ups, lift weights, and run certain distances. The logic of this test approach is that those who do better on these events are more physically fit, and thus better able to perform the physical tasks of the job in question.

This approach is problematic under the ADA, however, because an employer can only test for an applicant's ability to perform the essential functions of the job and most jobs do not directly require employees to do sit-ups or lift weights. Under current laws, physical ability testing usually results in some type of job simulation. For example, a physical ability exam for entry-level firefighters might require applicants to drag hoses, open fire hydrants, or climb ladders. Job simulations imply a content approach to test validation because the test components are direct samples of the job domain. This approach to physical ability testing is used extensively in the public sector.

Drug and Alcohol Testing

Based on the 1998 Annual National Household survey, 73 percent of all current illegal drug users 18 or older were employed in 1997. In response to the growing problem of drugs in the workplace (70 percent of all illegal drug users are employed) and related injuries and accidents, former President George Bush enacted the Drug-Free Workplace Act in 1988, which authorized the drug testing (or "biochemical surveillance") of federal employees under certain circumstances. Widely publicized estimates suggest that illegal drug use costs American businesses more than $60 billion annually. The cost impacts to businesses of drug use in the workplace based on congressional findings include a 66 percent higher absenteeism rate among drug users, 300 percent higher rate of health benefit utilization, 90 percent higher rate of disciplinary actions, a finding that 47 percent of workplace accidents are drug-related, and that employee turnover is significantly higher.

Preemployment screening of job applicants and testing as a part of a rehabilitation program are allowed by the act. In addition, the act requires that federal contractors and grant recipients satisfy certain requirements designed to eliminate the effects of elicit drugs from the workplace. In response to the act, all federal agencies established individual drug-use testing programs designed to ensure the safety and security of the government and the public. For example, the Department of Defense has instituted an employee assistance program that focuses on counseling and rehabilitation, in addition to self and supervisory referrals to substance abuse treatment clinics.

The act also provides that, for a drug-use testing program to be legal, the covered employers must post and distribute a policy statement explaining the unlawful manufacture, distribution, dispensation, possession, or use of controlled substances is prohibited. Discipline or sanctions against the offending employee are left to the employer's discretion. However, if a criminal conviction arises from a workplace

EXHIBIT 14–7   Executive Order 12564, September 15, 1986: Drug-free Workplace Act

I, Ronald Reagan, President of the United States of America, find that:

Drug use is having serious adverse effects upon a significant proportion of the national work force and results in billions of dollars of lost productivity each year;

The Federal government, as an employer, is concerned with the well-being of its employees, the successful accomplishment of agency missions, and the need to maintain employee productivity;

The Federal government, as the largest employer in the nation, can and should show the way towards achieving drug-free work places through a program designed to offer drug users a helping hand and, at the same time, demonstrating to drug users and potential drug users that drugs will not be tolerated in the Federal work place.

EXHIBIT 14–8   Benefits and Drawbacks of a Drug-free Workplace Policy (DFWP)

The Benefits

- Ridding the workplace of substance abuse can improve morale, increase productivity and create a competitive advantage.
- A comprehensive program may qualify an employer for discounts on workers' compensation and other insurance premiums.
- The prevention of a single accident or injury may pay for the entire program costs for several years.
- Some contractors may need to have a DFWP to be eligible for business.
- Many employers have successfully formulated policies which deal with ethical and privacy issues, and have successfully controlled their responsibility for, and the costs associated with, treatment and rehabilitation benefits.
- Unions have initiated DFWPs with employers to promote good public relations and recapture work for their members.
- Having a DFWP sends a very clear message to employees, their families and the community as to the company's position on illegal drug use.

The Drawbacks

- A DFWP can increase distrust between management and workers, and degrade morale and productivity in some workplaces.
- A comprehensive DFWP could add significantly to the cost of doing business.
- False accusations, misidentification of employees as drug users, unjustified dismissals and violation of confidentiality obligations could prompt burdensome litigation.
- Identifying substance users may entail an obligation to provide costly counseling and treatment for a relapsing condition. It is not always easy to contain the financial drain, and health insurance premiums could rise.
- A DFWP, particularly one that features drug testing, can raise serious ethical and privacy issues.
- Where the workplace is organized, the employer faces additional negotiations with the union.

Exhibit 14–8 Continued

Drug-Free Workplace Policy Checklist
1. What is our current company policy regarding the use of alcohol and other drugs?
2. How much of a drug or alcohol problem does our company have at the present time?
3. What is the nature of the problem (absenteeism, quality, productivity, safety, etc.)?
4. How much does this problem cost the company?
5. What type of DFWP would be most likely to improve the situation?
   a. urine testing
   b. impairment testing
   c. under the influence testing
   d. better supervision and quality control
   e. Employee Assistance Plan
   f. a combination of the above
6. If testing is involved, who will be tested?
   a. applicants
   b. employees in safety sensitive positions
   c. all employees
7. Under what circumstances will testing be done?
   a. pre-employment
   b. for cause
   c. random
   d. combination
8. What will be done with those who fail the test?
9. What action will be taken regarding those who refuse to be tested?
10. What would be the costs of such a program?
11. What would be the benefits? How much would the problems described in 3 & 4 above be reduced by the program? How great is the financial benefit of the reduction?
12. Do the projected benefits justify the costs?
13. Which proposed components of the DFWP are cost effective?
14. How do the company's employees feel about the proposed DFWP? Would they be more supportive of another option? Have we sought their input?
15. (If the company is organized) Has the proposed DFWP been negotiated with the union?
16. Is the proposed DFWP consistent with company values?
17. Is the proposed DFWP legal in the jurisdictions where it will be implemented?

Choosing a Policy
The first step in developing a policy is to decide whether to have a DFWP. Some employers may choose instead to judge employees simply on the basis of performance. Once a company has made a basic policy choice, it can consider in more detail the objectives it intends to achieve. There are a variety of possible motivations for pursuing such a program:
1. *Complying with legal requirements.* Under federal law, some employers are required to establish DFWPs, including engaging in drug (and possibly alcohol) testing.
2. *Reducing liability risks.* Having a DFWP may be viewed as assisting in the defense against certain legal actions, although DFWPs may also generate other kinds of claims.
3. *Reducing business costs due to accidents, absenteeism and ill health.* Eliminating drug use is seen as a way to promote safety and efficiency, improve the health of the workforce and curtail use of sick leave, medical benefits and workers' compensation.
4. *Ensuring the integrity of employees.* A potential cause of theft, pilferage and blackmail is removed, and workers' confidence in each other is enhanced.

EXHIBIT 14–8   Concluded

5. *Determining fitness for duty and corroborating evidence of misconduct.* A DFWP may help establish uniformity in standards of behavior and in discipline imposed. To establish the DFWP the employer must determine the proper balance between punitive and rehabilitative elements of the program. Being identified as substance abuser may lead to discharge, but there may also be an attempt at rehabilitating employees and returning them to duty.

6. *Assuring public confidence in the business.* The employer prevents embarrassment by taking genuine steps to deal with employees who are affected by substance abuse.

7. *Promoting a "drug-free" society.* Many employers, seeing themselves as responsible members of society, sense a moral obligation to support law enforcement efforts against illicit drugs. NIDA has stated its "belief that the fight against illegal drugs in the workplace is critical to the nation's war against drug use." It has encouraged private employers to adopt DFWPs.

Source: ABA Section of Labor and Employment Law, *Attorney's Guide to Drugs in the Workplace* (1996). Reprinted with permission.

substance abuse offense, the employer is required to administer an employment sanction, or advise and direct the employee to an approved substance abuse treatment program. To protect the employee's right to due process, the employer must educate the workforce of any drug/alcohol policy and testing procedures. In addition, laboratory and screening procedures must meet certain standards. In one case, *Fraternal Order of Police v. Tucker,* the court concluded that the employees were denied due process, because they were not informed of the basis of the employer's suspicion, and because they were not offered the opportunity to rebut the employer's claims.

NATIONAL TREASURY EMPLOYEES UNION V. VON RAAB
489 U.S. 656 (1989)

The United States Customs Service implemented a drug screening program which required urinalysis tests of service employees who wanted to be transferred or promoted to positions where there might be some contact with drugs, such as confiscation, or where the employee might have to carry a firearm or handle classified material. The program provides that the results of the test may not be turned over to any other agency without the employee's written consent. The petitioners, a federal employees' union and one of its officials, sued claiming a violation of the Fourth Amendment. The district court agreed and enjoined the program because the plan was overly intrusive without probable cause or reasonable suspicion. The court of appeals vacated the injunction, holding that this type of search was reasonable in light of its limited scope and the service's strong interest in detecting drug use among employees in certain positions. The Supreme Court affirmed in connection with positions involving contact with drugs and/or firearms but vacated and remanded the decision in regards to those positions which require handling of classified materials.

Kennedy, J.

In *Skinner v. Railway Labor Executives Assn.,* decided today, we held that federal regulations requiring employees of private railroads to produce urine samples for chemical testing implicate the Fourth Amendment, as those tests invade reasonable expectations of privacy. Our earlier cases have settled that the Fourth Amendment protects individuals from unreasonable searches conducted by the Government, even when the Government acts as an employer and, in view of our holding in *Railway Labor* that urine tests are searches, it follows that the Customs Service's drug testing program must meet the reasonableness requirement of the Fourth Amendment.

While we have often emphasized and reiterate today that a search must be supported, as a general matter, by warrant issued upon probable cause, our decision in *Railway Labor* reaffirms the longstanding principle that neither a warrant nor probable cause, nor, indeed, any measure of individualized suspicion, is an indispensable component of reasonableness in every circumstance. As we note in *Railway Labor,* our cases establish that where a Fourth Amendment intrusion serves special governmental needs, beyond the normal need for law enforcement, it is necessary to balance the individual's privacy expectations against the Government's interests to determine whether it is impractical to require a warrant or some level of individualized suspicion in the particular context.

It is clear that the Customs Service's drug testing program is not designed to serve the ordinary needs of law enforcement. Test results may not be used in criminal prosecution of the employee without the employee's consent. The purposes of the program are to deter drug use among those eligible for promotion to sensitive positions within the Service and to prevent the promotion of drug users to those positions. These substantial interests, no less than the Government's concern for safe rail transportation at issue in *Railway Labor,* present a special need that may justify departure from the ordinary warrant and probable cause requirements.

Petitioners do not contend that a warrant is required by the balance of privacy and governmental interests in this context, nor could any such contention withstand scrutiny. We have recognized that requiring the Government to procure a warrant for every work-related intrusion "would conflict with 'the common sense realization that government offices could not function if every employment decision became a constitutional matter.'"

Even where it is reasonable to dispense with the warrant requirement in the particular circumstances, a search ordinarily must be based on probable cause. . . . We think Customs employees who are directly involved in the interdiction of illegal drugs or who are required to carry firearms in the line of duty likewise have a diminished expectation of privacy in respect to intrusions occasioned by a urine test. Because successful performance of their duties depends uniquely on their judgment and dexterity, these employees cannot reasonably expect to keep from the Service personal information that bears directly on their fitness.

In sum, we believe that the Government has demonstrated that its compelling interests in safeguarding our borders and the public safety outweigh the privacy expectations of employees who seek to be promoted to positions that directly involve the interdiction of illegal drugs or who are required to carry a firearm. We hold that the testing of these employees is reasonable under the Fourth Amendment.

Case Questions

1. An approved drug-use test must be conducted within reasonable parameters. In *Capua,* the court determined that a urine collection process may not be reasonable if "done under close surveillance of a government representative [as it] is likely to be a very embarrassing and humiliating experience." Courts will generally balance the employee's rights against the employer's stated basis for the test and determine whether the cause of the test is reasonable and substantial. For

instance, in *Skinner v. Railway Labor Executives Assn.,* the Supreme Court stated that the railway employees had a reduced expectation of privacy due to the highly regulated nature of the industry. In addition, societal interests, such as safety and security of the railways, may outweigh the individual employee's privacy interests. When might this be the case?

2. Why do you think the Court made a distinction between positions involving contact with drugs and firearms and positions that require handling of classified materials?

The legality of drug testing relies, in part, on the reliability and effectiveness of the testing procedure itself. The most common form of employee drug-use screening test is an immunoassay test. The typical test kit will include a number of solutions (reagents) that are added to a urine sample. When the reagent containing a drug antibody is mixed with the urine, any drug-infected urine will become more dense. When the change in density is visible, the test result is positive. Confirmatory tests should then be administered. The test costs between $4.50 and $25.00 depending on the number of drugs that the employer wants to test.

The immunoassay test has several limitations. First, the test is subject to cross-reactivity, where the test detects small amounts of similarly structured drugs, some of which are not illegal. Second, the test does not evidence the time or quantity of ingestion, or the effects of the impairment on job performance. In addition, the test only investigates the presence of one drug at a time.

A second form of drug testing, testing hair follicles ("radioimmunoassay of hair"), has therefore become more popular among employers. This test works on the theory that substances are absorbed into the bloodstream and incorporated into the hair as it grows. A hair follicle test can purportedly determine the chronology and degree of the subject's drug use by reporting what was in the body at the time the hair was formed in the follicle. Any positive response is confirmed by a more sensitive gas chromatography/mass spectrometry test. The procedure involves cutting a small amount of hair from the subject, approximately one and one-half inches in length from the back of the head so as to remain physically unnoticed. The sample is placed in a collection envelope, which is immediately sealed and transported to a testing facility.

Because of the sampling technique, hair follicle testing is slightly less intrusive than are urinalyses. Many urinalysis examinations are monitored to prevent tampering or contamination; this type of intrusion into personal activities would not be required in a follicle exam. In addition, the window of detection opened by a follicle test is much greater than that of a urinalysis. The follicle test is reliable up to a period of approximately three months, compared with the one- to three-day window of reliability for urinalysis.

On the other hand, many of the arguments that arise in connection with urinalysis drug testing can be repeated here. Hair follicle testing provides much quantifiable information regarding the amount of drugs ingested, and the time over which the drugs were taken. Given its ability to reveal extensive information, follicle testing has been attacked as an unreasonable intrusion into the subject's private life in connection with unregulated and unrelated off-work activities. Decision makers should keep in mind the decision of the Sixth Circuit Court in *Baggs v. Eagle-Picher Industries, Inc.,* that represents a somewhat minority perspective on the issue of testing. In applying Michigan law, the court held that an employer can use "intrusive and even objectionable means to obtain employment-related information about an employee."

In a recent study performed by Steelcase Corporation, the firm found that the overall positive response rate jumped from 2.7 percent, when urinalyses were used to detect marijuana and cocaine usage, to 18.0 percent, when hair follicle testing was used. In follow-up interviews, individuals who tested negative for substance usage, according to the urinalysis, but positive, according to the follicle test, reported that they did actually use illegal substances some time within the three months prior to the examination.

One additional issue raised by drug and alcohol testing involves the Americans with Disabilities Act. The act, which applies to private sector employers, provides that individuals who currently use illegal drugs are not considered individuals with disabilities. However, if an employee or applicant is pursuing or has successfully completed a rehabilitation program, and demonstrates that they have a disability based on prior use, she or he is covered by the act and therefore entitled to reasonable accommodation. (See Chapter 13 regarding the ADA.)

The Drug-Free Workplace Act does not apply to private sector employers. An increasing number of private employers have implemented drug programs for their employees. According to congressional testimony given by Lawrence Bennett, a spokesperson for the Coalition for a Drug Free Greater Cincinnati, 98 percent of *Fortune* 200 companies have drug-free workplace programs in place. Private employers have generally followed the guidelines set forth in the act of 1989 in the institution of their own programs, and such programs have generally been upheld where reasonable procedures are followed. There do exist several occupation-specific regulations that restrict or require drug testing of employees. Where the government requires or actively encourages testing by the private sector, the testing may be subject to constitutional scrutiny. For instance, the Department of Transportation (DOT) requires private sector transportation employers to randomly drug test employees in safety or security-related positions. In addition, under certain circumstances, DOT requires preemployment and periodic testing, testing where reasonable cause exists, and subsequent to any accidents. An employee who tests positive is removed from her or his position and can only return after successful completion of a rehabilitation program. These requirements must meet constitutional requirements of privacy and due process, even though the testing is actually carried out by private employers.

On June 23, 1998, the House of Representatives passed the Drug-Free Workplace Act of 1998, aimed at providing small businesses—who often lack the resources and infrastructure to conduct employee drug tests—financial resources and technical assistance for implementing drug testing programs. The three purposes of the act are to (1) educate small business concerns about the advantages of a drug-free workplace; (2) provide financial incentives and technical assistance to enable small business concerns to create a drug-free workplace; and (3) assist working parents in keeping their children drug free. The Drug-Free Workplace Act of 1998 provides a $10 million grant program for nonprofit organizations that have the ability to provide technical assistance to small businesses in establishing drug-free policies.

Additionally, 23 states have enacted legislation designed to protect the privacy of private sector employees. These state laws vary in their approach; some states offer a great deal of protection for employees and may be classified as pro-employee (such as Connecticut, California, and Minnesota), while other states allow testing after satisfaction of only modest burdens and are classified as pro-employer (such as Utah).

It should be noted there are legal scholars who believe that the connection between the recreational use of drugs and low productivity is nonexistent. Some researchers have been shocked by low levels of drug-related absenteeism and terminations in their studies. Others have found no effect from drug use on worksite performance and have criticized misleading characteristics of pro-drug testing data. Instead, they contend that, even if the data were supportive of testing, drug testing ignores the presumption of innocence guaranteed to each individual. In many situations, a refusal to submit to a drug test is treated as an admission of drug usage.

Medical Testing

Many employers require preemployment, postoffer medical tests to ensure that the applicant is physically capable of performing the requirements of the position. Medical examinations are prohibited only prior to the offer to protect against wrongful discrimination based on a discovered disability. Pursuant to the Americans with Disabilities Act and the Vocational Rehabilitation Act, an employer may not reach an employment determination on the basis of a disability, where the applicant (or employee) is otherwise qualified for the position, with or without reasonable accommodation. (For more on disability discrimination, see Chapter 13.)

Medical examinations subsequent to the offer of employment but prior to the actual employment are allowed under the acts for the purpose of determining whether an employee is able to perform the job for which she or he has been hired. The acts require, however, that all employees within the same job category be subject to the medical examination requirement; individual applicants may not be singled out. In addition, all information generated through the examination process must be maintained in confidential files, separate from other general personnel-related information.

Subsequent to the applicant's employment, no medical examination may be required unless the test is job-related and justified by business necessity.

Genetic testing
Investigation and evaluation of an individual's biological predispositions based on the presence of a specific disease-associated gene on an individual's chromosomes.

Genetic Testing

Genetic testing is a scientific development that involves the use of laser and computer technology. Scientists make diagnostic predictions by locating a specific disease-associated gene on an individual's chromosomes. This type of testing evolved in the 1960s in connection with research regarding individuals who were "hypersusceptible" to certain chemicals used in certain workplaces. By testing an applicant's genes, the researchers were able to ascertain which applicants would be expected to experience negative reactions to various chemicals. Two decades later, Congress asked the Office of Technology Assessment (OTA) to conduct a study in the area. The OTA concluded in 1983 that "none of the genetic tests evaluated by the OTA meets established scientific criteria for routine use in an occupational setting. However, there is enough suggestive evidence to merit further research."

Today, with the tremendous advances in medicine and technology, employers who choose to use genetic testing would have tremendous amounts of information at their fingertips. Governments and private-sector firms are rushing to map the entire human genome for the purposes of preventing and treating countless health problems. However, there does not yet exist any federal legislation or regulations restricting the use of this personal, private, and potentially volatile information. The fear includes the concern that an employer might discover something about an individual's genetic makeup that points to the *potential* for a debilitating disease and therefore may choose not to hire the individual based on that potential, even though the person may never develop that disease. In addition, the individual might have no previous knowledge of her disposition towards the disease and, in fact, might not want to know. Should the employer let that person know the reasons for their failure to get the job? Taken to an extreme, genetic testing might allow society to separate individuals on the basis of their potential for disease—a result that should not be taken lightly. Simply because we have the ability to test for something, does that mean that we should?

Moreover, genetic testing is far from perfect. Researchers have discovered that some of the genetic differences found in the test might be due to damage to the genes from the test itself. Similarly, the tests (in their present technological state) evidence only the response of the sample to the presence of a certain toxic agent. The results show merely that the subject is more susceptible to that toxic agent than someone else. Only infrequently can the test show more than this mere susceptibility or potentiality.

One additional issue raised by genetic testing is based on the fact that the genetic irregularities that may substantially impair a major life activity may be considered protected disabilities under the Americans with Disabilities and Vocational

Rehabilitation Acts. A genetic test may only encourage discrimination based on myths, fears, and stereotypes about genetic differences.

In addition, at least 21 states prohibit or limit genetic testing as a matter of law. Except to determine an employee's susceptibility or level of exposure to potentially toxic chemicals in the workplace, employers in several states, including New Hampshire, Illinois, North Carolina, Rhode Island, Vermont and Wisconsin, are prohibited from using genetic testing as a condition of employment. Many states also prohibit discrimination and employment decisions made on the basis of genetic information.

HIV/AIDS Testing

Employers unreasonably fearful about the onslaught of **HIV** in the workplace and the effect it will have on their workforces are anxious to test their employees or applicants for the presence of HIV. However, the HIV test in the workplace is inappropriate for two reasons. First, for the test to be justified, it must serve a legitimate business purpose. Because HIV is not transmitted by casual contact of the sort that takes place in a work environment, an HIV test is improper for most positions. Second, the test only reports the subject's status as of several weeks, if not months, in the past. The test does not determine the HIV status of the individual as of the day of the examination. Therefore, unless the employer monitors and restricts the employee's off-work activities prior to the test and between testing, the inquiry is inefficient and ineffective.

In addition, an employer may not take an adverse employment action against an employee merely based on the knowledge that the individual is HIV-positive. That employee or applicant is protected by both the federal Vocational Rehabilitation Act as well as the Americans with Disabilities Act. These acts provide that an employer may not make an employment decision based on the individual's HIV status, where the person is otherwise qualified to perform the essential requirements of the position.

Frequently called the "AIDS Test," the HIV test does not actually test for **AIDS.** Instead, it tests for the presence of antibodies to HIV in the blood. If the first test performed—called the ELISA (Enzyme Linked Immunosorbent Assay)—is positive, a second ELISA test is performed to confirm the results. If that is positive, an additional test, the Western Blot, is conducted. One's body *may* take as long as six months to produce the HIV antibodies. A negative test result may be irrelevant if taken less than six months since the subject's last transmissive activity.

One area of HIV testing that has received a great deal of attention is the testing of health care workers (HCW) and the disclosure of their results. Several arguments can be made against mandatory testing of HCWs, but proponents of testing have a response for each. The first argument is that it is a waste of time and money to test workers, because the actual risk of HIV transmission is so small. In fact the chances of HCW transmission to a patient have been compared to the chances of a fatal accident occurring on the way to the hospital.

HIV
Human immunodeficiency virus, the virus that causes AIDS.

AIDS
Acquired immune deficiency syndrome, a syndrome in which the individual's immune system ceases to function properly and during which the individual is susceptible, in most cases fatally, to opportunistic diseases. AIDS is not transmitted through casual contact; to transmit the disease, there must be an exchange of fluids. The disease may be transmitted through sexual contact, during which there is an exchange of bodily fluids; needle sharing; or an exchange of blood.

As of June 30, 1998, the Centers for Disease Control and Prevention (CDCP) were aware of 54 health care workers (HCWs) in the United States who have had documented HIV seroconversion following occupational exposures, which means they tested negative for HIV infection around the time of exposure, but tested HIV positive within a year after the exposure. Another 133 HIV-infected health care workers have been classified as having possible cases of occupational transmission. These 133 health care workers have a history of occupational exposure to blood, other body fluids, or HIV-infected laboratory material and report no other risk factors for HIV infection, but do not have documentation of seroconversion after the occupational exposure. On May 6, 1991, *Newsweek* reported figures from the CDCP that the chances of a patient being infected with HIV from a health care worker are between 1 in 42,000 and 1 in 417,000.

Proponents of testing argue that the justification lies in the certainty that surgeons do cut themselves in surgery. In fact, a surgeon cuts a glove in approximately one out of every four cases and sustains a significant skin cut in 1 out of every 40 cases.

The second argument against testing is that the expense of testing these workers not only would take away from available funds for researching an HIV cure but would be excessive and unnecessary, due to the frequency of testing that would be necessary. Frequent testing is necessary, due to the test's inability to verify HIV status up until the date of the test. In fact, if an HCW were tested today, that test would evidence his or her condition as of six months prior to today. Because no one has yet suggested that the HCW disclose all transmissive activities since a time six months prior to testing, and because hospitals have not yet proposed testing on a daily basis (to prevent transmission as a result of the previous night's activities), testing appears to be a worthy cause but a futile effort.

Yet proponents question whether it is possible there is a way of testing that is both efficient and economical. Drug and HIV testing in the military is evidence that a mass mandatory testing program is possible. In fact, the military is able to test for HIV at a cost of less than $3 per test, with a false-positive rate of close to zero. Timely, inexpensive, and accurate tests are available; it is unlikely that their costs will exhaust research funds.

The third argument against testing is that, if testing becomes mandatory, it would act as a declaration our society has no faith or trust in HCWs. In effect, society would be testing the Hippocratic oath by which each HCW is required to abide every time an HIV test is administered. Many patients would refuse to see their doctor unless the results of the doctor's HIV test were available.

Proponents would respond, however, that even now many patients do not merely rely on the doctor's oath to make sure that they will receive professional treatment. News stories abound regarding unnecessary tests given to patients who have the money, and the failure to give certain tests or treatment to those who do not have the money. By making testing mandatory, society and lawmakers are recognizing that the health care industry should take affirmative steps to protect the public from sickness. A fundamental part of the Hippocratic oath is that a physician should cause no harm. Mandatory testing is one manner by which to guarantee this oath to the public.

An additional societal cost is the investment that society has made in training thousands of HCWs. This investment would be lost, causing a need to train replacements and to retrain the infected HCWs to preclude their burden on America's welfare system. The economic costs would be devastating to society in the additional form of increased health care costs. Moreover, the basic rights of all HCWs would be undermined. The right to privacy is a fundamental right, one that should not be revoked. Once the door to testing employees is opened for HIV testing, the borderline that protects employees and applicants from discriminatory tests will become blurred. If mandatory testing is invoked, the government will in effect be undermining its own efforts to stem discrimination against disabled employees and to ground policies in fact, rather than in fear.

Finally, the lives of thousands of HCWs and their loved ones will be shattered. The problems these people will face range from loss of friends to loss of employment to loss of insurance to loss of self-esteem. It is clear that the problem facing this industry comprises not only whether to implement mandatory testing but what to do if an HCW finds he is HIV-positive. The options facing the employee are few, at best.

GLOVER V. EASTERN NEBRASKA COMMUNITY OFFICE OF RETARDATION

686 F.Supp. 243 (D.Neb. 1988), affirmed 867 F.2d 461 (8th Cir. 1989)

Eastern Nebraska Human Services Agency implemented a policy, called the Chronic Infectious Disease Policy, which required certain employees to submit to mandatory testing for tuberculosis and HIV. The policy was enforced at all branches of the Agency, including the Eastern Nebraska Community Office of Retardation (ENCOR), which provides residential services for the mentally disabled. Staff members at ENCOR consistently deal with clients who bite, scratch, throw objects, hit, pinch, and have otherwise violent outbursts. The rationale for testing employees in certain positions at ENCOR is that these positions involve extensive contact with clients. A number of employees filed suit to enjoin the enforcement of the policy.

Stron, J.

[The court evaluated the low probability that even a positive response on the HIV blood tests may mean that the individual is infected, given the low incidence rate *at that time* for HIV in Nebraska. In addition, the court cited its understanding that, as a result of the foreboding message that accompanies a positive HIV test result, an individual may not wish to know if she is infected.] The evidence establishes that the risk of transmission of the AIDS virus from staff to client, assuming a staff member is infected with HIV, in the ENCOR environment is extremely low, approaching zero. The medical evidence is undisputed that the disease is not contracted by casual contact. The risk of transmission of the disease to clients as a result of a client biting or scratching a staff member, and potentially drawing blood, is extraordinarily low, also approaching zero. The risk of transmission of the virus from staff to client due to the staff member attending to a client's personal hygiene needs is zero. Further, there is no evidence of drug use or needle sharing at ENCOR, nor is there a problem of sexual abuse of clients by staff.

In short, the evidence in this case establishes that the risk of transmission of the HIV virus at ENCOR is minuscule at best and will have little, if any, effect in preventing the spread of HIV or in protecting the clients. Further, from a medical view, this policy is not necessary to protect clients from any medical risks.

Individuals have a reasonable expectation of privacy in the personal information their bodily fluids contain. Compulsory administration of a blood test "plainly involves the broadly conceived reach of a search and seizure under the Fourth Amendment."

The Court is convinced that the evidence, considered in its entirety, leads to the conclusion that the policy was prompted by concerns about the AIDS virus, formulated with little or erroneous medical knowledge, and is a constitutionally impermissible reaction to a devastating disease with no known cure. The risk of transmitting HIV at ENCOR does not justify the implementation of such a sweeping policy which ignores and violates the staff members' constitutional rights.

Case Questions

1. Note that the court in *Anonymous Fireman v. City of Willoughby* (779 F.Supp. 402 (N.D.Oh. 1991) upheld the city's policy of mandatory HIV testing for firefighters and paramedics as part of the city's annual physical examination and, in doing so, found no constitutional violations. Given the disparity among different courts' application of the Fourth Amendment to various factual situations, how would you construct your company's policy?

2. Given the fatality rate of HIV-positive individuals, is it relevant that the court found a "low probability" of infection following a positive response on the blood test? Is it critical to this decision that an individual may not want to know whether she or he is HIV-positive? Couldn't the hospital test and then not disclose to the person tested? Is that ethical?

3. If ENCOR is not allowed to test for HIV, how should it protect its residents from possible transmission?

Management Considerations

A workplace substance abuse program should incorporate (1) a written abuse policy that has been drafted after input from employees, (2) a supervisory training program, (3) an employee education and awareness program, (4) access to an employee assistance program, and (5) a drug testing program, where appropriate.

There are three possible corporate approaches for testing employees for ineligibility. First, the employer may establish mandatory testing, which requires that all employees be tested for drug or alcohol use, or some other form of ineligibility

EXHIBIT 14–9

The U.S. Department of Health and Human Services prescribes the following process by which to establish drug testing in a workplace.

1. Determine the need for drug testing in your work setting.
   - Examine the employee assistance program utilization.
   - Administer a confidential survey.
   - Conduct a cost benefit analysis. (Costs: initial screen plus confirmation tests, staffing and training; Benefits: potential savings from reduced sick leave, absenteeism, health benefits utilization.)
   - Assess health insurance utilization, accidents, safety complaints.
2. Develop a drug testing policy.
   - Consult legal resources.
   - Develop goal, rationale, limitations of drug testing.
   - Specific drugs to test. (Marijuana, cocaine, amphetamines, opiates, and phencyclidine (PCP) are those for which employees are most often tested.)
   - Set up disciplinary process and employee assistance program (EAP) referral process.
   - Specify details of collection, lab testing procedures, including chain of custody.
   - Set up conditions for designating sensitive positions where random testing.

when they enter a specific program or at the time of their annual physical. Second, an employer may implement "probable cause" testing, where an employer tests employees only if there is suspicion of ineligibility, and testing is implemented for the purpose of discovering a safety, conduct, or performance problem. Third, employers may implement random testing.

The decision about what method to use for testing will depend on the goals of the employer. Does it want to test its entire workforce? Or merely potential problem employees? In any case, an employer should look carefully at state and local laws in connection with specific test-related legislation, as well as at statutes regarding privacy and so on. Second, the employer should clearly articulate its policy regarding substance use, lie detectors, and other tests, as well as its purpose, the procedure by which this policy is enforced, and the appeals process. Third, the policy must be consistently implemented and diligently documented. Possible human and laboratory errors must be minimized. Fourth, all positive results should be confirmed with additional tests.

Exhibit 14–10

Company Drug Policy

Baxter has always had a strong commitment to its employees to provide a safe, healthy and productive work environment and to produce quality goods and services for its customers in an efficient manner. In light of that it is the company goal to achieve a work environment free of illegal drugs and substance abuse at all company locations.

While Baxter has no intention of intruding into the private lives of its employees, the company does expect employees to report for work in a condition to perform their duties. Baxter recognizes that employee off-the-job as well as on-the-job involvement with drugs can have an impact on the workplace and on our ability to accomplish our goal of a drug free work environment.

The following is the company's policy:

1. The use, sale, or possession of illegal drugs while on-the-job or on company property is a dischargeable offense. Illegal drugs will be turned over to the appropriate law enforcement agency and may result in criminal prosecution. Reporting for work with the presence of any illegal drug will result in an immediate suspension and, depending upon the circumstances, may result in discipline, including termination.

2. Pre-Employment Screening:

Beginning January 1, 1990 the company required mandatory drug testing for all job applicants. Applicants must consent to the drug screen. The failure to consent will result in a rejection of the individual's application. If the test results show the presence of an illegal drug in the body, it will result in not hiring the individual.

3. Current Employee Screening: Beginning no later than January 1, 1991 the company will require drug testing of current employees under the following circumstances:

Reasonable Suspicion:

Belief based upon objective facts or observations that could reasonably lead a supervisor/manager to suspect that an employee is using drugs. An example of reasonable suspicion would be an OSHA recordable accident. Employees testing positive will be suspended for two weeks without pay and will be referred to the EAP or other treatment program. To continue as an employee an agreement to follow the prescribed treatment program must be signed. The company may conduct periodic unannounced drug tests on the employee for a period of up to two years. The employee will be subject to termination after any subsequent positive drug screen.

Catastrophic Occurrences:

Any incident which results in greater than $4,400 of property, productivity or product loss or results in an injury to co-workers or public. Any employee testing positive and involved in a catastrophic occurrence will be subject to discipline including termination.

Safety Sensitive Jobs:

Safety sensitive jobs are those that are determined to be critical to the safety and welfare of our employees, property, product or community. Safety sensitive jobs are identified by the Division and approved by the Drug Screening Review Board. An employee testing positive in a safety sensitive job will be subject to discipline, including termination.

Universal or Announced Testing of Employee Groups:

Divisions/facilities have the option to do universal testing or announced screenings of employee groups. The company response to a positive drug screen will be the same as the response for Reasonable Suspicion.

4. The company may conduct unannounced searches for illegal drugs. Employees are expected to cooperate when such searches are conducted. If searches are conducted, a copy of the local search procedure must be posted in advance.

5. Before a facility implements any form of employee drug screening, an Employee Assistance Program (EAP) must be in place. The company offers the services of an EAP designed to help any employee whose personal problems may seriously affect his/her ability to function on the job or at home.

It is the responsibility of each employee to seek assistance from the EAP before drug problems lead to disciplinary action. Requests for assistance will be treated with the same degree of confidentiality as other requests for medical assistance.

6. Each operating unit/group is responsible for the development, implementation and administration of its own drug abuse procedures, as well as ensuring compliance with all applicable laws.

Information regarding the outcome of employee drug testing will remain confidential.

Source: Baxter Healthcare Corporation.

Management Tips

- Private sector employers are *not* generally restricted by the Fourth Amendment protection against unreasonable searches. Therefore, as a private employer, you are allowed to conduct searches under a lower standard. On the other hand, common law protections against invasions of privacy do apply in the private sector.

- You have an absolute right to determine whether someone is sufficiently healthy to do a job. The problem arises where your tests don't quite tell you that information or where you are testing for eligibility beyond the job's requirements. Make sure that your test will yield results that are relevant to the job in question.

- Health or eligibility testing should be conducted postoffer, preemployment.

- All tests should be validated; that is, they should be shown to test what they intend to test. Using an invalid test might subject you to liability.

- Restrict access to the information gained during testing. If you disclose the information to individuals who don't have a need to know it, you may be liable for an invasion of privacy or for defamation should the information turn out to be false.

- If you choose to try a polygraph test on workers, be wary of the restrictions imposed by the Employee Polygraph Protection Act.

- Since being HIV-free or AIDS-free is seldom (if ever) a BFOQ, testing for HIV is most likely to be unwarranted and a wrongful invasion of privacy.

Summary

- Testing for eligibility and ineligibility is a necessary component of the selection procedure. No employer would hire an unqualified employee if it knew the qualifications of the employee in advance of the hiring determination.

- Designing the appropriate preemployment tests in order to ensure applicants can perform the functions of the job is critical, not only to effective selection procedures but also to the prevention of liability for disparate results of your procedure.

Chapter-End Questions

1. Eule Ford was a police officer with the city of Pagedale, Missouri, police department. After working there for four years, he was appointed Pagedale's acting chief of police. One year later, Leatrice Dowd was appointed mayor and Alvin Wilson succeeded Ford as permanent chief of police. Ford and Dowd did not have a good relationship; Dowd instituted disciplinary

proceedings against him and fired him on several occasions (but the Pagedale board overturned the decisions each time). After Dowd heard a rumor that Ford was associating with a reputed drug dealer, she ordered that Ford undergo urinalysis testing and told him that failure to comply would result in serious disciplinary actions. The order requiring the testing stated that Dowd understood this rumor to mean that Ford was involved in "some type of illegal drug use and/or abuse." Ford complied with her order and all tests were found to be negative. However, Dowd's order remained in Ford's personnel file. When he later left the department and sought work elsewhere, he was unable to find employment as a result of this order in his file. Ford filed suit, claiming damages as a result of the city's wrongful and vengeful testing program. (*Ford v. Dowd,* 931 F.2d 1286 (8th Cir. 1991).)

2. After proposing a drug testing program, the FAA concluded that, while drug use is not widespread among commercial aviation personnel and there is no overwhelming drug problem in the industry, nevertheless there is concrete evidence of drug use in the commercial aviation sector. Consequently, the FAA decided that "in order to ensure that aviation safety is not compromised by a failure to detect drug users in the industry," it would establish a comprehensive random drug testing program. Aviation employees contested the testing, claiming a violation of their Fourth Amendment rights, given their contention that the tests were to be conducted without any reasonable basis for the search. What result? (*Bluestein v. Skinner,* 908 F.2d 451 (9th Cir. 1990).)

3. Sarah Borse alleges that she was employed by Piece Goods Shop, Inc., as a salesclerk for 15 years until she was fired on February 9, 1990. In January 1990, Piece Goods Shop, Inc., adopted a drug and alcohol policy requiring all employees to execute a consent to urinalysis screening for drug use as a precondition for continued employment. This consent also authorized the company to conduct searches of an employee's personal property located on company premises. Borse refused to sign the consent form, arguing that her

employer's drug and alcohol policy constituted an unreasonable interference with her right to privacy and a violation of her right to be free from unreasonable searches and seizures as guaranteed by the Constitution. (*Borse v. Piece Goods Shop, Inc.,* 758 F.Supp 263 (E.D.Pa. 1991).)

4. School bus attendant Juanita M. Jones was discharged because of her alleged marijuana use. She sued, challenging the constitutionality of drug testing by urinalysis. She believed the school system's mandatory drug testing of employees by urinalysis was a violation of the Fourth Amendment. The school contends that it maintains a responsibility to its students to ensure their safety on school buses by maintaining drug-free employees. (*Jones v. Jenkins,* 878 F.2d 1476 (D.C.Cir. 1989).)

5. Herman Smith was employed by Greyhound Lines for approximately 13 years as a clerk and was subject to the collective bargaining agreement of the union. He was responsible for receiving packages to be shipped from customers and either accepting cash or charging the transaction to the customer. On one occasion, Smith accepted two packages from a salesman and marked the receipt "charge." The salesman's company later claimed that the salesman had paid cash. Smith's terminal manager, Howard Kratovel, conducted an investigation, which seemed to show that the cash discrepancy was indeed Smith's fault. Smith was given a notice for discharge; but he was told that, if he took a polygraph test and passed, he would be reinstated with back pay. Smith signed a release, took the test, and he failed it. Smith filed a complaint against the company, alleging wrongful discharge, defamation, and invasion of privacy. (*Smith v. Greyhound Lines, Inc.,* 614 F.Supp. 558 (D.C. Pa 1984).)

6. Duke Power, in North Carolina, implemented selection requirements in 1965 that stated a potential employee needed to pass a mechanical aptitude test and a general intelligence test and have a high school diploma. There was no definitive attempt on part of the company to relate these new requirements to job requirements, since they did not affect current employees in any way. A lower district court did rule that the new requirements were permissible, because there was no evidence of discriminatory intent on Duke's part. However, statistics showed that 34 percent of white males in North Carolina at that time had high school degrees, compared to only 12 percent of black males that had high school degrees. Duke Power did emphasize the fact that Title VII allowed it to use the two tests as long as the tests were professionally developed. Were the new selection requirements discriminatory? (*Griggs v. Duke Power Co.,* 401 U.S.424 (1971).)

7. The District of Columbia's police department was charged with administering a racially discriminating test (Test 21) in recruiting new police officers. The charge was based on the fact that, although the police department did not have "intentional discrimination," Test 21 bore no relation to the job, and it screened out a disproportionate number of black applicants. The test had never been validated for job relevance, and a higher number of blacks did fail the test. The number of black officers on the police force was also not proportionate to the population mix in DC; however, the police department did show that over 44 percent of the new recruits had been black, and this figure was very close to the population mix within a 50-mile radius. The department also showed that it had consistently tried to enroll more blacks, but many of those who passed the test often failed to report for duty. Was Test 21 responsible for the low black population on the police force? (*Washington v. Davis,* 426 U.S. 229 (1976).)

8. Spurlock, a black flight officer, applied for a job with United Airlines and was rejected on his lack of two of the job requirements: a college degree and a minimum of 500 hours of flight service. Spurlock charged that these two requirements were discriminatory toward blacks, because the percentage of blacks in this country with college degrees was quantifiably less than the percentage of whites with college degrees, and, since whites had been in the industry longer, they would have a better chance of having the minimum 500-hour requirement. United defended its requirements by stating that both of these selection criteria were job related. United showed statistics that claimed applicants with a college degree were more apt to succeed in the classroom format of the preemployment training, and 500 hours' minimum was a reasonable predictor of employee success in the vigorous training program. Spurlock offered evidence on his behalf by showing that out of United's 5,900 flight officers only 9 were black; thus, there had to be some inherent discrimination in the selection process. (*Spurlock v. United Airlines,* 475 F.2d 216 (10th Cir. 1972).)

9. In response to the Drug-Free Workplace Act, the Department of Labor (DOL) instituted its Drug-Free Workplace Plan, which designated certain DOL positions as sensitive in regard to public health and safety or national security. Employees in these positions, called "testing-designated positions," could be subject to drug testing, including testing based on a reasonable suspicion of on-duty or off-duty drug use. The American Federation of Government

Employees sought to enjoin this type of testing. Will the DOL's plan hold up in court? (*AFGE v. Martin,* 969 F.2d 788 (9th Cir. 1992).)

10. How would you devise a drug testing program for a private sector workplace?

What would be the necessary components and what concerns would you have about its legality?

15 EVALUATION AND REGULATION OF JOB PERFORMANCE

Chapter Outline

SCENARIOS

SCENARIO 1

Mark Jonathan is the supervisor of 12 employees, most of whom generally perform adequate work in conformance with company job descriptions and standards. However, Mark has had problems in completing the performance appraisals of three employees.

The first employee is Gordy, a young man who went through a divorce during the past year. He was awarded custody of his children and has had a difficult time throughout this past year balancing his increased familial responsibilities with his job requirements. He has missed several important meetings as a result. Gordy has received two written warnings about his inadequate performance, and a poor year-end performance appraisal would mean an automatic dismissal. However, Mark is confident that Gordy will be able to successfully manage these two priorities in the coming year, if only given the chance. Does Mark draft an honest appraisal of his past performance with the knowledge that it would mean Gordy would lose his job according to company policy, or does he decide to use his "discretion" and offer a less than truthful assessment, knowing that it is in the company's best interest to retain this employee?

SCENARIO 2

Mark Jonathan's dilemma is accentuated by the fact that he is to review Julio, an Argentinean worker who holds a position similar to Gordy's. Julio is consistently late for work and has also received two written warnings about his inadequate performance. Mark has no idea why Julio arrives late, and, when asked, Julio offers no sufficient justification. If Mark writes a performance evaluation that highlights this poor behavior, similar to Gordy's, and terminates Julio but not Gordy (a white male), Mark is concerned about the potential for discrimination implications.

SCENARIO 3

Finally, Mark Jonathan must evaluate Rose, an employee who could be an adequate worker, except for the fact that she and Mark simply do not get along. As a result, Mark does not interact with her as much as he should to make a fair assessment of her abilities, and she hesitates to ask him questions because she does not enjoy associating with him. Consequently, she is unable to perform at the same level of those employees who constantly seek advice, supervision, and guidance. Does Mark evaluate her, given the potential for a biased appraisal, or does he admit to his superior that he is having a problem associating with an employee and cannot perform a satisfactory appraisal of his subordinate?

Performance Appraisals and Evaluation Schemes

Workplaces bring together employers and employees. Generally, employees wish to come into an organization and rise as high as they can go. Generally, an employer wishes to have qualified employees who can handle what must be done to accomplish the job. An employee who wants to progress within her or his employment organization does so by meeting the employer's expectations and doing so in an exemplary way. Employees hope to document support for their progression through **performance appraisals** (PAs). Employers wishing to have employees best suited for the job at hand must identify the best employee for promotion, demotion, retention, transfers, training, and raises. They hope to obtain the necessary information to do so through the periodic evaluation of employees. Disputes arise when an employer's expectations of the employee do not meet with the employee's understanding of the performance expected. These disputes are most often brought to light through the evaluation system.

Above all, the purpose of the performance appraisal should be to identify those characteristics the employer hopes the employee will accentuate and to dissuade the employee from exhibiting characteristics not in keeping with the organization's objectives. Performance appraisals have the potential for discriminatory effect, because discrimination may exist in the way the employer utilizes the evaluations as well as in the manner the appraisal is conducted.

Employers are not required to maintain poor performers. Termination as a result of inadequate work performance is justified by business considerations. It is the measure of adequacy that often results in an adverse impact or is the consequence of adverse treatment, which must be avoided by employers.

Of the many ways in which an employer may assess employees' performance levels, the most efficient and effective methods are those that utilize a variety of schemes to obtain the most complete job-related information.

Methods available include management by objective (MBO), which requires the manager and the employee to jointly set objectives that must be met within a specified time period. If the goal is not reached by the deadline as agreed, the employee's performance is deemed unsatisfactory. Another example of a performance appraisal system is the checklist system (weighted or nonweighted), which evaluates each employee according to a list of behaviors found to be related to job performance. In advance, the checklist is prepared (and weighted, if necessary) based on the effectiveness by job experts. A third approach is called the "summated scale," which requires supervisors to indicate how often the employee satisfies (how much the employee agrees, how strong the employee represents, and so on) each of several behavior-based statements, both desirable and undesirable.

Performance appraisal
A periodic assessment of an employee's performance, usually completed by her or his immediate supervisor and reviewed, at times, by others in the company.

Legal Implications of Performance Appraisal Systems

Given their potential for inherent subjectivity, as well as biased or skewed results, performance appraisal schemes are prone to abuse and criticism. It is undeniable that it is integral to the proper management of any workplace to have the ability to evaluate the performance of its employees, but there remain concerns regarding the efficacy and propriety of the evaluation systems available. The area of performance appraisal systems has been compared to a fire truck that is able to put out a fire only because its faulty brakes failed to stop the truck outside of the burning building. The truck instead roars directly into the building, dousing the flames as

---

EXHIBIT 15-1   Myths about Performance Evaluations

1. An employer can't be liable for giving a negative reference as long as it is based on a poor performance evaluation.
2. To accommodate individual employees' or applicants' needs (such as a disability), the employer must lower its standards or qualifications.
3. If the jobs of minority workers are dependent on their evaluation by other workers, bias cannot be eliminated.
4. As long as the employer believes that the employee understands the requirements or bases for the performance evaluation, the employer is not obligated to do anything further or to allow leeway in compliance.

---

it goes. "We, too, suffer from faulty equipment that may or may not help put out any 'fires.'"

Moreover, courts differ greatly in their decisions regarding similar performance appraisal methods; therefore, a conclusion is almost impossible about the propriety of any single method. What one is left with is merely direction.

Disparate Impact.   The legal implications of performance appraisals become relevant when their information is used as the basis for any employment-related decision. The Uniform Guidelines on Employee Selection Procedures apply to "tests and other selection procedures which are used as the basis for any employment decision"; therefore, the guidelines regulate the design and use of performance appraisals. Improper performance appraisal systems are those that do not fairly or adequately evaluate performance but, instead, perpetuate stereotypes that have an adverse impact on protected classes.

For example, the Supreme Court, in *Albemarle Paper Company v. Moody,* held that the paired-comparison standards (selecting the "better" of two employees) used by the employer as the basis for an empirical validation study were vague, prone to subjective interpretations, and thus discriminatory and unacceptable. Where a performance appraisal system has a disparate impact on a protected class, it is subject to high scrutiny by the courts.

Disparate impact may be determined by a number of methods, the most common of which is described in the guidelines as the "four-fifths rule" (discussed in Chapter 3). Recall that under the rule there is a presumption of discrimination where the selection rate (for any employment decision) of the protected group is less than 80 percent of the selection rate of the nonminority group. For example, if the number of males and females at a firm is equal, but the performance evaluation system results in promotions of 85 percent of the males and only 3 percent of the females, a court will presume discrimination, which may then be rebutted by the employer.

An employee disputing the performance appraisal may also prove a case using the disparate treatment analysis first articulated in *McDonnell Douglas v. Green.* The employee must show that he or she (1) is a member of a protected class, (2) suffered an adverse employment decision as a result of a performance evaluation,

(3) was actually qualified to perform the responsibilities of the position, and (4) was replaced by someone with similar qualifications who is not a member of a protected class.

As with other areas in which disparate impact is shown, the employer may still defend the system used if the performance appraisal was sufficiently job related. There must be some reasonable need for it, and some means by which to ensure its objectivity and fairness. If, for example, a checklist system is instituted, the employer must show that the person doing the checking is reasonably free of bias, and that the list itself is a fair representation of what is to be expected of the reasonable or "common" employee. This is called "validation" and is strictly regulated by the guidelines.

Disparate Treatment.   A performance appraisal may also result in disparate *treatment,* such as where a female employee is rated subject to different criteria than are the male employees. An example of this type of sexual stereotyping was at issue in the *Hopkins v. Price Waterhouse* case. In that case, a female accounting executive did not receive a promotion to partner based on her performance evaluation. During the evaluation, the plaintiff had been told that she needed to take a charm school course, maintain more social grace, walk, talk, and dress more like a woman, use less profanity, and act less "macho." The Supreme Court ruled in favor of the employee, even though the employer offered evidence of various nondiscriminatory bases for the denial of the partnership. The Court found that, as long as the sexual stereotype and discriminatory appraisal were "motivating factors" in the employer's denial, the motive was illegitimate. This was incorporated into Title VII in the Civil Rights Act of 1991 amending Title VII.

In connection with Scenario 1, where Mark Jonathan is considering his alternatives with regard to his evaluation of Gordy, Mark must consider the disparate treatment implications of his decision. If Mark bends the rules a bit for Gordy, in consideration of his recent divorce and other life-changing events, he may get into trouble unless he evaluates the life-changing events that take place in the lives of *each* of his subordinates. Failure to do so would result in him treating Gordy differently, simply because he knows about Gordy's situation. While this might be fine in Gordy's mind, the next person to come along might not be so happy about it. In Scenario 2, that is just what happens. Julio has a record similar to Gordy's. Suppose that he, too, has some difficulties in his life that have had an impact on his work performance. If Mark does not consider these difficulties, he would be treating Julio differently than he treated Gordy, resulting in disparate treatment.

Scenario

Scenario

Finally, in Scenario 3, we are faced with a situation where Mark and Rose do not get along, and she is therefore unable to perform at an adequate level. Since these circumstances are ripe for unintentional bias, Mark should probably remove himself from her evaluation process.

Scenario

It is important to be aware of these issues, even where the difference in treatment is not the result of any intentional wrongful discrimination. If Mark cannot show why there was a difference in the way he treated Gordy and Julio, it may be difficult to prove that it was not the result of discrimination.

Defamation.   What happens where the employer broadcasts to the world that an employee received a completely unsatisfactory appraisal? In this situation, faulty performance appraisals are not only subject to claims of discriminatory impact and treatment but also may give rise to actions for defamation, wrongful discharge, or negligent evaluation. Defamation may exist where the employer:

- States false and defamatory words concerning the employee.
- Negligently or intentionally communicates these statements to a third party without the employee's consent.
- Thereby subjects the employee to harm or loss of reputation.

In other words, if the employer makes a false statement during the course of an employee evaluation, and that evaluation is transmitted to a third party (such as a future employer), the employee may have a claim for defamation. A false evaluation does not necessarily contain false information, but it may evaluate the employee on improper criteria (data on which the employee was told she or he would not be rated).

An evaluation may also be considered false where the rater does not include information that would explain or justify a poor appraisal, such as the fact that the employee's poor task completion rate was due to a sight disorder, which has since been corrected. Finally, a false evaluation may exist where a rater revises a prior evaluation in an attempt to justify subsequent adverse action taken against the employee. Truth is a complete defense to defamation, and truth and honesty by raters should be ensured throughout the appraisal process.

One troublesome aspect of defamation in connection with the publication of performance reviews exists where a firm chooses to share the results of an internal investigation of performance with an enforcement entity. For example, E.F. Hutton conducted an internal investigation after it pleaded guilty in 1985 to 2,000 counts of mail and wire fraud. The firm found (and shared with the public) that, while the top officials of the firm were not involved in the wrongdoing, certain midlevel managers had improperly used their positions for personal profit.

One of these managers decided to sue the firm for $10 million on the basis of defamation. Though Hutton prevailed, the suit cost the firm enormous amounts of money in defense costs. As mentioned above, this manager was required to show that Hutton negligently published false statements about him. Hutton also argued that it had a qualified privilege to publish the results of internal investigations, so the standard was elevated to one including malice (plaintiff must show that the statement was made with actual knowledge of or reckless disregard as to its falsity).

Negligence
The omission to do something a reasonable person would do, when guided by those considerations that ordinarily regulate human affairs, or something that a prudent and reasonable person would not do.

Negligent Performance Evaluations.   An employee may have a claim against an employer for the employer's **negligence** in conducting a performance evaluation. The employee must be able to show a contract existed that provided for a performance evaluation. This may either be in the form of a formal employment contract or merely an agreement to include an evaluation in the criteria for promotion or merit salary increase. The liability of the employer stems from the common law doctrine that, where a party to a contract undertakes an obligation to perform certain obligations, the party becomes liable for any wrongdoing that results from the performance of that obligation.

The employee in *Schipani v. Ford Motor Co.* claimed that Ford Motor Company breached its contractual duty to evaluate in an objective manner. The court in *Schipani* held that an employer has a duty to exercise reasonable care in the course of employee evaluations. Failure to do so may give rise to a cause of action in tort for negligence.

A unique legal issue arises in connection with performance appraisals of individuals with disabilities. An employer is not required to lower quality or quality standards to accommodate a disabled employee, but it must do what is possible to enable the employee to perform her or his essential responsibilities, while not subjecting itself to an undue burden or hardship. The otherwise qualified employee who has a disability must be evaluated on reasonable job-related performance standards for the duties assigned to that position.

Anderson v. Boston School Committee
105 F.3d 762 (1st Cir. 1997)

A black former public school teacher, O'Neill, brought an action against the principal and the city school committee, alleging racial discrimination and various tort claims. During his employment, he was accused of breaking a lock in the art room where he worked. Although there were no consequences to this incident, they were noted on his performance evaluation. For the 1989 evaluation, his supervisor visited two of the classes in which the teacher taught and evaluated him on his skills. He was criticized for several factors but was also given satisfactory ratings for other factors. During the 1991 and 1992 evaluations, the teacher was given many "unsatisfactory" ratings and notes of inappropriate student conduct during his class. In a January 1992 incident, students complained to the principal about O'Neill's conduct. They claimed he made sexual advances to them and made inappropriate remarks. An investigation resulted and O'Neill was relieved of his duties and transferred pending hearing and resolution. O'Neill filed suit. The district court granted directed verdicts for defendants on all claims.

Coffin, J.

* * * *

[The court found dismissal of the discrimination charge proper.]

Plaintiff relies heavily on the four performance evaluations made of O'Neill to make out a jury case of defamation. But these, as well as statements concerning plaintiff's breaking a lock and his "erratic" behavior, are subject to the qualified privilege of an employer or supervisor to monitor, discuss, and attempt to improve subordinates' performance. Much of what plaintiff complains about was not contested. Much was obviously the Principal's opinion as to what was good or bad educational practice. But none of it could have been found to have been knowingly false or in reckless disregard of the truth.

[The court found the remaining grounds were proper for dismissal as well.]

Case Questions

1. Do you think an employer's statements made during a performance appraisal should be protected against libel and slander suits? Why or why not?

2. What precautions must an employer take in order to be able to claim a privilege in protecting these statements from libel and slander claims?

3. Although in this case there were concrete facts regarding the statements made in the evaluations, what about comments such as "Jon [the employee] is lazy" or "Irene [the employee] is a troublemaker, always questioning employer's authority for employment-related policies." Should these types of statements be protected from slander or libel?

JENSEN V. HEWLETT-PACKARD COMPANY
18 Cal.Rptr.2d 83(Cal. Ct. App. 1993)

An employee who did not agree with his performance evaluation filed suit against the employer for defamation.

Sonenshine, J.

Sean Jensen seeks reversal of a judgment in his defamation action against his former employer, Hewlett-Packard Company, and one of its supervisors, Rod Smith. The lawsuit involves a difference of opinion between the employer and employee about the quality of the employee's work. A supervisor, Hank Phelps, evaluated the employee, Jensen, as needing to improve his on-the-job performance in certain respects. Jensen took offense at the evaluation, claimed it was false, and accused Phelps of trying to hide his own incompetence. He demanded the evaluation be removed from his personnel file and challenged Phelps "to prove his various allegations to an impartial factfinder." Hewlett-Packard investigated the matter and sided with Phelps.

* * * *

As a prelude to our holding, we express our strong judicial disfavor for libel suits based on communications in employment performance reviews, particularly when, as here, the tort claim appears to be an attempted end run around the law. In light of the multitude of laws designed to protect the employee from oppressive employment practices, evaluations serve the important business purpose of documenting the employer's hiring, promotion, discipline and firing practices. Moreover, the laudable practice of evaluating employees is to be encouraged for other important reasons. The performance review is a vehicle for informing the employee of what management expects, how the employee measures up, and what he or she needs to do to obtain wage increases, promotions or other recognition. Thus, the primary recipient and beneficiary of the communication is the employee. Tangential beneficiaries are ordinarily, as in the case here, all part of a management group with a common interest, i.e., the efficient running of the business.

Clearly, there is a legitimate raison d'etre for such records, and management has an unquestioned obligation to keep them. We would therefore be loathe to subject an employer to the threat of a libel suit in which a jury might decide, for instance, that the employee should have been given a rating of "average," rather than "needs improvement," or that the employee had an ability, unrecognized and unappreciated by a foolish supervisor, to get along with and lead others.

Yet that result is exactly what Jensen intended to accomplish with his libel action against Hewlett-Packard: to have an "impartial factfinder" judge whether Phelps was "right" or "wrong" in his criticisms of Jensen, which is to say whether Jensen was more valuable to Hewlett-Packard than the employer was willing to acknowledge.

Based on the facts here, we hold that unless an employer's performance evaluation falsely accuses an employee of criminal conduct, lack of integrity, dishonesty, incompetence or reprehensible personal characteristics or behavior, it cannot support a cause of action for libel. This is true even when the employer's perceptions about an employee's efforts, attitude, performance, potential or worth to the enterprise are objectively wrong and cannot be supported by reference to concrete, provable facts. Moreover, where an employee alleges the employer's negative evaluations are feigned, the only potentially available remedy lies in contract, for breach of the implied covenant of good faith and fair dealing.

* * * *

The first ground raised by Hewlett-Packard was Jensen's failure to present facts demonstrating the evaluation statement was libelous. In defamation actions, it is entirely appropriate for the court to determine in the first instance "whether the publication could reasonably have been understood to have a libelous meaning."

"Libel is a false and unprivileged publication by writing . . . which exposes any person to hatred, contempt, ridicule, or obloquy, or which causes him [or her] to be shunned or avoided, or which has a tendency to injure him [or her] in his [or her] occupation." A publication "must contain a false statement of fact" to give rise to liability for defamation. A statement of opinion "cannot be false and is outside the meaning of libel." "[T]he

dispositive question . . . is 'whether a reasonable fact finder could conclude that the published statements imply a probably false factual assertion.'" The court examines the communication in light of the context in which it was published. The communication's meaning must be considered in reference to relevant factors, such as the occasion of the utterance, the persons addressed, the purpose to be served, and "all of the circumstances attending the publication."

Under the above standards, could any of the comments in Phelps's evaluation reasonably be interpreted as false statements of fact? No. First, we note the context: The communication was a 14-page evaluation of Jensen's performance, prepared by Phelps in the course of his designated duties as Jensen's manager. It was one of a series of evaluations, less favorable than those that preceded or followed it. It documented one manager's assessment of Jensen's work habits, interpersonal skills and level of effort, and it outlined the employer's expectations with regard to Jensen's improvement. It was presented to Jensen for his review and its contents were seen by or made known to a number of management people who participated in periodic employee-ranking sessions. Jensen was given the opportunity to respond to the evaluation, which he did. There is absolutely nothing in the attendant circumstances tending to show the document constituted anything but business-as-usual.

Next, the word "evaluation" denotes opinion, not fact. "Evaluation" is defined in Webster's Third New International Dictionary as ". . . the act or result of evaluating: JUDGMENT APPRAISAL, RATING, INTERPRETATION." To "evaluate" is " . . . to examine and judge concerning the worth, quality, significance, amount, degree, or condition of." The dictionary definition is not necessarily dispositive of the fact/opinion issue, but it certainly implies the defendants' intended legitimate purpose of the document, i.e., its use as a management tool for examining, appraising, judging and documenting the employee's performance.

Finally, we turn to the contents of the evaluation, none of which suggests Jensen lacked honesty, integrity or the inherent competence, qualification, capability or fitness to do his job, or that he had reprehensible personal characteristics. Three categories of comments are involved: ratings by which Phelps expressed a value judgment, such as "good," "acceptable" or "unacceptable," about Jensen's comparative level of skills, performance or attitude; directions in which Phelps advised Jensen that he was expected to develop or improve in various areas; and general remarks about Jensen's attitude toward his job responsibilities and his co-workers.

But even if the comments were objectively unjustified or made in bad faith, they could not provide a legitimate basis for Jensen's libel claim because they were statements of opinion, not false statements of fact. . . .

. . . It is poor policy to create an atmosphere of fear of liability which stifles management from exercising its "'fundamental prerogatives . . . to control the workplace and to retain only the best-qualified employees.'" Here, there is no claim that the negative evaluation was fabricated as a pretext for prohibited discrimination; rather there is only Jensen's unsubstantiated charge his supervisor's opinion was objectively wrong and subjectively feigned. We are compelled to conclude the court is an inappropriate forum for resolution of this grievance. No matter the denomination of the cause of action, employers should neither be required to justify performance evaluations by reference to objectively provable facts, nor subjected to fear of liability for good faith, but mistaken, judgments about the value of an individual employee to the business enterprise.

Case Questions

1. Would an employer be able to say anything on an evaluation and not be held liable?

2. Do you agree with this opinion? Why or why not?

3. What can a company do to protect itself from such libel suits?

ROWE V. GENERAL MOTORS CORP.
457 F.2d 348 (5th Cir. 1972)

General Motors employees Jake Rowe, Willie Williams, and Clarence Williams brought a charge of racial discrimination based on GM's practice of reaching promotion decisions by relying on the recommendations of foremen. This practice operated to discriminate against African-Americans and was held to be unlawful, even though the practice appeared to be fair on its face and General Motors had no intention to discriminate.

Henderson, J.

Until 1962, GMAD [GM's Atlanta plant] was wholly segregated with Blacks being limited to the few custodial jobs. In 1962, GM opened up all jobs to Blacks. Each of the three plaintiff employees sought promotion/transfer from their hourly jobs on the production lines to salaried jobs by using the "employee initiated" method [where employee makes an application directly to the personnel administrator]. Among other things, they base their charge of racial discrimination on the foreman referral system and claim that because they are Blacks, they have been hindered in obtaining the required recommendation of their immediate foreman and have therefore been unable to secure promotion.

It is clearly not enough under Title VII that the procedures utilized by employers are fair in form. These procedures must be fair in operation. Likewise, the intent of employers who utilize such discriminatory procedures is not controlling since "Congress directed the thrust of the Act to the *consequences* of employment practices, not simply the motivation."

We think it clear that the promotion/transfer procedures as applied violate Title VII in several particulars which can be briefly capsulated:

(i) The foreman's recommendation is the indispensable single most important factor in the promotion process.

(ii) Foremen are given no written instructions pertaining to the qualifications necessary for promotion. (They are given nothing in writing telling them what to look for in making their recommendations.)

(iii) Those standards which were determined to be controlling are vague and subjective.

(iv) Hourly employees are not notified of promotion opportunities nor are they notified of the qualifications necessary to get jobs.

(v) There are no safeguards in the procedures designed to avert discriminatory practices.

A brief consideration of some of the testimony of employees strengthens these conclusions. For example, Mr. Griswold, a foreman at GMAD, testified that he did not know what management was looking for in candidates for salaried jobs other than the job of foreman. Mr. Farnim, the GMAD Salaried Personnel Administrator, had to acknowledge that the methods for promotion/transfer at GMAD would enable an individual foreman, if he were so inclined, to exercise racial discrimination in his selection of candidates for promotion/transfer, and that, under the social structure of the time and place, Blacks may very well have been hindered in obtaining recommendations from their foremen since there is no familial or social association between these two groups. All we do today is recognize that promotion/transfer procedures which depend almost entirely upon the subjective evaluation and favorable recommendation of the immediate foreman are a ready mechanism for discrimination against Blacks, much of which can be covertly concealed and, for that matter, not really known to management. We and others have expressed a skepticism that Black persons whose positions are dependent directly on decisive recommendations from Whites can expect non-discriminatory action.

Case Questions

1. Is there any way to incorporate recommendations as a significant part of an employment evaluation scheme without suffering the same result as GM?

2. How can an employer ensure that its evaluation scheme is fair in operation, not just fair in form?

3. Do you agree with the skepticism expressed in the last sentence of the decision? Do you think things are significantly different than when the case was decided in 1972? That is, would the same language be appropriate in a decision today?

The Regulation of Work on the Job

Should an employee follow work-related rules? While this would appear to be a simplistic question, it has plagued employees for years. Suppose there is a workplace rule that an employee finds to be inconvenient? An employee will balance the cost of complying with the rule with the cost of noncompliance. If the employer greatly values compliance, even the slightest infraction may constitute grounds for dismissal. A different employer may allow minor infractions of "less important" rules but discharge employees for noncompliance with those deemed critical. How is the employee to know? What if, due to the personality differences of those who are in charge, it is handled one way in one department and another way in another department of the same business?

The compliance issue arises most frequently in connection with employer regulation of nonwork-related matters, such as physical appearance and off-work activities. (Physical appearance was discussed in Chapter 7.) We will address here the issue of work-related rules and their enforcement.

Research has found that employers may encourage greater conformity or discipline where the employer involves the workforce in the development of the regulations, clearly communicates to the employees the bases for the rules, and identifies and consistently applies the discipline that will be administered in the event of a transgression. In doing so, the employer displays respect for employees and their concerns relating to the matter under consideration. This is termed the "quality of worklife" approach to management decision-making that affects the employees' environment: increased involvement, responsibility, and autonomy.

It is not possible for an employer to identify everything that is prohibited in the workplace, or to describe precisely the type of conduct to be encouraged. However, a distinct, definitive policy regarding the intent or mission of the employer may suffice. For instance, a corporate statement that reads:

> It is our intent to create a work environment that is supportive of our company's objectives [outlined in a separate document]. To do so, it is critical that each employee respect her or his colleagues and coworkers. To this end, infringing on another's property or person will not be tolerated in any form, including theft, physical or verbal abuse, sexual misconduct or harassment, or other invasive or threatening acts by one employee against another.

Examples of more specific policies and work rules may include regulations regarding no smoking, appearance, rest period, or moonlighting policies and policies that prohibit employees from accepting work with an employer's competitor while working for the employer.

Finally, some rules may be considered by employers to be "understood"; however, it is better to obtain written confirmation from employees of that understanding. For instance, in a business that handles confidential information there may be a company policy requiring employees to sign nondisclosure documents. The firm, however, may neglect to require a signature on a conflict of interest form requiring disclosure to the company of any information that creates a conflict of interest for the employee.

Another example of a generally understood policy that should be reduced to writing is an employer's drug policy. Motivations behind written drug policies include the presentation of a clear management antidrug attitude, a statement of penalties or discipline in the event of a violation of the policy, and a specific and distinct deterrent from workplace drug use and abuse. The statement need not be complex or particularly lengthy but merely clear and firm.

An example of a drug-free workplace policy statement is:

> Liquor and drugs do not mix and should not be mixed with work. The abusive use of prescribed judgment- or ability-altering drugs or the use of non-prescription judgment- or ability-altering substances either while on the job or taken off the job but still impairing an employee's judgment or ability while on the job will not be tolerated. The first instance of a violation of this policy may be treated as a medical concern and the employee may be referred to an appropriate facility for treatment. Future violations may subject the employee to graduated discipline, up to and including, termination. The employer reserves the right to suspend graduated discipline if the exigencies of the situation call for such a suspension because of the nature of the infraction and its potential for harm to person or property.

Fairness in Regulating Behavior

As with other areas of employment regulation, work rules must be applied fairly and nondiscriminatorily. A policy that appears not to be discriminatory, though it has a disproportionate impact on a protected class, may be subject to scrutiny where it is not sufficiently business-justified. Similarly, a policy that treats members of a protected class differently than other employees is generally unacceptable, as would be a policy that applies to all employees but is only enforced against women and minorities or some other targeted group in a discriminatory fashion. Consistent application, therefore, is imperative.

Insubordination

One policy that is the subject of much litigation is the prohibition of insubordination. When an employee is **insubordinate,** the employee either defies or ignores orders or requests given by the employer. Since the determination of insubordination is generally a subjective analysis of appropriate behavior under given circumstances, the potential for inconsistent application and enforcement is great. For instance, it is obviously insubordination for an employee to ignore an employer's direct order to come to work on a specific day, or to perform a certain assigned task. But is it insubordination for an employee to gripe loudly about the employer to co-workers during lunch at the workplace? To gripe quietly? Is it insubordination for an employee's demeanor to be surly, defiant, or subtly challenging when the employee is unhappy with a workplace decision? Would it be more acceptable to tolerate such behavior from a female than a male? From a white than a black employee? Employers are constantly plagued with these subtle insubordination challenges.

To avoid problems in this area, an employer should identify precise situations that are considered to constitute insubordination, and should require, where

Insubordination
Acts or omissions by an employee that evidence a disrespect for the authority of her or his superior(s).

possible, corroboration for a supervisor's claim of insubordination. Failure to strictly regulate its application may result in personal bias ruling workplace relationships, instead of consistent standards of conduct doing so. For instance, an employer may constantly evaluate black employees as surly and insubordinate if they do not act "friendly" and "pleasant"; while white employees are simply deemed to be "having a bad day," though those days may be as frequent as the black employee's "bad attitude" days.

Limitations

There are exceptions, however, to these proscriptions on regulating workplace rules. For example, a seniority system may be facially neutral but result in an adverse impact. If the employer had traditionally hired only whites or males, and only recently had developed a more diverse workforce, such a seniority policy may adversely impact females and minorities because they will necessarily have less seniority than the white males. Nevertheless, Title VII specifically creates an exemption for bona fide seniority systems. The Supreme Court has held that a system is "bona fide" unless it was designed with the intent to discriminate or was closely associated with a system that already discriminates.

Discipline

As with any other area that involves actions taken toward employees, employee discipline is a sensitive domain, which must be approached with a critical eye. Regulation of employment decisions applies to any decision, whether involving retention, promotion, and raises, or demotion, termination, or other forms of discipline. All discipline decisions must be nondiscriminatorily applied and objectively administered. Discipline systems that have the purpose of educating the employee who is found to be in violation are generally considered by employees to be more "fair" and less arbitrary than traditional "punishment" systems of disciplinary action.

In general, a system that maintains consistency in application, that provides specific guidelines for attaining the varying levels of performance, and that communicates this information to employees is one likely to be deemed "fair." The fairer the system, the less likely it will come under attack from disgruntled employees.

Furthermore, the most effective and efficient method by which to ensure appropriate treatment of disciplinary action is to factually and completely document each action taken (whether such action was written or oral) and its background support. This assures employees of adequate feedback, and lawsuits will not hinge on the vagaries of a particular supervisor's memory. Where no documentation is maintained, there is no evidence that the employee was given the opportunity to redress the infraction or poor performance.

For example, you may recall from Chapter 6, Scenario 3, that a black female employee sued her employer for failing to give her negative feedback as part of her

Management Tips

- Documentation such as written performance appraisals can be your protection against wrongful lawsuits charging discrimination. As mentioned before, you are allowed to terminate someone for any reason *except* for certain prohibited reasons. As long as you document poor or deteriorating performance, you may generally terminate an individual on that basis and have protection against claims of discrimination.

- On the other hand, if you do conduct written performance appraisals, but treat workers with similar appraisals differently, you may be subject to charges of discrimination.

- Where performance appraisals are conducted by a manager on the basis of stereotypes or prejudice, you are subject to claims of either disparate treatment or disparate impact. Therefore, make sure that all supervisors undergo training in connection with nonbiased reporting and evaluations that are free from prejudgments.

- Make sure that there are precautions against inappropriate disclosures. An employer may be subject to claims of privacy invasions or defamation under certain circumstances.

- If your employee manual or other materials state that you will conduct appraisals, failure to conduct them may be a problem. Make sure that you are willing to live with the claims you make regarding the regularity of appraisals and other promises.

ongoing evaluation process. In fact, the employer had refrained from doing so in a misdirected effort to avoid a discrimination lawsuit. Since the employee did not receive the same opportunity to correct her performance as was offered to white employees, the court determined this practice to be discriminatory.

Documentation of discipline, as well as of appraisals, warnings, and commendations, should be retained in each employee's file and should be given to the employee to provide her or him with the opportunity to appeal the action.

Summary

Parameters within which an employer's evaluation techniques may be relatively safe from criticism follow:

- The employer should first describe precisely what is required of each position to be evaluated. An adequate description will include the following:

  1. Position title.
  2. Department or division in which the position is located.

  3. Title of supervisor (not name, as the individual may change while the supervisory position would not).
  4. Function or purpose of position.
  5. Scope of responsibility for accomplishing that purpose.
  6. Specific duties and responsibilities.
  7. Knowledge, experience, or qualifications necessary for performance of the above duties and

responsibilities (the connection should be apparent or explained).

8. Organizational relationship, persons to whom the employee should report, those employees who report to this supervisor, and those employees over whom the supervisor has direct supervisory responsibilities.

- There should be different appraisal forms for different job families, since each grouping would, presumably, require different qualifications.

- No "unwritten" qualifications should exist. These may have a disparate impact against those employees outside the "loop" of information, pursuant to which employees learn of the "real" way of obtaining promotions and other workplace benefits.

- The employer should communicate to its employees the nature, content, timing, and weight of the performance appraisal and ensure that the employees understand each of the standards pursuant to which they will be evaluated.

- The bases for the evaluation should be specific and job- or task-defined, rather than subjective, global measures of job performance. For example, a performance measure, such as "ability to finish tasks within specified time period," is preferable to "timeliness." "Suggests new approaches" would be preferable to "industrious." This is because the supervisor evaluating the individual is given baselines and vantage points, such as the schedules that she or he has given the employee, rather than being forced to reach a conclusion about the employee's timeliness in general.

- The employer should request justifications of ratings wherever possible. Some researchers have suggested that

documentation should be required only where a rating is extreme; however, this may be construed by the court as bending over backward only in those circumstances where the rating may be questioned. To the contrary, where an employer maintains a policy that each evaluation should be documented, the consistency of treatment is a defense in itself.

- The employer should take steps to determine the validity of each individual rater's scores. If the employee is able to establish adverse impact as a result of a performance appraisal system, the employer will have the opportunity to evidence that the appraisals are valid characterizations of the employee's performance. This validation is not possible where the raters do not maintain consistency, accuracy, and predictability in ratings. On the other hand, where the rating systems are objectively based, where the determinants are not subject to individual interpretations, where the employer utilizes more than one rater per employee evaluation, and where the employee has the opportunity for input and explanation, employers are less subject to court scrutiny of their performance appraisals.

- In addition to affording the employee the opportunity to be heard during the process, the employer should establish a formal appeals process, which the employee may follow subsequent to receipt of the final appraisal. This process may be implemented by the employer through its supervisors, a committee comprised of representatives from all levels of the company, or a committee comprised of the employee's peers. Under most circumstances, appeals processes act as a means to air differences and to explain misunderstandings, deterring later litigation.

Chapter-End Questions

1. Ford Motor has advised all of its employees that performance appraisals play an important role in employee promotions. Marquez has received excellent appraisals for the past 15 years and has been rated as promotable by his supervisors; however, he has not been promoted and his name has been removed from the list of promotable employees for no apparent reason. Marquez sues based on racial discrimination. Decide the case, telling what factors are used to justify the decision. (*Marquez v. Omaha Dist. Sales Office, Ford Division of Ford Motor Co.,* 440 F.2d 1157 (8th cir. 1971).)

2. Ray, a black worker, is instructed to switch positions with a white worker. Neither was satisfied with his new position; but Ray was the only one to lodge a complaint about the situation, and he threatened to refuse the reassignment order. There was no evidence that any employee had ever refused a job reassignment in the past. Ray was fired for insubordination in connection with his complaint regarding the reassignment and sues for racial discrimination. (*Ray v. Safeway Stores,* 614 F.2d 729 (10th Cir. 1980).)

3. Esther Harris, a black female, was hired at a Wal-Mart store as a checker/cashier. About six months after she was hired, she was promoted to be customer service manager (CSM). As a CSM, she was in charge of training, directing, and assisting the checkers, in addition to scheduling all breaks and lunches for the checkers. The CSM was also responsible for approving checks, overrings, refunds, and voids, as well as distributing money to each register, picking up money from each register, and meeting all the change needs of the registers. When Jim Harris, the store manager, was hired, he was told to combat the store's problems of high cash shortages

   and the cash control problems on the checkout lanes. Jim took action by issuing Esther a written notice for the reasons of cash shortages being abnormally high with no just cause, poor morale of checkers, and poor scheduling of breaks and lunches. Esther was consequently placed on disciplinary probation for 30 days. After a thorough investigation, Wal-Mart believed that there was just cause to believe that Esther was not competent as a CSM and transferred her to a position in the receiving department where she would have no cash handling responsibilities, but her pay remained the same. Her replacement was a white male who had extensive managerial training in two Wal-Mart stores. Esther claims that she was placed on probation because of her race. (*Harris v. Wal-Mart,* 658 F.Supp 62 (E.D.Ark. 1987).)

4. Rose White, a black female, had a high school education and began her state employment in 1972 as a clerk-stenographer with Juvenile Services. She received several promotions and was promoted to bookkeeper III by 1976. In 1977, she was promoted to accountant I, even though she did not have the required bachelor's degree in accounting or a related business field. (Her supervisor had requested the qualifications review committee to substitute her experience for education.) In 1978, White applied for the accountant II position, which required the same requisites as the accountant I position. Her competition, F. D. Smith, was a white male who also didn't meet the educational requirements of the position, but he did have an associate degree in business administration and some accounting and auditing experience. Smith received the position, and White claims that she was qualified because she was already an accountant I and that the accountant II

position was granted to an unqualified white male. (*Briggs v. Anderson,* 796 F.2d 1009 (8th Cir. 1986).)

5. Katie Jackson, an administrative assistant, was a black woman who was laid off by Ebasco Services Incorporated during the company's layoffs. She claims that her supervisor, Gueci, laid her off for racially discriminatory reasons; but Gueci claims that her discharge was based purely on a comparative review of other employees in the department. Gueci used Jackson's scores on her performance appraisals, generally 3s and 4s on a scale of 5, to prove that Jackson's performance was not sufficient enough to consider her retention as an employee. Jackson demonstrates the alleged fallacy in this argument by demonstrating that Gueci retained a white woman who was only qualified to be a secretary, whereas Jackson was a qualified administrative assistant. Gueci points out that Jackson received consistently low attendance scores on her performance evaluations, so he had to balance out all the information and make a subjective decision that went beyond the performance appraisals. *(Jackson v. Ebasco Services, Inc.,* 634 F.Supp. 1565 (S.D.N.Y. 1986).)

6. Four black employees of the Baltimore fire department charged the department with discriminatory promotion practices, which included discriminatory performance appraisals by the supervisors. Their claim contends that these practices were causing high attrition percentages among the black firefighters, because they felt that they were in dead-end jobs with no hopes for being promoted into supervisory positions. The department defends its practices by maintaining that only a small section of the performance appraisals were subjective supervisor evaluations. The firefighters claim that any subjectivity in the appraisals is discriminatory, because of the lack of

black supervisors, which creates an imbalance when the white supervisors subjectively judge the black firefighters. This was also given as a reason why there was a lack of blacks being promoted to supervisory positions. The department claims that most blacks often quit their jobs before earning an opportunity at a supervisory position; but the firefighters claim that blacks leave because they become aware of the futility of advancement caused by the discrimination inherent in the promotion procedures. (*Harder v. Mayor and City Council of Baltimore,* 359 F.Supp. 1187 (D.Md. 1973) modified by 486 F.2d 1134).

7. Shapolia was an electrician at the Los Alamos National Lab. In March 1987, Shapolia received a poor performance evaluation from his supervisor, Martin. In September 1987, pursuant to company procedures, Shapolia instituted review proceedings in an attempt to have the negative review removed from his file. The procedures require that an impartial review board of three individuals review the grievance. Shapolia contends that his evaluation and subsequent review were biased, because Shapolia was not a Mormon, but Martin was a Mormon, as was Whetten, one of the individuals on the review board. Consequently, Shapolia claims that he could not have received an unbiased review. Is he correct? (*Shapolia v. Los Alamos National Lab,* 992 F.2d 1033 (10th Cir. 1993).)

8. McNairn, a black female, was a typist in the Office of Equal Employment Opportunity and Civil Rights at the FDA. She was appointed to that position as a temporary employee, contingent on positive performance reviews. At the end of her temporary assignment, McNairn received a notice that she was eligible for promotion from GS-3 to GS-4; her supervisor, Ford,

informed her that he would not promote her, claiming her typing was not acceptable for a GS-4, but he extended her temporary assignment for one year. McNairn claims that the notice regarding her eligibility is conclusory, and that Ford discriminated against her based on her race in not following the recommendation of the notice. (*McNairn v. Sullivan,* 929 F.2d 974 (4th Cir. 1991).)

9. An individual contacts you in connection with a reference for one of your worst employees, who was just recently terminated for poor performance. This individual asks whether you believe the former employee will perform well in a similar position at a new company. What do you respond?

10. Using the same scenario as in problem 9, is your response different if the former employee was terminated for stealing, and the individual asks whether this employee can be trusted?

16 THE RIGHT TO PRIVACY AND OTHER PROTECTIONS FROM EMPLOYER INTRUSIONS

Chapter Outline

SCENARIOS

SCENARIO   1

Aravinda had been reading in the news lately of the skyrocketing costs of health care, particularly surrounding the HIV epidemic. She is concerned that her small 10-employee company would suffer a financial disaster if one of its workers contracted the virus since their insurance costs would increase. Therefore, she wants to conduct a confidential HIV test of each present employee and future applicant. Aravinda has several concerns. First, what if an individual refuses to take the test based on the grounds of invasion of privacy? Second, if someone tests positive, can Aravinda refuse to hire or to discharge her or him without violating federal law protecting employees with disabilities? Third, how can she otherwise protect against rising costs? Fourth, if an employee tests negative, but Aravinda decides to terminate the employee anyway, is she liable for the appearance that the employee is HIV-positive, and that Aravinda terminated her or him as a consequence of the test results? How can she ensure that the test results are kept confidential?

SCENARIO   2

Solange receives a "spam" e-mail asking her to go look at a certain website. Since she doesn't know who it is from or why she is receiving it, she clicks on the link and finds herself at a website devoted to XXX-rated videos. She is so perturbed by this occurrence that she spends a few moments looking around the website trying to find its site administrator. She intended to send off a message to this person asking them not to send her any more junk mail. After searching for several minutes with no luck, she leaves the website and goes back to reading her e-mail. A few days later, she is called into her manager's office and reprimanded for using employer-owned computer equipment for personal interests such as this XXX-rated video site. It seems that her manager was using a program that alerted him any time an employee perused certain inappropriate websites. She tried to explain, but left with a written reprimand in her hand and a copy in her files. She is furious not only at her manager's unwillingness to understand, but also the invasion of privacy posed by this computer monitoring. Does her employer have a right to monitor her computer use in this way?

SCENARIO   3

Abraham, a realtor, has three children, two of whom are in college. In order to earn extra money to help with college tuition payments, Abraham (who studied modern dance during his college career) found a job dancing in a club that caters specifically to women. While not exactly exotic dancing (he kept all of his clothes on), it wasn't ballroom dancing either. Celebrating during a bachelorette party, one of the partners of the real estate firm for which he worked caught sight of Abraham dancing. When he arrived at the office the next day, she called him into her office and ordered him to quit his night job She claimed that both clients and potential clients might see him there and he would lose all credibility as a realtor. Does she have a right to require Abraham to do this as a condition of future employment? (Presume that he is an employee and not an independent contractor.)

Are There Guarantees in Life?

Philosophers have argued that our society cannot maintain its core values without simultaneously guaranteeing the privacy of the individual. Edward Bloustein writes that "an individual deprived of privacy merges with the mass. His opinions, being public, tend never to be different; his aspirations, being known, tend always to be conventionally accepted ones; his feelings, being openly exhibited, tend to lose their quality of unique personal warmth and to become the feelings of every man. Such a being, although sentient, is fungible; he is not an individual."

Recent inventions and business methods call attention to the next step which must be taken for the protection of the person and for securing to the individual what Judge Cooley calls the right "to be let alone." Instantaneous photographs and newspaper enterprises have invaded the sacred precincts of private and domestic life; and numerous mechanical devices threaten to make good the prediction that "what is whispered in the closet shall be proclaimed from the house-tops."[1]

While the above concerns were first expressed over 100 years ago, they remain consistently valid in today's technologically advancing world. In a 1990 Harris poll, nearly three out of every four Americans agreed that they have "lost all control over how personal information about them is circulated and used by companies."

But do employees actually have a "fundamental right to privacy" as many believe? The answer to this question is not as easy as one might presume, given the wide recognition of employee rights in the workplace. The right to privacy may not be as fundamental as employees generally think. This is all the more important in these days of advancing information technology. Computer technology, though largely beneficial, can have a negative effect on employees if the easily obtained information is misused, incorrect, or misleading. Employers now have a greater capacity to invade an employee's privacy than ever before. Among other devices, there are chairs that can sense and record the time an employee spends at his or her desk, computer programs that measure employees' computer keystrokes to ensure they are as productive as they should be, phones that monitor employees' phone calls, and policies related to workplace communication to make sure they are work-related.

But perhaps there is presently a greater need for seemingly private information. Drug use in American industry costs employers approximately $60 billion per year in absenteeism and attrition, theft of employer property by employees is estimated at $10 billion per year, and failure to perform an intensive reference and background check of an applicant may cost the employer enormous amounts in litigation fees defending claims of negligent hiring.

Finally, in this time of increased competition in the global marketplace, each employee becomes all the more crucial to the workings of the company. An employer has a justified basis for attempting to choose the most appropriate and qualified person for the job; the means by which the employer obtains that information, however, may be suspect.

---

[1] Warren and Brandeis, "The Right to Privacy," 4 *Harvard Law Review* 193 (1890).

Because erosion of at-will employment was the dominant issue of the 1980s, scholars have predicted that privacy will be the main theme for the 1990s and beyond. This chapter will address the employee's rights regarding personal information and the employer's responsibilities regarding that information, as well as the employer's right to find out both job-related and nonrelated personal information about its employees. Chapter 14 previously addressed other issues regarding the legality of information-gathering through testing procedures.

Background

The US Constitution does not actually speak of privacy, but it has been read into the Constitution as a necessary adjunct of other constitutional rights we hold. The right to privacy was first recognized by the Supreme Court in *Griswold v. Connecticut,* when the Court held that a Connecticut statute restricting a married couple's use of birth control devices unconstitutionally infringed on the right to marital privacy.

The Court held a constitutional guarantee of various zones of privacy as a part of **fundamental rights** guaranteed by the Constitution, such as the right to free speech and the right to be free from unreasonable searches and seizures. The latter right is that on which many claims for privacy rights are based. The Court has held that under certain circumstances the required disclosure of certain types of personal information should be considered an unreasonable search. It has protected against the mandatory disclosure of personal papers, and it decided in favor of the right to make procreation decisions.

While baseless or unjustified intrusions, at first blush, may appear to be completely abhorrent in our society, proponents of the argument that employers can ask whatever they please argue that, if an employee does not want to offer a piece of information, there is something the employee is trying to hide. For example, why would an employee refuse to submit to a drug test if that employee is not abusing drugs? Do **private-sector** employers have the right to ask their employees any question they choose and take adverse employment actions against the employee if she or he refuses to answer?

Additionally, employees are concerned about the type of information gathered in the course of applying for and holding a job. Who has access to that information? What information may be deemed "confidential" and what does that mean to the employee?

Public-Sector Employee Privacy

The Constitution protects individuals from wrongful invasions by the state or by an entity acting on behalf of the government. Federal, state, and local employees are therefore protected in their right of privacy from governmental intrusion and excess.

Constitutional Protection

The Fourth Amendment.   For the Fourth Amendment's protection against unreasonable search and seizure to be applicable to a given situation, there must first exist

---

Fundamental right
A right that is guaranteed by the Constitution, whether stated or not.

Private sector
That segment of the workforce represented by private companies (companies that are not owned or managed by the government or one of its agencies).

Public sector
That segment of the workforce represented by governmental employers and governmental agency employers. In some situations, this term may include federal contractors.

EXHIBIT 16–1   Myths about Employee Privacy Rights

1. Employees have an absolute right to privacy in their workplace.
2. It is a breach of an employee's right to privacy for an employer to ask with whom the employee lives.
3. In the private sector, the Constitution protects employees' right to be free from unreasonable searches and seizures.
4. Without constitutional protection, employees in the private sector are left with no protection against invasions of privacy.
5. Once an employee gives information to an employer, the employer may use it for whatever purpose it desires.

---

a search or seizure. The Supreme Court has liberally interpreted "search" to include the retrieval of blood samples and other bodily invasions, including urinalyses, as well as the collection of other personal information.

For a search to violate the Fourth Amendment, that search must be deemed unreasonable, unjustified at its inception, and impermissible in scope. The Supreme Court in *O'Connor v. Ortega* held that a search was justified at its inception where the employer has

> reasonable grounds for suspecting that the search will turn up evidence that the employee is guilty of work-related misconduct, or that the search is necessary for a noninvestigatory work-related purpose such as to retrieve a file.

A search is permissible in scope where

> the measures adopted are reasonably related to the objectives of the search and not excessively intrusive in light of . . . the nature of the misconduct being investigated.

Generally, all searches that are conducted without a judicially issued warrant based on a finding of reasonable cause are held to be *per se* unreasonable. There are several exceptions to this rule, including searches incident to an arrest, some automobile searches, pat-down searches with probable cause to believe the subject is armed, and administrative searches of certain regulated industries.

In *Shoemaker v. Handel,* the court held that a drug-related urine test of jockeys without a warrant was acceptable because it satisfied the court's two-pronged test. The court held that (1) where there is a strong state interest in conducting the unannounced warrantless search and (2) where the pervasive regulation of the industry reduces the expectation of privacy, the search does not violate the Fourth Amendment. There are possible implications of this and related decisions on HIV or genetic testing in governmental workplaces and in employment in heavily regulated industries.

Finally, the employer may wish to conduct a search of employee lockers. Would this be acceptable? Under what circumstances is an employer allowed to conduct searches? A search may constitute an invasion of privacy, depending on the nature of the employer and the purpose of the search. The unreasonableness of a search is determined by balancing the extent of the invasion and the extent to which the employee should expect to have privacy in this area against the employer's interest in the security of its workplace, the productivity of its workers, and other job-related concerns.

Prior to any search of employer-owned property, such as desks or lockers, employees should be given formal written notice of the intent to search without their consent. Where the employer intends to search personal effects, such as purses or wallets, employees should be forewarned, consent should be obtained prior to the search, and employees should be made well aware of the procedures involved. Consent is recommended under these circumstances, because an employee has a greater expectation of privacy in those personal areas. These rights are significantly diminished where the employer is not restrained by constitutional protections.

When an employee is detained during a search, the employer may have a claim for false imprisonment, which is defined as a total restraint on freedom to move against the employee's will, such as keeping an employee in one area of an office. The employee need not be "locked" into the confinement to be restrained; but when the employee remains free to leave at any time, there is no false imprisonment.

The 5th and 14th Amendments.   The 5th and 14th Amendments also protect a government employee's right to privacy in that the state may not restrict one's rights unless it is justified. For instance, the Supreme Court has consistently held that everyone has a fundamental right to travel, free of government intervention. Where the state attempts to infringe on anything that has been determined to be a fundamental right, that infringement or restriction is subject to the **strict scrutiny** of the courts. For the restriction to be allowed, the state must show that the restriction is justified by a **compelling state interest.** Moreover, the restriction must be the least intrusive alternative available.

On the other hand, for those interests not deemed by the courts to constitute fundamental rights, a state may impose any restrictions that can be shown to be **rationally related to a valid state interest,** a much more lenient test.

To determine whether the state may restrict or intrude on an employee's privacy rights, it must first be determined whether the claimed right is fundamental. Two tests are used to make this determination. First, the court may look to whether the right is "implicit in the concept of ordered liberty, such that neither liberty nor justice would exist if [the rights] were sacrificed." Second is whether the right is "deeply rooted in this Nation's history and tradition."

While conception, child rearing, education, and marriage have been held to be within the area of privacy protected by the Constitution, other issues have not yet been addressed or determined by the Court, including the right to be free from mandatory preemployment medical tests. Moreover, the Court has found *no* general right of the individual to be left alone.

The Privacy Act.   Governmental intrusion into the lives of federal employees is also restricted by the Privacy Act of 1974. Much of the discussion in the area of employee privacy is framed by governmental response to the issue, both because of limitations imposed on the government regarding privacy as well as the potential for abuse. The Privacy Act of 1974 regulates the release of personal information about federal employees by federal agencies. Specifically, but for 11 stated exceptions, no federal agency may release information about an employee that contains the means for identifying that employee without the employee's prior written consent.

There are four basic principles addressed by the Privacy Act:

1. Employees should have access to their own personnel files, and there should be some way for them to find out the purposes for which the files are being used.

2. There should be some mechanism by which an employee may correct or amend an inaccurate record.

3. The employee should be able to prevent information from being inappropriately revealed or used without her or his consent, unless such disclosure is required by law.

4. The person who is in charge of maintaining the information must ensure that the files are not falling into the wrong hands and that the information contained within the files is accurate, reliable, and used for the correct reasons.

By affording the employee with these rights, Congress has effectively put the right of disclosure of personal information in the hands of the employee, at least when none of the 11 specified exceptions apply.

When one of the Privacy Act exceptions applies, the act dismisses the employee consent requirement, which gives the agency total control over the use of the file. The right to privacy is not absolute; the extent of protection varies with the extent of the intrusion, and the interests of the employee are balanced against the interests of the employer. Basically, the information requested under either the Privacy Act or the Freedom of Information Act is subject to a balancing test weighing the need to know the information against the employee's privacy interest.

The Ninth Circuit Court of Appeals has developed guidelines to assist in this balancing test. The court directs that the following four factors be looked to in reaching a conclusion relating to disclosure:

1. The individual's interest in disclosure of the information sought.

2. The public interest in disclosure.

3. The degree of invasion of personal privacy.

4. Whether there are alternative means of getting the information.

The Privacy Act grants employees two options for relief: criminal penalties and civil remedies, including damages and injunctive relief. The act also allows employees who are adversely affected by an agency's noncompliance to bring a civil suit against the agency in federal court.

Privacy Protection Study Commission.   The Privacy Protection Study Commission was formed by Congress with the purpose of studying the possibility of extending the Privacy Act to the private sector. In 1977, the commission concluded

EXHIBIT 16–2   Privacy Act of 1974

No Agency shall disclose any record which is contained in a system of records by any means of communication to any person, or to another agency, except pursuant to a written request by, or with the prior written consent of, the individual to whom the record pertains, unless disclosure of the record would be

1. To those officers and employees of the agency which maintains the record who have a need for the record in the performance of their duties.

2. Required under section 552 of this title; *(the Freedom of Information Act). (Note that this act does not apply to "personnel, medical, and similar files the disclosure of which would constitute a clearly unwarranted invasion of personal privacy.")*

3. Or a routine use as defined in subsection (a)(7) of this section and described under subsection (e)(4)(D) of this section; *(a purpose that is specifically compatible with the purpose for which the information was gathered).*

4. To the Bureau of the Census for purposes of planning or carrying out a census or survey or related activity. . . .

5. To a recipient who has provided the agency with advance adequate written assurance that the record will be used solely as a statistical research or reporting record, and the record is to be transferred in a form that is not individually identifiable.

6. To the National Archives of the United States as a record which has sufficient historical or other value to warrant its continued preservation by the United States Government, or for evaluation by the Administrator of General Services or his designee to determine whether the record has such value.

7. To another federal agency or to an instrumentality of any government jurisdiction within or under the control of the United States for a civil or criminal law enforcement activity if the activity is authorized by law, and if the head of the agency or instrumentality has made a written request to the agency which maintains the record specifying the particular portion desired and the law enforcement activity for which the record is sought.

8. To a person pursuant to a showing of compelling circumstances affecting the health or safety of an individual if upon such disclosure notification is transmitted to the last known address of such individual.

9. To either House of Congress, or, to the extent of matter within its jurisdiction, any committee or subcommittee thereof, any joint committee or subcommittee of any such joint committee.

10. To the Comptroller General, or any of his authorized representatives, in the course of the performance of the duties of the General Accounting Office.

11. Pursuant to the order of a court of competent jurisdiction.

that the Privacy Act should not be extended to private employers, but that private-sector employees should be given many new privacy protections. The suggested protections required a determination of current information-gathering practices and their reasons, a limitation on the information that may be collected to what is relevant, a requirement that the employer inform its employees to ensure accuracy, and a limitation on the usage of the information gathered both internally and externally.

The commission further found that certain issues demanded federal intervention and, for this reason, recommended that (1) the use of polygraph tests in employment-related issues be prohibited; (2) pretext interviews be prohibited; (3) the use of arrest or criminal records in employment decisions be prohibited except where otherwise allowed or required by law; (4) employers be required to use reasonable care in selection of their investigating agencies; and (5) the Federal Fair Credit Reporting Act provisions be strengthened. These recommendations have yet to be implemented by Congress, primarily due to private employers' vocal rejection of such an extension of federal law due to the cost of the implementation of the recommendations.

The commission has since established three general policy goals: (1) to attempt to create a balance between what an employee will divulge to the recordkeeping department and what that employee seeks in return for his information; (2) to find a manner by which to ensure fairness to all employees, in that the information that has been processed will not be used against them; and (3) to create and define rules regarding the type of information that may be disclosed and those to whom the information may be given.

Many large corporations have embraced privacy protection programs on their own in accordance with recommendations from the Privacy Commission and in anticipation of federal regulation. In light of this advance implementation, the privacy commission recommends that any program guarantee five basic employee procedural rights. The list includes:

- Notice
- Authorization
- Access
- Correction
- Confidentiality

Though the list seems rather specific, the problem lies within the depth and scope of each component.

Federal Wiretapping—Title III.   Title III, as amended (particularly by the Electronic Communications Privacy Act of 1986), is codified at Title 18 USC, Sections 2510–2521. These statutes provide privacy protection for and govern the interception of oral, wire, and electronic communications. Title III covers all telephone communications regardless of the medium, except that it does not cover the radio portion of a cordless telephone communication that is transmitted between the handset and base unit. The law authorizes the interception of oral, wire, and electronic communications by investigative and law enforcement officers conducting criminal investigations pertaining to serious criminal offenses, or felonies, following the issuance of a court order by a judge. The Title III law authorizes the interception of particular criminal communications related to particular criminal offenses. In short, it authorizes the acquisition of evidence of crime. It does not authorize noncriminal intelligence gathering, nor does it authorize interceptions related to social or political views.

Thirty-seven states have statutes permitting interceptions by state and local law enforcement officers for certain types of criminal investigations. All of the state statutes are based upon Title III, from which they derive. These statutes must be at least as restrictive as Title III, and in fact most are more restrictive in their requirements. In describing the legal requirements, we will focus on those of Title III since they define the baseline for all wiretaps performed by federal, state, and local law enforcement agencies.

In recent years, state statutes have been modified to keep pace with rapid technological advances in telecommunications. For example, New Jersey amended its electronic surveillance statute in 1993 to include cellular telephones, cordless telephones, digital display beepers, fax transmissions, computer-to-computer communications, and traces obtained through "caller-ID." Wiretaps are limited to the crimes specified in Title III and state statutes. Most wiretaps are large undertakings, requiring a substantial use of resources. In 1992, the average cost of installing intercept devices and monitoring communications was $46,492. Despite budget constraints and personnel shortages, law enforcement conducts wiretaps as necessary, but obviously, because of staffing and costs, judiciously.

Electronic Communications Privacy Act (ECPA).   At first, Title III was created to combat invasion of the government for eavesdropping in large part due to the Watergate scandal in the 1970s. Originally the federal statutes targeted government eavesdropping on telephone discussion without the consent of the speakers. The federal statute required the government agents to obtain a warrant before they could intercept any oral discussions. In late 1986, Congress increased the coverage by broadening the range of electronic communications, resulting in the ECPA.

The ECPA covers all forms of digital communications, including transmissions of text and digitalized images, in addition to voice communications on the telephone. The law also prohibits unauthorized eavesdropping by all persons and businesses, not only the government. In addition, the ECPA prohibits unauthorized access to messages in storage on a computer system, and unauthorized interception of messages in transmission.

Private-Sector Employee Privacy

Despite the fact that public and private employers have a similar legitimate need for information about applicants and employees to make informed decisions about hiring, promotion, security, discipline, and termination, privacy rights in the private sector of employment are limited; "the employment relationship generally denies any right to the employee who is arbitrarily treated [by his employer and is] . . . without a union or contract."

The distinction between the treatment of employees in the private and public sectors is one that is created by the constitutional requirement of *state action* as precedent to its application. The Constitution is a limitation made to curb *government* excesses.

Whether there should be a right to privacy in both the public and private sectors, employers suggest that the employee has three choices when faced with objectionable intrusions by employers: quit, comply, or object and risk termination. Employees argue that they are defenseless because of their economic condition and that their privacy in the private sector is subject to greater abuse precisely because there are no protections and the option to quit is unrealistic.

One explanation offered for the difference between public- and private-sector privacy protections is compliance-related costs. The implementation of the Privacy Act throughout its agencies costs the government relatively little, because it is conducting self-regulation.

By contrast, ensuring compliance within the private sector requires administration of the compliance and adjudication of violations. The Privacy Protection Study Commission found that requiring an employer to change its manner of maintaining and using records can drastically increase the cost of operation.

These costs include the costs of changing employment recordkeeping practices, removing relevant information from employment decisions, and implementing a social policy of employee privacy protection. These costs are not necessarily "burdensome" to the employer, however. One study found that protecting the rights of employees on a computer system could cost as little as $4 per person. Employers' concern for compliance costs may well be an unrealistic barrier to the development of regulations for privacy rights of private sector employees.

A second distinction between public- and private-sector employers offered to justify different privacy standards is that more stringent regulation is needed for government employees, because it is common for federal agencies to be overzealous in surveillance and information gathering. Private-sector employers, in contrast, do not generally have similar resources and, therefore, are unable to duplicate these invasive activities.

Common law
Law made and applied by judges, based on precedent (prior case law).

Other Bases for Right to Privacy in the Private Sector.   Private-sector employers are not bound by constitutional strictures. On a state-by-state basis, however, private sector employees may be afforded protection either by the **common law** or by statute. Many states provide common law tort claims, such as intrusion into seclusion, and other common law claims. Various torts addressed below have developed to protect individual solitude, the publication of private information, and publications that present personal information in a false light.

Statutory Claims.   State legislatures have responded to the issue of private-sector employee privacy in one of four ways:

1. Enacting legislation mirroring federal law regarding the compilation and dissemination of information.

2. Recognizing a constitutional right to privacy under their state constitutions. For example, California appellate courts have found employees terminated for refusing to submit to drug tests were wrongfully discharged in violation of the state's constitutional guarantee of a right to privacy. In Pennsylvania a court held that a drug test violates that state's policy against invasions of privacy where the methods

used do not give due regard to the employee's privacy, or if the test results disclose medical information beyond what is necessary.

3. Protecting employees only in certain areas of employment, such as personnel records or the use of credit information.

4. Leaving private-sector employees to fend for themselves while the federal laws and the Constitution afford protection to federal employees and those subject to state action.

Tort Law Protections/Common Law.   Courts in various states have developed case law, the common law, which identifies certain torts in connection with private-sector invasion of privacy. A **tort** is a legal wrong, for which the law offers a remedy. The torts of particular interest in this chapter include intrusion into solitude or seclusion, the publication of private information, defamation, and publication that places another in a false light.

Tort
Private (civil) wrong against a person or her or his property.

Publication as used in these torts means not only publishing the information in a newspaper or other mass media but generally bringing it to light or disseminating the information. Truth and absence of malice are generally not acceptable defenses by an employer sued for invasion of an employee's privacy, as they are, for instance, in connection with claims of defamation.

Intrusion into Seclusion.   To state a prima facie case for the tort of intrusion into seclusion, the plaintiff employee must show that:

- The defendant employer intentionally intruded into a private area.
- The plaintiff was entitled to privacy in that area.
- The intrusion would be objectionable to a person of reasonable sensitivity.

The intrusion may occur in any number of ways. An employer may:

- Verbally request information as a condition of employment.
- Require that its employees provide information in other ways such as through polygraphs, drug tests, or psychological tests.
- Require an annual medical examination.
- Ask others personal information about its employees.
- Go into private places belonging to the employee.

Any of these methods may constitute a wrongful invasion where it so invades the employee's private sphere that it would be objectionable to a reasonable person. On the other hand, if the employer can articulate a justifying business purpose for the inquiry/invasion, the conduct is more likely to be deemed acceptable.

In *Rogers v. Loews L'Enfant Plaza Hotel,* an employee was continually sexually harassed by her supervisor, including bothersome telephone calls to her home, during which he made lewd comments to her about her personal sex life. The sexual harassment evolved into harassment in the workplace, where the supervisor verbally abused her in front of her co-workers, kept important business-related information from her, and refused to include her in meetings. Her employer, refusing to take formal action, suggested that she change positions. The court determined that the telephone calls were not of a benign nature but, instead, were unreasonably intrusive and not normally expected. Further, the harassment constituted an intrusion into a sphere from which the employee could reasonably exclude the defendant. On these bases, the court found in favor of the employee.

In connection with scenario 1, Aravinda's decision in connection with the HIV tests may be governed, in part, by the law relating to employment testing, as discussed in Chapter 14, or disability discrimination, as discussed in Chapter 13 (since HIV is considered a disability under the Americans with Disabilities Act). On the other hand, the law relating to intrusion into seclusion would also have application here in terms of disclosure of the test results. If Aravinda discloses the results to anyone or, through her actions, leads someone to a belief about the employee's HIV status, she might be liable under this tort. In addition, it is important to consider that it is highly unlikely that Aravinda has any right to know any employee's HIV status as it is unlikely that the information would be job related. (Can you imagine what employment position might warrant this type of information? Is HIV status ever considered job related?)

O'CONNOR v. ORTEGA
480 U.S. 709 (1987)

In this case, the Court examines the issue of whether the search of an employee's office violated the Fourth Amendment to the US Constitution.

Respondent, a physician and psychiatrist, was an employee of a state hospital and had primary responsibility for training physicians in the psychiatric residency program. Hospital officials became concerned about possible improprieties in his management of the program, particularly with respect to his acquisition of a computer and charges against him concerning sexual harassment of female hospital employees and inappropriate disciplinary action against a resident. In particular, the officials thought that Dr. Ortega may have misled Dr. O'Connor into believing that the computer had been donated, when in fact the computer had been financed by the possibly coerced contributions of residents. Hospital officials were concerned with charges that Dr. Ortega had sexually harassed two female Hospital employees, and that he had taken inappropriate disciplinary action against a resident.

While he was on administrative leave pending investigation of the charges, hospital officials, allegedly in order to inventory and secure state property, searched his office and seized personal items from his desk and file cabinets that were used in administrative proceedings resulting in his discharge. No formal inventory of the property in the office was ever made, and all the other papers in the office were merely placed in boxes for storage. The employee filed an action against the hospital officials under 42 U.S.C. § 1983, alleging that the search of his office violated the Fourth Amendment. The trial court found that the search was proper in order to secure state property. The court of appeals held that the employee had a reasonable expectation of privacy in his office, thus the search violated the Fourth Amendment. The Supreme Court agrees.

O'Connor, J.

This suit under 42 U.S.C. § 1983 presents two issues concerning the Fourth Amendment rights of public employees. First, we must determine whether the respondent, a public employee, had a reasonable expectation of privacy in his office, desk, and file cabinets at his place of work. Second, we must address the appropriate Fourth Amendment standard for a search conducted by a public employer in areas in which a public employee is found to have a reasonable expectation of privacy.

* * * *

We granted certiorari and now reverse and remand.

* * * *

The Fourth Amendment protects the "right of the people to be secure in their persons, houses, papers, and effects, against unreasonable searches and seizures. . . . " Our cases establish that Dr. Ortega's Fourth Amendment rights are implicated only if the conduct of the Hospital officials at issue in this case infringed "an expectation of privacy that society is prepared to consider reasonable." . . .

Because the reasonableness of an expectation of privacy, as well as the appropriate standard for a search, is understood to differ according to context, it is essential first to delineate the boundaries of the workplace context. The workplace includes those areas and items that are related to work and are generally within the employer's control. At a hospital, for example, the hallways, cafeteria, offices, desks, and file cabinets, among other areas, are all part of the workplace. These areas remain part of the workplace context even if the employee has placed personal items in them, such as a photograph placed in a desk or a letter posted on an employee bulletin board.

Not everything that passes through the confines of the business address can be considered part of the workplace context, however. . . . The appropriate standard for a workplace search does not necessarily apply to a piece of closed personal luggage, a handbag or a briefcase that happens to be within the employer's business address.

* * *

Given the societal expectations of privacy in one's place of work, we reject the contention made by the Solicitor General and petitioners that public employees can never have a reasonable expectation of privacy in their place of work. Individuals do not lose Fourth Amendment rights merely because they work for the government instead of a private employer. The operational realities of the workplace, however, may make some employees' expectations of privacy unreasonable when an intrusion is by a supervisor rather than a law enforcement official. Public employees' expectations of privacy in their offices, desks, and file cabinets, like similar expectations of employees in the private sector, may be reduced by virtue of actual office practices and procedures, or by legitimate regulation. The employee's expectation of privacy must be assessed in the context of the employment relation. An office is seldom a private enclave free from entry by supervisors, other employees, and business and personal invitees. Instead, in many cases offices are continually entered by fellow employees and other visitors during the workday for conferences, consultations, and other work-related visits. Simply put, it is the nature of government offices that others—such as fellow employees, supervisors, consensual visitors, and the general public—may have frequent access to an individual's office. . . .

The undisputed evidence discloses that Dr. Ortega did not share his desk or file cabinets with any other employees. Dr. Ortega had occupied the office for 17 years and he kept materials in his office, which included personal correspondence, medical files, correspondence from private patients unconnected to the Hospital, personal financial records, teaching aids and notes, and personal gifts and mementos. The files on physicians in residency training were kept outside Dr. Ortega's office. Indeed, the only items found by the investigators were apparently personal items because, with the exception of the items seized for use in the administrative hearings, all the papers and effects found in the office were simply placed in boxes and made available to Dr. Ortega. Finally, we note that there was no evidence that the Hospital had established any reasonable regulation or policy discouraging employees such as Dr. Ortega from storing personal papers and effects in their desks or file cabinets, although the absence of such a policy does not create an expectation of privacy where it would not otherwise exist.

On the basis of this undisputed evidence, we accept the conclusion of the Court of Appeals that Dr. Ortega had a reasonable expectation of privacy at least in his desk and file cabinets.

Having determined that Dr. Ortega had a reasonable expectation of privacy in his office, . . . we must determine the appropriate standard of reasonableness applicable to the search. A determination of the standard of reasonableness applicable to a particular class of searches requires "balanc[ing] the nature and quality of the intrusion on the individual's Fourth Amendment interests against the importance of the governmental interests alleged to justify the intrusion." In the case of searches conducted by a public employer, we must balance the invasion of the employees' legitimate expectations of privacy against the government's need for supervision, control, and the efficient operation of the workplace.

* * *

The governmental interest justifying work-related intrusions by public employers is the efficient and proper operation of the workplace. Government agencies provide myriad services to the public, and the work of these agencies would suffer if employers were required to have probable cause before they entered an employee's desk for the purpose of finding a file or piece of office correspondence. Indeed, it is difficult to give the concept of probable cause, rooted as it is in the criminal investigatory context, much meaning when the purpose of a search is to retrieve a file for work-related reasons. Similarly, the concept of probable cause has little meaning for a routine inventory conducted by public employers for the purpose of securing state property. To ensure the efficient and proper operation of the agency, therefore, public employers must be given wide latitude to enter employee offices for work-related, noninvestigatory reasons.

We come to a similar conclusion for searches conducted pursuant to an investigation of work-related employee misconduct. Even when employers conduct an investigation, they have an interest substantially different from "the normal need for law enforcement." Public employers have an interest in ensuring that their agencies operate in an effective and efficient manner, and the work of these agencies inevitably suffers from the inefficiency, incompetence, mismanagement, or other work-related misfeasance of its employees. Indeed, in many cases, public employees are entrusted with tremendous responsibility, and the consequences of their misconduct or incompetence to both the agency and the public interest can be severe. . . . Public employers have a direct and overriding interest in ensuring that the work of the agency is conducted in a proper and efficient manner. In our view, therefore, a probable cause requirement for searches of the type at issue here would impose intolerable burdens on public employers. The delay in correcting the employee misconduct caused by the need for probable cause rather than reasonable suspicion will be translated into tangible and often irreparable damage to the agency's work, and ultimately to the public interest. Additionally, while law enforcement officials are expected to "schoo[l] themselves in the niceties of probable cause," no such expectation is generally applicable to public employers, at least when the search is not used to gather evidence of a criminal offense. It is simply unrealistic to expect supervisors in most government agencies to learn the subtleties of the probable cause standard. . . .

Balanced against the substantial government interests in the efficient and proper operation of the workplace are the privacy interests of government employees in their place of work which, while not insubstantial, are far less than those found at home or in some other contexts. . . . The employer intrusions at issue here "involve a relatively limited invasion" of employee privacy. Government offices are provided to employees for the sole purpose of facilitating the work of an agency. The employee may avoid exposing personal belongings at work by simply leaving them at home.

. . . We hold . . . that public employer intrusions on the constitutionally protected privacy interests of government employees for noninvestigatory, work-related purposes, as well as for investigations of work-related misconduct, should be judged by the standard of reasonableness under all the circumstances. Under this reasonableness standard, both the inception and the scope of the intrusion must be reasonable:

> Determining the reasonableness of any search involves a twofold inquiry: first, one must consider 'whether the . . . action was justified at its inception,' second, one must determine whether the search as actually conducted 'was reasonably related in scope to the circumstances which justified the interference in the first place.'

Ordinarily, a search of an employee's office by a supervisor will be "justified at its inception" when there are reasonable grounds for suspecting that the search will turn up evidence that the employee is guilty of work-related misconduct, or that the search is necessary for a noninvestigatory work-related purpose such as to retrieve a needed file. Because petitioners had an "individualized suspicion" of misconduct by Dr. Ortega, we need not decide whether individualized suspicion is an essential element of the standard of reasonableness that we adopt today. The search will be permissible in its scope when "the measures adopted are reasonably related to the objectives of the search and not excessively intrusive in light of . . . the nature of the [misconduct]."

* * * *

On remand, therefore, the District Court must determine the justification for the search and seizure, and evaluate the reasonableness of both the inception of the search and its scope.

Accordingly, the judgment of the Court of Appeals is REVERSED and the case is REMANDED to that court for further proceedings consistent with this opinion.

Case Questions

1. Do you think the standard of the search articulated in this opinion is the correct standard for determining whether a search violates the Fourth Amendment? Think of arguments for both perspectives—the employer and employee.

2. How can an employer protect itself from a claim of an unreasonable search conducted in the workplace? Note the court stated that a policy regarding this issue was not a determinative factor in determining the constitutionality of the search.

3. What could you do as an employee to protect yourself from a company search?

FRENCH V. UNITED PARCEL SERVICE, INC.
2 F.Supp.2d 128 (D. Mass. 1998)

Employee brought a claim for wrongful constructive discharge, invasion of privacy, and other torts after his employer kept seeking information about his mental state subsequent to an incident at an off-duty party.

O'Toole, J.

French began employment with UPS in March 1984. During the next fourteen years, he rose through the ranks to become Business Manager of the UPS facility in Chelmsford, Massachusetts. One night after completing his shift, French invited three fellow UPS employees from the Chelmsford facility to attend a beer festival. One of the employees, Daniel DeButts, was a supervisory employee but lower in rank than French. While at French's home, DeButts became intoxicated, emotionally volatile and uncontrollable. When he was left alone in French's garage to "dry out," he lost control, went into a violent rage and caused injury to himself. French and the two other employees found DeButts lying in the garage bleeding. An ambulance was called and DeButts was taken to a local hospital where he was treated and released after twenty-four hours.

Following the incident, French's supervisor, Clark, requested that French report it to his superiors at the Chelmsford facility. Believing that the incident was none of UPS's business. French initially decided not to do so. Clark continued to press French, and later French informed the division manager of operations, his superior, of the incident. French was put on leave pending an investigation. As a result of this suspension, French began treatment for depression. During the next several months while French was still on leave, UPS personnel demanded that French meet with them to discuss the incident. In addition, UPS repeatedly contacted the mental health professionals who were treating French for depression to determine his condition and prognosis

for recovery. At the end of the month, French was demoted to the position of supervisor. He returned to work but resigned about five weeks later because of the humiliation he felt in having to perform tasks that had not been his responsibility since the late 1980s. French brought this complaint, alleging four causes of action against UPS: invasion of privacy; reckless infliction of emotional distress; a violation of the Massachusetts Civil Rights Act; and wrongful constructive discharge.

* * * *

UPS has moved to dismiss all four counts of French's complaint. . . .

Count 1: Invasion of Privacy

The Massachusetts right of privacy statute provides that "[a] person shall have a right against unreasonable, substantial or serious interference with his privacy." To constitute an invasion of privacy, the invasion must be both unreasonable and serious or substantial. French alleges that UPS violated his right to privacy by: (a) insisting that he disclose details concerning an incident that occurred during off-work hours at his home; (b) repeatedly contacting his mental health providers without his consent; and (c) penalizing him, in the form of involuntary leave and demotion, for the incident.

(a) Requiring Disclosure about the Incident

For purposes of the Massachusetts Privacy Act, "private" facts are not necessarily simply those that are "not public," that is, not generally or widely known. Rather, [the Act] proscribes the "required disclosure of facts about an individual that are of a highly personal or intimate nature." The fact that a fellow employee drank too much at French's house is not a fact about French that is "highly personal or intimate." More importantly, the facts of what happened in the incident were not information that was "private" to French. Three other UPS employees took part in and observed the events, one of whom, Clark, was French's superior in the company hierarchy. Any of these persons was free to describe the incident; none had any apparent relationship with French that imposed some obligation of confidentiality. Indeed, as French's superior, Clark may even have owed UPS a duty to report, sua sponte, what he had observed. Be that as it may, it is surely unlikely that the Massachusetts courts would interpret § 1B to give French a right to prohibit Clark (or any one else who was present, including DeButts) from voluntarily disclosing what he had personally observed or done in connection with the incident. In short, the incident was simply not a "private" affair of French alone.

In addition, there are circumstances in which it is legitimate for an employer to know some "personal" information about its employees, so long as the information reasonably bears upon the employees' fitness for, or discharge of, their employment responsibilities. In the employment context "the employer's legitimate interest in determining the employees' effectiveness in their jobs [is] balanced against the seriousness of the intrusion on the employees' privacy." UPS has articulated legitimate business reasons for seeking information about the DeButts incident, including concerns about the soundness of judgment exercised by its supervisory employees in regard to alcohol abuse generally as well as in a particular setting where all participants were UPS employees. In light of these legitimate concerns, the company's questioning him about facts known to several other employees amounted, at most, to a de minimis intrusion into French's privacy, not actionable under the statute.

(b) Attempted Contact of Mental Health Care Providers

French also alleges that UPS "repeatedly contacted the mental health professionals who were treating the Plaintiff to determine his condition and prognosis for recovery. UPS made these contacts without the prior consent of the Plaintiff." The complaint does not allege that any private information was actually obtained by UPS. "Whatever unlawful invasion of privacy might have arisen if the defendant[ ] had obtained some of the information sought . . . , the short answer is that. . . . [t]he defendant['s] attempted invasion of privacy . . . failed." The Supreme Judicial Court has twice declined to decide whether the Privacy Act "reaches attempted interference with a person's privacy." The court has suggested that the statute may not reach attempts. Thus, [prior court rulings] rejection of the "failed" invasion as a basis for liability apparently continues to express the law of Massachusetts on this question.

(c) Suspension and Demotion

The employment actions UPS took against French—putting him on involuntary leave and then demoting him—were not themselves an invasion of his privacy within the scope of the statutory cause of action. If these actions were wrongful, it would have to have been for some other reason.

Therefore, French's claim for invasion of privacy must be DISMISSED.

Case Questions

1. Do you agree with the court's decision? Why or why not?
2. Why do you think the court determined the employer had a right to inquire about the incident that occurred off-duty?
3. Why do you think UPS was so concerned about an incident that occurred off-duty?

Public Disclosure of Private Facts.   To state a prima facie case for the tort of public disclosure of private facts, the plaintiff employee must show that:

- There was an intentional or negligent public disclosure
- of private matters, and
- such disclosure would be objectionable to a reasonable person of ordinary sensitivities.

The information disclosed must not be already publicized in any way, nor information the publication of which the plaintiff has consented. Therefore, in *Pemberton v. Bethlehem Steel Corp.,* publication of an employee's criminal record did not constitute public disclosure of private facts, because the criminal record did not contain private facts; it was information that was already accessible by the public.

The public disclosure must be either communication to the public at large or to so many people that the matter must be regarded as substantially certain to become one of public knowledge, or one of knowledge to a particular public whose knowledge of the private facts would be embarrassing to the employee. Therefore, publication to all of the employees in a company may be sufficient, while disclosure to a limited number of supervisors may not.

Several states have enacted legislation codifying this common law doctrine under the rubric of breach of confidentiality. Connecticut, for instance, has passed legislation requiring employers to maintain employee medical records separate from other personnel records. Other states have limited an employer's ability to disclose personnel-related information or allowed a cause of action where, through the employer's negligent maintenance of personnel files, inaccurate employee information is communicated to a third party.

YODER JR. V. INGERSOLL-RAND COMPANY A.K.A. ARO
31 F.Supp.2d 565 (W.D. Ohio 1997)

An employee brings suit against the employer for disclosing to the employee's mother that he had AIDS, The court dismissed this action for invasion of privacy and other claims.

Katz, J.

Lavern Yoder brought an action against his employer to recover for damages he alleged were caused as a result of Defendant's failure to keep his medical records confidential. Lavern Yoder was employed by Defendant as a tow motor driver. Around November 1993, Yoder learned that he was HIV-positive. Yoder made every effort to keep his HIV-positive status confidential from his employer because he was concerned that he might suffer adverse employment consequences if his employer or co-workers learned of his condition. In August 1995, Yoder's doctor recommended that he take a medical leave of absence because of stress-induced asthma. He obtained the necessary disability form. One side required completion by the employee; the other side required completion by the treating physician. After Yoder completed his information, the doctor completed his side but omitted the date of total disability. When the form was returned to Yoder, he forwarded the information to his doctor with an envelope with his employer's address on it. Yoder did not specifically direct it to the hourly disability coordinator, Mary Sullivan.

For reasons unknown to the parties, the envelope was returned to the employer undelivered to the doctor. The firm's procedure for mail without an individual name is for the mail clerk to open it. The mail clerk opened the envelope in order to determine where it should be routed, and read enough of its contents to find Yoder's name. The mail clerk did not read the document further. She replaced the Disability Benefit Request form in the envelope, placed that envelope in a large goldenrod interoffice envelope, put Yoder's name on the interoffice envelope, and routed it to him via his supervisor. Because Yoder was not at work that day, his supervisor received the interoffice envelope. The supervisor noticed that the inner envelope was addressed to the Medical College of Ohio, and thought it might contain urgent information. He did not open the envelope. Since Yoder was not at work, his supervisor gave the envelope to Yoder's mother, who also worked for the firm, and directed her to give to him. Later that day, Yoder's mother opened the envelope and read its contents. She learned from the Physician's Statement that he had AIDS. She had known her son was HIV-positive but did not know he had AIDS. Yoder brought a six-count complaint against the firm for permitting the unauthorized disclosure of his medical condition. Count three alleged the disclosure violated his Fourteenth Amendment right to privacy under the Constitution and count four alleged state common law claim for invasion of privacy. Both sides moved for summary judgment.

* * * *

D. Fourteenth Amendment Privacy Right

In Count III, Plaintiff alleges that the disclosure violated his Fourteenth Amendment right to privacy under the United States Constitution. However, the Fourteenth Amendment applies only to governmental action, and Defendant is not a governmental agency. Defendant's motion for summary judgment on Count III is granted.

E. Invasion of Privacy

In Count IV, Plaintiff brings a common law claim for invasion of privacy. . . .

Ohio courts recognize the tort of invasion of privacy to encompass four distinct types of wrongful acts: (1) intrusion into the plaintiff's seclusion, solitude, or private affairs; (2) public disclosure of private facts about the plaintiff with which the public has no legitimate concern; (3) publicity that places the plaintiff in a false light; and (4) appropriation of the plaintiff's name or likeness for the defendant's advantage.

Yoder alleges an invasion of privacy under the second theory, which is also known as the "publicity" tort. In order successfully to make out a claim under the "publicity" prong, Plaintiff must show five elements:

(1) there must be publicity, i.e., the disclosure must be of a public nature, not private;

(2) the facts disclosed must be those concerning the private life of an individual, not his public life;

(3) the matter publicized must be one which would be highly offensive and objectionable to a reasonable person of ordinary sensibilities;

(4) the publication must have been made intentionally, not negligently; and

(5) the matter publicized must not be a legitimate concern to the public.

Plaintiff can show neither the first nor the fourth element of this test. As to the first element,

Plaintiff can prevail only if he shows that the matter has been communicated to "the public at large, or to so many persons that the matter must be regarded as substantially certain to become one of public knowledge." It is not enough to show merely that the matter was communicated by the defendant to a third person. The record evidence indicates that Plaintiff's HIV/AIDS status was actually communicated to only one unauthorized person. Even if the Court accepts Plaintiff's argument that mail clerk Kornrumpf and supervisor Chroninger should be treated as having received the information because they had the opportunity to read Plaintiff's medical report, the information was communicated to three people at most. Three people do not constitute "the public at large." Plaintiff cannot meet the publicity prong of the test.

As to the fourth element, Plaintiff cannot show that Defendant, or its authorized agents, made the disclosure intentionally, even as to Plaintiff's mother. It is undisputed that nothing on the outside of the envelope received in the ARO mail room indicated that it contained a confidential medical record. Kornrumpf's testimony that she did not read the form beyond Plaintiff's name, and did not know that it was a confidential medical record, is undisputed. Chroninger's testimony that he did not read the form, and did not know

that it was a confidential medical record, is undisputed. It is a logical impossibility for a party intentionally to disclose information that it does not know it has. Furthermore, the disclosure would not have occurred without Plaintiff's mother's intervening act of opening and reading the medical records without authorization from Defendant. Plaintiff cannot meet the intent prong of the test. Defendant's motion for summary judgment on Count IV is granted.

* * * *

Plaintiff's motion for summary judgment is DENIED. Defendant's motion for summary judgment is GRANTED.

Case Questions

1. Do you think Yoder should have prevailed on his state law claim of invasion of privacy? Why or why not?

2. Do you think this case would have been decided differently if the mail clerk and Yoder's supervisor did read the doctor's statements?

3. How many people would have to read a sensitive document such as this to meet the "public disclosure" requirement for an individual to prevail on his or her claim?

Defamation.   In 1985, it was determined that one-third of all libel suits filed arose from a former employee's claim of bad references by a previous employer. Libel refers to defamation in a written document, while slander consists of defamation in an oral statement. Either may occur during the course of a reference process. And, while the prima facie case of defamation requires a false statement, even a vague statement that casts doubt on the reputation of an individual by inference can cause difficulties for an employer if it cannot be substantiated.

The elements of a claim for defamation include:

- false and defamatory words concerning employee,
- negligently or intentionally communicated to a third party without the employee's consent (publication), and
- resulting harm to the employee defamed.

One cautious solution to this problem area is to request that all employees fill out an exit interview form, which asks, "Do you authorize us to give a reference?" If the applicant answers yes, she or he should be asked to sign a release of liability for the company. One interesting form of defamation has evolved over the past decade. Ordinarily defamation arises from someone other than the defamed employee making defamatory statements about an employee. However, where an employee is given a false or defamatory reason for her or his discharge, the employee is the one who is forced to publicize it to prospective employers.

These circumstances give rise to a cause of action for defamation, termed *compelled self-disclosure,* because the employee is left with no choice but to tell the prospective employer the defamatory reasons for her or his discharge. Barring this result, the employee would be forced to fabricate reasons different from those given by the former employer and run the risk of being reprimanded or terminated for not telling the truth.

An employer may defend against an employee's claim of defamation by establishing the truth of the information communicated. While truth is a complete defense to defamation, it can be difficult to prove without complex paper management.

Employers may also be immune from liability for certain types of statement because of court-recognized privileges in connection with them. For example, an employer is privileged to make statements, even if defamatory, where the statement is made in the course of a judicial proceeding, or where the statement is made in good faith by one who has a legitimate business purpose in making the communication (e.g., ex-employer) to one who has a business interest in learning the information (e.g., a prospective employer). This privilege would apply where a former employer offers a good faith reference to an employee's prospective employer. (See additional discussion of liability for references, below.) Good faith means that the employer's statement, though defamatory, is not made with malice or ill will toward the employee.

LOVE V. UNIVERSITY OF CINCINNATI HOSPITAL
694 N.E.2d 1005 (Ohio Ct. Cl. 1997)

An employee sued for defamation and breach of contract after a former employer gave a prospective employer details of the employee's termination, despite an agreement that he would not do so.

Gartin, J.

Douglas Love was employed by the employer, University of Cincinnati Hospital, for a little over a year. The parties entered into a settlement agreement when Love resigned which stated that the University records would indicate that Love resigned to seek other employment. The agreement also stated that, in response to requests from outside the University, the University would volunteer only dates of employment, rates of pay, titles of positions held, and accomplishments in favor of Love, provided that such informational requests were directed only to Michael Grodi or Terry White. When Grodi was contacted by an employer considering Love for a position, in response to the question "would you consider rehiring Love if that were to become an option," Grodi informed her that he would not rehire Love because an unprofessional situation had developed between Love and the food service manager. When questioned further, Grodi stated that Love had a difficult time dealing with his coworkers, especially his subordinates. The prospective employer testified that, as a result of Grodi's remarks, she did not recommend Love for the position for which he was being considered nor did she forward his name to anyone else for consideration. A trial was held before a magistrate on Love's action for breach of a settlement agreement and defamation.

* * * *

It is axiomatic that a settlement agreement is a contract designed to terminate a claim by preventing or ending litigation and that such agreements are valid and enforceable by either party. Further, settlement agreements are highly favored in the law.

The words in the settlement agreement must be given their plain meaning. Any negative reference is contrary to the wording utilized in the settlement agreement. The magistrate finds that although [the prospective employer] could not hire plaintiff, she could have recommended him for the contract position; however, as a result of

Grodi's comments, she chose not to recommend him for the position. The magistrate finds that Grodi's comments did breach the settlement agreement, since he was to provide only "accomplishments in the favor of Love." Therefore, the magistrate finds that plaintiff's breach of contract claim was proven by a preponderance of the evidence.

As to the defamation claim, defendant proved by a preponderance of the evidence that plaintiff did have trouble getting along with at least two coworkers. Truth is a complete defense to a claim for defamation. [The relevant statute] states that, "[i]n an action for a libel or a slander, the defendant may allege and prove the truth of the matter charged as defamatory. Proof of the truth thereof shall be considered a complete defense." The magistrate finds that defendant was truthful in what was told to [the prospective employer] despite the fact that, pursuant to the settlement agreement, it should not have been communicated. Therefore, defendant shall prevail on the defamation claim. Based upon the above, judgment is rendered **in favor of plaintiff** on the breach of settlement agreement and **in favor of defendant** on plaintiff's defamation claim.

Case Questions

1. Who do you think "won" in this case?
2. As an employer, would you have handled this situation any differently? Why or why not?
3. Although the employer did not suffer any damages in this suit, can you foresee any problems this conduct could bring in the future?

Publication in a False Light.   The prima facie case of publication in a false light requires that: there was a public disclosure of facts that place the employee in a false light before the public if the false light would be highly offensive to a reasonable person, and the person providing the information had knowledge of or recklessly disregarded the falsity or false light of the publication.

Voluntary consent to publication of the information constitutes an absolute bar to a false light action. This type of tort differs from defamation where disclosure to even one other person than the employer or employee satisfies the requirements. The tort of publicizing someone in a false light requires that the general public be given a false image of the employee. In a false light action, the damage for which the employee is compensated is the inability to be left alone, while defamation compensates the employee for injury to her reputation in the public's perception.

Note that any of the above claims may be waived by the employee if the employee also publishes the information or willingly or knowingly permits it to be published. For example, in the *Cummings v. Walsh Construction Co.,* the employee complained of public disclosure of embarrassing private facts, consisting of information relating to a sexual relationship in which she was engaged with her supervisor. The court held that, where the employee had informed others of her actions, she waived her right not to have her supervisor disclose the nature of their relationship.

As with defamation, an exception to this waiver exists in the form of compelled self-publication, where an employer provides the employee with a false reason as the basis for termination and the employee is compelled to restate this reason when asked by a future employer the basis of departure from the previous job. Therefore, where the employer intentionally misstates the basis for the discharge, that employer may be subject to liability for libel, because it is aware that the employee will be forced to repeat (or "publish") that reason to others.

In *Lewis v. Equitable Life Assurance Society of the United States,* the court found the employer liable for defamation where it refused to offer a reference to the future employer of four former employees. The employees, therefore, were forced to explain the circumstances themselves. They had been terminated for "gross insubordination" as a result of their refusal to modify expenses reports. While the court of appeals noted that this decision could have a weighty impact on employers, it awarded the employees nearly $1 million in damages. The Supreme Court of Minnesota later slightly reduced the award.

Breach of Contract.   An employee may also contest an invasion of privacy by her or his employer on the basis of a breach of contract. The contract may be an actual employment contract, collective bargaining agreement, or one found to exist because of promises in an employment handbook or a policy manual.

Regulation of Employee's Off-Work Activities.   Employers may regulate the off-work activities of their employees where they believe that the off-work conduct affects the employee's performance at the workplace. However, control has been limited to what is sufficiently related to a legitimate business interest.

For example, drug testing in positions that affect the public safety, such as a bus driver, would not constitute an unlawful intrusion, because the employer's interest in learning of that information is justified. Where the attempted employer control goes beyond the acceptable realm, courts have upheld an exception to the employment-at-will doctrine based on public policy concerns for personal privacy or, depending on the circumstances, intentional infliction of emotional distress.

For instance, an employer may attempt to regulate those with whom an employee becomes romantically involved; under these circumstances, the employer would have to show that dating a coworker, for example, has an adverse effect on morale. Or where an employer prohibits employees from living with someone who is not the employee's spouse, the employer would have to show that this prohibition is somehow work-related.

Scenario

In connection with scenario three, does Abraham have to quit his nighttime dancing job? This is actually a difficult question and one that the courts have yet to answer. As long as Abraham can show that his dancing truly has no impact on his work (i.e., that the club is located in a different town from that of his clientele, or that the club has an excellent reputation for beautiful, artistic dancing styles), then he would not have to quit his night job. On the other hand, if Abraham's reputation is soiled by his connection with this club and his boss can show that his work has a negative impact on his ability to perform, then she may be justified in her ultimatum.

What Is the Scope of the Right to Privacy?

Not all information is protected by the right to privacy. An employer who is looking for an applicant with nursing experience may be justified in investigating an applicant's past employment history but not her marital status, husband's job history, or off-duty dress and grooming habits. Also, the privacy rights of applicants may be slightly different in degree than those of employees, due to the conception that applicants have less to lose than incumbent employees.

The greatest intrusions generally take place at the application stage. The applicant is most vulnerable to intrusions at this point, because, to obtain employment, the applicant will disclose an abundance of information, such as criminal records or familial relationships. Applicants are often asked to sign waivers that give permission to the prospective employer to collect and use any information the employer is able to locate.

Employer's Information-Gathering Process/Justified Use/Disclosure of Information

The above discussion focused on the scope of the privacy rights of the employee in connection with the dissemination of information. Privacy, however, can be invaded not only by a disclosure of specific types of information but also by the process pursuant to which the information has been obtained. An employer may be liable for its *process* of information gathering, storing, or utilization. Improper retrieval of information may be an invasion where the process of collection constitutes harassment, improper filing or dissemination of the information collected may leave the employer liable for defamation actions, and inappropriate use of data for other purposes than those for which it was collected may inflict other harms.

The collection or retrieval of information may occur in a variety of ways, depending on the stage of employment and the needs of the employer. For example, an employer may merely make use of the information provided by an applicant on her or his application form, or it may telephone prior employers to verify the data provided by the applicant. One employer may feel confident in an employee's educational background when she sees the employee's diplomas hung on the office wall, while a different employer may feel the need to contact prior educational institutions to verify attendance and actual graduation. On the more lenient end of the spectrum, the employer may rest assured that the employee is all that he states that he is on the application form, while, in more extreme situations, an employer may subject its employees to polygraph analyses and drug tests.

As is covered extensively in other chapters, employers are limited in the questions that may be asked of a potential employee. For example, an employer may not ask an applicant whether she or he is married, plans to have children, or the nature of her or his family's origin. These questions are likely to violate Title VII of the Civil Rights Act, because an employer is prohibited from reaching any employment decision on the basis of their answers.

In connection with the storage of the information collected, employers must be careful to ensure that the information is stored in such a manner that it will not fall into the "wrong" hands. If an improper party has access to the personal information, the employer, again, may be subject to a defamation action by the employee based on the wrongful invasion of her personal affairs. In today's world of advanced computer data storage, new issues arise that have not been previously litigated. For instance, where an item is stored in a computer, it is crucial to either close the file to all but those who have a correct entry code or to delete private information. Access to computer terminals throughout an office creates a problem concerning the dissemination of the private information and the control of access.

The employer offering the reference is responsible for its dissemination only to appropriate parties. A fax machine or postcard would be unacceptable means of transmitting a reference, since this would allow access by innumerable others. Similarly, an employer may get caught wrongfully disclosing information to an inappropriate individual in the case of the telephone reference. Failure to confirm the identity of the caller and purpose of the call may allow disclosure to one who otherwise should have no access to this information.

Electronic Monitoring or Surveillance of Employee Activities

With the dramatic increase in the use of technology in the workplace, several issues have recently developed surrounding the use of e-mail and the Internet. As of 1999, both areas are relatively undeveloped in the casebooks. Because of this, many state and district courts have dealt with the issues differently, or have not faced them at all.

Today, invasions of privacy in the workplace occur far more frequently than one might expect. In fact, while a 1993 study indicated that 30 percent of 1,000 firms surveyed had searched their employees' computer files, electronic mail, and voice-mail, subjecting more than 20 million employees to computer monitoring alone, a more recent study evidences the explosion of growth in its report that 67 percent of firms engage in monitoring.[2] The ACLU reports that the number of people subject to surveillance in the workplace has risen from 8 million in 1991 to more than 30 million in 1997.[3] Workers believe that something should be done to protect them. In a poll of more than 4,000 people, 90 percent favor legislation that would protect them from technological privacy invasions.[4]

While no related case has yet reached the Supreme Court, these actions have received lower court attention. As early as 1990, Epson America survived a lawsuit filed by a terminated employee who had complained about Epson's practice of reading all employee e-mail.[5] In that case, the court distinguished the practice of *intercepting* an e-mail transmission from storing and reading e-mail transmissions once they had been sent. However, relying on court precedent for protection is a double-edged sword. An employee–plaintiff in one federal action won a case against his employer where the employer had monitored the worker's telephone for a period of 24 hours in order to determine whether the worker was planning a robbery. The court held that the company had gone too far and had insufficient evidence to

[2]Amer. Mgmt. Assn., "More firms checking E-mail," www.amanet.org/research/specials/ monit.html. For a time comparison, see also Samuel Greengard, "Privacy: Entitlement or Illusion?" *Personnel Journal,* May 1996, p. 74; *see also* Andre Bacard, *"E-mail Privacy FAQ,"* www.well.com/ user/abacard/email.htm; Deborah Jacobs, "The Perils of Policing Employees," 19 *Small Business Reports,* no. 2 (Feb. 1994), p. 22 [Reports that more than one in five companies electronically eavesdrop on their employees]; Kristin Bell DeTienne, "Big Brother or Friendly Coach?" *The Futurist* (Sept./Oct. 1993), p. 33 [Reports that, in 1993, 26 million workers were subject to monitoring in their jobs, which will rise to 30 million by the year 2000.] American Management Association, Electronic Monitoring and Surveillance, Summary of Key Findings (1997). *See also,* American Civil Liberties Union, "New Study on Workplace Surveillance Highlights Lack of Protections, ACLU Says," press release (May 23, 1997); "Bawdy Bandwidth," *Chicago Tribune* (June 22, 1998), p. 4–1 [citing study by Euron Software, Inc. on workplace Internet surf abuse that found that 62 percent of companies that offer internet access to workers also monitor their use. One-third of those firms reported terminating employees for using the Internet to access pornography-related sites.] Note that workplace surveillance has occurred since the beginning of the employment relationship itself; only now (with the possibilities afforded by technological advances) have issues arisen that have never before been addressed. In addition, the potential for invasion is much greater as a result of new devices and techniques; consequently, an employee may be more concerned about surveillance than ever before.

[3]American Civil Liberties Union, "New Study on Workplace Surveillance Highlights Lack of Protections, ACLU Says," press release (May 23, 1997).

[4]B. Horovitz, "80% Fear Loss of Privacy to Computers," *USA Today* (Oct. 31, 1995), p. A1; *see also Ethics Officer Association, Technology & Ethics in the Workplace* (1998). [Study of 4,000 workers found that 75 percent believed invasion of privacy issues to be a primary concern.]

[5]No. SCW112749 Cal. Sup. Ct., L.A. Cty., 1989, *appeal den'd,* Sup. Ct. Ca., 994 Cal. LEXIS 3670 (6/29/94); James McNair, "When You Use Email at Work, Your Boss May Be Looking In," *Telecom Digest,* icg.stwing.upenn.edu/cis500/reading.062.htm, reprinted from *The Miami Herald.*

support its claims.[6] In another action, Northern Telecom settled a claim brought by employees who were allegedly secretly monitored over a 13-year period. In this case, Telecom agreed to pay $50,000 to individual plaintiffs and $125,000 for attorneys' fees.[7]

While, as stated earlier, there is little legislation that actually relates to these areas specifically, there is some statutory protection from overt intrusions, though the statute does not apply in all circumstances. The federal wiretapping statute, Title III of the Omnibus Crime Control and Safe Streets Act of 1968, as amended by the Electronic Communications Privacy Act of 1986 (18 U.S.C. §§2510–20), protect private and public sector employees from employer monitoring of their telephone calls and other communications without a court order.

There are two exceptions to this general prohibition. First, interception is authorized where one of the parties to the communication has given prior consent. Second, the "business extension" provision creates an exception where the equipment used is what is used in the ordinary course of business. An employer must be able to state a legitimate business purpose and there must be minimal intrusions into employee privacy.

Employee Internet Use

Monitoring is made simpler through an employee's use of a computer. Employers now customarily provide many employees with personal computers that are linked either to the Internet or, at least, to an internal network. Employers can monitor the computer user's activities. To the type of information that can be gathered, the Privacy Demonstration Page of the Center for Democracy and Technology can feed back to viewers information that it finds out merely because one has accessed the page. For instance, the page tells one individual viewer the type of computer that the viewer is using, the browser the individual is using, the server from which the viewer is operating and some of the pages the viewer has recently visited. While this information may not necessarily seem personal to some, consider the facts of scenario two. The employer in that case seems to be within its rights to monitor the use of its computers. While notice of this type of monitoring is recommended and may have a deterrent effect on inappropriate computer use (thus eliminating the need to actually conduct the monitoring), the law does not mandate notice in this situation.

Scenario

The need to monitor employees' usage becomes clear when one focuses on five areas of potential employer liability: defamation, copyright infringement, sexual harassment, discrimination, and obscenity.

As discussed previously in this chapter, the guidelines that apply to a general defamation claim also apply to issues surrounding the Internet. However, some

---

[6]Winn Schwartau, "Who Controls Network Usage Anyway?" *Network World* (May 22, 1995), p. 71.

[7]Bureau of National Affairs, "Northern Telecom Settles with CWA on Monitoring," *Individual Employment Rights* (Mar. 10, 1992), p. 1.

contend that the opportunity for harm is far greater. This is because employees and employers can easily disseminate information to a wide range of media. Not only can employers be subject to defamation claims by their own employees, but the far greater threat is the liability a company faces when an employee, as a representative of the employer, defames another individual using the Internet (with access provided by the employer) as the medium.

Further, firms are concerned about inappropriate use of web software such as when an employee downloads program files without compensating the creator, or where employees use copywritten information from the web without giving credit to the original author, thereby exposing the firm to potentially significant copyright infringement liability. Finally, when an employee downloads software programs from the web, the computer systems within the firm have the potential to be compromised by viruses or even unauthorized access.

Sexual harassment and discrimination by employees via the web are governed by the same general guidelines that were previously discussed in the chapters addressing sexual harassment and discrimination. However, many employees believe that once an e-mail message is deleted, it is permanently removed from the system. This is not the case. Because of this, e-mail sent on company time, with contents constituting sexual harassment or that might create a hostile working environment, or containing other forms of discrimination, may easily be discovered, both by the employer and opposing parties to litigation against the employer. E-mail is discussed in greater detail in the next section. Finally, obscenity becomes a critical issue, and the company may be placed at risk when employees download pornographic images while in the workplace.

Moreover, a firm might be concerned about the impression created when an employee visits various sites. Assume, for instance, that Firm A is involved in research and development. If its employees peruse specific locations of its competitors' sites, those competitors can learn which of its technologies interests Firm A's employees, thereby potentially having inadvertent access to the direction of Firm A's research and development.

Employers seem to have business justification for this type of monitoring—"If [the employer] sees you doing something on the screen that they think you can do in a quicker way, they can tell you. They can even tell you ways to talk to people, or they can tell you ways to do things quicker to end your [customer service] call quicker," says Kathy Joynes, a travel agent for American Express who works out of her home, but whose supervisor can shadow her computer screen at any time.[8]

Because of the overall potential liability for their employees' actions, employers should develop a formal policy or program regulating employee usage of the Internet. In addition to a formal policy, employers may choose to establish a process of monitoring their employee's Internet usage. This may involve tracking websites visited and the amount of time spent at each site with software programs designed

---

[8]Dan Charles, "All Things Considered: High-Tech Equipment in the Workplace," *National Public Radio* (Apr. 1, 1996).

for that specific purpose. This type of monitoring, however, is still in its infancy. Further, employers need to consider the employees' rights to free speech and privacy when developing such policies and systems.

Employee E-mail Usage

Employers' needs to monitor e-mail must be weighed against the employees' right to privacy. The employer is interested in ensuring that the e-mail system is not being used in ways that offend others, to harm morale, or for disruptive purposes. Likewise, an employer may choose to review e-mail in connection with a reasonable investigation of possible employee misconduct. Also, companies that maintain sensitive data may be concerned about disclosure of this information by disloyal or careless employees, apparently justifying this type of intrusion. In a suit filed in 1999 in San Francisco Superior Court, *NationsBanc Montgomery Securities v. Todd Haggerty,* NationsBanc sued its former employee, Haggerty. NationsBanc claimed that Haggerty and several other former employees, while employed at NationsBanc, downloaded proprietary documents and e-mailed them to the e-mail address of Haggerty's newly established business, a competitor of NationsBanc. Haggerty argued that his privacy was wrongfully invaded. No decision has yet been rendered.

While monitoring e-mail transmissions over telephone lines is forbidden by the ECPA, communications within a firm do not generally go over the phone lines and therefore may be legally available to employers. In addition, there are numerous exceptions to the ECPA's prohibitions, including situations where one party to the transmission consents, where the provider of the communication service can monitor communications, or where the monitoring is done in the ordinary course of business. In order to satisfy the ECPA consent exception, however, the employer's interception must not exceed the scope of the employee's consent. Employers must be aware, as well, that an employee's knowledge that the employer is monitoring certain communications is insufficient to be considered implied consent. To avoid liability, employers must specifically inform employees of the extent and circumstances under which e-mail communications will be monitored.

There are numerous ways in which an employer can meet its business necessity to monitor e-mail, protect itself from liability, and at the same time, respect the employees' legitimate expectation of privacy in the workplace. Employers should develop concise written policies and procedures regarding the use of company computers, specifically e-mail. The Society for Human Resource Management strongly encourages companies both to adopt policies that address employee privacy and to ensure that employees are notified of such policies. Any e-mail policy should be incorporated in the company policies and procedures manuals, employee handbooks, and instruction aids to ensure that the employee receives consistent information regarding the employer's rights to monitor employee e-mail. Additionally, a company could display a notice each time an employee logs on to a company computer indicating the computers are only to be used for business-related communication or explaining that the employee has no reasonable expectation of privacy in the electronic messages. Employers can also periodically send memos reminding employees of the policy.

"An employer has a strong defense to a potential invasion of privacy claim by an employee if the employer implements an e-mail policy that is both written and communicated to the employee, thereby stating that e-mail is for business purposes only and the employer may access the e-mail both in the ordinary course of business and if business reasons necessitate. Thus, an employer protects itself from lawsuits when it adopts an e-mail policy, notifies the employees of the policy, and faithfully adheres to it."[9]

Kevin Conlon, District Counsel for the Communication Workers of America, suggests these additional guidelines that may be considered in formulating an accountable process for employee monitoring.

1. There should be no monitoring in highly private areas, such as restrooms.
2. Monitoring should be limited to the workplace.
3. Employees should have full access to any information gathered through monitoring.
4. Continuous monitoring should be banned.
5. All forms of *secret* monitoring should be banned. Advance notice should be given.
6. Only information relevant to the job should be collected.
7. Monitoring should result in the attainment of some business interest.

As early as 1970, the US Department of Health, Education and Welfare developed principles along these same lines for a Code of Fair Employment Practices (CFEP), which includes five points. A review of these principles evidences attention to fundamental philosophical concerns such as a respect for individual autonomy and a congruent respect for business needs, as well as accountability.

The first CFEP principle is *openness,* meaning that maintenance or collection of personal information must be disclosed to the subject. The second principle is *disclosure.* A subject should be informed not only of the fact that information is to be collected, but also the contents of that information and the purposes for which it will be used. The third principle is the concept of *secondary usage,* which requires that information collected for one purpose may not be used for a second purpose. Fourth, the CFEP mandates that individuals have the right to *correction* of erroneous personal information. The fifth principle directs that firms maintain appropriate *security* surrounding the information collected in order to protect against misuse.

Failure to adhere to any of the above-stated principles may result in a violation of corporate integrity or a lack of accountability to those affected by the monitoring. If a manager consistently reviews all of her or his subordinate's e-mails with no notice to the individual workers and without regard to the business relatedness of the particular missives, the manager may acquire information that is completely

---

[9]Michael Traynor, "How Extensively Can an Employer Monitor Messages?" *National Law Journal,* Jan. 31, 1994, at S2, S3, citing *Bourke v. Nissan Motor Corp. in U.S.A.,* No. B068705 (Cal. App. 2d Dist., Div 5) (July 26, 1993).

unrelated to the person's job but that affects the way in which the manager treats the employee. For instance, through review of e-mail, a manager might find out that a worker is a member of a far-right Republican organization. The manager, a staunch Democrat, may allow this division between them to impact how she or he treats the worker. In the end, this result would be unprofitable for the business as a whole.

As is apparent from the above discussion, it is possible to implement a monitoring program that is true to the values of the firm and accountable to those it impacts—the workers. Appropriate attention to the nature and extent of the monitoring, the notice given to those monitored, and the ethical management of the information obtained will ensure a balance of employer and employee interests.

MICHAEL A. SMYTH V. THE PILLSBURY COMPANY
914 F.Supp 97 (G.D. Penn. 1996)

Michael Smyth worked for the Pillsbury Company. Pillsbury installed an electronic mail (e-mail) system in order to "promote internal communications between its employees." Pillsbury told its employees that e-mail transmissions were confidential and would not be intercepted or used by Pillsbury against its employees as grounds for termination. Smyth exchanged e-mails with his supervisor which were, in fact, intercepted by Pillsbury management. Three months later, Smyth was terminated for transmitting what it deemed to be "inappropriate and unprofessional comments" over its e-mail system. (The e-mails contained threats to "kill the backstabbing bastards" in discussions of management and referred to the company holiday party as the "Jim Jones Koolaid affair.")

Weiner, J.

Pennsylvania is an employment at-will jurisdiction and an employer "may discharge an employee with or without cause, at pleasure, unless restrained by some contract."

However, in the most limited of circumstances, exceptions have been recognized where discharge of an at-will employee threatens or violates a clear mandate of public policy. A "clear mandate" of public policy must be of a type that "strikes at the heart of a citizen's social right, duties and responsibilities."

Plaintiff claims that his termination was in violation of "public policy which precludes an employer from terminating an employee in violation of the employee's right to privacy as embodied in Pennsylvania common law." In support for this proposition, plaintiff directs our attention to a decision by our Court of Appeals in *Borse v. Piece Goods Shop, Inc.* In *Borse,* the plaintiff sued her employer alleging wrongful discharge as a result of her refusal to submit to urinalysis screening and personal property searches at her work place pursuant to the employer's drug and alcohol policy. After rejecting plaintiff's argument that the employer's drug and alcohol program violated public policy encompassed in the United States and Pennsylvania Constitutions, our Court of Appeals stated "our review of Pennsylvania law reveals other evidence of a public policy that may, under certain circumstances, give rise to a wrongful discharge action related to urinalysis or to personal property searches. Specifically, we refer to the Pennsylvania common law regarding tortious invasion of privacy."

The Court of Appeals in *Borse,* observed that one of the torts which Pennsylvania recognizes as encompassing an action for invasion of privacy is the tort of "intrusion upon seclusion." As noted by the Court of Appeals, the Restatement (Second) of Torts defines the tort as follows:

> One who intentionally intrudes, physically or otherwise, upon the solitude or seclusion of another or his private affairs or concerns, is subject to liability to the other for invasion of his privacy, if the intrusion would be highly offensive to a reasonable person.

Liability only attaches when the "intrusion is substantial and would be highly offensive to the 'ordinary reasonable person.'" Although the Court of Appeals in *Borse* observed that "the Pennsylvania courts have not had occasion to consider whether a discharge related to an employer's tortious invasion of an employee's privacy violates public policy," the Court of Appeals predicted that in any claim where the employee claimed that his discharge related to an invasion of his privacy "the Pennsylvania Supreme Court would examine the facts and circumstances surrounding the alleged invasion of privacy. If the court determined that the discharge was related to a substantial and highly offensive invasion of the employee's privacy, [the Court of Appeals] believe that it would conclude that the discharge violated public policy." In determining whether an alleged invasion of privacy is substantial and highly offensive to a reasonable person, the Court of Appeals predicted that Pennsylvania would adopt a balancing test which balances the employee's privacy interest against the employer's interest in maintaining a drug-free workplace. Because the Court of Appeals in Borse could "envision at least two ways in which an employer's drug and alcohol program

might violate the public policy protecting individuals from tortious invasion of privacy by private actors" the Court vacated the district court's order dismissing the plaintiff's complaint and remanded the case to the district court with directions to grant Borse leave to amend the Complaint to allege how the defendant's drug and alcohol program violates her right to privacy.

Applying the Restatement definition of the tort of intrusion upon seclusion to the facts and circumstances of the case *sub judice,* we find that plaintiff has failed to state a claim upon which relief can be granted. In the first instance, unlike urinalysis and personal property searches, we do not find a reasonable expectation of privacy in e-mail communications voluntarily made by an employee to his supervisor over the company e-mail system notwithstanding any assurances that such communications would not be intercepted by management. Once plaintiff communicated the alleged unprofessional comments to a second person (his supervisor) over an e-mail system which was apparently utilized by the entire company, any reasonable expectation of privacy was lost. Significantly, the defendant did not require plaintiff, as in the case of a urinalysis or personal property search, to disclose any personal information about himself. Rather, plaintiff voluntarily communicated the alleged unprofessional comments over the company e-mail system. We find no privacy interests in such communications.

In the second instance, even if we found that an employee had a reasonable expectation of privacy in the contents of his e-mail communications over the company e-mail system, we do not find that a reasonable person would consider the defendant's interception of these communications to be a substantial and highly offensive invasion of his privacy. Again, we note that by intercepting such communications, the company is not, as in the case of urinalysis or personal property searches, requiring the employee to disclose any personal information about himself or invading the employee's person or personal effects. Moreover, the company's interest in preventing inappropriate and unprofessional comments or even illegal activity over its e-mail system outweighs any privacy interest the employee may have in those comments.

In sum, we find that the defendant's actions did not tortiously invade the plaintiff's privacy and, therefore, did not violate public policy. As a result, the motion to dismiss is GRANTED.

Case Questions

1. Do you agree with the court's conclusion that, even if Smyth had a reasonable expectation of privacy of his transmissions, an interception would not be highly offensive to a reasonable person?

2. Are you sympathetic to an employer's reasons for wanting to intercept e-mail such as that involved in this case?

3. The court seems to be saying that, even though Pillsbury stated that it would not intercept e-mail, the employee should not have relied on this promise. Do you agree with this conclusion?

Waivers of Privacy Rights

On occasion, an employer may request that an employee waive her or his privacy rights as a condition of employment. This condition could be a **search.** A **waiver** would exempt the employer from liability for claims the employee may have as a result of privacy issues. While a valid waiver must be voluntarily given, requiring a waiver as an employment condition is a questionable approach. Employers maintain a superior bargaining position from which to negotiate such an arrangement, so voluntariness is questionable.

A search
A physical invasion of a person's space, belongings, or body.

Waivers exist at all stages of employment, from preemployment medical screenings to a waiver of age discrimination claims when being bought out of one's job at old age. Courts are not consistent in their acceptance of these waivers; but one common link among those that are approved is that there existss some form of consideration in which the employee receives something in return for giving up rights.

Waiver
The intentional relinquishment of a known right.

It has thus been held that the waiver at least be accompanied by an offer of employment. No waiver that is given by an applicant prior to a job offer would be considered valid and enforceable. Other requirements articulated by the courts include that the waiver be knowingly and intelligently given, that it be clear and unmistakable, in writing, and voluntary.

Management Tips

- Public sector employees are subject to protection by the Constitution and the Privacy Act; private sector employees are instead protected by common law and state-by-state restrictions on invasions of privacy.
- As an employer, you may search your employees' property where the employee does not have any expectation of privacy; the difficulty comes in determining where that expectation exists.
- Since many privacy protections exist on a state-by-state level, be sure to investigate the specific protections for which you are responsible in the states in which you do business.
- While it may appear reasonable for you to want to regulate certain off-work activities of your employees, be wary of over-restricting, since courts do not look on these regulations positively.
- You are less likely to find problems with a waiver of privacy rights where the waiver is accompanied by an offer of employment.
- When you do collect personal information about your employees, be sure to regulate access to this information, since unwarranted disclosure might constitute an invasion of privacy even where the original collection of information is allowed.

Summary

Basic rules that, if followed, may preclude employer liability for invasions of privacy:

- First, conduct an information audit for the purpose of determining those areas of the company's practices and procedures that have the potential for invasion, including what type of information is collected, how that information is maintained, the means by which the information is verified, who has access to the information, and to whom the information is disclosed. The audit should cover all facets of the organization's activities, from recruitment and hiring to termination. In addition, it may be helpful to ascertain what type of information is maintained by different sectors of the organization.

- Second, in connection with sensitive areas where the company maintains no formal policy, develop a policy to ensure appropriate treatment of data. It is recommended that a policy and procedure be maintained in connection with the ac-

quisition of information, the maintenance of that information, the appropriate contents of personnel files, the use of the information contained therein, and the conduct of workplace investigations. For instance, in connection with the maintenance of personnel files and the accumulation of personal information about company employees, the employer should request only information justified by the needs of the firm and relevant to employment-related decisions.

- Third, the information collected should be kept in one of several files maintained on each employee: (1) a personnel file, which contains the application, paperwork relating to hiring, payroll, and other nonsensitive data; (2) medical file, which contains physicians' reports and insurance records; (3) evaluation files, which contain any evidence of job performance including, but not limited to, performance appraisals; and (4) confidential file, which contains data relating to extremely sensitive matters that should not be disclosed except with express and specific authority, such as criminal records or information collected in connection with workplace investigations.

• Fourth, information should be gathered from reliable sources, rather than sources of questionable repute, such as hearsay, lie detector tests, and subjective indicators. Irrelevant or outdated material should periodically be expunged from these records as well.

• Fifth, publicize privacy policies and procedures and educate employees regarding their rights as well as their responsibilities.

Chapter-End Questions

1. Richard worked as a senior program analyst in a federal agency. In early February 1986, he requested a combination of his sick leave and annual leave until February 26 so he could prepare for and take the bar exam. On February 28, he requested administrative leave so he could satisfy a summons for jury duty. He was not scheduled to return until March 21. When he did not return on the 24th, his supervisor, Bennett, investigated and found out that Richard was still serving jury duty, but that his service began March 11, not February 28. When Richard returned, he was asked about this missing time, and he said that he was in his office most of the time. Further investigation did not fully corroborate this story. Bennett became suspicious about Richard's earlier leave and wrote to the board of law examiners to find out whether Richard had sat for the bar. The board confirmed that he had. When Richard found out about this investigation through later correspondence with the board, he filed suit against the agency, alleging a violation of the Privacy Act because Bennett had not collected this information directly from him. Who wins and why? (*Waters v. Thornburgh,* 888 F.2d 870 (D.C.Cir., 1989).)

2. Ponticelli was paid on a piecework basis and was responsible for recording the amount of her daily production. She was terminated after being accused of inflating her figures. She acknowledged the figures were inflated, but, she contends, not by her. Ponticelli's supervisor told her co-workers that she had been fired for inflating her numbers. Ponticelli filed suit against the supervisor on the grounds that he gave out conditionally privileged information to her co-workers by telling them of her discharge. The supervisor defends his comments by saying that he told her co-workers about her discharge to discourage them from making the same mistakes. Will Ponticelli be successful in her suit? Why or why not? (*Ponticelli v. Mine Safety Appliance Co.,* 247 A.2d 303 (R.I. 1968).)

3. Young, an employee with the Grand Gulf Nuclear Power Station, entered the hospital for unknown reasons. Her co-workers speculated that she was suffering from radiation exposure. To discourage concern regarding radiation, the employer informed the employees that Young's illness was related to a recent hysterectomy. Young sues for an invasion of privacy. Does she win? (*Young v. Jackson,* 572 S.2d 378 (Miss. 1990).)

4. Bodewig was a part-time checker for a Kmart store. During one particular sale, she and a customer, Golden, had a disagreement about the "sale" price of a particular item; the customer left her merchandise at the counter and went to check the listed price on the shelf. While waiting for the customer to return, Bodewig voided that sale and put

the merchandise aside to continue helping the other customers in line. When Golden returned, she accused Bodewig of taking $5.00 that she had left on the counter with her merchandise. Bodewig denied even seeing the money. The store manager searched Bodewig's coat pockets and did not find any money. He then balanced her cash drawer, and it balanced perfectly. Golden was still convinced that Bodewig had taken her money and continued to cause a loud scene. The store manager asked a female employee to accompany Bodewig to the washroom to strip-search her for the money. Bodewig was asked to strip down to her briefs, and there was no sign of any money. Golden claimed that she had between $500 to $600 in her purse; she wouldn't count it out, but she maintained her belief that Bodewig had stolen her money. Bodewig quit her job soon after this incident and filed charges based on invasion of privacy with the effect of emotional distress. Kmart claims that it did what was necessary to take care of the irate customer, and Bodewig did not resist the search at the time. Is Kmart's defense sufficient? (*Bodewig v. Kmart, Inc.,* 635 P.2d 657 (OR. 1981).)

5. David Patton, a merchandising manager for J.C. Penney Company, was having an intimate relationship with a co-worker. The store manager, McKay, told Patton that if he did not cease this relationship with a coemployee, his job would be in danger. Patton refused to break off his relationship, claiming that he did not socialize with this woman at work, and the relationship did not have an adverse effect on his performance as evidenced by his awards "Merchant of the Month" and "Merchant of the Year," both earned while dating this coemployee. The company had no specific written policies about dating co-workers; however,

McKay maintained that dating co-workers was not allowed and continued to threaten Patton's job. Finally, Patton asked for a transfer to another department because McKay threatened to discharge him for unsatisfactory performance. McKay denied the transfer and discharged him for unsatisfactory performance. Patton filed charges against the company and McKay that his discharge was outrageous conduct that violated his privacy. Did it? (*Patton v. J.C. Penney Co.,* 719 P.2d 854 (Ore. 1986).)

6. John Lambert, a pipefitter for the Dow Chemical Company, was severely injured on the job in a grinder explosion. The explosion lacerated the upper inside section of his left thigh, and he underwent several surgeries to have the damage repaired. During these surgeries, the doctors took several pictures of the wound in the various phases of its reparation process. Robert Vaughn, the safety director for Dow, acquired these pictures from the physicians without Lambert's permission and used them as visual aids in safety training and education programs. Lambert's name was unquestionably used in conjunction with these pictures; but Vaughn asserts that there was no malice, humiliation, or embarrassment intended on his part. One of the photographs used was an 8" × 10" color photo that was a closeup of the hole in Lambert's leg. Lambert filed a charge against Dow that Vaughn had invaded his right to privacy by using this picture without permission. Vaughn claims that the photograph was a medical record that Dow had access to as a private employer, and, since the photograph was used to educate other employees, the company was within its bounds. Was it? Why or why not? (*Lambert v. Dow Chemical Co.,* 215 So.2d 673 (La. 1968).)

7. Carol Kobeck, a night-shift worker for Nabisco, Inc., brought suit against the

company on the grounds that the company's violation of her privacy was the cause of her husband committing suicide. Kobeck's husband had called her at work one night and was told that she was not working that night. The next day, he went into the store because she had not yet come home. The assistant personnel manager, Carmical, confirmed that Kobeck had not worked the night before or for several other nights, when she had told her husband that she would be working, from which he deduced that she was having an affair with another man. Kobeck's husband confronted her that night and accused her of cheating. She denied the accusation, but that night her husband committed suicide and left a note, saying he killed himself because he loved her and wanted her to be happy. Kobeck charges Nabisco with violating her privacy by disclosing her schedule and attendance records to her husband without her knowledge or approval. (*Kobeck v. Nabisco, Inc.,* 305 S.E.2d 183 (Ga.App. 1983).)

8. Kristine Naragon was a graduate assistant in Louisiana State University at Baton Rouge's school of music. She mainly had teaching responsibilities and was often praised for her work and dedication. When the university discovered that she was a lesbian and was involved with a student, the school of music renewed her yearly contract but revoked teaching responsibilities and replaced them with purely research-oriented responsibilities. Naragon claims that her privacy rights and her freedom of association rights were violated because she is a lesbian, and she wants her teaching privileges restored. The university maintains that there was no obligation to renew Naragon's contract as it stood, and the university felt that her conduct with a student, lesbian or not, warranted less contact with the students. Naragon defends her conduct by showing that this student was not and never had been a student in her class. Was there an invasion of privacy by the employer? Why or why not? (*Naragon v. Wharton,* 572 F.Supp. 1117 (1983).)

9. John Bellamy filed suit against Mason's Stores, Inc., in Richmond, Virginia, on the grounds that his discharge from the company was based purely on his involvement in the Ku Klux Klan (KKK). Even though the company is a private employer, Bellamy claims that he cannot be fired for his association with the KKK, because it is a personal right that he pursues outside the work environment. Is Bellamy correct? (*Bellamy v. Mason's Stores, Inc.,* 508 F.2d 504 (1974).)

10. Swenson worked as a rural route mail carrier for the US Postal Service in California. In October 1985, she wrote letters to her representative and senator claiming that her postmaster deliberately undercounted rural route mail boxes, qualifying him for bonus and merit awards while forcing his workers to work off the clock. After the congressmen contacted the Postal Service, it responded with two letters, which form the basis of Swenson's Privacy Act claim. They disclosed private facts about her employment status, explaining that she had filed charges of sex discrimination as well as two grievances in response to warnings from her employer. Swenson claims that the disclosure of the information to the congressmen constituted a violation of the Privacy Act. Is she right? (*Swenson v. US Postal Service,* 890 F.2d 1075 (9th Cir. 1989).)

17 LABOR LAW

S C E N A R I O S

S C E N A R I O   1

Plastico Corporation hears through the corporate grapevine that its employees are unhappy with working conditions at the manufacturing plant and are looking into bringing in a union. In an effort to stop the plant's unionization, Plastico posts a notice on the lunchroom bulletin board stating that anyone found to be sympathetic to the unions will be terminated. Is this strategy permissible as a way for Plastico to discourage unionization?

S C E N A R I O   2

Zellico, Inc., is in the midst of a unionizing effort. In an attempt to counter the efforts, Zellico engages in several activities, including promising employees raises and bonuses if they do not form a union and sending out flyers about the evils of unionism, including workplace divisiveness and the possibility of corruption. Are Zellico's activities legal?

S C E N A R I O   3

Ace Company is frustrated. Its collective bargaining agreement with its largest union is about to expire. Ace wants to negotiate another contract with the union; however, the union has missed several negotiation meetings, and, when it does show up, merely sets forth contract proposals without any evidence to support its position. Even after repeated requests for evidence, and promises by union to produce it, none has been provided. What can Ace Company do?

S C E N A R I O   4

A nonunion company offers to form a partnership with its employees in order to decide what it can do to cut costs because of declining profits. Can the company do this?

Statutory Basis

Employees shall have the right to self-organization, to form, join, or assist labor organizations, to bargain collectively through representatives of their own choosing, and to engage in other concerted activities for the purpose of collective bargaining or other mutual aid or protection, and shall also have the right to refrain from any or all such activities. National Labor Relations Act, Section 7.

Coming Together on Issues

**Collective
bargaining**
Negotiations and
agreements
between
management and
labor about wages,
hours, and other
terms and
conditions of
employment.

Labor law is actually a very different and discrete part of the law than employment law, but it is important to be familiar with its basic history to have a more complete knowledge of the workplace. Labor law involves **collective bargaining** between employers and employees about issues in the workplace. Rather than each employee striking his or her own deal with the employer, the law now permits employees to do so in an organized and collective way. This was not always needed, nor was it always so. The agrarian nature of the economy in the United States was such that until the middle of the 18th century, the majority of working Americans worked on farms. In 1820, only about 12 percent of workers were employed in manufacturing. By 1860, that number increased to about 18 percent, and the location of manufacturing had shifted from private homes to factories. As this trend continued to grow so did the size of the labor class, and the basis for modern labor problems was created. Compounding the competitive nature of industry during this time was the simultaneous improvement of the transportation system. This served to allow products from other markets to compete with local products, thus decreasing the local demand and the profit margin of production. This was often offset by decreasing the wage of the worker. It was in this atmosphere that the earliest strikes took place.

An Historical Accounting

Labor law has a long and somewhat acromonious history in this country. Central to an understanding of the struggle between labor and management is understanding the role the courts played in shaping labor policy before the United States Congress enacted legislation that forms the basis for labor relationships today. There were four weapons of choice that business used to control early unionization efforts: criminal conspiracy laws, injunctions, antitrust laws, and constitutional challenges. A brief examination of these early antiunion efforts helps to explain how the balance between workers' rights and management's rights was ultimately reached.

Criminal Conspiracy Laws

In the 1800s, many courts considered activity by workers such as striking and picketing to be common law criminal conspiracies. Workers were convicted for trying to improve working conditions through union efforts. As early as 1806, employers in the shoemaking industry in Philadelphia discovered that they could enlist the aid of the courts by charging their unionized employees with criminal conspiracy. Thus, if a group of employees attempted to exert pressure on an employer to increase wages, they would be charged with criminal conspiracy and, if convicted, subject to imprisonment. Generally, the penalties imposed were fines rather than jail, but along with it came the threat of harsher sentences upon subsequent convictions. This acted to discourage and even eliminate union activity. This practice continued until 1842 when the landmark case of *Commonwealth v. Hunt* (see page 599) severely criticized the use of criminal conspiracy theory to discourage unionization.

COMMONWEALTH V. HUNT

45 Mass. (4 Metc.) 111 (Mass. 1842)

A lower court had found a group of shoemakers who belonged to a union guilty of conspiracy because they refused to work for an employer who hired a shoemaker who was not a member of their union. The Supreme Judicial Court of Massachusetts, in reversing the convictions of the seven shoemakers, found not only that it was not an unlawful activity to unionize but that the object of unions may be "highly meritorious and public spirited."

Shaw, J.

Without attempting to review and reconcile all the cases, we are of opinion, that as a general description, though perhaps not a precise and accurate definition, a conspiracy must be a combination of two or more persons, by some concerted action, to accomplish some criminal or unlawful purpose, or to accomplish some purpose, not in and of itself criminal or unlawful, by criminal or unlawful means. We use the terms criminal or unlawful, because it is manifest that many acts are unlawful, which are not punishable by indictment or other public prosecution; and yet there is no doubt, we think, that a combination by numbers to do them would be an unlawful conspiracy, and punishable by indictment.

Several rules upon the subject seem to be well established, to wit, that the unlawful agreement constitutes the gist of the offence, and therefore that it is not necessary to charge the execution of the unlawful agreement.

Another rule is a necessary consequence of the former, which is, that the crime is consummate and complete by the fact of unlawful combination, and, therefore, that if the execution of the unlawful purpose is averred, it is by way of aggravation, and proof of it is not necessary to conviction; and therefore the jury may find the conspiracy, and negative the execution, and it will be a good conviction.

And it follows, as another necessary legal consequence, from the same principle, that the indictment must—by averring the unlawful purpose of the conspiracy, or the unlawful means by which it is contemplated and agreed to accomplish a lawful purpose—set out an offense complete in itself; and that an illegal combination, imperfectly and insufficiently set out in the indictment, will not be aided by averments of acts done in pursuance of it.

From this view of the law respecting conspiracy, we think it an offence which especially demands the application of that wise and humane rule of the common law, that an indictment shall state, with as much certainty as the nature of the case will admit, the facts which constitute the crime intended to be charged. This is required, to enable the defendant to meet the charge and prepare for his defence, and, in case of acquittal or conviction, to show by the record the identity of the charge, so that he may not be indicted a second time for the same offence. It is also necessary, in order that a person, charged by the grand jury for one offence, may not be substantially convicted, on his trial, of another.

From these views of the rules of criminal pleading, it appears to us to follow, as a necessary legal conclusion, that when the criminality of a conspiracy consists in an unlawful agreement of two or more persons to compass or promote some criminal or illegal purpose, that purpose must be fully and clearly stated in the indictment; and if the criminality of the offence, which is intended to be charged, consists in the agreement to compass or promote some purpose, not of itself criminal or unlawful, by the use of fraud, force, falsehood, or other criminal or unlawful means, such intended use of fraud, force, falsehood, or other criminal or unlawful means, must be set out in the indictment.

We are here carefully to distinguish between the confederacy set forth in the indictment, and the confederacy or association contained in the constitution of the Boston Journeymen and Bootmakers' Society, as stated in the little printed book, which was admitted as evidence on the trial. Because, though it was thus admitted as evidence, it would not warrant a conviction for anything not stated in the indictment. It was proof, as far as it went to support the averments in the indictment. If it contained any criminal matter not set forth in the indictment, it is of no avail.

Now, it is to be considered, that the preamble and introductory matter in the indictment—such as unlawfully and deceitfully designing and intending unjustly to extort great sums, &c.—is mere recital, and not traversable, and therefore cannot aid an imperfect averment of the facts constituting the description of the offence. The same may be said of the concluding matter, which follows the averment, as to the great damage and oppression not only of their said masters, employing them in said art and occupation, but also of divers other workmen in the same art, mystery and occupation, to the evil example, &c. If the facts averred constitute the crime, these are properly stated as the legal inferences to be drawn from them. If they do not constitute the charge of such an offence, they cannot be aided by these alleged consequences.

Stripped then of these introductory recitals and alleged injurious consequences, and of the qualifying epithets attached to the facts, the averment is this: that the defendants and others formed themselves into a society, and agreed not to work for any person, who should employ any journeyman or other person, not a member of such society, after notice given to discharge such workman.

The manifest intent of the association is to induce all those engaged in the same occupation to become members of it. Such a purpose is not unlawful. It would give them a power which might be exerted for useful and honorable purposes, or for dangerous and pernicious ones. If the latter were the real and actual object, and susceptible of proof, it should have been specially charged. Such an association might be used to afford each other assistance in times of poverty, sickness and distress; or to raise their intellectual, moral, and social condition; or to make improvement in their art; or for other proper purposes. Or the association might be designed for purposes of oppression and injustice. But in order to charge all those, who become members of an association, with the guilt of a criminal conspiracy, it must be averred and proved that the actual, if not the avowed object of the association, was criminal. An association may be formed, the declared objects of which are innocent and laudable, and yet they may have secret articles, or an agreement communicated only to the members, by which they are banded together for purposes injurious to the peace of society or the rights of its members. Such would undoubtedly be a criminal conspiracy, on proof of the fact, however meritorious and praiseworthy the declared objects might be. The law is not to be hoodwinked by colorable pretenses. It looks at truth and reality, through whatever disguise it may assume. But to make such an association, ostensibly innocent, the subject of prosecution as a criminal conspiracy, the secret agreement, which makes it so, is to be averred and proved as the gist of the offence. But when an association is formed for purposes actually innocent, and afterwards its powers are abused by those who have the control and management of it, to purposes of oppression and injustice it will be criminal in those who thus misuse it, or give consent thereto, but not in the other members of the association.

Nor can we perceive that the objects of this association, whatever they may have been, were to be attained by criminal means. The means which they proposed to employ, as averred in this count, and which, as we are now to presume, were established by the proof, were, that they would not work for a person, who, after due notice, should employ a journeyman not a member of their society. Supposing the object of the association to be laudable and lawful, or at least not unlawful, are these means criminal? The case supposes that these persons are not bound by contract, but free to work for whom they please, or not to work, if they so prefer. On this state of things, we cannot perceive, that it is criminal for men to agree together to exercise their own acknowledged rights, in such a manner as best to subserve their own interests.

Suppose a baker in a small village had the exclusive custom of his neighborhood, and was making large profits by the sale of his bread. Supposing a number of those neighbors, believing the price of his bread too high, should propose to him to reduce his prices, or if he did not, that they would introduce another baker; and on his refusal, such other baker should, under their encouragement, set up a rival establishment, and sell his bread at lower prices; the effect would be to diminish the profit of the former baker, and to the same extent to impoverish him. And it might be said and proved, that the purpose of the associates was to diminish his profits, and thus impoverish him, though the ultimate and laudable object of the combination was to reduce the cost of bread to themselves and their neighbors. The same thing may be said of all competition in every branch of trade and industry; and yet it is through that competition, that the best interests of trade and industry are promoted. It is scarcely necessary to allude to the familiar instances of opposition lines of conveyance, rival hotels, and the thousand other instances, where each strives to gain custom to himself, by which he may lessen the price of commodities, and thereby diminish the profits of others.

We think, therefore, that associations may be entered into, the object of which is to adopt measures that may have a tendency to impoverish another, that is, to diminish his gains and profits, and yet so far from being criminal or unlawful, the object may be highly meritorious and public spirited. The legality of such an association will therefore depend upon the means to be used for its accomplishment. If it is to be carried into effect by fair or honorable and lawful means, it is, to say the least, innocent; if by falsehood or force, it may be stamped out with the character of conspiracy. REVERSED.

Case Questions

1. Why do you think it was necessary to dissolve the relationship between criminal conspiracy and the labor movement? What was the relationship given between criminal acts and employees' rights to control their environment at work?

2. Why do you think the court found that there was some good in organizing to affect the employer's policies? Explain.

3. Do you agree with the court's analysis in this case? Explain.

Despite *Commonwealth v. Hunt,* the criminal conspiracy trials retained some vitality until the 1890s. During this time, conspiracy trials were losing steam because of difficulty in getting juries to side with employers. Another method of discouraging unions was being developed which would prove equally difficult for labor.

Injunctions

Injunction
A court order requiring individuals or groups of persons to not perform certain acts that the court has determined will do irreparable harm.

Employers sought the use of **injunctions** to gain immediate relief from workers' activities. This legal action was encouraged and proliferated after 1895. In that year, the US Supreme Court issued a decision that upheld the constitutionality of the labor injunction. Armed with this potent legal support, judges were quick to apply this remedy to quash strikes and protests. They often committed abuses by wielding their power in personal ways. For example, when an injunction was sought, a judge would have to decide whether a union's objectives were lawful or unlawful. Judges outlawed many union activities this way. This was not always an issue of improper motivation; judges were left without legislative directives, and in their absence were free to use their own beliefs, attitudes, and prejudices to reach conclusions. Given the antilabor sentiment among the business class, which was the background of a good many judges of this period, the result was overwhelmingly against labor's attempt to organize.

Yellow dog contract
Agreement employers require employees to sign stating they do not belong to a union and will not join one. Now illegal.

This method came to a head in the case of *Hitchman Coal Company v. Mitchell,*[1] in which the Supreme Court declared that a labor injunction could be used to enforce a **yellow dog contract.** The yellow dog contract was a device used by antiunion employers to stop the progress of the union movement. It was the promise of a worker not to join a labor union while in the hire of an employer. Yellow dog contracts, used sparingly before *Hitchman,* proliferated afterward. Employees, often faced with no alternative employment options, were forced to sign a yellow dog contract. Later, if their employer was faced with a unionizing campaign, the employer could receive an injunction that would restrain anyone from encouraging these workers to join a union. This decision's hostile view toward organized labor dealt a harsh blow to workers seeking to organize. Its effects were felt until 1932, when yellow dog contracts were ended by Congress.

Antitrust Attacks

The early part of the 20th century saw declining competition and mammoth growth of industrialization. By 1930, nonagricultural occupations accounted for about 80 percent of the labor force. Business leaders saw the advantage of cooperation and began to establish price agreements, trusts, pools, and trade associations. These devices were intended to stamp out competition between rivals. Elimination of competition meant growth of huge and powerful corporations whose purpose was to monopolize. Once competition was eliminated, it was easy to control prices. Congress enacted the Sherman Antitrust Act in 1890 to eliminate monopolistic control of the nation's economy. After its passage, labor unions learned that the law limited a variety of their activities. Unions were prosecuted under various provisions which were interpreted to include them under the provisions that prohibited "Every contract, combination . . . or conspiracy, in restraint of trade. . ." When unions challenged the application of the Sherman Antitrust Act to their activities, the Supreme Court, in 1908, held that the Sherman Act applied to labor unions, giving business a new weapon to combat unionism. In addition, the case held that individual union

---

[1]245 U.S. 229 (1917).

members were responsible for the actions of its officers, making the rank-and-file liable for judgments against the union, and outlawed **secondary boycotts.** In response, unions organized themselves into a strong political force and in 1912 helped to elect Woodrow Wilson (who had pledged his support to the American Federation of Labor) as well as other democratic candidates. The Democratic Party soon fulfilled its promise to organized labor and in October 1914 the Clayton Act became law. Section six of that act provided that "nothing contained in the antitrust laws shall be construed to forbid the existence and operation of labor organizations" nor shall labor unions be held to be "illegal combinations or conspiracies in restraint of trade under the antitrust laws."

More importantly, the Clayton Act regulated the procedure by which a federal court could issue an injunction against labor. Some of the most important gains from labor's perspective were the requirement that an injunction not be issued without notice to the union, absent emergency circumstances; a jury trial for those members who were charged with a violation under the injunction; the requirement that a bond be posted by the party seeking the injunction and indemnifying the union if they were found to have acted lawfully; and the requirement that specific acts be enjoined and not just the activity of the union wholesale.

Secondary boycott
A work stoppage by employees who are not directly involved in the labor dispute. Done to show union solidarity.

Constitutional Challenges to Early Congressional Enactments

Early efforts by federal and state legislators to support organized labor were thwarted by the courts as a whole. Many state laws were declared unconstitutional by state supreme courts. Congress continued to recognize the rights of labor organizations and in 1898 passed the Erdman Act. The objective of the act was to set up a procedure by which conflicts in the railroad industry could be handled. Among other rights, it gave the railroad workers the right to self-organization and collective bargaining and outlawed the yellow dog contract. At this time Congress targeted railroad workers for protection largely because of the Pullman strike, which had so disrupted service in 1894. Feeling the need to ensure against further disruptions that had the effect of paralyzing the nation's transportation system, Congress thought it found a way to make this issue one of constitutional dimension by making it one of interstate commerce. However, when confronted with the issue of whether the Congress could regulate industry by regulating employer–employee relations in this way, the United States Supreme Court held that Congress could not and struck down this critical law. The Court was not partial to any laborers in particular. In 1918 and 1923, the Court struck down congressional laws that would have controlled the use of child laborers and legislation that would have given women a minimum wage when employed in industry.

Out of Necessity Comes Change

The start of World War I saw the first real movement away from antiunion sentiment. The need for uninterrupted production and for preventing wartime strikes was seen as critical for the greater national interest. President Woodrow Wilson formed the National War Labor Board for the purpose of peacefully resolving labor disputes. This precursor of the National Labor Relations Board (NLRB) embodied many of the tenets that were eventually adopted by the NLRB. While the war acted to create a moratorium on attacks on organized labor, it also served to show that peaceful efforts aimed at resolving labor disputes were possible. After World War I the National War Labor Board was dismantled, but the unmistakable effect was that it was a stepping stone toward recognition of the organized labor movement.

Congress continued to enact piecemeal legislation aimed at limited pockets of laborers, but in 1932, responding to the harsh effects of the Depression, Congress enacted the National Industrial Recovery Act (NIRA). This law put business in charge of regulating prices and production. Because the regulation of the market in this way was a clear violation of the Sherman Antitrust Act, the NIRA exempted any price control measure (called "codes") from the reach of the Sherman Act. In addition, the NIRA established a minimum wage and gave workers collective bargaining and other rights. Under the NIRA, the ranks of organized labor began to increase. It was under the umbrella of the NIRA that President Roosevelt created the National Labor Board in 1933 and bolstered its enforcement provisions in 1934. Both the NIRA and the Board operated successfully until a dispute with the automobile industry, which it could not settle, undermined labor's confidence in the Board to such an extent that it was effectively dismantled. In 1935, the NIRA was declared unconstitutional by the Supreme Court because, the Court held, neither the President of the United States nor any private group (such as the business entities given the power under the NIRA to control prices) had the constitutional authority to do what was required of them under the act.

It is against this backdrop that the modern labor movement was born. After this period in time, Congress was able to successfully enact legislation that has formed the basis of what we know as organized labor. Through a series of enactments which have shifted the balance of power first to the unions, then to employers, the balance that has been created is subject today only to refinement. (See Exhibits 17–1 and 17–3.)

At one point, labor unions enjoyed great popularity in the United States. In 1990, about 13 percent of the workforce was unionized, a decrease from former years, such as 1953 when the number was at the all-time high of just under 27 percent.

Due in part to such factors as the reduction in the labor force of traditionally heavily unionized industries, such as steel manufacturing, international competition, aggressive nonunionizing campaigns by employers, union concessions during downturns in the economy, and loss of jobs to other countries with cheaper labor the percentage has steadily decreased since the 70s.

Yet and still, labor unions are an important part of the workplace. In this chapter, we will discuss the basic laws addressing collective bargaining and what the laws require.

See Exhibit 17–2.

Labor Laws

Four main federal laws comprise the statutory basis for labor law and unionization. The legislation initiating a move toward collective bargaining in the United States began with restricting court responses to union activity and establishing the right of

EXHIBIT 17–1

Chronology

1940s-1960s *The postwar economic boom establishes the model for middle-class Americans' expectations of ever-rising earnings and job security.*

1956

William H. Whyte Jr. describes the emerging ethos of the corporate employee in his best-selling book, *The Organization Man*. According to an often-unspoken pledge of reciprocal loyalty, the company offered job security, rising earnings and generous fringe benefits in return for the employee's commitment to stay with the firm for his entire career.

●

1970s *Rising labor costs and growing competition from overseas suppliers prompt U.S. corporations to step up automation and set up plants in low-cost countries.*

1973

The steady rise in workers' earnings that has marked the postwar period comes to a halt after the first of a series of oil crises sparks inflation and slows economic growth.

1979

In the first phase of corporate restructuring, manufacturers begin cutting production jobs. General Motors, Ford and Chrysler will eliminate 350,000 jobs over the next decade.

●

1980s *Corporations eliminate millions of blue-collar jobs in an attempt to "restructure" their operations to become more competitive with foreign producers.*

1981-82

The worst recession since the Great Depression of the 1930s takes its greatest toll on the manufacturing industries of the Midwest, pushing unemployment among blue-collar workers to double-digit levels.

1985

IBM — hurt by mounting competition from foreign computer makers — begins cutting its work force.

1989

A wave of bank consolidations and closures begins, resulting in the loss of more than 100,000 jobs in that sector to date.

●

1990s *Restructuring begins to cut into white-collar employment as corporations eliminate many middle-management positions.*

July 1990

Recession begins, accelerating the pace of layoffs. While blue-collar workers continue to bear the brunt of unemployment, companies are for the first time cutting out entire layers of middle management to reduce labor costs and make their operations more flexible to changing economic conditions. As a result, white-collar unemployment spreads throughout U.S. industry.

August 1990

Sears, the nation's third-largest retailer, begins a cost-reduction program that will cut about 33,000 positions by the end of 1991.

1991

Restructuring accelerates. U.S. corporations announce more than a half million permanent staff cuts affecting both production and white-collar workers.

Nov. 26, 1991

IBM announces it will cut 20,000 jobs next year.

Dec. 18, 1991

General Motors says it will close 21 of its 125 North American plants and pare 74,000 positions, or 18 percent of its work force, over the next four years.

Jan. 7, 1992

Sears announces it will eliminate an additional 7,000 positions by automating customer-service tasks.

Jan. 21, 1992

United Technologies Corp. announces it will cut 13,900 jobs in its defense and civilian industries.

Feb. 4, 1992

Congress approves legislation providing an additional 13 weeks of unemployment compensation. President Bush, who blocked or vetoed two similar measures in 1991, signs the bill into law Feb. 7.

Feb. 24, 1992

General Motors names the first 12 of 21 plants to be closed in the U.S. and Canada. GM also posts a $4.45 billion loss for 1991 — the largest in American corporate history.

●

2000s *The global marketplace continues to transform American employment patterns.*

2005

According to the Labor Department, most of the 24.6 million new jobs that will be added to the U.S. economy over the 15-year period ending in 2005 will be high-skill positions requiring more training than most of the jobs they will replace.

Congressional Quarterly Researcher 2, no. 8 (February 28, 1992), p. 171.

EXHIBIT 17–2   Maquiladoras
Mexico's Cheap Labor Lures Firms

US Companies Take Jobs South

History—Mexico introduced maquiladoras in 1965. There are about 2,100 plants providing 500,000 jobs. More than 80 American companies have built assembly plants—among them, General Motors and Zenith Electronics.

How it works—US companies deliver raw materials and parts to the maquiladoras and receive finished goods, paying no taxes, and only a duty on the cost of labor. Workers are paid $5 to $7 a day. In the United States, the same jobs pay $8 to $15 an hour.

Results—The foreign exchange earnings, about $4 billion a year, are second only to the state-run oil industry.

Conditions—Some plants provide employees with cheap lunches, food coupons, health services, and housing aid, but many others are sweatshops that expose workers to toxic chemicals without protective gear or adequate ventilation.

Management—American companies say the flight south is a matter of survival. "Over the past 20 years, the US television industry has been under siege by foreign competitors," Zenith spokesman John Taylor said. "If we didn't have operations in Mexico, we would have been out of business years ago."

Labor—Mark Anderson of the AFL–CIO in Washington estimates 400,000 jobs that either existed in the United States or would have been created have moved to Mexico. "American companies don't advertise the fact they're closing their plants in the United States and moving to Mexico," he said. "We have gone from 10,000 jobs in 1975 to about 6,000," said Fred Gross, president of the United Auto Workers Local 292 in Kokomo, Indiana. "Based on what we've experienced . . . it's [the North American Free Trade Agreement being negotiated by the United States, Mexico, and Canada] going to send more jobs to Mexico."

S. Hayward, "Mexico's Cheap Labor Lures Firms," *State,* May 17, 1992, p. 1H.

employees to form labor organizations and to be protected against unfair labor practices at the hands of employers.

Until the Norris-LaGuardia Act of 1932 and the Wagner Act of 1935 (generally referred to as the National Labor Relations Act of 1935), employers had held virtually all the power. However, once that right to bargain collectively was created and unions established, the matter took on some rather sinister twists. Unions started feeling their power and often went overboard in using it.

This resulted in two other legislative measures to address the evolution of collective bargaining. The Taft-Hartley Act (also known as the Labor Management Relations Act) amended the Wagner Act in 1947 to establish unfair *union* practices, and the Landrum-Griffin Act of 1959 gave certain civil rights to union members and addressed corruption of union officials.

The Norris-LaGuardia Act

The Norris-LaGuardia Act was the first major labor law statute enacted in the United States. The opening section of the Norris-LaGuardia Act established that government recognized that the job to a worker is more important than a worker is to a

Exhibit 17–3   Union Role in Services Expanding

Many experts say that, following a sharp decline in clout and membership in the 1980s, labor
unions will need to evolve into providers of social and financial services if they are to survive.
One example would be the addition of alcohol and drug abuse prevention services to union
employee assistance plans. Some unions have already begun offering bargain financial
services to their members in the form of reduced-fee credit cards and checking accounts.
There are some bright spots on the horizon for labor unions. The failure of union-busting as a
management tool is reason for optimism. Still, private sector union membership and union
influence have weakened labor's bargaining position for workers' economic benefits. The
AFL–CIO has sought new recruits by creating a new membership category called an
"associate member." It also aired the "Union, yes" television advertising campaign to attract
workers. Many labor experts are guardedly optimistic about these revitalization attempts and
say that the scales of power still appear to be tilted in favor of management.

corporation. It recognized that the only real power workers had was in impacting
employers through numbers. An employer may not be disturbed when one worker
walks out, but most certainly will be when all or most workers do so. The Norris-
LaGuardia act endorsed collective bargaining as a matter of public policy. To implement this policy, Congress sharply curbed the power of the courts to intervene in
labor disputes, including curtailing use of the injunction. Norris-LaGuardia did not
give labor unions any new legal rights, rather, it allowed them more freedom to
operate free from court control and interference. This greatly facilitated labor unions
acting as effective collective bargaining agencies.

Section 4 of the act declares that no federal court has the power to issue any
form of injunctive relief in any case involving a labor dispute if that injunction
would prohibit any person who was participating in such a dispute from doing certain acts. Judges cannot restrain any strike, regardless of its objective, and cannot restrain picketing activities. Labor unions can provide relief funds to its strikers and
publicize its labor disputes, and workers could urge other employees to join the conflict. Norris-LaGuardia allows a union to act in defense of a person prosecuted for
his or her actions or to prosecute an action under their contract. A union can conduct meetings to promote the interests of workers. Norris-LaGuardia protected any
"labor dispute" even though parties did not stand as employer–employee with each
other, further encouraging collective bargaining.

Most importantly, while it did not directly outlaw yellow dog contracts, the act
declared that yellow dog contracts were inconsistent with US public policy and not
enforceable in any court in the United States. Later, the NLRB held that an employer
engaged in an unfair labor practice if it demanded that an employee execute such an
agreement.

The act also had significant impact in curbing prosecution under the antitrust
laws. In its statement of purpose, Congress claimed that the intent of the act was to
give labor what it thought it had received under the Clayton Act. Given the broadly
stated purpose of the act, the Supreme Court has broadly construed it, providing

unions with the opportunity to engage in activities calculated to effect the collective bargaining process. When Norris-LaGuardia limited the enforcement of yellow dog contracts and removed the impediments of workers to organize in a concerted fashion, the way was paved for enactment of the National Labor Relations Board three years later.

The Wagner/National Labor Relations Act

Of the four pieces of seminal labor legislation, it is the National Labor Relations Act (NLRA) that most consider to be the mainstay of union activity, since it established the right of employees to form unions, to bargain collectively, and to strike. Recall that at one time it had been illegal—in fact, criminal—for employees to join together in an effort to collectively bargain with employers.

The National Labor Relations Act

In order to avoid the unconstitutional delegation of legislative power, Congress, in enacting the NLRA, placed the administration of the act in the hands of the National Labor Relations Board (NLRB), an independent federal administrative agency, rather than in the hands of an industrial group; set up standards to govern the exercise of power delegated to that administrative agency; and provided for the judicial enforcement of the orders of that agency. The board was empowered to issue remedial orders, enforceable in the courts, to prevent commission of unfair labor practices. Five such unfair practices were outlined in Section 8 of the act. Under this section, it was an unfair labor practice to:

- interfere with, restrain, or coerce employees in the exercise of their rights;
- interfere with the formation of a labor organization;
- discriminate in the hiring or tenure of employment or discourage membership in a labor organization;
- retaliate for filing charges or testifying under the act;
- refuse to bargain with the representatives of the employees.

Notably absent from this act are unfair labor practices that might be committed by unions, although there were unfair labor practices listed that might be committed by employers. In the political climate that prevailed in 1935, the government placed its weight on the side of laborers because of the imbalance between corporate power and the labor market. The act was government's attempt to throw its weight on their side for the purpose of guaranteeing them the right to organize so they would be able to bargain on a more equal basis with employers.

Creation of the NLRB did not rest well with business, and for the first few years of its existence it survived a well organized and concerted attack challenging its constitutionality and the scope of its authority. Finally, in 1937 and 1938, the U.S. Supreme Court brought the avalanche of injunction suits against the NLRB to a halt in a series of rulings that found the authority of the board to determine whether an employer had engaged in an unfair labor practice was exclusive, subject only to subsequent judicial review after the board had issued its decision, and detailing the scope of the NLRB's legal powers. These decisions form the foundations of the NLRB that are still effective today.

With the constitutionality of the NLRB determined and the injunctions halted, the judicial proceedings during the third year of existence concerned themselves with the correctness of the NLRB's decisions and the power of the Board to fashion remedies. Certain principles of law were established, including that employees on strike were still employees; that employees striking because of an unfair labor practice are entitled to reinstatement, even if reinstatement makes it necessary to discharge employees hired to replace them; and that threatened economic loss does not justify the commission of an unfair labor practice. From 1935 to 1947 the courts developed a vast body of law dealing with labor issues.

The National Labor Relations Board

The NLRB is the independent federal agency that enforces labor laws in the private sector. Once sufficient interest has been indicated by the employees (usually by signing union authorization cards) the NLRB conducts elections to determine what union is to represent the employees in collective bargaining. The NLRB also decertifies unions that the employees no longer wish to have represent them, issues labor regulations, hears unfair labor practice cases at the agency level, and otherwise administers the NLRA.

In collective bargaining, employees with a **community of interests**—that is, similar workplace concerns and conditions—come together as a **bargaining unit** that the union will represent. The community of interests is based on such factors as similarity of the jobs the employees perform, similar training or skills, and so on. While the general rule is that at least two employees must be in a bargaining unit, an employer may agree to a one-person unit, such as for an on-site craftworker (e.g., a carpenter who belongs to a carpenter's union being employed at a worksite as the only carpenter).

Employees may unionize either by signing a sufficient number of authorization cards, by voting in a union during a union representation election, or, in some cases, by the NLRB ordering the employer to bargain with a union. NLRB supervises the union election and certifies the results. The employer cannot interfere in any way with the employees' efforts to form a union, as done in opening scenario 1.

Concerted Activity

Section 7 of the NLRA guarantees employees the right to engage in concerted activities for mutual aid or protection. Typical protected concerted activities includes union organizing, the discussion of unionization among employees, and the attempt by one employee to solicit union support from another employee. But concerted activity need not involve a union. Activities by groups of employees unaffiliated with a union to improve their lot at their workplace are deemed protected concerted activities.

Community of interests
Factors employees have in common for bargaining purposes.

Bargaining unit
The group of employees in a workplace that have the legal right to bargain with the employer.

Scenario

Concerted activity also covers activity by a single employee, even if no other employee joins him. The reasoning is that the protected status of such activity should not turn on whether another employee decides to join the activity. Not all concerted activity is protected, however. Acts or threats of violence are not given protection.

Unions

Unions are composed of nonsupervisory or nonmanagerial employees, including part-time workers. Specifically excluded from the NLRA are agricultural and domestic workers, independent contractors, and those employed by their spouse or parent.

The union's shop steward, elected by the members, is the intermediary generally between the union and the employer. He or she may collect dues, recruit new workers, and, if a union member feels something has gone wrong, or an unfair labor practice has been committed, the shop steward is usually the first to contact the employer and discuss the issue, hopefully having it resolved.

Many unions are formed with employees of a particular plant who may be part of a larger union network. For instance, the employees who process meat at a meat processing plant may organize and become the local branch or affiliate of an international meat processing labor organization, an **industrial union.** Rather than being organized at a particular workplace, unions also may be organized around a particular craft, totally detached from a particular workplace. In such cases, the **business agent** of the **craft union** (e.g., carpenters) represents the union craftworker's interest at a given jobsite. Employers will often contact the craft union when it needs the type of employees represented by that union.

Industrial union
Unions at a particular workplace.

Business agent
The representative of a union, usually craft.

Craft unions
Unions composed of skilled craftworkers not situated at any one workplace.

Mandatory subject of bargaining
Wages, hours, and other conditions of employment, which, by law, must be negotiated between labor and management.

Permissive subject of bargaining
Nonmandatory subjects that can be negotiated between labor and management.

Closed shop
Employer hires only union members.

Good Faith Bargaining

Under the NLRA, an employer is required to bargain in good faith with union representatives about wages, hours, and terms and conditions of employment. These are **mandatory subjects of bargaining.** While employers may actually bargain about other matters **(permissive subjects),** only a refusal to bargain about mandatory subjects of bargaining may form the basis of an unfair labor practice. (See Exhibit 17–4.)

At times, management and labor may differ on whether a particular matter is a mandatory subject of bargaining. If this disagreement is legitimate, it can form the basis of an unfair labor practice—for instance, a union may allege management has committed an unfair labor practice by refusing to bargain over a mandatory subject of bargaining such as wage increases. In *HHS,* the union demanded negotiations on the issue of the agency's new smoking ban.

If the matter proposed for negotiation is illegal, such as a proposal to have a **closed shop,** it is bad faith bargaining even to bring it up as a proposal, and management's refusal to bargain cannot be the basis of an unfair labor practice.

The law requires only that the parties bargain in good faith about appropriate matters, not that one party necessarily agree with the other's position and include it

EXHIBIT 17–4 Selected Collective Bargaining Agreement Clauses

Wages—including cost-of-living increases, production increases, learners' and apprentices' overtime.

Benefits—including vacations, sick pay, holidays, insurance.

Hours—including overtime and determinations about assignment.

Seniority—setting forth how employee seniority is determined and used.

Management security—employers may make their own decisions about how to run the business as long as they are not contrary to the collective bargaining agreement or law.

Union security—the union's legal right to exist and to represent the employees involved.

Job security—how employees will maintain employment, including procedures for layoffs, downsizing, worksharing, and so on.

Dues checkoff—right of a union to have the employer deduct union dues from employees' wages and turn them over to the union.

Union shop—requires all employees to join the union within a certain time of coming into the bargaining unit.

Modified union shop—requires that all new employees must join the union after an agreement becomes effective, as must any employees who were already union members; but those already working, who were not union members and do not wish to join, need not do so.

Maintenance-of-membership—employees who voluntarily join a union may leave only during a short window period prior to agreement expiration.

Agency shop—requires all employees of the bargaining unit to pay union dues, whether union members or not.

Grievances—sets forth the basis for grievances regarding conflicts over the meaning of the collective bargaining agreement and procedures for addressing them.

Exclusive representation—the union representative will be the only party who can negotiate with the employer about matters affecting bargaining unit employees.

Arbitration—the matters which cannot be otherwise resolved will be submitted to arbitration to be resolved by a neutral third party whose decision is usually binding.

Midterm negotiations—permits agreed-on topics to be reopened to negotiation prior to contract expiration.

No-strike, no lockout—parties agree that the employees will not strike or will only do so under limited circumstances, and employers will not engage in lockouts. Instead, the grievance procedure will be used to handle labor disputes.

in the collective bargaining agreement. The intent is to prevent management from unilaterally instituting workplace policies that closely affect workers without at least getting employee input and negotiating the matter. The fact that one side or the other does not receive what they want in the contract is not just cause for an unfair labor practice. As long as good faith bargaining takes place, there has been compliance with the statute.

An example of bargaining in bad faith might occur when, for instance, management comes to the bargaining table and denies a raise to employees without offering any evidence whatever as to why, and simply continues to reject the union's wage proposals. It could also occur if one side rejects proposals out of hand without making counterproposals to the other side. In opening scenario 3, the union missing negotiation sessions and setting forth unsupported proposals would subject it to an unfair labor practice charge. Of course, failing to show up for negotiations

Scenario

or refusing to sign the written agreement to which the parties orally agreed would also be bad faith bargaining. The case below demonstrates several ways in which the employer failed to bargain in good faith.

DEPARTMENT OF HEALTH AND HUMAN SERVICES V. FEDERAL LABOR RELATIONS AUTHORITY
920 F.2d 45 (D.C.Cir. 1990)

The employer announced it was creating a smoke-free workplace in all of its facilities and issued a smoking ban. The union wanted to negotiate over the policy. HHS argued that the smoking ban was legally nonnegotiable because it fell within the compelling need exception to the statutory duty to bargain. The court agreed with the union and required the agency to negotiate the smoking ban.

Silberman, J.

In May of 1987 HHS announced that it was creating a smoke-free working environment in all HHS facilities and in August of that year it issued personnel regulations implementing the smoking ban. Three local chapters of the NTEU attempted to negotiate over the policy, presenting proposals to accommodate smokers by establishing designated smoking areas within HHS facilities. Their proposals were consistent with the government-wide regulation issued by the General Services Administration (GSA), which calls for agencies to accommodate the needs of smokers by creating "smoking areas" that "do not impinge on the health of those who do not smoke," and instructs agencies to honor their collective bargaining obligations but allows an agency, in its discretion, to implement more stringent smoking regulations. HHS maintained, however, that the smoking ban was nonnegotiable under Title VII of the Civil Service Reform Act of 1978, commonly known as the Federal Service Labor–Management Relations Act, 5 U.S.C. 7101 et seq. (1988) (FSLMRA), because it fell within the compelling need exception to the duty to bargain created by U.S.C. 7117(a)(2).

HHS argued before the Authority that a complete ban on smoking in the workplace was essential to the performance of its mission to educate the public about the dangers of smoking. The agency claimed that it could not effectively persuade private-sector employers to create smoke-free work environments if it did not do so itself. Its credibility would be jeopardized, HHS claimed, unless it were free to set an example by creating for its own employees the healthiest working environment possible without being subject to the lengthy and uncertain collective bargaining process. Moreover, in light of the Surgeon General's 1986 report on the harmful effects of environmental tobacco smoke (ETS) and the difficulties of confining ETS so as not to endanger nonsmokers, such a ban was, in the agency's view, necessary to protect employees' health.

The FLRA determines that HHS had failed to meet its burden of demonstrating that a smoking ban in all HHS facilities was essential to the agency's mission within the meaning of the statute and its implementing regulations.

The Authority thought that a complete smoke-free working environment in all HHS buildings, while helpful or desirable as an aid to HHS's advocacy role, was not essential to the agency's mission of "performing research and informing the public on the hazards of smoking." And although the Secretary submitted materials to the Authority concerning the health hazards smoking causes its employees to show that "nothing less than a policy of a smoke-free environment can assure adequate protection of the occupants in Department-controlled building space," it would appear that this evidence was submitted merely to buttress the agency's claim that its credibility as an advocate would be undermined if it did not ban smoking completely in light of its knowledge of the harmful effect of smoking on its own employees.

In light of the government-wide GSA regulation, which permits smoking in designated areas in government buildings (and which also recognizes the collective bargaining obligations of government agencies on the question), HHS's position is of necessity focused on its unique governmental role as an advocate for policies throughout the country that the government itself has not yet accepted. It is primarily on this basis that HHS sought to establish the "compelling need" to ban smoking completely which would permit it to avoid collective bargaining on the issue. HHS argues to us, as it did before the FLRA, that it cannot perform its governmental mission (as properly understood) without a total smoking ban. As the FLRA, however, found that HHS could perform its mission without such a ban and that no "compelling need" therefore existed, the burden of HHS's argument in this court is that HHS, not the FLRA, is the expert on the articulation and performance of HHS's mission, and that it is consequently to HHS, and not to the FLRA, that this court should defer as to the nature and degree of the need for the regulation.

The difficulty with this argument is that it proves too much. We have repeatedly held that we must defer to the FLRA's interpretation of its own statute as against competing executive branch interpretations.

Once it is determined to whom deference is owed, there is not a good deal left to this case, because the term "compelling need" is not susceptible to precise measurement and we must therefore defer to any reasonable interpretation or application of it. The FLRA's regulation defines a need that is compelling as one that is to be distinguished from a need that is only "helpful" or "desirable."

Petitioner challenges that definition of compelling as too restrictive, but its challenge is lacking both analytical and legal support. The FLRA properly drew on the legislative history of the Act in determining that Congress meant "compelling need" to be a narrow exception to an agency's duty to bargain. But even aside from the legislative history, we do not take seriously the notion that the FLRA's distinction between helpful or desirable and compelling can be thought to be an unreasonable interpretation of the statute. Of course, what might be thought compelling (reasonably) to one person could be thought only helpful or desirable (reasonably) to another, but that is exactly why which agency gets deference is so important.

HHS further argues that even if the FLRA's regulation defining compelling need is reasonable, its application of that definition in this case is arbitrary. The FLRA, however, has consistently rejected similar agency arguments advanced to justify refusing to bargain over the scope of smoking bans.

Still, petitioner, pointing to the testimony of Surgeon General Koop that HHS simply cannot act as an effective advocate for a smoke-free workplace in the nation unless it creates such an environment within its own facilities, argues that the FLRA unjustifiably described its claimed "compelling need" as speculative. The testimony in question, however, is not a factual assertion; it is an opinion which the FLRA was not obliged to credit. To say that the FLRA was bound to accept the Surgeon General's testimony is simply another way of arguing that we (and the FLRA) should defer to HHS's judgment as to whether a complete smoking ban is essential rather than only helpful or desirable.

Perhaps because of the difficulties inherent in its case before the Authority, HHS shifts its focus on appeal to the argument that its "compelling need" stems from its concern for its employees' health—which is also, in HHS's view, essential to its mission. HHS barely preserved this contention below by pointing to its employees' health risk as part of its "good example" argument. But HHS goes so far in this court as to argue that the Occupational Safety and Health Act, which imposes on all agencies a duty "to provide safe and healthful places and conditions of employment," mandates the smoking ban. This argument was not even hinted at below so, of course, we may not entertain it.

In any event, we do not dispute, and we do not understand the FLRA to dispute, that all agencies are legitimately concerned with their employees' health. It is hard to see how it can be argued, however, that HHS's concern for its employees can be qualitatively different from that of other government agencies. Its health-based argument is consequently a collateral attack on the government-wide GSA regulation referred to above. That regulation, it will be recalled, governs smoking in federal buildings and requires that agencies accommodate the needs of smokers where feasible. Although an agency has discretion to "establish more stringent guidelines," the GSA regulation

instructs the agency to "meet its [collective bargaining] obligation." And to the extent that the GSA regulation gives HHS discretion regarding its smoking policy, HHS is obligated by the FSLMRA "to exercise that discretion through negotiation." With this backdrop, we think HHS has no basis to quarrel with the FLRA's refusal to designate a regulation prohibiting bargaining over smoking on HHS premises as arising out of "compelling need" because of concern with its employees' health. It would appear that HHS's quarrel is instead with the Administration. Petition for Enforcement GRANTED.

Case Questions

1. Since the union could actually decide during negotiations to make the smoking policy very restrictive, why do you think the agency fought so hard to have the matter taken out of negotiation?

2. What do you think of the agency's argument that its impact as the government agency responsible for information on smoking is lessened if it does not have a smoke-free environment for its employees?

3. Why do you think the court refused to accept this argument?

NLRB v. WEST COAST CASKET CO.
469 F.2d 871 (9th Cir. 1972)

Employer engaged in various acts in order to interfere with the union. The court deemed it an unfair labor practice for the employer to do so.

Hamley, J.

The Board's conclusions must be affirmed if, considering the record as a whole, the conclusions are supported by substantial evidence.

Prior to July 1, 1972, West Coast manufactured, sold, and distributed metal and wood cas-

kets at two plants in Los Angeles. In 1968, West Coast's president decided to discontinue some of its manufacturing procedures and to phase out one of the plants. During the first part of 1969, when West Coast alleges it had reached a point in its phasing out program at which it became necessary to lay off some of its workers, two unions began a joint program to organize the employees.

The Board found that West Coast, through Mrs. Selvin, its bargaining agent, refused to bargain in good faith with union representatives in violation of section 8(a)(5) of the Act. The unions were certified as the joint bargaining agents for West Coast's employees on June 24, 1969. Numerous unsuccessful attempts were made to reach agreement during the next five months. Mrs. Selvin cancelled many of the scheduled meetings and, on many occasions she refused to return phone calls from union representatives. She did not provide counter-proposals to the contract proposed by the union until October 16th, though she had promised to provide them by July 22nd. When the union representative informed West Coast's president of the lack of progress, the president states that he would leave these matters to Mrs. Selvin.

We find that there is substantial evidence supporting the Board's conclusion that West Coast violated section 8(a)(5). There is no duty to reach an agreement, but there is a duty to negotiate with a spirit of sincerity and cooperation. West Coast's acts, discussed above, show a lack of this "spirit" and, therefore, a violation of section 8(a)(5). We grant ENFORCEMENT of the Board's order.

Case Questions

1. If you were the agent, how would you have handled things differently?

2. Do you think it was sufficient for the president to handle this as he did? Why or why not?

3. What do you think led the employer to allow this situation, knowing that there were federal labor laws?

If agreement is not reached with the union after good faith bargaining is conducted, the union may then be free to advance to other alternatives it can exercise, up to and including strikes. Unions are also capable of engaging in refusals to bargain or bargaining in bad faith. It is not an activity engaged in only by management.

Duty of Fair Representation

Frequently when union members do not like the contract that results from collective bargaining negotiations, they will allege the union has breached its duty of fair representation. This duty, not formally defined in the statute and often used as a catchall allegation, requires the union to represent all employees fairly and nondiscriminatorily. If employees feel that one group has come out better than another in a contract, they will use the duty of fair representation as a basis for challenging the contract. The US Supreme Court speaks to this issue in the following case.

AIR LINE PILOTS ASSOCIATION, INT'L. V. O'NEILL
499 U.S. 65 (1991)

There was a bitter strike between the Air Line Pilots Association, International (ALPA), and Continental Airlines, Inc., after Continental filed for reorganization under Chapter 11 of the Bankruptcy Code and repudiated its collective bargaining agreement with ALPA. The strike went on for over two years, during which time Continental hired replacement workers and many pilots crossed the picket lines. Eventually the union negotiated a deal with Continental which allowed some of the striking pilots to return to work. However, the terms of the settlement were less favorable than a complete surrender to Continental would have been, particularly as it related to seniority for the striking pilots, which was the basis of their duty assignment system. The striking pilots did not like the deal which was struck between the union and management and alleged that in reaching the agreement, the union breached its duty of fair representation. The U.S. Supreme Court held that the union has done its job as long as the union's settlement with the employer is not "wholly irrational or arbitrary."

Stevens, J.

ALPA's central argument is that the duty of fair representation requires only that a union act in good faith and treat its members equally and in a nondiscriminatory fashion. The duty, the union argues, does not impose any obligation to provide *adequate* representation. The District Court found that there was no evidence that ALPA acted other than in good faith and without discrimination.

The union maintains, not without some merit, that its view that courts are not authorized to review the rationality of good-faith, nondiscriminatory union decisions is consonant with federal labor policy. The Government has generally regulated only "the *process* of collective bargaining," . . . but relied on private negotiations between the parties to establish "their own character for the ordering of industrial relations," . . . As we have previously stated, "Congress intended that the parties should have wide latitude in their negotiations, unrestricted by any governmental power to regulate the substantive solution of their differences."

There is, however, a critical difference between governmental modification of the terms of a private agreement and an examination of those terms in search of evidence that a union did not fairly and adequately represent its constituency. Our decisions have long recognized that the need for such an examination proceeds directly from the union's statutory role as exclusive bargaining agent. Just as fiduciaries owe their beneficiaries a duty of care as well as a duty of loyalty, a union owes employees a duty to represent them adequately as well as honestly and in good faith.

ALPA suggests that a union need owe no enforceable duty of adequate representation because employees are protected from inadequate representation by the union political process. ALPA argues that employees "do not need protection against representation that is inept but not invidious" because if a "union does an incompetent job its members can vote in new officers who will do a better job or they can vote in another union."

[W]e have repeatedly identified three components of the duty [of fair representation], including a prohibition against "arbitrary" conduct. Writing for the Court in the leading case in this area of the law, Justice White explained:

The statutory duty of fair representation was developed over 20 years ago in a series of cases involving alleged racial discrimination by unions certified as exclusive bargaining representatives under the Railway Labor Act, . . . and was soon extended to unions certified under the N.L.R.A. . . . under this doctrine, the exclusive agent's statutory authority to represent all members of a designated unit includes a statutory obligation to serve the interests of all members without hostility or discrimination toward any, to exercise its discretion with complete good faith and honesty, and to avoid arbitrary conduct.

Congress did not intend judicial review of a union's performance to permit the court to substitute its own view of the proper bargain for that reached by the union. Any substantive examination of a union's performance, therefore, must be highly deferential, recognizing the wide latitude that negotiators need for the effective performance of their bargaining responsibilities. For that reason, the final product of the bargaining process may constitute evidence of a breach of duty only if it can be fairly characterized as so far outside a "wide range of reasonableness," that it is wholly "irrational" or "arbitrary."

For purposes of decision, we may assume that the Court of Appeals was correct in its conclusion that, if ALPA had simply surrendered and voluntarily terminated the strike, the striking pilots would have been entitled to reemployment in the order of seniority. Moreover, we may assume that Continental would have responded to such action by rescinding its assignment of all the bid positions to working pilots. After all, it did rescind about half of those assignments pursuant to the terms of the settlement. Thus, we assume that the union made a bad settlement—one that was even worse than a unilateral termination of the strike.

Nevertheless, the settlement was by no means irrational. A settlement is not irrational simply because it turns out *in retrospect* to have been a bad settlement. Viewed in light of the legal landscape at the time of the settlement, ALPA's decision to settle rather than give up was certainly not illogical. At the time of the settlement, Continental had notified the union that all of the . . . bid positions had been awarded to working pilots and was maintaining that none of the strikers had any claim on any of those jobs.

The suggestion that the "discrimination" between striking and working pilots represented a breach of the duty if fair representation fails. REVERSED and REMANDED

Case Questions

1. Do you agree that the Court should not look into the substance of complaints about the union's duty of fair representation?

2. For the striking pilots who feel they were discriminated against, what are the drawbacks of the union?

3. Considering that the union had been on strike for over two years and management had hired replacement workers and non-striking employees, what sort of position do you think that management was in when negotiating with the union?

Collective Bargaining Agreements

If all goes well, bargaining between labor and management results in a **collective bargaining agreement.** This is the term for the contract that is reached between the employer and employees about workplace issues. There is no set form that this agreement must take, and it may be any length and contain any provisions the

Collective bargaining agreement
Negotiated contract between labor and management.

parties decide. (See Exhibit 17–4.) Job and union security is the main issue for employees, while freedom from labor strife, such as strikes, slowdowns, and work stoppages, is paramount for employers. Management will often wish to include a **management security clause,** stating that it has the power to run its business and make business decisions as long as it is not in violation of the collective bargaining agreement or the law.

Management security clause
Parties agree that management has the right to run the business and make appropriate business decisions as long as applicable laws are complied with.

Toward that end, in addition to wages and hours, collective bargaining agreements often also contain provisions regarding strikes, arbitration of labor disputes, seniority, benefits, employment classifications, and so on. Because things change, the agreement is only in effect for a specified period. Prior to expiration of that period, the parties will negotiate a new contract, to take effect when the old one ends.

Midterm negotiations
Collective bargaining negotiations during the term of the contract.

The collective bargaining agreement may also include a clause permitting **midterm negotiations.** These are negotiations during the life of the contract, rather than immediately prior to its expiration, about matters on which the parties have agreed they will permit interim negotiations. The parties may not be able to agree on a particular provision, and, rather than allow it to hold up the entire contract, will agree to come back together later to negotiate it. Alternatively, the parties may agree to midterm negotiations because the contract may cover a fairly long period, and the provision subject to midterm negotiation is one that may change quickly and need to be reviewed before the contract's expiration date.

Unfair Labor Practices

Refusal to bargain in good faith is not the only unfair labor practice that an employer can commit. Others include engaging in activities that would tend to attempt to control or influence the union, or to interfere with its affairs, and discriminating against employees who join or assist unions. Actual interference by the employer need not be proved for it to be considered an unfair labor practice. Rather, the question is whether the activity tends to interfere with, restrain, or coerce employees who are exercising rights protected under the law. (See Exhibit 17–5.)

As shown by *Polytech,* following, it is an unfair labor practice for employers to promise to give benefits, or, in the alternative, for employers to reduce benefits in an effort to discourage unionizing efforts. This is the basis for opening scenario 2.

2
Scenario

NLRB v. POLYTECH, INC.
469 F.2d 1226 (8th Cir. 1972)

Union claims employer committed an unfair labor practice in offering employees benefits if they would not unionize. The court agreed and enforced the NLRB's order.

Stephenson, J.

On August 4, 1969, immediately following a second attempt at union recognition by Bagwell, the union representative, McGowan held a meeting with his employees. While no concrete offers of specific benefits were made to the employees by McGowan, he did tell them that he did not intend to take things away from them that they had in the past with the owners they [the McGowans] bought the company from. Mrs. McGowan, in response to a question by an employee, indicated that if the employees were to receive certain benefits they would not need a union.

While employers may generally make their views about unions known and set forth their ideas as to what will happen to the workplace as a whole as a result of unionization, they should institute procedures for minimizing employee's fear of interference from the employer, such as secret balloting. Of course, employers should avoid questioning employees about their union sympathies, as this will tend to intimidate employees and be taken as interference with the union's activities, resulting in an unfair labor practice charge against the employer.

Employer contends that the statements made by McGowan and his wife at the August 4, 1969 meeting did not violate Section 8(a)(1) of the Act because they were (1) not made during an organizing campaign by the union and (2) protected free speech under Section 8(c) of the Act. Mr. McGowan's statement that he did not intend to take any benefits away from the employees that they had obtained from Polytech Co. [the previous owners], and Mrs. McGowan's comment that if the employees received similar benefits they would not need a union, fall within the "promise of benefit" clause of 8(c). The statements implicitly promised that the employees would receive benefits at least equal to those under the Polytech Company's contract with the union. The NLRB's order regarding this issue is ENFORCED.

Case Questions

1. Do you agree that the employer's statement would implicitly promise benefits? How would you change the statements so that they did not violate the law?

2. Do you think it is "fair" to prohibit employers from promising benefits to prevent unionization?

3. From the employee point of view, what are the drawbacks to permitting such promises?

Some employers are more aggressive in interfering with their employees' unionizing efforts.

DAVIS SUPERMARKETS, INC. V. NLRB
2 F.3d 1162 (D.C. Cir. 1993)

The owners of a supermarket whose employees at one of its outlets wanted to vote in a union interfered with the employees' organizing efforts and terminated several employees. The company was found by the NLRB to have committed unfair labor practices and the company vehemently disagreed. The court upheld the NLRB's decision and found in favor of the employees.

Mikva, C.J.

This multifarious case concerns the alleged efforts by Davis Supermarkets, Inc., ("the Company") to combat an organizing campaign by the United Food and Commercial Workers International union, Local Union 23, AFL-CIO-CLC ("Local 23") in the Company's Hempfield, Pennsylvania store in 1986. The National Labor Relations Board ("the NLRB" or "the Board") found that the Company had committed numerous unfair labor practices prohibited by sections 8(a)(1), 8(a)(2), and 8(a)(3) of the National Labor Relations Act ("the NLRA" or "the Act").

We will briefly summarize the main facts of the case and will relate additional facts as it becomes necessary to do so in analyzing the numerous issues we are asked to review. As will become apparent, our decision is largely fact-driven, as were the Board's determinations.

Davis Supermarkets, a family-owned corporation engaged in the retail grocery business, owns and operates a supermarket in Greensburg, Pennsylvania, and a supermarket in Hempfield Township, Pennsylvania. The Greensburg store has been open for approximately thirty years. The United Steelworkers of America ("Steelworkers") has represented the Greensburg employees throughout the period relevant to this case. The Hempfield store opened in 1984. When the events giving rise to this case commence in 1986, the Hempfield employees were unrepresented.

In March 1986, Local 23 launched a concerted organizing campaign in the Hempfield store, which employed more than one hundred men and women. Over the next few months, Donald Porter, an organizer for Local 23, met with various employees on and off the store's premises, urging them to sign authorization cards for Local 23. Some of the employees that he successfully recruited solicited authorization cards from other employees.

By April 19, 1986, a total of thirteen employees had signed authorization cards for Local 23. On that day, the Company summarily laid off eight workers, six of whom had signed authorization cards. In May, the Company fired or constructively fired two other employees who had signed cards. In July, the Company constructively discharged Linda Kunkle, who had also signed a card for Local 23.

On May 1, at two separate meetings with various employees of the Hempfield store, Bob Davis, the chairman of the Company's board of directors, told the assembled workers that he wanted them to sign authorization cards for the Steelworkers. After one of the meetings, a Steelworkers representative from the Greensburg store and an official of that union handed out Steelworkers contracts and authorization cards to the employees. Following the other meeting, two Steelworkers representatives from the Greensburg facility distributed Steelworkers contracts and cards.

On March 28, 1990, an Administrative Law Judge ("ALJ") found that the Company had violated the law by, among other actions: (1) firing or constructively firing nine employees for the purpose of discouraging union activity; and (2) urging employees to join the Steelworkers and permitting only that union to solicit employees in the Company's store.

The Company challenges the findings of unfair labor practices as to the nine firings, and the aiding of the Steelworkers at the Hempfield facility. The Board found the April 19 layoffs to be violations of section 8(a)(1) and 8(a)(3) of the Act. Section 8(a)(1) states, "It shall be an unfair labor practice for an employer . . . to interfere with, restrain, or coerce employees in the exercise of [self-organization and collective bargaining] rights guaranteed in section 157 of this title." 29 U.S.C. 158(a)(1). Section 8(a)(3) makes it an unfair labor practice for an employer "by discrimination in regard to hire or tenure of employment or any term or condition of employment to encourage or discourage membership in any labor organization." 29 U.S.C. 158(a)(3).

In assessing discriminatory discharge cases, we are required to use an approach known as the *Wright Line* test [after Wright Line, 251 N.L.R.B. 1083 (1980), enforced, 662 F.2d 899 (1st Cir. 1981)]. Under this approach, "where a termination is alleged to be improper, the NLRB General Counsel bears the burden of demonstrating that 'an antiunion animus' contributed to the employer's decision to discharge an employee." If the General Counsel makes this prima facie showing, the employer can nonetheless avoid an unfair labor practice finding by showing "by a preponderance of evidence that the worker would have been fired even if he had not been involved with the union."

The Company alleges that it fired the six employees for a variety of valid reasons, including "attitude problems," poor performance and consolidation in response to slow business. The Board did not find these explanations believable, in light of the shifting reasons offered for the dismissals, the lack of evidence of performance and attitude problems, the absence of prior warnings to the employees supposedly fired for such problems, and the quick replacement of the workers allegedly laid off for economic reasons with employees from the Greensburg store. The Board found instead that the firings were part of a strategy to suppress Local 23's organizing campaign.

The Company contends that the Board lacked substantial evidence to find that "antiunion animus" was the action motivation for the firings. To satisfy this requirement, the General Counsel generally must establish that the employer knew that the workers it laid off were involved in union activities. The Company maintains that on April 19, it was unaware of the union activities of any of the six employees, and that the General Counsel failed to show otherwise.

Despite the Company's assertions, there is considerable direct evidence that it knew of or suspected the pro-union sympathies of at least some of the workers. For example, about a year before she was fired, Shotts asked two managers about getting a union in the store, and the managers warned her not to talk about it any further. Also, on March 25, 1986, Welsh's immediate supervisor interrogated her about a Local 23 meeting that she had attended. As for the other employees, however, there is, as the Company maintains, scant direct evidence that the Company was aware they were union supporters when it discharged them.

The lack of direct evidence does not, however, necessarily render the Board's findings of antiunion motivation inadequate. The Board found substantial circumstantial evidence that the Company knew of the employees' union activities, and "although the Board may not base its decision on mere conjecture, the element of knowledge may be shown by circumstantial evidence from which a reasonable inference may be drawn." "Similarly, the Board may infer discriminatory motive from circumstantial evidence." Among the factors on which the Board may base such inferences are "the timing of the discharges in relation to the union activity [and] the simultaneous nature of otherwise unconnected dismissals."

Both the timing and the nature of the discharges in this case suggest anti-union motivations. The firings occurred just as Local 23's campaign was picking up steam, and the employees who worked in various different departments, were all dismissed on the same day for entirely disparate reasons. Furthermore, of the eight employees laid off, six were union supporters, and this occurred at a time when only thirteen out of more than one hundred employees had signed cards. In light of the summary and targeted nature of the dismissals and the Company's failure to come up with plausible legitimate reasons for them, there was probably sufficient evidence to find that the six firings were violations of the Act.

Nonetheless, there is a somewhat troubling lack of evidence that the Company even had the opportunity to learn of the union advocacy of several of the fired workers. Hilty and Garris, in particular, seem to have performed very few union-related actions on store premises within the sight of other people.

There is, however, an alternative and less problematic manner in which to assess the legality of these six layoffs. Although the General Counsel ordinarily must show that the employer was aware of the pro-union sentiments of a dismissed employee in order to establish an 8(a)(3) violation, he does not have to make such a showing if the dismissal is part of a mass layoff "for the purpose of discouraging union activity."

In other words, it is not necessary to establish the Company's awareness of each discharged worker's union advocacy, so long as the firing was part of a mass layoff.

The Board's finding of an unlawful mass layoff is clearly supported by substantial evidence. A supervisor told Defibaugh on April 19, the day of the firings, that "they heard the union was getting close to the number they needed for an election and they were getting rid of the troublemakers and the people with attitude problems."

We thus hold that the first part of the *Wright Line* test, requiring a showing that firings were motivated by anti-union animus, is satisfied under the mass discharge theory. According to the second part of the test, the employer can overcome the showing of anti-union motivation only by establishing, by a preponderance of the evidence, that "the discharge would have occurred in any event and for valid reasons."

The Board properly found that the Company failed to meet this burden. As we noted above the Company proffered allegedly valid reasons why each of the six employees was fired on April 19. The Board confidently rejected all of these explanations as inconsistent and implausible. "Under [the substantial evidence standard] our function is to determine only whether the agency could fairly and reasonably find the facts as it did." Because the Board's findings were clearly reasonable, we see no basis for overturning its conclusions. We therefore uphold the Board's determination that the six April 19 layoffs constituted unfair labor practices in violation of sections 8(a)(1) and 8(a)(3) of the Act.

In addition to the six April 19 firings, the Board also found three discharges or constructive discharges that occurred in later months to be violations of sections 8(a)(1) and 8(a)(3). Because the dismissals of Larry Miller, Charles Miscovich, and Linda Kunkle occurred on three different dates ranging from May to July, the mass discharge theory does not apply. In order to establish anti-union animus, the General Counsel was therefore required to establish that the Company was aware that each of the three employees supported Local 23.

We find that there is substantial evidence that the Company knew of the pro-union activities of these three workers. We also uphold the Board's conclusion that the firings were motivated only by anti-union animus.

Miller was discharged on May 14, 1986. The Company alleges that it fired Miller, a bagger and stockboy, because, while on break, he ate food that he had stolen from the store. The Board found, however, that the store manager who fired Miller never even asked him whether he had paid for the items. Moreover, neither of the two employees with whom Miller had been eating were similarly discharged. In light of the fact that Miller repeatedly spoke to Porter, Local 23's organizer, in the parking lot of the Hempfield store, and that the store manager once told Porter to leave Miller alone, there is substantial evidence that the Company knew of Miller's support of Local 23 and fired him for this reason.

Miscovich worked a day shift at the Hempfield store because he also had a night job at a gas station. In mid-May, shortly after Miscovich signed a Local 23 authorization card, the store manager began scheduling him for night shifts. When Miscovich reminded the manager of his situation, he responded that Miscovich had to work when told to or not work at all. After that, Miscovich was never able to work at the store again.

There is no doubt that the Company was aware of Miscovich's pro-union stance, for he was called to a May 12 meeting where Bob Davis, the chairman of the Company, told the assembled workers that he knew they had all signed authorization cards. There is substantial evidence to support the Board's conclusion that the Company constructively discharged Miscovich in violation of sections 8(a)(1) and 8(a)(3).

On July 26, Kunkle quit her job, after suffering through three weeks of inexcusable treatment. The Company transferred her from an office job to the meat department, reduced her hours, required her to stay in a back room and wrap meat, and forbade other employees to talk to her about anything except meat.

There is no doubt that the Company was aware of Kunkle's pro-union activities. Kunkle was an active and public Local 23 supporter who had signed an authorization card, solicited cards from other employees, and picketed the store to protest its unfair labor practices. The Company apparently photographed her picketing. More over, she was one of the employees present at the May 12 meeting where Bob Davis told the as-

sembled workers that he knew they had all signed authorization cards. We uphold the Board's finding that Kunkle was unlawfully constructively discharged. Unfair labor practices ruling UP-HELD.

Case Questions

1. Do the employer's violations seem clear to you? Why do you think the employer did not think they were so clear?

2. If you were the employer in a similar situation, and had read this case, what would you do when your employees wanted to unionize?

3. The employer here tried to promote one union over another, rather than trying to keep out unions altogether. Why do you think the employer tried to have the one union represent its employees rather than the other?

In another decision, what may have appeared to a company to be legitimate employee–management negotiations with nonunion employees was held to violate the NLRA. It is the basis for opening scenario 4.

Scenario

EXHIBIT 17–5 Management Unfair Labor Practices

- Trying to control the union or interfering with union affairs, such as trying to help a certain candidate get elected to a union office.

- Discriminating against employees who join a union or are in favor of bringing in a union or who exercise their rights under the law (e.g., terminating, demoting, or giving poor working schedules to such employees).

- Interfering with, coercing, or restraining employees exercising their rights under the labor law legislation. For instance, telling employees they cannot have a union or they will be terminated if they do.

- Refusal to bargain or refusal to bargain in good faith.

Electromation v. National Labor Relations Board
35 F.3d 1148 (7th Cir. 1993)

A nonunion company negotiated with its workers to resolve labor issues through "employee participation" or "employee–management" focus groups rather than a union. The court held that these committees constituted labor organizations and they were dominated by the employer thus constituting an unfair labor practice.

Will, J.

At the time of the events which gave rise to this suit, Electromation's approximately 200 employees, most of whom were women, were not represented by any labor organization. To minimize the financial losses it was experiencing at the time, the company in late 1988 decided to cut expenses by revising its employee attendance policy and replacing the 1989 scheduled wage increases with lump sum payments based on the length of each employee's service at the company.

In January 1989, the company received a handwritten request signed by 68 employees expressing their dissatisfaction with and requesting reconsideration of the revised attendance bonus/wage policy. After meeting with the company's supervisors, the company President, John Howard, decided to meet directly with employees to discuss their concerns. Accordingly, on January 11, 1989, the company met with eight employees—three randomly selected high-seniority employees, three randomly selected low-seniority employees, and two additional employees who had requested that they be included—to discuss a number of matters, including wages, bonuses, incentive pay, tardiness, attendance programs, and bereavement and sick leave policy, all normal collective bargaining issues.

Following this meeting, Howard met again with the supervisors and concluded that management had "possibly made a mistake in judgment in December in deciding what we ought to do" . . . [and] "that the better course of action would be to involve the employees in coming up with solutions to these issues." The company determined that "action committees" would be an appropriate

way to involve employees in the process. Accordingly, on January 18, 1989, the company met again with the same eight employees . . . and proposed the creation of action committees to "meet and try to come up with ways to resolve these problems; and that if they came up with solutions that . . . we believed were within budget concerns and they generally felt would be acceptable to the employees, that we would implement these suggestions or proposals." At the employees' suggestion, Howard agreed that, rather than having a random selection of employee committee members, sign-up sheets for each action committee would be posted.

On the next day, the company posted a memorandum to all employees announcing the formation of the following five action committees: (1) Absenteeism/Infractions; (2) No Smoking Policy; (3) Communication Network; (4) Pay Progression for Premium Positions; and (5) Attendance Bonus Program. Sign-up sheets were also posted at this time. Each committee was to consist of up to six employees and one or two members of management, as well as the company's Employee Benefits Manager, Loretta Dickey, who was in charge of the coordination of all the committees. Apparently, Dickey's role was primarily to facilitate the discussions between the company and its employees. Although the sign-up sheets also stated the goals of each action committee, no employees were involved in the drafting of any aspect of the memorandum or the statement of subjects that the committees were to consider. The company also unilaterally decided that two employees who had signed up for more than one committee would be limited to participation on only one committee.

Although the memorandum announcing the creation of the action committees declared that membership on each committee would be determined by the volunteer group for that committee, Dickey apparently made the final determination of which employees would participate on each committee. Five employees were eventually chosen to serve on each committee. The employees were not given an opportunity to vote on Dickey's selection of employee committee members. Each committee also included at least one supervisor or manager in addition to Dickey. According to Dickey, management expected that the employee members of the committees would "kind of talk back and forth" with the other employees in the plant because "anyone [who] wanted to know what was going on, they [could] go to these people." In order to keep other employees posted on the progress of the action committee work, at least one update memorandum was posted which described the activities of the action committees. The update memorandum was drafted by management without consultation with the employee members of each committee.

During the Attendance Bonus Committee's first meeting, Dickey and Electromation's Controller, Dan Mazur, solicited employee ideas regarding a good employee attendance award program. Their goal was to develop an attendance program which would be both affordable to the company and satisfactory to the employees. Through the discussions, the committee developed a proposal, which was declared by Mazur to be too costly and was not pursued further for that reason. Because the first proposal had been rejected, the committee developed a second proposal, which was deemed fiscally sound by Mazur. However, due to the intervening demand for union recognition, the second proposal was never presented to Howard and no responsive action by the company was ever taken.

On February 13, 1989, the International Brotherhood of Teamsters, Local Union No. 1049

(the "union") demanded recognition from the company. Until then, the company was unaware that any organizing efforts had occurred at the plant. In late February, Howard informed Dickey of the union's demand for recognition. Upon the advice of counsel, Dickey announced at the next meeting of each committee that, due to the union demand, the company could no longer participate in the committees, but that the employee members could continue to meet if they so desired.

Finally, on March 15, 1989, Howard formally announced to the employees that "due to the union's campaign, the Company would be unable to participate in the [committee] meetings and could not continue to work with the committees until after the [union] election." The union election took place on March 31, 1989; the employees voted 95 to 82 against union representation. On April 24, 1989, a regional director of the Board issued a complaint alleging that Electromation had violated the Act.

As they are described above, the facts in this case are largely undisputed. [In a hearing before an administrative law judge, it was] concluded that the Electromation action committees constituted labor organizations . . . that employees, supervisors, and managerial personnel served as committee members and that their discussions concerned conditions of employment . . . the company had organized the committees, created their nature and structure, and determined their functions . . . [and] the company had dominated and assisted the committees in violation of Section 8(a)(2) . . . [A]lthough management did not dominate the discussions, the committee meetings occurred on company property, the supplies and materials were provided by management, and the employee members were paid for their time spent on committee work.

The company appealed this decision to the Board . . . [contending] that the action committees were not labor organizations within the meaning of the Act and that they did not interfere with employee free choice. The company argued that no proposal from any action committee was ever implemented, that the committees were formed in the absence of any company knowledge of union activity, and that the committees followed a company tradition of employer-employee meetings.

The Board found that the action committees constituted labor organizations within the meaning of Section 2(5) of the Act, and that the company had dominated and assisted them within the meaning of Section 8(a)(2) and (1) that the only purpose of the committees was to deal with those conditions through a bilateral process involving both employees and management on the basis of employee-initiated proposals and that the employee committee members acted in a representational capacity within the meaning of the Act. Noting that (1) the employer initiated the idea to create the committees, (2) the employer unilaterally drafted the written purposes and goals statements of the committees, (3) the employer unilaterally determined how many members would compose each committee and that an employee could serve on only one committee at a time, and (4) the employer appointed management representatives to the committees to facilitate the discussions, the Board found that the company had violated Section 8(a)(2) and (1) of the Act by dominating the formation and administration of, and contributing financial and other support to, the action committees. In support of its findings, the Board also noted that the employer permitted the employees to conduct committee activities on paid time within a structure wholly designed by the employer.

The Board concluded on this evidence that the committees were the creation of the employer and that the impetus for their continued existence rested solely with Electromation. The Board agreed with the [administrative law judge] that the company did not effectively disestablish the committees upon receipt of the union's bargaining demand; that the purpose of the action committees was not to enable management and employees to cooperate to improve quality or efficiency, but rather to create in employees the impression that their disagreements with management had been resolved bilaterally, where in fact the employer

had imposed on its employees a unilateral form of bargaining in violation of Sections 8(a)(2) and (1). One Board member found that Section 8(a)(2) does not create obstacles for employers wishing to implement legitimate employee involvement programs, as long as those programs do not impair the right of employees to their free choice of a bargaining representative but emphasized that the employer's establishment of the committees in this case was illegal domination and support of a labor organization in violation of Section 8(a)(2) primarily because these committees placed the employer on both sides of the bargaining table to discuss the terms and conditions of employment, thus giving employees the illusion of a bargaining representative without the reality of one. Another member noted that the critical question is whether the entity is created with any purpose to deal with grievances, labor disputes, wages, rates of pay, hours of employment, or conditions of work and because the action committees' purpose was to address and find solutions for issues related to absenteeism, pay progression, attendance bonuses, and no smoking policies, he found a clear violation of Section 8(a)(2).

The Board's order requires the company to: (1) cease and desist from dominating, assisting, or otherwise supporting the action committees and in any like manner interfering with, restraining, or coercing employees in the exercise of their Section 7 rights; (2) disestablish the action committees; and (3) post an appropriate notice. Electromation has filed a petition to set aside this order.

An allegation that Electromation has violated Section 8(a)(2) and (1) of the Act raises two distinct issues: first, whether the action committees in this case constituted "labor organizations" within the meaning of Section 2(5); and second, whether the employer dominated, influenced, or interfered with the formation or administration of the organization or contributed financial or other support to it, in violation of Section 8(a)(2) and (1) of the Act. Each issue will be examined in turn.

A. The Action Committees Constituted Labor Organizations

Section 2(5) of the Act defines a labor organization as:

any organization of any kind, or any agency or employee representation committee or plan, in which employees participate and which exists for the purpose, in whole or in part, of dealing with employers concerning grievances, labor disputes, wages, rates of pay, hours of employment, or conditions of work.

Under this statutory definition, the action committees would constitute labor organizations if: (1) the Electromation employees participated in the committees; (2) the committees existed, at least in part, for the purpose of "dealing with" the employer; and (3) these dealings concerned "grievances, labor disputes, wages, rates of pay, hours of employment, or conditions of work."

With respect to the first factor, there is no question that the Electromation employees participated in the action committees. Turning to the second factor, which is the most seriously contested on appeal, the Board found that the activities of the action committees constituted "dealing with" the employer. We agree with the Board that the action committees can be differentiated only in the specific subject matter with which each dealt. Each committee had an identical relationship to the company: the purpose, structure, and administration of each committee was essentially the same. We note, in addition, that even if the committees are considered individually, there exists substantial evidence that each was formed and existed for the purpose of "dealing with" the company. It is in fact the shared similarities among the committee structures which compels unitary treatment of them for the purposes of the issues raised in this appeal.

Given the Supreme Court's holding that "dealing with" includes conduct much broader than collective bargaining, the Board did not err in determining that the Electromation action committees constituted labor organizations within the meaning of Sections 2(5) and 8(a)(2) of the Act.

Finally, with respect to the third factor, the subject matter of that dealing—for example, the treatment of employee absenteeism and employee bonuses—obviously concerned conditions of employment. We further agree with the Board that the purpose of the action committees was not limited to the improvement of company efficiency or product quality, but rather that they were designed to function and in fact functioned in an essentially representative capacity. Accordingly, given the statute's traditionally broad construction, there is substantial evidence to support the Board's finding that the action committees constituted labor organizations.

B. The Company Violated Section 8(a)(2) and (1) of the Act

Section 8(a)(2) declares that it shall be an unfair labor practice for an employer: to dominate or interfere with the formation or administration of any labor organization or contribute financial or other support to it: Provided, That subject to rules and regulations made and published by the Board pursuant to Section 6, an employer shall not be prohibited from permitting employees to confer with him during working hours without loss of time or pay. Section 8(a)(1) provides that it shall be an unfair labor practice for an employer: to interfere with, restrain or coerce employees in the exercise of the rights guaranteed in section 157 of this title. Section 7 in turn provides that: [e]mployees shall have the right to self-organization, to form, to join, or assist labor organizations, to bargain collectively through representatives of their own choosing, and to engage in other concerted activities for the purpose of collective bargaining or other mutual aid or protection, and shall also have the right to refrain from any and all such activities except to the extent that such right may be affected by an agreement requiring membership in a labor organization as a condition of employment as authorized in section 158(a)(3) of this title.

Electromation argues that the Board's ruling in this case implies that an employer violates Section 8(a)(2) whenever it proposes a structure whereby the employees and employer "cooperate," or meet together to discuss topics of mutual concern. The company thus asserts that the Board may find a violation of Section 8(a)(2) only where it finds that the employer has actually undermined the free and independent choice of the employees.

As the Board found, substantial evidence supports the finding of company domination of the action committees. First, the company proposed and essentially imposed the action committees upon its employees as the only acceptable mechanism for resolution of their acknowledged grievances regarding the newly announced attendance bonus policies. In response to perceived employee dissatisfaction with working conditions and a petition signed by 68 workers specifically protesting the changes in Electromation's attendance policy, the company unilaterally developed the concept of action committees. The record also clearly shows that the employees were initially reluctant to accept the company's proposal of the action committees as a means to address their concerns; their reaction was "not positive." Nonetheless, the company continued to press the idea until the employees eventually accepted. Moreover, although the company informed the employees that they could continue to meet on their own, shortly after Electromation removed its management representatives from the committees due to the union recognition demand and announced that it would not work with the committees until after the union election, several of the committees disbanded. It was on this basis that the Board reasonably concluded that the company created the action committees and provided the impetus for their continued existence.

The company played a pivotal role in establishing both the framework and the agenda for the action committees. Electromation unilaterally selected the size, structure, and procedural functioning of the committees; it decided the number of committees and the topic(s) to be addressed by each. The company unilaterally drafted the action committees' purposes and goal statements, which

identified from the start the focus of each committee's work. Also, as was pointed out during oral argument, despite the fact that the employees were seriously concerned about the lack of a wage increase, no action committee was designated to consider this specific issue. In this way, Electromation actually controlled which issues received attention by the committees and which did not. Although the company acceded to the employees' request that volunteers form the committees, it unilaterally determined how many could serve on each committee, decided that an employee could serve on only one committee at a time, and determined which committee certain employees would serve on, thus exercising significant control over the employees' participation and voice at the committee meetings. Also, although it never became a significant issue because so few employees signed up for the committees, the initial sign up sheets indicated that the employer would decide which six employees would be chosen as committee members where more than six expressed interest in a particular committee. Ultimately, the company limited membership to five and determined the five to serve. Also, the company designated management representatives to serve on the committees. Employee Benefits Manager Dickey was assigned to coordinate and serve on all committees. In the case of the Attendance Bonus Program Committee, the management representative— Controller Mazur—reviewed employee proposals, determined whether they were economically feasible, and further decided whether they would be presented to higher management. This role of the management committee members effectively put the employer on both sides of the bargaining table, an avowed proscription of the Act.

Finally, the company paid the employees for their time spent on committee activities, provided meeting space, and furnished all necessary supplies for the committees' activities. While such financial support is clearly not a violation of Section 8(a)(2) by itself, in the totality of the circumstances in this case such support may reasonably be characterized to be in furtherance of the company's domination of the action committees. We therefore conclude that there is substantial evidence to support the Board's finding of unlawful employer domination and interference in violation of Section 8(a)(2) and (1). NLRB ORDER ENFORCED.

Case Questions

1. Did the employer seem to intentionally violate the law? Explain.

2. What do you think would motivate an employer to prefer to deal directly with an employee participation group rather than a union?

3. Do you think it's harmful to put the employer on "both sides of the bargaining table?" Explain the pros and cons.

Strikes and Lockouts

The NLRA permits certain strikes by employees as a legitimate form of protest. When a union strikes, union members do not work but, instead, generally gather outside the employer's place of business and carry signs about the nature of the strike (**picketing**) and chant slogans. Engaging in such activity is for purposes of pressuring management to concede, bringing attention to the strikers' demands, gathering support, and discouraging others who may support the employer. For instance, a picket line may encourage shoppers going into a grocery store not to patronize the store where the clerks are on strike because wages are too low.

Legitimate strikes may be called by the union either for economic reasons or because of unfair labor practices. For instance, the employees may strike when a collective bargaining agreement expires or if the employees are attempting to force economic concessions from the employer. If employees strike for legally recognized reasons, their actions are protected under the NLRA and they retain their status as employees. Strikes not authorized by the union are called **"wildcat strikes"** and are illegal if they force the employer to deal with the employees, rather than the union, or impose the will of the minority, rather than the majority. They have been found not to be unlawful if they are merely to make a statement.

If the employer replaces the strikers, then once the strike is over, the strikers have a right to reinstatement if they offer an unconditional offer to return to work. If their jobs are occupied by replacement workers, then unfair labor practice strikers are entitled to be reinstated, but economic strikers are not.

Just as employees can stop working if they feel the need to strike to make their point, the employer can close the premises to employees and engage in a **lockout.** In a lockout, the employer curtails employment by either shutting down the plant or by bringing in temporary nonunion employees after laying off striking workers. Under the NLRA, the employer may not engage in lockouts as a way of avoiding bargaining or unionizing but, rather, as with strikes, to bring pressure to bear on the other side for legitimate purposes.

Many collective bargaining agreements contain **no-strike, no-lockout clauses,** which either prohibit or limit the availability of this action and, instead, agree to use

Picketing
The carrying of signs, which tell of an unfair labor practice or strike, by union members in front of the employer's business.

Wildcat strike
A strike not sanctioned by the union.

Lockout
Management does not allow employees to come to work.

No-strike, no-lockout clause
Labor and management agree that labor will not strike and management will not stage a lockout.

EXHIBIT 17–6   Types of Strikes

- *Economic strike*—used to exert pressure on the employer regarding economic issues. Also used for strikes resulting from any other reason than an unfair labor practice. Protected activity.
- *Unfair labor practice strike*—called by union because of an employer's unfair labor practice. Protected activity.
- *Sympathy strike*—employees of struck employer refuse to cross picket line. Whether protected depends on circumstances.
- *Sitdown strike*—employees illegally take possession of workplace during strike. Not protected activity.
- *Wildcat strike*—Strike not authorized by union. Generally not protected activity, but may be.
- *Intermittent strike*—strikes that occur from time to time and are not announced. Not protected activity.
- *Slowdown*—employees remain on the job and generally do not produce as much. Unprotected activity.

the grievance process to handle issues. In the case below, the court discusses legitimate purposes for which an employer can stage a lockout, and what happens if the workers are replaced with temporary employees during the lockout.

LOCAL 825, INT'L UNION OF OPERATING ENGINEERS V. NLRB
829 F.2d 458 (3d Cir. 1987)

Management engaged in a lockout and hired temporary employees to fill in during the lockout period. The union charged that the hiring of the temporary employees was an unfair labor practice. The court disagreed.

Mansmann, J.

Harter Equipment, Inc. (Harter), is a New Jersey corporation engaged in the sale, distribution and service of construction and lawn maintenance equipment. The union represents a unit of the company's employees, including parts and service department mechanics, "parts men"; a truck driver and a painter. Negotiations to renew the contract began on October, 1981. From the beginning, the company made it clear that it needed substantial cost concessions because it was oper-

ating at a loss. On the day the contract expired (December 1, 1981), the company submitted a "final" proposal providing, among other things, for certain wage reductions and a union security clause. The union rejected the proposal but indicated that the employees desired to continue working without a contract. Harter then refused to permit the employees to punch in or work. On December 4, the employees began picketing the company with signs stating they had been locked out.

Harter and the union continued to negotiate on the union security issue. However, after the withdrawal of proposals made by the union which had been accepted by the company, Harter decided to hire temporary replacements to complete service work already in the shop.

After temporary employees were hired, the parties continued to bargain but no final contract was consummated. The company continued to hire temporary replacements and the union continued to picket until April 1, 1982, when the unfair labor practice charge was filed by the union.

A lockout is not an unfair labor practice when used simply as a means of bringing pressure upon the union after an impasse in bargaining negotiations has been reached. After a hearing, an administrative law judge [ALJ] concluded that there had been no showing of anti-union animus, and that the company's lockout was instituted to bring economic pressure to bear upon the union. The ALJ reasoned that the lockout was neither inherently destructive of employee rights, inherently prejudicial to union interests, nor devoid of significant economic justification. The ALJ thus found that the use of replacements during the lockout was legitimate.

On appeal the National Labor Relations Board agreed with the ALJ. The Board held that absent specific proof of anti-union animus, an employer does not violate §8(a)(3) by hiring temporary replacements in order to engage in business operations during an otherwise lawful lockout, including a lockout initiated for the sole purpose of bringing economic pressure to bear in support of a legitimate bargaining position. This petition for review followed.

The Board's findings of fact are conclusive if supported by substantial evidence on the record considered as a whole, which we find it is. We turn now to an examination of whether the use of temporary replacements by Harter is inherently destructive of employee rights. The Court has defined conduct which is inherently destructive of employee rights as conduct which carries with it unavoidable consequences which the employer not only foresaw but which he must have intended. In that respect, the conduct would bear its own indicia of intent. We bear in mind that §8(a)(3) proscribes action impinging on the employees' rights to bargain collectively, strike, or engage in union activities.

In this case, the Company made it clearly known from the beginning of the negotiating sessions that while it desired an amicable renegotiation of its contract, it could not afford major wage concessions because of its declining economic fortunes. Indeed, many of the proposals suggested to the union contained less favorable terms than had been incorporated in the agreement due to expire. It was the company's intention to return the regular employees to work when the negotiations were completed, even though the advertisements for the temporary help did not state that the positions were temporary.

We cannot find that such use of temporary employees was inherently destructive of the employees' right to bargain collectively, strike, or engage in union activities. The use of the replacements during the lockout was a tactic chosen by the employer obviously to put pressure upon the union. Such pressure, however, affects the realities of the union's bargaining positions rather than any right as such to bargain collectively, strike or engage in other concerted activity. As the Supreme Court has noted for example, in respect to a strike, vis-à-vis lockouts, the union has no right to determine exclusively the timing and duration of all work stoppages.

The pressure Harter brought to bear in this case also was not destructive of the employees' rights due to the use of temporary employees. The court has previously noted three considerations in evaluating whether the use of temporary replacements had an inherently destructive or comparatively slight effect on employee rights. The court considered the duration of temporary employment and whether a definite date of termination had been communicated to the union and employees, and found that a definite date of duration for the temporary hires had been communicated. Second, the court noted that the option of returning to work was available to the employees upon their acceptance of the employer's terms, and third, the employer had agreed to continue in effect the union-security clause from the old contract.

In this case, the ALJ considered these factors and found that, although the advertisements for the replacement workers did not state that the positions were temporary, it was indeed the company's intention to return the regular employees to work at the conclusion of the dispute. In regard to the second factor, the ALJ found that the union could have returned its members to work on terms less profitable than desired. As for the union-security clause, the company had agreed to the latest of a series of union proposed security clauses, only to have it withdrawn by the union. Thus, the company in effect had agreed to such a clause.

Under these circumstances, we do not believe that the company's conduct was inherently destructive of employee rights. The "balance of power" between the union and the company may have tilted toward the company through the use of this type of pressure tactic, but as the Board noted, replacing the employees with temporary workers had no greater adverse effect on the right to bargain collectively than did the concededly lawful lockout.

Given this finding, "if the adverse effect of the discriminatory conduct on employee rights is 'comparatively slight' an anti-union motivation must be proved to sustain the charge if the employer has come forward with evidence of legitimate and substantial business justifications for the conduct." Thus, the "slight" impact on employee rights (to organize, etc.) which the conduct at issue arguably had, is negated if the employer has established a legitimate and substantial business justification for his conduct.

Here, that standard has been met. The ALJ specifically found that the Company was in financial straits and that the union was aware of its financial problems. Moreover, no temporary replacements were hired until six weeks after the commencement of the lockout, during which period no unit work was performed. These facts are not clearly erroneous. With respect to the application of legal precepts to the facts as found, we find that a legitimate business justification existed in this case and that no violation of §8(a)(1) or §8(a)(3) occurred. DENY the union's petition for review.

Case Questions

1. Do you agree with the court that this was legitimate pressure on the union?

2. What is the significance, to you, of the employer waiting six weeks before bringing in temporary replacements?

3. Is there an inherent imbalance between the relative positions of labor and management making a lockout more pressure-laden than a strike?

The Taft-Hartley Act

With the enactment of the NLRA and the subsequent gains made in unionism, the Taft-Hartley Act in 1947 was enacted as an amendment to the NLRA to curb excesses by unions. Most importantly, the Taft-Hartley Act changed the policies of the NLRA. No longer were all employers legislatively determined to be frustrating the organizational rights of their employees. Congress recognized that unions had grown so strong and powerful over the years that their activities required federal regulation. As such, unions were to have certain limitations placed on their activity.

Congress wanted employers, employees, and labor organizations to recognize one another's legitimate rights and made the rights of all three subordinate to the public's health, safety, and interest.

Section 7 was rewritten to recognize the right of an employee to refrain from concerted activity, including union activity. Like §8 of the Wagner Act, which enumerates unfair labor practices which could be committed by employees, §8 of the Taft-Hartley Act spelled out six unfair labor practices that could be committed by organized labor, (see Exhibit 17–7) thereby bringing unions under the regulation of the federal law. Under this section, it was an unfair labor practice for unions to:

1. restrain or coerce employees in the exercise of his or her rights or employers in the selection of his or her representatives for collective bargaining;
2. cause an employer to discriminate against an employee;
3. refuse to bargain with an employer;
4. engage in jurisdictional or secondary boycotts;
5. charge excess or discriminatory initiation fees or dues;
6. cause an employer to pay for goods or services that are not provided.

Before closed shops (employee must become a member of the union in order to obtain a job) were outlawed by the Taft-Hartley Act, states enacted right-to-work laws. This was done in response to the use of closed shops by unions to control dissenters by severing their union membership, without which they could not work in a closed shop. The NLRA permits states to have **right-to-work laws,** and about half of them do. In a right-to-work state, employment cannot be conditioned on union membership. Despite their nonparticipation in the union, the union must still represent these employees as a part of the bargaining unit. If a state is not a right-to-work state, the union and employer may have as a part of their collective bargaining agreement union security device a provision for a **union shop.** This provision, called a **"union shop clause,"** requires the employer to have all members or potential members of the bargaining unit agree that they will join the union within a certain amount of time (not less than 30 days) after becoming employed.

It is also permissible for the collective bargaining agreement to contain an **agency shop clause** that requires nonunion members to pay to the union the usual union dues and fees without joining the union and thereby becoming subjected to union rules. Some right-to-work laws do not allow this and, instead, permit nonunion employees of the bargaining unit to be **free riders**—that is, to receive union benefits without having to pay union dues or fees.

A frequent bone of contention with union members is the use of union dues for activities the members do not agree with. This is a particularly interesting question when it involves the agency shop, since employees who do not want to belong to the union must still pay to the union an amount equal to the union dues (often called a service fee). This is, of course, to prevent the problem of "free riders" who benefit from union activity, but do not contribute to the union's resources. In the case that follows, the US Supreme Court addressed the issue of what the union could use this money for.

Right to work laws
Permits employees to choose not to become a part of the union.

Union shop
Union and management agree that employees must be a member of the union.

Union shop clause
Provision in a collective bargaining agreement allowing a union shop.

Agency shop clause
Requires nonunion members to pay union dues without having to be subject to the union rules.

Free riders
Bargaining unit employees who do not pay dues but whom the union is still obligated to represent.

EXHIBIT 17–7   Union Unfair Labor Practices

- Refusal to bargain or bargaining in bad faith—that is, not attending bargaining sessions, not providing proposals, not providing necessary information.
- Coercing or restraining employees in exercising their rights to join (or not join) a union. This is not a problem if the union and employer have a provision in their collective bargaining agreement that states a nonunion member coming into the bargaining unit must join the union within a certain amount of time.
- Charging discriminatory or very high dues or entrance fees for admittance into the union.
- Threatening, encouraging, or influencing employees to strike in an effort to pressure the employer to join an employer organization, or to get the employer to recognize an uncertified union, or to stop doing business with an employer because of the employer not doing so.
- Influencing employers to discriminate against, or otherwise treat differently, employees who do not belong to the union or are denied union membership for some other reason than nonpayment of union dues or fees.

LEHNERT V. FERRIS FACULTY ASSOCIATION
500 U.S. 507 (1991)

Several members of a bargaining unit objected to the way their service fee funds were used, even though they were not members of the union in this agency shop. The Court addressed several different ways in which the money could and could not be spent.

Blackmun, J.

Michigan's Public Employment Relations Act (Act), provides that a duly selected union shall serve as the exclusive collective-bargaining representative of public employees in a particular bargaining unit. The Act, which applies to faculty members of a public educational institution in Michigan, permits a union and a government employer to enter into an "agency-shop" arrangement under which employees within the bargaining unit who decline to become members of the union are compelled to pay a "service fee" to the union.

Respondent Ferris Faculty Association (FFA), an affiliate of the Michigan Education Association (MEA) and the National Education Association (NEA), serves, pursuant to this provision, as the

exclusive bargaining representative of the faculty of Ferris State College in Big Rapids, Michigan. Ferris is a public institution established under the Michigan Constitution and is funded by the State.

Since 1975, the FFA and Ferris have entered into successive collective-bargaining agreements containing agency-shop provisions. Those agreements were the fruit of negotiations between the FFA and respondent Board of Control, the governing body of Ferris.

Subsequent to this Court's decision in *Abood v. Detroit Board of Education,* 431 U.S. 209 (1977), in which the Court upheld the constitutionality of the Michigan agency-shop provision and outlined permissible uses of the compelled fee by public-employee unions, Ferris proposed, and the FFA agreed to, the agency-shop arrangement at issue here. That agreement required all employees in the bargaining unit who did not belong to the FFA to pay a service fee equivalent to the amount of the dues required of a union member. Of the $284 service fee for 1981–1982, the period at issue, $24.80 went to the FFA, $211.20 to the MEA, and $48 to the NEA.

Petitioners were members of the Ferris faculty during the period in question and objected to certain uses by the unions of their service fees. Petitioners instituted this action, claiming that the use of their fees for purposes other than negotiating and administering a collective-bargaining agreement with the Board of Control violated rights secured to them by the First and Fourteenth Amendments to the United States Constitution.

The Court's decisions in this area prescribe a case-by-case analysis in determining which activities a union constitutionally may charge to dissenting employees, and set forth several guidelines to be followed in making such determinations. Chargeable activities must (1) be "germane" to collective-bargaining activity; (2) be justified by the government's vital policy interest in labor peace and avoiding "free riders," and (3) not significantly add to the burdening of free speech that is inherent in the allowance of an agency or union shop.

In arguing that these principles exclude the charges here, employees propose two limitations on the use by public-sector unions of dissenters' contributions. First, they urge that they may not be charged over their objection for lobbying activities that do not concern legislative ratification of, or fiscal appropriations for, their collective-bargaining agreement. Second, as to nonpolitical expenses, employees assert that the local union may not utilize dissenters' fees for activities that, though closely related to collective bargaining generally, are not undertaken directly on behalf of the bargaining unit to which the objecting employees belong. We accept the form proposition but find the latter to be foreclosed by our prior decisions.

The Court of Appeals determined that unions constitutionally may subsidize lobbying and other political activities with dissenters' fees so long as those activities are "'pertinent to the duties of the union as a bargaining representative.'" In reaching this conclusion, the court relied upon the inherently political nature of salary and other workplace decisions in public employment. "To represent their members effectively," the court concluded, "public sector unions must necessarily concern themselves not only with negotiations at the bargaining table but also with advancing their members' interests in legislative and other 'political' arenas."

This observation is clearly correct. Public-sector unions often expend considerable resources in securing ratification of negotiated agreements by the proper state or local legislative body. Similarly, union efforts to acquire appropriations for approved collective-bargaining agreements often serve as an indispensable prerequisite to their implementation. The dual roles of government as employer and policymaker in such cases make the analogy between lobbying and collective bargaining in the public sector a close one.

This, however, is not such a case. Where, as here, the challenged lobbying activities relate not to the ratification or implementation of a dissenter's collective-bargaining agreement, but to financial support of the employee's profession or of public employees generally, the connection to the union's function as bargaining representative is too attenuated to justify compelled support by objecting employees.

We arrive at this result by looking to the governmental interests underlying our acceptance of union-security arrangements. We have found such arrangements to be justified by the government's interest in promoting labor peace and avoiding the "free-rider" problem that would otherwise accompany union recognition. Neither goal is served by charging objecting employees for lobbying, electoral, and other political activities that do not relate to their collective-bargaining agreement.

Labor peace is not especially served by allowing such charges because, unlike collective-bargaining negotiations between union and management, our national and state legislatures, the media, and the platform of public discourse are public fora open to all. Individual employees are free to petition their neighbors and government in opposition to the union which represents them in the workplace. Because worker and union cannot be said to speak with one voice, it would not further the cause of harmonious industrial relations to compel objecting employees to finance union political activities as well as their own.

Similarly, while we have endorsed the notion that nonunion workers ought not be allowed to benefit from the terms of employment secured by union efforts without paying for those services, the so-called "free-rider" concern is inapplicable where lobbying extends beyond the effectuation of a collective-bargaining agreement. The balancing of monetary and other policy choices performed by legislatures is not limited to the workplace but typically has ramifications that extend into diverse aspects of an employee's life.

Perhaps most important, allowing the use of dissenters' assessments for political activities outside the scope of the collective-bargaining context would present "additional interference with the First Amendment interests of objecting employees." There is no question as to the expressive and ideological content of these activities. Further, unlike discussion by negotiators regarding the terms and conditions of employment, lobbying and electoral speech is likely to concern topics about which individuals hold strong personal views. Although First Amendment protection is in no way limited to controversial topics or emotionally charged issues, the extent of one's disagreement with the subject of compulsory speech is relevant to the degree of impingement upon free expression that compulsion will effect.

The burden upon freedom of expression is particularly great where, as here, the compelled speech is in a public context. By utilizing petitioners' funds for political lobbying and to garner the support of the public in its endeavors, the union would use each dissenter as "an instrument for fostering public adherence to an ideological point of view he finds unacceptable." The First Amendment protects the individual's right of participation in these spheres from precisely this type of invasion. Where the subject of compelled speech is the discussion of governmental affairs, which is at the core of our First Amendment freedoms, the burden upon dissenters' rights extends far beyond the acceptance of the agency shop and is constitutionally impermissible.

Accordingly, we hold that the State constitutionally may not compel its employees to subsidize legislative lobbying or other political union activities outside the limited context of contract ratification or implementation.

Employees' contention that they may be charged only for those collective-bargaining activities undertaken directly on behalf of their unit presents a closer question. While we consistently have looked to whether nonideological expenses are "germane to collective bargaining," we have never interpreted that test to require a direct relationship between the expense at issue and some tangible benefit to the dissenters' bargaining unit.

We think that to require so close a connection would be to ignore the unified-membership structure under which many unions, including those here, operate. Under such arrangements, membership in the local union constitutes membership in the state and national parent organizations.

The essence of the affiliation relationship is the notion that the parent will bring to bear its often considerable economic, political, and informational resources when the local is in need of them. Consequently, that part of a local's affiliation fee which contributes to the pool of resources potentially available to the local is assessed for the bargaining unit's protection, even if it is not actually expended on that unit in any particular membership year.

We therefore conclude that a local bargaining representative may charge objecting employees for their pro rata share of the costs associated with otherwise chargeable activities of its state and national affiliates, even if those activities were not performed for the direct benefit of the objecting employees' bargaining unit. This conclusion, however, does not serve to grant a local union carte blanche to expend dissenters' dollars for bargaining activities wholly unrelated to the employees in their unit. The union surely may not, for example, charge objecting employees for a direct donation or interest-free loan to an unrelated bargaining unit for the purpose of promoting employee rights or unionism generally. Further, a contribution by a local union to its parent that is not part of the local's responsibilities as an affiliate but is in the nature of a charitable donation would not be chargeable to dissenters. There must be some indication that the payment is for services that may ultimately inure to the benefit of the members of the local union by virtue of their membership in the parent organization. And, as always, the union bears the burden of proving the proportion of chargeable expenses to total expenses. We conclude merely that the union need not demonstrate a direct and tangible impact upon the dissenting employee's unit.

We turn to the union activities at issue in this case.

The Court of Appeals found that the union could constitutionally charge employees for the costs of a Preserve Public Education (PPE) program designed to secure funds for public education in Michigan, and that portion of the MEA publication, the *Teacher's Voice,* which reported these activities. Employees argue that, contrary to the findings of the courts below, the PPE program went beyond lobbying activity and sought to affect the outcome of ballot issues and "millages" or local taxes for the support of public schools. Given our conclusion as to lobbying and electoral politics generally, this factual dispute is of little consequence. None of these activities was shown to be oriented toward the ratification or implementation of employees' collective-bargaining agreement. We hold that none may be supported through the funds of objecting employees.

Employees next challenge the Court of Appeals' allowance of several activities that the union did not undertake directly on behalf of persons within employees' bargaining unit. This objection principally concerns NEA "program expenditures" destined for States other than Michigan, and the expenses of the *Teacher's Voice* listed as "Collective Bargaining" and "Litigation." Our conclusion that unions may bill dissenting employees for their share of general collective-bargaining costs of the state or national parent union is dispositive as to the bulk of the NEA expenditures. The District Court found these costs to be germane to collective bargaining and similar support services and we decline to disturb that finding. No greater relationship is necessary in the collective-bargaining context.

This rationale does not extend, however, to the expenses of litigation that does not concern the dissenting employees' bargaining unit or, by extension, to union literature reporting on such activities. While the union is clearly correct that precedent established through litigation on behalf of one unit may ultimately be of some use to another unit, we find extraunit litigation to be more akin to lobbying in both kind and effect.

Moreover, union litigation may cover a diverse range of areas from bankruptcy proceedings to employment discrimination. When unrelated to an objecting employee's unit, such activities are not germane to the union's duties as exclusive bargaining representative. We hold that the Amendment proscribes such assessments in the public sector.

The Court of Appeals determined that the union constitutionally could charge employees for certain public relations expenditures. In this connection, the court said: "Public relations expenditures designed to enhance the reputation of the teaching profession . . . are, in our opinion, sufficiently related to the unions' duty to represent bargaining unit employees effectively so as to be chargeable to dissenters." We disagree. Like the challenged lobbying conduct, the public relations activities at issue here entailed speech of a political nature in a public forum. More important, public speech in support of the teaching profession generally is not sufficiently related to the union's collective-bargaining functions to justify compelling dissenting employees to support it. Expression of this kind extends beyond the negotiation and grievance-resolution contexts and imposes a substantially greater burden upon First Amendment rights that do the latter activities.

Nor do we accept the Court of Appeals' comparison of these public relations expenses to the costs of union social activities chargeable to dissenters. We have held that the communicative content of union social activities, if any, derives solely from the union's involvement in them. "Therefore, the fact that the employee is forced to contribute does not increase the infringement of his First Amendment rights already resulting from the compelled contribution to the union." The same cannot be said of the public relations charges upheld by the Court of Appeals which covered "informational picketing, media exposure, signs, posters and buttons."

The District Court and the Court of Appeals allowed charges for those portions of the *Teachers' Voice* that concern teaching and education generally, professional development, unemployment, job opportunities, award programs of the MEA, and other miscellaneous matters. Informational support services such as these are neither political nor public in nature. Although they do not directly concern the members of employees' bargaining unit, these expenditures are for the benefit of all and we discern additional infringement of First Amendment rights that they might occasion. In short, we agree with the Court of Appeals that these expenses are comparable to the *de minimis* social activity charges.

The Court of Appeals ruled that the union could use the fees of objecting employees to send FFA delegates to the MEA and the NEA conventions and to participate in the 13E Coordinating Council, another union structure. The employees challenge that determination and argue that the meetings were those of affiliated parent unions

rather than the local, and therefore do not relate exclusively to the employees' unit.

We need not determine whether employees could be commanded to support all the expenses of these conventions. The question before the Court is simply whether the unions may constitutionally require employees to subsidize the participation in these events of delegates from the local. We hold that they may. That the conventions were not solely devoted to the activities of the FFA does not prevent the unions from requiring employees' support. We conclude above that the First Amendment does not require so close a connection. Moreover, participation by members of the local in the formal activities of the parent is likely to be an important benefit of affiliation.

The chargeability of expenses incident to preparation for a strike which all concede would have been illegal under Michigan law is a provocative question. At the beginning of the 1981–1982 fiscal year, the FFA and Ferris were engaged in negotiating a new collective-bargaining agreement. The union perceived these efforts to be ineffective and began to prepare a "job action" or, in more familiar terms, to go out on strike. These preparations entailed the creation by the FFA and the MEA of a "crisis center" or "strike headquarters."

Had the FFA actually engaged in an illegal strike, the union clearly could not have charged the expenses incident to that strike to dissenters. We can imagine no legitimate governmental interest that would be served by compelling objecting employees to subsidize activity that the State has chosen to disallow. Similarly, one might expect the State to prohibit unions from using dissenters' funds to threaten or prepare for such conduct. The Michigan Legislature, however, has chosen not to impose such a restriction, and we do not find the First Amendment to require that limitation.

The employees can identify no determination by the State of Michigan that mere preparation for an illegal strike is itself illegal or against public policy, and we are aware of none. Further, we accept the rationale provided by the Court of Appeals in upholding these charges that such expenditures fall "within the range of reasonable bargaining tools available to a public sector union during contract negotiations." The District Court expressly credited trial testimony by an MEA representative that outward preparations for a potential strike serve as an effective bargaining tool and that only one out of every seven or eight "job action investigations" actually culminates in a strike.

In sum, these expenses are substantially indistinguishable from those appurtenant to collective-bargaining negotiations. The District Court and the Court of Appeals concluded, and we agree, that they aid in those negotiations and inure to the direct benefit of members of the dissenters' unit. Further, they impose no additional burden upon First Amendment rights. The union may properly charge employees for those costs.

AFFIRMED in part and REVERSED in part, and REMANDED.

Case Questions

1. Do you agree with the Court's decision regarding funds spent for activities preparatory to a strike that could not legally take place? Does the Court's position make sense to you? Explain.

2. As an employer who has a unionized workplace, how would you feel about this decision?

3. Does the agency shop provision requiring nonunion members to contribute a service fee equal to the union dues make sense to you? Explain.

The Landrum-Griffin Act

Also known as the Labor Management Reporting and Disclosure Act, this legislation was enacted in response to congressional investigations into union corruption from 1957–59. After finding evidence of such corruption, the legislation was passed. Based on the investigative findings, the purpose of the law is to establish basic ways of unions operating to ensure a democratic process, to provide union members with a minimum bill of rights attached to union membership, and to regulate the activities of union officials and the use of union funds. (See Exhibit 17–8.)

Under the act, a bill of rights was provided for union members. Looking at some of the provisions of the bill of rights, one might think that they are so simplistic as to be taken as givens for an organization. However, keep in mind that the bill of rights was enacted in response to union abuses actually found during the two-year congressional investigation.

The Landrum-Griffin Act also set forth specific procedures to be followed when unions hold elections, including voting for officers by secret ballot, holding elections at least every three years (other times for different levels of the union, such as international officers), candidates being able to see lists of eligible voters, and procedures for having an election declared improper. Provisions were also enacted to safeguard union funds. Under the act, unions cannot use union funds for anything except benefiting the union or its members. Funds cannot be used to support union office candidates; and union officials, agents, employees, and so on cannot acquire financial interests that conflict with the union's. Stealing or embezzling union funds was made a federal crime by the law.

EXHIBIT 17–8   Union Members' Bill of Rights

Among other things, the law provides that:

- Union members have the right to attend union meetings, vote on union business, and nominate candidates for union elections.
- Members may bring an agency or court action against the union after exhausting union procedures.
- Certain procedures must be followed before any dues or initiation fee increases.
- Except for the failure to pay dues, members must have a full and fair hearing when being disciplined by the union.

Labor Relations in the Public Sector

Much of what has been discussed relates to the private sector. Of more recent vintage is the matter of collective bargaining in the public sector.

Federal Employees

Historically, there has been little legislation effecting the labor relations of public employees (federal, state, and local government employees). The NLRA has always exempted these employees. There is yet no uniform federal policy on public labor–management relations. Currently, however, over half of the 50 states and the District of Columbia have collective bargaining statutes covering most, if not all, public employees.

Over time, federal employees formed associations, but only postal workers were not powerless to influence their workplace. In 1962, President Kennedy established the right of federal employees to form and join unions. Since that time union ranks have increased among this sector.

Federal restrictions prevent federal unions from conducting direct bargaining over wages and benefits, and from striking. The Civil Service Reform Act of 1978 established the Federal Labor Relations Authority (FLRA) to administer federal sector labor law. This agency may be thought of as the federal counterpart to the private sector's National Labor Relations Board (NLRB).

State, County, and Municipal Public Employees

Most public employee organizations at the state, county, and municipal levels can be divided into three major categories—professional associations, craft unions, and industrial-type unions. Professional associations are composed of a wide variety of professionals. One of the largest segments of this population belongs to the National Education Association (NEA). This organization of public school teachers has over one million members, and in addition to teachers, consists of principals, administrators, and other school specialists. The Fraternal Order of Police does not consider itself a union, but many local lodges engage in collective bargaining, handle grievances, and represent the interests of their members to their employers.

Craft unions consist of such workers as the International Association of Firefighters (IAFF), which is an affiliate of the AFL–CIO. Another teachers union that considers itself part of the craft union is the American Federation of Teachers (AFT), which limits its membership to classroom teachers only. While craft unions are too numerous to count, many of them are familiar and have been in existence for nearly a century, such as the United Mine Workers and International Brotherhood of Electrical Workers.

The union that dominates the industrial-type union is the American Federation of State, County, and Municipal Employees (AFSCME), an affiliate of the AFL–CIO. These local unions may represent an entire city or county, or may represent a smaller unit of government, such as a department or a group of employees that cuts across many departments.

The AFL–CIO assists public workers' unions who affiliate with it through its Public Employees Department. This department, formed in 1974, has 33 affiliated unions which represent 4.5 million federal, state, and local government employees. These unions represent workers as diverse as schools, courts, regulatory agencies, hospitals, transportation networks, police, and firefighters. The AFL–CIO believes that state and local employees are the only workers in the United States who do not enjoy the basic right to enter into collective bargaining agreements with their employers. That is, there is no national legislation that gives these workers the right to enter into collective bargaining agreements. If they have the right, it is because the state in which they operate has enacted state legislation which permits it.

To many, the most important difference between the public and private collective bargaining is that the federal government and most state statutes do not contain the right of public employees to strike. This prohibition is grounded in the need to protect public health and safety (i.e., to prevent police officers or firefighters from being out on strike while crime rises or buildings burn), as well as the sovereignty doctrine deeming striking against a governmental employer as inconsistent with the government being the sovereign or highest authority.

State and federal employees have not always honored the prohibition on striking. While many ignored the prohibition, probably the most famous example was when the federal air traffic controllers, represented by the Professional Air Traffic Controllers Organization (PATCO), went on strike in 1981. One of the reasons the strike was so memorable was undoubtedly because newly elected President Ronald Reagan took a hard line and terminated 11,000 striking employees.

U.S. v. Professional Air Traffic Controller's Organization
653 F.2d 1134 (7th Cir. 1981)

PATCO Local No. 316 at Chicago's O'Hare Airport demanded an upgrade of the airport and a tax-free bonus of $7,500 for each air traffic controller. The Federal Aviation Administration refused to meet the demand. In response, from August 6–15, 1980, PATCO conducted a unified slowdown of airport traffic which resulted in several delays. The US sought an injunction on August 18, 1980, and the action was dismissed. The US appealed from the district court's decision holding that only the Federal Labor Relations Authority, not the district court, had the authority to enjoin such a strike.

Swygert, J.

Title VII of the Civil Service Reform Act of 1978 was enacted to provide a comprehensive statutory scheme for the regulation of federal labor-management relations. The statute created a new, independent agency, the Federal Labor Relations Authority (FLRA), which was to be primarily responsible for carrying out the purposes of Title VII. When Congress enacted Title VII, it adopted the language of section 19(b)(4) of the Executive Order [Executive Order 11491, as amended, which regulated federal labor–management relations prior to enactment of the Civil Service Reform Act] making it an unfair labor practice for a union "to call, or participate in, a strike, work stoppage, or slowdown." The reason for Congress's prohibition of strikes by federal employees was reiterated during the congressional debates on Title VII:

> The primary reason for Government services is to supply the public with certain essentials of life which cannot reasonably be supplied by the average citizen himself, or to him by private enterprise. Because these services are essential to the health, welfare and safety of the public, it becomes intolerable that they be interrupted.

Dismissing or indicting the air traffic controllers involved in the slowdown would not be a viable remedy for the Government. First, terminating a substantial number of controllers would seriously impair the FAA's ability to provide the public with this essential service; this is precisely the sort of result that the statutory provisions were intended to prevent. Second, indicting or terminating the controllers after a strike does nothing to prevent the strike and the serious consequences that would surely follow. Thus, the only remedy available to the Government that can prevent a strike is an injunction we conclude that an injunction is an available remedy. REVERSED and REMANDED.

Case Questions

1. In your opinion, based on the *PATCO* decision, should public employees have the right to strike?

2. Do you agree with Congress's assessment of why that right is not provided to public employees?

3. Given the court's language about the perils of terminating the air traffic controllers, why do you think President Reagan did so? What would you have done differently, if anything?

There are also differences between the private and public sector about what may be negotiated. While the US postal workers may do so, generally federal employees cannot bargain over wages, hours, or benefits. On the other hand, they can bargain about the numbers, types, and grades of positions, procedures for performing work or exercising authority, the use of technology, and alternatives for employees harmed by management decisions.

Management Tips

Dealing with unions can be a sticky business. The very idea is antithetical to many business owners who feel the business is theirs and that they should have full control. Giving over any control to employees through the unions and the collective bargaining process is not easy for them. Collective bargaining, is, however, the law. Following the tips below can help avoid problems.

- If employees decide they wish to unionize, do not try to negatively influence the decision.
- Do not assume any employee you speak to for the purpose of persuading employees not to unionize will keep the conversation confidential.
- Know the kinds of things the employer can legally do to influence the unionizing decision, and do only those things that are permissible.
- Once the union is in place, conduct all negotiations only with the union representatives. Avoid trying to make side deals with individual employees.
- Treat the collective bargaining process as one would any business activity. Do not invite unfair labor practice charges by engaging in activity which could be deemed a refusal to bargain in good faith.
- Know what the law requires—the employer need not do any more than the law requires in permitting the union to conduct its business. Know well what the employer can and need not do.
- Keep the lines of communication open between labor and management.
- Try to keep the "us versus them" mentality from having a negative impact on the collective bargaining process. It can be difficult to avoid, but if you can, it helps negotiations stay on an even keel, without letting egos get in the way.
- Play hard ball without setting management up for an unfair labor practice charge.

Summary

- The four main labor law statutes form a framework within which employers and employees may address workplace issues with some modicum of predictability.

- Laws paved the way for unionism by preventing courts from prohibiting union activity. These also provided a statutory basis with the Wagner or National Labor Relations Act; and they fine-tuned and addressed union abuses by the Taft-Hartley Act and the Landrum-Griffin or Labor Management Recording and Disclosure Act.

• Private employers and employees are free to negotiate upon mandatory as well as permissive terms of bargaining to determine matters of wages, hours, and other terms and conditions of employment.

Chapter-End Questions

1. After a bitter strike and boycott which included the use of "scabs" to replace workers in the walnut industry and strike-related violence, a returning worker who had been a quality control supervisor prior to the strike was placed in a seasonal packing position, a job with less status, because the employer was afraid that the replacement workers, some of whom were still on the job, would try to instigate violence against the returning workers. The workers claimed that the employer refused to place them in their prior positions because of retaliation for striking. Does the employer have an obligation to place workers in a position where there might be violence aimed at them? *Diamond Walnut Growers Inc. v. NLRB,* No. 95-1075, (D.C. Cir. 1997).

2. Bloom was hired to perform clerical work for Group Health Inc. Office and Professional Employees International Union Local 12 and Group Health had negotiated a collective bargaining agreement that contained a union security clause which stated that employees must be "members in good standing," which Bloom interpreted as requiring that he pay union dues. Upon filing a grievance with the NLRB, what is the likely outcome? *Bloom v. NLRB,* 30 F.3d 1001 (8th Cir. 1994).

3. Polaroid set up a committee called the Employee-Owners' Influence Council (EOIC). All employees were encouraged to become members. Of 150 employees who applied, 30 of Polaroid's 8,000 employees were selected by the company. They discussed such issues as medical insurance benefits, the Employee Stock Ownership Plan, and family and medical leave. Is this type of employee–management team in violation of the NLRA? *Polaroid v. NLRB,* 329 NLRB No. 47 (October 6, 1999).

4. In its employee handbook, an employer stated that it would do "*everything possible* to maintain the company's union-free status for the benefit of both our employees and [the Company]." Is this an unfair labor practice under the NLRB? *Aluminum Casting & Engineering Co v. NLRB,* 328 NLRB No. 2 (Apr. 9, 1999).

5. A truck driver who refused to drive a truck because he "smelled fumes" informed his co-worker of this fact. When the employee was disciplined for refusing to take the truck, he alleged that he was engaged in "concerted activity." What basis does he have for alleging this? *NLRB v. PALCO,* 1998 U.S. App. LEXIS 3521 (Dec. 21, 1998).

6. An employer was hiring employees after a strike. On employment applications, they asked the potential employees whether they belonged to a union. Was the employer engaged in an unfair labor practice? *Mathews Readymix, Inc. v. NLRB,* 165 F.3d 74 (D.C. Cir. 1999).

7. The employer engaged in the practice of photographing an employee engaged in picket line activity. Is this illegal surveillance, even though the activity was

"open and obvious," no action was taken against the employee, and the employer was preparing a defense regarding potential illegal secondary activity? *Clock Electric, Inc. v. NLRB,* 162 F.3d 907 (6th Cir. 1998).

8. What are the most important differences between public and private sector collective bargaining?

9. During contract negotiations, employer and union exchange information on the union's proposal for pay raises. The employer rejects the proposal. The employer is adamant and refuses to agree to the raises. The union alleges that this is an unfair labor practice, in that the employer is not bargaining in good faith. Is it?

10. The union strikes the employer in an effort to receive higher wages. The employer brings in workers to replace the striking employees. Agreement is finally reached between the employer and employees. Must the employer dismiss the replacement workers?

18　OCCUPATIONAL SAFETY AND HEALTH

Chapter Outline

S C E N A R I O S

S C E N A R I O   1

Jessie Caterez owned and operated a general construction business. He recently was successful in obtaining a bid to build a new athletic facility. Although his company could do most of the work, he needed to hire other contractors to do parts of the job, such as cement contractors and welders to lay the foundation of the building. He selected Cem-Steel as the subcontractor to lay the foundation and the steel work. During the cement work, Jane Sprint, an employee of Cem-Steel, was hospitalized due to the large number of cement particles she had inhaled. Her employer, Cem-Steel, had not provided protective mouth masks. The Occupational Safety and Health Administration (OSHA) cites Caterez for violation of its regulation about protective gear requirements. Is Caterez liable or Cem-Steel?

S C E N A R I O   2

Donna was the supervisor at a construction worksite. The company for whom she had worked had a rule that employees could not ride on the side of equipment vehicles because of the potential for physical harm. Donna posted signs about this and cautioned her workers, but they still hitched rides on any available vehicle. Shelly and Jack were on break and too tired to walk back to the main area of the worksite. So, Shelly jumped on one of the single-person forklift vehicles and Jack climbed aboard the side rails. Halfway back to the central area of the worksite, Jack fell off and was injured. The Occupational Safety and Health Administration (OSHA) cites the company for violation of its regulation about riding on vehicles. Is the employer liable?

S C E N A R I O   3

Paul Cronan had worked for New England Bell Telephone for 11 years when he discovered he had AIDS. While the telephone company agreed to let him continue working, his co-workers refused to pick up their assignments in the same office as Paul, and they demanded that someone from the phone company walk out to their trucks to deliver assignments. When the phone company refused, the employees walked off the job, claiming that they were being subjected to unsafe working conditions in violation of the general duty clause. What is the employer's duty?

S C E N A R I O   4

Hubert Steloik recently created a new, promising business—Chemical Corp. He found a niche in the market due to the recent desire of companies to recycle plastic. One chemical needed for this process was tphycioligycic, and not many chemical companies were providing the chemical. The company was up and running for approximately one year. Several of the employees handling tphycioligycic complained to the Director of Safety that their throats burned after working with the chemical for long periods

S C E N A R I O S

of time. Because not all of the employees handling the chemical complained about such side effects, the director did not take any action. Several weeks ago, one of the workers died due to breathing complications. OSHA investigated and issued a violation to Chemical Corp. for violating the general duty clause of the Occupational Safety and Health Act. The director later found out that the other chemical companies had not provided the chemical due to the chemical's hazardous nature, which was cited in one of the major industry publications two years ago. Steloik does not feel he should be liable because he was unaware of such risks. Will the violation stand?

Statutory Basis

Occupational Safety and Health Act

§654 (§5) Duties
    (a) Each employer—
        (1) shall furnish to each of his employees employment and a place of employment which are free from recognized hazards that are causing or are likely to cause death or serious physical harm to his employees;
        (2) shall comply with occupational safety and health standards promulgated under this Act.
    (b) Each employee shall comply with occupational safety and health standards and all rules, regulations and orders issued pursuant to this Act which are applicable to his own actions and conduct.

Safety at Work

Workplace safety seems like it might not be such a big deal—that is, of course, until you slip on a banana peel in the cafeteria at work and break your sacroiliac and you're laid up for 10 weeks with no income. Or you slip on spilled salad dressing in the kitchen of the restaurant for which you work and you can't continue to pay your tuition. Or you turn on your computer at the office and receive a severe shock that fries your nervous system and puts you in the hospital for weeks. Workplace safety is often perceived as the bailiwick of angry-looking union reps or blue-collar "working stiffs" who carry lunch pails to work. But it is a workplace issue that affects us all. *Each year* 6,000 Americans die from workplace injuries, another 50,000 workers die from illnesses caused by workplace exposure, and six million suffer nonfatal workplace injuries costing businesses over $110 billion.

    To further complicate matters, until fairly recently there was no comprehensive requirement that employers provide for the safety of workers on their premises toil-

EXHIBIT 18–1   Is It Really That Bad?

These statements were made by laborers explaining the conditions of their workplaces.

"You're breathing in all these chemicals, so you get all shriveled up, like Joey. You know he looks like an old man. He's all hunched up and he's only 40."

"I've been here when they put in large amounts of asbestos and the place is white with fumes. Chemical workers don't live long. You're bound to pick up something."

"My mask was defective, and I breathed in a whole lot of fasic [a type of acid]. When I took off my mask, the other guys were laughing at me. I couldn't understand what they were laughing at. Then I looked in a mirror and my face was all green. I lost my voice for three weeks. That fasic eats you away. You don't live long as a chemical worker."

"The whole safety program is a joke. We use to have meetings, and if we suggested anything that cost more than a hundred dollars the company would say, 'No, that's too expensive.' I said, 'What is this? Nothing is a safety problem if it costs more than a hundred dollars?' So after a while, I told them their whole safety program was a bunch of s—— and I refused to sit on the safety committee anymore."

D. Halle, *America's Working Man: Work, Home, and Politics among Blue-Collar Property Owners* (Chicago: University of Chicago Press, 1984), pp. 109–15. © 1984 by The University of Chicago. All rights reserved. Published 1984. Printed in the United States of America.

ing for them. Prior to the enactment of the Occupational Safety and Health Act in 1970, employers were only bound by the common law to provide employees with a safe place to work. However (as discussed in Chapter 22), employers also had the benefit of three common law defenses that allowed them to escape from liability in connection with 85 to 90 percent of industrial accidents: **contributory negligence, assumption of risk,** and the **fellow servant rule.**

Contributory negligence allows the employer to defend against the employee's injury suit by claiming that the employee contributed to the injury through his or her own negligence. The assumption of risk defense precludes the employee from recovering when the employee knows of a risk involved in the workplace and chose to chance not being injured and is in fact injured. The fellow servant doctrine permitted the employer to escape liability when the negligence was the fault of an employee, rather than the employer. The injured worker, consequently, did not find much protection from requirement that the employer provide a safe working environment.

While most states enacted occupational safety and health laws, these were not generally enforced. As an example of this lack of enforcement, one commentator cites that in 1970 there were only 1,600 inspectors ensuring compliance with state laws. Since there were three times as many fish and game wardens as safety inspectors, trout and quail were better protected than working men and women. In addition, workers' compensation statutes attempted to compensate the worker once the injury was sustained.

It is important to note that most of these statutes severely limit the recovery of the employee to medical expenses and only to a portion of lost wages. While under OSHA, although workers are still limited in their financial recovery to what they can

Contributory negligence
Defense to a negligence action based on the injured party's failure to exercise reasonable care for her or his own safety.

Assumption of risk
A defense to a negligence action based on the argument that the injured party voluntarily exposed herself or himself to a known danger created by the other party's negligence.

Fellow servant rule
An employer's defense to liability for an employee's injury where the injury occurred on the job and was caused by the negligence of another employee.

EXHIBIT 18–2   JUDICIAL INTERPRETATIONS OF THE OCCUPATIONAL SAFETY AND HEALTH ACT

"Responsibility under the Act for ensuring that employees do not put themselves into any unsafe position rests ultimately upon each employer, not the employees, and employers may not shift their responsibility onto their employees." *Caterpillar Inc. v. Occupational Safety and Health Review Commission,* 122 F.3d 437 (7th Cir. 1997).

"The Act's broad remedial scope is designed to 'assure as far as possible every working man and woman in the Nation safe and healthful working conditions.' As courts have determined, the Act's legislative history suggests that its primary focus was making places of employment, rather than specific employees, safe from work related hazards. This implies that 'once an employer is deemed responsible for complying with OSHA regulations, it is obligated to protect every employee who works in its workplace.'" *United States v. Pitt-Des Moines, Inc.,* 168 F.3d 976 (7th Cir. 1999)

obtain under workers' compensation laws, they may now obtain relief from hazardous situations in the form of correction of the circumstances by the employers.

State legislation regarding protection against hazards varied from state to state, so stringent legislation in one state merely pushed the employer to relocate to a more permissive state. No answer was left but to provide national standards. On December 29, 1970, President Richard Nixon signed into law the Occupational Safety and Health Act, attempting to assure safe and healthful working conditions for all employees and to preserve the human resources of the United States.

The act covers 85 million workers at more than 5 million workplaces. The act is clear regarding which employers are subject to its requirements—any employer that has employees and is in a business affecting commerce (most employers!). The act is slightly less clear, however, about which employees are covered.

There are basically two requirements that section 5(a) of the act imposes on employers to accomplish the goal of a safer workplace. First, the employer must comply with all of the safety and health standards dictated by the Department of Labor, generally called the "compliance" requirements. Second, the employer must "furnish to each of [its] employees employment and a place of employment which are

EXHIBIT 18–3   Myths about the Occupational Safety and Health Act

1. There is no need for the Act; employers want their employees healthy and thus productive, so they will necessarily provide a healthy workplace.
2. OSHA requirements are always costly.
3. Anyone working for an employer is covered under the Act.
4. Once an employer trains its employees regarding the use of a product, piece of equipment, and so on, the responsibility of that employer is concluded.
5. If there is no specific mention of a certain situation in the Act, then the Act does not cover that situation.

EXHIBIT 18–4A   Occupational Injury & Illness Incidence Rates per 100 Full-Time Workers (1) 1973–97(2)

Year (2)	Inj's&Ill's	Inj's&Ill's	Injuries	Injuries
SIC	Totl Cases (3)	LWCases (4)	Totl Cases (3)	LWCases (4)
1973	11.0	3.4	10.6	3.3
1974	10.4	3.5	10.0	3.4
1975	9.1	3.3	8.8	3.2
1976	9.2	3.5	8.9	3.4
1977	9.3	3.8	9.0	3.7
1978 (5)	9.4	4.1	9.2	4.0
1979 (5	9.5	4.3	9.2	4.2
1980	8.7	4.0	8.5	3.9
1981	8.3	3.8	8.1	3.7
1982	7.7	3.5	7.6	3.4
1983 (5)	7.6	3.4	7.5	3.4
1984 (5)	8.0	3.7	7.8	3.6
1985	7.9	3.6	7.7	3.6
1986	7.9	3.6	7.7	3.6
1987	8.3	3.8	8.0	3.7
1988	8.6	4.0	8.3	3.8
1989	8.6	4.0	8.2	3.9
1990	8.8	4.1	8.3	3.9
1991	8.4	3.9	7.9	3.7
1992 (6)	8.9	3.9	8.3	3.6
1993 (6)	8.5	3.8	7.9	3.5
1994 (6)	8.4	3.8	7.7	3.5
1995	8.1	3.6	7.5	3.4
1996	7.4	3.4	6.9	3.1
1997	7.1	2.1	6.6	2.0

Notes:

(1) The incidence rates represent the number of injuries and illnesses per 100 full-time workers and were calculated as: (N/EH) × 200,000, where n = number of injuries and illnesses; EH = total hours worked by all employees during the calendar year; and 200,000 = base for 100 equivalent full-time workers (working 40 hours per week, 50 weeks per year).

(2) Data for 1973–75 are based on the Standard Industrial Classification Manual, 1967 Edition; data for 1976–87 are based on the Standard Industrial Classification Manual, 1972 Edition; and data for 1988–97 are based on the Standard Industrial Classification Manual, 1987 Edition.

(3) Total lost workday cases involve days away from work, or days of restricted work activity, or both.

(4) Days-away-from-work cases include those which result in days away from work with or without restricted work activity.

(5) To maintain historical comparability with the rest of the series, data for small nonfarm employers in low-risk industries who were not surveyed were imputed and included in the survey estimates.

(6) Data exclude fatal work-related injuries and illnesses.

NOTE: Because of rounding, components may not add to the totals. Data for 1976–97 exclude farms with fewer than 11 employees.

Source: US Department of Labor, Bureau of Labor Statistics, News release, Thursday, December 17, 1998

EXHIBIT 18–4B   Injury and Illness Rate Chart 1973–1997

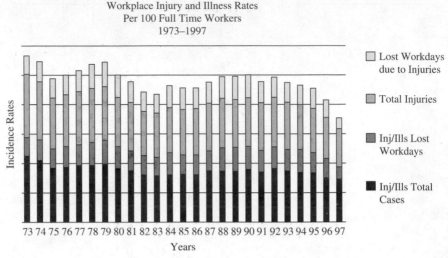

Workplace Injury and Illness Rates
Per 100 Full Time Workers
1973–1997

Data Source: Bureau of Labor Statistics Press Release USDL 98-494, Thursday, December 17, 1998.

free from recognized hazards that are causing or are likely to cause death or serious physical harm." This broad requirement is called the "general duty" clause, and traditional employer defenses are not often available.

Many employers contend that the mere breadth of the act is overwhelming and unnecessary. The standards promulgated under the act are often burdensome and, the employers argue, overcautious. Consequently, many argue that the act has not satisfied its stated purpose but has, instead, needlessly increased the cost of doing business. In response to such criticism, OSHA has increased its commitment to assist small businesses and to include all stakeholders in its efforts.

The act has, in fact, made a difference. Since 1970, when Congress created the Occupational Safety and Health Administration (OSHA), which administers the act, fatality rates have dropped, with the overall workplace death rate cut in half. More than 100,000 workers who might have died on the job did not because of improved safety and health.

The following case addresses the issue of whom the act covers; does the language in Section 5(a), which reads, "furnish to each of *its* employees . . . ," limit the liability of the employer to only those individuals who are actually employees of the cited employer?

UNITED STATES V. PITT-DES MOINES, INC.
168 F.3d 976 (7th Cir. 1999)

In this case, the court addresses a waiver of OSHA liability for worker injuries or death when work has been subcontracted out. The court determined that the subcontractee was liable also, even though the injured employee was employed by another.

Flaum, J.

In the construction of a postal facility, the USPS (United States Postal Service) hired Hyman/Power (HP) as the general contractor who, in turn, hired Pitt-Des Moines, Inc. (PDM) to fabricate and erect the structural steel for the project. PDM, in turn, subcontracted out part of the steel erection work to MA Steel. (In other words, USPS hired HP, who hired PDM, who hired MA Steel.) During part of the construction, steel beams were joined together and then hoisted to form the skeleton of the building. Under OSHA regulations, two bolts were required when joining the beams together before they could be hoisted. In the processes of hoisting steel beams a beam dropped killing two workers: one worker from PDM and one worker from MA Steel.

Although PDM received previous warnings about this OSHA regulation from Turner/Ozanne (a company hired to oversee the project), PDM did not alter their procedures. Rather, the company stated they were using a higher quality bolt and thus only one was required. When the Turner/Ozanne representative asked OSHA about this one-bolt process, they said that they were unaware of such practice and confirmed the representative's belief that two bolts were required. It was later determined by OSHA examiners that the cause of the beams falling was the lack of the two bolts. A jury consequently found PDM guilty of willfully violating OSHA safety standards resulting in the death of "any employee," namely Newsome of PDM and Thormeyer of MA Steel, and willfully violating an OSHA rule, known as the "training rule," requiring employers to instruct each of their employees in the safety regulations applicable to a given worksite. The counts were based on the violations that directly resulted in the death of the workers. PDM now appeals.

* * * *

The original indictment alleged that both Newsome and Thormeyer were employed by PDM. Prior to trial, the district court ruled that under the "multi-employer doctrine" the government only needed to prove that Thormeyer was an employee at the worksite; it did not need to prove that he was PDM's employee to establish a violation of OSHA. Following this ruling the government issued a superseding information containing the same charges as the indictment, but claiming that Thormeyer was employed at the worksite, but not by PDM.

* * * *

Multi-Employer Doctrine

Applying the multi-employer doctrine, the district court held that PDM could be liable for the death of Thormeyer without proof that he was PDM's employee so long as the government could show that he was an employee of the worksite exposed to the risk created by the contractor's safety violations. PDM now challenges this decision, claiming that the doctrine is inconsistent with the plain language of the Act and the purposes of the Act. However, none of PDM's objections to the district court's use of the doctrine are convincing. . . .

The doctrine holds that on multi-employer worksites, an employer who creates a safety hazard can be liable under the Act regardless of whether the employees threatened are its own or those of another employer on the site. Courts which have adopted the doctrine cite for statutory support the duties imposed on employers by Section 654(a) of the Act. These duties are two-fold:

> Each employer—
> (1) Shall furnish to each of his employees employment and a place of employment which are free from recognized hazards that are causing or are likely to cause death or serious physical harm to his employees.
> (2) Shall comply with Occupational Safety and Health standards promulgated under this chapter.

The first duty requires employers to protect their own employees from obvious hazards even when those hazards are not covered by specific safety regulations imposed by the Act. This duty is considered general because it asks employers to protect employees from all kinds of serious hazards, regardless of the source. Although general, the words "his employees" indicates that the duty imposed by 654(a)(1) is limited to an employer's own employees. Section 654(a)(2), on the other hand, contains no such limiting language. Courts have interpreted this provision as imposing a specific burden on employers to comply with and carry out the Act's safety standards regardless of whom in a given workplace is threatened by noncompliance. Unlike Section 654(a)(1), which imposes a general duty to a specific class, 654(a)(1) implies a specific duty to a more general class. Thus, courts have held that when an employer on a worksite violates a safety regulation, it can face liability under the Act regardless of whether those exposed to the resulting danger were the employer's own employees or those of another.

While Section 654(a)(2) provides the statutory basis for the multi-employer doctrine, courts garner additional support for it from the underlying purpose of the Act. The Act's broad remedial scope is designed "to assure as far as possible every working man and woman in the Nation safe and healthful working conditions." As courts have determined, the Act's legislative history suggests that its primary focus was making places of employment, rather than specific employees, safe from work related hazards. This implies that "once an employer is deemed responsible for complying with OSHA regulations, it is obligated to protect every employee who works in its workplace." Therefore, the combination of Section 654(a)(2)'s broad language and the goal of safer workplaces have led courts to conclude that the multi-employer doctrine is fully consistent with the Act.

* * * *

Next, while we are aware of no explicit authorization in the legislative history for the imposition of liability under the multi-employer doctrine, we have found none precluding it. As this court has observed, the congressional record relating to multi-employer job sites is sparse: "In enacting this law, Congress apparently gave little thought to the unique relationship which arises when employees of a number of different employers work in and around the same job site and are subject to the hazards which may exist at that site." In the absence of specific guidance, this court must attempt to render an interpretation of the Act which best fulfills the "stated congressional purpose in an equitable manner." Without the doctrine, employers could avoid OSHA liability for the hazardous conditions they create merely because the threatened or harmed workers—although their presence was entirely foreseeable and they are covered by the Act—happen to be on the payroll of another. Indeed this would be true even when, as here, the violating employer was the only one on the site who could reasonably have prevented the harm. We do not believe that this is the result Congress intended by enacting Section 654(a). We consider the multi-employer doctrine to be more consistent with the Act's broadly remedial purpose.

* * * *

While we consider this an appropriate basis for establishing an employer's potential liability, we emphasize that multi-employer liability has limits. While the Act seeks to create safer working environments, "it is clear that the Act is not nor could it be designed to eliminate all occupational accidents. Rather it is designed to require 'a good faith effort to balance the need of workers to have a safe and healthy work environment against the requirement of industry to function without undue interference.'" Because construction sites often entail different employees being exposed to hazards created by more than one employer, the affected employees on a worksite should be afforded the full protection of the Act regardless of their employer. Yet the class of employees who will trigger liability under the multi-employer doctrine should be limited to those with regular access to the areas controlled or directly impacted by the employer accused of violating a safety regulation. Although the logical class is composed of those on a given worksite, it may in certain circumstances be narrower. The doctrine is limited to exposure by the employees of the violating employer "or those of other employers engaged in a common undertaking." While we need not decide the exact contours of the doctrine here, it is enough to emphasize that at a minimum it excludes exposure by a "passerby or unrelated third persons."

This limitation, however, is not exceeded here, and it was appropriate for the district court to hold that PDM could be liable for the death of Thormeyer under the multi-employer doctrine. Thormeyer was employed as an ironworker on the Post Office worksite. His job was to follow PDM's raising gang and bolt up the connections they made. He belonged on the site and regularly

worked within the zone of danger created by any unsafe connections. Thormeyer was an entirely foreseeable victim of any willful safety violations PDM may have committed and thus easily fell within the multi-employer doctrine. AFFIRMED.

Case Questions

1. How far do you think this opinion goes? What would you do to protect your company from unexpected liability as a result of the exposure of other employer's employees to hazards at a worksite where your employees were working?

2. Would this opinion extend liability to individuals who were present at a worksite but not working?

3. The review commission, in a separate opinion, concluded that an employer at a multiemployer worksite is not responsible for safety hazards to its own or other's employees where:

    a. Those hazards have been created by another employer.

    b. The employer did not create and does not control the hazard.

    c. The employer does not have the expertise to correct or even to recognize the hazard.

    d. The employer has taken reasonable measures to protect its own employees from the hazards.

    Is this a reasonable solution?

In scenario 1, Caterez could be found liable due to the multiemployer doctrine. An employer is liable as long as the government can show that the employee at a worksite was exposed to the risk by the contractor's safety violations. An employer who creates a safety hazard can be liable under the act regardless of whether the employees threatened are its own or those of another employer on the site. Courts have held that when an employer on a worksite violates a safety regulation, it can face liability under the act regardless of whether those exposed to the resulting danger were the employer's own employees or those of another. In scenario 1, if it can be

Scenario

shown that Jane Sprint was exposed to the cement dust due to the contractor's safety violation of not providing the mask, Caterez can be held liable and would be the responsible party to handle the OSHA violation.

Procedure for Enforcement

Responsibility for enforcing the acts rests with the Occupational Safety and Health Administration (OSHA) under the auspices of the Department of Labor. The administration provides for inspections of the workplace by OSHA compliance officers, either as a result of complaints from employees, grievances filed by other sources, or reports of fatal or multiple injuries. Routine inspections in certain high-risk industries are also conducted by the officers. The act protects from retaliation against employees who file complaints, in that it prohibits an employer from discharging or discriminating against any employee who exercises any right afforded by the act.

To ensure that the inspectors are viewing the workplace in the same condition as that experienced by the employees, inspections are conducted without prior notice to an employer. In fact, anyone giving unauthorized advance notice of the inspection to the employer can be punished by a fine of up to $1,000. The officer will arrive at the worksite, ask to see the safety and accident records of the employer, conduct a "walk around" to visually inspect the site, and conclude by discussing with the employer any violations or concerns, as well as possible solutions to the problems.

Penalties

Penalties and "abatement orders" are assessed in connection with the officer's report. A nonserious or a serious violation may require payment of a penalty ranging from $0 to $1,000, while repeated or willful violations have a price tag of up to $10,000. Criminal sanctions and even higher fines are also possible where the employer acts willfully and causes the death of an employee. Congress is currently contemplating raising these fines.

Once imposed, some OSHA fines may appear to be minimal in light of the harm or potential for harm caused by the violation. However, it is important to realize that OSHA penalties are based on violations of standards and failure to comply, rather than the number or severity of injuries. While death may be the result of one violation of one OSHA provision, minor physical harm may result from a group of violations. The latter would likely result in a larger fine. In fact, if no willfulness can be shown, the maximum penalty for any violation is $7,000.

Standards

So, how does OSHA determine what standards to apply? The act provides for the creation of the National Institute for Occupational Safety and Health (NIOSH), which is the research arm of the Occupational Safety and Health Administration. The purpose of NIOSH is to conduct research in workplace health and safety and to formulate and make recommendations to the secretary of labor. If those recommendations are approved, then they may become the standards of conduct in connection with a certain industry.

For instance, NIOSH recently conducted a good deal of research in connection with the ergonomic and radiation hazards of computers in the workplace. This has become a significant area of worker concern, since more than 600,000 workers are injured on the job each year from repetitive motion injuries alone. In August 1992, NIOSH developed and recommended standards for employers to follow with regard to that segment of its workforce that may be at risk from ergonomic hazards. The administration then issued an Advance Notice of Proposed Rulemaking and requested comments on the proposed rules regarding ergonomics safety and a health management standard. When asked what were the reasons for the delay in moving forward with the standards, NIOSH responded that the reason for such long delays is the "numerous checks and balances" in the legal system for enacting regulations. "Research is certainly one of the issues. Research quality is always a subject of debate. NIOSH is doing its best to provide the research support, but it is a slow and deliberate process which is costly." (Until they are approved, workers *may* be able to recover under the general duty clause; see below.)

On the other hand, OSHA has just received approval from Congress to proceed with the development of "flexible, common-sense" ergonomics standards. This approval by Congress will pave the way for OSHA to publish a proposed ergonomic standard. OSHA's ergonomic standard could be far-reaching and controversial because it will directly affect all employers with regard to staffing, pace of production, equipment design, and function and physical design and layout of an employer's facility. In addition, this proposal would affect almost all employers, not only those with "high danger" sites.

Managerial Liability

Courts have ruled that when a corporate officer in a position of authority supervises the acts that resulted in an OSHA violation, she or he could be held individually criminally liable for the offense. However, the Department of Justice has been reluctant to enforce claims against individual decision makers, prosecuting only 4 out of 30 criminal cases referred to it by OSHA.[1]

Compliance Provisions

Specific Regulations

Some specific regulations seem to apply across the board to all types of employment environment. First, there are a number of specific requirements regarding the physical

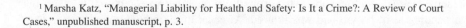

[1] Marsha Katz, "Managerial Liability for Health and Safety: Is It a Crime?: A Review of Court Cases," unpublished manuscript, p. 3.

layout of the worksite. Adequate safety measures must be taken, such as proper ventilation where necessary, adequate means of emergency exit if the need arises, safety nets, guard rails, and so on. Second, employees must be trained and informed (through classes, labels, signs) regarding protective measures, for everything from wearing protective devices, such as masks, to the proper use of chemicals. Third, medical examinations must be provided by the employer where an employee has been exposed to toxic substances.

In connection with the development of specific standards, OSHA can begin standards setting procedures on its own initiative, or in response to petitions from other parties. If it is determined that a specific standard is needed, any of several advisory committees may be called upon to develop specific recommendations. Recommendations for standards also may come from NIOSH, which conducts research on various safety and health problems, provides technical assistance to OSHA, and recommends standards for OSHA's adoption. Once OSHA has developed plans for a standard, it publishes these intentions in the Federal Register as a "Notice of Proposed Rulemaking." Some current areas of OSHA inquiry include workplace ergonomics, methylene chloride, nursing homes, silica tuberculosis, and workplace violence.

Continual-training requirement
OSHA requires that the employer provide safety training to all new employees and to all employees who have been transferred into new positions.

One of the most burdensome requirements on employers is the **continual-training requirement** in connection with the communication of workplace hazards. OSHA requires that employers adopt a program of continual training of its employees regarding safety in the workplace. Every time an employee is hired or transferred into a new position, even for just a day, the employer is required to provide safety training to that employee. A violation of this requirement is generally the most frequently cited type of violation on an annual basis. As a result, OSHA has made some effort to simplify the requirement and now supplies employers with material safety data sheets regarding various types of chemicals and the surrounding hazards associated with them.

Another area of regulation that impacts a large segment of the employment arena is a new group of requirements that deal with driver training, vehicle inspection, and seat-belt usage. Since more workers die as a result of vehicle accidents than from any other cause, a high priority has been placed on the formulation and enforcement of rules in this area. Sometimes the regulations are clear, but at other times the regulations may require interpretation. In the following cases, something as seemingly innocuous as the word "provided" required court interpretation.

USERY V. KENNECOTT COPPER CORP.
577 F.2d 1113 (10th Cir. 1977)

Nick Laboa, a highly skilled and experienced leadburner, constructed a makeshift scaffold to reach a leak 10 to 11 feet above the ground. While either working on this scaffold or ascending to it, he fell and was injured. After an investigation, the employer, Kennecott, was cited for failing to comply with OSHA regulations by not providing a ladder for Laboa to use in gaining access to the scaffold. The OSHA standard read as follows: "An access ladder or equivalent safe access shall be provided." In holding that Kennecott had not violated this provision, the commission interpreted "provided" as being synonymous with "made available."

Barrett, J.

The [Secretary of Labor] contends that this interpretation is incorrect because it is in derogation of the underlying purpose of the Act. The Secretary maintains that the commission erred in finding that Kennecott had complied with this regulation by simply providing its employees scaffold access ladders without *requiring* that they use them.

There is undisputed testimony that ladders were available to Kennecott's employees. It was also shown that some of the leadburners did not use them when ascending to their scaffolds and that Kennecott did not insist that such workers use the ladders for access to the scaffolds.

We hold that the Secretary's interpretation of the regulation is erroneous. Kennecott did comply with the regulation by providing ladders. It was not the purpose of the Act to make the employer the insurer of his employees' safety. The ultimate aim of the Act was not to prevent all accidents, but to provide American employees with safe and healthful working conditions "so far as possible." Certainly the Act requires employers to be diligent in protecting the health and safety of its employees; however, it does not hold the employer responsible for the prevention of all accidents. In addition, the Act does impose some responsibility for their safety on the employees, for "each employee shall comply with the occupational safety and health standards."

We do not agree that the Secretary may read "shall be provided" to mean "shall require use." In interpreting regulations, one must look at the plain meaning of the words used. The meaning usually attributed to the word "provide" is to furnish, supply or make available.

Case Questions

1. Is the plain meaning always the appropriate interpretation of a word in a statute? Is there ever a circumstance where it is more appropriate to look to the intent of the drafters of the statute, or perhaps to a different understanding that the employer had regarding the wording?

2. Do you agree that "provide" need not necessarily mean "to require to use?"

3. Would it have been fair or equitable to hold the employer responsible, as is usually the case in OSHA cases, for the failure of the worker to use a ladder to complete a certain job?

Emergency Temporary Standards

Section 6(a) of the act provides that the secretary of labor may establish **temporary standards** that will be effective immediately on publication in the Federal Register without having to go through the lengthy rulemaking process otherwise required by the act. The secretary is allowed to do so where he or she "determines (a) that

Emergency temporary standards
These standards are imposed by OSHA without immediately going through the typical process where an employee is exposed to grave danger from exposure to substances and the standards are necessary to protect employees from the danger.

employees are exposed to grave danger from exposure to substances or agents determined to be toxic or physically harmful or from new hazards, and (b) that such emergency standard is necessary to protect employees from such danger." The emergency standard is effective until regular standards are approved through the regular procedures or for six months, whichever is shorter.

Generally, the standard expires prior to the completion of the formal rulemaking process. In addition, courts hesitate to enforce temporary standards to the extent they enforce formal standards, because there may be insufficient notice given to the employers and there has been little opportunity for any critique or comment regarding the temporary standard. As a matter of fact, while some emergency temporary standards are put into place without opposition, every temporary standard that has been contested in court (whether for lack of proof, for insufficient danger, or for lack of proof of necessity) has been rejected by the courts.

General Duty Clause

General duty clause
A provision of the act requiring that employers furnish to each employee employment and a place of employment free from recognized hazards that cause or are likely to cause death or serious physical harm to the employee.

There was much discussion in Congress prior to the passage of the act relating to the act's **general duty clause.** The clause protects employees against certain hazards in the workplace, *where no other OSHA standard would address the condition.* Many representatives were concerned that the phrase as first proposed (merely that the employer must provide a safe and healthful workplace) was too vague to inform employers of what their actual obligations were, that it violated due process requirements, and that it did not have a mandatory penalty provision.

As a result, the House of Representatives proposed a more narrowly construed version; employers were to provide a workplace free from any hazards that are readily apparent and are causing or are likely to cause death or serious physical harm. The proposal also contained a provision for mandatory penalties for an initial citation under the clause. The clause, as passed, reads: "Each employer . . . shall furnish to each of his employees employment and a place of employment which are free from recognized hazards that are causing or are likely to cause death or serious physical harm to his employees."

Under the general duty clause, once it is found that a certain chemical used in an employer's manufacturing process causes reproductive harm, or perhaps damage to the employees' skin, for example, the employer must take steps to protect the employees and to provide a workplace free from these hazards. It is the employer's responsibility to be aware of these workplace hazards and to ensure that all employees are equally protected.

Recognizable Hazards

One of the most serious concerns of employers is determining what constitutes a "recognized" hazard. Imagine the employer's apprehension that a court some day in the future will rule that the effect of secondhand smoke in offices is a recognized hazard to other nonsmokers in that office. If that were the case, an employer may be liable to a nonsmoker who suffers a smoke-related injury because the employer did not provide a smoke-free environment in which to work. In anticipation of such a situation, many states have regulations on the provision of smoke-free working conditions.

A similar situation arose several years ago in connection with Johns-Manville and the exposure of its workers and others to the hazards of asbestos. A court held Johns-Manville, manufacturer of the asbestos, liable for the harms that resulted from the exposure.

On the other hand, during the discussion prior to the passage of the general duty clause by Congress, Representative Steiger made the following remarks:

> However, this requirement [general duty clause] is made realistic by its application only to situations where there are recognized hazards which are likely to cause or are causing serious injury or death. Such hazards are the type that can readily be detected on the basis of basic human senses. Hazards which require technical or testing devices to detect them are not intended to be within the scope of the General Duty requirement.

Governor Pyle, in his testimony on the clause, defined "recognized" as "obvious and admitted by all concerned." In the end, it appears that the definition most often adopted is that of Representative Daniels. Daniels claimed that a recognized hazard may take the form of actual knowledge when the employer actually knows of the hazard, or constructive knowledge if the industry recognizes the hazard even if the employer doesn't actually know of the hazard.

Scenario

When does an employer have "actual" knowledge? This can be shown in one of two ways. First, it can be shown through past safety practices or policies of the employer which evidence the employer knew there might be a hazard. For example, if an employer has issued a rule that all employees working in a certain area must wear a mask to prevent inhaling fumes from the chemicals with which they work, the rule might evidence the employer's actual knowledge that inhalation of the chemicals posed a risk. Second, actual knowledge may be shown where the hazard is so obvious that anyone would be aware of it. For instance, these days we are acutely aware that working with asbestos can be hazardous to one's health. Consequently, where a position requires asbestos exposure, that hazard may be so obvious that anyone would be aware of it.

One of the problems that has arisen in connection with the first example above is that an employer may be extra careful with its employees and protect them against any possible risk, rather than any known risk. In doing so, the employer may set standards higher than those necessary to protect the worker. If, however, the employer's standards and regulations are going to be held against her when the time comes to evaluate what hazards she was aware of, perhaps there would be less incentive to establish high standards in the first place.

The Occupational Safety and Health Administration review commission, however, discounts this concern by contending that few employers would abandon their safety procedures merely to avoid citation for a violation. What do you think? If you knew that your safety procedures may some day be used against you to prove that you were aware of a hazard, would you *ever* set a safety standard to protect against an unknown risk?

Barring actual knowledge, the employer may also be held responsible for knowledge of those hazards of which its entire industry is aware. An employer's knowledge may be inferred from an OSHA regulation that is issued to an industry about a certain hazard, or an industry publication citing a potential problem area, or a voluntary industry standard may be used against a specific employer who claims that he was not aware of the risk.

As discussed in the chapter on pregnancy discrimination, an interesting case arose a few years ago in connection with a protection policy. Recall that, in the *Johnson Controls* case, Johnson Controls was concerned that exposure to lead in the manufacturing process of its batteries would cause harm to females' reproductive capacities. As a result, women of childbearing age at Johnson Controls were barred from certain positions within the company. Unfortunately, those positions were also those with the highest pay. The employees sued, claiming that this type of protection from workplace hazard constituted unlawful discrimination under Title VII, since only females were barred from the higher paying jobs, when, in fact, males could just as well be affected by the exposure and were not barred.

CATERPILLAR INC. v. OCCUPATIONAL SAFETY AND HEALTH REVIEW COMMISSION
122 F.3d 437 (7th Cir. 1997)

An employee injured on the job resulted in a citation against the employer for a violation of the general duty clause. The employer appealed and the court affirmed that the employer willfully violated the clause.

Cummings, J.

Caterpillar Inc. ("Caterpillar") appeals a final decision of the Occupational Safety and Health Review Commission (the "Commission") that was issued September 4, 1996. The case arises out of an accident at Caterpillar's East Peoria, Illinois, facility involving the repair of a 6,000-ton forging press called the Erie 6000. The repair procedure required the use of a gear-pulling device on which were four steel studs, each weighing 35 to 40 pounds and measuring 42 inches in length and $1^3/_4$ inches in diameter. The accident occurred when a steel stud broke off during the repair operation and was propelled 121 feet, where it

hit an employee in the head, causing serious injury.

After the accident, the Secretary issued a citation alleging that Caterpillar willfully violated the "general duty clause" [Section 5(a)(1)] of the Occupational Safety and Health Act of 1970 (the "Act"). The Administrative Law Judge (the "ALJ") assigned to the case affirmed the citation and assessed a penalty of $30,000. Later, the Commission agreed with the ALJ that Caterpillar's violation of Section 5(a)(1) was willful, but concluded that a penalty of $49,000, the amount originally requested by the Secretary, was appropriate. Caterpillar appealed from the final order of the Occupational Safety and Health Review Commission that found employer violated the Occupational Safety and Health Act's (OSHA) general duty clause.

* * * *

. . . Ronald Williams, the day shift's lead repairman, met with his supervisor of three months, James Rhodes. . . . [P]rior to this time, Williams had held detailed discussions with his previous supervisor about his safety concerns regarding this type of operation and had made multiple suggestions regarding possible safety precautions. During his meeting with Rhodes, however, Williams suggested only that warning signs be posted and the area be cordoned off. Rhodes agreed and took care of the matter.

This was not the first experience Caterpillar had had with flying studs. In the spring of 1989, Williams and a crew removed the hub on the Erie 6000 press in order to fix the brake wheel. During the process one of the studs broke and a fragment flew 60 feet through the air, stopping finally when it hit a heavy metal cabinet. The force of the impact indented the cabinet three inches. Both maintenance foreman Clay Parker (Williams's supervisor prior to Rhodes) and the shop superintendent, Darrel Seeyle, were aware of the incident. The stud came within 20–25 feet of hitting Seeyle.

During a July 1989 pull, the crew removed the hub from the other side of the Erie 6000 press, with Williams again acting as leadman. Eight to ten studs broke and flew during this procedure, one of the studs flying 35 to 40 feet and leaving a half-inch dent in the metal of a crane (coincidentally, it was the accident victim in 1992, Dunn, who narrowly escaped injury from this stud).

As a result of these experiences, Williams had repeatedly requested, and repeatedly been denied, enhanced safety precautions. At various times, Williams suggested the use of [several devices, all of which were rejected as either too expensive or too time-consuming.]

* * *

The Act's "general duty" clause provides that each employer:

shall furnish to each of his employees employment and a place of employment which are free from recognized hazards that are causing or are likely to cause death or serious physical harm to his employees.

Commission precedent clearly establishes that a general duty clause violation requires the following elements: (i) the existence of a hazard likely to cause death or serious physical harm; (ii) the employer's recognition (i.e., awareness) of the hazard; (iii) the availability of feasible means to abate the hazard; and (iv) the employer's failure to implement the feasible means of abatement. Of these factors, at issue in this appeal is, first, whether Caterpillar was aware of the hazard of studs shooting into the workplace during the type of maintenance procedure on the Erie 6000 that took place in July 1992, and, second, whether Caterpillar failed to implement a feasible means of abatement. An OSHA violation is willful if it is committed with intentional disregard of, or plain indifference to, the requirements of the statute. A willful violation "is differentiated from other types of violations by a heightened awareness— of the illegality of the conduct or conditions—and by a state of mind-conscious disregard or plain indifference."

The Commission's finding of willfulness was based on its conclusion that, in accordance with "well settled" principles of agency law, an employer is imputed with its supervisor's knowledge of a hazardous condition, even if the supervisor subsequently departs the employ of the employer. . . . It found that Caterpillar was attempting to evade responsibility for its conduct by looking at the knowledge of Rhodes and its other new supervisory personnel in 1992, rather than looking back to the knowledge of the supervisors in place during the 1989 operations. In response, the Commission noted that it was Caterpillar's responsibility to disseminate to those entrusted with the health and safety of its employees the knowledge possessed by it regarding the "pervasive and continuing nature" of the flying stud problem. In other words, it concluded that Caterpillar's "heightened awareness" of the problem remained with the corporation despite any turnover in personnel.

After finding a "heightened awareness" of the problem, the Commission also concluded that Caterpillar showed a "plain indifference to employee safety" when it simply delegated authority to Williams, "whose prior safety concerns it had rebuffed. . . ." It noted that Caterpillar had both knowledge of the hazard and abundant resources to evaluate and abate it and found that Caterpillar's installation of the tape barrier and warning signs for the procedure at issue were not an "objectively reasonable means of abatement, especially where employees involved in the hub-pulling procedure were located within it."

Caterpillar claims that it took all steps required by the general duty clause when it put Williams, a skilled craftsman, in charge of the operation and relied on him to make appropriate safety recommendations to his supervisor, Rhodes. We agree with the Commission's analysis, however. The mere fact that Parker and Seeyle, who both indisputably were aware of the hazard, ceased to be Williams's supervisors before the 1992 pull does not cancel Caterpillar's knowledge (i.e., heightened awareness) of the risks of the operations and its responsibility for their impact on Williams and the safety of the operation. To hold otherwise would encourage corporate forgetfulness with possibly serious safety consequences. These supervisors consistently rejected Williams's recommendations for protecting workers from the flying studs. In light of these rejections, Caterpillar cannot now argue that it reasonably relied on Williams to ensure the safety of the hub-pulling operation in 1992.

We also find that the Commission's conclusion that such reliance showed a plain indifference to employee safety—a prerequisite to a finding of willfulness—is supported by substantial evidence and Commission precedent and is neither arbitrary nor capricious. The ALJ's findings of fact, as adopted by the Commission, demonstrate this. Caterpillar became aware as early as 1989 that when studs broke from the hub, fragments were propelled erratically in different directions and for different distances. Despite this knowledge, and despite two incidents in which employees were nearly struck by flying fragments, Caterpillar rejected or ignored the recommendations of the very person it had put on the projects to eliminate the hazard. Williams had neither the power nor the authority independently to implement his rejected safety measures, nor could he commit Caterpillar resources to the measures. Caterpillar cannot now claim that it is not guilty of a willful violation because it put Williams in charge of the pull operation and relied on his expertise. The fact that Williams did not suggest additional safety measures during the July 1992 operation appears understandable given the rejection of his many suggestions over the preceding three years, and it does not excuse Caterpillar's failure to implement additional safety measures. After all, "[r]esponsibility under the Act for ensuring that employees do not put themselves into any unsafe position rests ultimately upon each employer, not the employees, and employers may not shift their responsibility onto their employees."

Good faith efforts at compliance that are incomplete or not entirely effective can negate a willfulness finding provided that they were objectively reasonable under the circumstances. However, we agree with the Commission that in this case Caterpillar's decision in July 1992 to install warning tape and signs was not an objectively reasonable safety plan. As the Commission noted, the tape certainly offered no protection to employees working within the danger zone and Caterpillar had no way of knowing on July 16, 1992, that a 100-foot zone would be adequate, given that a previous stud had been shot out to 60 feet, stopping only when it slammed into a steel cabinet, leaving a three-inch dent (the safety zone of 40–60 feet on the sides only of the Erie 6000 on July 15, 1992, was without question inadequate). . . . Accordingly, the Commission's decision is AFFIRMED.

Case Questions

1. Do you think the penalty was appropriate in this case? Why or why not? Compare it to the penalty in the previous case, *United States v. Pitt-Des Moines, Inc.*

2. Do you agree with the court that Caterpillar should have been aware of the situation even after employee turnover of the previous supervisor, even though some of the employees currently working at the plant were aware of the dangers? Explain your answer.

3. Do you agree with Caterpillar's argument that it took all steps required by the general duty clause when it put Williams, a skilled craftsman, in charge of the operation and relied on him to make appropriate safety recommendations to his supervisor, Rhodes? Why or why not?

Likely to Cause Serious Physical Harm or Death

What does the term *likely* mean in connection with those risks that an employer must protect against? If there is a chance that 1 person in 1,000 may be harmed, does that mean that the risk is likely, or must 5 people out of 10 be at risk for harm to be "likely"? The Review Commission has stated that the harm need not be likely but *possible.* In fact, the commission has said that "the proper question is not whether an accident is likely to occur, but whether, if an accident does occur, the result is likely to be death or serious physical harm."

Current Problem Areas

Where a problem has recurred in the workplace, but no new OSHA standards have yet been developed to deal with this problem, employees are left to seek relief from the risk through the general duty clause. Think about areas of questionable risk that have been in the news lately. One area that has received a good deal of attention because of its fatal repercussions is HIV exposure. Individual employees have expressed concern regarding the safety of their exposure to HIV-positive co-workers or exposure to unsafe conditions where transmission may occur. There is no OSHA standard that directly addresses exposure to blood-borne pathogens, such as HIV, so the general duty clause may apply.

While the hazard of contracting HIV is a recognized hazard in general, within the workplace there are a few situations where an employee may be at risk of transmission from a co-worker. Consequently, an employee's claim that an unsafe environment exists merely due to the presence of an HIV-positive co-worker has little credence.

Scenario

A second area of rising concern for employers is the potential for ergonomic injuries in various occupations. Work-related musculoskeletal disorders (WMSDs) occur as a result of a repetitive motion which causes discomfort and sometimes the loss of use of the worker's arms, hands, wrists, knees, or other limb or joint.

WMSDs may result, for instance, where a computer word processor is not given sufficient break time away from the computer. Newspaper writers have complained of the inability to use their hands to type because of the pain that now results. WMSDs account for 34 percent of all lost-workday injuries and illnesses, according to the Bureau of Labor Statistics. Roger Stevens, chief ergonomist at OSHA, claims that WMSDs account for almost 50 percent of all worker compensation claims. OSHA has responded to this growing cry for protection from WMSDs in the workplace.

John Morrell & Company, a large meat-packing company, was fined $4.3 million by OSHA for poor conditions in its plants, including the repetitive requirements of its labor force. As a partial settlement of an OSHA claim, the firm has agreed to hire a neurologist and an ergonomist to oversee medical treatment at the plants. In a separate case regarding a newspaper office in Fresno, California's state OSHA office ordered that the employer comply with such specific standards as increased knee room for computer operators, more available work space at each work station, foot rests and arm rests, and adjustable terminals.

Other claims, however, have not been so successful. The probability of relief in any given case may turn upon the interpretation of "serious physical harm." Some interpreting the clause claim that intermittent pain or pain that fluctuates in severity or duration may not be sufficient to meet the "serious physical harm" standard.

Another, and we bet you'll think surprising, current problem area is workplace violence, up to and including workplace homicide. Would you believe that homicide is the second leading cause of fatal occupational injury in the United States? According to OSHA figures, nearly 1,000 employees are murdered and 1.5 million assaulted in the workplace yearly. There were 396,000 aggravated assaults, 51,000 rapes and sexual assaults, and 84,000 robberies. Retail workers were the most numerous victims, with 330,000 attacks each year, followed by police, who average 234,200 attacks. Can you imagine that it was more dangerous to work in retail than to be a cop?

While OSHA is not presently initiating rulemaking, it has developed guidelines and recommendations to reduce worker exposure to this hazard. Several workplace conditions associated with assaults have been identified, and control strategies have been implemented in several work settings.

Refusal to Work

Where an employee or a group of employees believes that the employer has violated its general duty to provide a safe working environment, the employees may refuse to work in that environment or to perform a given task. The employees' refusal must be based on a reasonable apprehension of death or serious injury, coupled with a reasonable belief that no less drastic alternative is available. If an employee chooses not to perform an assigned task as a result of this apprehension, the act prohibits an employer from discharging or discriminating against that employee.

Employer Reporting Responsibilities and Employee Rights

Reporting Requirements

Accidents do not "just happen," they are caused; and it is the goal of OSHA's reporting requirements that the causes are properly identified so future accidents will be prevented. Any employer covered by the act, with the exception of those with 11 or fewer employees, must maintain certain records for OSHA compliance. The records must contain the following information, must be reported on Form 200 produced by the Department of Labor, and must be posted for the employees to see each year from February 1 to March 1 (i.e., it need not be filed with the government but, instead, must be kept throughout the year and compiled for the February posting):

1. Incident date.
2. Category of illness, if applicable.
3. Description of incident.
4. Identification of affected employee.
5. Extent of illness or injury.
6. If incident was an illness, whether the employee was eventually transferred or terminated.

Within six days of an incident reported on Form 200, an additional record containing more complete information (Form 101) must be made and filed with OSHA. In addition, an incident involving fatalities or the hospitalization of five or more employees must be reported to the administration within 48 hours of the incident.

The determination of whether to report an illness or injury is relatively complicated. If the injury or illness does not result from a work-related cause, no report need be made. If the injury or illness is work related, then it must be reported as long as it is an illness, a death, or an injury that involves (1) medical treatment, (2) loss of consciousness, (3) restriction of work or motion, or (4) transfer to a different position. If the injury does not fit into one of these four categories, then no report needs to be made.

An illness or injury is considered work related if (1) it occurred on the employer's premises, (2) it occurred as a result of work-related activities, (3) the employee was required to be there by the employer, or (4) the employee was traveling to work or to a place he or she was required to be by the employer. If the activity does not fit into one of these categories, then it was not work related and no report needs to be made.

Because of their low risk of hazards, employers in certain industries are not required to file Forms 200 and 101. Among others, these industries include auto dealers, apparel stores, eating and drinking places, insurance offices, motion picture companies, legal offices, and educational services.

Employee Rights

To ensure the efficacy of the act, the act affords certain rights to employees. These rights are identified on OSHA poster no. 2203, which may be placed in the workplace. While employees must be informed of their OSHA rights by their employer, displaying this poster is not mandatory. Employee rights include requesting and participating in inspections, notice of an employer's violations or citations, access to monitoring procedures and results, and access to medical information.

Employer Defenses

Recklessness
Conscious disregard for safety; conscious failure to use due care.

Reckless Behavior

If hazardous circumstances occur at the employer's place of business, is the employer liable for any harm that results, no matter what? Would this be a fair rule? There are some rules in law that provide that, where an employer knew or should have known of a certain situation, then the employer is liable for the harm that results from that situation. For instance, in connection with a sexual harassment case, an employer is liable for the harassment where the employer knew of the harassing behavior or hostile environment, or where the employer *should have known* of the situation. Therefore, even if the employer did not know because it refused to see the problem, sometimes called the "ostrich defense," the employer will still be liable.

How does this apply to OSHA violations? If the employer had a stellar safety record, had gone for years without an incident or violation, had conducted on-the-job group safety meetings, had issued written handouts regarding the safety instructions and the requirements of the act, but *still* suffered an incident, do any of the previous precautionary measures lessen the employer's chances of being held liable for the resulting harm? Courts generally respond that employers may use prior precautions as a means to minimize their liability. If they did not allow this defense, OSHA would instead impose "strict liability" on employers—that is, liability no matter what steps the employer takes to prevent it; liability merely because it happened at the employer's worksite.

In *Horne Plumbing and Heating v. OSHRC,* the employer had done precisely what we just mentioned above in terms of precautionary measures; yet, when two men ignored the employer's instructions, as well as warnings from co-workers, and worked in an unsafe area of the site, they were killed. The court noted that, "A hazard consisting of conduct by employees, such as equipment riding, cannot be totally eliminated. A willfully reckless employee may on occasion circumvent the best conceived and most vigorously enforced safety regime. Congress intended to require elimination only of preventable hazards." The court found that the employer did everything possible to ensure compliance with the law, short of remaining at the worksite and directing the operations itself. Was this final effort required? The court responded that [citing a separate case]:

2
Scenario

While close supervision may be required in some cases to avoid accidents, it is unrealistic to expect an experienced and well-qualified [worker] to be under constant scrutiny. Such a holding by the Commission, requiring that each employee be constantly watched by a supervisor, would be totally impractical and in all but the most unusual circumstances, an unnecessary burden.

So, according to *Horne Plumbing,* the rule is that, where an employer takes all reasonable steps to prevent a hazard, but an employee's reckless disregard for the precautions causes him or her harm, the employer is relieved of liability for that harm. Instead, an employer will be held liable only for the foreseeable, plausible, and therefore preventable acts of its employees.

Also, note that companies with adequate safety programs in place are much less likely to be held responsible for the acts of their employees, whether reckless or merely negligent. On the other hand, where no safety program is in place, an employer is much more likely to be liable for injuries resulting from preventable accidents, even if it makes a good faith attempt to comply with the standard.

Physical or Economic Impossibility of Compliance

Perhaps the most difficult safety standards to enforce are those that command the greatest opposition from the employees. While the safety basis for most specific standards is apparent from the standard itself, and most employees adhere because of the potential hazards that would exist if they did not, there are some standards that employees contest. These standards would be those where the employees believe that the burden of complying is greater than the danger prevented by the compliance. Consequently, even though employers have rules about complying with that standard, it would be difficult to enforce without "policing" the employees.

In this situation, contrary to the above, noncompliance with the standard by the employees *is* foreseeable and predictable. The employer could not use the defense that the employees' actions were not expected or preventable. For example, in *Atlantic & Gulf Stevedores v. OSHRC,* the safety standard in question was an OSHA requirement that employees wear protective hard hats while on the job. The problem arose because only a small number of the longshoremen were willing to wear the hats. In addition, the longshoremen's unions opposed the hard hat requirement, so the secretary of labor had imposed a moratorium on the enforcement of the requirement for several years. Employers were threatened with wildcat strikes or walkouts if they attempted to fire those who did not comply. As a result, when Atlantic & Gulf Stevedores was cited for a violation of this OSHA requirement, it defended itself by claiming that compliance with the standard was not achievable.

The court compared this case to another where it concluded that the economic feasibility of a standard is relevant to its validity. An economically impossible standard would prove unenforceable, the court said, and the burden of policing a regulation uniformly ignored by a majority of industry members would prove to be overwhelming.

However, since the purpose of OSHA is to look for improvement in the techniques of industrial safety, many times its prescriptions for remedy are not appealing to those who must adhere to them. To remove this requirement would be akin to agreeing to an unsafe workplace, something that would be patently against the aims of OSHA. Therefore, the court held that the safety of the workforce is of greater importance than the burden of dealing with work stoppages. The employer should negotiate with the unions to be allowed to terminate those workers who do not comply and offer concessions in exchange for compliance. Barring agreement, the employer could apply to the secretary for a variance from the standard that would allow this employer to be free from compliance based on the specific situation at its worksite. A variance is a right given to the employer not to comply with the standard, either permanently or on a temporary basis, if the employer's work environment is at least as safe as if the employer had complied.

OSHA directs that employees comply with its requirements, but OSHA contains no penalty or fine provisions to use against an employee who does not comply. The responsibility to ensure employee compliance is left to the employer through discipline or termination.

Employee Reduction of Risk

While employees are obligated under OSHA to "comply with occupational safety and health standards and all rules, regulations, and orders," are they responsible to take extra measures to ensure their own safety?

In a case that preceded *Johnson Controls,* the court of appeals for the District of Columbia addressed the OSHA implications of fetal protection policies. Similar to *Johnson Controls,* in *Oil, Chemical, and Atomic Workers Int'l Union v. American Cyanamid Company,* the company had a fetal protection policy that prohibited fertile women from certain positions. The women sued claiming that, instead of making the workplace safe, the employer had attempted to get around the requirements of the act by requiring that the female employees undergo surgical sterilization so the worksite no longer presented a hazard to them. The issue in the case was whether such a requirement for the position was a violation of the act.

The court found that, where the situation could not be remedied (i.e., the company could not reduce the lead concentrations to a level that posed an acceptable

Exhibit 18–4

The OSH Administration produces many publications to offer guidance and direction to employers concerned about safety and health. The following are but a sampling of the many available by contacting the PSHA regional office in your area:

All about OSHA, OSHA Publication 2056.
How to Prepare for Workplace Emergencies, OSHA Publication 3088.
Hazard Communications Guidelines for Compliance, OSHA Publication 3111.
Hazardous Waste and Emergency Response, OSHA Publication 3114.

risk to fetuses), the sterilization option was an appropriate alternative. The company was not attempting to pass on to the employees the cost of maintaining an environment more hazardous than that allowed by law, but it was an attempt to permit the employees to mitigate costs to them imposed by unavoidable physiological facts. Since the workplace could not be made safe, employees had the choice of either not working in that workplace or undergoing the sterilization to make it safe for them. Note that this is different from the fetal protection policy in the gender chapter where the employer required females to show proof of infertility in order to be able to work there, but had no such requirement for men.

In order to better understand the court's thought process in this case, consider its actual language, included below.

OIL, CHEMICAL, AND ATOMIC WORKERS INT'L UNION
v. AMERICAN CYANAMID CO.
741 F.2d 444 (D.C. Cir. 1984).

In the case below, the court discusses fetal protection policies and whether they violate the OSH Act.

Bork, J.

. . . This, essentially, was the reasoning of the Review Commission. The Commission pointed out that the Act does not define the term "hazard" and turned to the legislative history for guidance. "Congressional floor debates, committee reports, and individual and minority views . . . are replete with discussions of air pollutants, industrial poisons, combustibles and explosives, noise, unsafe work practices and inadequate training and the like." From this, and other evidence of a similar nature, the Commission concluded that "Congress conceived of occupational hazards in terms of processes and materials which cause injury or disease by operating directly upon employees as they engage in work or work-related activities." The fetus protection policy, by contrast, does not affect employees while they are engaged in work or work-related activities. The decision to be sterilized "grows out of economic and social factors which operate primarily outside the workplace," and hence the fetus protection policy "is not a hazard within the meaning of the general duty clause." Id. We agree with this conclusion. Were we to decide otherwise, we would have to adopt a broad principle of unforeseeable scope: any employer policy which, because of employee economic incentives, left open an option exercised outside the workplace that might be harmful would constitute a "hazard" that made the employer liable under the general duty clause. It might be possible to legislate limitations upon such a principle but that is a task for Congress rather than courts. As it now stands, the Act should not be read to make an employer liable for every employee reaction to the employer's policies. There must be some limit to the statute's reach and we think that limit surpassed by petitioners' contentions. The kind of "hazard" complained of here is not, as the Commission said, sufficiently comparable to the hazards Congress had in mind in passing this law.

We are not prepared to speculate that, although Congress was thinking only about tangible hazards such as chemicals, it would, had it considered the subject, have decided that any employer-offered choice which leads to injury rather than discharge is a violation of the Act. That conclusion would have required a great deal of thought about unforeseen liabilities for employers and how far to let employees decide what is in their own best interest. It is not possible to say that, in all circumstances imaginable, Congress would have made employers liable for giving employees an option where the only feasible alternative was discharge. It seems to us safer, therefore, to confine the term "hazards" under the general duty clause to the types of hazards we know Congress had in mind.

Petitioners' argument may reveal a degree of uneasiness about the implications of their position. It is clear that American Cyanamid had to prevent exposure to lead of women of childbearing age, and, furthermore, that the company could not have been charged under the Act if it had accomplished that by discharging the women or by simply closing the Department, thus putting all employees who worked there, including women of childbearing age, out of work. The company was charged only because it offered the women a choice. Perhaps uncomfortable with the position that it was the offering of a choice that made the company liable, counsel for OCAW stated at oral argument that there would have been no violation if the company had simply stated that "only sterile women" would be employed in the Department because there would then have been no "requirement" of sterilization. We agree that such an announcement would not have involved a viola-

tion of the general duty clause, but we fail to see how that policy differs under the statute from the policy American Cyanamid adopted. An "only sterile women" announcement would also have given women of childbearing age the option of surgical sterilization. The only difference between this case and the hypothetical is that here the company pointed out the option and provided information about it. As petitioners frame the issue, therefore, violation of the general duty clause depends on the explicitness with which an employer phrases an option made available by its policy. It cannot be that the employer is better shielded from liability the less information it provides. It would, in any event, be difficult to find that distinction in the words of the general duty clause.

The case might be different if American Cyanamid had offered the choice of sterilization in an attempt to pass on to its employees the cost of maintaining a circumambient lead concentration higher than that permitted by law. But that is not this case. The company could not reduce lead concentrations to a level that posed an acceptable risk to fetuses. The sterilization exception to the requirement of removal from the Inorganic Pigments Department was an attempt not to pass on costs of unlawful conduct but to permit the employees to mitigate costs to them imposed by unavoidable physiological facts.

The women involved in this matter were put to a most unhappy choice. But no statute redresses all grievances, and we must decide cases according to law. Reasoning from precedent, congressional intent, and the unforeseeable consequences of a contrary holding, we conclude that American Cyanamid's fetus protection policy did not constitute a "hazard" within the meaning of the OSH Act.

Unlike *UAW v. Johnson Controls, Inc.*, in chapter 7, *Oil, Chemical, and Atomic Workers Int'l Union v. American Cyanamid Co.* dealt with the issue of whether OSHA can consider the company policy as a hazard to an employee's health. The court found that "[t]he decision to be sterilized 'grows out of economic and social factors which operate primarily outside the workplace,' and hence the fetus protection policy is not a hazard within the meaning of the general duty clause." Therefore, although these may appear to be contradictory rulings, the issues the courts were resolving were separate and distinct.

Where an employer cannot on its own make a workplace safe for its employees, but through the acts of its employees the workplace can be made safe, the employer is allowed to require those acts for anyone that chooses to work there. Instead of not offering the opportunity at all (taking away an option for the employees), the employer is merely allowing only those employees for whom the workplace would be safe to work there. There is no true requirement to undergo a sterilization process in the above case, but merely the offer that anyone who does or who can prove that she cannot bear children may work in that position. In the *Donovan* case below, the U.S. Supreme Court takes a look at the "economic" argument made by the employer.

AMERICAN TEXTILE MANUFACTURERS INSTITUTE, INC. v. DONOVAN
452 U.S. 490 (1981)

In this case, the U.S. Supreme Court dealt with the issue of whether OSHA must consider whether the cost of the standard it develops bears a reasonable relationship to its benefits. It determined that it does not have to have a reasonable relationship.

Brennan, J.

Congress enacted the Occupational Safety and Health Act of 1970 (Act) "to assure so far as possible every working man and woman in the Nation safe and healthful working conditions. . . ." The Act authorizes the Secretary of Labor to establish, after notice and opportunity to comment, mandatory nationwide standards governing health and safety in the workplace. In 1978, after much input, the Secretary, acting through OSHA, promulgated a standard limiting occupational exposure to cotton dust. Cotton dust is an airborne particle byproduct of the preparation and manufacture of cotton products, exposure to which induces a "constellation of respiratory effects" known as "byssinosis" or, in its more serious manifestations, "brown lung." This disease was one of the expressly recognized health hazards that led to passage of the Act.

Byssinosis is a serious and potentially disabling respiratory disease primarily caused by the inhalation of cotton dust. Byssinosis is a "continuum . . . disease," that has been categorized into four grades. In its least serious form, byssinosis produces both subjective symptoms, such as chest tightness, shortness of breath, coughing, and wheezing, and objective indications of loss of pulmonary functions. In its most serious form, byssinosis is a chronic and irreversible obstructive pulmonary disease, clinically similar to chronic bronchitis or emphysema, and can be severely disabling. At worst, as is true of other respiratory diseases including bronchitis, emphysema, and asthma, byssinosis can create an additional strain on cardiovascular functions and can contribute to death from heart failure. ("There is an association between mortality and the extent of dust exposure".)

Cotton manufacturers challenged the validity of the "Cotton Dust Standard." They contend that the Act requires OSHA to demonstrate that its Standard reflects a reasonable relationship between the costs and benefits associated with the Standard. The Secretary of Labor counters that Congress balanced the costs and benefits in the Act itself, and that the Act should therefore be construed not to require OSHA to do so. They interpret the Act as mandating that OSHA enact the most protective standard possible to eliminate a significant risk of material health impairment, subject to the constraints of economic and technological feasibility. We granted certiorari, to resolve this important question.

The principal question presented in these cases is whether the Act requires the Secretary, in promulgating a standard pursuant to the Act, to determine that the costs of the standard bear a reasonable relationship to its benefits. The cotton manufacturers urge not only that OSHA must show that a standard addresses a significant risk of material health impairment, but also that OSHA must demonstrate that the reduction in risk of material health impairment is significant in light of the costs of attaining that reduction. The Secretary, on the other hand, contends that the Act requires OSHA to promulgate standards that eliminate or reduce such risks "to the extent such protection is technologically and economically feasible." To resolve this debate, we must turn to the language, structure, and legislative history of the Act.

The starting point of our analysis is the language of the statute itself. The Act provides: "The Secretary, in promulgating standards dealing with toxic materials or harmful physical agents under this subsection, shall set the standard which most adequately assures, to the extent feasible, on the basis of the best available evidence, that no employee will suffer material impairment of health or functional capacity even if such employee has regular exposure to the hazard dealt with by such standard for the period of his working life."

Although their interpretations differ, all parties agree that the phrase "to the extent feasible" contains the critical language in the Act for purposes of these cases. The plain meaning of the word "feasible" supports the Secretary's interpretation of the statute. According to Webster's *Third New International Dictionary of the English Language 831* (1976), "feasible" means "capable of being done, executed, or effected." Thus, the Act directs the Secretary to issue the standard that "most adequately assures . . . that no employee will suffer material impairment of health," limited only by the extent to which this is "capable of being done." In effect then, Congress itself defined the basic relationship between costs and benefits, by placing the "benefits" of worker health above all other considerations save those making attainment of this "benefit" unachievable. Any standard based on a balancing of costs and benefits by the Secretary that strikes a different balance than that struck by Congress would be inconsistent with the command set forth in the Act. Thus, cost-benefit analysis by OSHA is not required by the statute because feasibility analysis is.

When Congress has intended that an agency engage in cost-benefit analysis, it has clearly indicated such intent on the face of the statute. Certainly in light of its ordinary meaning, the word "feasible" cannot be construed to articulate such congressional intent. We therefore reject the argument that Congress required cost-benefit analysis in the statute.

Even though the plain language of the Act supports this construction, we must still decide whether the general definition of an occupational safety and health standard, either alone or in tandem with the Act, incorporates a cost-benefit requirement for standards dealing with toxic materials or harmful physical agents. Section 3(8) of the Act, 29 U.S.C. §652(8) provides: "The term 'occupational safety and health standard' means a standard which requires additional requirements for issuance of a subcategory of occupational safety and health standards dealing with toxic materials and harmful physical agents: it required that those standards be issued to prevent material impairment of health to the extent feasible."

Congress could reasonably have concluded that health standards should be subject to different criteria than safety standards because of the special problems presented in regulating them. Not only does the legislative history confirm that Congress meant "feasible" rather than "cost-benefit" when it used the former term, but it also shows that Congress understood that the Act would create substantial costs for employers, yet intended to impose such costs when necessary to create a safe and healthful working environment. Congress viewed the costs of health and safety as a cost of doing business. Senator Yarborough, a cosponsor of the Williams bill, stated: "We know the costs would be put into consumer goods but that is the price we should pay for the 80 million workers in America."

When Congress passed the Act in 1970, it chose to place pre-eminent value on assuring employees a safe and healthful working environment, limited only by the feasibility of achieving such an environment. We must measure the validity of the Secretary's actions against the requirements of that Act. Accordingly, we AFFIRM IN PART, and VACATE IN PART.

Case Questions

1. Do you think OSHA's standard is fair? Unfair? Explain.

2. Given the standard, what do you think an employer can do to limit liability?

3. Do you think that it is possible that the standard adopted by the Court may have had something to do with the fact that the hazard was one which was the basis for passing the act in the first place?

"Greater Hazard" Defense

Employers may contend that compliance with a health or safety standard would subject the employees to a **greater hazard** than what is prevented by the compliance. For example, in one case, a citation was issued because a construction company failed to install a cable railing on the perimeter of the top of a building it was constructing. The employer presented evidence that the risk involved in constructing the railing would subject its employees to a greater risk than if the railing were not there. To assert this defense, however, an employer must show:

- The hazards of compliance with the standard are greater than the hazards of noncompliance
- Alternative means of protection are unavailable.
- A variance from the Secretary of Labor was unavailable or inappropriate.

Greater hazard defense
An employer may use the greater hazard defense to an OSHA violation where the hazards of compliance are greater than the hazards of noncompliance, where alternative means of protection are unavailable, and where a variance was not available.

Guidance?

The Occupational Safety and Health Act of 1970 makes employers responsible for the safety of the workplace. While OSHA regulates certain known hazards and industries under the General Duty Clause, the employer may be held liable for workplace hazards even if specific regulations do not exist. There are reporting requirements under the act, as well as enforcement procedures and penalties. Where employees reasonably believe that there is an immediate danger presented by a workplace hazard, they have the right to refuse to expose themselves to the hazard. Current problem areas that are not presently regulated but that present significant workplace hazards include ergonomic considerations as well as workplace violence. While some areas are very specific about their regulatory requirements, it is most helpful if the employer maintains a common-sense and comprehensive approach to workplace safety and health issues.

So how does a manager ensure that her or his company is not violating OSHA? There are, of course, a variety of practices that a manager can implement to protect its company from liability.

• There should be a standard procedure for investigating and recording accidents. If a standard procedure is in place, any employee who is involved in an incident will have guidance about the proper method of handling the incident. Without standard procedures, employees may do what they think is best, which may not always be in line with OSHA requirements.

• When an incident is investigated properly, perhaps the investigation will uncover the unsafe condition that led to the incident. In this way, the unsafe conditions can be remedied and additional accidents may be prevented.

• The manager should answer the following questions regarding any investigation and report: What happened and why? How might this be prevented in the future? To make sure that the actions of the employees or investigators are most effective, it is recommended that the company draft a form for the accident investigation report. The employer is then certain that all of the necessary information will be obtained.

• Once all of the information has been compiled and recorded, the manager must determine what action will be taken in response to the report. The action that led to the injury or accident may be eliminated from the workplace.

• Implement training or educational programs to teach employees about proper usage of materials or machines to prevent accidents.

• Determine whether more safety measures must be put in place to adequately protect the employees involved in that operation. (The chapter on workers' compensation has other workplace safety readings.)

As the administration has found that safety programs and policies that establish standard procedures regarding safety issues significantly reduce the number of incidents and violations at a work site, the Occupational Safety and Health Administration has issued voluntary program guidelines. The guidelines include the following recommendations:

1. An effective safety program should include provisions for the systematic identification, evaluation, and prevention or control of general workplace hazards, specific job hazards, and potential hazards that may arise from foreseeable conditions.
2. An effective safety program should look beyond legal requirements toward addressing all potential hazards.
3. An effective safety program will include the following four elements:
   a. Management commitment and employee involvement.
   b. Worksite analysis to identify present and potential hazards.
   c. Hazard prevention and control.
   d. Safety and health training.

Management Tips

- The purpose of OSHA is to provide a safe workplace; much of the Act is common-sense protection against harm for the employees.
- Remember: Complying with OSHA is cheaper than paying fines for noncompliance.
- Beware: Just because a situation is not specifically mentioned by the Act, this doesn't mean that the situation is not covered by OSHA. The General Duty Clause provides protection for employees from many hazards that are not covered by specific regulations.
- Since employee misuse is no defense to a safety violation, the best way to prevent these types of violations is to conduct exceptional training for all employees on all equipment.
- Employees have the right to refuse to work based on their reasonable concern about death or serious injury. Don't let a situation get to this point; take precautions in advance to allay concerns or to provide for a safe environment.
- In connection with economic impossibility of compliance as a defense to a violation, make sure that you have sufficient documentation to support the claim of impossibility.
- OSHA provides protection from liability for voluntary actions that an employee might take in order to help a co-worker in need of emergency physical help. In these situations, the employer will normally not be cited for its failure to train employees who perform "good samaritan" acts. However, an employer might be held liable if the "good samaritan" was an employee designated to perform this type of assistance by the employer or life-threatening accidents would be reasonably foreseeable in their position and they have not been instructed on how to respond.

Summary

Due to the lack of state legislation protecting employees against hazards, national standards were put into place through the Occupational Safety and Health Act. The act was passed to provide employees with a safe place to work with uniform standards. Since its passage over 100,000 fatalities have been prevented, due in part to OSHA efforts.

Enforcing the act rests with the Occupational Safety and Health Administration (OSHA) under the authority of the Department of Labor. Penalties and abatement orders can be assessed in connection with an OSHA violation. The penalties range from $0–$10,000 and can include criminal sanctions and higher fines where an employer acted willfully and caused an employee's death.

The process for determining standards is lengthy. OSHA can begin the standards-setting procedure on its own initiative or in response to petitions from other parties. Advisory committees may be called upon to develop specific recommendations. There are two standing advisory committees, the National Advisory Committee on Occupational Safety and Health (NACOSH) and the Advisory Committee on Construction Safety and Health. Recommendations may also come from the National Institute for Occupational Safety and Health (NIOSH) which conducts research on various safety and health problems, provides technical assistance to OSHA, and recommends standards of OSHA's adoption. Once standards are proposed, OSHA publishes these intentions in the *Federal Register,* and, in some cases, information will be solicited from interested parties on the proposal. A public hearing may be held on the proposal. After the comment period and public hearing, if one is held, OSHA will publish the full, final text of the standard in the *Federal Register* including the reasoning and rationale behind the standard. Due to the many steps involved, the process, as can be assumed, is time consuming.

There are differing types of regulations, specific regulations and the general duty clause of the act. Specific regulations generally apply across the board of all types of employers, such as adequate safety measures and the continual training requirement. The general duty clause of the act is broader and protects employees against certain hazards in the workplace where no other OSHA standard would address the condition. The clause states, "[e]ach employer . . . shall furnish to each of his employees employment and place of employment which are free from recognized hazards that are causing or likely to cause death or serious physical harm to his employees."

Most employers, except for those with 11 or fewer employees must maintain certain records for OSHA compliance. Employers in certain industries, due to their low risk of hazards, are not required to maintain such records.

Employers may have certain defenses to OSHA violations. The first, reckless behavior on the part of the employee, may be a defense when an employer took all reasonable steps to prevent a hazard but the employee's own reckless conduct created the accident. Physical or economic impossibility of compliance may be a defense to an OSHA regulation when a variance is issued by OSHA to allow the employer's noncompliance. Employee reduction of risk could be a defense where an employer cannot on its own make a workplace safe for its employees, but through the acts of its employees the workplace can be made safe. Lastly, the "greater hazard" defense applies where the safety standard would subject the employees to a greater hazard than what is prevented by the compliance.

Chapter-End Questions

1. A number of producers of benzene and benzene-containing products asked the OSHA Review Commission to review a new health standard, which limited occupational exposure to benzene to one part benzene per million parts of air and required employers to assure that no employee comes into physical contact with it. The Occupational Safety and Health Administration instituted the standard because benzene is a carcinogen (may be cancer-producing) for which there is no known safe level of exposure. The benzene producers contest the standard, arguing that the best available evidence does not show that the reduction of the permissible exposure level from 10 parts per million to 1 part per million is reasonably necessary or appropriate to provide safe or healthful employment. OSHA responds that its policy is to limit employee exposure to carcinogens to the lowest feasible level. How should this matter be reviewed? (*American Petroleum Institute v. OSHA,* 581 F.2d 493 (5th Cir. 1978, affirmed 448 U.S. 607.)

2. Titanium Metals produces titanium ingots in Nevada. Titanium is a highly flammable substance during processing and can be ignited by heat, sparks, friction, or striking other small particles. To minimize dust accumulation, the company installed a collecting tube on its machines and periodically washed the entire area surrounding the machines. One day, while a machine operator was using the machine in the normal way, an explosion and fire erupted and another employee was burned to death. The company was served with two OSHA violations: (1) for failure to provide nonsparking tools and equipment and (2) for allowing flammable accumulations of titanium. The company claims that the hazard posed by the metal is not a *recognized hazard,* which would trigger the employer's general duty. The titanium industry is still in its infancy (less than 30 years old) and no precise standards exist respecting the appropriate levels of dust accumulation. Also, never in its eight-year history has the company had such an explosion, so it was unprepared and it would have never expected death or serious injury. Are these acceptable defenses? (*Titanium Metals Corp. of Amer. v. Usery,* 579 F.2d 536 (9th Cir. 1978).)

3. Lactos Laboratories is an interstate manufacturer of animal feed concentrates. In the course of its manufacturing process, the company uses fish parts, which are treated with sulfuric acid when packaged. One night, a truck delivering the fish parts deposited the mixture into a Lactos tank, which overflowed into an adjacent room in the basement and filled it to a depth of 31 inches. The company used a pump to get rid of most of the overflow but ordered the employees to enter the room when the level had decreased 3–4 inches to clean up the remaining debris and to repair some pumps. The employees who entered were almost immediately overcome by hydrogen sulfide gas (caused when the sulfur came into contact with iron sulfide particles which had fallen from the ceiling), as were those who tried to help them. Lactos had no emergency equipment available and had taken no safety precautions to cope with accumulations of the gas. In the end, three employees died, and two were seriously injured.

   Lactos defended itself against violations cited by OSHA by claiming that the sulfide gas was an unforeseeable hazard. Do you agree? (*Brennan v. OSH Review Commission,* 494 F.2d 460 (8th Cir. 1974).)

4. In 1971, at a motel construction site operated by National Realty, Smith, a foreman with the company, rode the running board of a front-end loader driven by one of his subordinates, Williams. The loader stalled while going down a ramp and swerved off the ramp. Smith jumped from the loader but was killed when it toppled off the ramp and fell on him. National Realty had a policy at the time against equipment riding, but Williams did not order Smith off the vehicle because Smith was his superior. National Realty was later cited by OSHA, "in that an employee was permitted to stand as a passenger on the running board of a loader while the loader was in motion." National Realty claims that it did not "permit" Smith to ride the machine. What does NR need to prove to show that it did not "permit" this type of behavior? (*National Realty & Construction Co. v. OSHRC,* 489 F.2d 1257 (D.C. Cir. 1973).)

5. Employees at Whirlpool worked beneath an overhead conveyor transport. To protect employees from objects that continually fell from the conveyors, Whirlpool installed a wire mesh guard screen 20 feet above the plant floor. Maintenance employees spent several hours each week cleaning objects that fell from the conveyors onto the wire mesh. To perform this duty, the employees usually stood on the wire frames, but sometimes found it necessary to stand on the screen mesh itself. While the company's policy admonished the employees to stand only on the frames, several employees did not and fell through the mesh, sustaining injuries. Keller, an employee stationed in this position, refused to continue to clean the mesh, claiming that he had reason to believe such work would be dangerous. Is he allowed to stop his work? (*Whirlpool v. Marshall,* 100 S. Ct. 883 (1980).)

6. No employer intends to harm its employees. How would you define the term *willful* that would give rise to penalties of up to $10,000?

7. Worcester Polytechnic Institute (WPI) hired Francis Harvey & Sons as general contractor. SGH, an engineering firm, was hired to do certain structural engineering services in connection with the project. After a Harvey employee expressed concern to SGH via a telephone call about a potentially dangerous structural defect in the concrete flooring, he was told to continue his work. Later, the flooring collapsed and five workers were hurt. No SGH employees were working at the worksite. After a complaint was filed against SGH, SGH defended, claiming that the worksite was not a "place of employment" of the structural engineering firm and, consequently, OSHA did not apply. (*Reich v. Simpson, Gumpertz & Heger, Inc.,* 1993 WL 310699 (1st Cir. 1993).)

8. General Dynamics manufactures M-1 Abrams tanks for the Department of Defense. The tanks have internal hydraulics that leak during assembly so the workers use a solvent called Trichloro to clean up spills. In its gaseous state, the solvent may cause serious illness or death. The manner in which the tank repairers performed the cleanups was essentially a matter of the cleaning team's discretion, except that the tanks be ventilated when using more than one pint of solvent, since all tank repairmen were highly skilled. After a plant employee was overcome by fumes, and another died, OSHA issued a citation, claiming that General Dynamics violated the general duty clause. General Dynamics defended against the citation because it was acting in complete conformance with a separate OSHA section, which specifically set forth the limitations of employee exposure to

Trichloro. Is General Dynamics free from responsibility under the general duty clause where it is in compliance with a more specific proscription? (*International Union, UAW v. General Dynamics Land Systems Division,* 815 F.2d 1570 (D.C. Cir. 1987).)

9. Morello Brothers is a roofing company that has done business with the federal government for years. In 1984, Morello began to perform roofing services on a building that housed OSHA offices. Several OSHA employees noticed a variety of violations and issued citations. Morello attempted to remedy the situation. One month later, similar citations were again issued for noncompliance. Finally, on a third visit, OSHA found compliance insufficient and issued a citation for willful violation. Morello argues that there was no evidence of willfulness, even though similar violations went continually uncorrected. Is it correct? (*Brock v. Morello Bros. Construction,* 809 F.2d 161 (1st Cir. 1987).)

10. What is required to prove a section 5(a) violation of the general duty clause?

19 EMPLOYEE RETIREMENT INCOME SECURITY ACT

Chapter Outline

SCENARIOS

SCENARIO 1

Travis, the manager of operations at a large manufacturing firm, walks into his office on Monday morning to find his assistant Beth apparently upset. She informs him that she was recently diagnosed with hepatitis and filed a claim for medical costs with the company's insurer. She then found that, since the time of her diagnosis and after having informed the human resources division of that diagnosis, the company reduced its medical coverage and placed a cap of $2,000 on certain claims, including those for hepatitis. Beth contends that she is being discriminated against and that the company should not be able to reduce coverage just to avoid having to pay her present and future claims. Is she right?

SCENARIO 2

Kimberly's supervisor, Gordon, continually hounds and threatens Kimberly by saying, "if you don't work more hours, I'll have to fire you and you'll lose all of your pension benefits!" She doesn't want to lose her job but feels that this type of harassment is completely inappropriate. In fact, the added stress that Gordon has imposed on the workplace by his constant threats about her financial future has landed her in therapy. Kimberly wants to file a claim against Gordon and the firm for which she works, claiming intentional infliction of emotional distress. When she tells Gordon, however, he just laughs in her face saying that he and their employer are both immune from this claim since it is preempted by ERISA. Is he right, and what does this preemption mean to Gordon and the firm in terms of defenses and the costs of liability?

Background

Once an employee begins full-time employment, and in some cases part-time employment, many firms offer her or him the benefit of investing in their pension plan. Employees take a portion of their salary and invest it through their employer in a plan that provides funding for the employee's retirement. But then the employer goes bankrupt, or the employee switches jobs; what happens to all of this money the employee paid into that plan? Or assume an employee has excellent medical benefits with his present company, benefits of which he often takes advantage; is he tied to that company and discouraged from leaving because he is concerned that he will not find those benefits on his own or elsewhere? What about an employee who pays into a retirement fund through her employer, only to find there are insufficient funds for her to receive the benefits when she retires?

In 1974, as a result of concerns regarding the protection of pension benefits of workers who lost their jobs prior to retirement, Congress enacted the Employee Retirement Income Security Act (ERISA), a federal law that governs certain adminis-

EXHIBIT 19–1 Myths about ERISA

1. Your pension plans are not protected against the trustees who administer them.
2. No matter what, if you put money into a retirement plan, it will be there when you retire.
3. No matter what, if you put money into a retirement plan, it will not be there when you retire.
4. ERISA applies only to retirement or pension funds.

trative aspects of employee benefit and retirement plans. Congress had been concerned about the millions of employees and their dependents who were affected by employee benefit plans. Congressional findings reported that, to provide for the general welfare of employees, disclosure rules should be stronger and safeguards should be provided with respect to the establishment, operation, and administration of such plans (though ERISA does not require employers to provide any particular benefits). The findings further stated that, despite the enormous growth of employee benefit plans, many employees with long years of employment were losing anticipated retirement benefits due to the lack of vesting provision in the plans and the inadequacy of current minimum standards. Since employees and their beneficiaries were being deprived of anticipated benefits, Congress felt the need to establish minimum standards to assure the equitable character of such plans and their financial soundness. As the court found in *Smith v. CMTA-IAM Pension Trust,* "the underlying purposes of ERISA are to protect the interests of participants in employee benefit plans."

The purpose of ERISA, therefore was to encourage cautious, careful management of retirement funds by employers by providing them with tax benefits for doing so. Consequently, ERISA should be thought of as a tax incentive and not necessarily as a retirement issue. As we will see in the next section, ERISA coverage is not restricted to merely retirement plans but covers any type of promised benefit. ERISA is a complex act that is multifaceted. There are courses focusing solely on ERISA. Therefore, this chapter will focus on the basics of the act to give the reader a general understanding.

Statutory Basis

Employee Retirement Income Security Act

§1132. Civil Enforcement.
(a) A civil action may be brought—
    (1) By a participant or beneficiary—
    (B) to recover benefits due to him under the terms of his plan, to enforce his rights under the terms of the plan, or to clarify his rights to future benefits under the terms of the plan.

§1140. Interference with protected rights.

It shall be unlawful for any person to discharge, fine, suspend, expel, discipline, or discriminate against a participant or beneficiary for exercising any right to which he is entitled under the provisions of an employee benefit plan, or for the purpose of interfering with the attainment of any right to which such participant may become entitled under the plan.

Who Is Covered

An employer that offers welfare benefit plans to its employees, such as health insurance or retirement plans, is subject to certain requirements under ERISA. (See below for further explanation of types of plans.) ERISA covers most private-sector employee benefit plans. In general, ERISA does not cover plans established or maintained by governmental entities or churches. Also, ERISA does not cover plans maintained outside the United States primarily for the benefit of nonresident aliens.

Types of Plans to Which ERISA Applies

ERISA technically applies to **employee benefit plans,** which are defined in the act as "any plan, fund or program established or maintained for the purpose of providing medical, surgical or hospital care or benefits, or benefits in the event of sickness, accident, disability, death or unemployment, or vacation benefits." There are basically two types of plans that ERISA covers. The first type of plan covered by ERISA are welfare plans. A welfare plan is any plan, program, or fund that the employer maintains to provide: medical, surgical, or hospital care; benefits for sickness, accident, disability, or death; unemployment benefits; vacation benefits; apprenticeship and training programs; day care centers; scholarship funds; prepaid legal services; holiday or severance pay; and retirement plans. The other type of plan covered by ERISA are retirement or pension plans.

ERISA defines two general forms of pension plans: those with **defined contributions** and those with **defined benefits.** The former involves plans in which each employee has her or his own account and the benefits received at retirement are based solely on the principal and income contributed. The latter comprises all other plans but generally refers to plans where the amount the employee receives at retirement is specifically designated when the employee enters the plan. In defined contribution plans, the security comes from knowing the amount of principal that will be invested, while the security in defined benefit plans comes from knowing exactly how much will be paid in the end.

Requirements of a Qualified Plan

In order for a qualified plan to be valid, it must satisfy some general requirements. First, the plan must be permanent; that is, it cannot have a planned, definite

Employee benefit plans
A plan, fund, or program that has been established by an employer to cover benefits for its employees relating to medical or hospital care, death, unemployment, or vacation benefits.

Defined contribution plans
A plan that defines the amount of the employee contribution, without a specific amount to be recovered at retirement.

Defined benefit plan
A plan that defines in advance the amount to be recovered on retirement.

expiration date. Although the employer can change or terminate the plan, evidence that the plan was not a bona fide program from its inception will disqualify the plan. Second, the plan must be in writing and communicated to all employees. Third, the plan assets must be held in trust by one or more trustee(s). Fourth, the plan must be for the exclusive benefit of the employees and their beneficiaries. There can be no reversion of the trust's assets to the employer, other than forfeitures. Lastly, the plan must be established and maintained by the employer. Funding the program can result from employer or employee contributions or both.

ERISA Regulations

ERISA sets uniform minimum standards to ensure that employee benefit plans are created and maintained in a fair and financially sound manner. Also, employers must provide promised benefits and satisfy ERISA's requirements for managing and administering pension and welfare plans. There are two main important issues arising from ERISA compliance: reporting and disclosure, and fiduciary duties.

Reporting and Disclosure

ERISA requires the employer or plan administrator to provide information to each participant and beneficiary about retirement plans and welfare plans; this information must also be provided to the federal government under certain circumstances. The required information includes a summary plan description (SPD), identifying in understandable terms (1) the plan participants' and beneficiaries' rights, (2) benefits, and (3) responsibilities under the plan. Plan changes must also be addressed in the summary plan description. The SPD does not need to be submitted to anyone, but must be furnished when requested. However, an annual report must be filed containing financial and other information concerning the operation of the plan. Plan administrators must also furnish participants and beneficiaries with a summary of the information contained in the annual report. Certain plans may be exempt for the annual report requirement. For instance, the reporting and disclosures laws do not apply to welfare plans with fewer than 100 participants.

Fiduciary Duty

Fiduciary
One who holds funds in trust for another; one who holds a position of trust and confidence.

Prior to the enactment of ERISA, plan coordinators routinely abused the funds entrusted to them, often at the expense of the employees. For instance, the funds may have been offered as loans to selected people, with little or no interest in return and little or no security for the loans, thereby interfering with employees' ability to earn income from the otherwise proper investment of funds.

ERISA established a number of requirements, called "fiduciary standards," to prevent these abuses. Those authorized to make decisions about the placement and investment of the pension plan or those who offer the plan investment advice are considered **fiduciaries** and are held to a high standard of loyalty to the participants in the fund. Fiduciaries are legally obligated to act in the best interest of those to whom they owe a fiduciary responsibility, rather than acting in their own interest. Fiduciaries act in only a representative capacity for the participants—they are not allowed to act for their own benefit (considered a conflict of interest).

In lieu of investing or managing the fund in whatever manner they please, fiduciaries are directed to manage the fund with the "care, skill that a prudent [person] acting in like capacity and familiar with such matters would use in the conduct of an enterprise of a like character and with like aims." This provision requires that a plan trustee–administrator act in the best interests of the participants and with as much care as a reasonable person would use under the same circumstances.

Certain transactions between an employee benefit plan and "parties in interest," which include the employer and others who may be in a position to exercise improper influence over the plan, are prohibited by ERISA and may suffer penalties. Most of these types of transactions are also prohibited from the IRS. However, there are some statutory exemptions from the prohibited transaction rules, and the Departments of Labor and Treasury can authorize such exemptions through exemptions procedures.

Difficult questions often arise under this provision, however: questions such as how much risk the plan manager should assume when investing the principal or what types of investments might be otherwise appropriate. The answers to these questions have different impacts, depending on whether the fund is a defined contribution plan or a defined benefit plan. In the former, the amount of the contribution is set, but the amount that the individual receives upon retirement depends on the investment strategy of the plan manager. It is the plan manager, after all, who invests the contributions, and the employee who receives what is amassed over the years.

In a defined benefit plan, the amount the employee will receive on retirement is a set amount generally based on a formula. If the fund manager makes poor decisions, it is the fund that will suffer; if the manager invests wisely and the fund does better than expected, it is the employer who benefits, because the necessity for employee contributions to attain the level of the benefit defined may decrease.

This type of risk balancing led to employers withdrawing money from the overfunded defined benefit plans. Under the terms of those plans, the amount of benefits that were to be paid out was already determined; if the plan provided surplus money as a result of prudent investing during boom years, employers claimed that the money was theirs to do with as they pleased. Employee investors claimed that the employers should not be able to retrieve the money because that was to be the buffer for problem years when the fund was not so successful. In addition to a general standard of care as just discussed, ERISA provides specific requirements for diversification and a prohibition of conflicts of interest to assure relatively low-risk fund management. To further protect employees' interest, ERISA allows employees considerable access to information concerning the plan. Plan managers must provide participants with information of major alterations, summaries, annual reports on the financing and operation of the plans, and reports on the accrued status of their benefits.

Vesting
Acquiring a right
or an interest that
is irrevocable by
the donor.

Eligibility and Vesting Rules

ERISA requires that all employees of age 21 or over who have completed one year of employment must be covered by their employer's pension plan.

Vesting means acquiring rights. For instance, assume that Margaret tells Dianne that she will leave her home to Dianne in her will. Is Dianne's interest in Margaret's home vested? No, not until Dianne has acquired the rights to the home on the death of Margaret, when the will becomes effective. On the other hand, if Margaret leaves Dianne her home through an irrevocable trust, where Margaret has the right to use the home during her life, but the trust irrevocably gives the right to Dianne on Margaret's death, Dianne's right to the home is vested as soon as the trust is put into place and is irrevocable. Dianne's right may be vested, though she has no actual ownership interest yet nor any right to use the home until Margaret's death.

In connection with pension plans, the concept of vesting is much the same. ERISA provides that an employee's right to her or his pension benefit becomes 100 percent nonforfeitable after five years of employment or gradually nonforfeitable over seven years (20 percent per year beginning in the third year). The employee's right is vested after five years, but the employee may not obtain the money nor use it until retirement. Once an employee's rights in the plan are vested, the employee cannot lose the pension benefits, even if she switches employers.

Consolidated Omnibus Budget Reconciliation Act of 1985 (COBRA)

The promise of temporarily continued health care coverage when someone stops working was established by the Consolidated Omnibus Budget Reconciliation Act of 1985 ("COBRA") and was codified in ERISA. These COBRA provisions apply to group health plans provided by employers with 20 or more employees on a typical working day in the previous calendar year. COBRA gives participants and beneficiaries the right to maintain, at their own expense, coverage under their health plan that would be lost due to a change in circumstance, such as termination of employment. The cost of the benefit must be comparable to what it would be if the participant and beneficiary were still members of the employer's group. General notice informing the covered individuals must be given informing them of their rights under COBRA and describe the law.

ERISA, through COBRA, also regulates the portability of employer-sponsored insurance coverage for employees in job transitions. The Health Insurance Portability and Accountability Act (HIPAA), an amendment of ERISA, ensures the portability and availability of health care coverage by limiting the extent to which the preexisting exclusion may apply under a health care plan. Under the HIPAA, the exclusion of preexisting conditions may only be applied to conditions that were existing within the six months ending on the date of the individual's enrollment in the new plan. Plus, pregnancy is not to be considered a preexisting condition under any circumstances. Finally, the HIPAA provides that any condition is eligible for coverage after 12 months of "preexisting status" (or 18 months for individuals who enroll in a special enrollment period). The act provides that no one may be excluded from coverage because of past, current, or expected health status.

In addition, COBRA sets standards for the retrieval of pension funds by employers. Traditionally, the employer merely terminated the plan, took the excess funds, and began a new plan with fewer reserves. Under COBRA, to effectively terminate a plan and to retrieve excess funds, the employer must purchase a fully funded annuity for the plan beneficiaries who are already retired to guarantee the remainder of the payments, as well as create a new plan, adequately funded, for current employees.

VARITY CORP. V. HOWE
116 S.Ct. 1065 (1996)

At the time employer Varity Corporation transferred its money-losing divisions in its subsidiary Massey-Ferguson, Inc., to Massey Combines, a separate firm (they called the transfer "Project Sunshine"), it held a meeting to persuade its employees of these failing divisions to change benefit plans. Varity conveyed the impression that the employees' benefits would remain secure when they transferred. In fact, Massey Combines was insolvent from the day it was created and, by the end of its receivership, the employees who had transferred lost all of their nonpension benefits. The employees sued under ERISA, claiming that Varity breached its fiduciary duty in leading them to withdraw from their old plan and to forfeit their benefits. The District Court held for the employees, and the Court of Appeals affirmed.

Breyer, J.

. . . The second question—whether Varity's deception violated ERISA-imposed fiduciary obligations—calls for a brief, affirmative answer. ERISA requires a "fiduciary" to "discharge his duties with respect to a plan solely in the interest of the participants and beneficiaries." To participate knowingly and significantly in deceiving a plan's beneficiaries in order to save the employer money at the beneficiaries' expense, is not to act "solely in the interest of the participants and beneficiaries." As other courts have held, "[l]ying is inconsistent with the duty of loyalty owed by all fiduciaries and codified in section 404(a)(1) of ERISA."

Because the breach of this duty is sufficient to uphold the decision below, we need not reach the question of whether ERISA fiduciaries have any fiduciary duty to disclose truthful information on their own initiative, or in response to employee inquiries.

We recognize, as mentioned above, that we are to apply common-law trust standards "bearing in mind the special nature and purpose of employee benefit plans." But we can find no adequate basis here, in the statute or otherwise, for any special interpretation that might insulate Varity, acting as a fiduciary, from the legal consequences of the kind of conduct (intentional misrepresentation) that often creates liability even among strangers.

We are aware, as Varity suggests, of one possible reason for a departure from ordinary trust law principles. In arguing about ERISA's remedies for breaches of fiduciary obligation, Varity says that Congress intended ERISA's fiduciary standards to protect only the financial integrity of the plan, not the individual beneficiaries. This intent, says Varity, is shown by the fact that Congress did not provide remedies for individuals harmed by such breaches; rather, Congress limited relief to remedies that would benefit only the plan itself. This argument fails, however, because, in our view, Congress *did* provide remedies for individual beneficiaries harmed by breaches of fiduciary duty.

Case Questions:

1. What should Varity have done in order to avoid liability under ERISA?
2. How can an employee ensure that she or he knows all of the facts relevant to a question such as the one present in this case?
3. Why do you think Varity handled this in the way that it did?

Funding Requirements for Defined Benefit Plans

To ensure that adequate funds are available to the employees on their retirement, ERISA dictates how the plans should be funded throughout the years. Employers must fund the normal costs of the plan each year and amortize their employees' liabilities from previous service over not more than 40 years, and from formation of new plans over 30 years.

In addition, employers with defined benefit plans must purchase insurance from the Pension Benefit Guarantee Corporation (PBGC) to cover potential losses of benefits on the termination of a plan. The PBGC was established by ERISA. The pensions of retired workers are insured for the full amount owed, while the pensions of vested but still employed workers are covered only to the extent that their vested interests have accrued at the time the plan terminates.

Modification of Benefit Plans

When a firm considers modifying a retirement plan for its employees, it must be wary since the employees may have been making decisions in reliance on the original benefit plan. Even if a proposed plan offers greater benefits than those originally included, an employer has a fiduciary duty to notify all employees of the changes that might take effect once the employer gives the proposal "serious consideration." Consider the perspective of someone who is about to retire but who might have greater benefits if she simply waits a month or two until a new plan is implemented. She would prefer to know about the possibility, wouldn't she?

"Serious consideration" exists where the employer has a specific proposal under consideration, where it is being discussed by senior management with the authority to implement the changes, and where senior management is actually discussing it for purposes of implementation. A discussion by an employer is not deemed serious consideration where it represents simply gathering data or formulating strategies, commissioning studies, interacting with senior management regarding possible plan designs, or where it is being discussed in the abstract rather than in terms of practicalities.[1]

Where a plan is being given serious consideration, managers must truthfully and forthrightly offer the information to all employees. If notice of the possible changes are not given to employees, the firm should make eligibility for plan participation retroactive to the date of serious consideration.

Enforcement of ERISA

ERISA is enforced by the Department of Labor and the Internal Revenue Service (IRS) of the Department of the Treasury. The IRS is responsible for the requirements surrounding vesting and funding by removing tax-exempt status for those plans that violate vesting standards and by taxing the deficiencies in compliance with funding standards. The Department of Labor, on the other hand, administers the provisions with relation to disclosure, reporting, and fiduciary responsibilities. As discussed above, fiduciaries may be removed by the department for failure to act with due care or for engaging in an inappropriate conflict of interest.

Individual plaintiffs may file actions based on ERISA violations. ERISA preempts all state laws that relate to employee benefit plans, whether or not the situation contemplated by the state law is actually covered specifically in ERISA. Accordingly, state tort claims for tortious interference with employee benefit plans, state claims for intentional or negligent infliction of emotional distress in connection with the handling of disability benefits, and actions for unjust enrichment, for fraud, and for conversion are preempted by the act. The only form of relief for these types of injuries would be ERISA; state common law claims would not be appropriate. This is more of a burden on the employee than the employer:

1. "Bad faith" becomes a nonissue under ERISA, while it may be critical to a common law claim.
2. Certain defendants, such as the plan sponsor or claims review agents, cannot be sued.
3. There is no such thing as compensatory or punitive damages against the employer under ERISA, though they are available under tort law.
4. The process for a claim is slower.
5. There is no jury trial under ERISA as there would be under tort law.
6. Attorneys' fees and costs are recoverable.

In an effort to prevent subversion of the act's requirements, ERISA provides that an employee who is terminated "for the purpose of interfering with the attainment of any right to which the employee may become entitled" under ERISA has a claim based on section 510 of the act. That is, ERISA prohibits employers from

---

[1]*McAuley International Business Machines Corp.*, 165 F.3d 1038 (6th Cir. 1999).

Scenario

discharging employees merely to prevent their rights from vesting or to prevent them from receiving other benefits under the act.

Employers have the right to reduce or modify employee benefits (unless prohibited by contractual obligations), as long as similarly situated plan participants are treated alike. For instance, the employer may not reduce benefits for one full-time employee without similarly reducing the benefits for all similar employees. In order to prevail on a claim of a violation of section 510 of the act, in the case of discharge, the employee must prove that the employer terminated her or his employment with the "specific intent" to interfere with her or his benefit rights.

Owens v. Storehouse, Inc.
984 F.2d 394 (11th Cir. 1993)

Owens worked for Storehouse, Inc., a chain of retail furniture shops. In 1988, Storehouse instituted an employee benefits plan with a lifetime cap of $1 million for hospital and medical expenses per employee. Later that year, Owens was diagnosed with AIDS. Shortly thereafter, the insurance company notified Storehouse that they intended to cancel their policy because of the high incidence of AIDS in the retail industry generally and among Storehouse's employees in particular. (Five employees had AIDS.) The insurance company eventually agreed to continue Storehouse's contract, but only with a $75,000 deductible for AIDS-related claims, while it began coverage of all other claims at $25,000. Storehouse was concerned with this limitation and began to look for another insurer. It also decided that it would have a better chance of finding an insurer if it placed a $25,000 lifetime cap on AIDS-related medical claims. Owens sued his former employer claiming that its modification of the employee benefit plan to lower the lifetime cap for AIDS-related claims violated section 510 of ERISA.

Dubina, J.

ERISA does not prohibit a company from terminating previously offered benefits that are neither vested nor accrued. Unlike pension benefits, welfare benefit plans neither vest nor accrue. Instead, Congress intended employers to be free to create, modify, or terminate the terms and conditions of employee welfare benefit plans as inflation, changes in medical practice and technology, and the costs of treatment dictate.

Nevertheless, Beavers (Owen's personal representative after his death) argues that employers may not change the terms of their employee insurance programs to affect a particular illness once an employee has contracted that illness and begun making claims for it. Beavers thus reads into section 510 a latent vesting requirement that ripens upon the contraction of, and the submission of claims for, a particular sickness. Yet, section 510 contains no such requirement. Moreover, while an employer may contractually bind itself to fixed medical benefits, Storehouse did not do so here. Instead, it reserved the right to change or terminate the terms of its plan at any time. Absent contractual obligation, employers may increase or decrease benefits. Thus, Beavers has failed to demonstrate a statutory or contractual right under section 510 upon which a claim of discrimination would be based.

We also reject Beavers' contention that the plan modifications at issue here constitute the discrimination forbidden by section 510. As noted, section 510 targets discriminatory conduct designed to interfere with the exercise or attainment of vested or other rights under the plan or ERISA. It does not broadly forbid all forms of discrimination. Rather, it outlaws discrimination undertaken for purposes expressly made "impermissible" by the terms of the plan or statute. Thus, to prevail under section 510, a plaintiff must show that the alleged discrimination was designed either to retaliate for the exercise of a right or to interfere with the attainment to an entitled right. It is insufficient merely to allege discrimination in the apportionment of benefits under the terms of the plan.

To be successful, a plaintiff must present evidence of the employer's specific intent to violate ERISA; that is, evidence that the employer intentionally discriminated against an employee to retaliate for the exercise of a right or to interfere with the attainment of an entitled right, under the plan or ERISA. The record is devoid of any evidence of intentional discrimination.

First, the record demonstrates no retaliatory intent. It is uncontroverted that Storehouse acted to reduce plan costs at a time of financial hardship. Faced with the possibility of terminating its plan altogether or modifying it to incorporate a cap, Storehouse chose the latter. Contrary to Beavers' argument, Owens was not singled out for injurious treatment. Additionally, Owens was neither fired nor harassed. The plan modifications applied to all employees and included benefit caps for other illnesses.

Second, the record does not establish that Storehouse amended its plan to interfere with the attainment of any right to which Owens might have been entitled under section 510. The "right" referred to is not any right in the abstract. Rather it is one specifically conferred by the plan or by ERISA. As discussed, ERISA does not confer a right to particular health benefits.

We conclude that no statutory or contractual obligation prevented Storehouse from amending its employee welfare benefit plan to include a cap for AIDS-related claims.

Case Questions

1. Do you think the employer was legitimately attempting to protect itself from rising costs or loss of coverage, or making a statement about AIDS or gays and lesbians? Would it make a difference?

2. Can you think of any other type of illness that could be the basis of similar types of claims as the AIDS illness was here? Could an employer, for instance, similarly limit coverage of a disease primarily affecting a certain ethnic group, such as African-Americans and sickle-cell anemia?

3. Do you agree with the court that section 510 gives no right to which an employee may have been entitled? Why or why not?

INTER-MODAL RAIL EMPLOYEES ASSOCIATION V. ATCHISON, TOPEKA AND SANTA FE RAILWAY COMPANY

520 U.S. 510, 117 S.Ct. 1513 (1997)

An employer is sued for a violation of ERISA when it decreased the benefits due workers after the work was contracted out to another organization. Employees who declined to continue employment were terminated. The Supreme Court held that this constituted an ERISA violation.

O'Connor, J.

As employees of Santa Fe Terminal Services, Inc. (SFTS), a wholly owned subsidiary of Atchison, Topeka and Santa Fe Railway Co. (ATSF), the employees were entitled, among other things, to pension, health, and welfare benefits under SFTS-Teamsters Union collective bargaining agreements. The resulting benefit plans were subject to ERISA. Ultimately ATSF bid the work being done by SFTS to In-Terminal Services (ITS). ITS offered continued employment to the employees of SFTS, but provided fewer pension and welfare benefits. ITS then terminated SFTS employees who declined to continue employment with ITS. Employees filed suit, alleging that the terminations violated §510 of ERISA.

Section 510 of the ERISA makes it unlawful to "discharge, fine, suspend, expel, discipline, or discriminate against a participant or beneficiary [of an employee benefit plan] . . . for the purpose of interfering with the attainment of any right to which such participant may become entitled under the plan." The Court of Appeals for the Ninth Circuit held that §510 only prohibits interference with the attainment of rights that are capable of "vesting," as that term is defined in ERISA. We disagree.

* * * *

The Court of Appeals' holding that §510 bars interference only with vested rights is contradicted by the plain language of §510. ERISA defines a "plan" to include both "an employee wel-

fare benefit plan [and] an employee pension benefit plan," §1002(3), and specifically exempts "employee welfare benefit plan[s]" from its stringent vesting requirements, see §1051(1). Because a "plan" includes an "employee welfare benefit plan," and because welfare plans offer benefits that do not "vest" (at least insofar as ERISA is concerned). Congress's use of the word "plan" in §510 all but forecloses the argument that §510's interference clause applies only to "vested" rights. Had Congress intended to confine §510's protection to "vested" rights, it could have easily substituted the term "pension plan," for "plan," for the term "nonforfeitable" right, for "any right." But §510 draws no distinction between those rights that "vest" under ERISA and those that do not.

The right that an employer or plan sponsor may enjoy in some circumstances to unilaterally amend or eliminate its welfare benefit plan does not, as the Court of Appeals apparently thought, justify a departure from §510's plain language. It is true that ERISA itself "does not regulate the substantive content of welfare-benefit plans." Thus, unless an employer contractually cedes its freedom, it is "generally free under ERISA, for any reason at any time, to adopt, modify, or terminate [its] welfare pla[n]."

The flexibility an employer enjoys to amend or eliminate its welfare plan is not an accident; Congress recognized that "requir[ing] the vesting of these ancillary benefits would seriously complicate the administration and increase the cost of plans." Giving employers this flexibility also encourages them to offer more generous benefits at the outset, since they are free to reduce benefits should economic conditions sour. If employers were locked into the plans they initially offered, "they would err initially on the side of omission." Section 510 counterbalances this flexibility by ensuring that employers do not "circumvent the provision of promised benefits." In short, "§510 helps to make promises credible." An employer may, of course, retain the unfettered right to alter its promises, but to do so it must follow the formal procedures set forth in the plan. Adherence to these formal procedures "increases the likelihood that proposed plan amendments, which are fairly serious events, are recognized as such and given the special consideration they deserve." The formal amendment process would be undermined if §510 did not apply because employers could "informally" amend their plans one participant at a time. Thus, the power to amend or abolish a welfare benefit plan does not include the power to "discharge, fine, suspend, expel, discipline, or discriminate against" the plan's participants and beneficiaries "for the purpose of interfering with [their] attainment of . . . right[s] . . . under the plan." To be sure, when an employer acts without this purpose, as could be the case when making fundamental business decisions, such actions are not barred by §510. But in the case where an employer acts with a purpose that triggers the protection of §510, any tension that might exist between an employer's power to amend the plan and a participant's rights under §510 is the product of a careful balance of competing interests, and is most surely not the type of "absurd or glaringly unjust" result that would warrant departure from the plain language of §510.

* * * *

We therefore VACATE the judgment of the Court of Appeals and REMAND for proceedings consistent with this opinion.

Case Questions

1. Do you agree or disagree with this opinion? Why or why not? Think of it from the employer and employee perspectives.

2. How did the Court reconcile the difference between an employer's ability to reduce benefits to employees and the employees' rights to the benefits?

3. The court recognizes that ERISA does not regulate the substantive content of welfare-benefit plans. Do you think this opinion changes the employer's flexibility with regard to welfare-benefit plans?

It should be noted that some ERISA claims under section 510 may also be asserted under the Age Discrimination in Employment Act (ADEA). For instance, since benefits are more likely to become vested as a worker gains seniority and as seniority may be more likely with advancing age, employers attempting to avoid paying benefits may be more likely to terminate older workers, giving rise to a claim both under ERISA as well as the ADEA.

If the employee is legally terminated or loses benefit coverage due to a reduction in hours, COBRA requires that employers extend employee health insurance coverage for up to 18 months at the rates originally charged while the individual was still working for the employer. In this way, while the coverage is paid for by the employee, COBRA provides guaranteed coverage for an employee who leaves employment for a relatively short time where that person may have difficulty obtaining coverage.

Management Tips

- ERISA is a complicated statute that contains many specific regulations regarding the investment of retirement funds. Don't assume compliance; maintain consistent review.
- You do not *have to* provide retirement fund opportunities to your employees. If you *do,* however, ERISA applies.
- Since ERISA preempts all state laws relating to employee benefit plans, don't consider a state safe harbor where it is not in compliance with ERISA.
- Even though compensatory and punitive damages are not allowed against the employer under ERISA, they may be available under a common law tort claim.

Summary

Concerns that management must address in considering the management implications of ERISA:

- First, when organizing and implementing an employee benefit plan, the employer must ensure that the plan does not unjustly discriminate against individuals on the basis of a protected classification, such as race, gender, or age.
- Second, the employer must determine where the risk will lay in connection with a retirement benefit plan. If the risk is to be solely on the part of the participant/employee, a defined contribution plan is appropriate. However, any unexpected proceeds from the fund (due, perhaps, to excellent investment strategy or the economic climate) will then go to the participants. If the risk is to be placed instead on the employer, a defined benefit plan is more suitable. In that case, while

the employer assumes the risk that poor investment strategy may result in insufficient funds available when necessary (and consequently, the employer would have to contribute additional funds), any excess may be retrieved by the employer, as explained above.

- Third, the employer must determine vesting requirements and add any additional requirements. In one case, the employer's plan provided that, while funds would vest after a certain date, the participant would relinquish all rights if she or he worked for a competitor within one year after a voluntary termination.
- Fourth, the employer must name a trustee/fiduciary for the plan and ensure that the terms of any defined benefit plan are in accordance with those required by the statute.

Chapter-End Questions

1. Leigh and Dusek are beneficiaries of the Reliable Corporation Employee Profit Sharing Trust and former owners of the Reliable Corporation. The trust was originally created by the company as an

employees' profit-sharing trust that, until March 1978, held all of its funds in fixed-income money market investments. In late March, the trust invested approximately 30 percent of its assets in the stock of three companies; the trust administrators also held large personal interests in each of these three companies. The trust lost no money on the challenged transactions and in fact gained a return on the investment of 72 percent. However, the beneficiaries contest the transaction, claiming that the administrators violated their fiduciary duties by investing in companies where they, the administrators, would reap a personal benefit. In doing so, the beneficiaries argue, the administrators were acting in *their* interests and not necessarily in the best interests of the trust. The administrators made money, which they would not have otherwise made had they been making trust investments solely on the basis of what was best for the trust.

Note that the applicable ERISA section reads that "if ERISA fiduciaries breach their duties by risking trust assets for their own purposes, beneficiaries may recover the fiduciaries' profits made by misuse of the plan's assets." Decide the beneficiaries' claim in this case. What other information would you need? *(Leigh v. Engle,* 727 F.2d 113 (7th Cir. 1984).)

2. What is the difference between a defined contribution plan and a defined benefit plan?

3. Northwest Airlines decided to limit the benefit accruals of pilots once they became 60 years old. Seventeen pilots who were over 60 filed an action against the airline, alleging that the company's plan violated ERISA because pilots under 60 were to accrue benefits faster than pilots over 60. Are they correct? *(Atkins v. Northwest Airlines,* 967 F.2d 1197 (9th Cir. 1992).)

4. Does a plan violate ERISA if it refuses to allow same-sex unmarried couples to participate in the company-sponsored benefit plan?

5. A trustee of a pension plan is the owner and principal officer of the employer who sponsors the plan—a construction company.

The trustee contracted with his own company to build a restaurant on the land leased by the plan from an independent third party. The trustee caused the plan to pay additional fees to the company and himself that were not stated in the contract. Is this a violation of ERISA? *(Marshall v. Kelly,* 465 F.Supp. 341 (W.D. Ok. 1978).)

6. A trustee of a plan, who was also a participant, denied a discretionary payment of a lump sum accrued benefit to a participant who had terminated employment. What would be the argument that this was self-dealing? *(Fine v. Semet,* 514 F.Supp. 34 (S.D.Fl. 1981).)

7. Four individuals collectively owned an investment management company, an investment banking company, and a registered brokerdealer company. The investment management company managed assets for pension plans. Under agreements to raise capital for several unrelated companies, the investment banking company and the brokerdealer invested plan assets in exchange for a commission. Is this a prohibited receipt of consideration by a fiduciary in connection with transactions involving plan assets? *(Lowen v. Tower Asset Management Inc.,* 829 F.2d 1209 (2d Cir. 1987).)

8. Should an employee's salary, for purposes of profit sharing plan contributions, include bonuses in addition to base salary? *(Lowry v. Bankers Life and Casualty Retirement Plan,* 871 F.2d 522 (5th Cir. 1989).)

9. If an employer is reorganizing and the liability on its severance benefits plan will result as soon as the transfer of interest is made, can the corporation modify its benefits program to avoid that liability? *(Sulton v. Weirton Steel Division,* 724 F.2d 406 (4th Cir. 1983).)

10. Feinberg is a bookkeeper who had worked for Pfeiffer Company for 37 years at the

time the board decided to pass a resolution in her favor. The resolution stated that "she be afforded the privilege of retiring from active duty in the corporation at any time she may elect to see fit to do so on retirement pay of $200 per month for the rest of her life." She worked for two more years then retired. She was paid $200 per month for seven years, then the employer cut back when legal counsel advised the board that the money was a gift, rather than a legal obligation. Feinberg sued for breach of contract. What result? (*Feinberg v. Pfeiffer Co.,* 322 S.W.2d. 163 (Mo. Ct. App. 1959).)

20 IMMIGRATION REFORM AND CONTROL ACT

Chapter Outline

S C E N A R I O S

S C E N A R I O   1

Reina Guillen is an undocumented alien who entered the United States before January 1, 1982, making her eligible for legalization under the Immigration Reform and Control Act (IRCA). As an undocumented alien, she is currently unable to obtain a Social Security number. On her application for a job at the Pasadena Independent School District, she was not yet legalized and, therefore, inserted a fake Social Security number on the form. After the district discovered her false statements on the application form she was terminated. Is this an illegal discrimination by the employer?

S C E N A R I O   2

Gomez, the hiring manager at a Sizzler restaurant in Arizona, extended an offer to Rodriguez after having a long-distance telephone conversation with him while Rodriguez was in California working for a Sizzler restaurant there. On Rodriguez's arrival, Gomez asked to see evidence of Rodriguez's authorization to work in the United States. Rodriguez offered a driver's license and what looked like a Social Security card. Gomez did not look at the back of the card nor compare it to the example in the Immigration and Naturalization Service (INS) handbook. In fact, Rodriguez's card was a forgery, and the INS has assessed a fine against the Sizzler restaurant, claiming that Gomez knew or should have known that the card was a fake. Is Sizzler liable under IRCA?

Statutory Basis

Immigration Reform and Control Act of 1986
Sec. 274A(a)

(1) It is unlawful for a person or other entity:
   (A) to hire or to recruit or refer for a fee for employment in the United States an alien knowing the alien is an unauthorized alien with respect to such employment, or
   (B) to hire for employment in the United States an individual without [verification of employment eligibility].
(2) It is unlawful for a person or other entity, after hiring an alien for employment in accordance with paragraph (1), to continue to employ the alien in the United States knowing the alien is (or has become) an unauthorized alien with respect to such employment.
(3) A person or entity that establishes that it has complied in good faith with the [verification of employment eligibility] with respect to the hiring, recruiting or referral for employment of an alien in the United States has established an affirmative defense that the person or entity has not violated paragraph (1)(A).

Sec 274B(a)

(1) It is an unfair immigration-related practice for a person or other entity to discriminate against any individual (other than an unauthorized alien) with respect to the
hiring, or recruitment or referral for a fee, or the individual for employment or the
discharging of the individual from employment—
(A) because of such individual's national origin, or
(B) in the case of a protected individual [a citizen or authorized alien], because of
such individual's citizenship status.

Background

Prior to the enactment of the Immigration Reform and Control Act (IRCA), few restrictions were applied to US employers hiring illegal aliens or other undocumented
workers. Consequently, many seeking illegal entry to the United States for purposes
of finding a job had little trouble accomplishing just that; they would find the means
to get into the country, then have a relatively easy time locating employment. What
they may have to endure in seeking (and even finding) what many considered to be
undesirable employment was worthwhile, compared to the unemployment levels in
many of their countries of origin.

In an effort to protect employment of American citizens by reducing the number of illegal aliens, as well as to allow entry by aliens in areas where the nation's
economy would be helped, in 1986 Congress enacted the IRCA, later amended by
the Immigration Act of 1990. The IRCA requires an employer to inquire into the citizenship or residence status of all job applicants, and it specifically prohibits employers from hiring undocumented workers. The IRCA works in conjunction with a
number of other statutes addressing employment of aliens, including the Federal
Migrant and Seasonal Agricultural Worker Protection Act, which provides that no
farm labor employer may hire or use a worker who is an illegal alien. The Federal
Migrant Worker Act also requires employers to make a bona fide inquiry into the citizenship or residence status of each job applicant.

On September 30, 1996, President Clinton signed into law the Illegal Immigration Reform and Immigrant Responsibility Act of 1996 (IIRIRA), the most substantial change in immigration law in many years. This law basically revamped the
entire immigration process and introduced tougher penalties for any foreign national
who overstayed a visa in the United States, entered the country illegally, or worked
illegally. Under the act, any foreign national in the United States with a criminal history is treated in a more stringent manner. Its implications for the employment arena
are covered in Title IV of the act, "Enforcement of Restrictions Against Employment," which imposes a number of changes that affect employers. The most important change reduces the potential liability of employers under the provisions of the
IRCA regarding employer confirmation of worker's employment authorization and
identity (the "I-9" form).

In summary, the new act provides for three modifications to the IRCA. First, the new act provides employers who in good faith make technical or procedural errors in complying with the IRCA provisions an opportunity to correct those errors without penalty. Second, where an employer requests one or several documents that are required to confirm an employee's identity and authorization to work in the US or refuses to honor documents that reasonably appear to be genuine, this is now a violation only "if made for the purpose or with the intent of unlawfully discriminating against the employee on the basis of citizenship status or national origin." Third, the new act reduces the number of different documents that a worker can use to establish his identity and authorization to work in the United States. The case below is an example of the employment environment *before* the applicability of the act; though the court expressly states that the act merely clarified practices already in place. Consider the price suggested by the ALJ to be paid for what could have been an error of "overcompliance!"

ROBISON FRUIT RANCH, INC. v. UNITED STATES
147 F.3d 798 (9th Cir. 1997)

An employer was found by an administrative law judge to have violated the "document abuse" provision of the Immigration Reform and Control Act (IRCA), as it existed before its 1996 amendment, by asking applicants to provide two forms of identification when one would suffice. The court had to determine whether this action violates the IRCA.

Schroeder, J.

* * * *

The statute in question is 8 U.S.C. § 1324b(a)(6) as it existed during the 1990–93 period, when the events in question occurred. It then provided in pertinent part:

> [an employer]'s request, fr purposes of satisfying the requirements of [8 U.S.C. § 1324a(b)], for more or different documents than are required under such subsection or refusing to honor documents tendered that on their face reasonably appear to be genuine shall be treated as an unfair immigration-related employment practice relating to the hiring of individuals.

The statute was amended in 1996 to add an express requirement of discrimination. It now provides that the described documentary requests shall be treated as unfair employment practices "if made for the purpose or with the intent of discriminating against an individual in violation of paragraph (1)." Paragraph (1) is the statute's general anti-discrimination provision, which prohibits discrimination on the basis of national origin or citizenship status, except, of course, against an alien who is not authorized to work. See 8 U.S.C. § 1324h(a)(l). This provision constitutes a key protection against unfairness in the administration of the IRCA's requirement that employers verify that job applicants are either citizens or aliens authorized to work.

The material facts are not in dispute. Petitioner Robison is a family-owned fruit orchard in Idaho and employs a large number of migrant seasonal workers to harvest fruit. Many of the seasonal workers are aliens, and many do not speak or write English.

Central to an understanding of this case is Form I-9 itself. The form used by Robison during the period in question was the 1990 form that is attached as an addendum to this opinion. The form was revised in 1991. The revised form states expressly that employers cannot specify any particular document they will accept from employees. Robison, however, did not begin using the revised form until 1993, after most of the events in question here had occurred.

The purpose of the form is to verify the applicant's identity and eligibility to work. Section 1 of Form I-9, entitled "Employee Information and Verification," requires the applicant to attest to his work eligibility. Section 2 of the form, entitled "Employer Review and Verification," requires the employer to examine an applicant's documents and certify that the documents appear to be genuine and that the individual is eligible to work in the United States. The employee may present one document from List A or one document from each of Lists B and C. The documents on List A, such as an alien registration card (green card) or a U.S. Passport, establish both identity and work eligibility. The documents on List B, such as a driver's license, establish identity but not eligibility to work. The documents on List C, such as a social security card, establish eligibility to work but not identity.

Throughout the period in question, hiring at Robison Ranch was done primarily by the receptionist-bookkeeper and the office manager. The evidence showed that they commonly requested U.S. citizen applicants to show a driver's license and social security card. They requested alien applicants to show an INS document and a social security card. Some employees were requested to show "two forms of ID." The foreman who assisted Spanish speaking pickers or referred Spanish speaking applicants to the office commonly told them that they would need two forms of ID.

* * * *

In 1993, while investigating other charges, the Office of Special Counsel, Executive Office of Immigration Review, ("OSC") learned of Robison's practice of asking for specific forms of ID or for two forms of ID and determined that this practice violated the document abuse provision. Robison's transgression, as far as the OSC was concerned, was in telling applicants that two specific documents would be sufficient for verification purposes. In OSC's view, it was irrelevant that Robison did not intend to discriminate, but rather treated aliens and citizens the same. It was also irrelevant that Robison's practices did not in fact make it any more difficult for aliens to fill out the forms. It appears that the practice for which the government has prosecuted Robison is a nondiscriminatory and expeditious treatment of job seekers.

* * *

In contending that the statute does not require any showing of discrimination, the government looks in isolation at the language of § 1324b(a)(6) as it read prior to the 1996 amendments. That language, standing alone, did not express the discrimination requirement. Paragraph (1) of the statute, however, specifically proscribed discrimination in hiring. Paragraph (6) operated only by reference to paragraph (1): "For purposes of paragraph (1), [document abuse] shall be treated as an unfair immigration-related employment practice. . ." Section 1324b(a)(6) thus incorporates by reference the discrimination provision of § 1324b(a)(1). Paragraph (5) of that statute contained a similar incorporation of the discrimination requirement. It proscribed retaliation against employees who assert their rights under IRCA and provided that an individual "intimidated, threatened, coerced or retaliated against shall be considered . . . to have been discriminated against." 8 U.S.C. § 1324b(a)(5). Sections 1324b(a)(5) and (6) form part of the 1990 amendments to the Immigration Reform and Control Act, which were added in order to prevent IRCA's worker eligibility requirements from leading to discriminatory employment practices.

The statute's remedy and penalty provisions confirm that a violation of § 1324b was to be premised on a finding of discrimination. Sections 1324b(d)(1) and (2) stated that OSC investigations into unfair employment practices were to be premised on allegations of knowing and intentional discriminatory activity. And the penalty provision specifically applicable solely to subsection (a)(6), on which the instant penalties were based, provided for "a civil penalty of not less than $100 and not more than $1,000 for each individual discriminated against." Thus, no penalty may be imposed absent a finding of discrimination. Presumably, had Congress not intended violations to turn on the presence of discrimination, it would not have included the reference to discrimination both in this subsection and in § 1324b(a)(1).

The government contends that § 1324b(a)(6) does not require a showing of discrimination or harm. Rather, in the government's view, any specific document request can subject an employer to liability. For example, if the employer requests a driver's license and a social security card, the employer has requested both more and different documents than may be required. The employee could have shown only a U.S. Passport. Similarly, two different documents, such as a military identification and a birth certificate, could be produced to satisfy the requirement. The gov-

ernment's interpretation would mechanically subject employers to liability for naming documents when in fact the employer was attempting to assist the applicant in satisfying the requirements of Form I-9.

We hold that Congress intended a discrimination requirement in the 1990 statute and merely clarified the statute to state that intent in its 1996 amendment. The evidence unquestionably shows that the employment practices in this case did not create additional burdens to any class of applicants or constitute differential treatment of authorized aliens and citizens. The alien applicants were not specially burdened by the employer's requests. Robison simply requested documents the aliens were already using to complete the top portion of Form I-9 as well as the accompanying Treasury Form W-4, which requires a social security number. There could have been no discrimination, and the PETITION FOR REVIEW MUST BE GRANTED.

Case Questions

1. Do you think an intent to discriminate should be required in order to prevail in an alien discrimination suit? Why or why not?

2. Do you think that the burden to the alien is greater or less with the 1996 act? Why or why not?

3. Do you agree with the provisions in the 1996 act? Why or why not?

Under the IRCA, most of the more than 17 million legal alien workers are identified as "employees" and are due protection under the act. In this way, an employer may not avoid liability under the act by calling an alien worker an "independent contractor."

Unlike other federal employment-related statutes, the IRCA applies to all employers regardless of size. Violations of the act are prosecuted by the US Department of Justice. The act subjects violators to penalties of up to $2,000 per undocumented worker, and from $3,000 to $10,000 and possible imprisonment for subsequent violations or where a pattern or practice is established. Failure to main-

Exhibit 20–1   Myths about IRCA

1. The sole purpose of IRCA is to protect jobs for Americans and to keep alien workers out of the United States.
2. When you hire a worker, it is up to you to determine if that individual is an illegal alien or not. You must authenticate any documents presented and check all facts.
3. IRCA does not prohibit discrimination on the basis of citizenship.
4. IRCA is administered solely by the Federal Immigration and Naturalization Service.

tain adequate records for three years or one year after an employee leaves the employer may result in a $1,000 fine against the employer. In addition, the individual within the company who is responsible for checking and maintaining documentation may be liable as well.

Documentation

It was Congress's intent to prohibit undocumented aliens from obtaining employment in the United States. Congress placed the burden of checking the status of aliens on the employer. By doing so, it was contemplated that undocumented aliens would not be able to obtain employment and, therefore, may not have the same incentives to illegally enter the United States.

Employers must ask *all* job applicants (not just those surmised to be aliens) for documentation of employment eligibility to work in the United States. Appropriate documents include a US passport, birth certificate, or driver's license. It is only by asking all job applicants or employees for such documentation that employers can ensure that they are conforming to the requirements of the act. Employers are required to inspect verifying documents and establish employment eligibility within three business days of hiring an employee.

Scenario

The employer does not have to verify the authenticity of the documents presented. In fact, the 1990 amendments to the act specifically state that an employer may be wrongfully discriminating against an applicant if it refuses to honor documents that on their face reasonably appear to be genuine. Employers may also use a telephone verification system to check an applicant's alien registration number.

Employers must then fill out an "Employee Eligibility Verification Form," otherwise known as an I-9 form, which reports employee alienage status eligibility information to the Immigration and Naturalization Service. Employers must have I-9 forms on file for any employee hired after November 6, 1986.

To be held liable under the IRCA, the employer must have *knowledge* that the employee is an illegal alien. However, since the act imposes on the employer the duty to verify the legal employment status of all employees, failure to correctly verify such status may subject the employer to liability. In fact, the rule that establishes

EXHIBIT 20–2   Form I-9, INS

U.S. Department of Justice
Immigration and Naturalization Service

OMB No. 1115-0136
Employment Eligibility Verification

Please read instructions carefully before completing this form. The instructions must be available during completion of this form. **ANTI-DISCRIMINATION NOTICE. It is illegal to discriminate against work eligible individuals. Employers CANNOT specify which document(s) they will accept from an employee. The refusal to hire an individual because of a future expiration date may also constitute illegal discrimination.**

Section 1. Employee Information and Verification. To be completed and signed by employee at the time employment begins

Print Name: Last	First	Middle Initial	Maiden Name
Address *(Street Name and Number)*		Apt. #	Date of Birth *(month/day/year)*
City	State	Zip Code	Social Security #

I am aware that federal law provides for imprisonment and/or fines for false statements or use of false documents in connection with the completion of this form.	I attest, under penalty of perjury, that I am (check one of the following): ☐ A citizen or national of the United States ☐ A Lawful Permanent Resident (Alien # A _____) ☐ An alien authorized to work until ____/____/____ (Alien # or Admission # _____)
Employee's Signature	Date *(month/day/year)*

Preparer and/or Translator Certification. *(To be completed and signed if Section 1 is prepared by a person other than the employee.) I attest, under penalty of perjury, that I have assisted in the completion of this form and that to the best of my knowledge the information is true and correct.*

Preparer's/Translator's Signature	Print Name
Address *(Street Name and Number, City, State, Zip Code)*	Date *(month/day/year)*

Section 2. Employer Review and Verification. To be completed and signed by employer. Examine **one document from List A OR** examine **one document from List B and one from List C** as listed on the reverse of this form and record the title, number and expiration date, if any, of the document(s)

List A	OR	List B	AND	List C
Document title: _____		_____		_____
Issuing authority: _____		_____		_____
Document #: _____		_____		_____
Expiration Date *(if any)*: ___/___/___		___/___/___		___/___/___
Document #: _____				
Expiration Date *(if any)*: ___/___/___				

CERTIFICATION - I attest, under penalty of perjury, that I have examined the document(s) presented by the above-named employee, that the above-listed document(s) appear to be genuine and to relate to the employee named, that the employee began employment on *(month/day/year)* ___/___/___ **and that to the best of my knowledge the employee is eligible to work in the United States. (State employment agencies may omit the date the employee began employment).**

Signature of Employer or Authorized Representative	Print Name	Title
Business or Organization Name	Address *(Street Name and Number, City, State, Zip Code)*	Date *(month/day/year)*

Section 3. Updating and Reverification. To be completed and signed by employer

A. New Name *(if applicable)*	B. Date of rehire *(month/day/year) (if applicable)*

C. If employee's previous grant of work authorization has expired, provide the information below for the document that establishes current employment eligibility.

Document Title: _____   Document #: _____   Expiration Date (if any): ___/___/___

I attest, under penalty of perjury, that to the best of my knowledge, this employee is eligible to work in the United States, and if the employee presented document(s), the document(s) I have examined appear to be genuine and to relate to the individual.

Signature of Employer or Authorized Representative	Date *(month/day/year)*

Form I-9 (Rev. 11-21-91) N

EXHIBIT 20–2   Concluded

LISTS OF ACCEPTABLE DOCUMENTS

LIST A		LIST B		LIST C
Documents that Establish Both Identity and Employment Eligibility	**OR**	**Documents that Establish Identity**	**AND**	**Documents that Establish Employment Eligibility**

LIST A — Documents that Establish Both Identity and Employment Eligibility

1. U.S. Passport (unexpired or expired)

2. Certificate of U.S. Citizenship *(INS Form N-560 or N-561)*

3. Certificate of Naturalization *(INS Form N-550 or N-570)*

4. Unexpired foreign passport, with *I-551 stamp* or attached *INS Form I-94* indicating unexpired employment authorization

5. Alien Registration Receipt Card with photograph *(INS Form I-151 or I-551)*

6. Unexpired Temporary Resident Card *(INS Form I-688)*

7. Unexpired Employment Authorization Card *(INS Form I-688A)*

8. Unexpired Reentry Permit *(INS Form I-327)*

9. Unexpired Refugee Travel Document *(INS Form I-571)*

10. Unexpired Employment Authorization Document issued by the INS which contains a photograph *(INS Form I-688B)*

OR

LIST B — Documents that Establish Identity

1. Driver's license or ID card issued by a state or outlying possession of the United States provided it contains a photograph or information such as name, date of birth, sex, height, eye color, and address

2. ID card issued by federal, state, or local government agencies or entities provided it contains a photograph or information such as name, date of birth, sex, height, eye color, and address

3. School ID card with a photograph

4. Voter's registration card

5. U.S. Military card or draft record

6. Military dependent's ID card

7. U.S. Coast Guard Merchant Mariner Card

8. Native American tribal document

9. Driver's license issued by a Canadian government authority

For persons under age 18 who are unable to present a document listed above:

10. School record or report card

11. Clinic, doctor, or hospital record

12. Day-care or nursery school record

AND

LIST C — Documents that Establish Employment Eligibility

1. U.S. social security card issued by the Social Security Administration *(other than a card stating it is not valid for employment)*

2. Certification of Birth Abroad issued by the Department of State *(Form FS-545 or Form DS-1350)*

3. Original or certified copy of a birth certificate issued by a state, county, municipal authority or outlying possession of the United States bearing an official seal

4. Native American tribal document

5. U.S. Citizen ID Card *(INS Form I-197)*

6. ID Card for use of Resident Citizen in the United States *(INS Form I-179)*

7. Unexpired employment authorization document issued by the INS *(other than those listed under List A)*

Illustrations of many of these documents appear in Part 8 of the Handbook for Employers (M-274)

Form I-9 (Rev. 11-21-91) N

this requirement of knowledge specifically states that *knowing* "includes not only actual knowledge, but also knowledge which may be inferred through notice of certain facts and circumstances which would lead a person, through the exercise of reasonable care, to know about a certain condition."

Legal Status

At the time the IRCA was enacted, Congress recognized that, due to lack of enforcement of prior legislation, many illegal aliens were now living in the United States, had jobs, and raised families here. To locate and deport these aliens would be costly and largely inefficient. As a result, the IRCA offers legal documented status to aliens who illegally entered the United States prior to January 1, 1982, and continuously resided here since then. Dishonest reporting of alien status may result in a $2,000 fine against that untruthful individual and as long as five years in prison. However, it is critical to note that, in an effort to encourage the reporting of workplace discrimination and wage and hour violations, the investigation of these types of complaints may not include a review of an employee's I-9 form.[1]

Antidiscrimination Provisions

In contrast to Title VII, section 102 of IRCA *does* prohibit employers of four or more employees from discriminating against employees on the basis of their *citizenship* or *intended citizenship* when referring, recruiting, hiring, or discharging, and from hiring those not legally authorized for employment in the United States. However, IRCA also allows a preference for US citizens over legal aliens, and both groups have an evident preference over "unauthorized" or illegal aliens.

While aliens are guaranteed various rights pursuant to the Constitution, citizenship confers certain benefits only to those who are citizens and not to those who are legal aliens in the United States. For instance, while rights pursuant to the National Labor Relations Act and the Fair Labor Standards Act are available to citizens and aliens alike, government-provided benefits, such as Medicare and Medicaid, are limited to citizens.

Employers who may not be subject to Title VII's prohibitions because of their small size (Title VII only applies to employers of 15 or more employees) may still be sufficiently large to be covered by IRCA's antidiscrimination provisions; those employers with four or more employees may not discriminate on the basis of citizenship or intended citizenship. It is interesting to note that the National Labor Relations Board has held that illegal aliens are entitled to the same rights as legal work-

---

[1]Memorandum of Understanding Between Justice Department's Immigration and Naturalization Service and Labor Department's Employment Standards Administration, 227 DLR E-1, November 25, 1998.

EXHIBIT 20–3   Immigration Reform and Control Act of 1986

> Sec 274(a)(4) Notwithstanding any other provision of this section, it is not an unfair immigration-related employment practice for a person or entity to prefer to hire, recruit, or refer an individual who is a citizen or national of the United States over another individual who is an alien if the two individuals are equally qualified.

ers under the National Labor Relations Act and should be considered "employees" like all legal employees.

Fearing IRCA-related retribution in the form of enormous penalties to which an employer may be subjected for hiring illegal aliens, there have been complaints that some employers have been overzealous in complying with the IRCA. Applicants claim that they were discriminated against by employers merely because applicants were foreign looking or sounding and employers feared that the applicants were not authorized to work. This could be one of the backlashes nonnative citizens suffer as a result of stringent IRCA enforcement.

Also unlike Title VII, the Department of Justice, charged with prosecuting IRCA cases, has issued rules stipulating that intent to discriminate and knowledge are required to find an employer liable for a violation of section 102. Title VII does not require such intent. For example, if an employer maintains a policy that all workers must be available to work every day of the week, this policy, through no wrongful intent of the employer, may have the effect of discriminating against workers of certain religions who are not allowed to work on those days. No intent of the employer would need to be shown to find the employer liable for discriminatory practices under Title VII.

In IRCA cases, unlike in Title VII cases, the Department of Justice must show that the employer intended to discriminate. Consequently, IRCA claims are generally considered to be limited to disparate treatment, rather than disparate impact. Innocent or negligent discrimination is a complete defense to a claim of discrimination under IRCA.

Finally, unlike Title VII, the IRCA provides for an administrative hearing for violations. An administrative law judge may order the hiring or granting of other privileges and up to two years of back pay.

EXHIBIT 20–4

> IRCA's prohibition against employment discrimination:
>
> It is unfair immigration-related employment practice for a person or other entity to discriminate against any individual (other than an unauthorized alien) with respect to the hiring, recruitment or referral for a fee, of the individual for employment or the discharging of the individual from employment because of such individual's national origin, or in the case of a citizen or intending citizen . . . because of such individual's citizenship status.

League of United Latin American Citizens
v. Pasadena Independent School District
662 F.Supp. 443 (S.D. Tex. 1987)

Plaintiffs were three undocumented aliens, each of whom entered the United States prior to January 1, 1982. At the time of this action, they were eligible for legalization under the IRCA, but the legalization program had not yet been initiated. As a result, none of them had yet been able to obtain social security numbers. When they applied for employment as custodial workers at the Pasadena Independent School District, they inserted a fake social security number on the application. The District had a policy that falsifying information on an application would constitute grounds for refusal to hire or termination. This policy, however, was never communicated to the workers at the time of their application. The District terminated each of the employees as soon as the false statements were discovered.

McDonald, J.

When applied to those who are qualified for legalization, and who intend to become citizens, a policy of terminating undocumented aliens for no other reason than that they have given employers a false social security number constitutes an unfair immigration-related employment practice under §274B(a) of the Act. Only because of plaintiffs' citizenship status have they been unable to secure valid social security numbers.

Further, defendant's stated practice clearly contravenes the intent of Congress in enacting this law. In reporting the bill favorably to Congress, the House Judiciary Committee said of the antidiscrimination provision:

> The Committee does not believe barriers should be placed in the path of permanent residents and other aliens who are authorized to work and who are seeking employment, particularly when such aliens have evidenced an intent to become U.S. citizens. It makes no sense to admit immigrants and refugees to this country, require them to work and then allow employers to refuse to hire them because of their immigration (non-citizenship) status. Since Title VII does not provide any protection against employment discrimination based on

alienage or non-citizen status, the Committee is of the view that the instant legislation must do so.

Similarly, the Act would be manifestly unjust if it encouraged qualified aliens to come forward and to reveal their undocumented status only to have that very information serve as grounds for termination by employers. Under IRCA undocumented workers are given an opportunity to come forward, reveal their status, and apply for temporary residency, permanent residency and ultimately citizenship. The proposed application for legalization required that candidates list, among other things, their aliases, social security numbers used and employers.

It seems only logical that the INS will seek to verify this information with the employers of undocumented workers. Such verification will inform employers of falsifications that these workers have made, and, in the case of the School District, the result will be that the workers will be automatically terminated. In short, the application for legalization will lead to a revelation of falsifications made by undocumented aliens. Such revelations will in many cases lead to terminations.

Clearly, Congress did not intend to force qualified aliens to make the choice between exercising this right and risking termination of their employment. This Hobson's choice, however, is precisely the peril that defendant and others with similar policies would have the intended beneficiaries of this new law face.

Though not before the court, it is undoubtedly true that most employers have a policy of terminating employees who falsify their applications. Under ordinary circumstances, such a policy is justifiable and valid. It is an extraordinary circumstance, however, to have so many undocumented aliens working in the United States under false names and with invalid social security numbers. In the coming months and years, the administrative process established under the Act will have to reconcile many current employment practices with the new rights established under IRCA.

It is ordered that defendant immediately reinstate plaintiffs to the positions they occupied in defendant's employ immediately prior to their dismissal. Plaintiffs shall receive at least the same wages, benefits and other terms and conditions of employment that they received prior to their dismissals.

Case Questions

1. Why did the court seem to approve of the falsification? Couldn't the applicants simply have explained that they were undocumented aliens who were eligible for legalization, but who had not yet received social security numbers? Instead, they misled the employer and the employer has lost faith in their honesty.

2. What other solutions can be found to what seems to be a Catch-22?

3. Do you believe that the employees were fired for falsifying the information, or do you believe there were other reasons involved? Does the fact that the applicants were willing to make false statements of this type on their applications make them less trustworthy? Is this relevant to their ability to perform the jobs they applied for?

Where an employee believes that she or he has been discriminated against, the employer may identify a bona fide occupational qualification (BFOQ) that disqualified the employee or applicant from the position, raise, or privilege. There are two acceptable BFOQs statutorily allowed under IRCA:

1. English-language skill requirements that are reasonably necessary to the normal operation of the particular business or enterprise.

2. Or citizenship requirements specified by law, regulation, executive order, or government contracts, along with citizenship requirements that the attorney general determines to be essential for doing business with the government.

In connection with Reina's problem in scenario 1, she might not have a valid claim under IRCA for discrimination, since the reason for her termination is false representations on her application form, rather than her status as an undocumented alien. If she can show that the employer knew at the time of her termination that she lied about her social security number because she was an undocumented alien, and it fired her for her alien status, then she is more likely to have a claim.

Scenario

Employment of Foreign Nationals

Many companies hire foreign citizens for temporary or permanent employment in the United States based on specific need or availability. The United States maintains strict rules regarding the entry status of foreign nationals. For instance, permanent status is usually reserved for professional, service, technical, or managerial occupations. The Immigration Act of 1990 redefined quotas for entries for relatives, employment, and "diversity" visas. Quotas for job-based immigration were increased by the act from 54,000 to 140,000 per year. (Total immigration is limited to 700,000 per year until 1995 and 675,000 after 1995.) Work skills are emphasized in the immigration decision, so someone with a special skill is more likely to be granted a visa than one who duplicates skills readily available in the United States.

Traditionally, there were only two available categories for employment visas to work in the United States. The Immigration Act of 1990 established five new categories:

1. Priority workers, those with an extraordinary ability in the arts, sciences, education, business, or athletics, outstanding professors and researchers, and certain multinational executives and managers.

2. Members of professions with advanced degrees or aliens with exceptional ability.

3. Skilled workers, professionals, and other workers.

4. Special immigrants.

5. Employment-certain immigrants, who are seeking to immigrate to engage in a new commercial enterprise in which they will invest at least $1 million and that will create full-time employment for at least 10 citizens or permanent residents.

To apply for admission to the United States under these employment-related categories, an alien must first have a job offer as well as certification from the Department of Labor that (1) there are not sufficient US workers who are able, willing, qualified, and available at the place of intended employment and (2) the employment of the alien will not adversely affect the wages and working conditions of US workers similarly employed. This certification process takes about six months.

Enforcement

Five agencies are charged with the responsibility for enforcing IRCA. First, in connection with maintaining United States borders, inspecting the records that employers are required to keep regarding the citizenship status of their employees, and other measures designed to prevent illegal entry into the United States, the *Immigration and Naturalization Service* employs numerous agents to patrol borders and conduct inspections. These inspections may be the result of routine investigations by INS or as a result of a complaint filed with the INS by anyone else. Inspections are also conducted by the *Department of Labor* during its standard visit to employ-

Management Tips

- It is *your* responsibility to ensure the legal status of all of your employees. However, if you follow the requirements for determining status under IRCA, you are protected.

- You must request documentation from *all* employees, not just those you suspect to be of a different national origin or citizenship.

- Unlike Title VII, IRCA prohibits discrimination against workers because of their *citizenship or intended citizenship*.

- However, you *are* allowed to favor US citizens over legal aliens in employment decisions.

- Remember: You are statutorily allowed two BFOQs under IRCA—English language skill requirements and citizenship requirements.

- In verifying citizenship, do not request additional information or different information than the I-9 form requires. Adhering to the form provides the employer with a safe harbor from claims of discrimination in this area. In addition, wait to request the information and to fill out the forms until the employee has started work. In this way, you are protected from claims of discrimination that might arise on the basis of information you can gather from these documents (such as age, national origin, and so on). If you didn't have the information, you couldn't have made a decision on that basis.

ers to ensure compliance with equal opportunity and wage hour laws. The *National Labor Relations Board* is charged with investigating and prosecuting unfair labor practices. The *Department of Justice,* through the office of the attorney general, decides questions of legalization of alien workers and creates the procedures enforced by the INS and the Department of Labor during their investigations.

Finally, the *Secretary of Labor* deals with certifications of employees who fall under the category of foreign seasonal agricultural workers. These workers are allowed temporary entry to the United States for the purpose of working in agriculture on a temporary basis when crops so demand. Other agencies, such as the EEOC or the Occupational Safety and Health Administration, may become involved in an IRCA issue, depending on the type of employment practice at issue.

Summary

- To ensure that your company is complying with the complex procedures required by the IRCA, it is important to *identify one individual* who will be responsible for this compliance.

- This individual would be responsible for complying with and maintaining the I-9 forms, ensuring that no potential for discrimination exists in the hiring procedures, requirements, or job descriptions, and complying with regulations regarding the hiring of foreign nationals and coordinating their employment.

Chapter-End Questions

1. Noemi Romo, an unauthorized alien, was terminated by Todd Corporation in 1987, one month before the IRCA amnesty program went into effect whereby she would have been allowed to file an application for citizenship. Romo claims that she was discriminated against in violation of IRCA, because she was an "intending citizen." Todd, however, was under the mistaken belief that sanctions had already gone into effect for the employment of unauthorized aliens. Romo files an action claiming discrimination based on citizenship status. (*U.S. v. Todd Corp.,* 900 F.2d 164 (9th Cir. 1990).)

2. Three Latino employees were terminated by Sears because they did not possess green cards. They consequently filed an action against Sears, charging discrimination. (*EEOC v. Sears,* 885 F.2d 875 (9th Cir. 1989).)

3. The US Postal Service had a regulation that prohibited the employment of temporary resident aliens. Does this violate the IRCA? (*Tovar v. United States Postal Service,* 3 F.3d 1271 (9th Cir. 1993).)

4. Is a policy of terminating undocumented aliens for no other reason than they have given a false social security number an unfair practice under IRCA?

5. American Friends Service Committee (AFSC) is a Quaker organization employing more than 400 employees. AFSC does not comply with the I-9 form requirement and will not ask for identity and work authorization, because it believes that this practice violates the religious practices and beliefs of its members. Those beliefs require that AFSC "welcome—that they help and not show hostility to—the sojourner, stranger, the poor, and the dispossessed in their midst. They cannot deprive them of work simply because they may be strangers in this land." Do you believe that this is an adequate defense to a claim of noncompliance? (*American Friends Service Committee Corp. v. Thronburgh,* 941 F.2d 808 (9th Cir. 1991).)

6. The INS issued a citation to Big Bear Market, listing a number of recordkeeping violations, including 183 instances where no I-9s were maintained, and imposing fines. The company attempted to correct the violations but, due to a clerical oversight, 135 violations remained. Three months later, the INS returned and discovered the uncorrected errors; Big Bear was served with additional fines and protested, claimed that it had already been fined in connection with these violations and that it would again attempt to correct them. Are the additional fines enforceable? (*Big Bear Market v. INS,* 913 F.2d 561 754 (9th Cir. 1990).)

7. After an INS inspection, Mester Manufacturing received a citation for a violation of I-9 requirements in connection with 11 workers. Mester continues to employ these individuals for an additional two weeks and received a second citation and fine. How long would be a reasonable time to expect action from an employer and what would be the factors that you would look to? (*Mester Mfg. Co. v. INS,* 879 F.2d 561 (9th Cir. 1989).)

8. New York has a citizenship requirement for employment as a state trooper. New York argues that this was necessary because of the broad discretionary powers of the police in the areas of arrest, search, and seizure. Do they therefore fit within the category of important nonelected officials who participate directly in the execution of public policy? (*Foley v. Connelie,* 435 U.S. 291 (1978).)

9. Is this same argument (see question 8) relevant to public school teachers who teach government? The schools would argue that the teachers play a critical role in developing the students' attitude regarding government and an understanding of the role of citizens in our society. (*Ambach v. sNorwich,* 441 U.S. 68 (1979).)

10. Should an undocumented alien be considered an "employee" under the Fair Labor Standards Act so they can argue for minimum wage? (*Patel v. Quality Inn South,* 846 F.2d 700 (11th Cir. 1988).)

21 WORKERS' COMPENSATION

S C E N A R I O S

S C E N A R I O   1

Shelly slips and falls on a puddle of oil left by her co-worker Jeanne on the floor of the restaurant where they are both servers. Shelly is injured and incurs medical bills and three weeks away from work due to the fall. Betty, the restaurant owner, refuses to contribute to Shelly's medical bills or pay her for the time she was off, because Betty says the accident was caused by Jeanne, not Betty. Does Shelly have any recourse?

S C E N A R I O   2

After Manuel goes into a diabetic coma while at work, it is determined that he must stay in the hospital for a few weeks. Manuel files a workers' compensation claim. Is it allowed?

S C E N A R I O   3

Toni is injured on the job and is absent from work as a result. Toni's workers' compensation payments do not cover her outstanding bills, which have increased because of her injuries. The doctor tells Toni that her condition would be improved if she did not have to worry so much about her bills. Based on this, Toni requests an increase in her weekly workers' compensation benefit check. Is Toni's request granted?

Statutory Basis

> Compensation for temporary partial disability. Except as otherwise provided [herein], where the disability to work resulting from the injury is partial in character but temporary in quality, the employer shall pay or cause to be paid to the employee a weekly benefit equal to two-thirds of the difference between the average weekly wage before the injury and the average weekly wage the employee is able to earn thereafter, but not more than $233 per week for a period not exceeding 350 weeks from the date of injury. O.C.G.A. 34-9-262.
>
> "Injury" or "personal injury" means only injury by accident arising out of and in the course of the employment and shall not . . . include a disease in any form except where it results naturally and unavoidably from the accident. . . . "Injury . . . shall not include injury caused by the willful act of a third person directed against an employee for reasons personal to such employee. O.C.G.A." [Georgia Statutes Annotated] 34-9-1.

A Remedial History

Suppose you work in an office and one morning you come in, turn on the computer, and you receive an electrical shock that severely jolts you, nearly knocking you off your chair.

Think of the repercussions of this, financial and otherwise. Now imagine adding this: suing your employer to recover for the losses you suffered as a result of the injury on the job. Among other things, you must find a suitable attorney; find a means of paying the attorney at a time when you are least able, because of your injury; take time away from work to deal with the attorney and your injuries; wait for a court date, which may be a year or more away; and have the attorney gather evidence to support your claim that the employer is responsible for your injury.

When you finally get to court, you are subject to the results of the more formidable resources that the employer can probably afford, and also defenses that would prevent the employer from being liable for your injuries. Among other things, the employer may allege it was your **negligence** that caused the injury, or that it was the fault of some other employee.

Negligence
Failure to meet the appropriate standard of care for avoiding unreasonable risk of harm to others.

In the end, after all of your time, energy, and expense, you may lose. Or you may get much less of a judgment than you anticipated. Just when you need it most, you could also lose your job because you sued your employer. You would lose benefits to which your job may entitle you, such as health insurance.

Bleak scenario, isn't it? That is the reason for a system of state and federal workers' compensation statutes. That scenario was the reality in the workplace before such **no-fault** statutes were enacted to address primarily the issues of lost wages and medical expenses incurred in work-related injuries. The main reason for the statutes was to reduce the troublesome scenario the employee had to go through at such a difficult time. But the statutes are not unbalanced. There are benefits for employers also.

No-fault
Liability for injury imposed regardless of fault.

With workers' compensation statutes employees trade off potentially higher damages awarded after litigation, against the certainty of smaller benefits provided immediately. Also included is the guarantee of protection from employer retaliation for filing workers' compensation claims and the employer's inability to use the usual defenses against the employee to avoid liability for workplace injuries. The employee gets less in terms of benefits; but what there is, is certain if the workers' compensation requirements are met. The employer gains freedom from lawsuits for workplace injuries and the certainty of how much such injuries will cost them.

The overall effect is intended to make the workplace more efficient and to assist in the marketplace, since increased accidents mean lost time and lower production. Since workers' compensation statutes are remedial in nature, they are usually broadly construed to permit recovery where possible.

For the most part the system works. However, it is not without flaws. A common problem employers have is that they may routinely respond to inquiries from the workers' compensation office without giving them the closer inspection they deserve. Contributions for larger employers are based on their injury record, so premium contributions, which must be paid by the employer, increase when claims are filed. Without investigation of claims, unwarranted claims slip through, and this unnecessarily increases the employer's contribution. However, it is the experience of the industry as a whole that serves as the basis for premiums; thus, this may not be as crucial for smaller companies. Employer attention to workplace safety can greatly reduce accidents and resulting premiums and claims.

EXHIBIT 21–1   Employee Participation in Safety Programs Cuts Workers' Compensation Costs

---

By making employees responsible for a safe workplace, a General Electric plant in Columbia, MD, saved its plant, which varies from 850 to 1500 employees, $1.5 million in workers' compensation claims in a three-year period, according to John A. Jenkins, former manager of safety programs at the Columbia plant.

The Columbia General Electric plant manufactures electric ranges, and employees spend their days handling sheet metal parts. Injuries range from cuts, metal slivers and foreign substances in the eye to carpal tunnel syndrome. The system reduces costs and at the same time gives employees a sense of ownership in developing a safer work force.

Perhaps the most interesting feature of the safety program was the issuance of 2000 business-size safety warning cards used by employees. When a worker sees a coworker doing something unsafe, the worker silently hands that person a card and walks away. The card states that the recipient was observed performing an unsafe practice and should keep the card until he observes someone else working dangerously. At that point, he should present the card to that person. The card also states "P.S. I hope I don't get this back." As a result of the card program, employees are getting the message that they are responsible for their coworkers as well as themselves.

Each shop also has a safety team that works with the people in that section. Each team has a leader. The team is instructed in how to conduct complete walk-through inspections of their work areas with the same thoroughness of OSHA inspections. They look in, around and under work stations and conveyors, checking for unsafe practices and safety deficiencies. The team then makes a list of corrective actions for its area. Employees are assigned responsibility for the actions and time frames for completion. All corrective actions are then reviewed at a meeting with the plant manager, his staff and safety team.

Reprinted with the permission of *HRMagazine* published by the Society for Human Resource Management, Alexandria, VA.

A common source of dispute in workers' compensation cases arises from the two primary requirements of the workers' compensation statutes; that is, whether the injured person is an employee and whether the injury arose out of, or in the course of, employment. Both of these will be addressed in the chapter.

Workers' compensation is big business. An employer must be vigilant about providing a safe workplace and training so preventable workplace accidents are minimized. Some states are taking this very seriously. The California Corporate Criminal Liability Act may impose fines of up to $1 million on corporations for failure to notify employees of a "serious concealed danger" in the workplace. In addition, managers may also be fined and criminally prosecuted if they actually knew of a workplace condition that created a substantial probability of death, great bodily harm, or serious exposure to a hazardous substance. Again, employers should also keep a close watch on claims to ensure that only valid claims are permitted.

General Statutory Scheme

Schedule of benefits
The amounts and duration of payments a state provides for injuries under workers' compensation laws.

Workers' compensation plans basically provide compensation for time away from work and medical expenses related to on-the-job injuries. Employers pay into the system, which is administered by a state workers' compensation agent. Each state has a **schedule of benefits,** which tells how long an employee is to receive benefits (generally for a certain number of weeks) and the amount of benefits for a particular injury. The schedules also provide for the employee's death, or loss of the use of a limb. Employers usually arrange the payment of their workers' compensation contributions by taking out insurance or self-insuring. Self-insuring involves employers paying into a private fund of their own, while taking out insurance may be done through private or state insurance policies.

The amounts and time periods of benefit coverage vary from state to state. Nonpermanent injury benefit schedule amounts are usually based on some percentage of the employee's weekly wages, as demonstrated by the statute provided at the beginning of the chapter. There is a limitation on the amount to be received; and, once it is reached, the employer's statutory duty is fulfilled. Generally, in exchange for this immediate nonlitigated payment benefit, the employee does not sue the employer. However, there are states where employees may (under limited circumstances) sue the employer in addition to receiving workers' compensation benefits.

For instance, Florida has determined that, in sexual harassment cases, the workers' compensation statute will not be the exclusive remedy, because of the overwhelming public policy against workplace sexual harassment. In *The Ramada Inn Surfside and Adjusto, Inc. v. Swanson,*[1] the court, referring to *Byrd v. Richardson-Greenshields Securities, Inc.,* stated that "[a]pplying the exclusivity rule of workers' compensation to preclude any and all tort liability effectively would abrogate this policy, undermine the Florida Human Rights Act, and flout Title VII of the Civil Rights Act of 1964."

In concluding that workers' compensation should no longer be the exclusive remedy for workplace sexual harassment injuries, the court noted that

> workers' compensation is directed essentially at compensating a worker for lost resources and earnings. This is a vastly different concern than is addressed by the sexual harassment laws. While workplace injuries rob a person of resources, sexual harassment robs the person of dignity and self esteem. Workers' compensation addresses purely economic injury; sexual harassment laws are concerned with a much more intangible injury to personal rights. To the extent these injuries are separable, we believe that they both should be, and can be, enforced separately.

Workers' compensation statutes in some form or another have now been adopted in all states. A small minority of states have made them optional but, in doing so, generally prohibit employers who do not become a part of the state's workers' compensation plan from using the common law defenses if the employer is sued by the employee for negligence.

There is also federal coverage under other legislation, including the Federal Employers' Liability Act of 1908. This act limited the common law defenses an

---

[1]560 So. 2d 300 (Ct. App. Fl., 1st Dist. 1990).

Exhibit 21–2   Workers' Compensation Hot Issues in the '90s: Reducing Workers' Compensation Costs

In order to shed some light on the issues surrounding workers' compensation in the '90s, Commerce Clearing House interviewed Mr. Richard Victor, executive director of the Workers' Compensation Research Institute—a think tank specializing in public policy issues posed by workers' compensation.

CCH: What are some tips you can give employers to reduce their workers' compensation costs?

Mr. Victor: A balanced and effective cost containment program stands on three legs. One is to prevent injuries. The second is effective claims management because some injuries are inevitable no matter how good an employer's preventive program is. Workers should be brought back to work as expeditiously as possible. Sometimes that means creating bona fide work opportunities for employees who are not yet physically able to do their full jobs. But getting individuals back to the workplace tends to get them moving in the right direction. Also, containing medical costs is part of good claims administration.

The third leg is an often overlooked one, which is working with other employers, insurers and organized labor to improve the environment in which workers' compensation operates. The legislative and administrative system is workers' compensation. Increasingly in states, there are active workers' compensation reform efforts put together by coalitions of employers, insurers, and representatives of organized labor to improve the cost effectiveness and fairness of workers' compensation. Employers can do the best job of prevention and claims administration possible, but if the rules of the game are not cost-efficient and fair, then opportunities for cost savings are missed. (www. safetypays.com)

Reproduced with permission from *CCH Workers' Compensation Law Reports,* published and copyrighted by CCH Incorporated.

employer could use, rather than replacing virtually the entire common law approach to on-the-job injuries with a no-fault system. Later, the Federal Employee's Compensation Act in 1916 provided a workers' compensation scheme for US civil employees. The Longshore and Harbor Workers Service Compensation Act supplements state workers' compensation laws by providing benefits for employees in maritime employment.

Defenses

As previously mentioned, before workers' compensation statutes were enacted, the usual scheme of recovery for on-the-job injuries was for employees to sue the employer for negligence. The employer could defend by showing that the employer was not negligent or that:

• The employee was **contributorily negligent** by doing some act that fell below the reasonable standard appropriate for the circumstances, thereby contributing to the injury.

• The employee voluntarily assumed the risk (**assumption of the risk**) by knowingly engaging in an act that the employee knew could result in injury.

Contributory negligence
The injured party's injuries are due, in part, to the injured party's failure to meet a standard of reasonable care.

Assumption of the risk
Taking a chance that a known potentially harmful situation will not cause injury.

Fellow servant doctrine
Injury to an employee on the job is caused by the negligence of another employee.

Common law defenses
Contributory negligence, voluntary assumption of the risk, and fellow servant doctrine theories that could be used by an employer to prevent liability from attaching, before workers' compensation statutes were instituted.

• Or that the accident was the fault of some other employee's misdoings (**fellow servant doctrine**).

These are **common law defenses** to negligence. By contrast, workers' compensation laws impose liability on a no-fault basis. The employee who is injured on the job and meets the statutory requirements is able to file a workers' compensation claim and collect benefits, regardless of who is at fault. Thus, in opening scenario 1, the employer's defense of the fellow servant doctrine is of no avail in avoiding liability for the employee's injury. The employee may file a workers' compensation claim and collect, regardless of who was at fault.

Farmer v. Heard demonstrates what happens when an employee sues an employer for negligence rather than filing for workers' compensation. Keep in mind that none of the contentions in *Farmer* would be relevant in a workers' compensation claim.

Scenario

FARMER V. HEARD
844 S.W. 2d 425 (Ky. 1992)

Employee filed a negligence suit against the employer for injuries sustained when the employer did not warn employee not to disconnect a tractor from a loaded feed wagon. The court held for the employer, finding no negligence by the employer, and finding that the employee should have known of the obvious risk.

Shroder, J.

This is a tort action filed by a farm employee against his employer, the farm owner, for injuries sustained during the course of his employment. The trial court dismissed the employee's negligence claim by summary judgment on the ground that there was no showing that the injury was caused by the negligence of the employer. We affirm.

Heard is a self-employed farmer who operates his own farm. Farmer was employed and worked on Heard's farm from November 1, 1988 through June 1, 1989. During his seven-month employment, Farmer's job involved feeding and moving hogs, which included loading and unloading a feed wagon on a daily basis.

The feed wagon had four wheels aligned toward the wagon's center and its front weighted so

that the tongue would naturally sit down upon a jack located on the front of the wagon when unattached from a tractor. It should also be noted that the wagon being used by Farmer on the date of the accident was of a type designed for the purpose for which it was being used.

The day before the accident, Farmer had left the feed wagon attached to a tractor to be automatically loaded with feed during the evening. The following morning Farmer returned to find the wagon loaded but unhitched from the tractor. A co-employee, Mr. Bratcher, while attempting to hitch the wagon to the tractor, struck the tongue of the wagon with the tractor draw bar causing the wagon to tip backward and rest on its back end in a stationary position. In an attempt to set the wagon upright, Farmer climbed onto the tongue as Mr. Bratcher was lifting from the back of the wagon, but they were unable to set the wagon upright. As Mr. Farmer started to climb down from the tongue of the wagon, he slipped and fell, injuring his knee. Farmer's primary contention was that Heard had a duty to instruct his employees not to disconnect the tractor from the feed wagon when it was loaded.

Farmer contends that the trial court erred in granting summary judgment because a jury could reasonably find that Heard was negligent for failing to instruct his employees about the feed wagon and further, that Heard's alleged negligence was a proximate, substantial cause of Farmer's injuries. An employer is only under a duty to furnish an employee a reasonably safe place to work and is not an insurer of the employee's safety. The liability of an employer rests upon the assumption that the employer has a better and more comprehensive knowledge that the employees, and [the employer's liability] ceases to be applicable where the employee's means of knowledge of the dangers to be incurred is equal to that of the employer.

Here it is uncontroverted that Heard was not on the premises when the incident occurred, was not operating the tractor which caused the wagon to tip backward, nor did he instruct Farmer to climb upon the tongue of the wagon. Farmer also was familiar with the wagon, and stated that the wagon was in good working order and had no defects. More importantly, however, the evidence shows Farmer was not injured when the wagon tipped backward, but rather, as Farmer concedes, it was his voluntary act that led to his fall and resulting injuries. Consequently, we believe it was Farmer, not his employer, Heard, who was in a better position to appreciate that if he slipped and fell from the stationary feed wagon, an injury might result.

Farmer further argues that *Taylor v. Kennedy* [Ky. App., 700 S.W.2d 415 (1985)] controls the outcome of the case at bar. In Taylor, decomposed silage had been allowed to accumulate on the steps of a silo and plaintiff alleged that this hazard

directly caused him to slip and fall. In that case, due to conflicting testimony, the jury could determine if the employer was negligent for allowing the silage to remain, as it could be the cause of the injury. In this case however, there was no hazardous situation which injured Farmer. Farmer was not injured due to the wagon being unsteady or when the wagon tipped backwards, and there was no foreign matter on the wagon tongue to contribute to the hazard. Farmer created his own hazard when he climbed up on the tongue of the wagon, admittedly knowing that he had manure on his shoes, and fell from the wagon.

We further agree with the lower court that an unhooked wagon or a wagon in an upturned position does not present any hidden danger, but even if it did, since any danger was obvious under the facts of this case, Heard cannot be held liable since Farmer voluntarily exposed himself to such danger. Accordingly, we conclude Heard did not breach any duty and cannot be held responsible for an injury resulting from Farmer's voluntary action which created his own hazard.

Assuming arguendo that Heard had breached some duty to warn fellow employees as Farmer alleges, we believe Heard's failure to instruct would nonetheless be too remote to constitute the proximate cause of Farmer's injury. Before Farmer fell from the wagon tongue, the wagon was unhooked by another employee. Thereafter, the wagon was struck and tipped backwards by yet another co-employee. Only then did Farmer decide to climb on the wagon tongue with manure on his shoes and fail to hold on while stepping down. Given the chain of events outlined above, we conclude alleged failure to instruct was too remote and was not the proximate cause of Farmer's injuries. AFFIRMED.

Case Questions

1. Why do you think the employee sued the employer rather than filing a workers' compensation claim?

2. What effect do you think it has on the outcome that the injury was caused in part

because of manure on the employee's shoes, a common part of farm work with hogs?

3. Could the employer have done something to help avoid this injury? Explain.

Filing Claims

When an employee is injured on the job, the employee generally notifies the employer and files an injury report with the agency administering the state's workers' compensation system. The employer's insurance company generally handles it from there. If the employee is not satisfied with the amount to be received or the length of benefits, the employee may file a claim with the state agency and follow its procedures for challenging benefit decisions. Agencies generally have a system of quasi-judicial hearings to determine claims within the agency, and, if the employee is not satisfied, the case can be taken to court. Of course, in this event, much of the advantage of the workers' compensation system is lost, since one of the greatest advantages is quickly resolving claims without litigation.

Workers' compensation statutes generally contain antiretaliation provisions, which protect employees who file claims from being terminated or otherwise adversely affected as a result. In the absence of the antiretaliation provisions, if the jurisdiction is an employment-at-will state, the employer would be able to terminate the employee for filing a claim. However, antiretaliation provisions prohibit employers from doing so.

Who Is Covered

Not every employee is covered by workers' compensation statutes. Generally, agricultural and domestic workers are not. Also, depending on the state, there may be no coverage for state and local employees, charity employees, employees of small businesses, or casual employees. As the case below demonstrates, the issue of who the law applies to can become quite complicated.

GRACZYK V. WORKERS' COMPENSATION APPEALS BOARD
184 Cal. App.3d 997 (Cal. Ct. App. 1986)

A student athlete receiving financial aid at California State University at Fullerton was injured while playing varsity football for CSUF. One of the issues at trial was whether he was an employee of CSUF within the meaning of the California Labor Code. The Workers' Compensation judge found the player to be an employee of CSUF, but the decision was reversed upon reconsideration. The player appealed, contending that he should be considered an employee and thus covered under the workers' compensation statute. The Court of Appeals disagreed and held he was not an employee for purposes of the statute.

Lillie, J.

In applicant's second year at CSUF, he received an athletic scholarship in the amount of $1600 a year, payable in monthly installments. The athletic coach determined recipients of athletic scholarships based on athletic progress and value to the football team; and the scholarship funds were raised by alumni and business groups. Applicant had intended to continue playing on the football team even had he not received the athletic scholarship. The scholarship was for a full year and could not be terminated unless the recipient quit the team, dropped out of school, or failed to maintain academic standards.

The scholarship was intended to meet the costs of room and board, but there was no control over the manner in which the recipient spent it. Applicant understood that it was to be used for student expenses, and he so used it.

California's workers' compensation law is a statutory system enacted pursuant to constitutional grant of plenary power to the Legislature to establish a complete and exclusive system of workers' compensation. The right to workers' compensation benefits is "wholly statutory," and is not derived from the common law. This statutory right is exclusive of all other statutory and common law remedies, and substitutes a new system of rights and obligations for the common law rules governing liability of employers for injuries to their employees.

In enacting the workers' compensation law as an expression of the police power pursuant to the constitutional grant of plenary power, the Legislature defined employee status and defines persons excluded therefrom. An employee excluded from compensation benefits retains his right to maintain a civil action for damages against his employer.

The Legislature amended [the law saying that] "Employee" excludes [any] person, other than a regular employee, participating in sports or athletics who receives no compensation for such participation other than the use of athletic equipment, uniforms, transportation, travel, meals, lodgings, or other expenses incidental thereto. In 1981, the Legislature further amended [the law] by adding present subdivision (k) which provides that "'Employee' excludes . . . [any] student participating as an athlete in amateur sporting events sponsored by any public agency, public or private nonprofit college, university or school, who receives no remuneration for such participation other than [the above]."

The state has a significant, if not a compelling interest in defining the employer–employee status, such status in fact being the very cornerstone of the Legislature's enactment of a complete and exclusive workers' compensation system in exercise of its police power pursuant to the constitutional grant of plenary power. AFFIRMED.

Case Questions

1. In your view, should the statute have included student athletes rather than excluding them from coverage? Explain.

2. The court said that those excepted from the workers' compensation statute could still bring suit under civil law. Is this satisfactory as a course of action? Why or why not?

3. Does it matter to you that the financial aid went directly to the student to do with as he pleased, rather than going directly to pay for school? Should it change the outcome? Explain.

Covered Injuries

For covered employees, workers' compensation statutes apply to accidental personal injuries arising out of or in the course of employment. Accidental means the injury was not caused by someone's intentional tortious act, and the injury was not one of long standing. This is why Manuel's diabetes in opening scenario 2 would not be covered by workers' compensation. Since this is remedial legislation, personal injuries are broadly defined to include physical and mental injuries and diseases.

Sometimes this brings about surprising results. For instance, employees have been covered for what courts refer to as "psychic" (mental) injuries (requiring no physical manifestation) for situations as diverse as:

• A bus driver who happened on the scene of an accident in which there were fatalities and the driver had to stay until help arrived.

• A nurse becoming depressed after she heard the shots of a murder–suicide coming from a hospital room where she had just closed the door.

• An employee suffering stress from being wrongfully arrested for stealing from the employer.

On the other hand, there are limitations. Recovery of workers' compensation benefits were ***not*** allowed when

• a prison guard experienced stress from being held hostage in a prison riot.

• an employee wanted his high consumer debt, which resulted from the decrease in income due to his injuries, to be considered part of the rehabilitation costs, because his doctor said it would aid in the employee's rehabilitation for him not to have to worry about his indebtedness. This is the basis for opening scenario 3.

• an employee's back scar was not exposed to view.

• a husband's violinist wife was raped and murdered on the roof of the theater by a stagehand during an opera intermission.

• an employee choked to death on a peanut butter sandwich she brought from home and was required to eat at the premises during lunch break.

• a striking employee had a heart attack while walking a picket line.

Occupational diseases have not been covered as readily as other accidental injuries, because of the difficulty of fitting them into the traditional common-law notions of negligence and assigning liability, and, of course, because of the financial consequences to employers. One of the reasons employers are assigned to pay the premiums for workers' compensation is because on-the-job injuries are considered to be a cost of doing business, which the employer can readily pass on to the consumer. The theory is that occupational disease costs would be much too expensive to do so.

In recent years, there have also been requests for coverage for workplace sexual harassment. As you saw in Chapter 8 an employer is already subject to potential liability from permitting sexual harassment to occur. In addition to coverage under Title VII and applicable tort law, employees can also file a workers' compensation claim. It is generally an exclusive remedy, and, if the employee chooses to take this route, which many are now doing, the tort and Title VII case cannot also be brought. However, recall that some states, such as Florida, have determined that it is not the exclusive remedy. In the case below, the court explains why sexual harassment claims would be permitted under workers' compensation statutes.

THE RAMADA INN SURFSIDE AND ADJUSTCO, INC. V. SWANSON
560 So. 2d 300 (Ct. App. Fl., 1st Dist 1990)

Employee received temporary total disability and payment of medical bills for treatment for her psychiatric condition related to sexual harassment on the job. The employer appealed the decision, arguing that employee's emotional problems were not caused by the sexual intercourse with her supervisor. The compensation was allowed to stand.

Joanos, J.

The incident which forms the predicate for this appeal took place on March 30, 1988. In January 1988, employee was interviewed and subsequently hired for the position of lounge supervisor of The Ramada Inn Surfside. Mr. Darold Schonsheck, general manager of Ramada Inn Surfside, conducted the interview and made the hiring decision.

It is undisputed that (1) Mr. Schonsheck drove to employee's apartment to offer her the job; (2) Mr. Schonsheck frequently went to an eating establishment near employee's apartment; (3) employee and Mr. Schonsheck went out together for a drink after a Super Bowl party at the Ramada Inn; (4) Mr. Schonsheck went with employee to the liquor room at the Ramada Inn where employee was taking inventory; (5) on February 20, 1988, Mr. Schonsheck sent employee white roses for her birthday; (6) in March 1988, Mr. Schonsheck kissed employee on the lips in Ramada Inn elevator; (7) on March 30, 1988, Mr. Schonsheck engaged in sexual intercourse with employee; and (8) prior to employee's employment, Mr. Schonsheck had been involved in a sexual relationship with the former Ramada Inn lounge supervisor.

Employee's version of these events is that Mr. Schonsheck made her the recipient of unwelcome attentions and offensive touchings of her person. According to Mr. Schonsheck's version, employee was extremely flirtatious and generally sexually aggressive. The incident which is the focus of this appeal took place on March 30, 1988.

Employee testified that, on that date, she was working in the Ramada Inn lounge when Mr. Schonsheck told her he was going to view another hotel property as a possible business investment, and that she should meet him there to look over the property. Employee and Mr. Schonsheck drove to the hotel in separate cars. Employee said that, as she was looking over the restaurant and lounge area, she saw Mr. Schonsheck enter and walk over to the front desk. Mr. Schonsheck then walked over to employee, and at his suggestion, she accompanied him to inspect one of the guest rooms. The sexual intercourse which is the subject of the second issue took place in the hotel guest room. Mr. Schonsheck's account of the incident was that employee voluntarily drove her own car to the hotel where the sexual encounter occurred, and that she was the sexual aggressor.

Employee vehemently denied Mr. Schonsheck's allegation that she initiated the sexual activity, and denied that the sexual encounter took place with her consent.

Various witnesses testified that after March 30, 1988, employee became very tense and nervous, and began drinking on the job. Between June 16, 1988 through mid-September 1988, employee was hospitalized on three separate occasions for psychiatric treatment. Dr. Handel, employee's treating psychiatrist, diagnosed her condition as a severe major depressive disorder and adjustment disorder.

The doctor's testimony reflected that the initial history he received from employee indicated a possible suicide attempt in November 1987, an unhappy childhood with an alcoholic father, a divorce in the family, an unhappy marriage, and possible alcohol abuse. Although he had been referred to this background information, Dr. Handel's testimony reflects that he was still of the opinion that the condition for which he treated employee in 1988 was related to her obsession about returning to her job, and the conflict she felt due to the sexual encounter she had had with her boss. When asked whether employee's prior psychiatric problems could have caused her emotional disorder, Dr. Handel stated that the unfortunate episode of sexual intercourse at work played a greater role in employee's depression, and appeared to have prompted her three hospitalizations.

The employer and carrier first challenge the judge's finding that Dr. Handel's testimony causally related employee's emotional difficulties to her sexual contacts with her supervisor. Although section 440.02(1), Florida Statutes (1987), expressly proscribes workers' compensation benefits for "[a] mental injury due to fright or excitement only," severe work-related emotional disorders may be compensable where it is shown that the emotional disorder was occasioned by actual physical impact or trauma at the workplace.

Because we find the record supports the judge's finding that Dr. Handel concluded that the employee's emotional disorder was caused primarily by the sexual episode with her supervisor, we reject the employer and carrier's contention that employee's emotional condition and attendant hospitalization was caused by factors unrelated to the workplace sexual encounter. An examination of Dr. Handel's testimony in its entirety, demonstrates that although the opinions expressed are not set forth in a unified manner, Dr. Handel did, in fact, find that employee's emotional problems and three hospitalizations were caused primarily by the sexual contact with Mr. Schonsheck, within a reasonable degree of psychiatric probability.

The employer and carrier's second challenge is directed to the judge's finding that the sexual intercourse took place without employee's permission. We note at the onset that as the trier of fact, it is the function of the judge of compensation claims to determine the credibility of all witnesses, including the employee. In a similar vein, this court is not permitted to substitute its judgment for that of the judge with regard to a factual determination, so long as the judge's findings are supported by competent substantial evidence.

It is obvious that, in the context of this case, resolution of the voluntariness of the sexual episode turns upon the judge's evaluation of the credibility of employee and her supervisor. Here, the judge accepted employee's account of the incident and rejected that of Mr. Schonsheck. Since the judge had the opportunity to observe the demeanor of both witnesses during their testimony, her ability to assess the relative credibility of each is superior to our consideration of the transcribed testimony. In such circumstances, we decline to disturb the judge's factual determination that the sexual intercourse took place without the employee's permission.

Benefits are available under the Workers' Compensation Act for "injuries arising out of and in the course of employment." For an injury to arise out of and in the course of employment, "it must occur within the period of employment, at a place where the employee may reasonably be, and while he is reasonably fulfilling the duties of employment, or engaging in something incidental to it." In other words, "[t]o be compensable, an injury must arise out of employment in the sense of causation and be in the course of employment in the sense of continuity of time, space, and circumstances."

The record in the instant case reflects that the sexual encounter between employee and her supervisor arose out of and occurred during her employment as lounge supervisor of Ramada Inn Surfside. First, the episode occurred during the period of employment, in that it happened during employee's normal working hours. Second, the incident happened at the hotel where employee's supervisor directed her to go. Finally, the incident

transpired while employee was reasonably fulfilling the duties of her employment, in the sense that she purportedly was to assist her supervisor in the evaluation of a hotel property for possible investment purposes. For the foregoing reasons, we AFFIRM.

Case Questions

1. Do you think the court's decision is sound? Why or why not?

2. What do you think the employer could have done to avoid this?

3. Does this case tell you anything about how workplace decisions and potential liability claims go hand in hand?

Workers' compensation claims bring up diverse and interesting issues, such as whether criminal assault in the course of employment is something an employer is responsible for, or whether an employer takes on more of the responsibility for an employee's welfare when the employee is a minor. In *Slagle* the court had to contend with whether a minor's injuries were covered since they were sustained when he was criminally assaulted while returning home from work unexpectedly at 3 A.M.

SLAGLE V. WHITE CASTLE SYSTEM, INC.
607 N.E.2d 45 (Ohio 1992)

The minor employee was assaulted on the way home from work at 3 A.M. His parents sued the employer for, among other things, negligence in allowing the employee to leave at such a late hour. The court refused to hold the employer liable for the employee's injuries.

Petree, J.

Plaintiffs parents brought this action on behalf of their minor son, Ty Slagle, after Ty was criminally assaulted on his way home from working the night shift at defendant-employer's restaurant. The trial court ruled that the employer was immune from suit under the Ohio Workers' Com-

pensation Act because Ty's injuries were sustained in the course of his employment. Although we hold that plaintiffs' claims are not barred by the Ohio workers' compensation law, the judgment will be affirmed because plaintiffs are unable to show that the employer assumed a duty to protect Ty from criminal acts of third persons occurring off its business premises.

Ty Slagle was sixteen years of age when he applied for a job at a nearby White Castle restaurant. In addition to working weekday afternoons, Ty planned to work the night shift, 11:00 P.M. to 7:00 A.M., on Fridays and Saturdays. Concerned with their son's safety, Ty's parents discussed his proposed working hours with Marge Whittaker, a White Castle supervisor. During that conversation, Whittaker allegedly assured them that Ty would not be allowed to leave the restaurant during the night shift. With this understanding, Ty began working at White Castle in October. Although he usually walked to work for his afternoon shifts, his parents arranged transportation for the night shifts. On January 10, Ty was scheduled to work from 11:00 P.M. to 7:00 A.M. Several hours into the shift, Ty began to feel ill. At 3:15 A.M., he received the manager's permission to leave work early. Although he was offered a ride by several co-workers, Ty chose to walk home instead. Several blocks from the restaurant, Ty was robbed and assaulted by unknown assailants.

Employee filed this action alleging that the employer was liable for the injuries Ty sustained in the criminal assault. Essentially, plaintiffs alleged that the employer negligently allowed the employee to walk home late at night despite the risk that he might be criminally attacked.

The trial court granted summary judgment on each of the five negligence claims. Based on the special hazard rule in *Littlefield v. Pillsbury Co.* 453 N.E. 2d 570 (Ohio 1983), the court held that Ty's injuries were sustained in the course of, and arising out of, his employment and that the employer was therefore immune from all liability for these injuries. Plaintiffs appealed.

Under R.C. 4123.74, employers who comply with the Workers' Compensation Act are immune from damages for any injury sustained by an employee in the course of and arising out of the employment relationship. Likewise, an injury is compensable under R.C. 4123.54 if it is "received in the course of, and arising out of, the injured employee's employment." R.C. 4123.01(C). Thus, the tests for compensability and immunity are the same. If an unintentional injury is compensable under the Workers' Compensation Act, then the employer will be immune from any suit claiming damages for that injury.

The requirement that a compensable injury be received in the course of, and arising out of, the injured employee's employment is a conjunctive one. Each of the two elements must be satisfied before a claim will be allowed. As the employer points out, the latter element is satisfied in this case by the very nature of employee's claims. An injury arises out of the employment when there is a causal connection between the injury and the employment. A causal connection between the injury and employer's alleged breach of duty is also an essential element of any negligence claim. Because causation is an element essential to both compensability and negligence, proof sufficient for one purpose must necessarily establish the other.

To be compensable under the Workers' Compensation Act, an injury which arises out of the employment must also be sustained during the course of employment. This element refers to the time, place and circumstances of the injury. For employees with a fixed and limited place of employment, the course of employment is typically restricted to activities occurring on the employer's premises or within the immediately adjacent "zone of employment." Injuries occurring on the employer's premises are generally sustained in the course of employment. But injuries sustained while traveling to and from a fixed place of employment are not generally compensable because time spent commuting is considered a private activity, not one undertaken in the service of the employer.

Recognizing that Ty's injuries were not compensable under the general rule, the trial court relied on an exception to that rule fashioned by the Supreme Court in *Littlefield*. In that case, the court held that an injury sustained while commuting to and from a fixed place of employment was compensable if the employment created a special hazard or risk. "The special hazard rule applies where: (1) 'but for' the employment, the employee would not have been at the location where the injury occurred, and (2) the risk is distinctive in nature or quantitatively greater than the risk common to the public." The applicability of the special hazard rule typically turns on the second prong—whether the risk is distinctive in nature or quantitatively greater than the risk encountered by the general public. The risk of criminal assault on a public street, like the risk of traffic accidents, is shared equally by all citizens. We held that risks occurring late at night are not quantitatively different from those encountered by the general public. The same may be said for "high-crime areas." These are risks encountered by the public at large, not work risks distinctive to a given employment.

The trial court held that the risk of criminal assault was quantitatively greater for Ty than for the general public due to Ty's status as a minor. Even if we were to accept this somewhat doubtful proposition as true, the trial court's approach improperly shifts the focus from the nature of the risk to the characteristics of the person injured. A special hazard is a work-related condition or risk which is distinctive in nature or quantitatively greater than the risks common to the general public. The existence of such a risk does not depend upon the individual characteristics of the employee injured. It depends, instead, upon the nature of the risk or condition and whether that risk is greater for employees than it is for members of the general public. Ty's minority at the time in question has no impact upon this analysis. Because White Castle employees are no more susceptible to criminal assault than members of the general public walking down the same street, the special hazard rule does not apply. As Ty's injury was not sustained in the course of employment, the injury is not compensable and defendant is not entitled to immunity under R.C. 4123.74.

Although the trial court incorrectly ruled that the employer was immune from liability under the Ohio Workers' Compensation Act, we must affirm its judgment if it reached the right result, but for the wrong reasons. The existence of a duty owed by the defendant to the plaintiff is an essential element of any negligence action.

Many courts have recognized that there is no general duty to protect others from the criminal conduct of third persons absent some special relationship or circumstance.

Among the relationships which will give rise to a duty to protect others are those between a common carrier and a passenger, an innkeeper and a guest, and a landowner and persons invited upon the land. Undoubtedly, the relationship between an employer and an employee may also give rise to such a duty. However, that duty does not extend beyond the employment relationship. Ordinarily, an employer has no duty to protect its employees from injuries which occur while traveling to and from work. Because Ty's injuries were sustained outside the course of his employment, the employer had no duty to protect Ty based merely upon its status as Ty's employer.

Employee maintains that the employer owed an additional duty above and beyond its duties as an employer by accepting custody of a minor child. One who voluntarily takes custody of another is under a duty to protect the other against unreasonable risks of harm. When a person accepts custody of a child, that person stands in loco parentis to the child, accepting all the rights and responsibilities that go with that status. As it involves the ultimate physical and legal control of another, a custodial relationship is not entered into lightly. One who accepts custody of a child must voluntarily assume the duties and responsibilities of a parent towards that child. This is far beyond the degree of control and supervision typically exercised by an employer over a minor employee. To establish a custodial relationship between an employer and a minor employee, there must be proof that the employer voluntarily assumed the additional responsibilities of a custodian towards the child.

Plaintiffs also maintain that the employer may be found negligent per se based upon the breach of several statutorily imposed duties. Where a statute or city ordinance imposes upon any person a specific duty for the protection of others and the breach of that duty proximately causes injury to another, that person may be found negligent per se based upon the violation of the statutory duty. Of the five statutory sections cited by employee, three might arguably provide a basis for negligence per se. They are criminal statutes which apply to persons having custody of children under eighteen years of age who create a substantial risk to the child's health or safety by violating a duty of care, protection or support. The third statute applies to parents or guardians having legal custody of a minor who negligently allow the minor to violate the city curfew. The doctrine of neg-ligence per se applies only where there is a vio-lation of a legislative enactment by one required to obey it. As each of the three code sections relied upon by plaintiffs apply only to parents or custodians of minor children, proof that the employer assumed custody of Ty is an essential element of plaintiffs' negligence per se claims.

Here, plaintiffs have failed to produce any evidence which might convince reasonable minds that the employer assumed custody of their son. Whittaker's alleged promise that Ty would be "locked in" all night is simply insufficient to establish the requisite custodial relationship. Even construed most strongly for employee, it does not imply the assumption of a duty to protect Ty from a criminal assault committed by third parties off its business premises. As proof that the employer voluntarily assumed such a duty is an essential element of employee's claims, the employer is entitled to judgment as a matter of law. AFFIRMED.

Case Questions

1. Do you agree with the court's decision? Explain.

2. What do you think about the court's determination that the employer owed the minor no greater duty, even though the parents had specifically questioned the manager about the minor leaving at night and were assured that he would not be able to?

3. If you were the employer, based on this case, what would you do differently to avoid the possibility of a lawsuit?

"Of or in the Course of" Employment

One of the most frequently litigated areas of workers' compensation is whether the accident injuring an employee arose out of or in the course of employment. Having an injury occur at work does not necessarily mean that the injury is work related. For instance, if a diabetic employee goes into a coma while at work, as in scenario 2, this may have nothing whatever to do with work except that it occurred there. Though this is a remedial statute, and generally an attempt is made to find compensation for injured employees, the statutory requirements must still be met.

As you saw in *Slagle*, the "arising out of or in the course of" language generally requires the employee's injury be one that has a causal connection with the employee's employment and may involve the time, place, and circumstances of the accident. An employee can be injured off the premises and still have a valid workers' compensation claim if the employee was in the course of employment, just as she may receive an injury on the work premises and not be covered because it did not arise out of employment. The case below provides valuable insight into the considerations in such cases.

KARASTAMATIS V. INDUSTRIAL COMM'N
713 N.E.2d 161 (Ill. 1999)

An employee hired to help out at a church's Greek festival was injured while leading a Greek dance with others while on break. The court had to determine if his injury arose out of and in the course of employment for purposes of workers' compensation recovery. The court determined that it did not.

Rakowski, J.

Claimant was hired by a Greek Orthodox church to work at the church's annual picnic by putting up tents, driving a van, cleaning, and stocking beer and food. At 11:30 P.M., as the picnic was winding down, claimant went on break and joined picnic guests and other employees who were doing a Greek dance. While dancing, claimant fell and injured his knee. Under the circumstances, did the injury arise out of claimant's employment? Because we find that the risk of injury from dancing was personal to claimant and neither peculiar to his job nor a risk to which he was exposed to a greater degree than the general public, we conclude that the Industrial Commission properly determined that his injury did not arise out of his employment.

In order for claimant to recover, he must demonstrate that his injuries arose out of and in the course of his employment. "'In the course of' refers to time, place, and circumstances of the injury." For an injury to arise out of the employment:

"The risk of injury must be a risk peculiar to the work or a risk to which the employee is exposed to a greater degree than the general public by reason of his employment. An injury is not compensable if it resulted from a risk personal to the employee rather than incidental to the

employment." Thus, in order for an injury to arise out of one's employment, the risk must be: (1) a risk to which the public is generally not exposed but that is peculiar to the employee's work, or (2) a risk to which the general public is exposed but the employee is exposed to a greater degree. A peculiar risk is one that is peculiar to a line of work and not common to other kinds of work and one that is not common to the general public. One is exposed to a common risk to a greater degree than the general public when the circumstances of the employment "make the danger of receiving an injury an exceptional risk."

In the instant case, claimant's injuries did not result from some risk or hazard peculiar to his employment. Claimant was hired to set up and stock the picnic and serve beer and food. He was not hired to dance. The risk of injury from dancing was not peculiar to claimant's work or incidental to his employment "because it did not belong to, nor was it in any way connected with, what [claimant] had to do in fulfilling his contract of service." Claimant voluntarily exposed himself to an unnecessary danger entirely separate and apart from the activities and responsibilities of his job. His act of dancing was a personal act, solely for his own convenience; an act outside any employment risk. Further, claimant presented no evidence to show he was at an increased risk of injury from dancing because he was working at a picnic sponsored by a Greek church where his duties were to stock the picnic and serve food and beverages. Simply put, the risk of injury claimant was exposed to while dancing was neither peculiar to nor increased by the nature of his employment.

Because the Act utilizes "arising out of" and "in the course of" conjunctively, both elements must be present for claimant to be entitled to compensation. Even assuming, arguendo, that claimant's injuries occurred in the course of his employment, this is not sufficient to award compensation. Claimant must also show his injury arose out of his employment, that is, he must show the injury occurred as a result of some risk incidental to his employment. There is no evidence that the conditions of the employment or the premises caused claimant's injury nor is there any evidence that claimant was at an increased risk. Therefore, the Commission's decision find-

ing claimant's injuries did not arise out of his employment is not against the manifest weight of the evidence. AFFIRMED.

Case Questions

1. Does the outcome seem reasonable here? Why or why not?

2. If an employee is engaged in an activity, otherwise not harmful, which the employer would likely foresee (such as here, Greek dancing at a Greek festival), should the activity be considered within the scope of employment?

3. In analyzing the court's discussion of increased risk, think about what the court's decision might be if it involved, say, someone working at a grocery store slipping on a banana peel where the public is exposed to the same risk. Do you think the court's decision would be the same?

Another common area of litigation involving the issue of "arising out of or in the course of employment" is whether the employee is covered for injuries that occurred while the employee was on the way to or from work. In the case below, the court gives several reasons such injuries are not covered.

CAMBURN V. NORTHWEST SCH. DIST./JACKSON COMMUNITY SCHS.
592 N.W.2d 46 (Mich. 1999)

The court analyzes why the injury to a teacher injured on her way to a teaching seminar is determined not to arise out of or during the scope of employment for workers' compensation purposes.

Per Curiam

Employee teaches for the employer school district. Employee was injured in an automobile accident when she ran a stop sign on her way to a seminar sponsored by the intermediate school district. She sustained injuries that prevented her from working for the balance of the school year.

Employee's no-fault insurance carrier, intervenor ACIA, paid her wage-loss benefits, reimbursed mileage relating to treatment for her injuries, and covered her medical bills.

ACIA filed a petition for hearing, seeking reimbursement from the school district or its insurer, claiming that employee's injuries arose out of and in the course of her employment within the meaning of the Worker's Disability Compensation Act, MCL 418.101 et seq.; MSA 17.237(101) et seq.

Employee testified that the seminar was on cooperative learning and lasted three days, for which she was given paid leave by the employer. She testified that she intended to use what she learned for small group problem solving, especially for elementary math classes. She testified that she wished to attend the seminar because she had heard other teachers discuss it favorably. Although employee agreed that she was not required to attend the seminar, she testified that she felt her superiors expected teachers to engage in continuing education and that continuing education was a topic that came up during evaluations. Employee testified that the seminar was held at the intermediate school district office, which was closer to employee's home than the school at which she taught, although getting there required a different route. However, employee never attended the seminar because the accident occurred on her way to the first session.

Employee's immediate supervisor, principal Robert Badertscher, testified that attendance at seminars was not required of teachers. He did not request that employee attend the seminar and did not encourage her to do so any more than he encouraged his teachers generally to avail themselves of such opportunities. He explained that the intermediate school district provided such seminars without cost to teachers in the county, and, so, neither employee nor the employer paid for the privilege of employee's attendance. He estimated that approximately one-third of the teachers at his school had attended such seminars. Although he testified that attending such seminars did not provide any tangible benefit to the school or the school district, he conceded that a teacher's participation in seminars might benefit the teacher's students. He also conceded that attending seminars would be noted in a teacher's evaluation.

The general rule set forth in Larson's treatise and applied by the WCAB consists of a two-part test: (1) was the employer directly benefited by the employee's attendance; and (2) was attendance compulsory or at least definitely urged or expected as opposed to merely encouraged? This rule appears to be consistent with Michigan law.

In the instant case, the magistrate as factfinder determined that the employer (school district) was not directly benefited by the employee's attendance at the seminar, based on the testimony of Principal Badertscher, who stated that although the students might benefit from employee's attendance, the school would not. (Note again the Larson statement that "it is not enough that the employer would benefit indirectly through the employee's increased knowledge.") The magistrate also found, based upon Mr. Badertscher's testimony, that employee's attendance was not compulsory or at least definitely urged or expected, since he stated that he did not require attendance, he did not urge attendance, and that the only reason he asked employee if she was interested in attending the seminar was because of his desire that "all employees be the best they could be."

Employee's attendance at the seminar was not an incident of employment. This conclusion is dispositive and requires the denial of employee's claim.

The WCAC also affirmed the magistrate's alternative analysis, that even if attendance at the seminar had been an incident of employment, employee would still not be entitled to benefits because of the general rule that travel to and from work is not compensable and because employee fit none of the exceptions to that rule.

Stark v. L. E. Myers Co., 228 N.W.2d 411 (Mich. App. 1975) established four tests, and the magistrate found that none of these tests had been met by employee. As to the first test, the magistrate found, and it was undisputed, that the employer did not pay for or furnish the employee's transportation. As to the second test, the magistrate found, and it was undisputed, that employee's working hours would have begun when and if she had arrived at the seminar, and therefore the injury did not occur during or between working hours. As to the third test, the magistrate found that the employer did not derive a special benefit from the employee's activity at the time of the injury (the fact that employee was in the process of driving). As to the last test, the magistrate found that employee was not subjected to excessive exposure to traffic risks, because the seminar was being held at a site closer to employee's home than her normal school building.

Section 27.31(c) of Professor Larson's treatise states in pertinent part:

> As to the attending of conventions, institutes, seminars, and trade expositions, compensability similarly turns on whether claimant's contract of employment contemplated attendance as an incident of his work. It is not enough that the employer would benefit indirectly through the employee's increased knowledge and experience. . . .

* * *

> Employment connection may be supplied by varying degrees of employer encouragement or direction. The clearest case for coverage is that of a teacher who is directed to attend a teacher's institute. It is also sufficient if attendance, although not compulsory, is "definitely urged" or "expected," but not if it is merely "encouraged." Connection with the employment may also be bolstered by the showing of a specific employer benefit, as distinguished from a vague and general benefit, as when the attendance of an automobile mechanic at an examination given by the manufacturer permitted the dealer to advertise "factory-trained mechanic."

We note that in § 27.31(a) in his treatise Professor Larson summarizes a similar rule in cases when an employee is injured while undertaking educational or training programs to enhance the employee's own work proficiency.

Even if the school was directly benefited by employee's intent to attend the seminar, substantial evidence supports the magistrate's conclusion that attendance was neither compulsory nor definitely urged or expected. Instead, it was merely encouraged, and, as such, was not an incident of employment. Therefore, employee's injury did not arise out of and in the course of her employment.

We also agree that the magistrate properly denied ACIA's petition on the basis of her alternative analysis. The general rule is that injuries that occur while traveling to or coming from work are not compensable. However, a number of exceptions have been recognized where (1) the employee is on a special mission for the employer, (2) the employer derives a special benefit from the employee's activity at the time of the injury, (3) the employer paid for or furnished the employee transportation as part of the contract of employment, (4) the travel comprised a dual purpose combining the employment-required business needs with the personal activity of the employee, (5) the employment subjected the employee "to excessive exposure to the common risk," such as traffic risks faced by a truck driver on the way to his rig, and (6) the travel took place as the result of a split-shift working schedule or employment requiring a similar irregular nonfixed working schedule. Although employee argues that she was on a special mission for her employer, the magistrate's findings support a contrary conclusion. The magistrate found the school was not directly benefited by employee's attendance at the seminar and that the attendance was neither compulsory nor definitely expected. Moreover, even if employee's attendance at the seminar had been an incident of employment, her injury on the way to the seminar would not be compensable.

"When an employee, having identifiable time and space limits on his employment, makes an off-premises journey which would normally not be covered under the usual going and coming rule, the journey may be brought within the course of employment by the fact that the trouble and time of making the journey, or the special inconvenience, hazard, or urgency of making it in the particular circumstances, is itself sufficiently substantial to be viewed as an integral part of the service itself."

In the instant case, employee's off-premises journey was not an integral portion of the "special mission" she is assumed to be on for purposes of this alternative argument. Employee testified that the trip to the seminar was approximately the same length as the trip to her normal worksite, albeit over a different route. Therefore, even if employee's attendance at the seminar is considered to be the functional equivalent of being at work, employee's injury occurred while she was on the way to work and therefore is not compensable. AFFIRMED.

Case Questions

1. Does this decision seem "fair" to you? Explain.

2. How would you analyze the situation of the teacher's being informally expected to engage in opportunities for self-improvement to benefit the students, yet the employer not having responsibility for injuries incurred during such activities?

3. If the logical outcome of this decision is that teachers would be less likely to engage in opportunities to improve their teaching skills for the classroom, and the students are the ones who lose out, what might an employer do to prevent this?

Since the *Camburn* case seemed so close to being a covered injury, look at the case below to see one which is actually covered by workers' compensation law.

FLOYD V. FIRST CITIZENS BANK
512 S.E.2d 454 (Ct. App. N.C. 1999)

An employee who was injured while performing tasks related to coordinating the office Christmas party as requested by her supervisor attempts to have the injury covered by workers' compensation. The court permitted the coverage.

McGee, J.

Employee was employed by employer in December 1993 when she slipped and fell while buying bagels for an office Christmas breakfast that her boss had instructed her to coordinate for employer's entire city office, including all department heads. Employee suffered a serious back injury as a result of the fall. The Industrial Commission (Commission) found as a fact that employee's injury caused her to be disabled. The Commission concluded as a matter of law that employee's injury arose within the course of her employment and that she was entitled to workers' compensation disability benefits. Employer appeals.

The Commission found as a fact that employee "was instructed" by her supervisor to coordinate the breakfast. Employer disputes this finding, saying that "competent evidence does not exist" to support the finding. We disagree. The transcript of the Commission hearing includes employee's testimony stating, "I was asked to coordinate the breakfast for the main office[.]" Employee testified that because she had been asked to coordinate the event, her attendance was "absolutely" mandatory. Employee further testified, "It was . . . my job to coordinate it and do the breakfast, so I went and got the bagels for the breakfast." She also stated, "It was my job to coordinate and do this breakfast[.]" Employee testified that her supervisor "asked me to coordinate this, and so I followed through with coordinating it and making sure everything was there, and part of that was getting the bagels to the breakfast." Furthermore, employee's supervisor, Paul Ford, testified regarding the breakfast that employee "was asked to do it . . . to coordinate this event[.]" The Commission had ample competent evidence upon which to base its finding that employee's supervisor instructed her to coordinate the Christmas breakfast.

Employer also assigns error to the Commission's conclusion of law that employee's injury arose in the course of employment. To be compensable an accident must arise out of the course and scope of employment. Where the fruit of certain labor accrues either directly or indirectly to the benefit of an employer, employees injured in the course of such work are entitled to compensation under the Workmen's Compensation Act. This result obtains especially where an employee is called to action by some person superior in authority to him. . . . It appears clear that when a superior directs a subordinate employee to go on an errand or to perform some duty beyond his normal duties, the scope of the Workmen's Compensation

Act expands to encompass injuries sustained in the course of such labor. Were the rule otherwise, employees would be compelled to determine in each instance and, no doubt at their peril, whether a requested activity was beyond the ambit of the act. The order or request need not be couched in the imperative. It is sufficient for compensation purposes that the suggestion, request or even the employee's mere perception of what is expected of him under his job classification, serves to motivate undertaking an injury producing activity. So long as ordered to perform by a superior, acts beneficial to the employer which result in injury to performing employees are within the ambit of the act.

In the case before us, employee's injury occurred while employee was engaged in activity directly related to employer's request that she coordinate the Christmas breakfast. The Commission did not err in concluding that employee's injury arose in the course of employee's employment. AFFIRMED.

Case Questions

1. Can you see the difference between why there was coverage in this case and not in the last case? Explain.
2. As an employer, what would you do to avoid this liability?
3. Are there some situations that are simply an inevitable part of doing business and should be simply accepted and planned for? Explain.

Benefits

The benefits provided under workers' compensation statutes are divided into five categories based on the nature of the injuries, up to, and including, death. Of course, the amount of benefits varies, depending on the category and the state.

Medical Benefits.   The most-used category of benefits is medical benefits. This compensates the injured employee for the medical expenses related to the on-the-job injuries.

Temporary Total Disability.   This category is for wages lost due to temporary injuries, which cause the injured employee to miss work (usually after a certain waiting period, ranging from two to seven days), though not on a permanent basis. As previously stated, benefits vary from state to state, but most fall within the range of providing the injured employee with about two-thirds of the employee's wages.

Permanent Partial Disability.   This category addresses employees who are injured in a way that will not permit them to return to their old jobs, yet they may still be able to work in some other capacity. For instance, they may lose their eyesight and no longer be able to work at one type of job but can perform another. How much the employee receives is set by a schedule that accounts for the wages lost and also the injury, such as loss of right arm, loss of eyesight, loss of left arm, and so on.

Permanent Total Disability.   Injured employees falling into this category can no longer work, or they suffer major physical impairment.

Death.   Benefits to replace income are paid to the fatally injured employee's surviving spouse and children until the spouse remarries or dies and the children reach the age of majority specified by the statute. It may also help with burial expenses.

Management Tips

Workers' compensation claims are one of the things that an employer has at least some measure of control over in the workplace. It takes the employer thinking about the workplace in a somewhat different way, since the employer must try to foresee at least predictable hazards, but it is worth the effort in terms of decreased claims, less time lost from work due to injuries, and decreased employer contributions based on claims filed.

- Make employees aware of the importance of on-the-job safety considerations.
- Examine the workplace for obvious hazards and remove them; for instance, make sure lights are promptly replaced in dark stairways and there is no exposed wiring.
- When necessary, conduct training for employees in workplace safety matters.
- To the extent economically feasible, invest in equipment for employees that may decrease the incidence of work-related injuries (i.e., lower back support belts, computer wrist rests).
- Explore the possibility of time-release or financial incentives for those employees who exhibit exemplary workplace safety.
- Conduct periodic inspections of the workplace to check for hazards.
- Investigate all employee injury claims promptly.
- When workers' compensation claims are filed, do not routinely validate them without making sure the injury is actually work related.

Summary

• Workers' compensation statutes are the no-fault statutory scheme of providing medical costs and lost wages to employees for injuries incurred on the job.

• While coverage differs from state to state, in most, employees give up their right to sue the employer for negligence in exchange for having a certain specified time period of preset benefits provided on a no-fault basis.

• The statutes generally provide for permanent partial or total disabilities as well as death benefits.

• The injury must have arisen from or in the course of employment.

• Employers can do a great deal to help contain workers' compensation claims and costs.

Chapter-End Questions

1. Jill and JoAnna worked together at the concrete manufacturing plant. The two had been bickering with each other all during their shift because JoAnna thought Jill was trying to take her boyfriend. At the end of their work shift, Jill and JoAnna went to a bar located about a mile from the plant where they worked. While there, JoAnna assaulted Jill. Jill brings a workers' compensation claim. How will it be decided and why? *Stivison v. Goodyear Tire and Rubber Co.,* 687 N.E.2d 458 (Ohio 1997).

2. Kim was injured on the job. He went to the doctor for treatment and was killed in a traffic accident after leaving the doctor's office. Will Kim's family be able to recover survivor benefits? *Wyoming Workers' Safety and Compensation Div. v. Bruhn,* 951 P.2d 373 (Wyo. 1997).

3. During a paid break, Dennis left work and went across the street to purchase a gift for a supervisor who was being given an office party. On the way back, he was injured by a car at an intersection. Will Dennis be able to collect workers' compensation benefits? Why or why not? *Carrillo v. Liberty Northwest Ins.,* 922 P.2d 1189 (Mont. 1996).

4. Becky was hit by a vehicle while walking a picket line in front of her employer's place of business to protest working conditions. Will she be likely to receive workers' compensation benefits when she files? Why or why not? *Koger v. Greyhound Lines, Inc.,* 629 N.E.2d 492 (Ohio App. 1st Dist. 1993).

5. When Sylvia came to work for José, she requested to work only during the daytime and to be able to carry a gun because she had been harassed by her husband, from whom she was separated. José refused the request, and Sylvia was eventually injured when she was shot three times by her husband while she was at work. Sylvia filed for workers' compensation benefits. Will she be able to receive them? Explain. *Guillory v. Interstate Gas Station,* 653 So.2d 1152 (La. 1995).

6. Amada contracted with an exterminator to spray for cockroaches at his bar and grill each month. The exterminator sprayed and power-fogged the bar. The next day Su-Ling came in and washed down all the surfaces, immersing her hands and arms in buckets of water for two hours. She then had headaches, pain, seizures, blurred vision, and memory loss. Her doctor's diagnosis

was that she had organic brain damage due to toxic encephalopathy from poisoning. When Su-Ling filed a worker's compensation claim, Amada contested it, saying it was not work related and Su-Ling should not be able to receive benefits. At the hearing, there was conflicting testimony about what could have caused Su-Ling's injuries and how extensive her injuries were. For instance, one doctor said it could have come from alcoholism and that the damage was not permanent. Even though the testimony was conflicting, would it be permissible for the judge to accept the testimony favorable to Su-Ling and grant her the benefits? *Sheridan v. Catering Management, Inc.,* 558 N.W.2d 319 (Neb. App. 1997).

7. Hwan was an electronics salesperson. He maintained an office in his home and was expected to make calls on customers. While shoveling his driveway to clear the way so that he could make a call on a customer, Hwan suffered a heart attack. When he filed a workers' compensation claim, his employer refused the claim, saying that Hwan was only performing a domestic duty that did not qualify for benefits. Will Hwan be able to collect? *Tovish v. Gerber Electronics,* 642 A.2d 721 (Conn. 1994).

8. Mara is angry with Tjebi (Jeb'-bee) because Tjebi did not repay a loan Mara made to Tjebi several weeks ago. While at work, Mara and Tjebi start fighting and Tjebi is injured. If Tjebi files a workers' compensation claim, will he likely be granted benefits?

9. When José is sexually harassed at work by his supervisor and sues the supervisor in tort after collecting workers' compensation benefits, the supervisor uses as a defense the fact that workers' compensation was José's exclusive remedy. Is it?

10. What are some of the ways in which management can control the cost of workers' compensation?

22 Fair Labor Standards Act

Chapter Outline

S C E N A R I O S

S C E N A R I O   1

Fourteen-year-old Shamika wants to earn money to save toward college. She decides to deliver newspapers. Her mother objects, telling Shamika that she considers the job too dangerous and that, anyway, Shamika at 14 is underage for employment. Is Shamika's mom correct?

S C E N A R I O   2

When asked to work overtime, Kweisi tells his boss that, under the law, he is not required to work over 40 hours per week and declines the overtime. Is Kweisi correct?

S C E N A R I O   3

Derry, a new MBA graduate, is hired into a management job. It is Derry's first job as a professional. After several months, Derry finds he is leaving work later and later. Derry begins to resent that he works late, putting in more and more hours, and is not receiving any more than the originally agreed upon salary. He is contemplating legal action against his employer for violation of the Fair Labor Standards Act. Will it be worth his while to pursue this?

Statutory Basis

Every employer shall pay to each of his employees who in any workweek is engaged in commerce or in the production of goods for commerce, or is employed in an enterprise engaged in commerce or in the production of goods for commerce, wages at the following rates: . . . not less than $5.15 an hour beginning September 1, 1997. Sec. 6(a), Fair Labor Standards Act of 1938, as amended, 29 USC 201, et seq.

. . . No employer shall employ any of his employees for a workweek longer than forty hours unless such employee receives compensation for his employment in excess of the hours above specified at a rate not less than one and one-half times the regular rate at which he is employed. Sec. 7(a)(1), Fair Labor Standards Act of 1938, as amended, 29 USC 201, et seq.

Show Me the Money!

It may seem strange to us now, but there was a time when children as young as 8 and 10 years old and even younger were made to work until midnight and beyond to keep the wheels of the industrial revolution turning. There were no laws to regulate the maximum number of hours a child could be required to work or how much

EXHIBIT 22–1   How We Pay People

The national contract talks this summer between the Big Three auto companies and the UAW dramatically illustrate some of the major changes in employee compensation issues in the United States. Declining union membership, increased global competition, the aging of the work force are powerful forces that are changing the nature of how, and how much, we pay American workers.

The picture was far different 20, and even 10, years ago when UAW negotiators sat down with auto executives. In 1970 28 percent of the work force was unionized; today, 15 percent is.

How employers compensate their employees has always been shaped by social, economic, and legal currents. World War II accelerated the development of non-cash payments—paid holidays, vacations, insurance, and retirement programs—as compensation. What were once "fringe" benefits are now at the core of compensation. There is no doubt that today's employee has come to expect a broad array of benefits barely dreamed of by workers just a generation ago.

For employees, today's compensation packages appear to be more flexible, offering more choices than the static compensation packages of a decade ago. For America's six million business establishments, however, government policy is reducing flexibility and undermining their ability to tailor compensation schemes to meet the unique needs of their own work forces. Employees may find fewer benefits offered because employers cannot afford the cost of government-imposed directives.

Employee demographics, global competition, escalating health care costs, and legislative emphasis on mandated benefits are fashioning the practices of the present and the future.

No single factor is more powerful in forcing compensation changes than demographics. Whereas population grew at an annual 1 percent rate in the 12-year period from 1976 to 1988, it will grow by only 0.7 percent annually from 1988 to 2000. Concomitantly, the labor force will grow more slowly: 1 percent annually, compared to a 1.2 percent annual rate during the 1980 to 1988 period and a 2.6 percent rate of growth from 1970 to 1980.

With the slowing of the rate of young entrants into the work force, the age of the average employee will increase.

A dearth of young workers will increase competition for jobs, forcing compensation upward. Changing technology will necessitate retraining older workers, adding further pressure to employer costs.

Another demographic reality is that more employees will be women. By the year 2000, 61 percent of American working-age women will be employed, making up 47 percent of the work force. Of great significance is the fact that women who are entering the work force in these growing numbers are mothers. Employers will have to rethink benefit programs presently geared to a male-supported family structure. Benefit programs will have to accommodate the needs of two-earner families and single parents.

The states have added to the cost pressure by mandating that insurers provide certain benefits in insurance sold to employers or, in limited situations, that employers offer prescribed benefits.

Influenced by the forces identified above, there continues to be a move away from fixed (that is, nonvariable) basic wages or salaries toward benefits and supplemental pay arrangements. Indeed, real wages have declined for seven of the last ten years. When benefits increases are included, however, wage increases nearly kept pace with inflation.

Excerpted from W. J. Kilberg, *American Enterprise,* Sept/Oct 1990, p. 25. Copyright 1990 American Enterprise Institute. Dist. by NY Times Syndication Sales Corp.

employees were paid. Under the broad constitutional powers that Congress has to regulate interstate commerce, it passed a law to do so in 1938.

The law, now amended several times, is called the Fair Labor Standards Act (FLSA). The act set standards for the minimum age for workers, **minimum wages** they can make, and the rate at which they must be paid if they work over a certain amount of time during a work week. The act also prohibits pay differentials based solely on gender.

Minimum wage
The least amount a covered employee must be paid in hourly wages.

The purpose of the minimum wage laws is to ensure that all workers, especially those at the lower end of the pay scale, maintain at least a minimum standard of living that keeps them from poverty. Despite this, the Center on Budget and Policy Priorities concluded that the poverty rate among full-time, year-around workers rose from 2.5 percent in 1997 (2.345 million) to 2.9 percent in 1998 (2.804 million). Poverty is defined as a family of four earning less than $16,400 per year.

On the other hand, FLSA has been criticized as causing poverty in certain sectors of the workforce—for example, with unskilled minority teenagers, whom employers will not hire even at minimum wage, because it is deemed too high a price to pay for the contributions of this group, whose unemployment rate can run as high as 50 percent. A training wage of 85 percent of the minimum wage for certain groups is provided in an effort to encourage employment, but statistics for employment of certain groups remain low.

This chapter discusses the basic requirements of the Fair Labor Standards Act and how those requirements impact the workplace.

General Provisions

FLSA is administered by the US Department of Labor's Wage and Hour Division, which has authority to investigate, gather information, issue regulations, and enforce FLSA provisions. States also have wage and hour provisions administered by comparable state agencies. In addition to regulating child labor, wages, and hours, FLSA also requires employers to keep records on wages and hours, though there is no particular form in which such records must be kept. Violations, if willful, are crimes punishable by fines of up to $10,000, with second convictions resulting in possible imprisonment. Child labor violations carry civil penalties. FLSA contains antiretaliation provisions to protect employees who use FLSA, such as filing a complaint or participating in an FLSA proceeding.

If FLSA is violated by the employer underpaying employees, employees may recover back wages. There is a two-year statute of limitations, which stretches to three for willful violations. In the case below, the issue of willfulness arose regarding a claim for overtime compensation under the act.

ALABAMA A&M UNIVERSITY V. KING ET AL.
119 Lab. Cas. ¶ 35,538 (Ala. Civ. App. 1991)

Nine employees of Alabama A&M University who worked as residence hall counselors in female dormitories on campus alleged that they were due overtime pay for working 60-hour weeks for a two and a half year period. While FLSA requires payment of overtime for work in excess of 40 hours per week, executive, administrative, or professional employees are exempt from this provision. The university argued that the employees were administrative. The jury found for the employees, who then requested damages which would be greater if it was found that the university's actions were willful violations of FLSA.

Russell, J.

In the present action the trial court's initial instructions to the jury on the issue of willful violation of the FLSA included the following language:

> Unless you are reasonably satisfied from the evidence that the defendant university in failing to pay these plaintiffs overtime knew it was violating the statute, or that the defendant university in failing to pay these plaintiff's overtime showed reckless disregard for the matter of whether its failure to pay them overtime was a violation of the statute, then you cannot find that any violation which may have occurred was willful.
>
> If you are reasonably satisfied from the evidence that the plaintiffs were non-exempt employees, and that Alabama A&M either knew or showed reckless disregard to the matter of whether its conduct was prohibited by the Fair Labor Standards Act as to the plaintiffs, you would then find Alabama A&M guilty of willful violation of the Fair Labor Standards Act.

In a supplemental charge the trial court said that the reckless disregard standard requires an employer to make a reasonable effort to determine whether the plan it is following would constitute a violation of the law. Alabama A&M alleges the trial court's supplemental instruction to the jury

that the university was required "to make a reasonable effort" to determine its compliance with the law was legally incorrect and unquestionably prejudicial in that it allowed the jury to invoke too lenient of a standard in finding willful conduct.

The imposition of a duty upon Alabama A&M to "make a reasonable effort" to determine whether it was violating the requirements of the FLSA is contrary to the standard established by the U.S. Supreme Court. We find the jury charge was legally incorrect and prejudicial to the university. REVERSED AND REMANDED.

Case Questions

1. Should a high standard be imposed to find that the employer willfully violated the statute? Why or why not?
2. How should willfulness be established?
3. Does it make sense to you that an employer and an employee may differ over what type of employee the employer categorizes the employee as? Why or why not?

Covered Employees

Since FLSA was enacted pursuant to the powers of Congress to regulate interstate commerce, that requirement forms, in part, a basis for determining coverage. Actually, there are two types of coverage in FLSA: individual coverage and enterprise coverage. If the individual employee's job involves interstate commerce directly, such as an over-the-road truck driver traveling from state to state, or moving or preparing goods for interstate commerce, including phoning and using the mail, then the individual is covered. For enterprise coverage, all employees of a business will be covered if the business is engaged in interstate commerce or in producing goods for interstate commerce and meets a minimum gross annual income requirement. Retailers or service businesses must have annual income of at least $362,500 and other businesses $250,000 or more.

FLSA covers federal employees: Amendments to FLSA in 1966 and 1974 extended its coverage to most public employers, but gave rise to questions over the right of the federal government to regulate the compensation of state and local employees. After the US Supreme Court decided *Garcia v. San Antonio Metropolitan Transit Authority,* 469 U.S. 528 (1985) upholding Congress's power to do so, the US Department of Labor announced it would hold public employers to FLSA standards effective April 15, 1985 (later extended to November 1, 1985). State and local employees are covered under FLSA's child labor and equal pay provisions only if the service being conducted is a traditional government activity, such as police and fire protection or education. While most states have their own wage and hour laws, which can apply to state and local government employees, the minimum wage and overtime provisions of FLSA do not apply to them engaging in traditional government activities.

FLSA contains exemptions for several groups and they vary, depending on the area of FLSA being addressed. They will be discussed under the relevant FLSA sections.

REICH V. CIRCLE C. INVESTMENTS, INC.
998 F.2d 324 (5th Cir. 1993)

The court analyzes whether topless nightclub dancers who received no compensation except tips from customers are employees subject to FLSA or "business women renting space, stages, music, dressing rooms and lights from the club," not subject to the law. The court determined that they were, in fact, employees for FLSA purposes.

Reavley, J.

The secretary of labor alleges that a topless night-club has improperly compensated its dancers, waitresses, disc jockeys, bartenders, doormen, and "housemothers," and has failed to keep accurate records of the hours worked by its employees. The district court determined that the topless dancers and other workers are "employees" under the FLSA and that the club willfully violated its minimum wage, overtime and record-keeping provisions.

The dancers receive no compensation from the club. Their compensation is derived solely from the tips they receive from customers for performing on stage and performing private "table dances" and "couch dances." At the end of each night, the dancers must pay the club a $20 "tip-out," regardless of how much they make in tips. The club characterizes this tip-out as stage rental and argues that the dancers are really tenants. According to the club, the dancers are neither employees nor independent contractors, but are business women renting space, stages, music, dressing rooms, and lights from the club.

To determine employee status under the FLSA, we focus on whether the alleged employee, as a matter of economic reality, is economically dependent upon the business to which she renders her services, or in business for herself. To make this determination, we must analyze five factors.

The first factor is the degree of control exercised by the alleged employer. The district court found that the club exercises a great deal of control over the dancers. They are required to comply with weekly work schedules, which the club compiles with input from the dancers. The club fines the dancers for absences or tardiness. It instructs the dancers to charge at least $10 for table dances and $20 for couch dances. The dancers supply their own costumes, but the costumes must meet standards set by the club. The dancers can express a preference for a certain type of music, but they do not have the final say in the matter. The club

has many other rules concerning the dancers' behavior; for example, no flat heels, no more than 15 minutes at one time in the dressing room, only one dancer in the restroom at a time, and all dancers must be "on the floor" at opening time. The club enforces these rules by fining infringers.

The club attempts to de-emphasize its control by arguing that most of the rules are directed at maintaining decorum or keeping the club itself legal. The club explained that it publishes the minimum charge for table and couch dances at the request of the dancers to prevent dancers from undercutting each others' prices. Finally, it stresses the fact that it does not control the dancers' routines. We believe, however, that the record fully supports the district court's findings of significant control.

The second factor is the extent of relative investments of the worker and alleged employer. The district court found that a dancer's investment is limited to her costumes and a padlock. The amount spent on costumes varies from dancer to dancer and can be significant. The club contends that we should also consider as an investment each dancer's nightly tip-out, which it characterizes as rent. The district court rejected this argument, and so do we. It is the economic realities that control our determination of employee status.

Third, we must look at the degree to which the workers' opportunity for profit and loss is determined by the alleged employer. Once customers arrive at the club, a dancer's initiative, hustle and costume significantly contribute to the amount of her tips. But the club has a significant role in drawing customers. Given its control over determinants of customer volume, the club exercises a high degree of control over a dancer's opportunity for "profit." Dancers are far more closely akin to wage earners toiling for a living than to independent entrepreneurs seeking a return on their risky capital investments.

The fourth factor is the skill and initiative required in performing the job. Many of the dancers did not have any prior experience with topless dancing before coming to work at the club. They do not need long training or highly developed skills to dance at the club. A dancer's initiative is essentially limited to decisions involving costumes and dance routines. This does not exhibit the skill or initiative indicative of persons in business for themselves.

Finally, we must analyze the permanency of the relationship. The district court found that most dancers have short-term relationships with the club. Although not determinative, the impermanent relationship between the dancers and the club indicates non-employee status.

Despite the lack of permanency, on balance, the five factors favor a determination of employee

status. A dancer has no specialized skills and her only real investment is in her costumes. The club exercises significant control over a dancer's behavior and the opportunity for profit. The transient nature of the workforce is not enough here to remove the dancers from the protections of the FLSA. AFFIRMED.

Case Questions

1. Does any of the case surprise you? Explain.
2. If you were the club owner and did not want the dancers to be employees, after receiving this decision, how would you change things?
3. Do you think the dancers should have been considered employees? Why or why not?

Minimum Wages

When unions were legalized during the Great Depression, they immediately attempted to bargain for higher wages. John L. Lewis, the well-known president of the United Mine Workers (UMW), left the American Federation of Labor (AFL) and formed the Congress of Industrial Organizations (CIO) and the UMW struck for higher wages. The two organizations later linked up to form the AFL–CIO, and wages have always been an extremely important item on the collective bargaining agenda.

After World War II, the minimum wage law was established in hopes that it would avoid another depression. The advocates of the law, primarily unions and other workers, thought that a minimum wage would accomplish this by providing everyone with enough money on which to live without causing an economic harm to business owners.

Under FLSA, employers are required to pay covered employees a certain minimum hourly wage. Since September 1, 1997, the wage has been $5.15. In 1938, when FLSA was enacted, it was 25 cents per hour.

In addition to minimum wages, covered employees working over 40 hours per week are entitled to overtime pay of at least time and a half; that is, at least one and one-half times the covered employee's regular hourly wage rate.

Wage rates may be lower if, in accordance with appropriate regulations, an industry wage order makes them so in Puerto Rico, the Virgin Islands, or American Samoa. If the covered employee is an apprentice, learner, or disabled worker, then, under certain circumstances, she or he may receive less than the minimum wage if the employer obtains a certificate issued by the Department of Labor's wage and

EXHIBIT 22–2   Increasing the Minimum Wage: Help or Hindrance?

Congress and the White House have spent an inordinate amount of time wrangling over increasing the minimum wage. While the chief sticking point has been over the level the new minimum would be set at, insufficient attention has been paid to the key question: "How will the new minimum wage affect the American economy?"

There are a number of institutions facing fixed budgets as far as part-time help is concerned. Most colleges have work-study programs with which they are able to hire students to help professors. Academic departments have a fixed operating budget from which they must cover all of their expenses plus the hiring of work-study students. Another class of employees used is that of temporary service workers.

If there is an increase in the minimum wage, the limited budget cannot be expanded, so fewer students will be able to be hired with the fixed amount of funds available. Many of these students, in order to save money, are going to colleges which are supported by state governments. Will the state legislature add enough money to the schools' budgets so they can increase the departmental budgets, enabling these students to be hired?

More likely, a number of jobs which had been available to aid students suddenly will be gone. Some students who rely on that extra money to help them through the school year will have to drop out, and we will have lost an individual who might have been able to contribute a great deal to our world.

Businesses other than schools will also feel the crunch. Fast-food chains rely on part-time employees, generally high school students. To pay the higher wages, when there is no increase in the amount of output per worker, will mean the prices of their product will have to be increased to meet the added expense. This adds to the levels of inflation already present and does not satisfy the main aim of the increase, which is to raise the buying power of the individual. Meanwhile, the minimum wage will not affect those already earning above that level, except to lower the buying power of the dollars available to them.

The increase in these wages could affect our economic position overseas as well. The trade imbalance is fueled by wages which are higher than comparable salaries in other developed countries for jobs requiring similar skills. The minimum wage increase will tend to force other salaries above it higher in order to keep "equity" in the labor market. The higher wages will be reflected in prices, causing consumers to cut back on their demand for domestic products over nondomestic goods and resulting in a further increase in the U.S. trade deficit.

Government is like the camel which sticks its nose into a tent. After a while, the camel is the only one in the tent, and the other occupants have had to vacate. The minimum wage is becoming another of the inflationary aspects of the economy. Coupled with the savings and loan bailouts, the level of all debt, and low productivity, it well could be the act which pushes us into a recession.

Reprinted from *USA Today Magazine,* July copyright 1989 by the Society for the Advancement of Education Inc.

hour administrator. Exhibit 22–3 discusses the issue of low wages. Kilgore demonstrates that there may be problems with something as simple as even determining who receives minimum wages.

KILGORE V. OUTBACK STEAKHOUSE OF FLORIDA, INC.
160 F.3d 294 (6th Cir. 1998)

Employee servers who were required to pool their tips and have them redistributed to other types of employees who were not paid minimum wage challenge this practice as a violation of the minimum wage provision of the FLSA. The court permitted the arrangement.

Kennedy, J.

Outback's tip pooling arrangement requires its servers to contribute a share of their tips to a tip pool, which the restaurant distributes to hosts, bus persons, and bartenders. The servers' mandated contribution is three percent of their "total gross sales," which includes not only food and beverages, but also gift certificates and merchandise such as steak knives and T-shirts sold to customers at a server's assigned tables.

The restaurant paid its hosts and servers $2.125 per hour—one half the minimum wage at the time in question—with the required minimum wage difference made up through the tip pool arrangement. It was undisputed that hosts and servers never received less than the minimum wage for a workweek under this arrangement. Servers testified, however, that customer tips often fell short of the fifteen percent industry standard, and that Outback's tip pool requirement "routinely" required them to "tip out" more than thirty-five percent of the tips they actually received.

The FLSA, at 29 U.S.C. §203(m), permits employers to use a tip credit to account for up to fifty percent of the minimum wage but only with respect to "tipped" employees. The statute defines a "tipped employee" as "any employee engaged in an occupation in which he customarily and regularly receives more than $30 a month in tips." 29 U.S.C.§203(t). Section 203(m) also states that use of the tip credit this way "shall not

be construed to prohibit the pooling of tips among employees who customarily and regularly receive tips."

Employee servers and hosts allege that the required tip-out amount was impermissibly excessive, and, therefore, not "customary and reasonable" as required under Labor Department interpretations of the relevant statutory sections. They also contended that Outback's use of the tip credit to calculate the minimum wage was unlawful with respect to hosts because they did not qualify as "tipped employees."

Even though Outback prohibits hosts from accepting tips, they receive more than $30 a month in tips if tip pool receipts are included. Employees who receive tips from a tip pool are employees who 'receive tips' according to Department of Labor regulations, case law, and Department of Labor practices. Accordingly, the hosts meet the qualifications of Sections 203(t) and 203(m).

The hosts perform services to customers—greeting and seating, giving out menus, and sometimes "enhancing the wait" by serving food. These activities constitute sufficient interaction with customers in an industry where undesignated tips are common. Accordingly, the hosts are engaged in an occupation in which tips are customarily and regularly received and thereby qualify as tipped employees. AFFIRMED.

Case Questions

1. Do you consider the restaurant's pool tipping policy to be fair to the servers who received the tips? Explain.

2. Does the court's analysis make sense to you, that if hosts receive tips from the tip pot, then

they are employees who routinely receive tips? Explain.

3. Why do you think the employer uses this method of payment?

As mentioned, FLSA has exemptions, so not everyone is covered under the statute. At least 41 states have statutes that provide coverage for employees exempted under FLSA, with 16 states setting limits above those of the federal law.

Sometimes the rate of pay is not so clearcut. In *Casserly,* the court had to deal with whether employees on call should be able to receive overtime pay when it is beyond their regular 40-hour week.

Exhibit 22–3

EEOC Addresses Discrimination against Low-Wage Earners at Historic Public Meeting in Houston

In its second public forum outside the nation's capital this year, the U.S. Equal Employment Opportunity Commission (EEOC) held its monthly meeting in Houston on Tuesday, June 22, 1999, to hear testimony from expert witnesses on discrimination as it affects low-wage workers—particularly immigrants, minorities, and women.

The day-long meeting, held at Texas Southern University's Thurgood Marshall School of Law, attracted an outpouring of approximately 300 people, including community and business leaders, civil rights advocates and educators, state and local government officials, over a dozen print and electronic media outlets, as well as the public at large. The historic gathering marked another step in EEOC's ongoing effort to reach out to agency stakeholders, especially under-served communities, and expand its presence at the grassroots level.

"We left the Washington Beltway to listen carefully to experts and advocates at the local level who have first-hand knowledge about the problems facing low-wage workers," said EEOC Chairwoman Ida L. Castro. "The information we gathered will provide us with a solid foundation to develop our work plan so that together we can focus on these important issues."

During the meeting, three expert panels, including one affected individual, shared their experiences and insights on how best to break down the barriers to equal employment opportunity for low-wage earners. The Commission heard testimony from representatives of the following organizations: AFL-CIO; Asian Law Caucus; NAACP; Mexican American Legal Defense and Education Fund; Houston Immigration and Refugee Coalition; Texas Rural Legal Aid; Refugee Services Alliance; Wage and Hour Division, U.S. Department of Labor; and the Institute for Rehabilitation and Research. Also participating in the panel discussions were esteemed faculty members from the University of Texas.

Exhibit 22–3 (concluded)

Panelists discussed a number of issues affecting low-wage earners including wage bias, worker exploitation, industry trends, demographic and population changes, challenges faced by immigrants and undocumented employees, the role of organized labor, welfare-to-work programs, temp services and contingent workers, low job classification, and limited job opportunities for older workers and persons with disabilities.

In addition to the expert witnesses, the Commission heard testimony from Francisco Javier Guevera, a Mexican construction worker from Houston, who provided personal insights about his employment as a low-wage immigrant worker. The meeting "opened a whole new world" he said, because he previously had no knowledge about the laws enforced by EEOC, nor did he understand how to utilize the agency's complaint process.

"Due to a lack of education, cultural differences, and language barriers, too many low-wage workers are unaware of their rights, unfamiliar with EEOC's charge processing procedures, and unable to get a fair shot at the American dream," said Ms. Castro.

Among the recommendations made by the panelists were to increase enforcement attention to the agricultural, poultry, meat packing, construction, and restaurant industries; survey employees under the H-2A temporary farm worker program to ensure that employers are complying with the EEO laws; and monitor public works construction projects to safeguard against workplace bias.

"Too many employers continue to abuse and take advantage of low-wage earners because they are vulnerable to threats of retaliation and fear deportation," Ms. Castro said. "EEOC will enhance collaboration with stakeholders and provide more strategic enforcement to root out the bad actors and remedy egregious discrimination wherever and whenever it exists."

Under Chairwoman Castro's leadership, the Commission has made several major enforcement reforms which have increased the efficiency and effectiveness of agency operations. These include enhancing outreach, education, and technical assistance to stakeholders with a special emphasis on small and mid-sized employers as well as under-served communities; and revamping the agency web site to make information more accessible in a user-friendly format.

U.S. EEOC, June 24, 1999. http://www.eeoc.gov/press/6-24-99.html. Used with permission.

CASSERLY, ET AL. V. COLORADO
844 P.2d 1275 (Colo. App. 1992)

Employees, physician assistants for the state correctional facility, argued that they should be able to collect time-and-a-half overtime pay for the time over 40 hours that they are on call away from their jobs at the facilities. They make nearly $18 per hour as base pay, and the employer wants to pay them $1.75 per hour for "on-call time" rather than the time and a half that FLSA requires. The court agreed with the employees.

Metzger, J.

Plaintiff employees were employed as physician assistants at the State Correctional Facility at Canon City, Colorado. Each employee was assigned to a single facility for full-time duties requiring not less than 40 hours per week. In addition, on a rotating basis, each employee was required to provide emergency medical services to inmates after regular working hours. Employees were compensated at one and one-half their regular rate of pay for those hours they were physically present at a facility responding to a call.

Before November 1988, the employees were not paid for the time spent waiting for calls. After that time, defendants paid employees at a rate of $1.75 per hour as "on-call" pay.

During on-call periods, employees were required to respond to any of seven facilities covering an 8-mile radius within 20 minutes of receiving a call for services (if they determined that the call necessitated a physical response to a facility and could not be handled by telephone). The number and frequency of calls received during any on-call shift were not predictable.

The need to respond immediately to medical calls required employees to maintain a constant state of readiness. They did not engage in recreational activities during these hours, nor did they use this time for their own personal purposes. Employees testified that they did not shower, walk for recreation, cook meals, eat in restaurants, entertain guests, perform yard work, or attend sporting events during their on-call hours. Some employees rented motel rooms in Canon City in order to meet the response time requirements rather than going home during these shifts.

Employees claimed their time spent waiting for calls constituted hours worked pursuant to 29 U.S.C. 201-219 (1988), the Federal Fair Labor Standards Act (FLSA), and that they should be compensated at a rate of time and one-half for all hours spent on-call in excess of their regular 40 hours per week.

The employees filed a formal grievance with

defendants in March 1988 for overtime pay and supplied copies of state fiscal rules incorporating the provisions of the FLSA and affidavits detailing the restrictions imposed upon their lives while on-call. The grievance was denied.

The defendants contend the trial court erred in failing to follow the terms of an agreement alleged to exist between the Department of Corrections and the employees regarding compensation for waiting time. They further contend the court erred in finding that this agreement was against public policy. We find no error.

Defendants assert that, in March 1988, the Department of Corrections officials and the employees had agreed that time spent waiting for calls would be compensated at $1.75 per hour, and time spent when employees physically traveled to a facility responding to a call would be compensated at time and one-half. Thus, they argue, the trial court erred in refusing to consider the impact of this agreement on employees' FLSA claims. We reject this contention.

The trial court found that any agreement by the employees to provide on-call services for the Department of Corrections was not an agreement to perform those services without the compensation required by law. It correctly determined that, as a matter of law, an agreement entered into in good faith cannot supersede the FLSA or be used as a defense against employees' claims.

The FLSA's overtime requirement, 29 U.S.C. 207 (1988), has two purposes: (1) to encourage employers to hire additional workers rather than employ fewer workers for longer hours; and (2) to compensate employees who do work overtime for the burden of having to do so. The Act "forbids pay plans that have the effect of reducing the pay for overtime to less than one and one-half times the employees' regular rate, even though the plans may be acceptable to the employees involved."

Given the nature of the demands on the employees during their waiting time, we conclude, as did the trial court, that any agreement to pay them

$1.75 per hour (well below their average salary of nearly $18 per hour) would be contrary to the purpose of the FLSA and thus would violate public policy.

Defendants next argue the trial court erred in awarding overtime compensation to the employees for the time spent waiting for calls. We find no error.

The FLSA requires the payment of time and one-half of an employee's regular rate of pay for each hour worked in excess of 40 hours in any workweek. 29 U.S.C. 207(a)(1) (1988).

"An employee who is required to remain on call on the employer's premises or so close thereto that he cannot use the time effectively for his own purposes is working while 'on call.'" 29 C.F.R. 785.17 (1991). Whether "waiting time" is "working time" depends on the particular case and is a question of fact to be resolved by the trial court.

The test is whether the time is spent predominately for the employer's benefit or for the employee's benefit. If the time spent is predominately for the employer's benefit, the employee is "engaged to be waiting" and is entitled to compensation.

Renfro v. City of Emporia, 948 F.2d 1529 (10th Cir. 1991), illustrates the on-call standard under the FLSA. In *Renfro,* the Court of Appeals affirmed a summary judgment entered on behalf of firefighters who had alleged their "on-call" time was compensable. The City of Emporia had two fire stations and each station maintained a separate on-call list. Firefighters employed with the City were regularly scheduled to work six shifts of 24 hours each in a 19-day cycle, for a total of 144 hours. Each firefighter also appeared on a mandatory callback list for each 24-hour period following a regularly scheduled tour of duty. During this callback period, the firefighters were not required to remain at the station house premises. However, they were required to carry pagers and to return to work within 20 minutes if called or be subject to discipline. The number of callbacks firefighters received ranged from zero to 13 per day but averaged approximately four to five per day.

The firefighters argued that the on-call policy greatly restricted their personal activities. They asserted that, because of the 20-minute time constraint and the large number of callbacks, they could not go out of town, could not do simple things such as change oil or do other work on their cars, could not go to a movie or out to dinner for fear of being called back, could not be alone with their children unless they had a babysitter "on-call," could not drive anywhere with anyone when on call (i.e., they would have had to take separate cars in case of a callback), and could not participate in group activities for fear of being called away. The appellate court concluded that the trial court's findings were supported by the record and that its application of the FLSA was appropriate in determining that the firefighters were due overtime compensation for their "on-call" time.

Here, the trial court made ample findings to support its conclusion that the employees could not use on-call time effectively for their own purposes, and the evidence in the record fully supports this determination.

This evidence included the high number of calls received (ranging from 10 to 12 calls per weekday shift, up to 24 calls on a weekend shift), the number of facilities (7) and geographical radius (8 miles) involved, and the 20-minute response time required. The employees testified, as noted above, concerning the severe restrictions placed on their personal activities by the on-call status. Indeed, one physician assistant testified that he remained partially dressed and slept on a couch near the telephone rather than going to bed at night.

There is overwhelming evidence in the record demonstrating that waiting time was not spent in ways the employees would have chosen had they been free to do so. Hence, we will not disturb the trial court's finding that the employees could not use the time effectively for their own purposes and, thus, were "working" for purposes of the FLSA.

AFFIRMED as to the employer's liability.

Case Questions

1. Why do you think the employer thought the employees were not entitled to time-and-a-half pay for being on call over 40 hours?

2. Is there any way you can think of that the employer can get around paying time-and-a-half to the employees? Explain.

3. The employer agreed to pay the employees $1.75. Can you think of why an employer would do this?

The following are exemptions from both the wage and overtime provisions. Note that under FLSA some employees are exempt from the overtime provisions but not the minimum wage provisions; but because their salaries are generally higher, this may not present as much of a problem (for instance, executives or teachers).

Scenario

1. Outside salespeople, executive, administrative, and professional employees, including teachers and academic administrative employees in elementary and secondary schools. (This is why Derry is not correct in opening scenario 3).

2. Employees of certain individually owned and operated small retail or service establishments not part of a covered enterprise.

3. Employees of certain seasonal amusement or recreational establishments, messengers, full-time students, employees of certain small newspapers, switchboard operators of small telephone companies, sailors employed on foreign vessels, employees engaged in fishing operations.

4. Farm workers employed by anyone who used more than 500 person-days of farm labor in any calendar quarter of the preceding calendar year.

5. Casual baby-sitters and people employed as companions to the elderly.

REICH V. NEWSPAPERS OF NEW ENGLAND, INC.
44 F.3d 1060 (1st Cir. 1995)

In this case the court determines whether reporters who do general reporting for a small local newspaper are subject to the FLSA overtime pay requirements.

Torruella, J.

The Monitor is an award-winning small-city newspaper with a daily circulation in excess of 4,000 copies. Its reporters are assigned to tasks ranging from writing features to covering legislative, municipal, and town governments and agencies. The reporters work essentially unsupervised,

have authority and discretion over what they do and write, and decide how their assignments should be executed. Most of their time, however, is spent on "general assignment" work, and their writing is mainly focused on "hard news."

Even though its reporters work extended

hours, management at *The Monitor* discourages overtime. Rather, it prefers that its employees seek compensatory time. The secretary of labor asserts that *The Monitor*'s overtime policy violates the FLSA, and seeks a permanent injunction and back pay for the employees. *The Monitor* responds that the employees are exempt professionals.

The FLSA's overtime compensation provisions do not apply to professionals. The specific requirements of the exemption are not set forth in the statute. Rather, they are articulated in Department of Labor regulations and interpretations.

The regulation enumerates several types of professional exemptions, but only the "artistic professional" exemption, which applies to professionals working in a "recognized field of artistic endeavor," applies here. The regulation outlines both a short and long test for determining whether an employee qualifies as an artistic professional. The long test is applied to employees who earn weekly salaries of at least $170 but less than $250. Both tests demand that the employee's "primary duty" consist of work requiring "invention, imagination, or talent." The long test also requires that the employee's primary duty consist of "[w]ork that is original and creative in character." 29 CFR 541.3(a)(2).

The Monitor maintains that the district court erroneously applied the long test to three reporters whose weekly salary qualified them for analysis under the short test. This issue is not dispositive, however, because we believe the employees are exempt under either test.

The relevant portion of the short test requires us to determine (1) the employee's "primary duty," and (2) whether the performance of that duty requires "invention, imagination, or talent." Because the secretary stipulated that writing was the primary duty of these employees, the only issue remaining is whether their writing required "invention, imagination, or talent."

The day-to-day duties of the three reporters consisted primarily of "general assignment" work. Among other things, their stories covered public utility commission hearings; criminal and police activity; city and state legislative proceedings; business events, including compiling a list of people who had been promoted; and local art events. Rarely were they asked to editorialize about or interpret the events they covered. Rather, in the words of one of the employees, the focus of their writing was "to tell someone who wanted to know what happened . . . in a quick and informative and understandable way." Thus, these reporters were like the majority of reporters in that their work "depends primarily on intelligence, diligence, and accuracy." They were not performing duties that would place them in that minority of reporters whose work depends primarily on invention, imagination, or talent. Although some of their work product demonstrated creativity, invention, imagination, and talent, their writing did not exhibit these qualities on a day-to-day basis.

Our decision should not be read to mean that all journalism work is non-exempt. The determination of whether the exemption applies to a given employee depends on the specific duties and characteristics required by the position rather than its actual title. AFFIRMED.

Case Questions

1. Are you surprised by this decision?
2. Does this decision make sense to you?
3. Why do you think the employer chose to interpret the regulation as it did?

Maximum Hours

Scenario

Actually, FLSA does not limit the hours employees work, but, rather, sets standards for the hours constituting a normal work week for wage purposes. The statute then sets wage rates for hours worked over and above the normal week. The 40-hour work week and wage rate were discussed previously in the minimum wage section, as were the exemptions. That is why, in opening scenario 2, Kweisi is incorrect in telling his boss that the law does not require him to work over 40 hours per week. The law merely states that, if Kweisi does work over 40 hours, he must be paid time and a half for the time he worked in excess of 40 hours.

SHERWOOD V. WASHINGTON POST
871 F. Supp. 1471 (Dist. Ct. of D.C. 1994)

A newspaper reporter whose primary duties required invention, imagination, and talent is found to be exempt from the overtime requirement of the FLSA.

Johnson, J.

A former reporter for the *Washington Post* contends that the paper violated the FLSA by refusing to pay overtime for all hours worked in excess of 40 hours per week. The reporter's primary duty for the paper was to gather news and present it to readers in a clear, fair, balanced and expert fashion. He was also required to originate story ideas, piece together seemingly unrelated facts, analyze facts and circumstances, and present his stories in an engaging style. His fact gathering thus involved more than passively writing down what others told him. He was required to cultivate sources, utilize his imagination and other skills in seeking information, and continually develop his finely tuned interviewing skills. The reporter was required to advise his editors when he believed that particular topics might be newsworthy, and was expected to originate ideas for stories. He was the one primarily responsible for producing story ideas and following through on their investigation. The court finds that the duties of originating story ideas, and getting information to shape and develop stories, required invention, imagination and talent by the reporter. JUDGMENT FOR DEFENDANT.

Case Questions

1. Do you understand the difference between this case and the *Newspapers of New England* case? Explain.

2. Do you think there should be a distinction in FLSA between those who use their imagination, talent, and invention and those who do not, though they do the same thing such as work as reporters for a newspaper?

3. How would you change this FLSA scheme, if you could?

In *Moreau,* below, the US Supreme Court wrestled with the issue of whether sheriffs could receive **comp time** (see p. 762 margin note) rather than time and a half for overtime worked. This has become an increasingly heated topic for exempt employees who would not otherwise be entitled to overtime pay but wish to receive some form of compensation for working more than 40 hours per week.

MOREAU, ET AL. V. KLEVENHAGEN
508 U.S. 22 (1993)

A group of sheriffs wanted to be paid time-and-a-half rather than comp time for overtime under the FLSA. They alleged the statute allowing for comp time did not apply to them; thus, they should be paid overtime rather than comp time. The Supreme Court held that under FLSA they could lawfully be compensated with comp time rather than time-and-a-half for the overtime worked.

Stevens, J.

Because the text of the FLSA Amendments of 1985, 99 Stat. 70, codified at 29 U.S.C. 207(o) provides the framework for our entire analysis, we quote the most relevant portion at the outset. Subsection 7(o)(2)(A) states:

(2) A public agency may provide compensatory time [in lieu of overtime pay] only—

(A) pursuant to—

(i) applicable provisions of a collective bargaining agreement, memorandum of understanding, or any other agreement between the public agency and representatives of such employees; or

(ii) in the case of employees not covered by subclause (i), an agreement or understanding arrived at between the employer and employee before the performance of the work. . . .

Petitioners are a group of employees who sought, unsuccessfully, to negotiate a collective FLSA compensatory time agreement by way of a designated representative. The narrow question dispositive here is whether petitioners are "employees not covered by subclause (i)" within the meaning of subclause (ii), so that their employer may provide compensatory time pursuant to individual agreements under the second subclause.

Petitioner Moreau is the president of the Harris County Deputy Sheriffs Union, representing approximately 400 deputy sheriffs in this action against the County and its sheriff, respondent Klevenhagen. For several years, the Union has represented Harris County deputy sheriffs in various matters, such as processing grievances and handling workers' compensation claims, but it is prohibited by Texas law from entering into a collective-bargaining agreement with the County. Accordingly, the terms and conditions of petitioners' employment are included in individual form agreements signed by each employee. These agreements incorporate by reference the County's regulations providing that deputies shall receive one and one-half hours of compensatory time for each hour of overtime work.

The employees filed this action, alleging, inter alia, that the County violated the Act by paying overtime work with comp time, rather than overtime pay, absent an agreement with their representative authorizing the substitution. Employees contended that they were "covered" by subclause (i) of subsection 7(o)(2)(A) by virtue of their union representation, and that the County therefore was precluded from providing comp time pursuant to individual agreements (or pre-existing practice) under subclause (ii).

Employers find the language of the statute perfectly clear. In their view, subclause (ii) plainly authorizes individual agreements whenever public employees have not successfully negotiated a collective-bargaining agreement under subclause (i). Employees, on the other hand, contend that ambiguity in the statute itself justifies resort to its legislative history and the DOL regulations, and that these secondary sources unequivocally preclude individual comp time agreements with employees who have designated a representative. We begin our analysis with the relevant statutory text.

At least one proposition is not in dispute. Subclause (ii) authorizes individual comp time agreements only "in the case of employees not covered by subclause (i)." Our task, therefore, is to identify the class of "employees" covered by subclause (i). This task is complicated by the fact that subclause (i) does not purport to define a category of employees, as the reference in subclause (ii) suggests it would. Instead, it describes only a category of agreements—those that (a) are bargained with an employee representative, and (b) authorize the use of comp time.

Respondents read this shift in subject from "employees" in subclause (ii) to "agreement" in subclause (i) as susceptible of just one meaning: employees are covered by subclause (i) only if they are bound by applicable provisions of a collective-bargaining agreement. Under this narrow construction, subclause (i) would not cover employees who designate a representative if that representative is unable to reach agreement with the employer, for whatever reason; such employees would remain "uncovered" and available for individual comp time agreements under subclause (ii).

We find this reading unsatisfactory. First, while the language of subclauses (i) and (ii) will bear the interpretation advanced by respondents, we cannot say that it will bear no other. Purely as a matter of grammar, subclause (ii)'s reference to "employees" remains unmodified by subclause (i)'s focus on "agreement," and "employees . . . covered" might as easily comprehend employees with representatives as employees with agreements.

Second, employer's reading is difficult to reconcile with the general structure of subsection 7(o). Assuming designation of an employee representative, employer's theory leaves it to the employer to choose whether it will proceed under subclause (i), and negotiate the terms of a collective comp time agreement with the representative, or instead proceed under subclause (ii), and deal directly with its employees on an individual basis. If the employer is free to choose the latter course (as most employers likely would), then it need only decline to negotiate with the employee representative to render subclause (i) inapplicable and authorize individual comp time agreements under subclause (ii). This permissive interpretation of subsection 7(o), however, is at odds with the limiting phrase of subclause (ii) at issue here. Had Congress intended such an open-ended authorization of the use of comp time, it surely would have said so more simply, forgoing the elaborate subclause structure that purports to restrict use of individual agreements to a limited class of employees. Employer's broad interpretation of the subsection 7(o) exception is also in some tension with the well-established rule that "exemptions from the [FLSA] are to be narrowly construed."

At the same time, however, we find equally implausible a reading of the statutory text that would deem employees "covered" by subclause (i) whenever they select a representative, whether or not the representative has the ability to enter into the kind of agreement described in that subclause. If there is no possibility of reaching an agreement under subclause (i), then that subclause cannot logically be read as applicable. In other words, "employees . . . covered by subclause (i)" must, at a minimum, be employees who conceivably could receive comp time pursuant to the agreement contemplated by that subclause.

The most plausible reading of the phrase "employees . . . covered by subclause (i)" is, in our view, neither of the extreme alternatives described above. Rather, the phrase is most sensibly read as referring to employees who have designated a representative with the authority to negotiate and agree with their employer on "applicable provisions of a collective bargaining agreement" authorizing the use of comp time. This reading accords significance to both the focus on the word "agreement" in subclause (i) and the focus on "employees" in subclause (ii). It is also true to the hierarchy embodied in subsection 7(o), which favors subclause (i) agreements over individual agreements by limiting use of the latter to cases in which the former are unavailable.

This intermediate reading of the statutory text is consistent also with the DOL regulations, interpreted most reasonably. It is true that 29 CFR 553.23(b), read in isolation, would support the employees' view that selection of a representative by employees—even a representative without lawful authority to bargain with the employer—is sufficient to bring the employees within the scope of subclause (i) and preclude use of subclause (ii) individual agreements. So interpreted, however, the regulation would prohibit entirely the use of comp time in a substantial portion of the public sector. It would also be inconsistent with the Secretary's statement that "the question . . . whether employees have a representative for purposes of FLSA section 7(o) shall be determined in accordance with State or local law and practices." This clarification by the Secretary convinces us that when the regulations identify selection of a representative as the condition necessary for coverage under subclause (i), they refer only to those representatives with lawful authority to negotiate agreements.

Thus, under both the statute and the DOL regulations, employees are "covered" by subclause (i) when they designate a representative who lawfully may bargain collectively on their behalf—under the statute, because such authority is necessary to reach the kind of "agreement" described in subclause (i), and under the regulation, because such authority is a condition of "representative" status for subclause (i) purposes. Because we construe the statute and regulation in harmony, we need not comment further on the employees' argument that the Secretary's interpretation of the 1985 Amendments is entitled to special deference.

The employees' in this case did not have a representative authorized by law to enter into an agreement with their employer providing for use of comp time under subclause (i). Accordingly, they were "not covered by subclause (i)," and subclause (ii) authorized the individual agreements challenged in this litigation. AFFIRMED.

Case Questions

1. Why do you think the employer wanted to pay comp time rather than time-and-a-half?

2. Do you agree with the Court's assessment of the statutory language permitting the comp time? Explain.

3. Do you think that since this was a public employer the Court was more sensitive to the issue of public finances, accountability to the public, the need for containing costs, and the potential for abuse in overtime when the public's welfare is at issue? Explain.

Exhibit 22–4   Move to Lift Ban on Young Bat Boys, Girls Runs Counter to Child Labor Panel's Advice

Labor Secretary Robert Reich's announcement last week that he was moving to suspend restrictions on the hours that 14- and 15-year-olds may work as baseball bat boys and girls runs counter to a recommendation by an advisory panel established to review the child labor laws.

Reich's position accords with that of former Vice-President Dan Quayle, who unsuccessfully worked to lift the ban during his tenure in the Senate. Quayle had sought to amend the Fair Labor Standards Act after the Labor Department said bat boys and girls must be at least 16 years old because 14- and 15-year-olds may not work beyond 9:00 P.M. during the summer and 7:00 P.M. while school is in session.

Reich said last May 27 he was suspending enforcement of the DOL regulation for the remainder of the baseball season. "After a preliminary review, the current child labor policy, as it has been applied to batboys and batgirls, seems off base," he said.

Reich's move was prompted by the Savannah Cardinals' firing of Tommy McCoy, a bat boy under the age of 16. The Labor Department had alerted the team that McCoy's employment might pose a problem. The investigation had not proceeded any further before Reich decided to suspend enforcement while examining the rule.

Reich said an examination of whether "the child labor regulation in such a case is truly necessary" is "[c]onsistent with the current efforts to reinvent government, to make it more responsive and efficient." McCoy has since gone back to work for the Cardinals. It is "not the intent of the law to deny young teenagers employment opportunities, so long as their health and well-being are not impaired," Reich said.

Reich's move runs counter to the position adopted by the now-defunct independent Child Labor Advisory Committee. In 1989, the panel recommended and the Labor Department agreed that there should be no exception for hours and times of work for 14- and 15-year-olds working as bat boys and girls in professional baseball.

Linda Golodner, co-chair of the Child Labor Coalition, criticized Reich's move, voicing concern that it sets a precedent for other changes in the child labor regulations. Golodner, who headed the advisory panel, told BNA May 28 the coalition opposes any exceptions to allowing 14- and 15-year-olds to work longer hours, no matter how "glamorous" the industry.

Reprinted with permission from *Daily Labor Reports,* No. 103, pp A-13–A-14 (June 1s, 1993). Copyright 1993 by The Bureau of National Affairs, Inc. (800-372-1033). http://www.bna.com.

Comp time
Compensatory time. Time off given to an employee who works over a certain amount of hours. Given in lieu of overtime pay, generally to those who do not qualify for such pay.

Scenario

Child Labor Laws

FLSA sets minimum age standards for allowing children to work. Under the law, most cannot work before age 16, with 18 being the minimum age for hazardous jobs. The Department of Labor publishes a list of such occupations. Children between the ages of 14 and 16 may work at certain types of jobs that do not interfere with their health, education, or well being, such as the traditional newspaper deliverer set forth in opening scenario 1. Certain agricultural work is permitted also. States may have child labor laws even stricter than the federal, and, if so, they override federal law. Exhibits 22–3 and 22–4 indicate not only how important an issue this can become, but also how divided.

Management Tips

As you have seen, there are several unexpected ways in which an employer can unwittingly violate the Fair Labor Standards Act. Becoming familiar with the requirements of the law and knowing its limitations proves helpful, as do the following tips.

- Whenever an employee is not an adult, check to make sure the employee is working only in ways authorized by law, and hours dictated by law. Do not make exceptions.

- The purpose of time-and-a-half pay is to encourage employers to bring on extra employees when needed, rather than using present employees to take on extra duties or work extra hours. Keep this in mind when there is a pattern of excessive overtime pay. It may well indicate the need for additional employees.

- Be familiar with the employees exempted from wage and hour requirements so that wages are not paid out unnecessarily.

- Conduct periodic audits of the workplace to make sure employees are working as efficiently as possible so that overtime is limited only to what is necessary.

- Use the resources of the wage and hour offices if you run into a situation that seems unclear.

Summary

- FLSA is a comprehensive piece of legislation that governs wages, hours, and the employment of minors in the workplace and requires equal pay for both genders.

- While its coverage is far-reaching, it does provide exemptions.

- Employers are required to pay covered employees at least the minimum wage.

- Covered employees must be compensated at a rate of time and one-half their normal rate of pay for hours worked over 40 in one week.

- Children are prohibited from working if they are below a certain age, with exceptions.

- Be familiar with both the provisions of coverage as well as the exemptions, because violations may result in civil and criminal liability.

Chapter-End Questions

1. An employment placement agency employed Ursula as a staffing coordinator. Ursula received pay at straight-time rates for working any hours over 40. After resigning, Ursula claimed that the placement agency failed to pay her overtime wages as required by law. The agency claimed Ursula was an administrative employee who was exempt from overtime pay laws. Should Ursula receive the overtime pay? *Tift v. Professional Nursing Serv., Inc.,* 886 P.2d 1158 (Wash. App. Div. 1 1995).

2. A nonprofit religious organization derived most of its income from the operation of commercial businesses staffed by its "associates." These people, former drug

addicts and criminals, received no cash salaries, but were provided with food, clothing, shelter, and other benefits. Are these "associates" subject to the FLSA? *Tony and Susan Alamo Foundation v. Secretary of Labor,* 471 U.S. 290 (1985).

3. Truck drivers employed by a freight company were required to conduct safety inspections on their trucks and take them in for repair if they failed the inspection. They were not paid by the employer for doing this. Does FLSA require that they be paid? *Barrentine v. Arkansas-Best Freight System,* 450 U.S. 728 (1981).

4. A manufacturer agreed with the union to allow them to have their union representatives (president and vice president) work on union matters full time and be paid by the manufacturer. The manufacturer agreed to pay the employees for 40 hours per week plus an amount based on the average overtime worked by employees in their departments. The employees handled grievances and workers' compensation claims but performed no work for the manufacturer. The employees demanded time and a half for overtime pay for hours worked over 40, rather than the amount based on the average overtime worked by their department co-workers. The manufacturer refused to pay. Should the employees receive what they asked for, under FLSA? *Douglas v. Argo-Tech Corp.,* 113 F.3d 67 (6th Cir. 1997).

5. An ambulance service scheduled employees in 24-hour shifts, but only paid them for 13 or 14 hours of work. They deducted 8 hours for sleep and 3 hours for meals, even though they counted as little as 30 minutes as a meal break. The employees challenged this practice. Will they win? *Bayles v. American*

Medical Response of Colorado, Inc., 950 F. Supp. 1053 (D. Colo. 1996).

6. Churchill W. Allbright II runs a business in which he employs illegal immigrants from the age of 13 on to make shirts and pants. Allbright employs the workers, even at such young ages, because he knows they will not report him because of their immigration status. When Allbright is found to have violated the FLSA, the prosecutors request that criminal fines of $9,500 be imposed for each violation. Allbright does not think such fines can be imposed. Is he correct?

7. In the scenario in question 6, could Allbright be imprisoned for violating the FLSA? Explain.

8. Allbright finds that Benito, Juana, and Lao Tsu, three of his employees, were the cause of the discovery of FLSA violations. As a result, he terminates them. Do the employees have any recourse? Explain.

9. Thomas, an elementary school teacher, is resentful of the time he has to spend before and after school correcting papers, copying work sheets for students, and creating interesting and stimulating classroom bulletin boards for the children. Janella, an hourly employee at the local toy factory, tells Thomas that he should file a claim against his employer for violating the FLSA because when she works over a certain number of hours per week she is paid overtime, and Thomas should be too. What should Thomas do?

10. Sasha is employed as the Winston's babysitter when they must occasionally stay over in town because of their jobs. Sasha is becoming increasingly discontented with her wages, which are below minimum wage. What relief does the FLSA provide for Sasha?

abatement An action of stopping or removing.

abuse of process An intentional tort designed to protect against the initiation of legal proceedings for a primary purpose other than the one for which such proceedings were designed.

acceleration The shortening of the time for the performance of a contact or the payment of a note by the operation of some provision in the contract or note itself.

acceptance The actual or implied receipt and retention of what is tendered or offered.

accord and satisfaction A legally binding agreement to settle a disputed claim for a definite amount and its payment.

acquit To set free or judicially to discharge from an accusation; to release from a debt, duty, obligation, charge, or suspicion of guilt.

actionable Capable of being remedied by a legal action or claim.

act of God An occurrence resulting exclusively from natural forces that could not have been prevented or whose effect could not have been avoided by care or foresight.

adjudge To give judgment; to decide; to sentence.

adjudicate To adjudge; to settle by judicial decree, as a court.

ad litem During the pendency of the action or proceeding.

administrator The personal representative appointed by a probate court to settle the estate of a deceased person who died intestate (with out leaving a valid will).

adoption In corporate law, a corporation's acceptance of a contract by action of its board of directors, by which the corporation becomes liable on the contract.

adverse employment action Any action or omission that takes away a benefit, opportunity, or privilege of employment.

affidavit A signed writing containing statements of fact to whose accuracy the signing party has sworn. Used in a variety of judicial proceedings, including the motion for summary judgment.

affinity orientation Sexual preference.

affirm To confirm or uphold a former judgment or order of a court. Appellate courts, for instance, may affirm the decisions of lower courts.

affirmative action Intentional inclusion of women and minorities in the workplace based on a finding of their previous exclusion.

affirmative action plan A contractor's plan containing goals for representation of women and minorities in the workplace and timetables for accomplishing the goals.

Age Discrimination in Employment Act Prohibits discrimination in employment on the basis of age; applies to individuals who are at least 40 years old. Individuals who are not yet 40 years old are not protected by the Act and may be discriminated against on the basis of their age.

agency   A legal relationship in which an agent acts under the direction of a principal for the principal's benefit. Also used to refer to government regulatory bodies of all kinds.

agency shop clause   Requires nonunion members to pay union dues without having to be subject to the union rules.

agent   One who acts under the direction of a principal for the principal's benefit in a legal relationship known as agency. See **principal.**

aggrieved   One whose legal rights have been invaded by the act of another is said to be aggrieved. Also, one whose pecuniary interest is directly affected by a judgment, or whose right of property may be divested thereby, is to be considered a party aggrieved.

AIDS   Acquired immune deficiency syndrome, a syndrome in which the individual's immune system ceases to function properly and during which the individual is susceptible, most cases fatally, to opportunistic diseases. AIDS is not transmitted through casual contact; to transmit the disease, there must be an exchange of fluids. The disease may be transmitted through sexual contact, during which there is an exchange of bodily fluids, needle-sharing, or an exchange of blood or breast milk.

allegation   A statement of a party to an action in a declaration or pleading of what the party intends to prove.

allege   To make a statement of fact; to plead.

Americans with Disabilities Act   Extends Rehabilitation Act protection to employees in the private sector, with few modifications.

amicus curiae   Brief filed by a "friend of the court" who is not a party to the lawsuit but has an interest in the issues.

ancillary   Auxiliary to. An ancillary receiver is a receiver who has been appointed in aid of, and in subordination to, the primary receiver.

ancillary covenant not to compete   A promise that is ancillary to (part of) a valid contract whereby one party to a contract agrees not to compete with the other party for a specified time and within a specified location. Also called *noncompetition clause.*

answer   The pleading of a defendant in which he or she may deny any or all the facts set out in the plaintiff's declaration or complaint.

anticipatory breach   A contracting party's indication before the time for performance that he or she cannot or will not perform the contract.

appearance   The first act of the defendant in court.

appellant   The party making an appeal.

appellate jurisdiction   Jurisdiction to revise or correct the work of a subordinate court.

appellee   A party against whom a favorable court decision is appealed. May be called the *respondent* in some jurisdictions.

applicant   A petitioner; one who files a petition or application.

arbitrate   To submit some disputed matter to selected persons and to accept their decision or award as a substitute for the decision of a judicial tribunal.

argument   The discussion by counsel for the respective parties of their contentions on the law and the facts of the case being tried to aid the jury in arriving at a correct and just conclusion.

assault   An intentional tort that prohibits any attempt or offer to cause harmful or offensive contact with another if it results in a well-grounded apprehension of imminent battery in the mind of the threatened person.

assent   To give or express one's concurrence or approval of something done.

assignable   Capable of being lawfully assigned or transferred; transferable; negotiable. Also, capable of being specified or pointed out as an assignable error.

assignee   A person to whom an assignment is made.

assignment   A transfer or setting over of property or some right or interest therein, from one person to another.

assignor   The maker of an assignment.

assumpsit   An action at common law to recover damages for breach of contract.

assumption of the risk   A traditional defense to negligence liability based on the argument that the plaintiff took a chance that a known potentially harmful situation would not cause injury.

assurance   To provide confidence or to inform positively.

attachment   In general, the process of taking a person's property under an appropriate judicial order by an appropriate officer of the court. Used for a variety of purposes, including the acquisition of jurisdiction over the property seized and the securing of property that may be used to satisfy a debt.

attest   To bear witness to; to affirm; to be true or genuine.

attorney-in-fact   An agent who is given express, written authorization by her principal to do a particular act or series of acts on behalf of the principal.

at-will employment   An employment relationship where there is no contractual obligation to remain in the relationship; either party may terminate the relationship at any time, for any reason, as long as the reason is not prohibited by law (such as for discriminatory purposes).

authority   In agency law, an agent's ability to affect her or his principal's legal relations with third parties. Also used to refer to an actor's legal power or ability to do something. In addition, sometimes used to refer to a statute, case, or other legal source that justifies a particular result.

avoid   To nullify a contractual obligation.

back pay   Money awarded for the time an employee was not working (usually due to termination) because of illegal discrimination.

bad faith   A person's actual intent to mislead or deceive another; an intent to take an unfair and unethical advantage of another.

bankruptcy   The state of a person who is unable to pay his or her debts without respect to time; one whose liabilities exceed his or her assets.

bar   As a collective noun, it is used to include those persons who are admitted to practice law, members of the bar. The court itself. A plea or peremptory exception of a defendant sufficient to destroy the plaintiff's actions.

bargaining unit   The group of employees in a particular workplace who has rights to bargain with the employer under the law.

battery   An intentional tort that prohibits the harmful or offensive touching of another without his or her consent.

bench   Generally used as a synonym for the term *court* or the judges of a court.

beneficiary   The person for whose benefit an insurance policy, trust, will, or contract is established. In the case of a contract, the beneficiary is called a *third-party beneficiary.*

bequeath   In a will, a gift of particular property.

bid   To make an offer at an auction or at a judicial sale. As a noun, it means an offer.

bi-gender affinity orientation   Someone attracted to either gender.

bilateral contract   A contract in which the promise of one of the parties forms the consideration for the promise of the other; a contract formed by an offer requiring a reciprocal promise.

bona fide   Made honestly and in good faith; genuine.

bona fide occupational qualification (BFOQ)   Permissible discrimination if necessary to an employer's business and not based on pretext.

bona fide purchaser   An innocent buyer for valuable consideration who purchases goods without notice of any defects in the title of the goods acquired.

brief   A statement of a party's case or legal arguments, usually prepared by an attorney. Often used to support some of the motions described in the Resolution of Private Disputes chapter and also used to make legal arguments before appellate courts. Also, an abridgment of a reported case.

burden of proof   Used to refer both to the necessity or obligation of proving the facts needed to support a party's claim, and the persuasiveness of the evidence used to do so. Regarding the second sense of the term, the usual burden of proof in a civil case is a preponderance of the evidence, and in a criminal case it is proof beyond a reasonable doubt.

business agent   The representative of a union, usually craft.

business judgment rule   A rule protecting business managers from liability for making bad decisions when they have acted prudently and in good faith.

business necessity   Defense to a disparate impact case.

capacity   The ability to incur legal obligations and acquire legal rights.

case law   The law extracted from decided cases.

cause of action   A legal rule giving the plaintiff the right to obtain some legal relief once certain factual elements are proven. Often used synonymously with the terms *claim* or *theory of recovery.*

chancery   Equity or a court of equity.

charge   The legal instructions that a judge gives a jury before the jury begins its deliberations. In the prosecution of a crime, to formally accuse the offender or charge him or her with the crime.

charging order   A court's order granting rights in a partner's partnership interest to a personal creditor of the partner; a creditor with a charging order is entitled to the partner's share of partnership profits.

citation   A writ issued out of a court of competent jurisdiction, commanding the person therein named to appear on a day named to do something therein mentioned.

citation of authorities   The reference to legal authorities, such as reported cases or treatises to support propositions advanced.

civil action   An action brought to enforce a civil right; in contrast to a criminal action.

class action   An action brought on behalf of the plaintiff and others similarly situated.

closed shop   Employer hires only union members.

code   A system of law; a systematic and complete body of law.

collateral   Property put up to secure the performance of a promise, so that if the promisor fails to perform as promised, the creditor may look to the property to make him whole.

collective bargaining   Negotiations and agreements between management and labor regarding wages, hours, and other terms and conditions of employment.

collective bargaining agreement   Contract between labor and management, covering wages, hours, and other conditions of employment.

common law defenses   Contributory negligence, voluntary assumption of the risk, and fellow servant doctrine theories, which could be used by an employer to prevent liability from attaching, before workers' compensation statutes were instituted.

common law test of employee status   List of 20 factors to which the IRS looks to determine whether someone is an employee or an independent contractor. The IRS compiled this list from the results of judgments of the courts relating to this issue.

community of interests   Factors that employees have in common for bargaining purposes.

comparable worth   A Title VII action for pay discrimination, based on gender, in which jobs held mostly by women are compared with comparable jobs held mostly by men who are paid more than the women, to determine if there is gender discrimination.

comparative fault   Often used synonymously with comparative negligence. But also sometimes used to refer to a defense that operates like comparative negli-

gence but considers the plaintiff's and the defendant's overall fault rather than either's negligence alone.

comparative negligence   The contemporary replacement for the traditional doctrine of contributory negligence. The basic idea is that damages are apportioned between the parties to a negligence action in proportion to their relative fault. The details vary from state to state.

compensatory damages. See **damages, compensatory.**

complaint   The pleading in a civil case in which the plaintiff states his claim and requests relief.

concealment   In contract law, taking active steps to prevent another from learning the truth.

conciliation   Trying to reach agreement about a claim through discussion, without resort to litigation.

concurrent   Running with; simultaneously with. The word is used in different senses. In contracts, concurrent conditions are conditions that must be performed simultaneously by the mutual acts required by each of the parties.

condemn   To appropriate land for public use. To adjudge a person guilty; to pass sentence upon a person convicted of a crime.

condition   In contract law, a future, uncertain event that creates or extinguishes a duty of performance; a provision or clause in a contract that operates to suspend or rescind a party's duty to perform. In property law, a qualification or restriction annexed to a conveyance of lands, whereby it is provided that in case a particular event does or does not happen, or in case the grantor or grantees do or omit to do a particular act, an estate shall commence, be enlarged, or be defeated.

conditional acceptance   An acceptance of a bill of exchange containing some qualification limiting or altering the acceptor's liability on the bill.

conditional sale   The term is most frequently applied to a sale wherein the seller reserves the title to the goods, though the possession is delivered to the buyer, until the purchase price is paid in full.

condition precedent   A condition that operates to give rise to a contracting party's duty to perform.

condition subsequent   A condition that operates to relieve or discharge one from his obligation under contract.

confession of judgment   An entry of judgment on the admission or confession of the debtor without the formality, time, or expense involved in an ordinary proceeding.

confusion The inseparable intermixture of property belonging to different owners.

consent decree or consent order Used to refer to the order courts or administrative agencies issue when approving the settlement of a lawsuit or administrative action against some party.

consent restraint A security transfer restriction requiring a shareholder to obtain the consent of the corporation or its shareholders prior to the shareholder's sale of her shares.

consequential damages See **damages, consequential.**

consideration In contract law, a basic requirement for an enforceable agreement under traditional contract principals, defined in this text as legal value, bargained for and given in exchange for an act or promise. In corporation law, cash or property contributed to a corporation in exchange for shares, or a promise to contribute such cash or property.

constructive discharge Occurs when the employee is given no reasonable alternative but to terminate the employment relationship; considered an involuntary act on the part of the employee.

construe To read a statute or document for the purpose of ascertaining its meaning and effect, but in doing so the law must be regarded.

contempt Conduct in the presence of a legislative or judicial body tending to disturb its proceedings or impair the respect due to its authority, or a disobedience to the rules or orders of such a body, which interferes with the due administration of law.

continual training requirement OSHA requires that the employer provide safety training to all new employees and to all employees who have been transferred into new positions.

contra Otherwise; disagreeing with; contrary to.

contract A legally enforceable promise or set of promises.

contract of adhesion A contract in which a stronger party is able to dictate terms to a weaker party, leaving the weaker party no practical choice but to "adhere" to the terms. If the stronger party has exploited its bargaining power to achieve unfair terms, the contract is against public policy.

contribution In business organization law, the cash or property contributed to a business by its owners.

contributory negligence A traditional defense to negligence liability based on the plaintiff's failure to exercise reasonable care for his own safety.

conversion Any distinct act of dominion wrongfully exerted over another's personal property in denial of or inconsistent with her rights therein. That tort committed by a person who deals with chattels not belonging to her in a manner that is inconsistent with the ownership of the lawful owner.

counterclaim A legal claim made in response to the plaintiff's initial claim in a civil suit. Unlike a defense, the counterclaim is the defendant's affirmative attempt to obtain legal relief; in effect, it states a cause of action entitling the defendant to such relief. Often, the counterclaim must arise out of the occurrence that forms the basis for the plaintiff's claim.

counteroffer A cross-offer made by the offeree to the offeror.

countertrade A buyer's purchase of the seller's goods in exchange for the seller's agreement to purchase goods of the buyer or other person; usually required as a condition to selling goods to a foreign trade corporation.

course of dealing A sequence of previous conduct between the parties to a transaction that is fairly to be regarded as establishing a common basis for interpreting their contract.

covenant A contract; a promise.

covenant of good faith and fair dealing Implied contractual obligation to act in good faith in the fulfillment of each party's contractual duties.

cover To obtain substitute or equivalent goods.

craft union Unions composed of skilled craftworkers not situated at any one workplace.

credible As applied to a witness, competent.

creditor A person to whom a debt or legal obligation is owed, and who has the right to enforce payment of that debt or obligation.

crime An action prohibited by the state; a public wrong.

cross-action Cross-complaint; an independent action brought by a defendant against the plaintiff.

culpable Blameworthy; denotes breach of legal duty but not necessarily criminal conduct.

damages   The sum of money recoverable by a plaintiff who has received a judgment in a civil case.

   compensatory   Money awarded to compensate a party for direct losses.

   consequential   Damages that do not flow directly and immediately from an act but rather flow from the results of the act; damages that are indirect consequences of a breach of contract or certain other legal wrongs. Examples include personal injury, damage to property, and lost profits.

   incidental   Collateral damages that result from a breach of contract, including all reasonable expenses that are incurred because of the breach; damages that compensate a person injured by a breach of contract for reasonable costs he or she incurs in an attempt to avoid further loss.

   liquidated   Damages made certain by the prior agreement of the parties.

   nominal   Damages that are recoverable when a legal right is to be vindicated against an invasion that has produced no actual present loss.

   punitive   Money awarded over and above compensatory damages, designed to punish intentional wrongdoers and to deter them and others from engaging in similar conduct in the future.

   special   Actual damages that would not necessarily but because of special circumstances do in fact flow from an injury.

   treble   Three times provable damages, as may be granted to private parties bringing an action under the antitrust laws.

deal   To engage in transactions of any kind, to do business with.

debar   Prohibition from further participation in government contracts.

debtor   A person who is under a legal obligation to pay a sum of money to another (the creditor).

deceit   A tort involving intentional misrepresentation or cheating by means of some device.

decision   The judgment of a court; the opinion merely represents the reasons for that judgment.

declaration   The pleadings by which a plaintiff in an action at law sets out his cause of action. An admission or statement subsequently used as evidence in the trial of an action.

declaratory judgment   One that expresses the opinion of a court on a question of law without ordering anything to be done.

decree   An order or sentence of a court of equity determining some right or adjudicating some matter affecting the merits of the cause.

de facto   In fact; actual. Often used in contrast to *de jure* to refer to a real state of affairs.

defamation   An intentional tort that prohibits the publication of false and defamatory statements concerning another.

default   Fault; neglect; omission; the failure of a party to an action to appear when properly served with process; the failure to perform a duty or obligation; the failure of a person to pay money when due or when lawfully demanded.

defend   To oppose a claim or action; to plead in defense of an action; to contest an action suit or proceeding.

defendant   The party who is sued in a civil case, or the party who is prosecuted in a criminal case.

defense   A rule of law entitling the defendant to a judgment in his favor even if the plaintiff proves all elements of her or his claim or cause of action.

defined benefit plan   A plan that defines in advance the amount to be recovered on retirement.

defined contribution plan   A plan that defines the amount of the employee contribution without a specific amount to be recovered at retirement.

defraud   To deprive another of a right by deception or artifice.

de jure   According to the law; legitimate; by legal right.

delegation   In constitutional law and administrative law, a process whereby a legislature effectively hands over some of its legislative power to an administrative agency that it has created, thus giving the agency power to make law within the limits set by the legislature. In contract law, a transaction whereby a person who owes a legal duty to perform under a contract appoints someone else to carry out his performance.

demand   A claim; a legal obligation; a request to perform an alleged obligation; a written statement of claim. In corporation law, a request that the board of directors sue a person who has harmed the corporation; a prerequisite to a shareholder derivative suit.

demurrer   A civil motion that attacks the plaintiff's

complaint by assuming the truth of the facts stated in the complaint for purposes of the motion and by arguing that even if these facts are true, there is no rule of law entitling the plaintiff to recovery. Roughly similar to the motion to dismiss for failure to state a claim upon which relief can be granted.

de novo Anew; over again; a second time. A trial *de novo,* for example, is a new trial in which the entire case is retried.

de novo review A complete new look at an administrative case by reviewing court.

deposition A form of discovery consisting of the oral examination of a party or a party's witness by the other party's attorney.

detriment Any act or forbearance by a promise. A loss or harm suffered in person or property.

devise In a will, a gift of real property.

dictum Language in a judicial opinion that is not necessary for the decision of the case and that, while perhaps persuasive, does not bind subsequent courts. Distinguished from *holding.*

directed verdict A verdict issued by a judge who has, in effect, taken the case away from the jury by directing a verdict for one party. Usually, the motion for a directed verdict is made at trial by one party after the other party has finished presenting her or his evidence.

disability A physical or mental impairment that substantially limits one or more of the major life activities of an individual; a record of such impairment; or being regarded as having such an impairment.

disaffirm In contract law, a party's exercise of his power to avoid a contract entered before the party reached the age of majority; a minor's cancellation of his contract.

discharge Release from liability.

disclaimer A term in a contract whereby a party attempts to relieve itself of some potential liability associated with the contract. The most common example is the seller's attempt to disclaim liability for defects in goods that it sells.

discovery A process of information-gathering that takes place before a civil trial. See **deposition** and **interrogatory.**

dismiss To order a cause, motion, or prosecution to be discontinued or quashed.

disparate/adverse impact Effect of facially neutral

employment policy is deleterious for group protected by Title VII.

disparate treatment Treating similarly situated employee different from others because of prohibited Title VII factor.

divided court A court is so described when there has been a division of opinion between its members on a matter that has been submitted to it for decision.

donee A person to whom a gift is made.

duress Overpowering of the will of a person by force or fear.

duty to reasonably accommodate The employer's duty to try to find a way to avoid a conflict between workplace policies and an employee's religious practices or disability(ies).

EEO specialist Employee of EEO agency who reviews complaints for their merit.

emancipate To release; to set free. In contract law, a parent's waiver of rights to control and receive the services of a minor child.

embezzlement A statutory offense consisting of the fraudulent conversion of another's personal property by one to whom it has been entrusted, with the intention of depriving the owner thereof, the gist of the offense being usually the violation of relations of a fiduciary character.

emergency temporary standards These standards are imposed by OSHA where an employee is exposed to grave danger from exposure to substances and the standards are necessary to protect employees from the danger.

employee benefit plans A plan, fund, or program that has been established by an employer to cover benefits for its employees relating to medical or hospital care, death, unemployment, or vacation benefits.

en banc (in banc) By all the judges of a court, with all the judges of a court sitting.

equal employment opportunity (EEO) audit Periodic check to ensure a balanced workforce.

equitable relief Relief that is not in the form of money damages such as injunctions, reinstatements, promotion, and so on. Equitable relief is generally based on concepts of justice and fairness.

equity A system of justice that developed in England separate from the common law courts. Few states in the

United States still maintain separate equity courts, though most apply equity principles and procedures when remedies derived from the equity courts are sought. A broader meaning denotes fairness and justice. In business organization law, the capital contributions of owners plus profits that have not been distributed to the owners; stated capital plus surplus plus earned surplus.

error   A mistake of law or fact; a mistake of the court in the trial of an action.

essential functions of a position   The employer may not take an adverse employment action against a disabled employee based on the disability where the individual can perform the essential functions of the position, those tasks that are fundamental, not marginal or unnecessary, to the fulfillment of the position's objectives.

estop   To bar or stop.

estoppel   That state of affairs that arises when one is forbidden by law from alleging or denying a fact because of his previous action or inaction.

et al.   "And another" or "and others." An abbreviation for the Latin *et alius* meaning "and another"; also of *et alii,* meaning "and others."

evidence   That which makes clear or ascertains the truth of the fact or point in issue either on the one side or the other; those rules of law whereby we determine what testimony is to be admitted and what rejected in each case and what is the weight to be given to the testimony admitted.

exception   An objection; a reservation; a contradiction.

exculpatory clause   A clause in a contract or trust instrument that excuses a party from some duty.

executed   When applied to written instruments, synonymous with the word "signed"; more frequently, it imports that everything has been done to complete the transaction—that is, the instrument has been signed, sealed, and delivered. An executed contract is one in which the object of the contract is performed.

execution   1. A process of enforcing a judgment, usually by having an appropriate officer seize property of the defendant and sell it at a judicial sale. 2. The final consummation of a contract or other instrument, including completion of all the formalities needed to make it binding.

exemption   A release from some burden, duty, or obligation; a grace; a favor; an immunity; taken out from under the general rule, not to be like others who are not exempt.

exhaustion of administrative remedies   Going through the established administrative procedure before being permitted to seek judicial review of an agency decision.

exhibit   A copy of a written instrument on which a pleading is founded, annexed to the pleading and by reference made a part of it. Any paper or thing offered in evidence and marked for identification.

ex post facto   After the fact. The US Constitution prohibits *ex post facto* criminal laws, meaning those that criminalize behavior that was legal when committed.

facially neutral policy   Workplace policy that applies to all employees.

fellow servant doctrine   Injury to an employee on the job is caused by the negligence of another employee.

felony   As a general rule, all crimes punishable by death or by imprisonment in a state prison.

fetal protection policies   Policies an employer institutes to protect the fetus or reproductive capacity of employees.

fiction   An assumption made by the law that something is true that is or may be false.

fiduciary   One who holds goods in trust for another or one who holds a position of trust and confidence.

four-fifths rule   Minority must do at least 80 percent or four-fifths as well as the majority on a screening device, or presumption of disparate impact arises and device must be shown to be job related.

fraud   Misrepresentation made with knowledge of its falsity and intent to deceive. See **misrepresentation.**

free riders   Bargaining unit employees who do not pay dues, but the union is still obligated to represent them.

front pay   Money awarded for the time an employee would have been in a job had illegal discrimination not occurred.

fundamental right   A right guaranteed by the Constitution.

garnishee   Used as a noun, the third party who is subjected to the process of garnishment. Used as a verb, to institute garnishment proceedings; to cause garnishment to be levied on the garnishee.

garnishment A statutory proceeding whereby money, property, wages, or credits of the defendant that are in the hands of a third party are seized to satisfy a judgment or legally valid claim that the plaintiff has against the defendant.

gay A male attracted to other males; a generic term for homosexuals of either gender.

gender-plus discrimination Employment discrimination based on gender and some other factor such as marital status or children.

gender/sexual reassignment surgery The surgery required to change a person's gender.

gender stereotyping Assuming that all members of a particular gender must act a certain way based on preconceived notions and "norms."

general duty clause An OSHA provision requiring that employers furnish to each employee employment and a place of employment free from recognized hazards that cause or are likely to cause death or serious physical harm to the employee.

genetic testing Investigation and evaluation of an individual's biological predispositions based on the presence of a specific disease-associated gene on an individual's chromosomes.

goal Appropriate representation of women and minorities in the workplace, based on their availability in the workforce from which they are drawn.

good faith Honesty in fact; an honest intention to abstain from taking an unfair advantage of another.

goodwill The value of a business due to expected continued public patronage of the business.

greater hazards defense An employer may use the greater hazard defense to defend an OSHA violation where the hazards of compliance are greater than the hazards of noncompliance, where alternative means of protection are unavailable, and where a variance was not available.

guarantor A person who promises to perform the same obligation as another person (called the *principal*), on the principal's default.

guaranty An undertaking by one person to be answerable for the payment of some debt, or the due performance of some contract or duty by another person, who remains liable to pay or perform the same.

guardian A person (in some rare cases, a corporation) to whom the law has entrusted the custody and control of the person or estate, or both, of an incompetent person.

hearing The supporting of one's contentions by argument and, if need be, by proof.

HIV Human immunodeficiency virus, the virus that causes AIDS.

holding Judgment or decision of the court; has precedential effect. Distinguished from *dictum.*

hostile environment sexual harassment Sexual harassment in which the harasser creates an offensive or intimidating environment for the harassee.

i.e. That is.

illusory Deceiving or intending to deceive, as by false appearances; fallacious. An illusory promise is a promise that appears to be binding but that in fact does not bind the promisor.

immunity A personal favor granted by law, contrary to the general rule.

implied contract A contract that is not express, but instead created by other words or conduct of the parties involved.

incapacity A legal disability, such as infancy or want of authority.

inception Initial stage. The word does not refer to a state of actual existence but to a condition of things or circumstances from which the thing may develop.

inchoate Imperfect; incipient; not completely formed.

independent contractor A person who contracts with a principal to perform some task according to his own methods, and who is not under the principal's control regarding the physical details of the work. Under the *Restatement (Second) of Agency,* an independent contractor may or may not be an agent.

indictment A finding by a grand jury that there is probable cause to believe an accused committed a crime.

industrial union Unions at a particular workplace.

injunction An equitable remedy whereby the defendant is ordered to perform certain acts or to desist from certain acts.

in pari delicto Equally at fault in tort or crime; in equal fault or guilt.

in personam Against a person; for example, *in personam* jurisdiction.

in re   In the matter of.

in rem   Against a thing and not against a person; concerning the condition or status of a thing; for example, *in rem* jurisdiction.

in status quo   In the existing state of things. In contract law, the existing state of things at time the contract was made.

instrument   Formal or legal documents in writing, such as contracts, deeds, wills, bonds, leases, and mortgages.

insubordination   Acts or omissions by an employee that evidences a disrespect for the authority of her or his superior(s).

inter alia   Among other things.

interlocutory   Something not final but deciding only some subsidiary matter raised while a lawsuit is pending.

interpleader   An equitable remedy applicable where one fears injury from conflicting claims. Where a person does not know which of two or more persons claiming certain property held by him has a right to it, filing a bill of interpleader forces the claimants to litigate the title between themselves.

interrogatory   Written questions directed to a party, answered in writing, and signed under oath.

inter se   Between or among themselves.

intervening cause   An intervening force that plays so substantial a role in causing a particular plaintiff's injury that it relieves a negligent defendant of any responsibility for that injury. Also called *superseding cause.*

intervention   A proceeding by which one not originally made a party to an action or suit is permitted, on her own application, to appear therein and join one of the original parties in maintaining her cause of action or defense, or to assert some cause of action against some or all of the parties to the proceeding as originally instituted.

inter vivos   A transaction between living persons.

in toto   Wholly, completely.

in transitu   On the journey. Goods are as a rule considered as *in transitu* while they are in the possession of a carrier, whether by land or water, until they arrive at the ultimate place of their destination and are delivered into the actual possession of the buyer, whether or not the carrier has been named or designated by the buyer.

ipso facto   By the fact itself; by the very fact.

joint and several liability   Liability of a group of persons in which the plaintiff may sue any member of the group individually and get a judgment against that person, or may sue all members of the group collectively.

joint liability   Liability of a group of persons in which, if one of these persons is sued, he can insist that the other liable parties be joined to the suit as codefendants, so that all must be sued collectively.

jointly   Acting together or in concert or cooperating; holding in common or interdependently, not separately. Persons are "jointly bound" in a bond or note when both or all must be sued in one action for its enforcement, not either one at the election of the creditor.

judgment   A court's final resolution of a lawsuit or other proceeding submitted to it for decision.

judgment notwithstanding the verdict   A judgment made by a judge contrary to a prior jury verdict whereby the judge effectively overrules the jury's verdict. Also called the *judgment n.o.v.* or the judgment *non obstante veredicto.* Similar to the directed verdict, except that it occurs after the jury has issued its verdict.

judicial review   Court review of an agency's decision.

judicial review   The courts' power to declare the actions of the other branches of government unconstitutional.

jurisdiction   The power of a court to hear and decide a case.

jurisprudence   The philosophy of law. Also sometimes used to refer to the collected positive law of some jurisdiction.

jury   A body of lay persons, selected by lot, or by some other fair and impartial means, to ascertain, under the guidance of the judge, the truth in questions of fact arising either in civil litigation or a criminal process.

leading case   The most significant and authoritative case regarded as having settled and determined a point of law. Often, the first case to have done so in a definitive and complete fashion.

legal   According to the principles of law; according to the method required by statute; by means of judicial proceedings; not equitable.

levy   At common law, a levy on goods consisted of an officer's entering the premises where they were and either leaving an assistant in charge of them or removing them after taking an inventory. Today, courts differ as to what is a valid levy, but by the weight of authority there must be an actual or constructive seizure of the goods. In most states, a levy on land must be made by some unequivocal act of the officer indicating the intention of singling out certain real estate for the satisfaction of the debt.

libel   The defamation action appropriate to printed or written defamation, or to those that have a physical form.

liquidated damages   The stipulation by the parties to a contract of the sum of money to be recovered by the aggrieved party in the event of a breach of the contract by the other party.

litigant   A party to a lawsuit.

lockout   After an impasse is reached, management does not allow labor to come to work.

make-whole relief   Remedy for discrimination that attempts to put claimant in workplace position he or she would have been in had there been no discrimination.

management security clause   Parties agree that management has the right to run the business and make appropriate business decisions as long as all applicable laws are complied with.

mandatory retirement   Deemed illegal by the 1986 amendments to the ADEA, with few exceptions.

mandatory subject of bargaining   Wages, hours, and other conditions of employment, which by law must be negotiated between labor and management.

material   Important. In securities law, a fact is material if a reasonable person would consider it important in her decision to purchase shares or to vote shares.

memorandum   A writing.

midterm negotiations   Collective bargaining agreement negotiations that come before the end of the agreement is reached.

minimum wage   The amount a covered employee must be paid in wages.

misrepresentation   The assertion of a fact that is not in accord with the truth. A contract can be rescinded on the ground of misrepresentation when the assertion relates to a material fact or is made fraudulently and the other party actually and justifiably relies on the assertion.

mistrial   An invalid trial due to lack of jurisdiction, error in selection of jurors, or some other fundamental requirement.

mitigation of damages   A reduction in the amount of damages due to extenuating circumstances.

motion to dismiss   A motion made by the defendant in a civil case to defeat the plaintiff's case, usually after the complaint or all the pleadings have been completed. The most common form of motion to dismiss is the motion to dismiss for failure to state a claim on which relief can be granted, which attacks the legal sufficiency of the plaintiff's complaint. See **demurrer.**

motive   The cause or reason that induced a person to commit a crime.

mutuality   Reciprocal obligation of the parties required to make a contract binding on either party.

national origin   Individual's or individual's ancestor's place of origin (as opposed to citizenship), or physical, cultural, or linguistic characteristics of an origin group.

national origin discrimination project   It is unlawful for an employer to limit, segregate, or classify employees in any way that would deprive them of the privileges, benefits, or opportunities of employment.

negligence   Failure to meet the appropriate standard of care for avoiding unreasonable risk of harm to others.

negligence per se   The doctrine that provides that a conclusive presumption of breach of duty arises when a defendant has violated a statute and thereby caused a harm the statute was designed to prevent to a person the statute was designed to protect.

no cause   Finding that no basis for illegal discrimination existed.

no fault   Liability for injury is imposed regardless of fault.

nonsuit   A judgment given against a plaintiff who is unable to prove a case, or when the plaintiff refuses or neglects to proceed to trial.

no-strike, no-lockout clause   Labor and management agree that labor will not strike and management will not stage a lockout.

obiter dictum   What is said in passing; a rule of law set forth in a court's opinion, but not necessary to decide the case. See **dictum.**

objection   In the trial of a case the formal remonstrance made by counsel to something that has been said or done, in order to obtain the court's ruling thereon.

opinion   The opinion of the court represents merely the reasons for its judgment, while the decision of the court is the judgment itself.

parties   All persons who are interested in the subject matter of an action and who have a right to make defense, control the proceedings, examine and cross-examine witnesses, and appeal from the judgment.

party to be charged   The person against whom enforcement of a contract is sought; the person who is asserting the statute of frauds as a defense.

pass/fail barrier   Job requirement that acts to automatically screen out applicants if they do not meet the requirement and does not permit other qualifications to be considered.

performance appraisal   A periodic assessment of an employee's performance, usually completed by her or his immediate supervisor and reviewed, at times, by others in the company.

perjury   The willful and corrupt false swearing or affirming, after an oath lawfully administered, in the course of a judicial or quasi-judicial proceeding about some matter material to the issue or point in question.

permissive subject of bargaining   Nonmandatory subjects that can be negotiated between labor and management.

per se   In itself or as such.

petition   In equity pleading, a petition is in the nature of a pleading (at least when filed by a stranger to the suit) and forms a basis for independent action.

plaintiff   The party who sues in a civil case.

pleadings   The documents the party file with the court when they state their claims and counterarguments early in a civil case. Examples include the complaint and the answer.

polygraph   A lie-detecting device that measures biological reactions to individuals when they are questioned.

positive law   Laws actually and specifically enacted or adopted by proper authority for the government of a jural society as distinguished from principles of morality or laws of honor.

power of attorney   A written authorization by a principal to an agent to perform specified acts on behalf of the principal. See **attorney-in-fact.**

precedent   A past judicial decision relied on as authority in a present case.

preemployment testing   Testing that takes place before hiring (or sometimes after hiring but before employment) in connection with such qualities as integrity, honesty, drug and alcohol use, HIV, and other characteristics.

preponderance   Most; majority; more probable than not.

presumption   A term used to signify what may be assumed without proof, or taken for granted. It is asserted as a self-evident result of human reason and experience.

prima facie   At first sight; a fact that is presumed to be true unless disproved by contrary evidence.

prima facie case   A case sufficiently strong that, unless rebutted by the defendant in some fashion, it entitles the plaintiff to recover against the defendant.

principal   In agency law, one under whose direction an agent acts and for whose benefit that agent acts.

priority   Having precedence or the better right.

private sector   That segment of the workforce represented by private companies, companies that are not owned or managed by the government or one of its agencies.

privilege   Generally, a legal right to engage in conduct that would otherwise result in legal liability. Privileges are commonly classified as *absolute* (unqualified) or *conditional* (qualified). Occasionally, *privilege* is also used to denote a legal right to refrain from particular behavior (e.g., the constitutional privilege against self-incrimination).

privity of contract   The existence of a direct contractual relation between two parties.

process   Generally, the summons or notice of beginning of suit.

promissory estoppel   An equitable doctrine that protects those who foreseeably and reasonably rely on the promises of others by enforcing such promises when enforcement is necessary to avoid injustice, even though one or more of the elements normally required for an enforceable agreement are absent.

pro rata   Proportionate; in proportion.

proximate cause   A legal limitation on a negligent wrongdoer's liability for the actual consequences of his actions. Such wrongdoers are said to be relieved of responsibility for consequences that are too remote, or not the proximate result of their actions. Various tests for proximate cause are employed by the courts.

public sector   That segment of the workforce represented by governmental employers and governmental agency employers. In some situations, this term may include federal contractors.

punitive damages   See **damages, punitive.**

"qualified" for the position   Able to meet the employer's legitimate job requirements.

quantum meruit   As much as is deserved. A part of a common law action *in assumpsit* for the value of services rendered.

quasi-contract   The doctrine by which courts imply, as a matter of law, a promise to pay the reasonable value of goods or services when the party receiving such goods or services has knowingly done so under circumstances that make it unfair to retain them without paying for them.

quid pro quo sexual harassment   Sexual harassment in which the harasser requests sexual activity from the harassee in exchange for workplace benefits.

quota   Rarely used remedy for discrimination, requiring an absolute number of minorities or females to be hired or promoted.

reasonable accommodation   An accommodation to the individual's disability or religion that does not place an undue burden on the employer, which may be determined by looking to the size of the employer, the cost to the employer, the type of employer, and the impact of the accommodation on the employer's operations.

reasonable cause   Basis for finding illegal discrimination existed.

reasonable person standard   Viewing a situation from the perspective of a reasonable person in society at large.

reasonable victim standard   Viewing wrongful activity from the perspective of a reasonable person experiencing such activity.

recklessness   Conscious disregard for safety; conscious failure to use due care.

recordkeeping and reporting requirements   Title VII requirements for certain types of documents that must be maintained and periodically reported to EEOC.

respondeat superior   Holding the employer responsible for the torts committed by employees within the scope of business.

respondent/responding party   Person to whom an EEO claim is directed, usually the employer.

retroactive seniority   Seniority that dates back to the time the claimant was illegally treated.

reverse discrimination   Majority group member alleges adverse affect of affirmative action.

right to sue letter   Letter given by EEOC to claimant, permitting her or him to pursue the claim in court.

right to work laws   Permits employee to choose not to become a part of the union.

schedule of benefits   The amounts and duration of payments a state provides for injuries under workers' compensation.

screening device   Factor that is used to weed applicants from the pool of potential hirees.

search   A physical invasion of a person's space, belongings, or body.

Section 503 of the Rehabilitation Act   Requires affirmative action on the part of federal contractors and agencies to recruit, hire, and train disabled workers

service   As applied to a process of courts, the word ordinarily implies something in the nature of an act or a proceeding adverse to the party served, or of a notice to him.

set off   That right that exists between two parties, each of whom, under an independent contract, owes an ascertained amount to the other, to calculate their respective debts by way of mutual deduction, so that, in any action brought for the larger debt, the residue only, after such deduction, shall be recovered.

706 agency   State agency that processes EEO claims.

severe and pervasive activity   Harassing activity based on gender, which is more than an occasional act or so serious that it is the basis for liability.

slander   The defamation action appropriate to oral defamation.

specific performance   A contract remedy whereby the

defendant is ordered to perform according to the terms of her contract.

standing   The legal requirement that anyone seeking to challenge a particular action in court must demonstrate that such action substantially affects his legitimate interest before he will be entitled to bring suit.

stare decisis   A doctrine whereby a court is said to be bound to follow past cases that are "like" the present case on the facts and on the legal issues it presents, and that are issued by an authoritative court.

status quo   The existing state of things. In contract law, returning a party to status quo or "status quo ante" means putting him in the position he was in before entering the contract.

statute of limitations   A statute that requires that certain classes of lawsuits must be brought within defined limits of time after the right to begin them accrued or the right to bring the lawsuit is lost.

statutory employees   Individuals who are deemed to be employees by statutes, no mattser what the circumstances of their employment.

strict liability   Legal responsibility placed on an individual for the results of his actions irrespective of whether he was culpable or at fault.

sub nom.   Under the name of.

subpoena   A process for compelling a witness to appear before a court and give testimony.

summary judgment   A method of reaching a judgment in a civil case before trial. The standard for granting a motion for summary judgment is that there be no significant issue of material fact and that the moving party be entitled to judgment as a matter of law.

summary proceedings   Proceedings, usually statutory, in the course of which many formalities are dispensed with. But such proceedings are not concluded without proper investigation of the facts, or without notice, or an opportunity to be heard by the person alleged to have committed the act, or whose property is sought to be affected.

summons   A writ or process issued and served upon a defendant in a civil action for the purpose of securing her appearance in the action.

supra   Above; above mentioned; in addition to.

testimony   In some contexts, the word bears the same import as the word *evidence,* but in most connections it has a much narrower meaning. Testimony is the words heard from the witness in court, and evidence is what the jury considers it worth.

third-party beneficiary   A person who is not a party to a contract but who has the right to enforce it because the parties to the contract made the contract with the intent to benefit him.

timetables   Time limit attached to affirmative action goals.

tort   A private (civil) wrong against a person or her or his property.

tortfeasor   A person who commits a tort; a wrongdoer.

tortious   Partaking of the nature of a tort; wrongful; injurious.

transsexual   Someone who undergoes a change from one gender to another.

unconscionable   In contract law, a contract that is grossly unfair or one-sided; one that "shocks the conscience of the court." The Uniform Commercial Code expressly gives courts the broad discretionary powers to deal with such contracts.

under color of state law   Government employee is illegally discriminating against another as if it is a legitimate part of her or his duties.

underrepresentation/underutilization   Significantly fewer minorities or women in the workplace than relevant statistics indicate are available.

undue hardship   A burden imposed on an employer by accommodating an employee's religious conflict that would be too onerous for the employer to bear.

unilateral contract   A contract formed by an offer or a promise on one side for an act to be done on the other, and a doing of the act by the other by way of acceptance of the offer or promise; that is, a contract wherein the only acceptance of the offer that is necessary is the performance of the act.

union shop   Union and management agree that workplace employees must be members of the union.

union shop clause   Provision negotiated into a collective bargaining agreement that allows a union shop.

valid   Effective; operative; not void; subsisting; sufficient in law.

validation   Evidence showing that a test evaluates what it says it evaluates.

valuing diversity   Learning to accept and appreciate those who are different from the majority and to value their contributions to the workplace.

venue   A requirement distinct from jurisdiction that the court be so geographically situated that it is the most appropriate and convenient court to try the case.

verdict   Usually, the decision made by a jury and reported to the judge on the matters or questions submitted to it at trial. In some situations, however, the judge may be the party issuing a verdict, as, for example, in the motion for a directed verdict. See **directed verdict.**

versus   Against.

vest   To give an immediate fixed right of present or future enjoyment.

vicarious liability   The imposition of liability on one party for the wrongs of another. Also called *imputed liability.* For example, the civil liability of a principal for the wrongs his agent commits when acting within the scope of his employment. See **respondeat superior.** Such liability is also occasionally encountered in the criminal context (e.g., the criminal liability that some regulatory statutes impose on managers for the actions of employees under their supervision).

void   What is entirely null. A void act is one that is not binding to either party, and that is not susceptible of ratification.

voidable   Capable of being made void; not utterly null, but annullable, and hence that may be either voided or confirmed. See **avoid.**

waive   To throw away; to relinquish voluntarily, as a right that one may enforce, if he chooses.

waiver   The intentional relinquishment of a known right. It is a voluntary act and implies an election by the party to dispense with something of value, or to forgo some advantage that he or she might have demanded and insisted on.

workforce analysis   Appraisal of the workplace for finding the representation of women and minorities in all types and levels of employment.

yellow dog contracts   Agreements that employers have employees sign, stating they do not belong to a union and will not join one. Now illegal.

SEARCH THE WEB for further information on these chapter topics:

Additional web links can be found at the book's web site

CHAPTER 1

Ronald Reagan—www.whitehouse.gov
Tecumseh Products Co.—www.tecumseh.com
DOL Handbook on Whistle Blower Protections -
   www.dol.gov
Department of Defense—www.defenselink.mil
Defamation (Anti-Defamation League)—www.adl.org
Uniform Commercial Code—www.law.cornell.edu

CHAPTER 2

Federal Unemployment Compensation—
   www.doleta.gov
Medicare Information— epn.org
Social Security Administration—www.ssa.gov
Department of Labor—www.dol.gov
Internal Revenue Service—www.irs.ustreas.gov
Links Regarding Tax Reform—www.heritage.org
Department of Education—www.ed.gov
Internal Revenue Service—www.irs.ustreas.gov

CHAPTER 3

Title VII—www.law.cornell.edu
John F. Kennedy—www.whitehouse.gov
EEOC Regulations—www.dol.gov
EEOC Retaliation Guidance; EEOC Mediation—
   www.eeoc.gov
Department of Justice—www.usdoj.gov
Southwest Airlines—www.iflyswa.com

CHAPTER 4

Kraft Foods—www.kraftfoods.com
Office of Federal Contract Compliance Programs—
   www.dol.gov
National Organization for Women—www.now.org
The National Urban League—www.nul.org
Urban Institute—www.urban.org
Workplace Claims—www.pli.edu

CHAPTER 5

ACLU on Affirmative Action—www.aclu.org
Franklin D. Roosevelt—www.whitehouse.gov
Lyndon B. Johnson—www.whitehouse.gov
EO 11246—www.dol.gov
United Steelworkers of America—www.uswa.org
AFL-CIO—www.aflcio.org
Hudson Institute—www.hudson.org

CHAPTER 6

Texaco—www.texaco.com
Domino's Pizza—www.dominos.com

CHAPTER 7

New York Times—www.nytimes.com
Price Waterhouse Coopers—www.pwcglobal.com
Equal Pay Act—www.law.cornell.edu
Bureau of Labor Statistics—stats.bls.gov
DOL Handbook on FMLA—www.dol.gov

CHAPTER 8

United States Navy—www.navy.mil
Working Women—www.workingwoman.com
New York Times—www.nytimes.com
Hooters—www.hootersofamerica.com

CHAPTER 9

Bill Clinton—www.whitehouse.gov
CNN—www.cnn.com
Lesbian/Gay Rights: ACLU—www.aclu.org
AT&T—www.att.com
Gay and Lesbian Support Groups and Workplace
   Diversity Programs—www.hrc.org
Trans-Sexuality / Gender Reassignment Surgery—
   www.gpac.org
Constitution—www.house.gov
Human Rights Campaign—www.hrc.org
A.G. Edwards and Sons, Inc.—www.agedwards.com
Boeing—www.boeing.com

CHAPTER 10

Trans World Airlines—www.twa.com
Loyola University Chicago—www.luc.edu

CHAPTER 11

IRCA: Immigrants' Rights—www.aclu.org

CHAPTER 12

National Citizen Law Center—www.nsclc.org
Administration on Aging: Dept. Health and Human
   Services—www.aoa.gov
AARP—www.aarp.org
Age Discrimination in Employment Act—
   www.law.cornell.edu
Foremost Insurance—www.foremost.com

CHAPTER 13

Office of Federal Contract Compliance Programs
   Fact Sheet; The Rehabilitation Act of 1973—
   www.dol.gov